Strategic Management

Building *and* Sustaining Competitive Advantage

Robert A. Pitts
Gettysburg College

David Lei
Southern Methodist University

THOMSON
SOUTH-WESTERN

Australia · Canada · Mexico · Singapore · Spain · United Kingdom · United States

Strategic Management: Building and Sustaining Competitive Advantage, 3/e
Robert A. Pitts and David Lei

Dedication: To Our Parents and Our Students

VP/Team Director:
Mike Roche

Executive Editor:
John Szilagyi

Developmental Editor:
Denise Simon

Marketing Manager:
Rob Bloom

Sr. Production Editor:
Deanna Quinn

Manufacturing Coordinator:
Rhonda Utley

Media Technology Editor:
Vicky True

Media Developmental Editor:
Kristen Meere

Media Production Editor:
Karen Schaffer

Interior Design:
B. Casey

Cover Design:
B. Casey

Cover Image:
PhotoDisc, Inc.

Production House:
Michel Bass & Associates

Compositor:
Cover to Cover Publishing, Inc.

Printer:
Transcontinental

Printed in Canada

1 2 3 4 5 05 04 03 02

For more information contact South-Western, 5191 Natorp Boulevard, Mason, Ohio, 45040.
Or you can visit our Internet site at:
http://www.swcollege.com

Library of Congress Cataloging-in-Publication Data

Pitts, Robert A.
Strategic management : building and sustaining competitive advantage / Robert A. Pitts. David Lei--3rd ed.
p. cm.
Includes bibliographical references and index.
ISBN 0-324-11689-6 (InfoTrac)
ISBN 0-324-17705-4 (non-InfoTrac)
1. Strategic planning--United States--Case studies. 2. Industrial management--United States--Case studies. 3. Competition--United States--Case studies. I. Lei, David. II. Title

HD30.28.P528 2002
658.4'012--dc21

2002066814

Brief Contents

Contents

Preface

Strategic Management: Building and Sustaining Competitive Advantage, Third Edition, is designed as a text for the core classes taught as part of the strategic management or business policy component for majors in business. It should also prove useful to managers and professionals who wish to update or refine their knowledge of some vital issues in strategy through self-study.

As was the case with the first two editions, the objective of this book is to encourage the reader to develop an appreciation for and ability to understand the major drivers of strategy in organizations. There is no question that business organizations of all sizes must prepare for an increasingly complex future. Companies must deal with a variety of strategic, technological, and organizational issues on a daily basis, including such hot-button issues as corporate restructuring, mergers and acquisitions, global competition, rapid technological change, new methods to create value, strategic alliances, the emergence of new types of competitors, the rapid proliferation of the Internet, and the growing challenges of creating and serving new markets anywhere. All these forces work together to redefine the economic and competitive landscape of not only the United States but also the entire world. Despite the numerous strategic challenges posed by these developments, they also represent opportunities for companies of all sizes in all industries to create new sources of competitive advantage that will enable them to participate in and even shape how industries evolve in the times ahead. On the other hand, these same challenges also threaten to erode the long-held competitive advantages of companies that are either slow to react or unable to mount an effective response. Consequently, to survive and prosper in this new millennium, the need to *build and sustain competitive advantage* will be greater than ever. Every chapter in this book was written with a competitive advantage perspective in mind. We believe that even if a large number of readers were not to pursue a career in management per se, knowledge of how organizations conceive, formulate, implement, and adjust their strategies would assist the reader in gaining a stronger appreciation for some of the key issues, trade-offs, and decisions that managers must face. Thus, our central focus on competitive advantage provides the rationale driving every aspect of our book—from its organization and style to the selection and integration of concepts and illustrative examples.

The Organizational Architecture

Although the instructional approach of the first two editions has been retained, several major changes have been made in both coverage and organization. The field of strategic management is becoming a richer topic of study as we speak. Companies are continuing to innovate breakthrough products, services, technologies, and markets at ever-faster rates. They are planning and organizing their activities using new methods, techniques, and modes of operation. At the same time, their actions challenge researchers and teachers to become not only more keenly aware of these developments, but also more adept in explaining them in the classroom. We recognize and welcome this opportunity to bring forth a discussion of both the traditional and newly emerging characteristics that define our vibrant competitive environment.

One of our most significant changes in coverage is the enhanced focus on how the Internet is beginning to play a major role in shaping how industries evolve and how firms think about competing in this rapidly moving arena. Certainly, we dedicate much more attention to this topic to recognize the tremendous expansion of the Internet across every industry in the past few years. In our view, it is imperative that students and practitioners of business begin to understand the impact of the Internet, as well as its limitations, on how firms formulate and implement their strategies. Over time, the Internet, like many other technological advances, will be taken for granted and used as another means to boost productivity, to enhance communications, and to reach out to new customers. Thus, we present a new chapter (Chapter 5) to discuss how the Internet and the broader notion of e-business are beginning to reconfigure the way firms are creating and delivering value in many different industries. Likewise, the reorganization of many our chapters also serves to recognize the growing importance of this topic.

Throughout the entire book, we incorporate additional and more detailed material related to such cutting-edge topics as flexible mass customization, outsourcing, new product development methods, building virtual sources of advantage, the economic concept of network effects, harnessing disruptive technologies, change management, the notion of "co-opetition," network versus network competition, the rise and management of virtual organizations, and the emergence of modularity as a new principle of both product and organization design. All of these developments are redefining the way that companies build, sustain, and renew their individual sources of competitive advantage.

Apart from these salient changes, we retain the chapter sequence of the two previous editions. Yet, every chapter has been thoroughly updated to include some of the most recent, compelling, and revealing examples of firm-based strategies in action (up to the time of this printing). At the same time, we also introduce and present some of the latest theoretical concepts and frameworks that are widely discussed and researched in the strategic management/business policy field. This balanced approach allows us to ensure that we can maintain our powerful applications-driven focus with a solid grounding in research.

Part 1 examines the issue of *building competitive advantage*. Chapters 1 through 6 analyze the particular steps involved in identifying and building upon a firm's strengths and distinctive competencies to create sources of competitive advantage. We examine how firms across different industries formulate strategies that enable them to build on their strengths and distinctive capabilities to compete more effectively. Traditional ways of competing are less likely to be successful in the future as customers demand a higher level of product/service customization faster and at lower cost. Thus, many of the trade-offs associated with conventionally derived, generic competitive strategies may no longer be tenable over time. Instead, firms will need to compete along all three dimensions of value creation: low cost, high quality, and speed to market. Many firms have already recognized this likely development and, in response, have begun formulating alternative strategies based on mass customization, flexibility, and new ways to reach customers. As mentioned before, a completely new chapter on the Internet highlights some of the challenges and opportunities this new technological medium presents to both new and established firms. We also consider the development of other types of technologies that enable all firms to become more responsive to their customers' needs while planting the seeds for future competitiveness.

Part 2 focuses on *extending competitive advantage*. Chapters 7 through 9 examine the key roles of corporate strategy, global strategy, and strategic alliances in leveraging the firm's resources to deepen and reinforce its sources of competitive advantage. In particular, we bring forth additional research ideas from many fertile areas of the academic literature, including the resource-based approach to corporate strategy. This approach reveals how firms can use their distinctive capabilities and skills to leverage themselves into new arenas. Diversification and global expansion into new markets are not the only challenges and issues we cover; many companies are also actively restructuring and realigning their businesses to sharpen their competitive focus and to unlock latent sources of strategic and financial value. Thus, we also examine what firms need to consider when undertaking different forms of corporate restructuring (e.g., cost reduction programs, corporate spin-offs) to promote this value creation focus. The chapter on strategic alliances brings forth new material based on research and practice as well. For example, many firms find themselves developing strategic alliances with partner companies where they simultaneously collaborate and compete. Likewise, entire industries (e.g., automotive, airlines, software, telecommunications) appear to be regrouping into larger networks of firms that compete with other similarly organized networks. Allying and partnering with other firms will almost certainly become taken for granted as a normal part of strategic behavior.

Part 3 addresses the critical issue of *organizing for competitive advantage*. Chapter 10 deals with organizational structure, with a special emphasis on how alternative organization designs promote the simultaneous development of distinctive capabilities with speed and fast responsiveness to customers' changing needs. Chapter 11 explains the concept of the virtual organization in great detail. Traditional approaches to organization design have come under extreme scrutiny in recent years, as senior management in all industries begins to experiment and deploy new forms of network-based, horizontal organizational structures. We examine the critical success factors that managers must consider when they organize their firm's value-adding activities on a virtual basis. No less important, Chapter 11 also covers such vital topics as reward systems, performance evaluation criteria, and especially corporate culture. In particular, we focus extensively on how a firm's reward system and corporate culture can serve as a double-edged sword that can simultaneously promote and inhibit the implementation of new strategies. This is an especially important issue for firms that need to become adept and nimble as they respond to fast-changing industries and the rise of new competitors.

Part 4 deals with issues that revolve around *sustaining and renewing sources of competitive advantage*. The three chapters of this section explore vital issues that are the underpinnings of managing and sustaining growth, being receptive to new technologies and ideas, and maintaining profitability. Chapter 12 deals specifically with such issues as managing interrelationships among the firm's businesses to provide enduring sources of corporate-wide synergy, while balancing the need for fast responsiveness to changes in the competitive environment. The growth of multipoint competition, technological convergence among industries, and the simultaneous need for rapid adaptation to new environmental developments create a high level of organizational tension between coordination and autonomy. Chapter 13 deals extensively with the broader issue of how best to understand and implement strategic change. In particular, the increasingly popular notion of building learning organizations that utilize and enact upon change to create new forms of distinctive competencies will become paramount for firms in many industries facing hypercompetitive environments. In Chapter 14, we examine a host of new and leading-edge management practices that enable firms to reinvent themselves in the wake of faster environmental change. Topics such as corporate reengineering, flexible manufacturing systems, Internet-based technologies, and even newer forms of organization design are analyzed.

Instructional Approach

Within this organizational framework, our coverage of strategic management utilizes a variety of approaches to examine the topic of competitive advantage. To maintain continuity with the expanding research in the field, we have based our presentation and discussion of key concepts on a thorough review of the theoretical and empirical literature from strategic management. To maintain relevancy and applicability for managerial practitioners, we illustrate our presentation with numerous "strategic snapshots" and examples of organizations operating within a variety of different industries. Wherever possible, we use up-to-date, real-world examples to demonstrate how organizations from multiple settings deal with the many complex issues surrounding competitive advantage. Numerous industries (e.g., financial services, consumer packaged goods, telecommunications, airlines, retailing, electronics, computers, restaurants, automotive, entertainment, software, multimedia) that are either on the leading edge of change or facing many of these strategic challenges are examined in detail.

Key Content Features of This Text

In keeping with the spirit of competitive advantage, our book provides a distinctive edge to our customers and users. Within the context of our advantage-driven focus, seven key themes are addressed and reinforced throughout the book:

- Distinctive competence
- Quality
- The Internet
- Globalization

- Managing change
- Innovation
- Ethics

Distinctive competence represents a key pillar of competitive advantage and forms the backdrop for every chapter of the book. We discuss the concept of distinctive competence in great detail. Organizations can thrive only to the extent that they perform some activity(ies) better than their competitors. *In the long term, a firm is only as profitable as it is distinctive. Likewise, a strategy is only as useful as it is distinctive.* Identifying and building those special resources, capabilities, and skills that make a firm special, and even unique, form the basis for competitive advantage. Achieving and maintaining distinctiveness thus becomes a key, ongoing task facing every manager and employee within a firm.

Quality is another vital ingredient of competitive advantage that is reinforced in many places throughout the text. Although numerous firms began implementing total quality management (TQM) efforts during the 1980s, these efforts have met with mixed success, even to this day. To sustain competitive advantage, building quality products alone is insufficient. Firms also need to build and support quality-oriented cultures, thinking, and management practices in all of their organizational activities. In addition, firms need to practice continuous improvement so that they are able to constantly reach for higher levels of excellence. As we enter the new millennium, the ability of firms to produce high-quality products, services, and organizational processes will become a given, as all firms are expected to be competitive in this dimension. Yet, building quality products *and* processes remains an ongoing journey.

There is little doubt that the Internet has become a real driver of technological change in almost every industry. The Internet has given rise to a number of unprecedented business opportunities, such as the growth of digital media, new forms of entertainment, new channels of retailing, the convergence of telecommunications with computer networks, and on-line services that enable customers to access voice, video, data, and other services at decreasing cost over time. At the same time, firms are using the power of the Internet to redesign their organizations to take advantage of the technology's real-time information power and data to stay on top of environmental developments, while simultaneously enhancing internal organizational communications and coordination. Many companies are using the Internet to build newer sources of virtual advantage.

Many of the world's national markets are becoming more uniform, and opportunities to enter new markets are increasing. Globalization is becoming a permanent force in every person and every organization's life. Despite recent economic recessions both at home and abroad, customers around the globe are becoming savvier and possess more discretionary buying power. As a result, we will all be living in a "global village" in which a growing range of consumer and industrial products/services will be continuously redefined, tailored, and customized to each person's tastes and preferences. Globalization, however, requires firms to deal with a host of unfamiliar elements, including customers in distant locations, governments pursuing different agendas, and competitors possessing unusual capabilities. Globalization also brings with it the rise of very different competitors, many of them backed by home governments and industrial policies that may drastically alter the competitive environment.

As environmental change accelerates in future years, a firm's ability to respond to change will become an increasingly vital ingredient to competitive advantage. Sources of competitive advantage developed in one time period may rapidly become obsolete as new technologies, competitors, and customer needs change overnight. However, previous investments in core competencies and skills may actually erect their own barriers to learning new technologies and skills. How companies can sustain their strategies and growth paths into the future remains an ongoing strategic and organizational challenge that pervades our book. We provide a thorough examination of the kinds of responses that firms will be increasingly called upon to make, the problems they may confront when attempting to achieve effective response, and approaches for dealing with such problems.

Throughout our book, we place a great emphasis on understanding how firms across many industries innovate products, services, and value-creating processes to build and sustain advantage. In many industries, firms are beginning to realize that they need to create new products and services faster and more efficiently to preempt what future competitors might bring to the marketplace. Competing on time is considered an essential building block of an effective strategy in every industry. This innovation-driven theme pervades every chapter in our book by focusing on how the latest developments in computer technology, service operations, lean production, flexible manufacturing, and Internet-driven distribution systems are compelling firms to become more nimble and agile in implementing and redesigning their strategies. At the same time, firms must become increasingly vigilant of new, "disruptive technologies" that could fundamentally alter the value chain and the value proposition they offer to their customers. This text provides many examples of how firms have introduced new product and service offerings across the telecommunications, financial services, restaurant, retailing, transportation, health care, manufacturing, consumer electronics, software, entertainment, and multimedia industries.

Society has long imposed censure on firms that fail to meet minimum standards of ethical behavior. However, societal expectations are increasing and will continue to do so in future years. Behavior that conforms to high ethical standards will therefore be increasingly rewarded and indeed necessary for competitive survival. Managers cannot make decisions about their firms' strategies in a vacuum. The needs of different stakeholders (e.g., shareholders, employees, communities) must be evaluated and considered when formulating and implementing strategies. Thus, we provide a broad coverage of different types of ethical dilemmas that are likely to surface in every organization as strategic managers wrestle with the issues we discuss.

New to This Edition

In our quest to ensure that instructors, students, and other readers receive an outstanding coverage of the major issues defining strategic management, we have attempted to capture and present many of the most recent economic, technological, organizational, and regulatory developments that have transpired in the business world since the publication of our previous second edition. Certainly, any instructor in strategic management knows that new developments from every industry occur daily—many of which will have a lasting impact on the competitive environment. Yet, we believe that some key emerging and evolving concepts are significant enough to warrant more intensive coverage in this third edition. *Strategic Management*, Third Edition, discusses and examines a number of major ideas that are becoming focal points for how companies are realigning their strategies and organizations. Among these are the following:

- Internet-driven strategies and business models
- The potential sources of virtual advantage when competing in the marketspace, as well as the marketplace
- The increasingly popular notion of modularity in product and organization design
- The economic concept of network effects
- The growth and application of knowledge webs
- The rise of simultaneous cooperation and competition, described by some researchers as "co-opetition"
- Network versus network forms of competition
- The need to understand, monitor, and respond to competence-changing or disruptive technologies
- Management practices of virtual organizations
- The critical link between reward systems and strategy
- How corporate culture and dominant mindsets give rise to both strength and inertia
- Additional research findings and changes in how companies deal with the generic strategies of differentiation, low-cost leadership, and focus
- The continued search for coherent corporate strategies based on inimitable resources

We believe that our balanced pedagogical approach of providing a strong applications focus, combined with a thorough review of the theoretical and empirical academic literature (continuously revised and improved from our two previous editions), will help the reader understand many of these evolving concepts in a succinct and direct manner.

Our Distinctive Edge

Of the fourteen chapters in our book, nine are especially distinctive, containing material that we emphasize when compared with other strategic management texts. Examples include the following:

Chapter 4: Opportunities for Distinction: Building Competitive Advantage

Understanding the trade-offs among various competitive strategies
Developing new competitive strategies based on mass customization
The rise of product design modularity and its impact on fast response
Competing to understand and to create new market segments
Life cycle dynamics and its impact on different forms of competitive advantage

Chapter 5: Competing on the 'Net: Building Virtual Advantage

How the Internet is transforming the way we compete
The different types of Internet-based business platforms
How business-to-business differs from business-to-consumer platforms
Economic characteristics of Internet-based competition
The concepts of network effects, disintermediation, and value chain compression

Chapter 6: Shifts in Competitive Advantage: Responding to Environmental Change

How change affects a firm's distinctive competence
Competence-changing and disruptive technologies
Rise of new Internet-driven and alternative distribution channels
Changes in related or neighboring industries
Strategies and responses designed to accommodate change

Chapter 7: Corporate Strategy: Leveraging Resources to Extend Advantage

Revisiting the resource-based view of corporate strategy
Competence-based focus that forms the pillar of synergy
Key tests for diversification success
Corporate restructuring and the rise of spin-offs to unlock value

Chapter 9: Strategic Alliances: Teaming and Allying for Advantage

Types of strategic alliances
Competence-based competition and learning
Multipartner consortia arrangements
Network versus network competition
The rise of "co-opetition"
Alliance benefits/costs/risks
Japanese *keiretsu*/Korean *chaebols*
Using alliances to deskill competitors

Chapter 11: Attaining Integration for Advantage

The rise of hybrid network organizations
Key characteristics of virtual organizations
Management practices in virtual organizations
The impact of reward systems on strategy implementation
Performance evaluation and its impact on strategy
Corporate cultures and strategy implementation
The double-edged characteristic of corporate cultures
How dominant approaches give rise to dominant mind-sets

Chapter 12: Balancing Cooperation and Autonomy: Managing Interrelationships

Synergy and corporate-wide competitive advantage
Technological convergence
Multipoint competition
Factors promoting high levels of interunit cooperation
Factors promoting the need for greater autonomy
New developments in technology "fusion"

Chapter 13: Managing Strategic Change: Building Learning Organizations

The concept of a learning organization
Management practices of learning organizations
Organization designs to promote learning
Implementing strategic change
Avoiding corporate ossification and competitive decline
Steps to promote change in static and "dinosaur" organizations

Chapter 14: Redefining Advantage

Building quality cultures
Continuous improvement
Understanding and managing advanced, flexible manufacturing
New approaches to product development and commercialization
Reengineering and business process redesign
Internet-driven supply chain management and manufacturing systems
The continued growth of horizontal, networked organizations

Learning-Based Features of This Text

To maximize the learning value of this text, we have organized each chapter using a common format that introduces and reinforces key strategic management concepts and terms. Each chapter includes the following organizational features:

- **Learning objectives.** At the beginning of every chapter, a series of learning objectives helps readers identify key points and ideas. These objectives provide a step-by-step process that guides the reader through the chapter's material.
- **Opening Strategic Snapshots.** Each chapter begins with an opening mini-case(s), known as strategic snapshots. These are designed to introduce the different environmental settings, strategies, and actions that relate to an issue surrounding competitive advantage. We use companies from a variety of different industry settings, including Boeing, Cisco Systems, Coca-Cola, Eastman Kodak, Kellogg, 3M, Nordstrom, IBM, Ford Motor Company, Tyco International, and Sony. The purpose of these cases is to show how a specific company applies the concepts and principles presented in that chapter, providing a useful bridge between real-world practices and the concepts discussed throughout the book.
- **Key terms.** Key ideas and terms that are vital to understanding strategic management are boldfaced throughout the book and defined in the margins. A glossary at the end of the text provides a review and handy summary of these terms and definitions.
- **Chapter summary.** Each chapter ends with a summary that is directly linked to the learning objectives. These summaries are presented in a bullet-point format to reinforce key concepts, tools, and ideas discussed in the chapter.
- **Exercises and discussion questions.** At the end of most chapters, students are encouraged to think about what they have learned through the use of discussion questions, exercises, and even the Internet to see how companies are competing in today's fast-changing environment. Internet exercises are easily identified by a logo that appears next to the exercise.

- **Examples.** In addition to the opening cases, each chapter includes many up-to-date examples of how different organizations tackle a particular issue related to competitive advantage. These examples are designed to supplement the opening cases and to reinforce the reader's learning. A comprehensive company and subject index are provided at the end of the text to facilitate easy accessibility to the examples discussed throughout the book.

The Package

Instructor's Resource Guide with Test Bank

The *Instructor's Resource Guide with Test Bank* (ISBN 0-324-11690-X), written by Michael D. Ensley at the University of North Carolina, Charlotte, is much more than an instructor's guide. This all-in-one instructional resource has learning objectives, key terms and concepts, lecture notes, an overview of the chapter material, supplementary resources, and test questions for each chapter.

PowerPoint Slides

A complete set of PowerPoint slides developed by John P. Orr at Cameron University supports each chapter. The slides include the chapter figures, additional figures, and text slides and are available for downloading from this book's Web site at **http://pitts.swcollege.com**.

InfoTrac College Edition®

Each new copy of *Strategic Management* comes with a card entitling students to free access to InfoTrac College Edition, an on-line database—updated daily—of full-text articles from hundreds of scholarly and popular periodicals, including *Newsweek, Academy of Management Executive, Harvard Business Review, Fortune*, and the *Journal of Management*. Use InfoTrac to give your students the opportunity to build their research skills or point them to particular articles of your own choosing. To get started, go to **http://www.infotrac-college.com**.

Web Site

Visit our Web site at **http://pitts.swcollege.com/** where you will find interactive quizzes, InfoTrac resources, PowerPoint slide presentations, and other valuable materials for both the instructor and student.

Turner Learning/CNN Video: Management and Strategy

Available on VHS cassette, forty-five minutes of video segments from the Cable News Network (ISBN 0-324-17170-6) are free to adopters of *Strategic Management*, making it easy to bring the real world into the classroom and providing numerous opportunities to relate strategic management concepts to stories in the news. This videotape comes with a guide containing topic keys and other special pedagogical features to facilitate discussion.

Other Resources

- **Global Corporate Management in the Marketplace: An Online Simulation in Business Strategy.** Developed by Ernest R. Cadotte, of the University of Tennessee, Knoxville, and Innovative Learning Solutions, Inc. In this Internet-based simulation (ISBN 0-324-16866-7), students team up to manage a new venture formed to spearhead the introduction of a new line of microcomputers into global competition. Along the way, they experience a full range of value chain decisions and learn what drives performance up or down. Comprehensive success criteria are presented to each team in the form of a "balanced scorecard." Excellent tutorials and help screens complete the picture. Learn more at **http://marketplace-simulation.com**.

- **Strategic Management in the Marketplace: An Online Simulation in Business Strategy.** Developed by Ernest R. Cadotte, of the University of Tennessee, Knoxville, and Innovative Learning Solutions, Inc., *Strategic Management in the Marketplace* (ISBN 0-324-16867-5) is a compact alternative to *Global Corporate Management*, with fewer decision periods to play through, fewer potential markets to explore, and fewer product lines to manage.
- **The Global Business Game: A Simulation in Strategic Management and International Business.** Developed by Joseph Wolfe, Professor Emeritus of the University of Tulsa, and Experiential Adventures LLC. This newly revised CD-ROM-based game (ISBN 0-324-16183-2) crosses over all areas of business, with dedicated chapters on marketing, operations management, and accounting/finance.
- **Strategize! Experiential Exercises in Strategic Management.** Written by Julie I. Siciliano, of Western New England College, and C. Gopinath, of Suffolk University. Constructed around seventeen unique action-oriented "Strategy Sessions," *Strategize!* (ISBN 0-324-06653-8) presents a range of experiential exercises and projects for use in class or out. (An accompanying Instructor's Manual is also available.)

Acknowledgments

This is probably the most important and fun part of this book. We want to express our deep appreciation to the many people who provided assistance in the creation of this text. We remain indebted first and especially to our mutual friend, John W. Slocum, Jr., a current colleague of one of us and a former colleague of the other, for his genius in bringing us together to work on this project. John's guidance, help, and inspiration have been vital to not only this third edition but also the second and especially the first. In fact, it is no exaggeration to say that John has spent dozens of hours reading some of the earlier drafts of our chapters, making recommendations and helping us demystify some of our academic writing tendencies. Because of his own enormous base of publishing experience, we benefited from John's knowledge of how the writing, revision, and publication cycle works in practice. Through his insight, we learned a variety of very helpful techniques that made our writing experience much more enjoyable and certainly more efficient. John's helpful counsel at critical points and his ready willingness to review many early chapters of all our editions have contributed substantially to this effort. In addition, John's advice about content development, style, and creation of learning exercises proved absolutely invaluable in helping make this third edition much more readable and valuable to the student's ongoing learning efforts. John has served as a valuable role model, a ready source of assistance and advice, and, most important, a truly valued friend.

The highly professional attitude of the many people at South-Western (a division of Thomson Learning) has greatly enhanced the pleasure of writing this book. We have enjoyed our ongoing relationship with John Szilagyi and Denise Simon, who have given us invaluable guidance and advice on how best to improve our efforts. Our experience in working with John has been especially fun and rewarding. Denise oversaw many aspects of developing this third edition. Likewise, a warm thank you is due to Rob Bloom, who has diligently worked with his many colleagues in the sales department to promote our book to universities and business schools. Finally and especially, our senior production editor, Deanna Quinn, has done an absolutely splendid job of managing the rapid flow of copyediting and page proofs during the production phase of this book. In fact, Deanna has worked with us for the first, second, and third editions of our book and should be especially commended for all of her first-rate efforts over the past several years; she has become the paragon of fast turnaround, efficiency, dedication and innovation. Doubtless, she has been a real inspiration for us and certainly has borne the cumulative effects of many years' listening to the second author's barrage of jokes, continuous requests for schedule clarifications, and need for continuous production feedback.

We would like to thank all of the external production services who contributed to this edition, especially Michael Bass & Associates (project management), Cover to Cover

Publishing, Inc. (composition), Laura E. Larson (copyeditor), Thomas Torrans (proofreader), Asterisk, Inc.* (artwork), and Robert Swanson (indexer).

We would also like to thank the numerous colleagues in the fields of strategic management, technology management, and organizational behavior who have encouraged us to pursue and deepen our efforts in working on this project. These include Michael A. Hitt of Arizona State University; Michael E. McGill, executive vice president of Associates First Capital (and formerly of Southern Methodist University); Charles R. Greer of Texas Christian University; Richard A. Bettis of the University of North Carolina at Chapel Hill; Joel D. Goldhar of Illinois Institute of Technology; and Mariann (Sam) Jelinek of William and Mary College. A number of our colleagues from business and industry have also contributed their invaluable insights and support to ensure that our examples and ideas were accurate, timely, and on target. More important, all of these colleagues have become our friends along the way.

Furthermore, we would like to acknowledge and thank our colleagues who reviewed *Strategic Management* as this new edition was in development:

Amy Beattie, Champlain University
Eldon H. Bernstein, Lynn University
Thomas M. Box, Pittsburgh State University
Timothy W. Edlund, Morgan State University
Alan B. Eisner, Pace University
Robert R. Edwards, Arkansas Tech University
Dennis J. Pollard, California State University, Fullerton
Robert Wharton, Western Kentucky University

We would also like to thank the people who read and commented on *Strategic Management* in its various earlier incarnations. These colleagues provided valuable suggestions that helped to refine the content and instructional approach: Kenneth E. Aupperle, B. R. Baliga, Joyce M. Beggs, Kimberly B. Boal, Garry D. Bruton, Charles M. Byles, James J. Chrisman, Marian Clark, Mary Coulter, Peter S. Davis, Derrick E. Dsouza, Golpira Eshghi, Ari Ginsberg, Freda Zuzan Hartman, F. Theodore Helmer, J. Kay Keels, David R. Lee, William M. Lindsay, Franz T. Lohrke, John P. Loveland, Timothy A. Matherly, Paul H. Meredith, Wilbur N. Moulton, William F. Muhs, Newman S. Peery, Jr., Jesus A. Ponce-De-Leon, W. Keith Schilit, Dean M. Schroeder, Terrence C. Sebora, Chris Shook, Charles B. Shrader, Marilyn L. Taylor, John Clair Thompson, Larry C. Wall, and Jack W. Wimer.

We want to thank as well our respective academic institutions—Gettysburg College and Southern Methodist University—for their encouragement and support of this effort. In particular, we thank Judy Hepler and Rosalyn Sterner of Gettysburg College and Edith Benham, Billie Boyd, Wanda Hanson, Linda Lang, Jeannie Milazzo, and Nancy Williams of Southern Methodist University for their exceptional dedication, cheerful personalities, formidable work ethics, and all-around help in putting this manuscript through many stages of rewriting, editing, copying, and retyping. The second author thanks Dean Al Niemi for promoting an intellectual environment conducive to the revision and production of this book.

Finally, a special thanks is due to all of the students with whom we have had the pleasure and honor of associating and teaching over many years. It is they who are our fountains of youth, as they have the opportunity to learn from the past and to create a better future.

Robert A. Pitts
David Lei

PART 1

Building Competitive Advantage

CHAPTER 1

The Strategic Management Process

Chapter Outline

Strategic Snapshot: **Evolution of the Restaurant Industry**
Introduction
The Strategy Concept
- The Basis of Strategy
- Charting a Direction: Determining and Setting Strategic Goals
- The Strategic Management Process
- Business and Corporate Strategies
- Strategic Imperatives

Responsibility for Strategic Management
- Characteristics of Strategic Decisions

Who Are Strategic Managers?
What Decision Criteria Are Used?
- Key Stakeholders
- Difficulties in Accommodating Stakeholders

Why Study?
- Candidate Seeking Employment
- Employee or Manager

Summary

What You Will Learn

- The importance of strategy and why it matters to organizations
- The key roles of vision, mission, and goals in shaping an organization's future
- The four stages of the strategic management process
- The concept of a SWOT analysis
- The concepts of corporate and business strategies
- The central role of ethics in strategy
- The different stakeholders of an organization

Evolution of The Restaurant Industry[1]

Ever since Ray Kroc purchased the rights to use the McDonald brothers' idea of serving fast-cooked, low-cost hamburgers, French fries, and chocolate shakes to customers in 1955, the restaurant industry has never been the same. Since that time, the McDonald's restaurant chain has grown to become a $40 billion business (2000 systemwide sales). Its famous golden arches are a familiar sight across the United States and increasingly much of the world. More broadly speaking, the fast-food restaurant has become a highly complex industry in its own right. Companies such as McDonald's, Burger King, Wendy's, KFC (Kentucky Fried Chicken), Taco Bell, and Domino's Pizza are well-known American and global brand names. All of these restaurant firms typically target customers willing to pay for a low-cost meal with a minimum of service and maximum convenience.

The Fast-Food Restaurant Environment

Despite its continued high growth, competition in the fast-food restaurant industry is increasingly fierce; newer rivals enter the picture to serve both existing tastes and the rise of new segments. For example, restaurant chains such as Bennigan's, Brinker International (better known for its flagship chain, Chili's Bar & Grill), and TGI Friday's are trying to capture customers who want larger and more "deluxe," gourmet hamburgers with table service and a more diversified menu. Their offerings are significantly different (and more expensive) from those provided by McDonald's, Burger King, Wendy's, and Jack in the Box—all of which compete fiercely for the fast-food segment of the restaurant industry. Other firms, such as Cracker Barrel, KFC, Pizza Hut, Domino's Pizza, La Madeleine, Papa John's International, Little Caesar's, Sbarro, and Taco Bueno, are attempting to stake out positions in the nonhamburger segment of the industry, where they do not have to compete directly with industry giant McDonald's and other established hamburger-based chains with long-standing market positions.

Behind the rapid rise in the number of fast-food restaurants are some important trends that may change the way the industry competes. Two key macroeconomic factors are redefining this industry. First, most people are becoming more health-conscious and selective about what and how they eat. In particular, newer forms of "leaner" cuisine that emphasize balanced nutrition and good taste are dramatically changing the way restaurants are preparing and marketing their offerings. The baby-boom generation that grew up after World War II powered the enormous growth of McDonald's and other hamburger joints. As this generation grows older, it is increasingly turning away from hamburgers and more toward ethnic foods, such as Chinese, Italian, or Tex-Mex, or regular sit-down meals offering healthier fare at such fast-expanding restaurants as the La Madeleine chain and the variety of restaurants offered by Brinker International (e.g., Chili's, Macaroni Grill, On The Border).

The second major trend defining this industry is that the average American family continues to eat about half of its meals outside of home—an ongoing trend that became entrenched during the 1990s. Although this development would seem to suggest that the restaurant industry can continue to grow at a rapid pace, Americans are becoming much more selective about what they want. In general, not only are people becoming more health-conscious, but they are seeking value from their meals as well. This has been particularly more evident with the recent economic downturn in 2001–2002.

In response to these broader changes in population demographics and economic spending patterns, the more traditional fast-food chains have persisted in trying to conceive new "value-based meals," or "value pricing," that seek to bundle different food offerings under one lower price. At the same time, restaurants have offered a new selection on their menus, featuring items that are claimed to be "heart-healthy," or "lighter fare" for those who are watching their weight. Many existing and newly entering restaurant chains find these changes in demand and tastes an opportunity, since it means that more health- and value-conscious customers are willing to try new types of leaner food, such as rotisserie-cooked chicken as opposed to fried chicken. Thus, the numerous changes in the way people choose their meals are having a significant impact on how these restaurant chains formulate their strategies and compete with new rivals.

Sample Competitors

Let us now look at three different competitors in the fast-food restaurant industry and see how they deal with both their competitors and the larger changes taking place among their customers.

McDonald's. McDonald's is one of the oldest and perhaps the best known of all fast-food restaurant companies. Some of its most popular food offerings range from small hamburgers to such market hits as the Big Mac, Quarter Pounders, its great-tasting French fries, and rich chocolate shakes. In many ways, McDonald's is considered the bellwether industry leader because of its enormous reach within the United States and around the world. Many Wall Street analysts view McDonald's as a proxy for the overall restaurant industry, since it is viewed as the "price leader" in defining value for customers. When McDonald's offers a special promotion, all of its fast-food rivals must respond by matching a lower price.

McDonald's competes by offering the same basic types of food offerings in each of its restaurants, all prepared to the same exact specifications of heat, time, weight, size, and presentation. By requiring each restaurant to follow certain procedures in cooking food and serving customers, McDonald's can ensure a consistent level of quality and service throughout its system. These procedures and guidelines also help McDonald's become a low-cost producer, since each restaurant does not have to "relearn" how to cook its food and serve its customers. In effect, the procedures and basic menus used in each McDonald's restaurant are interchangeable with outlets in other parts of the country. Thus, a customer eating a hamburger at a McDonald's in San Francisco will notice little difference from a hamburger served at a McDonald's in New York or elsewhere.

To compete against rivals such as Burger King, Jack in the Box, and Wendy's, McDonald's focuses on providing fast service with consistent quality and generally low prices. This formula has made McDonald's the largest fast-food provider in the United States and one of the most consistently profitable.

Brinker International. Brinker International is better known for the growing variety of restaurants that it operates, including Chili's Bar & Grill, Macaroni Grill, and On The Border, to name a few. However, Chili's is the largest restaurant chain under Brinker management. It is probably best known for its deluxe hamburgers, and it certainly competes very differently than McDonald's in trying to win customers. Instead of copying McDonald's formula for low-priced, standardized food with no table service, Chili's has taken the opposite approach. Founded by legendary restaurateur Norman Brinker, Chili's was designed to make eating out a fun and warm experience. Although people pay more to eat at Chili's, customers receive friendly table service with a menu that highlights the many different ways a hamburger can be cooked and served. Its famous gourmet hamburgers are offered with various cheeses, mushrooms, and sauces, generous French fries, and other extras that make for a distinctive, satisfying, but reasonably priced meal.

Despite its high-quality offering, Chili's is certainly not just a hamburger-only restaurant. A customer's selection is not limited solely to hamburgers; large salads, small steaks, grilled chicken dishes, seafood, pasta, and other fare are also available. These offerings cater to more health-conscious customers who still want the fun of eating at Chili's without the high calories or fat content of hamburgers. Still, if customers should feel the need, generous portions of desserts are also offered to round out the meal. Chili's wants to make its customers feel that eating out can be a fun and relaxing experience. The company emphasizes customer service by training its people to be extremely responsive to customer needs and to get to know their regular customers better.

Tricon Global Restaurants. Tricon is best known for the three different fast-food restaurant chains it operates and manages: Pizza Hut, KFC (formerly Kentucky Fried Chicken), and Taco Bell. Once a part of PepsiCo, Tricon became an independent firm in 1997 when PepsiCo decided to exit from the fiercely competitive restaurant business. Although Tricon is not a familiar name to most customers, its restaurants most certainly are. All three units have decades of experience competing with McDonald's and other restaurant chain giants. Instead of competing directly with McDonald's or Chili's, Tricon's three different businesses—KFC, Taco Bell, and Pizza Hut—target three nonhamburger segments of the restaurant industry.

For example, KFC offers its traditional, distinctive-tasting fried chicken recipes, along with its golden rotisserie-cooked chicken to serve both the conventional fast-food and the growing health-conscious segments. Although KFC is a leader in the chicken segment of the restaurant industry, it faces consistently tough competition from Chick-Fil-A, Church's, Popeye's, and other smaller chicken-based restaurants. The growing popularity of rotisserie-cooked chicken also threatens the high profitability of KFC's traditional fried chicken meals. To meet these competitive threats, KFC has now begun to offer value-priced meals that feature fried chicken with mashed potatoes or biscuits for a new lower price.

Tricon's Taco Bell unit seeks to carve out a position in the growing Tex-Mex fast-food segment. The higher population growth in the Southwest and the Sunbelt has contributed to making Tex-Mex food more popular throughout the United States. In turn, Taco Bell has benefited by offering different types of tacos, enchiladas, fajitas, and other similar foods through its convenience-oriented outlets. Taco Bell competes with other Mexican-style food chains, such as Taco Bueno and numerous smaller Mexican restaurant chains found in the Southwest. For much of the 1990s, Taco Bell was one of Tricon's fastest-growing and most profitable businesses, although in recent years its growth has slowed considerably as competition in this market segment intensified.

Pizza Hut has traditionally competed by offering restaurant-style, sit-down pizza meals. Pizza Hut's most distinctive food offering is its specialty pan pizza, which has a special taste and texture. In recent years, Pizza Hut has been a strong performer for both previous owner PepsiCo and current owner Tricon. In fact, Pizza Hut is now experimenting with a variety of different types of pizzas in different parts of the country in order to satisfy more local tastes. Although Pizza Hut retains the largest market share in this segment, it faces fierce competition from new companies such as Domino's Pizza and Little Caesar's. Most recently, Pizza Hut's toughest competitor appears to be coming from Papa John's International, a small company that has grown by leaps and bounds over the past decade. All of Pizza Hut's competitors try to offer a different approach to customers. To carve out its own market, Domino's Pizza competes against Pizza Hut by offering only home delivery of pizza, rather than sit-down service. Little Caesar's, on the other hand, competes primarily through innovative advertisements and specially priced pizzas for both pickup and delivery; it does not offer sit-down service, either. Papa John's International offers home delivery, advertises aggressively, and claims to use only the freshest ingredients. To meet these competitive challenges, Pizza Hut refocused its operations more on home delivery service and offers free breadsticks, salads, and even soft drinks in order to win over more customers. Pizza Hut even took Papa John's International to court in 1999 and 2000 in a dispute over food claims and the luring away of existing restaurant franchise owners.

Multiple Strategic Issues

As an example of some of the different issues facing each type of company, we can look at how the major competitors view and manage their restaurant operations. For both McDonald's and Brinker International, restaurants are their primary business. However, the two companies differ in some important ways. For the most part, McDonald's defines its business through its hamburger-focused offerings to customers, with a particular focus on consistency, good value, and a standardized approach to managing operations. In this sense, McDonald's has a much more targeted approach to growing its business. Brinker International, however, operates a number of different restaurant chains—each designed to reach a different type of customer who wants to satisfy a different type of meal preference or taste. What people want from Chili's may indeed be different from what they want from Macaroni Grill or On The Border. Thus, Brinker International must formulate a strategy for each of its restaurant chains in order to reach out to multiple markets.

When Tricon was part of PepsiCo, restaurants were just one portion of a larger company that also includes Frito-Lay snacks and its traditional soft drinks. Thus, PepsiCo did not actually compete in the restaurant industry; its various units (KFC, Taco Bell, and Pizza Hut) did. Consequently, senior management at PepsiCo were asking themselves how well did their various restaurant businesses fit with their other snack food and soft drink units. Throughout much of the 1980s and 1990s, the restaurant business was an important part of PepsiCo's overall strategy. Increasing competitive pressures and slowing of the restaurant industry's overall growth rate, however, made it increasingly difficult for Pepsi-

Co to compete effectively in the industry. The strategic benefits that PepsiCo could once bring to the restaurant industry—marketing prowess, low-cost source of beverages, shared advertising expenditures, and shared management—became difficult to sustain when PepsiCo's beverage business began to lose significant market share to arch rival Coca-Cola, especially in markets outside the United States. By the mid- to late 1990s, severe competition and declining profit margins on both fronts—beverages and restaurants—made it increasingly difficult for PepsiCo to compete effectively in both businesses simultaneously. Deciding that it needed to sharpen its competitive focus and to raise capital for its beverage business, PepsiCo's senior management decided to sell its restaurant operations as a way to exit the restaurant business.

McDonald's appears to be taking a very different approach from that of PepsiCo. In 2000, McDonald's purchased Boston Market, a restaurant chain that enjoyed very high growth in the early 1990s. However, Boston Market (better known to some people as Boston Chicken, its previous name) faced growing difficulties by offering home-style cooking at low prices. Fast growth also saddled Boston Market with considerable debt that became very burdensome. When Boston Market ultimately shuttered many of its operations in 2000, McDonald's took the bold step of purchasing the company. Now, McDonald's faces some key strategic issues that are very different from how it previously managed its hamburger-focused business in past years.

Introduction

As the preceding examples illustrate, firms must compete with each other to gain their customers' business. Yet, not all firms will necessarily compete with one another in the same way. Each firm is likely to devise its own *strategy* to deal with its competitive rivals, to serve its particular base of customers, and to act on the changes that impact the way it operates. Each firm's strategy needs it to develop a *competitive advantage* that enables it to compete effectively. **Strategy** refers to the ideas, plans, and support that firms employ to compete successfully against their rivals. Strategy is designed to help firms achieve competitive advantage. In the broadest sense, **competitive advantage** is what allows a firm to gain an edge over its rivals. Competitive advantage enables a firm to generate successful performance over an extended period of time. Throughout this book, which focuses on the concepts of strategy and competitive advantage, you will learn how firms from a variety of different industries, settings, and situations develop strategies to achieve competitive advantage. Activities undertaken to achieve this end form the basis of the strategic management process.

strategy: Refers to the ideas, plans, and support that firms employ to compete successfully against their rivals. Strategy is designed to help firms achieve competitive advantage.

competitive advantage: Allows a firm to gain an edge over rivals when competing. Competitive advantage comes from a firm's ability to perform activities more distinctively or more effectively than rivals.

Competitive rivalry characterizes economic activity not only in our own country but throughout the free world as well, and it is rapidly replacing government planning across most of the globe. Much organized activity outside the realm of business and commerce is also highly competitive. Nonprofit enterprises such as colleges, churches, and charities, for example, generally face numerous rivals eagerly seeking the same students, parishioners, and contributors. Because rivalry is such a pervasive aspect of so many different kinds of activity, the concepts developed in this text will be useful to managers operating in a wide range of settings. How to deal with competitive rivalry is the primary question addressed in this book.

In this first chapter, we show how strategy can help a firm deal with competition in an industry. We examine the concept of strategy and introduce the notion of strategic imperatives. We then examine the basic ingredients that make up the strategic management process and show how different situations will influence the strategic imperatives facing firms. In the later sections, we identify the various responsibilities of senior management in the strategic management process, along with the issues of stakeholders and ethics.

The Strategy Concept

From a traditional or historical perspective, the term *strategy* reflects strong military roots. Military commanders employ strategy in dealing with their opponents. Throughout human history, numerous military theorists, including Sun Tzu, Alexander the Great, Karl von Clausewitz, Napoleon, Stonewall Jackson, and Douglas MacArthur, have contemplated and written about strategy from many different perspectives.[2] The fundamental premise of strategy is that an adversary can defeat a rival—even a larger, more powerful one—if it can maneuver a battle or engagement onto terrain favorable to its own capabilities and skills.

distinctive competence: The special skills, capabilities, or resources that enable a firm to stand out from its competitors; what a firm can do especially well to compete or serve its customers.

In this book, we use the term **distinctive competence** to describe those special capabilities, skills, technologies, or resources that enable a firm to distinguish itself from its rivals and create competitive advantage. Ideally, a firm's competence or skill is so distinctive that others will not be able to copy it readily. Capabilities and skills that are valuable in business include such activities as innovative product design, low-cost manufacturing, proprietary technology, superior quality, faster response to customer needs, and superior distribution. Thus, a firm may have several areas of activity or skill that lead to competitive advantage. Competitors in the restaurant industry, for example, use a variety of methods for building competitive advantage, including warm and friendly service and gourmet hamburger recipes (Brinker International's units, including Chili's), consistent quality and low-cost operation (McDonald's), and identification of new marketing segments (Tricon and PepsiCo).

terrain: The environment (or industry) in which competition occurs. In a military sense, *terrain* is the type of environment or ground on which a battle takes place. From a business sense, *terrain* refers to markets, segments, and products used to win over customers.

Terrain refers to the environmental setting in which an engagement with an adversary takes place. In the military realm, terrain may be a plain, a forest, a marsh, or the mountains. The characteristics of each of these settings influence which type of troops or deployments can be used most effectively. In the world of business, competitors do not confront each other directly on a battlefield as armies do. Rather, they compete with each other in an industry environment by targeting market segments and attempting to win customers. It is customers who determine, each time they make a purchase, which competitors "win" and which ones "lose." The industry environment thus constitutes the ultimate *terrain* on which business competition takes place.

Because most industries contain numerous customers displaying different needs, firms generally have many different possible terrains from which to choose. Consider the restaurant industry, for example. It contains a number of different groups of customers: those wanting low-cost meals, people desiring gourmet hamburgers, and individuals preferring ethnic or health-conscious menus, as well as those who prefer a special dining experience. Each group thus constitutes a different segment or terrain on which rivals compete. Furthermore, each of these groups can be further divided into smaller subgroups of customers with even more specific needs and characteristics. For example, ethnic food runs the entire range from Chinese to French to Mexican. Each of these individual segments has somewhat different competitive characteristics that define the subterrain.

The Basis of Strategy

The essence of strategy is to match strengths and distinctive competence with terrain in such a way that one's own business enjoys a competitive advantage over rivals competing on the same terrain. In the military realm, the strategic imperative for commanders is to select a battlefield favorable to their force's particular strengths and unfavorable to the adversary. A cavalry or highly mobile armored force, for example, should try to fight on flat, open ground where its speed and maneuverability can be put to good use. Units skilled in guerrilla tactics, by contrast, should try to encounter the enemy in dense woods or in the mountains—terrains that favor a hide-and-strike capability. Military strategy thus aims at achieving a favorable match between a military force's internal strengths and the external terrain on which it operates (see Exhibit 1-1).

Military Strategy

EXHIBIT 1-1

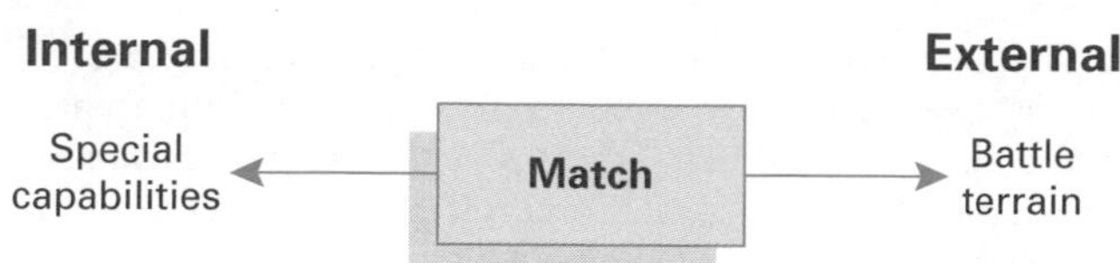

Competitive strategy for organizations likewise aims at achieving a favorable match between a firm's distinctive competence and the external environment in which it competes. However, the nature of this match is more complex in the business sphere. Unlike military conflict, competition in business does not always have to result in a win-lose situation. Industry rivals frequently have the opportunity to improve their strengths or skills as competition unfolds. In addition, the value of their distinctive competences that lead to competitive advantage can also decline over time as a result of environmental change. Because of these possibilities, competitive strategy involves not just one but several different imperatives. The most important of these are to discover new opportunities, avert potential threats, overcome current weakness, sustain existing strength, and apply strength to new fields (see Exhibit 1-2).

Business Strategy

EXHIBIT 1-2

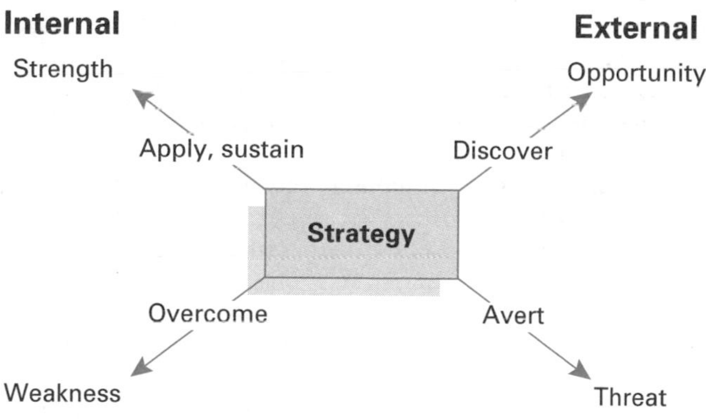

Every firm faces the need to deal with these strategic imperatives on a continuous basis. However, some imperatives will be more dominant at a given point in time, depending on the individual firm's particular situation. Before a firm can determine which imperatives are most important, it must have a strong sense of self-knowledge, purpose, and direction.

Charting a Direction: Determining and Setting Strategic Goals

Any organization needs an underlying purpose from which to chart its future. If organizations are to compete effectively and serve their customers well, they need to establish a series of guideposts that focus their efforts over an extended time period. These guideposts will help the firm clarify the purpose of its existence, where it is going, and where it wants to be. Strategies are unlikely to be effective without a sense of direction.

vision:
The highest aspirations and ideals of a person or organization; what a firm wants to be. Vision statements often describe the firm or organization in lofty, even romantic or mystical tones (see *mission; goals; objectives*).

Vision. A vision relates to the firm's broadest and most desirable goals. A **vision** describes the firm's aspirations of what it really wants to be. Visions are important because they are designed to capture the imagination of the firm's people and galvanize their efforts to achieve a higher purpose, cause, or ideal. Some of the most effective visions are those in which the firm seeks to excel or lead in some activity that bond all of its people together with a common purpose. Visions should have a strong emotional appeal that encourages people to commit their full energies and minds to achieving this ideal.

Examples of powerful visions that have changed and redefined entire industries include that of Cable News Network (CNN), now a part of AOL Time Warner. Founded in 1981 by Ted Turner to provide twenty-four-hour news coverage, CNN prospered by aggressively pushing forward its new television format that would ultimately become the fastest news source for corporations and even national governments. Even under new owner AOL Time Warner, CNN's vision remains to be the best and most reliable news source on any topic, anywhere, anytime. For example, during the Gulf War of 1990–1991, world leaders, including Iraq's Saddam Hussein, reportedly tuned in to CNN to receive the most accurate and up-to-date coverage of Operation Desert Storm.

In the restaurant industry example, McDonald's and Brinker International have prospered by pursuing their own visions of what they think the restaurant industry should offer to consumers. The founder of McDonald's Corporation, Ray Kroc, promoted a vision of McDonald's as being the leading provider of moderately priced, quality food to anyone, anywhere. Brinker International, on the other hand, has prospered by pushing forward a different vision of restaurant service; it believes each meal should be a fun and exciting experience.

In the beverage industry, Coca-Cola has a powerful vision that has galvanized the firm's efforts in defining much of the beverage and soft drink industry. Coke wants to make sure that "a Coke is in arm's reach" of any customer, no matter where that customer is around the world. This simple but mighty vision has defined the essence of Coke's purpose and its strategy of entering and serving many markets around the world. No market is too small for Coke to carry out its vision.

In the telecommunications and computer networking industries, Cisco Systems leads in developing state-of-the art equipment that brings the Internet to everyone—businesses, governments, large organizations, and consumers in the home. A company that is barely fifteen years old, Cisco Systems has grown to become one of America's technology leaders and most valuable companies. Under CEO John Chambers, Cisco has a vision that all of the world's activities will eventually be strongly influenced and impacted by the Internet. Over the next few years, Cisco envisions that most business transactions will occur over the Internet, as will a significant portion of job training and education, stock trading and investments for individuals, as well as even health care through telemedicine. Cisco's vision of the Internet can be summarized in its often-quoted commercials: "Are You Ready?" To make its vision happen, Cisco has been extremely aggressive in growing its businesses, especially by acquiring a vast number of promising, start-up firms that are developing cutting-edge technologies.

Corporate visions are often lofty and even surrounded by a high level of idealism or romanticism. They provide a consistency of purpose that gives the organization a reason to exist. However, visions do not lay out the actual strategies, steps, or methods by which the firm will pursue its purpose. Missions, on the other hand, are intended to provide the basis for fulfilling a vision.

mission:
Describes the firm or organization in terms of its business. Mission statements answer the questions "What business are we in?" and "What do we intend to do to succeed?" Mission statements are somewhat more concrete than vision statements but still do not specify the goals and objectives necessary to translate the mission into reality (see *vision; goals; objectives*).

Mission. A firm's **mission** describes the organization in terms of the business it is in, the customers it serves, and the skills it intends to develop to fulfill its vision. Visions that capture the organization's purpose and ideals become more concrete and "real" in an organization's mission. Missions are more specific than visions in that they establish the broad guidelines of how the firm will achieve or fulfill its vision over a certain time period. Firms will translate their vision into a *mission statement* that sets the firm's boundaries and provides a sense of direction. Mission statements spell out in a general way some key pillars of building a strategy—the firm's customers, the firm's principal products or services, and the direction that a firm intends to move over a future time period.

For example, the mission at McDonald's can be summarized in four letters originally conceived by founder Ray Kroc and his earliest franchises: QSCV (quality, service, cleanliness, and value). The mission of McDonald's (at both corporate headquarters and in individual restaurants) is to implement each of these four policies to satisfy its customers. High quality of food, fast and courteous service, clean restaurants, and affordable prices are guiding pillars that lay the foundation for all of McDonald's Corporation's strategies and organizational practices. By carrying out this simple mission statement, McDonald's can translate its vision into reality.

Goals and Objectives. Mission statements are designed to make the organization's vision more concrete and real to its people. However, mission statements still do not provide the tangible goals or objectives that must be met to achieve a firm's broader purpose. Thus, goals and objectives are needed to provide a series of direct, measurable tasks that contribute to the organization's mission. **Goals** and **objectives** are the results to be achieved within a specific time period. Unlike the mission statement that describes the firm's purpose more generally, goals and objectives designate the time period in which certain actions and results are to be achieved. Examples of goals and objectives include the following: achieving a 30 percent market share gain in two years, increasing profitability by 15 percent in three years, and developing a new product in six months. Goals and objectives are powerful tools that break the mission statement into very specific tasks, actions, and results throughout the organization. Each part of the organization is likely to have its own set of goals and objectives to accomplish within a specified time period. When put together, all of these smaller goals and objectives should bring the organization's mission into fruition.

goals:
The specific results to be achieved within a given time period (also known as *objectives*).

objectives:
The specific results to be achieved within a given time period (also known as goals). Objectives guide the firm or organization in achieving its mission (see *vision; mission*).

strategic management process:
The steps by which management converts a firm's values, mission, and goals/objectives into a workable strategy; consists of four stages: analysis, formulation, implementation, and adjustment/evaluation.

SWOT analysis:
Shorthand for strengths, weaknesses, opportunities, and threats; a fundamental step in assessing the firm's external environment; required as a first step of strategy formulation and typically carried out at the business level of the firm.

The Strategic Management Process

A management process designed to achieve the firm's vision and mission is called a **strategic management process**. It consists of four major steps: analysis, formulation, implementation, and adjustment/evaluation (see Exhibit 1-3).

Analysis. The strategic management process begins with careful analysis of a firm's internal strengths and weaknesses and external opportunities and threats. This effort is commonly referred to as **SWOT analysis** (strengths, weaknesses, opportunities, and threats).

Strategy Management Process — EXHIBIT 1-3

Analysis	External environment	Opportunities, Threats
	Internal environment	Strengths, Weaknesses
Formulation	Mission	Customers to be served Competencies to be developed
	Policies	Goals, guidelines for major activities
Implementation		Organization structure, systems, culture, etc.
Adjustment/ Evaluation		(Cycle to earlier steps)

McDonald's uses SWOT analysis regularly to assess consumer desire for new types of foods. This analysis identified increasing customer desire for new types of food and hamburgers that are "healthier" or have a lower fat content as compared to McDonald's current offerings. McDonald's top management recognizes the rising health consciousness of the American public as a potential *opportunity* to expand its service to customers. To exploit this opportunity, McDonald's developed, tested, and then offered a variety of new offerings, including at one point a fat-free hamburger, chicken sandwiches, and different salads that would be instrumental in meeting this need. Had McDonald's not continued its efforts to undertake these modifications, its sales would likely have suffered as a consequence. Consumers' rising health consciousness also represents a potential *threat* to McDonald's as well as a potential opportunity. Failure to respond to this development could erode McDonald's competitive position in the industry.

McDonald's *strengths* are its fast, efficient service and its low-cost operations. These strengths give the company a well-known, commanding reputation among many segments of the U.S. population. Moreover, McDonald's spans the entire nation with its golden arches and distinctive restaurant architecture, giving each outlet a special, recognizable presence. McDonald's value-pricing policies instituted several years ago offer a combination of large sandwich, French fries, and large drink for a lower price than if these items were purchased individually. They were designed to overcome a weakness that customers perceived McDonald's food as becoming more expensive over time. These numerous sources of strength, together with aggressive pricing, allow McDonald's to compete effectively with other national hamburger-based chains, such as Burger King and Wendy's, and regional hamburger outlets, such as Carl's Jr. in California and Sonic in the South.

Formulation. Information derived from SWOT analysis is used to construct a strategy that will enable the firm to articulate and pursue a coherent mission. A strategy must be formulated that matches the external opportunities found in the environment with the firm's internal strengths. For each firm, this matchup or coalignment is likely to be different. To gain maximum competitive advantage, individual firms need to identify the activities they perform best and seek ways to apply these strengths to maximum effect. Effective strategy formulation is based on identifying and using the firm's distinctive competences and strengths in ways that other firms cannot duplicate. This is key to building competitive advantage.

McDonald's strategy has long been based on the firm's distinctive competence in serving its customers quality food at reasonable prices. That has enabled McDonald's to become an extremely formidable player in the restaurant industry. The Chili's unit of Brinker International, on the other hand, has formulated a strategy based on providing highly personalized and warm service to each customer. Its approach is designed to make each dining experience memorable with the hope that customers will return frequently. A sit-down meal at Chili's is, however, more costly than a meal at McDonald's. Yet, both firms are prospering in the industry by formulating strategies that use their strengths to pursue somewhat different opportunities in the environment.

Implementation. A key aspect of an organization's mission is a commitment to develop the distinctive competence and strengths needed to achieve the mission. Once an organization has made such a commitment, it must then take steps to implement this choice. Implementation measures include organizing the firm's tasks, hiring individuals to perform designated activities, assigning them responsibility for carrying out such activities, training them to perform activities properly, and rewarding them if they carry out responsibilities effectively. At McDonald's corporate headquarters, implementation involves determining such issues as the franchising fees and compensation policies for its restaurants, hiring policies that individual McDonald's restaurants will use, and an organizational structure that facilitates efficient operations. In the case of individual McDonald's restaurants within the network, implementation focuses on such matters as hiring able-bodied individuals, training employees to perform specific tasks, motivating employees to perform tasks properly, and treating customers courteously and efficiently.

Adjustment/Evaluation. The industry environment within which a firm operates inevitably changes over time. Also, a firm's performance may fall below desired levels. Either event compels a firm to reexamine its existing approach and make adjustments that are necessary to regain high performance. Mechanisms must be put into place to monitor potential environmental changes and alert managers to developments that require modification of mission, goals, strategies, and implementation practices.

For example, competition and growth in the restaurant industry may change significantly with the advent of an economic recession that limits people's disposable income. Although fancier restaurants are more likely to suffer from an economic downturn than McDonald's, such a change will also affect McDonald's, though in different ways. More people may initially be inclined to eat at McDonald's because of its value-pricing policies. However, a prolonged recession may lead to a reduction in volume, causing McDonald's to slow down expansion of new restaurants. This development, in turn, will lead to a slower growth of McDonald's earnings in the future.

The issues that managers confront when conducting the strategic management process will differ according to the competitive environments their firms face, the internal strengths and weaknesses they possess, and the number of other businesses their firms operate. Consequently, each firm needs to tailor its strategic management process in ways that best suit its own specific context and situation. Firms such as PepsiCo, which operate other businesses in addition to restaurants, faced strategic issues beyond that of McDonald's and Chili's, which compete only in the restaurant industry. In addition, each firm's strategy is likely to change as its environment and industry evolve over time. Thus, firms need to remain constantly attuned to developments and changes in the environment that may warrant further adjustment of their strategies.

Business and Corporate Strategies

To appreciate the comprehensiveness of the analytic approach we will take, consider the organizational chart in Exhibit 1-4. It shows the organizational arrangement used by many firms that operate multiple businesses, as PepsiCo did before it divested its restaurant business. These types of firms are known as **diversified** or **multibusiness** firms. In contrast, firms such as McDonald's and Papa John's International are known as **single-business** or **undiversified firms**. As indicated in Exhibit 1-4, the major subunits of a diversified, multibusiness firm are entire businesses. Each individual business generally operates in its own specific competitive environment and thus requires a separate **business strategy**. Business strategy attempts to answer the question "How do we build competitive advantage for this particular business?" or "How should we compete?" For example, the business strategy pursued by KFC, previously a division of PepsiCo and now part of Tricon, is to provide different types of food based on its famous chicken recipes. By limiting itself to offering primarily chicken-centered recipes, KFC does not compete directly with McDonald's in the larger restaurant industry. Thus, KFC can focus its efforts on competing for an attractive but separate segment that matches its mission and distinctive competences. Some ways that KFC builds competitive advantage include its highly memorable advertising ("finger-lickin' good"), its proprietary recipes (original, extra crispy, skin-free, rotisserie golden chicken), and its ability to share marketing expenses and skills with its sister units Pizza Hut and Taco Bell.

Diversified, multibusiness firms also need a higher-level strategy that applies to the organization as a whole. Strategy at this higher level is known as **corporate strategy**. Corporate strategy deals with the question "What set of businesses should the organization operate?" PepsiCo's decision to sell its restaurant business in 1997 is an issue of corporate strategy. Thus, corporate strategy was a dominant issue in the minds of PepsiCo's senior management when it considered and acted on such questions as these: Should PepsiCo even have a presence in the restaurant business? If so, what new restaurant (or other) businesses should PepsiCo enter? If not, how should PepsiCo exit the restaurant business to sharpen its focus on its beverage and Frito-Lay snack food businesses? PepsiCo's managers are still

diversification: A strategy that takes the firm into new industries and markets (see *related diversification; unrelated diversification*).

multibusiness firm: A firm that operates more than one line of business. Multibusiness firms often operate across several industries or markets, each with a separate set of customers and competitive requirements (also known as a *diversified firm*). Firms can possess many business units in their corporate portfolio.

single-business firm: A firm that operates only one business in one industry or market (also known as an *undiversified firm*).

undiversified firm: A firm that operates only one business in one industry or market (also known as a *single-business firm*).

business strategy: Plans and actions that firms devise to compete in a given product/market scope or setting; addresses the question "How do we compete within an industry?"

corporate strategy: Plans and actions that firms need to formulate and implement when managing a portfolio of businesses; an especially critical issue when firms seek to diversify from their initial activities or operations into new areas. Corporate strategy issues are key to extending the firm's competitive advantage from one business to another.

EXHIBIT 1-4 Multibusiness Enterprise

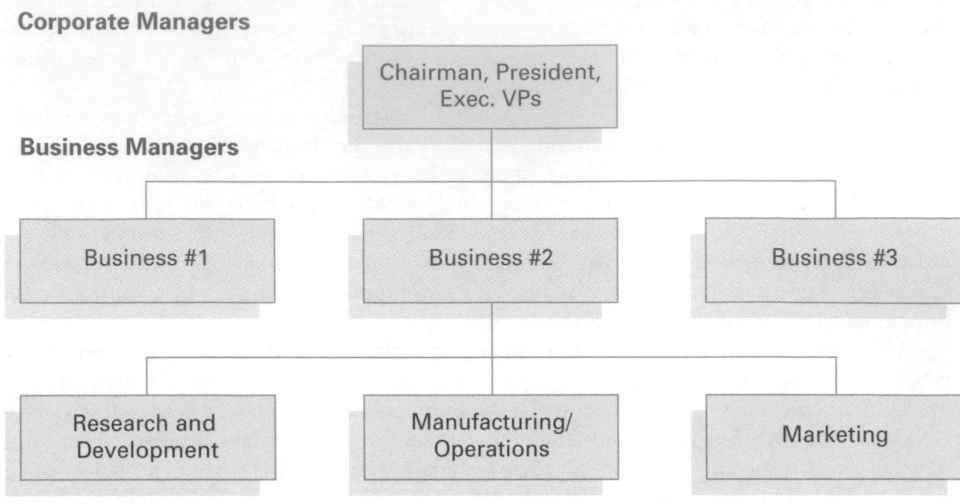

asking themselves many of the same corporate strategy questions as related to their current businesses. What resources can PepsiCo's various businesses usefully share to apply and sustain competitive advantage? How can the marketing skills developed at Frito-Lay be used to help the beverage unit and vice versa?

Strategic Imperatives

Firms facing different strategic situations must generally deal with quite different strategic imperatives. Three common strategic situations and their corresponding strategic imperatives are summarized in Exhibit 1-5.

Sustain Advantage. In many industries, large established firms possess substantial knowledge, highly refined distinctive competences, knowledge of their customers' needs, and considerable experience in competing in their respective industries and individual segments. However, changes in the environment can seriously erode these advantages. Consequently,

EXHIBIT 1-5 Different Strategic Imperatives

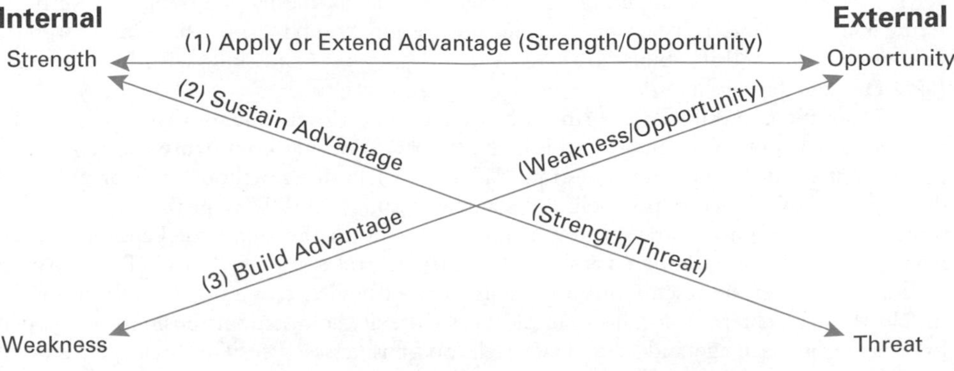

environmental change represents a potential threat to established firms. A major strategic imperative facing such firms is to sustain advantage in the face of environmental threat.

In recent years, McDonald's (as well as its larger rivals, such as Burger King and Wendy's) has had to deal with this kind of strategic imperative. First, the growing health consciousness of American consumers means that McDonald's cannot rely solely on its traditional hamburger-centered menus for sustained growth. Second, the rise of new competitors makes McDonald's expansion difficult without considering their response. These developments compel McDonald's to devise alternative strategies to sustain high performance and profitability in the fast-food restaurant industry. These include offering salads and lower-priced "value" meals to halt the erosion of its market base.

Build Advantage. Chili's situation is very different from McDonald's. As a much smaller competitor, it lacks McDonald's enormous size, pervasive market presence, and extensive operating experience. The strategic imperative it faces is to build advantage to overcome this initial weakness. To satisfy this imperative, a firm must generally seek market opportunities that do not force it to compete directly with its larger and more powerful rivals. It will generally need to achieve some type of distinction in customers' eyes by offering innovative product features, providing superior service, creating a unique experience, using novel distribution channels, or promoting an unusual image. Such an approach may enable it to satisfy some customers without triggering massive retaliation from well-established rivals. Chili's has adopted this approach by focusing on sit-down customers who want fun, friendly service, and good food. Although its restaurant menus initially had a strong hamburger-oriented focus, Chili's now offers alternative meals—such as grilled chicken, salads, and other foods—designed to appeal to different tastes and health-conscious consumers. Chili's has also differentiated itself from McDonald's by offering superior customer service. These modifications enable it to operate without subjecting itself to head-on competition from McDonald's for the same customers.

Extend Advantage. Some firms discover that the capabilities they have developed in one business can be used in another. Entry into the new arena enables them to extend advantage beyond their original domain. PepsiCo found itself in this situation when it concluded that the capabilities developed in its beverage and snack food businesses could be usefully applied to restaurants. These capabilities include extensive knowledge of customer buying habits, market segmentation skills, and market research and advertising prowess. Acting on this belief, it acquired such well-known restaurant chains as KFC, Taco Bell, and Pizza Hut during the 1970s and 1980s.

Over time, PepsiCo, like many other firms that diversified into new areas, discovered that transferring skills from one business to another is a very complicated organizational endeavor. Oftentimes, senior management cannot implement the sharing of skills or capabilities from one business to another very effectively or quickly. The economic and organizational costs of managing multiple businesses can often outweigh the potential benefits. PepsiCo suffered from this difficulty. Also, by the mid-1990s, competition in the restaurant industry had become much fiercer and required a new set of skills such as fast product innovation and franchising expertise to compete effectively. These skills were significantly different from those possessed by PepsiCo. Having concluded that it was unable to provide its restaurant businesses significant assistance and value, PepsiCo ultimately spun off its restaurants to shareholders as a separate corporate entity.

Text Overview: The Key Challenge of Competitive Advantage. These three challenges provide the primary organizing framework for this text. These strategic imperatives apply to all firms in all industries. See Exhibit 1-6 for a summary of how the different chapters in this book fit into this framework.

Chapter 2 begins as the first of four chapters that focus on building advantage. It examines the issue of the business environment. Firms compete in two basic types of environment: the general environment and the more specific, industry-competitive environment. We discuss the five forces that determine an industry's structure and how that structure influences the potential for profitability.

EXHIBIT 1-6 Chapter Organization

Strategic Challenge	Key Strategic Management Issues	
Building Advantage (Business Strategy)	Ch. 2	The Competitive Environment: Assessing Industry Attractiveness
	Ch. 3	Firm Capabilities: Assessing Strengths and Weaknesses
	Ch. 4	Opportunities for Distinction: Building Competitive Advantage
	Ch. 5	Competing on the 'Net: Building Virtual Advantage
	Ch. 6	Shifts in Competitive Advantage: Responding to Environmental Change
Applying/Extending Advantage	Ch. 7	Corporate Strategy: Leveraging Resources to Extend Advantage
	Ch. 8	Global Strategy: Harnessing New markets to Extend Advantage
	Ch. 9	Strategic Alliances: Teaming and Allying for Advantage
Organizing for Advantage	Ch. 10	Designing Organizations for Competitive Advantage
	Ch. 11	Attaining Integration for Advantage
Sustaining and Renewing Advantage	Ch. 12	Cooperation and Autonomy: Managing Interrelationships
	Ch. 13	Managing Strategic Change: Building Learning Organizations
	Ch. 14	Redefining Advantage

In Chapter 3, we present tools to analyze internal strengths and weaknesses. The concept of the value chain is presented, and we also discuss some generalized sources of competitive advantage that apply to firms well established within an industry.

In Chapter 4, we consider how firms develop their competitive strategies. While each firm must formulate its own set of competitive strategies that best match its situation, most business is developed using one of the three basic strategies: low-cost leadership, differentiation, and focus. The crucial role of quality and how the product/market life cycle influences these generic competitive strategies are also presented.

Chapter 5 presents some new issues brought about by the massive growth of the Internet. For example, the notion of e-commerce has become quite popular in recent years. However, the Internet presents numerous opportunities and challenges for organizations to build new sources of competitive advantage. As the Internet assumes a permanent place in our lives, every organization must understand how the Internet can significantly change the way it offers products and services to their customers.

Chapter 6 examines the impact of environmental changes and driving forces on sources of competitive advantage. A competitive advantage developed in one period may not often be as valuable in later time periods. Potential changes in technology, distribution channels, government regulations, and other factors require firms to formulate strategies to deal with change.

Chapter 7 is the first of three chapters that focuses on extending advantage. It introduces the three basic routes firms can take to expand their scope of operations: vertical integration, related diversification, and unrelated diversification. This chapter stresses the point that diversification strategies must be based on the extent to which the firm's distinctive competence can be used to enter new lines of businesses. We also examine some steps that firms can take to reinvigorate their core businesses and operations through restructurings and other measures designed to enhance competitive advantage.

Chapter 8 presents the crucial topic of global strategy. Firms can expand their operations abroad by using global strategies. The economic basis of global strategies and their benefits and costs are analyzed.

Chapter 9 focuses on strategic alliances. In many industries, firms can no longer afford to assume all the risks of developing new products or entering new markets on their own. In fact, almost every large and medium-sized organization will use alliances in some way during their existence. Strategic alliances enable firms to share the risks and costs of new commercial endeavors, but they also raise important trade-offs that management needs to consider.

Chapter 10 is the first of two chapters that focuses on strategy implementation. Strategy implementation is concerned with building an organization to achieve desired advantage. In this chapter, we examine the basic dimensions and types of organizational structure. A well formulated strategy needs a well-designed structure to support it.

Chapter 11 also covers some key topics related to strategy implementation. In the first part of the chapter, we focus specifically on the growth of networked and virtual organizations. These new formats are designed to help firms become more responsive to fast-changing technologies and customer needs. The balance of the chapter discusses the pivotal roles of reward and performance measurement systems, shared values, and corporate culture in generating high performance. These management practices, or organization designs, strongly influence and may even constrain the implementation of a firm's current and future strategy.

Chapter 12 is the first of three chapters focusing on sustaining and renewing advantage. Sustaining advantage means being able to generate high performance consistently over an extended period of time. Chapter 12 focuses on developing distinctive competence by promoting internal interrelationships among different business units. Crucial in this equation is how to strike the right balance between cooperation and autonomy of the firm's various subunits.

Chapter 13 deals with a topic that borders on life-or-death issues for organizations—the process of managing change. Although this is a seminal topic in its own right, we focus more specifically on how firms can become learning organizations. Learning organizations use change as an opportunity to create new sources of competitive advantage, especially as industry environments become faster moving. The concept of a learning organization is still evolving. Since most companies find organizational change a difficult process to manage, we present some steps senior management can take to make the change process easier.

Chapter 14 presents some of the latest developments that are helping firms to sustain and redefine their sources of competitive advantage. Total quality management (TQM), continuous improvement programs, and building quality cultures are vital steps in helping firms renew their competitive advantages. In addition, we consider how firms can redesign their business processes through reengineering and examine some of the benefits and costs associated with it. We also discuss how the latest advances in manufacturing and distribution (Internet) technology are enabling firms to become nimbler and more responsive. These advances are helping transform what companies are doing to design new products and services, as well as to provide them to their customers. In particular, the Internet is also playing a crucial role in linking up manufacturing and service operations with product designers, suppliers, distributors, and even directly to customers. Finally, we look at the emerging "horizontal" organization and how it is different from structures found in most firms today.

Responsibility for Strategic Management

Lower-level employees in an enterprise often possess considerable specialized expertise about such issues as technology, customers, and marketing. This gives them an excellent vantage point from which to identify opportunities and threats and to assess a firm's strengths and weaknesses. One might therefore expect senior managers would turn over to them considerable responsibility for conducting the strategic management process. In fact, senior managers do share such responsibility with employees, at least in part. However, top managers generally must play a primary role because of the large financial outlays associated with strategic decisions, the long-term impact of such decisions, and the considerable controversy that such decisions often provoke.

Characteristics of Strategic Decisions

Large Financial Outlay. Decisions reached through the strategic management process often commit a firm to significant investment of funds. For example, in the high-technology semiconductor (chip) industry, the decision to build a new factory can cost a firm up to $3 billion. In 2001, U.S. semiconductor giant Intel spent over $7.5 billion on capital expenditures alone. Intel sees this huge outlay as a way to learn and apply ever more sophisticated manufacturing techniques to design faster and more powerful chips. In the next few years, a new chip plant will likely cost upward of $5 billion. Other industries face similar situations where high capital expenditures are required to compete in the industry. With its decision to build the Saturn manufacturing plant in Tennessee, General Motors (GM) committed as much as $5 billion over a ten-year period on factory equipment, training, new tools and dyes, robotics, and so forth. Now, GM is trying to use what it learned from the Saturn experience to revolutionize automobile manufacturing in its other divisions; Saturn has already become the "teacher" that shows other GM divisions, such as Chevrolet and Pontiac, how to build small cars effectively. Rolling out a new advertising campaign to promote a new pizza brand at Pizza Hut could cost well over $300 million over several years, with little guarantee that the promotion will be successful. Decisions by Procter & Gamble, Cisco Systems, Citigroup, Microsoft, American Express, Pfizer, Coca-Cola, and PepsiCo to develop new products, launch advertising programs, and acquire other companies often involve very large sums. These are therefore critical strategy issues that fall within the realm of top management.

Long-Term Impact. Decisions reached through the strategic management process are often difficult to reverse. Strategic decisions therefore commit an organization to a particular course of action for an extended period of time. A decision to build a manufacturing facility, for example, involves choices about location, size, manufacturing technology, training programs, and choice of suppliers. Many factors are difficult to alter once a facility has been built. Investment in physical assets, such as a factory, is just one of many decisions that have a long-term impact. Other hard-to-reverse decisions include acquiring another company, forming a strategic alliance, the creation of industry-wide technical standards for new products, and the amount to spend on research and development to foster innovation.

How a firm allocates resources to strengthen its competitive position thus requires both judgment as well as disciplined analysis. Considerable time is generally needed to make changes; during the interim, a firm may not be able to respond to customers' needs or the challenge brought on by new technologies or rivals. Likewise, a decision not to invest in some key activity can also impose its own set of costs. For example, IBM's initial inability to expand capacity quickly to produce its highly popular Think Pad notebook computer gave Japanese competitors easy entry into this extremely profitable segment. In many industries, investments in fixed assets are often considered "irreversible." Unsuitable facilities are also often so specialized that they cannot be sold except at a substantial loss. For example, oil companies such as ChevronTexaco, Royal/Dutch Shell, and BP Amoco are saddled with numerous refinery operations that are quickly becoming obsolete because of new technology and numerous environmental regulations introduced throughout the 1990s. Cleaning up these refineries will add tremendous costs to these firms, thus raising the cost of gasoline for consumers. While these firms might like to liquidate some of their facilities, doing so may be difficult; few buyers are likely to be interested in these specialized and increasingly obsolescent assets. Not all strategic decisions are irreversible, but most exert a long-term impact on the organization. Top managers therefore become involved in strategic decisions in an effort to avoid costly mistakes, but there is no guarantee of their success.

Controversial Nature. Strategic decisions often engender controversy among the firm's managers and employees. Consider a decision by Olympus Optical to customize camera products to meet the needs of individual customers. Sales personnel are likely to favor such a policy, since customization improves their ability to meet customer needs and thereby increases sales volume. It would enable customers to buy different types of cameras with different types of lenses and other features according to their experience level, personal budgets, and color or model preferences. Manufacturing personnel at Olympus would likely resist this move, however, since customization of products significantly complicates the production task, thereby increasing manufacturing costs. Senior managers must oversee and manage controversies of this sort to prevent disagreements from escalating into time-consuming arguments and to ensure that decisions ultimately reached reflect the needs of the overall enterprise.

In recent years, the strategic actions of some companies have invited considerable scrutiny by the government, as well as by investors who question the efficacy of some expenditures. For example, Microsoft faced an inquiry from the Department of Justice in recent years over its economic behavior and massive expenditures to promote the use of Internet Explorer as part of its software offerings for personal computers. Competitors such as Sun Microsystems, AOL Time Warner, and other smaller firms have charged that Microsoft deliberately spends prodigious sums of money to encourage customers to move away from products offered by rivals, thereby creating a de facto monopoly in key aspects of the software business.

Likewise, many people have questioned the significant marketing expenditures undertaken by U.S. pharmaceutical firms to promote products and brand awareness among consumers. Some people in Congress, as well as public interest groups, wonder why companies such as Pfizer, Pharmacia, AstraZeneca, Merck, and Schering-Plough advertise their products so aggressively, yet at the same time they have not reduced the price of their drugs. At the same time, pharmaceutical firms are fighting price controls and the specter of increasing government regulation as their profit margins face continued pressures from new competitors, generic drugs, and the high costs of research.

In another realm, investors have increasingly become more vocal about what management should do to build competitive advantage. Particularly in the last few years, investors are becoming more active in voicing their opinions about key strategic decisions. For example, investors may signal their approval or dislike of a company's decision to acquire another firm. Consider the case of Hewlett-Packard in 2001. Investors responded very coolly to H-P's announcement that it wanted to merge with Compaq Computer. Believing that the two companies would not make a suitable fit, investors sold off their shares in Hewlett-Packard, thus revealing their distaste for the merger.

In the managed care industry, investors also frowned on Aetna's series of decisions in the late 1990s to acquire its rivals, such as Prudential HealthCare, NYLCare, and other health maintenance organization (HMO) firms. Because Aetna faced significant difficulties and cost overruns when attempting to integrate its acquisitions, investors became less confident in senior management's ability to build new sources of competitive advantage and profitability.

Who Are Strategic Managers?

There are two kinds of senior managers most directly responsible for strategy: business managers and corporate managers. **Business managers** are in charge of individual businesses. In a diversified, multibusiness firm (such as IBM), the executives in charge of individual businesses (such as electronic commerce, semiconductors, personal computers, networking systems, storage systems, and consulting) are business managers. These

business managers: People in charge of managing and operating a single line of business.

executives go by a variety of titles, including business manager, general manager, division manager, and strategic business unit manager. The president and chairperson of a single business enterprise (e.g., Papa John's International, Domino's Pizza, or McDonald's) are also business managers.

corporate managers: People responsible for overseeing and managing a portfolio of businesses within the firm.

Corporate managers are responsible for portfolios of businesses. Consequently, corporate managers exist only in multibusiness firms. The president and chairperson of a multibusiness enterprise are corporate managers. Multibusiness firms containing large numbers of businesses often assign executives to positions midway between individual businesses and these senior executives. Each such individual oversees a subset of the firm's total portfolio of businesses. Since each of these individuals has supervisory responsibility for several businesses, these executives are considered corporate managers as well. They go by a variety of titles, including group vice president, executive vice president, and sector executive.

Both business and corporate managers play pivotal roles in the strategic management process. They are the key people who bring all other assets into play when competing with other firms. They also represent the highest levels of authority within the firm or subunit. As a result, they exert enormous influence over the company's capital expenditures to build new plants or to acquire other companies, chart the future direction of the firm's growth, and direct the firm's efforts toward emerging market opportunities. Top managers often serve as the spokespersons for their firms when dealing with the media over such issues as breakthrough technologies, new product rollouts, or potential allegations against the company by shareholders, customers, or communities. Thus, top managers perform multiple tasks at the highest level of an organization and bear the highest responsibility for their firm's strategies and actions.

At the same time, customers, investors, employees, and even the public at large depend on the judgment, experience, and skills of these managers to compete both fairly and within the law. For the vast majority of companies in the United States, senior managers continue to work long hours formulating strategies and action plans that aim to satisfy their customers, reward their investors, develop their employees, and foster a larger sense of public trust. However, business is not immune from scandalous activities that can mar the reputation of entire industries for an extended period of time. Consider the recent series of events that surround the collapse of the Enron Corporation, an energy giant that had tremendous ambitions to expand into a variety of businesses. When Enron declared bankruptcy in November 2001, it not only cost investors a tidy sum but also inflicted a calamity on its employees. These people believed that they were working for a firm with a bright future. Moreover, almost all employees had their retirement assets tied to the value of Enron stock, and they were prevented from selling their stock at a crucial time when the company's fortunes were rapidly declining. When Enron ultimately collapsed, all of these employees faced dire financial futures. At the same time, many senior executives were able to sell their stock in the months ahead before the true depth of Enron's financial troubles surfaced in the news. Scandals such as these put American business on the defensive, since the public becomes more skeptical, and even cynical, about the motives (and even the integrity) of senior management.

What Decision Criteria Are Used?

The strategy concept helps managers deal with competitive realities. However, competition is not the only factor managers must consider. They must also weigh the needs of stakeholders when making strategic decisions. In the chapters that follow, we will explore some of the dilemmas managers face when attempting to consider the needs of various stakeholders. By way of introduction to this material, let us briefly identify key stakeholders of business organizations and the difficulties senior managers often face when attempting to accommodate stakeholders' needs.

Key Stakeholders

Among the most important stakeholders of any business organization are shareholders, customers, workers, the communities in which firms operate, and top managers themselves.

Shareholders. Shareholders provide the equity capital to finance a firm's operation. Therefore, they have a vital stake and say in its welfare. Although most shareholders are interested in earning a return on their investment, individual shareholders may have differing preferences for the timing of returns (some being interested in immediate benefits, others in long-term returns), varying tolerances for risk taking (some preferring to strictly limit risk, others to assume more risk to reap potentially higher returns), and differing needs for maintaining control of the firm. Feasible strategic alternatives often will have a different impact on these different dimensions. Senior managers must strive to select an approach that reflects the relative importance shareholders attach to each dimension.

How top managers deal with shareholders' concerns is becoming increasingly important to the fate of companies and to the careers of top managers. A growing number of chief executive officers (CEOs) at leading firms have been dismissed in recent years because of their inability to generate sufficient return to their shareholders. For example, companies such as General Motors, Ford Motor Company, Sears, JCPenney, 3M, Honeywell International, Procter & Gamble, and The Home Depot have sought new CEOs in the past few years to deal with new challenges that face their respective firms. Even IBM had to replace its CEO in the early 1990s as it sought to chart a new direction in the wake of fast-changing technology and customer needs. Louis Gertsner, IBM's CEO from 1993 to 2002, crafted a strategic balancing act that sought to build new sources of competitive advantage for "Big Blue" in the wake of a changing computer industry, while ensuring that the company remained responsive to its shareholders' needs for steady dividends. Shareholders exercise important powers, enabling them to oblige top executives to take the necessary steps to maintain or restore profitability of the firms they manage. Senior management owes a **fiduciary responsibility** to their shareholders. A fiduciary responsibility means that managers must act in the financial interest of shareholders, since shareholders directly or indirectly hire the top management of a company.

fiduciary responsibility: The primary responsibility facing top management—to make sure the firm delivers value to its shareholders, the owners of the firm.

At the same time, shareholders take on a degree of financial risk by investing in company stock. For example, a number of well-known companies declared bankruptcy in the wake of serious economic difficulties. Companies such as Kmart (retailing), Montgomery Ward (retailing), Finova (financial services), and Global Crossing (telecommunications) are just a few firms that have experienced very grave competitive issues.

Customers. As noted earlier in the discussion of the concept of strategy, competition requires that firms satisfy the needs of customers or go out of business. A firm's responsibility to customers does not simply end there, however. Customers are often unaware of many aspects of the products and services they buy. Product quality, integrity, and safety are absolutely essential issues that managers must consider when designing and selling products or services to the buying public. A firm failing to consider such factors risks loss of reputation, potentially onerous legislation, costly liability litigation, and even imprisonment of managers. To avoid such risks, senior managers must keep their broader responsibilities to customers in mind when making strategic decisions.

Employees. Employees typically seek a wide range of benefits that managers must consider when making strategic decisions. These include adequate compensation, benefits, safe working conditions, recognition for accomplishment, and opportunity for advancement. Careful attention to such needs can sometimes produce spectacular results. Leading high-technology firms such as Cisco Systems, Intel, Microsoft, Xerox Corporation, Dell Computer, EMC, and Apple Computer, for example, treat their employees exceptionally well by giving them generous benefits, flexible work hours, and even day care for their children. These progressive companies have achieved considerable success producing state-of-the-art products and technical solutions that are consistently in high demand. By contrast, many U.S. airline companies (e.g., Continental Airlines, Delta Air Lines, and American Airlines) have experienced difficult relations with their employees. High labor costs severely eroded the long-term profitability of almost every major U.S. airline. Over time, management's initiatives to cut labor costs resulted in decreased employee morale, shoddier service, and poor management–labor relations. Workers crippled some airlines—specifically Eastern Airlines during the late 1980s—with protracted strikes costing the company millions of dollars.

Employees at many companies also serve in the dual role of shareholders as well. For example, the retirement plans used in many companies (known as 401[k] plans because of the tax code) are used to provide a means for employees to save for their futures. However, many of these plans contain a significant amount of company stock, thus directly tying the fate of employees to that of their companies. Over time, however, increased government regulation, triggered in part by the Enron scandal, will likely allow employees to take on less risk as they build their retirement assets.

Communities. Communities rely on firms for tax revenue, employee income to sustain the local economy, and financial and other support for charitable and civic organizations. They are also adversely affected when a firm's facilities pollute the air, burn down, or close down. Thus, communities have a vital stake in the health and integrity of firms operating within their borders. Since communities have legislative authority, they are in a strong position to enforce their wishes. Senior managers must therefore keep community needs in mind when formulating strategies. Cummins Engine, a leading manufacturer of diesel engines for trucks and construction equipment, has paid careful attention to community needs. It works closely with the city of Columbus, Ohio, the site of its corporate headquarters. Cummins is a leading contributor to many civic activities in Columbus; it also is one of the few companies that does not avoid paying a high level of taxes to the city to fund numerous municipal programs. Ben and Jerry's Ice Cream works with neighboring communities in its home state of Vermont to promote a clean environment and social programs. Eastman Kodak works closely with government officials in Rochester, New York, the site of its corporate headquarters, to design community self-improvement programs that enable people to learn skills through education. Corporate and city/state managers often meet together to discuss vital economic and social issues that affect the needs of workers and people in the larger community.

Senior Managers. To lead their organizations and implement strategy effectively, senior executives must be personally enthusiastic and committed to the direction of their firms. Managers often have varying preferences for goals such as a firm's size (over $100 million in annual sales), growth rate (at least 20 percent per year), the areas in which a firm competes (high-tech businesses only), and location of facilities (global operations). Top managers need to consider their own personal skills and experiences in developing strategies so that they can feel committed to the course the firm is pursuing. Above their own needs, of course, must come needs of shareholders when evaluating and developing strategies that affect the long-term value of the firm.

Difficulties in Accommodating Stakeholders

The task of accommodating stakeholder needs is complicated by several factors. First, as even this cursory overview indicates, stakeholders have a great variety of needs. Second, the relative strength of such needs is often difficult to determine. The willingness of shareholders to accept risk, for example, or a community's tolerance for pollution is often exceedingly difficult to judge. Third, individuals within each stakeholder group often have conflicting needs. For example, as noted previously, individual shareholders may have different risk reward preferences: some desiring a risky strategy with high potential returns; others prefer a more conservative approach, even if it offers lower returns. Perhaps most difficult of all are conflicts that arise between stakeholder groups. Shareholders, for example, may favor reducing water pollution control expenditures to increase short-term profitability, while the community in which a firm operates disapproves of such a step because of its increased risk of water contamination.

Conflicts such as these are often called **ethical dilemmas** because they pit the needs of one stakeholder group against those of another. Ethical dilemmas can occur during the strategy selection process and pose some of the most troublesome strategic issues managers confront. To resolve them, managers must carefully weigh the claims of contending parties, a complex task requiring great sensitivity, balance, and judgment. It is not our purpose here to provide definitive guidance in this area. However, it is useful to mention three criteria managers must consider when assessing conflicting stakeholder claims: legal obligations, expectations of society, and personal standards of behavior.

ethical dilemmas: Difficult choices involving moral, legal, or other highly delicate issues that managers must weigh and balance when considering the needs of various stakeholders. Ethical dilemmas work to shape and sometimes constrain a firm's ability to take certain actions.

Legal Obligations. At the very minimum, managers must devise strategies that are within the law. Failure to do so can lead to severe consequences such as fines, public censure, and even imprisonment. For example, bond traders at several investment banking and securities firms in the United States, Japan, Singapore, and elsewhere engaged in a wide range of speculative illegal activities to corner various commodity markets during the 1990s. Such blatantly illegal actions have exerted a high cost on both the firms and their managers. Many of these traders eventually found themselves imprisoned, while the firms (e.g., Daiwa Securities, Barings, Sumitomo) themselves came under extreme scrutiny by different governmental agencies in the United States and abroad.

Societal Expectations. Managers must also strive to meet the broader expectations of the communities in which they operate, even when such expectations are not explicitly codified into law. Failure to do so can lead to costly litigation. Unfortunately, many companies have taken actions that cost their trust with the public. For example, thousands of patients sued pharmaceutical giant American Home Products for medical conditions that well may have resulted from the taking of some controversial diet drugs during the 1990s. Even more astounding was the constant refusal by tobacco companies to acknowledge a key link between smoking and cancer. Even through much of the 1990s, executives from tobacco companies vociferously defended their companies' viewpoints that smoking was not a major factor related to the high incidence of lung cancer. As a result, the government began to investigate the marketing, product development, and advertising practices of tobacco companies; public pension and retirement funds sold their shares in tobacco companies as a sign of protest; and numerous states began to sue the companies for reimbursement of smoking-related health costs. Over time, the tobacco companies were forced to change their marketing practices and to pay huge sums to different states as part of a larger tobacco settlement that cost the industry tens of billions of dollars. Yet, the tobacco companies face continued legal difficulties as some cancer patients are suing the same companies in court. In the early part of the 1990s, other companies faced a number of different issues related to societal expectations of corporate behavior. The numerous lawsuits that confronted Dow-Corning over the safety of its silicone breast implants emphasize to all firms the importance of prioritizing such issues as safety, health, due diligence, and other social responsibility matters. Dow-Corning spent hundreds of millions of dollars and precious time in court defending its reputation and safety practices and paying fines.

Repeated failure to meet societal expectations often inspires the public to take corrective action in the form of additional legislation. All too frequently, such regulation imposes an even greater burden on firms than socially responsible behavior would have imposed in the first place. These regulations often subject firms to more detailed disclosure requirements, time-consuming paperwork, and stricter product safety and testing practices.

Personal Standards. Senior executives can implement strategy effectively only if they feel comfortable with the actions that the strategy entails. A final ethical criterion for judging strategic decisions is thus managers' own personal standards of behavior. Such standards are generally influenced by the laws and the expectations of the communities in which organizations operate; however, they also reflect many personal factors, such as each manager's upbringing, religious convictions, values, and personal life experiences. These, too, must be brought to bear on strategic decisions.

The task of resolving ethical dilemmas is complicated by changes in ethical criteria that occur over time. Legislation governing child labor, worker safety, and job discrimination, for example, has changed markedly over the years; so have societal expectations about such issues as air and water pollution, treatment of minorities, and sexual harassment. To avoid adopting strategies that will soon be obsolete, managers must anticipate rather than simply react to such changes.

Standards of behavior also vary widely across geographic boundaries. German law, for example, requires firms to provide workers formal representation on the board of directors; U.S. law imposes no such requirement. Test requirements for new pharmaceuticals are very onerous in the United States but are significantly less rigorous in many other countries. As a result, drugs whose efficacy and safety have not been fully established by U.S. standards can be legally sold in many other locations. Payoffs to managers and key government officials are illegal in the United States but are common business practice in other locales. Managers operating abroad must decide which standards to apply in resolving ethical dilemmas: those prevailing in their home country or those of the countries within which they operate. The need to consider such differences will be even more critical over the next decade as industries and firms become more global in scope. Meeting the laws, societal expectations, and cultural traditions of regions around the world will be as important to corporate success as meeting the needs of individual communities at home. Becoming a successful global competitor compels firms to think carefully about their actions and the reputations they project in other lands.

Why Study?

What benefit can you derive from studying strategic management? If you are currently a senior manager, the benefit is clear: you can immediately apply the knowledge you will gain. Individuals on track to move into senior management positions will likewise benefit. For many readers, though, that eventuality may be a long way off. However, there are two roles that most readers will soon assume for which an understanding of strategic management can be useful: a candidate seeking employment and an employee or manager within an organization.

Candidate Seeking Employment

Someone seeking employment must assess the long-term career opportunities offered by potential employers. Strategic management can assist in this task by enabling a candidate to evaluate a prospective employer's competitive position, the soundness of its strategy, and its future prospects. This knowledge can help a candidate avoid employers that may soon be forced to retrench because of competitive difficulties. It can also provide an edge in the recruitment process; candidates can distinguish themselves from others by showing an interest in and a deep understanding of a company's strategic situation. Demonstrating an awareness of the competitive dynamics of the industry in which a prospective employer operates, the environmental changes affecting its industry, and the challenges these developments pose improves an individual's chances of employment success. Likewise, it is important that prospective employees, as well as current managers and employees, understand some of the key factors that drive the basis for competition in their industry. A heightened awareness of how companies compete, how technologies change, and the decisive role of customers in deciding the fate of companies will help all people become more sensitive as to how they contribute value to their employers. This book will provide a foundation for this kind of awareness.

Employee or Manager

Entry- or lower-level employees and managers are often closer to the action in the specialized areas of a firm's operations than top managers. Consequently, they are in a better position to detect developments with potential implications for strategy. By keeping abreast of such matters, understanding the implications of new developments, and communicating their judgments upward, lower-level employees can provide valuable service to their superiors and senior managers. An understanding of strategic management will help lower-level employees and managers fulfill this function.

Lower-level employees and managers need to understand strategic management for a second important reason. They are critically responsible for implementing company strategy within their own particular spheres of activity. While superiors will normally provide some guidance on how to do this, their directives cannot anticipate every possible contingency. As a result, lower-level employees and managers must make many decisions on their own. To do so in a way that reinforces rather than undermines what top management is trying to accomplish, lower-level employees need to understand a company's strategy and the requirements it imposes for their particular activities.

A growing awareness and appreciation for strategic thinking can help all employees understand how changes in the industry environment can ultimately affect their company's competitive posture. The need for continuous strategic thinking becomes especially important as every organization in every industry confronts a variety of challenges each day, including new technologies, new forms of competition, changes in regulations, and shifting customer needs. As managers and employees become better versed in understanding the impact of their firms' strategies, they can also play an even stronger role in helping learn, build, and sustain new sources of competitive advantage. Likewise, a growing familiarity and comfort with strategic thinking can help managers and employees advance within their careers. As managers and employees gain increasing levels of responsibility and authority, they will need to be able to think strategically, especially as it relates to allocating scarce resources, people, and time to complete their projects and tasks. Thus, strategic thinking and strategic concepts are by no means the sole domain of senior management; quite the contrary—anyone in any position can benefit from learning and applying key strategic principles to their own roles and lives.

Summary

- Strategy is a powerful concept designed to help firms gain a competitive advantage over rivals. It involves two key choices: the customers a firm will serve and the competences and strengths it will develop to serve customers effectively.
- A firm's choices must reflect its strengths and weaknesses relative to rivals and the opportunities and threats presented by its external environment. Analysis of these four elements is referred to as SWOT analysis.
- All firms must deal with the strategic imperatives facing them according to their own individual situations.
- The management process designed to satisfy strategic imperatives is called a strategic management process. It consists of four major steps: analysis, formulation, implementation, and adjustment/evaluation. The issues that managers confront when carrying out these steps will be unique to each firm, depending on the imperatives and situations it faces.
- Because strategic choices frequently involve a large financial outlay, have long-term impact on an organization, and generate considerable controversy among organizational members, top or senior managers generally play a primary role in determining such decisions.
- Executives most directly responsible for strategic decisions are business managers and corporate managers. A business manager is in charge of an entire business; a corporate manager oversees a portfolio of businesses.

- Competitive advantage is one important criterion by which to assess strategic decisions. It is not the only such criterion, however. Strategic decisions must also satisfy the numerous and often-conflicting needs of various stakeholders: shareholders, customers, employees, communities in which firms operate, and top managers.
- Knowledge of strategic management is useful not only to those who currently occupy or will soon occupy top management positions but also to individuals seeking employment with organizations operating in a competitive environment and to lower-level personnel employed by such organizations.

Endnotes

1. Data and facts for the restaurant industry were adapted from the following sources: "Wendy's See Future Growth in Acquisitions and Ventures," *Wall Street Journal*, February 11, 2002, p. B4; "Pie in the Sky: Is Domino's Pizza Worth All the Trouble to Gain Capital?" *Forbes*, September 17, 2001; "McDonald's to Give More Information about Its Ingredients," *Wall Street Journal*, August 14, 2001; "Restaurant Companies' Good Times Slow Down," *Wall Street Journal*, July 10, 2001; "There's Life in the Old Bird Yet," *Business Week*, May 14, 2001, pp. 77–78; "High Court Rejects Review of Pizza Hut's Lawsuit against Rival," *Wall Street Journal*, March 20, 2001; "Taco Bell Chief Has New Tactic: Be Like Wendy's," *Wall Street Journal*, February 23, 2001, pp. B1, B4; "Jack in the Box: This Chain Really Does Think Outside the Box," *Investor's Business Daily*, February 6, 2001, p. A12; "Thirsty for Growth at Pepsi," *Business Week*, October 16, 2000; "McDonald's Breaks with Franchisee Curb," *Wall Street Journal*, October 10, 2000, p. B10; "PepsiCo Renews Pact to Supply Beverages to Tricon Locations," *Wall Street Journal*, June 30, 2000; "PepsiCo's New Formula: How Roger Enrico Is Remaking the Company," *Business Week*, April 10, 2000; "Restaurant Chains Feast on Great Expectations," *Wall Street Journal*, January 17, 2000; "Burger King Seeks New Sizzle," *Wall Street Journal*, April 14, 1999, pp. B1, B6; "Getting off Their McButts," *Business Week*, February 22, 1999, pp. 84–88; "Tricon Is Serving Up a Fast-Food Turnaround," *Wall Street Journal*, February 11, 1999, p. B10, "Burger King Takes on Tweens Role on Cable," *Wall Street Journal*, January 11, 1999, p. A27; "McDonald's Profit Rises 7.4% as Strength in U.S. Offsets Pressure in Asian Markets," *Wall Street Journal*, October 20, 1998, p. B11; "McDonald's Starts Over: Reinventing the Arch," *Fortune*, June 22, 1998, p. 34; "At McDonald's, a Case of Mass Beaniemania," *Wall Street Journal*, June 5, 1998, p. B1; "McDonald's Problems in Kitchen Don't Dim the Lure of Franchisees," *Wall Street Journal*, June 3, 1998, p. A1; "McDonald's Veggie Burger Is Being Tested in the U.S.," *Wall Street Journal*, May 22, 1998, p. A4; "McDonald's Makes Changes in Top Management," *Wall Street Journal*, May 1, 1998, p. A3; "McDonald's Chief Concedes Fast Growth Last Year Took Firm's Focus off Basics," *Wall Street Journal*, April 9, 1998, p. B10; "Does McDonald's Deserve a Break?" *Business Week*, March 3, 1998, p. 13; "McDonald's: Can It Regain Its Golden Touch?" *Business Week*, March 9, 1998, p. 70; "Like Tacos for Quarter-Pounders," *Business Week*, February 23, 1998, p. 47; "McDonald's, in Break from Tradition, Sets Ambitious Target for Profit Growth," *Wall Street Journal*, November 11, 1997, p. A5; "Restaurants: Fast-Food Spinoff Enters Pepsi-Free Era," *Wall Street Journal*, October 7, 1997, p. B1; "McDonald's Arches Lose Golden Luster," *Wall Street Journal*, September 3, 1997, p. C1; "McDonald's Weighs Whether to Drop Arch Deluxe Adult Burger from Menu," *Wall Street Journal*, August 20, 1997, p. A3; "Pepsi's Eateries Go It Alone," *Fortune*, August 4, 1997, p. 27; "Ads the Burger King Way," *Wall Street Journal*, July 14, 1997, p. B2.

2. Many discourses on strategy have evolved over the course of human history. Military history has provided some of the richest sources and "roots" for many concepts underpinning business strategy. Some early examples of discourses on military strat-

egy and history include the following: Sun Tzu's *Art of War*, trans. Samuel Griffith (London: Oxford University Press, 1963); *The Military Maxims of Napoleon*, trans. David G. Chandler (London: Freemantle, 1901; republished, New York: Macmillan, 1987); and Clausewitz's *On War*, from the original German version, *Vom Krieg* (New York: Knopf, 1993). A readable overview of some interesting military strategy concepts with direct relevance to the management of organizations is John Keegan's *The Mask of Command* (New York: Viking Penguin, 1988).

CHAPTER 2

The Competitive Environment: Assessing Industry Attractiveness

Chapter Outline

What You Will Learn

- The nature of the general environment, also known as the macroenvironment
- Macroenvironment influences over competition between firms and organizations
- The nature of the industry environment, also known as the competitive environment
- The five forces that make up the industry environment: barriers to entry, supplier power, buyer power, the availability of substitutes, and rivalry among firms
- The concept of strategic groups
- Techniques companies use to monitor changes in the environment

The Personal Computer Industry in 2001[1]

Ever since its introduction to the public in 1981, the personal computer (PC) has become a mainstay in the office, laboratory, factory floor, home, our briefcases, and now even our cars. The omnipresence of the PC in many ways symbolizes our full arrival in the information or cyberspace age, where the convenience, low cost, versatility, power, speed, and infinitely growing applications of computing power are taken for granted. In fact, twenty years after the PC's debut, the industry is already highly mature, and many analysts are saying that the days of the PC as we know it are numbered. Although many market research firms in years past have claimed that other types of electronic devices will ultimately replace the PC, so far it remains the dominant computing device that most people will use in their day-to-day lives for the foreseeable future. However, the inner workings and technological capabilities of the PC have dramatically changed in ways that were unimaginable as recently as seven years ago.

Let's consider what the PC offered back in the early to middle 1990s. Back then, the average PC had very little memory (sixteen megabits of RAM), little in the way of sound or video playback quality, and no CD-ROM. Hard drives contained approximately 100 megabits (a tiny fraction of today's sixty- to seventy-gigabit hard drive capacities), and most people stored their data on 5.25- or 3.5-inch floppy disks. Only around 1992–1993 did PCs begin to widely incorporate a mouse driver that helped users circumvent the difficulties of relying solely on a keyboard to enter instructions. Users physically had to type in commands to make their computers work. Equally important, PCs were stand-alone devices—for all practical purposes, the Internet did not exist for the public, and the word *modem* remained foreign to most people. What modems that did exist were extremely slow by today's standards, and e-mail had yet to become the popular messaging system that it is today.

In sum, the PC was for the longest time a clumsy-looking, boxlike device that could not interact or connect with other computers, and it operated on software that users frequently loaded up through floppy disks. Most people thought that the word *windows* referred to glass that you could see through in buildings. A highly advanced machine, including monitor and extra disk drive space, would cost consumers close to $3,000.

Today, the PC has metamorphosed to such an extent that, for under $800, a person can buy a sophisticated machine that runs Windows 2000 or XP, has an ultrafast Intel Pentium 4 processor, preloaded with 128 to 512 megabits of RAM (memory), standard CD-ROM or DVD drive, and fast, easy connections to the Internet. In fact, current PCs are more versatile than even the ones produced just a few months ago. Instead of being solely a clumsy, boxlike device, they can now be found in almost every configuration and size, with the latest PCs now designed to look like avant-garde furniture. Each new generation of PC, with substantially more power, speed, and versatility than its predecessor, hits the store shelves or Web sites approximately every twelve to eighteen months.

The growing versatility of PCs to perform a wide array of functions (e.g., standard computing, e-mail, fax capabilities, Internet access, video games, home monitoring systems, video and audio entertainment, moviemaking, CD recording, desktop publishing) is transforming the PC into a multifunctional "network appliance" that serves as the integrated brain of many once-separate conventional appliances and tools. PCs from Apple Computer, for example, enable users to even engage in digital recording, thus allowing consumers to make their own movies at home.

More powerful microprocessors (Intel's line of Pentium III and Pentium 4 chips, Motorola's G4 Processor) and software operating systems (Microsoft's Windows 95, 98, 2000, and XP; and Apple's Macintosh system) developed through the years have made it possible for almost anyone of any age and background to learn to use the PC in a matter of hours. Learning the PC has become so much easier because many of the latest software advances no longer require customers to engage in mind-numbing installation and programming of their machines using hard-to-read, cumbersome instruction manuals. Even the most rudimentary PC sold today (for under $400) can surf the Internet, do your taxes, transmit e-mail, play video games, do spreadsheets, and even allow you to download MP3 files or listen to CDs.

At the same time, however, the average price of personal computers has continued to drop 10 to 20 percent every year. Since 1997, the biggest growth of PCs has occurred in models selling for under $1,000 (also known as the sub-$1,000 PC), which now pack as much power and speed as models that once sold for over $3,500 in 1995–1996. The sub-$1,000 PC in 1998–1999 typically offered a host of standard features, including a fast microprocessor, a built-in software operating system, a CD-ROM drive, stereo speakers, and numerous "ports" to hook up a variety of different computer peripherals, such as scanners, printers, digital cameras, and other novel items. Now, these same features are found on machines that cost less than $800.

The growing power and popularity of PCs, however, are testament to how fast an industry can develop and change over ever-shorter periods of time. Xerox Corporation conceived the first "true" personal computer, according to most analysts, during the mid-1960s. It was hard to use, designed for scientific applications, and certainly not as user-friendly or versatile as we expect today. However, not until companies such as Apple Computer, IBM, Compaq Computer, and others entered the market did the PC become the taken-for-granted product that it is today. The arrival of the Intel microprocessor—the "brains" of the PC—and powerful operating system software (from Apple Computer and Microsoft) triggered the PC explosion that has lasted for over twenty years. Let us examine some of the factors that have dramatically shaped the PC industry over the past ten years and continue to do so.

Intensely Fierce Competition

By early 2002, there were primarily six makers of PCs: Dell Computer, Compaq Computer, Hewlett-Packard, Gateway, IBM, and Apple Computer. Companies such as Toshiba, Sony, and Acer still participate in the U.S. market but have comparatively little share. For all practical purposes, all of these companies (with the exception of Apple) are known as "box makers" or assemblers in the industry—they incorporate microprocessors made by either Intel or Advanced Micro Devices (AMD) and Microsoft software into a plastic or metal casing, and then they ship them out to buyers or directly to consumers. Among these players, price-based competition is extremely fierce, and PC makers are doing whatever they can to squeeze out ever-thinner margins in order to survive. As margins continue to shrink and the industry slows down, Dell Computer appears to be sustaining its lead over the other PC makers. Compaq Computer, Hewlett-Packard, Gateway, and IBM are in the midst of reevaluating just how committed they are to the PC business. Apple Computer, on the other hand, is a lone standout in this industry; it writes and develops its own software (the Macintosh system) to compete with Microsoft, and it tries to become the design trendsetter for the industry. While the company is profitable, it has a very small share of the total market, since its computer software is not compatible with the vast majority of PCs that use the Microsoft Windows operating system. Many of Apple's latest computers are built with novel designs, such as a cube or even a piece of fine furniture, to help distinguish them from other more standardized offerings.

However, this industry is one in which companies can easily enter and disappear just as quickly. Names such as AST Research, Packard Bell, Zenith Electronics, Texas Instruments, Tandy, Commodore, Micron Electronics, and others were once major players but have since quit the industry. At the beginning of 2002, the top five PC makers—Dell Computer, Compaq Computer, Hewlett Packard, Gateway, and IBM—commanded nearly 64 percent of the U.S. market, after having squeezed out many of the players mentioned above after years of competition.

Dueling but Consolidating Standards. The PC industry currently has two competing software operating system standards. One operating system, backed by Apple Computer, is known as the Macintosh operating system. It is extremely user-friendly and runs on proprietary software, which means that the software for an Apple PC will not run on any other computer. The "brains" of the Apple PC is a family of microprocessors made by Motorola. For several years, Apple's highly distinctive Macintosh system commanded premium prices, but its exclusive nature sharply limited Apple's total market share to about 4.2 percent at the beginning of 2002.

The other PC camp (and certainly the more dominant industry standard) is based on Microsoft's Windows operating system. The Windows operating system is based on using an alternative set of software instructions and icons that allow for significant ease of use and efficient organization of the PC's functions. In many ways, the tremendous growth of the PC industry throughout the past decade can be traced to the several versions of the Windows operating system (3.0, 3.1, Windows 95, Windows 98, 2000, XP) that have greatly eased the way consumers can operate their machines. Windows makes it possible for users to load a variety of different programs into their PCs with fast speed and a high level of convenience. Because of the tremendous popularity of Microsoft's Windows operating system, literally thousands of different broad-based software applications (e.g., word processing, spreadsheet, Internet access, etc.) have been designed to use Microsoft's format to make the computer more versatile. Moreover, Microsoft, in sharp contrast to Apple, freely licenses its Windows operating system (and its earlier DOS operating system) to any other PC maker willing to pay a royalty fee. Throughout the 1980s and 1990s, this licensing policy attracted scores of new computer manufacturers and software designers seeking to capture early profits generated by the popularity of Microsoft's various operating systems. Thus, the popularity of Microsoft's operating systems became overwhelming and now represents well over 90 percent of the PC market.

Ease of Entry and Manufacture. PCs are easy to manufacture (assembly of premade parts), although some of the highest-quality machines may use customized parts. For example, the "average" PC requires only an Intel microprocessor (or equivalent AMD) as its central processing unit, a hard disk drive (which provides long-term storage of programs and data), a CD-ROM or DVD drive (for audio/video play and downloads of extremely memory-intensive software programs), a few printed circuit boards, a keyboard, and a monitor. In effect, these six hardware components are so easy to source and assemble that PC manufacture has become almost a cottage industry. With the exception of the microprocessor and the software (which is protected), all other PC components are standard, off-the-shelf items that almost anyone can purchase and assemble. Thus, new firms are easily able to enter the industry, as a few have done in late 1999 (e.g., eMachines, PeoplePC).

Still, it is tough to distinguish one firm's machine from that of another. Economies of scale in PC production are moderate, but the availability of manufacturing capacity and standardized, off-the-shelf technology makes assembly easy and inexpensive. Aside from the microprocessors and the software operating systems (both of which can be readily purchased or licensed), few proprietary technologies or techniques are involved in PC manufacture or distribution. What may keep even more firms from entering the PC industry is the brand recognition (e.g., Hewlett-Packard, Dell) and access to distribution channels (e.g., IBM) that existing firms already enjoy.

Numerous Distribution Channels. PCs can be purchased from almost any large merchandiser, especially those specializing in consumer electronics products. Most important, customers can more easily purchase PCs through the Internet. Dell Computer thrives in this industry through its creative marketing campaigns that offer custom-built PCs that can be ordered through the telephone or the Internet. In fact, Dell Computer got its start in the business by offering computers for sale through an 800 number. Ordering through the Internet has become much more commonplace in the last few years, as customers can contact Compaq, Gateway, IBM, Hewlett-Packard, and others directly through their Web sites. In fact, the growth of the Internet as an alternative distribution channel has made it possible for PC manufacturers to begin imitating Dell's strategy of delivering custom-made machines for individual customers according to their need for speed, power, number of different peripherals (e.g., scanners, printers, DVD, video cards), and price range.

Strong Buyers

The PC industry is full of knowledgeable and powerful buyers. With hundreds of suppliers to choose from, customers are ruthless in their search for higher value and better quality. Until about 1990, the majority of PC buyers were large and small businesses that used the machines to increase their productivity. Now, the weight of buyers is shifting toward people purchasing PCs for the home, with many families looking to purchase a second or even third PC for entertainment or dedicated Internet use. Regardless of what the PC is used for, the consumer is demanding and savvy. Technical vocabulary to describe computer parts and functions is no longer the domain of engineers or specialized salespeople. PCs have already become similar to color television sets during the 1970s and VCRs during the 1980s, with most customers fully aware of what options they need and how much those features should cost. Since most PCs have a minimum standard of quality, power, speed, and memory, competition turns largely on price.

To many customers, brand name has become less important over time. A key issue for the industry is that customers have become conditioned to think and to expect that PC prices will drop dramatically from one year to the next.

Knowledgeable buyers also mean that some customers will not base their purchase decision solely on price. This is particularly true for business and corporate buyers, who often want superior maintenance, software upgrades, and repair service. In most cases, businesses will purchase either directly from large PC manufacturers (Compaq, Dell, Hewlett-Packard, IBM) or from value-added resellers who will perform much of the maintenance, warranty work, and system upgrades when new technologies or software applications enter the market. Thus, there are opportunities for some PC makers to stake out important market niches with customers who seek additional security and fast service for their machines.

Strong Suppliers

Microchips. Some of the most important suppliers to the PC industry are the manufacturers of microprocessors, memory and graphics chips, and printed circuit boards, which represent the guts of the machine. Large chip makers with the capability and manufacturing prowess to make both PC components and the PC itself include Intel, Advanced Micro Devices (AMD), IBM, Motorola, Toshiba of Japan, Via Technologies of Taiwan, and a host of smaller semiconductor manufacturers. Even Sun Microsystems' line of UltraSparc microprocessors could be used for high-end desktop computers that serve as engineering workstations. Some companies additionally provide many of the specialized graphics and digital signal processing chips used in PCs—such as Nvidia and Texas Instruments—but do not actually directly participate in the PC industry themselves. Nvidia, for example, is probably better known for making the graphics chips that power Microsoft's Xbox video game console. For the most part, however, Intel and AMD vie with one another to sell microprocessors to PC manufacturers, while a larger number of firms supply the memory chips (DRAMs) needed for PCs (e.g., Micron Technology, Samsung Electronics, Toshiba, NEC, Hynix Semiconductor).

Computer Peripherals. Computer peripherals broadly include all hardware components and add-ons necessary to make the PC more complete and fully versatile. These include such important components as disk drives, monitors, scanners, printers, CD-ROM drives (to play music or to download software), DVD (digital video disks that play movies or store data), video cards (that make full-motion video possible on the screen), and even digital cameras (to take pictures that do not require conventional film). These peripheral components have become increasingly vital to how customers use their PCs to move beyond standard computing tasks. In fact, adding ever more powerful peripherals is an important way for PC makers to distinguish their machines from rivals and to attempt to slow down price-based competition. However, the prices of many peripherals (especially scanners, monitors, and printers) are themselves dropping 20 percent or more every year as well.

Important disk drive suppliers to the PC industry have included companies such as Seagate, Quantum, Western Digital, Applied Magnetics, and Read-Rite. IBM, in particular, has innovated a number of key advances in designing and building ultra-small disk drives that can hold unprecedented amounts of data (e.g., 100-gigabit drives). IBM is also a leading supplier of key storage components to both its own PC unit, as well as to Dell Computer. Major manufacturers of printers include Hewlett-Packard, Canon, Seiko-Epson, and Lexmark, all of whom are technological leaders in this critical peripherals business. The traditional names in consumer electronics—Sony, Philips, Matsushita, and others—are key players that make many of the CD-ROM and DVD components. In sum, suppliers of all key PC components, from chips to circuit boards to hardware components, are large and have the technological prowess to enter the industry should they choose to do so.

A Budding Potential for Substitutes

Although few direct substitutes currently exist for standardized PCs at today's low prices, the potential clearly exists for new products and technologies to redefine and reshape the way PCs are designed, made, sold, and used. Even smaller PCs have already made major inroads into this market, as we are now witnessing with the explosion of laptop, notebook-sized computers. Laptop models are more stylish and can replace the bulky monitors and keyboards associated with conventional PCs. However, the real growth in substitute products will likely occur with the growing availability of hand-held, palm-top computers or personal digital assistants (PDAs) that can perform many PC functions without a keyboard. These hand-held machines, such as those popularized by Palm and Handspring, may very well signify the rise of new types of wireless network appliances that eventually replace other devices such as the cellular phone, the pager, and even the laptop itself over time.

Other potential substitutes include the video game consoles made by Nintendo, Sony, and even Microsoft. Today's leading-edge video game consoles already come with Internet connectivity, Intel-class microprocessors, extremely sophisticated graphics chips, and DVD drives. Some analysts have speculated that video game consoles may become the primary electronic appliances that young children and adolescents will use in their most formative years. Thus, these future buyers will likely demand that future PCs or other electronic devices are as simple to operate as their game consoles.

Introduction

environment: All external forces, factors, or conditions that exert some degree of impact on the strategies, decisions, and actions taken by the firm.

Managers need to understand the strong influence the environment exerts on their firm's strategies and operations. A firm's **environment** represents all external forces, factors, or conditions that exert some degree of impact on the strategies, decisions, and actions taken by the firm. This chapter focuses on the task of environmental analysis and its pivotal role in strategy formulation.

Every firm in every industry exists in an environment. Although the specific types of environmental forces and conditions vary from industry to industry, a number of broad environmental forces exert an impact on the strategies of every firm. In this chapter, we focus on two types of external environments: the broader macroenvironment and the industry-specific, competitive environment. In the first section, we selectively examine several key factors and conditions that make up the broader macroenvironment and discuss how they relate to all firms, regardless of industry. In the second section, we analyze a more industry-specific type of environment, the firm's competitive environment. The competitive environment refers to the forces and conditions directly relevant to the industry in which a firm competes. In other words, the competitive environment focuses on the particular factors that define a specific industry setting. We then examine the concept of strategic groups. Strategic groups help reveal specific differences in competitive behavior among firms within an industry. In the last section, we discuss techniques that firms can use to monitor their external environments to formulate their strategies.

The Macroenvironment

macroenvironment: The broad collection of forces or conditions that affect every firm or organization in every industry (also known as *general environment*).

general environment: The broad collection of forces or conditions that affect every firm or organization in every industry (also known as *macroenvironment*).

The **macroenvironment**, also known as the **general environment**, includes all of those environmental forces and conditions that have an impact on every firm and organization within the economy. As such, the macro- or general environment represents the broad collection of factors that directly or indirectly influence every firm in every industry. Consider, for example, such general environmental developments as the aging workforce, the rising trend toward greater health consciousness, changing cost of capital or interest rates, the growing use of technology in all types of products and services, declining birthrates, the impact of terrorism, and growing foreign competition. These factors shape the long-term environment in which all firms must operate. Some factors represent long-term shifts, such as the aging of the U.S. population, the incorporation of new technology to transform products, and the growing prevalence of foreign competition. Other factors have shorter-term impact, such as interest rates, changes in household purchasing power, and exchange rates.

Of course, firms generally cannot control the macroenvironment. Moreover, these factors are often difficult to predict with any real precision. Although numerous factors make up the general environment, several developments that will impact all firms in some way in the twenty-first century will be our focus here. Specifically, we will consider developments in the demographic environment, the political environment, the social/cultural environment, the technological environment, and the global environment.

The Demographic Environment

Demographics describe the broad characteristics of people that make up any geographic unit of analysis, such as nation, state or region, or county/prefecture. The importance of changes in demographics lies in their influence on the eventual makeup of each firm's workforce, on human resource practices, on marketing, and on the growth of the firm. Let us examine some key demographic trends that are now redefining the United States.

Perhaps one of the most important and lasting changes over the past thirty years in the United States has been the steady arrival and participation by women in the workforce. Already, women make up close to half of the workforce, and their numbers are expected to continue to grow as they find ways to balance the pursuit of a professional career with choices about raising families. Clearly, women have made substantial gains in numerous professions once dominated by males, such as law, accounting, management consulting, engineering, and other high-paying occupations. However, they remain extremely underrepresented at the highest level of management in the vast majority of companies today.

Women have begun to make their presence felt on boards of directors and the ranks of chief executive officers (CEOs) of large U.S. firms. For example, in late 2001, such companies as Hewlett-Packard, Avon Products, Exodus Communications, Xerox Corporation, and Lucent Technologies had women as CEOs. Anne Mulcahy, CEO of Xerox Corporation, hopes that in the future all women will be able to break through the "glass ceiling" that appears to limit how far women can advance within their firms, no matter how capable they are. Women from all types of industries and firms are increasingly forming their own professional networks to provide mentoring, career advice, and new career opportunities to one another. Still, despite the substantial gains made in the late 1990s, women still are confronted with decisions about careers and families that their male counterparts have not typically faced. Many companies recognize the enormous talent and contribution of their female managers and workforces, and have begun instituting new type of family-friendly programs (e.g., child care, flexible leaves, new types of employee benefits) that are designed to support and retain this vast reservoir of talent. Firms such as IBM, Johnson & Johnson, Procter & Gamble, Eastman Kodak, and Ford Motor Company are just a few of leading U.S. companies taking concrete steps to offer real opportunities for their female managers to grow.

Another important demographic factor is the changing racial composition of the United States. A major ongoing challenge for managers of minority descent is to create sustainable personal networks that allow them to interact with people inside and outside the firm. By creating a strong network, a manager is better able to leverage his or her knowledge, experience, and personal relationships to open up new opportunities for advancement.[2] On a broader theme, America is becoming much more diverse. For example, the Hispanic population is growing much faster than other racial groups and represents nearly one-third of the local population in many states such as California, Arizona, and Texas. Asian Americans also make up a growing percentage of the U.S. population.[3] While the United States has confronted and benefited from rising tides of immigration in previous decades (e.g., 1840–1860; 1890–1910; 1970s), the massive influx of people from different ethnic and religious backgrounds also presents a new set of imperatives for U.S. companies. For example, with the rising numbers of immigrants from South and Southeast Asia, many U.S. firms are capturing the enormous engineering and software design skills of highly trained professionals and scientists who are looking for a better life in this country. Companies located in California's Silicon Valley in particular are hotbeds of innovation—some of the newest ideas and technologies in recent years are also coming from new immigrants who are taking great risks to create new businesses. From the perspective of the restaurant industry case of Chapter 1, one can easily imagine how the rising levels of affluence among different ethnic groups are likely to promote not only more ethnic food restaurants but also a greater demand within the restaurant industry in general.

The average age of the U.S. population is steadily rising. The combination of declining birthrates and longer life expectancy—made possible by improved health conditions—is a trend that will have direct impact on the availability of labor within the U.S. economy. An aging population means that more resources will likely be devoted to health care and medical expenses. Since many senior citizens in the United States tend to be relatively affluent, an aging population implies that more people will have more discretionary income to spend on vacations, resorts, and hobbies. From the restaurant industry case of Chapter 1, one can see how a fast-growing aging population has been a significant influence on the evolution of the restaurant industry. Legions of baby boomers who are more health-conscious have shifted their dietary preferences away from fast food and more toward sit-down meals at restaurants whose menus offer a wide selection of healthy foods.

Unfortunately, an aging population also means that some elderly people who are less well off will spend a significant portion of their lives worried about their financial means. In particular, the rising population of senior citizens has also placed significant pressures on the pharmaceutical industry to rein in the prices of some key drugs that help treat cardiovascular and other diseases. In recent years, the government has explored the potential of instituting new policies that may mimic price controls on a broad range of drugs. While price controls will likely devastate the profitability of the pharmaceutical industry, they will also have the unintended effect of suppressing innovation as drug companies retreat from expensive research and development (R&D) expenditures that they may not be able to recoup. All of the drug companies are listening to what their customers and the government are saying, and a number of them are offering specially designed pricing to help senior citizens purchase prescription drugs through new discount programs targeted to them. For example, in 2002, GlaxoSmithKline, Pfizer, and Novartis began to institute significantly lower prices for senior citizens who earn below certain income thresholds.

The Political Environment

Within the United States, the political environment affects business in many ways. For example, in recent years, the government significantly reduced the number of regulations that once shaped many industries. The airline, financial services, and telecommunications industries faced less regulation during the 1990s, thus prompting new entrants and new technologies to redefine how firms compete for business. This trend of deregulation has facilitated greater customer choice for new products and services, thus significantly changing the nature and profitability of many of these industries. Other industries have instead become more regulated. For example, the savings and loan (S&L) debacle that cascaded in to more than $500 billion in losses during the late 1980s resulted in new government regulations concerning bank and S&L activity. New regulations related to electric utilities, pensions, retirement plans, and audits by accounting firms will have an important impact on firms in this decade.

Many of these regulations have come into place because of the scandalous events surrounding the bankruptcy of the Enron Corporation in November 2001. Once listed in the top ten of Fortune 500 companies in 2000, Enron's fortunes began to unwind as the company engaged in many dubious accounting and business practices that were designed to hide the losses and risks that it was taking. By apparently concealing losses and certain projects in the form of limited partnerships, Enron gave the impression that it was profitable, despite the fact that many of its far-flung investments exposed the firm to a variety of risks. Many of the company's finances were hidden in "off-balance sheet" statements that were difficult to understand, even for Wall Street investors and analysts. To make matters worse, Enron's accounting auditors from Arthur Andersen destroyed key documents in order to eliminate the "paper trail" that showed what the oil and gas giant was doing. As the company's stock price dropped from a peak of $90 a share to less than a dollar in several months, Enron's middle managers and employees were prevented from selling their shares at the same time that senior executives were able to sell their stock positions. The debacle surrounding Enron opened numerous investigations by Congress, the Securities and Exchange Commission, and law enforcement agencies. Even as investigations by the federal government began in earnest in spring 2002, Enron continued to blatantly shred documents in ways that defied adherence to the law. In 2002 and 2003, it appears that the government may institute even more stringent regulations concerning how firms can compel their managers and employees to invest in company stock in their retirement plans. Thus, government regulation can directly shape the way firms conduct their business across many industries.[4]

A major regulatory trend affecting all U.S. businesses is the renewed emphasis on protecting the environment. With the passage of the Clean Air Act in 1990, more U.S. companies must make environmental protection a crucial part of their long-term strategies, not just an afterthought. For example, many automobile makers (such as General Motors), appliance manufacturers (such as General Electric), and chemical makers (such as DuPont and Dow Chemical) are substituting new types of coolants for the ozone-depleting chemicals used in refrigeration and air-conditioning systems. Semiconductor manufacturers such as Intel, Texas Instruments, Lucent Technologies, and IBM are spending more money on devising new ways to recycle the pollutants that are produced when making microchips. More companies are beginning efforts to recycle their wastes to avoid dumping in saturated landfills. Many steel and utility companies are adopting new types of clean-air manufacturing technologies that prevent contaminants and noxious odors from even entering the air.

At the same time, the costs of the regulations have become so burdensome in some industries that some companies are beginning to close down mines and factories in order to save costs. These closures, in turn, have put many people out of work, leaving them with few economic opportunities. Many companies have decided to relocate their manufacturing facilities outside the United States, partially because of the rising costs and burdens of complying with new forms of regulations. This trend has been especially notable in traditional, "heavy" industries that utilize significant amounts of fossil fuels, petroleum, and other natural resources to create products for consumer and industrial end markets (e.g., plastics, chemicals, synthetic fibers, steel, aluminum). The renewed public and governmental concern with protecting the environment is challenging U.S. business to incorporate environmentally friendly strategies as part of their long-term planning.[5]

Other recent political developments in the United States that affect business include changes in the tax codes, greater assistance to people with disabilities, and new laws that protect people from sexual harassment. Each of these developments has a direct impact on how firms conduct their activities within the economy. Tax codes can enhance or deter investment, depending on the nature of the law. The Americans with Disabilities Act of 1990 is designed to help those with disabilities secure greater employment access and assistance in performing their jobs. In today's environment, changing mores, values, and laws increase the seriousness of sexual harassment as a criminal and civil offense. All of these developments are challenging U.S. business to make the economy and workplace more open to all. Throughout the chapters in this book, we will show how different U.S. companies are responding to the needs of different people and constituencies or stakeholders, such as customers, employees, shareholders, suppliers, and communities.

A new political development confronting the United States is the growing risk that the country faces from military and terrorist actions on American soil. On September 11, 2001, a group of terrorists of Middle Eastern origin orchestrated an attack on America that resulted in the destruction of the Twin Towers of the World Trade Center, as well as an attack on the Pentagon in Washington, D.C. After hijacking four commercial jets operated by American Airlines and United Airlines, the terrorists inflicted a huge loss of life and economic damage on the United States by using the planes as missiles to attack their targets. A planned simultaneous attack on the White House was foiled after the passengers on the fourth jet overpowered the hijackers, resulting in the plane's crash in western Pennsylvania. As the United States enters this new decade, the risk of terrorist actions will likely continue to grow as terrorists and their supporters look for ways to hurt American interests around the world.

Domestically, the terrorist attack already has fundamentally changed the way many industries operate. For example, the airline, hotel, gaming, and travel industries have incurred huge financial losses resulting from travelers who canceled trips and meetings throughout the country. More profoundly, the six major U.S. airline companies (American Airlines, United Airlines, Continental Airlines, Delta Airlines, Northwest Airlines, and USAirways Group) collectively laid off a hundred thousand employees. The losses endured by the airlines were so severe that the Bush administration and Congress worked together to offer an emergency financial rescue package to help the airlines get back on their feet. For the fourth quarter of 2001, American and Continental lost close to a billion dollars alone for that period, while Northwest Airlines and USAirways Group also registered huge losses.[6] Still, financial distress for the industry will likely continue for an extended period as they cut back on their routes and add new security procedures that will slow down the pace of their operations.

Hotel and gaming companies such as Marriott International and MGM/Mirage have also incurred significant losses as travel dropped. Security firms, however, became inundated with business as companies, airlines, and the government sought new means to protect their employees from new types of nefarious attacks.

The Social/Cultural Environment

The social/cultural environment represents the set of values, ideals, and other characteristics that distinguish members of one group from those of another. Firms need to be aware of how social and cultural factors can directly affect the way they manage their operations, particularly human resources and marketing. For example, managers need to be increasingly aware of and sensitive to the values and ideas of people from different upbringing and backgrounds.

One of the most important developments in the social/cultural environment is the need for greater diversity awareness and training. With the rapidly changing composition of the U.S. workforce, managers and employees must understand how to manage an increasingly heterogeneous work environment. The need for programs that help managers think about diversity issues becomes especially important as a greater number of women and racial minorities enter the workforce.[7]

Another key development in the social environment is the apparently steady erosion of the U.S. educational system. Particularly in inner cities, many students are floundering and thus becoming less employable in U.S. businesses. This trend is alarming, not only because there are fewer young people in the U.S. population as a result of demographic changes, but also because these new employees often are underskilled, which places a greater burden on business to offer remedial training to help young people learn the skills they need to become productive employees. Recently, the Bush administration has passed a new set of legislation through Congress that is designed to tighten educational standards for schools. Also, this same legislation will compel annual testing of student competency in many grade levels so that parents and teachers can see how their children are progressing in educational achievement.

Finally, a key issue all companies will increasingly face over the next few years is the growing demand by managers and employees for more flexible working arrangements. More and more people are now caring for elderly parents, many of whom depend on their sons and daughters to perform both routine and emergency-related care. In a related vein, many working parents need a more flexible schedule to enable them to take care of children during off-school or other unusual hours. This development alone has prompted many companies, such as AT&T, IBM, and Xerox, to offer either corporate day care facilities or increased employee benefits that enable managers and employees to better cope with child care needs. As a growing number of women enter and advance in the workforce, the issue of providing child care will become an increasing challenge for all U.S. businesses.[8]

Technological Developments

New technologies are dramatically reshaping the way American business competes. In just the last few years, for example, several new technologies have begun to transform the workplace and the home once again. The rise of such new offerings as Internet services, faster semiconductors, digital video disk (DVD) players, voice recognition, new types of wireless phones, new biotech-based drugs, and even more efficient automotive engine designs present U.S. companies with a plethora of opportunities to grow their businesses. At the same time that new technology brings forth new products and services, existing products become obsolete and dated even faster. Consider the rapid obsolescence of cellular phones, pagers, fax machines, personal digital assistants (PDAs), and videocassette recorders (VCRs)—products that were considered state-of-the-art in 1998 are now so commonplace that companies have moved to develop new generations of products with features that far transcend their predecessors. The massive growth of the Internet, which allows people to order merchandise and services and to communicate with other people on-line, has already begun to redefine the nature of many industries. Communications technology, in particular, is making it possible for people to relate to each other in ways that make the traditional notions of distance and geography potentially obsolete. New manufacturing technologies in the factory are improving product quality, accelerating turnaround time, reducing inventory costs, and giving firms unprecedented flexibility. In a broader context, new technologies are now making themselves felt in many routine activities, such as overnight mail, electronic commerce, and computers that recognize handwriting and voice.

The explosive growth of new technologies has redefined the U.S. business landscape and presented many opportunities for both entrepreneurs and established firms to create new products for new markets. The rise of new technologies has also spawned entirely new industries within the U.S. economy, such as biotechnology, genomics, specialty semiconductors, voice recognition software, biodegradable plastics, digital media, genetically engineered seeds, factory automation, Internet services, and artificial intelligence. Few of these industries were considered commercially viable even as recently as 1995.

The rapid rise of new technologies also presents many significant challenges. For example, technology can threaten to make some people's jobs obsolete, as is now happening in highly automated steel mills. Growing levels of factory automation displace unskilled and semiskilled labor from once high-paying jobs. The technological challenge is present even in high-paying white-collar positions. Computer programs and spreadsheets redefine the way accountants and financial analysts perform their work. The Internet is transforming how customers order products and services, enabling them to purchase directly from manufacturers and service providers on-line. This development presents a challenge to businesses such as brokers, travel agencies, florists, and other economic entities that previously served as intermediaries between customers and firms providing products and services. In the medical sector, technology is redefining the way doctors perform surgery by providing faster and safer ways to treat diseases and injuries. Advanced robotic technology makes it possible to perform surgery on patients using state-of-the-art "virtual" computers that assist the doctor with continuously updated information and new surgical tools. This growing availability of technology to enhance health care also raises the costs of medical services.

These technological developments challenge the U.S. economy to become more productive and creative in its use of resources. The rapid pace of technological change is likely to continue, as both entrepreneurs and existing firms find new ways to use technology to improve their products and competitiveness. Constant and intense innovation of new products, services, production processes, and distribution capabilities increasingly will become the basis for future growth in the United States and elsewhere. Technological developments represent a real opportunity for firms with the skills to understand and apply them; they simultaneously represent genuine threats for those firms that are slow and cannot adjust to new advances. Throughout this book, we will show how different types of technologies offer new opportunities and challenges to firms in various industries.

The Global Environment

Firms in every industry are facing the rising tide of globalization. Put simply, the world is becoming a smaller place each day, and U.S. businesses need to think about selling and producing goods for customers, no matter where they may be located. Globalization presents an exciting opportunity for many companies, as companies like Coca-Cola,

General Electric, Intel, Cisco Systems, Caterpillar, Boeing, Citigroup, American Express, AT&T, IBM, and Colgate-Palmolive have learned. These companies have developed thriving operations outside the United States and now derive an increasingly high proportion of their revenues from these operations. The rise of new markets outside the United States means many more jobs for U.S. exporters, such as General Electric, Boeing, Caterpillar, and Merck. More prosperity and growth in places such as Brazil, China, India, Russia, and Eastern Europe mean more jobs for U.S. employees and greater opportunities for U.S. firms willing to serve those markets.[9]

At the same time, globalization presents many challenges, of course. As markets become more open, many U.S. industries will feel fierce competitive pressures from more efficient manufacturers abroad. Already, several U.S. industries are reeling from the onslaught of global competition, including shipbuilding, textiles, electronic assembly, toys, and steel. Even high-technology U.S. industries such as memory chips, telecommunication equipment, software, biotechnology, office equipment, and fiber optics are facing significant challenges from competitors abroad.

Globalization can accelerate changes within and across industries. In the auto industry, for example, the unrelenting pressure from Japanese automakers has contributed to the steady decline of market share by U.S. manufacturers over the past two decades. Thus, while Japanese manufacturers held less than 7 percent of the U.S. automobile market in 1972, their share had increased to 25 percent by 1998, after peaking as high as 28 percent in the early 1990s. Now, both Japanese and U.S. automakers face growing pressures from reinvigorated Korean manufacturers who have begun to make steady inroads into the U.S. market. At the same time, General Motors, Ford, and the Chrysler unit of DaimlerChrysler face rising difficulties trying to hold onto their U.S. market shares as the lower cost of foreign currencies make imports more competitive in the United States. Consequently, numerous American autoworkers have been laid off during the past decade, and the trend still continues unabated in 2002.

Not only the automakers but also other companies in the steel, aluminum, memory chip, and aircraft industries face the constant need to restructure their operations to meet the challenge of intensified global competition. Likewise, the suppliers to these industries face similar challenges. Companies that supply glass, rubber, steel, and other automobile parts have also been forced to become more efficient and quality-conscious or close their doors. In sum, foreign competition has obliged the U.S. automotive and other industries to make better products without large employment increases and adjustment costs.

Globalization may also lead to additional financial exposure to U.S. corporations when local economies suffer recessions or major political changes. In 1997, a recession that led to a marked downturn of several Far Eastern and Southeast Asian economies resulted in significant profit declines for many American companies, particularly those selling high-technology products. Although recovery ultimately occurred, the investments in factories and distribution facilities made by U.S. firms exposed them to increased financial risks stemming from volatile foreign exchange rates, currency devaluations, and the loss of purchasing power by local customers. More recently, the near total collapse of the economy in Argentina resulted in significant losses to such U.S. banks as Citigroup, J. P. Morgan Chase, and FleetBoston Financial Corporation. Many of these banks were compelled to write off significant loans they made to large Argentine businesses, as well as to the national government. Some U.S. manufacturers also incurred losses in Argentina as they were unable to sell their capital goods to customers who could no longer afford to pay in dollars.[10]

On top of these changes, many sectors of U.S. industry are becoming more global in their own right. Consider again the automotive sector. Chrysler merged with German giant Daimler-Benz in a huge trans-Atlantic merger in July 1998 to form DaimlerChrysler. This transaction spurred other acquisitions by Ford (e.g., Volvo's automobile unit, Land Rover) and by General Motors (e.g., Saab of Sweden, higher equity stakes in Japan's Isuzu, Suzuki, and Fuji Industries) throughout Europe and Asia. Elsewhere, the financial services industry witnessed the cross-Atlantic mergers of many banking and insurance firms that are looking to expand operations in both regions. For example, Dutch, French, and British insurance firms are looking to merge with their U.S. counterparts, as well as with banks in order to expand their presence here and to lower the cost of their capital. Even the telecommunications and publishing industries have become more global, as European and American firms form cross-border ties that include alliances as well as outright mergers. One such relationship is the growing relationship between Qwest Communications International with Dutch telecommunications firm KPN, NV. Both telecom firms are looking to expand the opportunities to develop new means to transmit voice and data communications across trans-Atlantic markets. The venture, known as KPNQwest, also allows KPN to receive significant new technologies and funding to help the Dutch firm become more competitive to compete against such larger European behemoths as Deutsch Telecom, Vodafone PLC, and BT.[11]

Many countries and regions of the world seek to consolidate their national markets into larger trading blocs in which member countries receive preference for imports and purchases. This development presents difficulties for firms operating outside those blocs. For example, the rise of the European Economic Community (EEC) raises difficulties for U.S. firms in such critical industries as commercial aircraft, automobiles, chemicals, computers, agriculture, and electronics. The rise of the Euro as a common European currency to be shared among the majority of European nations also presents an indirect challenge to the U.S. economy, as it enables European firms to achieve greater critical mass and currency stability in their operations back home. Countries such as France, Germany, Italy, and the United Kingdom have begun to think about economic battle plans that facilitate greater coordination of activities among their countries' large industrial firms to counter feared U.S. economic dominance, especially in certain high-tech markets such as aerospace, defense, automotive, communications, and high-technology arenas.

Interest in economic consolidation of markets is also growing in the Western Hemisphere. In the mid-1990s, the United States and every other country in the Western Hemisphere (except Cuba) began working on a plan to create a free-trade zone that would extend from Alaska to Argentina by 2005. Already, the United States has offered Chile an opportunity to join the newly created North American Free Trade Agreement. NAFTA was inaugurated in 1994 to create a free-trade zone between Canada, the United States, and Mexico. Some of these discussions face new difficulties, however, as Argentina recently faced enormous difficulties in meeting its foreign debt obligations. In December 2001, Argentina defaulted on its sovereign debt and faced numerous rioters in the street who were protesting the economic downturn in that country. Neighboring country Brazil faces its own pending economic issues as its exports become less competitive to other South American countries. Still, several Far Eastern and Southeastern Asian countries are engaged in similar discussions designed to create free-trade zones among such economic dynamos as Singapore, Indonesia, Thailand, and other Asian countries.

The global environment is so important to U.S. business that we will devote an entire chapter to analyzing different types of strategies that U.S. firms can adopt to compete more effectively in an increasingly borderless world.

Assessing the Impact of the General Environment

Firms need to be aware of developments in the general environment as both opportunities and threats. For example, the same environmental trend or development can have dramatically different implications for different industries. Consider the rising consciousness of the need to protect the environment. For industrial companies, meeting the need may add to their costs of doing business. For manufacturers of steel, aluminum, and copper—such as Nucor, Alcoa, and Phelps-Dodge—meeting this need means formulating new strategies and designing new processes that will protect the environment while these companies produce products vital to the economy. Steelmakers face the same pressures to clean up the environment as do aluminum processors and copper refiners. On the other hand, companies such as Waste Management and Hewlett-Packard are more likely to view rising environmental consciousness as an opportunity rather than as a threat. It will likely provide Waste Management an upturn in demand for its efficient waste removal services, while high-tech electronics instrument maker Hewlett-Packard will feel an indirect rise in demand for its measurement products, since laboratory and diagnostic equipment will be needed to track wastes and to find new ways to remove them safely. Thus, the same environmental trend can have different effects on firms in different industries.

Developments in the general environment can also have a differential effect on competitors within a single industry. For example, the ongoing deregulation and convergence of financial services now enables securities firms, such as Merrill Lynch and Fidelity Investments, to offer services similar to those of banks. Deregulation of the trucking and airline industries accelerated a "shakeout" of less efficient firms in favor of more efficient ones. Combined with large financial losses, deregulation decreased the number of airlines in the United States. However, deregulation has steadily increased the number of firms willing to become major players in the telecommunications industry. For much of the late 1990s, the telecom industry witnessed the massive entry of new types of competitors offering different technologies and products to "wire" the country with Internet-based services. Potential regulatory changes that affect the cable television and telecommunications industries may make it possible for consumers to access Internet and telephone service from their cable television providers, and vice versa. In addition, consumers are already finding ways to broaden their access to hundreds of television channels through the rise of digital satellite television transmission, regulated by the Federal Communications Commission (FCC). These new technologies enable consumers to gain the benefits of cable TV without a separate hookup in their homes. Thus, a single economic or political development can shift the balance of power and the makeup of entire industries.

Therefore, developments in the general environment can have intended and unintended effects on firms within and across different industries. The general macroenvironment can be regarded as a large pond in which hundreds of different firms live. When a stone is tossed into the pond, it creates ripple effects that all firms will feel. Either directly or indirectly, these ripple effects benefit some firms while hurting others.

competitive environment: The immediate economic factors—customers, competitors, suppliers, buyers, and potential substitutes—of direct relevance to a firm in a given industry (also known as *industry environment*).

industry attractiveness: The potential for profitability when competing in a given industry. An attractive industry has high profit potential; an unattractive industry has low profit potential.

industry structure: The interrelationship among the factors in a firm's competitive or industry environment; configuration of economic forces and factors that interrelate to affect the behavior of firms competing in that industry.

The Competitive Environment

The general environment contains forces and developments that affect all firms within the economy. In addition to these forces, managers must also deal with forces whose effects are limited to their more immediate competitive environment. In this section, we examine the critical dimensions of the competitive environment. The **competitive environment** includes the key forces shaping competition in an industry. Analysis of the competitive environment for any given firm is concerned with assessing how these forces affect the attractiveness of the industry. **Industry attractiveness** refers to the potential for profitability that results from competing in that industry. Each industry's attractiveness, or profitability potential, is a direct function of the interaction of various environmental forces that determine the nature of competition.

The Five Forces Model of Industry Attractiveness

The competitive state of an industry exerts a strong influence on how firms develop their strategies to earn profits over time. Although all industries are competitive, the nature of this competition can differ significantly between industries. For example, competition in the airline industry is somewhat cutthroat and occurs by way of price wars, while firms in the desktop printer industry often compete through enhanced product features and new models.

Competition in an industry is determined by its own particular structure. **Industry structure** refers to the interrelationship among five different forces that drive behavior of firms competing in that industry. How firms compete with one another in any given industry is directly related to the interaction of these five key forces. As initially developed by Michael Porter, these five forces are as follows:

- The threat of new entrants into the industry
- The bargaining power of customers
- The bargaining power of suppliers
- The intensity of the rivalry among firms within the industry
- The potential for substitute products or services

Porter's *five forces* model is one of the most effective and enduring conceptual frameworks used to assess the nature of the competitive environment and to describe an industry's structure. This chapter draws heavily from his work on competitive industry analysis.[12] Exhibit 2-1 shows how these five forces interrelate to determine an industry's attractiveness. A highly attractive industry is one in which it is comparatively easy to make profits; an unattractive industry is one where profitability is frequently low or consistently depressed. The interrelationships among these five forces give each industry its own particular competitive environment.

To perform well, managers need to know how to identify and analyze the five forces that determine the competitive structure of their industries. By applying Porter's five forces model of industry attractiveness to their own industries, managers can gauge their own firm's strengths, weaknesses, and future opportunities.

Threat of New Entrants

A firm's profitability will tend to be higher when other firms are blocked from entering the industry. New entrants can reduce industry profitability because they add new production capacity and can substantially erode existing firms' market share positions. To discourage new entrants, existing firms can try to raise barriers to entry. **Barriers to entry** represent economic forces (or "hurdles") that slow down or impede entry by other firms. Common barriers to entry include (1) capital requirements, (2) economies of scale, (3) product differentiation, (4) switching costs, (5) brand identity, (6) access to distribution channels, and (7) promise of aggressive retaliation.

barriers to entry: Economic forces that slow down or prevent entry into an industry.

Capital Requirements. When a large amount of capital is required to enter an industry, firms lacking funds are effectively barred from entry, thus enhancing the profitability of existing firms in the industry. For example, large investments are needed to build plants or establish brand awareness among customers of existing firms in the personal care products industry. Few firms have sufficient resources to sustain this kind of investment; as a result, entry has been limited in the past several years. Lack of vigorous entry is one reason why industry-wide profitability for pharmaceuticals, personal care products, and software tends to remain fairly high. On the other hand, the situation is quite different for the trucking and shipping industry in which anyone with sufficient funds can lease trucks for a short period of time. In part because little capital is required for entry, numerous competitors are thus able to enter the industry with relative ease. The same economic condition also holds for firms competing in the restaurant and dry cleaning/laundry, and commercial linen industries, where capital requirements to set up operations tend to be comparatively less.

Economies of Scale. Many industries are characterized by economic activities driven by economies of scale. **Economies of scale** refer to the decline in the per-unit cost of production (or other activity) as volume grows. A large firm that enjoys economies of scale can produce high volumes of goods at successively lower costs than a smaller rival. Knowledge of this fact tends to discourage new entrants. Consider, for example, the semiconductor industry. Larger companies, such as IBM, Intel, National Semiconductor, Motorola, and Texas Instruments in the United States, enjoy substantial economies of scale in the production of advanced microprocessors, communication chips, and integrated circuits that power cellular phones and video games. This cost advantage deters entry of most other firms seeking to produce these chips. (We will discuss the economic basis for scale advantages in Chapters 3 and 4.)

economies of scale: The declines in per-unit cost of production or any activity as volume grows.

EXHIBIT 2-1 Porter's Five Forces Model of Industry Attractiveness

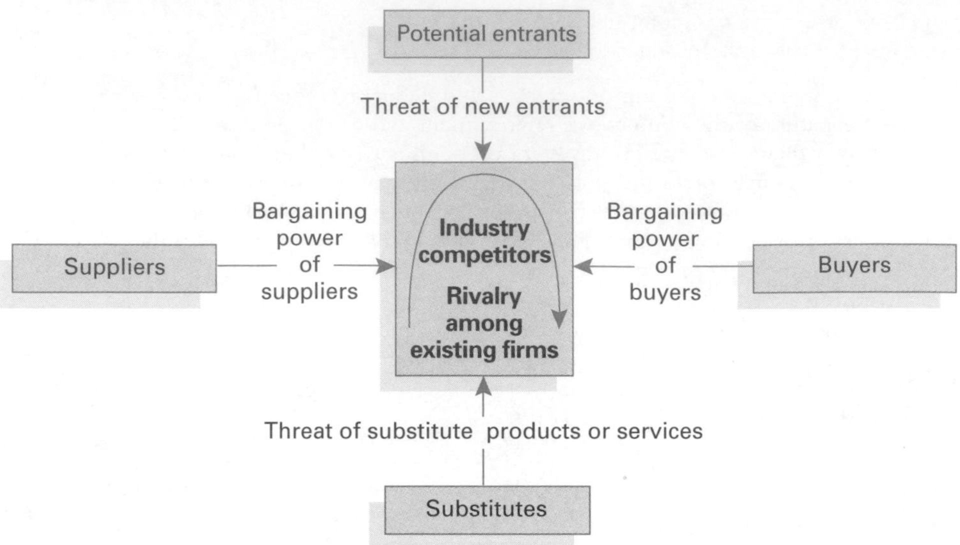

Barriers to Entry
- Economies of scale
- Proprietary product differences
- Brand identity
- Switching costs
- Capital requirements
- Access to distribution channels
- Absolute cost advantages
- Proprietary learning curve
- Access to necessary inputs
- Government policy
- Expected retaliation

Determinants of Rivalry
- Industry growth
- Fixed (or storage) cost/Value added
- Intermittent overcapacity
- Product differences
- Brand identity
- Switching costs
- Concentration and balance
- Informational complexity
- Diversity of competitors
- Exit barriers

Determinants of Substitution Threat
- Relative price/Performance of substitutes
- Switching costs
- Buyer propensity to substitute

Determinants of Supplier Power
- Differentiation of inputs
- Switching costs of suppliers and firms in the industry
- Presence of substitute inputs
- Supplier concentration
- Importance of volume to supplier
- Cost relative to total purchases in the industry
- Impact of inputs on cost or differentiation
- Threat of forward integration relative to threat of backward integration by firms in the industry

Determinants of Buyer Power
- Bargaining leverage
- Buyer concntration vs. firm concentration
- Buyer volume
- Buyer switching costs relative to firm switching costs
- Buyer information
- Ability to backward integrate
- Substitute products
- Pull-through
- Price sensitivity
- Price/Total purchases
- Product differences
- Brand identity
- Impact on quality/Performance
- Buyer profits
- Decision makers' incentives

Product Differentiation. Product differentiation is another factor that limits entry into an industry. **Product differentiation** refers to the physical or perceptual differences that make a product special or unique in the eyes of customers. It is a tool firms can use to "lock in" customer loyalty to their products. Differentiation works to enhance entry barriers because the cost of overcoming existing customers' buying preferences and loyalties and genuine product differences may be too high for new entrants. (We will discuss product differentiation more explicitly in Chapter 4.)

product differentiation: The physical or perceptual differences that make a product special or unique in the eyes of the customer.

Switching Costs. To succeed in an industry, new entrants must be able to persuade existing customers to switch from current providers. To make a switch, buyers may need to test a new firm's product, negotiate new purchase contracts, train personnel to use the equipment, or modify facilities for product use. Buyers often incur substantial financial (and psychological) costs in switching between firms. When such switching costs are high, buyers are often reluctant to change. For example, the software industry enjoys significant profitability in large measure because of the enormous difficulties in switching from one type of computer operating software to another. High switching costs in moving away from Microsoft's Windows operating systems used in personal computers and corporate servers powered the company's stunning growth over the past decade in the software industry.

Brand Identity. The brand identity of products or services offered by existing firms can serve as another entry barrier. Brand identity is particularly important for infrequently purchased products that carry a high dollar cost to the buyer. Oftentimes, a brand will signify in the customer's mind that the product is reliable and worth the value paid. New entrants often encounter significant difficulties in building up brand identity, since to do so they must commit substantial resources over a long period of time. Consider the history of the Japanese automobile industry in the United States. During the 1970s, companies such as Toyota, Nissan, and Honda had to spend huge sums on advertising and new product development to overcome the American consumers' preference for domestic cars. Only by doing so could these manufacturers gain market share against the Big Three's existing dominance. These Japanese firms have spent close to three decades trying to earn the loyalty of American buyers through superior product quality and frequent advertising. Now, the sway of such brands as Lexus, Infiniti, and Acura have given Japanese automakers considerable power in the automobile industry by virtue of these strong brands. American consumers have shown their preference for these brands by giving them high marks in annual surveys of automobile quality conducted by numerous market research firms, such as J. D. Power and Associates.

Access to Distribution Channels. The unavailability of distribution channels for new entrants poses another significant entry barrier. Oftentimes, existing firms have significant influence over a market's distribution channels and can retard or impede their use by new firms. For example, consumer packaged goods and personal care products companies depend on using their distribution-based clout to capture the market share and mind share of consumers. For example, Procter & Gamble fills its distribution channels with a broad range of products (e.g., Tide, Crest, Folger's, Charmin) and spends considerable resources to keeping store shelves well stocked. New entrants faced with this entrenched distribution expertise must offer aggressive promotions that ultimately are extremely expensive. The fewer the distribution channels available for any given product, the higher is the cost of entry for a new entrant. Conversely, the enormous difficulties facing U.S. manufacturers seeking to enter the Japanese and other Far East markets shows how limited access to distribution can effectively shut out new entrants.

Promise of Aggressive Retaliation. Sometimes, the mere threat of aggressive retaliation by incumbents can deter entry by other firms into an existing industry. For example, when Dr Pepper (now a unit of Cadbury-Schweppes) attempted to go national during the 1960s and 1970s, aggressive retaliation by both Coca-Cola and PepsiCo kept it from penetrating many markets outside its Texas home base. Dr Pepper found itself defending its own markets in the South from Coke and Pepsi, which retaliated because of Dr Pepper's entry into their midwestern and northern markets. Entry by firms in other industries, such as photographic film, hospital supplies, and motor oil, is often deterred by the threat of aggressive, massive retaliation.

Bargaining Power of Buyers

Buyers of an industry's products or services can sometimes exert considerable pressure on existing firms to secure lower prices or better service. This leverage is particularly evident when (1) buyers are knowledgeable, (2) they spend a lot of money on the industry's products, (3) the industry's product is not perceived as critical to the buyer's needs and, (4) buyers are more concentrated than firms supplying the product. Buyers are also strong when the industry's product tends to be undifferentiated or has few switching costs and when they can enter the supplying industry fairly easily themselves.

Buyer Knowledge. Buyers lacking knowledge about the true quality or efficacy of a product are handicapped when bargaining with product suppliers. A skilled supplier can sometimes convince buyers to pay a high price, even for a product that may not be too different from those of its competitors. Suppliers selling to unsophisticated buyers thus can command higher profits over time.

In the software and electronics instruments industries, for example, these products are often so complex that users have little ability or time to compare them to competitive offerings. Companies such as Agilent Technologies, Perkin-Elmer, and Keithley Instruments, for example, have developed a highly specialized base of knowledge and experience in designing sophisticated laboratory and testing instruments that are sold to universities, government agencies, and other firms that conduct their own research endeavors. Likewise, in the software industry, consumers often rely on the advice of engineers, distributors, and specialized technical service firms to assess their particular needs. For these and other reasons (including switching costs, specialized skills, and patents), software and electronics instruments firms can sustain strong profitability.

Conversely, when buyers have sufficient knowledge and information to evaluate competitive offerings, their bargaining power grows. Competitors then have less ability to charge premium prices, and industry profitability is lower. Airline passengers, for example, can easily evaluate airline service and offerings. For all practical purposes, most travelers regard any given airline as a substitute for another. Since computerized reservation systems are now linked directly with travel agents and with customers through the Internet, pricing information is freely available for customers to compare. This means that every airline must begin to match competitive discounts offered by other airlines or risk the possibility that it would lose more business from unsold seats. As a result, no airline can raise fares without experiencing a drop in traffic, which helps explain a major factor as to why its industry profitability typically has suffered.

Purchase Size. Buyers have less incentive to pressure suppliers for a low price when a small purchase is involved, since even a large percentage reduction in price has little impact on total purchase cost. Smokers, for example, pay less than $3 for a pack of cigarettes. As a result, many are relatively unconcerned with price. This circumstance enables cigarette producers such as Philip Morris to charge high prices on brand products, which leads to consistently high profitability for the tobacco industry. Rapid growth of lower-priced cigarette brands, extremely high health consciousness, government intervention, and legislative actions/lawsuits, however, strongly suggest that industry-wide profitability will decline significantly over the next several years.

Firms have less ability to charge a premium price when they produce big-ticket items, since even a small reduction or increase in price then has a big impact on total purchase cost. Refrigerators and dishwashers, for example, involve a large dollar outlay, so buyers often shop hard to find the best deal. This fact helps explain why the appliance industry's profitability has remained comparatively low, since competitors (e.g., Maytag, Whirlpool, General Electric, Amana, Electrolux) fight hard for every sale to a customer.

Product Function. When products serve a critical function, buyers will pay premium prices to obtain them. The pharmaceutical industry is a case in point. When people are sick or injured, the price of pharmaceuticals means little to them. This attitude is particularly evident when patients have health insurance that protects them from paying the full price for medications. In effect, prescription and over-the-counter drugs are important to people's health and are likely to command high prices because of their necessity. This fact contributes heavily to the drug industry's comparatively high profitability over the past two decades. Over time, however, the growing threat of price controls and government intervention in the form of health care reform legislation could reduce industry-wide profitability.

Concentration of Buyers. When buyers are more concentrated than firms supplying the product, suppliers often have alternatives when seeking buyers. Buyers can then often obtain better terms on price and service. For example, large firms in the computer and automobile industries have traditionally been able to bargain heavily with key suppliers to these industries because they are more concentrated than their suppliers. Computer and automobile firms can also command better prices because they offer the prospect of large volume purchases from their suppliers. A concentration of buyers over suppliers is also found in the agricultural sector. Firms such as Archers Daniel Midland (ADM), Farmland Industries, Corn Products International, and Cargill can command strong bargaining power over farmers and the farm cooperatives that supply them with corn and wheat. In the health care industry today, many firms are banding together to establish health insurance purchasing cooperatives. These cooperatives enable firms to purchase health insurance for their employees on better terms than individual firms could command.

Undifferentiated Products. Buyers also tend to have strong bargaining power when they purchase standardized, undifferentiated products from their suppliers. They can easily change suppliers without incurring significant switching costs. This phenomenon raises their bargaining power. Consider, for example, the purchase of steel by automakers. For the most part, steel remains largely an undifferentiated commodity. Thus, General Motors, Ford, and DaimlerChrysler can easily obtain high discounts from their suppliers.

Buyer Entry into the Industry. Buyers' bargaining power is increased if they can potentially enter the industry from which they are currently buying. If buyers decide to make those items for themselves that they now purchase, they can exert strong bargaining power over the supplying industry. This method is known as *backward integration* (and will be discussed at length in a later chapter).

Bargaining Power of Suppliers

Conversely, suppliers can influence the profitability of an industry in a number of ways. Suppliers can command bargaining power over an industry when (1) their products are crucial to a buyer, (2) they can erect high switching costs, and (3) they are more concentrated than buyers. Suppliers also possess a certain amount of power over an industry when they can potentially enter it themselves.

Products Crucial to Buyer. If suppliers provide crucial products or inputs to buyers, then their bargaining power is likely to be high. Consider, for example, the semiconductor industry's supply relationship with firms making PCs. Because microprocessors and other specialized chips are critical to PC operation, chip suppliers can often pass on increases in chip prices to PC makers. For example, Intel has consistently been able to reap huge (but recently declining) profits from the sale of its Pentium line of microprocessors to Dell Computer, Compaq, Hewlett-Packard, and IBM. Since the microprocessor remains the central brain of the PC, Intel is able to capitalize on its strong supply position.

Products with High Switching Costs. When buyers incur a high cost for switching from one supplier to another, then suppliers will possess high bargaining power over buyers. For example, software providers possess bargaining power over the firms that need their operating systems to run computers and other applications. Switching from one software provider to another will often require buyers to undergo expensive modification of their computer systems.

In the heavy machinery and machine tool industry, product specifications and tolerances for different kinds of machinery make it difficult to switch from one supplier to another. This difficulty often means that the buying firm has to shut down an entire factory before it can install another machine made by another supplier—an extremely costly proposition. Suppliers of these products and components therefore enjoy high bargaining power over buying firms.

High Supplier Concentration. When suppliers are more concentrated than buyers, they tend to be in a better bargaining position over prices. As shown in the personal computer industry example, the comparatively few suppliers of chips relative to the number of PC makers means that PC makers are consistently absorbing the price increases passed on by their suppliers. The pharmaceutical industry is another case in which comparatively few firms produce each specific type or class of drug. This supplier concentration gives drug producers considerable bargaining power over physicians, wholesalers, and hospitals.

The poultry industry, as another example, has a high supplier concentration in relation to buyers such as restaurants and food distributors. A comparatively few number of firms are in the chicken-processing business, such as Pilgrim's Pride, Tyson Foods, and Perdue Chickens. These firms can pass on price increases to buyers, such as KFC, Popeye's, Church's, other restaurants, food companies, and grocery stores.

Suppliers' Ability to Enter the Buying Industry. When suppliers can fairly easily enter the industry they are supplying, their bargaining power is increased. Buyers are then reluctant to bargain too hard for price reduction because they may cause suppliers to enter the industry. For example, if chip makers such as Intel or Advanced Micro Devices decided to make PCs, their entrance into the PC market would even further depress the profitability of the PC industry. The ability to move into a buyer's industry thus helps maintain high profitability for suppliers. This action of moving into a buyer's industry is known as *forward integration* (and will be discussed extensively in a later chapter).

The Nature of Rivalry in the Industry

The intensity of rivalry in an industry is a significant determinant of industry attractiveness and profitability. The intensity of the rivalry can influence the costs of supplies, distribution, and attracting customers and thus directly affect profitability. The more intensive the rivalry, the less attractive is the industry. Rivalry among competitors tends to be cutthroat and industry profitability low when (1) an industry has no clear leader, (2) competitors in the industry are numerous, (3) competitors operate with high fixed costs, (4) competitors face high exit barriers, (5) competitors have little opportunity to differentiate their offerings, and (6) the industry faces slow or diminished growth.

Industry Leader. A strong industry leader can discourage price wars by disciplining initiators of such activity. A primary tool for exercising such discipline is a retaliatory price reduction by the leader itself. Because of its greater financial resources, a leader can generally outlast smaller rivals in a price war. Knowing this, smaller rivals often avoid initiating such a contest. The comparatively high profitability of the personal care products industry is due in part to the strong price leadership exercised by giant Procter & Gamble. If an industry has no leader, price wars are more likely and industry profitability generally lower. The historically low profitability of the steel, paper, memory chip, homebuilding, and waste management industries is due in part to the absence of a clear leader in these industries.

Number of Competitors. Even when an industry leader exists, the leader's ability to exert pricing discipline diminishes as the number of rivals in the industry increases as communicating expectations to players becomes more difficult. Also, an industry with many players is more likely to contain mavericks whose ideas about how to compete may not reflect industry norms and expectations. Such firms are often determined to go their own way in spite of persuasion or signaling by an industry leader. For these reasons, industry profitability tends to fall as the number of competitors grows. The trucking industry's historically low profitability can be attributed in part to the large number of firms operating in the industry.

Fixed Costs. When rivals operate with high fixed costs, they feel strong motivation to utilize their capacity and therefore are inclined to cut prices when they have excess capacity. Unless industry demand is highly elastic, price cutting causes profitability to fall for all firms in the industry. For this reason, profitability tends to be lower in industries characterized by high fixed costs.

The profitability of the metals industry (e.g., steel, aluminum, copper, iron) is depressed in part from this cause. Most costs of operating highly integrated steel mills—plant setup, equipment, smelting, casting, and fabrication—are essentially fixed because of the nature of the conversion and heating process. In the steel, copper, iron, and aluminum industries, cost efficiency is highly dependent on full capacity utilization. Moreover, the plant and equipment used to produce steel and aluminum are extremely expensive. Steel companies are therefore prone to price reductions in order to keep their plants at full utilization, since capacity shortfalls mean they must bear the entire weight of their high fixed cost. Once one firm begins to cut prices, others generally must follow suit. The resulting price wars have depressed industry profitability for many years, if not decades.

The airline industry is another arena where competitors face very high fixed costs. Aircraft, terminals, maintenance facilities, long-term lease agreements, and other assets cannot be added or deleted quickly to adjust to short-term demand fluctuations. Thus, airlines often must engage in extensive price-cutting behavior to amortize their fixed costs, regardless of how many passengers and planes are used at any given point in time.

Exit Barriers. Rivalry among competitors declines if some competitors leave an industry. Firms wanting to leave may be restrained from doing so by barriers to exit, however. Profitability therefore tends to be higher in industries with few exit barriers. Exit barriers come in many forms. Assets of a firm considering exit may be highly specialized and therefore of little value to any other firm. Such a firm can thus find no buyer for its assets. This discourages exit. A firm may be obliged to honor existing labor agreements or to maintain spare parts for products already in the field. In addition, discontinuing the activities of one business may adversely affect a firm's other businesses that share common facilities. When barriers to exit such as these are powerful, competitors desiring exit may refrain from leaving. Their continued presence in an industry exerts downward pressure on the profitability of all competitors.

High exit barriers have contributed to the low profitability of integrated steel producers. Profitability of such producers in recent years has been significantly below that of many industries. Their profitability has been low in part because many integrated producers are controlled by national governments, particularly in Europe. Government owners are notoriously reluctant to liquidate unprofitable facilities since doing so results in bigger transfer payments (to support unemployed workers), voter dissatisfaction, and political unrest. To avoid these difficulties, government owners often keep mills operating even when doing so has meant selling output at prices below cost. Such behavior has depressed profitability for all integrated producers worldwide. Even in 2002, the U.S. steel industry faces continuing challenges from foreign steelmakers, many of which continue to receive government aid in some form to promote production and employment at home.

Product Differentiation. Firms can sometimes insulate themselves from price wars by differentiating their products from those of rivals. As a consequence, profitability tends to be higher in industries that offer opportunity for differentiation. The high profitability of the software, pharmaceutical, sporting equipment, and medical supplies industries results in part from the many opportunities these fields offer for product differentiation. Profitability tends to be lower in industries involving undifferentiated commodities such as textiles, memory chips, trucking, and railroads.

Slow Growth. Industries whose growth is slowing tend to face more intense rivalry. Slower rates of growth pervade many industries, including automobiles, digital phones, insurance, broadcasting, advertising, retail financial services, real estate, and personal computers. As industry growth slows, rivals must often fight harder to grow or even to keep their existing market share. The resulting intensive rivalry tends to reduce profitability for all.

Threat of Substitutes

A final force that can influence industry profitability is the availability of substitutes for an industry's product. To predict profit pressure from this source, firms must search for products that perform the same, or nearly the same, function as their existing products. In some cases this search is quite straightforward. Real estate, insurance, bonds, and bank deposits, for example, are clear substitutes for common stocks, since they represent alternate ways to invest funds. Identifying substitutes for a ski resort presents more difficulty, however, since services as diverse as gambling casinos, cruise ships, and foreign travel are potential substitutes.

Consider the case of electronic mail as a substitute for the U.S. Post Office and other overnight delivery services such as Federal Express and United Parcel Service (UPS). The growing spread of the Internet, private computer intranets, and other forms of digital communications that allow users to communicate and to conduct business with one another has a direct substitution effect on the mail and overnight package business. The threat of substitutes is great in many high-tech industries as well. For example, the digital filmless camera represents a direct substitute threat that could substantially erode market shares of Eastman Kodak and Fuji Film. Wireless digital telephones are a substitute threat for conventional, ground-wired telephones. In turn, new forms of digital phones are a substitute for older analog-based cellular phones. In the long term, advances in biotechnology threaten to create substitutes for many drugs currently used to treat disease.

Having identified substitutes for an industry's product, firms must then judge their potential to depress industry profitability. As a general rule, a substitute will threaten industry profitability if it can perform the function of an industry's product at a lower cost or perform the same function better at no increase in cost. Particularly worrisome are substitutes whose price or performance characteristics are improving over time. Oil posed this kind of threat to gas in the 1980s and 1990s. The price of oil had been declining relative to that of gas, causing some gas users to switch to oil to power electric utility plants. Effort by gas producers to stem this trend may have helped this sector become slightly more profitable as utilities look for cleaner ways to generate electricity. A similar situation confronts firms in the telecommunications industry. For example, an increasingly large number of customers can now make long-distance calls through their personal computers by way of Internet service providers. Over time, the software features of Microsoft's and AOL Time Warner's browsers will allow customers to communicate with other people through voice as well as e-mail formats. Instant Messenger, offered by AOL, in one example could become a very powerful substitute offering that threatens the very foundation of the long-distance businesses of many telecommunications firms.

Strategic Groups and the Industry Environment

Up to this point, our focus has been on analyzing the forces that drive *industry-wide profitability*. As we have seen, Porter's five forces model is extremely powerful in helping us understand the specific economic forces and conditions that determine industry profitability. Yet, managers often need a more detailed analysis and information of an industry. To develop effective competitive strategies, managers need to understand how their own firm's particular strategic posture will relate to building or maintaining profitability within the industry. Within any given industry, each firm's particular competitive strategies and behaviors are likely to be different than those of its rivals. In other words, even though companies in the same industry may face similar pressures from suppliers, buyers, and substitutes, in practice they may actually behave differently in reaction to these forces. Competitors within a single industry may be quite dissimilar. Firms within a single industry could differ in terms of their product attributes, emphasis on product quality, type of technology used, type of distribution channel used, type of buyer sought, and other characteristics. Thus, firms are likely to respond to environmental forces in ways that best fit their own individual strategic postures and competitive strategy.

The focus of this section is to examine the concept of strategic groups.[13] **Strategic groups** are groups of firms that pursue similar types of strategies within the same industry. Management may find benefit in being able to classify firms within an industry into strategic groups. Such analysis can aid them in understanding which firms pursue similar types of strategies. Strategic groups exist because of strong economic forces acting within an industry that constrain firms from easily switching from one competitive posture or position to another. Generally, firms within a strategic group face similar economic conditions and constraints that differ from those of firms located in other strategic groups.

strategic groups: The distribution or grouping of firms that pursue similar strategies in response to environmental forces within an industry. Firms within the same strategic group will tend to compete more vigorously with one another than with firms from other strategic groups.

Strategic groups are important because they represent a valuable link between studying the behavior of an entire industry and the behavior of individual firms that compose the industry. To study the characteristics of every firm within the industry can be arduous and time-consuming. Strategic groups analysis enables managers to aggregate firms into groups of firms showing similar characteristics. It is therefore a useful tool to help managers understand and compare their own firm's strategic postures and actions with their rivals.

Defining the Strategic Group

Most industries can be decomposed into several different strategic groups. Firms within each strategic group might be similar to one another in terms of any number of different key attributes, such as (1) product line breadth, (2) type of technology used, (3) type of buyer served, (4) relative emphasis on product quality, (5) type of distribution channels used, and (6) number of markets served. Thus, many different attributes or dimensions can be used to classify firms into a strategic group. Most important, managers must choose those dimensions that are most salient and relevant to their own particular industry. Some competitive dimensions (e.g., type of distribution channel used and product line breadth) may be more salient for some industries (e.g., packaged foods, soft drinks, beer, cereals, and personal care products), while other dimensions (e.g., product function and type of technology used) may be more useful in other industries (e.g., semiconductors, medical equipment, and sporting goods). Thus, constructing meaningful strategic groups that effectively capture different firms' strategic postures requires a careful selection of those dimensions that best describe their industry's environment. Choosing the right dimensions depends on both industry knowledge and managerial experience in dealing with customers and competitors.

Thus, managers may experiment with a number of different dimensions to assess properly the strategic groups in their competitive environment.

Strategic Groups in the Personal Computer Industry

Exhibit 2-2 portrays one way of defining the strategic groups within the PC industry. The dimensions chosen for this particular analysis include product quality and speed of customization/delivery to customer. We could have examined the PC industry using other dimensions, such as level of product quality versus price, or customer support versus price. Using product quality and speed of distribution for dimensions in our analysis, six strategic groups appear within the PC industry.

EXHIBIT 2-2 Strategic Groups in the Personal Computer Industry

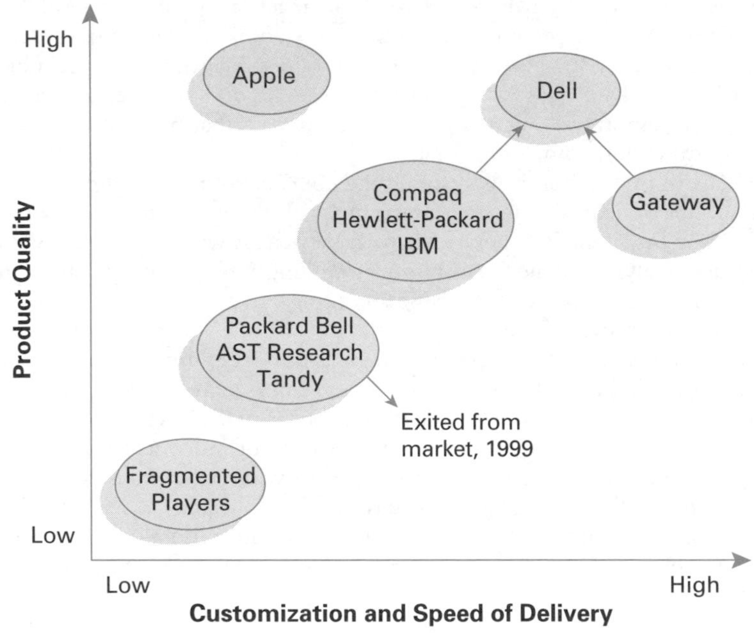

The first group, composed of one company, is Apple Computer. That Apple Computer makes up its own group is not surprising, given its high user-friendly nature and the sophistication of its distinct Macintosh operating system quality. Later product generations of Apple's computer line, such as the recently introduced iMac models, have continued to reinforce customers' perceptions of Apple's high quality. However, Apple's models are not available directly from the manufacturer but must be purchased through a value-added reseller or electronics retailer. As a result, it is comparatively difficult to add custom features to Apple's product line. Apple's use of a different operating system from that used by other PC makers helps insulate it from fierce rivalry; at the same time, it also limits how much market share Apple can stake out in this industry (approximately 4 to 5 percent). Nevertheless, Apple's cutting-edge models still attract a very loyal audience who use the firm's latest technologies to create digital movies and a host of other applications that are not widely available in Windows-based PCs.

The second group, defined by Dell Computer, represents a powerful combination of both high product quality and very fast speed of delivery of a custom-built product to the customer. In fact, Dell's strategy of combining high product quality with speed of customization has been so successful that many other firms are attempting to copy its strategy (especially Gateway, IBM, and Compaq). However, Dell has been able to distinguish itself from its competitors by keeping its production system and inventories exceptionally lean and simultaneously working with key suppliers to incorporate the latest advances in chips, peripherals, and other components that drive product quality higher. Moreover, Dell keeps its distribution costs low by encouraging customers to order their computers through a toll-free number or directly through the Internet. This enables Dell to avoid the cost of selling through department stores, electronics retailers, and other types of resellers.

Compaq Computer, Hewlett-Packard, and IBM attempt to pursue both high product quality and customization of PC features to customers' specific needs. However, these three manufacturers still rely heavily on selling their products through electronics stores and to business customers, through value-added resellers who perform much of the final stages of customizing the product according to each individual customer's specifications (usually for corporate buyers). Although all three firms have begun to sell their computers directly to their customers through toll-free numbers and via the Internet, they cannot move as quickly as Dell in pursuing this strategy for fear it will alienate their current distribution partners who help them perform product upgrades and other services. Still, many analysts believe that over the next few years Compaq and IBM will continue to take on Dell directly by selling more custom-built PCs through their own Internet sites. IBM has offered service guarantees and warranties that help improve the perceived quality of its products, although it has recently decided not to make its own PCs anymore. Instead, IBM has contracted out the assembly of its personal computer line to Sanmina-SCI, a leading contract electronics manufacturer. Ironically, IBM manufactures many of the semiconductors, displays, disk drives, and power supplies that go into its line of PCs, as well as for Dell! Yet, IBM still cannot quickly adjust its own internal production system to sudden and rapid changes in demand. Compaq, for the most part, still manages the production of its PCs closely, but it has also showed signs of relying on other electronics manufacturers to do more of the work. Among all three players are unrelenting price wars in which a company attempts to undercut the offering price of its competitors.

Gateway constitutes a fourth strategic group that focuses on building custom-order PCs largely for the home market. In many critical areas, Gateway is attempting to catch up with industry leader Dell Computer by adopting a lean production process in which key suppliers build and ship it components as they are ordered. To serve the broader individual market, Gateway in the past has attempted to keep its prices lower than those of Dell by using cheaper Intel Pentium or Celeron chips (or rival chips manufactured by AMD). Now, the company has moved to rely solely on Intel for its microprocessor needs. Customers purchase Gateway computers through the company's toll-free number. They can also go to selected Gateway retail outlets in some U.S. cities. Gateway's presence in the business market is more limited, largely because its customer service center is focused on serving the individual market. In fact, at the beginning of 2002, Gateway announced that it would begin lowering the prices of its machines in order to compete more effectively with Dell Computer and other rivals that had slowly eaten away some of its market share during the latter half of 2001. The company has also begun to close some of its less profitable stores in order to prepare itself for a long struggle with other PC firms.[14]

A fifth strategic group may effectively be described as PC makers providing acceptable quality computers with standard features through conventional distribution channels. For all practical purposes, however, this group has disappeared in the past few years, since customers are increasingly demanding high quality machines with the latest features offered at low prices. Included in this group were such rivals as AST Research, Tandy, and Packard Bell. Their computers, while reliable, often did not include the fastest chips or the most versatile CD-ROM or DVD drives and video and sound cards. Also, these firms did not attempt to customize their products according to each individual customer's needs; rather, their machines were sold through department stores and electronics retailers with the same standard features for all customers. As a result, it was difficult for customers to order custom-made machines directly from them. Losses mounted for all of these companies, and each completed its withdrawal from the market by 1999.

The final strategic group may be described as a collection of small, fragmented PC makers that border on simple assembly, almost cottage-industry operations. These include such upstarts as eMachines and PeoplePC. Even here, however, the fate of these companies is in some doubt because they are unable to offer fast delivery of custom-made machines with the latest features. Their lack of brand name recognition and their use of standardized technology keep these small PC makers in an unattractive strategic group.

Implications of Strategic Group Analysis

Strategic groups are useful in describing the competitive behavior of firms within an industry. The first thing to note is that competition *within* a strategic group is often more heated than that *between* strategic groups. In other words, firms that are similar, and thus placed in the same strategic group, generally compete against one another more intensely than against firms in different strategic groups. Largely, this phenomenon results from the fact that firms within the same strategic group display similar product characteristics and strategic behavior. As a result, it is difficult for rivals to distinguish themselves easily from one another. Oftentimes, they are compelled to use price wars to steal market share from their competitors. For example, Compaq, Hewlett-Packard, and IBM compete fiercely against one another in the same type of distribution channel. They are also playing "catch-up" to Dell Computer in offering custom-built machines to customers over the Internet. While all three firms ultimately aim to become more agile and responsive like Dell Computer, they tend to regard each other as the more immediate "enemy." Part of the reason why firms within the same strategic group tend to compete more fiercely with each other is their similarity of offerings or their lack of skills and opportunities to make themselves distinctive. Consequently, members within a strategic group are likely to pursue a similar competitive strategy to attract the same targeted group of buyers.

Strategic groups can shift over time, so managers must continue to be aware of how firms may differ in their future competitive postures and strategies. As we have seen in the past few years, an entire strategic group has effectively disappeared, as AST Research, Tandy, and Packard Bell exited the industry. Strategic groups appear to be shifting again in this business, as IBM, Compaq Computer, and Hewlett-Packard try to imitate Dell's successful strategies. However, Dell appears to have become even more dominant because it is able to engage in price wars and yet remain profitable through its lean production, distribution channels, and supply system. Customers are even beginning to associate Dell Computer with their PC needs because of the company's innovative marketing and advertising campaigns. At the same time, both Compaq and Hewlett-Packard appear to have stalled in 2001 and 2002 because of the overall economic difficulties that accompany a national recession. Also, merger talks between Compaq and Hewlett-Packard occurred during 2001 and 2002 as both companies sought to gain greater size advantages to compete in the PC and other businesses. IBM, for its part, has steadily withdrawn from the PC business in terms of actively manufacturing all of the parts and components needed to make the device. Although businesses and consumers can still buy IBM-labeled PCs, and the company will continue to service them, IBM is now a maker of PC components, but not the entire PC itself.

So far in 2002, Apple is beginning to reassume the role that it pioneered for itself in the early 1980s—developing trendy and fashionable PCs that stand out from the crowd. Apple believes that many of its loyal customers will continue to buy its machines not only for its high quality but because they wish to make a "fashion statement" as well. The company's most loyal customers are typically publishers, graphic designers, and creative artists who love the feel of Apple's unique designs and the versatility of its Macintosh operating system. Yet, Apple has already developed a new operating system that enables users to switch back and forth between the Macintosh and Microsoft's Windows operating systems. While this innovation makes Apple's product even more distinctive and of higher quality in the eyes of consumers, it could potentially change how Apple competes against other Windows-formatted PC firms.

What are some broader lessons about strategic group analysis that can apply to a variety of different industry conditions? Let's examine how changes in the environment can have a marked impact on the evolution of strategic groups and the firms that compose them.

- First, strategic groups can shift over time as the needs of customers or different technologies evolve in the marketplace. As we can see from the personal computer industry, it appears that Compaq, Hewlett-Packard, and IBM are moving toward adopting some of the exact same strategies that have made Dell Computer so successful in years past. As the three other firms become more successful in building custom-made computers and selling through the Internet, they are likely to find themselves moving directly into Dell's once isolated strategic group. Thus, rivalry will intensify (as is the case when firms become more similar to one another), and therefore managers should not assume that membership in a particular strategic group permanently locks the firm into a fixed strategy. With sufficient resources and focus, firms can enter and exit strategic groups over time. Customers, however, are benefiting in a major way—they are getting custom-made personal computers for steadily less cost and higher performance.
- Second, entire strategic groups and the firms that compose them can emerge or disappear over time. As we see from the personal computer industry, the strategic group that was made of firms that built low- to midrange PCs eventually fell by the wayside. As customers became more savvy, it became difficult for AST Research, Packard-Bell, and others to continue to rely on their previous strategies. In the future, we might expect that Gateway could face a similar fate if it is not successful in closing the gap with Dell Computer and the other rivals. Thus, as the environment changes, the competitive conditions that define a strategic group may work against an entire collection of firms, resulting in the group's long-term decline if competitive conditions intensify.
- In recent years, one of the more enduring trends that have defined a growing number of industries is the hastening pace of consolidation. Competitors are now seeking to buy or merge with their rivals to limit the effects of fierce price wars that negatively impact profitability. Consider, for example, the financial services industry. Companies such as J. P. Morgan Chase, Bank of America, Citigroup, First Union, and Morgan Stanley have been buying up their immediate competitors, as well as firms that once operated in completely different strategic groups. As commercial bank firms acquire companies in the investment banking and insurance arenas, strategic groups are becoming larger. Although groups may appear to be stable for the short term, competition will likely increase as bigger rivals muscle in on the turf of other like-minded firms. Thus, consolidation within and among industries can also markedly redefine the underlying stability and membership of strategic groups.
- Finally, the personal computer industry illustrates an important strategic lesson that will be examined in great detail throughout the balance of this book. As the Dell Computer example reveals, a firm can only build and sustain competitive advantage (and profitability) to the extent that it remains distinctive from its rivals. Competitive advantage and profitability are a direct function of distinctiveness. Or, put in another way, to the extent that customers begin to view each firm's offerings as interchangeable with that of other firms, the growing lack of distinctiveness directly means that profitability will likely suffer as well.

Strategic Application of Five Forces Analysis to the Personal Computer Industry

Let us now use the five forces model to analyze the structure and attractiveness (profitability) of the PC industry. To illustrate the potency of these five forces, let us apply these concepts to examine how the PC industry has evolved in recent years. What profitability pressures would these five forces exert on firms operating in this market?

New Entrants

Barriers to entry in the PC industry are low. Entry into this market would be fairly easy for several reasons. First, capital requirements for PC assembly are modest. Second, customers face few switching costs when changing suppliers and probably would not hesitate to buy a Windows-formatted operating system PC from a new supplier if the price were right. This makes competition very intense. In fact, some Internet start-up firms in 1998 and 1999 offered stripped-down PCs free to customers who subscribed to an Internet service provider for an extended multiyear contract. These entrants deployed many of the same strategies that cellular telephone companies implemented during the 1990s: give away the hardware for free in exchange for long-term customer commitment to purchasing a service for several time periods. Third, product differentiation and economies of scale are elusive in this industry. Numerous small firms can easily and quickly enter this business through subassembly and subcontracting their manufacturing activities. The presence of so many competitors in this market would thus depress profitability.

Direct Competitors

PC firms have engaged in cutthroat pricing to maintain and even grow their market shares in the past few years, especially as the sagging economy deterred consumers from buying more expensive models. Also, PC assembly involves few exit barriers, so competitors experiencing profit problems could exit fairly quickly. Yet, product differentiation is much less favorable. Product differentiation is likely to be increasingly difficult to achieve as PCs become more and more like a commodity. Potential opportunities for differentiation do exist to the extent that designers and manufacturers continue their efforts to miniaturize the PC and pack it with more versatile features, such as faster CD-ROM drives, Internet access, DVD, and video cards. However, these are temporary advantages. For its part, Apple Computer has relied on innovative designs and software to stand out successfully from the crowd. Still, broader opportunities for differentiation are fleeting, since manufacturers of components and peripherals freely sell such add-ons to any PC manufacturer willing to pay for them. Thus, competition among PC suppliers has increasingly turned on price (even with those machines packed with added-on features), exerting enormous downward pressure on profitability.

Buyers

Users are increasingly knowledgeable about PCs and increasingly inclined to regard them as a commodity. Many buyers (especially individuals and families) are starting to purchase second and third PCs for the home, in much the same way that they purchased multiple color television sets and VCRs for home entertainment use. These characteristics will lead buyers to be increasingly price conscious when shopping for PCs. This sensitivity to price, in turn, will exert strong downward pressure on the profitability of PC producers.

Suppliers

Suppliers of memory chips, microprocessors, integrated circuits, and other key peripherals and components are comparatively few and concentrated. Intel and AMD dominate the microprocessor side of the business and have used their strong bargaining power to capture much of the profits in the PC business. Likewise, Microsoft's dominant position in software, and the fierce protection of its intellectual property, allows it to capture a large share of the profit as well. For these reasons, suppliers are in a good position to negotiate effectively with PC producers, thereby exerting strong downward pressure on their profitability.

Substitutes

Perhaps the most immediate potential substitute for the PC currently is the development of the so-called "network computer" or NC technology. Developed and promulgated by an alliance of several firms (led by Oracle and Sun Microsystems), the NC could become a potent substitute if large corporations ever decide to purchase them in substantial quantity. NCs differ from personal computers in that they do not possess a hard drive and other peripherals now taken for granted with today's PCs. Instead, network computers are tied together through a centralized network of larger servers that house many of the software applications that must now be loaded individually into each PC. As might be expected, if the potential growth for network computers does materialize, it will likely occur because corporate buyers will seek ways to streamline their spending on information-technology products. More corporate buyers may be attracted to network computers because they may feel that they will not have to upgrade their computers periodically as often as they did during the 1990s. Network computers, however, will not likely become a significant substitute threat for home users of PCs, since such users need all of the peripherals and software applications installed directly in their machines to perform their tasks.

More recently, the emergence of smaller, hand-held personal digital assistants (PDAs) has attracted some interest among leading-edge PC users, but their high cost and limited software applications contribute to a limited market presence. However, the rise of new hand-held personal computers that can recognize handwriting and even voice commands may become important substitutes in the near future. This technology could become a real threat to the current PC industry if PDAs are thought of as advanced consumer electronics products that combine Internet access with other new communication features. Already, the latest offerings from Palm, Handspring, and even Nokia provide many of these functions. Palm's latest device offers secure e-mail services through its newest hand-held wireless computer. Not be outdone, Handspring is also rolling out a series of products that can serve also as a cellular phone as well.[15] In another vein, America Online, a unit of AOL Time Warner, is beginning to explore the viability of providing Internet access through non-PC consumer electronic devices. It has begun to partner with Sony of Japan to develop new types of Internet-access and communication devices. At the same time, Microsoft's Xbox game system, Sony's Playstation series of video game consoles, as well as Nintendo's GameCube, are starting to display computing, software, communication, and video capabilities that are mimicking that of many new PCs.

In summary, these developments do not bode well for sustained high profitability in the PC industry. Many of these have already materialized and have caused a number of competitors to exit the industry. In summary, the PC industry is rapidly becoming less attractive over time, especially since customers begin to view the PC as a commodity. Equally important, competitors appear to be mimicking each other's strategies, thus strongly suggesting that it is becoming even harder to maintain distinctiveness in this industry.

Techniques to Monitor the Environment

To keep abreast of rapid environmental changes, firms need to monitor their environment continually. **Environmental scanning** refers to gathering information about external conditions for use in formulating the firm's strategies. Scanning is an important ongoing activity because it helps managers understand and oversee potential changes in market demand, industry rivalry patterns, the rise of potential substitute products, and general macroenvironmental forces that may have long-term effects on the firm.

environmental scanning: The gathering of information about external conditions for use in formulating strategies.

Scanning can occur at several levels. Broad-based scanning focuses on spotting new trends or changes in the general macroenvironment. For example, PC makers examine the potential growth of new markets outside the United States to develop and sell computers. Industry-level scanning is often much more specific in intent and scope. Managers and technical personnel from rival firms frequently visit their competitors, buy their products, and then break them down to see what progress competitors have made in such areas as product quality and new product features. In another example, airline personnel often take trips on competing airlines to assess service quality, timeliness of departure, and general maintenance. Managers from different department stores, hotels, banks, and other service establishments perform similar types of monitoring activities to gauge their competitors' strengths, skill levels, and focus. This type of scanning effort is also known as **competitor intelligence gathering**. Competitor intelligence gathering includes getting information on potential products under development, new technologies that may be incorporated in existing products, new markets to enter, service quality, and responsiveness. In other words, competitor intelligence gathering seeks to acquire as much information as can be found legitimately to help firms better track, understand, and deal with their competitors. Continuous scanning and intelligence gathering can help firms better understand their environments and their competitors to identify new opportunities for future improvements as well as possible threats to a firm's existing competitive position.

competitor intelligence gathering: Scanning specifically targeted or directed toward a firm's rivals; often focuses on a competitor's products, technologies, and other important information

Firms can gather huge amounts of information about their competitors from numerous public sources. For example, newspaper interviews and stories, trade magazines, and research results published in journals all can be valuable sources of information about competing firms. Broader economic or industry-level data can be found through many computer databases, such as Gartner Group, Compustat, Bloomberg, WSJ.com, CNNfn, and Valueline, which provide financial data for individual firms and their industries. Trade shows and conventions often represent opportunities for firms to display their best products and thus can be useful sources of information for their rivals as well.

Ethical Dimensions

This chapter shows how a firm can improve profitability by careful selection of the industry and strategic groups in which it competes. Careful positioning can enable it to charge higher prices and limit rivalry. But are these objectives really proper? Should firms charge as high a price as the market will bear? Are there limits to the means firms should take to limit competition? These questions have ethical ramifications too complex to discuss in detail here. However, in closing this chapter, we reflect briefly on two critical ethical issues: legal requirements and long-run consequences of preserving industry-wide profitability.

Legal Requirements

Society enacts laws constraining the actions firms can take to limit competition, gouge customers, or otherwise take advantage of stakeholders. The United States, for example, has a vast network of regulations governing the claims firms can make about their products, the actions they can take to limit supply, and their ability to collude with competitors. At the very least, all firms must satisfy these legal requirements. Unfortunately, legislation is often so complex that meeting its mandate is difficult in practice.

Long-Run Consequences

When building barriers to entry in the areas discussed earlier, firms must look beyond the present to the long-run consequences of their actions. As an example, consider a decision to charge what the market will bear. Such a policy may boost a firm's profitability in the short run but at the same time alienate customers so that they defect as soon as an alternate source of supply becomes available. Price gouging can seriously injure a firm's long-run position. For example, a number of consumer groups have accused oil companies of engaging in price-gouging behavior when gasoline was in short supply during the summers of 2000 and 2001. Behavior not in society's best interest can have another kind of adverse long-run consequence: it can invite additional government regulation. Indeed, most laws currently on the books in a wide range of areas (financial disclosure, product safety, food and drug safety, contract requirements, and advertising claims) were enacted to eliminate abuses that were widespread at the time. To head off imposition of additional legal restrictions, managers must avoid abusive behavior giving rise to them.

Whether a particular behavior is abusive is sometimes difficult to determine, however. To explain the high prices charged by pharmaceutical firms, for example, managers claim that these high drug prices are needed to generate funds for further drug development. However, an increasing number of those who pay the bill—employers, state and local governments, and the public at large—are objecting to high pharmaceutical prices in the face of large profits. Negative sentiment is now so strong that some sort of legislation is likely. If enacted, it may be also be counterproductive to the point that drug companies have fewer incentives to invest in exploring and developing new treatments. This is an especially potent issue as Congress begins to consider the possibility of offering prescription drug coverage in its Medicare programs.

Summary

- Analysis of the external environment is vital for firms to identify opportunities and threats. The external environment may be examined from two different levels of analysis: the general macroenvironment and the more specific industry-level, competitive environment.
- The general macroenvironment describes those forces and conditions likely to affect all firms in the economy. The general environment includes such forces as the demographic environment, the political environment, the social/cultural environment, technological developments, and the global environment. These forces can have a stronger impact on some firms than on others.
- The competitive environment describes those forces and factors that characterize the specific industry conditions in which a firm competes. These forces often have immediate and direct effect on the firms in an industry.
- Porter's five forces model describes the key factors that influence an industry's environment. These forces include (1) the threat of new entrants, (2) the bargaining power of buyers, (3) the bargaining power of suppliers, (4) the intensity of rivalry, and (5) the potential threat of substitutes.
- Industry attractiveness defines the potential for profitability from competing in that industry. An attractive industry is one in which a high potential for earning profits exists. An unattractive industry is one with few opportunities to earn high profits.
- Strategic groups consist of those firms with similar strategic postures and competitive characteristics within an industry.
- Strategic group analysis helps managers develop competitive strategies for their firms within the context of the industry.
- Intensity of rivalry is often stronger among firms within a strategic group than among firms from different strategic groups.
- Environmental scanning is a set of techniques that allows managers to better understand and to track developments within the environment. An important scanning technique is that of competitor intelligence gathering.

Exercises and Discussion Questions

1. After the United States suffered through its worst attack on home soil on September 11, 2001, how do you think most companies will begin thinking about and planning to protect their people? What will the impact of September 11 be on firms that supply the commercial airline, hotel, gaming, and travel industries? If you were a supplier, what would be some things that you are likely to consider doing?
2. Around the world, people in many nations have not yet felt or realized the benefits of instituting economic policies that promote free enterprise at home and less restrictive trade abroad. If foreign governments increasingly turn away from these policies, what will likely be the impact on American companies? If you were the CEO of McDonald's, what strategies and actions would you consider taking? On the other hand, if you were Caterpillar, Ford Motor Company, or IBM, what would you be doing also?
3. Clearly, the personal computer industry is beginning to slow down dramatically after twenty years of phenomenal growth. What other industries do you see sharing similar characteristics with the PC industry? Do you think Palm and Handspring are likely to face the issues that now confront Compaq Computer, Hewlett-Packard, and Gateway? Are the changes taking placing in the personal computer industry likely to occur in the same way in other industries, such as consumer packaged goods or processed foods? What are some important differences between the PC industry and the consumer packaged goods industry?
4. As customers become ever more knowledgeable about the products they buy, they become more demanding about what they want from companies. How do you think companies should plan for the eventuality that customers become smarter and more savvy over time? Which firms appear to have a good grasp on how to understand their customers' evolving needs over time?

Endnotes

1. Data and facts for the personal computer industry were adapted from the following sources: "Dell Does Domination," *Fortune*, January 21, 2002, pp. 71–75; "On to the Living Room! Can Microsoft Control the Digital Home?" *Business Week*, January 21, 2002, pp. 68–72; "As PC Industry Slumps, IBM Hands Off Manufacturing of Desktops," *Wall Street Journal*, January 9, 2002, pp. B1, B4; "Dell Soars above Rival Amid Slump in Market for PCs," *Wall Street Journal*, January 18, 2002, p. B4; "Apple's 21st Century Walkman," *Fortune*, November 12, 2001, pp. 213–220; "Technology Grows Up," *Wall Street Journal*, October 25, 2001, pp. B1, B3; "Handspring Plans Line of Hybrid Devices," *Wall Street Journal*, October 15, 2001, p. B7; "Nokia Expects New 5510 Mobile Phone to Boost Popularity of Mobile Internet," *Wall Street Journal*, October 15, 2001, p. B7; "The New Computer Landscape," *Wall Street Journal*, September 6, 2001, pp. B1, B8; "Windows XP Pricing Looks Good for Consumers," *Wall Street Journal*, September 6, 2001, p. B4; "H-P's Deal for Compaq Has Doubters as Value of Plan Falls to $20.52 Billion," *Wall Street Journal*, September 5, 2001, pp. A3, A14; "Hewlett Packard Deal Will Hurt Component Suppliers," *Wall Street Journal*, September 5, 2001, p. B6; "As More Buyers Suffer from Upgrade Fatigue, PC Sales Are Falling," Wall Street Journal, August 24, 2001, pp. A1, A4; "Compaq to Give AOL Edge on XP PCs," *Wall Street Journal*, July 27, 2001, p. B2; "How Dell Fine-Tunes Its PC Pricing to Gain Edge in a Slow Market," *Wall Street Journal*, June 8, 2001, pp. A1, A8; "Dell Dethrones Compaq as Global PC Sales Leader," *Investor's Business Daily*, April 23, 2001, p. A6; "No Cartwheels for Handspring," *Business Week*, April 2, 2001, pp. 56–58; "Price War Squeezes PC Makers," *Wall Street Journal*, March 26, 2001, pp. B1, B3; "IBM Turns around Its PC Unit,

Though Skeptics Still Call It a Drag," *Wall Street Journal*, February 15, 2001, pp. B1, B4; "Market for Hand-Held Computers Doubled in 2000," *Wall Street Journal*, January 25, 2001, p. B6; "Market Declines for PCs," *Dallas Morning News*, January 20, 2001, p. 3F; "Domestic Growth in PC Market Hits Slowest Rate in 7 Years," *Wall Street Journal*, January 19, 2001, p. B3; "Chips Designed to Prod PC Sales," *Investor's Business Daily*, January 18, 2001, p. A4; "Palm, Microsoft Extend Rivalry to Wireless Arena," *Investor's Business Daily*, November 20, 2000, p. A6; "Many Current PCs Are Already Able to Record Music on Compact Discs," *Investor's Business Daily*, October 11, 2000, p. A6; "After AutoPC's Hard Ride, Detroit Tries Rebooting In-Car Computers," *Wall Street Journal*, October 4, 2000, pp. B1, B4; "Hand-Held Makers Spring Free from Parent," *Investor's Business Daily*, October 4, 2000, p. A12; "AOL to Roll Out Devices That Get You on the Internet without Requiring a PC," *Wall Street Journal*, April 16, 1999, p. B7; "DVDs Are Making Biggest Hit with Computer Buyers," *Wall Street Journal*, April 15, 1999, p. B4; "PC Matinee: The Race Is On to Make Web a Cyber-Cinema," *Wall Street Journal*, March 2, 1999, pp. B1–B4; "Beyond the PC," *Business Week*, March 8, 1999, pp. 79–88; "Will Pentium III Revive the Pricey PC?" *Business Week*, February 22, 1999, p. 38; "Compaq to Unveil New Presarios," *Wall Street Journal*, January 8, 1999; "From Microsoft Corp.: PC-Centric Gadgets Are a Little Too Tricky," *Wall Street Journal*, December 24, 1999, p. B1; "Is the PC Dead? Not Even Close," *Fortune*, December 21, 1998, p. 211+; "Dell Profit Jumps 55%, Beats Estimates," *Wall Street Journal*, November 13, 1998, p. A3; "Gadgets Move in on PC's Turf," *Wall Street Journal*, November 12, 1998, p. B1; "Intel Is Pushing for Simpler Personal Computers," *Wall Street Journal*, November 4, 1998, p. B6; "PC Demand Is Offset by Shrinking Prices," *Wall Street Journal*, October 26, 1998, p. B6; "IBM Plans to Unveil Aptiva Model for $599," *Wall Street Journal*, October 23, 1998, p. B5; "Pesky White Boxes Take Bigger Slice of PC Sales," *Investor's Business Daily*, October 21, 1998, p. A10; "Sony Plays on PC Margins as It Awaits Convergence," *Investor's Business Daily*, October 5, 1998, p. A10; "Gateway's Unusual Move: When Direct Meets Retail," *Investor's Business Daily*, September 29, 1998, p. A10; "Worldwide PC Shipments Expected to Rise 11% in '99," *Wall Street Journal*, September 25, 1998, p. B5; "AMD Chip May Cut Prices of Laptop," *Wall Street Journal*, September 22, 1998, p. B6; "PC Makers Equip Laptops with Latest Pentium II Chip," *Wall Street Journal*, September 10, 1998, p. B6; "Big PC Makers in Taiwan Post Sizable Gains," *Wall Street Journal*, September 8, 1998, p. B9F; "A PC in Your Car?" *Fortune*, September 7, 1998, p. 112+; "Dell Computer Looks to Hit a Home Run," *Investor's Business Daily*, August 20, 1998, p. A8; "Sun and IBM Release an Operating System in the Java Language," *Wall Street Journal*, August 5, 1998, p. B5; "The ABCs to Today's PC Bus? Spell It USB," *Investor's Business Daily*, July 31, 1998, p. A1; "Apple Introduces iMac, a Fast and Potent PC with a Sleek New Look," *Wall Street Journal*, July 30, 1998, p. B1; "Compaq Says Cheapest PCs Are Most Profitable," *Wall Street Journal*, July 14, 1998, p. B5; "Windows 98 Sales Exceed Pace of 95 Predecessor," *Wall Street Journal*, July 9, 1998; "How Low Can PCs Go? Not Much Lower," *Investor's Business Daily*, June 12, 1998, p. A1; "Packard to Offer Laptops Minus Explorer Icon," *Wall Street Journal*, June 1, 1998, p. B5; "Dell Delivers; HP Eats Crow," *Fortune*, May 25, 1998, p. 158; "PC Playing Field Tilts in Favor of Dell," *Wall Street Journal*, May 21, 1998, p. B8; "PC Makers Push Ahead on Windows 98," *Wall Street Journal*, May 19, 1998, p. B6; "The Squeeze Is on for PC Makers," *Fortune*, April 13, 1998, p. 182+; "Chip May Drive PC Prices under $400," *Wall Street Journal*, April 6, 1998, p. A4; "PC Makers Are Suffering from an Identity Crisis," *Investor's Business Daily*, March 19, 1998, p. A8; "Apple's Rise Is Tied to Marketing Strategy, New Products and Healthier Outlook for Products," *Wall Street Journal*, March 18, 1998, p. C2; "How IBM Turned around Its Ailing PC Division," *Wall Street Journal*, March 12, 1998, p. B1; "Are You Ready for PC-TV Convergence?" *Investor's Business Daily*, March 9, 1998, p. A1; "Can a Sub-$1,000 PC Meet Your Needs?" *Investor's Business Daily*, February 2, 1998, p. A1; "The Under $1,000 PC Offers All the Basics, But You May Need More," *Wall Street Journal*, December 11, 1997, p. B1; "PC Show Features Nerves and Wish List," *Wall Street Journal*,

November 14, 1997, p. B3; "IBM to Introduce $999 PC to Compete with Rivals," *Wall Street Journal*, November 6, 1997, p. B9; "Dell's Growth Seen Outpacing the Rest of the Industry," *Wall Street Journal*, September 5, 1997, p. B3; "Dell Fights PC Wars by Emphasizing Customer Service," *Wall Street Journal*, August 15, 1997, p. B4; "Dell Computer to Sell Workstations at Prices Below Competitors'," *Wall Street Journal*, July 28, 1997, p. B6; "Scanning Your Snapshots into a Printer?" *Business Week*, July 28, 1997, p. 88C; "A New Color Scanner That Makes Easy Work of Photos and Papers," *Wall Street Journal*, July 24, 1997, p. B1; "PC Makers, Intel to Unveil Scaled-Back NetPCs," *Wall Street Journal*, June 16, 1997, p. B7; "Intel to Unveil Its Pentium II Chips, Setting New Speed Standard for Rivals," *Wall Street Journal*, May 5, 1997, p. B8; "PC Market's Worldwide Growth Slowed during First Quarter," *Wall Street Journal*, April 28, 1997, p. B4; "Bargain PCs Thrill Buyers, Worry Makers," *Wall Street Journal*, February 24, 1997, p. B1; "Compaq Rethinks PC Design to Launch the Basic $999 Model," *Wall Street Journal*, February 20, 1997, p. B1; "PC Industry Is Underwhelmed by Network Machines," *Wall Street Journal*, November 22, 1996, p. B4.

2. See, for example, "Isolation at Top Hurts Minorities When Layoffs Hit," *Wall Street Journal*, January 29, 2002, pp. B1, B8.

3. See, for example, W. B. Johnston, "Global Work Force 2000: The New World Labor Market," *Harvard Business Review* (March–April 1991): 115–127.

4. See "Enron Collapse Has Congress Backing off Deregulation," *Wall Street Journal*, January 29, 2002, p. A22.

5. See, for example, A. J. Stern, "The Case of the Environmental Impasse," *Harvard Business Review* 69 (May–June 1991): 14–29. For an overview of how companies can formulate a strategic framework to think about environmental issues, see F. L. Reinhardt, "Bringing the Environment Down to Earth," *Harvard Business Review* 77, no. 4 (July–August 1999): 149–157.

6. See "Northwest, USAirways Continue Industry's Losing Streak," *Wall Street Journal*, January 18, 2002, p. B6; "American Air, Continental Report Losses Totalling Almost $1 Billion," *Wall Street Journal*, January 17, 2002, p. A4.

7. R. D. Dickinson, "The Business of Equal Opportunity," *Harvard Business Review* 70 (January–February 1992): 46–54.

8. See B. Avishai, "What Is Business's Social Compact?" *Harvard Business Review* 72 (January–February 1994): 38–48. Also see "When a Parent Needs Care," *Parade*, January 29, 1995, pp. 4–6.

9. See S. A. Zahra, "The Changing Rules of Global Competitiveness in the 21st Century," *Academy of Management Executive* 13, no. 1 (1999): 36–42.

10. See, for example, "FleetBoston Weighs Quitting Argentina, Cheapest Option but Politically Riskier," *Wall Street Journal*, January 18, 2002, p. A3.

11. See "KPN Chief Becomes Bellwether for European Telecoms," *Wall Street Journal*, January 29, 2002, p. A14.

12. See, for example, M. E. Porter, *Competitive Strategy* (New York: Free Press, 1980); M. E. Porter, *Competitive Advantage* (New York: Free Press, 1985); and M. E. Porter, "Towards a Dynamic Theory of Strategy," *Strategic Management Journal* 12 (Winter 1991): 95–117.

13. Early discussion of strategic groups is included in M. E. Porter, *Competitive Strategy* (New York: Free Press, 1980), chap. 7. Some of the most recent empirical work examining strategic groups include the select following: A. Fiegenbaum and H. Thomas, "Strategic Groups and Performance: The U.S. Insurance Industry, 1970–1984," *Strategic Management Journal* 11 (March 1990): 197–215; A. Fiegen-

baum, D. Sudharshan, and H. Thomas, "Strategic Time Periods and Strategic Groups Research: Concepts and Empirical Examples," *Journal of Management Studies* 27 (March 1990): 133–148; W. C. Bogner and H. Thomas, "The Role of Competitive Groups in Strategy Formulation: A Dynamic Integration of Two Competing Models," *Journal of Management Studies* 30 (January 1993): 51–68; R. E. Caves and P. Ghemawat, "Identifying Mobility Barriers," *Strategic Management Journal* 13 (January 1992): 1–13; M. J. Tang and H. Thomas, "The Concept of Strategic Groups: Theoretical Construct or Analytical Convenience?" *Managerial and Decision Economics* 13, no. 4 (1993): 323–330; K. O. Cool and I. Dierickx, "Rivalry, Strategic Groups and Firm Profitability," *Strategic Management Journal* 14, no. 1 (1993): 47–59; M. A. Peteraf, "Intraindustry Structure and Response towards Rivals," *Journal of Managerial and Decision Economics* 14 (1993): 519–528; R. Wiggins and T. Ruefli, "Necessary Conditions for the Predictive Validity of Strategic Groups: Analysis without Reliance on Clustering Techniques," *Academy of Management Journal* 38 (1995): 1635–1655; R. K. Reger and A. Huff, "Managerial Categorization of Competitors: Using Old Maps to Navigate New Environments," *Organization Science* 7 (1996): 22–39; D. Nath and T. S. Gruca, "Convergence across Alternative Methods for Forming Strategic Groups," *Strategic Management Journal* 18, no. 9 (1997): 745–760; M. Peteraf and M. Shanley, "Getting to Know You: A Theory of Strategic Group Identity," *Strategic Management Journal* 18, Special Issue (1997): 165–186; D. Dranove, M. A. Peteraf, and M. Shanley, "Do Strategic Groups Exist? An Economic Framework for Analysis," *Strategic Management Journal* 19, no. 11 (1998): 1029–1044.

Recent work on strategic groups has continued to examine their relationship with other measures of performance. See, for example, J. D. Osborne, C. I. Stubbart, and A. Ramaprasad, "Strategic Groups and Competitive Enactment: A Study of Dynamic Relationships between Mental Models and Performance," *Strategic Management Journal* 22, no. 5 (2001): 435–454; A Nair and S. Kotha, "Does Group Membership Matter? Evidence from the Japanese Steel Industry," *Strategic Management Journal* 22, no. 3 (2001): 221–235; T. D. Ferguson, D. L. Deephouse, and W. L. Ferguson, "Do Strategic Groups Differ in Reputation?" *Strategic Management Journal* 21, no. 12 (2000): 1195–1214.

14. See "Gateway May Announce More Store Closings," *Wall Street Journal*, January 24, 2002, p. B6.

15. See "Palm Device Sorts E-Mail in Real Time," *Wall Street Journal*, January 28, 2002, p. B6.

CHAPTER 3

Firm Capabilities: Assessing Strengths and Weaknesses

Chapter Outline

What You Will Learn

- The strategic tool known as the value chain
- The use of the value chain in evaluating an organization's internal strengths and weaknesses
- The differences between primary and supporting value-adding activities
- The concept of competitive advantage
- The concept of distinctive competence
- Some important economic sources of competitive advantage

Pizza Hut[1]

Pizza Hut, a division of Tricon Global Restaurants, is one of the largest sellers of pizza in the world. As such, it enjoys unique advantages not available to smaller rivals. These advantages have contributed significantly to its success during its years of growth over the past two decades. Although new competitors have clearly made significant market share gains in the restaurant industry, Tricon's Pizza Hut unit has been able to continue growth, although at a more moderate pace. Among the most important advantages Pizza Hut enjoys as a result of its leadership position are the following:

- **Location:** As the first competitor to establish a facility in many high-traffic areas, it has been able to preempt some of the most desirable restaurant locations.
- **Reputation:** The company has been in existence for a long time. In addition, it offers new types of pizza combinations in different markets. This allows Pizza Hut to maintain a high level of brand awareness.
- **Purchase discounts:** Its large-scale purchase of advertising time and food ingredients enables it to enjoy quantity discounts not available to smaller competitors.
- **Interrelationships:** Its interrelationships with other units of Tricon Global Restaurants, including Kentucky Fried Chicken (KFC) and Taco Bell, enable Pizza Hut to gain significant negotiation leverage with advertising firms to conduct jointly sponsored marketing campaigns. In addition, all three restaurant chains were once part of PepsiCo, the nation's second largest provider of beverages and the leader in snack foods through Frito-Lay. Even though all three restaurants have formally separated from PepsiCo since 1997, they still closely work with PepsiCo to secure lower cost beverages and other supplies from their former parent. These advantages are often less available to smaller rivals operating as single business firms.

Even with these many strengths, Pizza Hut's ability to maintain a dominant market share has repeatedly faced numerous challenges, especially from tough competitors such as Domino's Pizza, Papa John's International, and a host of locally owned restaurants that have strong roots in their respective communities. During the early 1980s, Pizza Hut miscalculated badly when it did not pursue the opportunity to supply the growing demand for home delivery of cooked pizza. This decision left the home delivery niche open to competitors, many of whom are better able to serve customers in this fast-growing but established niche. Although Pizza Hut still operates its traditional line of sit-down restaurants, it is now playing catch-up to Domino's Pizza and other home-delivery firms that have flourished in recent years. Now, Pizza Hut's primary strategic direction is to build a nationwide network of pizza preparation facilities that are solely dedicated to home delivery. Whether the company can retake some of the market share it has lost to Domino's Pizza and Papa John's International, however, remains an open question.

General Motors Corporation[2]

Despite its status as the world's largest automobile manufacturer, General Motors has faced numerous strategic and operational challenges over the past two decades, suffering a steady decline in market share (from 50 percent in 1979 to 26.6 percent in July 2001). Although the company is attempting to "reinvent itself" by offering highly advanced vehicles and newer car designs, General Motors (GM) remains caught in a quagmire of different issues, including flat productivity, difficult relations with workers, obsolete production facilities, and organizational practices that impede major improvements in product quality. Why has GM performed so poorly over the past two decades? The most likely factors are several weaknesses that continue to plague General Motors, despite numerous attempts to revitalize and improve its operations.

Flat Productivity Gains and Higher Costs

Even though GM's wage costs are now roughly comparable with those of Toyota and other competitors, GM has experienced difficulties in capturing major improvements in productivity growth over the past two decades. How well a company improves its productivity determines its long-term competitiveness vis-à-vis its rivals. Simply put, productivity is a measure of how much labor and capital is required to produce a given unit of output. Over time, successful companies should be able either to steadily produce more output with the same level of labor or capital or to find ways to reduce some of its labor and capital costs. While GM has taken major strides in the past three years to improve employee productivity, the company is still playing catch-up to such Japanese competitors as Toyota and Honda, who are better able to design, develop, manufacture, and distribute a new car in less time.

The original source of GM's lagging productivity can be attributed to the fairly large wage gap that resulted from lower wages paid to Japanese workers in the 1980s. However, as the wage gap has narrowed or even closed in recent years, GM's employee productivity per car in most instances has not yet caught up to its foreign and, in some cases, domestic rivals. When compared with Ford and Chrysler as recently as 1998, GM's employee productivity per car was still anywhere from 40 to 60 percent lower. Still, the company's productivity improvement efforts are beginning to pay off. Some analysts believe that GM has caught up to Ford in productivity in March 2001 for the first time in many years. Part of the reason for this change has been Ford's recent quality problems that have plagued a number of cars and sport-utility vehicles (SUVs) over the past two years.

Growth in productivity typically stems from a number of different factors, many of them directly related to how well the car is designed, the type of equipment used, and, especially, the management and motivation of the workforce. In addition, other factors can influence productivity, including the costs and procedures involved in ordering materials from suppliers. In particular, the numerous labor difficulties that all U.S. makers have experienced over the past decade, combined with difficulties in learning and adapting new technologies to the workplace, reveal just how interwoven labor relations and new technology are with productivity gains. Some of the factors that drive (or impede) productivity gains include the following:

- **Design:** How GM and other U.S. competitors approach product design is a significant reason why productivity gains are difficult to sustain. GM tends to design a new car model from the ground up, using a "clean sheet of paper" to redo all aspects of the car. This often means that components that were successfully used in an earlier line of cars are often not reused in a new one. Japanese manufacturers, in contrast, attempt to improve continuously the quality and durability of all the components used in their cars. If proven components work from year to year, they are incorporated in new cars, thus saving the manufacturer from spending large sums to test a new part.
- **Process technology:** When building a new factory, GM spends prodigiously on new robots, computer-aided technology, ultraclean paint rooms, and other "hardware" that make up the backbone of the factory. However, it often takes a long time to make sure that all parts of the factory are working together in a coordinated, synchronized manner. To make sure that this happens, GM needs to cultivate the knowledge and skills of its workers and technical personnel. However, GM's history of difficult labor relations has made workers fearful that the new technology is ultimately designed to replace them. As a result, workers have little interest in bringing the latest equipment up to speed.
- **Workforce motivation:** A huge problem for General Motors (and also for Ford and Chrysler Group) is the legacy of poor management–labor relations. To cut costs, GM closed dozens of U.S. plants in the 1990s. At the same time, to improve quality and focus, each GM plant has become more specialized in the activity that it performs. Thus, a strike at a plant that makes a critical component in one region of the country can have "ripple effects" that cause part shortages throughout GM's manufacturing network. In fact, a

labor confrontation over pay and benefit issues at a GM plant that makes steering components resulted in a nationwide shutdown of GM factory assembly operations in the summer of 1997. The decades-old practice and mind-set whereby GM would view the United Auto Workers (UAW) as the "enemy" rather than as a partner continue to sorely test and aggravate labor relations.

- **Procurement costs:** Another ongoing issue for GM is the high costs of paperwork when ordering materials, components, and suppliers from its vast network of suppliers in the United States and around the world. For almost all of GM's purchases, forms must be filled out in triplicate and often signed and countersigned to ensure that they are approved at different ranks or locations in the company. GM spends over $85 billion a year to order and work with a base of some thirty thousand suppliers. Overhauling the management of this vast network is now a top priority for GM, which is looking to use the Internet as a means of streamlining its ordering practices. However, getting approval from all parts of the company to use the Internet to accelerate orders, to lower costs, and to build on-line relationships with suppliers requires a "buy-in" and a change in mind-set from managers that will likely take a long time.

Lack of Focus in Manufacturing

Until the recent past, GM has traditionally made more (and bought less) of the components it uses to assemble cars than its rivals. GM must therefore spend more on factories, plants, and equipment than its competitors to build these components. The high cost of capital spending directly contributes to lower productivity gains. General Motors' internal parts-making unit, known as Delphi Automotive Systems, produces a whole range of different components and parts, ranging from automotive electronics to power trains and engines. However, Delphi faces many of the same labor-related and productivity problems that plague GM's automotive assembly operations. While a high degree of self-contained manufacturing can sometimes be an advantage, it turned out to be a weakness for GM. High wages and worker alienation also plague GM's component facilities, so the components they supply are often more expensive and less conveniently delivered than similar items available from outside suppliers. Oftentimes, outside suppliers can make components at far less cost and better quality than GM can. To remedy this issue, GM has begun to steadily seek more work from outside suppliers and to foster a better relationship with them to jointly design new components for the future. To ensure that it is able to lower the cost of its components and parts, GM is seeking to reduce the amount of work that it performs in-house. In fact, GM went as far as to make Delphi Automotive Systems an independent company in 2000 by selling the firm directly back to its shareholders. Delphi must now compete for GM's business in the same manner as any other external supplier.

Bureaucratic Delays

Because of its large size, GM experiences greater difficulty making and implementing decisions than its smaller competitors. This often slowed its adaptation to changes in the industry environment, such as the advent of new fuel cell technologies, the demand for minivans during the 1980s, and the growth of SUVs in the 1990s. For example, GM lagged behind Japanese rivals in seizing new opportunities to incorporate electronics and new computerized engine management technologies to improve fuel efficiency and performance during the early 1990s. Product development and design remain complex issues at GM, since they require the contribution, skills, and input from a number of different departments. However, GM's traditional approach to product development, which is often characterized by bureaucratic delays and infighting, frequently resulted in car designs and models that customers find dull and unexciting. Recognizing that most buyers of GM cars could not easily distinguish among the company's various lines of cars (e.g., Chevrolet, Pontiac, Buick), GM discontinued its Oldsmobile brand in December 2000 to give more focus to those brands that had higher market reach.

Introduction

To identify opportunities and to neutralize threats in the external environment, managers must thoroughly evaluate their firm's potential capabilities to compete. A significant part of successful strategy formulation depends on a careful assessment of the firm's strengths and weaknesses. This task requires each firm to conduct an internal analysis to determine those activities it can perform better than its competitors. Finding those activities or resources that allow the firm to perform in ways that other competitors cannot do as well is one key to developing effective strategies. Even though numerous rivals may compete in the same industry environment, some firms are likely to perform some activities better than others. Thus, each firm has its own particular set of strengths and weaknesses that influences how it competes.

This chapter examines the concept of firm capabilities and internal analysis of strengths and weaknesses. Developing effective strategies requires managers to understand how each firm's strengths and weaknesses may differ from those of competitors. These differences lay the foundation on which each firm bases its own strategy in the competitive environment.

We begin by examining the concept of the value chain. The value chain is an analytical tool that helps firms understand how their primary and supporting activities can be used to create value. It is the starting point to help firms identify their strengths and weaknesses. We will then apply the value chain analysis tool to examine the types of activities that occur in two different industries: pizzas and automobiles. In a later section, we discuss other issues related to developing firm capabilities outside the value chain, such as financial analysis and internal organization.

The Value Chain

To understand how a firm builds its capabilities to compete, one must identify the specific types of activities that make up the firm's competitive posture. Every firm engages in numerous activities that, in sum, determine its competitiveness in serving customers in the marketplace. These activities create economic value. A useful analytical tool for portraying and analyzing these activities is the value chain shown in Exhibit 3-1.[3] The **value chain** describes all of the activities that make up the economic performance and capabilities of the firm. It portrays activities required to create value for customers of a given product or service. As such, the value chain is an excellent framework by which managers can determine the strengths and weaknesses of each activity vis-à-vis the firm's competitors.

The value chain classifies each firm's activities into two broad categories: primary activities and support activities. **Primary activities** relate directly to the actual creation, development, manufacture, distribution, sale, and servicing of the product or service offered to the firm's customer. These activities represent the key tasks a firm performs to produce and deliver a product or service to a customer. **Support activities** refer to those tasks that contribute to or assist the firm's primary activities. In other words, support activities work to enhance or to help the functioning of primary value-adding activities. The combination of both primary and support activities determines the firm's basis for adding value. By breaking up the firm's value chain into discrete, isolated centers of activity, managers can assess whether they are performing each activity in ways that are better than that of their competitors (e.g., lower cost, better quality, faster delivery). In other words, it is not enough to say that one firm is better than another in some overall way; the value chain allows managers to compare their firm's specific activities with the same activities performed by competitors. Thus, comparing a firm's chain with that of competitors can provide valuable insight into each firm's individual strengths and weaknesses.

Activities in the value chain can be characterized as being upstream or downstream. **Upstream activities** occur far away from the consumer, closer to the firm's suppliers. In other words, upstream activities are performed in the early stages of the value-adding

value chain: An analytical tool that describes all activities that make up the economic performance and capabilities of the firm; used to analyze and examine activities that create value for a given firm.

primary activities: Economic activities that relate directly to the actual creation, manufacture, distribution, and sale of a product or service to the firm's customer (see *support activities*).

support activities: Economic activities that assist the firm's primary activities (see *primary activities*).

upstream activities: Economic activities that occur close to the firm's suppliers but far away from the consumer. Examples include inbound logistics, procurement, manufacturing, and operations (see also *downstream activities*).

EXHIBIT 3-1 The Value Chain

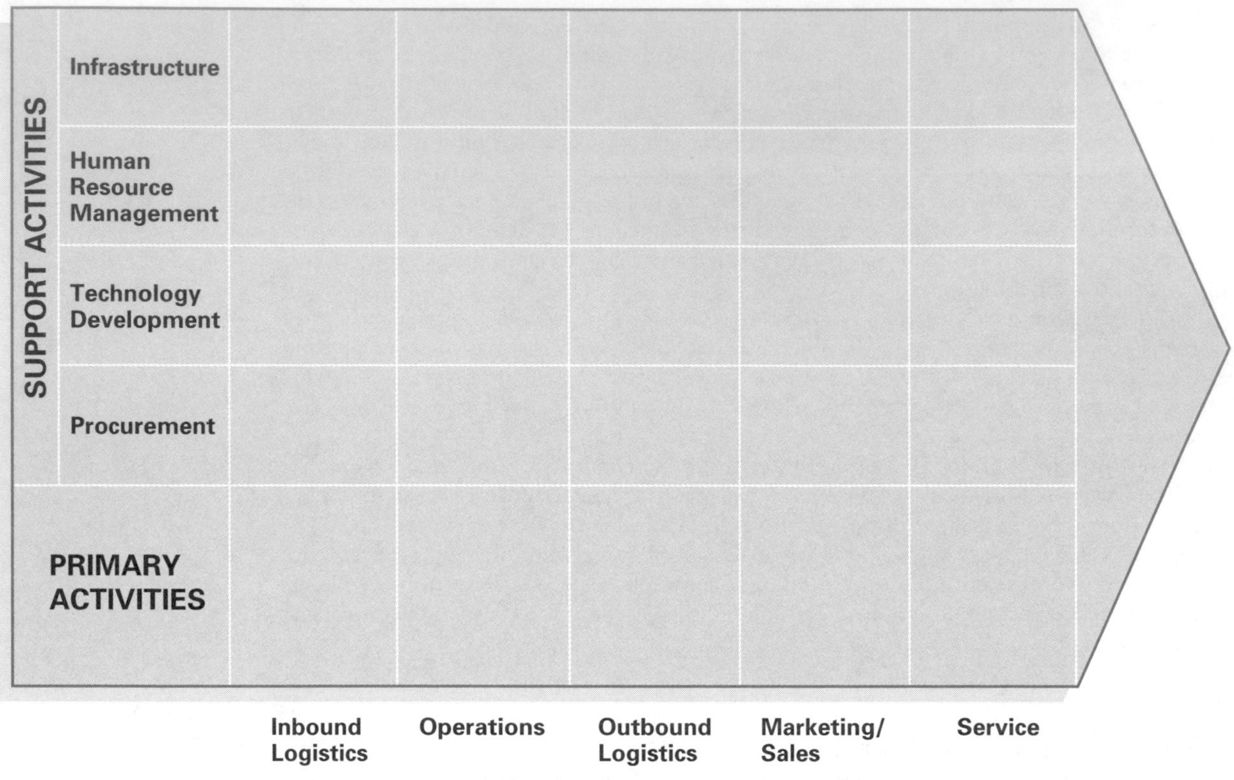

Reprinted/Adapted with the permission of The Free Press, a division of Simon & Schuster, Inc., from *Competitive Advantage: Creating and Sustaining Superior Performance*, by Michael E. Porter. Copyright © 1985 by Michael E. Porter.

downstream activities: Economic activities that occur close to the customer but far away from the firm's suppliers. Examples include outbound logistics, distribution, marketing, sales, and service (see also *upstream activities*).

process. **Downstream activities** occur closer to the firm's buyers. Downstream activities add value to those inputs that were processed through earlier upstream value-adding activities.

Primary Activities

The sequence of activities through which raw materials are transformed into benefits enjoyed by customers is called primary activities. These activities are shown along the bottom row of Exhibit 3-1. Five major activities make up this sequence: inbound logistics, operations, outbound logistics, marketing/sales, and service. Working together, these five activities determine the key operational tasks surrounding the product or service.

- *Inbound logistics*: In most industries, the transformation process begins with conveyance or delivery of raw materials to a firm's manufacturing (or service) facilities.
- *Operations*: Inputs are transformed into products.
- *Outbound logistics*: Products are shipped to distributors or to final users.
- *Marketing/sales*: Users are informed about products and encouraged to buy them.
- *Service*: Once in the customers' hands, products are installed, repaired, and maintained.

Let us now examine more closely the specific tasks and operational procedures that make up these five primary activities.

Inbound Logistics. As the words imply, inbound logistics deal with the handling of materials and inventory received from the firm's suppliers. The typical operational procedures and tasks surrounding inbound logistics include warehousing, storage, and control of raw materials or managing component flows from different suppliers. Inbound logistics are considered a primary activity because they represent the beginning of the firm's value-adding conversion of inputs. Inbound logistics represent a major source of direct costs to the firm; thus, new techniques and improvements in inventory control, storage, and materials handling can dramatically improve a firm's cost position in this activity. For example, a reduction in inventory and storage costs over time can have a major positive impact on a firm's cost position. Differences in storage and inventory costs relative to one's competitors can add up to a significant competitive strength or weakness.

In many firms, inbound logistics require significant capital investment. The location and management of warehouses, and the inventory held in them, are important areas in which to focus cost control and efficiency. Many manufacturers around the world have taken numerous steps in recent years to improve the efficiency and reduce costs involved with inbound logistics activities. At General Electric, for example, the huge major appliances (dishwashers, refrigerators) plant at Louisville, Kentucky, uses highly automated bar coding, sorting, and inventory checking systems that enable GE to move components and parts quickly from the railhead to its factory. Parts and components do not sit idle in warehouses for long. Fast movement of components and inventory greatly reduces the operating costs for the entire Major Home Appliance Group business.

Improvements in inbound logistics activities are not confined to manufacturing firms. For example, both United Parcel Service (UPS) and Federal Express (now a unit of FedEx Corporation) have built strong competitive positions by using techniques that promote superefficient, time-responsive sorting of packages and overnight mail. Both firms expect their business to grow substantially with the rise of on-line ordering and delivery through the Internet and e-commerce. Likewise, hospitals depend on smooth, well-honed ordering and delivery systems to ensure that critical supplies of pharmaceuticals, medical supplies, and surgical instruments are available on a daily basis. Banks and financial service firms depend on extremely automated, real-time, and efficient inbound, computer-driven logistics to manage, coordinate, and track the flow of payments and funds that enter their systems for different purposes such as check clearance, credit card payments, investments, and cash management.

Operations. Operations are the activities and procedures that transform raw materials, components, and other inputs into finished end products. In other words, operations concerns itself with the generation, manufacture, and/or production of products and services. Specific task activities in the operations realm include stamping, machining, testing, fabrication, and assembly in manufacturing-based settings. In a broader sense, any type of *processing* activity that results in a product or service is the heart of the firm's operations. Operations also represents the dominant upstream activity in many firms. Success in managing and improving upstream operations over time represents a critical source of leverage in building or reinforcing a firm's ability to compete in a sustained manner. Differences between firms conducting similar types of operations may result from relative age of equipment, type of technology used, size of plant, economies of scale, degree of automation, productivity levels and gains, wage rates, and possible improvements resulting from longer experience.

For many service businesses, operations is concerned directly with the provisioning of a service to its customers. For telecommunications firms, operations is focused on managing and updating the vast network of routers, switches, and other gear that is at the backbone of communications and the Internet. For health care providers, operations represents a multifaceted set of activities, ranging from emergency room care, to surgery, to postoperative care, and to direct personal care of patients. Operations in a financial services firm could relate to check clearing and automated teller machines (ATMs) for banks, trading securities for brokerages, and transmitting funds and clearing credit transactions for banks and credit card processors.

In many ways, how a firm manages its production/transformation operations will strongly influence the entire firm's competitive posture. For example, in the chemical, oil refining, and paper industries, the dominant production mode is that of continuous flow processes. Continuous flow processes are characterized by rigid and dedicated production systems geared to the standardized production of a single or limited range of products. These capital-intensive processes are costly to operate and hard to switch between products; they represent very large fixed costs for the firm. Any disruption of a continuous flow process generates enormous downtime costs for the firm. As a result, firms in industries whose dominant production mode is that of continuous flow processes are likely to develop strategies that recognize the nature of the production process's high fixed costs, rigidity, and lack of flexibility in switching to alternative products.

The considerable focus and effort that firms have placed on implementing total quality improvement (TQM) in manufacturing and service spawned new technologies and practices that allow firms to improve the efficiency and quality of their operations-based activities. Consider, for example, the illustration of Nucor in the steel industry. Unlike integrated steel mills such as Bethlehem Steel, USX's U.S. Steel unit, and AK Steel, Nucor built up a significant competitive position in the steel industry by focusing on minimills. These mills are superefficient and can produce a ton of steel of significantly better quality for less cost than older integrated mills. Investment in highly responsive and efficient minimills has enabled Nucor to sustain its profitability for many years, even when the industry moved into downturns and recessions. The focus on improving operations has certainly not been limited to the heavy manufacturing sector. Motorola, a leading manufacturer of semiconductors, electronic components, and cellular telephones, has made enormous strides by simultaneously improving the responsiveness, cost efficiency, and quality of its manufacturing process during the 1990s. Motorola views sustained investment and improvement in advanced manufacturing technologies as central to its ability to compete.

Outbound Logistics. Outbound logistics refers to the transfer of finished end product to the distribution channels. The focus in outbound logistics is on managing the flow and distribution of products to the firm's immediate buyers, such as wholesalers and retailers. Activities and procedures associated with outbound logistics include inventory control, warehousing, storage, and transport of finished products. As is the case with inbound logistics and operations, improvements in efficiency and responsiveness of outbound logistics can greatly aid the firm's competitive posture. Firms can build competitive strengths based on their ability to lower the costs of outbound distribution and to enhance responsiveness.

Procter & Gamble (P&G) over the past several years has made major efforts to improve the efficiency and turnaround of its outbound logistics activities. By linking up more closely with key wholesalers and retailers (e.g., Wal-Mart Stores), P&G has accelerated the timely delivery of goods that retailers have trouble stocking. By making extensive use of bar-coding technology, P&G and its key buyers balance the flow of inventory and goods between P&G's warehouses and the retailers' store shelves. This responsive distribution system becomes an overwhelming competitive strength for P&G and helps the company track which products are in particularly high demand. Conversely, a close understanding of how its products are distributed gives P&G a better understanding of how to work with its buyers to improve everyone's margin over time.

Marketing and Sales. Marketing and sales activities include advertising, promotion, product mix, pricing, specific distribution channels, working with wholesalers, and sales force issues. Marketing is vital in helping the firm determine the *competitive scope* of its value-adding activities. For example, some firms may decide to concentrate their efforts on a specific market segment or niche, while other firms may want to pursue a more broadline product strategy. Thus, marketing becomes a vehicle by which the firm can develop specific competitive postures and strategies to serve a variety of segments or niches within the industry. Marketing activities deal extensively with pricing issues as well. The price of a firm's product can be an important signal or indicator of the firm's value-creating capabilities; a product's price becomes a surrogate measure of what value the firm is delivering to the market. Marketing activities also represent a central part of the firm's downstream value-adding activities; planning in these activities is oriented toward meeting the needs of immediate buyers and the final consumer.

Clearly, numerous companies have built extensive competitive positions and strengths based on their superior approaches to managing marketing activities. Companies such as Coca-Cola, McDonald's, PepsiCo, Pfizer, American Home Products, Bristol-Myers Squibb, Schering-Plough, and American Express come to mind as leading corporate examples of firms that have built effective competitive strengths based on excellence in marketing activities. Pharmaceutical firms, in particular, have begun direct marketing campaigns to promote their leading-edge products, as well as to encourage customers to ask their physicians if certain types of drugs are appropriate for them.

Service. Customer service is a central value-adding activity that a firm can seek to improve over time. During the 1990s, an increasing number of companies began redefining the way they manage their customer service activities. Value is more often defined in the *eyes of the customer* rather than by what the firm thinks it has created. Thus, customer service has become a vital means to compete in any industry environment. Customer service includes such activities and procedures as warranty, repair, installation, customer support, product adjustment and modification, and immediate response to customer needs.

Customer service is so important as a competitive weapon because it enables a firm to create value immediately before the customer's eyes. How well the firm conducts these tasks will strongly impact the customer's preference for buying from the firm again in the future. Both FedEx and UPS thrive in the overnight delivery business because of their superior approaches to customer service. Both firms also allow and even encourage customers to track the status of their packages and deliveries through the Internet. Conversely, the U.S. Postal Service, which offers a similar overnight delivery service, has only just begun to match what FedEx and UPS can offer in terms of Internet-based tracking systems. Despite the enormous size and reach of the postal system, many business customers still prefer to rely on FedEx and UPS for managing their critical deliveries and urgent package shipments.

Companies in every industry ranging from telecommunications to hotels, industrial equipment, and hospitals are rethinking and reinventing the ways they perform customer service activities. For example, many current reengineering efforts are devoted to improving how firms meet their customers' needs. **Reengineering** means redefining the way firms organize their operations to improve responsiveness to customer needs. For example, at most telecommunications companies, customers can now call one number and get all of the information they need about their account from one customer service representative. In the past, customers had to dial separate numbers for different requests, such as telephone installation, equipment repair, leasing, purchase, and account adjustments.

reengineering: The complete rethinking, reinventing, and redesign of how a business or set of activities operates.

Perhaps the most important source of technological change that has transformed the very notion of fast and responsive customer service is the Internet. Barnes & Noble, L.L. Bean, Xerox, IBM, General Electric, Dell Computer, Fidelity Investments, Charles Schwab, and Wells Fargo are among the firms that have begun to lead the way in using the Internet as a competitive weapon to dramatically improve their customer service operations. By creating sophisticated Web sites, many companies are encouraging their current and potential customers to use the Internet as a means to gather information, select their desired products, and order products through on-line, instantaneous transactions. In the financial services industry, for example, many securities brokerage operations (e.g., Fidelity, Schwab, Merrill Lynch, Morgan Stanley Dean Witter) have built state-of-the-art, secure Internet sites that enable customers to set up accounts, transfer funds, and invest in stocks and other investment vehicles from their computer screens. Eventually, all of their competitors have done the same to provide convenient service to customers. In fact, entirely new companies such as Ameritrade and E*Trade have become thriving, vibrant competitors to existing financial service firms by offering customers low-cost commission and transaction fees through the Internet to trade stocks.

In the most advanced form of Internet-driven customer service, companies such as IBM, Intel, Dell Computer, General Electric, and Amazon.com are using the Internet to link up directly and transfer a customer's order to their distribution centers, factories, and even suppliers for immediate processing, billing, and delivery. Dell Computer, for example, can receive and process a customer's order for a highly customized personal computer over the Internet and have it shipped and delivered in less than four days. Amazon.com, a company that did not exist as recently as 1995, has become a major retailer of books, compact discs (CDs), videos, toys, and other items through the Internet. By allowing customers to order any book or music CD in print, Amazon.com offers customers a fast, secure, and easy way to purchase these items (often at prices lower than those of existing brick-and-mortar competitors) without leaving the comforts of their home.

The Internet is becoming a powerful tool that companies and organizations in every industry are using to make themselves more responsive to the needs of their customers. The Internet has become an important economic driver of distribution, marketing, and service for all types of firms, even those in less technologically intensive industries. For example, grocery store chains are beginning to harness the power of the Internet to enable customers to order food and other items for fast delivery. Some analysts are predicting that by the middle of this decade, on-line transactions on the Internet may become anywhere from 25 to 33 percent of total revenues.

Support Activities

The remaining activities of the value chain are undertaken to support primary activities. They are therefore referred to as support activities. Support activities help the firm improve coordination across and achieve efficiency within the firm's primary value-adding activities. Support activities are located across the first four rows in Exhibit 3-1 and include procurement, technology development, human resource management, and firm-level infrastructure.

- *Procurement*: Inputs are secured for primary activities.
- *Technology development*: Methods of performing primary activities are improved.
- *Human resource management*: Employees who will carry out primary activities are recruited, trained, motivated, and supervised.
- *Infrastructure*: Activities such as accounting, finance, legal affairs, and regulatory compliance are carried out to provide ancillary support for primary activities.

Since each primary activity generally requires assistance in each of these four areas, the value chain includes four cells above each primary activity, one for each category of support activity. Let us examine how each of these four support activities contributes to building the firm's capabilities.

Procurement. Procurement refers to purchasing the necessary inputs, resources, or components for the firm's primary value-adding activity. The purchasing function involves specific procedures such as billing systems, methods for dealing with suppliers and vendors, and information systems about different components and parts. Even though it is a support activity, the purchasing function can significantly enhance the firm's cost position relative to its competitors. Improved procurement practices enable the firm to gain significant economies of scale and higher bargaining power over suppliers if the firm coordinates its procurement across different functions and even businesses.

Technology Development. Technology is found in every value-adding activity within the firm. Given the rapid technological changes that are present in almost every industry (e.g., new forms of communications, software, Internet), this support activity has assumed enormous importance in every firm. Technology in firms today transcends the conventional wisdom that it is primarily focused on research and development (R&D). Although most firms still have engineering and R&D staffs devoted to exploring and using new sources of technology, in practice, technology is developed and used in countless ways throughout the firm. It can be the software found in computers, the standard operating procedures used to manage a factory, the human know-how employed in developing, manufacturing, and selling products, the layout of the factory, the sophisticated nature of the firm's Internet capabilities, and the laboratory equipment involved in the firm's value-adding activities. Technology is pervasive in both upstream and downstream activities of the firm.

Technology is concerned with both *product* development and *process* development. **Product development** refers to the conception, design, and commercialization of new products. For example, the design of new aircraft, more sophisticated microchips, better-tasting potato chips, and faster-heating, microwave-oriented convenience foods all represent different types of product development. Even though the end products are completely different, they are all based on the firm's ability to conceive and design new product ideas. **Process development**, on the other hand, refers to the development and use of new procedures, practices, or equipment to improve the value-adding activity itself. For example, the development of new assembly and packaging techniques, the use of new factory layouts to reduce work-in-process (WIP), the creation of a new medium to deliver advertising, and the improvement of inventory tracking systems represent some different ways to conduct process development. The aim of process development is to adapt new techniques or to improve existing methods of conducting value-adding activities.

product development: the conception, design, and commercialization of new products.

process development: The design and use of new procedures, technologies, techniques, and other steps to improve value-adding activities.

Many companies have refocused efforts on technology development to improve their value-adding activities. For example, Allen-Bradley (a unit of Rockwell International), a leading U.S. producer of motor controls, has developed new techniques to use factory automation that have dramatically reduced the unit costs of new motor components. Likewise, competitors in the pizza restaurant business are investigating new types of pizzas that they can offer their customers; they are also looking at investing in faster, state-of-the-art ovens to improve consistency. General Electric has invested large sums to introduce new forms of flexible automation and materials handling that lower the production costs and improve the quality of its dishwashers and refrigerators. These firms are investing steadily in technology—product and process—to find new sources of competitive strength.

Human Resource Management. Human resource management refers to working with people throughout the firm. These activities focus on recruiting, hiring, compensating, and training people to perform their jobs within the firm. As with technology development, human resource management receives considerable attention from top management because of its strategic role in helping the firm learn and build new types of competitive skills. Human resource management activities thus affect every aspect of the firm's value-adding activities.

When conducted properly, human resource management enables the firm to cultivate the skills necessary for competitive success. Although managers typically tend to think of investments in terms of capital budgets and physical, durable assets, continuous investment in the firm's people represents a more enduring way to build the firm's capabilities. Managers and employees are the most flexible and capable assets firms have. By providing the right levels of training, firms can assign people to perform different tasks, thus enhancing job satisfaction, efficiency, and quality. However, assessing the direct costs of investing in human resource activities is often difficult, since factors such as employee turnover and morale are hard to measure.

Successful human resource management is often a key factor in determining a firm's competitive strengths. As a result, hotels and restaurants need to ensure that their employees are well trained and know the correct procedures for treating guests. Direct customer service activities, in particular, require extensive training. Professional service firms, such as accounting, architecture, management consulting, and legal firms, depend heavily on the human resource function to recruit, select, and hire the right people that make up the workforce.

Firm Infrastructure. Infrastructure include such activities as finance, accounting, legal affairs, information systems, and payroll. These activities assist all of a firm's value-adding functions, so it is difficult to put an accurate dollar figure on their worth to the firm. Since infrastructure costs are hard to isolate, they are often called *overhead expenses.* Although many firms seek to cut infrastructure expenses during business downturns, such activities can be important sources of competitive strength. For example, in highly regulated industry environments, such as electric utilities, telecommunications, financial services, and pharmaceuticals, the firm's legal department can be as critical to success as operations, outbound logistics, marketing, or technology development activities. Understanding legislation and government regulations may be just as important as designing new types of drugs or pricing long-distance telephone calls. Thus, infrastructure activities cannot be ignored when formulating competitive strategies.

Pizza Industry Value Chain

Let us now apply the value chain concept to a service setting, using the pizza restaurant industry as our reference point (see Exhibit 3-2).

Primary Activities

The value chain in this industry begins with transport of foodstuffs, such as dough, cheese, and pasta, from suppliers to restaurants (inbound logistics). Materials are then con-

EXHIBIT 3-2 Pizza Restaurant Industry Value Chain

		Inbound Logistics	Operations	Outbound Logistics	Marketing/ Sales	Service
SUPPORT ACTIVITIES	Infrastructure	Obtain funds, carry out accounting and payroll functions, and perform other administrative tasks for each activity.				
	Human Resource Management	Supervise truck drivers and warehouse personnel	Supervise kitchen personnel		Supervise advertising personnel	Supervise waiters
	Technology Development	Improve truck routing and warehouse methods	Develop new menu items; improve oven design		Discover new promotional materials	Improve restaurant layout
	Procurement	Buy trucks; lease warehouse space	Buy dough, cheese, ovens, and other supplies		Buy TV time	Buy tables, chairs, silverware to equip restaurant
PRIMARY ACTIVITIES		Transport dough, cheese, etc., to restaurants	Cook pizzas; make salads; prepare other menu items		Develop advertising copy	Serve food to restaurant customers

verted in each restaurant's kitchen into items such as pizza and salads (operations), which are then served to customers (service). In addition, customers must be persuaded to seek restaurant service (marketing/sales). Note that outbound logistics is not a part of this industry's value chain since customers come to a pizza restaurant to be served. Indeed, outbound logistics is, to a large degree, significantly absent from the value chain in many service industries, including hospital services, tax preparation assistance, and higher education.

Support Activities

Let us now examine the support these activities require.

Procurement. Trucks and warehouse space must be procured to perform inbound logistics activity; ovens and foodstuffs to perform operations; TV advertising to perform marketing/sales; and tables, chairs, and silverware to provide restaurant service. Since restaurant firms do not generally produce these inputs themselves, they must procure them from outside vendors. Identification of suppliers for these inputs, evaluation of supplier offerings, and negotiation of purchase terms are major procurement activities in this industry.

Technology Development. Movement of materials to restaurant sites can be improved by streamlining warehousing methods, kitchen operation by designing better ovens, marketing/sales by devising more effective advertising copy, and restaurant service by improving restaurant design. Opportunities for technology development thus exist in each primary activity of the industry.

Human Resource Management. Personnel responsible for inbound logistics, for operations and service, and for marketing must be hired, trained, and supervised.

Infrastructure. Finally, those involved in primary activities need financing and budgeting assistance, accounting activities, and legal affairs. These are infrastructure activities.

Automobile Industry Value Chain

To illustrate the value chain in a manufacturing context, consider the automobile industry (see Exhibit 3.3).

Primary Activities

The value chain in this industry begins with transport of components from suppliers to auto assembly facilities (inbound logistics). Components are then assembled into finished autos (operations), and the finished cars are shipped to dealers (outbound logistics). Finally, dealers sell cars to customers (marketing/sales) and maintain the products owned by customers (service).

Support Activities

These primary activities require assistance in each of the support areas noted previously.

Procurement. Trucks and warehouse space must be procured to perform inbound and outbound logistics; machinery, raw materials, and components to operate factories; media

EXHIBIT 3-3 Automobile Industry Value Chain

		Inbound Logistics	Operations	Outbound Logistics	Marketing/Sales	Service
SUPPORT ACTIVITIES	Infrastructure	Obtain funds, carry out accounting and payroll functions, and perform other administrative tasks for each activity.				
	Human Resource Management	Supervise truck drivers and warehouse personnel	Supervise assembly workers	(Same as inbound logistics)	Supervise advertising and sales personnel	Supervise maintenance personnel
	Technology Development	Improve truck loading procedures and warehouse methods	Improve product design and assembly process	(Same as inbound logistics)	Improve selling methods	Improve maintenance procedures
	Procurement	Buy trucks; lease warehouse space	Buy components and assembly equipment	(Same as inbound logistics)	Hire advertising agency; buy media time	Buy tools for maintenance personnel
PRIMARY ACTIVITIES		Transport components to assembly facility	Make and assemble components into autos	Transport autos to dealers	Advertise, promote, and sell autos	Maintain and repair autos

advertising space to conduct marketing/sales; and specialized tools, lubricants, parts, and diagnostic machines to provide auto service. Identification of suppliers for these inputs, evaluation of supplier offerings, and negotiation of prices are procurement activities. Note that procurement does not deal with the physical movement of goods or "logistics." Rather, it focuses on identification of suppliers, evaluation of supplier offerings, and negotiation of purchase terms.

Technology Development. Inbound and outbound logistics activities in the auto industry can be improved by redesigning the flow of component and finished product inventories in warehouses and transportation facilities. Auto firms can improve their operations by simplifying product design, introducing automated manufacturing techniques, utilizing robots and computers, and redesigning factories to make work easier and more satisfying for employees. Marketing and sales can be improved through designing better advertising copy, while service activity can be improved by instituting more efficient repair procedures, training service personnel to be more responsive to customer needs, and installing more sophisticated diagnostic equipment. Activities undertaken to achieve such improvement are designated technology development.

Human Resource Management. Personnel performing primary activities must be recruited, trained, developed, and supervised. Human resource management, through its activities, helps improve product quality, innovation, and productivity.

Infrastructure. Primary activities require capital budgeting, financing, accounting, legal affairs, governmental affairs, and other administrative assistance. These infrastructure activities help automakers finance expansion, communicate with shareholders, and work with the government in implementing new types of environmental and fuel efficiency regulations.

The Value Chain as Part of a Business System

So far, we have seen how different activities make up the value chain. A firm need not always perform every single activity of the value chain. Indeed, most firms do not. The subset of value chain activities that a firm actually performs is referred to as its *business system*.[4] To illustrate, let us return to Pizza Hut and General Motors.

Pizza Hut

Pizza Hut's business system includes only a portion of the activities contained in its industry's value chain (see Exhibit 3-4).

Primary Activities. Suppliers deliver raw materials to Pizza Hut's restaurants. Consequently, Pizza Hut performs little inbound logistics activity. Pizza Hut's restaurant business

Pizza Hut's Business System EXHIBIT 3-4

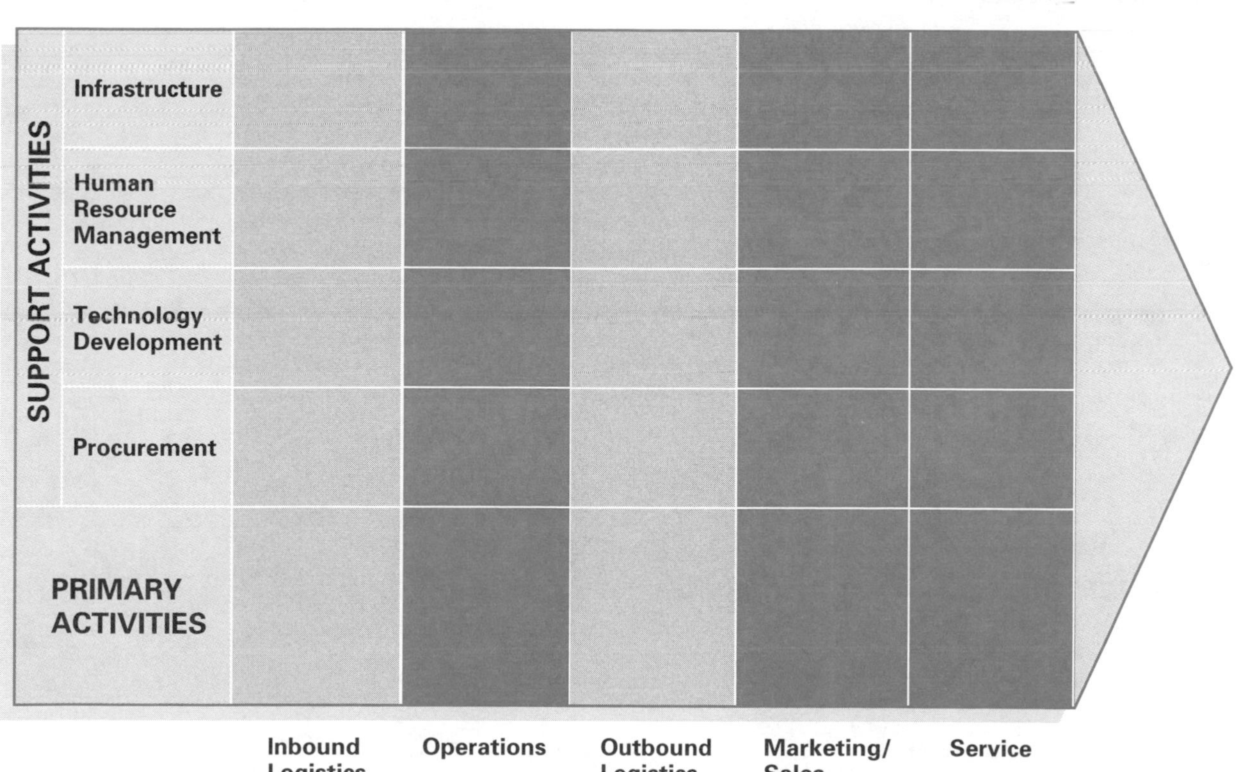

Reprinted/Adapted with the permission of The Free Press, a division of Simon & Schuster, Inc., from *Competitive Advantage: Creating and Sustaining Superior Performance*, by Michael E. Porter. Copyright © 1985 by Michael E. Porter.

performs no outbound logistics at all since customers come to its facilities to be served. However, Pizza Hut is extensively involved in operations (food preparation), marketing/sales (mainly advertising), and service (serving restaurant customers). These three activities are therefore integral parts of its business system.

Support Activities. Pizza Hut conducts procurement activity for each of its primary activities. For example, it procures dough, cheese, ingredients, and ovens for operations; TV advertising time for marketing/sales; and tables, chairs, and silverware for service. It also conducts technology development activity for each primary activity. For example, Pizza Hut devotes considerable effort to improve pizza-making procedures, to enhance advertising copy, and to streamline restaurant design. It also conducts extensive human resource management and infrastructure activities for each primary activity. These support activities are therefore integral parts of its business system.

General Motors

General Motors' business system is shown in Exhibit 3-5. As indicated, it includes many but not all activities of the automobile industry value chain.

Primary Activities. GM makes many of its own components, warehouses them, and transports them to its assembly sites. However, it also purchases an increasing number of components from outside suppliers. This number is certain to grow as Delphi Automotive

EXHIBIT 3-5 General Motors' Business System

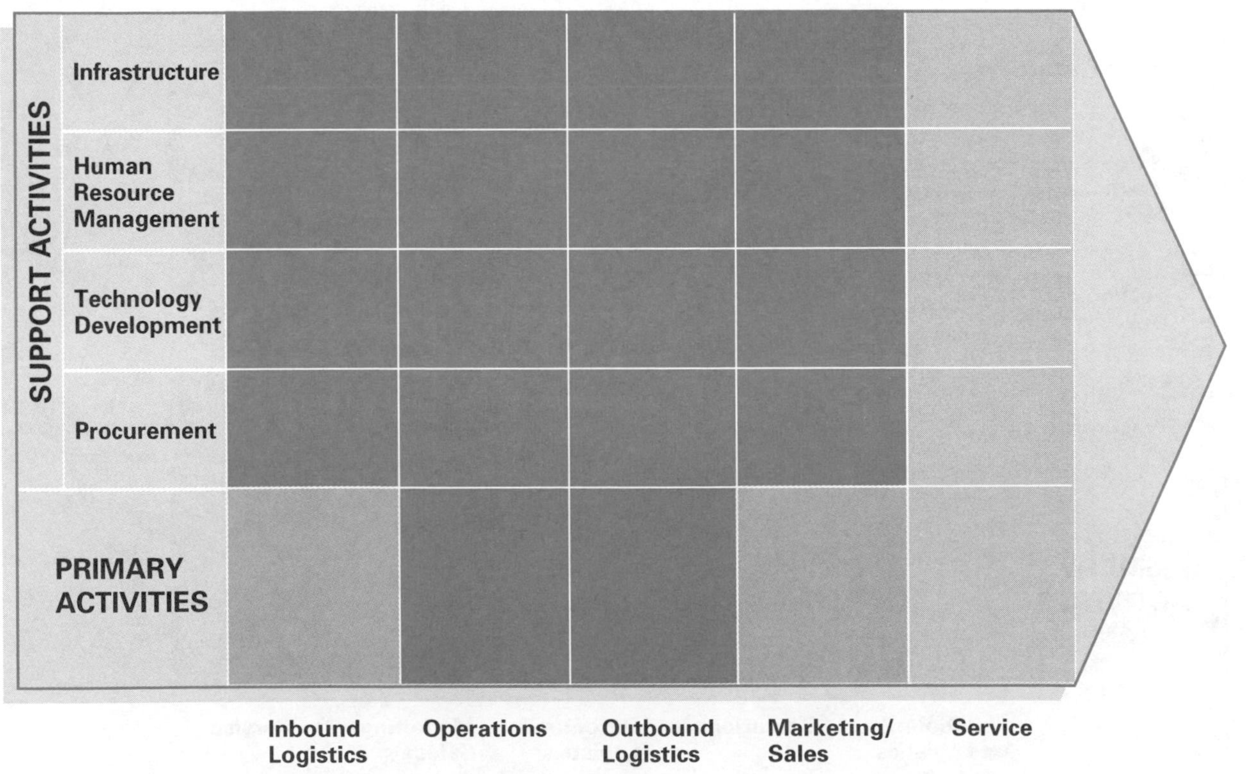

Systems has become a fully independent company that is no longer part of GM. These purchased components are generally delivered to GM's facilities by other firms, such as trucking and railroad companies. Consequently, GM performs some, but not all, inbound logistics activity associated with its business. It builds and assembles components into automobiles and delivers finished autos to dealers; therefore, it is extensively involved in both operations and outbound logistics. GM advertises its products but leaves the actual selling up to its dealers; it thus performs only a portion of the marketing/sales activity associated with its industry. Independently owned dealers maintain and repair GM vehicles, so GM is not significantly involved in auto service.

Support Activities. Procurement activities for GM include purchase of components for cars, factory equipment from machine tool and electronics companies, automotive paints and coatings from chemical firms, and lubricants and supplies from oil and chemical companies. General Motors devotes considerable effort to technology development for its key value-adding activities. For example, it is attempting to improve internal warehousing and factory inventory control through just-in-time (JIT) techniques. GM has invested heavily in new forms of factory automation and software to improve both product quality and the responsiveness of its factories. GM also commits substantial resources and effort to managing the human resource function. For example, it must work closely with the union leadership to create new labor contracts. Within individual plants, GM attempts to cooperate with workers to find new ways and insights to build better cars. Finally, it has an extensive group of people working in legal affairs and government relations. In recent years, the company has spent considerable time working with consumer groups and government safety boards.

Capability Drivers

Once a firm's various activities have been identified using the value chain, an analyst interested in strategy must then assess the firm's capability in performing each activity. Any activity that the firm can perform more efficiently than its rivals (because fewer resources are required) or more effectively than rivals (because greater customer benefits are produced with the same resources) constitutes a strength. Similarly, activities that the firm performs less efficiently and effectively than rivals constitute weakness. The specific attributes and practices that determine efficiency and effectiveness differ markedly across industries. For example, the practices that enable the Walt Disney Company to excel in theme park operations are very different from those underpinning Intel's success in microprocessors. As a result of these differences, it is difficult to provide general guidance to a strategy analyst on what to look for when trying to assess a firm's strengths and weaknesses. However, guidance is possible at a more general level. In most industries, enduring competitive strength (i.e., strength that cannot be easily duplicated or imitated by rivals) derives from a few fundamental capability drivers. **Capability drivers** represent broad routes to achieving competitive strength regardless of the particular industry setting in which a firm operates. By assessing capability drivers underlying an activity, an analyst can often gain valuable insight into whether a firm possesses strength in performing the activity. In this section, we examine four common capability drivers—first-mover status, scale, experience, and interrelationships—and consider the kinds of competitive strength provided by each.

capability drivers: The basic economic and strategic means by which a firm builds an underlying source of competitive advantage in its market or industry. Examples of basic capability drivers include first-mover advantages, economies of scale, experience effects, and interrelationships among business units.

First-Mover Status

Early entrants to an industry sometimes enjoy benefits that are not available to firms arriving later. These benefits are referred to as **first-mover advantages**.[5] Common benefits in this category are patent protection, a government license, superior location, channel access, supply access, and reputation (see Exhibit 3-6). In most instances, firms attempting

first-mover advantages: The benefits that firms enjoy from being the first or earliest to compete in an industry.

EXHIBIT 3-6 Common First-Mover Advantages

- Patents
- License
- Location
- Channel access
- Supply access
- Reputation

to exploit a first-mover advantage must move quickly to penetrate its market and stake out its position. More often than not, first-mover advantages allow a new firm to seize the initiative early on, but the firm must be able to reinforce its position through sustained investment and continuous innovation. Because established firms have operated in the competitive environment for longer periods of time, they often possess commanding, but not impenetrable, advantages over new entrants in these areas.

Patent Protection. Established firms sometimes own patents on important technology. They enjoy a strong competitive advantage over new entrants that must either circumvent the patented technology or develop a new one on their own. Xerox Corporation, for example, held early patent rights to the xerographic duplicating process. These rights gave it a strong advantage over other entrants during the long period over which the patents applied. In the pharmaceutical industry, patents are a critically important source of advantage, since they legally protect the chemical composition of a drug from unauthorized duplication by other firms. For example, Smith Kline (now part of a larger entity known as GlaxoSmithKline) introduced a new type of ulcer medication known as Tagamet during the 1970s. Having received patent protection from the government, Smith Kline enjoyed considerable profits from Tagamet until the patent expired in the mid-1980s. Other firms were prohibited from copying Smith Kline's patented formulas for making Tagamet. The same patent protection capability gave Eli Lilly and Pfizer significant competitive advantages in depression and blood pressure medications, respectively, in the 1990s. Patents thus represent a very strong source of competitive advantage in the pharmaceutical and other science-based industries.

Licenses. A government license is needed to operate some businesses. Licenses are necessary, for example, to operate an airline, a radio or TV station, an electric generation facility, and a gas distribution company. Governments often limit the number of licenses they make available. Once all available licenses have been issued, new entrants may be blocked from entering an industry or, if allowed to enter, may be forced to operate at a disadvantage. Thus, early holders of licenses have a significant competitive advantage over later entrants. Most recently, the U.S. government over the past three years has auctioned off a large portion of the radio frequency spectrum that it once reserved for its own security uses. Many bidders from the telecommunications industry, particularly wireless firms such as Verizon Wireless and NextWave Communications, bought frequencies for use in their own plans to offer high-speed data and voice communications.

Location Sites. In some industries, a suitable location is an important source of competitive advantage. A waterfront site, for example, may be useful to a boat dealer; a site near a busy intersection is often useful for a fast-food operator. By entering an industry early, leaders can sometimes preempt the best locations. Later entrants must often make do with less attractive sites.

Channel Access. Large, established firms sometimes lock up the most desirable channels of distribution. New entrants or smaller existing firms then have difficulty finding outlets for their products, and they must often engage in extensive promotions and negotiations with wholesalers and retailers to obtain suitable shelf space. For example, new entrants in the packaged goods field—canned goods, beverages, breakfast cereal, diapers, personal care products—often face this challenge. The chief distribution channels for such products are supermarkets. Because of limited capacity, supermarkets often restrict the amount of shelf space they devote to each product category to just two or three brands, giving preference to well-known brands that can generate the most volume. Because of this policy, smaller firms and new entrants often experience difficulty getting their products on the shelf.

Supply Access. Established firms can sometimes monopolize critical supplies. Later entrants then experience difficulty securing inputs for their own operations. U.S. Steel, for example, once controlled the world's richest iron ore deposits. Exclusive access to this valuable resource gave it a formidable advantage over newcomers forced to rely on more costly supplies that often required high transportation costs.

Established firms do not necessarily have to own a resource to enjoy exclusive access. A long-term supply contract can sometimes produce the same benefit. Large food processors, for example, sometimes dominate supply by entering into long-term contracts with groups or cooperatives of farmers in a region. In the Midwest, companies such as Pillsbury, General Mills, Kellogg, Carnation, Archer-Daniels-Midland (ADM), and Cargill are large purchasers of wheat and corn. They often buy huge amounts of wheat and corn through long-term contracts with farmers for use in making processed foods. This practice can make it difficult for a small processor to secure low-cost supplies.

Reputation. Many customers have already used products made by established firms. If satisfied, they will often seek out the same brand when making subsequent purchases. Even customers who have not yet tried an industry's product will often be familiar with a well-known brand and therefore may give it higher preference when making their first purchase. Established firms thus often enjoy a significant reputation advantage over later entrants. For example, customers are more likely to place a higher degree of trust with brand-name products and medications rather than "generic" versions if the price differential is not too great. Similarly, business travelers will often prefer to fly with a more established, larger airline than to fly an upstart carrier that has little track record.

Scale of Operation

Large, established firms produce, sell, and advertise in greater volume than smaller firms and later entrants. Their greater volume allows them to take advantage of economies of scale within many primary and supporting value-adding activities. Research has shown that as the scale of many business activities increases, the cost of carrying them out per unit of output declines.[6] This phenomenon is shown in Exhibit 3-7. Among the most important contributors to economies of scale, shown in Exhibit 3-8, are specialization, fixed-cost spreading, purchase discounts, and vertical integration.

Specialization. As the scale of an activity increases, more employees are needed to carry it out. The more employees who are involved in performing an activity, the greater are the opportunities for individuals to specialize. Since specialization fosters expertise, increasing scale often enhances productivity.

Fixed-Cost Spreading. Many fixed costs (e.g., technology development and automated production equipment) do not increase proportionally as an activity expands in size. These costs can therefore be spread over a larger number of units as an activity increases, resulting in declining per unit cost. Because large firms can operate activities on a big scale, they often have greater opportunity to spread and amortize fixed costs than smaller rivals or later entrants.

Purchase Discounts. Since large purchasers frequently enjoy high bargaining power, suppliers frequently extend them quantity discounts. Greater volume—and therefore

EXHIBIT 3-7 Economies of Scale

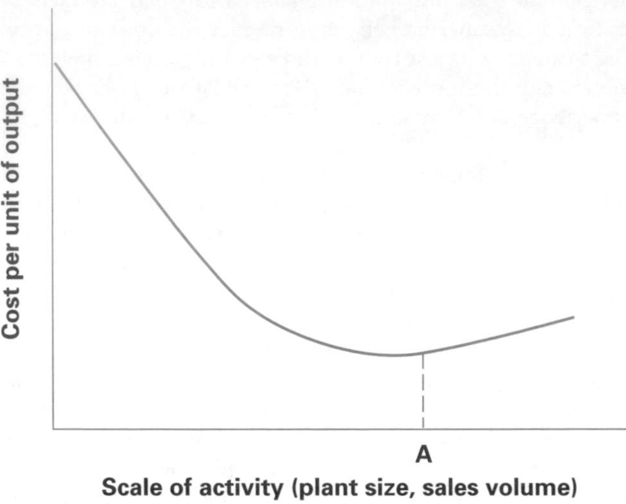

EXHIBIT 3-8 Major Contributors to Economies of Scale

- Specialization
- Fixed-cost spreading
- Purchase discounts
- Vertical integration

greater profit—allows suppliers to offer large, established firms in the industry major discounts on components, inputs, and other raw materials, which may not be available to smaller rivals.

Vertical Integration. Vertical integration refers to the expansion of the firm's value chain to include activities once performed by its suppliers and buyers. By manufacturing inputs itself, a firm can eliminate the potentially high costs associated with locating suppliers, evaluating the quality of their products, negotiating purchase contracts, and litigating disputes. A large firm is usually in a better position than a smaller one to make its own inputs, since it consumes inputs in greater volume and can therefore operate larger, more efficient facilities to produce them. Similarly, large firms are often in a superior position than smaller firms or new entrants to undertake activities that its buyers once performed. Thus, large established firms are in a better position than smaller rivals to reduce a variety of different costs by pursuing vertical integration. (Vertical integration is discussed more fully in Chapter 7.)

economies of experience: Cost reductions that occur from continuous repetition of activities that allow for improvement with each successive act (also known as *experience curve effects* or *learning curve effects*).

Experience

As an organization's experience in carrying out an activity increases, the cost of performing the activity often declines on a per-unit basis. Cost reductions of this sort are called **economies of experience.**[7] Continuous repetition of activities that allow for improvements with each successive repetition is the basis of economies of experience. Established firms have more opportunity than later entrants to make such improvements since they typically have greater experience conducting and improving their activities.

A typical experience curve, also known as a learning curve, is shown in Exhibit 3-9. Its vertical axis is the same as an economies of scale curve, cost per unit of output. Its horizontal axis is different, however; it depicts the number of units processed (that is, produced, sold, or serviced) since a firm began performing that activity. This variable is customarily referred to as **cumulative volume**. The most important processes that facilitate declining costs with growing cumulative volume are employee learning, product redesign, and process improvement (see Exhibit 3-10).

cumulative volume: The quantity that a firm has produced since the beginning of that activity, up to this point in time.

Employee Learning. As employees repeat activities, they learn how to carry them out more quickly and accurately. The net result is continuing improvement in both productivity and quality as employees' experience base expands. For example, workers in factories learn how to use their tools better, how to set up equipment more quickly, and when to perform equipment maintenance to avoid breakdown. This is why the know-how and insight provided by employees can become valuable "hidden" assets. This source of knowledge avoids costly mistakes when designing and implementing new technologies.

Among the first to study this phenomenon systematically were engineers at Wright-Patterson Air Force Base in Ohio. As they studied contractors building aircraft for the U.S. Air Force, they noticed that the labor time needed to assemble an aircraft of a particular type tended to decline as more and more aircraft of the same type were produced. In fact, a systematic relationship was discovered. The number of direct labor hours utilized in assembling each aircraft tended to decline by about 20 percent with each doubling of cumulative volume. Thus, if 3,000 direct labor hours were required to produce the first unit

Economies of Experience

EXHIBIT 3-9

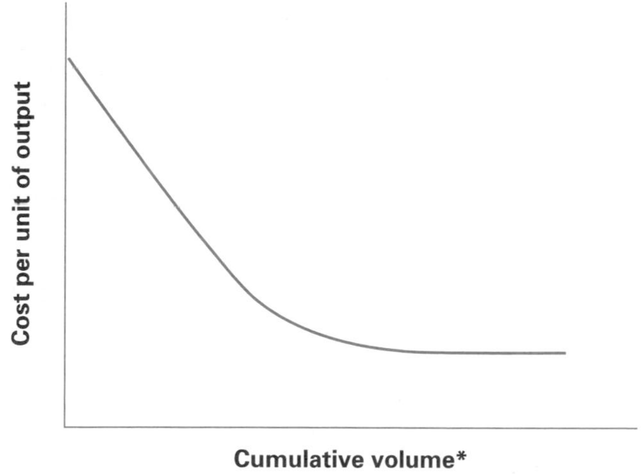

*Number of units produced (or sold, serviced, developed, etc.) since commencing an activity.

Major Contributors to Experience Benefits

EXHIBIT 3-10

- Employee learning
- Product redesign
- Process improvement

of an aircraft model, only about 2,400 hours (0.80 × 3,000) would be needed for the second, 1,920 hours (0.80 × 0.80 × 3,000) for the third, and so on. Observers attributed this decline to learning on the part of employees involved. Similar declines have been observed in a wide range of manufacturing and service settings.

Product Redesign. As a firm's engineers become more familiar with the way a product is manufactured, they can often redesign components that cause problems in later assembly, reduce the number of components needed to make the product, and substitute better materials. These changes not only reduce manufacturing costs but help improve product quality as well. For example, large Japanese manufacturers of consumer electronics such as Sony, Hitachi, Matsushita, Sharp, Sanyo, and Toshiba have successfully engaged in ongoing programs of redesigning each new generation of television set to use fewer but better components. Color television tuners that first employed vacuum tubes subsequently used transistors and now integrated circuits that combine many functions on a single chip. Similarly, telecommunications equipment companies such as Nokia, Ericsson, Motorola, and Samsung are designing increasingly more versatile cellular phones that use fewer semiconductors to transmit and receive signals of all types. It is expected that digital cellular phones will eventually incorporate such features as digital cameras, MP3 players, and other attributes to enhance the device's overall functionality.

Process Improvement. Increasing experience also enables engineers to improve the process by which a product is manufactured through such means as changing the work flow and altering equipment design. Continual small improvements in these areas can, over time, not only reduce manufacturing cost but enhance product quality and reliability as well. For example, Toyota Motor Company of Japan encourages its employees to identify new ways of improving manufacturing processes that reduce turnaround and work-in-process times. Lower work-in-process times can result in lower costs for carrying inventories and supplies needed for final car assembly. Continuous improvement of Toyota's manufacturing equipment and work flow enables the Japanese firm to accelerate time-to-market for new car models and to reduce its inbound logistics, operations, and outbound logistics costs. Design costs go down, manufacturing proceeds more smoothly, and customers are more satisfied, even as Toyota is able to develop a new car model faster with fewer glitches. This practice has enabled Toyota to increase its productivity significantly over all the U.S. automakers over the past decade.

Interrelationships

Competitive advantage can also come from interrelationships with other businesses of the same firm. Interrelationships enable a firm's businesses to transfer resources and share activities among each other. We will discuss these mechanisms at length in later chapters. By way of introducing that material, let us briefly examine the chief benefits these two mechanisms can provide.

Resource Transfer. If one business possesses a resource of value to another, transfer of the resource across the two businesses can provide a potentially valuable competitive advantage. Many different kinds of resources are potential candidates for such transfer: cash, personnel, information, and different forms of knowledge or expertise in particular.

To illustrate the value of transferring expertise between businesses, consider the interrelationships among PepsiCo's different businesses. Personnel in its soft drink and other beverage businesses are highly skilled in such activities as market research, market segmentation, consumer promotion, and TV advertising. Other units of PepsiCo, such as Frito-Lay, can use these skills in their businesses. By drawing on this expertise, PepsiCo's non–soft drink businesses (e.g., Tropicana) enjoy an advantage not available to rivals lacking this kind of interrelationship.

Activity Sharing. Two or more businesses can sometimes share a common activity, thereby eliminating unnecessary duplication and high activity costs. Sharing permits operation of value-adding activities on a larger, more efficient scale than would be possible for any single business acting on its own. In effect, sharing a critical resource enables the firm to exploit potentially significant cost savings among a number of businesses, or to enhance and deepen the skills needed to compete. Large, diversified firms with established market positions in several different industries or market segments share activities in numerous ways to create competitive advantage. For example, most of PepsiCo's businesses make heavy use of TV advertising. By pooling their advertising effort, they can combine multiple products within the same message, achieve quantity discounts on purchase of TV time, and create bargaining power with media firms. Similarly, 3M's overall competitive position among a number of different businesses—tapes, weather stripping, automotive finishing products, sandpaper, and specialized paints—is significantly bolstered when the company is able to share its highly proficient R&D skills and marketing to accelerate product innovation and to lower its costs. By pooling the knowledge and skills from different businesses, 3M can achieve the critical mass of talent to investigate new opportunities for innovation.

Assessing Competitive Advantage

Generally, only a few value-adding activities of established firms qualify for the advantages previously noted. Firms contemplating entry must therefore carefully examine each value-adding activity of established firms to determine where there may be opportunities to exploit any potential weaknesses or oversights. In this section, we present some considerations and guidelines for assessing established firms' strengths and potential sources of competitive advantages.

First-Mover Advantages

In practice, only a few activities of the value chain generally qualify for first-mover advantages (see Exhibit 3-11). For example, in most industries only operational activities can derive much benefit from patent protection, since such protection generally applies to product design, product formulas, or manufacturing processes. Patents, however, cannot prevent competitors from attempting to do something different. Particularly in manufacturing processes, rivals and new entrants may sometimes be able to substitute a new or different process for the patented one. Thus, for the vast majority of products, patents do not represent complete protection from imitation. Similarly, a government license is likely to be needed to perform only a few activities of the value chain. Included in this category are outbound logistics activity (e.g., a radio station or a cellular telephone operator needs a license to transmit its signal), service (restaurants often need a license to process and sell food), and operations (a waste disposal company needs a license to operate a toxic waste dump). These activities are therefore the most likely to benefit from first-mover advantage.

First-mover advantages carry their own set of disadvantages. For example, changes in technology or buying patterns can render an early mover's advantage obsolete. During the early 1980s, minimills took advantage of major advances in steel-casting technology that made the larger, integrated steel companies' processes obsolete. In the retailing industry, large department stores such as Sears and JCPenney pioneered the concept of offering a wide range of merchandise at reasonable cost to consumers. Yet, later entrants such as Wal-Mart Stores and other discounters were able to seriously erode the first-mover benefits of the larger, diversified department stores. Over the past ten years, Sears and JCPenney were forced to undertake extremely expensive and time-consuming renovations and revamping of their merchandise mixes to win back customers they lost to other retailing entrants. Some competitors, such as Montgomery Ward and Ames Department Stores, were

EXHIBIT 3-11 Activities Frequently Benefiting from First-Mover Advantages

SUPPORT ACTIVITIES — **Infrastructure**					
Human Resource Management				Reputation	
Technology Development		Patent protection; license			
Procurement		Supply access			
PRIMARY ACTIVITIES		Patent protection; license	License	Location; channel access; reputation	Reputation; license
	Inbound Logistics	**Operations**	**Outbound Logistics**	**Marketing/ Sales**	**Service**

Reprinted/Adapted with the permission of The Free Press, a division of Simon & Schuster, Inc., from *Competitive Advantage: Creating and Sustaining Superior Performance*, by Michael E. Porter. Copyright © 1985 by Michael E. Porter.

eventually forced out of business because they could not readily adapt to the changing retailing environment.

Scale and Experience Advantages

To enjoy significant advantage from scale or experience, an activity must generally meet four requirements as shown in Exhibit 3-12: it must be centralized, it must be susceptible to scale or experience, it must be properly implemented, and the resulting benefits must be proprietary.

Centralization. Activities operated on a decentralized, fragmented basis cannot achieve significant critical mass; hence, they will rarely enjoy significant economies of scale. Decentralized activities will also rarely achieve significant experience curve benefits, since such benefits come from repetition of an activity by the same group of employees over many cycles. Thus, centralization of activities is generally a prerequisite before firms can reap the benefits of economies of scale and cumulative experience effects.

Susceptibility. Since economies of scale are derived from such characteristics as specialization, spreading fixed costs, and quantity discounts, activities that provide opportunity for these processes to occur are particularly susceptible to producing scale advantage. In prac-

Requirements for Achieving Scale and Experience Advantage

EXHIBIT 3-12

• Centralization	• Activity must be centralized
• Susceptibility	• Activity must be susceptible to the processes that produce scale and experience benefits
• Implementation	• Activity must be properly implemented
• Proprietary	• Benefits of scale and experience must be proprietary

tice, value-adding activities differ widely in providing such opportunity. Manufacture of a standardized product, for example, provides considerable opportunity for these processes to occur, thus promoting scale economies. Manufacture of custom-made products, on the other hand, generally offers few such opportunities, although recent developments in new technology may be relaxing this constraint. As a result, most custom-made products are significantly less susceptible to scale benefits.

One factor that complicates the assessment of scale susceptibility is the variation in scale benefits that occurs when scale of an activity increases. Consider most types of manufacturing activities, for example. They lend themselves to economies of scale as long as scale does not exceed a certain point. However, beyond this point, diseconomies of scale set in. This means further increase in scale then produces an increase rather than a decrease in unit cost. The letter *A* in Exhibit 3-7 indicates this point. Diseconomies of scale sometimes occur when the scale of an activity becomes very large because employees involved in the activity become bored and disgruntled as their jobs become more specialized and they experience increasing communication problems as their numbers grow. Many observers suspect that GM suffers extensively from these difficulties. It is also likely to be a primary reason why GM is looking to reduce the amount of in-house manufacturing that it performs.

Because beyond some point an increase in scale often raises rather than lowers unit cost, benefits that large firms can realize from increasing the scale of their activities are limited. However, for many activities, this point is not reached until considerable output is attained. Large, established firms are therefore often able to derive some scale advantage over smaller rivals in performing at least a few activities of the value chain.

Let us now consider susceptibility of activities to experience benefits. Since such benefits emanate largely from employee learning, product redesign, and process improvement, activities that provide significant opportunity for these processes to occur are the most likely to enjoy experience advantage. Manufacture of a standardized product, for example, provides ample opportunity of this sort and thus is often quite susceptible to experience benefits. Production of custom-made products, by contrast, provides somewhat less such opportunity, so is generally less conducive to experience benefits.

Effective Implementation. While scale and experience provide firms with opportunities to develop competitive advantage, such benefits do not come automatically. Managers must work hard to achieve them through effective implementation of activities. General Motors' failure to realize scale and experience advantages despite its position as world leader of the automobile industry has resulted in part from serious implementation problems over a long period of time.

Proprietary Access. Established rivals can derive competitive advantage from scale and experience only if they retain proprietary access to the resulting benefits. Unfortunately, rivals can often easily imitate or develop substitutes for such benefits, thus neutralizing some of the early entrants' advantages. To illustrate, consider Pizza Hut's development of new menu items. Pizza Hut centralizes this activity to operate it on a larger scale than smaller rivals. However, rivals can easily copy or imitate new menu items as soon as Pizza

Hut introduces them. Because Pizza Hut does not have proprietary access to menu innovations, it derives little competitive advantage from operating menu development activity on a large scale.

The situation is somewhat different with Pizza Hut's procurement of TV advertising time. In particular, the interrelationships that Pizza Hut can share with sister businesses KFC and Taco Bell enable Pizza Hut to enjoy significant discounts on media purchases. This benefit is more proprietary because smaller rivals cannot capture the discounts Pizza Hut receives nor duplicate them on their own. By way of its internal interrelationships, Pizza Hut thus enjoys an important scale advantage over smaller rivals in this area.

The Growth of the Internet and Competitive Advantage

The momentous rise of the Internet as a key distribution and marketing channel will redefine the basis of many firms' strategies to reach their customers in almost every industry. A more complete discussion on the Internet's influence and effect on competitive strategy will be discussed in Chapter 5. However, any discussion on the sources of competitive advantage would be remiss without at least briefly mentioning some of the initial changes brought about by this new technology medium.

In many situations, companies are using the Internet as a way to reach their customers directly, oftentimes bypassing existing brick-and-mortar distribution channels, wholesalers, and, in some cases, even retailers. The emerging behavior of customers who currently use the Internet for on-line information gathering and product/service purchases signifies that many businesses will need to start thinking about how the Internet will likely impact their existing sources of competitive advantage and the way they reach and serve their customers.

Although the growth in Internet-driven, electronic commerce is still in its takeoff phase, it is becoming clear that the Internet allows many companies to offer a high level of service for their customers. Many firms, such as L.L. Bean, Dell Computer, General Electric, IBM, Intel, and Fidelity Investments, have designed Web sites that allow potential customers to search for product information, part numbers, technical specifications, and other data on a real-time basis. Increasingly, most Web sites enable customers to place an order for products, services, or parts and pay for them electronically through secure data encryption methods. Both UPS and FedEx, for example, offer Web sites that enable its customers to track the status and location of overnight package shipments using standard Web site browsers (e.g., Microsoft Internet Explorer, Netscape Communicator, etc.).

Some firms have created even more technologically sophisticated Web sites that serve as an on-line, electronic catalog and ordering system that provides extremely customized product and service offerings according to what has been negotiated between the customer and the firm. For example, General Electric, Cisco Systems, and Intel are working to make their Web sites fully integrated and compatible with their customers' ordering, procurement, and logistics systems, thus allowing these companies to learn much about their customers' needs and use that information to offer other customized services that other competitors would find difficult to imitate.

In the retailing industry, the meteoric rise of on-line book and CD retailer Amazon.com represents a major threat to such established brick-and-mortar book retailers as Borders Group and Barnes & Noble. The economic appeal of Amazon.com to individual customers lies not only in the upstart firm's lower cost structure but also in its ability to tailor future publishing and music offerings to each customer's individual tastes. Amazon.com's revenues are just starting to grow, and it is not expected to reach more consistent profitable growth until 2003. On the other hand, Barnes & Noble has already created and deployed its own interactive Web site to deal with Amazon.com's entry and is hoping that customers will use both its retail stores and its on-line services to search for and to purchase books in print.[8]

From a value chain–based perspective, the Internet is making every activity potentially open to price bidding from alternative suppliers. In this sense, the Internet is particularly useful to new entrants. These firms can use the Internet to provide products and services at lower costs than established firms, who often have high fixed costs of existing distribution facilities and relationships. Even though the Internet provides customers with a wide-ranging capability to search for free information about products, services, and prices, established firms that recognize the power of the Internet can also invest in this new technology as an opportunity to strengthen their existing customer relationships and thus erect potentially higher switching costs over time. Companies such as Cisco Systems, Dell Computer, General Electric, IBM, and Intel are actively pushing to make their Web sites more interactive and even more "plugged in" to their customers' on-line ordering systems and operations. To minimize the effects of cannibalizing their existing distribution relationships, several of these firms are offering to let their distributors take on more of the after-sales service and warranty work through "preferred provider" and "value-managed relationships." By designing and implementing new Internet-driven electronic commerce technologies that lower their customers' costs of gathering information and doing business, all of these firms are hoping to protect and even reinvent their sources of competitive advantage by providing faster and more customized forms of service.

Diagnosing Pizza Hut's Capabilities

Assessing internal strengths and weaknesses is a highly complex task for several reasons. First, many firms generally perform numerous types of value adding activities. Second, firms can derive several different kinds of advantage in performing each activity. Third, a variety of different economic or technical requirements must be satisfied before the various sources of competitive advantage can be realized.

To illustrate the complex nature of analyzing strengths and weaknesses, let us revisit Pizza Hut in an attempt to perform a summary analysis to demonstrate the power of internal analysis of strengths and weaknesses. Our objective is to identify the major advantages Pizza Hut enjoys over other rivals in each of the four areas discussed earlier. Exhibit 3-13 summarizes these advantages.

First-Mover Advantages

Many consumers have personal experience with Pizza Hut's restaurants. Even individuals who are not frequent consumers of pizza are often aware of Pizza Hut. They have become familiar with the company as a result of passing Pizza Hut units on the highway, testimonials from acquaintances, and the company's extensive TV advertising. In recent years, Pizza Hut has developed advertisements that are linked to blockbuster movies. This awareness predisposes them to consider Pizza Hut when selecting a restaurant. The firm thus enjoys a significant, though declining, reputation advantage over other firms.

On the other hand, Pizza Hut enjoys little first-mover advantage in other value-adding activities. Possession of a license to operate, for example, means little, since any firm willing to enter the industry can easily obtain one in most areas. Consequently, Pizza Hut probably enjoys no first-mover advantage in this area. Patents are unimportant in this industry, since food-making technology and restaurant procedures are well known and easy to imitate. Pizza Hut thus enjoys no significant advantage in this area, either. While its restaurant sites are excellent, Pizza Hut enjoys only modest location advantage, since good alternative locations are still available in most areas. More important, other competitors such as Domino's Pizza and Papa John's International compete with Pizza Hut for new facilities in fast-growing suburban areas. Competitors can purchase from the same suppliers, so Pizza Hut enjoys no proprietary access to supplies. These considerations all point to the

EXHIBIT 3-13 Pizza Hut's Sources of Competitive Advantage

		Inbound Logistics	Operations	Outbound Logistics	Marketing/Sales	Service
SUPPORT ACTIVITIES	**Infrastructure**					
	Human Resource Management					
	Technology Development					
	Procurement		Procurement of food (S)		Procurement of TV time (S,I)	
PRIMARY ACTIVITIES					Reputation (FM); advertising (S,I)	

likelihood that this company enjoys no significant first-mover advantages except perhaps a small edge in reputation.

Scale Advantages

Pizza Hut's primary value-adding operational activity of preparing food and its service activity of serving restaurant customers are both carried out on a decentralized basis within individual restaurants. Consequently, Pizza Hut derives few scale benefits in these two areas. On the other hand, it may derive some scale-based advantage from its TV advertising activity. Advertising tends to be centralized, is highly susceptible to economies of scale (since TV advertising costs can be spread over Pizza Hut's many units), and produces benefits that are highly proprietary (since competitors cannot immediately appropriate such benefits). Pizza Hut thus enjoys a significant marketing/sales advantage over smaller or newly entering rivals.

Let us now consider support activities. Procuring food, since such activity is mostly centralized, is highly susceptible to economies of scale (because of quantity discounts) and produces benefits that are proprietary (since smaller competitors cannot achieve similar discounts). Pizza Hut's other support activities fail to satisfy one or another of the requirements for scale. Technology development is limited as an advantage because rivals easily imitate improvements resulting from it. Human resource management activities are confined within restaurants and therefore are highly decentralized, while infrastructure activities are not very susceptible to meaningful scale. Consequently, Pizza Hut probably enjoys few if any scale advantages outside advertising and procurement.

Experience Benefits

Since activities that Pizza Hut centralizes either are not very susceptible to experience benefits, such as procurement, or produce benefits that cannot be kept proprietary (e.g., technology development), Pizza Hut probably enjoys few significant experience advantages over smaller rivals.

Interrelationships

Pizza Hut enjoys several benefits from interrelationships with other Tricon businesses, such as KFC and Taco Bell. It can pool certain procurement activities—obtaining silverware, restaurant furnishings, ovens, and other materials—with those of other Tricon businesses and achieve purchase discounts. It can draw on marketing expertise from PepsiCo's beverage business, in which Tricon's restaurants still enjoy a close commercial relationship. PepsiCo possesses very strong capabilities in the area of consumer marketing. Pizza Hut can also negotiate advertising rates jointly with KFC and Taco Bell, thus enhancing its bargaining power and sharing advertising costs. These benefits provide it a significant marketing/sales advantage over smaller or nondiversified rivals.

Achilles' Heel of Established Firms

Thus far we have focused on potential advantages that established firms may enjoy over smaller rivals because of first-mover advantages, scale, experience, and interrelationships. These advantages do not come without trade-offs, however. Established firms tend to suffer from a distinct weakness that smaller rivals and new entrants can often avoid. Because of their large size and entrenched practices, they are often slower to respond to environmental change. Pizza Hut, for example, was late in responding to consumer demand for home delivery of pizza. In much the same way, General Motors was slow in responding to increased consumer demand for smaller automobiles.

Let us examine Pizza Hut's predicament in more detail. Consider how Domino's Pizza dramatically changed the competitive environment of the pizza industry during the mid-1980s, making substantial inroads by focusing its efforts on the one part of the industry's value chain that Pizza Hut (and everyone else) largely ignored—that of outbound logistics. Pizza Hut and other established pizza restaurants based their competitive strategies on the key assumption that customers preferred coming to restaurants to be served. Domino's Pizza redefined the competitive balance of the industry by developing a strategy based on home delivery. Domino's Pizza developed a formidable source of competitive advantage by focusing its efforts on that part of the value chain (outbound logistics) the rest of the industry ignored. By doing so, Domino's Pizza seized the initiative from Pizza Hut and was able to stake out a large market share position. To keep its effort concentrated on home delivery, Domino's did not set up restaurants, thereby minimizing its on-site customer service. This was possible because customers generally called from home for pizza to be delivered.

While value chain analysis can help both established firms and those contemplating entry identify strengths and weaknesses, it is unfortunately static in nature. Firms often base their strategies on the assumption that current strengths and weaknesses will persist in the future. Larger firms, in particular, are often saddled with significant fixed costs, investments, and methods of operation that impede fast response to new developments. However, to make the value-chain analysis meaningful on an ongoing basis, managers need to challenge such assumptions about the competitive environment. New competitors that can change the "rules" of competition in an industry (e.g., growth of the Internet and electronic online commerce; the rise of new technologies that transform an industry) can often make major inroads the way that Domino's Pizza did if existing firms become overreliant on existing sources of competitive advantage without challenging themselves to think about how the future may evolve.

Inflexibility and slow response in the face of environmental change is the Achilles' heel of large, established firms. This may be an important issue for many businesses to consider as new technologies, changes in market demand, the widening influence of the Internet, and new competitors take root in every industry. We will examine this weakness in more detail in later chapters on sustaining and redefining advantage.

Assessing the Financial Position of Competitors

comparative financial analysis: The evaluation of a firm's financial condition across multiple time periods.

ratio analysis: The use of a proportion of two figures or numbers that allow for consistent comparison of performance with other firms.

The strategic tools and concepts presented in this chapter can only go so far in assessing a firm's strengths and weaknesses relative to competitors'. A more thorough assessment of the firm's capabilities also requires analysis of the firm's financial position. **Comparative financial analysis** compares a firm's financial condition to that of competitors for two or more time periods. The objective of comparative financial analysis is to assess a firm's financial health. Managers use income statements, balance sheets, and other financial data and projections to compare their firm's financial position with that of other firms in the same industry.

The most common approach to financial analysis is through ratio analysis. **Ratio analysis** selects two vital figures or indicators and expresses them as a proportion that allows for comparison with other firms over time.[9] Financial ratios serve as important indicators of financial health. The most common types of financial ratios focus on profitability, liquidity, activity, and leverage. Key ratios are defined in each category in Exhibit 3-14.

EXHIBIT 3-14 Comparative Financial Analysis: Key Ratios

Type	Examples	Measures	Indicators
Profitability	Return on Equity (ROE)	$\frac{\text{Profit after taxes}}{\text{Shareholders' Equity}}$	Productivity of firm's value-adding activities
Liquidity	Current Ratio	$\frac{\text{Current Assets}}{\text{Current Liabilities}}$	Measure of financial solvency
Activity	Asset Turnover	$\frac{\text{Sales}}{\text{Total Assets}}$	Asset use efficiency
	Inventory Turnover	$\frac{\text{Sales}}{\text{Inventory}}$	Turnaround of inventory
Leverage	Debt/Equity Ratio	$\frac{\text{Liabilities}}{\text{Shareholders' Equity}}$	Corporate financing; financial risk; default risk

return on assets: Net income divided by total assets.

return on equity: Net income divided by stockholder equity.

Profitability can be measured through any number of return-based ratios, such as **return on assets** (net income divided by total assets), **return on equity** (net income divided by shareholders' equity), and **return on capital** (net income divided by total capital). All three return ratios are common measures of **return on investment** (ROI). These return ratios are considered the most important indicators of profitability because they indicate how productively firms are using their resources.

Liquidity is an indicator of the firm's ability to make payments to suppliers and creditors. A common measure of liquidity is the **current ratio**, which is current assets divided by current liabilities. A firm with a comparatively low current ratio presents a problem for creditors who fear it may not be able to meet its short-term obligations. The firm may use variations of the current ratio that factor out inventory, since inventory often cannot be sold quickly. Inventory is less liquid than cash. High liquidity means the firm can meet all of its financial obligations.

The firm's **activity ratios** refer to efficiency in handling inventory or other assets. Many activity ratios are also known as **turnover ratios**. For example, *asset turnover* is calculated by dividing sales by total assets; it gives a rough measure of the firm's ability to generate sales for any given level of assets. *Inventory turnover* is measured by sales divided by inventory. This ratio gives a sense of how well the firm is managing its inventory.

A firm's **debt ratio** measures the firm's leverage. Debt ratios measure the extent to which the financing of the firm's activities is based on debt or equity. It measures the financing provided by creditors in relation to that provided by stockholders or owners. One of the most common measures of leverage is the ratio of debt to equity. A high ratio of debt to equity means the firm has borrowed considerable sums in relation to shareholder investment. High leverage, or high debt to equity, works to the firm's benefit if it can use the borrowed funds to produce gains (create value) that are higher than the firm's after-tax borrowing costs. Conversely, high leverage can cripple a firm if its value-adding activities generate returns that are less than the firm's after-tax cost of borrowing. Note that leverage can also increase earnings per share (EPS), but high leverage can make EPS relatively more volatile.

The use of all these ratios requires care in interpretation. For example, an excessively high ROI measure not only may mean high profitability but also could suggest that the firm is not investing sufficiently to build up its competitive strengths. Ratios have limited meaning if managers do not compare them to competitors in the same industry. Moreover, ratios must be assessed over relevant time periods to be meaningful. Cyclical or business upturns and downturns can distort an individual firm's ratios unless they are viewed within the context of the entire industry. To use ratios effectively, managers should also compare an individual firm's ratios with respect to average ratios for the industry. Each industry is likely to have its own set of historically based, average ratios with which the firm can compare its own ratios.

return on capital: Net income divided by total capital.

return on investment: Net income divided by total investment.

liquidity: The ability of a firm or business to pay or meet its obligations (e.g., debt payments, accounts payable) as they come due. The more liquid the firm, the easier its ability to meet these obligations.

current ratio: A measure used to assess a firm's ability to make payments to its short-term creditors; current assets divided by current liabilities.

activity ratios: Measures used to assess the efficiency of a firm's use of assets (e.g., sales divided by assets).

turnover ratios: Measures that assess the speed with which various assets (inventory, receivables) are converted into cash.

debt ratio: A measure of a firm's leverage; the amount of debt it possesses divided by stockholder equity.

Ethical Issues

In this chapter, we have examined methods of analysis that enable managers to assess the strengths and weaknesses of firms competing in an industry. In closing, let us consider some of the ethical issues associated with this effort. To conduct strength and weakness analysis, managers need detailed information about how rivals operate. They must therefore exert serious effort to obtain such information. In doing so, however, they must be careful not to overstep the bounds of ethical behavior. Consider the following means that firms commonly use to learn about and appropriate their rivals' advantages.

Examining Competitors' Products

One way to gain proprietary information about a protected technology is to knock down and carefully study each firm's new products. Since new products are generally available to all who wish to purchase them, few would object to the propriety of this practice.

Questioning Competitors' Employees

Another approach to obtaining proprietary information about a competitor is to talk to employees of a competitor's organization. Such questioning or "probing" can take place in many different settings—during professional meetings, on the golf course, at cocktail parties, or in other social settings. Some would argue that this kind of questioning is proper so long as those seeking information clearly identify themselves as representatives of a rival firm. But what if they do not? Is it ethical to question employees from a rival organization under some other guise—that of a curious third party, for example?

Using Consultants

Yet another approach to securing information about a competitor is to hire a consultant to gather such data. Some may feel that this method absolves a firm of blame if information is inappropriately obtained. However, if a consultant uses improper means to obtain such information, is its client wholly blameless?

Engaging in Industrial Espionage

industrial espionage: Systematic and deliberate attempts to learn about a competitor's technologies or new products through secretive, and often illegal, ways.

Still another approach to obtaining information about a rival is to pay a fee to an employee of a rival organization to supply such information. This practice is called **industrial espionage**. Few managers would justify this practice on ethical grounds. Furthermore, the practice is illegal in most countries, including the United States, carrying significant penalties if discovered.

Nevertheless, some unscrupulous firms employ it to obtain information about competitors. In September 2001, Procter & Gamble admitted to engaging in espionage against one of its competitors, European consumer packaged goods firm Unilever. Apparently unbeknownst to Procter & Gamble's senior management, several managers and employees undertook a clandestine effort to learn about the ingredients of Unilever's shampoo. Procter & Gamble employees would search through Unilever's garbage in an effort to identify how Unilever was developing its product. To the company's credit, however, Procter & Gamble's CEO openly admitted that his company was engaging in this practice, once the issue was disclosed to him. The company then immediately informed Unilever about its own self-investigation and has offered to settle the issue outside court.[10]

"Pirating" Employees

pirating: Hiring individuals from a competitor specifically to gain their knowledge (also known as *raiding*).

raiding: Hiring individuals from a competitor specifically to gain their knowledge (also known as *pirating*).

Yet another method of obtaining information about rivals is to hire individuals from rival organizations who have access to such information. This practice is often referred to as employee **pirating** or **raiding**. Many argue that this practice is justifiable as long as information possessed by new hires is general in nature. However, new hires often come with specific knowledge about former employers' strategic plans, new product intentions, or other confidential information. High-level managers are particularly likely to possess such information.

This practice has becoming increasingly common in Silicon Valley, the San Jose, California, region. Silicon Valley has become proliferated with hundreds of innovative firms doing cutting-edge research and product development in the fields of semiconductors, software, Internet technology, advanced imaging, and other high-technology products. Because qualified technical and managerial talent is often short, firms will often seek to "raid" other firms, including their competitors, for the people they need to manage their operations. This kind of pirating can often result in a firm's losing their critical talent and skills to a competitor in a short period of time. In some industries, however, firms have required that their departing managers sign noncompete agreements that preclude them from working with their competitors for an extended period of time. Some of these noncompete agreements even include clauses that prohibit departing managers or employees from encouraging their colleagues to leave with them to another firm.

Conclusion

The tools described in this chapter are useful for identifying a firm's strengths and weaknesses relative to competitors. Such information is not the only input needed to formulate strategy, however. As noted in Chapter 1, strategy formulation involves finding an appropriate fit between strengths and weaknesses on the one hand and opportunities and threats on the other. To formulate an effective strategy, the opportunities and threats appearing in the firm's external environment must therefore also be first identified. How to go about making this identification and how to match a firm's strengths and weaknesses to opportunities and threats presented to it are topics explored in depth in subsequent chapters.

Summary

- Firms need to undertake a thorough analysis of their own internal strengths and weaknesses to lay the foundation for building effective strategies.
- The activities of all firms in an industry can be studied through an analytical tool known as the value chain. A value chain identifies and isolates the various economic, value-adding activities that occur in some way in every firm.
- The value chain can highlight the strengths and weaknesses of firms competing in the industry. It distinguishes between primary activities and support activities. Primary activities are directly concerned with the conversion of raw materials, inputs, and designs into products or services that are then sold to customers. Support activities assist primary activities in carrying out their functions and tasks. A firm's business system consists of the subset of value chain activities that it actually performs.
- A major task of the strategic management process is to match the conditions of the external environment with the firm's internal strengths and weaknesses. If a firm can perform an activity or activities particularly well relative to its competitors, it then possesses a distinctive competence. A distinctive competence enables the firm to build its own source of competitive advantage. The choice of which strategies to pursue should be based on using and exploiting the firm's competitive advantage.
- In any industry, established firms are likely to enjoy prevailing strengths as compared with firms entering later. In particular, larger established firms, and especially industry leaders, often enjoy advantages derived from first-mover, scale, experience, or interrelationship benefits. These benefits may provide initial sources of competitive advantage; however, competitive advantage from these sources is significant only when specific requirements are met.
- Understanding the financial position of the firm is as important as knowing its value chain. The financial position of the firm can and should be measured in many different ways. Four common measures of financial position are financial ratios that examine profitability (return), liquidity, activity, and leverage. These ratios should be compared with rivals in the same industry and over the same time periods of interest.
- Companies engage in industrial espionage in an attempt to learn about competitors' strategies, products, technologies, and future plans. In most countries, this practice is illegal.

Exercises and Discussion Questions

1. Using the Internet, visit the Web site for General Motors **(www.gm.com)**. What are some initiatives that GM appears to be taking that could resuscitate its

competitive advantage? In particular, how does GM want to deal with its suppliers, distributors (dealers) and final customers such as ourselves?

2. What are some fundamental trade-offs that large companies are likely to face? In particular, do economies of scale come with their own sets of costs?
3. Assume the role of an entrepreneur who has a burning desire to get into the pizza business. What value-adding activity would you focus on to build your own source of competitive advantage? How would you compete with the sit-down restaurants, as well as with the firms that focus on home delivery? Are there any other routes to building competitive advantage that have not yet been discovered?

Endnotes

1. Data for this strategic snapshot were adapted from the following sources: "Restaurant Companies' Good Times Slow Down," *Wall Street Journal*, July 7, 2001; "High Court Rejects Review of Pizza Hut's Lawsuit against Rival," *Wall Street Journal*, March 21, 2001; "Raw Deal: Take-and-Bake Pizza May Not Sound Appetizing, But Papa Murphy's Undercuts Rivals by Taking Out Seats, Delivery—and Cooking," *Forbes*, December 25, 2000; "PepsiCo Renews Pact to Supply Beverages to Tricon Locations," *Wall Street Journal*, June 30, 2000; "Papa John's and Pizza Hut Found Guilty in Ad Suit," *Wall Street Journal*," November 19, 1999; "For Pizza Hut, a New Pie-in-the-Sky Ad Strategy," *Wall Street Journal*, September 30, 1999; "Pizza Hut Test-Markets Charging a Delivery Fee," *Wall Street Journal*, September 20, 1999; "With All of This Fizz, Who Needs Pepsi?" *Business Week*, October 19, 1998; "Pepsi Has Lost Its Midas Touch in Restaurants," *Wall Street Journal*, July 18, 1994, pp. B1, B4.

2. Data for the GM Strategic Snapshot were adapted from the following sources: "GM Product Guru Prepares to Overhaul Auto Maker's Development of New Models," *Wall Street Journal*, January 28, 2002, p. A4; "Cruising for Quality," *Business Week*, September 3, 2001, pp. 74–75; "GM Shifts into Overdrive in Luxury Sport-Sedan Race," *Wall Street Journal*, August 17, 2001, p. B4; "Rivals Are Catching Up to the Big Three," *Wall Street Journal Europe*, August 14, 2001, p. 8; "GM Appoints an Industry Guru To Fix Its Lineup," *Wall Street Journal*, August 3, 2001, pp. B1, B4; "Raytheon Locks on New Market for Night Vision," *Wall Street Journal*, June 27, 2001, p. B4; "Imports to Detroit: Eat Our Dust," *Fortune*, June 11, 2001, pp. 151–154; "Tailoring World's Cars to U.S. Tastes," *Wall Street Journal*, January 15, 2001, pp. B1, B6; "After Decades of Brand Bodywork, GM Parks Oldsmobile—For Good," *Wall Street Journal*, December 13, 2000, pp. B1, B4; "GM Tests a Web-Based Ordering System, Seeking to Slash Custom-Delivery Time," *Wall Street Journal*, November 17, 2000, p. B4; "GM Sees Internet as Means to Make It Fast and Flexible," *Investor's Business Daily*, October 27, 2000, p. A5; "How GM, Ford Think Web Can Make Splash on Factory Floor," *Wall Street Journal*, December 3, 1999, pp. A1, A8; "GM Will Connect Drivers to the World Wide Web," *Wall Street Journal*, November 3, 1999, pp. B1, B4; "Reviving GM," *Business Week,* February 1, 1999, pp. 114–122; "Delphi Pushes a Peace Program" *Business Week*, February 1, 1999, p. 122; "GM Turns to Computers to Cut Development Costs," *Wall Street Journal*, October 12, 1998, p. B4; "Toyota Revamps Platforms for Shift to Exports If Local Markets Fail," *Wall Street Journal*, October 7, 1998, p. A17; "GM to Announce Major Reorganization; Wagoner to Lead Merged Operations," *Wall Street Journal*, October 6, 1998, p. A8; "GM's Cadillac Aims to Stem Market-Share Slide," *Wall Street Journal*, September 28, 1998, p. B9K; "General Motors to Take Nationwide Test Drive on Web," *Wall Street Journal*, September 28, 1998, p. B4; "GM, Isuzu Investing $320 Million to Build Advanced Diesel Engines for GM Pickups," *Wall Street Journal*, September 9, 1998, p. A4; "GM: It'll Be a Long Road Back," *Business Week*, August 17, 1998; "GM's Chairman Plans Sweeping Changes," *Wall Street Journal*, August 6,

1998, p.A3, A6; "Wide Gap Exists between GM, Rivals in Labor Productivity, Report Says," *Wall Street Journal*, July 16, 1998, p. A4.

3. For an excellent and seminal discussion of this topic, see M. E. Porter, *Competitive Advantage* (New York: Free Press, 1985), 36–61. Also see K. Cool and J. Henderson, "Power and Firm Profitability in Supply Chains: French Manufacturing Industry in 1993," *Strategic Management Journal* 19, no. 10 (1998): 909–926; C. B. Stabell and O. D. Fjeldstad, "Configuring Value for Competitive Advantage: On Chains, Shops and Networks," *Strategic Management Journal* 19, no. 5 (1998): 413–438; R. Normann and R. Ramirez, "From Value Chain to Value Constellation," *Harvard Business Review* 71, no. 4 (1993): 65–77; M. Hergert and D. Morris, "Accounting Data for Value Chain Analysis," *Strategic Management Journal* 10, no. 2 (1989): 175–188; C. G. Armistead and G. Clark, "Resource Activity Mapping: The Value Chain in Service Operation Strategy," *Service Industries Journal* 13, no. 4 (1993): 221–239.

4. This notion was initially developed by McKinsey & Company, management consultants.

5. See, for example, R. Kerin, R. Varadarajan, and R. Peterson, "First-Mover Advantage: A Synthesis, Conceptual Framework, and Research Propositions, *Journal of Marketing* 56, no. 4 (1992): 33–52; B. Mascarenhas, "First-Mover Effects in Multiple Dynamic Markets," *Strategic Management Journal* 13, no. 3 (1992): 237–243; M. B. Lieberman and D. B. Montgomery, "First-Mover Advantages," *Strategic Management Journal* 9 (1988): 41–58; R. Rosenbloom and M. Cusumano, "Technological Pioneering and Competitive Advantage: The Birth of the VCR Industry," *California Management Review* 29, no 4 (1987): 51–76. Also see M. B. Lieberman and D. B. Montgomery, "First-Mover (Dis)Advantages: Retrospective and Link with the Resource-Based View," *Strategic Management Journal* 19, no. 12 (1998): 1111–1126; P. Vanderwerf and J. F. Mahon, "Meta-Analysis of the Impact of Research Methods on Findings of First-Mover Advantage," *Management Science* 43, no. 11 (1997): 1510–1519; C. Nehrt, "Timing and Intensity of Environmental Investments," *Strategic Management Journal* 17, no. 7 (1996): 535–547.

6. See, for example, J. A. Buzacott, ed., *Scale in Production Systems* (New York: Pergamon, 1982). An excellent examination of scale and related effects in promoting competitive advantage is M. B. Lieberman, "The Learning Curve: Technological Barriers to Entry and Competitive Survival in the Chemical Processing Industries," *Strategic Management Journal* 10 (1989): 431–447. Earlier work that looks at scale and learning effects include P. Ghemawat, "Capacity Expansion in the Titanium Dioxide Industry," *Journal of Industrial Economics* 33 (December 1984): 145–163; M. E. McGrath and R. W. Hoole, "Manufacturing's New Economies of Scale," *Harvard Business Review* (May–June 1992): 94–102; B. J. Seldon and S. H. Bullard, "Input Substitution, Economies of Scale and Productivity Growth in the U.S. Upholstered Furniture Industry," *Applied Economics* 24 (September 1992): 1017–1026; S. C. Kumbhakar, "A Reexamination of Returns to Scale, Density and Technical Progress in U.S. Airlines," *Southern Economic Journal* 57 (October 1990): 425–443; M. J. Farrell, "Industry Characteristics and Scale Economies as Sources of Intra-Industry Trade," *Journal of Economic Studies* 18 (November 1991): 36–58; A. Seth, "Sources of Value Creation in Acquisitions: An Empirical Investigation," *Strategic Management Journal* 11 (1990): 431–446; G. Forestieri, "Economies of Scale and Scope in the Financial Services Industry: A Review of Recent Literature," *Financial Conglomerates*, Organization for Economic Cooperation and Development (1993): 63–124.

7. The landmark work that first examined the effects of cumulative learning and experience curve effects within large firms is found in The Boston Consulting Group, *Perspectives on Experience* (Boston: Author, 1972). Examples of research that empirically tested this phenomenon include A. Spence, "The Learning Curve and Competition," *Bell Journal of Economics* 12 (1981): 49–70; R. J. Gilbert and R. G. Harris, "Investment Decisions with Economies of Scale and Learning," *American Economic*

Review 71 (May 1981): 172–177; M. B. Lieberman, "The Learning Curve, Diffusion and Competitive Strategy," *Strategic Management Journal* 8 (1987): 441–452; R. H. Hayes, S. C. Wheelwright, and K. B. Clark, *Dynamic Manufacturing: Creating the Learning Organization* (New York: Free Press, 1988); L. Argote and D. Epple, "Learning Curves in Manufacturing," *Science* 247 (February 23, 1990): 920–925; P. S. Adler and K. Clark, "Behind the Learning Curve: A Sketch of the Learning Process," *Management Science* 37 (March 1991): 267–282; C. Koulamas, "Quality Improvement through Product Redesign and the Learning Curve," *Omega* 20 (March 1992): 161–168; F. Malerba, "Learning by Firms and Incremental Technical Change," *Economic Journal* 102 (July 1992): 845–860; H. Gruber, "The Learning Curve in the Production of Semiconductor Memory Chips," *Applied Economics* 24 (August 1992): 885–895; B. Bahk and M. Gort, "Decomposing Learning by Doing in New Plants," *Journal of Political Economy* 101 (August 1993): 561–584.

8. See, for example, "My, What Big Internet Numbers You Have," *Fortune*, March 15, 1999, pp. 114–120. "Amazon.com Sales More Than Triples Boosting Online Bookseller's Shares," *Wall Street Journal*, January 6, 1999, p. B7. "Amazon.com," *Business Week*, December 14, 1998, pp. 106–112; "Internet Retailers Take on Amazon.com with Shopper Connection Online Mall," *Wall Street Journal*, November 25, 1998, p. B6; "Some Big Companies Long to Embrace Web but Settle for Flirtation," *Wall Street Journal*, November 4, 1998, pp. A1, A14; "Bertelsmann's New Media Man," *Fortune*, November 23, 1998, pp. 176–186; "Mating Game: Worried Web Players Rush to Pair Up," *Wall Street Journal*, October 8, 1998, p. B4; "CDnow and N2K, Online Music Retailers, and Rivals of Amazon.com, Plan Merger," *Wall Street Journal*, October 7, 1998, p. B6; "Bertelsmann to Buy a 50% Interest in Web Bookseller," *Wall Street Journal*, October 7, 1998, p. B6; "Time Warner Erects an Internet Superstore," *Wall Street Journal*, September 14, 1998, pp. B1, B4.

9. See, for example, S. Eilon, "Analysis of Corporate Performance," *Business and Economic Review* (Summer 1987): 20–29; and L. J. Gitman, *Basic Managerial Finance* (New York: HarperCollins, 1992).

10. See "P&G's Covert Operation," *Fortune*, September 17, 2001, pp. 42–44; also see "The Prying Game," *Fortune*, September 17, 2001, p. 235.

CHAPTER 4

Opportunities for Distinction: Building Competitive Advantage

Chapter Outline

What You Will Learn

- The three types of "generic" competitive strategies that can be used to build competitive advantage, including low-cost leadership, differentiation, and focus
- The benefits and costs of pursuing each type of generic strategy
- The rise of mass customization as a new strategy
- The role of quality as a key pillar of any competitive strategy
- The evolution of strategic considerations over a product's life cycle

Nordstrom, Inc.[1]

Competition among firms in the retailing industry has always been fierce. Within the department store segment, large nationwide chains such as JCPenney, Sears, May Department Stores, and Federated Department Stores have strengthened their presence in ever-expanding malls throughout the country. May Department Stores and Federated, in particular, operate a collection of different store brands, many of which were acquired over the past two decades as a wave of consolidation reshaped the department store landscape.* All of these firms operate large stores that offer a wide merchandise selection where they can leverage their distribution strengths. With the growth of computerized, real-time inventory tracking systems, many of these chains have invested in new technologies that enable them to keep track of customer demand patterns while lowering their inventory costs through streamlined ordering systems. By capturing significant economies of scale in their procurement and distribution activities, the large consolidated chains have been able to steadily accumulate cost savings, some of which are passed on to their customers.

While consolidation has dominated the landscape of the retailing industry in recent years, a number of retailers have attempted to compete by offering superior service and emphasizing upscale, high-quality products. These include such smaller firms as Neiman Marcus Group and Saks. However, there was one firm that every competitor sought to imitate when learning how best to provide customer service. Considered one of the finest retailers in the United States, Nordstrom has always prided itself on the exceptional customer service that it offers to its customers. In fact, the very name *Nordstrom* has become synonymous with quality, intimate service, and personal charm. Throughout the company's history, family management led the company over the past hundred years to set the standards for the finest possible customer service that could be delivered in-person.

With deep roots in Seattle, Nordstrom originally began its operations as a shoe retailer in 1901. For the first sixty-seven years of its history, Nordstrom sold only shoes throughout the Pacific Northwest. In 1968, the family began to add women's fashions and other clothing lines to its merchandise assortment. The company began to expand nationally during the 1990s, with over seventy full-line stores in every region. In 2000, Nordstrom rang up sales of $5.5 billion, earning $102 million in net profit.

The defining hallmark of Nordstrom's approach to retailing has been its obsessive focus on customer service. In fact, the vast majority of the company's managers all started their careers by working on the sales floor where they learned and refined the fine art of delivering highly personalized service. Sales associates always put the needs of their customers first. In fact, they are expected to notify customers of impending sales events and special offers through personal phone calls or notes in the mail. These loyal customers frequently returned to make future purchases of an expanding line of fashions, shoes, accessories, and maternity wear. In turn, Nordstrom rewards its sales associates with compensation that is often significantly higher than what competitors offer; more important, Nordstrom follows a policy of promoting from within its own ranks. The company believes that it can preserve and improve its distinctive customer service only by ensuring that its managers have fully embraced the concept through personal sales experience. In addition, Nordstrom is known for its caring human resources practices. It offers a generous family leave program for future mothers and allows time off for employees to care for other family members as well. See Exhibit 4-1 for these defining characteristics of Nordstrom's service-driven strategy.

Nordstrom's singular focus on customer service enabled the firms to vault over its competitors in customer loyalty, sales per square foot, and earnings growth during the 1980s and early 1990s. However, the changing retailing environment posed significant challenges for Nordstrom of late. Many of Nordstrom's stores have become

*Some of the stores affiliated with May Department Stores include Lord & Taylor, Foley's, Strawbridge's, Kaufmann's, and Hecht's, to name a few. Federated Department Stores include such stores as Macy's, Bloomingdale's, Rich's, and Goldsmith's.

Nordstrom's Differentiation from Department Store Chains

EXHIBIT 4-1

SUPPORT ACTIVITIES						
Infrastructure			Strong legacy of family emphasis on service			
Human Resource Management			Promotion from within for managers; Caring practices		Development of service culture	Training on service expectations; service rewarded
Technology Development			Development of new ordering systems		Customer loyalty programs; Internet sales	Make Internet as user-friendly as possible
Procurement		Emphasis on high fashion labels				
PRIMARY ACTIVITIES			Smaller stores; higher store density; narrower product line		Higher prices; Emphasis on classic designs	Personalized, friendly, customer-first policy
		Inbound Logistics	Operations	Outbound Logistics	Marketing/ Sales	Service

bigger as it offers a broader line of merchandise in new regions of the country. Although the company has invested considerable resources to expand nationally, it is encountering new operational challenges as its competitors began to invest heavily in new computer-driven ordering and distribution technologies. Even as the company expanded rapidly, family management at Nordstrom believed that it could replicate its intimate customer service strategy at each store to compete effectively.

Until recently, Nordstrom operated over twelve different buying centers to procure merchandise for its stores. This often meant that each region would place its own separate orders, thus losing any potential scale benefits from shared buying. Also, the firm has lagged behind its competitors in installing real-time inventory tracking systems that enable the firm to automatically reorder merchandise where needed. Equally important, Nordstrom's dispersed buying and ordering systems meant that buyers could not communicate with one another about what particular market trends were taking shape, nor could they fine-tune the right mix of fashionable offerings for increasingly savvy customers.

To counter some of these difficulties, Nordstrom attempted to combine both contemporary clothing (lots of color, trendy prints) with classical styles and brand names across its departments. This meant that high-fashion labels were sold alongside house brands and other less well-known labels in the same clothing category. Over time, customers became confused with what Nordstrom was offering, because the merchandise mix appeared to be diluted and offered mixed messages, rather than promoting its traditional upscale, classical taste. When interviewed by market research firms, some customer groups felt that Nordstrom had become overly formal (store piano players often wear tuxedos) while lagging other stores in offering cutting-edge fashions. In recent years, Nordstrom was also perceived as overemphasizing its reach toward younger customers (loud hip-hop music in many stores) at the expense of its more loyal, baby-boomer shoppers.

As Nordstrom enters the new century, the firm is in the midst of investing in many of the same technologies that have enabled its competitors to better track and order inventory. At the same time, Nordstrom continues to focus on offering superior customer service, even as it begins to provide merchandise designed for middle-income shoppers. Nordstrom stores still remain synonymous with beautiful designs and helpful people, but the company still struggles with its "backroom" operations where managing expenses has become particularly important as customers become more price-sensitive. While the Nordstrom family continues to reign over the company, some market analysts believe the firm needs to attract new, outside talent that can provide more experience to better manage its technology investments. Nordstrom's legendary promote-from-within policy has also come under question from some analysts, who believe that the company's obsessive focus on superior service may have limited the kind of professional backgrounds and experience that could flourish in the company's ranks. In fact, Neiman Marcus and Talbot's have made serious inroads into Nordstrom's customer base, as the two competitors offer classic merchandise with improving service. Moreover, many upscale customers prefer discounts to highly pampered service, especially during times of economic uncertainty.

To counter some of these challenges, Nordstrom has begun to offer its merchandise at its new Nordstrom.com Web site, with a strong emphasis on shoes—the same line of merchandise that was the foundation for the company's early growth. However, Nordstrom's family management still asserts that superior customer service will remain the ultimate trump card over its competitors. As the company moves into a new competitive era, it will have to balance its traditional focus on customer service with alternative approaches to capture new customers who may want something beyond personalized service.

Introduction

In Chapter 3, we presented an overview of some of the generalized sources of competitive advantage that established firms within an industry are likely to possess. Although first-mover, scale, experience, and interrelationship advantages are important, especially for large firms, in practice companies of all sizes need to build their own specific sources of competitive advantage based on their distinctive competences. Each firm is likely to possess its own set of distinct strengths and weaknesses among its set of value-adding activities. Developing a distinctive competence that builds on a firm's strengths while minimizing its weaknesses enables a firm to lay the foundation for a sustainable competitive advantage. In this chapter, we explore the opportunities and routes available for firms to build competitive advantage over their rivals.

We begin by examining the concept of competitive advantage as it applies to specific value-adding activities performed by the firm. Competitive advantage arises when a firm can perform an activity that is distinct or different from that of its rivals. Superior earnings can only come from distinction. Therefore, a strategy is only as useful as it is distinctive. Generally speaking, there are three sources of competitive advantage: low-cost, differentiation, and focus. However, other emerging sources of competitive advantage have also surfaced for firms that seek to provide improved customer value through customization of product and service offerings.

We also analyze the advantages and disadvantages that accompany each approach to building competitive advantage. We explore each of these "generic" strategies in separate sections and point out the benefits and costs associated with each one. In the last section, we investigate how competitive strategy depends significantly on the product life cycle. We consider how sources of competitive advantage may shift over the span of the product life cycle as well.

Routes to Building Competitive Advantage

Competitive strategies must be based on some source of competitive advantage to be successful. Companies build competitive advantage when they take steps that enable them to gain an edge over their rivals in attracting buyers. These steps vary: for example, making the highest-quality product, providing the best customer service, producing at the lowest cost, or focusing resources on a specific segment or niche of the industry. Regardless of which avenue to building competitive advantage the firm selects, customers must receive superior value than that offered by its rivals. Providing superior value to customers also translates into superior financial performance for the firm. Numerous studies demonstrate that firms providing superior value in the form of lower-cost products or services or distinctive, high-quality products are able to sustain high profitability and competitive advantage.[2]

Competitive advantage is developed at the *industry* or *business* level of analysis. Recall that *business-level strategy* focuses on how to compete in a given business or industry with its different types of competitors aiming to sell to the same or similar group of customers. In practice, competitors within an industry may be companies with no other lines of business (single-business firms) or business units belonging to larger, diversified companies that operate across many industries. Analysis at the business or industry level is the basis for building competitive advantage.

Firms have long attempted to build competitive advantage through an infinite number of strategies. Competitive strategies are designed to help firms deploy their value chains and other strengths to build competitive advantage. Thus, in practice, each company formulates its specific competitive strategy according to its own analysis of internal strengths and weaknesses, the value it can provide, the competitive environment, and the needs of its customers.

Although there are as many different competitive strategies as there are firms competing, three underlying approaches to building competitive advantage appear to exist at the broadest level. They are (1) low-cost leadership strategies, (2) differentiation strategies, and (3) focus strategies. These strategies are depicted in Exhibit 4-2. These three broad types of competitive strategies have also been labeled **generic strategies**. All three generic strategies are designed to achieve distinction relative to a rival.[3] Let us now examine how each generic type of competitive strategy can build competitive advantage.

generic strategies: The broad types of competitive strategies—low-cost leadership, differentiation, and focus—that firms use to build competitive advantage (see low-cost leadership, differentiation, focus strategies).

Low-Cost Leadership Strategies

Low-cost leadership strategies are based on a firm's ability to provide a product or service at a lower cost than its rivals. The basic operating assumption behind a low-cost leadership strategy is to acquire a substantial cost advantage over other competitors that can be passed on to consumers to gain a large market share. A low-cost strategy then produces a competitive advantage when the firm can earn a higher profit margin that results from selling products at current market prices. In many cases, firms attempting to execute low-cost strategies aim to sell a product that appeals to an "average" customer in a broad target market. Oftentimes, these products or services are highly standardized and not customized to an individual customer's tastes, needs, or desires.

low-cost leadership: A competitive strategy based on the firm's ability to provide products or services at lower cost than its rivals.

A central premise of the low-cost leadership strategy is the following: By making products with as few modifications as possible, the firm can exploit the cost reduction benefits that accrue from economies of scale and experience effects. Low-cost leadership strategies can also flourish in service businesses as well. In these arenas, firms attempt to capture economies of scale in information systems, procurement, logistics and even marketing.

Examples of firms that have successfully used a low-cost leadership strategy to build competitive advantage include Whirlpool in washers and dryers, Black and Decker in power

EXHIBIT 4-2 Generic Strategic Approaches to Build Competitive Advantage

Target Market	Competitive Advantage: Defined by Cost	Competitive Advantage: Defined by Distinctiveness
Industry-wide (Broad)	**Low-cost leadership**	**Differentiation**
Specific Niche or Segment (Narrow)	**Cost-based focus**	**Differentiation-based focus**

tools, BIC in ball point pens, Wal-Mart in retailing, Gillette in razor blades, Texas Instruments and Intel in semiconductors, Samsung in color television sets, Sharp in flat-panel screens and LCD technology, Citigroup in credit card services, Emerson Electric in power drives and tools, and DuPont in nylon and other synthetic fibers.

Building a Low-Cost Advantage

The low-cost leadership strategy is based on locating and leveraging every possible source of cost advantage in a firm's value chain of activities. As Exhibit 4-3 shows, numerous opportunities are available for firms seeking to build cost-based advantages among their primary and supporting value-adding activities. Once a firm pursuing a low-cost leadership strategy has discovered an important source of cost improvement and reduction, however, it must then seek new ways to lower its activity costs even further over time. In other words, the sources of low-cost advantage are not enduring or sustainable without continuous improvement and ongoing searches for improved process yields, streamlined product design, or more efficient means of delivering a service.

cost driver: A technological or economic factor that determines the cost of performing some activity.

Building a cost-based advantage thus requires the firm to find and exploit all the potential cost drivers that allow for greater efficiency in each value-adding activity. A **cost driver** is an economic or technological factor that determines the cost of performing some activity. Important cost drivers that shape the low-cost leadership strategy include (1) economies of scale, (2) experience or learning curve effects, (3) degree of vertical integration, and even (4) location of activity performance. Firms can tailor their use of these cost drivers to build low-cost leadership across different value-adding activities.

In pursuing a cost-based advantage, no firm can obviously ignore such product attributes as quality, service, and reliability. If it does, its offering may become so unacceptable that consumers will refuse to buy it or will buy it only if the price is reduced to a level below what is needed to sustain profitability. A firm pursuing a cost-based advantage must therefore strive to achieve some degree of quality *parity* or *proximity* with other firms that have defined the standards of product quality valued by customers.[4]

Economies of Scale and Experience Effects. Economies of scale and experience curve effects (as initially discussed in Chapter 3) enable firms to successively lower their unit costs as both capacity and experience grow. Economies of scale and experience curve effects are particularly significant in the inbound logistics, operations, outbound logistics,

Competitive Advantage Based on Low-Cost Leadership — EXHIBIT 4-3

SUPPORT ACTIVITIES	Infrastructure	Centralized cost controls				
	Human Resource Management	Intensive training to emphasize cost saving means; encourage employees to look for new ways to improve methods				
	Technology Development	Economies of scale of R&D and technology development; learning and experience amortized over large volume				
	Procurement	Purchasing from numerous sources; strong bargaining power with suppliers				
PRIMARY ACTIVITIES		Large shipments; massive warehouses	Economies of scale in plants; experience effects	Bulk or large order shipment	Mass marketing; mass distribution; national ad campaigns	Centralized service facilities in region
		Inbound Logistics	Operations	Outbound Logistics	Marketing/ Sales	Service

procurement, and technology development activities of the value chain. For example, large factories (e.g., steel mills, semiconductor plants) and service delivery centers (e.g., overnight delivery facilities, database management, centralized reservation systems, call centers) often have operating systems characterized by high fixed costs and capital-intensive processes that are sensitive to economies of scale. Experience effects are important in these activities, too, because employees have opportunities to become more proficient in performing their tasks over time. For example, workers in a factory or scientists in a laboratory setting often become better accustomed to performing their work over time so that output yield rises with greater familiarity. In another vein, procurement and technology development costs (associated with research and development, or R&D) can also be shared and spread among a variety of different products and activities. For instance, improving the coatings used to create weather stripping and tape products can help create new adhesives for automotive and aerospace applications. All of these activities are based on significant scale or experience drivers that lower unit costs. Firms that are able to build a low-cost strategy on both scale and experience effects can thus reap higher returns for products sold at market prices.

Vertical Integration. Vertical integration is an economic concept that refers to the degree of control a firm exerts over the supply of its inputs and the purchase of its outputs. For example, when an automobile manufacturer acquires a steelmaker (a key supplier of crucial materials needed to produce cars), it is pursuing one form of vertical integration. Here, the car company is attempting to control a supply source. Similarly, when the automobile manufacturer purchases a car rental firm, it is pursuing another form of vertical integration. In this case, the automobile company is extending its control over an important buyer of its products. Extending control over sources of supply (upstream operations) or buyers (downstream operations) is vertical integration.

Firms may find that different approaches to vertical integration enable them to produce at low costs, although the nature of this relationship requires some explanation. Vertical integration can be an important cost driver, depending on the nature of the firm's product, degree of technological change, the relative strength of buyers and suppliers in that industry, and other external factors. How it contributes to building cost-based competitive advantage depends on the specific situations facing the firm. (Although a brief overview of vertical integration is presented here, this topic is covered much more extensively in Chapter 7 on corporate strategy.)

High levels of vertical integration help firms control all of the inputs, supplies, and equipment needed to convert raw materials into the final end product. In many instances, a high degree of vertical integration allows the firm to leverage scale and experience effects from one activity to another. For example, vertical integration is prominent in the oil refining, paper, and steel industries, where the firm is better able to control costs and potentially reduce total costs for all of the firm's activities by bringing many production or conversion activities in-house. For oil, paper, and steel companies, the transaction costs of dealing with numerous external suppliers and buyers are removed, which often results in large cost savings, greater predictability of supplies, and greater production efficiency. **Transaction costs** refer to the costs of finding, negotiating, selling, buying, and resolving disputes with other firms in the open market. Thus, high vertical integration is a significant cost driver when products and technologies tend to remain fairly stable over long periods of time. For example, Matsushita Electric Industrial of Japan is highly vertically integrated in the manufacture of televisions, VCRs, DVD players, office equipment, and medical equipment. Matsushita makes the circuit boards, switches, semiconductors, controls, wiring harnesses, plastic casings, and power supplies that become important components for its end products (e.g., consumer electronics products). By performing most of these activities in-house, Matsushita can reap substantial cost advantages through numerous value-adding activities of components and activities that directly "feed" into its final products.

transaction costs: Economic costs of finding, negotiating, selling, buying, and resolving disputes with other firms (e.g., suppliers and customers) in the open market.

In other situations, firms can sometimes achieve a strong cost advantage by having very little vertical integration. By deliberately choosing *not* to perform certain activities in-house, a firm avoids the start-up and fixed costs that often accompany high integration. Firms can thus seek to lower their costs by buying more than they make. By concentrating its effort on lowering the costs of pursuing one or two sets of activities, the firm may avoid high fixed-cost capital investments in other parts of the value chain. This approach to minimal vertical integration is particularly well suited for firms in rapidly evolving industries. Firms do not seek to invest in those product technologies or production processes that could become obsolete in a short time. For example, low levels of vertical integration have served fast-growing Dell Computer well in the rapidly evolving personal computer (PC) industry. Making chips and designing software are expensive activities, so Dell does not invest in these areas. By devoting its effort to assembling and distributing personal computers, the firm avoids many of the fixed costs that come with vertical integration. In fact, Dell benefits significantly from its lack of vertical integration, since it can purchase key components and computer peripherals from a number of different suppliers and thus contain its inventory and production costs. These savings translate directly into enhanced profitability margins and faster response to individual customer needs.

Other firms producing high-technology products have begun to transform their own operations to emphasize less vertical integration of many operational and manufacturing-based activities. For example, developers of advanced digital cell phones, such as Ericsson, NEC, Motorola, and Samsung, are focusing their efforts on design and marketing activities. In turn, they are relying on contract manufacturers (e.g., Flextronics, Solectron, Sanmina-SCI, Celestica) to perform many of the component manufacturing and assembly operations. As the features in cell phones continue to change rapidly, less vertical integration enables NEC, Motorola, and Ericsson to become more responsive to fast-evolving market trends. Thus, firms can pursue a low-cost strategy with either high levels *or* low levels of vertical integration, depending on the nature of the industry and the competitive environment.[5]

Location of Activities. The actual location where a value-added activity is performed may be a significant cost driver in determining a firm's cost advantage. Perhaps one of the best examples of how location can be used to build cost-based competitive advantage is Toyota's strategy for dealing with its suppliers in the automobile industry. To keep inventory costs minimal and quality of parts high, Toyota works with key suppliers to build their component factories near its own assembly plants. By having suppliers' factories close to its own assembly plants, Toyota can implement just-in-time (JIT) inventory management. This means that Toyota can receive the parts it needs almost immediately without the costs of holding inventory. This "lean production" strategy enables Toyota to further reduce the costs of building and assembling cars. Moreover, lean production and just-in-time inventory practices enable both Toyota and its key suppliers to continuously improve the quality of their products. In addition, all of the components must be of the highest production quality standard, since neither Toyota nor its suppliers can afford a shutdown because of defects or missing parts. Inbound logistics costs at Toyota are thus reduced substantially, since little inventory sits in the warehouse. In addition, operations run more efficiently and seldom experience a shutdown due to unscheduled deliveries or poor-quality components/parts. Toyota practices its lean production approach in both Japan and the United States, where it has begun large-scale production of mid-sized automobiles and pickup trucks for the American market over the past decade.

In a similar vein, location is a vital strategic cost driver for Federal Express, a unit of FedEx Corporation. By centralizing all inbound and outbound logistics or distribution activities near its Memphis headquarters, FedEx can achieve tremendous economies of scale and experience in sorting the overnight packages and letters that are key to its business. Because Memphis is centrally located in the United States, FedEx can use its location-based strategy to develop its low-cost, highly efficient air-flying routes across its entire system.

Benefits and Costs of Low-Cost Leadership Strategies

Low-cost leadership strategies carry their own set of advantages and disadvantages to firms that practice them. Many of the advantages associated with low-cost leadership strategies are based on the relatively large size of the companies pursuing them. However, the disadvantages associated with low-cost strategies may outweigh some of the benefits.

Advantages of Low-Cost Strategies. The appeal of the low-cost leadership strategy is based on the strong relationship that appears to exist between high market share and high profitability. Numerous studies have found that firms with high market share, for various reasons, can command above-average industry profitability over extended periods of time.[6] Some of the empirical findings that appear to explain, at least partially, the relationship between high market share and profitability include economies of scale, risk avoidance by customers, strong market presence, and focused management.[7]

Risk avoidance by customers means that buyers who are currently familiar with the low-cost leader's products are unlikely to switch to a competing brand of a similar product, unless that brand has something very different or unique to offer. Thus, low-cost producers that achieve a dominant market share position may induce risk aversion on the part of the industry's buyers. Customers often prefer to buy from well-known, dominant-share companies because they feel these firms will be around a long time after their purchase. This reasoning is particularly true for products that are costly or require after-sales service, such as electrical products, computers, and appliances. Emerson Electric, a leading firm in developing a broad range of electrical motors, drives, tooling, and other components, has built a commanding market position in these products. Emerson's emphasis on being the "best-cost producer" in any given category means that it invests in state-of-the-art manufacturing processes to strive for ever-higher efficiencies. At the same time, industrial customers that use Emerson's products feel the company's commitment to its businesses and know that components and after-sales service will be available.

Strong market presence means that low-cost firms are able to "convince" their competitors not to start price wars within the industry. This means that low-cost firms can set the stage for pricing discipline within the industry. In turn, prices are kept stable enough over time to ensure that all firms in the industry maintain some degree of profitability. Attempts to establish pricing discipline were used by leaders in the U.S. steel, aluminum, and heavy machinery industries during the 1960s. The arrival of intense global competition, however, has made this type of discipline difficult to enforce in most manufacturing industries today.

Low-cost firms are often able to keep potential competitors out of the industry through their price-cutting power, which can generate substantial obstacles to firms contemplating entry into the industry. In other words, low-cost leadership strategies, when effectively implemented and understood by potential entrants, constitute a very effective barrier to entry that governs industry rivalry. For example, Intel currently dominates the production of microprocessors that serve as the "brains" for personal computers. By investing heavily in the latest generation of new technologies and processes, Intel has become the lowest-cost producer of these microprocessors. Its cutting-edge manufacturing skills complement its fast product development cycles. Other competitors such as Via Technologies' Cyrix unit and Advanced Micro Devices (AMD) are serious players in this industry, but Intel has enormous power to lower the prices of its popular Celeron, and Pentium 4 classes of chips in advance of its rivals' entry. Intel's price-cutting power and manufacturing skill thus slow down the ability of other chipmakers to grab significant market share from Intel. However, even Intel must continually remain vigilant as a reinvigorated AMD continues to chip away at Intel's market share in not only the lowest-priced segments but also some midrange microprocessor segments.

Low-cost firms also have the advantage of being able to sustain price increases passed on by their suppliers. By operating at more cost-efficient levels of production, low-cost firms can more easily absorb increases in the prices of components or ingredients used in their products. For example, Hershey Foods, a low-cost producer of chocolates and candies, is probably in a better position to absorb increases in cocoa prices than other smaller chocolate and candy manufacturers.

Disadvantages of Low-Cost Strategies. Cost-based strategies are not without their disadvantages, some of them rather extreme. The biggest disadvantage associated with low-cost leadership is the high level of asset commitment and capital-intensive activities that often accompanies this strategy. To produce or deliver services at low cost, firms often invest considerable sums of resources into rigid, inflexible assets and production or distribution technologies that are difficult to switch to other products or uses. Thus, firms can find themselves locked in to a given process or technology that could rapidly become obsolete. Such was the case with Timex Watch Company during the 1960s and 1970s when the company was the low-cost producer of mechanical watches. When quartz and digital watches became popular during the late 1970s, Timex was so committed to its mechanical watch and process technology that it could not easily adapt to technological change.

A huge disadvantage facing low-cost firms is that cost reduction methods are easily imitated or copied by other firms. Cost advantages, particularly in standardized production or service delivery processes, are often short-lived and fleeting. U.S. steelmakers were caught in this situation during the 1970s when they faced the rising tide of cheaper Japanese steel imports. In fact, many Japanese steelmakers were able to leapfrog ahead of U.S. companies by innovating an even more advanced manufacturing process called continuous casting that made U.S. processes using open-hearth furnaces obsolete. Japanese steelmakers were able to forge better-quality steel at lower costs than comparable U.S. plants. What made the situation even worse for U.S. companies was their failure to reinvest in new technologies; companies such as U.S. Steel, Bethlehem Steel, and National Steel believed their low-cost production was a long-standing, enduring advantage. Now, Korean steelmakers are adopting more innovative steel fabrication technologies to undercut even their Japanese competitors. Korean steel companies, such as Posco, have found new techniques to lower steel production costs even further, thus making it difficult for Japanese and U.S. firms to respond effectively.

More important, companies fixated on cost reduction may blind themselves to other changes evolving in the market, such as growing customer demand for different types of products, better quality, higher levels of service, competitor offerings, and even declining customer sensitivity to low prices. Over the past three years, Intel now faces this growing dilemma in the microprocessor business that it still dominates. Although no other firm can match Intel's enormous manufacturing prowess, massive R&D and capital expenditures, and brand identity for its Celeron, Pentium III, and Pentium 4 line of chips, Intel has come under increasingly fierce assault recently from Advanced Micro Devices for microprocessors designed for the sub-$1,000 and sub-$600 personal computer (PC) market. Despite Intel's commitment and continuous investment in microprocessors, its large size eventually blindsided it to the arrival of less expensive microprocessor offerings made by competitors who were still willing to compete in a different and unprotected segment of the PC industry. In 2002, the company is expected to roll out twenty-five to forty new chips a year. In 2001, despite Intel's overwhelming 80 percent commanding market share of microprocessors sold to the entire PC industry, the company was in a distant second place for less expensive chips used in PCs near the $600 price.[8] More important, Intel's near-obsession with the microprocessor segment may have blinded it to new opportunities unfolding in the communications, analog, and networking segments of the semiconductor industry. Thus, firms obsessed with low costs may find themselves ambushed by competitors taking a different strategy designed to outflank a dominant industry player. Also, low-cost leadership strategies may result in a firm's missing new developments that may redefine an industry's future structure.

In practice, a low-cost leadership strategy usually allows room for only one firm to pursue this strategy effectively. When numerous firms compete with one another to become the low-cost producer, the result is outright warfare in which everyone in the industry bleeds. In a short period of time, rivals build enormous amounts of excess capacity that depress industry-wide profitability. Consider, for example, the highly competitive environment of the airline industry in the United States over the past ten years. Large carriers, such as AMR's American Airlines, UAL Group, Continental Airlines, Northwest Airlines, Delta Air Lines, and USAirways, have attempted to lower their unit costs by expanding the range of markets they serve. Some of these firms have even attempted to merge in order to strengthen their market positions and even further lower their costs (e.g., UAL Group's United Airlines and USAirways Group near-merger in 2001; American Airlines' consummated merger with TWA in July 2001). However, during the time competitors have attempted to undercut each other, customers have become accustomed to buying deeply discounted tickets. Even highly profitable Southwest Airlines is now feeling the pressure of excess capacity in the short-haul markets it once dominated. On the East Coast, for example, Delta Express and USAirways' Metrojet service are fighting Southwest's entry into this market by forming their own low-cost affiliates. However, it remains to be seen whether these two firms can fully execute their low-cost strategies given the constraints imposed by a high-cost labor structure.[9] In this brutal state within the airline industry, many firms such as America West, TWA, and Northwest Airlines have sought bankruptcy protection, sometimes on multiple occasions. More mergers and consolidations are likely for this industry, especially as it grapples with the enormous losses of 2001.

Differentiation Strategies

Another strategic approach to building competitive advantage is that of pursuing differentiation strategies. **Differentiation** strategies are based on providing buyers with something that is different or unique, that makes the company's product or service distinct from that of its rivals. The key assumption behind a differentiation strategy is that customers are willing to pay a higher price for a product that is distinct (or at least perceived as such) in some important way. Superior value is created because the product is of higher quality, is technically superior in some way, comes with superior service, or has a special appeal in some perceived way. In effect, differentiation builds competitive advantage by making customers more loyal—and less price-sensitive—to a given firm's product. Additionally, customers are less likely to search for other alternative products once they are satisfied.

differentiation: Competitive strategy based on providing buyers with something special or unique that makes the firm's product or service distinctive.

Differentiation may be achieved in a number of ways. The product may incorporate a more innovative design, may be produced using advanced materials or quality processes, or may be sold and serviced in some special way. Often, customers will pay a higher price if the product or service offers a distinctive or special value or "feel" to it. Differentiation strategies offer high profitability when the price premium exceeds the costs of distinguishing the product or service. Examples of companies that have successfully pursued differentiation strategies include Prince in tennis rackets, Callaway in golf clubs, Mercedes and BMW in automobiles, Coors in beer, Beretta in guns, Brooks Brothers and Paul Stuart in classic-cut clothing, Diners Club/Carte Blanche in credit cards, Bose in stereo speakers, American Express in travel services, J. P. Morgan Chase in investment banking, Krups in coffee makers and small kitchen appliances, and Benetton in sweaters and light fashions.

Building a Differentiation-Based Advantage

Firms practicing differentiation seek to design and produce highly distinctive or unique product or service attributes that create high value for their customers. Within the firm, differentiation-based sources of competitive advantage in value-adding activities can be built through a number of methods. Exhibit 4-4 portrays some sources of competitive advantage that a differentiation strategy can provide.

An important strategic consideration managers must recognize is that differentiation does *not* mean the firm can neglect its cost structure. While low unit cost is less important than distinctive product features to firms practicing differentiation, the firm's *total* cost

EXHIBIT 4-4 Competitive Advantage Based on Differentiation

		Inbound Logistics	Operations	Outbound Logistics	Marketing/Sales	Service
SUPPORT ACTIVITIES	Infrastructure	Try to coordinate activities tightly among functions; build quality into organizational practices				
	Human Resource Management	Treat employees as special team members; emphasize design incentives that promote quality				
	Technology Development	Heavy R&D expenditures to make distinctive or even unique products; refinement of high quality manufacturing and technology processes; emphasis on excellence, world class quality				
	Procurement	Selective purchasing from best or world class suppliers				
PRIMARY ACTIVITIES		Use of best materials, parts, and components	Extremely fine quality manufactured workmanship emphasized	Fast delivery to distributors; extra care in packaging and transport	Special, distinctive ads; Technical sales and know-how	High emphasis on treating customer as special individual; Fast and courteous special service

Reprinted/Adapted with the permission of The Free Press, a division of Simon & Schuster, Inc., from *Competitive Advantage: Creating and Sustaining Superior Performance*, by Michael E. Porter. Copyright © 1985 by Michael E. Porter.

structure is still important. In other words, the costs of pursuing differentiation cannot be so high that they completely erode the price premium the firm can charge. Firms pursuing differentiation must still control expenses to balance somewhat higher costs with a distinctive edge in key activities. The cost structure of a firm or business pursuing a differentiation strategy still needs to be carefully managed, although attaining low-unit costs is not the overriding priority. A firm selecting differentiation must therefore aim at achieving cost parity or, at the very least, *cost proximity* relative to competitors by keeping costs low in areas not related to differentiation and by not spending too much to achieve differentiation. Thus, the cost structure of a firm practicing differentiation cannot be that far above the industry average. Also, differentiation is not an end in itself; companies must continue to search for new ways to improve the distinctiveness or uniqueness of their products/services.

7-Eleven (formerly Southland Corporation) has practiced differentiation to avoid direct competition with large supermarket chains. It offers consumers greater convenience in the form of nearby location, shorter shopping time, and quicker checkout. It achieves these benefits by designing a business system within the value chain that is different from that of supermarket chains in several key respects: smaller stores, more store locations, and narrower product line. Its approach is higher cost than that of supermarket chains, so 7-Eleven must ordinarily charge higher prices to achieve profitability. However, customers are generally willing to pay a premium in exchange for the greater convenience 7-Eleven provides. 7-Eleven still strives for cost parity, however, by buying merchandise in bulk and keeping close control of inventory. Its current management team is placing renewed emphasis on cost reduction by introducing computerized ordering and tracking systems in U.S. stores for even better product turnaround and inventory control.

Starbucks Coffee has grown at an annual rate exceeding 30 percent over the past decade as it rolls out its distinctive and specialized blends of coffee throughout the United States. Once a Seattle-based coffee-bean retailer that pioneered the concept of uniquely blended coffees, Starbucks has grown to almost 1,800 outlets throughout the country and is currently opening up a new location almost every day. For the unique flavor of Starbucks' premium coffees and ice coffee drinks, the company can charge upward of $2 to $3 per serving. To remain ahead of other competitors such as Dunkin' Donuts and even smaller specialized coffee chains, Starbucks has begun to roll out an increasing number of different types of beverages that capture and retain its premium image. The Starbucks concept and image have become so popular that it is now serving new types of cold, fruit-flavored drinks like Tiazzi to expand beyond coffees alone. More recently, it has begun to sell many of its ice coffee drink mixes (e.g., Frapuccinos) through grocery store chains and other retailers.[10]

Maytag Corporation has practiced differentiation successfully to distinguish itself from such larger rivals as General Electric and Whirlpool in the major home appliance industry. The company offers a full line of washers, dryers, stoves, and refrigerators that is bolstered by ongoing efforts at continuous improvement and new product development. Its television commercials feature a Maytag repairman who often has nothing to do while on call. Maytag seeks to attract customers at the higher end of the appliance market with superior quality and value offered to buyers. One of its most recently introduced new products is an extremely energy-efficient washing machine known as the Neptune, which has begun to generate high margins in an industry characterized by fierce rivalry and discounting to major wholesalers and retailers. Later versions of the Neptune are utilizing state-of-the-art "smart" technology to self-diagnose potential mechanical problems before a costly repair is needed. Future versions of the Neptune are believed to incorporate Internet-access technology that will automatically place a service call once a problem is detected. Because of the company's focus on new product development, continuous quality improvement, and premium pricing, Maytag's margins rose during the late 1990s, and it has been able to insulate itself from General Electric and Whirpool's scale-based advantages.[11]

In almost all differentiation strategies, attention to product quality and service represents the dominant routes for firms to build competitive advantage. For example, firms may improve a product's quality or performance characteristics to make it more distinctive in the customer's eyes, as Lexus does with its sleek line of automobiles or Tiffany & Company does with its broad line of jewelry and gift items. The product or service can also embody a distinctive design or offering that is hard to duplicate, thus conveying an image of unique quality, as with Krups coffee and espresso makers or with American Express in travel services and charge cards. After-sales service, convenience, and quality are important means to achieve differentiation for numerous firms, such as for IBM in computer and electronic commerce technology or Hewlett-Packard in desktop printers and digital imaging technologies.

Technologically advanced products offer a natural route to pursue differentiation; new features convey a sense of quality that enables firms to distinguish themselves from competitors, as Sony has done with great success in its Walkmans, Discmans, Trinitron television sets, and now Playstation 1 and 2 video game systems. However, these same technologies also require the firm to remain on the cutting edge of innovation and quality to accelerate new product development and to stay in touch with customer's needs and market trends.

It is not unusual for firms practicing differentiation to invest in production processes that use specially designed equipment that makes it hard for rivals to imitate the product's quality. Olympus Optical's fine camera lenses are one example. Olympus's skills in fine optics and lens grinding make it difficult for other competitors to rapidly imitate its fine quality of cameras, microscopes, and other laboratory instruments that command premium prices throughout the world.

Any potential source of increased *buyer value* represents an opportunity to pursue a differentiation strategy.[12] Buyer value can be increased or made more distinctive through several approaches, including (1) lowering the buyer's cost of using the product, (2) increasing buyer satisfaction with the product, and (3) modifying the buyer's perception of value. Of course, these three approaches to increasing buyer value are not mutually exclusive; a distinctive product or service that lowers buyers' direct costs can certainly increase their level of satisfaction as well. Nevertheless, increasing buyer value on any dimension usually means a need to reconfigure or to improve other activities within the firm's value chain.

Lowering Buyer Cost. One important means of lowering the buyer's cost to attain differentiation is through designing products that require less time, energy, or other physical, emotional, or financial costs on the part of the customer. For example, Canon, Minolta, Ricoh, and Sharp of Japan have built extremely reliable and durable photocopying machines that do not require lengthy and costly downtime to service. By using better-designed and better-quality components, the Japanese copier companies made substantial inroads into Xerox's market share in the United States. These machines enabled customers to save considerable sums in repair and downtime costs. Canon, in particular, has been able to turn Xerox's recent weaknesses into its advantage by offering cutting-edge color copying technologies and printers that are easy to service and expandable according to the user's needs. Companies serving other industrial buyers are constantly seeking ways to lower the costs to users of their services, components, or parts. Steel companies, for example, are wrapping their flat-rolled steel shipments in plastic to prevent the metal from rusting while being transported to automobile stamping factories, thus eliminating the need for rework in the customer's plant.

In the consumer market, major appliances such as air conditioners, refrigerators, and washers and dryers are made more energy-efficient each year, thus reducing the consumer's energy costs. The introduction of electronic controls also enable customers to reduce the cost of these appliances' use, as sophisticated sensors regulate the amount of energy, hot water, and detergent needed to achieve a desired effect. For example, increasingly better and higher energy-efficient and reliable appliances are what allow Maytag to pursue a successful differentiation-based strategy, despite heavy competition from Whirlpool and General Electric. In general, one can expect that major appliances and consumer electronics products will significantly increase their use of "smart technology," which provides self-diagnostic routines and even warn the user of impending failure.

Lowering costs for buyers is a significant competitive advantage for firms that can redesign their products that simply the number of steps involved in their use. Reducing the costs of inconvenience and other "hassle" factors can raise a product's appeal. For example, flexible contact lenses produced by Johnson & Johnson's Vistakon division are designed for long-term use without the need for daily removal and washing. By designing ultrathin contact lenses that are flexible and less irritating, Vistakon can charge a premium price because customers are saved from the "aggravation" costs that come with daily washing and rinsing.

Increasing Buyer Satisfaction. Another way to achieve differentiation is to increase the satisfaction of the buyer consistently, which usually means increasing the performance and quality characteristics of a product over that of a rival's. For example, manufacturers of tennis rackets, such as Head, Prince, and Wilson, race each other in providing better, more powerful, lightweight rackets based on new composite materials such as graphite and even titanium. Players using these rackets can deliver more forceful volleys than with older and heavier steel or wood rackets. Sporting equipment—bicycles, protective gear, tennis rackets, golf clubs—incorporating advanced materials do not reduce the buyer's costs in using the product; instead, the higher performance of the product enhances buyer satisfaction. For example, a number of companies in the golf equipment business (e.g., Callaway Golf, Karsten Manufacturing) are making their mark in customers' minds by offering clubs with new designs (e.g., Big Bertha, Ping) that enable even an average or occasional player to enjoy the game more.

In the food industry, companies continuously search for new ways to increase buyer satisfaction. Mustards, mayonnaise, steak sauces, ketchup, teas, coffee creamers, and soft drinks are frequently reformulated, redesigned, and repackaged to serve every possible niche segment that may exist. The rising popularity of newly introduced ethnic foods makes differentiation a natural strategy for companies such as H. J. Heinz, ConAgra, Bestfoods, Campbell Soup, and Del Monte to pursue. Reaching out with distinctive tastes and new brands enable these firms to bypass direct pricing competition with each other while enhancing a new appealing food category to customers in different markets. For example, differentiation enables firms to target their offerings to different niches according to regional tastes and preferences. Certain customers prefer their food preparations with a distinctive "kick" or spice level; others prefer a milder version. Hebrew National hot dogs, for example, proclaim the fact that they are made entirely of natural meat products and do not have the same fillers that are found in other companies' offerings. This emphasis on wholesome, natural products not only helps Hebrew National hot dogs remain popular with its traditional kosher-oriented market but also make inroads into other market segments as well. Regardless of the actual market segment, meeting these needs provides further opportunity to enhance differentiation. These products do not serve to lower the buyer's costs but do increase buyer satisfaction by meeting some need.

In another powerful example of how differentiation can create new products and the basis for future innovation, 3M's enormous success in the coatings, adhesives, and office supplies markets is based on designing innovative products that solve needs that future customers have not even articulated. For example, 3M's Post-It notes, flexible weather stripping products, Scotch tapes, glass sealants, Scotchgard, carpet cleaners, and other products are designed to solve many customers' practical office and household needs. The success of 3M's products is based on fulfilling a need that in many cases customers had not even anticipated. The firm's ability to successfully leverage its powerful differentiation strategy has also enabled the firm to pioneer many critical thin-film technologies and applications now in use in various electronics industries. For example, an ultrathin application of 3M's coatings technology is the basis for the electronic substrate and film that form the core of today's compact disc (CD) and digital video disk (DVD) technology. 3M's substrate captures the laser beam that reads the digitally encoded data from the disk format and translates it into an analog signal (e.g., video, sound, data).

Increasing Buyer's Perceived Value. Finally, firms may find opportunities for differentiation by increasing the buyer's *perceived* value of the product or service. This task is much trickier, since the firm must attempt to "manage" how customers perceive its product. Differentiation strategies based on perceived value alone are extremely difficult to carry out. For example, Burger King (once affiliated business unit of Diageo, PLC) continues to blitz the airwaves with television advertisements designed to promote the better value and better-tasting food it offers as compared with McDonald's and other fast-food restaurants. A promotion during the late 1990s announced that Burger King had the most popular-tasting French fries. However, Burger King's market share has remained relatively constant, and in some regions share has declined, despite its introduction of new ads and repackaged food products. People can determine relatively easily whether Burger King's new approach to value and service is truly different or more of a perception.

On the other hand, American Express has been successful in expanding and growing its travel-related services business through carefully shaping the public's perception of value and security that it receives from AMEX. Security and peace of mind are defining themes that AMEX has used to heighten differentiation of its travelers' checks and other products. The company reinforces the security theme by showing how travelers abroad will always feel safer when using American Express travelers' checks and through familiar television advertisements that feature vacationers caught in exotic locales with competitors' travelers' checks that cannot be easily cashed or replaced. American Express is even implementing a personal security-based differentiation strategy as it embraces the Internet to serve its customers better. Through the company's Web site, card members can get preferred access to sporting and other entertainment events. More important, American Express recognizes the high level of importance that customers place on their financial privacy. The company has invested in state-of-the-art technology that now allows customers to access their accounts and to surf the Internet without revealing who they are.

Perceived value is often directly related to the lack or incompleteness of information possessed by consumers. Consumers without sufficient knowledge of the product or competing offerings eventually become smarter over time, so perceptions of value alone are unlikely to sustain a higher price premium. For example, people selling antiques often encountered a wide degree of price variance and acceptance by consumers before the advent of the Internet and on-line auction systems. Differentiation strategies based on increasing perceived value alone will not endow the firm with durable competitive advantage, since rivals can easily match and even exceed what the firm attempts to do. Of course, firms able to produce truly distinctive products that lower the buyer's costs or improve product performance have an easier time increasing perceived value.

Toyota's strategy for differentiating the Lexus automobile is based on all three aspects of increasing buyer value. First, because of their exceptional quality of manufacturing and use of the latest technologies, Lexus automobiles have high resale value, low service needs, and comparatively high fuel economy for luxury cars. These attributes reduce both the direct costs of ownership and the "aggravation" costs to consumers of frequent servicing. Second, Lexus automobiles directly increase buyer satisfaction through the use of genuine wood paneling, advanced sound systems, leather seats, easy-to-access controls, numerous safety features, and high engine performance. The latest Lexus models even offer a number of standard, integrated electronic applications that allow drivers to use a satellite-assisted technology to help them navigate unfamiliar surroundings. Even more advanced features include Internet access and DVD-assisted navigation systems that cover the entire country. Smart technology also tracks the maintenance of each Lexus vehicle to anticipate and diagnose potential mechanical problems before they occur, thus saving drivers the stressful experience of breakdowns in traffic or in unsafe areas. Finally, Lexus has continued to produce an ongoing series of distinctive and memorable ads that, in one example, feature a Lexus car moving at speeds in excess of 120 miles per hour on a test platform, with no champagne glasses falling from an arrangement placed on the hood of the car. These ads reinforce the perception of how stable and well built Lexus cars are. Other ads demonstrate the exceptional quality, soundproofing, and road-handling characteristics of Lexus cars. These frequent advertisements, in combination with high annual customer satisfaction ratings, increase both the actual and perceived value of the car.[13]

Benefits and Costs of Differentiation Strategies

Differentiation strategies, when carried out successfully, reduce buyers' price sensitivity, increase their loyalty, and reduce the extent to which they search for alternative products. Compared with firms pursuing low-cost leadership strategies, firms practicing differentiation strategies are willing to accept a lower share of the market in return for higher customer loyalty. Yet, differentiation strategies come with their own set of advantages and disadvantages.

Advantages of Differentiation. A big advantage behind the differentiation strategy is that it allows firms to insulate themselves partially from competitive rivalry in the industry. When firms produce highly sought-after, distinctive products, they do not have to engage in destructive price wars with their competitors. In effect, successful pursuit of high differentiation along some key product attribute or buyer need may allow a firm to carve its own strategic group within the industry. This has been particularly the case in the food preparations industry, where large manufacturers try to avoid direct price-based competition with one another through frequent product differentiation and new product introductions.

A major advantage behind differentiation is that customers of differentiated products are less sensitive to prices. In practice, this attitude means that firms may be able to pass along price increases to their customers. Although the price of Lexus automobiles has risen steadily over the past several years, demand for these cars also continues to rise, as does buyer loyalty. The high degree of customer satisfaction with Lexus cars has translated over to the sport utility vehicle segment, where vehicles command a far higher price and profit. Buyer loyalty means that successful firms may see a substantial increase in repeat purchases for the firm's products.

Another advantage is that strategies based on high quality may, up to a point, actually *increase* the potential market share that a firm can gain. One landmark study noted, in fact, that competitive strategies based on high product quality actually increased market share over time. The combination of both high quality and higher market share resulted in significantly increased profitability. Product quality often leads to higher reputation and demand that translate into higher market share.[14]

Finally, differentiation poses substantial loyalty barriers that firms contemplating entry must overcome. Highly distinctive or unique products make it difficult for new entrants to compete with the reputation and skills that existing firms already possess. Nordstrom's ability to woo and retain customers in the cutthroat fashion and clothing retailing industry enabled the leading-edge store chain to anticipate its customers' needs and to offer them special promotions before they became available to the general buying public. Nordstrom's focus on superior customer service has, until recently, allowed the firm to sell top-of-the-line brands that offer a much higher margin than brands targeted to the middle market.

Disadvantages of Differentiation. A big disadvantage associated with differentiation is that other firms may attempt to "outdifferentiate" firms that already have distinctive products by providing a similar or better product. Thus, differentiation strategies, while effective in generating customer loyalty and higher prices, do not completely seal off the market from other entrants. Consider the market for steak sauces in the food industry. Once a competitor develops a particular flavor of steak sauce, its rivals can easily meet that challenge with their own offerings. In fact, excessive product proliferation can even hurt a firm's attempt to differentiate, since customers may become confused with the wide variety of offerings. For example, H. J. Heinz's recent moves to offer ketchup with different colors may have backfired, as some buyers are turned off by the prospect of putting purple or green ketchup on their French fries. The attempt to outdifferentiate another rival's moves occurs frequently in the radio broadcasting industry. Frequently, a station will adopt a format that emphasizes a particular theme: oldies, light rock, rock from the 1970s, pop, easy listening, country, or Top 40. However, the initial gains that any given station makes are difficult to sustain, because competing stations can dilute this message with their own variation of a theme. Most recently, some radio stations are attempting to reach a previously underserved market segment, such as the growing Hispanic or African American audience. Companies such as Radio One are buying stations in different parts of the country that have a strong African American presence. Radio One hopes that its distinctive music offerings and programs will enable it to capture a disproportionate share of advertising dollars of products that target the African American market.[15] Thus, unless differentiation is based on the possession of some truly proprietary technology, expertise, skill, service, patent, or specialized asset, a firm runs the risk of being outmaneuvered by an even shrewder competitor.

Another disadvantage of differentiation is the difficulty in sustaining a price premium as a product becomes more familiar to the market. As a product becomes more mature, customers become smarter about what they want, what genuine value is, and what they are willing to pay. Price premiums become difficult to justify as customers gain more knowledge about the product. The comparatively high cost structure of a firm practicing differentiation could become a real weakness when lower-cost product imitations or substitutes hit the market. Consider, for example, the recent travails that beset Callaway Golf. Despite the enormous popularity of its Big Bertha golf club design that made swinging and hitting the ball easier, Callaway Golf was unable to sustain a huge market share position in the golf equipment business because other competitors eventually followed with similar, but somewhat different, designs or variations on the same theme. Even existing golf equipment providers, such as Wilson, innovated their own sets of large-head golf clubs that eroded Callaway's once-distinctive identity in the marketplace. Callaway's differentiation strategy yielded fewer benefits as new entrants seized the initiative away from the innovator and started producing similar clubs at lower cost.

Differentiation also leaves a firm vulnerable to the eventual "commoditization" of its product, service offering, or value concept when new competitors enter the market or when customers become more knowledgeable about what is available. Over time, firms that are unable to sustain their initial differentiation-based lead with future product or service innovations will find themselves at a significant, if not dangerous, cost disadvantage when large numbers of customers eventually gravitate to those firms that can produce a similar product or service at lower cost.

Finally, firms also face a risk of overdoing differentiation that may overtax or overextend the firm's resources. For example, Nissan Motor of Japan during the past decade became so obsessed with finding new ways to differentiate its cars that it produced more than thirty types of steering wheels for its line of cars and a broad line of engines, all of which eventually confused customers and made manufacturing costly. Nissan recently announced a sharp reduction in the number of steering wheel sizes, optional accessories, and other features in its cars to lower its operating costs. In 2000, Nissan reduced the number of core automobile platforms to seven in order to reduce the high cost of overlap and design. Excessive differentiation can seriously erode the competitive advantage and profitability of firms as rising operating costs eat into price premiums that customers are willing to pay.

Focus Strategies

focus strategies: Competitive strategies based on targeting a specific niche within an industry. Focus strategies can occur in two forms: cost-based focus and differentiation-based focus.

The third generic strategy is known as a focus strategy. **Focus strategies** are designed to help a firm target a specific niche within an industry. Unlike both low-cost leadership and differentiation strategies that are designed to target a broader or industry-wide market, focus strategies aim at a specific and typically small niche. These niches could be a particular buyer group, a narrow segment of a given product line, a geographic or regional market, or a niche with distinctive, special tastes and preferences. The basic idea behind a focus strategy is to *specialize* the firm's activities in ways that other broader-line (low-cost or differentiation) firms cannot perform as well. Superior value, and thus higher profitability, are generated when other broader-line firms cannot specialize or conduct their activities as well as a focused firm. If a niche or segment has characteristics that are distinctive and lasting, then a firm can develop its own set of barriers to entry in much the same way that large established firms do in broader markets.

Building a Focus-Based Advantage

Firms can build a focus in one of two ways. They can adopt a cost-based focus in serving a particular niche or segment of the market, or they can adopt a differentiation-based focus. As previously shown in Exhibit 4-2, focus strategies are different from low-cost leadership and differentiation strategies in terms of the scope of the target market. Within a particular targeted market or niche, however, a focused firm can pursue many of the same characteristics as the broader low-cost or differentiation approaches to building competitive advantage. Thus, many of the sources of competitive advantage discussed earlier for cost and differentiation also apply to focus strategies at the niche or segment level. It is important to remember that focus strategies attempt to pursue low-cost or differentiation with respect to a much narrower targeted market niche or product segment. Thus, the resources and skills that the firm or business uses must be specialized as well.

What do Krispy Kreme Doughnuts, Solectron, Magna International, Southwest Airlines, American Iron Horse, Bang and Olufsen, Nucor, Chaparral Steel, Aaon, and Patek Philippe have in common? These firms have adopted a well-defined focus/specialization strategy that has enabled them to earn high profits in industries that are fundamentally unattractive or fast changing. All of these companies have reconfigured their focus-driven value chain to emphasize either differentiation or cost-based sources of competitive advantage. Each of these companies has targeted a particular type of buyer or product segment that other broader-line competitors cannot serve as well. In effect, firms with highly refined focus/specialization strategies have developed a distinctive competence in defending their niches from larger firms that have difficulty understanding or serving their target customers.[16]

An upstart that appears to be pursuing a tightly focused strategy is Krispy Kreme Doughnuts. Its Original Glazed doughnuts are so wildly popular that people have been known to stand in line for hours to get them in the morning. Following careful cost controls, Krispy Kreme is now busy expanding its network of some two hundred franchises around the nation. Unlike other franchised operations that eventually had financing difficulties (e.g., Boston Chicken, a.k.a Boston Market), Krispy Kreme initially concentrated on its wholesale business in order to lower its earlier debt. Now, the firm is in the midst of creating different variations of its Original Glazed doughnut to sell at premium prices.

Solectron is a highly specialized manufacturer of circuit boards used in personal computers and other electronic devices. It has followed a focused strategy of building low-cost, but well-manufactured, circuit boards for other PC manufacturers and assemblers that have decided to outsource this particular operation. In effect, Solectron has built a commanding presence in a particular cost activity of the personal computer industry value chain that other larger firms cannot perform as well. This strategy has won it many admirers and customers who prefer not to undertake some of the more mundane manufacturing tasks that are required for components and peripherals to fill out their product needs. Recently, Solectron has begun expanding contract manufacturing operations to meet the needs of firms in the cellular phone and personal digital assistant (PDA) industries as well. Solectron operates lean and extremely efficient manufacturing facilities that build circuit boards according to the designs provided by such personal computer firms as Compaq Computer, Gateway, IBM, and others. In effect, contract manufacturing enables Solectron to carve a highly defensible niche from broader-line players with significantly higher cost structures.

In a remarkable turnaround for American manufacturing, Mitsubishi Electric in June 1998 announced that it, too, would outsource many of its manufacturing operations for printed circuit boards and other components to Solectron. In 2001, even Sony of Japan announced that it also would utilize Solectron's well-honed manufacturing skills to outsource production of components for cellular phones and even video game consoles. In the past, large Japanese companies such as Mitsubishi and Sony would have never even considered utilizing the manufacturing services of an American company.[17] In recent years, however, Solectron has begun to face growing competitive pressures from similar contract manufacturers such as Flextronics, Sanmina-SCI, and Celestica—all of which have begun to offer manufacturing services to large firms in different high-technology industries.

In the automobile industry, outsourcing has become an important trend in which the Big Three (DaimlerChrysler, Ford, and General Motors) manufacturers have delegated an increasing amount of manufacturing work to more specialized firms that have the expertise to design, produce, and supply an entire component or subassembly. Magna International, one of the world's largest and probably lesser-known firms in the automobile component business, makes the bumpers and fascias that are found on many of General Motors' and DaimlerChrysler's cars. Today's bumpers and front grilles are much more sophisticated than those of previous decades, since these components are made with advanced, engineered plastics that require specialized molding and shaping technology. Magna's distinctive competence is its ability to work with a range of different types of engineered plastics and other advanced materials to make fashionable, low-cost, and safe bumpers for large automakers that will in turn assemble them into their cars. Some analysts believe that Magna International will eventually be able to design and develop an ever more sophisticated range of automotive subassemblies for manufacturers throughout the North American market.

Southwest Airlines is the lowest-cost operator in the airline industry. The airline industry is perhaps one of the least attractive industries in which to compete. Fixed and operating costs are very high, and buyer loyalty remains fairly low. Yet, Southwest has pursued a successful focused/specialization strategy by building a distinctive competence in serving short-haul routes, rather than fighting major airlines for a losing share of long-distance flights. Southwest Airlines practices low-cost policies in almost every activity of its value chain. Its planes are frugal, its offices are spartan, and it does not serve fancy meals on its planes. Moreover, its procurement policies are also frugal; it buys only one type of plane (Boeing 737s) to keep maintenance costs low and to use common spare parts. Fast turnaround of aircraft is one key to Southwest's success in sustaining its low costs. Yet, to promote a high degree of customer service, Southwest carefully recruits the people that it believes have the best attitude that reflects the company's fun and efficient way of doing business. Colleen Barrett, Southwest Airlines' president, feels that it is Southwest's way of selecting and managing its people that gives the firm a uniquely low-cost structure, despite the comparatively high pay that it offers. The major airlines are wary of Southwest, since Southwest offers the lowest fare on any route that it chooses to serve and can seriously erode route profitability for other higher-cost airlines. In effect, competitors such as American Airlines, Continental Airlines, and UAL are forced to lower their fares in response to Southwest's initiative.

American Iron Horse is a fast-growing start-up company that has begun to compete with legendary motorcycle manufacturer Harley-Davidson in a major way. This company, based in Fort Worth, Texas, has begun to design and hand-produce top-of-the-line motorcycles that offer more power and finesse than comparable Harley models. Taking advantage of the fact that Harley-Davidson remains unable to meet all of the demand for its legendary, fast, and powerful motorcycles, American Iron Horse has focused its strengths on building bikes that come close to full customization. The company has found a profitable niche within a niche in the motorcycle industry. The company offers big engines, custom wheels, and powder-coated frames (which resist chipping and metal fatigue) that are put together in a factory dedicated to handmade craftsmanship. In a recent test by some popular motorcycle magazines, bikes made by American Iron Horse offered excellent performance at reasonable prices.[18]

Bang and Olufsen is an innovative Danish designer and manufacturer of stereo systems. These stereo systems have a distinctive flat shape, silver color, and design flair that looks ultramodern. These expensive stereo systems are sold to music and stereo hobbyists who prefer to avoid the more mass-produced look of Japanese equipment. Bang and Olufsen has carved out a defensible niche through its innovative designs that allow it to stand on its own against fierce Japanese consumer electronics companies.

Nucor was one of America's most successful steel companies during the 1980s and remains so today. By producing steel from scrap and recycled metal through minimills, Nucor and its competitor Chaparral Steel are profitable entities in an industry that is declining and debt-ridden. Unlike larger, integrated steel mills, both Nucor and Chaparral can produce smaller quantities of steel at lower cost and can remain profitable even when the economic growth slows or declines. Nucor's use of innovative casting technology to process scrap steel at low cost has enabled the firm to dominate the production of wire rods that are used in the construction and building industries. As both Nucor and Chaparral continue to invest in newer mill technologies, they are will likely be able to produce the higher-quality sheet steel that is used in home appliances and automobiles at potentially lower cost than some of the older integrated mills.[19]

Aaon is a leading manufacturer of semicustomized air-conditioning systems for large corporations. The company has grown over 20 percent a year over the past three years by tailoring the design of its air-conditioning systems to include features that are not available on lower-end and lower-priced machines. Aaon has succeeded against such major companies as American Standard's Trane division, Lennox, United Technologies' Carrier unit, and York. Recently, the company seized over 12 percent of the $1.4 billion rooftop air-conditioning systems that are found atop department stores, and other corporate customers. Aaon's prices are only slightly higher than that of lower-priced units, but about a third of truly customized systems. To sustain its growth, Aaon is now seeking to provide air-conditioning solutions to schools and hospitals.[20]

Founded in 1839 by a Polish aristocrat and a French watchmaker, Patek Philippe is one of the world's finest brands for luxury watches. In the highly competitive watch industry, Patek Philippe is one of the few companies that has been able to withstand the forces of consolidation. The company's lowest-priced watch starts at $3,000 and can easily climb into the millions. Production is limited to just thirty thousand per year, and the company closely guards its reputation to protect it from counterfeiters. A watch owner is encouraged to contact the company to check on the historical archives and production data to determine the origin of his or her timepiece. Patek Philippe's newest watch, the Star Caliber set, has over eleven hundred parts fitted into a watch case that is no bigger than three inches in diameter and a little over an inch high. Both faces of the double-sided watch are adorned with filigree and jewels. The company spent over seven years and dedicated ten of its 180 watchmakers to design the Star Caliber since 1993.[21]

The number of examples of companies finding and building niche-based focus strategies is growing. For example, in many parts of the United States, an increasing number of microbreweries have begun operations. These small breweries are designed to brew beer in limited quantities and cater to a specific taste or regional market. Although these breweries represent no real threat to national breweries such as Anheuser-Busch and Miller (a unit of Philip Morris), they could carve out a significant local market presence in cities such as Seattle and San Francisco.

Benefits and Costs of Focus Strategies

By finding and serving a narrow market niche, firms that practice focus strategies often can remain highly profitable, even when the broader industry appears to be unattractive. Firms that practice focus/specialization strategies look for a niche and avoid deviating from it. Concentration of resources and effort to serve and defend a niche makes the focused/specialized firm less vulnerable to major changes in the industry's competitive environment. Yet, even a focus/specialization strategy brings its own set of advantages and disadvantages.

Advantages of Focus Strategies. The biggest advantage of a focus strategy is that the firm is able to carve a market niche against larger, broader-line competitors. Some firms pursuing this strategy have even been able to locate niches within niches (e.g., handcrafted, Oriental musical instruments), thus further insulating themselves from the attention and efforts of larger, industry-wide players that cannot serve the niche as well. Thus, defensibility and avoidance of direct, price-based competition are big advantages that accrue to a focus/specialization strategy.[22]

In many cases, a focus/specialization strategy enables a firm to improve other sources of value-adding activities that contribute to cost or differentiation. Consider, for example, the case of McIlhenny Company. Its expertise with Tabasco sauces gives it some ability and detailed knowledge of how to make Bloody Mary mixes as well. Thus, focus/specialization strategies may enable firms to utilize their specialized distinctive competence or set of assets to create new niches. Solectron's growing expertise with electronics-based manufacturing from work outsourced by larger firms has given the firm valuable experience and even critical mass to take on larger projects that move beyond the personal computer industry and into other electronics segments, such as cellular phones and telecommunications equipment. Magna International's growing experience with bumpers and front-end systems has given it the capability to design entirely new subsystems and assemblies at costs and quality levels that are by some measures superior to that of in-house production by the Big Three automakers.

Disadvantages of Focus Strategies. The biggest disadvantage facing the focus/specialization strategy is the risk that the underlying market niche may gradually shift more toward characteristics of the broader market. Distinctive tastes and product characteristics may blur over time, thus reducing the defensibility of the niche. This may be particularly the case when tastes and preferences, once considered exotic or nouveau at an earlier period, become more widely accepted and even imitated by larger market segments. A related risk is the potential for broad-line competitors to develop new technological innovations or product features that may redefine the buying preferences of the niche. For example, the growing use of flexible, advanced manufacturing technology makes it possible for larger firms to produce ever-smaller quantities of products that could be used to serve a variety of market niches or segments. This is also already happening in the designer and leather clothing market, in which Levi Strauss is now using cutting-edge computer-aided design (CAD) technologies, once relegated to industrial and engineering applications, to create new one-of-a-kind clothing patterns and designs according to each individual customer's tastes. Also, larger broad-line competitors could become swifter and faster in responding to market changes, thus enabling them to practice some variation of a focus/specialization strategy as well.

Strategic Application to Nordstrom

One of Nordstrom's current strategic challenges is how best to maintain its superb customer service, while deciding how best to reduce its cost structure through better inventory and distribution cost controls. Thus, Nordstrom must carefully balance its traditional intimate service approach with improved operations to attain cost parity with its rivals. Also, despite Nordstrom's reputation for superior service, many young customers feel the stores are too formal in their appearance and often lack the kind of cutting-edge fashions that ordinarily do not mix well with Nordstrom's traditional line of classic-cut clothing.

To attract these younger customers, Nordstrom in recent years began to tone down the formality of its displays and interior store décor, and it also started selling fashions targeted specifically for a much younger crowd. The attempt to win over this new audience may have seriously diluted Nordstrom's reputation for top-of-the-line quality, as customers became confused about what Nordstrom was offering. Even more nimble competitors such as Neiman Marcus Group and Talbot's are beginning to make serious inroads into Nordstrom's traditional market base, as the boomer market becomes turned off from some of the avant-garde fashions designed for the twenty-something segment. However, it is the boomer market that provides the vast majority of Nordstrom's current revenues.

A greater long-term threat to Nordstrom, though, is the renewed emphasis by larger retailing chains to provide better levels of customer service through buyer affiliation and reward programs, as well as improved training of sales personnel to enhance personal attention to customers. The larger chains are able to implement these steps as they continue to reap the benefits of cutting-edge computer-based inventory management systems that allow them to respond quickly to changing fashions and market needs. This emphasis on using advanced technology to lower inventory and distribution costs will serve the large retailing chains well, especially in economic downturns. As the larger chains adopt strategies that emphasize cost reduction, they will need to attract a larger number of customers in order to pay down the fixed costs of making such technology investments.

As growing numbers of people seek better value from their purchases, even the larger chains such as May Department Stores and Federated will attract customers that once predominantly shopped at Nordstrom. Thus, differentiation strategies do not allow a firm to endure a "war of attrition" for a long period, especially when the firm's costs are significantly higher than that of its rivals.

An Emerging View of Strategy: Mass Customization for Best Value

Increasingly, companies in every industry and from every part of the world need to find new ways to satisfy their customers' quest for ever-increased value and performance. Although each of the basic generic strategies—low-cost leadership, differentiation, and focus—provides the basis for building a source of competitive advantage, the long term viability of any single approach rests on a firm's ability to provide new sources of value continuously. As an industry evolves and innovation flourishes, firms must provide more value to their customers while controlling costs and even perhaps lowering their prices over the long term. With respect to the value chain (discussed in Chapter 3), firms will have to devise new, innovative solutions to create and deliver value and productivity in each and every stage of their business system. Finding new ways to accelerate the creation and delivery of improving value will become the next battleground for firms in all industries. Ideally, companies will begin to formulate and execute those business strategies that enable them to deliver unique sources of value and solutions to their customers quicker and faster, rather than simply a product or service that can be readily imitated or copied. The way firms create and deliver a product or service will become just as important as the offering itself.

Our perspective is that reliance on any single, generic strategy (low-cost, differentiation, or focus) in itself will not endow the firm with a sustained capability to innovate new sources of value more quickly and more efficiently over time. Firms will need to provide a variety of different value "bundles" or solutions to their customers. Speed, rapid response, customized offerings, low cost, and innovation can no longer be trade-offs in future business strategies. In effect, competitive advantage will increasingly require firms to offer *fast response* and *best source of value* to each market segment or customer targeted. However, each basic, generic strategy imposes a set of limitations and constraints that make it difficult for firms to respond rapidly to sudden changes in customer demand, technological improvements, or product/service features along some key dimension: speed, cost, or variety. Instead, we believe that other types of business strategies will likely emerge over the next several years that will come close to delivering a new, value-driven and value-solution concept of competitive advantage: mass customization.

Mass customization is an evolving strategic capability that allows firms to produce an increasing variety of products or services while simultaneously lowering their costs. At its best, mass customization seeks to combine the positive benefits of low-cost and differentiation strategies while reducing the negative effects. Mass customization, when understood and exploited, provides the basis for fast response, creation of best value solutions, and a high degree of flexibility to serve new customers and segments with future innovations. In effect, a business strategy based on mass customization enables firms to reconcile and even remove some of the trade-offs that are conventionally associated with pursuing each generic strategy alone.[23]

mass customization: The capability to produce a growing variety or range of products at reduced unit costs. Mass customization is a strategic competitive weapon that helps firms to expand the range of their product offerings and modifications without incurring the high costs of variety.

The principle behind mass customization rests on a growing set of advanced technological, distribution, and marketing capabilities that enable firms to produce products or deliver services to smaller and smaller segments while simultaneously lowering their unit costs. Traditional manufacturing and service operations typically confronted an economic trade-off in which lower unit costs required a high degree of product or service standardization. Conversely, differentiation strategies often left the firm competitively vulnerable to rivals that could provide a comparable bundle of value at lower costs. However, mass customization is an increasingly viable way to avoid these trade-offs. Some of the most important economic drivers that facilitate the potential of mass customization strategies include (1) the rise of advanced manufacturing technology, (2) the rapid use of modular product design techniques, (3) the growth of the Internet as a distribution channel, and (4) market segmentation tools and techniques (e.g., data mining) that enable firms to locate and uncover previously unserved customer needs and market niches.

Advanced Manufacturing Technology

State-of-the-art advances in manufacturing technology, such as the introduction of computers into product design and factory work, have made it possible to substantially reduce the amount of time it takes to commercialize a new product from the lab to the market. Moreover, computers in manufacturing have also boosted quality significantly, as machines and processes are integrated through common databases and routines that simplify procedures and reduce the scope and potential of human error. Perhaps the most significant contribution of advanced manufacturing technologies to mass customization strategies is their ability to produce a wider scope, or envelope, of variety using the same design and production equipment to serve a growing number of market segments and differentiated needs. In effect, advanced manufacturing systems provide the basis to transfer the benefits of low-cost production (once confined to extremely standardized product designs) to an expanded range of product offerings and families. Thus, firms have the technical capability to produce more quantities in more ways that previously were not possible. (The full organizational and human impact of using advanced manufacturing technologies to create new sources of competitive advantage will be presented in Chapter 14.)

Levi Strauss has successfully used CAD systems to help design customized, one-of-a-kind leather outfits for its customers. Using an engineering workstation and advanced software, Levi Strauss can measure a customer's specific contours, body shape, weight, and preferences to create a customized pattern that becomes the basis for a perfectly fitting leather suit or dress in a short time. A customer's color and style preferences, as well as his or her body measurements, are then directly input into a computer that is electronically linked to a highly flexible stitching and finishing operation. Currently, most Levi Strauss outlets carry somewhere between eighty to one hundred different varieties of jeans and outfits. With the use of its new manufacturing and customization capability, the company feels that it will have somewhere between four hundred and five hundred different variations out on the shelves in the near future. Levi Strauss can thus provide the customer an individual, personalized sense of best value, while preserving a relatively low cost of operations.

modularity:
An element of product design that allows for the mixing and matching of different components and parts that all share the same interface or means of connecting with one another. A product exhibits modularity if its constituent parts can be rearranged among themselves or with additional parts that share the same pattern of linkage.

Modular Product Designs

In many industries, the design and manufacturing of products (and even services) have taken on a new concept—that of modularity. **Modularity** refers to the capability of mixing and matching different components and product features together to create a customized offering. The key to successful modularity in product design is to ensure that the individual components that make up the final end product can be rearranged in any number of ways so as to increase variety. However, modularity requires that the underlying components and product features share a common set of design interfaces or "protocols," to guarantee that they can be mixed and matched without costly retooling or extensive modification.[24] Connectivity among different parts that use a standard linkage is key.

One company that has taken modularity as a core design competence is Mattel in the fiercely competitive toy industry. The company envisions that its young female customers will soon be able to custom-design their own dolls (e.g., Barbie) and other toys through modular choices of clothing, hair coloring, skin texture, and other desired attributes. Already, Mattel has produced large numbers of custom-ordered Barbies for major retailers that have special accounts with the firm (e.g., Toys "R" Us and organizations that want the doll for their own promotion packages).[25]

Modularity of product and component design is what drives Dell Computer's fast-turnaround manufacturing capability. Dell generates tremendous revenues and profits from its ability to mix and match personal computer components according to what each individual customer wants. In effect, by maintaining a very flexible supply and manufacturing system, Dell can custom-build each computer and price it according to what the customer wants. All of the standardized components are made by key suppliers who design these parts according to computer industry specifications. These common standards (e.g., universal serial bus [USB] ports) allow for full interoperability across manufacturers and user applications (e.g., memory cards slots in laptop computers that can perform multiple functions).

Internet-Driven Distribution Systems

The rise of the Internet as a powerful distribution channel over the past several years testifies to the enormous leverage that customers have over firms in choosing and purchasing their products and services. The growth and spread of the Internet means that customers can become much closer to their firms and expect from them a level of speed and response that was previously not possible. For example, firms in the airline, travel services, financial services, music distribution, and book retailing businesses are now facing new rivals that are using the Internet to circumvent preexisting barriers to entry to reach new customers (see Chapter 5 for an extended discussion of this topic).

The Internet is a powerful economic driver that is now compelling firms to link up their product and service offerings more closely with their customers. Since customers effectively face very little switching costs (see chapter 2) when they surf the Web to find alternative product or service providers, it is incumbent upon firms to significantly upgrade and improve their distribution capabilities to exploit this new "real-time" virtual marketplace. The Internet has transformed the marketplace into a "marketspace" in which customers can freely select and demand the best possible "value bundle" or "value solution" from firms willing to tailor and modify their offering according to individual taste.

Service industries have been the first to adopt the Internet as a key vehicle to provide for mass customization strategies, but product based firms are increasingly using the Internet to get a better feel of what their customers want. In fact, some firms are moving ahead to use the Internet to provide custom-ordered coupons for individuals who sign up for company-sponsored services. For example, a number of upstart Internet-based firms are offering customers the ability to order CDs over the Web without the hidden markup charged by conventional retailers to cover their overhead costs. Also, some of the most innovative Web-based music outlets (e.g., RealNetworks) are beginning to allow customers to create their own customized music selections by directly downloading any number of recordings by any series of performing artists (subject to legal restrictions on copyright and permissions) onto their hard drives or rewritable compact disc systems (CD-R). Procter & Gamble is in the midst of offering special coupons and promotional discounts to customers through the Internet. Toy firm Mattel is even using the Internet to encourage young children to custom-order the toys and dolls they want according to their unique preferences. The data gathered from the Internet are then directly fed into Mattel's manufacturing and supply operations. Thus, the growing use of the Internet to capture each customer's individual preferences, combined with advanced manufacturing and modular product designs, create new possibilities for making mass customization strategies a reality for the next century.

New Market Segmentation Techniques

New statistical techniques developed by market research firms and computer software companies are now allowing marketers to identify previously hidden market segments and customer needs that were not easily found through traditional research techniques. For example, a new artificial intelligence program, known as *data mining*, enables firms to search for new market segments and latent demand for product and service offerings that have not yet been developed or are in testing stages. Data mining allows companies to search for patterns through massive amounts of research data to find correlations and results that the human mind and more rigorous hypothesis testing previously excluded.

The use of computers and bar coding has made it much easier now to further identify segments within established segments. In other words, groups of consumers sharing similar purchasing and buying habits can be further defined and isolated into even smaller subgroups for the purposes of better identifying and capturing new ways to provide value. Through the use of new segmentation techniques, companies are no longer compelled to design a product that fits "an average customer" (as was the case with low-cost leadership strategies) but can now customize product attributes and features more aligned or in sync with the needs of much smaller market segments.

Distinctive Competence Revisited and Why Quality Dominates

The preceding discussion of generic strategies captures a more generalized, "big picture" view of how different strategic approaches can be used to build competitive advantage. In reality, each firm will custom-design and formulate its own set of competitive strategies that will approximate many of the characteristics we have analyzed. Yet, two themes seem to pervade our discussion of building competitive advantage: the role of distinctive competence and why quality dominates successful performance.

The Role of Distinctive Competence

To build and sustain competitive advantage, all three generic strategies require firms to develop a distinctive competence in performing its value-added activities. Recall that a distinctive competence is something a firm does especially well compared to its rivals. Developing a distinctive competence is a key pillar of competitive strategy. *A well-designed strategy is one that develops a distinctive competence in some key activity and then leverages it to create a competitive advantage over other firms. A firm's strategy is only valuable to the extent it builds distinction.* The significance of a distinctive competence is that it endows the firm with a unique capability, skill, or resource that gives it an edge over its competitors. This edge is critical in pursuing new market or product opportunities in the environment.

Broad characterizations of a distinctive competence include the following: quality manufacturing processes, superior service, fast product development, brand management techniques, specialized distribution systems, specialized knowledge of customer buying patterns, and technology-based or human resource skills and assets that are hard for rivals to duplicate. Investment in the firm's distinctive competence should be guided by the firm's underlying approach to building competitive advantage. Regardless of the specific type or nature of the distinctive competence, a firm needs to search for ways to improve it continuously over time. Firms need to be aware of potential substitutes or threats to its distinctive competence and to think of ways to reinforce, redefine, or rejuvenate it. Thus, the development and sustenance of a distinctive competence should be the foundation of any strategy formulation effort.

The Importance of Quality

Another principal theme that surrounds our examination of competitive advantage is the central role that quality plays. Regardless of what product or service a firm offers, quality is key to building and sustaining competitive advantage and therefore should be a vital part of the firm's competitive strategy. Despite the numerous characterizations and definitions of quality, firms should view and design their own competitive strategies around the basic concept of customer-defined quality. **Customer-defined quality** represents the best value a firm can put into its products and services for the different market segments and niches it serves. *Every product for each market segment should offer and deliver the highest value to customers in that segment.* These products or services should culminate in an optimal combination of cost, function, utility, and value for that segment.

customer-defined quality: The best value a firm can put into its products and services for the market segments it serves. Customer-defined quality is more important to competitive strategy than what the firm thinks its quality should be.

Efforts to manage quality require developing a set of strategies, setting goals and objectives along with action plans, and carrying out other steps in the strategic management process. An increasing number of senior managers are now discovering the strong link between quality and profitability. A quality orientation has become paramount in many companies not only because of fierce global competition but also because of the recognition that quality leads to a better reputation, more purchases, and a sustainable competitive advantage. A major study of excellent firms conducted by Peters and Waterman during the early 1980s found that the most successful firms had an obsession with quality, service, and reliability of their products.[26] Despite the utmost, paramount importance of quality, many U.S. firms are still struggling to achieve total quality in their products.[27]

An emphasis on high quality works in two ways to sustain competitive advantage and profitability. Exhibit 4-5 captures the underlying relationship among quality, market share, differentiation, and profitability that has been found empirically in research studies.[28] A strategy based on quality enhances market share, which in turn raises firm profitability in part because of the firm's ability to exploit some degree of economies of scale. Quality also works along another dimension: it enhances the possibilities for differentiation that in turn generate higher returns. In effect, regardless of the specific type of generic strategy a firm pursues, quality is central to high performance and competitive advantage. This premise does not mean that the low-cost leadership strategy cannot work over time; rather, firms practicing low-cost leadership strategies require senior management to devote at least part of their attention and investment toward building quality products and services.

A major cost for many firms practicing low-cost leadership strategies is the amount of inspection and rework that accompanies mass production. However, studies have shown that performing the task right the first time sharply reduces the firm's future costs in terms of scrap, waste, rework, and warranty obligations. Thus, in the interest of maintaining low-cost leadership, firms can practice quality management and techniques from the perspective of cost control as well.[29]

The Relationship between Quality and Competitive Advantage

EXHIBIT 4-5

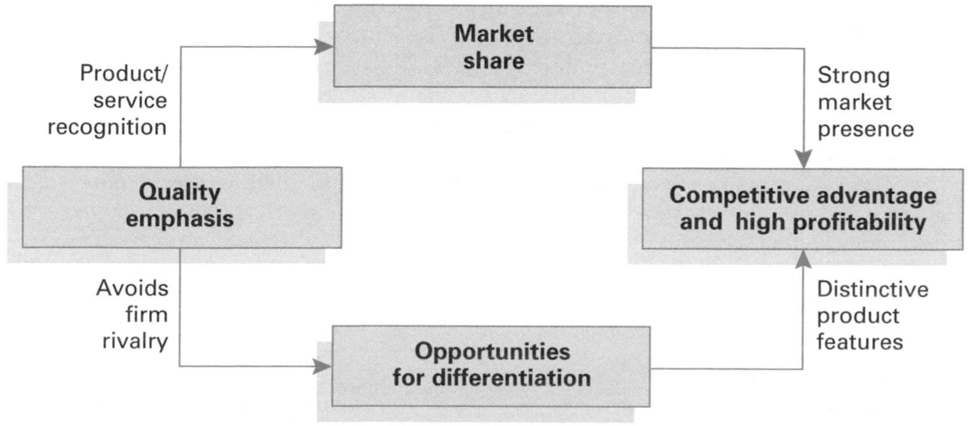

Commitment to quality serves to boost performance and competitive advantage for all types of firms practicing different strategies. The greater the attention paid to quality as a cornerstone of competitive strategy, the higher is the likelihood of building and sustaining advantage. Designing products and services that people really want leads to high performance as well. Quality therefore becomes an essential ingredient in managing a business and the people involved. It is not enough to build quality products; management must also lead in building quality organizations. We will discuss the issue of building quality-driven organizations in a later chapter on redefining advantage.

Strategy and Competitive Advantage over the Life Cycle

The strategy a firm selects depends on both the industry environment and its own distinctive competences and strengths. Yet, the evolution of the industry environment can have a marked impact on how firms build different sources of competitive advantage.[30] In this section, we examine the impact of the product life cycle on formulating competitive strategies.

The product life cycle exerts significant influences on both the competitive dynamics of the industry environment, and on the sources of competitive advantage that may be most effective in designing a competitive strategy.[31] As products (and their markets) move from introductory stages, through growth and maturity, and then into the decline stage, the strategic setting for competing within the industry changes. Exhibit 4-6 portrays the impact of each life cycle stage on strategic considerations and policies facing the firm. Note that as the industry environment progresses toward maturity and decline, the industry experiences a growing tendency to consolidate and shake out some of the weaker competitors. Also, each generic strategy will impose a different set of strategic requirements on firms as they evolve through the life cycle. Let us now briefly examine the impact of each life cycle stage on developing competitive strategies.

Introductory Stage

This early or emerging stage of the product's life cycle is often characterized by pioneering firms attempting to get their innovative products accepted by the market. A key strategic task facing the firm is to create product awareness within the market. In many cases, pioneering firms are able to establish important sources of competitive advantage based on their first-mover status.[32] First-movers often gain market share rapidly and early over the competition and thus can build initial competitive advantage as the product concept begins to penetrate the market. Many strong sources of competitive advantage are derived from patents and other proprietary technologies. However, first-mover status by itself does not mean that the firm will always retain its advantage; firms possessing first-mover status must continue to invest in product designs and ultimately in cutting-edge process technologies to sustain advantage as the life cycle evolves.

In many industries, pioneering firms are often more focused on their products than on the processes. This stage is characterized by an enormous degree of uncertainty over the technology to be used in the product; the nature, number, and type of future competitors; as well as the risk aversion and lack of awareness by potential customers. Competing product designs and prototypes are likely to proliferate as firms jockey with one another to define a future industry or technical standard for customer use and adoption. Buyers of products in the introductory phase of the life cycle must be convinced of the new product's merits. Therefore, firms search for new types of buyers and regions to become early adopters. In many cases, the new product offers the prospect of a substitute for an existing product or way of doing things.

EXHIBIT 4-6 The Impact of the Product Life Cycle on Sources of Competitive Advantage

Stage	Introductory	Growth	Mature	Decline
Nature of competitive rivalry	Limited focus on competitors; product is center of attention	Firms stake out key positions in market	Firms try to survive shakeout; many exit or fail	Remaining firms seek to reduce intensity of competition
Nature of entry	Pioneering firms define industry	Large scale entry by firms seeking profits	Growth slows and entry is less attractive	Few, if any, entrants
Product technology	Emerging, untried technology. No dominant design is set in most cases	Competing designs hope to set industry standard	Dominant design for industry, few modifications	No real product change
Process technology	General purpose equipment and tools for flexibility	Growing investment in specialized tools/assets	Emphasis on efficiency and volume production; high automation	Processes do not change; may become exit barrier if rigid or capital intensive
Marketing emphasis	Focus on innovators; volatile prices that have no set level	Build growing product and brand awareness; prices begin to decline	Promote to as many segments as possible; prices are more stable	Marketing emphasis changes to preserving existing share position. Prices steady or declining
Investment intensity	Very high—needed to build business	Massive expenditures to reinforce position	De-emphasis on adding new capacity	Begin gradual exit and even divest activities
Profitability levels	Generally unprofitable, lots of cash needed	Moving to higher profits; cash flow negative or uneven	Peak profits; cash is high	Profits decline; cash flow declining rapidly

TIME

As the industry environment approaches maturity and decline stages, cost efficiency becomes important. It is generally difficult to find new opportunities for differentiation.

Consider the development of software for personal computers. Each time a new software product comes out (word-processing software, spreadsheets, graphics, statistics), it becomes a substitute for a preexisting method or product (calculators, adding machines, copy print, mainframe computers) performing the same function. Thus, buyers must feel that the new product offers significant value in substituting or complementing what they are already doing. The same economic logic also drove the innovation and eventual proliferation of DVD players in the market during the late 1990s. DVD players are increasingly regarded as not only a substitute for traditional VCRs but also a component that can be readily used with personal and laptop computers. The stunning clarity of DVD players' images, plus their ability to play traditional compact discs, makes these devices especially appealing to the market.[33]

Some of the strategic problems facing firms in the introductory phase include (1) difficulty in accessing and obtaining resources or raw materials, (2) challenge in defining quality controls, (3) uncertainty in articulating a standard or set of value-providing features that customers will clearly accept, (4) high initial production and marketing costs, and (5) the potential response of established firms.

The development of new products or services often requires new skills, technologies, and raw materials that may be difficult to obtain. For example, advanced composite materials for building graphite tennis rackets and golf clubs were initially scarce; much of this material was high priced and went to government defense projects.

A major technical and marketing problem facing pioneering firms is also defining and producing a high-quality product. For example, new software or video games with unforeseen "bugs" or glitches can easily destroy the value of the firm's innovations if buyers are turned off. This was the series of events that plagued the introduction of first-generation personal digital assistants by Apple and Sharp in 1993. Both companies' offerings, the Apple Newton and the Sharp Wizard, were difficult to operate and the software was slow. Not until the advent of the Palm operating system and smaller versions of PDAs did the market really blossom. In almost all industries, initial entrants face high production, development, and marketing costs. Unit costs will be high until fixed costs of production can be spread over greater volume. Economies of scale and cumulative experience effects do not usually decrease costs until after considerable volume is produced.

Articulating a set of technical standards or features that customers will come to accept is a major challenge for any firm developing early products or services. While pioneering firms may have the initial advantage of defining what the product or service should provide, it is in no way guaranteed that customers will be satisfied with what they are offered. In practice, firms will find that they will have to devote considerable resources and expenses to change and modify their original prototypes and designs to fit more in line with what their customers will want. What complicates this matter is that other competing firms will likely do the same thing, with the end result being that the product design ultimately accepted by the market may very well be quite different (and thus require different skills) from that originated by a pioneering firm. This is a major reason why pioneering firms are often unable to sustain an early advantage as the product, service, or technology unfolds.

This series of difficulties appear to be a significant factor in slowing down Palm, Inc.'s growth as its hand-held digital assistants become more widely accepted in the marketplace. Although the size of the original Palm Pilot has remained fairly constant over the past three years, customers have been demanding that the company add new features to make the device more versatile. New-generation Palm Pilot machines include expansion slots for additional memory, as well as potential link-ups with digital cellular phones. However, the widespread popularity of hand-held computer operating systems and hardware has attracted the interest of Microsoft, which has significant ambitions to further extend its own Pocket PC technology to challenge Palm more directly in the marketplace. Microsoft's size and relationships with established customers (e.g., Hewlett-Packard) make it a formidable threat to Palm. Newer versions of Microsoft's hand-held computers (including one named Merlin) are expected to have many of the same features as those produced by Palm.[34]

Finally, a huge uncertainty hanging over these firms is the potential reaction of established firms facing the prospect of substitute products. New industries, such as biotechnology, represent a long-term threat to established pharmaceutical and other life-science companies. Thus, biotechnology firms must gauge the response and potential impact of countermoves by established players. In the automobile industry, a high level of uncertainty faces firms that are developing and pioneering electric cars that operate on batteries and other alternative, advanced fuel cell technologies. Batteries and long-lasting fuel cells threaten to replace many of the current electrical and even drive-train components found in today's cars. The fast-evolving multimedia industry, which hopes to substitute new forms of technology for today's stand-alone personal computers, televisions, and other consumer electronics, represents a potentially enormous threat (as well as opportunities) for firms such as AOL Time Warner, Sony, Philips Electronics, Intel, General Electric, Motorola, IBM, and other giants. Thus, new entrants and pioneers must always think about and design a strategy that recognizes the potential countermoves that established firms could deploy against them.

Growth Stage

The growth stage of the life cycle is characterized by an increasing level and intensity of competitive rivalry. More firms seek to enter the industry because they believe the new product will be a commercial success. The new product or service is generally taking off, and industry growth surges. Profitability also dramatically increases, but competing businesses will consume vast amounts of cash to build new factories, to serve new customers, and to refine the product's features and quality.

In the growth stage of the life cycle, numerous firms emerge, each trying to establish its own design or format as the industry standard. Firms will try to stake out and expand key portions of the market by offering what they believe is the best-valued product or service for their customers. In fact, the demand for the product may be growing so fast that it causes a shortfall of capacity. As firms invest in new factories, plants, and equipment, the process technology will become increasingly specialized and dedicated to producing a given type of design or format. However, increased specialization is expensive and requires large volumes to justify its cost.

In many industries such as video games, pharmaceuticals, advanced telecommunications systems, and even new pet food products, firms will spend prodigiously to build brand awareness. In fact, the growth stage offers some of the best opportunities for firms to formulate differentiation-based strategies. Sufficient growth and profitability enable firms to look for new ways to avoid direct, head-to-head competition. Quality becomes a key driver in attracting and retaining customers and distinguishing rivals from one another. As profitability grows, however, many firms will be inclined to begin charging a premium price for their products. Rising prices, high industry profitability, and the rapid entry of new competitors set the stage for an eventual "shakeout" of many weaker firms. Some of the strategic problems confronting firms in the growth stage of the life cycle include (1) the need to deal with potential excess capacity, (2) the search for new product applications, and (3) rising buyer power.

Firms in the growth phase are likely to spend large sums on new capital equipment and factories. High market growth rates and demand create a tendency for many firms to overinvest in capital equipment. When growth eventually begins to slow, industry-wide overcapacity eventually hurts the entire industry. For any one firm, however, overinvestment in capital equipment represents a major and possibly continuing drain on cash. Each firm needs to judge carefully the timing of its own capacity additions and to calculate the potential capacity expansion made by rivals. High growth may actually set the stage for a much less attractive industry resulting from overcapacity. For example, the large number of firms now producing and selling different types of digital cellular telephones, CD players, and video games signals the growing possibility of excess capacity that will plague these industries as they mature. This trend has already devastated the telecommunications industry as dozens of new competitors in the local and long-distance markets were forced out of business during the high-technology recession of 2001. Other more recently established telecom firms such as Qwest Communications, Level 3 Communications, Williams, and Global Crossing have added so much fiber optic capacity that bandwidth has essentially become almost a "free" commodity.

Firms also must deal with the growing challenge of finding and developing alternative applications for the new product. The costs associated with finding new product applications—engaging in more R&D and testing activities for a smarter and well-established market—are likely to rise. Instead, firms perhaps should consider devoting more R&D effort and resources toward improving product quality and the cost efficiency of their production processes.

The growth stage is also the period during which buyers become increasingly more knowledgeable about the different designs, standards, and formats of a product. Thus, buyer power is likely to rise just as growth begins to level off. Since the product is no longer truly new or novel, buyers will pay more attention to brands and images. Strong buyer power means that firms will have to spend more effort and resources in marketing and promotional activities that maintain differentiation.

Sometimes, firms wait too long before they recognize the strength of buyers' power and delay their response to rivals' price cuts. This points to a significant potential weakness for those firms hoping to extend their differentiation-based strategies and advantages over the product's life cycle. As a product or service concept evolves through the growth phase and enters the mature phase, the viability of sustaining differentiation-based advantages begins to require ever more effort, since cost control and more focused, process-driven management issues will begin to predominate. As the Nordstrom example reveals, firms engaged in differentiation strategies need to ensure that they have a sufficient degree of effort dedicated to cost control in order to reach at least a strategic cost parity with those firms already executing a low-cost leadership strategy. For those firms practicing low-cost leadership strategies, stronger buyer power is a signal that they need to become more cost-conscious about their operations and seek new ways to create and extend value solutions without compromising their internal operational efficiencies.

Mature Stage

The mature stage of the cycle is where the majority of U.S. businesses are located. Market growth is slow in the mature stage. A dominant design or industry standard defines the product technology in the industry, and buyers are knowledgeable about the product. Process technologies at this time become highly specialized, and cost efficiency becomes extremely important in determining profitability. Other key characteristics of maturity include a stronger emphasis placed on competition based on cost and price, difficulty in finding new opportunities for differentiation, a "shakeout" of weaker competitors, and more stable prices. Opportunities for differentiation still exist, but they are more difficult to pursue because buyers are familiar with competing firms' products. Declining differences between products of competing firms generally means an increased similarity in pricing.[35] Strategic issues and problems facing firms competing in mature industries include (1) excessively emphasizing price wars to utilize capacity and gain small market share and (2) finding new markets for mature products.

Many mature industries, such as airlines, automobiles, aluminum, packaged foods, personal care products, diapers, and industrial equipment, are characterized by occasionally fierce fights among existing rivals to gain additional market share. Since the prospect for actual market growth of the industry is virtually nil, an increase in one firm's market share must ordinarily come at the expense of another firm. Thus, firms competing in mature industries must monitor and prepare for occasional, if not frequent, price wars between existing firms. Oftentimes, the end result of such price wars is a lowering of the entire industry's overall profitability.

Some firms will initiate a price war to dislodge potentially weaker rivals; others need to lower prices to sell more products to use existing production capacity. For example, airfare wars were increasingly common over the past ten years as stronger major airlines sought to dislodge weaker carriers from the industry. In the aluminum and steel industries, firms cut their prices to continue operating at near capacity. The high-capital intensity of these industries means that firms continue to produce as long as they can meet their variable costs. Paradoxically, long-term profitability for all the firms involved in the industry will likely suffer. A big strategic issue facing most mature businesses is how best to deal with dedicated and rigid production processes or technologies that have few alternative uses.

Firms in mature industries need to engage in efforts to locate other faster-growing markets for their products. Expanding globally represents a useful option for many firms that face the prospect of maturity in their home markets. For example, Crown Cork and Seal, a leading firm in the metal can industry, faces an extremely mature and structurally unattractive industry environment in the United States. It prospered in the mature, domestic market because its specialized technology worked on a wider range of thin and thicker metals to make bottle caps and other containers in ways that other companies could not. Realizing the cost pressures of competing domestically, Crown Cork and Seal has utilized numerous opportunities to set up operations and sell metal cans and bottle caps to many rapidly growing markets throughout Asia, Latin America, and elsewhere. The firm has remained a consistently profitable company, not only because of its differentiation-based focus strategy but also because of its aggressive sales in new markets.

The example of Crown Cork and Seal also shows that firms can still manage to execute differentiation-based strategies in a mature life cycle stage, but they need to be careful in managing their costs and search for new opportunities to extend their sources of competitive advantage to new arenas. Many other firms, such as Corning, 3M, Cisco Systems, Eastman Kodak, Coca-Cola, PepsiCo, General Electric, and even the large U.S. automakers, are shifting their strategic focus to overseas markets that are rapidly growing and where maturity is a long time away. Even small regional firms, such as bakeries, are moving into Mexico and other developing markets to take advantage of rapid growth to complement mature operations back in the United States.[36] Thus, global expansion offers many mature businesses the opportunity to continue their operations and to increase profitability.

Decline Stage

Every product at some point in time reaches the decline stage of the life cycle. Decline results when demand for the product drops, when the number of substitute products increases, and when customer needs shift or change. Many entire products and industries have disappeared over past decades as a result of declining markets such as buggy whips, nonelectric typewriters, wooden agricultural plows, mechanical automobile brakes, rotary dial telephones, and black and white televisions in the United States. Other industries that are clearly approaching decline in the United States include shipbuilding, coal mining, textiles, and brass implements.[37] Products that currently appear to be on a fast decline include cassette tape recorders and even VHS format VCRs. The decision of whether to continue competing in a declining industry should be based on an objective assessment of the firm's viability and what returns the owners of the firm or business can gain from a sale.

Most firms cannot survive profitably in a declining industry. Not only is the industry structure deteriorating, but also rivals are confronted with numerous potential exit barriers that make smooth exit difficult. Exit barriers can result from earlier excessive investment in a specialized process technology that has yet to be paid for, emotional commitment by managers to a given business, and natural resistance by workers, managers, and the society in which they reside to shutting down plants. The presence of strong exit barriers means that firms will continue to compete fiercely with one another for a declining share of the market. In this environment, firms must consider several different strategic options: immediate divestiture or sale of the business, harvesting, or focusing on some niche.

Divestiture and sale of the business to other owners is often more difficult than it appears. Exit barriers often make leaving quickly difficult. More important, many firms are unable to sell assets at a price high enough to recoup some of the residual investment value. Attempts to divest and sell the business quickly often encounter resistance from workers and political pressure from communities intent on saving jobs. Thus, divestiture and sale, while viable economic options, may not be entirely easy steps. Many firms currently seeking to exit the defense industry, for example, face great pressures from communities concerned with preserving jobs in a declining market.

Harvesting means gradually "disinvesting" in the business. In other words, management deliberately and calculatingly runs the business into the ground so as to maximize the cash flows that can be extracted from future product sales in a declining market. Investment is stopped, maintenance is reduced, and employees are gradually let go. Harvesting strategies, however, are not without their downside. As might be expected, businesses that harvest often suffer from extremely poor employee morale. It is usually better to sell off the business (even when there are exit barriers) rather than to engage in extended harvesting. (We will discuss harvesting in greater detail in Chapter 6.)

Finally, a declining business could search for some niche in which to survive. This option, too, is highly problematic, since by nature a niche affords only enough room for one firm or business to serve it. Motorola has pursued a declining niche strategy in deciding to stick with the basic transistor business. Since integrated circuits and advanced semiconductors have long replaced basic transistors in most electronic applications, many of the original firms producing basic transistors have finally exited. Motorola is now the last niche producer of basic transistors that still have a tiny market (mostly hobbyists) in the United States.

Life Cycle Dynamics and Competitive Advantage

The evolution of the product life cycle can exert a major influence on how a firm applies its distinctive competence to competing along the various life cycle stages. Although the life cycle may be used to describe the evolution of a broad product class, product derivatives or spin-offs may indeed have their own particular life cycles. Managers need to recognize that each subset or subfamily of a given broad product type can indeed progress through its own stages of life cycle dynamics.

Let us consider the broadly defined semiconductor industry during the period of 1997 to 2001 as an illustration. Each product has its own individual life cycle characterized by introductory, growth, mature, and declining phases. The one-gigabit memory chip, for example, is currently in the introductory phase of the life cycle. A number of competitors such as IBM, Toshiba, Infineon Technologies (a unit 80 percent owned by Germany's Siemens), Samsung, and Motorola are working on commercializing and improving the chip's performance before offering it to the personal computer and other industries. This new design has yet to undergo rigorous quality testing or widespread commercial use at the time of this writing. However, the 64- and 256-megabit memory chips, incorporated in the latest personal computers and other electronic equipment, moved into different phases of the growth cycle around 1999. Demand for the 64-megabit chip originally was greater than manufacturing capacity at the time it was first unveiled in 1995, although the recent high-technology recession and the meltdown of the telecommunications industry has limited market interest in the 256-megabit chip. Even before 1997, the earlier 16-megabit memory chips used in personal computers and other electronics have become more mature if not declining products. Personal computer and other electronics makers still buy and use them for existing products, but their continued usefulness and applicability will become more limited over time. Since 1997, however, the 1-megabit, 4-megabit, and 256-kilobit (256K) chip represent a series of memory products that are clearly in the decline phase. Few electronics firms even use them for cutting-edge computer applications, and even fewer are committed to producing them.

Other types of semiconductor products, such as microprocessors, have their own separate life cycles within the industry. For example, in 1997 Intel's popular Pentium II microprocessor sat somewhere between the introductory and growth phases of the life cycle. The Pentium II began to incorporate MMX technology that allowed for faster multimedia (e.g., sound, video, graphics) applications. By early 1998, the original Pentium series that was unveiled in late 1994 had become obsolete, while the Pentium II and the even newer Pentium III variations became the expected de facto industry standard microprocessor for personal computers. The original Pentium family of microprocessors has greatly proliferated along many different performance levels according to speed and frequencies (measured in megahertz). Now, Intel's Pentium III lines of microprocessors, however, are currently fully mature and are primarily used to create derivative applications of lower-priced Celeron chips for the sub-$1,000 and sub-$600 PC markets. Today, newer variants of the Pentium 4 line of microprocessors are rapidly becoming the standard in most PC and server applicants. By late 2002, even the Pentium 4 will become mature as Intel's new line of Itanium chips roll out. Intel may plan to segment the microprocessor market even further, with faster Pentium 4 chips (upward of two-gigahertz clock speed) designed for PCs, while the Itanium will go into large corporate servers and workstations.

Thus, a firm can use the life cycle concept and its various stages as an approximate basis for defining the next generation of technology and products the market will likely need and use. True forecasting with the product life cycle, however, is extremely difficult, since future generations of products (and substitutes) could evolve in unanticipated ways. Most important, the next generation of products could have a much shorter or more compressed life cycle than current products. Despite these uncertainties, Intel has been consistently successful in using life cycle dynamics as the basis for rapidly designing and producing successive waves of ever-more powerful microprocessors.

Let us examine Exhibit 4-7, which displays the types of skills that are needed to compete in the semiconductor industry. Toward the early stages of any chip's life cycle, factors such as design expertise, creativity, and product innovation are important sources of competitive advantage. New ways to think about designing chips, the creation of electronic "silicon layers" to form the chip's architecture, the incorporation of new materials, and techniques to improve processing speed, logic, or memory are the technological drivers that stimulate innovation and competitive advantage early on. Manufacturing expertise, process technology, and cost controls are less important than excellence in product design early in the life cycle. As the chip evolves and matures, however, the relative importance of design expertise, creativity, and product innovation becomes less significant as the primary sources of competitive advantage for that particular generation of chip. Instead, manufacturing expertise, process technology, yield improvement, and cost control become the significant technological and cost drivers that define subsequent sources of competitive advantage. As the current generation of a given chip matures, mastery and excellence in manufacturing techniques tend to become much more important than design improvements as the basis

Life Cycle Dynamics and Sources of Competitive Advantage in the Semiconductor Industry — EXHIBIT 4-7

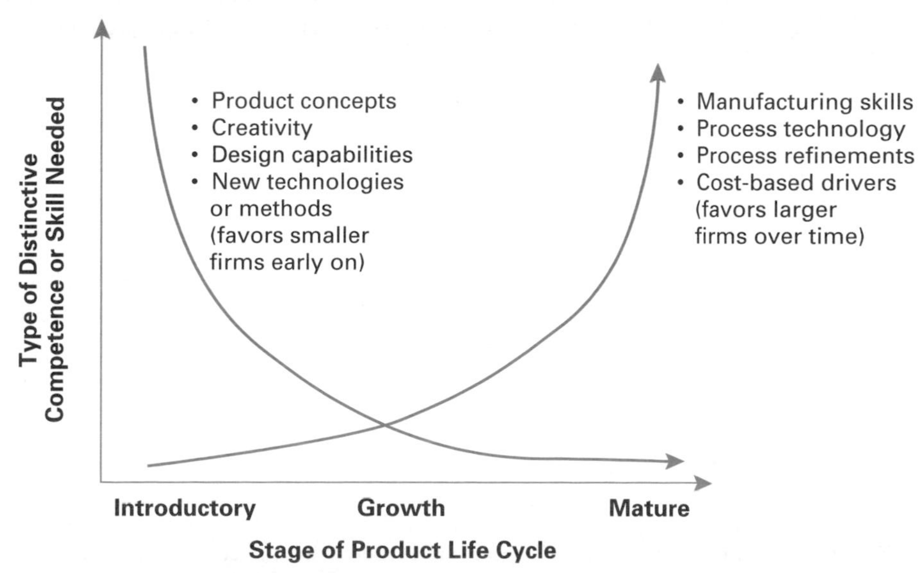

for building competitive advantage, since cost, experience, and volume-based advantages become the basis for competing in a fast maturing market. By the time any given chip generation enters the decline stage, firms will have already begun working on, introducing, and commercializing the next product generation.

The dynamics of evolution portrayed in Exhibit 4-7 have significant implications for many small U.S. semiconductor firms. Small semiconductor companies such as Nvidia, TriQuint Semiconductor, Vitesse Semiconductor, Broadcom, Microchip Technology, and Integrated Device Technologies are hotbeds of design innovation that seek to provide new forms of communications chips that either speed up the Internet or provide greater bandwidth. They specialize in pioneering and using cutting-edge technologies to design new types of logic, signal processing, and other application-specific chips. Thus, their distinctive competences are based on design excellence that serves them well in the early stages.

However, these firms typically do not have the funds, the size, the capital investment, or the technical competence to engage in large-scale commercialization and manufacture of microprocessors on their own. Many have relied on outsourcing the manufacturing of their microprocessors to larger, dedicated chip "foundry" firms with clear distinctive competences in skills such as cost control, process and yield improvement, and manufacturing scale economies. In fact, many semiconductor firms have flourished in recent years by outsourcing their manufacturing or maintaining a very lean production system without significant capital investments. These firms have instead concentrated their scarce capital and resources to focus on what they do best: innovative designs, creativity, and pushing the limit of technology. In Silicon Valley, they are known as "fabulous fab-less" companies because of their lack of manufacturing operations. Some of the representative firms include Altera and Xilinx (programmable logic devices); Nvidia (graphics chips); PMC-Sierra and Broadcom (communication chips for cable modems); and MIPS Technologies (customized microprocessors and embedded memory chips integrated with advanced logic chips). More often than not, these companies have established a strong production, division-of-labor relationship with semiconductor "foundries," such as Taiwan Semiconductor Manufacturing Company (TSMC) and United Microelectronics Company (UMC), both of which are Taiwan-based firms that provide contract manufacturing services.

On the other hand, larger U.S. firms such as Lucent Technologies, Intel, Motorola, IBM, and Texas Instruments have significant distinctive competences in manufacturing excellence and process technologies that can dramatically lower the costs of semiconductor manufacturing. (These same firms also have significant design capabilities and a few are also manufacturing partners to some of the innovative firms listed previously.) These manufacturing-based competences represent enduring sources of competitive advantage as the microprocessor (and logic or memory chip) enters maturity. The cost-based and quality-based advantages possessed by the larger companies enable them to "ramp up" production quickly.

By examining the life cycle dynamics for communications chips (and even microprocessors to some extent), we see that smaller semiconductor firms, such as ARM Holdings, Rambus, Integrated Device Technology, Nvidia, and Broadcom, formulate competitive strategies that build on their design-based distinctive competences. They avoid investing large sums in manufacturing processes that they are unlikely to master as well as dedicated chip "foundries" in Taiwan or large U.S. firms such as IBM, Motorola, and Texas Instruments.

Conversely, although the large U.S. semiconductor firms have significant design capabilities in their own right (e.g., Texas Instruments' line of digital signal processors [DSPs], Motorola's line of 88000 microprocessors), their distinctive competences in manufacturing excellence and process technology nicely complement the design-based competences of small firms. It is no accident that large companies such as Intel, IBM, Texas Instruments, STMicroelectronics (the former SGS-Thomson), and Motorola are beginning to look toward the smaller, design-oriented firms for new sources of innovation in semiconductor technology to supplement their own internal R&D. In many cases, the larger U.S. firm will invest to buy an equity stake in the smaller design firm to fund its research and to learn about new opportunities in communications and other chip applications. In other words, smaller semiconductor design "boutiques" are concentrating and limiting their efforts to designing new generations of communications chips and specialized application products as their core business activity. These design competences represent real sources of competitive advantage in the early stages of the life cycle (design flair is vital) but become less valuable as the chip matures (where cost predominates). Instead of attempting to learn and to build an untried competence in later stages of manufacturing, they continue to invest in their design-based sources of competitive advantage. Conversely, the Taiwanese chip "foundries" have manufacturing strengths that represent real sources of competitive advantage as the chip matures. At the same time, large U.S. firms that possess both design and manufacturing strengths are looking toward the smaller boutiques as hotbed centers of advanced research and product ideas.

Consequently, firms in different industries need to consider how their distinctive competence can be used to build competitive advantage according to life cycle dynamics. As the semiconductor example reveals, design-based competences outweigh manufacturing skills early on. As the microprocessor, memory, or logic chip begins to mature, manufacturing and process technology become correspondingly more important than design skills in building and sustaining competitive advantage. This pattern of life cycle dynamics applies to each subsequent generation or class of chips as well.

In other industries, different patterns reflect the economic drivers that define competitive advantage across the life cycle. In the video game industry, for example, Sega, Sony, and Nintendo have been strong competitors in designing wildly popular games. After they design their games, both companies leverage their marketing and distribution strengths to reach every possible electronics outlet, department store, and toy shop. Creativity is a driver of competitive advantage early on, but mass marketing techniques become vital to high profitability as a game approaches maturity. To capitalize on some new technologies, Sony's recent entrance into the video game industry through its technologically advanced Playstation system enables Sony to leverage its quality and differentiation-based skills to become a major force in new-generation games that are sufficiently different from what Sega and Nintendo offer. Sony's ability to leverage its marketing and new technology is crucial to stimulating buyers' potential interest in new game formats such as the Playstation.

Life cycle dynamics, however, should not serve as a substitute for effective strategy formulation. Companies should not use the life cycle concept as a road map to predict how broader industry or technological changes are likely to evolve. In fact, excessive devotion to life cycle thinking can lead a firm down dangerous paths. For example, U.S. consumer electronics manufacturers during the early 1970s, such as General Electric, Motorola, RCA, Sylvania, and Zenith, believed that the radio and color television set were highly mature products that had little future. These U.S. companies thought that the future of consumer electronics was largely predictable and unprofitable; in turn, they shut down their factories and sold off many of their operations. Sony, on the other hand, took a different view. It redesigned the basic transistor radio to incorporate a sleeker, more elegant design that consumers could use when walking, exercising, or performing other routine tasks. This product became known as the Walkman, and Sony was able to jump-start and regenerate an entirely new product life cycle in the consumer electronics industry. Therefore, firms should be aware of life cycle dynamics in their own industries but not use them as a substitute for strategy.

Ethical Dimension

In this chapter, we have examined how firms can formulate different types of competitive strategies to build competitive advantage. Competitive advantage and high profitability come from delivering superior value to customers through desirable products. Regardless of the individual competitive strategy it selects, a firm must ensure that its products and services are sold with integrity. Thus, the competitive strategy a firm ultimately adopts must also satisfy ethical criteria. Ethical standards differ from society to society and among individuals within a particular society. They also evolve over time. Consequently, generalizations are difficult. However, most U.S. managers operating today would agree that, at the very least, a firm should strive to satisfy a worthy customer need, to supply a safe product, and to provide honest information about its offering.

Worthy Need

Some consumer desires may be less worthy of satisfaction than others. Consequently, even highly profitable businesses may be hard to justify on an ethical basis. Most managers would judge businesses involving illegal narcotics, illegal gambling, falsely labeled nutritional products, deliberately shoddy products, and financial scams as part of this category. In other cases, judging worthiness is not so straightforward. For example, some record companies such as AOL Time Warner are comfortable operating businesses that produce violent films and music (a source of major controversy and parent concern in the late 1990s); other managers would be uncomfortable in this kind of business. Because of these differences, management may be unable to specify precisely which consumer needs constitute ethically worthy targets deserving of attention. Rather, each management group must consult its own collective conscience to arrive at a sound judgment.

Safe Product

All firms have an obligation to provide safe products to customers. Companies that fail to meet this requirement often face serious consequences. Consider, for example, C. R. Bard, a manufacturer of medical equipment. Its chairman and five other current and former managers were indicted in 1993 as a result of difficulties with the company's heart catheter, a wire with a balloonlike end used to open clogged arteries.[38] The Justice Department found that in about fifty instances, the tip of Bard's catheter broke off within a patient's coronary artery during medical procedures. On some of these occasions, doctors were obliged to perform emergency heart surgery to remove the broken tip. The Justice Department charged that Bard officers had concealed test data revealing serious product malfunction. Bard agreed to pay a $61 million fine to settle these charges.

In a related vein, several pharmaceutical companies during the past several years were the targets of class-action lawsuits alleging that their drugs were unsafe. American Home Products faced considerable litigation in 1998 over the potential side effects that resulted from its Redux diet drug (also known as Fen-phen). In 2001, Bayer AG of Germany withdrew its Baycol cholesterol-lowering drug after noting that a disproportionate number of deaths accompanied its use.

The issue of product safety has become especially significant in the wake of a massive recall by Ford Motor Company in 2001 to replace the Firestone tires that equip its popular line of Explorer SUVs. Over two hundred people are believed to have died from accidents that resulted from either potentially faulty tires made by Bridgestone/Firestone or potential design flaws in the Ford Explorer. While Ford has been aggressive to recall any Explorer using Firestone tires, Bridgestone/Firestone has been somewhat slower to react to the market's outcry over its potentially defective tires. The company has acknowledged that manufacturing problems in its Decatur, Illinois, plant did result in some tires' losing their treads, but it feels that a significant portion of the responsibility belongs with the Ford Explorer design.

Ample Information

All firms have an obligation to provide customers with ample information about new products or services. In some industries, this requirement is codified into law. Manufacturers of packaged foods, for example, must provide a full list of ingredients on their package labels, while issuers of common stock must warn investors in a detailed written prospectus about potential risks associated with an offering. Procter & Gamble managed this issue of ample information carefully by informing consumers of the potential risk that its new fat substitute product, Olestra, may introduce. For some people, Olestra (as used in potato chips and other foods) may cause digestive distress.

The obligation to inform customers about products does not end with legal requirements, however. Where customer ignorance about a product is high and the potential damage that a product can inflict on customers is large, firms must often go beyond legal requirements. Failure to fully inform customers under such conditions constitutes a serious ethical lapse that can cause damage to a firm's reputation as well as considerable expense.

Prudential Insurance Company's experience with limited partnerships in the early to mid-1990s is a case in point. A relatively late entrant to the securities industry, it attempted to build market share. As part of this effort, its securities unit sold $8 billion worth of limited real estate and energy partnerships to about four hundred thousand investors. Subsequent slumps in both markets, coupled with adverse tax law changes, caused many of these partnerships to fail. A Securities and Exchange Commission (SEC) investigation concluded that Prudential had made "false and misleading statements" to investors when selling these investments. While Prudential neither admitted nor denied these allegations, it agreed in October 1993 to pay $371 million to settle the charges.[39]

Summary

- Competitive strategies must be based on some source of competitive advantage for success. A company must possess an advantage that enables it to perform an activity(ies) or task(s) better than its competitors. Every part of the value chain should be examined for opportunities to build competitive advantage.
- All firms compete with other rivals for customers at the *industry* or *business* level. Competitors may be small entrepreneurial start-ups, established single-business firms, or business units of a larger, diversified corporation.
- Competitive strategies may be analyzed from three generic categories: low-cost leadership, differentiation, and focus/specialization. Each type of strategy is designed to build competitive advantage in a different way.
- Low-cost leadership strategies are based on producing a product or service at a lower cost than that of rivals. A low-cost strategy builds competitive advantage through economies of scale, experience curve effects, and other factors to gain a large share of the market.
- Differentiation is based on enhancing the distinctiveness or uniqueness of a product or service. Differentiation builds competitive advantage by making customers more loyal, less price-sensitive, and less willing to consider other product alternatives.
- Focus strategies aim to sell products or services to a narrow or specific target market, niche, or segment. Focus builds competitive advantage through high specialization and concentration of resources in a given niche.
- In the future, firms will be compelled to offer improved sources of value to their customers faster, better, and at lower cost. Mass customization enables firms to use new technologies (manufacturing, Internet, modular product designs, and market segmentation) to respond faster to customers' needs and to provide new sources of value continuously. The combination of all four emerging technologies will make mass customization a new strategy to tailor-make and serve individual customers.
- Regardless of which strategy a firm selects, high quality is an essential pillar of competitive advantage. Quality builds high market share and distinction; both lead to high profitability.
- The product life cycle is an important factor that influences how firms develop their competitive strategies. Each stage of the life cycle presents different issues with which the firm must deal. As a product progresses through the life cycle, certain skills and competences play a more important role than others in building

competitive advantage, depending on the life cycle stage and the nature of the industry.

Exercises and Discussion Questions

1. What kind of trade-offs does a firm face when it chooses a particular type of generic strategy (low-cost leadership, differentiation, or focus)? How does the choice of a generic strategy ultimately affect the kind of people the firm would hire for its management team? What kind of skills would be needed for a firm pursuing low-cost leadership? Are these skills different from those needed to support a differentiation or focus strategy?

2. Look up the Web sites for three different airlines (e.g., American Airlines, Delta Air Lines, and Continental Airlines). In this chapter, we described the airline industry as brutal and extremely competitive. What have these three carriers attempted to do using the Internet? How does the ability to make reservations directly on their Web sites contribute value to you? What kind of generic strategy are the airlines hoping to pursue using their Web sites? In your judgment, is it sustainable over the long haul?
3. What are some disadvantages that come from large size? What are some industries in which large firms have encountered difficulties competing with smaller firms?
4. How do you see the product life cycle affecting the nature of competition within an industry? What types of competitive actions seem to be most important at each life cycle stage? Use the current evolution of DVD players as the basis for your discussion. What do you think DVD players will look like in five years?
5. Using the Internet, look up the Web site for Starbucks Coffee. How would you evaluate Starbucks' position in the product life cycle for specialized coffees? Do you believe Starbucks is well positioned to compete as this market continues to evolve? What are some things that this firm needs to think about as it continues to grow at the pace that it has in recent years?

Endnotes

1. Data for the Nordstrom Strategic Snapshot were adopted from the following sources: "Macy's Tries a CD to Draw Teen Shoppers," *Wall Street Journal*, August 2, 2001; "Can Nordstroms Find the Right Style?" *Business Week*, July 30, 2001; "Nordstrom Cites Slowing Economy for Drop in Profit," *Wall Street Journal*, February 23, 2001; "Slaughter in the Aisles," *Forbes*, January 8, 2001; "The 100 Best Companies to Work For," *Fortune*, January 8, 2001; "In Return to Power, the Nordstrom Family Finds a Pile of Problems," *Wall Street Journal*, September 8, 2000; "Nordstrom Cleans Out Its Closets," *Business Week*, May 22, 2000; "In Retailing, Bricks Beats Bytes," *Wall Street Journal*, January 6, 2000; "Heard in the Northwest: Nordstrom Sags as Analysts Fault Store Merchandise," *Wall Street Journal*, December 15, 1999; "Filling Big Shoes," *Forbes*, November 15, 1999; "Nordstrom to Start Web Unit with Cash from Two Venture Capital Concerns," *Wall Street Journal*, August 25, 1999; "Nordstrom Tries to Cut Costs While Maintaining Service," *Wall Street Journal*, April 8, 1999.

2. See, for example, W. K. Hall, "Survival Strategies in a Hostile Environment," *Harvard Business Review* (September–October 1980): 75–85. A good discussion of the antecedents of high performance can be found in R. E. Caves, B. T. Gale, and M. E. Porter, "Interfirm Profitability Differences," *Quarterly Journal of Economics* (November 1977): 667–675; C. S. Galbraith and C. H. Stiles, "Firm Profitability and Relative Firm Power," *Strategic Management Journal* 4 (1983): 237–249; G. S. Day,

"Strategic Market Analysis and Definition: An Integrated Approach," *Strategic Management Journal* 2 (1981): 281–299. Also, the use of firm-specific assets and resources to capture higher profitability can be found in K. Cool and I. Dierickx, "Rivalry, Strategic Group and Firm Performance," *Strategic Management Journal* 14 (1993): 47–59; M. J. Chen and D. Miller, "Competitive Attack, Retaliation and Performance: An Expected-Valency Framework," *Strategic Management Journal* 15 (1994): 85–102.

Some of the more recent work examining this area include the following sample pieces: C. Lee, K. Lee, and J. M. Pennings, "Internal Capabilities, External Networks, and Performance: A Study on Technology-Based Ventures," *Strategic Management Journal* 22, issues 6–7 (2001): 615–640; J. Gimeno and C. Y. Woo, "Multimarket Contact, Economies of Scope, and Firm Performance," *Academy of Management Journal* 42, no. 3 (1999): 239–259; W. J. Ferrier, K. G. Smith, and C. M. Grimm, "The Role of Competitive Action in Market Share Erosion and Industry Dethronement: A Study of Industry Leaders and Challengers," *Academy of Management Journal* 42, no. 4 (1999): 372–388; K. Smith, C. M. Grimm, G. Young, and S. Wally, "Strategic Groups and Rivalrous Firm Behavior: Towards a Reconciliation," *Strategic Management Journal* 18 (1997): 149–157; M. Chen, "Competitor Analysis and Inter-Firm Rivalry: Toward a Theoretical Integration," *Academy of Management Journal* 21 (1999): 100–134; J. A. Baum and J. J. Korn, "Competitive Dynamics of Interfirm Rivalry," *Academy of Management Journal* 39 (1996): 255–291. A more detailed review of the academic literature can be found in the next endnote, which more specifically covers the topic of generic strategies.

3. This section draws heavily on the excellent treatment of generic strategies by M. E. Porter, *Competitive Strategy* (New York: Free Press, 1980), and his second work, *Competitive Advantage* (New York: Free Press, 1985), chaps. 1, 3, and 4. An excellent academic treatment of generic strategies may be found in C. W. L. Hill, "Differentiation versus Low Cost or Differentiation and Low Cost: A Contingency Framework," *Academy of Management Review* 13, no. 3 (1988): 401–412. Empirical tests of generic strategies have been an important research area. Some sample works include R. Amit, "Cost Leadership Strategy and Experience Curves," *Strategic Management Journal* 7 (1986): 281–292; G. G. Dess and P. S. Davis, "Porter's Generic Strategies as Determinants of Strategic Group Membership and Organizational Performance," *Academy of Management Journal* 27 (1984): 467–488; R. E. White, "Generic Business Strategies, Organizational Context and Performance," *Strategic Management Journal* 7 (1986): 217–231; L. Kim and Y. Lim, "Environment, Generic Strategies, and Performance in a Rapidly Developing Country: A Taxonomic Approach," *Academy of Management Journal* 31 (1988): 802–827; E. J. Zajac and S. M. Shortell, "Changing Generic Strategies: Likelihood, Direction and Performance Implications," *Strategic Management Journal* 10 (1989): 413–430; V. A. Zeithaml, A. Parasuranam, and L. L. Berry, *Delivering Quality Service* (New York: Free Press, 1990); J. Beath and Y. Katsoulacos, *The Economic Theory of Product Differentiation* (Cambridge: Cambridge University Press, 1991); E. Mosakowski, "A Resource-Based Perspective on the Dynamic Strategy-Performance Relationship: An Empirical Examination of the Focus and Differentiation Strategies in Entrepreneurial Firms," *Journal of Management* 19, no. 4 (1993): 819–839.

4. See Porter, *Competitive Advantage.*

5. See, for example, K. R. Harrigan, *Strategies for Vertical Integration* (Lexington, Mass.: Heath, 1983). An excellent literature review of vertical integration can be found in J. T. Mahoney, "The Choice of Organizational Form: Vertical Financial Ownership versus Other Methods of Vertical Integration," *Strategic Management Journal* 13 (1992): 559–584.

6. Some of the landmark academic pieces on this topic include S. Schoeffler, R. D. Buzzell, and D. F. Heany, "Impact of Strategic Planning on Performance," *Harvard Business Review* (March–April 1974): 137–145; R. D. Buzzell, B. T. Gale, and R. Sultan, "Market Share—A Key to Profitability," *Harvard Business Review* (January–

February 1975): 97–106. An excellent overview of the research literature documenting the different relationships between market share and various levels of profitability can be found in R. D. Buzzell and B. T. Gale, *The PIMS Principles: Linking Strategy to Performance* (New York: Free Press, 1987). These authors present an overview of the research findings that attempt to explain the relationship between share and industry profitability. Also see J. E. Prescott, A. K. Kohli, and N. Venkatraman, "The Market Share—Profitability Relationship: An Empirical Assessment of Major Assertions and Contradictions," *Strategic Management Journal* 7 (1986): 377–394; N. Varaiya, R. Kerin, and D. Weeks, "The Relationship between Growth, Profitability, and Firm Value," *Strategic Management Journal* 8 (1987): 487–497 and N. Capon, J. Farley, and S. Hoenig, "Determinants of Financial Performance: A Meta-Analysis," *Management Science* 36, no. 10 (1990): 1143–1159.

Later work addressing this issue includes the following: S. Davies and P. Geroski, "Changes in Concentration, Turbulence, and the Dynamics of Market Shares," *Review of Economics and Statistics* 79 (1997): 383–391; C. Banbury and W. Mitchell, "The Effect of Introducing Important Incremental Innovations on Market Share and Business Survival," *Strategic Management Journal* 16 (1995): 161–182.

7. See Buzzell and Gale, *The PIMS Principles*.

8. See "Intel, AMD Lay Out Strategies to Boost Sales, Spur Growth," *Wall Street Journal*, August 29, 2001, p. B4; "Intel Fights AMD with Faster Chips, Steep Price Cuts," *Wall Street Journal*, August 22, 2001, p. B6; "Intel Researchers Build Tiny Transistors That Could Sharply Boost Chips' Speed," *Wall Street Journal*, June 11, 2001, p. B2; "Intel Aims New Chips at High-End Market," *Wall Street Journal*, May 21, 2001, p. B9; "Intel inside the War Room," *Business Week*, April 30, 2001, p. 40; "Intel Is Banking on Pentium 4 Ads to Revive Sales," *Wall Street Journal*, February 15, 2001, pp. B1, B4; "Intel Price Cuts May Slice into AMD's Market Gains," *Wall Street Journal*, October 17, 2000, pp. C1, C4; "Intel Mounts Response to Sub-$1,000 PC Pressure," *Wall Street Journal*, August 21, 1998, pp. A3, A9; "Many Firms Would Switch from Intel to Rival Chip Makers, Survey Finds," *Wall Street Journal*, August 5, 1998, p. B7; "Intel Steps Up Production of Next Level of Sub-$1,000 Celeron Microprocessor," *Wall Street Journal*, July 22, 1998, p. B3.

9. See "Southwest Rivals on East Coast Copy Its Formula for Success," *Dallas Morning News*, September 20, 1998, pp. 1H–2H; "Continental, Southwest Ills Send Airline Stocks Reeling," *Wall Street Journal*, December 9, 1994, p. B4.

10. See "Reheating Starbucks," *Business Week*, September 28, 1998, pp. 66–68.

11. "Maytag Says Profit Again Will Surpass Analyst Estimates," *Wall Street Journal*, September 10, 1998, p. B10.

12. I. C. MacMillan and R. G. McGrath, "Discovering New Points of Differentiation," *Harvard Business Review* (July–August 1997): 133–145.

13. See "Why Toyota Wins Such High Marks on Quality Surveys," *Wall Street Journal*, March 15, 2001, pp. A1, A11.

14. See L. W. Philips, D. R. Chang, and R. D. Buzzell, "Product Quality, Cost Position and Business Performance: A Test of Some Key Hypotheses," *Journal of Marketing* 47 (Spring 1983): 26–43.

15. See "Radio One Deploys an Urban Beat to Make Revenue Jump," *Wall Street Journal*, August 29, 2001.

16. See "Specialized Firms Stick to the Straight and Very Narrow," *Wall Street Journal*, May 19, 1989, p. B2.

17. "Why Some Sony Gear Is Made in Japan—By Another Company," *Wall Street Journal*, June 14, 2001, pp. A1, A10; "Solectron Becomes a Force in Stealth Manufac-

turing," *Wall Street Journal*, August 18, 1998, p. B4; "Solectron to Take Over Manufacturing of Some Mitsubishi Electric Products," *Wall Street Journal*, July 30, 1998, p. A6.

18. See "Hot Rod Rivalry: Cycle Mania Has Company Rolling," *Dallas Morning News*, September 6, 1998, p. 1H, 3H.

19. See "An All-New Cast: Nucor's Attempt to Make Steel Sheets without Huge Rolling Mills May Boost an Ailing Industry," Forbes, April 16, 2001, pp. 318–320.

20. "When Cool Heads Prevail," *Business Week*, June 11, 2001, p. 114.

21. See "Patek Philippe Is Luxuriating in Independence," *Wall Street Journal*, December 11, 2000, p. B18.

22. See, for example, C. Y. Woo and A. C. Cooper. "The Surprising Case for Low Market Share," *Harvard Business Review* (November–December 1982): 106–113; and R.G. Hammermesh, M. J. Anderson, and J. E. Harris, "Strategies for Low Market Share Businesses," *Harvard Business Review* (May–June 1970): 95–102. Also see C. Y. Woo, "Market-Share Leadership—Not Always So Good," *Harvard Business Review* (January–February 1984): 2–4; M. J. Chen and D. C. Hambrick, "Speed, Stealth and Selective Attack: How Small Firms Differ from Large Firms in Competitive Behavior," *Academy of Management Journal* 38, no. 2 (1995): 453–482; and A. Fiegenbaum and A. Karnani, "Output Flexibility—A Competitive Advantage for Small Firms," *Strategic Management Journal* 12 (1991): 101–114.

23. The concept of mass customization has become more popular as the basis for rethinking some of Porter's unidimensional, generic strategies. For example, see B. J. Pine, B. Victor, and A. C. Boynton, "Making Mass Customization Work," *Harvard Business Review* (September–October 1993): 108–121, for an early introduction to the concept. The use of advanced manufacturing technologies to undertake mass customization and integrated low-cost/differentiation strategies is explained in D. Lei, M. A. Hitt, and J. D. Goldhar, "Advanced Manufacturing Technology: Organization Design and Strategic Flexibility," *Organization Studies* 17, no. 3 (1996): 501–523.

24. See M. A. Schilling, "Toward a General Modular Systems Theory and Its Application to Interfirm Product Modularity," *Academy of Management Review* 25, no. 2 (2000): 312–334; C. Baldwin and K. Clark," Managing in an Age of Modularity," *Harvard Business Review* 75 (September–October 1997): 84–93; R. Sanchez and J. Mahoney, "Modularity, Flexibility, and Knowledge Management in Product and Organizational Design," *Strategic Management Journal* 17 (1996): 63–76; R. Langlois and P. Robertson, "Networks and Innovation in a Modular System: Lessons from the Microcomputer and Stereo Component Industries," *Research Policy* 21 (1992): 297–313.

25. See "The Customized, Digitized, Have-It-Your-Way Economy," *Fortune*, September 28, 1998, pp. 114–124.

26. See T. Peters and R. Waterman, *In Search of Excellence* (New York: Harper & Row, 1982).

27. See, for example, "Ford Says Last Year's Quality Snafus Took Big Toll—Over $1 Billion in Profit," *Wall Street Journal*, January 12, 2001, pp. A3, A6.

28. See Philips, Chang, and Buzzell, "Product Quality, Cost Position and Business Performance." Also see Buzzell and Gale, *The PIMS Principles*, for a brief overview of the literature using the PIMS database.

29. See, for example, P. Crosby, *Quality Is Free* (New York: McGraw-Hill, 1979); and D. A. Garvin, *Managing Quality* (New York: Free Press, 1988). A landmark work on quality is that by W. E. Deming, *Out of the Crisis* (Cambridge, Mass.: MIT Center for Advanced Engineering Study, 1986).

30. See, for example, C. R. Anderson and C. P. Zeithaml, "Stage of the Product Life Cycle, Business Strategy, and Business Performance," *Academy of Management Journal* 27 (1984): 5–24; J. G. Covin and D. P. Slevin, "New Venture Strategic Posture, Structure, and Performance: An Industry Life Cycle Analysis," *Journal of Business Venturing* 5 (1990): 123–135.

31. See R. A. Thietart and R. Vivas, "An Empirical Investigation of Success Strategies for Businesses along the Product Life Cycle," *Management Science* 30 (December 1984): 1405–1423. Also see D. C. Hambrick and D. Lei, "Towards an Empirical Prioritization of Contingency Variables for Business Strategy," *Academy of Management Journal* 28 (1985): 763–788; and C. Hofer, "Towards a Contingency Theory of Business Strategy," *Academy of Management Journal* 18 (1975): 784–810.

32. A landmark work in this area is R. A. Kerin, P. R. Varadarajan, and R. A. Peterson, "First-Mover Advantage: A Synthesis, Conceptual Framework and Research Propositions," *Journal of Marketing* 56 (October 1992): 33–52. Also see R. Makadok, "Can First-Mover and Early-Mover Advantages Be Sustained in an Industry with Low Barriers to Entry/Imitation?" *Strategic Management Journal* 19, no. 7 (1998): 683–696; C. Brown and J. Lattin, "Investigating the Relationship between Time in Market and Pioneering Advantage," *Management Science* 40, no. 10 (1994): 1361–1369; L. Huff and W. Robinson, "The Impact of Leadtime and Years of Competitive Rivalry on Pioneer Market Share Advantages," *Management Science* 40, no. 10 (1994): 1370–1377; P. Golder and G. Tellis, "Pioneer Advantage: Marketing Logic or Marketing Legend," *Journal of Marketing Research* 30 (1993): 158–170; M. B. Lieberman and D. B. Montgomery, "First-Mover Advantages," *Strategic Management Journal* 9 (1988): 41–58; and M. Lambkin, "Order of Entry and Performance in New Markets," *Strategic Management Journal* 9 (1988): 127–140.

33. See "DVD Gains on Tape, but Economics Have Hollywood in a Tizzy," *Wall Street Journal*, February 5, 2002, pp. A1, A6; "For Now, at Least, DVD Sales Are Soaring as Prices Drop," *Wall Street Journal*, September 11, 2001, p. B4.

34. See "How Palm Tumbled from Star of Tech to Target of Microsoft," *Wall Street Journal*, September 7, 2001, pp. A1, A4.

35. See, for example, D. C. Hambrick, "High Profit Strategies in Mature Capital Goods Businesses: A Contingency Approach," *Academy of Management Journal* 26 (1983): 687–707; and D. C. Hambrick, "An Empirical Typology of Mature Industrial-Product Environments," *Academy of Management Journal* 26 (1983): 213–230.

36. See "Bakers Find Acquisition Is Now the Recipe for Growth," *Wall Street Journal*, June 16, 1994, p. B4.

37. See, for example, K. R. Harrigan, *Strategies for Declining Industries* (Lexington, Mass.: Heath, 1985).

38. "C. R. Bard's Chairman and Five Others Are Indicted in Heart-Catheter Scandal," *Wall Street Journal*, October 18, 1993, p. A4.

39. See "Prudential Sets Accord to End Partnership Case," *Wall Street Journal*, October 22, 1993, p. C1.

CHAPTER 5

Competing on the 'Net: Building Virtual Advantage

Chapter Outline

What You Will Learn

- How the Internet is redefining the basis of competition in many industries
- The basic types of Internet-driven business platforms: business-to-business, business-to-consumer, and consumer-to-consumer
- The economic conditions that give rise to different Internet-driven business applications
- The concepts of disintermediation, value compression, and network effects
- The critical success factors that underpin the notion of virtual advantage
- What established firms need to think about when migrating to the Internet

Amazon.com[1]

Ever since its beginning, Amazon.com has been considered the leading on-line retailer. Over the past seven years, Amazon has grown by leaps and bounds to become one of the biggest sellers of books, compact discs (CDs), videos, gifts, and even electronic products on the Internet. Founded in 1994 by Jeff Bezos, Amazon.com initially started selling books by offering over a million titles that included most of the English titles in print. Amazon offered book customers a significant discount to list price, and it was able in most cases to ship books out within a day or two upon receiving the order. By the end of 2000, Amazon.com's revenues reached over $2.7 billion, with growth coming from a variety of different revenue streams, becoming the largest on-line retailer. Although the company at this time has just reached pro forma profitability in the fourth quarter of 2001, Amazon expects to reach its long-term profit goals in the next few years. At present, it is believed that Amazon has over three million book titles listed.

Amazon first sold books in the summer of 1995 by offering customers a selection of over a million titles (books in print). This selection of available titles was far greater than any traditional book retailer (e.g., Barnes & Noble, Borders, Waldenbooks) was able to provide at the time; even the largest conventional bookstores carry about 150,000 titles in stock. Amazon attracted a huge customer following as readers loved the enormous array of titles, the discounted pricing, and the ease with which people can search for their titles and order securely over the Internet. Of growing importance, Amazon even allowed readers to communicate their thoughts and reviews about a book on the company's Web site. For each title that is available on Amazon's site, customers have the opportunity to provide their comments. Thus, any given reader is free to provide his or her thoughts about the book and other prospective customers can read those reviews.

Customer Convenience

Amazon also provides a high level of personalized service for its virtual customers. Every book that Amazon carries also shows how the expected delivery time, ranging from one to two days to four to six weeks, depending on how readily available the item is. More important, Amazon offered a high degree of convenience and security for customers. It was one of the first companies to offer credit card transactions over the Internet and explain in great detail the lengths the company will go to in order to preserve security.

Customers are free to browse throughout Amazon's vast Web site and are encouraged to place the books of interest into a virtual shopping cart. Once a customer is ready to check out, he or she enters an e-mail address and creates a personal password. First-time customers need to enter their billing and credit card information, shipping address, and other items to create a personal profile. Each time the customer revisits Amazon.com, the Web site then retrieves the customer's personal profile in order to expedite the ordering process.

The personal profile serves three purposes. First, it saves customers time from reentering all of the billing information, shipping address, and other data needed to complete the transaction. Second, the profile allows Amazon to make recommendations of other books in which the reader might be interested. Third, it allows customers to view their entire purchase history with Amazon.com. This feature gives customers the ability to recall which books they may have ordered either for themselves or as gifts for other people. Amazon has also made it easy to shop for gifts as well, since the Web site also allows buyers to choose gift wrap and the ability to send a virtual greeting card as well.

Of course, throughout the entire browsing and shopping process, customers are free to change their order anytime during their virtual visit, and even if they leave the site, their shopping cart will still be there, containing the items that were previously selected. Once an order is entered and verified by the customer, Amazon sends an e-mail back to the customer confirming what the customer ordered. Later, as Amazon ships the order out, it will then send another e-mail indicating how long to expect delivery and what items might be back-ordered.

Fast Turnaround

To ensure that books are widely available to Amazon's growing legions of customers, the company has worked closely with publishers and other suppliers to devise a fast ordering system that is based on a highly efficient inventory management system. From its earliest days, Amazon has worked closely with Ingram Books, a large nationwide wholesale distributor, to build an instantaneous book-shipping system. Once Amazon had a confirmed order from a customer, it would then order the title needed from Ingram, who in turn would ship the book out immediately. By working closely with Ingram, Amazon was able to reduce some of the inventory costs that would accompany storage of millions of book titles.

In mid-1997, Amazon.com opened its own huge warehouses on both U.S. coasts in order to reach customers even faster. Although this step now means that Amazon will have to stock some of its own inventory, the company felt that it needed to offer even faster customer service and delivery times. Even with its own warehouses, however, Amazon typically stocks only a small portion of its own inventory. Publishers, in turn, work closely with Amazon because the company shares very detailed sales information with them each week. Publishers also like Amazon's Web site where customers can provide their own input; this helps publishers gain an early sense about a new book title's likely sales and reader interest. Amazon.com still works closely with Ingram Books and other distributors, who continue to play an important role in providing fast deliveries of books and other hard-to-stock items to the company. By working with both publishers and distributors of books, Amazon has become a leading customer for shipping companies such as United Parcel Service (UPS).

Expansion and Growth

By 2001, Amazon.com had over thirty-five million customers around the world. The fast growth of Amazon in book retailing enabled the company to branch out into other retailing arenas as well. When the company offered its shares to the public in summer 1997, Amazon also began to sell CDs. Now, the company offers well over a hundred thousand music titles on its site. In 1999, Amazon also began selling DVDs, consumer electronics, toys, and even computer software. Customers can purchase all of these items with the same degree of ease, convenience, and security as they can with books. At the beginning of 2000, Amazon even considered setting up a credit card business, in which the company can utilize its massive marketing and customer database as a vast wellspring of information. However, because Amazon realizes that customers value their privacy and security, the company will not sell its database information to other marketing firms.

In one of the most important strategic shifts for the company, Amazon announced a series of alliances with traditional brick-and-mortar retailers to solidify its presence and to expand its product offerings during the past few years. In one of the biggest retailing arrangements ever announced for the toy retailing industry, Amazon.com joined forces with Toys "R" Us in August 2000 whereby Amazon will sell and warehouse a wide range of toys that are purchased and owned by the retailer. Both Amazon.com and Toys "R" Us share in the revenues earned from items purchased from Amazon's Web site. For Toys "R" Us, the relationship with Amazon is envisioned to help boost the company's sales in a "parent-friendly way." In fact, over the past few years, Amazon and Toys "R" Us have formed three separate on-line ventures to sell different types of toys and baby products to families. Most parents feel that shopping for toys with their children can sometimes become a trying experience, especially with long lines during the holiday season. On the other hand, parents may be more inclined to shop for toys through Amazon's Web site, since it is more convenient and allows the parent to control the shopping experience.

Even the types of products that Amazon is now offering has become complex and technically sophisticated, as compared with the company's traditional line of books and CDs. For example, Amazon entered into a relationship with Circuit City in July 2001 that is designed to greatly enlarge the range of consumer electronics devices that customers can buy from Amazon. Customers using Amazon's Web site will have the option of either ordering directly from Amazon or buying from Circuit City's broader array of merchandise. At present, customers have to go to a Circuit City store to pick up their purchase, but both companies are intent on offering home delivery in 2002. Circuit City will pay Amazon.com a small percentage on sales that are directed toward the electronics retailer.

Also in July 2001, Amazon announced that it would commence selling personal computers (PCs) through its Web site as well. Some analysts feel that the technical nature of PCs, and the high level of customer support needed to assist buyers, would overstretch Amazon's capabilities. To succeed in this particular market,

Amazon may be required to set up is own technical support departments, which are costly undertakings even for established PC firms such as Dell Computer and Gateway.

In September 2001, Amazon.com also announced a new relationship with Target Corporation, the nationwide discount retailer. This move is designed to help Amazon sell such items as home furnishings, sporting goods, and luggage, and both companies will share in the revenues.

As Amazon.com continues to strive for sustained levels of profitability in the next few years, the company has already set the standard for what consumers can expect from the Internet. In fact, Amazon has proved so successful in selling books and CDs over the 'Net that its longtime traditional competitor, Borders Group, decided to shut down its own Web site. In April 2001, Amazon announced that it would take over Borders' Internet-based operations. Borders had struggled with creating its own competing Web site for three years, and it never came close to matching Amazon's success. By the end of the fourth quarter of 2000, Borders had sold under $10 million worth of books, compared with $512 million for Amazon.com during the same period. Many financial analysts and strategists believe that Amazon.com will become an increasingly attractive partner for many traditional brick-and-mortar firms that have struggled with creating their own Internet Web sites to serve their customers. A few have predicted that Amazon.com might even form a close relationship with other such giant retailers as Wal-Mart Stores in the near future.

Introduction

In our previous chapters, we have seen how firms are attempting to build distinctive competence to create value for their customers. As technology and customer needs continue to evolve, so will the competitive drivers and underlying sources of competitive advantage that shape each firm's strategy. One of the most profound changes currently under way is the enormous growth of the Internet. Across all industries, the Internet has already begun to change the way that companies think about the way they do business. In fact, the Internet has spawned the creation of an entirely new medium in which companies can better reach and serve their customers.

This chapter is dedicated to understanding the impact of the Internet on building competitive advantage. Indeed, the Internet poses a significant opportunity, as well as a challenge, to both new entrants and established firms in their ongoing efforts to achieve distinction. In particular, the Internet is beginning to change how firms compete with one another, manage their value-creating activities, and develop new sources of competitive advantage. In short, the Internet has become an indispensable competitive tool.

We begin by examining how the Internet is transforming the relationship between companies and customers. We analyze the key characteristics of Internet-driven competition, attempting to highlight those industries that are especially shaped by the Internet's growth. We will also consider the different types of Internet-based business models that have evolved over the past few years. These include such variants as business-to-business, business-to-consumer, and consumer-to-consumer platforms that differ in how the Internet is used for business applications. Next, we focus on how the Internet can exert a dramatic impact on competitive strategy and advantage. We examine such evolving developments as disintermediation, changes in the firm's value chain, and the concept of network effects. Generally speaking, companies will have to compete in ways that emphasize faster response to customer needs, a high degree of personalized service, and a dramatic reduction in transaction costs in their activities. These ingredients are necessary to help build what might be termed virtual advantage. Finally, we assess how the Internet has challenged the way established firms manage their businesses, as well as their strengths and weaknesses when adopting this new technological medium.

Characteristics of Internet-Driven Competition

The growth of the Internet has the potential to transform how every firm relates to its customers and suppliers across a wide spectrum of industries. As the Amazon.com case reveals, the Internet is already becoming a huge force in the retailing industry, as customers can now order everything from books to pet foods without visiting a traditional, physically located store. Other industries feeling a similar impact from the Internet include financial services, airlines, travel services, broadcasting, and publishing. In short, the Internet provides a new medium by which companies can meet and support customers' needs regardless of distance and time. By using new technology to generate and transmit vast amounts of information, the Internet is now linking together customers, suppliers, employees, transportation companies, and other economic entities to provide real-time information on products and services, pricing, and availability.[2] Equally important, the Internet opens up new opportunities to create business relationships with almost anyone around the world. In general, the Internet offers the following opportunities:

- It can establish a direct link to customers and suppliers that lowers the cost of not only products and services but of activities required to support the transaction.
- It lets companies reduce the number of middlemen involved in order to reach the customer. In short, the Internet allows companies to bypass other firms that are in the value chain. For example, record label companies can begin to sell music directly to customers without going through traditional retailing outlets.
- It enables companies to access new customers in new markets in ways that were not possible with traditional distribution channels. Additionally, the Internet can help companies develop new products and services in ways that better match specific customers' needs. For example, large retailing firms can now sell their merchandise to people in rural areas where the small population size would not ordinarily justify the building of a store in that location. Likewise, financial service firms are now offering their customers information on how best to invest their money across a variety of different financial instruments, all of which can be accessed securely through the Internet.
- It allows companies to acquire real-time, valuable information on customers' needs and their likely buying patterns. Thus, the Internet can assist companies in their efforts to design or offer products and services to meet customers' needs faster. For example, Internet-based travel service firms can use a customer's previous purchase and flying history to send personalized e-mails informing him or her about future discounts on airfare to travel to his or her most frequent destinations.

The Rise of Internet-Based Business Platforms

Consequently, the massive growth and proliferation of the Internet in just the past few years has given rise to a new business vocabulary to describe this phenomenon. To better comprehend and utilize the Internet for their own business activities, many firms have actively invested in cutting-edge Internet-related technologies to take advantage of the opportunities mentioned above. Creating Web sites on the Internet is just one small part of a company's effort in this new arena. In fact, companies around the world are investing billions of dollars to build up an entire new set of firm infrastructure, such as advanced computer systems, customer databases, real-time information sharing systems, and Internet-based ordering/tracking systems that provide the customer with both convenience and security of performing transactions on line. Some business commentators and analysts have labeled these companies' efforts as either electronic business or electronic commerce activities (e-business or e-commerce for short). Briefly speaking, **e-business** (or e-commerce)

e-business: The use of Internet-based technologies to transform how a business interacts with its customers and suppliers.

is the use of advanced Internet-driven technology to transform how a firm interacts with its customers and suppliers. On a broader level, e-business can incorporate all or parts of a transaction between a buyer and a seller. In its most sophisticated application, e-business can perform the entire range of value-adding activities to support a customer's request through the Internet. This includes supplying information about a company's products and services through an on-line catalog, providing real-time pricing, allowing for direct and secure payment of funds from the customer, enabling the customer to check on his or her order and delivery status, and managing the logistics of delivering the actual end product or service to the customer at his or her location. Of course, many specific customer needs cannot be met entirely through the Internet, such as professional services (e.g., medicine, law, veterinary services, architecture) or those in which a high degree of live, personal interaction is required (e.g., choice of wedding gowns, automotive repair work). Even in these businesses, though, companies can still use many aspects of Internet technologies to facilitate their activities, such as scheduling customer requests, managing inventory, billing, and record keeping.

Not all Internet-driven businesses are the same, however. In fact, the way that firms sell products and services to retail customers is quite different from how firms use the Internet to work with its suppliers and other business partners. In addition, there are some Internet-based businesses that effectively allow customers to relate directly to one another, often in the form of on-line auction houses whereby customers are able to transact with other customers. The three most common Internet-based platforms are (1) business-to-business, (2) business-to-consumer, and (3) consumer-to-consumer. (See Exhibit 5-1.)

EXHIBIT 5-1 Major Types of Internet Commerce Platforms

- **Business-to-Business:** Designed to help firms streamline costs and efforts to work with other firms, especially suppliers. Examples abound in chemicals, automotive, aerospace, metals, and plastics.
- **Business-to-Consumer:** Provides a new medium and channel to reach customers with greater emphasis on convenience, customization, and speed. Early examples include books, music, toys, airline tickets, and financial services.
- **Consumer-to-Consumer:** Allows consumer to interact directly with other consumers to match needs. Auction sites, employment/job searches, and hobby interests are some primary examples.

Business-to-Business Platforms. The basic idea behind the business-to-business (B-to-B) Internet platform is that firms are looking for ways to radically lower the transaction costs of working with suppliers. As discussed in Chapter 3, transaction costs involve searching, negotiating and working with suppliers or other companies (in the marketplace) in order to provide inputs or services that the firm cannot or does not provide for itself. During the late 1990s, companies of all sizes, including General Electric, Cisco Systems, Honeywell, General Motors, Ford, and United Technologies, have invested heavily in new on-line information systems that tightly link their operations with those of their key suppliers. By using the Internet to foster closer communications and cost sharing with their suppliers, all of these firms are hoping to achieve major reductions in both the cost of their supplies, as well as the time required to process the paperwork and other documentation that accompanies a highly complex ordering system. Some companies, such as General Electric and General Motors, work with thousands of suppliers, each one of which often has its own set of forms and procedures involved with ordering parts and other needed inputs. In fact, the most likely benefit arising from Internet-driven B-to-B platforms will be potential cost savings amounting to billions of dollars every year for America's largest companies by streamlining processes that often require hundreds of people to track and monitor shipments, billing, payments, and deliveries each day. For example, by working together with suppliers to design, share, and implement common ordering and parts-numbering systems, U.S. automakers are looking to slice as much as $3 billion per year in back-room processing costs.

Most B-to-B Internet platforms and sites focus on achieving substantial cost reductions within a given industry. This is not unexpected, since each industry often exhibits its own specific ordering patterns and ways of doing business that were shaped from many years of growth and management practice. For example, a variety of different B-to-B initiatives have sprung up over the past two years, including such Internet sites as Chemdex.com and Chemconnect.com (for linking together buyers and sellers in the chemical industry), Plastics.com (for the plastics industry), Emetals.com and Esteel.com (for the metallurgical industry), and even MyAircraft.com for aerospace parts (a joint initiative by Honeywell and United Technologies). Oftentimes, these Internet sites will even bring together competitors to fund the Internet platform, since it is in each firm's interest to ensure that a standardized ordering, billing, and payment system applies to suppliers who may actually sell to a number of different competitors in the industry.

Business-to-Consumer Platforms. Business-to-consumer (B-to-C) Internet platforms are those designed by individual firms to help reach and serve their retail customers. The vast majority of recent Internet-based businesses that were created in the late 1990s were based on numerous variants of the B-to-C platform. Amazon.com, for example, is a leading practitioner of a B-to-C strategy, in which Amazon hopes to sell books, CDs, videos, toys, and even electronic products to customers around the world. The company's approach to serving customers has set the standard for what customers have come to expect when shopping on-line: convenience, security, wide product availability, and fast turnaround of orders and shipments. By the end of 2001, all of the major retail chains had developed their own versions of B-to-C Internet platforms that complement their own traditional brick and mortar retail sites.

Business-to-consumer Internet platforms differ significantly from those designed for business-to-business transactions. First, most of these Web sites are designed to serve customers who may not be able to or desire to visit a physical retail site. Customers typically can receive the same merchandise that they would ordinarily buy in a regular store.

Second, each company will typically create its own Web site and Internet platform for its own use. Unlike the business-to-business Internet platform, whereby several competitors will join together to create the Web site and ordering system, the business-to-consumer platform is really another separate channel that each company creates for its own purposes. Often, retailers will want to keep their own Web sites distinctive and reflective of their own merchandise, their own pricing structure, and their own special offers that they provide to their customer base.

Third, business-to-consumer Internet platforms are designed to be easy to use so as to enhance the customer's experience and to facilitate repeat business. In the consumer-based retailing environment, customers are free to switch among different Web sites in much the same way that they can do comparison shopping among different stores. There are no real switching costs for consumers to shop across a variety of different Internet-based retailers. However, with business-to-business Internet sites, the economic objective is somewhat different. When dealing with suppliers and other business partners, firms are looking to use the Internet to lock in their suppliers and to share costs and other critical data. Thus, firms are hoping to use the Internet not only to lower the costs of their supplies and inputs but also to reduce the coordination costs involved with complex ordering and purchase requirements. Many firms are hoping to use the business-to-business Internet platforms to raise the switching costs of their suppliers and thus lock them in with preferred pricing, ordering, or delivery arrangements.

Literally hundreds of different B-to-C retailers are on the Internet. For example, Amazon.com's most potent competitor so far includes that of Barnes & Noble's barnesandnoble.com, a rival seeking to sell an equally broad range of books, videos and other gift items. Other B-to-C retailers include the "brick-and-click" sites of L.L. Bean,

Lands' End, Petopia.com, Petsmart.com, and Tiffany.com—all of which lead in providing a high degree of convenience and ease when using these sites.

Customer-to-Customer Platforms. The third most prevalent Internet business platform focuses on providing an easy way to engage in customer-to-customer transactions. Unlike B-to-B and B-to-C, these Web sites are not attempting to buy or to sell inputs or merchandise from one economic entity to another. On the other hand, customer-to-customer (C-to-C) Internet platforms are designed to bring together people who ordinarily would have no other way to sell their own goods to prospective buyers. In many ways, these sites are akin to electronic auction houses or flea markets, where buyers and sellers negotiate their own prices through bids that are taken through the Internet.

One of the best-known customer-to-customer Internet platforms is that of e-Bay, which allows customers to place their own goods for bids by other buyers through a vast collection of different categories (e.g., books, toys, historical artifacts, golf clubs, sports memorabilia, comic books, antiques, etc.). Prospective sellers place a description of their items, as well as photographs, for listing on e-Bay's Web site. In turn, buyers at their convenience can place bids for what they think the item is worth; e-Bay, in turn, makes money by charging a small percentage fee off each transaction, just as any auction house would in a traditional non-Internet environment.

How Traditional Business Differs from E-Business

While the Internet will continue to reshape how firms interact with their customers and suppliers, there are some significant differences between traditional and Internet-driven business practices. Some of the most important ones are listed in Exhibit 5-2.

EXHIBIT 5-2 Key Differences between E-Business and Traditional Business

E-Business	Traditional Business
• Always open and on—24/7	• Limited by time constraints/schedules
• No geographical boundaries	• Physical location important
• High pricing transparency	• Uneven availability of pricing
• Decisions have fast impact	• Decisions take time to implement
• Immediate competitor response	• Competitor response time lagging
• Customer has more power	• Supplier usually has more power
• Easy to compare rival offerings	• Effort required to compare offerings
• Firm is part of larger value network	• High distance between firms with suppliers and customers
• Convenience and cost are key—defined by customer	• Convenience and cost defined by supplier in many cases

Around-the-Clock Availability. Businesses in more traditional settings, such as retailing and financial services, are limited by existing time constraints, imposed because of tradition, legal requirement, or economics. For example, retailing chains in most parts of the country do not operate on a twenty-four-hour basis, simply because too few customers make purchases in the late hours of the night or early morning. Those that do, such as a select number of grocery store chains in major cities, offer this service as a convenience to their customers, but usually incur higher labor and operating expenses.

One of the biggest changes brought about by the Internet is the ability to service customers' needs twenty-four hours per day, seven days a week. On-line businesses are always open and able to accept customers' requests for information or to receive their orders. For example, Amazon.com's entire range of product offerings from books and CDs to gifts and toys are available for customers to evaluate and purchase around the clock. Once a customer places an order, even in the wee hours of the morning, he or she will automatically receive an e-mail confirmation of the order's receipt and likely delivery time.

No Geographical Boundaries. Because of the ubiquitous nature of the Internet, businesses can now interact with customers and suppliers no matter where they may be. Consider the case of General Electric. This huge U.S. provider of aircraft engines, plastics, medical equipment, and financial services works with customers and suppliers anywhere around the world. In fact, GE actively uses the Internet to search for promising new suppliers wherever they may be. At the same time, GE's advanced Internet-based technology enables it to serve its customers anywhere at anytime. In fact, many of GE's latest medical equipment have an on-line internal diagnostic feature that automatically notifies a GE repair center in advance of when the equipment is likely to fail. This prevents hospitals and clinics from incurring costly mechanical breakdowns and helps GE schedule preventive maintenance requests automatically through the Internet.

Widespread Availability of Pricing Data. The Internet makes pricing of goods and services fully transparent to customers and suppliers worldwide. For example, customers can readily compare the prices of such services as airline tickets, hotel rooms, car rentals, and entertainment using different on-line travel service firms, such as Expedia.com or Travelocity.com. Pricing data is not limited to services alone. In fact, several on-line companies are using the Internet to make comparison shopping among different makes of automobiles much easier. Firms such as automallusa.com, vehix.com, and autobytel.com, for example, allow customers to compare the costs of new and used vehicles in their area. All customers need to do is to enter in their ZIP code, their make and model of vehicle desired, and they are provided with pricing data for that vehicle and participating dealer information.

The impact of full pricing transparency helps business customers secure the needed raw materials and components that they need from their business suppliers as well. For example, chemical and steel companies in their respective industries have come together in a series of joint initiatives to provide on-line product "catalogs" that also match buyers' needs with suppliers' inventory. Buyers can compare the industrial offerings that different suppliers make available and then negotiate an acceptable price through the Internet.

Immediate Competitor Response. One of most telling effects of the Internet has been to accelerate dramatically a competitor's response to a company's moves. For example, when one competitor announces a price cut over the Internet, its competitors will almost immediately follow and match it. Conversely, when an on-line retailer is the first to provide a highly sought-after product (e.g., a wildly popular toy for the December holiday season), other retailers are forced to respond in order to secure their own toy supplies so as to not lose their customers. Thus, the Internet has compelled every firm to respond faster to its competitors' actions.

More Information Power for the Customer. Another major change brought about by the Internet is that customers have access to a huge array of information than was previously ever available. They now have the ability to compare product offerings easily from a large number of suppliers, and they can potentially make more informed decisions before they buy. Chat rooms enable prospective customers to speak with other customers to discuss product quality and features on-line. Customers can even contact firms directly to inquire about specific product attributes, delivery times, and other related matters. Some advanced Web sites even allow customers to visit new homes on the market through advanced 3-D images on the Internet. In sum, as customers gain more access to product and pricing information, they are in a much better position to negotiate with suppliers.

Equally important, customers can now freely access information on a wide range of topics from a number of different sources. For example, people can now use the Internet as a real-time encyclopedia to look up and research almost any topic, ranging from health issues (e.g., WebMD.com), to locate restaurants in a given city, to find out weather conditions, and even to search for real estate in different parts of the country. In effect, information that was previously hard to find is now becoming widely available and, in most cases, even offered free.

Economic Drivers of Internet-Based Competition

As we are currently seeing, companies in every industry are using the Internet to reshape their business activities. By offering an entirely new way to reach their customers and suppliers, the Internet is also beginning to even change the underlying economic structure of some industries. In fact, in certain industries the Internet's impact has been especially profound. It is no accident that some of the earliest arenas most affected by the Internet include retailing, travel services, financial services, publishing, and media. Products and services such as pet supplies, office supplies, mutual funds, and airline tickets are among the first businesses that were directly influenced by the Internet. While there are numerous economic drivers that determine how the Internet will impact an individual product or service, some of the most important considerations include the following attributes (see also Exhibit 5-3).

EXHIBIT 5-3 Key Drivers of Internet-Based Business Models

- High information intensity
- Wide product selection
- Customer understands the nature of product/service
- Customer value customization/convenience
- Product pricing highly transparent
- Product availability fluctuates
- Customer able to compare offerings on product variations

digitization: The conversion of information into binary form (0s and 1s). Digitization is a key reason why information-based industries are rapidly moving to the Internet.

High Information Intensity. One of the most important drivers of Internet-based competition is the extent to which a product or service can be digitally transmitted over computer and telecommunication networks. **Digitization** refers to the conversion of information into digital or binary (0s and 1s) form. Anything that can be transmitted over traditional communication media (e.g., print, radio, television, magnetic tape) can be converted into digital form and thus is susceptible to Internet-based competition. This means that all information-intensive businesses, especially financial services, travel reservations, and publishing, lend themselves to digital transmission, since this data can easily be converted into binary form for computer processing and storage. In particular, the Internet has a huge sway over companies such as AOL Time Warner (which owns CNN, Warner Music, and *Time* magazine), for example, since news, entertainment and publishing represent information that is constantly updated and replenished. Brokerage companies such as Merrill Lynch, Fidelity Investments, and Charles Schwab use the Internet not only to serve their customers but also to relay and process financial information that is literally updated each second of the day. News and financial information can be downloaded daily. As the costs of digital storage and transmission drop rapidly, information-rich products of any kind are likely to be found on the Internet.

In the most extreme situations, the Internet can transform or even eliminate entire businesses. Encyclopaedia Britannica, for example, faced precipitously declining sales of its traditionally hardbound books that were becoming more expensive every year. Now, the company is making the encyclopedia freely available over the Internet. In return, Britannica hopes to survive by charging advertisers a fee for listing their products on its company Web site. Each time a reader searches for an entry in the on-line version of *Encyclopaedia Britannica*, he or she will also see advertisements offering other products.

Wide Product Selection. When there is a wide selection of products, the Internet often becomes an important medium to reach customers. For example, the enormous number of books and CDs makes it difficult for individual stores, even the large chains, to stock all that customers may want to purchase. Shelf space is very limited for most retailers. The costs of purchasing and holding such a large inventory becomes prohibitive, even for the largest chains such as Borders and Barnes & Noble. More important, traditional retailing chains may only stock the books and music that are the most popular (and therefore most likely to sell), thus leaving many selections unavailable for customers. On the other hand, it is easy for Amazon.com to offer books and music through the Internet because it ships products to customers only when the company has received a firm order. Customers are purchasing an increasing number of other products such as toys and videos for much the same reason. In a similar vein, automobile dealers will participate in such Internet-based initiatives as autobytel.com and automallusa.com in order to reach a broader base of customers. At the same time, prospective car buyers use these sites to reduce the effort required to search for the car they want to buy at the right price.

Well-Understood Products. The Internet is a powerful driver of competition in those industries where customers understand the nature of the product. For example, airline tickets, hotel rooms, office supplies, and pet supplies lend themselves to sales over the Internet because buyers know what they are purchasing. Often, these products are not complex and do not require extensive trial by customers. Moreover, these products do not change over time and typically are highly mature. In the case of the pet food industry, many retailers have sprung up over the past few years to supply customers with products with which they are already familiar. Petopia.com and Petsmart.com offer frequent shoppers additional discounts for the foods and supplies that their pets consume on a regular basis. Purchasers like the fact that they can order their pet care products from these sites without much hassle and receive a discount as well. Likewise, on-line travel service companies such as Priceline.com, Expedia.com and Travelocity.com offer a wide array of airline tickets and hotel rooms through the Internet, and customers do not hesitate buying from these firms because they know what they are receiving.

Fluctuating Product Availability. The Internet is well suited to sales of products whose availability changes rapidly, even on a day-to-day basis. For example, customers will frequently use the Internet to browse different on-line retailers and auction sites to search for hard-to-find toys and video games during the December holiday season. Also, customers can use the Internet to search for out-of-print books that traditional book retailers are unlikely to carry. Business customers frequently use the Internet to purchase hard-to-locate products or inputs that they need for their own operations. For example, automotive manufacturers will frequently use the Internet to widen their search for vendors of specialty plastics or electronics that may not be readily available from their established suppliers. Often, industrial buyers who face highly fluctuating availability of components will use the Internet to scour the world for other suppliers that can provide an immediate shipment or a back-up source of supply.

On the other hand, certain types of products and services cannot be easily sold or provided over the Internet. Products that require extensive after-sales support, such as sophisticated electronic or medical equipment, are often sold face to face. Buyers will often have numerous technical questions and will usually request demonstrations on-site. Although companies such as General Electric and United Technologies will use the Internet to help schedule preventive maintenance or even provide on-line diagnostic testing, initial product sales typically require a close working knowledge of the buyer's needs. Products that require personal customer trial also do not lend themselves to easy on-line sales. This explains why it is difficult to sell clothing and shoes over the Internet, since sizes may vary across manufacturers. Customers also prefer speaking directly with informed salespeople when buying materials or products for highly complex activities, such as installing new kitchen appliances or building a swimming pool. In these situations, customers will probably feel comfortable receiving advice from more experienced professionals, rather than attempting to explain something over the Internet or even the telephone.

The Internet's Impact on Competitive Strategy

The rise of the Internet has also heralded a major change in how companies formulate their competitive strategies. As speed and fast response to competitors' moves become essential to compete, the Internet has redefined the competitive environment in a number of different ways. Some of the most significant changes on competitive strategy that the Internet has brought about include (1) disintermediation, (2) modifying the value chain's structure, and (3) network effects on competition. (See Exhibit 5-4.)

EXHIBIT 5-4 Impact of the Internet on Competitive Strategy

- **Disintermediation:** Removal of distributors or middlemen that separate provider from consumer
- **Value Chain Effects:** Redefinition and shifts in what firms do to provide value to customers; may involve more outsourcing and a greater focus on personal service. Also may promote the rise of "infomediaries"—information providers that serve as industry sources of pricing, products, and suppliers.
- **Rise of Network Effects:** More profound in technology-driven products, less prevalent in retailing activities or businesses

Disintermediation and Redefinition of the Value Chain

disintermediation: The bypassing of middlemen and other economic entities that once separated firms from their customers.

One change of great magnitude is the growing extent of disintermediation in many industries. Briefly stated, **disintermediation** refers to the bypassing of middlemen or other economic entities that once separated firms from their customers. In other words, firms can now use the Internet to sidestep distributors, wholesalers, and even retailers in order to sell products and services directly to customers. Thus, as disintermediation takes root across different industries, the value chain will also change to reflect this "compression" of activities. As firms attempt to use the Internet to sell directly to their customers, they will be performing many activities that were once in the domain of other entities that served roles as economic intermediaries. Also, a different type of electronically connected intermediary will likely become an important force in many industries' value chains.

Effect on Distributors. In the airline industry, we are now witnessing the process by which airline companies are disintermediating travel agents on a nationwide scale. As firms such as American Airlines, United Airlines, and Delta Air Lines start selling their tickets directly to consumers over the Internet, they are simultaneously removing a big portion of revenues that travel agents once shared before the Internet became so pervasive. This ongoing push by the airlines to direct sales of tickets, combined with steady reductions in the amount of commissions they pay to travel agents, has resulted in an enormous shrinkage in the number of travel agents that exist in the United States today. At the same time, a new form of intermediary has risen to take the place of traditional travel agencies. These are the on-line travel service firms that serve as giant clearinghouses that match customers with airlines, hotel chains, vacation cruise lines, and car rentals. Firms such as Travelocity.com, Expedia.com, Orbitz, and Priceline.com provide a different source of value from travel agents because they can update their real-time databases on pricing, capacity, and availability instantaneously. They also allow customers to search for the best possible price on different carriers from the convenience of their own chosen location (e.g., at home, work, via cell phone, etc.).

Disintermediation has also occurred in a number of other industries as well, such as in music and personal computers (PCs). Record label companies (e.g., Sony, Vivendi Universal, Bertelsmann) are now experimenting with ways to sell music on-line to their customers through the Internet. This means that listeners may not have to visit CD music retailers in the future if the companies continue to push in this direction.

Also, several PC manufacturers are attempting to sell computers directly to consumers, at the risk of alienating their long-time wholesalers and distributors that used to be their exclusive partners. For example, both Compaq Computer and Hewlett-Packard have attempted to emulate Dell Computer by offering some variants of their PCs directly to consumers over the Internet. Dell Computer, as we have seen in Chapter 2, has always sold its PCs directly over the phone or the Internet and thus is not pursuing a direct disintermediation strategy since it has never relied on wholesalers and retailers as part of its strategy.

In many commodity-based industries such as energy, metals, and plastics, the Internet has actually given way to the rise of a new type of an industry-specific intermediary (the B-to-B platform) that supplements traditional supply and distribution channels. In addition to helping firms dramatically lower their procurement, ordering and other transaction costs, these platforms also help serve to link up buyers and sellers for products and inputs within a given industry. For example, Web sites such as Chemconnect.com, Chemdex.com, and Emetals.com represent digital clearinghouses that serve to match buyers and sellers of commodities whose prices and availability can fluctuate significantly in a short time span. These intermediaries also provide real-time information about the state of pricing trends in the industry. By serving as an on-line exchange or hub that matches buyers and sellers, they are effectively taking on important new distribution-related activities in their respective industry's value chain.

Effect on Value Chains. In general, the Internet accelerates the process of disintermediation across industries because it is much easier for suppliers and customers to communicate with one another. Thus, the number and composition of wholesalers and retailers for many consumer-based products and services will change dramatically in the next few years. More important, customers prefer in many cases to deal directly with manufacturers or service providers, since they often can purchase the products at lower cost (without paying the additional mark-up that accompanies traditional retailing channels). Manufacturers and service providers will sometimes attempt to sell directly to consumers because it helps them even out their production or capacity requirements. Airline companies, for example, will offer special fares on their Web sites that can only be purchased on the Internet in order to fill up planes that appear to have fewer passengers than they anticipated. Manufacturers will sell computers and other electronic equipment for much the same reason—to reduce the amount of inventory they are holding. Thus, in some industries, the value chain may become further compressed as firms and customers interact more closely than before. To continue to survive, wholesalers and retailers, however, will probably have to invest more of their resources and time to building up their service capabilities, especially for those products that require significant after-sales technical support.

At the same time, there will likely be a rise in the number of new types of Internet-based intermediaries that play an important role in matching customers with suppliers, especially in the commercial business-to-business realm. While these platforms can do much to lower procurement costs and further link up firms with key suppliers, they also exercise an increasingly important role as an information hub for the industry. These new economic entities have been described by some researchers as "infomediaries"—companies that specialize in the acquisition and widespread dissemination of real-time information to customers. For those industries that utilize these new types of B-to-B electronic platforms or hubs, the value chain will actually become more efficient as buyers and sellers can interact with one another using real-time information to get the best possible pricing and availability of key products or inputs. In addition, the B-to-B platform can provide a high degree of ordering, billing, and payment consistency and paperwork reduction among the key firms and suppliers within an industry.[3]

Network Effects on Competition

Changes in the industry's value chain, as well as the critical strategic role that information plays in Internet-driven businesses, lay the foundation for some firms to grow very quickly. In fact, some companies may be able to use the power of the Internet to reshape the competitive dynamics of an entire industry. One of the most important characteristics of Internet-driven competition is the prevalence of what some economists call network-based effects. **Network effects** refer to the phenomenon in which the value of any product or service rises as more people use it. The notion of a network effect stems from the observation that as more people use a given product (e.g., telephone, fax machine, Internet), then the value of being connected to it will rise also. Information-rich products and services often exhibit high network effects. For example, computer operating system software (e.g., Microsoft's Windows 2000 and XP) has a very strong network effect because as more people use it, the more likely that other software applications will be developed for it. Over time, this makes the software more valuable to the people who own it, since they can take advantage of future offerings based on this platform. Likewise, for companies that develop computer software, network effects often means a potentially very profitable product. Once the fixed costs of developing software are paid off, each and every additional sale represents pure profit. Network effects in the software business help to explain the enormous profitability that Microsoft was able to capture by ensuring that its Windows operating system became the standard for the entire industry.[4]

network effects: An economic condition in which the value of a product or service rises as more people utilize it.

For Internet-based businesses, network effects may play an important role in how firms leverage critical mass to build new sources of competitive advantage. America Online (a unit of AOL Time Warner), for example, appears to have captured a large and growing share of subscribers who use its service to access the Internet. By winning over thirty million subscribers, America Online's AOL service is increasingly seen as the de facto standard that has defined the high level of customer ease and convenience for on-line services. AOL has attracted a growing subscriber base over the past few years, even as it began to raise its subscription fees. Thus, AOL's dominant position could strengthen further, as network effects reinforce the company's critical mass in Internet services. Already, the company is able to offer a vast array of information-based offerings from such sister business units as CNN, Warner Music, and other assets of the larger AOL Time Warner company. Other companies will be forced to design their own Internet service features based on the quality levels set by AOL. More important, AOL's strong market position gives the firm enormous leeway and initiative in designing new types of innovative services for its subscriber base. For example, AOL's Instant Messenger service is thought to be the foundation for a new type of telephone service that bypasses traditional telecommunications providers. If AOL is successful in pushing its Instant Messenger service as a new form of Internet-based telephony, then AOL's position is likely to become even stronger, since it can offer its subscribing customers the equivalent of free local and long-distance telecommunications over its system.[5]

The desire to secure powerful network effects has led many Internet-based businesses to expand rapidly in order to build on first-mover advantages. As you may recall from Chapter 3, first-mover advantages are the benefits that a firm enjoys from being the first to enter a market. Many Internet-based retailers, for example, expanded so fast in 1999 and 2000 that they were hoping to capture network effects by establishing a very sizable and well-recognized presence in cyberspace. By aggressively advertising their presence and offering products at exceptionally lower prices, many Internet firms such as Petopia.com, Pets.com, Staples.com, and eToys hoped to become the dominant standard for their respective industry's Web site. In fact, an entirely new set of business models was created in which many companies hoped to become the dominant, overwhelming firm in that industry. Yet, network effects proved hard to sustain, since it is difficult to lock in customers in such a way that they would shop exclusively at only one company's Web site. These first-mover advantages were largely illusory, because a host of competitors entered the market at the same time. As a result, many of these initiatives failed. Network effects tend to exist only when customers have a strong need to connect with a given provider's standard, technology, product architecture, or method of operation. To sustain network effects, companies have to rely on an increasing number of long-term, if not permanent, customers. Customers using Internet-based retailers, however, typically do not face high switching costs that are an important basis for strong network effects. Thus, there are comparatively few, if any, network effects for firms engaged solely in Internet retailing.

This extremely fast growth resulted in huge economic and organizational challenges related to the fixed costs of running the business. In many cases, revenue growth was artificially depressed, because these firms often sold products at such a low price that it was tantamount to giving the products away. Other companies offered special discounts where customers did not pay the costs for shipping and delivery, thus forcing companies to spend precious cash on activities that represented an extra financial burden. Still other firms provided special incentives to customers who brought in referrals of their families and friends to purchase on-line. These incentives also represented major hits to profitability, since these companies had to develop special software and databases to track the referrals, as well as provide even larger discounts to their most frequent shoppers.

The cumulative effect of rapid expansion, combined with the apparent lack of network effects, resulted in a massive number of bankruptcies and business collapses for Internet retailers in 2001 and 2002. Dozens, if not hundreds, of Internet-based retailing sites have shuttered operations because they could not turn a profit.[6] One of the most stunning collapses in this arena includes the long list of companies that attempted to create an on-line grocery shopping service. Internet-based firms such as Webvan, Groceryworks.com, and Peapod attempted to bring a high level of convenience and ease to customers who did not want to hassle with the long lines of purchasing groceries in traditional retailing outlets. However, all three of these firms suffered from extremely high fixed costs resulting from large investments in warehouses, distribution and sorting facilities, advanced computer systems, and trucks for shipment. Moreover, the high degree of perishability of many items meant that these firms had to sell their items quickly, often at steep discounts in order to avoid a high level of inventory. By 2002, all of these companies had either filed for bankruptcy or were purchased by other firms.[7]

The Internet and Virtual Advantage

The phenomenal rise of business activities on the Internet is beginning to create a new set of rules and playbook in order to build competitive advantage. Concepts such as disintermediation, first-mover advantages, and network effects are some of the broad drivers of Internet-based competition. However, each individual firm still needs to build its own set of distinctive activities that become the basis for a competitive advantage. Although the Internet has clearly modified the structure and dynamics of some industries, the principles of competitive advantage remain the same. A company can only be as profitable as the distinctiveness of its value-creating activities.

Because the Internet has made it possible for firms to interact with their suppliers and customers in many new ways, it is imperative that companies build sources of competitive advantage that apply information and knowledge in new ways. At the same time, they must focus on a limited number of activities around which they can build strong distinction. This combination of applying knowledge and well-defined activity focus lays the foundation for what we term virtual advantage. **Virtual advantage** refers to the ability of firms

virtual advantage: A type of competitive advantage based on speed, fast turnaround, and deep knowledge of customers' needs to create value faster than what competitors can do, often by focusing on a few core value-adding activities to leverage speed, fast turnaround, and knowledge of customers' needs to create and deliver value faster than one's competitors by focusing on a few core value-adding activities. Oftentimes, firms building sources of virtual advantage will rely heavily on their business partners and suppliers to undertake the remaining value-chain activities that they have chosen not to perform. Building virtual advantage is especially critical for Internet-based businesses because the barriers to entry, particularly in on-line retailing, are fairly low. However, the concept of virtual advantage is not exclusive only to Internet-based firms; brick-and-mortar companies can also develop sources of virtual advantage when they apply speed, turnaround and customer knowledge to innovate or to create products faster and at lower costs than their competitors as well. For example, Dell Computer's dominant position in personal computers (see Chapter 2) resulted from the company's ability to build virtual advantage by customizing PCs and delivering them fast to its customers. Dell relies heavily on its key suppliers to deliver key components and parts in order to minimize its inventory holding costs and the need to build expensive warehouses and storage facilities. Some of the most important components of virtual advantage are discussed in the following sections. (See Exhibit 5-5.)

EXHIBIT 5-5 Emerging Generic Sources of Virtual Advantage

- Speed of response
- Fast turnaround
- Deep knowledge of customer
- Customization of offering
- High convenience to customer
- Consistency of customer service
- Customer controls the relationship

Speed and Fast Turnaround

Lean operations that place a high premium on fast turnaround of inventory are a must for Internet-based businesses. Ideally, the firm would stock very little inventory (if any at all) and work closely with its suppliers to ensure that products are available for immediate shipment once an order is received. Suppliers and logistics firms (e.g., UPS, FedEx) must be tightly integrated with the firm's scheduling, ordering, and delivery systems. Equally important, financial and operational information must be gathered, collated, synthesized, and processed quickly at each activity stage. In particular, business processes related to ordering, shipping, billing, and accounts payable must function on a real-time basis. By updating these processes instantaneously, the firm can provide full information to both its suppliers and customers about the status of orders and deliveries. This information forms the nucleus for the firm's ability to track emerging patterns of market demand as well as to provide a high level of personalized service to each customer. All customer support functions should be at the center of a company's database and technical infrastructure.

Customer Knowledge and Intimacy

Customer service will become a critical, if not the most important, factor that Internet-based businesses must develop and cultivate. These businesses must offer high levels of customer service simply because many customers will initially be reluctant to make on-line purchases for such reasons as security, lack of reputation, lack of personnel to answer questions, and so forth. As recent upstarts, most on-line retailers lack significant experience that would significantly lower its cost structure over time (see Chapter 3). In fact, Internet-based businesses must go beyond simply offering fast and efficient service; they must attempt to foster a high level of customer intimacy with shoppers. **Customer intimacy** refers to a deep knowledge of what motivates a customer to buy. These include factors such as his or her specific needs, decision-making processes, and receptiveness to trying new products. The result of pursuing customer intimacy is a high degree of customer loyalty in return. Because most on-line retailers operate in a virtual environment (lacking physical stores), customer intimacy becomes an essential competitive tool that helps these firms attempt to differentiate themselves from traditional retailers. To provide a high level of customer intimacy, retailers need to provide a high degree of customization, convenience and security, and an ability to anticipate customers' future needs.[8]

customer intimacy: A deep knowledge of what motivates a customer to buy; often used in the context of fostering a high degree of communication with the customer to earn his or her loyalty.

Customization. On-line retailers and providers of service need to provide a high level of product and service customization in order to win over their customers. In fact, offering customized products and services enables the on-line provider to give customers a higher degree of control in managing the relationship. For example, many on-line travel service firms such as Travelocity.com and Expedia.com encourage customers to create their own ideal vacation packages from a variety of different airlines, hotel firms, vacation cruise lines and car rental firms. All customers need to do is to provide their dates and times of their proposed vacation, the amount they wish to spend, and where they want to go. The travel firms' advanced search and matching software will then attempt to create a series of different vacation sites that leaves the choice entirely up to the customer to accept.

Financial service firms offer a high degree of customization in the kinds of products they offer to their on-line customers. For example, American Express, Fidelity Investments and Charles Schwab offer a vast array of different products and services that customers can use to create their own financial plans based on their personal priorities. Both firms offer hundreds of different mutual funds, as well as annuities, brokerage accounts, stock research, insurance products, retirement accounts, access to their 401(k) plans, and even estate-planning tools. Fidelity and Schwab will even offer products from competing firms in order to help customers find the best possible value for their own objectives. Customers are encouraged to freely browse through and select those offerings that best match their financial profile based on the information they provide (e.g., age, years to retirement, college funding for children, long-term care, etc.). These "smart" Web sites will also provide a sample of different investment plans depending on each customer's risk preferences and likely future needs.

Some companies will take customization a step further and develop a strategy based on personalization. **Personalization** is the creation of a unique mix or set of products and services designed for a specific individual's needs. The objective behind personalization-based strategies is to treat each customer, no matter where he or she may be, as a truly distinct individual that deserves high personal attention and respect. For example, on-line pet supply retailers such as Petopia.com and Petsmart.com encourage customers to provide information about the specific needs and eating habits of their pets. Once information about a pet (or pets) is entered into the company's database, Petopia.com will send periodic e-mails informing the pet owner of special deals on health products, toys, and food for that special companion. Some of these Web sites even offer a continuous replenishment program in which customers can prearrange deliveries of pet food, litter, and other supplies according to their individual pet's habits.

personalization: The creation of a unique mix or set of products and services catered to a specific individual's needs.

Customers can also use some companies' Web sites as a virtual calendar to remind them of important events during the year. For example, on-line clothing retailers Lands' End and L.L. Bean have advanced Web sites that offer customers the choice of individualized gift selections that have been preselected according to important anniversary or birthdays in their family. L.L. Bean's Web site will even provide a large amount of helpful information about how to best use the company's products for specific uses, such as camping, mountain climbing, and biking. L.L. Bean strives to provide the same high quality of personalized service on its Web site that customers come to expect from visiting its retail locations.

In effect, personalization strategies attempt to treat *each customer as a market segment of one*. Moreover, Internet retailers are hoping that as customers feel more comfortable with the shopping experience and are treated with a high level of service, then they will be more likely to purchase more higher-priced products when they revisit the site.

Convenience. Internet-based businesses need to design their business processes from their customers' perspective. Both business-to-business and business-to-consumer platforms need to make convenience, security, and user-friendliness the defining features of the customer's experience with the Web site. In effect, the best Web sites are those that *encourage the customer to learn and to help him- or herself perform transactions*. Customers should be able to find product information, enter their orders securely, access their previous purchase history, find out about their orders' status, and determine when the products will be shipped and delivered. Unlike traditional businesses, in which customers often are routed from one department to another to find information or to resolve problems, Internet business platforms need to have a total customer focus whereby every possible question or concern that the customer may have can be addressed immediately through the click of a mouse. In fact, customers should be able to access the same information and troubleshooting procedures that are available to the company's own technical personnel.

This issue could present a huge problem for established firms, since preexisting computer hardware systems ("legacy systems") need to be synchronized and meshed with Internet-based systems. For example, customers who use the Internet today may want to access their own purchase histories from years ago. These records are likely to be stored in a different computer system or, worse yet, in paper form that has not been digitally archived. For traditional businesses especially, the Web site should be fully integrated into the company's preexisting call centers, telephone-based sales departments, physical retail or service locations, and even into the company's shipping and delivery locations. During the late 1990s, many firms were spending prodigious sums of money in their attempt to standardize and harmonize their computer storage, databases, and ordering systems to make them all Internet-compatible. In the most ideal configuration, customers should be able to switch effortlessly between a company's Web site and a call center for service or inquiries.

Companies such as General Electric, Dell Computer, and Cisco Systems are among the leaders in providing a great amount of convenience when buyers use their Web sites. Both business and retail customers receive a high degree of service and help, regardless of the media that they use to contact the company. Cisco Systems has even gone as far as to promote the creation of Web-based "communities," in which Cisco's customers are encouraged to communicate with one another on how best to use Cisco's router and other networking products for maximum benefit. Cisco believes that its customers know the most about the company's products and feel that customers will actually receive more satisfaction and value from being able to communicate with the people who really know how to use them—other satisfied Cisco customers. In a similar vein, General Electric is beginning to integrate its toll-free technical support call center with its Web site. Users of GE equipment ranging from aircraft engines to advanced medical equipment (MRI and CT scanners) to plastics can receive the same high degree of customer support and help from either the Web site or the telephone call center. Troubleshooting ideas and recommendations are updated continuously for access by users to either medium.[9] *In short, consistency in treating the customer is key; customers should be able to receive the same high degree of service regardless of how they approached the company—through Web sites, call centers, or personal one-to-one service.*

Strategic Application to Amazon.com

Let us now examine the extent to which Amazon.com's strategies and approaches to customer service support some of the ideas presented above. First, consider the issue of how Amazon's business model differs from that of traditional retailers. Amazon offers customers the ability to access its Web site and to order products twenty-four hours a day, seven days a week. The company also sells books, CDs, toys, gifts, and consumer electronics around the world, so it is not confined to a single geographical location. Moreover, Amazon hopes its customers will participate in the buying process. Customers are encouraged to write reviews about books they have purchased. In turn, Amazon's Web site shows a prospective buyer what other readers have bought in the past. This gives the potential buyer a broader view of other books that may suit his or her reading needs. Amazon believes that it should provide customers with all the information that they will need about a book, CD, video, or any other product to make a satisfying purchase.

In terms of building sources of virtual advantage, Amazon.com has done much to adopt the key concepts of speed, fast turnaround, customer knowledge and intimacy, and a clear focus on key value-adding activities. For example, Amazon works closely with publishers and distributors to ensure that it can secure and ship books and CDs once a customer places an order. Most important, Amazon has specifically taken steps to build convenience, ease of use, security, privacy and transaction efficiency in its Web site. The company has anticipated every potential challenge that a customer may face when using an Internet-based retail site and advises at each step of the transaction what he or she needs to do. Customers can even find out the status of their orders immediately upon placing it by tracking the shipment's progress through a direct link to one of Amazon's logistics partners (e.g., UPS). In addition, Amazon sends an e-mail immediately to a customer once an order is placed. This e-mail message will provide details of the exact cost of the purchase, how payment was made, and the estimated time for delivery. Moreover, customers can freely contact Amazon through its Web site to modify or even cancel any order that they just made. Amazon also lets customers view their previous transaction history, as well as show which books and other items were purchased as gifts for other people. Moreover, customers can ask Amazon to wrap their gifts and even send out a personal card that the buyer will inscribe. Thus, Amazon has clearly defined its strategy around the key competitive drivers of customer convenience and intimacy.

Amazon's approach to customization and personalization of the shopping experience makes it easy and convenient to do business with the firm. By offering the highest level of personalized service possible through the Internet, Amazon has won millions of loyal customers from around the world.

Are there limitations behind Amazon's strategy? While its strategy is fixated on providing superior customers service and fast turnaround, the company just barely became pro forma profitable during December 2001. CEO Jeff Bezos believes that Amazon will attain significant profitability sometime during late 2002 or 2003. In fact, Amazon has consumed vast amounts of cash over the past six years to build up its highly sophisticated computer-driven infrastructure that is closely linked with those of suppliers, publishers, distributors, and even shipping firms.

Some of Amazon's most recent agreements with Circuit City, Toys "R" Us, and Target Corporation may well represent mixed blessings. On the one hand, the relationship developed with Toys "R" Us complements Amazon.com well, since the company has become a major toy retailer in its own right. Both Toys "R" Us and Amazon.com will mutually benefit from the relationship because it allows both firms to share in the costs of developing new Internet sites for baby toys and other emerging products. Also, the two firms will share in the costs of shipping and inventory—two issues that are particularly difficult for toy retailers around the December holiday season.

On the other hand, the relationships with Circuit City and Target take Amazon.com into a completely new direction. In particular, the decision by Amazon to offer consumer electronics and PCs compels the company to begin offering customer service and technical support for products that are highly complex, especially when compared with books, CDs, videos, and toys. PCs especially require a high degree of direct customer support to resolve technical issues, since troubleshooting is difficult to do over the phone or over the Internet.

In other words, Amazon's strategy is best suited for those products that are well understood by its customers and from which customers like to search among a wide product selection to find what they want. The Internet works best when customers can search through a vast array of information quickly and conveniently; servicing personal computers and electronic equipment require very different skills that Amazon does not have. However, if Amazon were to work closely with other companies that possess such skills (e.g., Dell Computer, Gateway, Hewlett-Packard), then it might be able to overcome this potential weakness. On the other hand, this means that Amazon must devote even more scarce resources to working with other companies that may not have the same approach to customer knowledge and intimacy for which Amazon has become the recognized leader.

The Internet and Established Firms

One of the most critical challenges facing an established firm is how best to harness the power of the Internet without disrupting its existing relationships with key customers, distributors and other people that contributed to the firm's success in the past. In many cases, the advent of Internet will compel firms to rethink and redesign many of their business processes and approaches to creating value, simply because new on-line competitors can often move much more quickly than established incumbents.

Perhaps the single greatest impact of the Internet has been to make many parts of an industry's value chain open to competitive price bidding by another provider. In particular, upstart companies in almost every industry are using the Internet as a way to overcome traditional barriers to entry, especially in distribution and marketing. This is what Amazon.com is doing to such traditional retailers as Barnes & Noble and Borders Group. As newcomers build on-line, electronic distribution channels, they often can provide products and services at lower cost than established competitors that may have sunk considerable fixed costs into their existing, conventional distribution channels and relationships. The rise of the Internet, therefore, poses a very difficult challenge and dilemma to established firms, forcing them to assess carefully the degree to which they are willing and able to reconfigure their value chains rapidly to take advantage of the Internet's growing capabilities.

Although manufacturers can now serve their customers directly through the Internet, doing so exposes them to the severe risk of alienating their long-standing relationships with current distributors. This is the dilemma that PC companies Hewlett-Packard and Compaq Computer now face as they try to imitate many of the Internet-driven direct sales models of Dell Computer. On the other hand, new upstart competitors may force established firms to use the Internet as an alternative or complementary form of distributing products and serving their customers. Companies will feel compelled to respond, if only to meet the challenge and appeal of Internet-driven convenience and ease of use.

Even in the business-to-business competitive environment, the Internet is making great strides in reshaping how firms engage in their ordering, procurement, and delivery activities. Producers of industrial products are facing the same prospect of Internet-driven competition that is already a standard fixture for consumer-based retailing and travel services. Plastics, aircraft parts, and even metals are facing the prospect that the Internet is converting the physical marketplace into one huge, computer-based, "auction" system, in which customers can readily and freely compare the product/service offerings and the respective prices offered by different providers.

Providers of highly standardized products and services, in particular, face perhaps the greatest challenge in adjusting to the Internet's rapid-change environment. For example, Priceline.com, a Web site dedicated to enabling customers to bid on low-cost airfares, is causing more price-based competition within the airline industry through its real-time capability to track the various changes in airfares that all carriers have set for their various routes. In effect, Priceline.com and other Internet sites that allow customers to conduct a free search for information and to bid on pricing are beginning to redefine the sources of competitive advantage that many established firms have relied on for years to attract and retain customers. To counter such moves, established airlines such as American and Delta have designed their own Web sites that allow registered frequent fliers to take advantage of 'Net-based savings and special fares/promotions that customers can access only through the airline's Web site and a personal frequent flier number and password.

As established, incumbent firms begin to grapple with both the opportunities and challenges posed by the Internet, they will steadily begin to invest in new technologies, strategies, and organization designs that will help them bridge the gap between previous management practices and the growing expectations of their customers. Recently, some traditional brick-and-mortar firms have encountered significant obstacles when attempting to implement some of their Internet-based initiatives. For example, Kmart has launched its BlueLight.com Web site to provide discounted pricing and fast delivery of many items that the nationwide retailer also offers in its chain of stores. (The BlueLight reference stems from the company's long practice of offering a special in-store discount for those items that are advertised under a flashing blue light, usually in the middle of the store.) However, the Web site has been plagued with serious difficulties in coordinating its inventory management with logistics firms. Moreover, customers have come to view BlueLight.com as simply another extension of Kmart itself, which has come under sharp attack from many financial analysts for poorly stocked merchandise and uneven service in its stores. In January 2002, Kmart was forced to reorganize under the Chapter 11 provisions of the bankruptcy code.

Competing with new strategies and new technologies to serve customers over the Internet represents just one of many challenges that established incumbent firms face when attempting to adjust to new environmental developments. We will discuss some of the issues in detail in many of our ensuing chapters.

Summary

- The key characteristics of Internet-driven competition include (1) forming a direct link between firms and their customers and suppliers, (2) shrinking the number of middlemen between firms and their customers, (3) enabling customers to access new customers in new markets, and (4) helping companies gain access to real-time information on customers' needs, buying patterns, pricing, product availability, and so forth.
- There are three primary types of Internet-based businesses. These include business-to-business (B-to-B), business-to-consumer (B-to-C), and consumer-to-consumer (C-to-C) platforms. Each platform is based on a different economic rationale to reduce costs and to serve customers.
- Internet-driven businesses differ from traditional businesses along several key dimensions, including (1) around-the-clock service, (2) the lack of geographical boundaries, (3) widespread availability of pricing data, (4) immediate customer response, and (5) more information for customers and greater ability to use it.
- Four economic factors amplify the Internet's impact on competition and strategy, including (1) high information intensity, (2) wide product selection, (3) products that customers understand and know, and (4) fluctuating availability of products.
- The Internet can reshape an industry along three key dimensions by bringing about (1) disintermediation, (2) changes in the structure of the industry's value chain, and (3) network effects on competition.
- Disintermediation refers to the ability of firms to bypass their wholesalers and distributors in order to reach and serve their customers directly. In many industries, this means that the number of middlemen will contract sharply in coming years.
- The Internet can remake the structure of the value chain in many industries. In consumer-driven industries, the number of wholesalers and distributors will likely shrink, and those that remain will have to perform high levels of customer service to survive. In business-to-business applications of the Internet, new B-to-B platforms will serve not only to reduce transactions costs between buyers and sellers but also as electronic clearinghouses to provide real-time information on pricing and to match buyers' needs with sellers' offerings.
- Network effects occur when the value of a product or service actually grows when more people use it. Network effects relate to the notion that as more people are connected, the value of the underlying product, service, technology, or platform rises. Companies that can harness network effects in their products or services will likely dominate their industries and earn huge profits.
- Firms can build virtual advantage when they use speed, fast turnaround, and customer intimacy and knowledge to create value faster than their competitors. Oftentimes, this means that the firm will concentrate its efforts on a few core value-adding activities, while suppliers and other business partners perform the others.

- Personalization is the creation of a unique mix or set of products to meet an individual customer's specific needs.
- Established, incumbent firms must use the Internet to transform their value-adding activities, but at the same, continue to serve their customers through established distribution channels and relationships. This will prove to be an exceptionally difficult balancing act for most firms.

Exercises and Discussion Questions

1. Imagine yourself as the owner of a florist shop who sells to local customers. What are some things that you can do to use the Internet to help bolster your business? What are some issues you need to consider when other national florist distribution chains (e.g., FTD) begin using the Internet to broaden their reach? How would you use the Internet to become even closer to your customers yet reach out to new ones who do not know of your presence?
2. What are some real advantages for the airline industry as it begins to sell airline tickets directly over the Web? Conversely, if you were a travel agent, what would be some steps you could take to reverse recent industry trends? How could you use the Internet to provide more value and knowledge to your customers?
3. Over the long term, what kinds of products and services best lend themselves to selling over the Internet? What are some critical factors that may influence the applicability of the Internet to these products and services? Is education a product or service that lends itself well to the Internet? What kinds of education might work best?
4. How do you see the future of patient care changing with the advent of telemedicine? What are some major advantages that the Internet can bring to speed up patient care in the future? What might be some difficulties that slow down the use of the Internet in the field of medicine?

Endnotes

1. Facts and data for Amazon.com were adapted from the following sources: "Alliance of Amazon, Target Is Expected for Sale of Products Over the Internet," *Wall Street Journal*, September 11, 2001, p. A4; "Amazon.com Is Offering Discounts on Some Sales of Electronic Goods," *Wall Street Journal*, August 22, 2001; "Amazon Signs Deal With Circuit Cit in Bid to Boost Its Electronics Business," *Wall Street Journal*, August 21, 2001, p. B4; "Amazon.com Inc.: Online Store to Be Opened with Toys 'R' Us," *Wall Street Journal*, July 30, 2001; "Do PCs Compute for Amazon?" *Investor's Business Daily*, July 24, 2001, p. A5; "Amazon.com Inc: Web Retailer Starts Area to Buy Software," *Wall Street Journal*, June 26, 2001; "Amazon Adds an Online PC Store," *Business Week*, June 18, 2001; "Toys 'R' Us to Launch Baby-Products Store on Amazon's Web Site," *Wall Street Journal*, May 23, 2001; "Borders Deal Bolsters Amazon's Strategy," *Wall Street Journal*, April 12, 2001, p. B13; "Amazon to Run Borders Web Operations, as Internet Retailer Seeks More Share," *Wall Street Journal*, April 11, 2001; "Amazon.com Actively Hunts for New Partnerships," *Wall Street Journal*, March 26, 2001; "Amazon + Wal-Mart = Win-Win," *Business Week*, March 19, 2001; "Amazon and Wal-Mart Have Discussed an Alliance, but No Deal Is Likely Soon," *Wall Street Journal*, March 7, 2001; "Amazon Plans to Charge Publishers Fee for Online Recommendations," *Wall Street Journal*, February 7, 2001; "Diving into Amazon," *Forbes*, January 22, 2001; "Amazon: Cheaper—But Cheap Enough?" *Business Week*, December 4, 2000; "Amazon.com, Toys 'R' Us Agree to Combine Online Toy Stores," *Wall*

Street Journal, August 11, 2000; "Seeing Clearly through the Amazon Jungle," *Business Week*, July 31 2000; "Amazon.com Sets Sights on Overseas Marketplace," *Wall Street Journal*, July 20, 2000; "Back to Being Amazon.Bomb," *Fortune*, June 26, 2000; " Amazon.com's Amazing New Products," *Business Week*, June 5, 2000; "Amazon's Greatest Feat: Swimming in Red Ink," *Business Week*, March 20, 2000; "Suddenly, Amazon's Books Look Better," *Business Week*, February 21, 2000; "Amazon.com, in Yet Another Expansion, Will Launch Credit Card with NextCard," *Wall Street Journal*, November 11, 1999; "Amazon.com to Sell Software Online, Promises More Product-Line Expansions," *Wall Street Journal*, November 9, 1999; "Amazon vs. Everybody," *Fortune*, November 8, 1999; "Amazon.com Throws Open the Doors," *Business Week*, October 11, 1999.

2. An enormous amount of information about the Internet has sprung up in recent years. A new category of business publications focuses exclusively on the Internet, including such magazines as *Fast Company, E-Company, Red Herring*, and *Wired*. Some of the more recent academic pieces on the advent of the Internet include the following representative works. R. Amit and C. Zott, "Value Creation in E-Business," *Strategic Management Journal* 22, Special Issue (2001): 493–520; S. Zaheer and A. Zaheer, "Market Microstructure in a Global B2B Network," *Strategic Management Journal* 22, no. 9 (2001): 859–873; P. M. Lee, "What's in a Name.com? The Effects of '.com' Name Changes on Stock Prices and Trading Activity," *Strategic Management Journal* 22, no. 8, (2001); R. Wise and D. Morrison, "Beyond the Exchange: The Future of B2B," *Harvard Business Review* 78 (November–December 2000): 86–98; D. Kenny and J. F. Marshall, "Contextual Marketing: The Real Business of the Internet," *Harvard Business Review* 78 (November–December 2000): 119–130; F. F. Reichheld and P. Schefter, "E-Loyalty: Your Secret Weapon on the Web," *Harvard Business Review* 78 (July–August 2000): 105–114; S. Kaplan and M. Sawhney, "E-Hubs: The New B2B Marketplaces," *Harvard Business Review* 78 (May–June 2000): 97–103; P. Evans and T Wurster, *Blown to Bits: How the New Economics of Information Transforms Strategy* (Boston: Harvard Business School Press, 1999); W. C. Kim and R. Mauborgne, "Creating New Market Space," *Harvard Business Review* 77 (January–February 1999): 83–94; R. Kraut, C. Steinfield, A. Chan, B. Butler and A. Hoag, "Coordination and Virtualization: The Role of Electronic Networks and Personal Relationships," *Organization Science* 10, no. 6 (1999): 722–740; P. Evans and T. Wurster, "Getting Real about Virtual Commerce," *Harvard Business Review* 77 (November–December 1999): 84–94; S. Ghosh, "Making Business Sense of the Internet," *Harvard Business Review* 76 (March–April 1998): 125–135.

3. See, for example, S. Zaheer and A. Zaheer, "Market Microstructure in a Global B2B Network," *Strategic Management Journal* 22, no. 9 (2001): 859–874.

4. See C. Shapiro and H. Varian, *Information Rules* (Boston: Harvard Business School Press, 1999). An excellent work that discusses the foundation of network effects is W. B. Arthur, *Increasing Returns and Path Dependence in the Economy* (Ann Arbor: University of Michigan Press, 1994). Also see M. Sawhney and D. Parikh, "Where Value Lives in a Networked World," *Harvard Business Review* 79 (January 2001): 79–90; K. P. Coyne and R. Dye, "The Competitive Dynamics of Network-Based Businesses," *Harvard Business Review* 76 (January–February 1998): 99–111.

5. See, for example, "AOL Is Anywhere, Everywhere," *Investor's Business Daily*, December 14, 2000, p. A6; "AOL Talks with Sony and Toyota," *Wall Street Journal*, December 12, 2000, p. A21; "Time Inc. to Relaunch Its Time Digital, in Sign of Strategy after AOL Merger," *Wall Street Journal*, January 9, 2001, p. B2; "Creating a New Media Concept," *Wall Street Journal*, March 9, 2001, p. B1; "AT&T's Sweeping Cable Access Attracts AOL," *Wall Street Journal*, July 26, 2001, p. B7.

6. See, for example, "E-Biz: Down But Hardly Out," *Business Week*, March 26, 2001, pp. 126–133; "EToys to Close Web Site, Seek Protection," *Wall Street Journal*, February 27, 2001, p. A8.

7. See, for example, "Webvan Joins List of Dot-Com Failures," *Wall Street Journal*, July 10, 2001, pp. A3, A6; "Traditional Grocers Feel Vindicated by Webvan's Failure," *Wall Street Journal*, July 11, 2001, p. B4.
8. See M. Treacy and P. Wiersema, "Customer Intimacy and Other Value Disciplines," *Harvard Business Review* 71 (January–February 1993): 84–96.
9. See "GE Reshuffles Its Dot-Com Strategy to Focus on Internal 'Digitizing,'" *Wall Street Journal*, May 4, 2001, pp. B1, B4.

CHAPTER 6

Shifts in Competitive Advantage: Responding to Environmental Change

Chapter Outline

What You Will Learn

- How and why a firm's competitive advantage can change over time
- Some important sources or triggers of change
- Strategies that firms can undertake to respond to change

Delivery of On-Line Music[1]

The growth of the Internet has brought significant change to a variety of different industries in the United States and globally. One of the industries most profoundly affected by the Internet is the music industry, as customers now have the opportunity to purchase music on-line rather than through traditional retailing channels. Thus, the delivery of on-line music (through a variety of formats) represents a significant change in how record label companies deal with new technology and new methods of distribution that threaten to challenge how music is created, packaged and sold to customers. Some doomsayers went as far as to predict that the availability of on-line music will eventually spell the death of conventional CDs sold by the record companies.

Physical Capture of Music

Throughout the music industry's history, record labels companies such as Vivendi Universal, Warner Music (a unit of AOL Time Warner), EMI Group, Sony Music (a unit of Sony), and Bertelsmann AG have built strong market positions by selling and publishing all genres of music to customers through a physical storage medium of some type. In earlier years, music was stored and played in prerecorded formats, such as vinyl records (LPs) and magnetic tapes (e.g., eight-track and cassettes). In 1982, Sony and Philips Electronics jointly introduced a new format of music storage known as the compact disc (CD), thus giving us stunning clarity and audio fidelity. The advent of the CD, however, also meant that music was now recorded and stored in digital form, where each and every sound in a given audio track was converted into binary form (using 0s and 1s) as a means to improve fidelity and to reduce background noise. The biggest impact of the CD during the late 1980s and early 1990s was that sales of traditional vinyl records and cassette tapes plummeted dramatically over the succeeding years. In fact, most music retailers today do not carry vinyl records in any form, and sales of cassette tapes are relegated to a small corner of the store.

The "digitization" of music, however, also triggered a series of important changes in other related industries as well. New consumer electronic devices such as CD players began to displace sales of phonographs and tape players. More important, digitization of music meant that record label companies needed to invest in a whole new set of skills and technologies in order to ensure that customers were able to get the highest-quality music possible. Many of the skills and technologies involved are computer related, thus compelling the record label companies to invest in state-of-the-art manufacturing facilities that can process millions of CDs in a "clean room," highly automated environment. For consumers, digitization also heralded potentially significant changes in how people listened to music. As technology evolved to the point where CD players could be hooked into personal computers by way of CD-ROM drivers, consumers could also listen to music while they were engaged in other computer-based activities, either at home or on the job. Thus, people could begin to enjoy music when working on their PCs, in addition to driving, reading, exercising, or doing other tasks.

The fact that music, until very recently, was recorded and stored in physical form only by the record label companies helps to explain much of the music industry's relatively high profitability. To secure a steady "pipeline" of music to reach its customers, record label companies would sign contracts with a large number of promising artists and performers in exchange for royalties paid to them. More important, artists and performers often sign long-term contracts with the record label companies, often for a period of years at a time. This means that a very popular performing group or artist (e.g., The Beatles, Elton John, Mariah Carey, Gloria Estefan, Garth Brooks, Brittany Spears, The Back-Street Boys) will produce a very rich stream of income for the record company. Predicting which type of music or which performing group will become a success in the future, however, is almost an impossible task. In fact, for many record labels, 80 percent of the recordings made do not make money. To protect themselves from excessive financial losses, the record label companies hedged their financial risk by deducting production and marketing costs from the artists' and performers' initial royalties. If the record company is unable to sell a sufficient number of recordings to recoup this up-front cost, the artists and performers will receive no payment. If the recording turns out to be a real winner, the royalties paid to artists and performers will grow correspondingly.

For consumers, the physical storage of music on a CD format also highlights a major strength of the record label companies. These firms are able to predetermine which selections of recorded music that consumers can buy on any given CD; also, they are able to roll out future CDs of popular artists and performers according to the companies' marketing timetable. Artists and performers typically record a stream of different performances and hits, and the record companies then disperse the most popular tracks among a number of different CDs. This means that consumers will very often pay the full price for a CD with a dozen or more tracks of prerecorded music, when, in fact, what attracted consumers to buy the CD was only one or two of the most popular tracks.

The Arrival of Web Music

The massive growth of on-line, Web-distributed music over the past few years actually has its roots in a series of important technical achievements that began in the early 1990s. The digitization of music into CDs during the previous decade also made possible the "compression" of music into computer files as well. In 1992, the Motion Picture Experts Group (also known as MPEG) developed a standard for condensing audio into a well-defined computer format. This standard ultimately became known as MP3 (which refers to the layer 3 of MPEG1 code). Three years later, a company that would become better known as RealNetworks pioneered a new type of software that made it possible to engage in "audio streaming." Streaming is the process by which listeners can hear music one digital bit at a time. In practice, streaming recreates music or other audio by stringing together the series of binary 0s and 1s (digital computer form) into audible form. This technology dramatically took off around 1996–1997 as the Internet became more widely accessible to personal computers. However, Internet connections were often haphazard, especially with dial-up modems that were the predominant basis of how most people accessed the Net. Downloading an entire two-minute song in MP3 required six minutes using a traditional phone modem and thus became impractical to most people. Because Internet transmission speeds were relatively slow during that time, streaming-based technology made it impossible for listeners to hear music without consuming a vast amount of computer memory and processing time to store downloaded music on their own PCs. By early 1998, however, faster and more reliable Internet transmission speeds made it possible for listeners to download entire music and audio files (in MP3 format) onto their PCs. Downloading an entire song now became much easier and faster to do.

The strategic situation facing record companies became increasingly more complex and challenging by 1999. First, a series of new developments in the consumer electronics industry made it possible for music listeners to store and hear music without relying entirely on conventional CDs. For example, MP3 players made by Diamond Multimedia and a host of other firms, allow users to download and carry MP3 music files anywhere they want. Second, new companies created a variety of different software to download music and to open up the compressed digital file. Internet users could in fact download most of these "digital players" for free, including Real Audio, Liquid Audio, WinAmp, and Microsoft's Media Player. Third, the evolution of CD-ROM drives in computers became more technologically advanced. PCs are now equipped with CD drives that can not only read files from the disc but write files as well. Thus, consumers are now able to create and "burn" their own custom-made CDs on their computers. In fact, consumers can now store music in digital MP3 format by using their PCs as a giant "digital jukebox;" and they can then copy whatever files they choose directly onto blank CDs for replay in the car or in traditional CD players. Finally, because MP3 music is stored in digital form, it was now possible for listeners to literally send music files by e-mail to their friends and other listeners. (See Exhibit 6-1 for a contrast of how traditional CD music differs from Web-based forms.)

The cumulative effect of all these new developments was that music, for all practical purposes, was becoming a free good that was distributed over the Internet without any restrictions or controls imposed by the record label companies. In the very worst case, listeners received music free through many Web sites, including the one of the most popular requested ones—Napster. MP3 files can be copied repeatedly with no degradation of audio quality. Moreover, the proliferation of MP3 files gave rise to music piracy on a vast scale. Record label companies lost billions of dollars in royalties as

EXHIBIT 6-1 The Rise of New Music Platforms

CD-Based	MP3-Variants
• Captured in disc form	• Portable in digital code form
• Dependent on retailers to sell	• Downloadable directly through the Internet
• Companies determine/select offerings on CD	• Listener chooses what he or she wants to pay for
• Requires advanced manufacturing to produce discs	• Listener able to "burn" discs through PC/other device
• Pricing set by label company	• Pricing varies by demand/popularity
• Marketing and promotion drive disc sales	• Music "communities" may evolve over chat rooms on Web

MP3 files were beamed across the Internet, and very few listeners may have actually paid for what they received. The massive use of Napster by college students to access and to trade music, for example, contributed to a surge in Internet use during 1999. Even more foreboding to the record companies was the development of even more sophisticated downloading software, such as Gnutella and other "peer-to-peer" sharing formats that do not utilize central computer servers for storage. In fact, continuing improvements of all types of technology presented a real challenge for record companies. MP3 players are rapidly falling in price. PC hard drives and other storage devices are sold for a mere pittance when compared with earlier generation products. Audiophiles are now connecting their traditional stereos with their PCs. New wireless forms of Internet transmission even now make it possible to download and hear MP3 files in cars and elsewhere. Moreover, the real issue for record label companies is that it has become much more difficult for them to decide when and where listeners are able to purchase and enjoy the music they actually want to hear. Music is no longer encapsulated in a physical form (CD or tape) whose tracks are preselected and determined by the record companies.

Response Initiatives

All of the record label companies realized the threat that on-line music represented to sales of conventional CDs. More important, the rampant piracy of copyrighted music threatened to erode their future profitability as listeners became further emboldened to download a blossoming list of MP3 files using a variety of different devices. On the one hand, the record companies need to protect their copyrights and intellectual property. On the other hand, these companies recognize that music storage and distribution have changed to an irreversible degree.

Recognizing this development, all of the major record label companies (Universal Music, Sony, EMI Group, Warner Music, and Bertelsmann AG), as well as a host of different technology companies (e.g., software) came together to form the Secure Digital Music Initiative (SDMI) to devise new technology standards that would enable digital distribution of music but continue to protect copyrights. To protect their intellectual property even further, several record label companies and a number of different performers in 1999 sued MP3.com and Napster in federal courts, charging them with copyright piracy. In several cases that were brought to trial in 2000, both MP3.com and Napster lost a series of important court decisions. Later in 2000, a federal judge ordered Napster to shut down its operations permanently until it can figure out a way to charge customers for each music track downloaded.

Although all of the record companies engaged in extensive litigation to bring the piracy problem under control, a number of them began to undertake steps to incorporate the new technology into their own business models. For example, three major record companies—Warner Music, EMI Group, and Bertelsmann AG—joined together with RealNetworks to license their music offerings on using RealNetworks' digital technology. Forming a new company called MusicNet, the venture will act as a distributor of digital music files to other companies wanting to offer music subscription services over the Internet. In some ways, MusicNet will act like a traditional wholesaler by letting other on-line distributors charge their own fees to listeners.

Not to be outdone by its competitors, Vivendi Universal paid $372 million to buy out MP3.com in May 2001. Universal Music Group (a unit of Vivendi) hopes to use MP3.com's technology to help compete with the new subscription-based technology developed by RealNetworks and the MusicNet initiative. Universal also inked a deal with Sony Music to form Pressplay, a competing digital subscription service that is designed to match MusicNet. These deals are especially significant for the industry, since they reveal the extent to which the record companies are beginning to use digital distribution in their own plans to expand their music offerings over the Internet. In addition, Bertelsmann AG even formed a strategic relationship with Napster itself during the early months of 2001. This deal, however, appears to have backfired since many of Bertelsmann AG's artists and performers were outraged that the company would join forces with an outfit that many people consider to be the "pariah" of the industry.

Now, all of the record companies are beginning to sell digital files of their music, as either whole albums or individual tracks, in a downloadable format to listeners. At the same time, record label companies are strengthening their efforts to work together to prevent piracy and to jointly coordinate their legal strategies to protect their copyrights. Most recently, the Recording Industry Association filed suit to prevent the spread of a new Web-enabled file sharing system called Morpheus, which appears to have many characteristics of Napster. Morpheus will allow PC users to share music and other files through a new peer-to-peer electronic transmission system, which also poses another threat to the intellectual property of entertainment companies. New digital encryption technologies can better ensure that listeners pay for the music that they download and still be unable to make illegal copies for distribution over the Net to other people.

Eastman Kodak and Digital Photography[2]

As we enter the next century, consumer photography is also undergoing a revolutionary technological change. Eastman Kodak is a global leader in developing chemical-based film. Even though its biggest competitor, Fuji Photo of Japan, sells lower-priced film, as recently as 1996, Kodak commanded upward of 60 percent of the U.S. market for all makes of consumer film. Kodak's shares are even higher in the industrial and medical film segments. Yet throughout the 1990s, double-digit growth in the chemical-based film market slowed dramatically, leaving Eastman Kodak in a real struggle to redefine its core technologies and products in the wake of technological change, revitalized competitors, the advent of the Internet, and different customer tastes.

Kodak must now deal with the major challenge presented by the arrival of new competitors who are accelerating the transition of chemical-based imaging to new electronic and digital imaging techniques that will change the way consumers use their cameras and how manufacturers link up the camera with other technological applications. Although Kodak still holds a large number of patents that protect both its core, proprietary silver-halide film coatings technology and many advances in digital imaging, the company now faces challenges from emerging technologies that threaten its chemical-based investments over the past century.

Semiconductors and Digital Imaging

Two particular agents of change threaten Kodak's traditional technology. The first is the growing use of semiconductors in cameras and other imaging equipment. During the 1990s, cameras incorporated ever-more powerful semiconductor chips to improve picture quality and product performance. In particular, the rise of so-called flash memory has become a direct substitute for chemical-based film. Flash memories serve to store a series of images on a disk or memory card that is then easily inserted into a personal computer for long-term storage, imaging manipulation, and eventual printing. Cameras that incorporate these and other state-of-the-art chips use microprocessors and microcontrollers to control focus and shutter speed. As these chips improve, these new cameras have given weekend photography amateurs a growing ability to match the quality of professional photographers.

The second development facing Kodak is the rise of digital imaging technology. More important, new advances in electronics now mean that cameras and other imaging equipment, such as X-rays, can store images as digital, binary codes. By storing images in digital, binary codes, people are able to transfer their pictures and images onto optical disks similar to those used in current personal computers. This ability means that customers can now manipulate images for clearer pictures, accentuate shadows or lines, and even make wholesale changes of the picture's background. The use of video compression algorithms together with faster, smarter electronics heralds a new type of imaging technology, whereby digital images can be stored with different degrees of clarity and resolution, depending on what applications are used later. In fact, many of these digital images can not only be stored on a computer or optical disk but also be downloaded and shared through the Internet. Consequently, the production and use of cameras and film development methods are becoming more similar to the technologies used to make compact disks, optical disks, semiconductors, and even software techniques for image manipulation. These technologies defined the evolution of the personal computer, consumer electronics, and computer peripherals industry. The power to edit photographs on a computer or television screen, for example, means that photographers can custom-build and assemble their own set of pictures; only the user's imagination defines how far the technology can be applied. Camera buffs, advertisers, copy editors, medical diagnosticians, and other industrial users will find many new uses for digital imaging methods to capture, store, and manipulate images. In particular, the rapid ability to digitize an image and send it through the Internet allows for fast capture and translation of images for medical applications (second opinions), insurance claims, real estate (virtual sales), and other forms of video transmission. This transformation of imaging at Eastman Kodak from chemical-based to digital, electronic-based methods is depicted in Exhibit 6-2.

Currently, most electronic and digital imaging techniques cannot achieve the fine degree of resolution of chemical-based film. The number of tiny dots—known as *pixels*—in any square area determines the clarity of the image. The more dense the pixels, the finer is the resolution. Even though chemical-based films still outclass their digital counterparts in image clarity and fineness, many firms are steadily improving charged coupled devices (CCDs), digital compression techniques, algorithms, flash memory density, and software interpolation

EXHIBIT 6-2 Transformation of Imaging at Eastman Kodak

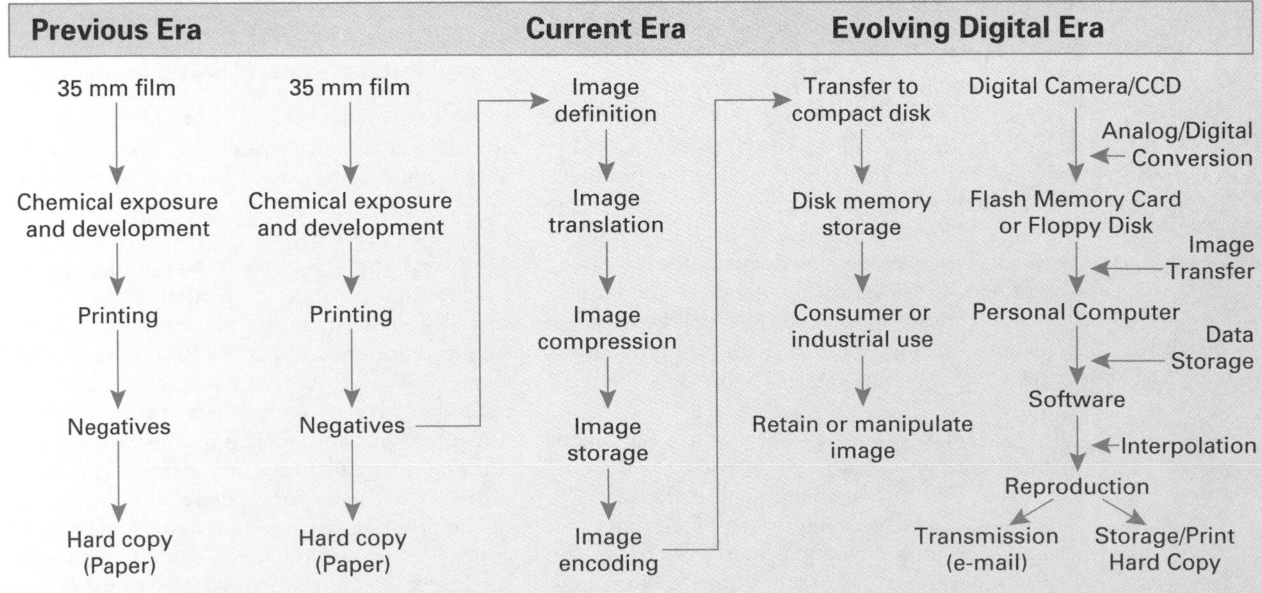

techniques that will make it possible for electronic imaging to reduce the quality gap with chemical-based film imaging. Some analysts have already predicted that the quality gap for all practical purposes has already closed. Once this digital-based technology catches up, consumer and industrial users will no longer have to wait to develop their photos. Consumers already are taking and developing pictures with digital, filmless cameras.

Impact of New Technology on Kodak

The full magnitude of the new technology's threat to Eastman Kodak is difficult to grasp. Many rivals investing in new technologies include Japanese consumer electronics giants Canon, Toshiba, Ricoh, Sony, Epson, and Sharp. Epson, in particular, has developed its own line of digital cameras under the Photo PC brand, in which the flash memory card is directly inserted into a personal computer accessory card interface for immediate image capture. Other rivals that have demonstrated a strong, compelling interest in the arena include Hewlett-Packard, Polaroid, Motorola, IBM, and Intel, all of which have strong semiconductor and/or imaging technologies in their own right. Hewlett-Packard's advanced software and controller chips are already used in state-of-the-art laser and ink-jet printers, while Intel's flash memory and microprocessor businesses are natural potential entrants into the digital imaging industry. Even U.S. chemical giant DuPont has expressed an interest in imaging technologies that take advantage of its new strengths in advanced materials related to imaging. Either way, Kodak faces both domestic and foreign competitors who have mastered and utilized advanced digital imaging techniques learned from their own respective core businesses. These technologies, in turn, could conceivably be used to design and to produce new, "smart" electronic or digital-based cameras that store images on semiconductor chips. In fact, as early as 1984, Sony attempted to introduce its digital-based camera known as the Sony Mavica. It floundered because of poor images from first-generation technology. However, the product reveals the depth of Sony's skills and commitment to commercializing this new technology. The newest generation of Sony's Mavica, reintroduced in 1997, has proven to be extremely popular since images are directly stored onto a floppy disk.

Thus, Eastman Kodak during the 1990s faces a challenge and dilemma of monumental proportions. Kodak must now learn new semiconductor and digital-based imaging technologies that depart from its chemistry background and traditional technology. In the most extreme case of this threat, consumers can practically capture images with a digital filmless camera and download these images directly on the Internet, thus completely bypassing all of Kodak's traditional film business offerings.

To begin meeting the growing needs of people who use electronic/digital imaging, Kodak has even begun to move beyond its current Photo-CD developing process. Photo-CD allows consumers to put their film negatives on optical disks, which can then be viewed on a television screen. However, from Kodak's marketing perspective, this process has proved expensive and uncertain, as the image is still inextricably linked with a CD-like device that remains cumbersome to use. Competing flash memory cards may generate considerably more consumer interest, since they require even fewer stages of complexity.

Searching for an Effective Response

The next stage of photography and film development has already begun to unfold. Kodak has developed an Internet site that allows customers to drop off their film at a finishing lab, only to have the pictures available to them on the Internet through a special Web account with Kodak. This on-line service, known as PhotoNet, enables customers to develop their film cartridges or have negatives scanned into the system to be available the next day on the Internet. Customers can then download these 'Net-based images into their PCs or send them to friends and family through e-mail.

To help learn how better to compete in the semiconductor and digital-imaging arenas, Kodak formed a joint venture with Intel in May 1998 to codevelop new flash memories specifically for digital imaging applications. It is simultaneously working with Motorola to develop superior flash memory technology. These flash memory cards will pave the way for Kodak to compete more directly with Epson, Sony, and other firms that have similar ambitions. Already, Kodak has pushed through a new flash-derivative product that uses conventional 3.5-inch floppy disks as the "digital film" that captures images, although its storage capacity remains limited at this time and Sony has an initial lead. Kodak also entered into an array of relationships with Microsoft, Adobe Systems, Hewlett-Packard, and even a few Silicon Valley start-ups (e.g., Live Picture) to understand better how these new technologies will evolve. It has a significant ownership stake in an upstart firm known as PictureVision, which has developed a system to allow a consumer's film to be developed by a photo-finishing lab and then delivered to the customer through Kodak's Web site on the Internet. To further strengthen its hold over this technology, Kodak also entered into a partnership arrangement with America Online to ensure that its Web site is prominently displayed for potential users.

These moves represent important learning steps for Kodak in revitalizing its skills along a series of new technologies. Whether Kodak's growing experience with making newer disc and flash memory-related devices will help it compete in the professional and consumer video market remains difficult to assess. If Kodak becomes successful in learning and applying newer, digital-based imaging technologies, then the photography giant could become an important player in such newly emerging industries as multimedia, Internet-based transmission, advanced color printers, software interpolation, and advanced color optics.

Currently, Kodak's newest DC215 Zoom Digital Camera has become one of the world's most popular digital cameras. Also, Kodak's newest mc3 digital camera combines video and music (MP3) together with a digital camera. The company is beginning to invest further in the next-generation technology for digital displays, including a new format called organic light-emitting diodes (OLEDs), which are brighter and thinner than conventional transistor-based displays. New products in Kodak's labs include a sixteen-megapixel CCD that is capable of capturing up to eight times the amount of visual information of today's standard digital cameras. At the same time, Kodak has strengthened its relationship with America Online to allow faster transmission of video attachments. It has also begun to work with Cisco Systems and Motorola to produce a new wireless communications standard that will be able to support high-speed Internet transmission. Another relationship with Scientific-Atlanta, the world's leading cable set-top box manufacturer, is designed to help customers work with digital photography Web sites without using a personal computer.

Introduction

Firms that have built substantial sources of competitive advantage often enjoy high levels of profitability. Yet, as we have seen in numerous examples, industries can change quickly. Although the product life cycle is an effective tool that describes how an industry evolves, numerous other factors can also drive change. As we have seen from the last chapter, the rise of the Internet poses significant challenges as well as opportunities to established firms. New developments in the environment can threaten a firm's distinctive competence and existing sources of competitive advantage if the firm does not or cannot respond to change.

Determining when and how to respond to environmental change is the subject of this chapter. We begin by examining different triggers of change that can seriously erode a firm's distinctive competence and sources of competitive advantage. Then, we explore the options available to firms in their response to these changes. Finally, we consider the factors that influence the selection of these options.

New Developments Affecting Competitive Advantage

Changes in the industry environment can have marked effects on firms' sources of competitive advantage. These changes represent *triggers*, or new developments that can redefine the way firms compete. In some instances, the developments are industry-wide and substantially alter the nature of competition and the long-term structure of the industry. Changes in government regulations (e.g., deregulation in electric utilities, financial services, and telecommunications) can have major intended and unintended effects on the industry. Other developments may be "spillover" effects resulting from changes occurring in a neighboring or related industry (e.g., the impact of digital images and flash memories or charged coupled devices on chemical-based film). Developments or triggers that frequently change the nature of competition and sources of competitive advantage include (1) new technology, (2) new distribution channels, (3) shifts in economic variables, (4) changes in related industries, and (5) changes in government regulation.

New Technology

In any industry, a firm invests considerable resources in the technologies used in its value-adding activities. The choice of technology determines the materials, designs, methods, processes, and equipment used to carry out its activities. Over time, a firm learns and builds a considerable base of expertise in dealing with the technologies that directly impact its value chain configuration (business system). Often, these technologies involve both products and processes. Recall that *product technologies* relate to the product's design, patents, and components, and *process technologies* refer to plant and equipment, operational methods and practices, and manufacturing improvements. The emergence of a new or superior product or process technology represents a potential threat to existing sources of competitive advantage, since it can undermine the value of a current distinctive competence.

On a general level, all firms face the potential threat of obsolescence. This problem is especially salient, however, for pioneering firms that defined current industry standards or practices. When new technologies threaten to undermine a current product standard or process technology, they are known as competence-changing technologies. **Competence-changing technologies** are advances that could redefine an industry's structure and technological format. In many situations, competence-changing technologies represent substitutes for existing industry processes and methods.[3] For example, Eastman Kodak faces a competence-changing threat from digital imaging technologies, which are unlike its established competences in silver-halide film technologies. In the automobile industry, ceramic-based engines and even sophisticated hybrid fuel cells, as well as battery-powered systems, promise the possibility of better efficiencies and performance than internal combustion engines. They represent competence-changing technologies for all U.S., European, and Japanese players that build gasoline and diesel technologies. Broad examples of competence-changing technologies are described in the following sections.

competence-changing technology: A technology that markedly changes or redefines the structure of an industry; often new processes or innovations that disrupt and erode the market for existing products.

New Materials. Fiber-optic cable made of glass is rapidly replacing copper as a medium for transmitting telecommunication signals. This development enables new competitors like Corning Incorporated and Lucent Technologies to enter the telecommunications supply field in a major way. In addition, these new materials create opportunities for both Corning and Lucent to shape the kinds of capabilities and offerings that telecommunications companies can offer to their customers. In another example, newly engineered plastics are replacing steel and other metal parts in automobiles and heavy machinery. Composite body panels, doors, and dashboards made of synthetic fibers and plastics, for example, can be found in almost all cars. These materials help reduce the weight and cost of automobiles. Their development creates important opportunities for chemical manufacturers that produce these plastics and for the firms that use them. Some of the most exciting developments in new materials include the use of "smart technology," which enables hybrid alloys to deflect stresses and fractures that would cause failure in traditional metals.

New Manufacturing Techniques. In the steel industry, minimills use an alternative technology to make steel rather than the traditional open hearth method. Using this new low-cost manufacturing technology, new entrants such as Nucor and Chaparral Steel have achieved spectacular success. By using scrap iron and metal, minimills avoid the high fixed costs of more traditional, integrated steelmakers, such as U.S. Steel and Bethlehem Steel to produce steel wires, rods, and beams used in the construction and road-building industries. The older firms depend on much larger mills and higher ore-based processing costs. In another case, many firms in the plastics industry are using new types of liquid-injection molding technologies to produce plastic products. These machines inject hot plastic liquids into molds directly to make parts, components, and toys more quickly and efficiently than past methods. This development provides new entrants to the industry a valuable opportunity for technology differentiation.

Both Kodak and record label firms such as Vivendi Universal, Sony, EMI Group, AOL Time Warner, and Bertelsmann AG faced threats of competence-changing technologies in the 1990s and 2000s respectively. As noted in the opening cases, these firms built their original business models around older technologies. They achieved distinctive competence and substantial competitive advantage in these areas. Digital-based technologies promise to change the way images are created, transferred, stored, manipulated, and even transmitted along today's information media. New music formats such as MP3 and other variants promise to make music freely available over a wide range of Internet-driven media and new devices.

The steel, plastics, watch, and film industries are not the only settings to have experienced this kind of technological change. As shown in Exhibit 6-3, superior technology has emerged in a wide range of settings. In each of the industries shown, a new technology eventually surpassed the traditional one in terms of market acceptance. Firms unable or unwilling to build expertise in the new areas experienced erosion and, in some instances, extinction of their market positions.

EXHIBIT 6-3 Emergence of New Technology

Industry	Old Technology	New Technology
Electronics	Transistors	Integrated circuits
Shoe materials	Leather	Engineered polymers
Appliances	Discrete controls	Fuzzy logic
Airframes	Steel, Metal	Composite materials
Automobile engines	Aluminum	Ceramics
Automobile body frames	Welded pieces	Unibody, single piece construction
Computers	Mainframes	Personal computers Networked systems
Medical equipment	Stand-alone x-ray	CAT scans, MRI
TV manufacturing	Handcrafted	Automated insertion tools
Cameras	Silver-halide film	Flash memory cards

New Distribution Channels

Established firms must monitor their distribution and marketing activities to detect potential threats or opportunities to their current distribution methods. Distribution represents a vital component of every industry, and certainly any change in the method or channel used could redefine the basis of future competitive strategies. In the late 1990s, perhaps the single greatest change in distribution channels now affecting every industry and organization was the growing use of the Internet to provide on-line ordering, distribution, sales, and even manufacturing. More broadly, the Internet is also forcing existing firms in the travel agency, real estate, financial services, office supplies, and airline industries to rethink how best to reconfigure their distribution and marketing systems to serve their customers (see Chapter 5).

A broad understanding of how alternative distribution systems evolve can help the firm better scan its environment for new developments or competitors. In many instances, the arrival of a new distribution channel or method often signals the entry of a new competitor. Certainly, for Barnes & Noble and Borders Group, the arrival of Amazon.com on the Internet signifies a potentially dangerous threat because the upstart can sell to anybody who has access to the World Wide Web. While distribution channels continue to evolve, each step of their evolution means that established firms must likely deal with a set of new entrants. These entrants will probably use a different business model and value proposition to win over customers.

Pitney Bowes, a company best known for making postage machines, is now facing a similar type of challenge from the rise of the Internet. For over seventy years, Pitney Bowes has provided a valuable service to many businesses through the durable machines that allow them to issue the right amount of postage needed to mail letters and packages on their own. Companies prepurchase the amount of postage they want from the U.S. Postal Service. In turn, the Postal Service gives each customer's postage machine an assigned number that designates permission to issue postage on his or her outgoing mail. However, by late 1998, new upstarts using the Internet have begun to challenge Pitney Bowes' long held dominance in the postage machine market. Companies such as E-Stamp, StampMaster, and others attempted to design Web sites that enable customers to pay for postage over the Internet, download a customer-specific set of coded data into their computers, and then print it out on mailing labels and envelopes. In effect, the Internet, with the permission of the U.S. Postal Service, now allows customers to print their own stamps.[4] In turn, Pitney Bowes has introduced its own version of user-friendly, Internet-based software to help customers order prepaid postage with greater ease.

From the on-line music example, many record label companies were unaware of how new distribution channels (besides the Internet) actually helped pave the way for the arrival of new competitors. The record label companies did not initially realize that telecommunications firms (which manage much of the 'Net), as well as consumer electronic firms that develop and sell digital phones and other electronic devices, were highly influential in promoting the use of personal computers, cell phones, MP3 players, and hand-held computers as alternative ways of listening to music. These new platforms increasingly do not require the use of compact discs as the sole means to store music.

Kodak is also embracing the Internet as a means to reach its customers more quickly and lucratively. Using its new PhotoNet technology, Kodak has developed a Web site that enables customers to sign up for an account in which the images from their pictures and negatives will be available to them through the Internet. Customers now can drop off their film cartridges at Kodak-affiliated outlets (drugstore chains, grocery chains, camera outlets, and convenience stores) and receive the images on the Web. Once the images are available to customers, they can choose which ones to download to their own PCs or to send to other people through e-mail. America Online and PictureVision are two firms that have become important partners for Kodak in this evolving Internet-based venture.

Firms in many other industries have found their existing sources of competitive advantage threatened by the arrival of new methods of distribution, even those that are not specifically Internet driven. Brokerage houses, such as Merrill Lynch and Citigroup's Smith Barney, have been hurt by the growth of discount brokers. Discount brokers such as Fidelity Investments, Charles Schwab, and Quick & Reilly have eroded the once-dominant position of established, full-service brokers by offering lower-cost commissions on stock and bond trades. These discount brokers, in turn, face the problem of dealing with on-line brokerage firms, such as Ameritrade, E*Trade, and other upstarts, that can directly access their customers. In addition, since they tend to have small research departments (if any), their overhead costs are lower, and they can pass these savings on to consumers.

In a similar vein, network television leaders such as Disney's Capital Cities/ABC unit, Viacom's CBS unit, and GE's NBC unit have been threatened by new cable, pay-per-view, and home video outlets, where competing offerings have sliced market share for networks expecting large numbers of viewers. NBC is rethinking its current approach and business model in the broadcasting industry to preempt some of these threats.[5]

Department stores are also coming under siege from newly emerging Internet and television-based shopping (e.g., Home Shopping Channel and QVC Network). Newly emergent distribution channels sometimes enable firms, particularly later entrants, to reach neglected customers. Combining both Internet access and traditional catalog sales has enabled upstarts such as Lands' End, Early Winters, Touch of Class, and L.L. Bean to reach customers whose specialized needs are not effectively satisfied by existing brick-and-mortar department stores and discount chains. When a television viewer or computer user surfing the Web sees a product or service that is of interest, the viewer simply calls a toll-free telephone number or downloads ordering and billing information on the Internet to purchase the item.

More recently, Blockbuster Entertainment's nationwide franchises in videotape rentals face the long-term challenge of pay-per-view programming coming from cable, telecommunications, and satellite companies. These alternative means of distributing movies and entertainment threaten Blockbuster's current distinctive competence in offering low-cost video rentals. Families can watch movies directly through expanded forms of cable television, where desired films are available instantaneously. Thus, telecommunications and satellite companies could make most of Blockbuster's current distribution channels obsolete by offering direct, pay-per-view movies, sporting events, and other entertainment avenues to customers. The rise of pay-per-view technology, as well as the advent of DVD sales, means that customers will be increasingly able to rent or pay for movies without going to a Blockbuster outlet.

Economic Shifts

Changes in the basic economic parameters or structure of an industry can dramatically shift the nature of competitive advantage. Consider the current difficulties facing Japanese automobile and electronics manufacturers, for example. Their highly advanced, quality-driven, Japan-based manufacturing facilities once enjoyed an enormous cost advantage over U.S. factories and competitors. Rising wages of Japanese workers, a dramatic slowdown in the domestic economy, and severe fluctuations in the value of its currency (the yen) have combined to undermine many Japanese firms' advantage substantially over the past decade. Now Japanese manufacturers are taking aggressive steps to reduce costs through such means as automation, outsourcing, reduced number of product variations, and shifting manufacturing to facilities outside of Japan, particularly through aggressive investments in Southeast Asia. In fact, Japanese investment in this region has grown so dramatically that economic downturns and recessions in many Southeast Asian economies (e.g., Indonesia, Thailand, Malaysia, Singapore) in the late 1990s affected the profitability of Japanese firms. The same developments have strengthened the market and cost positions of General Motors, Ford, and DaimlerChrysler—both in the United States and in other export markets. Thus, sharp swings or changes in the exchange rate, domestic demand, commodity prices, or even the receptivity of trade partners can dramatically alter the competitive advantage of firms across many industries.

Changes in Related or Neighboring Industries

related industry: An industry that shares many of the same economic, technological, or market-based drivers or characteristics as another.

Sometimes, shifts in one industry's competitive environment may be precipitated or triggered by changes in a neighboring or related industry. A **related industry** is one that shares many of the same economic, technological, or market-based drivers or characteristics. For example, consumer electronics and personal computers may be thought of as related, since these two industries often rely on the same type of mass market distribution channel, incorporate many of the same electronic components, and even manufacture key components or peripherals in the same factories. Increasingly, the telephone, Internet, and computer-networking industries are becoming more related since they share the same basic telecommunications architecture and are growing more linked together through the use of common information transfer technologies (e.g., routers, bridges, and packet switches). Even the cable TV business is becoming more similar to the telecommunications industry as well.

In a similar vein, the rise of so-called digital media reflects the growing recognition that traditional content media (television, publishing, broadcasting, radio, and music) are becoming ever more interwoven with new forms of Internet and satellite distribution systems that allow for growing digitization of traditional media forms (e.g., print, broadcast, paper, and tape). These two sectors, content and communications, are becoming more related as both industries increasingly look to one another to access customers and markets more cheaply and effectively. The massive growth of Internet "portals," such as Yahoo!, Terra Lycos, and Microsoft Network, reveals the growing convergence between content providers and communication channels/distribution. Content providers are increasingly dependent on new forms of technology to create and deliver value to customers; communication-based firms need content providers to expand their array of offerings to the public. Perhaps the recent merger of America Online with Time Warner to form AOL Time Warner in 2000 best exemplifies this trend in which communications and content are becoming increasingly interwoven.

Let us consider a hypothetical example of how changes in one industry can trigger changes in another. Take the relationship between leather shoes, the tanning industry, and chemicals. Countries such as Italy and Brazil have large and profitable shoe industries because their manufacturers often can purchase large quantities of high-quality, processed leather from long-standing tanning firms. The high quality and output of Brazilian and Italian shoes are based not only on the economies of scale and experience effects that established shoe firms have built up but also on the close relationships they have developed with tanning firms. Innovations in tanning leather are likely to have been passed on to shoe makers; conversely, shoe firms have probably suggested ways to improve the tanning process. However, if a chemical firm were to develop a cheaper, alternative material that could be used to make more durable and comfortable shoes, then growing use of this new material could dramatically change the competitiveness of the Brazilian and Italian shoe industries. First, the arrival of a substitute material would reduce the amount of leather that Brazilian and Italian shoe factories purchase from tanning firms over time. Thus, tanning firms would face an enormous amount of new competition and a sharp drop-off in business. Second, a new chemical material might be used in new ways to make even less costly shoes. If the chemical material lends itself to more efficient or perhaps automated means of production, then this material would threaten the existing cost advantages and investment in equipment by Brazilian and Italian firms. The growing availability of the new chemical-based material might also encourage entry by other shoe firms into the niches currently served by the existing firms, since cheaper shoe materials would lower the cost of differentiation. Thus, technological, economic, or other developments in a related industry can trigger marked changes and shifts in sources of competitive advantage in another industry.[6]

Changes in Government Regulation

Actions taken by the government can markedly shift or threaten the sources of advantage needed to compete in an industry. For example, the U.S. government's imposition of high tariffs on Japanese motorcycle imports in the 1970s damaged the competitive position of Japanese manufacturers such as Kawasaki, Honda, and Yamaha. More recently, quotas imposed in the early 1990s on Japanese auto imports, especially minivans, threatened Honda, Toyota, and Nissan, forcing them to increase U.S. manufacturing capacity more rapidly to remain competitive in this country. Likewise, the Clean Air Act of 1990 threatened to render obsolete many U.S. oil refinery operations because of the extremely high costs required to meet new regulations. The proposed global Kyoto Accord that committed national signatories to reduce their emissions and use of carbon-based fuels is a regulation of such magnitude that it is expected to cause considerable financial distress to companies in many industries; this is one reason why the United States has not been a signatory to this agreement.

Changes in antitrust regulations can alter the competitive dynamics in an industry. For example, the recent sparring and court battles between Microsoft and the Department of Justice reduces Microsoft's near monopoly power over the PC software industry, especially as it relates to Internet search engines. This agreement makes it easier for personal computer manufacturers to use Internet search engines software made by other firms (in particular, AOL's Netscape Communications). Moreover, PC makers are not required to pay as much in royalties to Microsoft as in the past. Even though the U.S. government is not looking to break up Microsoft into a series of smaller companies, the Department of Justice in 2002 was still evaluating alternative means to sanction the company for what it believes to be monopolistic practices. The impact of this agreement has not yet been felt in either the PC or the software industry, but it is likely to stimulate further effort by other software firms seeking to design new forms of PC operating systems.

A significant degree of deregulation was occurring in many industries within the United States during the late 1990s. For example, deregulation of the telecommunications industry, through the Telecommunications Act of 1996, makes it legally possible for local phone companies (e.g., Regional Bell Operating Companies such as SBC Communications, Verizon Communications, and Bell South) to enter the long-distance market once held solely by larger interexchange carriers that are the heart of the national telephone system (e.g., AT&T, Sprint, WorldCom). Likewise, the same act enables cable television companies (e.g., Cox Communications, Comcast, Cablevision) to enter the telephone and data transmission markets directly as well. Deregulation of this industry has already promoted a tremendous degree of consolidation pressures among existing, incumbent firms. For example, AT&T agreed to purchase cable giant Tele-Communications Inc. (TCI) in May 1998 to enter the cable television and possibly the local phone market. Likewise, Bell Atlantic merged with GTE to form Verizon Communications, while Qwest Communications International bought US West (both deals completed in 2000). Other Regional Bell Operating Companies (RBOCs) are now in the midst of their own consolidation, with SBC Communications (formerly known as Southwestern Bell) purchasing West Coast giant Pacific Telesis and Ameritech (completed in 1999). WorldCom and Sprint are also speeding up their acquisitions of cable and wireless cable companies to offer local phone service and high-speed Internet access, and they even attempted to merge in the summer of 2000. The federal government, however, intervened and prevented the merger from happening because of potential antitrust reasons.

Response Options

Firms can respond to environmental developments in three fundamentally different ways: by prospecting, defending, or harvesting (see Exhibit 6-4). Each approach aims at a specific objective, requires specific adjustments, and has varying advantages and drawbacks.

Prospecting

prospecting: An activity designed to help the firm search, understand, and accommodate environmental change; a proactive attempt by a firm to make an environmental change favorable to itself (see *defending*).

The most aggressive approach a firm can adopt to deal with environmental change is to strive to be the first to accommodate it. Since the objective is to acknowledge and exploit the new development first, we refer to it as **prospecting**.[7] The actions required of a prospector vary depending on the nature of the environmental development involved. Consider the emergence of new, potentially superior product technology—the kind of change that Kodak faced in the mid-1990s. A prospector experiencing this kind of development must strive to be the first competitor to launch a product incorporating the new technology. To achieve this end, it will need to undertake a series of initiatives. These include conducting research into the new technology, designing prototypes that incorporate the new approach, retooling manufacturing equipment to produce the new design, and promoting finished products once they are ready for market.

Implementing Strategic Response

EXHIBIT 6-4

Response Option	Typical Implementing Actions
Prospect	Develop new distinctive competence Initiate R & D in new technology Learn new manufacturing processes Learn how to design and promote new product
Defend	Preserve existing distinctive competence Reduce price on existing product Increase promotion of existing product Intensify R & D in existing technology

From a historical perspective, consider the issues facing Timex Watch Company, a leading U.S. watch company during the 1970s. Timex faced enormous competitive pressures from new competitors using electronic and digital-based technologies. These technologies represent substitute offerings that steadily displaced mechanical watches, the heart of Timex's product line. One response option for Timex is to engage in prospecting. A prospecting strategy designed to penetrate and secure a portion of the electronic watch market would involve significantly higher levels of investment in learning new forms of electronics and in adopting highly automated tooling processes. These tools would fabricate and assemble quartz and light-emitting diode (LED) components. Eventually, they would displace standard mechanical parts of winding gears, spring wheels, and turning movements. Understanding the new product, learning the new process technologies, and designing a new promotional campaign would represent significant changes in both managerial attention and focus. Pioneering would also cause Timex's existing distinctive competence in mechanical watches to become less relevant over time. Equally important, Timex would have to make capital expenditures in many high fixed-cost investments before uncertainties surrounding the electronic watch would be resolved.

In the currently fast-changing semiconductor industry, many firms in the late 1990s and the early part of this decade have attempted to become prospectors. Firms such as National Semiconductor, Taiwan's Via Technologies, and Britain's ARM Holdings are developing new industry and technological standards that attempt to combine many once disparate functions onto a single sliver of silicon. These standards promise to improve a product's performance on some critical dimension, such as processing speed or compatibility with different types of computer operating systems, consumer electronics, and even Internet applications.

Probably the best example of prospecting in this industry currently includes Transmeta and Applied Micro Circuits. Transmeta has been working on a series of microprocessor designs (code-named Crusoe) that are designed to provide as much power as some of Intel's Pentium III processors with half the power consumption. Transmeta's initial productions of microprocessors have found their way into laptop computers made by Toshiba and NEC of Japan.

In the communications chip sector, Applied Micro Circuits is a leading firm that is developing semiconductors based on germanium, a different core material from the silicon substrate that is at the foundation of most chips. Applied Micro is looking to harness the power of germanium to improve the speed of communications and video transmissions over the Internet and other telecom media.

Other smaller companies such as Integrated Device Technologies (IDTI) and Advanced Micro Devices (AMD) have begun to challenge Intel through prospector-type strategies by offering new microprocessor designs that provide "system-on-a-chip" capabilities. AMD's line of Duron chips is designed to outflank and ambush Intel in the emerging market for microprocessors and controllers in the consumer electronics and sub-$1,000 (and now the sub-$600) personal computer market. Advanced Micro, in particular, has begun to steadily chip away at Intel's total market share and dominance of the microprocessor market (at about 80 percent share in late 2001), although the firm more often than not loses money in its fight. These firms implemented prospector-type strategies more effectively by targeting a niche that Intel either ignored or was unable to respond to effectively.

When formulated and implemented effectively, prospecting enables a firm to gain a head start in exploiting a new development or market trend, thereby securing first-mover, surprise, and timing advantages over later entrants. Prospecting therefore could help a firm preserve its industry position that might erode if it failed to respond. However, prospecting is not without substantial risks, as demonstrated by AMD's battle with Intel. If an anticipated change or development never materializes, or if it evolves in an unanticipated direction, or if the product or service conceived is inadequate, the investment made by a prospector could be partially or wholly lost.

Defending

defending: An activity designed to help the firm shield or insulate itself from environmental change (see *prospecting*).

Another approach to dealing with an environmental change is to make a deliberate choice not to accommodate it. Instead, the firm seeks to defend its traditional business from the development's potentially adverse effects. The chief objective in **defending** is to protect a firm's traditional business from direct or collateral damage brought about by a new development.[8] One of the most common actions to defend a business's current position is a price cut. By lowering price, an established firm can sometimes sustain sales of its traditional product despite stiff competition from a new product or substitute. Recently, Philip Morris engaged in a series of massive price cuts in its premier Marlboro brand of cigarettes to counter the effects of lower-priced generic and off-brand cigarettes that were beginning to erode its margins. By cutting prices aggressively, Philip Morris is hoping to slow down the inroads of generic cigarette makers who must themselves lower their own margins to capture new buyers. Price warfare is also extremely common among consumer nondurable products such as soft drinks, snacks, and other food products. Established firms hope to protect their core market positions and brand recognition from inroads by other firms or new entrants practicing their own form of prospecting in a given segment. PepsiCo's unit Frito-Lay, for example, is now aggressively defending its market position in salt-based snack foods through "value pricing" that enables it to slow the prospecting efforts of generic products made by other food companies.

Another common defensive move is increased promotion. By beefing up its advertising outlay, a defender can delay consumer acceptance of a new approach. One firm that has relied extensively on increased promotion is AT&T in the long-distance industry. AT&T's heavy promotional efforts are designed to ward off the discounting strategies used by WorldCom, Sprint, and other long-distance carriers. AT&T is hoping that consumers associate its corporate name with a higher level of quality and reliability than would be found with a smaller, less experienced firm. Traditional broadcasting networks, such as NBC in television and Clear Channel Communications in radio, are aggressively increasing promotion of their offerings, stars, and new shows to ward off the potential erosion brought about by new digital mediums and Internet transmission technology.

Intensified development or refinement of a traditional or upgraded technology can also help defend an established firm's position by enhancing the attractiveness of its traditional product. Motorola has followed this strategy in its wireless radio business by incorporating the latest advances in microchips to upgrade the two-way radios used for police and emergency services systems. It is now pursuing this same technology improvement strategy to fend off the prospecting moves by such competitors as Nokia, Ericsson, and Qualcomm in the digital phone market. Newer chips and circuit designs make Motorola's offerings more efficient and modernized and give them greater versatility. On the other hand, Motorola's efforts in the wireless satellite phone business followed a prospector-based strategy. Even though Motorola's investment in Iridium and Teledesic (two leading satellite infrastructure firms that promised users the ability to make a call to anybody around the world) was a commercial failure, the company became highly proficient in making satellites for other uses.

While defending enables a firm to avoid the prospecting risks already described, it subjects the firm to risk of another kind. Some environmental developments and changes are so powerful that even the most vigorous defense cannot thwart them. This result is particularly likely if the defending firm faces a radical shift in competence-changing technology or new distribution channels. In particular, many retailing firms are facing this kind of threat and encroachment from Internet-driven commercial firms that seek to gain access to new customers without investing in the traditional "brick-and-mortar" infrastructures and costs. Books, sporting goods, video rentals, travel agencies, and even brokerage firms are faced with a tidal wave of change brought about by compressed and cheap Internet distribution systems. Even pharmacies and drugstores are facing a new threat in the Internet space with the arrival of new health care Web sites that promise low prices and speedy delivery. New technologies or Internet distribution systems threaten to render obsolete the firm's initial investment in its distinctive competences, brand names, market positions, and other sources of competitive advantage. Defending against such major shifts can lead to serious loss of competitive position, regardless of later steps taken to reorient the firm's strategy.

Similarly, today's VCRs may be fading rapidly in the wake of new DVD players and other formats. DVD technology enables the viewer to capture double the clarity and resolution of traditional videotapes. When these new devices allow users to record their music and video on advanced DVD-R systems in the next few years, the market for existing VCR systems, videotapes, and movies will likely plummet. Customers' expectations and demand patterns will likely drive the rapid adoption and diffusion of this new technological standard in both home and commercial settings as the price of DVD technology drops. Thus, the advent of new, more versatile DVD technology means that both VCRs and existing CD formats are likely to fade rapidly in the near future. Defending strategies to ward off the advances of DVD firms are likely to be futile in the long run.

Harvesting

A third general option for a firm facing an environmental shift is to harvest its business while it still has time to do so. The objective of **harvesting** is to generate as much cash from a business as possible before the adverse consequences of an environmental threat materialize. As mentioned in Chapter 4, a key difficulty associated with harvesting is high exit barriers facing the firm. Exit barriers usually exist in the form of dedicated production equipment, specialized assets, and other sunk costs, some of which may have not been completely paid for (amortized). As a result of such barriers, exit often costs as much as investing in new equipment to serve another possible niche or segment.

harvesting: The systematic removal of cash and other assets from a slow-growth or declining business; may be thought of as "milking" a business before it loses all its value.

To harvest a business, a leader must take actions opposite of those described for defending: increase the price of its products and reduce expenditures for such things as research, maintenance, and advertising. Westinghouse Electric during the late 1980s and early 1990s pursued a modified version of this harvesting strategy by selling factories gradually to Asea-Brown-Boveri (ABB) in the power distribution business. Believing that power distribution represents a declining industry, Westinghouse has gradually sold off the product lines associated with heavy-duty transformers and power relays used for high-voltage grids. In the meantime, Westinghouse used the cash to prop up its other industrial and commercial businesses.

Despite its availability as a response option, gradually harvesting a business is generally a poor strategic approach to managing change. Usually, selling assets to a willing buyer if possible is better, because other owners and managers may be able to derive additional value out of assets that would otherwise be "stripped" in harvesting. This situation confronted the Sylvania division of GTE (now part of Verizon Communications) during the early 1980s, when GTE decided investment in consumer electronics represented a major distraction from its core telephone businesses. Eventually, GTE sold its Sylvania line of color televisions to a competitor.

Harvesting also means that the firm must devote considerable managerial effort to a declining business when that effort could be better spent looking for more attractive businesses. General Electric decided against harvesting its consumer electronics group by selling the entire business outright to Thomson, S.A. of France, in exchange for the French firm's medical electronics business and a large cash infusion.

Generic Change Situations

A key pillar of strategic management is that managers have the ability to make adjustments to their firms' strategies following an environmental change. In reality, constraints imposed by the competitive environment, the needs of different stakeholders, and the organization itself may limit senior management's degree of "maneuvering room" needed to undertake rapid adjustments. Nevertheless, adjustment to environmental change requires considerable managerial judgment in deciding what type of response will best navigate the firm through a change or modification of strategy. In selecting one of three response options—prospecting, defending, or harvesting—a firm must balance two critical factors: the magnitude of the threat posed by an environmental development and a firm's ability to adjust to the development.

Magnitude of Threat

Some environmental developments have only modest impact on a firm's core business. Growth of a small specialty niche within an industry is a case in point. Such a development may cause defection of only a few of the established firms' traditional customers. When new niches remain small and confined, the need to adapt is relatively minor. For example, the rise of Polaroid in instant photography resulted in limited inroads into Kodak's business. Although customers were initially fascinated with the concept of instant photography that did not require long waiting times for film development, the poor picture quality of Polaroid's instant photography technology limited its appeal to a wide base of Kodak customers. On the other hand, this situation is unlike one in which a development threatens the very foundation of an established firm's business and sources of competitive advantage. Failure to adjust can then bring about rapid and severe loss of market position. With the growing use of digital imaging technologies by upstart entrants, this appears to be happening in a variety of different distribution-intensive industries.

Ability to Adjust

Adjusting to an environmental development or shift generally obliges a firm to build some sort of new skills and competences. To offer customers new ways of sampling and purchasing music, for example, the record label companies need to develop a new competence in digital security, encryption, and telecom-based skills that allow for fast downloads and easy use. Similarly, Eastman Kodak will need significantly greater investment, competence, and experience with semiconductors, display technologies, and digital imaging techniques to make a successful transition to new forms of digital photography. Before attempting such an adjustment, however, firms must assess their ability to develop the necessary new competence and skill set.

New types of distinctive competences and skills required for adjusting to an environmental shift can come in many forms. For example, skills in software engineering and mathematical algorithms would help record label companies better understand and manage the complexity of offering music over the Internet. A strong presence in color televisions and display screens would help an electronics manufacturer quickly adjust to developing laptop and notebook computers. Experience and competence in applied chemistry and blending techniques can be valuable skills for a consumer nondurables firm in making new types of laundry detergent or stain removers (as is the case for Procter & Gamble, Unilever, Henkel, as well as Clorox). Telecommunications expertise is becoming a necessity for firms seeking to establish a strong presence in all types of emerging digital media industries, in which new forms of content and publishing are combined into interactive multimedia platforms and transmitted along fiber-optic cables. A strong ability to manage networks (e.g., routers and switches) can greatly assist a telecommunications or content firm in dealing with the fast growth and demand for information.

In assessing the capability for adjustment, a firm must often reconfigure its entire value chain or business system to develop a broad range of new skills. Finding and building a new distinctive competence is extremely difficult, since significant resistance to change is likely to occur within the organization. Ironically, established firms may experience more difficulty in creating an entirely new distinctive competence than would a new entrant. Established firms are likely to have their own managerial practices and ways of thinking that can complicate the adjustment to a new technology, distribution channel, or other shift. This difficulty that established firms may face in implementing change is known as **inertia**. Inertia is an important factor that inhibits fast response to environmental developments, particularly for large, well-established firms in mature industries facing new types of technologies and competitors. Sometimes, the best approach to developing a new distinctive competence required for adjustment is a clean sheet of paper that "frees" management from the cognitive maps and mental constraints imposed by long experience with an existing technology or distribution setup.[9] In other words, the existence of older distinctive competences and sources of competitive advantage may erect real cognitive and economic adjustment barriers to learning new ones.

inertia:
The difficulty that established firms face when trying to adjust to change; inhibits fast response to new developments in the environment

The underlying tone of our discussion so far has implied that an environmental development or shift usually poses a threat to existing sources of competitive advantage. On the other hand, new developments can also represent opportunities for firms willing and able to recognize and adjust to them. Established firms that already possess many of the skills needed to make the adjustment may find that the new development opens up markets previously unavailable to them. In other words, adjustment efforts could pave the way to unforeseen prospecting opportunities. For example, the rise of multimedia-based technologies that could revolutionize the design, manufacture, and distribution of television sets, CD players, personal computers, hand-held computers, personal digital assistants (PDAs), cable television, set-top boxes, Internet connections, DVD technology, and telecommunications poses a dual threat and opportunity for companies such as Sony, Hewlett-Packard, Motorola, IBM, AT&T, WorldCom, Cisco Systems, Handspring, and Philips Electronics. On the one hand, those firms with a strong base of experience and skills in semiconductors and computers, such as IBM and Motorola, may find that they have many of the ingredients and "raw materials" necessary to participate and compete in a broader multimedia industry. As a result, this new development could represent an opening to serve markets that previously did not exist. Similarly, Sony and Philips Electronics possess many of the distinctive competences and insights needed to design, manufacture, distribute, and market consumer electronics and Internet hardware (e.g., devices for WebTV) that would appeal to a broad array of global markets. The manufacturing and marketing "muscle" of these two firms could propel multimedia and Internet access technologies and products into many new markets. AT&T's and WorldCom's commanding positions in telecommunications and advanced transmission networks endow them with a unique set of skills and market that digital media industries will need to reach the Internet. Both firms have access to the transmission technologies that would allow for interactive cable television and new forms of entertainment. Finally, Cisco Systems' exceptionally strong position in designing new switches and routers to underpin Internet communications systems enables this fast-moving computer-networking firm to provide equipment for Internet and video transmissions, even across existing telecommunications infrastructures. Thus, even though the rise of multimedia and digital media formats represents a potential threat to each of these players in terms of technological shifts and new entry, its arrival also means an opportunity for each of the firms to apply their existing distinctive competences and skills to this emerging arena. Each firm's current sources of competitive advantage would need some adjustment to enable the firm to compete fully and effectively in the emerging industry. However, successful adjustment and learning of new competences and skills in addition to existing skills would enable each of these firms to prospect in a completely new, related, or potentially redefined industry.

Common Change Situations

Let us now combine these two dimensions—ability to adjust and magnitude of threat—to form the matrix shown in Exhibit 6-5. The figure depicts four generic change situations distinguished on the basis of the magnitude of the opportunity or threat posed by environmental change and the ability of a firm to deal with developments brought about by change. An established firm facing environmental change will generally need to respond differently to each of these situations.

EXHIBIT 6-5 Major Response Options

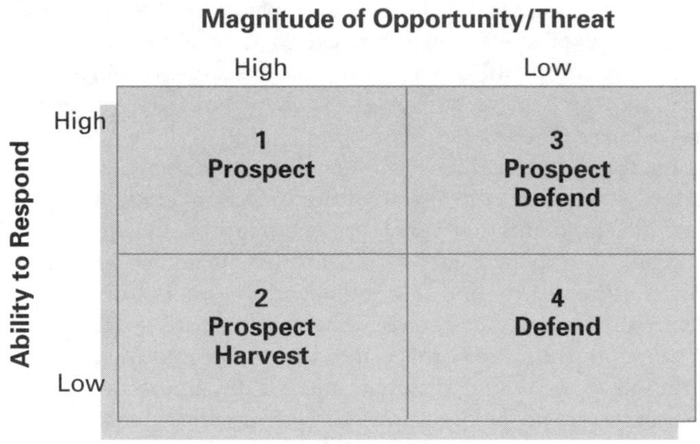

Ability to Respond \ Magnitude of Opportunity/Threat	High	Low
High	1 **Prospect**	3 **Prospect** **Defend**
Low	2 **Prospect** **Harvest**	4 **Defend**

Cell 1. A firm in this kind of situation faces a serious environmental development. The development could result in permanent loss of competitive position if the firm fails to respond. However, the firm possesses the ability to respond. When these two conditions are present, then a firm should try to establish itself quickly in the new area, meaning it should prospect. Any other approach would enable rivals to gain the lead in responding to the development by giving them the first-mover, experience, and scale advantages that a hesitant or late-responding firm would have trouble matching.

Intel in the late 1990s faced this predicament when designing microprocessors for the sub-$1,000 PC market. If it failed to respond to the new system-on-a-chip microprocessor technologies introduced by Advanced Micro Devices, Intel would face vastly more powerful, ambitious, and aggressive competitors seeking to break its stronghold on conventional microprocessors to serve higher-priced machines in both the consumer and commercial marketplaces. However, Intel has a strong commitment and the distinctive competences necessary to develop its own chip-based design and manufacturing skills for a segment that it concedes it neglected earlier in the decade. The firm began shipping its own version of a cheaper microprocessor named Celeron that complements its higher-priced lines of Pentium III and Pentium 4 microprocessors. Intel is thus pursuing a prospector strategy in the low-end, sub-$1,000 PC market by offering a new line of chips for a growing market segment. So far, Intel's response, although somewhat belated, has been to gain some share back from its smaller competitors.[10]

Microsoft in a similar way has responded to the demands for customized and open-systems software through its new line of Windows 98, Windows 2000, Windows XP, Windows NT (which stands for "New Technologies") and Windows Pocket PC products. Customers have increasingly demanded new forms of software that can work across IBM, Apple, Compaq Computer, and other proprietary systems. Failure to meet its customers' requests would leave Microsoft vulnerable to new entrants. The new Microsoft Windows 98 and NT product lines are designed to allow machines from different manufacturers—IBM, Digital Equipment (now part of Compaq Computer), Hewlett-Packard, and Sun Microsystems—to "talk" with one another. More recently, Windows Pocket PC, as adopted by such manufacturers as Hewlett-Packard and Casio, has given rise to new digital network appliances that work across and link up with copiers, computers, personal digital assistants, network devices, telephones, and other office equipment through a common software language using a streamlined version of Windows. To reinforce its lead, Microsoft is heading a consortium of twenty different companies (including software, computer, and office equipment manufacturers) to design their hardware offerings around variants of Microsoft's proprietary software language codes. This step helps Microsoft's corporate customers gain access to new products first, and it keeps other software providers at bay.

In the aerospace industry, Boeing confronts a situation similar to those facing Intel and Microsoft. The advent of a powerful competitor in Europe, Airbus Industries, has challenged Boeing with new types of commercial jet aircraft. An emerging technological development and challenge also exist. The rise of new technologies incorporating fly-by-wire controls (replacing hydraulics) threatens Boeing's skills in its current line of aircraft designs and manufacturing skills. Boeing has been quick to invest in, learn, and apply these new electronics-driven technologies for use in its new line of 777 aircraft. These new aircraft, incorporating the latest technological advances, became available for customers in 1996 and 1997. With competition between Boeing and Airbus now intensifying, Boeing is now planning to develop a whole new line of subsonic jet aircraft that promise to greatly slice down the amount of traveling time. These subsonic jets are designed to fly almost as fast as the speed of sound, but be able to land in smaller airports for travelers' convenience.

Cell 2. The most difficult situation confronting an established firm occurs when an environmental development or shift poses a major threat to its sources of competitive advantage, but the firm lacks the ability to respond. Timex faced this kind of situation when the electronic revolution swept through its industry in the 1970s. The new technology threatened to revolutionize manufacture of low-priced watches. Consequently, if Timex failed to respond, it risked serious loss of competitive position. Timex possessed little electronic capability, and thus it lacked the ability to make an effective response.

IBM's mainframe business faces growing competition from the personal computer, client-server, networking, and workstation markets. Its difficulties point out the real dangers of how competence-changing technologies can dramatically redefine the basis of competitive advantage within an industry. Distribution channels have also changed markedly in the industry. Although IBM retains great technological expertise to compete in these newer markets, it remains burdened by older management practices that do not easily support the newer strategies of speed and agility required in the personal computer and networking markets. In fact, IBM's efforts in the PC business, despite gaining significant share, are still trailing the actions and strategies of Dell Computer and even Hewlett-Packard. It is widely believed that IBM continues to lose money by trying to make and sell its own line of PCs.

During the 1970s and 1980s many integrated U.S. steelmakers (U.S. Steel, Inland, National, Armco, LTV, Bethlehem) suffered from two types of shifts. First, domestic minimills used nonunion labor and cheaper scrap metal to gain market share. They produced lower-cost steel and responded more quickly to customer changes in demand, since they tended to operate closer to their customers. Second, more efficient and modernized plants in Korea and Japan eroded away U.S. technological leadership. The U.S. steel industry failed to invest consistently in new oxygen-based furnaces and continuous casting processes. On the other hand, Japanese and Korean producers spent large sums on R&D to improve the steel-making process by introducing new forms of temperature controls and quality improvement techniques. The U.S. steel industry fell behind when its open-hearth furnace technology could not produce the high-quality steel demanded by its key customers. Auto and appliance makers then began to buy the improved steel needed in making cars, motors, components, and appliance frames from ultramodern Korean and Japanese plants.

An industry currently undergoing massive changes is the U.S. health care system. The U.S. hospital industry during the 1990s faced many of the environmental shifts that signify a cell 2 predicament. Overcapacity and investment in high-technology equipment have forced many U.S. hospitals, both private and public, to operate with large losses. In addition, hospitals also face wrenching demands for lower costs, improved efficiency, and quality care made by managed care firms, traditional insurance companies, doctors, patients, and the federal government. Even worse, reimbursements for hospital care have been declining so fast over the past several years that many hospitals are close to bankruptcy. Even the well-funded hospitals in large cities are facing enormous budgetary problems as Medicare and other government programs slash the amount they pay to hospitals for care of indigents and senior citizens.

This kind of pressure for cost containment and technological improvement are also impacting physicians and other care providers in a major way, as the U.S. health care system adjusts to the demands of managed care systems and markedly fewer hospitals in existence. These factors dramatically increase the traditional hospital's cost base. Already, many doctors are performing specialized or rapid-recovery medical services and care in facilities outside traditional hospitals. Known as *carve-outs*, these physician-owned and physician-managed facilities are beginning to compete with hospitals for the more lucrative lines of care (e.g., cardiology, ophthalmology, oncology, radiology, diagnostic testing). Moving these activities out of the hospital helps lower the costs for patients and managed care firms. In this way, patients receive care and managed care/insurance providers do not incur the high costs of using traditional hospital facilities. Medical procedures that are now performed more frequently outside of the hospital include cataract and minor skin surgeries.

However, these trends have been devastating to hospital finances. To deal with this development, many hospital chains (particularly those managed by Columbia HCA and Tenet) have restructured, consolidated, and even merged their operations. Columbia HCA's noteworthy acquisition and restructuring moves of many hospitals around the country during the 1990s are designed to reposition hospitals so they can gradually slim down their operations, gain economies of scale in key activities (particularly information processing, pharmaceutical purchases, and government reimbursement of Medicare fees), and thus lower their fixed costs.

One approach for a firm in this kind of situation is harvesting—extracting cash from a business before adverse consequences take full effect. Harvesting represents an extreme and generally undesirable solution, since it deliberately and methodically reduces a once healthy business to extinction. Moreover, environmental developments and shifts often proceed so rapidly that harvesting yields only a limited amount of cash, potentially far less than if the business were sold outright. A more viable solution for leaders in this kind of situation is vigorous prospecting. While prospecting is clearly difficult for a firm that lacks the necessary skills and resources, limited forms of prospecting should still be considered, especially if such activity can be performed in conjunction with another firm. By channeling effort in this direction, firms are sometimes able to develop the needed expertise to respond to environmental change. To succeed, they must initiate prospecting efforts early, long before adverse developments threatening their businesses fully materialize, as Barnes & Noble and Borders Group are attempting to do in the wake of Amazon.com's challenge. Concentration of effort is key, although senior management may resist the need to do so. Prospecting almost always means commitment of resources to some uncertain endeavor, resources that are in demand by other areas within the organization. Unfortunately, serious organizational obstacles often impede this sort of initiative, as was the case with the domestic steel and television industries during the 1980s and possibly many hospital systems in the late 1990s. As a result, firms that are either unwilling or unable to recognize the need for early prospecting find themselves unable to handle serious competitive challenges later.

A firm facing the need to prospect quickly can sometimes shorten the time required to develop new competences and skills by teaming up with a partner who already possesses new skills. Timex, for example, might have obtained the electronic-based technologies it needed by working with an electronic component manufacturer such as Texas Instruments or Motorola (with which it now has a joint technology development relationship). It would then have had instant access to the new forms of skills or technologies needed to make the adjustment. Conversely, Timex potentially could have licensed existing electronic technologies from other firms that were either unaware or uninterested in entering the watch market.

Cell 3. A firm in this situation has the capability to respond to an environmental change, so prospecting is a fully viable option. Prospecting is not immediately urgent, however, since not doing so will not result in serious erosion of the firm's competitive advantage. Defending to reinforce a firm's current distinctive competences and skills is an equally viable option. Merrill Lynch's decision to avoid excessive commitment to the LBO (leveraged buyout) sector during the 1980s is a cell 3 response. In the wake of massive corporate restructurings, powerful LBO firms, such as KKR (Kohlberg, Kravis and Roberts), carved up this market. Instead, Merrill Lynch reinforced its core brokerage business and its expertise in the consumer market for financial planning and investments. It invested in new computer technologies and expanded its traditional product offerings in the stock and bond markets. Merrill also maintains a host of smaller positions in asset management, mutual funds, and other lines of businesses. Merrill's strong brokerage franchise, wide consumer recognition, and computer-based investments allow it to enter many new financial service areas without facing undue environmental risk from existing competitors. However, Merrill appears to be facing a dilemma concerning how best to deal with the advent of new Internet-based online technologies.

Partnering or allying with other firms is a highly effective cell 3 response strategy that enables a firm to prospect and defend simultaneously. For example, in the music industry, many record label companies formed relationships with RealNetworks and MP3.com to learn how best to harness the Internet to manage digital distribution. The MusicNet and Pressplay alliances formed by the record label companies are indicative of the kind of prospecting that is needed to bring in new skills and insights to help regain competitiveness.

In the telecommunications industry in the late 1990s, AT&T undertook a broad prospecting initiative by forming alliances with scores of different firms to help the company adapt to a changing industry environment. The company also purchased two major cable companies (TeleCommunications, Inc. and MediaOne Group) and Internet-oriented firms (e.g., ExciteAtHome) to learn how to compete in emerging Internet technologies and markets. Ultimately, these were costly endeavors that saddled AT&T with tremendous debt. By 2002, AT&T had retreated from its cable investments by selling its Broadband unit to Comcast. Alliances with other firms can help AT&T prospect into new businesses while still using its competences and skills in information management and telecommunications. At the same time, however, AT&T's long-distance services are coming under intense price pressure from other competitors, such as WorldCom and Sprint, and even from local phone companies in some regions (e.g., Verizon Communications in New York State). By responding with new discount calling plans, AT&T is simultaneously defending its traditional long-distance telephone business from WorldCom and Sprint's continuous assaults, as well as likely threats from deregulated local phone companies.

However, while AT&T realizes that defending its long-distance business through discounting is a viable option in itself, a cell 3 combination of prospecting and defending is needed to create and exploit new sources of competitive advantage, particularly as the traditional telephone industry is converging with Internet and other forms of telecommunications. First, prospecting efforts help AT&T find new types of businesses that could utilize and reinforce its existing telecommunications services. Second, prospecting helps AT&T understand and develop the skills to serve and compete in newly emerging technologies, such as on-line video games, wireless local-loop service, entertainment, interactive cable television, and very high-speed Internet access. These new industries can readily borrow from AT&T's distinctive competences in information processing and managing advanced fiber networks. By forming alliances to learn how other firms compete in these areas, AT&T will be better able not only to adjust to technological shifts in related or neighboring industries but to participate in them as well. Third, maintaining a strong defense of its current long-distance transmission business against new competitors such as MCI WorldCom and Sprint helps AT&T retain its overwhelming market share (50+ percent) that provides an important source of brand awareness among its customers. Time, however, may not be on AT&T's side in the long run, especially if the company feels that it cannot compete as effectively as new entrants that bring even newer technology to the marketplace.

Cell 4. A firm in this situation lacks the capability to respond to an environmental development, but the development poses only a modest threat to its position. Under these conditions, a firm should generally avoid prospecting, for several reasons. First, prospecting is expensive since it requires development of new competences and skills significantly different from those the firm currently possesses. Second, given the firm's current lack of skill in the new area, a prospecting effort that fails may be extremely costly. Third, since the environmental development poses only a modest threat, a decision not to prospect will not seriously undermine the firm's competitive health. A firm facing this kind of situation should therefore avoid prospecting and instead concentrate its resources to defend its position by reinforcing existing sources of competitive advantage. Fourth, the technology involved in prospecting may be uncertain. Even if the firm can learn a new technology, it may have to commit a disproportionate amount of resources to do so.

General Electric's Major Home Appliance Group (MHAG) faces a cell 4 type of threat. As environmental regulations gradually restrict the amount and type of CFC-based (chlorofluorocarbon) chemicals that can be used in refrigeration and air-conditioning systems, firms are beginning to develop substitute coolants. Innovative firms such as Bose (the manufacturer of high-end automobile stereo systems) have designed cooling systems based on acoustics and semiconductor technologies. Even though these new concepts are beginning to threaten GE's core skills and distinctive competence in rotary and reciprocating compressors (the heart of most refrigerators), they are still years away from being effectively commercialized. More improvements will be needed for use in large home appliances. In turn, GE has decided to defend by renewing its commitment to improve the efficiency, quality, and durability of its current compressor line.

A similar cell 4 situation faces the Big Three automakers—General Motors, Ford, and DaimlerChrysler—in their continued use of internal combustion engines to power automobiles. Although new types of electric, hybrid fuel cell, and battery-powered cars are currently in development, they are not expected to be available for wide commercial use for a number of years. At present, battery and electric-powered cars do not have the staying power, performance, or long running times of more conventional gasoline-powered engines, although this will likely change during the decade. Vigorous prospecting will eventually be required, although all of the automakers are committed to developing advanced fuel cell technologies for use in the early part of the decade.

Uncertainty

Thus far, we have generally ignored the issue of uncertainty associated with environmental change. In reality, environmental change and responding to it are usually fraught with great uncertainty. The changing situations in digital music distribution at present and Eastman Kodak in the 1990s exemplify the degree of uncertainty that established firms face when confronted with new developments. Uncertainty surrounds the impact of new developments on a firm's existing sources of competitive advantage and on its ability to learn new skills and competences.

Impact of Environmental Development

From our current perspective, anyone could surmise that consumer acceptance of new formats of digital music ultimately depended on the speed of Internet connections, convenience and ease of use, and the cost relative to conventional CDs. Even though technology continues to progress, a fair degree of uncertainty still surrounds both Internet speed and the cost of incorporating new types of electronics to make this media more easily accepted by the broader marketplace. In addition, some performing artists may feel the Internet can potentially result in the mass piracy of their performances.

Consider first the issue of Internet speed. As downloading music files becomees faster and easier, the growth of digital music will surge. Second, the acceptance of digital music will likely depend on how fast the cost for MP3 players, CD burners, and other new forms of consumer electronics will decline in the next few years. If history is any indication, these "hardware" products typically follow steep price curves wherein they become less expensive over time as the devices mature. However, if the record label companies begin developing their own digital recording and playback formats independently of each other, then there is a growing risk that future digital distribution systems may require consumers to bear either significant monetary costs or inconvenience to gain access to digital music.

Finally, with respect to performing artists, the Internet is a double-edged sword. On the one hand, it allows customers to sample their music and bring the performing artist much greater awareness by the public. On the other hand, the proliferation of the Internet means that performing artists (and their record companies) now must compete for a share of cyberspace that is always growing. It is possible to envision hundreds of thousands of music tracks on the Internet. This means that even popular bands and upcoming songs could become overwhelmed by the sheer amount of music available over the Net. Unless there are new ways to sift through all the information and music samples that are out there, some consumers may feel that searching for Internet-based music may not be worth the trouble.

Now, Eastman Kodak faces a parallel set of uncertainties concerning the rise of electronic photography. Consumer acceptance of charged-coupled devices (CCDs), flash memories, personal computer networking cards, and later formats of digital "film-free" photography depends greatly on the fineness and quality of image resolution. Also the cost of the new equipment is a big question. Product acceptance ultimately depends on how customers feel about the new technology and its cost, thus introducing significant uncertainty into the planning process. Advances by Kodak rivals, such as Epson's Photo PC and Sony's newer versions of its Mavica technology, make it difficult to respond effectively because competitors' moves will often depend on their own technological trajectories and views of the market.

Ability to Adjust

If the record companies decide to embrace new digital music formats fully, they can initially benefit from their well-known brand names, sponsorship of popular bands, worldwide distribution network, and sophisticated promotional abilities. These sources of competitive advantage would not guarantee success in the new field, however. To become a potent competitor or leader in digital music formats, Vivendi Universal, Sony, Bertelsmann AG, and Warner Music would need skills in areas such as encryption, digital compression techniques, and telecom-based skills. Sony and AOL Time Warner, in particular, have other businesses within the same firm that could offer some of these technical skills. However, other firms that specialize in these areas can potentially offer superior technology (Verisign, RealNetworks, Qwest Communications). These companies possess the skills that would complement what record labels can offer. By forming a partnership or alliance with firms such as these, the record label firms might be able to overcome some of the technical obstacles involved. As noted in the initial example, MusicNet and Pressplay represent new initiatives by the record label companies to learn how best to compete on the Internet.

Eastman Kodak today confronts a similar set of questions concerning its adjustment ability. One of Kodak's key problems is that its current competence in digital imaging technology is not significantly better than that possessed by Hewlett-Packard, Intel, Motorola, Canon, Sharp, or Epson. These firms have major sources of competitive advantage in their brand names, proprietary processes, and miniaturization technology, honed through fierce competition in the instrumentation, semiconductor, consumer electronics, office equipment, and imaging industries. Firms competing in these related or neighboring industries are likely to develop new product technologies and manufacturing processes that could eventually be applied to digital imaging. Since Eastman Kodak is not a significant player in consumer electronics or office equipment, it has little potential to transfer or share skills from other businesses to its imaging unit, despite its current command and ownership of many digital imaging patents. Kodak must now deal with the strategic dilemma of learning how to apply uncertain technologies for next-generation consumer photography and imaging, without excessively cannibalizing or destroying its current core chemical and film coatings businesses. This dilemma is a major source of organizational uncertainty.

If significant uncertainty surrounds a new development, the best initial course may be simply to investigate the development to learn more about it. Investigating involves learning about developments in related or neighboring industries, finding out what other competitors are doing, studying technology research, developing prototypes of new products, and conducting market research. Investigating enables firms to avoid making a large investment that may ultimately be unsuccessful. However, simply investigating poses another kind of risk: a firm that spends too much time investigating a new development risks losing the lead to more aggressive competitors.

Another potentially better approach is to allocate small resources to establishing *skunk works* whose sole purpose is to better understand new technology. These skunk works would thus engage in a variety of R&D activities, as well as reverse engineering, active searching for new product development approaches, and streamlining existing technologies to improve upon a competitor's development. Firms can sometimes establish small divisions or business units whose sole purpose is to prospect and experiment with new technologies with the hope that they can capture some new insights and develop a new product, service, process, or distribution channel within enough time to recover from a competitor's moves. An even more novel approach would be to form a direct relationship with prospective competitors to learn jointly the potential benefits of emerging core technologies. This strategy would be particularly useful for a company in a substantially weaker position, since it has little to lose and much to gain.

Ethical Dimension

What balance should top managers strike between the alternative objectives of prospecting, defending, or harvesting? Should top managers seek to "get ahead of the curve" and sell a currently prosperous business before being confronted with the decision to harvest? How much should senior management tilt their judgment toward prospecting versus defending? Clearly, no single answer is applicable to firms in different types of change situations. The decision to prospect or to defend hinges heavily on the nature of the environmental development, the firm's ability to adjust, and the extent to which the firm or business can devote sufficient resources to make the adjustment. Unfortunately, senior management in many firms start addressing and acting upon these issues only when their backs are against the wall. Nevertheless, the decision to prospect, defend, or harvest depends significantly on the degree of uncertainty and risk that senior management feels that the firm can bear.

Many prospecting efforts involve considerable short- to medium-term risk. Sufficient funds must be devoted to exploring and investing in new technologies, skills, distribution channels, and other future sources of competitive advantage that may not bear fruit for several years. However, failure to respond to an environmental development will often subject the firm to another kind of long-term risk—the risk that the firm will eventually lose all of its existing sources of competitive advantage and never recover. Regardless of which strategic option is invoked, the balance between risk and return inherent within each of these response options should also factor in the needs of different stakeholders.

The task of reconciling stakeholder needs with respect to risk and return is complicated by the fact that top managers are one stakeholder group whose interests are factored into this equation. Unfortunately, their needs sometimes conflict with those of other stakeholder groups, particularly with those of shareholders. Managers are sometimes tempted to give their own needs undue weight when making a decision.[11] Succumbing to this temptation raises potentially serious ethical questions, since managers have a fiduciary responsibility to act on behalf of shareholders. To understand the nature of this problem, let us briefly contrast the risk and reward preferences of top managers and shareholders.

Risk Preference

Institutions—pension plans, mutual funds, and insurance companies—hold a majority of shares of public companies. Let us therefore put ourselves in the place of an institutional shareholder. The holdings of institutions are generally widely diversified. For example, a mutual fund commonly holds shares in more than a hundred different firms. Because their holdings are so diverse, institutions stand to suffer only minor loss if an effort to prospect or to enter a new market undertaken by one of the companies in their portfolio ultimately fails. Institutions can thus tolerate considerable prospecting risk.

Now let us consider managers of companies owned by institutions. They are often held accountable when new ventures fail. Such failure can result in termination of their employment, problems securing employment with other firms, and severe psychological hardship. Managers thus stand to suffer serious professional and personal hardship from failure of ventures for which they are responsible. As a consequence, they may be inclined to be more risk-averse over the short to medium term and therefore avoid vigorous prospecting efforts.

Return Preference

The payoff from success of high-risk prospecting efforts is also generally different for managers and shareholders. Top managers of most public companies own only a small portion of the equity of the firms they oversee. As a result, their reward from successful new ventures is limited mainly to such things as enhanced compensation and improved career prospects. These benefits are important. However, they pale next to those that shareholders can derive from new venture success. Consider, for example, Bill Gates, founder and major shareholder of Microsoft, the spectacularly successful Seattle-based computer software company. His original investment of a few thousand dollars in 1980 has grown into an ownership position worth more than $90 billion in market value in the middle of 2001. He and the many institutional investors holding Microsoft shares have thus reaped enormous returns from this high-risk venture.

These considerations suggest that managers often have more to lose and less to gain from high-risk/high-return ventures than shareholders. As a consequence, managers are often tempted to forego such projects in favor of lower-risk/lower-return efforts. In other words, defending becomes a natural outcome or response because of the way senior management is itself rewarded. Requests by lower-level managers to engage in prospecting initiatives often meet significant resistance and must be justified by the presence of a direct and immediate threat. The status quo becomes preferable, since operating the firm on "cruise control" is much easier. Managers who succumb to this temptation often end up putting their own interests above those of shareholders, thereby potentially sidestepping their fiduciary duty to shareholders.

The extent to which risk avoidance may inhibit top managers of public companies from exploiting potentially lucrative opportunities is difficult to judge. Nevertheless, this factor has likely played some role in the spectacular declines of one-time giants like General Motors and IBM. Both companies have displayed a consistent pattern of avoiding high-risk but potentially lucrative new niches in their industries. Prospecting became difficult because of the enormous inertia these two large companies had developed. General Motors, for example, paid little attention to rapidly growing demand for small, fuel-efficient autos during the 1970s and 1980s. As a result, other firms—most notably, Japanese competitors—

now dominate this important segment. IBM has displayed a similar reluctance to exploit emerging opportunities in its industry, letting other firms pioneer and eventually dominate such lucrative niches as computer services, software for personal computers, advanced graphics software, network servers, and new forms of operating systems.

The issue of harvesting a business also presents another ethically related dilemma in the sense that this particular response option can be demoralizing to lower-level managers and employees in the firm. Harvesting involves the gradual dissolution of the business, which inevitably results in people losing their jobs over time. Selling the business outright may offer some of the affected managers and employees at least some potential for continued employment with another owner who could better identify valuable uses for the underlying assets. Also from a shareholder perspective, harvesting is usually less desirable than selling the firm or business. Selling the business, even with associated exit barriers, releases existing capital from increasingly less productive uses.

Summary

- Environmental change and developments can significantly alter an industry's competitive environment. Moreover, new developments or shifts can sometimes dramatically affect the value and threaten existing sources of competitive advantage.
- Competence-changing technologies are advances that could redefine an industry's structure and technological format.
- The growth of the Internet as a new distribution system has fundamentally changed the way firms in both product and service industries can now reach and meet their customers' needs. The Internet will likely become an important competitor to firms in many existing industries as customers face fewer switching costs, greater convenience, and easy access to competitors' offerings.
- Environmental changes or developments in related or neighboring industries can eventually make themselves felt in any given industry. Oftentimes, technological, distribution, or demand changes in one industry can have ripple effects that ultimately require a shift in a firm's strategy, resource allocation, and sources of competitive advantage in another.
- Firms facing new developments or shifts can respond in three fundamentally different ways: prospecting, defending, or harvesting.
- Selection of the appropriate response option should be based on the magnitude of the opportunity or threat that the change presents and the firm's ability to adjust.
- High levels of uncertainty accompany environmental developments. When uncertainty is extremely high, it is sometimes preferable to investigate the change first until a clearer picture emerges. Spending an excessive amount of time investigating, however, can result in costly response delay.

Exercises and Discussion Questions

1. Using the Internet, look up the Web site for Blockbuster Entertainment. What are some steps that Blockbuster has taken to protect its huge investment in music retailing by using the Internet? How does its Web site differ from that of Vivendi or Sony? What type of strategy is Blockbuster pursuing by using the Web? Is it prospecting or defending?

2. Now, look up the Web sites for Vivendi and Sony. How do these two Web sites differ from each other and from Blockbuster's? In your judgment, are there any particular attributes in Vivendi and Sony's Web sites that enable these firms to sustain doing business using the Internet alone? What type of strategies are these three firms pursuing? What should they do in the future?

@ 3. The rise of digital photography remains an ongoing challenge for Eastman Kodak. Look up Kodak's Web site and describe some of the investments that it has made recently in learning how to compete in this era. How would you describe Kodak's strategy in this emerging digital photography arena? In what areas does the Web site suggest that Kodak is prospecting? What are some different approaches that Kodak has used in its prospecting strategy?

@ 4. Visit the Web site of E-Stamp and that of the U.S. Postal Service. What other services would you recommend that these two entrants provide to broaden the appeal of their strategy? Now look up Pitney Bowes on the Web. What should this company do to help it compete against the new entrants?

5. Which type of firm appears to be better able to carry out a prospecting strategy—large or small? What are some key attributes that prospectors need to have, regardless of size?

Endnotes

1. Facts and data for examining this strategy snapshot were adapted from the following sources: "Dysfunctional Discs," *Dallas Morning News*, February 21, 2002, p. 3D; "Vivendi Seeks Respect from U.S. Investors," *Wall Street Journal*, February 12, 2002, pp. A12, A14; "Vivendi Universal Prospers in Hard Times for Media Firms," *Wall Street Journal*, December 18, 2001, p. B8; "Entertainment Industry Sues to Curtail Web Music-Sharing System Morpheus," *Wall Street Journal*, October 4, 2001, p. B9; "Vivendi to Begin Releasing CDs Equipped With Technology to Deter Digital Piracy," *Wall Street Journal*, September 26, 2001, p. B2; "Online Music: Can't Get No . . . ," *Business Week*, September 3, 2001, pp. 78–80; "Sony, Warner to Back Protection Standard," *Wall Street Journal*, July 17, 2001, p. B7; "Sony to Unveil Online Music Studio," *Wall Street Journal*, June 18, 2001, p. B8; "Vivendi Universal Is Betting on Future of Wireless Movies and Music," *Wall Street Journal*, May 24, 2001, pp. B1, B4; "Vivendi Universal to Buy MP3.com for $372 Million in Cash and Stock," *Wall Street Journal*, May 21, 2001, pp. A3, 12; "Plugging into the Web Is a Jarring Experience for the Music Industry," *Wall Street Journal*, April 12, 2001, pp. A1, A10; "Music Companies Plan to Team Up with RealNetworks," *Wall Street Journal*, April 3, 2001, p. B8; "Download, Downshift and Go: MP3 Takes to the Road," *Wall Street Journal*, February 27, 2001, pp. B1, B4; "Tech Firms to Announce Improvements in Delivery of Internet Audio and Video," *Wall Street Journal*, December 11, 2000, p. B12; "Napster Alliance Boosts Prospects for Encryption," *Wall Street Journal*, November 2, 2000, p. B1, B20; "Bertelsmann Deal Marks Alternative Web Strategy," *Wall Street Journal*, September 25, 2000, p. A20; "Warner Music Will Join Digital-Download Market," *Wall Street Journal*, September 11, 2000, p. B14; "Bertelsmann, in Online Play, to Buy CDNow," *Wall Street Journal*, July 20, 2000, pp. B1, B4; "Now the Napsterization of Movies," *Wall Street Journal*, July 17, 2000, pp. B1, B7; "AOL Agrees to Use Software Made by RealNetworks," *Wall Street Journal*, July 13, 2000, p. B14; "Making Music Together on Web Becomes Reality," *Wall Street Journal*, July 6, 2000, pp. B1, B10; "Can the Record Industry Beat Free Web Music?" *Wall Street Journal*, June 20, 2000, pp. B1, B4; "MP3.com Plans to Store CD Copies on Web Site," *Wall Street Journal*, January 13, 2000, p. B11.

2. Facts and data for Eastman Kodak were adapted from the following sources: "Kodak Advances in Market Share of Digital Cameras," *Wall Street Journal*, December 21, 2001, p. B2; "Price Wars, Shift to Digital Photos Leaving Kodak Out of the Picture," *Investor's Business Daily*, March 19, 2001, p. A1; "Y Factor: A Camera That Tapes and Plays," *Washington Post*, March 24, 2001, pp. E1, E8; "Kodak Streamlines Units to Be Nimbler in Digital Age, and Names Coyne to Post," *Wall Street Journal*, October 24, 2000, p. A3; "Kodak Hires Web Guru to Develop Its Digital Plans," *Wall Street Journal*, October 9, 2000, pp. B1, B6; "Kodak's Digital Moment," *Forbes*, August 21, 2000,

pp. 106–111; "How Sony Beat Digital Camera Rivals," *Wall Street Journal*, January 29, 1999, pp. B1, B4; "Kodak Is Rolling Out Digital Photo Processing in CD-ROM Disks," *Wall Street Journal*, February 9, 1999, p. A4; "Kodak's Cool Digital Pix Site," *Fortune*, September 28, 1998, p. 285; "Shutterbugs, It May Be Time to Go Digital," *Business Week*, September 28, 1998, p. 122E8; "A New Microchip Ushers in Cheaper Digital Camera, *Wall Street Journal*, August 21, 1998, p. B1; "Kodak Agrees to Buy Imation's Unit in Medical Imaging for $520 Million," *Wall Street Journal*, August 4, 1998, p. B2; "Digital Cameras Come into Sharper Focus," *Investor's Business Daily*, July 23, 1998, p. A1; "Digital Ice Focuses on Cleaner Images," *Wall Street Journal*, July 16, 1998, p. B6; "Kodak and AOL Are Expected to Unveil Pact Allowing Digitized Photos On Line," *Wall Street Journal*, May 19, 1998, p. B16; "Kodak, Intel Join to Make Slimmer, Cheaper Cameras," *Wall Street Journal*, May 1, 1998, p. B6; "Digital Artists Link Up with Talent Agencies," *Wall Street Journal*, March 16, 1998, p. B9; "Kodak to Buy PictureVision in Bid to Lift Internet Photo Business," *Wall Street Journal*, February 12, 1998, p. B10; "Kodak Is Focused, All Right, But It's a Wide Focus," *Business Week*, December 15, 1997, p. 14; "Smile, You're on Intel Camera," *Business Week*, November 10, 1997, p. 6; "Kodak Buys Picture Network," *Wall Street Journal*, July 24, 1997; "Kodak Is Launching Service on Internet to Store, Print Photos," *Wall Street Journal*, August 26, 1997, p. B18; "HP Pictures the Future," *Business Week*, July 7, 1997, p. 100; "Eastman Kodak to Unveil Low-Priced Digital Camera," *Wall Street Journal*, p. B4; "Kodak in Pact with Microsoft to Offer Faster Ways to Send Images by Computer," *Wall Street Journal*, May 29, 1996, p. B8; "Digital Imaging Had Better Boom before Kodak Busts," *Fortune*, May 1, 1995, pp. 80–85; "Photos on Your Desktop," *Forbes*, March 27, 1995, p. 118; "Kodak's New Focus," *Business Week*, January 30, 1995, pp. 62–68; "The Times of Your Life: As Many Times as You Want, *Business Week*, January 30, 1995, p. 68; "Kodak Licenses Quicker System for Photo CD," *Wall Street Journal*, January 18, 1995, p. B3; "Kodak Reorganizes Its Sales Force at Imaging Group," *Wall Street Journal*, January 24, 1995, p. B4; "Kodak to Change Marketing Strategy for Low-End Film," *Wall Street Journal*, December 9, 1994, p. B3; "Kodak to Reorganize Imaging Division to Emphasize Electronic Technology," *Wall Street Journal*, February 24, 1994, p. A8.

3. The effects of new technologies on firm capabilities have received significant treatment in the research literature. The following sample research pieces are representative of some of the work undertaken in recent years. See F. T. Rothaermel, "Incumbent's Advantage through Exploiting Complementary Assets via Interfirm Cooperation," *Strategic Management Journal* 22, nos. 6–7 (2001): 687–700; M. Song and M. M. Montoya-Weiss, "The Effect of Perceived Technological Uncertainty on Japanese New Product Development," *Academy of Management Journal* 44, no. 1 (2001): 61–80; C. E. Helfat and R. S. Raubitschek, "Product Sequencing: Coevolution of Knowledge, Capabilities and Products," *Strategic Management Journal* 21, nos. 10–11 (2000): 961–980; R. S. Rosenbloom, "Leadership, Capabilities and Technological Change: The Transformation of NCR in the Electronic Era," *Strategic Management Journal* 21, nos. 10–11 (2000): 1083–1105; W. J. Orlikowski, "Using Technology and Constituting Structures: A Practice Lens for Studying Technology in Organizations," *Organization Science* 11, no. 4 (2000): 404–428; M. Tripsas and G. Gavetti, "Capabilities, Cognition, and Inertia: Evidence from Digital Imaging," *Strategic Management Journal* 21, nos. 10–11 (2000): 1147–1162; C. M. Christensen, "Will Disruptive Innovations Cure Health Care?" *Harvard Business Review* 78 (September–October 2000): 102–117; C. M. Christensen and M. Overdorf, "Meeting the Challenge of Disruptive Change," *Harvard Business Review* 78 (March–April 2000): 66–77; "B. Dyer and X. M. Song, "Innovation Strategy and Sanctioned Conflict: A New Edge in Innovation," *Journal of Product Innovation Management* 15 (1998): 505–519; L. Kim, "Crisis Construction and Organizational Learning: Capability Building in Catching-Up at Hyundai Motor," *Organization Science* 9, no. 4 (1998): 506–521; C. M. Christensen, *The Innovator's Dilemma* (Boston: Harvard Business School Press, 1997); S. L. Brown and K. M. Eisenhardt, "The Art of Continuous

Change: Linking Complexity Theory and Time-Paced Evolution in Relentlessly Shifting Organizations," *Administrative Science Quarterly* 42, no. 1 (1997): 1–34; M. W. Lawless and P. Anderson, "Generational Technological Change: Effects of Innovation and Local Rivalry on Performance," *Academy of Management Journal* 39, no. 5 (1996): 1185–1127; D. Dougherty and C. Hardy, "Sustained Product Innovation in Large, Mature Organizations: Overcoming Innovation-to-Organization Problems," *Academy of Management Journal* 39, no. 5 (1997): 1120–1153; D. Dougherty and T. Heller, "The Illegitimacy of Successful New Products in Large Firms," *Organization Science* 3 (1994): 200–218; K. M. Eisenhardt and B. M. Tabrizi, "Accelerating Adaptive Processes: Product Innovation in the Global Computer Industry," *Administrative Science Quarterly* 40 (1995): 84–110; J. L. Bower and C. M. Christensen, "Disruptive Technologies: Catching the Wave," *Harvard Business Review* (January–February 1995): 43–53; C. J. G. Gersick, "Pacing Strategic Change: The Case of a New Venture," *Academy of Management Journal* 37 (1994): 9–45; T. Amburgey, D. Kelley, and W. Barnett, "Resetting the Clock: The Dynamics of Organizational Change and Failure," *Administrative Science Quarterly* 38 (1993): 51–73; H. Haveman, "Between a Rock and a Hard Place: Organizational Change and Performance under Conditions of Fundamental Environmental Transformation," *Administrative Science Quarterly* 37 (1992): 48–75; R. Henderson and K. Clark, "Architectural Innovation: The Reconfiguration of Existing Product Technologies and the Failure of Established Firms," *Administrative Science Quarterly* 35 (1990): 9–30; W. Mitchell, "Whether and When: Probability and Timing of Incumbents' Entry into Emerging Industrial Subfields," *Administrative Science Quarterly* 34 (1989): 208–230. Additional work on technological change and sources of competitive advantage can be found in D. Lei, "Competence Building, Technology Fusion and Competitive Advantage: The Key Roles of Organizational Learning and Strategic Alliances," *International Journal of Technology Management* 14, no. 2 (1997): 208–237; G. Dosi, "Technological Paradigms and Technological Trajectories," *Research Policy* 11 (1982): 147–162; J. Galbraith, "Designing the Innovating Organization," *Organizational Dynamics* 10, no. 3 (1982): 5–25.

4. "It's Digital, It's Encrypted—It's Postage," *Wall Street Journal*, September 21, 1998, pp. B1, B6.

5. "Reinventing CBS," *Business Week*, April 5, 1999, pp. 74–82; "GE's NBC Unit Is Seeking to Expand in Cable as Broadcast Economics Soften," *Wall Street Journal*, July 17, 1998, p. B3.

6. Shifts in the sources of competitive advantage in one industry can occur rapidly, particularly if changes are triggered by a related or adjacent industry. See M. E. Porter, *Competitive Strategy* (New York: Free Press, 1980), for a discussion of neighboring industries. To examine the ramifications of change across industries and their impact on entire national economies, see M. E. Porter, *The Competitive Advantage of Nations* (New York: Free Press, 1991).

7. This term was originally used by R. E. Miles and C. C. Snow in their groundbreaking study of the way businesses deal with environmental change: *Organizational Strategy, Structure and Process* (New York: McGraw-Hill, 1978). Some of the more recent research studies that have tested and utilized the Miles and Snow typology include the following: S. F. Slater and E. M. Olson, "Strategy Type and Performance: The Influence of Sales Force Management," *Strategic Management Journal* 21, no. 8 (2001): 813–830; C. Homburg, H. Krohmer, and J. Workman, "Strategic Consensus and Performance: The Role of Strategy Type and Market-Related Dynamism," *Strategic Management Journal* 20, no. 4 (1999): 339–358; W. James and K. Hatten, "Further Evidence on the Validity of the Self-Typing Paragraph Approach: Miles and Snow Strategic Archetypes in Banking," *Strategic Management Journal* 16, no. 2 (1995): 161–168; S. F. Slater and J. Narver, "Product-Market Strategy and Performance: An Analysis of the Miles and Snow Typology Types," *European Journal of Marketing* 27, no. 10 (1993): 33–51; D. Dvir, E. Segev, and A. Shenhar, "Technology's Varying

Impact on the Success of Strategic Business Units within the Miles and Snow Typology," *Strategic Management Journal* 14, no. 2 (1993): 155–161; S. Zahra and J. Pearce, "Research Evidence on the Miles-Snow Typology," *Journal of Management* 16, no. 4 (1990): 751–768; J. Conant, M. Mokwa, and P. R. Varadarajan, "Strategic Type, Distinctive Marketing Competencies, and Organizational Performance: A Multiple Measures-Based Study," *Strategic Management Journal* 11, no. 5 (1990): 365–383; S. W. McDaniel and J. Kolari, "Marketing Strategy Implications of the Miles and Snow Strategic Typology," *Journal of Marketing* 51, no. 4 (1987): 19–30.

8. This term is also one developed by Miles and Snow in *Organizational Strategy, Structure and Process*.

9. See G. Hamel and C. K. Prahalad, "Strategic Intent," *Harvard Business Review* (May–June 1989): 63–76.

10. See "Intel, AMD Lay Out Strategies to Boost Sales, Spur Growth," *Wall Street Journal*, August 29, 2001, p. B4; "Intel Chip Is Cited in AMD Price Cut, Rambus Stock Rise," *Wall Street Journal*, August 28, 2001, p. B4; "Intel Researchers Build Tiny Transistors That Could Sharply Boost Chips' Speed," *Wall Street Journal*, June 11, 2001, p. B2; "Intel Aims New Chips at High-End Market," *Wall Street Journal*, May 21, 2001, p. A9.

11. See an excellent discussion of this problem by T. Goss, R. Pascale, and A. Athos, "The Reinvention Roller Coaster: Risking the Present for a Powerful Future," *Harvard Business Review* (November–December 1993): 97–108.

PART 2

Extending Competitive Advantage

Chapter 7 *Corporate Strategy: Leveraging Resources to Extend Advantage*

Chapter 8 *Global Strategy: Harnessing New Markets to Extend Advantage*

Chapter 9 *Strategic Alliances: Teaming and Allying for Advantage*

CHAPTER 7

Corporate Strategy: Leveraging Resources to Extend Advantage

Chapter Outline

What You Will Learn

- The concept of corporate strategy
- The notion of a "resource-based view" of corporate strategy
- How effective corporate strategy can be used to extend and leverage a firm's distinctive competence
- The broad types of corporate strategy, including vertical integration, related diversification, and unrelated diversification
- Economic forces that motivate the pursuit of different corporate strategies
- How to balance the benefits and costs of diversification
- Benefits of sharing and leveraging resources among businesses or activities
- Costs accompanying diversification and the limitations of sharing
- Why companies undertake corporate restructuring
- How spin-offs and divestitures represent a form of restructuring designed to regain focus

The Kellogg Company[1]

Perhaps one of the best-known companies in the United States, the Kellogg Company has begun to shift its focus away from being the country's largest producer of ready-to-eat cereals and other breakfast food items that have traditionally been synonymous with the company. The company has a long history, having got its start in Battle Creek, Michigan, where Dr. John Harvey Kellogg originally pioneered the cereal flake as a way to provide grain-based foods to cure indigestion. His brother, Will Keith Kellogg, developed innovative packaging that would preserve cereal flakes for a long period. This enabled the company to begin shipping prepackaged cereal on a nationwide basis. In turn, this spawned the growth of a tremendous cereal empire, in which Kellogg would dominate this market for many decades.

By the 1990s, however, times would change for Kellogg. Although the company remains highly profitable, Kellogg faced numerous strategic challenges. The company earned $587 million in net income on $6.95 billion in revenues for 2000. Even with such highly recognized brands as Kellogg's Corn Flakes, Frosted Flakes, Special K, Raisin Bran, Rice Krispies, Eggo waffles, Pop-Tarts toaster pastries, and Nutri-Grain cereal bars, the company has faced increasingly tough competition from other packaged foods producers such as General Mills, PespiCo's Quaker Oats line of cereals, Philip Morris's Kraft foods unit (Post line of cereals), and Ralcorp Holdings (a big manufacturer of private-label, generic brands). More important, eating cereal at breakfast is no longer an important part of many Americans' lives when they wake up in the morning. As a result, in the past decade, Kellogg has watched its earnings growth slow down, while its market share in cereals dropped from 37 percent to 33 percent. Other food items such as croissants, bagels, yogurt, and energy bars have made serious inroads into the market for cereals; in fact, one in five Americans now does not even eat breakfast. When people do eat breakfast, only 35 percent eat cereal, while many prefer to consume hot breakfast items at such fast-food restaurants as McDonald's and Burger King. To the extent that people are eating cereal, many of them are switching to cheaper, private-label or generic alternatives.

Many of the challenges facing Kellogg, however, resulted from breakfast consumption trends that slowly took shape over the past decade. Traditionally, Kellogg would introduce a new line of cereal or breakfast food item with an expensive, marketing promotion that would emphasize the newness of the product. Unlike its competitors, Kellogg generally prefers not to compete on the basis of price. Although consumers sometimes enthusiastically greet Kellogg's new cereal products (e.g., Raisin Bran Crunch), they often care more about the price of the product, rather than who made it. However, the company is beginning to significantly change its long-standing approach to product development and marketing. In January 1999, Kellogg promoted Carlos Gutierrez as its new CEO to resuscitate the company's profitability and to lead the company into new directions. A Cuban-born émigré who believes that Kellogg needs to become more innovative, Gutierrez is seeking to inject faster growth into the company.

Moving into Vegetarian and Alternative Foods

One of Gutierrez's earliest moves in 1999 was to purchase Worthington Foods for $307 million, a leading natural foods company that develops soy-based products and other vegetarian foods. Other products made by Worthington Foods include veggie burgers and soy-based hot dogs and corn dogs. Worthington's best-known brand is Morningstar Farms, which holds over 50 percent market share of vegetarian and nonmeat alternative food products in U.S. supermarkets. With the acquisition of Worthington, Kellogg is now able to participate in the fast-growing organic and natural foods segment, which has grown at a 20 to 25 percent clip in recent years.

The purchase of Worthington Foods by Carlos Gutierrez shows how he intends to find growth for Kellogg in noncereal foods products. Worthington's skills in developing vegetarian foods, as well as its strong supermarket position, will help Kellogg accelerate the creation of its own line of new health food products. Some of these ideas include dry pasta, fiber-coated potato chips, and even a line of frozen entrées. Many of these food products will be vitamin enhanced or fiber enriched to help lower blood cholesterol levels.

Finding Growth through Snack Foods

Perhaps the biggest and most important acquisition to date is Kellogg's purchase of Keebler Foods for $3.86 billion in October 2000. Keebler is one of the largest snack food companies in the United States, making such well-known products as Cheez-It crackers, Club crackers, and a broad line of cookies (e.g., Chips Deluxe, Fudge Shoppe). The company is also highly recognized through its famous television advertisements that feature its Keebler Elves making and delivering fresh cookies. Kellogg's acquisition of Keebler has transformed the combined entity into a $10 billion breakfast and snack food company. With Keebler's product lines, Kellogg will now derive only 40 percent of its sales from breakfast cereals, as opposed to 75 percent from just a few years ago. More important, Keebler brings to Kellogg not only the potential for much higher earnings growth but also a new set of product development and distribution skills that can help the company breathe new life into its existing brands.

Under Keebler's CEO Sam Reed, the company proved itself to be very successful in finding ways to jump-start growth for many of its cookie and cracker products. For example, Keebler was able to grow sales of Cheez-It by 81 percent since 1996 by modifying serving sizes and by offering it through new means of distribution. Keebler has also led the food industry in offering cookies and other snack foods in smaller, single-serving portions. These smaller portion sizes may be more profitable than larger-sized boxed cookies and crackers, since Keebler can stock some of its cookies near the candy displays at the grocery checkout lines. Customers often make these purchases on a spur of the moment and are less likely to think about comparing the prices to other competitors' offerings.

Kellogg is also hoping to acquire a new set of distribution skills from its acquisition of Keebler Foods. In particular, Keebler excels in a different type of packaged-foods distribution system than what Kellogg has traditionally relied on. For many decades, Kellogg has relied heavily on selling its breakfast cereals through wholesalers and food brokers, who in turn would serve supermarket chains. Because brokers and store personnel would be responsible for shelving the products and handling merchandising issues (e.g., displays, in-store promotions, location of products along aisles), it often takes anywhere from six to eight weeks before a new Kellogg breakfast product would reach supermarkets' shelves. This lengthy and time-consuming process would often allow competitors, such as General Mills and Ralcorp Holdings, to gain valuable time and insight into what Kellogg would be offering. Even worse, General Mills would be able to rapidly develop its own line of competing products that would take away the initial product enthusiasm and momentum from Kellogg.

Keebler Foods, on the other hand, has developed its own direct-to-store distribution system that bypasses wholesalers and food brokers. Keebler's method of distribution speeds its products on trucks directly to the store. Equally important, Keebler's food representatives handle in-store shelving of products and other merchandising issues. Thus, Keebler brings to Kellogg a new way of managing the distribution of food products, especially for those items that have short shelf lives (spoils easily) or are sold in smaller, single-serve portions (e.g., crackers and cookies). In particular, Keebler has begun using its distribution system to serve other channels besides supermarkets, including vending machines and convenience stores, where single-serve portions are most likely to be sold. In addition, customers shopping at convenience and gasoline stores are less likely to be as price-sensitive as they are in traditional supermarkets.

As part of the larger Kellogg Company, both Worthington Foods and Keebler Foods will bring the potential for new growth and opportunities to broaden the scope and depth of Kellogg's distribution system. Already, Keebler is managing the distribution of such traditional Kellogg products as Rice Krispies Treats and Nutri-Grain snack bars. Even before acquiring Keebler, the company had already begun introducing single-serve portions of these and other food products to reignite sales. Keebler, on the other hand, will now able to better handle and sell these existing Kellogg products through its own direct-to-store distribution system. Morningstar Farms, the leading brand that comes from Worthington Foods, remains the leader in vegetarian, nonmeat foods. Kellogg, on the other hand, offers both Worthington and Keebler much in the way of new product R&D capabilities and the use of its new $75 million development facility near headquarters. Already, new product development is accelerating as Kellogg begins to introduce a new product for the market each month. Some of the most recent innovations include peanut butter and chocolate

Rice Krispies, Pop-Tarts that are divided into small pieces for toddlers, and muffins in the shape of bread slices so that they can be toasted like traditional Pop-Tarts. Kellogg will continue to look for ways to make its other products more vitamin enhanced, while continuing to expand the Morningstar Farms line of healthier products to the fast-growing organic foods market segment.

Even after these two major acquisitions, Kellogg still continues to search for new high-growth opportunities. In November 1999, Kellogg sold its Lender's Bagels business to Aurora Foods for $275 million. Acquired originally in 1996, Lender's Bagels turned out to be a difficult acquisition for Kellogg, since fewer people ate frozen or refrigerated bagels. Instead, most consumers would purchase them at bagel shops that sold them fresh. Kellogg had originally hoped to acquire a bagel business in the belief that it could capture that segment's fast growth during the early 1990s. In June 2000, Kellogg acquired Kashi Company, a maker of breakfast cereals that use natural ingredients without sugar or artificial products. Kellogg believes that Kashi can help reinforce the company's new product strategy for the natural foods business and is an important complement to its Worthington acquisition.

Tyco International[2]

One of the fastest-growing and perhaps least well-known companies in the United States is Tyco International, a firm that acquires businesses in such widely different markets as medical products, fire and security systems, flow control equipment, and electronic components. Under CEO Dennis Kozlowski, Tyco International has become a $30 billion company in just less than ten years. Since 1992, Tyco has grown by acquiring over two hundred companies of varying sizes and has grown its earnings over 25 percent per year. The company has recently boasted that it aims to become a $100 billion company by 2006 and accelerate earnings growth to 30 percent per year.

The span of Tyco's many current operations is bewildering; for example, it operates a large fiber optic network crossing the Atlantic, runs sewage and water treatments plants around the world, manages burglar alarm and fire security systems throughout the United States, and produces a wide array of medical products, including surgical gloves, sutures, and vascular care products. Although many Wall Street analysts believe that Tyco cannot continue to grow at its fervent pace, they are quick to point out that under Kozlowski, the company has followed a consistent pattern in identifying companies that it wants to acquire and in following a well-defined roadmap to integrate them smoothly with the rest of Tyco's operations. For almost all of the company's acquisitions over the past decade, Tyco has looked for companies with business units that have a solid foundation but suffer from a high-cost structure. These businesses must also fit well within an existing Tyco product or business line to gain or reinforce a critical mass of activities. Some of Tyco's legendary strategies for identifying and acquiring businesses are considered here.

A Finely Tuned Acquisition Strategy

More often than not, the search for proposed acquisition targets actually begins with ideas that operating managers have to improve their own market's growth potential. Tyco looks at over a thousand different targets per year, but each one is assessed on how well it can contribute to the company's earnings once acquired. Both small and large companies are considered, usually in industrial or commercial markets where Tyco's managers can assess the extent where there are opportunities to reduce costs dramatically and to build on complementary strengths. In particular, Tyco looks for ways to quickly remove overlapping management positions and organizational layers that slow down communications and fast decision making. Once a potential company acquisition is isolated, Tyco's internal management prepares a business renewal and turnaround plan whose objectives include immediate growth in earnings and vastly improved productivity. Tyco then informs the company of its intentions and begins to work on negotiating an acquisition price to close the deal. However, Tyco will not pursue hostile takeovers by buying the target company's share in the open market, especially since CEO Kozlowski feels that hostile takeovers will compel Tyco to overpay for an acquisition. Once the company is acquired, Tyco's management immediately goes to work in cutting costs and implementing its prepared turnaround plan to boost productivity and earnings in just one year. Frequently, though, this approach means that Tyco will lay off thousands of managers and support personnel to streamline the decision-making process and to speed up internal communications.

Tyco also takes some very important steps to integrate the acquired unit carefully into the rest of Tyco's businesses. Kozlowski prefers to delegate considerable latitude and freedom to all of Tyco's business unit managers, since he believes that they are in the best position to formulate and implement strategies for their respective markets. Tyco interviews and evaluates all of the senior managers that accompany the newly acquired unit. The company generally prefers to keep managers who exhibit strong ambition and a direct, even blunt, approach to solving problems. Tyco will also shut down what it considers wasteful uses of resources in the form of lavish corporate headquarters and perks that managers in other companies enjoy. Internal meetings are infrequent and kept short, whereas managers are expected to communicate and work closely with their customers. At the same time, Kozlowski closely monitors the financial performance of each Tyco business through an internal computerized reporting system that tracks each unit's sales, profit margins and order rates. In turn, Tyco provides a generous compensation system that evaluates each manager's performance solely on how well his or her unit performs. Bonuses that are several times that of base pay are not uncommon. However, managers who do not perform are quickly let go.

A Broad Array of Businesses

Tyco International's acquisition of over 200 different companies and businesses has positioned the company into four broad lines of business. Each line of business, in turn, seeks continued growth and dominant market share in the segment that it serves, usually by pursuing a low-cost leadership strategy. This emphasis on attaining a dominant market position is the underpinning of Tyco's search for acquisitions. Almost all of Tyco's acquisitions during the 1990s have been designed to purchase firms that offer a complementary line of products that dovetails with an existing Tyco business. Many of these acquisitions allow Tyco to further consolidate and reduce the number of competitors within a given industry or market segment, thus enhancing Tyco's ability to negotiate prices with customers. Three of Tyco's more prominent lines of business are described in the following sections.

Medical Products. Tyco's substantial market presence in this line of business includes such products as disposable gloves, sutures, syringes, vascular care and urology products, and even high-tech catheters to treat the heart. In 2001, Tyco Healthcare generated revenues close to $7.1 billion. Throughout the 1990s, Tyco acquired a number of different companies in this field, including Kendall, Sherwood-Davis & Geck, and U.S. Surgical. The acquisition of Sherwood from American Home Products, Inc., for $1.77 billion in January 1998, helped Tyco gain considerable strength in the area of disposable medical products. The $3.3 billion purchase of U.S. Surgical in May 1998 helped reposition Tyco in medical products used for minimally invasive techniques. Some of U.S. Surgical's product line includes cauterizing devices, sutures, and ultrasound diagnostic devices. Most recently in 2001, Tyco bought up Mallinckrodt, Inc., a leader in disposable medical supplies. Tyco's medical line of business has gained a fierce reputation for grabbing market share from its competitors. Also, it appears that Tyco's medical unit is moving toward higher value-added technologies, rather than the disposable medical products that defined the business's earlier investments.

Electronics Products. In its largest acquisition ever, Tyco acquired AMP, Inc., for $11.3 billion in November 1998. AMP is one of the nation's biggest manufacturers of electronic connectors and switches that are at the foundation of many high-tech products. AMP, based in Harrisburg, Pennsylvania, has long been considered the industry leader in providing all types of devices that insulate and connect different types of wiring harnesses used in such products as computers, building controls, appliances, and large factory automation systems. At the time, Tyco's acquisition of AMP ($5.75 billion in revenues) helped the company grow its revenues to upward of $22 billion. Many of AMP's largest customers include firms that are generally in mature industries. However, Tyco gains access to a new set of customers, some of them in high-tech industries that utilize AMP's advanced line of connector products.

The acquisition of AMP plays well to Tyco's emphasis on buying companies that are typically focused in mature industrial or commercial segments that are ripe for consolidation. CEO Kozlowski believes that Tyco can help AMP become even more efficient in its operations and, at the same time, become more responsive to the quick changes in product designs and shipments that customers in high-technology industries demand. After acquiring AMP, Tyco proceeded to shut down and consolidate many of AMP's 325 smaller factories, many of which were out-of-date and did not produce at high volumes. Now the biggest part of Tyco Electronics, AMP is in the midst of a massive reorganization of operations that also includes significant layoffs of personnel.

Another major acquisition for Tyco's electronics unit came with the purchase of Raychem Corporation in May 1999 for $2.94 billion. Raychem, which had annual revenues of $1.8 billion, is an important U.S. producer of connectors and many high-tech electronic components, including flat-panel displays and other sophisticated devices used in appliances, telecommunications, automotive and aerospace applications. The acquisition of Raychem strongly complements Tyco's purchase of AMP and other smaller companies, such as Sigma Circuits (acquired in June 1998 for $57 million), to make Tyco Electronics the overwhelming market share leader for connectors. In addition, acquiring AMP and Raychem helps Tyco gain market share in several lines of components that are vital to the telecommunications and other high-tech industries. Likewise, in November 2000, Tyco purchased the power systems unit of Lucent Technologies for $2.5 billion. Lucent, a telecommunications equipment maker that had been suffering sharp declines in business, sold the unit to Tyco to focus on its core optical and wireless equipment businesses. For Tyco, the acquisition of Lucent's power systems unit helps further broaden the company's range of offerings. CEO Kozlowski hopes that these moves will also help reduce the cyclical nature of making highly mature electrical products.

A focus on migrating toward higher-tech products may already be paying off for Tyco Electronics. In December 2000, Tyco began working with Furukawa Electric of Japan to build sophisticated optical fiber connectors that are used in telecommunications systems. These components will not only be sold to other telecommunications companies but also be used in Tyco's own undersea telecom cables that are managed by its TyCom subsidiary.

Security Systems. Another major line of business for Tyco International is its fire and building security systems unit. With revenues over $5.5 billion, this security business has grown extensively through acquisitions as well. The largest acquisition in this unit was Tyco's purchase of ADT Limited for $6.2 billion in 1997. Now known as ADT Security Services, this Tyco unit is best known as one of the nation's largest home security monitoring companies that offer police, fire, and ambulance dispatch services. It also serves many commercial customers who need a similar kind of electronic security and monitoring. ADT, itself, had grown extensively through the 1990s by purchasing a number of smaller, regional home-security companies to expand its national reach and brand recognition. In April 1998, Tyco purchased the Wells Fargo Alarm unit from Borg-Warner, a Chicago-based diversified manufacturer for $425 million. The Wells Fargo unit also serves thousands of commercial and residential customers throughout the United States and, when combined with ADT, helped Tyco become a market share leader in this category. Tyco also makes many electrical alarms and other physical products that are used in advanced electronic monitoring systems.

More recently, Tyco continued its relentless acquisition pace by buying three additional security alarm businesses. In December 2000, the company acquired Simplex Time Recorder for $1.15 billion to strengthen its market position in its fire and security business. Simplex makes components and devices that are used in monitoring systems. In May 2001, Tyco purchased the electronic security alarm business from Cambridge Protection Industries for $1 billion. Tyco said it would combine Cambridge's security network with that of its ADT Security Services unit. In August 2001, Tyco purchased Sensormatic, a Florida-based firm that specializes in making devices that prevent shoplifting from stores. Although it cost Tyco $2.2 billion, it broadens the company's reach into more specialized areas of providing commercial security.

Recent Initiatives

Until 2002, Tyco International has been consistently on the prowl for acquisitions to grow its businesses and revenues. However, in 1999 and 2000, the company's aggressive acquisitions recently caught the eye of federal regulators, who began to investigate the company's accounting practices. The Security and Exchange Commission (SEC) asked for documentation on how Tyco accounted for all of its expenses and acquisition-related charges over the past six years. Because Tyco had taken some aggressive restructuring charges to account for layoffs and plant closures, federal regulators became concerned that the company may have overstated its actual returns and profitability to investors. Ultimately, the SEC closed its inquiry into Tyco's accounting methods in July 2000, but investors became concerned that the company would no longer be able to sustain such a high growth rate.

In a move toward financial services, the company purchased commercial lender CIT Group for $9.2 billion in March 2001. Before this acquisition, almost all of Tyco's previous purchases were confined to industrial and commercial businesses that were used to help lower costs or to reinforce market share for an existing Tyco unit. CEO Kozlowski acknowledged that the CIT acquisition is a different move for the company, but he felt that it would help Tyco offer financing to corporate customers that prefer to avoid banks. Unlike other Tyco acquisitions in which the company had a sizable pool of managerial and operational talent, the CIT deal placed Tyco in a business where it has comparatively little in-house expertise in commercial finance. Moreover, CIT offered few complementary benefits to Tyco's other units, since there were few opportunities to share physical assets or to consolidate an existing line of business. Investors were unhappy with the deal and sold off Tyco shares.

In what is perhaps one of the most significant reversals of corporate strategy in recent years, Tyco International announced in January 2002 that it would propose breaking itself up into four separate companies to "unlock shareholder value." Facing renewed pressures for better accounting transparency, as well as ongoing difficulties in capturing synergies from operating in so many different businesses, CEO Kozlowski acknowledged that Tyco could perhaps serve its shareholders better by becoming more focused. As a result, he is planning to split Tyco into four companies, each of which is dedicated to a clear line of business: electronics and security systems, health care products, fire protection, and financial services. While the timetable for the breakup has been in flux, Kozlowski realizes that investors have had great difficulty valuing Tyco as the company became more complex and diversified. Likewise, it became extremely difficult for Tyco to share costs across all four lines of businesses in a way that produced significant corporate wide sources of competitive advantage, since each line of business dealt with a different product and customer base.

Many analysts believe that several key parts of Tyco, such as its recently acquired CIT Group, will become attractive acquisition targets for other companies, such as General Electric, American International Group (AIG), FleetBoston Financial Services, and even United Parcel Service (UPS). Even though the remaining pieces of Tyco will compete independently, analysts continue to believe they will be strong competitors in their respective industries because of their large size and previous growth by acquisitions that occurred during the past decade.

Introduction

Thus far, most of our examination of competitive advantage has been from the standpoint of a firm operating a single business within an industry. We are now ready to broaden our view. A firm can develop new capabilities by expanding into other segments, businesses, or industries. Such expansion is guided by corporate strategy. **Corporate strategy** in this book refers to the identification of opportunities and the allocation of resources to develop and extend the firm's competitive advantage to other activities or lines of businesses. In its most powerful application, corporate strategy is more than the sum of the firm's individual business unit strategies; it seeks to leverage the firm's distinctive competence from one business to new areas of activity. The issues surrounding corporate strategy are different and significantly more complex than those for a firm operating a single business in one industry. Corporate strategy requires managers to establish a coherent, well-defined direction that guides the allocation of resources into new areas of activity.

corporate strategy: Plans and actions that firms need to formulate and implement when managing a portfolio of businesses; an especially critical issue when firms seek to diversify from their initial activities or operations into new areas. Corporate strategy issues are key to extending the firm's competitive advantage from one business to another.

Corporate strategy is an important but often misunderstood area of management. An overwhelming number of the Fortune 500 companies operate more than one line of business. In fact, recent research shows that the average Fortune 500 company has positioned itself in about ten different businesses. Such expansion, however, is not easy. One landmark study found that more than half of all acquisitions made by thirty-three large corporations prior to 1975 were subsequently divested by 1985.[3] Moreover, many of the large Fortune 500 companies that have attempted to enter new lines of businesses (General Electric, IBM, General Mills, Sears, American Express, and AT&T) have encountered serious difficulties in building and extending their competitive strengths even to businesses and industries that they knew well. The key issue of corporate expansion into new activities or businesses may be viewed as follows: *Is a firm's competitive advantage in one business or area of activity strengthened by the firm's presence in another?* Identifying activities or businesses that satisfy this requirement is the focus in this chapter.

First, we examine the concept of what resources are important to formulating a coherent corporate strategy. Ideally, well-formulated corporate strategies are based on utilizing and leveraging resources that enable the firm to create distinctive sources of value and advantage over a long time period. Managers need to build their corporate strategies on those resources—assets, skills, and capabilities—that are hard for other firms to duplicate. Second, we consider the various routes to expanding the number of businesses a firm operates. Third, we look at specific types of corporate strategies that enable firms to leverage their resources and skills to extend their competitive advantage to new areas of activity. We focus our attention on the issue of diversification in particular. Fourth, we then consider the chief benefits and costs associated with each type of expansion, especially as it concerns diversification. Finally, we offer guidelines to help firms achieve the benefits of expansion into new areas while avoiding its costs.

The Concept of Resources in Corporate Strategy

Corporate success in extending sources of competitive advantage to new arenas—products, businesses, and market segments—depends heavily on how well firms have developed and cultivated those assets, skills, technologies, and capabilities to create a set of distinctive competences and resources that are significantly different from those of its competitors. In many ways, the central issue that relates to building competitive advantage at the business-unit level—leveraging a distinctive competence to create a competitive advantage—is fundamentally no different an issue than that for companies trying to compete across multiple businesses. However, managing a diverse set of multiple business units, particularly those involving market positions among different industries, significantly adds to the complexity of operations.

Building and leveraging sources of competitive advantage among multiple business units within a diversified firm thus calls for a different perspective that recognizes the inherent complexity of managing resources, skills, technologies, and capabilities across the firm's different subunits. When considering the issue of corporate strategy, firms need to understand how their broader collection of resources contributes not only to leveraging their distinctive competences among internal businesses but also to competing against other firms as well. In many ways, successful corporate strategy is based on identifying those resources that enable a firm to build systemwide advantage among its businesses in ways that other firms cannot readily imitate or duplicate. During the 1990s, this **resource-based view of the firm** is becoming more important to understanding corporate strategy.[4] From this perspective, corporate strategy will be successful only to the extent that the firm possesses and leverages those resources (assets, skills, technologies, and capabilities) that share a number of important characteristics.

resource-based view of the firm: An evolving set of strategic management ideas that place considerable emphasis on the firm's ability to distinguish itself from its rivals by means of investing in hard-to-imitate and specific resources (e.g., technologies, skills, capabilities, assets, management approaches).

First, a firm's resources should ideally be so distinctive that they are hard for competitors to imitate or duplicate. The more distinctive or hard to imitate the resource, the less likely there will be direct competition in that arena. If a resource (skill, technology, or capability) is hard to imitate, then any future profit stream and competitive advantage is likely to be more enduring and sustainable. Conversely, those resources that are easy to imitate will generate only temporary value, since other firms can readily copy that skill. Over the long term, however, few corporate resources will sustain their hard-to-imitate qualities unless firms continue to invest and upgrade them at a rate faster than what other competitors can do. As we noted in Chapter 4, it is difficult for the vast majority of firms in the semiconductor industry to sustain their distinctive resources and skills over a long period of time when new entrants and competitors come out with ever newer designs, manufacturing processes, and advanced materials as the technology evolves through its life cycle stages. On the other hand, an organizational capability for fast innovation such as that found at Hewlett-Packard, Sony, or Procter & Gamble might be considered a valuable resource that is hard to imitate.

Second, a firm's resources should also be highly specialized and durable. This feature can often represent a double-edged sword. Highly specialized assets and skills can produce long-lasting value, but they can also be very rigid and hard to change when new technologies or demand patterns arise. Some of the most specialized and durable assets can also limit a firm's ability to respond to environmental changes, as we have seen in the Eastman Kodak situation. On the other hand, some of the best examples of where highly specialized and durable resources have created sustainable advantage over long time periods include such assets as brand names and patents. Brand names such as Walt Disney, Procter & Gamble, Sony, Nokia, IBM, Frito-Lay, Honda, American Express, Intel, and Microsoft provide these firms with a durable, lasting degree of staying power and freedom to maneuver, even when their respective markets may be fast moving. Patents, especially those in the pharmaceutical and chemical industries, are another way in which specialized and durable resources can be readily used and reused to build and leverage new sources of competitive advantage. Both brand names and patents may be significant resources in helping firms formulate and implement their corporate strategies, since they are enduring over an extended period of time.

Third, firms need to monitor the environment so that their corporate resources do not suffer from easy substitution from other competitive providers of similar value-adding activities. In other words, even when a firm's set of resources is hard to imitate and highly durable, senior managers need to remain aware of potential substitute threats from firms in other industries that may bring to bear an entirely different set of assets, skills, technologies, and capabilities to the current industry or arena. Over the long term, however, emerging products, services, or technologies that could serve as substitutes are likely to surface in any industry. Yet, many firms have invested in learning new sets of skills and capabilities that enable them not only to deal effectively with the emerging substitute threat but also to embrace the substitute as part of the firm's redefined strategy. For example, until 1994, Microsoft had not really developed a well-thought-out strategy for dealing with such pioneering upstarts as Netscape Communications and others who were riding the first wave of the Internet. By late 1995, realizing the potential threat that Netscape's Web browser products could eventually substitute for many of its existing stand-alone, desktop applications, Microsoft completely shifted its strategy and made the Internet a central part of its corporate strategy to extend its software design and applications skills to learning and building new businesses. Now, Internet-driven initiatives have become a central focus for all of Microsoft's newest product development efforts, including Windows 2000 and Windows XP, its latest personal computer operating system that makes it easy for users to combine traditional PC tasks with those of the Internet.

Using many of these resource-based perspectives, we now begin to examine how firms can develop various types of corporate strategies for leveraging their sources of competitive advantage into new arenas.

Alternative Routes of Corporate Strategy

Firms usually begin their existence serving just one or a few niches. At some point during their evolution, many expand beyond their initial base or core business.[5] Such expansion increases the diversity of customers a firm serves, the number of products it produces, and the technologies it must learn and manage. This pattern is therefore broadly referred to as *expanding the scope of operations.* **Scope of operations** refers to the extent of a firm's operations across different activities, products, and markets. Corporate strategy is concerned with selecting the products, markets, and industries in which to extend the firm's distinctive competence.

scope of operations: The extent of a firm's involvement in different activities, products, and markets.

Expansion into other activity areas is considered successful when the firm's distinctive competence is strengthened by moving into new areas.[6] Recall that a firm's *distinctive competence* refers to what it can do particularly well vis-à-vis its competitors. Distinctive competence is rooted in such attributes as a central technology, resource, expertise, or skill that the firm uses to create and add value. From the perspective of corporate strategy, if a firm can successfully apply and extend its distinctive competence to new activities, products, or markets, then it can develop competitive advantage across multiple businesses. The most common routes to enlarging the firm's scope of operations are expansion into new stages of the industry value chain and expansion into new businesses and industries (see Exhibit 7-1).

EXHIBIT 7-1 Common Avenues to Enlarging the Firm's Scope of Operations

- Entrance into new stages of activity (i.e., vertical integration)
- Entrance into new businesses/industries (i.e., industry-based diversification)

vertical integration: The expansion of the firm's value chain to include activities performed by suppliers and buyers; the degree of control that a firm exerts over the supply of its inputs and the purchase of its outputs. Vertical integration strategies and decisions enlarge the scope of the firm's activities in one industry.

backward integration: A strategy that moves the firm upstream into an activity currently conducted by a supplier (see *vertical integration; forward integration*).

forward integration: A strategy that moves the firm downstream into an activity currently performed by a buyer (see *vertical integration; backward integration*).

New Stages

Firms may expand their scope of operations to include different stages or levels of value-adding activity within the same industry. Expansion into an earlier or later stage of a firm's base industry is usually referred to as vertical integration. We briefly discussed **vertical integration** in previous chapters as a source of competitive advantage for a single-business firm. Yet, vertical integration is also a corporate strategy issue, since it involves enlarging the scope of what the firm does to include other value chain activities. It can take two basic forms: backward integration and forward integration. **Backward integration** moves the firm into an activity currently carried out by a supplier. **Forward integration** moves the firm closer to its customers.[7] In its earliest days, Standard Oil (Exxon) integrated backward when it moved into oil production from its initial base in refining. It integrated forward when it began retailing gasoline through its own service stations.

During the 1980s, AT&T pursued a strategy of wide-spanning vertical integration as it invested in new technologies that enabled it to design and build advanced computer and communications equipment. At the same time, AT&T began to provide new types of wireless, Internet, and other telecommunications services directly to its customers. AT&T also became synonymous with high-tech innovations and cutting-edge research through its Bell Laboratories unit. This unit developed thousands of different ideas and patents, including the transistor, which laid the foundation for many electronic and consumer products today. During the 1980s and early 1990s, AT&T built strong positions in semiconductors (chips), lasers, digital coding schemes, and fiber optics that are key components required to build long-distance switches and networks, hand-held computers, and transmission hardware. These components represented the building blocks AT&T thought were necessary to make its own equipment without relying on external suppliers. Thus, expansion into these high-tech areas represented backward integration for AT&T. On the other hand, investing in cellular phone networks, local telephone services, and Internet access allowed AT&T to get closer to its customers by offering services without an intermediary or middleman. In particular, when AT&T received regulatory approval to offer new wireless services in different regions of the United States, it allowed the company to offer a full range of phone services to customers without going through a local phone company. This move is forward integration.

New Businesses and Industries

Backward and forward integration do not take a firm beyond its initial industry, often represented by a line of business within the firm. **Diversification** does, however. Diversification involves entry into fields where both products and markets are significantly different from those of a firm's initial base.[8] There are two basic types of diversification: (1) related and (2) unrelated.[9]

diversification: A strategy that takes the firm into new industries and markets (see *related diversification; unrelated diversification*).

Related diversification occurs when a firm expands into businesses similar to its initial business in terms of at least one major function (manufacturing, marketing, engineering) or type of skill used (e.g., microelectronics, packaging, surface coatings, thin-film technologies, display screens). Related diversification is thus concerned with extending the firm's distinctive competence to other lines of business.

related diversification: A strategy that expands the firm's operations into similar industries and markets; extends the firm's distinctive competence to other lines of business that are similar to the firm's initial base (see related industry; *unrelated diversification*).

Unrelated diversification is expansion into fields that do not share any functional or skill-based interrelationship with a firm's initial business. Unrelated diversification therefore involves entry into new industries that share no distinctive competence with the firm's initial business.

unrelated diversification: A strategy that expands the firm's operations into industries and markets that are not similar or related to the firm's initial base; does not involve sharing the firm's distinctive competence across different lines of business (*see related diversification;* related industry).

To illustrate related diversification, consider Microsoft's recent expansion into the video game industry with the introduction of its Xbox game console. Software and video games are different products used by different customers, so this strategy represents industry diversification. The two businesses, however, do share similar skills in software technologies (generating computer programs and codes to run on machines), similar product research and development skills (the need for fast innovation in both industries), and even similar technological platforms (ensuring that future video games work on a range of different electronic appliances). These characteristics thus make Microsoft's strategy more like related diversification. In a similar vein, Kellogg's acquisition of Worthington Foods and Keebler Foods also represents a form of related diversification. Health-oriented, soybean-based vegetarian foods, crackers, and cookies are products often consumed by different customers, although they are still food products. Cereal and breakfast food items, vegetarian products, and snack foods share a similar set of distribution requirements (managing wholesaler channels and working with supermarkets and other retail outlets), similar skills in product development (finding better tasting foods), and similar skills in marketing (engaging in market research, cross-promotional activities, developing advertising). For Kellogg's these activities represent key aspects of a related strategy.

On the other hand, consider Intel's recent moves to establish a Web-hosting business. During the late 1990s, Intel hoped to dominate a market where small and midsized businesses would outsource their Web sites and Internet networks to a third-party company. A Web-hosting business requires a company to manage a vast telecommunications network that links companies' Web sites with other companies, customers, suppliers, and people using the Internet. Building data centers and "server farms" (groupings of thousands of computers to manage Internet data flows) took Intel far from its semiconductor manufacturing expertise. The value chain configuration required to manage Web-hosting activities is very different from those involved in semiconductor manufacturing. Managing a Web-hosting business requires Intel to operate a business that is more similar to a telecommunications company, rather than a fast-moving, highly precise manufacturing business. Thus, Intel's move into this area constitutes unrelated diversification.[10]

Broad Types of Corporate Strategies

These three expansion routes lead to three broad types of corporate strategies. In this section, we examine in detail these three types of corporate strategies: (1) vertical integration, (2) related diversification, and (3) unrelated diversification. These strategies provide very different opportunities to extend distinctive competence. Each of these three corporate strategies is based on a specific economic motive as it relates to enlarging the firm's scope of operations. Each of these corporate strategies has different implications for the way that companies can extend their distinctive competence into new areas of activity.

Vertical Integration

Vertical integration allows the firm to enlarge its scope of operations within the same overall industry. Vertical integration is characterized by the firm's expansion into other parts of the industry value chain directly related to the design, production, distribution, and/or marketing of the firm's existing set of products or services. Many companies practice vertical integration in some way. Companies engage in vertical integration primarily to strengthen their hold on resources deemed critical to their competitive advantage. Vertical integration is an important strategy for firms that face great uncertainty, especially as it concerns their sources of supply or future buyers of their products. Moreover, vertical integration enables the firm to reduce the external transaction costs of working with numerous suppliers and customers. Recall from Chapter 4 that *transaction costs* are those costs involved in finding, buying, selling, negotiating, and overseeing activities with other firms in the open market. Lower transaction costs are especially important for firms when high economic uncertainties make external long-term contracts costly.[11]

full integration: Vertical integration that seeks to control every activity in the value chain. In full integration, firms bring all activities required to design, develop, produce, and market a product in-house (see *partial integration*).

partial integration: Vertical integration that is selective about which areas of activity the firm will choose to undertake. In partial integration, firms do not control every activity required to design, develop, produce, and market a product (see *full integration*).

Full versus Partial Integration. Firms can vertically integrate in varying degrees. Some firms may attempt full integration. **Full integration** occurs when the firm seeks to control all stages of the value chain related to the final end product or service. In the automobile industry, a potential example of full integration would be Ford Motor Company's owning everything from the coal mines used to make steel; the steel mills that make body panels, doors, engines, and car frames; the glass used in windshields; all the way to the dealerships that finance and sell cars to customers.

On the other hand, firms can also attempt a limited form of vertical integration known as partial integration. **Partial integration** refers to a selective choice of those value-adding stages that are brought in-house. For example, Ford Motor Company could achieve partial integration by owning the engine and assembly plants necessary for making cars but selling off the coal plants and steel mills to other firms that may be more efficient than Ford in managing those operations. In the past few years, Ford has gradually sold off its parts-making operation to focus on product design, assembly, and core engine-manufacturing operations. Firms exhibit some degree of partial integration when they attempt to control strategically important or valuable activities but rely on external providers to outsource activities that do not match their competitive strengths.

Backward Integration. The direction of vertical integration may be as important as its degree. Backward integration can allow firms to convert a previously external supplier into an internal profit center. Consider AT&T's strategy in the early 1990s. By amassing its own in-house chip development capability, AT&T lessened its reliance on external suppliers of a component vital to manufacturing its higher-value products, such as the phones, switches, and other devices that incorporate these chips. When AT&T previously bought chips and other electronic devices from outside firms, it was dependent on these suppliers.

Backward integration is particularly common in industries where low cost and certainty of supply are vital to maintaining the firm's competitive advantage in its end markets. For example, drug companies often exhibit high levels of backward integration to ensure supply of necessary chemical ingredients for their pharmaceuticals. On the other hand, firms competing in industries defined by rapid product and technological change are likely to avoid extensive backward integration, fearing that the high fixed capital costs associated with backward integration will reduce the flexibility needed to respond to rapid change.

Forward Integration. Forward integration is designed to help the firm capture more of the value added in the product or service offered to the customer. For example, when American Express sells travelers' checks and other financial services through its travel agencies, it is seeking to capture those customers who might otherwise buy their travelers' checks and insurance from banks and other firms. Similarly, when General Motors, Ford, and Chrysler bought large stakes in nationwide car rental firms such as Hertz, National, Budget, Dollar, and Thrifty, they sought to achieve forward integration. The Big Three wanted to capture some of the profits not only from the rental agencies' purchase of their cars but also from the customers who rent those cars on an intermittent basis.

A desire to forward integrate into lower-cost medical delivery and prescription services motivated pharmaceutical giant Merck to purchase distribution powerhouse Medco Containment Services in 1993. Merck is one of the world's leading developers and producers of brand-name proprietary drugs. During the late 1980s, more and more customers and physicians began to use off-brand generic drugs that often were lower priced than Merck's products. Many of these generic drugs were sold through large, competing drug wholesalers, such as McKesson HBOC, Cardinal Health, Bergen Brunswick, Advance Paradigm, PCS, Express Scripts, and Medco. Unlike Merck, these firms do not develop or patent drugs on their own but primarily acquire their products from other leading drug companies. Merck decided that it could not afford to allow its drug prices to be severely undercut. In 1993, Merck's decision to acquire Medco, one of the largest drug wholesalers in the United States, enabled Merck to distribute its own drugs more cheaply because of Medco's vast distribution network to physicians, retailers, and pharmacies. Through this move, Merck believed it could retain customers interested in buying drugs through discount channels. In a similar move, pharmaceutical competitor Eli Lilly in 1994 made its own acquisition of PCS, another leading drug distribution system. Lilly believed that ownership of PCS would enable it to negotiate better pricing terms with other large retailers and managed care firms that wanted to take steps to limit annual price increases of new drugs.[12]

Thus, vertical integration strategies extend the firm's scope of operations to other activities within the same industry. Basically, all vertical integration strategies are motivated to some extent by (1) accessing vital resources, both backward toward suppliers and forward toward customers, (2) extending the firm's control over critical value-adding activities directly concerned with its core products or services, (3) reducing uncertainty of relying on external suppliers or buyers, (4) ensuring a more stable or efficient flow of value-adding activities within its own operations and key processes, and (5) capturing profits that might otherwise leave the firm. The cumulative potential benefit of vertical integration strategies is that they tend to reduce the economic uncertainties and transaction costs facing the firm, at least in the short term.

Vertical integration strategies are not without their disadvantages, however. They can sometimes lead a firm to overcommit scarce resources to a given technology, production process, or other activity that could then lock the firm into eventual obsolescence. In addition, excessive vertical integration may also weigh down the firm with significantly high fixed costs, leaving it vulnerable to an industry downturn. Vertical integration can also pose problems of meshing different capabilities and skill sets. For example, Eli Lilly did not realize that managing extensive drug distribution channels through its PCS acquisition would require a very different set of skills as compared to pharmaceutical R&D and marketing. The PCS unit eventually became a drag on Lilly's financial performance in 1995 and 1996.[13] Eventually, Lilly sold off the PCS unit, and it later merged with Advance Paradigm in 1999, a leading pharmacy benefit manager (PBM) firm. The new company, now known as Advance PCS, is a leading drug distributor that works closely with pharmacies and managed care plans to ensure that pharmaceuticals are stocked using highly responsive inventory management systems. Its major competitors include Express Scripts, Amerisource Bergen, and Cardinal Health. In a similar move in February 2002, Merck announced that it, too, would separate its core pharmaceutical unit from its Medco unit. By divesting itself of Medco, Merck hopes to gain renewed focus on its huge drug development business. It ultimately realized the two businesses' requirements for success were very different.

Likewise, vertical integration can also pose problems of balancing capacity and throughput in the firm's operations. These disadvantages are particularly amplified for those firms attempting full integration. For example, if Ford Motor Company should attempt to own its own set of coal mines, steel mills, and assembly plants and dealerships to a much greater degree than rival DaimlerChrysler, then an economic recession would have much more devastating effects on Ford than it would on DaimlerChrysler. Ford's higher level of fixed costs threaten to keep Ford in the red longer than DaimlerChrysler, which would not be as burdened with excess capacity and other problems.

On the other hand, for many companies in the petroleum and other resource-extractive industries, the benefits of full integration outweigh the disadvantages. For companies such as ExxonMobil, ChevronTexaco, Phillips Petroleum, and Royal Dutch Petroleum, control over all stages of oil exploration, drilling, production, refining, and marketing is important. Any significant disruption in supply or distribution would send shock waves throughout the entire company.[14]

Related Diversification

Related diversification is perhaps the most important corporate strategy discussed in this chapter for a number of reasons. First, related diversification is an increasingly common corporate strategy found in large companies worldwide. Many Fortune 500 firms are pursuing some variant of related diversification, and interest in this strategy is growing in Europe and the Far East. In particular, many companies outside the United States are seeking to realign their operations in such a way as to achieve greater focus and more productive use of their assets. For example, German and Japanese companies such as Siemens, NEC, Hitachi, Fujitsu, and Toshiba are recently attempting to shed businesses and activities that do not support a renewed focus on their core competences.

Second, related diversification is directly concerned with extending the firm's distinctive competence or set of firm-specific resources into new lines of business and industry, as opposed to limiting the firm's scope of operations to within the same industry. Recall that a firm's distinctive competence is a central technology, resource, or skill that it uses to design, develop, produce, or market its products. Related diversification offers firms the potential to extend and leverage their distinctive competences/resources into new industries that share common characteristics. Third, related diversification poses a highly complex set of issues for managers, since the resources and skills used to guide related diversification strategies are often the key to obtaining corporate synergy. **Synergy** exists when the whole of the company is greater than the sum of its parts. In other words, related diversification creates value not only in the firm's individual businesses but across the entire firm as well. For these reasons, related diversification represents perhaps the single most important trend defining current corporate strategy today.

synergy:
An economic effect in which the different parts of the company contribute a unique source of heightened value to the firm when managed as a single, unified entity.

Focus on Synergy. Related diversification is an extremely attractive and potent strategy that aims to extend the firm's distinctive competence (technologies, resources, innovation, skills) to areas of activity in other lines of businesses or industries. The primary economic motive for related diversification is that firms can create new sources of value by extending and applying their distinctive competence across a wide array of similar businesses and activities. Related diversification works to extend a firm's distinctive competence by building a *corporate-level, firm-specific, resource-based* source of competitive advantage. Corporate-level advantage occurs when value is created both in a firm's individual business units, and system-wide across a firm's businesses. Thus, the goal of related diversification is to achieve synergy. This objective is realized when the value of the whole firm is greater than the discrete value of its individual business units.

Focus on Internal Development. Firms can attempt related diversification through various channels. For example, firms could (1) identify and exploit an underlying technology or skill that defines the way a product is designed or manufactured; (2) start up new products or services where key value-adding activities can be shared across a wider base; (3) develop and commercialize new products that borrow from the firm's brand name recognition, manufacturing prowess, or R&D capability; or (4) acquire new businesses that closely match and complement the firm's existing strengths or distinctive competence in its original activity. Note that the most common steps to achieve synergy are through internal development as opposed to acquiring other firms or businesses. Internal development seeks to share or transfer the firm's resources and skills to other business units.

Numerous examples of related diversification can be found in every industry. In particular, many firms competing in different sectors of high-technology practice related diversification. For example, Sharp Corporation of Japan pursues related diversification when it develops and produces a broad line of calculators, desktop copiers, television sets, and video camcorders. Sharp's set of distinctive resources includes its highly specialized competence in precision manufacturing skills, expertise with liquid crystal display (LCD) technology, flat-panel technology, miniaturization, and an organizational capability for fast product development. All of Sharp's product groups share a common need and access to these distinctive resources. By extending its manufacturing skills from calculators to camcorders, Sharp expands its manufacturing base and experience to new products. In turn, Sharp creates value by being able to lower its manufacturing costs even further by spreading them over a wider base of products. Sharp's products are not only similar in using related LCD and flat-panel display components, but they also lend themselves well to similar marketing by way of mass distribution channels, such as Best Buy, Circuit City, and other electronic superstores.

Hewlett-Packard also pursues a related diversification strategy. It is probably best known by consumers for its highly popular inkjet and laser printers, digital imaging products, as well as for its personal computers. However, Hewlett-Packard (H-P) also develops and produces calculators, software, supercomputers, and new multimedia and Internet technologies for the broader consumer and commercial markets. Hewlett-Packard's distinctive competence/resource is its capability to undertake rapid development and fast innovation of cutting-edge products. This distinctive competence allows H-P to develop internally and build a rapid succession of winning products for a variety of end markets. By producing high-quality calculators, Hewlett-Packard further refines its product development skills and technical expertise used to design new types of controllers for laser printers. Having a strong market presence in consumer electronics and office equipment helps reinforce Hewlett-Packard's position in building its Internet-oriented businesses and vice versa. H-P is even developing consumer-friendly, Internet-based electronic appliances, such as portable MP3 players that can be easily connected with cellular phones and personal digital assistants (PDAs).

Building Synergy in Related Diversification

Central to related diversification is the notion of building *mutually reinforcing, closely fitting* business units. The task of related diversification is to identify and leverage the firm's distinctive competence and resources (assets, technology, capabilities, and skills) across closely fitting businesses to create new sources of value that form the basis for building synergy. Strategic fit occurs when the value chains of different business units are similar enough to create a corporate-wide basis for competitive advantage.

Identifying Fit. The first step in building synergy is identifying the potential for close fit among the firm's different businesses. For example, in the case of Sharp, the precision manufacturing skills, flat-panel display technologies, and innovative R&D used in making microwave ovens, DVD players, and notebook computers also apply to office equipment (e.g., copiers). For SBC Communications, this company's future service offerings increasingly build on its recent investments in advanced transmission networks, Internet services, electronic commerce applications, and even data transmission and networking for commercial buyers. By leveraging and combining skills from one business to another, SBC has been able to offer its customers a full range of telecommunications and electronic-commerce applications.[15] Motorola has brilliantly succeeded in leveraging its distinctive competence in semiconductor manufacturing and development to compete in the fast-paced cellular telephone, communications equipment, and networking technologies businesses. Motorola has been able to transfer its proprietary manufacturing skills and techniques from one line of business to another, resulting in fast product development and low-cost, high-quality products.

Finding a close fit to build synergies is not easy. Oftentimes companies will discover that their distinctive competences do not lend themselves well to application in other industries or markets. For example, Marriott Corporation found that its expertise in providing high-quality food in its family-oriented restaurants, cafeterias, and hotels did not give it much capability to compete in top-of-the-line gourmet restaurants. Similarly, Black and Decker's excellent reputation for high-quality appliances and tools designed for do-it-yourselfers did not automatically translate into higher sales of power tools aimed at professional contractors and construction firms. AT&T discovered a similar problem in 1995. Skills in R&D and manufacturing (now in Lucent Technologies) did not readily apply to managing and operating an advanced telecommunications network that could handle the huge surge and demand for Internet-based traffic, electronic commerce, and other services. AT&T's skills in product development did not in any way guarantee a success in understanding how newer forms of data-networking technologies could redefine the telecommunications and Internet backbone business almost overnight. Thus, a crucial first step for managers undertaking related diversification is to assess how well the firm's distinctive competence lends itself to direct application to other markets or industries. *The firm's distinctive competence should be leveraged for competitive advantage across all of its business units.*

Making the Competence Hard to Imitate and Durable. The second step in building synergy is to make the firm's distinctive competence and resources (assets, technologies, capabilities, and skills) as distinctive as possible from the competition and enduring over a long period of time. Firms engaging in related diversification need to invest continuously in their distinctive competence or corporate resources so that they become difficult for competitors to imitate and thus preserve the competence's or resource's long-term value. The more distinctive the firm's set of resources (capabilities, skills, and technologies), the more difficult it is for competitors to copy and imitate the firm's strategy. A truly distinctive skill or competence will enable the firm to lower costs, enhance differentiation, or accelerate learning in ways faster or better than its competitors.

Related diversification works best when firms can build a competence that is so distinctive and utilized systemwide that it is nearly impossible for competitors to duplicate it. Durable, specialized assets or skills are a key pillar in attaining successful related diversification. In the case of 3M, its proprietary and durable skills in applied chemistry, coatings, adhesives, and thin-film technologies make it difficult for competitors to imitate the quality of 3M's products; yet these same skills allow 3M to develop future sets of related products with greater ease and lower cost. For example, few people ordinarily know that all of the transdermal medical delivery products (e.g., Nicoderm or "patches" that are applied to the skin) are actually made by 3M for drug companies. Transdermal medical products share the same technologies that 3M uses to develop specialized coatings and adhesive products for other industries. Likewise, in the Sharp and Hewlett-Packard examples, few companies could have easily mustered or quickly copied the precision manufacturing or fast product development skills of both companies. An organizational capability for fast innovation or quality manufacturing is hard to imitate and constitute a specialized and durable resource that lasts over many product generations and life cycles. Firms with very distinctive competences are well positioned to create potentially new sources of value and competitive advantage across their businesses that will be difficult for competitors to imitate and copy.

Managerial Fit. Finally, a strong fit among the different managers that run the underlying businesses is important. Managers with similar levels of entrepreneurial qualities, technical knowledge, marketing savvy, or engineering backgrounds provide an important foundation for building synergies. A convergence of managerial mind-sets can reduce the coordination costs among the businesses. Transfer or rotation of managers across different business units can help solidify the firm's management fit. The more closely fitting and related the various business units are, the more important a tight managerial fit becomes. This fit helps management understand both the characteristics of individual businesses and the overarching distinctive competence of the firm. Value creation at both business and corporate levels becomes easier when managers work jointly to develop ways to extend the firm's distinctive competence across businesses. For example, managers at PepsiCo often rotate their positions throughout the company in order to learn how other PepsiCo businesses function. Corporate management believes that transferring and rotating managers among various business units will help provide a new set of insights and a "total view" of the entire company's operations.

Thus, related diversification strategies are designed to extend the firm's distinctive competence and corporate resources to other products, businesses, and industries. Related diversification aims to create synergy, whereby the firm leverages its distinctive competence to achieve a mutually reinforcing, tight fit among its businesses. When pursued successfully, related diversification enables the firm (1) to lower its costs across a wider base of activities; (2) to increase or heighten the differentiation of its businesses; and (3) to accelerate learning and transfer of new technologies, skills, or other capabilities at a rate faster than if the business units remained separate.

Unrelated Diversification

Although the majority of Fortune 500 firms are now emphasizing related diversification, many firms during earlier periods engaged in a corporate strategy of unrelated diversification. Unrelated diversification occurs when a firm seeks to enter new industries without relying on a distinctive competence to link up business units. These firms were popularly known as conglomerates. **Conglomerates** are firms that practice unrelated diversification. Unlike related diversification, unrelated diversification is *not* based on any distinctive competence or central set of hard-to-imitate corporate resources. Consider, for example, the case of Allegheny-Teledyne, a large conglomerate. Allegheny-Teledyne has extensive defense electronics businesses, financial services, stainless steel (through its Allegheny-Ludlum acquisition in 1996) industrial products, consumer goods (e.g., Water Pik toothbrushes), and machinery. The company does not attempt to share an underlying technology or skill among these various businesses.

conglomerates: Firms that practice unrelated diversification (see *unrelated diversification*; holding company structure).

During the 1970s, the list of unrelated diversified firms or conglomerates was long and included such names as Teledyne, Textron, Litton Industries, Gulf and Western (now part of Paramount Communications, a unit of Viacom), American Can (now Primerica, which has recently merged with financial services firm Citigroup), and ITT. Although some of these firms are still found in the Fortune 500 listings, their proportional representation of large U.S. companies has declined significantly in the past fifteen years. In particular, conglomerate firms have largely divested themselves of many disparate businesses over the past twenty years so that comparatively few exist.[16]

Unrelated diversification, or conglomerate-based strategies, became popular during the 1960s and 1970s. Companies such as Textron, ITT, Litton Industries, LTV, and others bought firms in such far-ranging industries as steel, textiles, typewriters, movie studios, household appliances, and silverware. Any conceivable business that appeared to be attractive for future growth was a candidate for acquisition. Conglomerates grew by way of acquiring other companies, instead of developing core skills internally. Because unrelated diversification does not rely on a distinctive competence, companies are free to purchase existing firms with already established market positions. Some of the methods by which firms pursue unrelated diversification include (1) buying high-performing companies in an attractive industry, (2) buying cash-poor companies that could utilize additional funds for a quick turnaround, (3) buying a company whose seasonal and cyclical sales patterns would provide stability to the firm's total cash flow and profitability, and (4) buying a largely debt-free company to improve the acquiring firm's borrowing power. Note that these methods do not attempt to identify and to extend a distinctive competence from one business unit to another. The primary corporate resource used among these subunits is financial leverage. In addition, the only linkage between newly acquired and preexisting business units is that of financial sharing and budgeting, as opposed to technological or skill-based resources.

Perhaps the two best examples of how unrelated diversification as practiced in the 1990s is giving way to renewed focus are that of Tenneco and Textron. Some of Tenneco's disparate businesses in the early part of the decade included farm and construction equipment (J. I. Case), natural gas pipelines, shipbuilding (Newport News Shipbuilding), chemicals and materials (Albright and Wilson), automotive parts, and containers/packaging (Packaging Corporation of America). Tenneco acquired these businesses over the past twenty years in the belief that diversity brought stability of earnings. The farm equipment business, for example, operates on a cycle different from the shipbuilding or packaging businesses. During a recession, for example, farm equipment sales plummet, while automotive parts go up (mostly because people keep their older cars longer). By 1992, Tenneco pushed each business unit to lower its costs to compete better in its own industry. However, this effort has proved difficult at Tenneco, since quality improvement and cost reduction efforts in one business are not easily transferred to another. In April 1994, Tenneco decided to put 35 percent of its J. I. Case farm equipment subsidiary up for sale to the public. Because Case has recovered from its early 1990s recession, Tenneco now wants to use the cash from this sale to improve its overall corporate balance sheet. The cash would be used to reduce corporate debt. By late 1995, Tenneco's packaging subsidiary (the PCA unit) undertook several large acquisitions of other companies to double its size over the next five years. Through 1996 and 1997, Tenneco continued to reduce the enormous scope of its diversification breadth. The Newport News Shipbuilding Company was sold off in late 1996 and is now part of Northrop Grumman. Even though General Dynamics had signed an agreement to acquire Newport News, Northrop Grumman launched a hostile takeover bid to thwart it.[17] Once farm equipment maker Case Corporation became fully independent from Tenneco, other companies also investigated acquiring it. Ultimately, New Holland N.V. purchased Case Corporation to strengthen its competitive position vis-à-vis Caterpillar and other large firms in the construction and farm equipment industries. The merger of New Holland N.V. and Case Corporation in November 1999 resulted in a new entity known as CNH Global N.V., which also sells agricultural and construction equipment under the Steyr, Fiatallis, International Harvester, and Fiat-Hitachi brand names.

In July 1998, Tenneco announced that it would formally separate its remaining automotive and packaging operations. Even further, Tenneco divided PCA's packaging business into even more narrowly defined paperboard and specialty materials units that will serve their respective markets using their own resources.[18] Packaging Corporation of America is now a very key player in the paperboard and plastic container businesses, while Tenneco Automotive will likely become an acquisition candidate for other auto parts companies seeking to consolidate their position in this industry.

Another company that practices unrelated diversification is Textron. At the height of its diversification posture, some of Textron's most well-known businesses included business jets (Cessna), helicopters (Bell Helicopter), golf carts and sporting equipment (E-Z-Go), chain saws (Homelite), lawn mowers (Jacobsen), watch bands (Speidel), disability insurance (Paul Revere), consumer finance (Avco), aircraft parts (Accustar), tank and aircraft engines (Lycoming), and industrial fasteners. In 1998, Textron sold its Avco insurance and consumer finance subsidiaries to Associates First Capital, a financial powerhouse that was recently part of Ford Motor Company. Associates First Capital, now itself part of Citigroup, bought Avco Financial Services because it represented a complementary fit to its own commercial and credit card financial services businesses. Textron's current corporate strategy is to allocate some $1 billion to buy new businesses, mostly on the industrial side, that are clearly dominant in their industries.[19]

Although Tenneco and Textron represent examples of companies that have pursued full-blown conglomerate strategies, there are other examples of firms that still attempt to undertake unrelated diversification in a more limited manner. Consider, for example, the case of Schlumberger Ltd., one of the world's largest and best-known oil services firm. Schlumberger specializes in developing the technologies that are required to help oil exploration companies discover, exploit, and manage the wells that are drilled in the search for petroleum. Some of Schlumberger's advanced products include electronic wireline monitoring systems (used for well measurement and control); bits, muds, and packs (used for drilling); and seismic technologies (used to calibrate geological surveys and to test for well stability). In February 2001, Schlumberger purchased Sema PLC, an Anglo-French software, outsourcing and systems integration firm for $5.2 billion. Schlumberger believes that its acquisition of Sema will help the oil services giant use the Internet to manage the complex process of gathering critical information to monitor oil drilling and well management operations. Sema will also help Schlumberger develop a new line of "smart cards" that can store all kinds of information for consumer and commercial uses. *Smart cards* are plastic cards that have microchips embedded within them. Ultimately, the company hopes to be able to provide totally integrated information solutions to other companies also. Many observers have noted that Schlumberger's investments in nonoil areas have failed in the past and that Sema ultimately requires a different kind of skill set than what Schlumberger possesses.[20]

Likewise, Tyco International appears to be pursuing a variation of unrelated diversification as well. Although not as far reaching and expansive as the conglomerates of years past, Tyco's four line of businesses—electronic products, medical products, security systems, and flow and valve products—do not share many similar characteristics or skills among these units. Cost savings at the corporate level are hard to obtain because true sharing of resources does not exist. Even though CEO Dennis Kozlowski has pushed each of his four businesses units to become a low-cost leader in their respective businesses, the primary growth mechanism has been overwhelmingly through external acquisition (over two hundred in the past ten years), rather than through internal development. In addition, Tyco's recent acquisition of CIT Group to enter the highly competitive world of commercial financing and lending adds a completely new line of business to the company's mix.

Beating the Market. The examples of Tenneco and Textron also point out some of the problems in pursuing an unrelated diversification strategy. For example, Tenneco's desire to grow its containers/packaging business by using funds acquired from selling J. I. Case is a bet that the packaging subsidiary is likely to be a growing and profitable long-term business. However, senior management cannot always accurately predict how each individual business is likely to perform in the future. Also, senior management cannot effectively formulate the specific, competitive strategies required for each business and market. The economic motive of unrelated diversification is that the corporation creates value to the extent that it is able to identify attractive acquisition or new business opportunities faster than the market can. Trying to even out the business cycle swings across different industries requires precise resource allocation and timing to ensure that the value acquired from new businesses justifies their acquisition costs. This task is difficult to accomplish at best.

Rise of a Conglomerate Discount. Unrelated diversification strategies assume that senior management can predict which businesses will do well over time. In other words, the economic rationale for conglomerates is based on the financial market's acceptance of senior management's judgment and selection of acquisition candidates that appear to be attractive for the future. The basic source of value in a conglomerate is senior management's ability to time the market to buy and sell businesses. This task generally proves to be difficult to perform consistently, because senior management cannot stay abreast of day-to-day operations in each individual business. In addition, throughout the 1990s, many conglomerate firms suffered because of the high debt costs incurred to buy businesses.

Several researchers have pointed out the existence of a so-called *conglomerate discount*, whereby the sum of the individual parts is greater than the value of the whole.[21] In fact, poorly managed conglomerate firms appear to provide *dysynergy*, in which individual businesses may actually be worth more on their own rather than when placed under a larger corporate umbrella with other unrelated units. In other words, unrelated diversification strategies can actually destroy value instead of creating it. Senior management often cannot lower costs, enhance differentiation, or accelerate learning in the conglomerate's vast array of businesses.

During the 1990s, however, senior management at many conglomerate firms began to recognize the strong tendency by the market to discount these firms' values. To counter this tendency, companies such as Litton Industries, ITT, Allegheny-Teledyne, Textron, and Tyco International have begun a process of divesting themselves of some of their businesses. Moreover, these same companies are trying to become more focused by limiting their acquisitions to only those businesses that appear to have some potential for synergies. Thus, conglomerates may become more related over time. Litton Industries, for example, has even considered placing some of its defense electronics businesses for sale, since it may no longer have the critical mass needed to compete in some key segments of the fast consolidating defense industry.[22]

Acquisitions over Internal Development. The unrelated diversification strategies of conglomerates are designed to acquire, hold, and sell businesses in various industries without the benefit or guide of an underlying distinctive competence. Unrelated, or conglomerate-based, diversification is based entirely on acquiring and selling different parts of the firm to maximize corporate profitability. When compared with related diversified firms, unrelated firms grow and contract primarily through asset acquisitions and divestitures. Unrelated diversification presents little opportunity to grow by developing new businesses internally. Senior management is not focused on identifying and extending a distinctive competence that can be leveraged across businesses. Nevertheless, when pursued successfully, unrelated diversifiers can maintain a high level of corporate growth and profitability. The biggest disadvantage of this strategy rests on the assumption that senior management will be able to beat the market consistently in identifying and purchasing attractive businesses in other industries.

Corporate Strategies Compared

So far, we have examined three different types of corporate strategies: vertical integration, related diversification, and unrelated diversification. The basic differences between these three strategies are important enough to reiterate. Vertical integration is based on extending the firm's scope of operations to other value-adding activities within the same industry. Unlike related or unrelated diversification, vertical integration is concerned primarily with improving efficiency and the core operations of the firm's existing activities. It does not extend the firm's distinctive competence to activities in other industries or businesses.

Related and unrelated diversification represents two corporate strategies that do extend the firm's scope of operations beyond the initial industry. Both of these diversification strategies move the firm into new areas of activity that represent different competitive conditions, products, and markets. Related diversification is based on extending the firm's distinctive competence among closely fitting businesses. Firms pursuing this strategy seek to use their existing resources (assets, skills, capabilities, and expertise) as a way to build and extend competitive advantage across different businesses and markets. By doing so, they are hoping to increase the value of the entire firm, thereby generating synergy. Unrelated diversification also takes the firm beyond the initial industry. However, it does not require a distinctive competence to identify and select new areas of activity. Acquiring and selling businesses remain the dominant focus of the unrelated diversification strategy.

Diversification is directly concerned with extending the firm beyond its original industry. The next section considers the major benefits that diversification can provide. Diversification can provide a firm three different kinds of benefits: (1) more attractive terrain, (2) access to key resources, and (3) opportunity to share activities among businesses (see Exhibit 7-2).

More Attractive Terrain

New terrain may be more attractive than that of a firm's base business for several reasons (see Exhibit 7-2A).

Benefits of Diversification — EXHIBIT 7-2

A. More attractive terrain
- Faster growth
- Higher profitability
- Greater stability

B. Access to resources
- Physical assets and access to markets
- Technologies and skills
- Expertise

C. Sharing of activities
(any business system activity)

Growth

New terrain may be growing more rapidly, thus providing opportunity for more rapid expansion, economies of scale, and learning new skills. Entry into high-growth areas gives the firm access to potential new sources of technologies and skills. In time, these resources could become the basis for future industries. This search for growth by way of extending technologies into new products and markets is particularly appropriate for related diversification strategies.

Kellogg's concern about the declining margins it was facing in its traditional breakfast cereals business motivated the firm to consider its most recent diversification moves. As competition heated up in the cereals business, Kellogg also found that fewer Americans were eating cereal as part of their breakfast regimen. This prompted Kellogg to move into other food products that could help compensate for its sluggish growth in breakfast foods. The same growth logic also applies to Tyco International's long list of acquisitions as it sought to enter more promising businesses. Even though the markets that Tyco entered were not considered high growth, they offered Tyco the opportunity to streamline the cost structure of its newly acquired units and thus help Tyco even out some of the cyclical nature of mature, industrial businesses. AT&T's earlier attempts to diversify away from its traditional telephone business enabled management to counter some of the reduced growth prospects of the long-distance business. In addition, advanced computers and consumer electronics represented growing businesses that use many of AT&T's newest technological developments in advanced materials, lasers, and software. By staking out new positions in these two growing industries, AT&T sought to define new industry standards for future products (e.g., customized software to operate future computers and electronics hardware) that could potentially use considerable amounts of AT&T technology.

Companies such as IBM, DuPont, Toshiba, and Hitachi are also diversifying their core operations to search for newer growth opportunities. In the case of IBM, the slow growth of revenues from its core mainframe business means that IBM must carefully identify and select new emerging product and market opportunities in which to invest (e.g., semiconductors, networking systems, servers, miniaturized disk drives, advanced routers, electronic commerce, software platforms, Internet-related businesses). For example, IBM has extended its extremely precise manufacturing techniques used for semiconductors to enter such related areas as making ultradense disk drives, compact disc etching equipment, flat-panel display screens, and even advanced lasers and optics used in telecommunications. DuPont, realizing that many of its fiber businesses are approaching maturity (Nylon, Dacron), has extended its knowledge of synthetic fibers into the composite materials business (e.g., Kevlar, Mylar, Tyvek), and, most recently, agribusiness (genetically engineered seeds using biotechnology). DuPont has also exited from its low-growth upstream petroleum operations by divesting its Conoco oil unit. In addition, DuPont sold its small pharmaceutical business to Bristol-Myers Squibb in July 2001 for $7 billion. At the same time, it is working to reinvigorate its core polyester and polyethylene operations. In fact, DuPont has begun working with Teijin Corporation of Japan to explore new ways to consolidate operations in these businesses.[23] Japanese electronics giants Toshiba and Hitachi are seeking to revitalize their growth by diversifying away from their mature core power generation, memory chip, and mainframe computer businesses. The growth in these businesses has slowed considerably in recent years, and several of these firms, including Hitachi and Fujitsu, have decided to exit the mainframe business.

Profitability

The desire for higher profitability also leads firms to search for new terrain. New terrain may be less competitive, thereby enabling a firm to earn a higher rate of return. Fewer competitors mean that firms often have "breathing room" to improve their profitability and to innovate new, related products. Consider the following examples. The cost of developing ever-faster microprocessors is becoming an extremely costly endeavor, even for Intel, which has traditionally led the semiconductor industry. Competition from Advanced Micro Devices, Transmeta, and Via Technologies has recently taken a significant toll on Intel's earnings. At the same time, Intel believes that there are new opportunities to utilize its semiconductor technology and skills that are more profitable, such as building communications chips for Internet and consumer applications. This motivation explains why Intel has purchased over twenty companies in the past few years at it searches for a more attractive market in which to compete. By diversifying into new fields, Intel hopes to resuscitate its profitability and to capture new market segments.

Despite its wide range of successful consumer products, Procter & Gamble continues to feel strong competition from such companies as Colgate-Palmolive, Clorox, Unilever, and other firms in its traditional consumer nondurables and personal care products businesses. Unrelenting pressure to cut costs, to accelerate product development, and to streamline operations has taken a toll on P&G's earnings in recent years. This explains why P&G at one point seriously considered acquiring a large pharmaceutical company to diversify its earnings, even entering the bidding process to purchase Warner-Lambert Company, before Pfizer finally acquired the firm. In August 1999, P&G purchased Iams Company, a leading pet foods maker that has a fiercely loyal customer base. P&G hopes to use its formidable distribution skills and base to help sell Iams in other channels besides those of pet supply stores and veterinarians' offices.[24]

In another example, Japanese producers of DVDs, VCRs, cellular phones, and television sets are beginning to feel low-cost pressure from Korean firms (Samsung, Lucky-Goldstar) in their core consumer electronics businesses. This pressure is prompting firms such as Sharp, Sony, Canon, and Matsushita to develop new technologies that allow them to enter higher profit areas, including office equipment, factory automation, electronic instruments, semiconductors, and household appliances (related diversification). Movement into these new areas gives the Japanese firms an opportunity to sidestep some of the fierce competition that characterizes many segments of the consumer electronics industry.

Stability

Finally, new terrain may be more stable than a firm's base business in terms of the cyclical nature and fluctuations of output. Firms sometimes face huge price swings in their core business, which lead to distortions in both production planning and pricing of the firm's product. Diversification into businesses with different industry cycles may allow a firm to generate more predictable levels of sales and profits. Entering other businesses to counterbalance the core business's output swings can even out the company's total revenue and profit picture. By expanding into a field with more stable characteristics, a firm can sometimes move away from problems in its core business. Unrelated diversification is particularly concerned with stability of earnings from different businesses. Textron and Tenneco have used this strategy since the mid-1970s, and both Schlumberger and Tyco appear to be practicing it today for this reason as well.

Access to Resources

A second common motive for diversification is a desire to secure access to resources. By acquiring a firm that possesses a scarce resource or market position, a firm can significantly improve its own competitive position. Similarly, a firm that possesses a critical resource can often improve the position of another business by acquiring and transferring the resource to it. Resources frequently acquired and transferred in this way are physical assets, technologies, and expertise (see Exhibit 7-2B).

Physical Assets

Diversification can be prompted by firms seeking access to the physical assets, such as manufacturing plants or distribution centers that complement the firms' original businesses. Firms will often buy another company because the physical assets utilized by its previous management were undervalued, or firms will acquire other businesses because of the scarcity or uniqueness of the assets involved. For example, Sony of Japan acquired U.S. entertainment assets during the late 1980s (Columbia Pictures and CBS Records). Part of the reason for these acquisitions was the Japanese giant's desire to secure the large film libraries whose values were likely to grow in the future. Films and television shows made by Columbia Pictures represented important assets because they are becoming critical pieces of the emerging multimedia and cable television industries. The films, television shows, and documentaries possessed by movie studios represent the "content" or "software," that is likely to flow along the future Internet-driven information highway and interactive television sets. Matsushita also purchased MCA Universal in the late 1980s but was forced to retreat from the business in 1995 when the synergies between electronics and entertainment proved illusory.

In the past decade, WorldCom has become a major player in the telecommunications industry by acquiring numerous other smaller firms to gain access to their physical assets. From 1987 to 1997, WorldCom has grown substantially by acquiring such firms as Metromedia Communications, Resurgens Communications, WilTel Network, and Advanced Telecommunications to acquire state-of-the-art fiber optic networks that were laid out by these and other firms. In 1996, WorldCom acquired MFS Communications to secure that firm's enormous Internet "backbone" that is now becoming the basis for the nation's data transmission network. Through its UUNet subsidiary, MFS Communications allows WorldCom to layer its own physical telecommunications network with that of the Internet in major cities. Acquiring all of these firms enabled WorldCom to amass an enormous amount of telecommunications assets and skills in a short time. Moreover, it strengthened WorldCom's market position and power by enabling it to consolidate a number of smaller firms into a larger entity. In September 1998, WorldCom merged with MCI Communications to become the nation's leading Internet "backbone" company and second-largest long-distance company. In 2000, WorldCom even attempted to merge with Sprint, the nation's third-leading long-distance company. However, federal regulators blocked the deal because they feared it would overly restrict competition in this industry.[25]

Technologies

Technological advances provide the underlying basis for innovating and commercializing new products. Developments in new technologies, such as robotics, display screens, microelectronics, software, genetic engineering, and advanced composite materials, represent the building blocks of future industries. Diversification is an important way for firms to learn, to extend, or to acquire new technological resources that could have serious future impact on their businesses, especially for firms practicing related diversification.

Many industries are becoming more related because of the sheer intensity and use of technology involved. For example, United Technologies, a leading provider of jet engines (Pratt & Whitney), elevators (Otis), flight systems and helicopters (Hamilton Sundstrand and Sikorsky), building systems (Carrier), and microelectronics, is facing a growing technological convergence among its businesses. All of these individual businesses are becoming more related because of the growing degree that microelectronics, hydraulics, and control systems play in making UTC's products function. The control technology used to develop avionics and aircraft cockpits is similar to those in the air-conditioning, heating, lighting, and security systems found in many modern office buildings. Thus, technology developed in one core business can often be leveraged and extended to other fields far beyond the original industry. Also, by offering a variety of different products as one combined set of "technology solutions" to its aerospace customers, UTC can provide a full array of skills in ways that other less diversified companies cannot do so as efficiently. UTC, in fact, has found that diversification also helped the company maintain a strong market position in businesses that have robust cash flows that come from selling spare parts and advanced services.[26]

Diversification can help firms improve the operating posture of their core businesses. For example, in 2000, America Online merged with Time Warner to combine Internet, print, publishing, music, cable television, and film production into one company. AOL Time Warner, as the new company is known, is now in a better position to compete across a variety of different media channels, including through such well-known outlets as CNN, *Time*, *Fortune*, HBO, and Warner Brothers. For America Online, the deal with Time Warner gives it important access to a variety of different "content" businesses that will help attract more subscribers to its on-line Internet service. For Time Warner, the merger with America Online helps the staid publishing, entertainment, and music giant learn how to compete in the fast-moving digital information business. In addition, Time Warner gains valuable access to AOL's important Internet-related businesses, such as Netscape Communications' new range of browsers and encryption technologies.

Cisco Systems is another example of a firm that has obtained needed resources through diversification. Ever since the firm went public in 1990, Cisco Systems has strengthened its leading technological and market position in providing network equipment solutions to firms in the telecommunications and Internet-related industries. In the past five years alone, Cisco has made over sixty acquisitions of firms that possess a proprietary technology or capability in the field of bridges, hubs, routers, and software management tools that allow data to be transmitted throughout the world along fiber optic, Internet networks. Some of Cisco's most important acquisitions include Grand Junction Networks (September 1995), StrataCom, Inc. (April 1996), Granite Systems (September 1996), LightSpeed International (December 1997), NetSpeed (March 1998), Fibex Systems, Sentient Networks, and GeoTel (all in April 1999). Later in 1999, Cisco acquired Cerent Technologies and Monterrey Networks for $10 billion. These two companies lead in state-of-the-art optical networks and switches that are expected to be at the heart of tomorrow's communication network. In 2000, Cisco acquired some twenty companies in the fields of wireless Internet technologies and optical networking. All of these firms have developed critical computer networking technologies that enable Cisco to blend its offerings with those of the acquired firms to provide customers with a full array of technologies and advanced products. Cisco's growth strategy has been so successful that it is now able to offer telecommunications carriers many products and technologies that were once developed by other companies such as Lucent Technologies, Nortel Networks, and Alcatel.[27]

Medtronic, Inc., is one of the world's leading manufacturers of medical devices, cardiac defibrillators, and heart pacemakers. The company has also diversified in recent years to gain access to new technologies to develop state-of-the-art surgical and disease treatment products. For example, some of its acquisitions include Xomed (ear/nose/throat surgery products), Sofamor Danek (spinal surgery tools), and Arterial Vascular Engineering (cardiac stents). All of these products complement the kind of specialized R&D that Medtronic has been refining for many years. In the future, Medtronic believes that its next-generation pacemakers and defibrillator devices will employ advanced information-based technologies to warn a patient's doctor of an impending heart attack or dangerously irregular heartbeat patterns. Medtronic is developing pacemakers that incorporate state-of-the-art wireless telecommunications chips that automatically either dial 911 or use the Internet to contact a patient's physician in case the patient's heart develops some type of abnormality—a major improvement in ongoing treatment of chronic diseases that can save lives before heart attacks or other syndromes become too serious to be treated easily. Thus, Medtronic is devoting a high proportion of its R&D to learning and building on new types of semiconductor and related technologies to strengthen and leverage its existing competitive position. In addition, Medtronic has also developed its own line of products designed to treat Parkinson's disease with electrical brain stimulation devices. In May 2001, Medtronic spent $3.7 billion to acquire MiniMed Inc. and Medical Research Group, two companies that have developed innovative new insulin pumps to help diabetic patients regulate the flow of insulin. Both MiniMed and Medical Research Group will help Medtronic strengthen its market position by harnessing new electronic and mechanical-based technologies to assist patients to better treat their chronic disease conditions.[28]

Expertise

Expertise possessed by a business in the form of information, knowledge, or skill has already been paid for. It therefore represents an essentially free good and invaluable resource to another business that can utilize it. If two such businesses merge, expertise possessed by one can be transferred to the other, producing potentially important economic benefits, especially if the expertise is highly specialized, durable, and hard to imitate. This extension of knowledge and expertise between companies forms a vital ingredient of the synergy behind diversification. In many ways, knowledge and expertise represent the best types of resources on which to build and extend new sources of competitive advantage. Knowledge and expertise are increasingly intangible (nonphysical) and based in organizational capabilities, meaning that they cannot easily be copied or imitated by competitors. Over time, competitors can learn the secrets behind new manufacturing plants and distribution channels, but it is much more difficult to imitate a competitor with distinctive knowledge or expertise. Knowledge-based assets, such as reputation, marketing know-how, brand names, patents, quality improvement skills, scientific testing, and fast product development teams, take time to accumulate and to grow. They are also highly specialized and tend to last a long time. This time requirement makes these characteristics especially distinctive, perhaps even unique, to the firm possessing them. Firms with such knowledge and expertise-based resources are well situated to extend their own distinctive competences into new areas of activity, since the uniqueness of such knowledge makes it hard for competitors to follow rapidly.

In the pharmaceutical industry, many leading drug firms are beginning to purchase small, vibrant biotechnology companies to supplement their own R&D efforts. Many small biotechnology companies, such as Amgen, Genentech, Immune Response, and others, were originally formed by small groups of scientists. They were specially trained and skilled in new cutting-edge technologies, such as genetic and molecular engineering. Large pharmaceutical firms' interests in acquiring many of the smaller biotechnology firms are based on the latter's distinctive knowledge and skills, which are essential to developing drugs against cancer, AIDS, hereditary diseases, and other ailments.[29] Companies such as Eli Lilly, Pfizer, Merck, Pharmacia & Upjohn, and American Home Products are continuing to investigate new biotechnology developments in order to develop safer and more effective drugs, especially those for cancer, diabetes, and other hard-to-treat conditions. Several biotechnology firms have become important established firms in their own right. Amgen, for example, has become the market leader in developing new forms of biotech-based treatments that help combat blood sepsis and clot formation during heart attacks. It is also a leader in inflammation and soft-tissue repair drugs.

General Motors' acquisition of Electronic Data Systems (EDS) in 1986 was motivated by a similar technology transfer consideration. EDS's core competence is data processing and systems integration. Systems integration helps computers, software, and machines from different vendors "talk" to one another. GM planned to introduce EDS's computer systems integration technology to make GM's factories work more smoothly and more compatibly, thereby making GM's factories more responsive and cost efficient when changing car models or tooling. GM reasoned that EDS's expertise in systems integration would make its factories more flexible and computer driven. However, the potential synergies between the two companies never really materialized. Ultimately, General Motors sold off its EDS unit to the public in a complex transaction spanning 1995 and 1996.

In the financial services industry, the purchase by American Express of Shearson, Lehman Brothers, IDS, and other financial firms during the 1980s stemmed from its need for expertise in investment and merchant banking. American Express's core business was that of providing high-quality travel and limited financial services to an upscale customer base. By expanding and acquiring Shearson, Lehman Brothers, and E. F. Hutton during the 1980s, American Express instantly transformed itself into a leading Wall Street financial powerhouse. A similar motivation prompted Primerica to purchase the Travelers insurance group in 1993. In 1998, Travelers merged with Citibank to form a giant financial services powerhouse that combines banking, insurance, brokerage, asset management, and other operations. The combination of the two firms, known as Citigroup, allows for transfer of expertise and knowledge of financial services, distribution, and other businesses that are increasingly technological and knowledge-based. Citigroup itself is now looking for new acquisition candidates to help it become even bigger in key financial service segments. For example, it acquired Associates First Capital to enter the commercial financing and leasing industry in late 1999. With diversified interests across a wide array of businesses, Citigroup now competes with megabanks (e.g., J. P. Morgan Chase, Bank of America), brokerages (e.g., Merrill Lynch, Morgan Stanley Dean Witter), and even some insurance firms (e.g., Prudential, Metropolitan Life, John Hancock) to provide financial services.

New product expertise like EDS's system integration skills or American Express's investment banking skills is not the only kind of expertise that can be usefully transferred from one business to another. Resources in virtually any functional area (production, marketing, or human resource management) or core skill (miniaturization, molding technology, packaging, or thin-film extrusion) are a candidate for this kind of transfer. These skills ideally should be highly specialized, durable, and applicable to reinforcing the firm's distinctive competences. Many of these functional area or core skills represent the basic building blocks of each firm's distinctive competence. Examples of successful diversification involving transfer of expertise are shown in Exhibit 7-3.

Sharing Activities

A third common motive for diversification is a desire to share one or more value chain activities among businesses. Such sharing avoids unnecessary duplication. It also enables businesses to operate activities on a larger scale than would be possible for any single business operating on its own. Sharing an activity produces greater economies of scale and thus lowers total costs. Equally important, sharing also offers the prospect for faster learning and application of new skills and technologies. Effective sharing of key resources among business units lays the foundation for building strong, highly inimitable core competences.

To illustrate, consider Kellogg's acquisition of Keebler Foods. Keebler's direct-to-store distribution system provides an important skill that could benefit Kellogg's endeavors to sell its ready-to-eat products and single-serve products more quickly and with less cost. At the same time, Keebler benefits from Kellogg's internal R&D and strong supermarket distribution channels. Both companies offer skills that allow for considerable sharing, which in turn helps Keebler to sell more of its products in Kellogg's traditional supermarket channels, while Kellogg is now able to learn how to compete in direct distribution systems. By diver-

Sharing Expertise among Businesses

EXHIBIT 7-3

Company	Partial List of Businesses	Shared Expertise
Hewlett-Packard	Computers/workstations Calculators Laser printers Digital imaging Engineering systems Microprocessors	• Engineering skills • Rapid product development • Distinctive manufacturing quality • Leverage design skills
Banc One	Nationwide system of low-cost, super-efficient banks	• Efficient management of banking activities (especially electronic data processing) • New product introduction (e.g., leasing, commercial lending)
Nutri/system	Weight loss centers Cosmetic dentistry centers	• Operation of retail centers devoted to enhancing physical appearance
KOA	Campgrounds Printing shops	• Franchising expertise • Selling franchises to small investors
PepsiCo	Soft drinks (Pepsi, Mountain Dew) Snack food (Frito-Lay) Gatorade (Quaker Oats) Tropicana juices	• Distribution systems • Marketing research • Segmentation skills • Consumer advertising • Brand development • Advertising
Medtronic	Heart devices Insulin pumps Spinal surgery Nervous system disorders	• Shared R&D skills • Wireless initiatives • Advanced technologies for less invasive treatments

sifying into snack foods, Kellogg added a business that could share the expense of this important activity. Joint conduct of distribution helps both the cereals and snack foods businesses in two ways. First, it avoids unnecessary duplication. Second, it enables the two businesses to mount a more concerted distribution effort than would be possible for either business acting alone.

Sharing remains a vital part of 3M Corporation's diversification strategy, especially of technologies and product applications that utilize skills based on coatings and adhesives. Production and R&D skills and insights gained from making superstrong adhesives are likely to be effective in developing more popular products as Post-It Notes. Also, 3M's R&D laboratories encourage scientists to work on a broad array of projects that have potential application to future lines of products that combine insights from a number of different disciplines. Technology is freely shared throughout the company, while businesses are free to pursue those opportunities that best fit their own marketing plans. Moreover, 3M scientists are encouraged to share their insights and breakthroughs and even to lead in new product development activities using their ideas. This approach to product development makes it difficult for competitors to imitate. Thus, technology sharing at 3M reduces the costs of entering related businesses that borrow upon an underlying coatings, adhesive, or thin-film competence.

In the early 1990s, AT&T's Bell Laboratories shared breakthrough technologies among numerous product groups. Improved chips that boost long-distance transmission quality are also used in AT&T's videophone, computer, and consumer electronics businesses. Technologies that improve sound quality are applicable to enhancing the quality of video images when transmitted over phone lines. (This technique is known as *data compression.*) AT&T's expertise with new microchip applications used for cellular phones can be used for network switching equipment. Advanced lasers are another technology that enhances the prospect for sharing among product groups. Different types of laser technology are used in products ranging from optical-based storage devices to new forms of signal transmission and consumer electronic goods.

Sharing becomes a vital part of diversification when skills learned in one business can be transferred to others. Virtually any activity in the value chain is a potential candidate for such sharing. Exhibit 7-4 provides several illustrative examples. Firms that can learn new skills or technologies and then share activities among businesses can reinforce their competitive advantage. Because sharing has its own challenges, it will be covered in a later chapter devoted to building and managing interrelationships.

EXHIBIT 7-4 Sharing Activities among Businesses

Firm	Partial List of Businesses	Key Shared Activity
3M	Sandpaper, tapes, fabric treatments, sealants, weatherstripping, Post-It Notes, medical patches, signs	Technology development: coatings adhesives, thin-film substrates, advanced membranes
Philip Morris	Cigarettes, packaged foods, consumer nondurables	Marketing: distribution, advertising, market research, promotion
IBM	Semiconductors, computers, network systems, disk drives, software, electronic commerce	Technology: silicon etching, systems integration, advanced materials, miniaturization Marketing: distribution, Internet, sales force, consulting
Fidelity Investments	Mutual funds, brokerage, securities, annuities	Operations: network management, telecommunications, internal logistics Marketing: distribution, sales, service, Internet, e-commerce

Costs of Diversification

Thus far we have considered only the benefits of diversification. Let us now turn to its costs. Diversification often imposes costs arising from (1) ignorance about newly entered fields, (2) neglect of a diversifier's core businesses, and (3) effort exerted to coordinate the businesses that result from diversification (see Exhibit 7-5).

Costs of Diversification — EXHIBIT 7-5

- Ignorance (about newly entered fields)
- Neglect (of core business)
- Coordination
  - communication
  - compromise
  - accountability

Cost of Ignorance

A firm that diversifies into a new area generally knows less about the new field than competitors. It is therefore less able to articulate consumer needs, predict technology developments, and foresee environmental shifts. This deficiency puts it at a disadvantage when compared with more experienced competitors, increasing the likelihood that it will miss important opportunities and make costly errors. General Electric's purchase of RCA in 1986 illustrates these problems. One of RCA's businesses was the NBC television network. Broadcasting is fast moving and dependent on personalities, managing relationships, fads, and trends. By contrast, GE's core businesses include such items as power generators, jet engines, financial services, medical equipment and plastics that have unique competitive characteristics. Not surprisingly, GE experienced initial troubles understanding and learning the broadcasting business.

Sony's purchase of Columbia Pictures in 1989 mirrored many of the same problems. As a giant electronics firm with a strong engineering flavor to its corporate culture, Sony was unable to manage effectively its newly acquired U.S. entertainment unit for several years because it was a completely different kind of business. Competitive advantage in entertainment depends much more on relationship-building, while success in electronics mandates tight quality control, focused product development, and product-driven sources of innovation that do not readily transfer to businesses that promote experiences and visual images.

Cost of Neglect

To carry out a diversification program, a firm's senior managers must deal with a host of issues. They must first decide that diversification is desirable. Since this is a critical decision, they must work with key individuals inside and outside the firm before reaching a conclusion. Consultants and investment bankers are outsiders who can advise top management in diversification issues. This effort takes time and can potentially distract attention from core businesses.

Once a decision to diversify has been made, top managers must decide how to enter the new area. If entry is by way of internal development, they must find managers to head up the new business. If acquisition is the route, they must identify suitable targets for purchase. Top managers must then integrate and manage the new unit after purchase. These activities significantly reduce the effort they can devote to a firm's original business. These problems are especially likely to occur in firms that engage in unrelated diversification into new industries. Consider the following two situations.

During the 1980s, Chrysler Corporation (now part of DaimlerChrysler) faced this problem with its high-profile, unrelated acquisitions of defense electronics, commercial aircraft, and financial services firms. These moves distracted Chrysler from its main auto business, thus diluting its cash flow and slowing its momentum in designing new cars. This lapse enabled Ford to gain further ground on Chrysler in the auto market and almost precipitated another collapse of Chrysler's core automotive business in 1991.

ITT's core telephone business eroded during the 1970s and 1980s when it acquired such businesses as Hartford Insurance, Sheraton Hotels, Rayonier forestry products, and other financial services and defense outfits. ITT's effort to understand and nurture the various businesses it had acquired caused it to neglect its telecommunications business. ITT completely withdrew from the growing telecommunications business by selling the remaining stakes of its original core business to France's Alcatel. Even after numerous restructurings during the 1990s, ITT continued to face difficulties that resulted from managing multiple sets of businesses, including schools for technical education, automotive products, and hotel reservation systems.

Costs of Cooperation

To share a common resource, two businesses must cooperate with each other. Achieving cooperation often entails substantial costs. This issue is especially important to senior managers in firms engaged in related diversification. Among the most significant costs are those of (1) communication, (2) compromise, and (3) accountability.

Cost of Communication. To share an activity, businesses must reach agreement on such issues as objectives for the activity, resources to be allocated to it, scheduling of new products, assignment of personnel to use, and a reporting structure for personnel. These vital issues can significantly affect the performance of each business. Managers in the businesses need to communicate, perhaps extensively, to resolve these issues. The time devoted to such communication is a cost that businesses must incur to share an activity.

To illustrate, consider the sharing of resources between Kellogg's breakfast foods and its recently acquired vegetarian foods and snack foods businesses. These three businesses must determine what types of product development, marketing, and distribution the firm will pursue jointly. Scheduling of different product testing and marketing initiatives needs to be resolved among the businesses to determine priorities. The three businesses must also decide from which division product and marketing specialists will come and how to divide the expenses.

To illustrate further, consider General Electric's Major Home Appliance Group. It uses plastics and motors produced by other GE divisions. The scheduling of plastics and motors production must be closely coordinated with the assembly of dishwashers. Motors must sometimes be customized to the particular speeds of dishwashers, while plastic tubs that go into dishwashers may need additional coatings and other protection from harsh dishwashing liquids. The businesses involved must communicate extensively about these issues.

Time Warner (now part of AOL Time Warner) had to devote considerable resources to coordinate its activities when it sought to jointly produce and conduct news operations with its Cable News Network (CNN) subsidiary. When it acquired Turner Broadcasting and CNN in September 1995, Time Warner wanted to orchestrate and leverage the full range of information gathering, analysis, production, distribution, and marketing activities to deliver the latest news and information across all types of media (e.g., broadcasting, cable, Internet, print, and publishing). Together with *Time*, *Fortune*, and *Entertainment Weekly* magazines, CNN would provide cutting-edge news reporting along with Time Warner's full line of popular news-oriented publications. Unfortunately, synchronizing the two operations with their different management styles, news gathering techniques, and editorial approaches made for an initially difficult combination.[30]

Many Japanese firms, currently suffering in the wake of a domestic recession and slow growth throughout Southeast Asia, are now finding that a significant cost accompanying their broad-based diversification strategies is the need for frequent and extensive communication among managers from many businesses. Companies such as Toshiba, Mitsubishi, Mitsui, and Sumitomo have been slow to respond to changing environments and new sets of customer needs in part because of their internal need to communicate, often at great length, among managers. Even as many Japanese firms currently struggle with their ongoing efforts to slim down their operations, they have proved very reluctant to abandon entire lines of businesses to improve their focus. Only recently have several major Japanese firms decided to exit such tough businesses as memory chips, mainframe computers, and even some types of consumer electronics.[31]

Cost of Compromise. Businesses involved in coordination will sometimes place different priorities on development projects. Decisions ultimately reached may therefore involve compromises that do not fully satisfy the needs of one or both businesses. Compromises can result in political frictions and reduced strategic flexibility for both businesses. For example, designing and making a particular line of dishwashers might be more time-consuming if plastics and motors provided by other GE units are used than if components are purchased from outside suppliers. Fine-tuning and calibrating dishwasher motors may require additional time and testing, especially if the motors were originally designed for other purposes. Internally supplied plastic dishwasher tubs may need an additional sealant and may cost more. On the other hand, outside suppliers might be faster, more responsive, or more skilled in making dishwasher components. Oftentimes, external suppliers will offer key products and components at a deep discount with the hope of capturing more business in the future. For managers at GE's Major Home Appliances Group, obtaining components internally would then involve a compromise for GE's dishwasher businesses.

IBM currently faces important issues and costs that result from the need to find the right balance of compromise and coordination among its many different businesses. IBM's most recent strategy is to become a full-service provider of all types of computer, electronic-commerce, and technology solutions to firms in every industry. However, the pace of product development within IBM often moves at different speeds. IBM Microelectronics, for example, leads the semiconductor industry in developing new types of microchips that use copper-based technologies that speed up processing speed at lower cost. Its software group excels in creating new electronic-commerce platforms that integrate supply chain, procurement, and logistics management across different parts of a client company's operations. These businesses typically move at a rapid pace because they must respond to fast-changing environmental developments within their respective industries. However, other IBM businesses, such as mainframe computers, may not move so quickly, since these products' architectures and standards tend to have long life cycles. Managers in these units often think in terms of years, rather than months, to design next-generation products. This means that IBM managers must spend a great deal of time to coordinate the product development efforts of multiple units and technologies to ensure that IBM's products enter the market at the right time. Compromises among the different businesses are often required to ensure that each unit understands the timing and strategic imperatives facing the others. Thus, to be able to provide customers with a full range of solutions, IBM managers must often try to coordinate the product development, production, and sales activities of their many units to ensure that customers receive the best mix of products at a price they are willing to pay. Managers must also speak and negotiate with one another about pricing and sharing costs. This is a complex organizational task that occasionally gives the impression that IBM is slow to respond to customers' needs. Sometimes, IBM managers may be compelled to use products from competitors if customers demand them to do so.[32]

AT&T faced significant costs related to compromise and coordination among its telecommunications, electronics, and networking equipment businesses in the mid-1990s. Both the long-distance telephone and the networking equipment units competed with one another for investment dollars each year, with the result that neither business felt it had sufficient funds to build market share and to continue new product or service development. Moreover, both businesses felt they had insufficient autonomy to compete in their respective core markets as managers needed to consult with one another frequently about pricing, strategy, equipment use, and competitor responses. The network equipment and electronics side of AT&T, in particular, felt it was losing significant business to competitors such as Nortel Networks, Motorola, Alcatel, Siemens, Ericsson, and others that could move more quickly to meet their telecommunications customers' needs. In addition, competitors were unwilling to purchase significant quantities of AT&T equipment, despite its high quality, because they felt they would be helping a competitor in the long-distance telephone business.

Cost of Accountability. When a business operates independently, its managers can be held accountable for results. Accountability is reduced if a business is asked to cooperate with other units, since its performance will then be influenced, perhaps to a large degree, by compromises it makes to work with other units. Also, the help it receives from them will affect its results. For example, if GE's Major Home Appliance Group uses plastics and materials from other GE units, then the costs of goods sold for dishwashers are mostly based on internal prices that may be different from market prices. A manager's performance can then no longer be strictly equated with financial results of the business's operations; instead, performance must be judged in part on other subjective factors. Such evaluations complicate the job of senior managers by requiring them to consider these subjective factors when measuring a manager's performance. Subjective evaluations in turn can create motivational problems, since subordinates will sometimes disagree with evaluations made at higher levels. This disparity can lower morale and reduce motivation to perform.

Maximizing Benefits, Minimizing Costs

Diversification thus involves a series of important trade-offs (see Exhibit 7-6). It can sometimes produce important benefits due to more attractive terrain, resource transfers, and activity sharing. However, it also imposes potentially formidable costs stemming from ignorance, neglect, and reduced accountability. To achieve a favorable balance between these opposing elements, top managers charged with diversification must try to maximize benefits while minimizing costs.

EXHIBIT 7-6 Balancing the Benefits and Costs of Diversification

Diversification Benefits ⟷	Diversification Costs
• More attractive terrain	• Ignorance
• Access to key resources	• Neglect
• Sharing resources	• Coordination

Achieving Powerful Diversification Benefits

Let us now consider the conditions leading to powerful advantages for each kind of diversification benefit discussed previously (see Exhibit 7-7).

More Favorable Terrain. Some stakeholders may derive important benefits from a firm's expansion into more favorable terrain. Consider, for example, workers of a firm currently operating in a declining industry saddled with high fixed costs and underutilized capacity, such as coal mining or sugar refining. Unless such a firm can increase its market share, its employees will be laid off as the level of activity declines over time. Expansion into a more rapidly growing field enables a firm to avoid this situation by providing employment opportunities for workers no longer needed in its core business. Managers can also benefit from expansion, since it brings them expanded responsibility, greater career challenge, and higher compensation.

Shareholders are much less likely to benefit from diversification designed solely to improve terrain, however. Shareholders can improve terrain on their own simply by pur-

Conditions Leading to Powerful Diversification Benefits

EXHIBIT 7-7

A. Achieving more attractive terrain
(This is rarely a source of powerful benefits for all stakeholders.)

B. Transferring resources which are . . .
- competitively important to receiving businesses
- difficult for receiving businesses to duplicate on their own
- hard for competitors to imitate

C. Shared activities must be . . .
- large in dollar terms
- susceptible to economies of scale and experience

chasing shares in other firms already operating in desirable new areas. To help shareholders, *diversification must produce benefits that they cannot achieve by diversifying their own portfolios.* Again, the key issue underscoring diversification's performance is the following question: Does a company reinforce and improve its distinctive competence by entering another area? Only if the answer is yes can diversification benefit shareholders. Diversification undertaken solely to improve terrain is thus a mixed bag, producing benefits for some stakeholders, but not for others (Exhibit 7-7A). Indeed, diversification with this sole objective in mind will often be a losing proposition for shareholders, because it imposes various costs—ignorance, neglect, reduced accountability—without providing offsetting benefits that shareholders cannot achieve on their own. Whether top managers should proceed with diversification despite this potentially unfavorable trade-off will depend on the relative importance they attach to shareholder needs relative to those of other stakeholder groups. This issue is complicated by the fact that top managers are one of the groups that most benefits from diversification. Therefore, they are often least able to make an objective decision.

Resource Transfers. Diversification that transfers resources between two businesses can provide important benefits to shareholders, since shareholders cannot reproduce resource transfers simply by diversifying their own portfolios. These benefits will tend to be large when three conditions are present (Exhibit 7-7B). First, a transferred resource must be *competitively important* to the receiving business. It can be competitively important by either significantly reducing the receiving business's costs or by enhancing its uniqueness in some important way. Also, a transferred resource must be *difficult to duplicate* by the receiving business acting on its own, meaning that the receiving business could not develop the resource by itself because of high cost, time, lack of skills, or other factors. Finally, the resource should be sufficiently *specialized and durable* to produce value over long time periods.

Whether these three conditions are satisfied in any particular instance is often difficult to assess. Consider General Motors' acquisition of EDS in 1986, for example. GM's managers expected that EDS's highly specialized skills in managing technology and computers would significantly improve GM's ability to automate its factories, and thus build better-quality cars using advanced robotics. Their expectation went unmet, however. EDS's computer-oriented skill set proved to be of little use to General Motors, mainly because of its high cost and limited applicability to factory automation systems. The resource was not valuable in enhancing GM's cost, differentiation, or capability to generate new knowledge. Resources transferred between GM and EDS therefore had little beneficial impact on either company's competitive position.

Often diversifiers learn only through trial and error what capabilities may be useful to other businesses. Consider KOA, for example. It is the nation's largest operator of campgrounds, with more than seven hundred franchised units throughout the country. Its first diversification involved the acquisition of Gardner, Inc., a manufacturer of recreational vehicles (RVs). KOA was actively purchasing RVs at the time for use in its Stay & Tow program, so it could provide Gardner a captive market. KOA felt its own camping expertise would be useful to an RV manufacturer. This expectation went largely unfulfilled, however. Success in the RV business requires sophisticated assembly skills, which KOA, a service enterprise, totally lacked. KOA possessed little expertise it could transfer to Gardner. Unable to improve Gardner's performance, KOA eventually sold the subsidiary at a loss. KOA's next major diversification was more successful. It acquired Sir Speedy, Inc., a large network of franchised printing shops. While Sir Speedy operated outside the camping industry, it faced challenges similar to those that KOA had already mastered through many years of experience operating its franchised campground network, including selling franchise rights, negotiating franchise contracts, training new franchisees, and overseeing geographically dispersed units. These skills are highly specialized and useful to a number of different franchising-related opportunities. By transferring distinctive skills and know-how in these areas, KOA has been able to improve Sir Speedy's competitive position significantly.

Activity Sharing. The sharing of an activity between two or more businesses will produce a powerful benefit when two distinct conditions are satisfied (Exhibit 7-7C). First, the activity being shared must involve a *large dollar outlay*. Without this prerequisite, even a major reduction in the activity's cost will have little impact on total business expense. Most staff-related, nonoperational activities (accounting, legal, finance) fail to meet this requirement. Sharing them among businesses therefore rarely produces powerful benefits. This is a big reason why conglomerate-type diversification tends to produce little lasting value or competitive advantage. By contrast, activities such as operations, sales, advertising, procurement, and technology development often involve substantial financial outlays. Thus, even a small percentage reduction in their cost can have a major impact on total business expense.

Second, a shared activity must also be *susceptible to economies of scale and experience*. Only through this susceptibility will sharing the activity among businesses produce significant benefits for the businesses involved. Recall that the susceptibility of a firm's activities to economies of scale and experience varies greatly. For example, automated tooling, molding, die-casting, fabrication, and managing information networks are activities that typically display high economies of scale. On the other hand, gourmet cooking, construction of new buildings, and interior décor are activities that often depend upon meeting a customer's exact specifications, thus limiting the potential to capture significant economies of scale.

Limiting Diversification Costs

In addition to trying to maximize diversification benefits, diversifiers must also attempt to limit diversification costs. A diversifier can take certain steps to contain each of the diversification costs noted earlier in the chapter (see Exhibit 7-8).

Cost of Ignorance. One way to limit the cost of ignorance is to confine diversification to *familiar fields*, which are areas close to a firm's base business. New segments or new stages of a firm's core industry generally satisfy this requirement, since they usually involve products, technologies, and a general environment similar to those of a firm's original business. Carefully implemented related diversification also satisfies this requirement.

Entering new areas through internal development rather than by acquisition can also limit costs of ignorance. This step is an important key to the success of the related diversification strategy. Internal entry provides a firm with opportunities to build up its investment gradually in a new area, thereby limiting risk in early stages when ignorance is the greatest. By the time investment reaches a critical mass, a firm using internal entry will often have learned enough about a new business to avoid serious missteps. Diversification by acquisition, however, often requires a firm to make a substantial investment up front, before it has had time to learn much about a new field. In this situation, acquiring relatively small firms can limit some of the difficulties involved in learning and gaining experience with a

Limiting Diversification Costs

EXHIBIT 7-8

Limit Costs of Ignorance by . . .

- entering familiar fields
- centering new areas internally rather than by acquisition

Limit Costs of Neglect by . . .

- ensuring new businesses fit easily with existing ones
- leveraging a distinctive competence systemwide

Limit Costs of Cooperation by . . .

- carefully managing the sharing of activities
- designing organizational support systems that promote interrelationships

new field. Large acquisitions in a familiar field can especially pose significant management and integration problems for firms. This happened to many companies in the managed care, broadcasting, financial services, railroad, and telecommunications industries during the late 1990s, even as they pursued related diversification. In particular, this challenge often confronts managers pursuing an unrelated diversification strategy. The cost of miscalculation can then be much greater and harder to reverse.[33]

For example, even though General Electric faced significant difficulties in attempting to integrate its NBC broadcasting unit during the 1980s (by way of acquiring RCA), GE has done much better when it has confined its acquisitions to businesses that it already knows. In July 2001 alone, GE acquired three different companies, each of which complements an existing line of business. In the medical field, GE acquired Data Critical, a key manufacturer of wireless and Internet-driven systems for transmitting health care data. This acquisition will help GE make much of its medical equipment Internet-ready so that technicians and medical personnel can then transfer patient findings and data with fewer steps and greater ease. GE also acquired Heller Financial, a firm that is well positioned in the fields of commercial financing, equipment leasing, and real estate finance in July 2001. Heller will help GE Capital become more competitive as the unit offers its commercial customers a broader array of financial service products. Finally, GE acquired a business unit that makes equipment to transmit voice, video and data from Nortel Networks to help it boost its GE Industrial Systems unit. GE Industrial Systems will use the technology from Nortel to design some key components for next-generation telecommunications equipment.[34]

Cost of Neglect. A diversifier's base business is most likely to be neglected when crises occur in one or more of its newly entered businesses. This situation occurred with Eastman Kodak when problems arose in its Sterling Drug acquisition in 1988. Kodak discovered that skills required for researching and producing pharmaceuticals were substantially different from those used to develop new films. Kodak's efforts to improve Sterling Drug's performance caused it to neglect important aspects of its film business, especially new product development. Eventually, Kodak sold its wide-ranging pharmaceutical operations in a number of different transactions in 1994 and 1995. These moves represented a serious strategic distraction for Kodak. Kodak's acquisitions also cost the company valuable time and resources that could have been devoted to learning about digital technologies, something that was already available as far back as the mid-1980s. Instead, Kodak hoped to use its acquisitions as a way to compensate for the steadily declining earnings of its traditional film business.

Sony's purchase of Columbia Pictures in 1989 resulted in senior managers refocusing their time and commitment to integrate the newly acquired entertainment unit within Sony's corporate umbrella of operations. However, the significant effort required to learn about how the entertainment business operates resulted in neglect of the firm's core electronics operations. Capital once allocated to new product development and process improvements in consumer electronics was siphoned off to produce blockbuster movies, many of which were financial failures, from 1992 to 1995. By late 1995, realizing the potential effects of neglect on its core operations, Sony refocused its investment and managerial priorities on learning new forms of digital, video game, and Internet-driven technologies needed for consumer electronics. These moves, by contrast, have been much more successful, since they are based on harnessing Sony's creative and fast product development skills in electronics, a more familiar field.

Intel's move to enter the Web-hosting and consumer electronics businesses over the past few years has resulted in significant difficulties for the company's core semiconductor business. As Intel tried to build its Web-hosting business for corporate customers, it became distracted from the significant progress that its arch rival AMD was making. By the end of 2001, AMD had seized upward of 20 percent of the microprocessor market, and appeared to be gaining on Intel in the more lucrative market for corporate servers as well. At the same time, Intel tried to compete in the consumer electronics business by designing such gadgets as digital cameras, home networking devices, and even MP3 digital music players. By October 2001, Intel announced that it would retreat from consumer electronics to concentrate on its core semiconductor business. Many analysts also believe that Intel will eventually leave the Web-hosting business as well to conserve resources.[35]

To avoid neglect of their core businesses, top managers must take steps to reduce the likelihood of new crises in their newly entered businesses. Crises in newly entered businesses will tend to be fewer and of smaller magnitude when diversification is confined to familiar fields and achieved through internal entry rather than by acquisition. Thus, diversifying firms can avoid costs of neglect and ignorance by following the same two guidelines.

Cost of Cooperation. To transfer resources and share activities, businesses must cooperate with each other. Some cooperation costs therefore inevitably accompany these benefits. Such costs can be minimized, however, by careful design of a diversifier's administrative systems. We will focus on this subject in a later chapter that examines the management of interrelationships.

Alternatives to Diversification: Corporate Restructurings

Diversification is one potentially useful remedy available to a firm operating in a troubled industry. However, it is not the only remedy. In fact, diversification for its own sake can produce significant managerial difficulties, destruction of shareholder value, dilution of corporate resources and distinction, and long-term problems in recovering firm competitiveness. The difficulties that confronted such firms as American Express, Aetna, Sears, Sony, General Electric, General Motors, McKesson HBOC, and others in recent years testify to the significant managerial challenges posed by complex or overly ambitious diversification strategies. When diversification is likely to produce fewer benefits (in the form of resource transfers and activity sharing) than costs (from ignorance, neglect, and cooperation), then some other solution to industry decline should be pursued. Equally important, when diversification has failed to produce sustainable increases in long-term shareholder value and new ways to use the firm's set of distinctive competences and resources, action is needed to induce a renewed focus on the firm's core business.

corporate restructurings: Steps designed to change the corporate portfolio of businesses to achieve greater focus and efficiency among businesses; often involve selling off businesses that do not fit a core technology or are a drag on earnings.

Fortunately, alternatives and remedies for excessive diversification exist. Many of these efforts can be broadly described as corporate restructurings. **Corporate restructurings** involve changing the firm's portfolio or mix of businesses to become more efficient and focused in key activity areas.[36] Particularly worthy of consideration are (1) selective focus and (2) divestitures and spin-offs of noncore units (see Exhibit 7-9). Both forms of corporate restructurings are designed to help senior managers rebuild sources of competitive advantage in their core businesses. Simultaneously, restructurings help shareholders (the firm's owners) gain improved value and financial performance from a tighter focus.

Steps in Corporate Restructuring — EXHIBIT 7-9

- Selective focus on carefully chosen activities or niches
- Divestitures and spin-offs

Selective Focus

By carefully targeting new segments, a firm may be able to expand its market share even though the industry in which it operates is in decline. The ease of increasing market share will depend on the tenacity of competitors. If competitors are tough, as often occurs when fixed costs are high, market share will be difficult to gain. However, if competitors have lost interest in an industry, as is often the case in maturing or declining industries, gains in market share are more feasible. Selective focus also fits a careful acquisition strategy.

Perhaps the one firm that best exemplifies a strategy of carefully identifying and targeting new market segments is Southwest Airlines. From its original core base in the Southwest and California markets, Southwest overcame the worst problems of an airline by targeting new short-haul routes in the Northeast where it can make a sustainable penetration of airports or metropolitan areas that were previously underserved. After completing its acquisition of Morris Air to reach the Rocky Mountain region in 1994, Southwest began to duplicate its successful short-haul strategy in the dense metropolitan cities of the East. For example, in 1996, Southwest entered the East Coast market by establishing a base area in Baltimore, a city often bypassed by other larger carriers. Later, Southwest moved into Providence, Rhode Island, to use that facility as a way of avoiding direct competition with larger established carriers that use Boston's Logan Airport as their core hub. Now, Southwest has begun to challenge the major airlines in the New York area by offering service from a small airport in Long Island.

Motorola pursued a strategy of selective focus in the field of conventional transistors and simple electronic components. As more sophisticated electronic devices are shrink-wrapped into microchips, few companies have any interest in building simpler electronic devices from an earlier age, including stand-alone transistors, resistors, capacitors, and even vacuum tubes. Motorola continued to stake out this obsolescent, declining part of the electronics industry as other competitors leave. In turn, Motorola became one of the world's largest suppliers of simple, stand-alone, electronic devices. Even Motorola has realized that in order to maintain a tight focus on its core advanced semiconductor and communications businesses, it can no longer devote considerable resources and attention to older products. In 1998, Motorola folded its discrete semiconductor business into a new company known as On Semiconductor that now operates independently.

Acquisitions of smaller firms in market niches that complement a firm's existing core business interests may help build the kind of critical mass needed to overcome problems of a declining industry. By focusing on specialized segments in its existing industry, a firm can sometimes maintain steady sales and profitability despite overall industry decline. Crown Cork & Seal has taken this approach in the metal can industry. Industry sales have declined in recent decades as a result of inroads made by substitute packaging materials, such as plastic, paper, and glass. Crown Cork & Seal continued to dedicate itself entirely to metal containers for a long period of time. It concentrated its product development efforts on those segments unaffected by substitute materials, such as bottle caps and crowns. Crown Cork & Seal's selective focus also includes hard-to-hold applications, such as aerosols, and customers in developing countries where the newer materials have not yet penetrated. This selective focus has enabled Crown Cork & Seal to far outperform American Can and Continental Can, whose diversification programs have had disastrous results.

During the mid-1990s, many firms in the managed health care industry were undertaking a similar set of strategies designed to serve different specialized segments of this industry. In late 1996, for example, Aetna purchased U.S. Healthcare, a leading managed care and health maintenance organization (HMO) provider. The combination of the two firms was designed to give both critical mass as well as the ability to create new products and services for customers in different health plans around the nation. Although the merger of the two firms has brought some major problems with integration (especially in computers, information systems, and infrastructure), the two firms have surfaced to become a major player in the managed care market. Aetna has even acquired other managed care firms, such as New York Life's NYLCare unit and Prudential's health care unit (after divesting certain regions for competitive reasons). However, it appears that Aetna may have seriously overextended its strategy. Integrating NYLCare and Prudential HealthCare proved even more daunting, and costs ballooned in ways that management never predicted. Employers and other customers of Aetna's health plans began to balk at the insurance firm's poor coordination of activities, while doctors revolted against the firm's lower reimbursement rates for patient care. In 2001, Aetna actually fell behind such other competitors as UnitedHealth Care, WellPoint Health Networks, and CIGNA in the race to win over new customers in the fast-consolidating managed care industry. Another large insurance firm with significant managed care interests is that of CIGNA, which purchased its smaller rival Healthsource in 1997. The acquisition of Healthsource gives CIGNA access to complementary markets where it did not offer coverage before. The combination of both firms' managed care offerings enables CIGNA to gain significant bargaining power and economies of scale to negotiate with employers, hospital chains, pharmaceutical firms, and pharmacy benefit managers.

At the same time, however, CIGNA is steadily growing its managed care business through carefully focused internal development and growth of new markets, thus avoiding some of the major integration problems that continue to bedevil Aetna. WellPoint Health Networks is also growing through careful internal development and acquisition of small managed care firms throughout the country. Based in California, WellPoint works to develop good relations with hospitals, physicians, employers, and patients who utilize its managed care HMO and PPO networks. Under CEO Leonard Schaeffer, WellPoint has become a leader in offering innovative health insurance solutions to large and small businesses, and has gained important market share in its newly acquired territories in many parts of the United States.[37]

Divestitures and Spin-offs

spinning off: A form of corporate restructuring that sells businesses or parts of a company that no longer contribute to the firm's earnings or distinctive competence.

Yet another powerful and increasingly used means of corporate restructuring for a firm confronting the challenges of diversification is that of divesting or "spinning off" parts of the company. **Spinning off** businesses means selling those units or parts of a business that no longer contribute to or fit the firm's distinctive competence. Spin-offs can involve sales of assets to another firm or to the public in the form of a new stock offering. The major purpose of a spin-off or divestiture is to unlock the hidden value of assets or businesses that floundered with excessive diversification and reduced corporate focus. In recent years, literally hundreds of firms across a wide array of industries have undertaken major corporate spin-offs of noncore or maturing assets in order to increase shareholder value and renew focus. Exhibit 7-10 presents some of the more prominent spin-offs over the past few years in different industries.

Spinning off businesses and other assets can help the firm regain a stronger sense of focus and unlock critical funds by divesting assets whose value has plateaued or declined as a result of ignorance or neglect. Firms can utilize the cash generated from spin-offs to invest in emerging or future technologies that better leverage or revitalize their distinctive competences. For example, DuPont in June 1998 announced that it would spin off its petroleum business, Conoco, to the public to refocus on its life sciences and pharmaceutical businesses. Procter & Gamble in October 2001 announced that it would divest its Jif peanut butter and Crisco cooking oil units by selling them to the family-run J. M. Smucker Company for $810 million. This move allows P&G to concentrate its resources on those businesses that it believes to have greater growth potential, while allowing J. M. Smucker to gain critical market share in the peanut butter and shortening businesses. In addition, J. M. Smucker will be able to devise new marketing programs that combine its strong positions in the jellies and jams with its peanut butter offerings.[38] *Spin-offs enable firms to reverse their*

Key Corporate Spin-offs in Recent Years

EXHIBIT 7-10

Firm	Spun-off Unit	Industry/Intent
Baxter Healthcare	• Allegiance	• Divest low margin, mature medical supply unit
AT&T	• Lucent Technologies	• Separate telecom equipment maker from telecommunications service firm
PepsiCo	• Tricon Global Restaurants	• Free up KFC, Taco Bell, Pizza Hut into new unit
Ralston-Purina	• Ralston Ralcorp.	• Separate animal feed business cereals business
Ford	• Associates First Capital	• Divest commercial lending unit to focus on automobile business
	• Visteon Corp.	• Divest of part-making unit
Monsanto	• Solutia	• Frees up Monsanto to focus on biotechnology
DuPont	• Conoco	• Use cash from spin-off to focus on life sciences
ICI	• Zeneca	• Separation of commodity chemical and agribusiness units
Sprint	• 360 Communications	• Separation of long distance and cellular, wireless network
Marriott International	• Host Marriott	• Separation of hotel management and real estate businesses
General Mills	• Darden Group	• Divest restaurant unit to focus on core foods business
Sears	• Allstate Insurance • Coldwell Banker • Dean Witter • Discover	• Divest four financial services units to focus on retailing
American Express	• Lehman Brothers	• Separation of brokerage/ underwriting unit from travel services
Eastman Kodak	• Eastman Chemical	• Focus on digital photography and imaging
CBS	• Westinghouse industrial businesses	• Renew focus to become a pure play media company
US West	• MediaOne Group	• Separation of cable and distribution business from telecommunications unit
AT&T	• AT&T Broadband	• Focus on core long-distance business
Tyco International	• 4 business units	• Increase transparency to shareholders
Citigroup	• Travelers unit	• Divest of some noncore property/casualty business
Lucent Technologies	• Agere Systems	• Divest of chip-making unit to focus on wireless and optical segments

(continued)

EXHIBIT 7-10 Key Corporate Spin-offs in Recent Years *(continued)*

Firm	Spun-off Unit	Industry/Intent
Merck	• Medco Containment	• Focus on core drug development activities
H. J. Heinz	• Weight Watchers unit	• Focus on condiment and flavorings business
Hewlett-Packard	• Agilent Technologies	• Focus on printing, digital imaging, and computing systems
AMR Corp.	• The Sabre Group	• Divest of software and reservations systems
General Motors	• Delphi Automotive Systems	• Divest of auto part-making unit

diversification postures that may have resulted in reduced corporate focus or dilution of their distinctive competences. These corporate restructurings enable firms to "downscope" the wide degree of diversification that became unwieldy and cumbersome over time. When firms can no longer generate value from acquired or internally developed businesses, spinning off these units is preferable to retaining underutilized assets. Consider, for example, the following recent major corporate spin-offs of the past few years.

Eastman Kodak's core imaging business has suffered from high costs of neglect resulting from senior management's diversification into chemicals and pharmaceuticals. To regain its focus, Eastman Kodak spun off its Eastman Chemical unit as a newly formed, independent company to its stockholders in 1993. Eastman Chemical is now a completely separate company from Eastman Kodak, with its own management team, board of directors, markets, and products. Kodak's senior management believed it could create more value for its shareholders by making the chemical unit an independent firm. In addition, Kodak sold its pharmaceutical business to various firms for a total of $7.7 billion throughout 1994 and 1995. These proceeds were then used to reduce Kodak's large mountain of debt and to reinvest in its core imaging and photography business. The prescription drug business was sold to its joint venture partner Sanofi of France in July 1994, while Smith Kline Beecham bought Kodak's over-the-counter drug business. Johnson & Johnson purchased Kodak's medical diagnostic business in September 1994. For both chemicals and pharmaceuticals, Kodak has acknowledged that it could not adequately develop these businesses in conjunction with its core imaging businesses. Divesting and spinning off these units has enabled Eastman Kodak to regain its focus to develop new technologies and products in advanced electronic and digital-based imaging.[39]

In 1997, PepsiCo spun off its $10 billion restaurant unit (including KFC, Taco Bell, and Pizza Hut) as a new company known as Tricon Global Restaurants. Pepsi's senior management realized that competing in restaurants would become a highly capital-intensive endeavor, with more money being diverted away from its core beverages and Frito-Lay snack food businesses. The highly profitable and cash flow–rich earnings from Frito-Lay were being diverted to a restaurant unit that faced a higher cost of capital and significantly tougher competition from revitalized pizza chains (e.g., Domino's Pizza, Papa John's International, Little Caesar), ethnic food chains (e.g., Taco Bueno), and even from small players in the fiercely competitive chicken market (e.g., Popeye's, La Madeleine). Moreover, the restaurant business was slowing as the entire industry entered a period of slow-growth maturity. In addition, coordination and communication between the restaurant group with the rest of PepsiCo's operations were difficult at best. More important, other restaurant chains were reluctant to purchase Pepsi beverages (in the highly lucrative fountain business) because they felt that they would be indirectly helping their competitors (KFC, Taco Bell, and Pizza Hut). Thus, PepsiCo's ability to create further value in the restaurant unit, and vice versa, deteriorated and no longer provided a rationale for its earlier diversification strategy. Although the current PepsiCo is now half the size it once was in 1995, it is significantly more profitable, with the bulk of revenues and net income coming from its flagship Frito-Lay unit. CEO Roger Enrico and his management team are now working to leverage joint marketing initiatives and programs to coordinate both Frito-Lay's and Pepsi's use of internal resources to fight Coke. In April 1999, PepsiCo also undertook a spin-off of its domestic bottling unit to give it greater focus and responsiveness to the marketplace. The company concedes it has underinvested in its bottling unit for several years because there were so many other competing demands for its cash. PepsiCo's senior management believes that Coca-Cola's 1986 spin-off of its bottling unit into a separately managed and traded Coca-Cola Enterprises unit freed up a tremendous amount of cash and galvanized Coke's focus to invest more singularly in key marketing and promotion activities that directly contributed to its competitive advantage. Thus, over time, one can expect PepsiCo to pursue further corporate restructurings that may involve additional spin-offs and selective acquisitions to bolster its position in the beverage and snack food industries. Its most recent large acquisition has been that of Quaker Oats, which Pepsi bought in December 2001 for $14 billion. PepsiCo is hoping to use Quaker's Gatorade brand of sports drinks to push further into the noncarbonated beverage market.[40]

In a period of two years, an emerging retailing giant known as CVS has undertaken a massive series of spin-offs designed to give it critical mass, renewed focus, and cash to fund growth in its core pharmacy retailing business. Originally known as Melville Corporation, this holding company as late as June 1995 operated a wide array of retailing businesses with such well-known names as Thom McAn (shoes), Linens N' Things (textiles and furniture coverings), Kay-Bee Toys (children's toys), Wilson's (leather goods and accessories), and This End Up (furniture stores). Deciding that the company would concentrate only on managing and revitalizing its fast-growth pharmacy operations, Melville sold off its various retailing businesses in a series of spin-offs over the next two years. In December 1995, Melville sold off its Kay-Bee Toy store chain to Consolidated Stores for $315 million. In that same month, it also sold off its Wilson's leather goods chain to its management group who wanted to manage the unit independently. In June 1996, Melville sold off its This End Up, Thom McAn, and a leasing company to both a newly formed management group and shareholders. By December 1996, Melville formally renamed itself CVS to give customers, shareholders, and Wall Street analysts a sense of renewed focus and reduced scope of operations.

Westinghouse Electric underwent a series of dramatic restructurings and corporate spin-offs over the past several years that ultimately resulted in the company's transformation into a broadcast network giant and eventual sale to Viacom. After having purchased CBS in September 1995 for $7.5 billion, senior management led by CEO Michael Jordan decided to completely revamp Westinghouse and make the newly acquired CBS broadcasting and television business its core business and primary driver of future growth. In December 1995, Westinghouse sold off its Knoll Group furniture offerings to Warburg Pincus Ventures for $565 million. In March 1996, Westinghouse sold its Electronic Systems Group, a major defense subcontractor, to Northrop Grumman for $3.8 billion. In December 1996, in a move designed to bolster CBS's position in key urban radio broadcasting markets, Westinghouse purchased Infinity Broadcasting for $4.9 billion. In September 1997, two deals were consummated that strengthened CBS's position as a new media company. The Thermo King commercial refrigeration unit was sold to Ingersoll-Rand ($2.5 billion). Simultaneously, Westinghouse bought American Radio Systems for $2.6 billion to strengthen both CBS and Infinity's market share. Finally in December 1997, Westinghouse sold off its original, historically core power generation business to Siemens of Germany. In that same transaction, Westinghouse formally renamed itself CBS Corporation and changed its stock ticker to reflect its corporate makeover and restructuring. In 1999, Viacom purchased CBS in its entirety to strengthen its market position in the consolidating broadcasting other media businesses. Under CEO Sumner Redstone, Viacom hopes to integrate CBS with its Paramount Communications filmmaking unit to create a fully integrated entertainment giant. Viacom also owns MTV, Blockbuster Entertainment, Nickelodeon, Simon and Schuster (book publishing), and Showtime (a premium cable channel).

Most poignantly, AT&T undertook one of the biggest divestitures and spin-offs in corporate history in September 1995. Realizing that the costs of communications, compromise, and coordination among its multiple business units were high (despite the earlier benefits of an integrated, technologically focused strategy), AT&T broke itself up into three separate companies: AT&T (core telecommunications business), Lucent Technologies (networking equipment, electronics, photonics, semiconductors, and Bell Labs), and NCR (mainframe computers). Once a highly competitive enterprise, AT&T had become cumbersome and slow to respond to new challenges from faster, more focused competitors. Now, AT&T, NCR, and Lucent Technologies are free to compete as independent entities. Ironically, NCR may be the best performing unit from the older AT&T. At one point NCR manufactured small computers and electronic cash registers, but it has become an important player in the fast-evolving data warehousing and storage industry. Lucent Technologies, while exhibiting strong growth through the 1990s, fell behind such important competitors as Cisco Systems, Juniper Networks, and Nortel Networks in 2000 and 2001. By overly focusing on building older circuit-switched equipment for traditional telephone carriers, Lucent missed significant market opportunities to use its Bell Laboratories technologies to develop state-of-the-art optical networks and switches for more advanced applications. Once considered a Wall Street high-flyer because of its fast rising stock price, Lucent's shares are now worth less than they were when the firm became independent in April 1996.

AT&T itself is undergoing a series of restructurings designed to help bolster the firm's fast-declining earnings. In 2000 and 2001, under CEO C. Michael Armstrong, AT&T has even proposed breaking itself up into four independent businesses: business services, consumer long distance, cable, and wireless. Already, the wireless unit of AT&T is quasi-independent from AT&T, since it trades as its own tracking stock. Many observers predict that AT&T Wireless will eventually be spun off as its own independent company when market opportunities or buyers surface. While AT&T attempted to gain market share in its core telecommunications business by acquiring a variety of different cable companies (e.g., Tele-Communications, Inc., and MediaOne Group), the company substantially overpaid for the assets and transmission rights that it did receive. More important, local regulators often imposed strict conditions on AT&T's use of its cable assets, including that the company make its assets available to competitors who wanted to sell their own Internet service and "content." In addition, AT&T did not realize the extent to which customers would be reluctant to spend the high dollars necessary to make its cable investments and Internet projects pay off. Even worse, AT&T has now considered the sale of its cable assets (under the name AT&T Broadband) at a price that might not even be half of what the company paid for them in 1998 and 1999. Other cable companies (e.g., Comcast), and local telephone companies (e.g., Bell South) have expressed an interest in buying AT&T Broadband. Even AOL Time Warner is considering a bid to buy out AT&T Broadband. By late 2001, AT&T, however, decided to sell its Broadband unit to Comcast, which will become the nation's largest cable operator. There is a genuine possibility that AT&T may even cease to exist as an independent company sometime in the next few years.[41]

One of the biggest corporate restructurings in late 1999 was Hewlett-Packard's spin-off of Agilent Technologies to divest itself of its traditional electronic instruments businesses. Hewlett-Packard believed that it needed to sharpen its focus on developing next-generation Internet-oriented technologies, such as electronic commerce solutions, digital imaging, and advanced computer solutions. In addition, H-P felt that it needed to concentrate its resources on continuing to build state-of-the-art laser and inkjet printers, as well as committing to its personal computer business. By June 2000, Hewlett-Packard completed its spin-off of Agilent into a fully independent company with forty-three thousand employees. Agilent Technologies is a recognized world leader in such fields as semiconductor test equipment, measurement instruments, fiber optic components, and even tools used in the biotechnology field. The skills required for developing these innovative products are quite different from those used for laser printers and networking applications for the Internet. Agilent's DNA microarray technology offers leading-edge solutions that enable scientists to accelerate the development of new genetically engineered drugs. DNA microarray technology is also an important tool that is used to isolate genes in living organisms in order to determine how disease processes and mutations are initiated. Some of Agilent's other promising R&D activities include new "bubble technology" that improves the speed and productivity of fiber optics–based communication systems. Agilent's bubble technology is seen as an important competitor to Corning Incorporated's photonics products that will power next-generation telecommunications networks.[42]

Other firms in the late 1990s that have spun off businesses to renew their focus include Ralston-Purina (Ralcorp Holdings—private-label cereals, Protein Technologies—biotechnology applications, and AgriBrands International—animal feed businesses), Monsanto (its Solutia commodity chemicals business), Rockwell International (automotive, industrial and semiconductor units), Ford Motor Company (Associates First Capital financial services unit), Sears Roebuck (financial services units Allstate, Coldwell Banker, and Discover), General Mills (its restaurant unit known as the Darden Group), DuPont (Conoco oil unit), American Express (Lehman Brothers financial brokerage unit), ITT (automotive, Rayonier forestry and paper products, hotels, and entertainment units), General Motors (Delphi Automotive Systems), Ford Motor Company (Visteon Corporation), AMR (The Sabre Group), and Dun and Bradstreet (financial publishing and database businesses). In the vast majority of these transactions, these spin-offs enabled both the remaining core business and the newly independent spin-off or sold unit to compete better in the marketplace. The high costs of diversification (ignorance, neglect, compromise, and communication) had seriously outweighed the benefits of competing across multiple businesses and industries.

Strategic Application to Kellogg and Tyco International

To what extent do Kellogg's and Tyco International's corporate strategies support our prescriptions? Although sufficient space to analyze both companies' entire corporate strategy and diversification experiences is not available here, a brief look at a single instance for each will highlight some of the ongoing dilemmas and issues surrounding diversification.

Let us first consider some of the recent moves undertaken by the Kellogg Company. By acquiring Keebler Foods, Kellogg has diversified into new food businesses that share several characteristics with its core breakfast food business. As such, Kellogg is engaging in related diversification. This move took Kellogg into new areas where the company could learn new skills and develop new products to reverse the declining earnings and market share position of its traditional cereal products. On the other hand, acquiring Keebler did not really move Kellogg too far into new or completely unfamiliar terrain, since Kellogg has considerable experience in developing and marketing prepackaged food products. This acquisition opens up opportunities for Kellogg to learn new skills from Keebler. Keebler's renowned skills in reinvigorating growth in mature brands (such as its 1996 experience with Cheez-It) will greatly assist Kellogg as it tries to devise new product mixes and marketing programs to boost the sales of both existing and newly created cereals. In addition, Keebler offers Kellogg considerable expertise in the area of direct-to-store distribution systems, especially for convenience stores and gas stations where Kellogg has virtually no presence. Keebler already handles many of Kellogg's smaller, single-serve portions of such traditional branded products as Nutri-Grain granola bars that are often sold in the same way that candy bars are. Thus, Keebler's direct-to-store distribution system has considerable potential to complement Kellogg's traditional wholesaler and brokerage-based distribution methods. However, meshing two types of distribution systems within the same company will cause Kellogg to deal with the costs of coordination and compromise. Kellogg will need to take special care not to alienate its traditional wholesale channels as it begins to deploy Keebler's direct-to-store systems. One way for Kellogg to do this is to initially limit Keebler's skills toward those nonsupermarket channels that are already accustomed to this type of arrangement. Over time, however, Kellogg will eventually have to work with supermarket chains and its wholesalers in order to slowly introduce the direct-to-store system so that it can sell newer and fresher products without generating considerable inventory. At the same time, Kellogg offers Keebler a much bigger R&D platform in which to experiment and to develop new types of recipes for future packaged goods.

With Worthington Foods, Kellogg enters fairly new terrain—that of vegetarian and soy-based products with which it has little experience. In addition, customers who purchase vegetarian products are likely to be different from those who purchase Kellogg's traditional breakfast products. This means that opportunities to closely share and coordinate marketing programs may be more difficult than initially presumed. More important, Kellogg needs to work closely with Worthington's management to learn how to sell to health-conscious customers, who may have different demographics and marketing requirements. Since Kellogg's acquisition of Worthington Foods is comparatively large, there is inherently more risk and cost associated with making the deal work. On the other hand, Kellogg will be able to transfer important R&D and marketing skills to help Worthington develop new products for its Morningstar Farms brand. These skills are clearly valuable to Worthington and difficult for it to develop on its own quickly. However, if Kellogg's R&D and marketing skills are not completely applicable, then the costs with such diversification may prove too high. For example, Kellogg acquired Lender's Bagels in 1996 for $400 million, only to sell it three years later for $275 million. Lender's Bagels required a different set of marketing skills, especially since customers were beginning to eat freshly baked bagels offered by doughnut and specialty bagel shops. Kellogg's acquisition of the Kashi Company, on the other hand, holds the seeds for potentially much more successful related diversification, since Kashi is a small company and already makes different types of natural-grain cereal products, a better fit with Kellogg's traditional core business.

With Tyco International, the strategic picture is significantly more mixed. In many ways, Tyco International is practicing many of the same strategies that characterize the traditional conglomerates that have relied on unrelated diversification to grow revenues and earnings. Tyco's four lines of businesses are very different from one another and do not offer many opportunities to share resources, technologies, or even customers. As a result, true synergies in the form of revenue sharing among such disparate, unwieldy units is very difficult. Although CEO Dennis Kozlowski has stressed the importance of acquiring companies and businesses that closely fit Tyco's existing business units, many of the firm's most recent acquisitions have been comparatively large, thus posing an additional risk. Thus, even though Tyco International practices unrelated diversification at the corporate level, it is attempting to become somewhat more related within each line of business. Each line of business is attempting to become the low-cost leader in its respective field. For example, Tyco's medical products, electronics, and security systems businesses are major competitors in their own market segments. They have been fairly successful at seizing market share from other competitors, but through price-based competition, as opposed to innovation. They are also helping further consolidate the medical products, electronics, and security monitoring industries at a fast pace, thus reducing the number of firms competing in those fields. Over time, a consolidating industry may give firms more negotiating leverage with their customers. More recently, these units have been searching for acquisition targets that will help them move to more technically sophisticated, higher value-added products. Tyco has also tried to limit the costs of coordination among businesses by giving business unit managers considerable autonomy to run their own operations. Even here, however, the emphasis on cost reduction means that each business unit becomes more focused on its own market, thus limiting opportunities to build any scale at the corporate level.

Yet, despite Tyco's unrelenting search for ways to reduce costs and improve efficiency, the company is still taking on major risks by moving into unfamiliar terrain. The acquisition of CIT Group in March 2001 shows how Tyco is moving into completely different businesses without much benefit of sharing internal resources. Since the CIT Group is engaged in commercial financing and lending activities, there are comparatively few opportunities for Tyco to share physical or technological resources with any of the other four lines of business. Investors have recently become more skeptical about Tyco's strategy and growth prospects. While enormous credit should be given to CEO Kozlowski for growing the company's revenues and earnings so fast (market capitalization rose to $90 billion in 1999 from only $2 billion in 1992), many analysts are wondering just how fast Tyco can continue to grow. Also, the SEC's investigation into Tyco's accounting practices may suggest that the company is relying on one-time or extraordinary restructuring charges as a way to "manage its earnings." Even though the SEC has cleared Tyco of any wrongdoing, investors may be starting to think of Tyco International as a conglomerate firm, and beginning to value it accordingly.

The recent swirl of accounting controversies, combined with the operational difficulties that Tyco International has confronted in achieving true corporate-wide synergies, has resulted in the company doing a major about-face in its overall corporate strategy. CEO Dennis Kozlowski announced in early 2002 that Tyco would break itself into four separate companies through a complex divestiture process that involves both spin-offs and asset sales to other companies. For example, CIT Group, the financial services business that Tyco most recently acquired in 2001, was among the first to go. Many other financial services companies are eagerly looking at CIT Group, since this unit can provide more synergies to them than it could to such a diverse company as Tyco. Because cost savings can go only so far to build a business, Tyco faced the looming challenge of sustaining its high earnings growth rate from its feverish pace of acquisitions. Shareholders, in turn, became more skeptical about the company's highly touted growth prospects, simply because they knew that a highly complex pattern of unrelated diversification could produce no lasting synergies at the corporate level. Each line of business (electronics, fire protection, health care, financial services, security systems) faces a different group of customers who require a different set of products. Therefore, attempting to share resources such as R&D, manufacturing, distribution, marketing, and sales and service would be a difficult, if not impossible, task—simply because the underlying nature of the businesses is so different. Shareholders thus began to attribute a growing conglomerate discount to Tyco as the company became ever more unwieldy and unrelated, despite the management's efforts to achieve substantial cost savings. As a result, Tyco has attempted to transform itself in recent years into a much smaller but more focused company.

Summary

- Corporate strategy deals with the issue of enlarging the firm's scope of operations to new areas of activity or businesses.
- The most important issue behind corporate strategy is this question: Does a firm improve its competitive advantage by entering new areas of activity?
- Successful diversification requires firms to utilize distinctive competences and resources in new ways. Resources (e.g., skills, assets, technologies, capabilities) should be hard to imitate, specialized, and durable to produce value and profits over a long period of time.
- A firm can enlarge the scope of its operations by entering new segments, new stages, new product areas, and new industries. Scope enlargement can be accomplished by vertical integration, related diversification, and unrelated diversification.
- Vertical integration may occur through partial or full integration. Backward integration moves the firm closer to its sources of supply. Forward integration moves the firm closer to its customers.
- Related diversification extends the firm's distinctive competence into new industries that are similar to the firm's original business.
- Unrelated diversification is not based on the firm's underlying distinctive competence.
- Diversification enables a firm to secure more attractive terrain, to access resources not otherwise available, and to share activities on a potentially economical basis.
- Diversification imposes costs. These costs arise because diversifiers are often ignorant about newly entered fields, neglect their base businesses, and must expend cooperative effort to transfer resources and share activities among businesses.
- Diversification will be fruitful only when the benefits generated by diversification outweigh the related costs.

- Transferring a resource between two businesses will produce a significant benefit if the resource is competitively important to the receiving business and is difficult for the receiving business to develop on its own.
- Sharing an activity between two or more businesses will produce a significant benefit when the activity involves a large dollar expenditure and is highly susceptible to economies of scale and experience.
- A diversifier can sometimes contain diversification costs by confining diversification to familiar fields and by diversifying internally rather than by acquisition.
- When analysis reveals that diversification will most likely produce greater costs than benefits, a firm operating in a troubled industry should undertake corporate restructurings.
- Possibilities include increasing market share and selective focus, as well as divesting and spinning off noncore operations or businesses.
- Spinning off noncore or less related businesses help produce renewed focus on remaining core operations. It also helps shareholders capture the full value of assets being used by management.

Exercises and Discussion Questions

@ 1. Using the Internet, look up the Web site for General Electric. How many different businesses does General Electric have? What appears to be the underlying basis for General Electric's strength in many of its business units? What type of diversification strategy would you say General Electric is pursuing?

@ 2. Now look up the Web site for Harris Corporation. Look up the company's annual report for 1999 and 2000. How many different businesses does Harris have? How does Harris's management of these businesses differ from that of General Electric? How does CEO Parmer hope to build shareholder value and new sources of distinctive competences at Harris? What type of diversification strategy would you say Harris is pursuing? Are there any particular types of trade-offs that Harris needs to consider?

@ 3. Look up the Web site for Viacom Corporation and find its most recent annual report. What is CEO Sumner Redstone attempting to accomplish with Viacom's position in the entertainment and multimedia industries?

4. Throughout this chapter, we noted that unrelated diversification, or conglomerates, appear to be declining in popularity throughout the United States. On the other hand, this particular type of diversification strategy appears to be extremely widespread in Mexico, Brazil, South Korea, Japan, and even some countries throughout Europe. In Mexico, companies are organized along a "Grupo" structure. Why do you think unrelated diversification and the proliferation of conglomerate-type companies are so prevalent in Mexico, Brazil, and other nations? What does the presence of so many conglomerates seem to say about the nation's underlying financial institutions and the role of shareholders in the management of these companies? What is the real contribution of senior management in conglomerate-type firms in Mexico and elsewhere?

@ 5. AT&T is currently undergoing another wave of strategic restructuring. Using the Internet, check out the status of AT&T now. Why is the company seeking to break itself up into four parts? How is the telephone industry different from the cable industry? Why do you think AT&T wants to sell off its wireless business unit? Does it make sense? What are some factors that you need to consider in assessing the company's potential?

6. When managers within a firm share activities to achieve related diversification, they must also compromise on some issues in order to make the sharing successful. What issues, in particular, appear to be the basis for making sharing successful in a related diversified firm? How can these same issues cause a potentially successful strategy to slip?

Endnotes

1. Data for the Kellogg Company case were adapted from the following sources: "Snap, Crackle, Plop: Cereal Is a Sore Subject in Battle Creek, Michigan," *Wall Street Journal*, August 27, 2001; "How to Make a Frozen Lasagna (with Just $250 Million)," *Fortune*, April 30, 2001; "Kellogg, General Mills Battle over Bars," *Wall Street Journal*, March 27, 2001; "Thinking Out of the Cereal Box," *Business Week*, January 15, 2001; "Keebler Acquisition Trims Near-Term Profit Forecast," *Wall Street Journal*, November 29, 2000; "Kellogg to Buy Keebler Foods for $3.86 Billion," *Wall Street Journal*, October 27, 2000; "Keebler Auction Is Said to Draw Interest from Kellogg, Danone," *Wall Street Journal*, October 17, 2000; "Kellogg Spurts into Lead," *Business Week*, October 9, 2000; "Kellogg Agrees to Buy Kashi Co.," *Wall Street Journal*, June 30, 2000; "Kellogg Promotion Creates Corn Flakes Craze," *Wall Street Journal*, May 17, 2000; "Kellogg, Salton Form Alliance," *Wall Street Journal*, April 25, 2000; "Why the Cereal Business Is So Soggy," *Fortune*, March 6, 2000; "Kellogg's Net Surges Despite Slight Decline in Its Sales of Cereal," *Wall Street Journal*, January 28, 2000; "Granola Hits the Big Time," *Business Week*, January 10, 2000; "General Mills Passes Kellogg Co. as Leader Based on Cereal Volume," *Wall Street Journal*, December 30, 1999; "Kellogg to Buy Mondo Baking," *Wall Street Journal*, December 21, 1999; "Kellogg Completes Acquisition," *Wall Street Journal*, November 24, 1999; "Kellogg Company: Ensemble Line of Foods Axed Because of Poor Results," *Wall Street Journal*, November 22, 1999; "Kellogg Posts Third-Quarter Net Loss, but Results from Operations Improved," *Wall Street Journal*, October 29, 1999; "Food Firms to Tout Health Benefits of Soybeans," *Wall Street Journal*, October 26, 1999; "Kellogg Plans to Go Vegetarian in Deal for Worthington," *Wall Street Journal*, October 4, 1999; "Breakfast King Agrees to Sell Bagel Business," *Wall Street Journal*, September 28, 1999; "Food Makers, amid Bland Performance, Are Facing Heat to Cook Up Mergers," *Wall Street Journal*, September 13, 1999; "Kellogg Profit Jumps 7.7% as Growth in Convenience Foods Offsets Cereal Woes," *Wall Street Journal*, July 30, 1999; "Kellogg Cranks Up Its Idea Machine to Grow," *Fortune*, July 5, 1999; "Kellogg May Close Part of Cereal Plant, Cut Jobs in Michigan," *Wall Street Journal*, June 18, 1999; "Outside the Box: Kellogg's New Boss, Carlos Gutierrez," *Forbes*, June 14, 1999.

2. Data for Tyco International were adapted from the following sources: "Tyco Seems to Back Off from Breakup," *Wall Street Journal*, February 14, 2002, pp. A3, A8; "Tyco Pledges to Hasten Breakup Efforts," *Wall Street Journal*, February 7, 2002, pp. A3, A12; "Tyco Breakup Gets Razzed by Investors," *Wall Street Journal*, January 24, 2002, pp. C1, C9; "Tyco Aims to Boost Shareholder Value with Breakup," *Wall Street Journal*, January 23, 2002, p. A4; "Amid Enron's Fallout, and a Sinking Stock, Tyco Plans a Breakup," *Wall Street Journal*, January 23, 2002, pp. A1, A4; "Tyco Acquisitions in Fiscal Year 2001 Lead to Job Cuts," *Wall Street Journal*, August 14, 2001; "Tyco to Buy Sensormatic Security Firm in Deal Valued at $2.2 Billion," *Wall Street Journal*, August 6, 2001; "Tyco Posts 22% Rise in Earnings, Expects Strong Full-Year Results," *Wall Street Journal*, July 19, 2001; "Tyco Closes $1 Billion Purchase," *Wall Street Journal*, July 6, 2001; "Tyco Just Got Bigger—Again," *Business Week*, June 11, 2001; "Tyco Affirms Accord to Acquire C. R. Bard in a $3.1 Billion Deal," *Wall Street Journal*, May 31, 2001; "The Most Aggressive CEO," *Business Week*, May 28, 2001; "The Real Trouble with Tyco: Rose-Colored Glasses," *Fortune*, May 28, 2001; "Tyco to Buy Cambridge Security-Systems Business," *Wall Street Journal*, May 18, 2001; "Tyco Breaks Out of Its Mold," *Business Week*, March 26, 2001; "Tyco Shares Drop 8% as Investors React Skeptically to the CIT Deal," *Wall Street Journal*, March 14, 2001; "Tyco to Buy Scott Technologies," *Wall Street Journal*, February 6, 2001; "Tyco's Net Income Rises 29% as Sales Show 21% Increase," *Wall Street Journal*, January 18, 2001; "Dennis Kozlowski: Tyco International," *Business Week*, January 8, 2001; "Tyco, Furukawa Electric Ink Licensing Deal for Optical Interconnects," *Fiber Optic News*, December 11, 2000; "Tyco to Buy Simplex Time Recorder," *Wall Street Journal*, December 5, 2000; "Tyco to Buy Lucent Unit for $2.5 Billion," *Wall Street Jour-*

nal, November 14, 2000; "The Conglomerator Wants a Little Respect," *Forbes*, October 16, 2000; "Kozlowski's Cosmos: The Tyco Universe Is Constantly Expanding," *Forbes*, October 16, 2000; "Tyco's Profit Soars on Strong Revenue at Electronics Unit," *Wall Street Journal*, July 20, 2000; "SEC Enforcement Arm Ends Its Inquiry into Accounting at Tyco International," *Wall Street Journal*, July 14, 2000; "Tyco Agrees to Buy Mallinckrodt Inc. for $4.2 Billion," *Wall Street Journal*, June 29, 2000; "Tyco International Agrees to Buy Unit of Thomas & Betts," *Wall Street Journal*, May 8, 2000; "Tyco: The Road Back," *Business Week*, April 10, 2000; "Lion's Share: For Plastic Hangars, You Almost Need to Go to Tyco," *Wall Street Journal*, February 15, 2000; "Tyco to Build Vast Undersea Cable Network," *Wall Street Journal*, January 18, 2000; "Lucent to Sell Gear to Tyco," *Wall Street Journal*, January 18, 2000; "Tyco Annual Report Holds No Surprises about Accounting," *Wall Street Journal*, December 14, 1999; "Probe of Tyco's Accounting Hits Its Stock," *Wall Street Journal*, December 10, 1999; "Tyco Buys Siemens Unit," *Wall Street Journal*, November 24, 1999; "Tyco Revamps Its Option Program for Top Executives," *Wall Street Journal*, November 15, 1999; "Tyco's Accounting Faces Renewed Criticism," *Wall Street Journal*, November 1, 1999; "Is Tyco after Bard?" *Business Week*, October 25, 1999; "Tyco International to Buy AFC Cable in $578 Million Deal," *Wall Street Journal*, September 1, 1999; "Tyco Plans to Lay Off 24% of Work Force at Its Raychem Unit," *Wall Street Journal*, August 25, 1999; "Tyco International Lays Off 9,350; Plans 7,000 Additional Cuts," *Wall Street Journal*, August 11, 1999; "Tyco Reaches Agreement to Buy AMP in Stock Swap Valued at $11.3 Billion," *Wall Street Journal*, November 23, 1998; "Tyco Completes Deal to Buy U.S. Surgical, Names Unit President," *Wall Street Journal*, October 2, 1998.

3. See, for example, M. E. Porter, "From Competitive Advantage to Corporate Strategy," *Harvard Business Review* 66 (May–June 1987): 43–59. Another study by D. J. Ravenscraft and F. M. Scherer, *Mergers, Selloffs and Economic Efficiency* (Washington, D.C.: Brookings Institution, 1987), found comparable results.

4. An excellent discussion of the underpinnings of the resource-based view of the firm may be found in B. Wernerfelt, "A Resource-Based View of the Firm," *Strategic Management Journal* (September–October 1984): 171–180; J. B. Barney, "Firm Resources and the Theory of Competitive Advantage," *Journal of Management* 17 (1991): 99–120; K. R. Conner, "A Historical Comparison of Resource-Based Theory and Five Schools of Thought within Industrial Organization Economics: Do We Have a New Theory of the Firm?" *Journal of Management* 17, no. 1 (1991): 121–154; R. M. Grant, "The Resource-Based Theory of Competitive Advantage," *California Management Review* 33, no. 3 (1991): 114–135; I. Dierickx and K. Cool, "Asset Stock Accumulation and Sustainability of Competitive Advantage," *Management Science* (December 1989): 1504–1511; R. Hall, "The Strategic Analysis of Intangible Resources," *Strategic Management Journal* 13 (1992): 135–144; R. Amit and P. Schoemaker, "Strategic Assets and Organizational Rent," *Strategic Management Journal* (January 1993): 33; M. A. Peteraf, "The Cornerstones of Competitive Advantage: A Resource-Based View," *Strategic Management Journal* (March 1993): 179; J. A. Black and K. B. Boal, "Strategic Resources: Traits, Configurations and Paths to Sustainable Competitive Advantage," *Strategic Management Journal* 15 (1994): 131–148; D. J. Collis and C. A. Montgomery, "Competing on Resources: Strategy in the 1990s," *Harvard Business Review* (July–August 1995): 118–125; J. A. Robins and M. Wiersema, "A Resource-Based Approach to the Multibusiness Firm," *Strategic Management Journal* 16 (1995): 277–299.

   The development of additional theories surrounding the concept of resources has progressed markedly over the past several years. Examples of academic pieces that have furthered knowledge in this area include the following sample works: R. Makadok, "Toward a Synthesis of the Resource-Based and Dynamic Capability Views of Rent Creation," *Strategic Management Journal* 22, no. 5 (2001): 387–402; S. D. Hunt, *A General Theory of Competition: Resources, Competences, Productivity, Economic Growth* (Thousand Oaks, Calif.: Sage, 2000); J. G. Combs and D. J. Ketchen,

"Explaining Interfirm Cooperation and Performance: Toward a Reconciliation of Predictions from the Resource-Based View and Organizational Economics," *Strategic Management Journal* 20 (1999): 768–888; T. C. Powell, "Information Technology as Competitive Advantage: The Role of Human, Business and Technology Resources," *Strategic Management Journal* 18, no. 5 (1997): 375–405; C. Oliver, "Sustainable Competitive Advantage: Combining Institutional and Resource-Based Views," *Strategic Management Journal* 18 (1997): 607–713; C. Helfat, "Know-how and Asset Complementarity and Dynamic Capability Accumulation: The Case of R&D," *Strategic Management Journal* 18 (1997): 339–360; K. R. Conner and C. K. Prahalad, "A Resource-Based Theory of the Firm: Knowledge versus Opportunism," *Organization Science* 7 (1996): 477–501; J. A. Black and K. B. Boal, "Strategic Resources: Traits, Configurations and Paths to Sustainable Competitive Advantage," *Strategic Management Journal* 15 (1994): 131–148.

An interesting debate about the validity of the resource-based view of the firm can be found in the following: R. L. Priem and J. E. Butler, "Is the Resource-Based View a Useful Perspective for Strategic Management Research?" *Academy of Management Review* 26, no. 1 (2001): 22–40; J. Barney, "Is the Resource-Based View a Useful Perspective for Strategic Management Research? Yes," *Academy of Management Review* 26, no. 1 (2001): 41–56; R. L. Priem and J. E. Butler, "Tautology in the Resource-Based View and the Implications of Externally Determined Resource Value: Further Comments," *Academy of Management Review* 26, no. 1 (2001): 57–66.

Some empirical research pieces that have utilized or tested the resource-based view include the following representative sample works: Y. E. Spanos and S. Lioukas, "An Examination into the Causal Logic of Rent Generation: Contrasting Porter's Competitive Strategy Framework and the Resource-Based Perspective," *Strategic Management Journal* 22, no. 10 (2001): 907–934; M. A. Hitt, L. Bierman, K. Shimizu, and R. Kochhar, "Direct and Moderating Effects of Human Capital on Strategy and Performance in Professional Service Firms: A Resource-Based Perspective," *Academy of Management Journal* 44, no. 1 (2001): 13–28; P. L. Yeoh and K. Roth, "An Empirical Analysis of Sustained Advantage in the U.S. Pharmaceutical Industry: Impact of Firm Resources and Competition," *Strategic Management Journal* 20, no. 7 (1999): 637–753; E. Mosakowski, "Managerial Prescriptions under the Resource-Based View of Strategy: The Example of Motivational Techniques," *Strategic Management Journal* 19 (1998): 1169–1182; M.V. Russo and P. A. Fouts, "A Resource-Based Perspective on Corporate Environmental Performance and Responsibility," *Academy of Management Journal* 40 (1997): 534–559; A. Madhok and S. Tallman, "Resources, Transactions and Rents: Managing Value through Interfirm Collaborative Relationships," *Organization Science* 9, no. 3 (1998): 326–339; M.V. Russo and P. A. Fouts, "A Resource-Based Perspective on Corporate Environmental Performance and Profitability," *Academy of Management Journal* 40, no. 3 (1997): 534–559; K. M. Eisenhardt and C. B. Schoonhoven, "Resource-Based View of Strategic Alliance Formation: Strategic and Social Effects in Entrepreneurial Firms," *Organization Science* 7, no. 2 (1996): 136–150; D. Miller and J. Shamise, "The Resource-Based View of the Firm in Two Environments: The Hollywood Film Studios from 1936 to 1965," *Academy of Management Journal* 39, no. 3 (1996): 519–543; S. Maijoor and A. Van Witteloostujin, "An Empirical Test of the Resource-Based Theory: Strategic Regulation in the Dutch Audit Industry," *Strategic Management Journal* 17, no. 7 (1996): 549–569; J. Robbins and M. F. Wiersema, "A Resource-Based Approach to the Multibusiness Firm: Empirical Analysis of Portfolio Interrelationships and Corporate Financial Responsibility," *Strategic Management Journal* 16 (1995): 277–299.

5. One of the first to systematically examine this phenomenon was Alfred D. Chandler's *Strategy and Structure* (Cambridge, Mass.: MIT Press, 1962). His later work also examines the benefits of garnering additional economies of scale, scope, and efficiencies in A. D. Chandler, *Scale and Scope: The Dynamics of Industrial Capitalism* (Cambridge, Mass.: Harvard University Press, 1990). Also see R. Rumelt, *Strategy, Structure and Economic Performance* (Cambridge, Mass.: Harvard University Press, 1974).

6. The concept of distinctive and core competences has begun to redefine the way researchers and practitioners look at their corporate diversification strategies. Further excellent reading on this subject may be found in C. K. Prahalad and G. Hamel, "The Core Competence of the Corporation," *Harvard Business Review* (May–June 1990): 79–93; G. Hamel and C. K. Prahalad, "Corporate Imagination and Expeditionary Marketing," *Harvard Business Review* (July–August 1991): 81–92; A. A. Lado, N. G. Boyd, and P. Wright, "A Competency Model of Sustained Competitive Advantage," *Journal of Management* 18 (1992): 77–91; and G. Hamel and C. K. Prahalad, "Strategy as Stretch and Leverage," *Harvard Business Review* (March–April 1993): 75–85. Prahalad and Hamel's numerous articles on the topic can be found in their summarized book version entitled *Competing for the Future* (Boston: Harvard Business School Press, 1994).

   The notion of core competence, distinctive competence, and core skills can also be found in a landmark work by K. Andrews, *The Concept of Corporate Strategy* (Homewood, Ill.: Dow Jones-Irwin, 1971). Core competences can also be dynamic; see, for example, D. Lei, M. A. Hitt, and R. A. Bettis, "Dynamic Core Competences through Meta-learning and Strategic Context," *Journal of Management* 22, no. 4 (1996): 549–569. Also see D. J. Teece, G. Pisano, and A. Shuen, "Firm Capabilities, Resources and the Concept of Strategy," working paper, University of California at Berkeley, no. 90-9, 1990; G. Stalk, P. Evans, and L. E. Shulman, "Competing on Capabilities: The New Rules of Corporate Strategy," *Harvard Business Review* (March–April 1992): 57–69; and M. A. Peteraf, "The Cornerstones of Competitive Advantage: A Resource-Based View," *Strategic Management Journal* 14 (1993): 179–191. An excellent treatment of core skills and competences may be found in H. Itami, *Mobilizing Invisible Assets* (Cambridge, Mass.: Harvard University Press, 1987). An excellent piece that discusses and empirically tests the notion of distinctive competence is R. Makadok and G. Walker, "Identifying a Distinctive Competence: Forecasting Ability in the Money Fund Industry," *Strategic Management Journal* 21, no. 8 (2000): 853–864.

   Also see the following theoretical and empirical research pieces examining different aspects of core competences and firm capabilities: A. Wilcox King and C. P. Zeithaml, "Competencies and Firm Performance: Examining the Causal Ambiguity Paradox," *Strategic Management Journal* 22, no. 1 (2001): 75–98; C. E. Helfat and R. S. Raubitschek, "Product Sequencing: Co-evolution of Knowledge, Capabilities, and Products," *Strategic Management Journal* 21, issues 10–11: 961-979; D. C. Galunic and S. Rodan, "Resource Recombinations in the Firm: Knowledge Structures and the Potential for Schumpeterian Innovation," *Strategic Management Journal* 19, no. 12 (1998): 1193–1201; W. J. Duncan, P. M. Ginter, and L. E. Swayne, "Competitive Advantage and Internal Organizational Assessment," *Academy of Management Executive* 12 (1998): 6–17; D. J. Teece, G. Pisano, and A. Shuen, "Dynamic Capabilities and Strategic Management," *Strategic Management Journal* 18, no. 7 (1997): 509–533; D. Lei, M. A. Hitt, and R. Bettis, "Dynamic Core Competences through Meta-Learning and Strategic Context," *Journal of Management* 22, no. 4 (1996): 549–569; R. M. Grant, "Prospering in Dynamically Competitive Environments: Organizational Capability as Knowledge Integration," *Organization Science* 7 (1996): 375–387; J. P. Liebeskind, "Knowledge, Strategy, and the Theory of the Firm," *Strategic Management Journal* 17, Special Issue (1996): 93–107; R. Henderson and I. Cockburn, "Measuring Competence: Exploring Firm-Effects in Pharmaceutical Research," *Strategic Management Journal* 15 (1994): 63–84; G. Pisano, "Knowledge, Integration, and the Locus of Learning: An Empirical Analysis of Process Development," *Strategic Management Journal* 15, Special Issue (1994): 85–100; R. Reed and R. J. DeFillippi, "Causal Ambiguity, Barriers to Imitation, and Sustainable Competitive Advantage," *Academy of Management Review* 15 (1990): 88–102; M. A. Hitt and R. D. Ireland, "Relationships among Corporate Level Distinctive Competencies, Diversification Strategy, Corporate Structure and Performance," *Journal of Management Studies* 23 (1986): 401–416; M. A. Hitt and R. D. Ireland, "Corporate Distinctive Competence, Strategy, Industry and Performance," *Strategic Management Journal* 6 (1985): 273–293.

7. An excellent treatment of this subject appears in K. R. Harrigan, "Formulating Vertical Integration Strategies," *Academy of Management Review* 9, no. 4 (1984): 638–652. The strengths and weaknesses of different vertical integration approaches may also be found in K. R. Harrigan, "Matching Vertical Integration Strategies to Competitive Conditions," *Strategic Management Journal* 7 (1986): 535–555; O. E. Williamson, *The Economic Institutions of Capitalism* (New York: Free Press, 1985); S. Balakrishnan and B. Wernerfelt, "Technical Change, Competition and Vertical Integration," *Strategic Management Journal* 7 (1986): 347–359; R. E. Caves and R. M. Bradbury, "The Empirical Determinants of Vertical Integration," *Journal of Economic Behavior and Organization* 9 (1988): 265–279; M. B. Lieberman, "Determinants of Vertical Integration: An Empirical Test," *Journal of Industrial Economics* 39 (1991): 451–466. Also see R. G. Buzzell, "Is Vertical Integration Profitable?" *Harvard Business Review* (January–February 1983): 92–102; M. E. McGrath and R. W. Hoole, "Manufacturing's New Economies of Scale," *Harvard Business Review* (May–June 1992): 94–103, to see how technological changes can make different forms of manufacturing-based integration possible; as well as R. Normann and R. Ramirez, "From Value Chain to Value Constellation: Designing Interactive Strategy," *Harvard Business Review* (July–August 1993): 65–77.

The relationship between vertical integration and external dependence is discussed by J. M. Pennings, D. C. Hambrick, and I. C. MacMillan in "Interorganizational Dependence and Forward Integration," *Organization Studies* 5 (1984): 307–326. An outstanding overview of the relationship between vertical integration and internal firm costs is R. D'Aveni and D. J. Ravenscraft, "Economies of Integration versus Bureaucracy Costs: Does Vertical Integration Improve Performance?" *Academy of Management Journal* 37, no. 5 (1994): 1167–1206; G. Walker and D. Weber, "Supplier Competition, Uncertainty, and Make-or Buy Decisions," *Academy of Management Journal* 30 (1987): 589–596; G. Walker, "Strategic Sourcing, Vertical Integration, and Transaction Costs," *Interfaces* 18, no. 3 (1988): 62–73; R. J. Maddigan and J. K. Zaima, "The Profitability of Vertical Integration," *Managerial and Decision Economics* 6 (1985): 178–179; A. R. Burgess, "Vertical Integration in Pharmaceuticals: The Concept and Its Measurement," *Long Range Planning* 16, no. 4 (1983): 55–60.

Also see S. White, "Competition, Capabilities, and the Make, Buy, or Ally Decisions of Chinese State-Owned Firms," *Academy of Management Journal* 43, no. 3 (2000): 324–341; L. Poppo and T. Zenger, "Testing Alternative Theories of the Firm: Transaction Cost, Knowledge-Based, and Measurement Explanations for Make-or-Buy Decisions in Information Services," *Strategic Management Journal* 19 (1998): 853–877; T. Robertson and H. Gatignon, "Technology Development Mode: A Transaction Cost Explanation," *Strategic Management Journal* 18 (1997): 515–531.

8. During the 1980s and 1990s, a plethora of research literature has covered the diversification issue. Excellent reviews can be found in R. A. Johnson, "Antecedents and Outcomes of Corporate Refocusing," *Journal of Management* 22 (1996): 437–481; R. E. Hoskisson and M. A. Hitt, "Antecedents and Performance Outcomes of Diversification: A Review and Critique of Theoretical Perspectives," *Journal of Management* 16, no. 2 (1990): 461–509; R. E. Hoskisson, M. A. Hitt, and C. W. L. Hill, "Managerial Risk Taking in Diversified Firms: An Evolutionary Perspective," *Organization Science* 2 (1991): 296–314; V. Ramanujam and P. Varadarajan, "Research on Corporate Diversification: A Synthesis," *Strategic Management Journal* 10 (1989): 523–552.

The strategic management research literature is replete with studies examining the impact of diversification on corporate performance and innovation. Some representative works include the following: M. Lubatkin, W. S. Schulze, A. Mainkar, and R. W. Cotterill, "Ecological Investigation of Firm-Effects in Horizontal Mergers," *Strategic Management Journal* 22, no. 4 (2001): 335–358; G. Ahuja and R. Katila, "Technological Acquisitions and the Innovation Performance of Acquiring Firms: A Longitudinal Study," *Strategic Management Journal* 22, no. 3 (2001): 197–220; J. M. Geringer, S. Tallman, and D. M. Olsen, "Product and International Diversification among Japanese Firms," *Strategic Management Journal* 21, no. 1 (2000): 51–80; L.

Capron, "The Long-Term Performance of Horizontal Acquisitions," *Strategic Management Journal* 20, no. 11 (1999): 987–1018; Y. Amihud and B. Lev, "Does Corporate Ownership Structure Affect Its Strategy towards Diversification?" *Strategic Management Journal* 20, no. 11 (1999): 1063–1070; D. J. Denis, D. K. Denis, and A. Sarin, "Agency Theory and the Influence of Equity Ownership Structure on Corporate Diversification Strategies," *Strategic Management Journal* 20, no. 11 (1999): 1071–1076; M. A. Hitt, R. E. Hoskisson, and H. Kim, "International Diversification: Effects on Innovation and Firm Performance in Product-Diversified Firms," *Academy of Management Journal* 40, no. 4 (1997): 767–798; M. A. Hitt, R. E. Hoskisson, R. A. Johnson, and D. D. Moesel, "The Market for Corporate Control and Firm Innovation," *Academy of Management Journal* 39, no. 5 (1996): 1084–1119; R. E. Hoskisson, M. A. Hitt, and C. W. L. Hill, "Managerial Incentives and Investment in R&D in Large Multiproduct Firms," *Organization Science* 4 (1993): 325–341; M. A. Hitt, R. E. Hoskisson, R. D. Ireland, and J. S. Harrison, "The Effects of Acquisitions on R&D Inputs and Outputs," *Academy of Management Journal* 34 (1991): 693–706; P. G. Simmonds, "The Combined Diversification Breadth and Mode Dimensions and the Performance of Large Diversified Firms," *Strategic Management Journal* 11 (1990): 399–410.

9. One of the earliest to use these terms was R. Rumelt, *Strategy, Structure and Economic Performance* (Cambridge, Mass.: Harvard University Press, 1974). A vast literature has ensued over the past twenty years examining the impact of different related and unrelated diversification strategies on performance. Some of the representative works include R. A. Bettis, "Performance Differences in Related and Unrelated Diversified Firms," *Strategic Management Journal* 2 (1981): 406–415; B. Baysinger and R. E. Hoskisson, "Diversification Strategy and R&D Intensity in Large Multiproduct Firms," *Academy of Management Journal* 32 (1989): 310–332; A. Lemelin, "Relatedness in the Patterns of Interindustry Diversification," *Review of Economics and Statistics* 64 (1982): 646–657; K. Palepu, "Diversification Strategy, Profit Performance and the Entropy Measure," *Strategic Management Journal* 6 (1985): 239–255; C. K. Prahalad and R. A. Bettis, "The Dominant Logic: A New Linkage between Diversity and Performance," *Strategic Management Journal* 7 (1986): 485-501; C. A. Montgomery, "Product-Market Diversification and Market Power," *Academy of Management Journal* 28 (1985): 789–798; M. Lubatkin and R. C. Rodgers, "Diversification, Systematic Risk and Shareholder Return: A Capital Market Extension of Rumelt's 1974 Study," *Academy of Management Journal* 33 (1989): 454–465; H. Singh and C.A. Montgomery, "Corporate Acquisition Strategies and Economic Performance," *Strategic Management Journal* 8 (1987): 377–386; D. J. Teece, R. Rumelt, G. Dosi, and S. Winter, "Understanding Corporate Coherence: Theory and Evidence," working paper, University of California at Berkeley, July 1992; P. R. Nayyar, "On the Measurement of Corporate Diversification Strategy: Evidence from Large U.S. Service Firms," *Strategic Management Journal* 13, no. 3 (1992): 219–235; R. E. Hoskisson and R. A. Johnson, "Corporate Restructuring and Strategic Change: The Effect on Diversification Strategy and R&D Intensity," *Strategic Management Journal* 13 (1992): 625–634; C. W. L. Hill, M. A. Hitt, and R. E. Hoskisson, "Cooperative versus Competitive Structures in Related and Unrelated Diversified Firms," *Organization Science* 3 (1992): 501–521; R. E. Hoskisson, M. A. Hitt, R. A. Johnson, and D. Moesel, "Construct Validity of an Objective (Entropy) Categorical Measure of Diversification Strategy," *Strategic Management Journal* 14 (1993): 215–235; C. A. Montgomery, "Corporate Diversification," *Journal of Economic Perspectives* 8 (1994): 623–632; R. E. Hoskisson, R. A. Johnson, and D. D. Moesel, "Corporate Divestiture Intensity in Restructuring Firms: Effects of Governance, Strategy, and Performance," *Academy of Management Journal* 37 (1994): 1207–1251; P. J. Lane, A. A. Cannella, Jr., M. H. Lubatkin, "Agency Problems as Antecedents to Unrelated Mergers and Diversification: Amihud and Lev Reconsidered," *Strategic Management Journal* 19, no. 7 (1998): 555–578; M. Farjoun, "The Independent and Joint Effects of the Skill and Physical Bases of Relatedness in Diversification," *Strategic Management Journal* 19, no. 7 (1998): 611–630; R. Kochhar and M. A. Hitt, "Linking Corporate Strategy to Cap-

ital Structure: Diversification Strategy, Type, and Source of Financing," *Strategic Management Journal* 19, no. 6 (1988): 601–610; D. D. Bergh and M. W. Lawless, "Portfolio Restructuring and Limits to Hierarchical Governance: The Effects of Environmental Uncertainty and Diversification Strategy," *Organization Science* 9, no. 1 (1998): 87–102; J. E. Bethel and J. P. Liebeskind, "Diversification and the Legal Organization of the Firm," *Organization Science* 9, no. 1 (1998): 49–67.

10. See, for example, "Intel Unleashes Its Internal Attila," *Fortune*, October 15 (2001): 168–184; "Intel: Can Craig Barrett Reverse the Slide?" *Business Week*, October 15 (2001): 80–90.

11. A solid discussion of transaction costs in corporate strategy may be found in G. R. Jones and C. W. L. Hill, "Transaction Cost Analysis of Strategy-Structure Choice," *Strategic Management Journal* 9 (1988): 159–172.

12. See "Merck Officials Say Medco Deal Aiding Growth," *Wall Street Journal*, November 30, 1994, p. B8; "Changing Minds: Owning Medco, Merck Takes Drug Marketing the Next Logical Step," *Wall Street Journal*, May 31, 1994, pp. A1, A5.

13. See "Merck to Shed Medco, Its Drug-Benefits Unit, in Bid to Boost Stock," *Wall Street Journal*, January 22, 2002, pp. A1, A8; "Lilly Rides a Mood Elevator," *Business Week*, November 11, 1996, p. 63.

14. See "Merger to Leave Much Room for Chevron Texaco to Grow," *Wall Street Journal*, October 9, 2001, p. B14.

15. See, for example, "SBC Making Some Connections," *Investor's Business Daily*, April 26, 2001, p. A5.

16. Despite their steadily declining numbers, interest in conglomerates has taken a new twist. See, for example, "A New Mix: Conglomerates Make a Surprising Comeback—with a '90s Twist," *Wall Street Journal*, March 1, 1994, pp. A1, A6; J. R. Williams, B. L. Paez, and L. Sanders, "Conglomerates Revisited," *Strategic Management Journal* 9, no. 5 (1988): 403–414.

    An interesting academic study that has examined the decline of conglomerate-type firms is D. D. Bergh, "Predicting Divestiture of Unrelated Acquisitions: An Integrative Model of Ex Ante Conditions," *Strategic Management Journal* 18, no. 9 (1997): 715–731; G. F. Davis, K. A. Diekmann, and C. H. Tinsley, "The Decline and Fall of the Conglomerate Form in the 1980s: The Deinstitutionalization of an Organization Form," *American Sociological Review* 59 (1991): 547–570. One of the first pieces to examine the nature of conglomerate firms is Y. Amihud and B. Lev, "Risk Reduction as a Managerial Motive for Conglomerate Mergers," *Bell Journal of Economics* 12 (1981): 605–617. Also see J. R. Williams, B. Paez, and L. Sanders, "Conglomerates Revisited," *Strategic Management Journal* 9 (1988): 404–414.

17. See "Newport News Says It Will Reconsider Bid from Northrop," *Wall Street Journal*, October 8, 2001, p. A4.

18. Data adapted from "Adding Up All of Tenneco's Many Parts," *Wall Street Journal*, August 9, 1991, p. A4; "Tenneco Restructuring Is Over, but Doubts Remain," *Wall Street Journal*, September 8, 1992, p. B4; "Tenneco Plans to Sell 35% of Case Unit to Public, on Revival in Agriculture," *Wall Street Journal*, April 27, 1994, p. A2; "Tenneco Packaging Subsidiary Weighs Making Acquisitions as Big as $1 Billion," *Wall Street Journal*, October 11, 1994, p. B10; "Tenneco Plans to Divide Operations; As Many as Three Concerns to Result," *Wall Street Journal*, July 22, 1998, p. A6.

19. "Acquiring by the Book," *CFO* (February 1999): 25–26; "Textron Gives Henkel No. 2 Job, Putting Him in Line for CEO Post," *Wall Street Journal*, July 23, 1998, p. B10.

20. See "Schlumberger to Find Out If Oil and High Tech Mix," *Wall Street Journal*, February 15, 2001, p. B4.

21. See, for example, M. C. Jensen and R. C. Ruback, "The Market for Corporate Control: The Scientific Evidence," *Journal of Financial Economics* (April 1983): 7–23.

22. See "Litton Studies Possible Sale of Businesses," *Wall Street Journal*, October 23, 2000, pp. A3, A17.

23. See "DuPont Cajoles Independent Units to Talk to One Another," *Wall Street Journal*, February 5, 2002, p. B4; "Bristol-Myers Reaches Agreement to Buy DuPont Drug Business for $7.8 Billion," *Wall Street Journal*, June 8, 2001; "DuPont Plans Sale of Unit Developing Pharmaceuticals," *Wall Street Journal*, December 15, 2000; "DuPont Co.: Apparel, Fiber Businesses to Be Combined into Unit," *Wall Street Journal*, October 31, 2000; "Flat DuPont Needs to Find Right Mix of Businesses," *Wall Street Journal*, May 8, 2000; "DuPont Returns to More-Reliable Chemical Business—Plans for Biotech, Drug Divisions Fizzle as Mergers Change Landscape," *Wall Street Journal*, February 23, 2000; "Teijin to Form a Venture to Produce Polyester Film," *Wall Street Journal*, February 4, 1999; "DuPont Moves Away from Polyester, Putting Bulk of Business in Ventures," *Wall Street Journal*, April 16, 1999, p. B8; "Engineering the Future of Food," *Fortune*, September 28, 1998, pp. 128–144; DuPont Gets FDA Clearance for AIDS Drug," *Wall Street Journal*, September 21, 1998, p. B4; "Grains That Taste Like Meat?" *Business Week*, May 25, 1998, p. 44; "DuPont Is Paying Merck $2.6 Billion to Buy Out 50% Stake in Drug Venture," *Wall Street Journal*, May 20, 1998, p. B4; "DuPont Plans to Shed Conoco Oil Unit," *Wall Street Journal*, May 12, 1998, p. A2; "DuPont's Pioneer Hi-Bred Stake," *Wall Street Journal*, September 19, 1997; "DuPont to Buy Ralston-Purina Unit in Building Dirt-to-Dinner Biotech Line," *Wall Street Journal*, August 25, 1997, p. A8.

24. See "Warm and Fuzzy Won't Save Procter & Gamble," *Business Week*, June 26, 2000; "After Gobbling Up Iams, P&G Finds People Who Have Bones to Pick," *Wall Street Journal*, June 14, 2000; "P&G Is Out to Fetch Distribution Gains for Iams Pet Food," *Wall Street Journal*, January 6, 2000, p. B4; "Stirring Giant: P&G Is on the Move," *Wall Street Journal*, January 24, 2000; "P&G to Buy Iams: Will Pet-Food Fight Follow?" *Wall Street Journal*, August 12, 1999.

25. See "When a Merger Fails: Lessons from Sprint," *Fortune*, April 30, 2001, pp. 185–186.

26. See "United Technologies' Otis, Carrier Units Gain Importance amid Aviation Crisis," *Wall Street Journal*, September 28, 2001, p. B6.

27. See "Cisco Tops $100 Billion in Market Capital," *Wall Street Journal*, July 20, 1998, p. B5.

28. See "Medtronic to Buy MiniMed and Medical Research," *Wall Street Journal*, May 31, 2001, pp. A3, A4.

29. See, for example, "SmithKline Beecham Enters Genetic-Diagnostics Race," *Wall Street Journal*, September 3, 1997, p. B4; "Biotech Companies Abandon Go-It-Alone Approach," *Wall Street Journal*, November 21, 1995, p. B4.

30. "CNN and Time Are Facing a Bumpy Road to Synergy," *Wall Street Journal*, August 14, 1998, pp. B1, B4.

31. See, for example, "Sony and NEC, Slow to Eliminate Weak Lines, Cut Profit Forecasts," *Wall Street Journal*, October 1, 2001, p. A18. Also see "Japanese Chip Makers End Love Affair with the D-RAM," *Financial Times*, August 13, 2001, p. 22; "Turnaround at Mitsubishi Motors Could Prove Difficult," *Wall Street Journal*, March 6, 2001, p. A14; "How Japan's Toshiba Got Its Focus Back," *Wall Street Journal*, December 28, 2000, A6, A7.

32. See, for example, "IBM Unveils High-End Computer Server," *Wall Street Journal*, October 4, 2001, p. B7; "Content Management Is Top Goal of IBM," *Wall Street Journal*, October 1, 2001, p. B4; "IBM Plans Energy-Efficient Chip to Counter High Electricity Costs," *Wall Street Journal*, October 1, 2001, p. B4.

33. See, for example, "More and More, Mergers of 90's Are Becoming Today's Spinoffs," *Wall Street Journal*, February 6, 2002, pp. C1, C7; "Big Mergers of '90s Prove Disappointing to Shareholders," *Wall Street Journal*, October 30, 2000, pp. C1, C21.

34. See "Merger Machine: Can GE Keep Growing through Deals?" *Wall Street Journal*, July 31, 2001, pp. C1, C2.

35. See "Intel Plans to Pull Back Diversification Effort," *Wall Street Journal*, October 22, 2001, p. B5.

36. A number of studies have addressed the issue of restructuring and the impact on competitive advantage. Some of the following works are representative of the recent studies examining this topic: L. Capron, W. Mitchell, and A Swaminathan, "Asset Divestiture Following Horizontal Acquisitions: A Dynamic View," *Strategic Management Journal* 22, no. 9 (2001): 817–844; S. Chang and H. Singh, "The Impact of Modes of Entry and Resource Fit on Modes of Exit by Multibusiness Firms," *Strategic Management Journal* 20, no. 11 (1999): 1019–1036; R. L. DeWitt, "Firm, Industry, and Strategy Influences on Choice of Downsizing Approach," *Strategic Management Journal* 19, no. 1 (1998): 59–80; J. L. Stimpert and I. M. Duhaime, "Seeing the Big Picture: The Influence of Industry, Diversification, and Business Strategy on Performance," *Academy of Management Journal* 40, no. 3 (1997): 560–583; S. J. Chang, "An Evolutionary Perspective on Diversification and Corporate Restructuring: Entry, Exit, and Economic Performance during 1981–1989," *Strategic Management Journal* 17, no. 11 (1996): 587–611; C. C. Markides, "Diversification, Restructuring and Economic Performance," *Strategic Management Journal* 16, no. 2 (1995): 101–118; M. A. Hitt, B. W. Keats, H. F. Harback, and R. D. Nixon, "Rightsizing: Building and Maintaining Strategic Leadership and Long-Term Competitiveness," *Organizational Dynamics* 23, no. 2 (1994): 18–32; R. E. Hoskisson, R. A. Johnson, and D. D. Moesel, "Corporate Divestiture Intensity in Restructuring Firms: Effects of Governance, Strategy and Performance," *Academy of Management Journal* 37, no. 5 (1994): 1207–1251; E. H. Bowman and H. Singh, "Corporate Restructuring: Reconfiguring the Firm," *Strategic Management Journal* 14, Special Issue (1993): 5–14; P. A. Gibbes, "Determinants of Corporate Restructuring: The Relative Importance of Corporate Governance, Takeover Threat and Free Cash Flow," *Strategic Management Journal* 14, Special Issue (1993): 51–68; J. E. Bethel and J. Liebeskind, "The Effects of Ownership Structure on Corporate Restructuring," *Strategic Management Journal* 14, Special Issue (1993): 15–32; M. A. Hitt and R. E. Hoskisson, "Strategic Competitiveness," in *Applied Business Strategy*, ed. L. Foster (Greenwich, Conn.: JAI, 1991), 1–36; F. R. Lichtenberg, "Industrial De-Diversification and Its Consequences for Productivity," *Journal of Economic Behavior and Organization* 18 (1992): 427–438; H. O'Neill, "Turnaround and Recovery: What Strategy Do You Need?" *Long Range Planning* 19, no. 1 (1986): 80–88; M. A. Hitt and B. W. Keats, "Strategic Leadership and Restructuring: A Reciprocal Interdependence," in *Strategic Leadership: A Multiorganization-Level Perspective*, ed. R. Phillips and J. G. Hunt (New York: Quorum, 1992), 45–61.

37. See, for example, "WellPoint Agrees to Buy RightChoice for Cash, Stock, Totaling $1.3 Billion," *Wall Street Journal*, October 19, 2001, p. B8.

38. See "It's a Natural: P&G Sells Jif to J. M. Smucker," *Wall Street Journal*, October 11, 2001, B1, B12.

39. See, for example, "Eastman Chemical Company Is Developing Its Own Image," *Wall Street Journal*, November 14, 1994, p. B4; "Kodak, Flush with Cash, Plans to Buy Up to $4.76 Billion in Debt Outstanding," *Wall Street Journal*, October 4, 1994, p. A4.

40. See, for example, "A Touch of Indigestion," *Business Week*, March 4, 2002, pp. 66–68; "PepsiCo Inc. Gains in Soda Market as Coca-Cola's Shares and Sales Slip," *Wall Street Journal*, March 1, 2002, p. B5; "Pepsi Names Chief of New Bottling Unit," *Wall Street Journal*, September 25, 1998, p. A3; "Revamped PepsiCo Still Needs to

Conquer Wall Street," *Wall Street Journal*, July 27, 1998, p. B3; "PepsiCo Looks at a Spinoff for Bottling," *Wall Street Journal*, July 24, 1998, p. A3.

41. See, for example, "AT&T's Long, Troubled Trip Back to Its Past," *Wall Street Journal*, December 21, 2001, pp. B1, B4; "Say Goodbye to AT&T," *Fortune*, October 1, 2001, pp. 135–146; "AT&T in Talks to Sell Long-Distance Units," *Wall Street Journal*, September 28, 2001, p. B6; "AOL Makes Offer for AT&T Broadband," *Wall Street Journal*, September 10, 2001, pp. A3, A10; "Disney Opposes Deal to Combine AOL with AT&T Cable Assets" *Wall Street Journal*, September 11, 2001, p. A4; "AT&T's Plan for Breakup May Change," *Wall Street Journal*, March 27, 2001, pp. C1, C2; "AT&T Intends to Spin Off Liberty Media," *Wall Street Journal*, November 16, 2000, pp. A3, A14; "AT&T: Disconnected," *Wall Street Journal*, October 26, 2000, pp. B1, B4, "Once Corporate Icon, AT&T Finally Yields to a Humbler Role," *Wall Street Journal*, October 26, 2000, pp. A1, A12.

42. See "H-P's Agilent Spinoff Greeted Warmly on Wall Street, as Stock Climbs 41%," *Wall Street Journal*, November 19, 1999; "The Secret's Out: It's Agilent Technologies," *Semiconductor International* 34 (1999); "Old H-P Unit Adjusts to Life with New Name," *Wall Street Journal*, July 29, 1999.

CHAPTER 8

Global Strategy: Harnessing New Markets to Extend Advantage

Chapter Outline

What You Will Learn

- Why companies need to develop strategies to expand across national borders
- The key environmental factors that promote the need to expand into overseas markets
- The two basic strategies used for expanding overseas, including global strategy and multidomestic strategy
- Balancing the benefits and costs of overseas expansion
- How companies can continue to grow by becoming global players

The Boeing Company[1]

Throughout much of the last decade, Boeing has attempted to maintain its lead as the world's largest commercial aircraft manufacturer, and also serve as America's premier exporting company. Boeing's wide line of famous aircraft, such as the 737, 747, 757, 767, and ultramodern 777 jets, are used by most nations' commercial airlines. From the 1970s to the present, Boeing stands as a symbol of American industrial might in what is perhaps one of the most global industries around. It has remained America's number one exporter for the past five years and derived more than half of its total $51.3 billion in 2000 sales from customers outside the United States. Despite growing competition from its major European competitor, the Airbus Industries consortium,* Boeing was able to post substantial earnings of $2.3 billion, while continuing to invest enormous sums (approximately 5 percent of sales, down from recent years) in R&D for new aircraft. Although Boeing's dominance in the commercial aircraft industry remains significant, the company is beginning to feel the competitive heat from a reinvigorated Airbus in many of its large aircraft market segments (e.g., 747 and the new 777 aircraft). In some ways, Airbus has seized the competitive initiative in this enormous industry, as it begins to design and develop the world's largest line of commercial aircraft—the A380. In terms of market share based on revenues, Boeing still appears to command roughly 60 percent of the world market for large jets. But by the middle of 2001, the unthinkable began to happen at Boeing; Airbus had a much larger order backlog for large jets (1,602 units on order) compared with Boeing's 1,451. As both companies continue to vie for global dominance of commercial jet aircraft, this aspect of Boeing's strategy—competing in global markets—is the focus of our interest here.

Since its beginnings in 1916 and throughout its long history, Boeing has consistently spent large sums to maintain the high pace of innovation required for designing successful aircraft. During the 1970s and 1980s, Boeing's overriding corporate objective was to remain the dominant force in every segment of the commercial aircraft industry. Boeing's airframe families include the 727 and 737 aircraft for short-range flights, the 757 and 767 for medium-range flights, and the widely successful 747 for intercontinental flights. During the 1980s and early 1990s, however, Boeing has faced a series of growing competitive challenges from both Airbus and McDonnell-Douglas, two companies that aspired to loosen Boeing's grip over global markets. Airbus, with the ongoing assistance of sponsoring European governments, has steadily increased its market position at Boeing's expense by winning several key customers' orders for state-of-the-art aircraft that utilize new fly-by-wire controls with advanced electronics. In September 2000, Airbus won a stunning coup by signing up Singapore Airlines to order its gigantic, 650-seat Airbus A380 model, a plane that will cost the European company upwards of $10 billion in R&D costs. By January 2001, a number of other airlines, including Qantas Airways, Air France, Virgin Atlantic, as well as General Electric's aircraft leasing unit, placed orders for the A380. Industry observers note that Airbus, once an R&D and marketing laggard to Boeing, now appears to have both innovation and sales momentum on its side.

Having long realized that Airbus would eventually reach the point of matching Boeing's capabilities in R&D and advanced manufacturing, Boeing took the bold step of purchasing its other U.S. rival, McDonnell-Douglas, in a complex transaction that required government approval through much of 1997. McDonnell-Douglas has traditionally sought to challenge Boeing's dominance of the medium-range aircraft market, but now its expertise in this area greatly complements Boeing's product line (the 717 and 737 line of planes) to fight Airbus for smaller and medium-sized aircraft for customers in emerging and developing markets, as well as for short distance, point-to-point travel between

---

*Airbus Industries is 80 percent owned by EADS (European Aeronautic Defense and Space Company), with the other 20 percent owned by BAE Systems of the United Kingdom. EADS, in turn, is jointly owned by France's Aerospatiale Matra SA (37.9 percent), Germany's DASA Aerospace unit of DaimlerChrysler (37.9 percent), and Spain's Construcciones Aeronauticas SA (4.2 percent). Previously organized as a loose consortium or alliance among these four companies, Airbus effectively became a centralized company in 1999.

congested airports in the United States and elsewhere. Still, with the steady rise of Airbus and potentially new entrants from Japan, China, and elsewhere, Boeing realized that purchasing McDonnell-Douglas was not enough to forestall the rise of its massive European rival. Instead, Boeing is seeking to reinvent itself by investing in new types of manufacturing technology that aim to slice down the amount of time it takes to develop and build next-generation aircraft. By adopting some of the same techniques that the Japanese have developed to accelerate product development in the automobile industry, Boeing is experimenting with new materials and processes that will greatly reduce the number of steps to construct an aircraft, while simultaneously raising the productivity of its factories. The high fixed costs of investing in new techniques and materials, however, means that Boeing must sell and receive firm orders from customers around the world to support such an expensive undertaking. To accomplish its cherished goal of industry dominance, Boeing identified several critical factors that are the pillars of its global strategy: sustaining advanced research, seeking quantum leaps in manufacturing efficiencies and process improvement, focused global marketing, and continuous product enhancement and investment.

Advanced Research and Development (R&D)

The cost of designing and developing a new generation of aircraft is rising exponentially. Every new plane costs more than double its predecessor to commercialize successfully. Since 1970, Boeing has consistently spent well over $1 billion per year in designing and testing new models of aircraft, such as its famous 747s, 757s, and 767s. Boeing's newest line of aircraft, the huge 777, cost the company more than $4 billion and four years' development effort before a single plane was built in 1995. Now, as the Airbus A380 development program proceeds, the costs have ratcheted even higher. An entire new line of aircraft can easily cost upward of $9 billion—even more as new composite materials and superstrong metallic alloys are developed to lighten the aircraft's weight. These huge development expenditures serve as a nearly insurmountable barrier to entry and keep many other competitors from entering this industry on their own.

More important, Boeing's commitment to learning and deploying state-of-the-art R&D and advanced technologies enables the company to learn and use the latest developments in computer-aided design (CAD), metallurgy, electronics, and composite materials. The company is streamlining its R&D activities so that engineers from different parts of the company are able to use a common set of computers and software programs to accelerate product development and to share results. Previously, Boeing used over 450 different computer systems to run tests and experiments, resulting in an overly complex, cumbersome, and time-consuming process that cost years in development time.

Manufacturing Efficiencies and Process Improvement

A second pillar vital to supporting Boeing's global dominance of commercial aerospace is the firm's centralization of production activities to achieve low-cost economies of scale in production. Manufacturing and assembly of key aircraft components are highly capital-intensive operations whose costs need to be spread over a wide base of aircraft models. To capture high economies of scale and high quality, Boeing has concentrated most of its key component, assembly, and systems integration operations near its main plant in Washington. All assembly operations take place in Boeing's plant in Everett, Washington, which covers more than forty square acres of factory and laboratory space. This one plant alone can assemble more than four hundred planes a year, or about 65 percent of total world demand.

Even though Boeing has consistently managed its costs carefully, the company remains dedicated to investing in the latest manufacturing, advanced materials, and electronics-based technologies to further strengthen its hold over the global market. Throughout 2000 and 2001, Boeing continued to apply advanced production techniques into its manufacturing system—a decade-long process that began with the introduction of new facilities that utilized new materials and methods to build aircraft wing panels in 1992. For the past several years, Boeing has been able to build new wing panels for its wide-body aircraft in ten days, as opposed to eighty days in the past. However, even these sizable gains are not enough. Boeing believes that it must attain quantum leaps in efficiency and cost reduction to counter Airbus' new manufacturing platforms, especially as key airline customers are demanding lower cost planes during tougher economic times. The company is rethinking its entire manufacturing process approach to drive costs out of the system at every level—from inventory that sits on factory floors to the number of welds and rivets (and the man-hours needed) to build a plane. Yet, as the company continues to strive for even more productivity, Boeing is experimenting with new types of composite materials, such as carbon fiber and advanced plastic resins. Composite materials are new substances designed to replace metal beams and parts in constructing the aircraft's frame. Over time, Boeing is counting on these newly engineered materials to radically simplify its manufacturing process and simultaneously strengthen and reinforce its planes. Carbon fiber and other advanced resins reduce the weight of the aircraft, thus saving on fuel consumption. Boeing is also investigating the use of engineered plastic alloys and resins to help reduce, and eventually, eliminate the number of welds and rivets that are needed to construct the fuselage and other aircraft body sections. In the future, both Boeing and its competitor Airbus envision a time when an entire aircraft's fuselage and other key sections are made from a single piece of advanced composite material. This practice is already common in the recreational boat industry, where an entire boat's hull is constructed from one piece of carbon fiber.

To improve Boeing's total cost reduction efforts, the company remains in the midst of learning and implementing just-in-time (JIT) management of inventory, flexible product designs and tighter management of close relationships with suppliers. These techniques, learned by benchmarking the best practices of competitors in the automobile industry, allow for faster customization of aircraft models according to specific customers' needs while lowering costs simultaneously. By 1998, Boeing was able to assemble a state-of-the-art 777 aircraft in thirty-seven days instead of seventy-one. Now, the company is using moving assembly lines to help improve worker productivity and buying parts only when they are needed for assembly. This step saves hundreds of millions of dollars in inventory costs in parts of components that used to sit in the factory until they were assembled.

Global Marketing

The third pillar supporting Boeing's global strategy is its dedication to aggressive and highly focused marketing. Boeing prides itself on having developed aggressive global marketing teams. These teams are able to match any customer's needs with Boeing's wide line of aircraft, while also providing generous financing terms and pricing to win the customer. The choice of a particular aircraft model is vital to the customer, since it commits the buyer not only to the operating range of the aircraft but also to the parts, service, and maintenance costs that are needed to keep the plane afloat. Effective marketing of aircraft requires a highly sophisticated, knowledgeable, and well-trained sales force. To keep Airbus and newly emerging rivals (e.g., Embraer, Bombardier) at bay, Boeing attempts to reach potential new customers before its rivals.

Equally important, Boeing works closely with each and every customer in terms of customer satisfaction, aircraft pricing, leasing costs, and service requirements. Financing the aircraft (e.g., purchase vs. long-term leasing) has become a critical lever in the firm's global marketing efforts. Boeing's sterling reputation in providing immediate, worldwide service is another key competitive advantage. Service is key to keeping customers satisfied since any downtime with maintenance failures or lack of parts means huge costs for the customer. With the world's most prestigious airlines, Boeing will go to almost any length to make sure that it retains their business. For example, with such well-known global carriers as British Airways, Lufthansa, and Japan Airlines, Boeing has even set up satellite offices near these airlines' headquarters to make sure they receive the latest technical developments and immediate servicing of their aircraft.

Continuous Product Improvement and Investment

The fourth pillar supporting Boeing's global strategy is continuous improvement and product quality enhancement. To maintain its market position, Boeing constantly searches for new ways to upgrade its aircraft models to accommodate the changing needs of its customers. For example, Boeing has several variations of its widely popular 737 line of short-range aircraft to meet the special needs of regional low-cost carriers such as Southwest Airlines. The acquisition of McDonnell-Douglas's MD-80 line of smaller aircraft (now redesignated as the 717) enables Boeing to fill out its product line with streamlined aircraft designed for short and medium-haul markets. Variations of each aircraft model offer advanced features, but without sacrificing the commonality of design that makes for easy servicing and parts requirements. Offering product enhancements and upgrades enables Boeing not only to experiment with new aircraft derivatives, but also to understand more closely and provide for its customers' special needs.

Most recently, to blunt Airbus's renewed vigor and assertive position in the market, Boeing has committed significant resources to extend the life of its popular 747 line of wide-body aircraft to offer a lower-cost alternative to Airbus's new A380. Even more important, Boeing has begun developing an entirely new line of aircraft to be known as the Sonic Cruiser. The Sonic Cruiser will utilize many of Boeing's advanced manufacturing processes to build a plane that will travel just under the speed of sound. Believing that more airlines and passengers wish to fly from one point to another faster, the company is looking to make the Sonic Cruiser available by 2006 to 2008. Boeing thinks that as countries further open their skies to more airlines and greater availability of flight schedules, passengers will want to fly directly to smaller airports, rather than change planes and transfer at large centralized airport hubs. The Sonic Cruiser is designed to carry two hundred to three hundred passengers over distances as long as 6,300 miles. By flying near the speed of sound, it can slice an hour or two off a long flight. Using an advanced delta-wing design, the Sonic Cruiser will incorporate the use of advanced composite materials, carbon fibers, and newly engineered resins throughout the body of the plane.

The Coca-Cola Company[2]

Perhaps no product is more global than Coca-Cola, or Coke. Customers from St. Louis to São Paulo to St. Petersburg and the world over love the taste of Coca-Cola and are demanding more of it. Yet, the secret behind Coca-Cola's enormous popularity and market success lies in the Coca-Cola Company's continuing efforts to innovate new products and to enter new markets, no matter how prohibitive they seem initially. If one product comes close to setting the standard and symbol for a truly global product, Coca-Cola must surely rank near the top.

The Coca-Cola Company (also known as Coke) is one of the world's most profitable beverage companies. In 2000, its $20.46 billion in total sales earned nearly $2.18 billion in profits for the company, making Coke one of the most profitable large U.S. companies in recent history. In the United States, it retains the top spot for soda sales, with over 44.1 percent of the overall $60.2 billion beverage industry, while Pepsi captured 31.4 percent. What is more startling about Coke is that nearly 75 percent of its profits come from overseas, with Japan as its biggest profit center. Worldwide, Coke employs more than seven hundred thousand people in its value creation and distribution system (with some thirty-seven thousand in the United States). Coke has more than eight million wholesalers, retailers, and distributors selling a broad range of cola and other soft drink products. From giant, megastore retailers to individual vendors and vending machines, Coke is distributed in almost every way imaginable. The company can produce in excess of twenty-eight billion cases of soft drinks a year, and is seeking to expand this capacity by 5 to 10 percent in its newly growing markets such as Eastern Europe, China, Latin America, and parts of the former Soviet Union. Coca-Cola products are clearly stunning successes, but what is equally remarkable is that the company itself has continued to grow around the world, although at a somewhat slower rate in the past few years.

Unlike its arch rival PepsiCo, Coke has remained extremely focused on its beverage businesses. While PepsiCo has restructured its international operations, divested its restaurant units (KFC, Taco Bell, and Pizza Hut are now in a newly created spin-off known as Tricon Global Restaurants) and invested more heavily in its snack food (Frito-Lay) operations, Coke now avoids entering businesses that do not relate to beverages. At one point Coke owned a 49 percent stake of Columbia Pictures but sold its holdings to Sony Corporation in 1989 for a large profit. Earlier, in the mid-1980s, Coke attempted to enter the wine and coffee businesses but found that they did not fit Coke's style of marketing and strategic mission.

Coke defines its strategic mission as making sure that its products are "within an arm's reach of desire," no matter where that customer may be. This overriding strategic direction forms the basis of its far-reaching strategy to reach every part of the world. Coke believes globalization is the key to its future because of the five billion people (or customers, in Coke's view) who can share in the quality and message that Coke brings. What makes Coke's globalization push so potent is that its late chairman and CEO, Roberto Goizueta, personally exemplified and embodies Coke's strong global flavor. A chemical engineer born in Cuba, Mr. Goizueta worked in a Coca-Cola plant prior to his arrival in the United States in the early 1960s. Until Mr. Goizueta's untimely death in 1997, Coke continuously pushed the frontier and aggressively entered newly developing markets.

Even now under new leadership (Chairman Douglas Daft), Coke stays remarkably patient in developing new products and entering new markets. In China, for example, Coke committed over twenty years and several million dollars before it became a major presence and turned a profit. In fact, Coke sees serving the developing markets of China, India, Russia, and Eastern Europe—about half the world's population—as pivotal to its future success. Most of these regions have only just begun to open up their economies to the global market.

More important, Coke sees itself not only as the producer and distributor of soft drinks but also as a messenger of good feelings, such as joy and laughter, refreshment, fun, a new start, sports, and music. As such, the cornerstone of Coke's global strategy is to do whatever it takes to create opportunities to reach customers with exciting new products that fit their tastes, however they may want them. Crucial elements of Coke's global expansion include (1) a unifying message, (2) global distribution, (3) new products, and (4) community involvement.

A Unifying Message

Coke believes that success in the global marketplace demands not only high-quality, instantly visible products but also a central theme, symbol, or idea that binds together its products with its customers and distributors. For American travelers going to new places, Coke symbolizes a friendly reminder of home. For people in newly developing markets, Coke represents a potential avenue and opportunity to enjoy prosperity. The image of Coca-Cola as a beverage, outlined by flowing white letters in a red background, symbolizes instant refreshment and awareness, no matter where you are in the world. Yet, Coke sees its trademark as more than simply a medium for advertising; the Coca-Cola label ought to convey a deeper message of fun, refreshment, and joyful memories to people who consume it.

Global Distribution and Business Systems

Central to Coke's mission of being within arm's reach of its customers is its globe-spanning distribution system. The global Coca-Cola distribution system functions as a well-oiled machine, in which seven hundred thousand employees work together to produce and distribute Coca-Cola products in every market. Coke's distribution system relies heavily on a combination of both wholly owned subsidiaries and long-standing partnerships with local bottlers and distributors that share the same common passion toward Coke's products. Coke's distribution system varies across every country and region that it serves, although the company prefers to own as many of its facilities where possible to improve timely delivery and logistical concerns. Most important, Coke tries to achieve the maximum market penetration in every market through extensive market research, inventory control, and ownership of key bottling and distribution channels. No outlet is considered too small to sell Coca-Cola products. In Japan, for example, Coke has advertised in local retailing trade magazines and even presented seminars to mom-and-pop stores on the virtues and profits of selling Coca-Cola. As such, marketing activities, with the exception of the company's corporate-wide image, tends to be managed locally. Coke's distribution pipeline includes everything from concentrate and bottling plants to vending machines, restaurant sales, grocery stores, and even soft drink stands in every conceivable market.

Coke tends to rely heavily on dedicated local managers and personnel to oversee significant distribution operations. In the United States, for example, Coca-Cola Enterprises is a separate company that handles distribution of all Coke and affiliated products throughout the country. Coca-Cola Enterprises, in turn, franchises many local bottlers and distributors to handle the flow of Coke products through the system. In overseas markets, Coke has aggressively bought or established new bottling facilities to further extend its reach and to deny access to its rival Pepsi. Most recently in late 1996, Coke was able to break Pepsi's once-strong position in Venezuela by acquiring new bottlers in that critical growth market. Franchising is important, especially in Coke's more distant locations, where local managers and owners are better attuned to their markets' specific needs. In newly developing markets such as

China and Eastern Europe, Coke relies on a combination of company-owned bottlers and distributors and local joint ventures to understand and to serve more distant customers better.

New Products and New Variations

Coke spends large sums annually to conduct market research to locate potential new markets. Successful market research in every major country or region of the world allows Coke to carefully match the taste of its products with local preferences. Market research also enables Coke to produce numerous variations of its underlying beverage products. For example, in Europe, Coke developed Coke light to compete not only with its own mainstream Coke products but also with new soft drink products from Pepsi and other producers. In Spain, Coca-Cola is often used as a mixer for wines. In Japan, Coke introduced such new products as Georgia Ice Coffee and Cafe Au Lait Premium products to enter a new market segment. Also, Coke introduced beta carotene–enriched VegitaBeta and Bonaqua-flavored mineral water in Japan during 1992. Through the early 1990s, Coke introduced two new drinks tailored specifically for the Australian market—Lift and Skysurfer. In Indonesia, Coke sells strawberry-, pineapple-, and even banana-flavored sodas. Coke also sports a broad range of soft drink products, such as Sprite, New Coke, Coke light, Fanta, Diet Coke, and Mello Yellow in the United States, as well as Minute Maid orange juice. Amazingly, Coca-Cola USA represents less than a third (33 percent) of total worldwide sales. Yet, in all of these and other markets, regular Coke in its familiar red-and-white label is always available to serve as the basis for the company's worldwide recognition.

In addition to offering such a wide variety of tastes, Coke offers an incredible array of beverage sizes, ranging from the omnipresent two-liter bottles to aluminum cans and glass bottles of varying sizes. By offering a countless assortment of sizes and tastes of its broadly expanding product line, Coke keeps local store shelves, vending machines, and other distribution outlets well stocked. Paradoxically, offering a wide variety of tastes and sizes keeps the product price low to the customer and limits the effective actions of other beverage competitors.

Community Involvement

A key pillar to Coke's global strategy is its strong belief in local community involvement. Coke believes good marketing goes beyond traditional advertising and distribution. Coke's distribution system is committed to making Coca-Cola products part of every community. This means that Coke, its local bottlers, and many of its distributors are active supporters of community activities ranging from sports and holiday celebrations to local charities.

Recent Initiatives

Over the past ten years, Chairman Douglas Daft believed that the company had become slower to respond to local challenges and competitors' moves, as managers in some regions were forced to get some operating decisions cleared by corporate headquarters in Atlanta. Even advertisement decisions sometimes required corporate approval, thus slowing the company's ability to respond. In reality, many local managers felt that they could no longer act on their own, even if they had the authority to do so. This additional reporting process, in turn, may have hurt the company's long-term competitiveness. For example, Coke faced a real marketing and public relations disaster in 1999 when several Belgian children apparently got sick from beverage cans that were processed by a local Coke bottling unit. The company's initial response to this crisis was slow, because management did not feel that their quality control systems might have been out of sync. More important, four nations in the European Community ordered Coke products off the shelf, and the company was forced to spend over $100 million on a massive recall. This crisis forced the company to realize that it needed to streamline its decision-making process.

By 2001, the company has appeared to recover from some of its earlier European difficulties. In fact, Coke has begun launching its own line of Powerade drinks for the European market in a renewed show of confidence. Although Powerade was originally designed to challenge Pepsi's Gatorade line of products in the United States (acquired from Quaker Oats in 2001), Coke hopes that Powerade will allow it grab market share from five smaller European competitors. Coke also sees Powerade as another product that will help it boost the sales of another sports drink known as Aquarius, also sold heavily in Europe. Coke is trying to position Powerade as a drink that people drink during their sports activities, while Aquarius is sold as an after-sports drink. Thus, Coke faces some risk of cannibalization in selling similar types of products at the same time. As in the United States,

Coke is trying to sell Powerade to surfers and skateboarders, who are becoming more active in Europe as well.

Coke's strong global presence has given the company considerable latitude to introduce new products according to local tastes. Although the company remains committed to ensuring that it listens to its customers, it has even gone beyond that to implementing an even more attentive "think local, act local" strategy. In effect, Coke has begun reorganizing itself in such a way that local managers have even more autonomy to formulate and implement strategies for their individual markets. The benefits of reinvigorating local managers to act on their own may be paying off in Japan. In 2000, Coke developed over seven new brands of energy drinks, waters, and teas for Japan and several other Asian markets. Japan is unique for the sheer number of vending machines that exist in the country (over six million). Canned coffees and teas often outsell cola-based beverages. To make sure that the company protects its Japanese market position, Coke formed teams of marketing people to find the best possible drink ideas and authorized the local managers to devise how best to meet those needs. Managers can even buy out a local brand if it fits Coke's long-term strategy in that region. In fact, Coke's Japan-based beverage team even gets calls for advice from all around the world on how best to proceed. Money for R&D is now spent not only in major markets such as the United States, Japan, and Europe but also in the smaller but fast-growing Asian markets.

Coke is also looking to expand some of its non-carbonated beverages in a careful manner in the United States. In early 2001, Coke acquired two small makers of "new-age beverages." One company, known as Planet Java, is a maker of specialty coffee drinks. The other acquisition involved Mad River Traders, Inc., which develops teas, juices, lemonades and gourmet soda drinks. Most recently, Coke has investigated the possibility of acquiring Odwalla, a leading maker of fresh fruit and vegetable juices. Odwalla also makes dairy-free shakes and a blend of other soy-based vegetable drinks, too. All of these recent U.S.-based initiatives are helping Coke to move into a new line of health-oriented beverages.

Introduction

This chapter focuses on how firms can develop strategies for global expansion that extend their competitive advantage to worldwide markets. For firms in almost every imaginable industry, the need to think about strategies for global expansion and operations is rising fast. In fact, in some industries (e.g., high fashion, Hollywood movies, and Internet-driven, on-line businesses) where products are in such high demand, the need to think about global expansion begins on day one. Rapidly changing technologies, the growth of computer networks that make the Internet ever-more pervasive around the world, the rise of new competitors from newly developed markets, the global desire for exciting new products and services, and the availability of new sources of production make global strategy issues a critical consideration for senior managers in all types and sizes of companies. Business leaders from North and South America, the Far East, and Europe all agree that going global is essential to their future business success. Yet, few managers actually agree on which factors are most important in pursuing successful global expansion strategies.[3]

globalization: Viewing the world as a single market for the firm; the process by which the firm expands across different regions and national markets. On an industry level, globalization refers to the changes in economic factors, such as economies of scale, experience, and R&D, that make competing on a worldwide basis a necessity.

At the same time, however, globalization can introduce its own set of economic and organizational challenges. Competing in many parts of the world often requires the firm to establish facilities and goodwill in new markets, a very time-consuming task. Also, managing far-flung operations can tax the best company's organizational efforts, since global strategies place a premium on attaining a balance between meeting customers' needs in different part of the world with maintaining cost parity with competitors. In other words, the term *globalization* often conjures up different images in the minds of people from different industries. In this book, we define **globalization** as viewing the entire world as a potential market or source of inputs for the firm.

The issue of globalization is a complex one. Firms operating in many national markets face different strategic considerations and issues than do firms operating solely in their home market. Developing effective global expansion strategies requires managers to think beyond their home market and into many markets. When carefully understood and matched to their firm's products and practices, global expansion strategies can dramatically help firms extend their distinctive competence and sources of competitive advantage to new markets.

We begin by examining the environmental changes and factors that accelerate the trend toward globalization in many industries. Second, we focus on the broad types of global expansion strategies that firms can undertake to expand their operations overseas. Third, we look at the benefits and costs that underscore global operations and examine how managers can balance the risks and rewards inherent in each type of global strategy. Finally, we examine some of the ethical issues that surround globalization. As firms move to set up operations abroad, managers begin to realize that other cultures sometimes have their own interpretation of what constitutes sound business practices and ethics.

Environmental Factors That Accelerate Globalization

Over the past two decades, companies in a growing range of industries have looked overseas to expand their operations. Industries ranging from semiconductors to consumer electronics, automobiles, computers, watches, tools, medical equipment, aerospace, and others have also seen global competitors from other nations make serious inroads into the United States. Some of the most important environmental factors that promote globalization within and across industries are the following: (1) narrowing of demand characteristics among countries and regions; (2) escalating costs of R&D; (3) pressures for cost reduction and higher economies of scale; (4) the rise of government "industrial" policies that promote globalization; (5) the reduction of factor/capital and labor/costs in many markets; (6) the availability of new distribution channels; and (7) lower transportation, communication, and storage costs.[4] (See Exhibit 8-1.)

Factors Promoting the Globalization of Industries — EXHIBIT 8-1

- Narrowing of demand characteristics
- Escalating costs of R&D
- Cost reduction pressures and economies of scale
- Government industrial policies
- Reduction of factor costs (e.g., labor, capital)
- Rise of new distribution channels
- Reduction of transportation, communication, and storage costs
- Internet access
- Reduction of tariffs worldwide

Narrowing of Demand Characteristics across Markets

One of the most important factors promoting faster globalization is the rising level of incomes and awareness of new products and services in regions around the world. Since the 1970s, rising prosperity in countries such as Brazil, Chile, China, South Korea, Taiwan, Singapore, South Africa, Saudi Arabia, Greece, and Turkey has vastly increased the amount of disposable income available for purchasing new products. In addition, more mature markets, such as Europe, North America, and Japan, have been experiencing steadily rising incomes as well, albeit at a slower rate. Even though many countries still exhibit varying rates of economic development, the rise of new middle classes in once-underdeveloped nations has opened up new markets for products such as Sony Walkmans, Levi's jeans, McDonald's restaurants, Coca-Cola, and even Motorola or Nokia cellular phones and pagers. Entirely new markets are being created over a span of a few years. For example, the rising level of prosperity in China has created a middle class that is almost a third the size of that of the United States. The country is installing as many new telephone lines each year as there are in the state of California. Products and services that once were confined primarily to wealthier people in the United States and Europe (e.g., financial services, luxury automobiles, commercial banking, golfing equipment, tennis rackets, cellular phones) is now available to anyone, anywhere around the world who can afford them. In fact, rising prosperity around the world is opening up huge new markets annually—to firms willing to enter and serve them—populated by millions of wealthier people. In the new millennium, even greater opportunities may abound. The economic stabilization of Latin America, the opening up of Eastern Europe, and the massive growth of new middle classes in Indonesia, India, and Southeast Asia are all contributing to the marked rise of incomes, aspirations, and business opportunities for designing and selling new products.

Increasing demand worldwide has direct and more specific effects on the competitive nature of many industries. In some industries, globalization of demand means a leveling of demand patterns, whereby people's desires for products and services are becoming steadily more homogeneous. **Homogeneity of demand** means that regardless of where customers are physically located, buyers are likely to want the same kind of product or service with certain similar features. In other words, customers are becoming increasingly similar in some industries where tastes, preferences, and desires for certain product attributes are converging into one larger, more homogeneous market. Demand characteristics in one region are likely to be nearly, if not altogether identical to those characteristics found in another region. For example, in the cellular phone industry, companies such as Motorola of the United States, Fujitsu of Japan, and Nokia of Finland are designing, producing, and selling hundreds of thousands of these devices to customers worldwide, with few substantive changes in the way the products look or function.

homogeneity of demand: Similarity of demand patterns and wants across customers, regardless of where they are located.

Perhaps the best example of the growing homogeneity of demand in the consumer electronics industry is the Sony Walkman. Consumers in New York, Nanjing, and Nairobi are all likely to be wearing the same style of headsets and listening to music from a radio/cassette player that is interchangeable across markets. However, a product does not necessarily have to be tangible to be wanted by millions of global consumers. For example, blockbuster movies and television shows produced by Hollywood studios are clearly hits wherever they are shown worldwide. See Exhibit 8-2 for examples of products with worldwide markets and increasingly shared tastes and uses.

Homogeneity of demand, however, is perhaps more prevalent in industries that produce and sell products that serve as *components* to some other product or cannot be truly differentiated in their use. For example, semiconductors, telecommunications equipment, and other electronic devices are clearly designed to serve the same purpose and function, no matter where the end user is located. Microprocessors run computers, telephones, and even automobile engines, regardless of where the end product is located. Fiber optics transmits telephone calls across regions, countries, and continents, no matter what language is spoken. Commercial aircraft, such as the Boeing 747 and 777, serve the same purpose of carrying passengers and freight, whether they are sold to American Airlines, Air France, or Aerolineas Argentinas. Homogeneity of operating standards, such as software and word-processing systems, also contributes to rising globalization of these industries. Witness the impact of Microsoft's various operating systems (Windows 98, Windows 2000, Windows NT) in shaping the evolution of future add-on software, video games, and other programs by other software design companies throughout the world. Other industries exhibiting a growing convergence of tastes and demand characteristics include certain types of automobiles (luxury, sport utility, four-wheel drive, and sporty segments), soft drinks (Coke vs. Pepsi), and even high fashion to some degree (the prevalence of Italian-cut suits in Europe, Asia, and the Americas), where a growing common desire for high-quality products transcends languages, ethnic differences, political systems, and religions.

Examples of Growing Homogeneity of Demand — EXHIBIT 8-2

- Communications equipment
- Cellular phones
- Sony Walkmans
- Levi's jeans
- Commercial banking
- Financial services
- Color televisions, VCRs, and DVDs
- Semiconductors
- Machine tools
- Computers
- Pharmaceuticals
- Construction equipment
- Commercial aircraft
- Hollywood films
- Television shows
- Data and computer networks

Escalating Costs of Research and Development

The exponentially rising costs of research and development (R&D) in some industries make it absolutely essential for companies in these industries to sell their products globally. For example, in recent years, Boeing and Airbus now face costs up to $10 billion to design a new model or line of commercial aircraft. In this industry, neither Boeing nor Airbus can afford to design a line of aircraft solely for manufacture and distribution in its home markets; the R&D costs involved are too high. High R&D costs mean that firms must *leverage their R&D costs* across a greater volume of products that inevitably must be sold across many markets. For example, Boeing's new 777 line of aircraft has been so expensive to develop that the company first had to secure orders from various national airlines before a single plane was built. Airbus is finding that it, too, must secure definite orders and commitments to use its Airbus A380 model before the company can even develop the plane.

The semiconductor, biotechnology, pharmaceutical, and composite materials industries also face a similar economic imperative of rising R&D costs. In 2001, Intel alone spent $7.5 billion for both research and capital equipment, despite the fact that the semiconductor industry went into a downturn for much of the year. Intel realizes that it must not only prepare for next generation chips regardless of the immediate economic climate but also establish facilities to sell its chips on a global basis. Its next generation Itanium chip (previously code-named Merced) was so complex and expensive that Intel developed it in conjunction with Hewlett-Packard, which committed significant design expertise to the project. In the biotechnology and pharmaceutical industries, designing a new line of anticancer drugs is a costly proposition. The research and development costs of testing, developing, and finally commercializing new medications can easily exceed $800 million, so selling globally as fast as possible is a must. Companies that manufacture "new wave" materials, such as hybrid composites used in tennis rackets (graphite), golf clubs (titanium, tantalums, and carbon fibers), engineering resins and alloys (super strong composite metals or engineered plastics), and new synthetic fibers (advanced polyester blends) must also amortize their R&D costs over a global volume of business. For example, graphite tennis rackets are expensive to develop and sell, but few people in one market alone are likely to buy enough of them to justify a firm's initial investment in that business. Likewise, carbon fiber developed for the aerospace business needs to be produced on a global basis to justify the massive investment in these complex manufacturing plants. Companies in this and other industries must view the entire world as their market before they can undertake costly product development. Thus, firms in industries that face rising R&D costs accelerate the broader trend toward globalization. See Exhibit 8-3 for examples of global, R&D-intensive industries.

EXHIBIT 8-3 Examples of R&D-Intensive Industries

- Semiconductors
- Software
- Biotechnology
- Communications systems
- Pharmaceuticals
- Commercial aircraft
- Electronics
- Composite materials
- Advanced imaging systems
- Medical equipment
- Fiber optics

Rising Economies of Scale and Cost Pressures

minimum efficient scale (MES): Level of production volume that a factory must reach before it achieves full efficiency.

Many industries are currently exhibiting rising levels of economies of scale in production. For example, the steel industry is characterized by a high minimum efficient scale (MES). **Minimum efficient scale** refers to the production volume at which a plant must operate to achieve full efficiency. New integrated steel mills that turn out high-quality, continuously cast steel face rising levels of MES to the point where a brand-new steel mill must be able to produce a sizable fraction of total world demand before it breaks even. South Korea's newest integrated steel mill, owned and operated by the Pohang Iron and Steel Company (POSCO), can produce high-quality steel for export at 75 percent of the cost of comparable U.S. integrated mills. However, POSCO's plant is so huge that it must produce approximately 3 percent of total world demand before it achieves full efficiency. Thus, high economies of scale in production mandate high-volume exports to other nations, thus accelerating globalization of the industry.

Global economies of scale can also promote related experience curve effects in production. Experience curve effects (see Chapter 3) resulting from global volume production are important, because they can help firms to reduce costs even further. In technologies where costs decline from both cumulative volume and learning, firms may be more inclined to sell more products across different regions. As costs decline, the company will be better able to price its product to penetrate new markets. In addition, faster learning and experience means that the company will be able to remain at a lower cost position than its rivals for an extended period. Economies of scale is clearly an important factor in most information-driven industries, because once the fixed costs are amortized, there is enormous profit in selling to new markets and new customers. Computer hardware and their components exhibit significant economies of scale, especially in storage and memory devices. The economies of scale and cumulative experience effects gained by Japanese automakers, such as Toyota, Honda, and Nissan, have helped these companies penetrate both the U.S. and European markets, while sustaining the momentum of global volume production. See Exhibit 8-4 for examples of products in industries with rising economies of scale.

Role of Government Policy

Government policy can often accelerate the trend toward globalization in one or a group of industries. For example, the rise of Japanese integrated steel producers during the

Examples of Rising Economies of Scale/Cost Pressures

EXHIBIT 8-4

- Steel
- Automobile engines
- Color television tubes
- Semiconductors
- Fiber optics
- Office equipment
- Telecommunications
- Aircraft
- Chemicals

1960s and 1970s was largely due to the coordination and preferential tax treatment (particularly in depreciation) accorded to steelmakers by the government. Companies such as Nippon Kokan, Nippon Steel, Sumitomo Metal, and others were encouraged by the government to share their technological innovations and to build steel mills that exhibited ever-higher minimum efficient scale (such policies can, of course, have a very mixed blessing when these industries enter a protracted cyclical downturn, as is the case with Japan now). In turn, many of these steel companies started to export to the United States, where older mills owned by a variety of existing and previous firms, such as U.S. Steel, Bethlehem Steel, Jones and Laughlin, and National Steel, could not compete as effectively.

Numerous tools of government policy, such as subsidies, preferential tax treatment, and other support for critical industrial sectors can accelerate the trend toward globalization. "Industrial policies" such as these are fairly common in the Far East and Latin America, where governments often intervene in ways to promote their strategic industries. Until very recently, for example, South Korea's government provided generous subsidies or indirect loans to its electronics and semiconductor companies (e.g., Samsung), which in turn are able to invest in newer equipment and larger plants for export. Europe's numerous government-sponsored collaborative projects in semiconductors, aircraft, and other industries (e.g., JESSI and Airbus Industries) have spurred the rise of pan-European global competitors that are seeking to challenge U.S. and Japanese strongholds in a number of industries. Thus, government policy can accelerate the rise of new global competitors in industries by removing some of the initial impediments to globalization. Exhibit 8-5 presents some industries in the United States, Japan, and Europe that have been the recent focus of government-backed initiatives or industrial policies.

Examples of Government Initiatives to Promote Industrial Development

EXHIBIT 8-5

USA → Sematech (semiconductors)

Japan → Steel, Computers, Autos, Artificial Intelligence, Advanced Materials, Aerospace

Europe → Semiconductors, Aerospace, Automobiles, Advanced Lasers, Optics, Defense

Conversely, government policy can impede the trend toward globalization in some industries. Subsidies to weak domestic producers, protectionist measures such as tariffs, quotas, and other import limitations can actually prolong the decline of certain industries that are ripe for global competition. For example, many governments protect their domestic producers of agriculture, textiles, steel, electronics, and other businesses that in many cases would ordinarily have been subject to global competitive pressures earlier were it not for protective policies. Even government-sponsored "industrial policies" can backfire in unintentional ways. For example, South Korea's generous support of its numerous semiconductor manufacturers caused a massive oversupply of memory chips during the late 1990s that hurt competitors from around the world, including its own. Two of its own domestic producers of memory chips, Lucky-Goldstar and Hyundai Electronics, were unable to remain profitable without domestic subsidies. Hyundai Electronics, now known as Hynix Electronics, has repeatedly turned to its creditors for extensions on loan payments and has even sought debt relief. Japan's long-cherished policy of promoting its own industrial growth has resulted in serious economic distortions, especially as many of its export-oriented companies confront currency fluctuations and overcapacity in many industries. In fact, several Japanese electronics companies, such as Hitachi, NEC, Toshiba, and Fujitsu, during the past two years have been forced to resort to layoffs across their disparate businesses, an amazing turnabout for a country that has long prided itself on preserving a policy of lifetime employment at its largest companies.

Change in Factor Costs around the World

One of the most important factors that have accelerated the globalization of different industries is the prevalence of low-cost labor and resources in different parts of the world. Low-cost labor attracts companies from other countries to set up operations in the hope of lowering the cost of their end products. During the 1960s and 1970s, many U.S. companies such as General Electric, United Technologies, Westinghouse Electric, Ford, Texas Instruments, and General Motors established factories and other production facilities throughout the Far East and Latin America to take advantage of lower labor costs to manufacture consumer electronics and automotive components. Many textile, small appliance, housewares, and toy manufacturers have also opened up overseas operations because of low labor costs as well. Toy companies, such as Mattel and Hasbro, and garment makers/retailers Liz Claiborne, Evan Picone, and Bloomingdale's have significant production and sourcing operations in the Far East that enable them to offer high-quality goods at lower cost. The presence of these companies has also helped stimulate the development of local economies, which, in turn, have become important customers and competitors in different industries.

In fact, the sustained growth and increased prosperity of the Mexican border areas near California and Texas have resulted from massive investment by both U.S. and Japanese firms to establish assembly plants in the region to take advantage of lower labor costs. These assembly plants, known as *maquiladoras*, play a vital role in bringing new technology and new opportunities for Mexico, which in turn has spawned a whole new set of suppliers and distributors in the region.

U.S. investment in Mexico is certainly not confined to the border area alone. For example, General Motors and Ford build some of their most popular-selling vehicles deep inside Mexico, in places such as Ramos Arizpe (GM), Monterrey (GM and Ford), and Hermosillo (Ford and Volkswagen). Japanese automotive firms have established a strong presence in many of the same places to serve both the Mexican and U.S. markets with greater local presence.

The continued presence and attraction of low-cost, skilled labor in China, India, Indonesia, and other Southeast Asian countries have recently encouraged many Japanese producers to build factories in this region during the 1990s, since labor has now become a scarce and high-cost commodity in Japan. In fact, some economic analysts have noted that the Japanese have built as much manufacturing capacity in Southeast Asia as exists in all of

France. Many well-known Japanese products, such as Sony's television sets and Matsushita Electric's air conditioners, are made in China, Singapore, Thailand, and elsewhere.

Lower costs of energy and other resources can also accelerate globalization. Metal smelting and fabrication costs for aluminum, copper, iron, and other resources are highly sensitive to processing costs. Dramatically cheaper costs of energy may encourage miners and producers of these metals to shift their value-adding functions to cheaper locations. For example, the mining of bauxite (the ore that becomes aluminum) takes place globally, but its processing into higher, value-added metal parts and components occurs closer to aluminum's end markets, where energy, transport, and distribution costs are lower. Many U.S. firms are locating some of their most sophisticated operations according to where they can find abundant sources of highly skilled, technical personnel. Countries such as Taiwan, India, and Israel are becoming important engineering and development centers for key skills such as software and computer design. For example, Texas Instruments (TI) has established a state-of-the-art software development site in Bangalore, India, to work with a rich source of exceptionally skilled technical expertise. TI's engineers in India communicate with their U.S. and European counterparts by way of the company's proprietary satellite transmission system that offers real-time communication. In fact, software competency in India has become so sophisticated that almost all U.S. and European computer and telecommunications companies have established operations in both Bangalore and around the country. Because of the nation's rich educational traditions and rigorous educational standards, India has become a world leader in producing some of the highest quality software talent found anywhere. Even India, though, is not immune to global competition in this extremely advanced industry. Japanese companies such as NEC and Omron Electronics are now starting to tap into China, which over the last decade has begun educating and graduating legions of software engineers.

The trend of tapping into the world's abundant pools of ever-rising talent will likely accelerate as companies further invest and implement new internal computer networks that use the Internet to link up their disparate subsidiaries into a cohesive, real-time information system. In turn, companies that use the Internet to build strong relationships with local talent can often take advantage of important first-mover advantages, not only in developing new technology, but also in understanding how local market conditions may differ. Motorola, Intel, and other U.S. semiconductor firms have set up R&D facilities in Israel to accelerate new product design and testing activities. Taiwan is fast becoming the center of PC production and development expertise for such companies as Compaq Computer, Gateway, and other U.S. firms. Equally important, Taiwan in just the past four years has become the epicenter for much of the world's semiconductor fabrication and testing processes. Companies unheard of as recently as 1997 (e.g., Taiwan Semiconductor Manufacturing, United Microelectronics, Via Technologies) now do much of the production work for such U.S. and European semiconductor firms as Altera, Xilinx, Broadcom, Vitesse Semiconductor, and even Philips Electronics.

Rise of New Distribution Channels

The rise of new distribution channels can also accelerate globalization of product trends. For example, the rise of hypermarts—huge supermarkets—in Germany and other parts of Europe has greatly increased the availability of American-made products (e.g., Tex-Mex food) that ordinarily would have had a much more limited market presence. New distribution channels that supplement or replace more costly existing channels may indirectly act to stimulate demand for newer products. For example, the rise of the Toys "R" Us chain in Japan not only lowered the cost of Japanese-made toys for the local population, but also brought in competing imports from U.S. and other Far Eastern toy makers. The rise of department store chains (Sears and JCPenney in Brazil and Mexico), discount houses (Wal-Mart in Canada and Kmart in Eastern Europe), and specialized, low-cost retailers (Toys "R" Us in Japan, The Home Depot in Chile) is hastening the convergence of tastes and the demand for new global products that are made elsewhere. In Mexico, Wal-Mart has become an important domestic competitor for the hard-earned pesos of Mexican consumers who are attracted to the company's wide product offerings and low prices. Operating in conjunction with its Mexican partner Cifra SA, Wal-Mart has even outmuscled other U.S. firms as Sears and JCPenney in setting up similarly large stores throughout Mexico as it did in the United States.

Overall Reduction in Transportation, Communication, and Storage Costs

The expanding availability of lower-cost transportation has helped stimulate the globalization of many industries. For example, few people probably realize that the United States is the largest importer of fresh flowers and tulip bulbs from South America and the Netherlands. Although fresh-cut flowers would seem to represent the one product least subject to global shipment and export (because of perishability), the ability to mass produce and to ship flowers on airplanes overnight to the United States has instantly transformed the growing of flowers and plants into a new global business. Growing and shipping flowers has become an important industry for many South American countries such as Ecuador and Peru. Custom-made Swiss chocolates and candies are now often shipped directly from Switzerland to the United States to serve niche markets in New York and other cities. The greater availability of low-cost, overnight transportation is not limited to specialty products either. Caterpillar, the leading U.S. manufacturer of construction equipment, routinely promises and delivers replacement parts to its distributors anywhere around the world in less than forty-eight hours. More broadly, the long-run decline in real costs of transportation over the past thirty years has been a fundamental, although subtle, factor that has accelerated globalization across every type of industry.

Communication costs also decline each year. Most recently, the single greatest accelerating factor that promotes globalization and homogeneity of demand is the Internet's presence in every corner of the globe. The massive proliferation of personal computers, state-of-the-art communication networks using fiber optics, and the establishment of huge "server farms" has brought the Internet to some of the most remote villages of the world. New satellites, electronic mail and broadband-based video communications connect the world more tightly than could have ever been imagined as recently as five years ago. Fiber optics that transmit voice, video, and data over telephone lines, combined with wireless communications over a growing range of the electromagnetic spectrum, have lowered the cost of communications every year. Communications technology has advanced to the point where IBM is now actively designing and installing voice recognition chips able to translate languages over the telephone without the need for a translator. New search engines (e.g., Yahoo! and Netscape) on the Internet enable information access from a variety of different global and domestic sources using multiple languages. During the late 1990s, this technology has already far surpassed conventional mail in terms of commercial application and the amount of communications sent.

Storage costs have also declined along with transportation and communication costs in recent years. Improvements in inventory control, such as just-in-time (JIT) production and scheduling, and innovations in containerization and intermodal shipping have contributed to the decline in storage cost for durable products. Merchant ships now routinely carry boxed "containers" that are then directly hooked on to the back of trucks or loaded onto specialized railway wellcars or flatcars (which in turn lowers transport costs even further). This simplification of transportation and storage of products across vast reaches of ocean and land contributes greatly toward faster globalization. For example, shipping companies such as Maersk of Denmark, NYK and K-Line of Japan, Sea-Land of the United States, and Hapag-Lloyd of Germany work closely with other shippers and railroad companies in each country to ensure that containers are off-loaded from ships and quickly loaded onto trucks or rail cars for fast delivery. Many of these companies have even begun deploying advanced Global Positioning System (GPS) technologies to provide customers with the ability to instantaneously track the location and status of their shipment anywhere around the world. These companies also find that utilizing GPS technologies helps them to use their containers far more productively by reducing the time they sit empty or in port. Exhibit 8-6 summarizes some of the key triggers that have lowered the costs of transportation, communications, and storage over the past decade.

Examples of Declining Transportation, Communication, and Storage Costs — EXHIBIT 8-6

Transport costs
- Containerization
- Intermodal shipping/rail
- Air freight

Communication costs
- More global long distance carriers
- Better ways to transmit voice, video, and data
- Internet access everywhere

Storage costs
- Refrigeration
- Just-in-time inventory
- Reduction of perishability
- Supply chain management
- Virtual production/design

Strategies for Global Expansion

Firms need to address two basic questions when thinking about developing effective strategies for competing globally: (1) *How can we extend our advantage by competing across many markets?* and (2) *How do we minimize our vulnerabilities and maximize our opportunities when competing globally?* The first question focuses on the issue of leveraging a critical resource, distinctive competence, or competitive advantage from one market to another. In the examples of Boeing and Coca-Cola, even though the products are vastly different, both companies realize that competing globally is an effective and necessary way to extend and reinforce their multiple sources of competitive advantage. Thus, the underlying issue behind global expansion is similar to that of expanding across industries in corporate strategies. Global expansion strategies concentrate on matching the firm's distinctive competence and line of products with the markets it will serve.

The second question addresses a different issue. Here, the focus is on building and managing global operations in a way to counter the actions and moves of other global competitors. Since global competition by its very nature involves strategies and actions that cut across multiple markets, the actions of a competitor in one market could very well present both vulnerabilities and opportunities in other markets. Individual global expansion strategies will thus require particular practices and ways of managing operations to deal with competitors' actions.

In other words, the issues surrounding global expansion strategies are similar to corporate strategy issues discussed in the preceding chapter. In corporate strategy, the decision to enter new activities, industries, and businesses should be based on the extent to which enlarging the firm's scope of operations reinforces and extends its distinctive competence. That issue was summarized in the question: Does a firm's presence in one set of activities or businesses benefit from expansion into another set? When examining globalization, a similar question exists: *To what degree does expansion into different regional markets help extend and reinforce the firm's distinctive competence?*

Global expansion involves creating and running large operations in markets outside the firm's home base. We now focus on two fundamentally different global expansion strategies for competing across multiple markets. One of the most important strategic choices firms must make is deciding whether to compete on a global basis or a multidomestic basis.[5] Firms pursue a **global strategy** when they seek to operate with worldwide consistency and a highly standardized approach across different markets. Firms pursue a **multidomestic strategy** when they adjust their products and operations according to each country or market they serve. Each strategy, to a large extent, is shaped by the economic requirements of the industry and the product.

global strategy: A strategy that seeks to achieve a high level of consistency and standardization of products, processes, and operations around the world; coordination of the firm's many subsidiaries to achieve high interdependence and mutual support.

multidomestic strategy: A strategy that seeks to adjust a firm's products, processes, and operations for markets and regions around the world; allows subsidiaries to tailor their products, marketing, and other activities according to the needs of their specific markets.

Global Strategy

Over the past decade, many companies have adopted global strategies because their markets have moved toward increasing standardization. Popular images of firms pursuing a global strategy, for example, include huge Japanese firms acting as economic juggernauts seeking to dominate every market in which they compete, or legendary IBM (Big Blue) developing and manufacturing all of the computers used in the world. In reality, a number of specific industry-driven factors have prompted firms from around the world to develop a global strategy. These factors include growing homogeneity of demand, rising economies of scale, increasing technological intensity of new products, the pressure to amortize high costs of R&D or other proprietary investments, and the need to avoid duplication of critical value-adding activities. These industry drivers oblige the firm to compete along a highly standardized and consistent manner across different markets.

A global strategy emphasizes operating with worldwide consistency and standardization at low relative cost. Firms pursuing a global strategy view all of their markets and subsidiaries as being *highly interdependent* and *mutually supporting* to achieve a high level of internal cohesion and consistency. Key to pursuing a global strategy is an integrated view of building and extending sources of competitive advantage that link up all of the firm's operations to create a unified value-adding delivery system. Firms undertaking a global strategy view each market in which they compete as a platform to learn new skills and techniques that are then applied in other markets. In other words, when a firm pursues a global strategy, actions or results that occur in one market can directly affect the others. This approach enables firms to maximize the benefits of exploiting worldwide economies of scale, rising technology intensity of new products, and growing homogeneity of demand. Moreover, a global strategy helps firms extend their distinctive competences to build leverage across markets. The mutually interdependent, systemwide view of a global strategy is shown in Exhibit 8-7. Firms pursuing global strategies tend to undertake the following actions to build leverage across markets: (1) standardize products as much as possible, (2) build their plants and factories in locations that maximize systemwide global competitive advantage, (3) leverage their technology across many regional markets, (4) coordinate marketing and sales worldwide, and (5) compete against other global competitors through cross-subsidization. (See Exhibit 8-8.)

Product Standardization. Global firms seek to standardize their products and designs as much as possible. In a full-blown global strategy, a high level of product standardization is essential not only to sell aggressively to markets that are increasingly homogeneous but also to capture low-cost economies of scale in production. In turn, standardized products often convey the image of design excellence, global acceptance, and world-class quality, as demonstrated by such highly regarded products as Sony Trinitron television sets, Minidiscmans, Walkmans, Citizen and Seiko watches, Panasonic VCRs, Motorola and Nokia phones, Hewlett-Packard calculators and laser printers, Toyota and Ford automobiles, and Caterpillar and Komatsu heavy construction equipment. Companies seek a high level of product

Global Strategy of Expansion — EXHIBIT 8-7

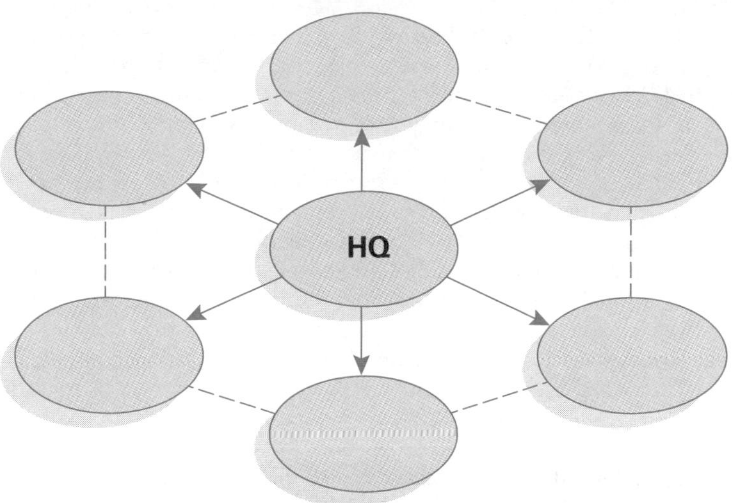

- Systemwide approach to competing worldwide
- Mutually interdependent subsidiaries
- Centralized control and reporting of activities
- Facilitates cross-subsidization policies across markets

Key Characteristics of a Global Strategy — EXHIBIT 8-8

- Standardized products
- Global economies of scale in key components and activities
- Leverage technology across many markets
- Global coordination of marketing and sales systemwide
- Cross-subsidization policies to respond to competitive moves by other global strategy firms

design standardization (with some minor adaptation or variation according to local power requirements, laws, or sizes) because it enables them to produce global volumes at low cost. Moreover, well-conceived and standardized product designs do much to increase the firm's marketing image. A strong image eases the firm's entry task of producing another line of products to serve the same markets in later periods.

In the case of Boeing, standardization of product designs is a predominant feature of the commercial aircraft industry. Although Boeing may produce different models of its 737, 747, 777, and other lines of aircraft, each aircraft line is manufactured and assembled in sequenced lots according to standardized product specifications. Components are fully standardized and shared across different aircraft wherever possible. Moreover, the demand for commercial aircraft tends to be highly uniform across buyers. Although individual aircraft may exhibit small differences—the design of the insignia for different national carriers and the layout of the first-class and coach cabins—these differences do not compromise Boeing's ability to produce its aircraft at low cost according to standardized airframe designs. Boeing's reputation for product excellence and durability, highly refined assembly techniques, and commitment to global service enhance its prospects to open additional markets for its aircraft.

Locating Plants to Maximize Systemwide Advantage. Another central facet of a global strategy is to maximize the total systemwide competitive advantage of the firm across multiple regional markets. Global strategy firms must invest in the newest production technologies to reap the benefits of economies of scale from serving all of its markets. Key to doing so is locating plants, factories, laboratories, facilities, and other crucial infrastructure in those worldwide sites that maximize the firm's sources of global leverage and scale economies. In other words, the decision to build plants and factories is based not only on the economics of serving individual local markets but also on maximizing the firm's competitive advantage and economies of scale across all of its subsidiaries and markets. For example, firms may locate some plants in low-cost countries to further reduce labor costs (as is the case with the textile or consumer electronics industries); they may locate their most sophisticated plants closest to their most important markets (cellular phone, construction equipment and automotive industries); or they may build only one or two giant, world-scale plants to serve the entire global market (steel and semiconductor companies). Thus, the decision to locate plants and laboratories globally is predicated on a systemic view of extending and leveraging the firm's scale-driven production base across all of its key markets, as opposed to scattering plants across many markets in a host of countries.

Ford Motor Company, for example, centralizes the production of many standardized engines and components in the United States but builds many of its transmissions and drive-train parts in Brazil and Mexico, where the cost of engineering and building such complex parts is lower. On the other hand, some of Ford's newest multivalve engines come from Ford factories and affiliates in Japan, where a greater abundance of multivalve technology and advanced production techniques is available. Cars that are to be sold in the United States are assembled here, while cars destined for Europe are assembled in locations throughout Britain and Germany. Thus, Ford's decisions to build and locate plants and facilities around the world are based on maximizing the firm's overall objective of being competitive and a low-cost producer for each critical component of the car.[6] In recent years, Ford's luxury line of Lincoln LS cars now shares the same chassis and drivetrain platforms with those used for the Jaguar XJS. Even though Ford seeks to maintain the unique identities of its European automotive acquisitions (Jaguar, Aston Martin, Volvo Cars), the company still actively searches for ways to use a common set of suppliers to lower its total procurement costs. Ford will even share components among all lines of vehicles (U.S. and European) to the extent that they do not compromise the unique experience that a customer feels when driving that particular line or type of car.

IBM also pursues a global strategy in its various computer, networking, consulting, and semiconductor operations. Many of IBM's mainframe computers are designed and built in the United States, but its most advanced laptop, notebook-sized computers are built in IBM facilities located in Japan, where there is an abundance of skills and expertise in manufacturing flat-panel display screens. On the other hand, IBM's line of personal computer products is built in several key locations in Korea, Taiwan, the United States, and Japan to take advantage of greater expertise and lower production costs for such core components as monitors, hard disk drives, operating software, and power packages. Conversely, IBM also supplies key components to a number of other PC firms as well, thus helping it gain economies of scale in semiconductors, disk drives, displays and power systems. These components are actually more profitable for IBM than the PC itself. Over the past few years, IBM is now facing the paradoxical situation wherein it is cheaper for the company to supply the parts for PCs rather than to make the entire PC itself.

In the Boeing example, the majority of Boeing's aircraft manufacturing and assembly operations takes place in its flagship plant in Everett, Washington, as well as in St. Louis and Long Beach where the company has refurbished some of McDonnell-Douglas's preexisting facilities. In facilities around Seattle, 65 percent of total world demand for commercial aircraft can be assembled in that one region. The size and sophistication of Boeing's recent manufacturing investments exemplify Boeing's commitment to economies of scale in component manufacture and final airframe assembly. Advanced machining and metal-cutting operations needed for aircraft wings are located in nearby supporting plants, while centralized development laboratories and facilities provide new composite or resin materials that help further reduce the weight and eventual cost of operating the plane. Also central to Boeing's enormous base of production expertise is the company's commitment to total quality management and continuous improvement. Boeing is constantly searching for new techniques that steadily improve the cost, quality, and durability of its airframes. Novel assembly techniques are continuously explored and tested to see if they can further reduce waste to speed up development time.

Leveraging Technology across Multiple Markets. Rising technological intensity of new products makes them correspondingly more expensive to develop and commercialize. High R&D costs that accompany more sophisticated products mean that global production volumes are necessary to recoup the firm's initial outlays. R&D represents a huge fixed cost in which large amounts of money and time are spent to test and finally develop a new product. Only by selling to the entire world can firms recoup their development costs. Thus, firms possessing highly proprietary technologies or distinctive, hard to imitate R&D skills and facilities often seek to blitz the world with their products.

For example, Honda Motor Company of Japan retains a distinctive technological capability in small combustion engine design and manufacture. Because of its expertise, Honda has been able to design and market engines for use in outboard motor boats, generators, lawnmowers, motorcycles, snowblowers, and, of course, its best-selling line of cars in the United States and Japan. The existence of a technological competence or skill encourages the firm to develop a full-blown global strategy, in which new applications of the underlying skill help build reputation, market share, and a global presence.

In highly scientific industries, such as pharmaceuticals, biotechnology and specialty plastics or chemicals, firms possessing highly proprietary technologies or patents on their products have also pursued a global strategy. Patents give the firm a temporary monopoly over its product, and thus entering worldwide markets greatly raises the firm's earnings potential.

In the commercial aircraft industry, Boeing pursues a global strategy because the cost of developing each new generation of aircraft is enormous. For example, the new 777—for which orders were taken before a single plane was manufactured—is equipped with extremely advanced technical features, such as fly-by-wire controls and avionics that perform many electronic control functions. Equally important, all of the parts and components for the 777 were designed and tested on computer before a single prototype of the plane was built. Instead of building costly and time-consuming models, Boeing used computers to electronically preassemble all of the plane's components. It also used digital imaging to locate the problem areas within the plane that could become difficult for mechanics to service. The advanced R&D and proprietary computer-assisted design (CAD) techniques possessed by Boeing provide it the capability to serve markets around the world.

Worldwide Marketing Efforts. Most marketing efforts by their very nature must be carried out within individual local markets. Marketing requires close contact with customers to ensure that the firm meets their needs. Yet, some marketing activities lend themselves well to supporting a global strategy. The most obvious case would be a centralized, global marketing team or sales force that specializes in selling highly sophisticated, expensive products that are purchased infrequently. In some industries, such as aircraft, power generation equipment, and telecommunications, a common sales force travels the globe in providing customers with specifications, costs, and individual features of the products. For example, in the power generation equipment industries, General Electric, ABB, Siemens, Toshiba, and Mitsubishi use global marketing and sales teams to compete with one another in selling large nuclear plants or intricate turbines that are used in hydroelectric and coal-burning electricity plants. The sales task is often highly complex, in that it involves discussing the specifications of the project with the customer over a lengthy period. Moreover, the number of people who have the detailed, technical knowledge behind such complex products and projects is few. This scarcity compels companies such as General Electric and ABB to rely on the same marketing team to travel the world in search of customers for power generation equipment.

Boeing and other commercial aircraft manufacturers have centralized their marketing efforts as well. Whether the customer is in Saudi Arabia, China, Brazil, or Japan, Boeing will send the same team that is knowledgeable about Boeing aircraft and their specifications to meet with potential customers. In this way, Boeing spreads the fixed costs of a highly sophisticated, technically fluent sales force over its many markets.

cross-subsidization: Using financial, technological, and marketing resources from one market to fight a competitor in another; involves extensive use of "parry and thrust" tactics to gain new market positions.

Competing by Cross-Subsidization. Firms pursuing a global strategy often engage in a policy known as cross-subsidization. **Cross-subsidization** refers to using the financial resources and technological skills learned from one market to fight a competitor in another. It is a powerful process that enables firms competing globally to build leverage across markets by transferring funds, skills, low-cost production, or market insights from one market to another. Cross-subsidization, in its most sophisticated form, is the deployment of resources and products across markets to maximize opportunities to build leverage. The presence of several large, global firms competing for the same market often indicates a strong potential for cross-subsidization. For example, Japanese and South Korean consumer electronics firms practice cross-subsidization in the sale of televisions and VCRs globally. The earnings they receive from their home market often allow them to fund expensive promotion efforts in the United States and Europe. Simultaneously, the marketing skills and techniques they learn from selling in one overseas market help them refine their techniques to enter another. Thus, cross-subsidization, when carried out effectively, enables firms pursuing a global strategy to build on success in one market to penetrate and fight competitors in another. Some authors have termed this type of global, cross-subsidization fight as "parry and thrust," which is also the phrase used to describe how fencers maneuver around one another when searching for weakness and advantage.[7] The careful coordination of the actions of its subsidiaries through cross-subsidization allows firms to achieve a systemwide view of competition and market share.

Cross-subsidization is a vital tool that enables firms to deal with the second issue of global expansion: How do we minimize our vulnerabilities and maximize our opportunities against the actions of similarly minded competitors? Cross-subsidization is directly concerned with the actions of competitors across shared markets. The actions and earnings of Sony in the European television market, for example, may have direct effects on the way it will compete in the U.S. market. Sony could use the potentially high profits earned from Europe to develop a new line of less costly televisions to penetrate the U.S. market even further, thus escalating its fight with other firms jockeying for the American market. Based on Sony's capability to use cross-subsidization in this manner, existing competitors in the U.S. market such as Toshiba, Sanyo, Sharp, Lucky-Goldstar, Samsung, General Electric, and Matsushita Electric have reason to watch and monitor Sony's moves in Europe and all of its other markets. Conversely, Sony needs to keep a watchful eye on Matsushita Electric, which may seek to build share in both the United States and adjacent markets. Matsushita's large domestic market in Japan and growing presence in Latin America will give Matsushita a source of funds that it could use to battle Sony elsewhere, perhaps in Southeast Asia or the Middle East. Thus, the competitive moves of firms that practice cross-subsidization resemble a global game of chess, whereby a move anywhere on the board (world markets) will eventually have ripple effects elsewhere.

Boeing's early 1990s strategy against global competitors Airbus and McDonnell-Douglas shows how cross-subsidization applies even when an industry has only three competitors. Both Boeing and Airbus sought to build market positions around the world, while McDonnell-Douglas was largely concerned with protecting its U.S. market base. Boeing frequently offers superior financing, servicing, and other buying incentives to its vital European customers, such as Lufthansa and Air France. A strengthened position in Europe gives Boeing more room to maneuver against Airbus in its home base. By selling more planes to European customers, Boeing squeezes Airbus's cash position and market share. On the other hand, Airbus is likely to offer its own set of superior and possibly more attractive financing terms to its customers in North America, such as United Airlines and American

Airlines. If Airbus is successful (and it has become even more so in recent years), then it gains a valuable beachhead from which to penetrate Boeing's home market with other types of aircraft in the future. Airbus has even secured commitments from FedEx to purchase its A380 aircraft for cargo shipment applications. Thus, Boeing and Airbus are engaged in constant parrying and thrusting into each other's markets.

Note that McDonnell-Douglas, a weak third player in the 1980s and early 1990s, was largely unable to move against Boeing or Airbus successfully, since its excessive reliance on the U.S. commercial market gave it little leverage against either firm elsewhere. Thus, it is no accident that both Airbus and Boeing gained strength at the expense of McDonnell-Douglas, since its lack of a global presence handicapped it against better armed competitors. Boeing's recent acquisition of McDonnell-Douglas occurred at a time when McDonnell-Douglas could no longer afford to commit vast sums of money into development expenditures for a market base that was increasingly squeezed by two larger competitors practicing cross-subsidization.

Thus, global strategies are designed to link the firm's operations in many markets into a systemwide perspective for building and extending competitive advantage. Global strategy seeks to exploit technologically driven sources of leverage. Leverage results when the firm can extend and transfer its skills and resources across markets that are interdependent and mutually reinforcing. When pursued successfully, global strategy maximizes a firm's opportunities to transfer its products, processes, and competences from one market to another.

Multidomestic Strategy

A multidomestic strategy is often the preferred way to compete when regional markets contrast with one another in terms of consumer tastes and preferences and competitive conditions. The more diverse the regional or national market condition, the greater is the appeal of the multidomestic strategy. A multidomestic strategy is really a collection of country or region-based strategies, where each region or country (defined by the firm's economic reach and organizational approach) possesses its own set of value-adding activities or value chains. Popular images of firms pursuing a multidomestic strategy, for example, include various sizes and tastes of Maxwell House coffee or Snapple teas in China, India, and other locales where these offerings are considered new and perhaps exotic products. Nestlé's assortment of chocolate candies that are mixed to suit varying tastes in different countries also represents a multidomestic strategy. A number of economic and industry-driven factors promote the use of multidomestic strategies for a given industry. These industry drivers include heterogeneous demand patterns across markets, few economies of scale in production, high product transportation costs, variations in distribution channels across markets, and the need to source products locally because of perishability, legal requirements, or specific types of ingredients or components.

Firms pursuing a multidomestic strategy adjust and tailor their products and practices to the individual needs of each market. As opposed to a global strategy, a multidomestic strategy treats each market independently and separately. Firms pursuing multidomestic strategies also view competitive challenges in the context of local conditions and therefore do not attempt to form a completely unified, systemwide approach to building and extending competitive advantage. Key to a successful multidomestic strategy is treating each market as a unique arena from which to differentiate the firm's products as much as possible from those of local producers or other multidomestic competitors. Thus, value chains in one market may be significantly different from value chain configurations designed for another market with very different economic or environmental settings. In other words, *a firm pursuing a multidomestic strategy must deal with the very real possibility that each market will require its own value chain, with few opportunities to share costs or activities among them.* The lack of sufficient economies of scale across multiple markets is a critical industry factor that promotes a multidomestic strategy. The multidomestic strategy's independent and separate treatment of markets and subunits is shown in Exhibit 8-9.

Although firms undertaking a multidomestic strategy can sometimes transfer what they have learned from one market to another, this transfer is difficult to do on a consistent

EXHIBIT 8-9 Multidomestic Strategy of Expansion

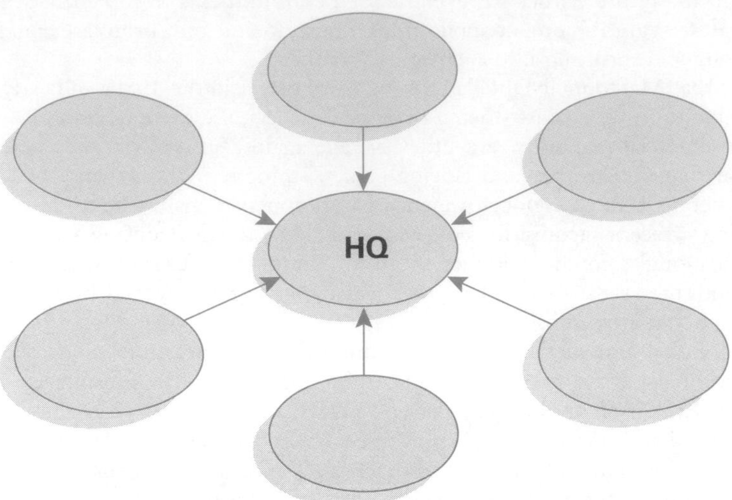

- Competitive advantage built in each separate national or regional market
- Markets and subunits treated independently from one another
- Controls of activities are decentralized, reporting back to headquarters

basis because of the numerous value chains dedicated to each market. Because the individual markets are often so unlike one another, the firm must essentially retrace its steps to build competitive advantage in each market, making it difficult to leverage highly tangible skills or resources across markets. Firms pursuing a multidomestic strategy tend to exhibit the following practices to build competitive advantage in each market: (1) adapt and change their products frequently, (2) conduct key value-adding activities and operations in each market locally, (3) coordinate marketing and sales within individual markets, and (4) leverage a brand name or reputation globally to build image. (See Exhibit 8-10.)

EXHIBIT 8-10 Key Characteristics of a Multidomestic Strategy

- Customization or frequent adaptation of products for each separate market
- Few systemwide opportunities for economies of scale
- Value-adding activities performed and duplicated in each market
- Coordination of marketing and sales within each market
- Quality and image across markets are important sources of competitive advantage

Frequent Product Adaptation. Central to the multidomestic strategy is frequent product adaptation and modification to match the specific tastes and consumer preferences of a firm's individual markets. In stark contrast to a global strategy, in which product standardization often conveys the image of quality, frequent product adaptation in a multidomestic strategy is required because the product or service does truly differ along some critical attribute across markets. Superior quality in such products as food, beverages, banking, clothing, and even some categories of industrial goods and supplies is not based on standardized features, but rather on how closely the products fit the targeted market. For example, most competitors in the food processing and consumer nondurable industries, such as Procter & Gamble, H.J. Heinz, General Mills, Philip Morris, and PepsiCo all practice some variation of a multidomestic strategy. Tide detergent, Heinz ketchup, Marlboro cigarettes, and Pepsi cola drinks, to note a few examples, are actually quite different, depending on where you purchase the product. Other industries characterized by a high level of multidomestic competition include textiles, brewing, automotive motor oils, local telephone services, and personal banking. In each of these cases, the product or service in question is customized to the individual market segment that is targeted.

In a multidomestic strategy, each firm seeks to identify the most important attributes of a product to a specific market and then to closely tailor its offerings to that market. McDonald's restaurants are found worldwide, but the servings offered in a restaurant in France or Germany, for example, are likely to differ significantly from those in the United States and Japan. McDonald's serves beer and a particular menu of sandwiches in its German restaurants, while in Japan it offers a special kind of fish sandwich and beverages that taste unlike those in the United States. In the personal care and cosmetics industry, firms such as Estée Lauder, Procter & Gamble, Revlon, and Lancôme often customize the blends that become ingredients used for eye makeup, face creams, cleansing solutions, and other care products. A cosmetic company must often consider such region-specific factors as the daily amount of sun, water hardness or acidity conditions, skin complexions, and likely personal habits of customers in deciding how to tailor its products to each market.

Product adaptation is sometimes necessary because of local laws and regulations stipulating that certain products use a high percentage of domestic content. For example, certain segments of the machine tool industry are multidomestic in nature because host governments demand that multinational firms produce a given portion of their product using local labor and supplies of materials. This is particularly the case for those industries that a local government considers strategic or vital to its national development. Thus, although machine tools such as lathes and drills would ordinarily exhibit economic characteristics favoring a more global strategy, local restrictions can sometimes make a multidomestic strategy the best alternative for a firm serving local markets.

Coke practices a high degree of product adaptation and modification across every market it serves. Rapid product testing, introduction, and adaptation are the hallmarks of Coke's product strategy worldwide. Product testing and development are performed in each individual market, since market research for one country or region is unlikely to show trends that are identical to another market. In the United States, Coke is best known for its Coca-Cola, Diet Coke, Sprite, Diet Sprite, and Mello Yellow carbonated beverages. Although Coke offers its cola-based drinks in a similar form and taste in Japan and Europe, the sweetness levels are altered from one market to the next. Also, Coke develops and introduces new brands in many of its markets besides the United States. For example in Japan, the company has pioneered and sold large quantities of its beta carotene–based beverages aimed at a specific health-conscious segment. In Australia, flavored carbonated beverages sold under the brand names Skysurfer and Lift are unlike beverages that people are accustomed to in the United States. The sizes of containers that Coke uses for its beverages vary greatly across regions. Even the size of aluminum cans used for convenience packaging of Coke's products is adjusted.

Local Value-Adding Activities. Another key facet of the multidomestic strategy is to perform all critical value-adding functions locally. In effect, a pure multidomestic strategy is an aggregate collection of many separate value chains, each of which is found within the market it serves. Each market has its own R&D, manufacturing, and marketing functions to perform the value-adding activities needed to compete there. Thus, firms in multidomestic industries tend to produce or source their products locally. Several economic factors promote the need to establish separate value-adding activities in each market, including high perishability of product, the lack of economies of scale in production, and high transportation costs resulting from a low value-added/weight ratio.

High perishability is often a factor promoting multidomestic strategies. **Perishability**, in the broadest sense, occurs when a product or service is not used by a certain time. The most obvious case of high perishability as a significant strategic factor is the food-

perishability: The loss of economic value that occurs when a product or service is not used within a given time period, often used to describe the ease with which a product spoils or decays; a major economic consideration that promotes the use of multidomestic strategies.

processing industry, in which eggs, meat, and dairy products spoil rapidly, in days if not hours. The need for extensive refrigeration, warehousing, and careful packaging is best performed in local facilities, since transportation costs associated with moving highly fragile or perishable products are prohibitive. Perishability is the primary reason why milk (which actually exhibits a high degree of consistency worldwide) is not a global industry.

The lack of significant production economies of scale is a major factor in keeping manufacturing activities within each regional market. Many products still do not offer sufficient global economies of scale to warrant central production. For example, leather and tanning products still remain largely multidomestic in nature, although some Brazilian and Italian firms are starting to export large quantities of their fine quality shoes to Europe, the United States, and other markets. The building controls industry is another example where the need to adapt and produce parts locally outweighs any large economies of scale in components. Companies such as TRW, United Technologies, Honeywell, and General Electric tend to manage their building controls businesses in a multidomestic approach, since it is easier to build or source low-voltage transformers and other mature electrical supply products locally. Other products by their very nature must be built locally, such as engineering-intensive projects. Engineering, contracting, and construction companies such as Bechtel, Morrison-Knudsen, and Halliburton's Brown and Root subsidiary often establish local offices to manage their projects under contract. The "components" or raw ingredients used for their products and services (reinforced cement and gravel) are products and supplies best provided locally. High cost prohibits their shipment, but, more important, local rock and mineral conditions dictate what kinds of materials can be used for a particular project. Even though these firms have world-class engineers (located both locally and around the world) who are highly mobile, the need to deal with the customer on a day-to-day basis for several years after the contract is signed means that the actual building, servicing, and management operations remain local.

Another factor that favors the multidomestic strategy is *low value-added/weight ratio*. Perhaps the best example of a low value-added/weight ratio product is that of reinforced cement, mentioned in the preceding paragraph. Cement is a highly standardized product with numerous uses. It also faces a market with homogeneous demand. Yet, the costs of shipping reinforced concrete anywhere is prohibitive. That is why even in the United States, local highway projects, shopping centers, office buildings, and subway construction use cement that is actually manufactured or mixed on-site. Its use of ingredients with a low value-added/weight ratio is also why most construction and building industries remain a multidomestic industry throughout the world. On the other hand, architectural and engineering talent is becoming more global in nature, since technical knowledge and experience can easily be leveraged from one project to another. Other products that exhibit a low value-added/weight ratio include unprocessed farm crops (wheat, corn, oats), raw pulp, and other intermediate products that are refined into more valuable products farther down the value chain.

Coke's global distribution system is actually a collection of many distribution and bottling centers located around the world. Each nation or region that is a market for Coke's broad range of products houses a Coke concentrate plant and bottling/packaging facility. Thus, when Coca-Cola seeks to enter a new market, it must also invest in the corresponding value-adding processes related to concentrate mixing and bottling, as well as distribution of the final product. The nature of soft drink concentrate, while valuable in making different types of beverages, does not lend itself to world-scale production located in one or two plants. Soft drink concentrate does exhibit some degree of perishability. Governments in local countries also prefer that Coke establish local beverage concentrate production and facilities within their countries to boost employment. Moreover, unprocessed concentrate has a low value-added/weight ratio that, when combined with perishability, prohibits costly shipment over long distances.

In addition, the bottling of Coca-Cola and other soft drink products is clearly a multidomestic industry in itself. First, the nature of packaging activities means that glass bottles and aluminum cans must be procured. Glass breaks easily, thus making it troublesome to ship over long distances at high cost. Aluminum cans consume a lot of space when shipped. Thus, the containers used to package Coke's numerous product offerings by themselves favor local sourcing and production. Second, bottling activities do not lend themselves well to significant economies of scale and experience curve effects, giving Coke little incentive to centralize the production of glass or aluminum containers. Third, the storage of the final Coca-Cola or soft drink products requires considerable space and inventory management. Inventories of perishable or fragile products are often best managed at the local site by managers who are more knowledgeable about which specific drinks are preferred by people in that particular market. Thus, local management helps avoid production and inventory surges or fluctuations that raise costs.

Local Distribution Channels. Firms competing in multidomestic industries must understand and manage a broad range of distribution channels. Each country is likely to have its own distinct way of distributing products throughout its economic system. Even across Europe, stark differences in the distribution and shopping habits can be observed within individual nations. In Germany, a large volume of products is sold through huge hypermarts that are even bigger than the shopping warehouse clubs found in the United States. In Italy, on the other hand, the distribution channels are highly complex and convoluted. Instead of large supermarkets and hypermarts, small retailers (almost overwhelmingly family owned) tend to dominate distribution, even in large cities such as Milan and Florence. Numerous middlemen and wholesalers make it difficult for firms to sell their products without maintaining substantial operations there. France and Great Britain contrast with Germany and Italy in that distribution channels are even more region-specific within the same country.

Multidomestic firms develop their own distinctive strategies for each market's distribution channels and other unique, region-specific features. Procter & Gamble, for example, has its own sophisticated, computer-driven warehousing system that ships vast quantities of Tide detergent and other products to its German wholesalers and retailers quickly. On the other hand, Procter & Gamble relies on an array of middlemen to manage the inventory flow of Tide to reach customers in Italy and France. In recent years, P&G has restructured its European operations in an attempt to centralize more of its product development and distribution activities to cater to a greater, pan-European market. New products are designed to serve a broader market base, although so far the reception has been mixed. Entrenched middlemen, wholesalers, and retailers in a number of countries, plus shifting currency exchange rates, complicate P&G's ability to price its products uniformly across the continent.

Procter & Gamble's largest competitors (e.g., Colgate-Palmolive, Unilever, Henkel, and Kao of Japan) have confronted similar problems in trying to develop a wider, pan-European strategy. Like Procter & Gamble, Nestlé has attempted to concentrate its efforts on key products that appear to attract large, similar segments from different markets. Its white chocolate candy bars, for example, are a hit in both the United States and Europe. On the other hand, some of Nestlé's other products, such as instant chocolate drinks, confront more traditional multidomestic issues, such as separate distribution systems for highly perishable products. Kmart, the large U.S. discount retailer, commenced operations during 1995 in Prague, Czech Republic, after having bought out an existing retailer a few years back. It is finding that despite the Czech population's zeal for lower-priced goods and imports, managing the distribution system that brings products into its flagship stores is an arduous task, particularly in a nation that was previously more accustomed to state-run distribution systems where pricing flexibility and wide product choice were nonexistent. Kmart must deal with a host of middlemen and other distribution players (often relics of previous state ownership) that eats into its cost advantage.

Coke believes that marketing and distribution is best managed at local levels, where knowledgeable managers and personnel have the inside track to identify and sidetrack potential problems involved with shipment of Coke's products. Coke conducts extensive market research and testing of its products for every market. Coke's distribution system in each nation runs the gamut from vending machines in isolated hotels and gas stations, to soft drink stands, to huge supermarkets (where they exist). For each distribution channel, Coke develops a specific distribution strategy to ensure that its products reach maximum coverage for a given area. Although Coke prefers that its local managers and affiliates manage the details of each operation, Coke ensures that managers understand the company's values and commitment to product quality and to treating its customers right. Aside from these two guiding imperatives, Coke gives its distribution and marketing people free rein over developing specific regional strategies.

Leveraging a Global Brand Name. Multidomestic strategies by their very nature require firms to locate their key value-adding activities in each market they serve. Yet, firms pursuing multidomestic strategies can still attempt to build sources of leverage and competitive advantage across markets. The most important source of leverage for each firm comes from cultivating and extending its well-known quality image to new products and markets. Many of the companies that practice multidomestic strategies (e.g., Nestlé, H. J. Heinz, Kellogg, Procter & Gamble, Unilever, McDonald's, PepsiCo, and Philip Morris, to name just a few) have tried to develop and foster their own corporate images of quality that help with entry into new markets. On the one hand, the nature of these firms' product offerings/foods, restaurants, laundry detergents, soft drinks and beverages, and personal care products/makes local value-adding activities a necessity. On the other hand, these firms have been careful to build up a strong corporate association with high product quality. Thus, markets around the world can come to expect a certain level of high quality with McDonald's restaurant offerings, with PepsiCo's soft drinks and snack foods, and with P&G's or Henkel's laundry detergents and soaps. Even though each firm's products are multidomestic, these companies can still develop strong global images. In effect, a strong quality reputation provides competitive strength in each local market and helps provide a unifying framework for developing a global brand franchise.

Coke is a leading practitioner of standardizing its image so that people around the world realize the quality of the product they are buying. It believes that its contour-shaped bottles and red-and-white logo surrounding Coca-Cola should convey not only a low-cost source of refreshment, but also other deeper emotions, such as joy, laughter, and personal renewal. To support high quality and a corporate image of refreshment, Coke carefully selects the managers and personnel who work with the company in its many markets. Because it prefers to delegate local marketing strategy to individuals, the company must be sure that the people it hires have a passionate dedication to Coke's products and, more importantly, its quality values. Another commitment that reinforces Coke's global image of quality and refreshment is the company's long-standing support of charitable and community-oriented programs that promote health and other human virtues. Coke hopes the acceptance of its products will be as universal as the desire for good health and happiness around the world. Coke remains a huge sponsor of many sporting events, such as soccer matches throughout the developing world. In addition, it contributes generously to health research and foundations to improve the human body and spirit in its many markets. By giving back substantial sums to the communities it serves, Coke continues to embellish its global quality image.

Thus, multidomestic strategies are an aggregate collection of the firm's many distinct and discrete operations in multiple markets. Unlike a global strategy, a multidomestic strategy does not explicitly seek to link up markets and subsidiaries through shared technologies, products, and processes. Even as the Internet begins to connect a firm's local subsidiaries into an integrated information and communication platform, the specific strategies and marketing programs for each subsidiary still remain largely autonomous. The needs of satisfying local customers often continue to outweigh the gains of centralized coordination of subsidiary actions and local strategies. Instead, firms that compete multidomestically do so on a market-by-market basis. Each subsidiary is free to formulate and execute its own strategies for the market it serves, since pricing, local tastes and customs, regulations, distribution channels, product differences still represent major strategic considerations. Leverage in a multidomestic firm is not based on shared technologies, products, or production processes, but rather on creating a well-known, high-quality, worldwide image.

Benefits of Global Expansion

Global expansion can help the firm achieve numerous benefits. Whether its strategy is global or multidomestic, global expansion can create numerous sources of value and help the firm reinforce its competitive advantage. Some of the most important value-creating benefits of global expansion include (1) market growth and expansion, (2) the recovery of investment costs, (3) the creation of a strong image, and (4) accelerated learning and transfer of new knowledge and skills (see Exhibit 8-11).

Benefits of Global Expansion — EXHIBIT 8-11

- Market growth and expansion opportunities
- Recovery of R&D and investment costs
- Creation of a distinct image
- Accelerated learning and transfer of new skills

Market Growth and Expansion

Globalization allows firms to overcome the limits of domestic growth. For U.S., European, and Japanese companies in particular, global expansion is a necessity because many domestic markets are maturing and growth rates are slowing down. Numerous sectors of the U.S. economy, including service-oriented businesses, such as fast foods, packaged goods, grocery store chains, beverages and even telecommunications, are not growing as fast as they used to. On the other hand, the opening of vast new markets in China, Eastern Europe, and Latin America means that U.S. firms such as McDonald's, Colgate-Palmolive, Safeway, and SBC Communications can continue to grow and create new sources of value. Thus, companies can expand globally to achieve benefits similar to diversifying into new industries; they can maintain their growth momentum and extend their competitive advantage in new markets.

Globalization also enables the firm to outperform local domestic competitors in their home markets. When a firm expands globally, it develops new insights and identifies new product opportunities that may not be available to competitors who remain domestic in orientation. The trials of going abroad help the firm refine and reinforce its competitive advantage. The lack of global awareness was a big problem with the Big Three automakers during the 1970s and 1980s. Although General Motors and Ford had substantial European operations, senior management in the United States was primarily concerned with "milking" the domestic market. Japanese competitors, such as Toyota, Nissan, and Honda, on the other hand, were looking to expand beyond their small domestic base. They made deep inroads into the U.S. market that not only persist, but also continue to grow even today. Although Ford has made great strides to globalize its operations and enter new markets, General Motors and Chrysler until recently still remain handicapped because they have comparatively fewer operations outside the United States than does Ford. Chrysler now has enormous global reach through its merger with Daimler-Benz, while GM has large equity holdings of other car companies (e.g., Saab, Fuji Motor, Isuzu, Suzuki).

Through global expansion a firm can realize the related benefit of keeping competitors at bay and effectively barring them from cross-subsidizing into the firm's home market. For example, Caterpillar maintains a small presence in Japan to keep tabs on Komatsu, its most important competitor in the construction, earth-moving, and heavy equipment industry. If Caterpillar did not maintain even a small presence in Japan, Komatsu would likely feel less constrained about taking on Caterpillar more aggressively in the

United States and other national markets. IBM Japan serves an extremely valuable purpose for all of IBM. Having a major presence in Japan helps IBM learn critical new technologies that can be applied to its entire line of computer and semiconductor products. More important, IBM Japan serves to constrain the actions of such key competitors as Fujitsu, Toshiba, NEC, and Hitachi. Despite fierce competition from these companies, IBM Japan serves as a vital "strategic window" that IBM can use to monitor its competitors. Most recently, IBM Japan in 2001 is actually beginning to gain significant market share from Fujitsu and NEC in mainframe computers. In September 2001, IBM Japan's efforts in rebuffing its competitors were so successful that Fujitsu has even announced that it will no longer make IBM-compatible mainframe computers—an effort that Fujitsu once considered to be its core undertaking during the 1970s and 1980s.

In a similar vein, Xerox once owned 50 percent of Fuji-Xerox Corporation. Fuji-Xerox played a major role in helping the U.S. copier giant learn how to compete using such Japanese manufacturing techniques as lean production, total quality management, and just-in-time inventory systems. As Xerox Corporation almost went into financial collapse during the 1980s, many observers believe that Fuji-Xerox's presence in Japan helped Xerox not only to learn how to make better copiers but also to constrain the actions of fierce Japanese competitors such as Canon, Sharp, Minolta, and Ricoh. Even though Xerox recently sold off part of its interest in Fuji-Xerox to restructure its domestic U.S. operations, the company still retains a 25 percent share of Fuji-Xerox to keep abreast of new technologies and manufacturing techniques.

On the other hand, both Zenith and Goodyear operated at a substantial disadvantage in the color television and tire industries in the face of competitors that leveraged attacks on the U.S. market from other national markets. Zenith faced this problem when confronted by Japanese producers of televisions who could undercut Zenith in the United States by subsidizing their operations from home and elsewhere. Eventually, Zenith was completely defeated in the market share wars for color television sets and was eventually bought out by Korean competitor Lucky-Goldstar. Michelin was able to seize significant market share from Goodyear and other domestically oriented tire firms by using its European and Canadian operations as a springboard to subsidize a bold and aggressive entry into the U.S. market. Thus, firms need to formulate and implement global expansion strategies so that they can match the cross-subsidization and "parry and thrust" moves of their competitors.

Recovery of Investment Costs

Globalization is a powerful method to help recover the investment costs required for new products and processes. As noted earlier, selling at global volumes is a requirement for innovation in many industries. The recovery of huge investments for R&D and production facilities is an overwhelming incentive for firms in high-technology industries to expand globally. Semiconductor, pharmaceutical, aircraft, communication and medical equipment, advanced materials, and other industries need global markets to build sufficient economies of scale to recover their sunk costs. Multidomestic firms also can recover investments in brand names by expanding globally. Although multidomestic firms do not share the same economies of scale that global firms do, companies such as Coca-Cola, Nestlé, Colgate-Palmolive, and Unilever have invested heavily into their brand names that are effectively intangible assets that can be applied abroad. **Intangible assets** represent firm-based resources, skills or other hard-to-imitate assets that are not physical in form. These can include investments in brand equity, human talent, a unique approach to product development, means to foster innovation, and other resources that help make the firm distinctive.

intangible assets: Resources based on skills or other hard-to-imitate assets that are not physical in form; examples include brand equity, fast product development, management techniques, proprietary means of developing knowledge, innovation, and so forth.

Creation of a Strong Image

Both multidomestic and global firms enhance their image when they expand globally with quality products. A strong image works as an investment that can ease entry into new markets later, thus extending a competitive advantage over time. In other words, a strong, globally recognized image becomes an intangible but vital building block of competitive advantage that lays the foundation for creating future value. For many firms, their brand names and quality image have become almost synonymous with their distinctive competences, and thus represent durable but intangible assets that serve to implement an "umbrella" strategy.

Consider the wide line of products that Sony uses to enter new markets. Because Sony's television sets and other consumer electronics are so well built and engineered, new Sony products, such as electric shavers, food mixers, and even air conditioners, are likely to receive a warm reception in new markets as well. Sony's distinctive competence in designing and producing high-quality, technically advanced consumer electronics and gadgets (a key aspect of a global strategy) thus "spills over" into emerging high-tech household appliances and new markets. Consequently, Sony's task of entering new markets with new products becomes much easier over time, since Sony's highly burnished image helps extend its competitive advantage in unforeseen ways. Sony's image thus serves as an umbrella that protects its new products from fierce competition and consumer skepticism. For example, Sony's rapid rise to challenge both Nintendo and Sega in the fiercely competitive video game business stems from many consumers' experience and belief that a Sony-made product will consistently be world-class. As Sony begins to enter other electronic and Internet-driven arenas, the company's strong brand equity allows it to lower the cost of entry and risk in pursuing new ventures. In other words, strong brand equity and images are fixed investments in value-creating assets; reputation and quality give these firms (both global and multidomestic) a decided and enduring competitive advantage, which facilitates new market entry. This same emphasis on building and sustaining a strong brand equity and presence for packaged foods and beverage companies has also enabled many U.S. multinational giants establish strong market positions overseas.[8]

The American Express Company also realizes the benefits of a well-known and well-defined image that brings forth the idea of quality, security and safety. One of American Express's strategic missions is to create the "world's most respected brand name." Travelers around the world recognize the reliability and quality that are behind the blue, square American Express logo. Although each American Express region pursues its own specific advertising and marketing (multidomestic strategy), all travel offices follow a common set of procedures to help people in need (common practices to reinforce quality and image). Travelers or tourists who encounter trouble can go to an American Express office for emergency replacement of travelers' checks or lost or stolen credit cards. In addition, all American Express offices are equipped to send emergency telegrams and messages to families, consulates, and other contacts of the people in need.

Accelerated Learning

One of the most important benefits of globalization is the ability to learn and transfer new knowledge within the firm. Global and multidomestic firms, through their exposure to numerous environments, products, and markets, are constantly receiving vast amounts of information concerning competitors, customers, and new technologies. Firms with large operations become storehouses of new knowledge and skills, especially if they possess distinctive competences in core R&D, production, or marketing techniques. The need to seek a return on proprietary technologies and brand names encourages expanding firms to design new products and to enter new markets. In turn, by doing so, firms accumulate new insights that can be used to generate products for other markets. Global and multidomestic firms acquire their knowledge and skills from high-intensity competition with other global and domestic firms

The effect of global competition on these firms is the building of a substantial value-adding infrastructure that allows for faster transfer of ideas, insights, and skills across their subsidiaries. Such information has helped global companies such as Sony, Texas Instruments, Nokia, and IBM to develop a range of products that flow through these firms' vast R&D, production, and distribution systems. Similarly, multidomestic firms such as Coca-Cola,

Nestlé, Procter & Gamble, Diageo, Henkel, Electrolux, and PepsiCo can take advantage of the insights and new ideas learned from one market to enter new markets under a well-recognized global umbrella of brands.

Costs of Globalization

Although global expansion strategies can provide firms with huge benefits, managing overseas operations also involves substantial costs. Many of these expansion-related costs are organizational. Coordinating operations across multiple, diverse markets generates significant tensions and pressures within a company. Also, companies are exposed to the volatilities and idiosyncrasies of operating in different markets. Thus, while regions of the world are still prospering, others, such as Southeast Asia during the late 1990s, have suffered recessions. As Southeast Asia entered a difficult period of recession and recovery, many U.S. firms with extensive operations there, such as 3M, Boeing, and IBM, reeled from the effects of lessened demand.[9]

In many ways, global expansion can present a double-edged sword, since such expansion can often expose firms to different types of economic cycles and practices they would not have ordinarily incurred with a more domestic approach.[10] Nonetheless, as markets become more integrated and as technology links people from around the world through cheap communications, the costs of global expansion should still be viewed in the context of building a wide base of firm capabilities and planting the seeds for new sources of competitive advantage that will ideally give the firm significantly more growth when market demand becomes more homogeneous, technologically similar, or when emerging markets recover. Thus, even though economic conditions in one part of the world may be less than favorable, they also create opportunities for firms willing to strengthen their positions by buying out their joint venture partners or increasing management control over ventures and activities in that region.

For example, despite the great turmoil and recessionary pressures that confronted firms competing in Southeast Asia, many Japanese firms continued to invest in local operations in Thailand, Malaysia, Singapore, and other nations because they believe it is an opportunity to further strengthen their investment hold and market position when other foreign rivals are contemplating exit. Management in several Japanese firms believes that Southeast Asia's troubles open up opportunities to solidify their market positions even at a time when they are likely to lose money in the short term. For example, Nissho Iwai Corporation, a leading Japanese trading corporation, recently increased its ownership of Thai Central Chemical Republic Co., a leading fertilizer firm in the region. Nissho Iwai increased its ownership stake from 24 percent to 42 percent by purchasing additional shares in Thai Central Chemical at a substantial discount. Moreover, other Nissho Iwai–affiliated companies have also increased their ownership of the same firm to over 11 percent, thus giving Nissho Iwai effective control over its Thai partner's operations. In another case, Honda Motor Company says it will use its Thailand-based operations to increase exports of its Honda Accord models to Australia and New Zealand to take advantage of the region's depreciating currency effects. Honda believes the regional downturn is temporary and is willing to continue investing there, despite short-term profitability pressures.[11]

A few U.S. firms have begun to view their joint ventures in Asia as opportunities to increase their presence at a time when domestic competitors in Korea, Indonesia, Thailand, and elsewhere are feeling the pressures from recessionary downturns. Great Lakes Chemical, a leading U.S. specialty chemical manufacturer, expanded its equity stake in Miwon Chemical of Korea. The two companies have operated a joint venture in Korea for a number of years, but management at Great Lakes Chemical believes it can further expand its presence throughout Asia by forming additional joint ventures with companies that need a partner for financial and technological assistance. Parker Hannifin, a leading U.S. manufacturer of industrial controls and fluids, viewed the economic difficulties in Asia as a buying opportunity. In March 1998, Parker Hannifin bought out two majority-owned joint venture stakes from its long-standing partner, H S Group of Korea. By selling out, H S Group receives badly needed cash, while Parker Hannifin gains control of some key plants that manufacture air-conditioning components.

Other U.S. firms have noted that the Asian economic downturn offers tremendous opportunities to gain access to markets that were previously difficult to penetrate. For example, in January 1999, GE Capital, a unit of General Electric, bought over $6 billion worth of assets from Japan Leasing Corp., a unit of Long-Term Credit Bank of Japan. Likewise, GE Capital also purchased Koei Credit Company and Lake Credit, two Japanese lenders in the subprime market in 1998. GE Capital hopes that its investment in Asian companies will enable it to earn significant returns in the next few years.

In a similar move to bolster its Southeast Asian market presence, U.S. foods company H. J. Heinz bought out its Indonesian joint venture partners in the local food processing industry. Heinz believes that growth in Southeast Asia will continue in the future, but the current recessions offers significant opportunities to acquire new assets to compete in the future. In fact, Heinz strengthened its position in the Japanese market by forming a tighter alliance with another Japanese food producer, Kagome Company, that has strong distribution advantages in its own home market. Kagome is Japan's largest producer of tomato-processed foods and vegetable juices, which are natural complements to Heinz's enormous strengths and market presence for ketchup, seasonings and other condiments. Heinz has also solidified its relationship with other Asian companies, such as Universal Food Corp. and Southeast Asia Food, both of the Philippines.[12]

Among the most serious costs often associated with globalization are those arising from (1) strategic leverage, (2) loss of flexibility, and (3) efforts required to coordinate businesses across market lines (see Exhibit 8-12).

Costs Associated with Global Expansion — EXHIBIT 8-12

Costs of strategic leverage
- Sustained investment required
- Preserving and extending image

Costs of flexibility
- High interdependence of subsidiaries (and businesses)
- Change or development affecting all markets

Costs of cooperation
- Compromise
- Accountability

Cost of Strategic Leverage

One of the more significant costs imposed on a firm by global expansion is the cost of identifying and leveraging sources of competitive advantage across diverse, multiple markets. Identifying points of leverage requires the firm to focus on critical value-adding activities. These are applied to build and sustain advantage across its markets. Building systemwide leverage applies especially to global strategy firms. In these companies, leverage comes from interdependent and mutually supporting subsidiaries working together. However, the costs of building leverage are also present with multidomestic firms, although in a different way. In these firms, leverage comes primarily from cultivating strong brand images, as opposed to technology-driven investments in global firms. Because the sources of leverage are distinct for global and multidomestic firms, the costs of building leverage will depend upon the strategy employed.

Successful global strategies require firms to manage and view their subsidiaries as a single system, not as a loose collection of national markets. Shared production forces managers to allocate resources and investments according to criteria that support the firm's competitive advantage. The biggest cost of leverage in global firms is the sustained, continued investment in a key source of competitive advantage. In other words, resources committed to a particular competence or skill are likely to require sustained investment over time. Thus, building leverage in global firms imposes on managers an ongoing need to fund one or more key resources. In the case of Boeing, investment funds are needed to support the company's commitment to leading-edge electronics, manufacturing, and lean production techniques that are used across all its models of aircraft. New technologies, such as fly-by-wire controls that replace hydraulic controls and composite materials that substitute for aluminum and metal, are viewed as critical levers that help Boeing achieve a stronger competitive advantage over Airbus and potential entrants from the Far East and Japan.

In multidomestic firms such as Coca-Cola, Nestlé, Procter & Gamble, Hershey Foods, PepsiCo, and McDonald's, leverage comes from global brand recognition based on high-quality products that cater to local market tastes. However, the nature and cost of leverage in multidomestic firms does not come from making expensive, technology-driven investments that are shared across subsidiaries. Instead, leverage in multidomestic firms arises from the cumulative market successes of many subsidiaries' efforts over time. The biggest cost of building leverage in multidomestic firms is ongoing investment that *preserves and extends the image.*

Loss of Flexibility

An important cost associated with globalization is the potential loss of flexibility in managing operations. Across all industries, quick responsiveness to market needs is vital to building new sources of competitive advantage. This need for responsiveness applies in every industry from consumer electronics to advanced composite materials, where new technologies allow scientists to custom design hybrid materials made of both new plastics and metals. Expanding globally raises the risk that the firm will lose its ability to respond to new technological or market trends that could be critical in creating new, valuable products. The potential loss of flexibility could occur in both global and multidomestic firms, although the kind of flexibility lost will depend upon the specific strategy employed.

In firms pursuing global strategies, the loss of flexibility is likely to result from the high level of interdependence and shared investment found between subsidiaries. Because the actions of one subsidiary may affect the behavior of another, the response time to adjust to new market developments slows considerably in global firms. Managers need to communicate and convince their counterparts in other subsidiaries why a particular market development should receive attention. Even though advances in e-mail and the Internet have linked subsidiary operations more closely, these technologies can introduce so much information that they actually overwhelm managers' priorities and cognitive ability to process it. Information pouring in on a daily basis may lose its sense of urgency. What may be vital or urgent to one subsidiary manager may not be to another. Thus, the immediate, day-to-day priorities confronting each subsidiary may cause systemwide inflexibility in response to a potential threat.

Consider IBM's situation in mainframe computers. IBM knew for a long time that personal computers (and now the Internet and client-server architecture) would eventually displace mainframe computers in many applications. Yet, IBM's huge systemwide investment in plants, laboratories, and distribution facilities geared to making and servicing large mainframe computers slowed down its response to this new trend. IBM's loss of flexibility in dealing with new environmental developments that threatened its systemwide investments resulted in the company's slow recognition of the personal computer threat. Even though this inflexibility cost the company valuable lost time and market share, IBM eventually was able to undertake the transition to new technologies and investments that allow it to gain strength against Japanese and European competitors in the industry.

In firms pursuing multidomestic strategies, the loss of flexibility occurs differently. Unlike global firms, multidomestic firms can respond quickly to changing product needs within their own markets. But multidomestic firms are less able to respond to a change that may affect all of its markets simultaneously. Subsidiaries that operate as discrete, stand-alone units, such as those found in Coca-Cola, 3M, Colgate-Palmolive, Henkel, Unilever, PepsiCo, and Procter & Gamble, have sufficient local resources, initiative, and incentive to respond promptly to local market changes. On the other hand, a multidomestic firm faces a potentially serious problem if a new technology renders its existing products obsolete across all of its markets. For example, if Coke were confronted by a new technological development that extended the shelf life of soft drink concentrate, then it would almost certainly need to restructure its numerous multidomestic distribution arrangements to take advantage of this change. Instead of organizing multidomestically as it does now, Coke would be forced to consider adopting a more global strategy. This move, in turn, would likely undermine goodwill and initiative among Coke's many local distributors and bottlers.

Similarly, if a multidomestic firm were to confront a crisis in any of its served markets, then how the company responds to that crisis can have far-reaching effects on its markets elsewhere. More recently, Coke faced a massive crisis in its Belgian operations in 1999 when several children initially became sick after they consumed what they believed were spoiled Coke products. The company's initial reaction to this threatening event was slow, since management genuinely believed that its strongly managed operations could not have resulted in contaminated ingredients or poorly bottled products. Senior management from the U.S. tried to "micromanage" the problem from headquarters in Atlanta. However, local managers felt that they needed to clear proposed action with headquarters, thus delaying the company's responsiveness. Since it appeared to Belgian authorities that Coke was not taking the issue seriously, they immediately ordered their own health investigation into the matter, thus dealing a serious blow to Coke's statements on quality. Belgium and three other countries immediately ordered all Coke products off the shelves of supermarkets. When senior management finally realized the gravity of the crisis and sent teams to investigate the root causes of the illness, the company lost considerable market share and confidence among many European customers—at the same time that Pepsi began increasing its European production. Ultimately, Coke was forced to do "damage control" through extensive local advertisements and worked out an agreement with the Belgian and other concerned governments to arrange for ways to help the afflicted consumers and to restore confidence. The crisis ultimately cost the company over $100 million and forced the company to give away hundreds of thousands of half-liter bottles of the product in Belgium, France, and Germany.

Thus, multidomestic firms face a potential loss of flexibility in terms of dealing with new developments that span multiple markets at the same time. As Coke now tries to refocus its worldwide operations with a broad reorganization, the company still seeks to preserve its focus on local markets without diluting the overall brand equity and image of the company.

Costs of Cooperation

Global strategies, in particular, require a high level of cooperation and coordination among business units and subsidiaries to achieve systemwide leverage. Cooperation is especially relevant for global firms practicing cross-subsidization policies across numerous markets in efforts to dislocate other global competitors. Yet, achieving cooperation can engender significant costs of its own. These include (1) costs of compromise and (2) costs of accountability. To a large extent, multidomestic strategies do not generate high costs of compromise and accountability. Because these firms do not have a systemwide perspective for building competitive advantage, they are not subject to many of the costs associated with high cooperation.

Costs of Compromise. Global firms allocating scarce resources to develop new technologies and investments must often compromise on what goals and products should proceed first and where key operations should be located. A huge semiconductor or automobile engine plant, for example, is likely to engender debate within the company on which markets to target first, how much to produce for each market, how long the product should be produced, and which subsidiaries should bear the costs of the plant. In addition, considerable debate is likely to take place over the plant's location. Some managers might wish their subsidiary to be the one that houses this plant, since it may generate internal prestige among their colleagues and allow it to control a significant portion of components used by other subsidiaries. Yet, these same managers are probably unwilling to assume the full costs of the plant, since much of the plant's output will be shared among other subsidiaries and markets. The costs of compromise include, for example, long committee meetings, time spent negotiating between subsidiary managers, and deciding how to share critical resources and their internal pricing.

In multidomestic firms, the goals and specific products of each subsidiary are determined according to that subsidiary's market conditions. Subsidiaries are independent from one another and are less likely to engage in debate about shared resources or joint projects across subsidiaries. Still, such debate tends to occur within each subsidiary over issues on how best to serve its local market.

Costs of Accountability. Global firms also face the issue of accountability of their subsidiaries. Building competitive advantage systemwide means that some subsidiaries must bear a higher cost of R&D or new product development, for example, than other subsidiaries. Some subsidiaries will also gain less benefit from such efforts than others. These discrepancies mean that using a uniform set of measures to assess the performance of each manager may cause some subsidiaries to appear to be underperforming. In reality, subsidiaries investing heavily in new equipment will appear to be high cost units, while those firms that invest little will have higher profitability and greater cash flow. In particular, shared resources and costs, as well as joint development efforts, will distort the financial performance of each subsidiary. For multidomestic firms, calculating the costs and returns of each subsidiary is an easier task. The independent nature of the subsidiaries within multidomestic firms enables performance evaluations to be specific to each subsidiary. As each subsidiary is responsible for its own market (and thus its own set of value-creating activities), it is easier for senior management to isolate and evaluate each subsidiary's contribution to the firm's overall profitability.

Strategic Application to Boeing and Coca-Cola

Let us now summarize by examining how Boeing and Coca-Cola's strategies fit the underlying patterns of a global or multidomestic strategy. Clearly, the description and analysis of Boeing indicate that this aircraft manufacturer pursues a full-blown global strategy. The high R&D costs associated with each line of aircraft forces Boeing to seek global customers because of the need to spread out its huge development and manufacturing costs. Moreover, Boeing concentrates its production and development activities in several key plants in the United States, most of which are adjacent to one another to lower costs even further. Boeing seeks global production and assembly economies of scale across all its products. Components and aircraft models are standardized as much as possible to ensure commonality of parts and ease of maintenance and service. In addition, Boeing's marketing strategy is global. It uses highly trained and technically fluent global sales force teams that search the world for new customers and opportunities to sell and service its aircraft. Boeing also practices a high degree of cross-subsidization in its ongoing global competition with Airbus. Its purchase of McDonnell-Douglas in 1998 is a testimony to Boeing's successful culmination of a cross-subsidization strategy against a weaker number three competitor. More important, McDonnell-Douglas brings its own set of distinctive experience, capability, and talent in medium-range aircraft that will be useful for serving emerging and developing markets. By aggressively pricing and offering a full range of services to its existing and emerging European customers, Boeing hopes to reinforce and sharpen its attack on its rival on Airbus's home European turf.

Conversely, Boeing must be careful to defend its existing U.S. base from Airbus's wooing of American carriers, such as United Airlines, United Parcel Service, FedEx, and American Airlines. Recently, in 1997 and 1998, Airbus has become much more effective in using cross-subsidization to enter the U.S. market by winning significant orders from Northwest Airlines and USAirways. More important, pursuing a global strategy is no guarantee of an eternally strong market position, as Boeing has begun to discover over the past few years. Airbus is a much stronger competitor than it was in the past, thanks in part to a recent reorganization that streamlined communications and brought about vast improvements in operational efficiencies. More important, Airbus is gaining in many ways because of its ability to cross-subsidize effectively the penetration of one market with cash flow earned from another. In Europe, Airbus for the first time has secured an order potentially worth up to $20 billion from longtime Boeing customer British Airways. Airbus has also successfully wooed away some previous Boeing customers to sign up for the future Airbus A380, a risky undertaking for the European competitor.

By some accounts, Airbus has already taken the lead in developing several new types of manufacturing processes that help reduce the weight of next-generation aircraft. Part of Airbus's success in this area stems from the fact that it was forced to invest in the latest manufacturing technology simply to catch up with Boeing during the early part of the 1990s. Although Boeing has engaged in a decade-long effort to revitalize its manufacturing, it still must deal with the high costs of inflexibility that result when the company must decide how best to utilize the talent and facilities acquired from its McDonnell-Douglas acquisition. For both Boeing and Airbus, the continued fight for the skies is a testament to both the effectiveness of both companies, as well as the high risks that accompany a desire to dominate a truly global industry.

Conversely, Coca-Cola is steadfastly pursuing a strongly multidomestic strategy. In fact, under Chairman Douglas Daft, the company is giving even more authority and autonomy to managers in local markets. Unlike Boeing, Coca-Cola uses a specific strategy for each market it serves. More often than not, each Coca-Cola subsidiary devises its own local strategy, advertising, marketing, and other sales techniques to better serve its customers. Coca-Cola's global distribution and bottling system is really a collection of local distributors, bottlers, wholesalers, and retailers, all of whom share a commitment to preserving and enhancing Coca-Cola's product quality and corporate image. Because of the high cost and perishability of shipping cola concentrate to distant regions, Coke has established local production and bottling facilities in each market. This practice helps create employment and a rising skill base in all of Coke's markets and fosters goodwill with local governments, managers, and personnel. Coca-Cola has grown by leaps and bounds in following this strategy, as numerous local firms aspire to be part of the Coca-Cola bottling and supply network. It scored a major victory against PepsiCo in November 1996 when Coke was able to woo over the bottling operations of the Cisneros family, the largest soft drink bottler and distributor in Venezuela.

At the same time, however, the pursuit of a multidomestic strategy is no guarantee that developments in one market cannot adversely affect another, even though each market has its own subsidiary and its own strategy. The recent difficulties that Coke confronted with Belgian authorities over its slow reaction to an emerging crisis caused shockwaves throughout the company's operations around the world. While the company was eventually able to regain its market footing in Belgium, it required an enormous marketing effort and work with local health authorities to stabilize the situation, plus public apologies for the situation. Thus, multidomestic strategies still require a coordinated effort by the entire company to preserve its brand equity and image. Damage in one market can easily cause ripple effects in other markets if the company is not careful, as Coke eventually discovered in Europe.

Today, Coke remains committed to maintaining the quality and integrity of its operations, even those of local bottlers affiliated with the company. Although distribution channels vary significantly from region to region, and even within a single country, Coke seeks to build distribution muscle, technologies, and capabilities according to what will best serve that market's needs in ways that also limit the actions of other competitors. Coca-Cola's pursuit of its strategic mission (a Coke "within an arm's reach of desire") means that it must design its production and marketing strategy region by region, market by market. At the company's most recent organizational shift, Coke is reemphasizing the need to regain its nimbleness and agility—something that can only be done when local managers have the discretion and authority to act on their own. More important, local managers will not have to consult with corporate headquarters in Atlanta to design their own marketing programs or to develop their own new products. In fact, R&D funds will now be distributed around the world according to how fast markets are growing and what competitors are doing. This reorganization in many ways returns Coke to its original mission—fast responsiveness is needed to "think locally, act locally." Yet, the cumulative sum of all the actions taken by Coke's numerous subsidiaries, distributors, bottlers, and affiliated employees results in one of the world's strongest overall brand images and one of this country's most valuable companies.

Balancing Global and Multidomestic Approaches

The illustrations of Boeing and Coca-Cola clearly represent two distinct, almost polar opposite strategies or approaches to expanding globally. Boeing's full-blown global strategy fits an economic environment where homogeneity of demand, huge R&D costs, rising economies of scale, and proprietary manufacturing technologies define the competitive parameters. Coca-Cola, on the other hand, employs a multidomestic strategy to compete in each market separately. With the exception of cultivating a strong corporate quality image, Coca-Cola relies heavily on local managers, producers, marketing research staffs, distributors, and wholesalers to develop the best-fitting region-specific strategies. Coke's multidomestic approach works well, given its need for extensive product customization, rapid new product development, reduction of high transportation costs, minimization of potential perishability problems and accommodation to wholesale and retail distribution differences found throughout the world. Yet, an increasing number of firms around the world are looking to combine the benefits of both global and multidomestic strategies when expanding globally. A hybrid or blended strategy that seeks to combine the benefits of both global and multidomestic approaches is growing in a number of companies producing consumer electronics, automobiles, personal care products, and even financial services and high fashion. Let us examine how a few companies in these industries have attempted to move toward a blended global/multidomestic strategy to secure the benefits of both.

Automobiles: Combining Global Scale with Local Response

Several leading companies in the automobile industry are moving toward a blended global/multidomestic strategy to balance low-cost production with high product customization and fast response to local markets. One of the most important considerations facing the global automotive industry is that it is difficult to build a single model with few variations to serve the entire world. Despite the fact that an increasing number of vehicles share a common platform (e.g., unitized body, chassis, drivetrain, braking systems), buyers are increasingly looking for distinctive, if not unique, styling. Ford, DaimlerChrysler, Toyota, Mazda, and Honda are among a growing number of firms seeking to build critical core components of their cars, such as engines, transmissions, air conditioning compressors, and fuel-injection systems, in world-scale facilities to lower their unit costs. On the other hand, these same companies are looking to use design talent and assembly sites in local markets to perform much of the automobile design work and car assembly tasks for individual markets. By producing scale-sensitive components in one or two key plants and assembling the final product in local markets, these auto firms are hoping to combine the benefits of global and multidomestic approaches.

Consider the illustration of the Honda Accord, one of the most popular cars in the United States.[13] Honda produces its various lines of engines, transmissions, and other components for the Accord in scale-efficient plants in Japan to reduce costs and to share proprietary manufacturing processes across auto-part families. Advanced automobile engines often require extremely costly development of new materials (aluminum heads and magnesium-alloy engine blocks) that demand global volume to cover R&D costs. On the other hand, all of the Honda Accords sold in the United States are now assembled in plants in Ohio and elsewhere. Engines and transmissions are shipped from Japan and assembled in the United States, often with a high mix of U.S.-made parts, such as glass and rubber, from local manufacturers. Thus, Honda seeks to blend the benefits of a global strategy for its core scale-sensitive and technology-intensive components (to secure low-cost production and shared development of advanced designs) with a multidomestic strategy for assembly and distribution of the finished car (the final product comes together in local markets).

Honda's evolution to combining both aspects of a global and multidomestic production strategy is leading the way in the automotive industry. More recently, Honda originally decided to make all of its highly popular CR-V line of vehicles in Japan. But because of currency fluctuations and the need to better understand U.S. consumers, Honda has decided to make some of its vehicles in the U.S. Moreover, because Honda also faces a potential overcapacity problem in Europe, Honda will actually begin to make some CR-Vs in Britain, and then reexport them to the United States. In turn, Honda will start making a hatchback version of its popular Civic in the United States and begin shipping them to Europe. The reason Honda has been so effective in being able to ship to the location of production around the world is because of the company's commitment and investment to building highly flexible factories that are capable or switching from one car model to another without significant retooling or downtime. Both Honda and its arch rival Toyota are now capable of putting a new model into production in as little as three months.

The automobile industry is also under considerable pressure to consolidate in the wake of rising technology costs, growing economies of scale, and the need to develop distribution and sales infrastructures in many parts of the world simultaneously. In the past few years, the pace of consolidation has accelerated. Joint ventures and strategic alliances to share costs, access new markets, and develop new core technological platforms for future car models have been long-standing practices within the industry (see Chapter 9). More recently, however, many firms in the global automotive industry are beginning to merge and acquire their competitors so as to achieve the critical mass and scale economies to invest in new engine and production technologies, brand names, alternative energy sources, advanced batteries, and market share-building programs needed for competitive advantage.

For example, Ford purchased Volvo Cars from Volvo SA of Sweden to strengthen its position in the luxury car market. General Motors now fully owns Saab SA, once a 50-50 joint venture with Saab-Scania of Sweden. GM has also bought a 20 percent equity stake in Fuji Motors of Japan, the maker of Subaru automobiles, and even bought a controlling stake in South Korea's Daewoo Motors. Citroen and Peugeot of France have combined to form PSA Group, a new entity that has invested heavily in telematics (a technological platform that integrates the Internet and other communications technology into cars). In May 1998, Daimler-Benz of Germany, best known for its Mercedes line of luxury and high-end automobiles, purchased Chrysler for a price up to $40 billion in one of the largest cross-border mergers in history. The combined firm, known as DaimlerChrysler, has begun working together on developing state-of-the-art engines and electrical power systems that will be the basis for environmentally friendly cars of the future. The company is envisioned to be a "transglobal company" that aims to combine the benefits of global scale economies with an intimate approach to serving each market's unique needs.[14] Although the two firms have no intention of combining their brand names when competing in different markets, management from both companies will be looking to each other for ways to save on product development costs and to streamline manufacturing efficiencies. In particular, Chrysler will gain access to Daimler's state-of-the-art technology and development in advanced fuel cell batteries and alternative (e.g., hydrogen/oxygen) energy sources. More recently, however, the scale and size of this merger have brought about its own set of complex issues. In particular, transferring managers across these two proud organizations has resulted in serious costs of compromise and accountability as DaimlerChrysler endeavors to forge a truly global strategy for this industry. These coordination issues have become particularly exacerbated recently as the automotive industry faces growing overcapacity worldwide and reduced demand.[15]

Personal Care Products: Matching Local Response to Global Development

A growing number of companies producing personal health care products appear to be moving away from a pure multidomestic strategy to a blended multidomestic/global strategy. Personal care products such as diapers, shampoos, and toothpastes still clearly require a strongly multidomestic focus to tailor activities to local market conditions. Rapid product introduction and product customization still essentially define the basis of competitive success in regional markets. Yet, consumer products firms such as Unilever, Colgate-Palmolive, Procter & Gamble, Henkel, and Kao are developing new R&D facilities that can obtain some of the benefits of shared product development and testing across national markets. The R&D costs of developing new personal health care products that use, for example, new mixtures of chemicals and environment-friendly and less perishable ingredients are rising. This trend means growing opportunities for companies that will consider adopting a more global approach to develop and test future products. For example, Procter & Gamble has several key R&D facilities in Europe, Japan, and the United States to share research, product development, and testing. Japanese competitor Kao has staked out R&D facilities in the United States, Europe, and Southeast Asia to avoid duplication of product development efforts. Kao, for example, acquired the Andrew Jergens company in the U.S. to strengthen its technical and marketing reach. Both firms are using a network of globally situated laboratories to develop high-value products for their global operations.

Consider the illustration of Bausch & Lomb in the contact lens and eye-care industry. Bausch & Lomb is a leading firm in the development and production of contact lens, sunglasses, and associated cleaning solutions for markets worldwide. Bausch & Lomb has conducted its operations on a strictly multidomestic basis because of its goal of developing and cultivating a strong local presence in each market. The company realized that customers had to become more aware of the quality standards and image of Bausch & Lomb's products before people would trust their eyes to them. Working with and supporting local opticians and distributors have been critical to competitive success. Local managers knew best how to understand and penetrate their markets. Moreover, the shape and fit of a pair of glasses actually depends on the contours of a person's nose and cheekbones, characteristics that vary markedly around the world. Thus, Bausch & Lomb has endeavored to produce and market eye care products in each of its regional markets separately. More recently, Bausch & Lomb has begun to develop new contact lenses based on expensive proprietary technologies developed in key laboratories in South Korea, Japan, and the United States. These advances enable Bausch & Lomb to formulate a more global approach to its strategy.

These examples point to the growing likelihood that firms in a number of industries will move to implement some combination of a blended global/multidomestic strategy to expand their overseas operations. Balancing the dual need for low-cost economies of scale with fast-response product customization will be a significant factor in determining competitive advantage and success. The Honda example shows a firm in a traditionally scale-sensitive industry beginning to learn some of the benefits of competing multidomestically. Alternatively, firms in the personal care products industry are now realizing some of the benefits of using some aspects of a global strategy for their product development activities.

Ethical Dimensions

Globalization presents significant strategic opportunities for firms willing to take the risk of going overseas and committing themselves to serving customers worldwide.[16] Yet, global expansion obliges a firm to deal with a wide range of competitors, customers, and market needs, thereby compelling it to deal with a broad range of ethical beliefs and practices. Many of these beliefs and practices contrast starkly with those found in U.S. firms. The issue of ethics when competing globally is becoming especially noteworthy in the late 1990s, as we witness the assortment of values found around the world.

Much of the current interest in ethics that accompanies global expansion can be traced to the numerous scandals in Europe and the Far East that occurred during the 1980s and continued through the 1990s. For example, a major scandal in London's posh Lloyd's of London insurance firm surfaced when numerous investors were defrauded by Lloyd's agents who allegedly expropriated funds for their own use. In 1989 and 1990, several stock market scandals and insider-trading scams took place in France and Germany, while in 1995, several major financial firms were taken to the brink of disaster because of alleged insider training and misuse of funds to engage in global commodities speculation (e.g., Sumitomo Metals, Daiwa Securities of Japan). Despite all of the effort the United States has devoted to making insider trading illegal here (e.g., the investigation of Michael Milken's bond trading), officials in Europe have a different perspective on what constitutes the ethical boundaries of insider trading.

In 1997 and 1998, Japan faced its own set of political and economic scandals rocking its closely knit financial and industrial establishment. Several politicians were forced to step down from office and face indictments because they allegedly received payoffs from construction interests, the local Yakuza (the Japanese "mob"), and industrial companies seeking preferential treatment in the allocation of government contracts. In fact, several leading Japanese brokerage firms pleaded guilty to having loaned considerable sums of money in secret deals to underworld characters. Yet, despite having committed apparently extremely serious criminal acts, many of the officials investigated and indicted received only minor punishments because Japan has not acted on its recently adopted set of formal regulations, laws, or ethical codes of conduct that prohibit these activities.

The differences in attitudes and what defines ethical practices across nations is strongly rooted in public expectations and local history. In the United States, ethical behavior transcends what is simply considered legal or even legitimate. Managers, employees, suppliers, and even customers are implicitly expected to follow their own personal codes of conduct that prohibit embezzlement, insider trading, and a host of other practices that most of us take for granted as somehow "crossing the line." In many other nations, however, practices such as preferential treatment to long-standing financial and business partners, gift giving, relaying insider information, and other actions are considered discreet and appropriate ways of smoothing business relations between people who know each other well. Although criminal investigation and prosecution has accelerated in Europe for insider trading and other corporate transgressions, the pace of reform to a large extent is slower in the Far East, where local customs and traditions mandate that close ties require a different set of standards be applied to "insiders" and "outsiders."

Differences in business ethics across the globe are rooted in the way ethics is defined. In the United States, where individualism defines many of our institutions and legal codes, ethics is strongly based on personal behavior and attitudes that condemn actions that clearly do not fit the spirit of what was intended, even if these actions are not overtly illegal. People are expected to decide what is right and wrong largely through their own moral beliefs and conscience. In effect, when a company does something perceived as wrong, employees often feel great discomfort. In many other countries with less strongly rooted individualism, the distinction between company and individual actions may be more vague. In other words, individual managers in Europe and the Far East may perhaps be more likely to conform their own beliefs to that of their companies' needs. The role of the individual is not as well defined or cherished in Europe and elsewhere. Thus, managers may be more inclined to overlook ethical breaches committed for company-related goals as opposed to personal goals, since the company might benefit from these actions in the long term. In the Far East, the distinction between individual employee and company is even more vague. Many workers in Japan, Korea, and elsewhere see themselves as "industrial soldiers," where their primary function is to carry out their companies' strategy, mission, and other objectives to whatever extent they best can. As recipients of generous corporate benefits, these workers will often do whatever they feel is necessary to preserve and to strengthen their company's strategies, including the potential use of industrial espionage. Whistle-blowers and similar individuals would be perceived as troublemakers and socially isolated from other people in the company.

The net effect of these divergent ethical beliefs and practices around the world is that U.S. firms in particular face great dilemmas when dealing in other nations. The business practices of competing firms may even conflict with practices of U.S. firms. Moreover, what constitutes legal or ethical behavior may be specific to different situations. U.S. companies, for example, are prohibited from offering bribes to foreign officials because of the Foreign Corrupt Practices Act passed in the mid-1970s. Unfortunately, many global competitors of these U.S. firms may not face the same restriction when competing for lucrative contracts in third-party countries. These countries often have more liberal definitions of what defines gift giving as opposed to bribes and payoffs. In many cases, U.S. managers will face great moral dilemmas in designing ethical and appropriate strategies to counter such actions. On the one hand, securing a lucrative contract may be imperative to building market share and profitability. Yet, on the other hand, U.S. managers realize they are held to a difficult standard, one that is often more restrictive and that calls upon the individual to make a personal judgment when ethical boundaries are less clear.

The cumulative effect of these contrasting ethical backgrounds and beliefs is the likelihood of more government regulation in the United States and elsewhere. Governments in many cases are being forced to scrutinize the actions of firms and individuals more closely because of growing public outrage at blatantly unethical acts and transgressions. For example, in Japan, the Liberal Democratic Party (LDP) has never really regained its firm control over parliament (the Diet) and the confidence of the Japanese people as a result of its scandal-plagued administrations during the 1990s. Many LDP politicians have campaigned on the need to restore public confidence in the government and to take action to bring about a recovery of the Japanese economy. However, few prime ministers or elected officials have demonstrated much vigorous action to attain these objectives. The ethical transgressions in the United States, Britain, France, Germany, and Japan during the 1980s and 1990s will probably result in increased governmental scrutiny and regulation of large, multinational firms operating at home and abroad.

Summary

- Global expansion enables firms to build and extend their sources of competitive advantage to new markets.
- Firms need to consider global expansion because of increasing demand around the world, rising R&D costs to develop new products, growing economies of scale, the change in factor (labor and capital) costs, and greater ease of communications, transportation, and storage.
- Global expansion strategies are of two basic types: global and multidomestic. Industry drivers are important factors that influence the firm's choice of a global or multidomestic strategy.
- Firms pursue a global strategy when they seek to operate with worldwide consistency, standardization of products and practices, and a systemwide perspective to extend competitive advantage.
- Firms pursue a multidomestic strategy when they adjust their products and operations according to the particular markets being served.
- Benefits of global expansion include entering fast-growing markets, recovering investment costs, creating a strong image, and accelerating learning and knowledge transfer.
- The expense of building leverage, potential inflexibility, and the challenges of cooperating across subsidiaries are all costs of global expansion.
- Many companies are currently formulating their own strategies that combine the benefits of both global and multidomestic approaches. The imperative to combine

these strategies becomes especially relevant as companies strive to find the right balance between the need to serve different customers with efforts to reduce costs of operations and other activities.

Exercises and Discussion Questions

1. What are some important environmental and economic factors that firms must consider when choosing to compete in global markets? How can these factors be significantly different from those facing the firm in its domestic market?
2. The growth of the Internet has been a major factor that has substantially reduced the costs of communications around the world. What are some things that a small firm can do to use the Internet as a tool to enter global markets? Can a small firm that shrewdly uses the Internet still become an important global player?
3. Most recently, many U.S. firms have sustained losses in profits and market share as the economies of Southeast Asia have entered a recession. If you were a consultant to 3M, for example, what are some steps that you would recommend to senior management to protect your market position and perhaps even use the recession to your advantage?
4. As new technologies make mass customization strategies more commonplace, which type of overseas expansion strategy is likely to dominate in the future: global or multidomestic? What are some attributes of mass customization strategies that make them particularly powerful weapons in the fight for global market share and position?

Endnotes

1. Facts and data were adapted from the following sources: "Boeing Hopes Its Futuristic Jet Will Deliver Extra Lift," *Wall Street Journal*, February 27, 2002, p. B3; "With Airbus on Its Tail, Boeing Is Rethinking How It Builds Planes," *Wall Street Journal*, September 5, 2001, pp. A1, A16; "Boeing to Install New Landing Aids in Cockpits," *Wall Street Journal*, August 29, 2001, p. A4; "Airbus Signs Up Partners to Help Build Jumbo Jet," *Wall Street Journal*, June 21, 2001, p. A14; "At Paris Air Show, Boeing-Airbus Deal Has New Twist," *Wall Street Journal*, June 15, 2001, p. B4; "Boeing Is Near Deal with Some Airlines to Test In-Flight E-mail, Internet Access," *Wall Street Journal*, June 11, 2001, pp. A3, A14; "Boeing Plans Longer-Range Model of 747," *Wall Street Journal*, April 13, 2001, pp. A3, A6; "Commercial Jetmakers Project Optimistic Trajectory," *Wall Street Journal*, April 12, 2001, p. B4; "Airbus Revamp Brings Sense to Consortium, Fuels Boeing Rivalry," *Wall Street Journal*, April 3, 2001, p. A1, A8; "Rumble over Tokyo," *Business Week*, April 2, 2001, pp. 80–81; "With Market Share Rising, Airbus Opens a Charm Offensive in U.S.," *Wall Street Journal*, March 6, 2001, pp. B1, B8; "Boeing Plans to Build Smaller, Faster Jet," *Wall Street Journal*, March 30, 2001, pp. A3, A8; "Airbus's Parent Posts Net Loss of $815.8 Million for Full Year," *Wall Street Journal*, March 20, 2001, pp. A14, A17; "Boeing Wins Order from Singapore Air in Coup over Rival," *Wall Street Journal*, February 15, 2001, p. A15; "Taking Tons Off the World's Biggest Passenger Jet," *Wall Street Journal*, January 19, 2001, pp. B1, B4; "Boeing Considers Innovative Jet to Rival Airbus," *Wall Street Journal*, January 19, 2001, p. A4; "Boeing-Airbus Battle Grows Hotter as Stakes Rise For Air Supremacy," *Investor's Business Daily*, January 17, 2001, p. A1; "At Boeing, an Old Hand Provides New Tricks in Battle with Airbus," *Wall Street Journal*, January 10, 2001, pp. A1, A12; "Boeing Weighs Giving Japan 747X Wing Job," *Wall Street Journal*, January 2, 2001, pp. A3, A18; "How to Build a Really, Really, Really Big Plane," *Fortune*, March 5, 2001, pp. 145–154; "Boeing Is Set for Record in 777 Orders," *Wall Street Journal*, November 27, 2000, pp. A3, A6; "Boeing vs. Boeing,"

Fortune, October 2, 2000, pp. 147–160; "Shakeups: Can a New Crew Buoy Boeing?" *Business Week*, September 14, 1998, p. 53; "Airbus to Raise Base Price of Aircraft by 3%, Following Boeing's 5% Increase," *Wall Street Journal*, September 8, 1998, p. A4; "The Best Defense Is a Good Offense," *Business Week*, September 7, 1998, p.42; "Boeing Nears Decision on Assembling," *Wall Street Journal*, August 7, 1998; "Boeing Production Takes Wing," *Business Week*, July 13, 1998, p. 46; "Boeing Is Placing Focus on Smaller, Cheaper Airliners," *Wall Street Journal*, July 6, 1998, p. A22; "Airbus Partners Make Pact to Form Single Company," *Investor's Business Daily*, March 30, 1998, p. A1; "Boeing Plans to Make Drastic Changes to Slash Development Time for Aircraft," *Wall Street Journal*, February 11, 1998, p. B2; "Boeing Hits an Air Pocket," *Business Week*, January 19, 1998, p. 40; "Boeing's Big Problem," *Fortune*, January 12, 1998, p. 96; "A Jumbo Jolt at Boeing," *Business Week*, November 30, 1997, p. 50; "Boeing May Spend $1 Billion to Develop Expanded 747's to Combat Airbus Planes," *Wall Street Journal*, September 10, 1997, p. A6; "Boeing-McDonnell Gets a Thumbs Up," *Business Week*, August 4, 1997, p. 42; "Strategies: Boeing at Your Service," *Business Week*, July 14, 1997, p. 32; "Five Airlines Unveil Expanded Alliance That Links Various Customer Services," *Wall Street Journal*, May 15, 1997, p. A8; "The Next Wave: Global Forces Push Europe's Firms, Too, into a Merger Frenzy," *Wall Street Journal*, April 4, 1997, p. A1; "Airbus Lines Up Superjumbo Partners, Examines Boeing-McDonnell Merger," *Wall Street Journal*, February 5, 1997, p. A12; "Boeing's 747 Decision Shifts Rivalry with Airbus," *Wall Street Journal*, January 22, 1997, p. A3; "Airbus Partners Reach Agreement for Centralized Company by 1999," *Wall Street Journal*, January 6, 1997, p. A9; "Airbus Begins Marketing Superjumbo at a Price Similar to Boeing's Models," *Wall Street Journal*, November 5, 1996, p. A5; "McDonnell Douglas Courted by Daimler-Benz to Join Airbus Efforts to Develop Jet," *Wall Street Journal*, May 14, 1996, p. A4; "Boeing's New Dream Machine," *Fortune*, February 19, 1996, p 104; "Airbus May Have to Alter Its Course to Remain Competitive," *Wall Street Journal*, January 11, 1996, p. A10.

2. Facts and data for the Coca-Cola case were adapted from the following sources: "Coke to Launch Powerade Drink in Europe," *Wall Street Journal*, October 16, 2001, p. B11E; "Coke Holds Talks to Buy Odwalla to Expand Noncarbonated Beverages," *Wall Street Journal*, October 22, 2001, p. B8; "Coca-Cola Is Expected to Name New Chiefs of Global Groups in Management Shake-Up," *Wall Street Journal*, July 30, 2001, p. B8; "Coca-Cola, Gates Help Step Up Assault on AIDS," *Wall Street Journal*, June 20, 2001; "Coke to Appoint Veteran to Bolster Its Operations," *Wall Street Journal*, July 23, 2001; "Coke and Pepsi Escalate Their Water Fight," *Wall Street Journal*, May 18, 2001; "Coke Aims to Revive 'Feel Good' Factor," *Wall Street Journal*, April 20, 2001; "Guess Who's Coming to the Cola Wars," *Fortune*, April 2, 2001; "New Diet Coke Campaign Plays Up Sex," *Wall Street Journal*, March 23, 2001; "Repairing the Coke Machine," *Business Week*, March 19, 2001; "How a Coke Ad Campaign Fell Flat with Viewers," *Wall Street Journal*, March 19, 2001; "Coke to Launch Juice Targeting Tropicana," *Wall Street Journal*, March 15, 2001; "New President of Coca-Cola Ventures, Heyer, Plans to Expand Product Lines," *Wall Street Journal*, March 8, 2001; "Coke Will Hire AOL Executive to Oversee Unit," *Wall Street Journal*, March 7, 2001; "Coke and P&G Meet over Snacks," *Business Week*, March 5, 2001; "Coke's 'Think Local' Strategy Has Yet to Prove Itself," *Wall Street Journal*, March 1, 2001, p. B4; "Coke Retains Top Spot in U.S. Soda Sales," *Wall Street Journal*, February 16, 2001; "Coke to Acquire Maker of Coffee, Bottled Drinks," *Wall Street Journal*, January 12, 2001; "Milk Is Also the Real Thing," *Business Week*, January 8, 2001; "My Pepsi Challenge," *Fortune*, November 27, 2000; "For Coke, Local Is It," *Business Week*, July 3, 2000; "Making Coke a Better Place to Work," *Business Week*, June 12, 2000; "Coke Hit," *Business Week*, May 29, 2000; "Things Could Go Better at Coke," *Business Week*, May 15, 2000; "The Big Spill Coke's CEO Doug Daft Has to Clean Up," *Business Week*, March 6, 2000; "Now, Coke Is No Longer It," *Business Week*, February 28, 2000; "Is Doug Daft the Real Thing?" *Business Week*, December 20, 1999; "Things Go Pricier with Coke," *Business Week*, November 29, 1999; "Have a

Coke and Smile Please," *Business Week*, August 30, 1999; "Coke's Boss Doesn't Get It," *Business Week*, August 8, 1999; "Crunch Time for Coke: His Company Is Overflowing with Trouble," *Fortune*, July 19, 1999; "Coke's Hard Lesson in Crisis Management," *Business Week*, July 5, 1999; "Things Aren't Going Better with Coke," *Business Week*, June 28, 1999; "I'd Like to Teach the World to Sell," *Business Week*, June 7, 1999; "Coke's Problems Are of Its Own Making," *Business Week*, May 17, 1999; "Now That's a Pepsi Challenge," *Business Week*, May 3, 1999; "Aggressive Push Abroad Dilutes Coke's Strength as Big Markets Stumble." *Wall Street Journal*, February 8, 1999, pp. A1, A8. "Soft Drinks: Tropicana—A New Way for Pepsi to Squeeze Coke," *Business Week*, August 3, 1998, p.78; "Cola Wars on the Mean Street," *Business Week*, August 3, 1998, p.78; "New Sweetener: Pepsi Pounces, Coke Ponders," *Wall Street Journal*, July 1, 1998, p. B1; "Coke Expects Volume Gains to Be Strong," *Wall Street Journal*, March 31, 1998, p. A3; "Coke's Market Share Rises to 43.9% as PepsiCo Slips," *Wall Street Journal*, February 13, 1998, p. A4; "Coke Expected to Sponsor World Cup Soccer Matches," *Wall Street Journal*, January 30, 1998, p. A6; "What Other CEOs Can Learn from Goizueta," *Business Week*, November 3, 1997, p. 38; "Can His Successor, Douglas Ivester, Refresh Coca-Cola?" *Wall Street Journal*, October 20, 1997, p. B1; "Where Coke Goes from Here," *Fortune*, October 13, 1997, p. 88; "Coke vs. Dr Pepper: A Sticky Battle," *Business Week*, June 16, 1997, p. 45; "Coke and Pepsi May Call Off a Pricing Battle," *Wall Street Journal*, June 12, 1997, p. A3; "Coca-Cola Powerade Takes on Gatorade as It Becomes NHL Official Sports Drink," *Wall Street Journal*, June 2, 1997, p. B5; "Why Pepsi Needs to Become More Like Coke," *Fortune*, March 3, 1997, p. 26; "PepsiCo Draws New Battle Plan to Fight Coke," *Wall Street Journal*, January 27, 1997, p. B1; "For Coca-Cola in Japan, Things Go Better with Milk," *Wall Street Journal*, January 20, 1997, p. B1; "Coca-Cola Plans to Launch Grapefruit-Flavored Soda," *Wall Street Journal*, January 14, 1997, p. B4; "Coca-Cola Co. Sees Continuing Growth in Global Volume," *Wall Street Journal*, December 20, 1996, p. A5; "Coca-Cola Plans Splashy Rollout of Citrus Soda," *Wall Street Journal*, December 16, 1996, p. B1; "Coke Pours into Asia," *Business Week*, October 21, 1996, p. 22; "Tried and True vs. New: Pepsi and Coke Swallow Different Brew," *Wall Street Journal*, January 10, 1996, p. B5; "Coke's Monster Bottler Has Latin Fizz," *Fortune*, December 11, 1995, p. 205; "The New Champ of Wealth Creation," *Fortune*, September 18, 1995, p. 131; "Coke, Blockbuster in Pact Covering Soft-Drink Sales," *Wall Street Journal*, July 6, 1995, p. B5; "Coke Contours New Ads to Fit 'Cultural Icon' of Shapely Bottle," *Wall Street Journal*, February 14, 1995, p. B12.

3. An excellent landmark work that first investigated the relationship between headquarters and subsidiaries as the foundation of a global strategy is by J. M. Hulbert and W. K. Brandt, *Managing the Multinational Subsidiary* (New York: Holt, Rinehart & Winston, 1980). Also see A. M. Rugman and A. Verbeke, "Subsidiary-Specific Advantages in Multinational Enterprises," *Strategic Management Journal* 22, no. 3 (2001): 237–250; T. S. Frost, "The Geographic Sources of Foreign Subsidiaries' Innovations," *Strategic Management Journal* 22, no. 2 (2001): 101–124; S. Watson O'Donnell, "Managing Foreign Subsidiaries: Agents of Headquarters, or an Interdependent Network," *Strategic Management Journal* 21, no. 5 (2000): 525–548; J. M. Birkinshaw and N. Hood, "Multinational Subsidiary Evolution: Capability and Charter Change in Foreign-Owned Subsidiary Companies," *Academy of Management Review* 23, no. 4 (1998): 773–795; J. H. Taggart, "Strategic Shifts in Multinational MNC Subsidiaries," *Strategic Management Journal* 19, no. 7 (1998): 663–681; J. Birkinshaw, N. Hood, and S. Jonsson, "Building Firm-Specific Advantages in Multinational Corporations: The Role of Subsidiary Initiative," *Strategic Management Journal* 19, no. 3 (1998): 221–242; G. S. Yip, *Total Global Strategy: Managing for Worldwide Competitive Advantage* (Englewood Cliffs, N.J.: Prentice-Hall, 1992); C. A. Bartlett and S. Ghoshal, "What Is a Global Manager?" *Harvard Business Review* (September–October 1992): 124–133; and R. F. Maruca, "The Right Way to Go Global: An Interview with Whirlpool CEO David Whitwam," *Harvard Business Review* (March–April 1994):

150–160; M. Schrage, "A Japanese Giant Rethinks Globalization: An Interview with Yoshihisa Tabuchi," *Harvard Business Review* (July–August 1989): 70–76; G. Hedlund, "The Hypermodern MNC: A Heterarchy?" *Human Resource Management* 25 (1986): 9–36.

4. An enormous amount of literature has developed in the past several years on global strategy. The following seminal pieces have provided much of the groundwork for this chapter. For a study on how firms become more global or multinational over time, a landmark study is J. M. Stopford and L. T. Wells, Jr., *Managing the Multinational Enterprise* (New York: Basic Books, 1972), and M. Z. Brooke and H. L. Remmers, *The Strategy of Multinational Enterprise: Organization and Finance* (London: Longman, 1970). Within the strategic management literature, for example, see T. Hout, M. E. Porter, and E. Rudden, "How Global Companies Win Out," *Harvard Business Review* (September–October 1982): 98–108. Also see B. Kogut, "Designing Global Strategies: Comparative and Competitive Value-Added Chains," *Sloan Management Review* 26 (1985): 15–28; M. E. Porter, "Changing Patterns of International Competition," *California Management Review* 28 (Winter 1986): 9–40; S. Ghoshal, "Global Strategy: An Organizing Framework," *Strategic Management Journal* 8 (1987): 425–440; S. Ghoshal and C.A. Bartlett, "The Multinational Corporation as an Interorganizational Network," *Academy of Management Review* 15 (October 1990): 603–625. Excellent books that survey the requirements for success in global strategies include C. A. Bartlett and S. Ghoshal, *Managing across Borders: The Transnational Solution* (Boston: Harvard Business School Press, 1989); M. E. Porter, *The Competitive Advantage of Nations* (New York: Free Press, 1990); C. K. Prahalad and Y. L. Doz, *The Multinational Mission: Balancing Local Demands and Global Vision* (New York: Free Press, 1987); Y. Doz and C. K. Prahalad, "Managing DMNCs: A Search for a New Paradigm," *Strategic Management Journal* 12, Special Issue (1991): 145–164; N. Nohria and C. Garcia-Pont, "Global Strategic Linkages and Industry Structure," *Strategic Management Journal* 12, Special Issue (1991): 105–124; H. V. Perlmutter, "The Tortuous Evolution of the Multinational Corporation," *Columbia Journal of World Business* 4, no. 4 (1969): 9–18; J. Fayerweather, *International Business Strategy and Administration* (Cambridge, Mass.: Ballinger, 1978); J. H. Dunning, *International Production and the Multinational Enterprise* (London: Allen & Unwin, 1981); P. J. Buckley and M. C. Casson, *The Economic Theory of the Multinational Enterprise* (London: Macmillan, 1985); A. K. Sundaram and J. S. Black, "The Environment and Internal Organization of Multinational Enterprises," *Academy of Management Review* 17 (1992): 729-757; P. M. Rosenweig and J.V. Singh, "Organizational Environments and Multinational Enterprise," *Academy of Management Review* 16 (1991): 340–361. The economics of globalization are shown in C. W. L. Hill and W. C. Kim, "Searching for a Dynamic Theory of the Multinational Enterprise: A Transactions Cost Model," *Strategic Management Journal* 9 (1988): 93–104; B. Mascarenhas, A. Baveja, and M. Jamil, "Dynamics of Core Competencies in Leading Multinational Companies," *California Management Review* 40, no. 4 (1998): 117–132.

Some critical studies that have examined different modes of global competition, entry strategies, and the relationship with financial performance and firm-based innovation include the following: H. Barkema and F. Vermeulen, "International Expansion Through Start-up or Acquisition: A Learning Perspective," *Academy of Management Journal* 41, no. 1 (1998): 7–26; J. H. Taggart, "Strategy Shifts in MNC Subsidiaries," *Strategic Management Journal* 17, no. 7 (1998): 663–682; M. A. Hitt, R. E. Hoskisson, and H. Kim, "International Diversification: Effects on Innovation and Firm Performance in Product-Diversified Firms," *Academy of Management Journal* 40, no. 4 (1997): 767–798; S. Tallman and J. T. Li, "Effects of International Diversity and Product Diversity on the Performance of Multinational Firms," *Academy of Management Journal* 39, no. 1 (1996): 179–196; J. F. Hennart and Y. R. Park, "Greenfield versus Acquisition: The Strategy of Japanese Investors in the United States," *Management Science* 39 (1993): 1054–1070; K. Roth, "International Configuration and Coordination Archetypes for Medium-Sized Firms in Global

Industries," *Journal of International Business Studies* 23 (1992): 533–549; K. Roth, D. Schweiger, and A. Morrison, "Global Strategy Implementation at the Business Unit Level: Operational Capabilities and Administrative Mechanisms," *Journal of International Business Studies* 22 (1991): 361–394.

More recent work includes the following studies examining the impact of globalization: J. W. Lu and P. W. Beamish, "The Internationalization and Performance of SMEs," *Strategic Management Journal* 22, Issues 6–7 (2001): 565–586; S. J. Chang and P. M. Rosenzweig, "The Choice of Entry Mode in Sequential Foreign Direct Investment," *Strategic Management Journal* 22, no. 8 (2001): 747–776; D. G. McKendrick, "Global Strategy and Population Level Learning: The Case of Hard Disk Drives," *Strategic Management Journal* 22, no. 4 (2001): 307–334; Y. Luo and S. H. Park, "Strategic Alignment and Performance of Market-Seeking MNCs in China," *Strategic Management Journal* 22, no. 2 (2001): 141–156; E. Autio, H. J. Sapienza, and J. G. Alameda, "Effects of Age at Entry, Knowledge Intensity, and Imitability on International Growth," *Academy of Management Journal* 43, no. 5 (2000): 909–924; J. M. Geringer, S. Tallman, and D. M. Olsen, "Product and International Diversification among Japanese Multinational Firms," *Strategic Management Journal* 21, no. 1 (2000): 51–80; S. Thomsen and T. Pedersen, "Ownership Structure and Economic Performance in the Largest European Companies," *Strategic Management Journal* 21, no. 6 (2000): 689–705; S. A. Zahra, R. D. Ireland, and M. A. Hitt, "International Expansion by New Venture Firms: International Diversification, Mode of Market Entry, Technological Learning, and Performance," *Academy of Management Journal* 43, no. 5 (2000): 925–950; P. P. McDougall and B. Oviatt, "International Entrepreneurship: The Intersection of Two Research Paths," *Academy of Management Journal* 43, no. 5, pp. 902–908; A. Delios and W. J. Henisz, "Japanese Firms' Investment Strategies in Emerging Economies," *Academy of Management Journal* 43, no. 3 (2000): 302–323; A. Delios and P. W. Beamish, "Geographic Scope, Product Diversification and Corporate Performance of Japanese Firms," *Strategic Management Journal* 20, no. 8 (2000): 711–727; L. G. Thomas III and G. Waring, "Competing Capitalisms: Capital Investment in American, German and Japanese Firms," *Strategic Management Journal* 20, no. 8 (2000): 729–739; Y. Pan and P. S. K. Chi, "Financial Performance and Survival of Multinational Corporations in China," *Strategic Management Journal* 20, no. 4 (1999): 359–374.

5. T. Levitt, "The Globalization of Markets," *Harvard Business Review* (May–June 1983): 92–102. Also see M. E. Porter, ed., *Competition in Global Industries* (Boston: Harvard Business School Press, 1986).

6. S. Wetlaufer, "Driving Change: An Interview with Ford Motor Company's Jacques Nasser," *Harvard Business Review* 77 (March–April 1999): 76–91.

7. See, for example, G. Hamel and C. K. Prahalad, "Do You Really Have a Global Strategy?" *Harvard Business Review* (July–August 1985): 139–148. Also see C. K. Prahalad and Y. L. Doz, *The Multinational Mission: Balancing Local Demands and Global Vision* (New York: Free Press, 1987).

8. See, for example, R. Kerin and R. Sethuraman, "Exploring the Brand Value-Shareholder Value Nexus for Consumer Goods Companies," *Journal of the Academy of Marketing Sciences* 26, no. 4 (1998): 260–273.

9. See, for example, "3M Expects Earnings to Decline Due to Asia's Turmoil," *Wall Street Journal*, June 16, 1998, p. B4.

10. "U.S. Firms' Global Prowess Is Two-Edged," *Wall Street Journal*, August 17, 1998, pp. C1, C2; "To Battle Asian Slump, Multinationals Import Lean-and-Mean Ways," *Wall Street Journal*, August 19, 1998, pp. A1, A6.

11. See "Many Japanese Firms Cling to Troubled Southeast Asia," *Wall Street Journal*, September 18, 1998, p. A8.

12. See "H. J. Heinz, Japan's Kagome Agree to Investments as Part of Alliance," *Wall Street Journal*, July 26, 2001, p. B11; "U.S. Firms Reassess Asian Joint Ventures," *Wall Street Journal*, September 23, 1998, pp. A2, A10; "GE Capital's Tokyo Treasure Hunt," *Business Week*, February 18, 1999, p. 39.

13. See "Fickle Consumers Force Auto Makers to Be More Flexible," *Wall Street Journal*, September 10, 2001, p. B8; "Tailoring World's Cars to U.S. Tastes," *Wall Street Journal*, January 15, 2001, pp. B1, B6; "Honda to Halt Civic, Accord Exports to the U.S.," *Wall Street Journal*, September 20, 1993, p. B5; "Toyota Is Expected to Build New Car at Kentucky Plant," *Wall Street Journal*, October 12, 1993, p. A18; "A New Export Power in the Auto Industry? It's North America," *Wall Street Journal*, October 18, 1993, pp. A1, A5; "Japan's Car Makers Seek Solutions from U.S. Big Three," *Wall Street Journal*, November 15, 1993, p. B4; "Ford Aggressively Increases Its Visibility in Japan as U.S. Brands Make Inroads," *Wall Street Journal*, February 11, 1994, p. A6; "Toyota Studies Fourth North American Plant," *Wall Street Journal*, February 10, 1995, p. A3.

    A recent academic piece that examines the role of global product development is M. Subramaniam and N. Venkatraman, "Determinants of Transnational New Product Development Capability: Testing the Influence of Transferring and Deploying Tacit Knowledge Overseas," *Strategic Management Journal* 22, no. 4 (2001): 359–378; also see L. Thomas and K. Weigelt, "Product Location Choice and Firm Capabilities: Evidence from the U.S. Automotive Industry," *Strategic Management Journal* 21, no. 9 (2000): 897–910; A. K. Gupta and V. Govindarajan, "Knowledge Flows within Multinational Corporations," *Strategic Management Journal* 21, no. 4 (2000): 473–496; M. Subramaniam, S. Spear, and H. K. Bowen, "Decoding the DNA of the Toyota Production System," *Harvard Business Review* 77 (September–October 1999): 96–108; S. R. Rosenthal and K. J. Hatten, "Global New Product Development: Preliminary Findings and Research Propositions," *Journal of Management Studies* 35, no. 6 (1998): 773–796; S. Ghoshal, H. Korine, and G. Szulanski, "Interunit Communication in Multinational Corporations," *Management Science* 40, no. 1 (1994): 375–384.

14. See "Eaton: DaimlerChrysler Will Be 'Transnational,'" *Wall Street Journal*, August 31, 1998, p. B8.

15. See, for example, P. Ghemawat and F. Ghadar, "The Dubious Logic of Global Megamergers," *Harvard Business Review* 28 (July–August 2000): 64–74; "For Two Car Giants, a Megamerger Isn't the Road to Riches," *Wall Street Journal*, October 27, 2000, pp. A1, A8. Also see "DaimlerChrysler Turnaround Seems to Be Going in Reverse," *Wall Street Journal*, October 11, 2001, p. B4; "DaimlerChrysler Ponders 'World Engine' in Bid to Transform Scope into Savings," *Wall Street Journal*, January 8, 2002, pp. A3, A4.

16. An excellent article that examines the globalization of business ethics is D. Vogel, "The Globalization of Business Ethics: Why America Remains Distinctive," *California Management Review* 35, no. 1 (1992): 30–49.

CHAPTER 9

Strategic Alliances: Teaming and Allying for Advantage

Chapter Outline

What You Will Learn

- The characteristics of a strategic alliance
- Why companies around the world are forming strategic alliances
- The different broad types of strategic alliances, including licensing, joint ventures, and multipartner consortia
- The benefits and costs of entering into strategic alliances
- How to balance the need for cooperation with competition

IBM's Global Alliance Strategy[1]

Throughout the 1990s, International Business Machines (IBM), the world's largest computer company, entered into a wide array of strategic alliances with numerous partners in the United States, the Far East, and Europe. During the past twenty years, IBM, popularly known as Big Blue, has shifted from relying on mainframe computer products for its huge revenue base ($88.4 billion in 2000). Already, IBM is a leading provider of many leading-edge products and services such as advanced semiconductors, hand-held communicators, storage devices and servers, mainframe computers, software development tools, Internet e-commerce tools, personal computers, disk drives, telecommunications equipment, and corporate Internet and Intranet Web sites. Many of these technologies require more than one firm to perfect and to rush to market. This development is especially revealing as twenty-first-century technologies become more expensive and risky to develop.

Strategic alliances will play a key role in helping IBM reshape these technologies. Altogether, IBM has formed more than five hundred strategic alliances (of varying degrees of complexity) with partners around the world. These strategic alliances involve not only shared marketing and software development efforts, but also major commitments of investment funds to build ultra-modern facilities that are beyond the financial means of any one company. Exhibit 9-1 portrays some of the most significant alliance relationships that IBM has entered as of February 2002.

IBM's initiatives to form a broad collection of strategic alliances with different firms did not materialize in a short time. In fact, IBM's array of strategic alliances represents an ongoing process of working with partners from every part of the world in almost every industry for twenty years or more. IBM's current alliance strategy in large measure is due to several key driving factors: (1) to enter new markets, (2) to block other key rivals from encroaching on its core U.S. market too quickly, (3) to shorten product development time, and (4) to learn new technologies to serve new customers across different industries.

IBM's Early Alliances: Responding to Japan

During the 1980s, many of IBM's alliances were predicated on preventing large, well-funded Japanese firms from penetrating too deeply in IBM's core mainframe markets. Japanese rivals in the computer business, such as Fujitsu, NEC, Hitachi, and Toshiba, possess comparable technologies and skills in many key products and technologies. Unlike IBM, however, these firms were highly experienced in learning new technologies and skills from their strategic alliance partners, which enabled them to reduce greatly the development time needed for successive product generations. In many ways, working with Japanese companies became a necessity, not a matter of choice, for IBM. The Japanese government originally had insisted that IBM share its mainframe computer technology with Japanese rivals in order to be able to sell in Japan. Moreover, IBM was worried that if it did not maintain a presence in Japan, then its Japanese rivals would have a free hand to develop new technologies and compete directly in the United States where IBM's position might be threatened. NEC, Fujitsu, and Toshiba, in particular, had partnered with a host of U.S. and European firms in earlier days (e.g., General Electric, Honeywell, TRW, Control Data, Bull, Olivetti) to learn how to compete in the computer business during the 1970s and 1980s.

IBM's alliances with these Japanese firms were designed not only to help IBM penetrate the Japanese market but also to limit the degree to which they could easily access the U.S. market on their own. Moreover, these alliances gave IBM a valuable window by which IBM could monitor the technological progress and learning of its Japanese partners. Even though IBM worked with NEC, Fujitsu and Toshiba, IBM simultaneously competed with them to develop new technologies and to accelerate product development.

Alliance Initiatives During the 1990s: Rebuilding Competitiveness

Motorola. IBM has worked with Motorola on many key emerging technologies over the past decade, and these alliances have been instrumental for both companies to learn and apply new technologies, particularly in the area of

IBM's Alliance Strategy

EXHIBIT 9-1

IBM

Personal Computers
- Matsushita (Low-end PCs)
- Ricoh (Hand-held PCs)

Computer Hardware/Screens
- Toshiba (Display tech)
- Mitsubishi (Mainframes)
- Canon (Printers)
- Hitachi (Large printers)

Factory Automation
- Texas Instruments
- Sumitomo Metal
- Nippon Kokan
- Nissan Motor

Telecommunications
- NTT (Value-added networks)
- Motorola (Mobile data nets)

Business Platforms
- i2 Technologies
- Oracle
- Siebel Systems
- Ariba

Health Care
- Pfizer
- Microsoft

Semiconductor Technology
- Micro Technology
- Motorola (X-ray lithography)
- Motorola (Micro-processor designs)
- Sematech (U.S. Consortium)
- Siemens (16 M and 64 Megabit chips)
- Apple Computer (Operating systems and multimedia technology)
- Etec/Applied Materials (Electron beam technology)
- Toshiba & Siemens (256 Megabit chips)
- Toshiba (Flash memories)
- Advanced Micro Devices (Microprocessors)
- Silicon Valley Group (Photolithography)
- Xilinx (PLD technology)
- Seiko Epson (advanced ASICs)
- Transmeta (production agreement)
- Novellus Systems (copper interconnects)
- Sony & Toshiba (three-way venture in advanced processors)
- Intel & Motorola (three-way venture in deep ultraviolet (DUV) technology)

Software and Processing
- Microsoft
- Oracle
- Sun Microsystems
- Silicon Graphics
- Metaphor
- Hewlett-Packard
- Netscape Communications

Customer Linkages
- Mitsubishi Bank
- Eastman Kodak
- Baxter Healthcare
- Xerox
- Integrion

Consumer Electronics
- Philips Electronics
- Sega
- Blockbuster Entertainment
- Sony
- Nintendo

semiconductors and new forms of communications equipment. Some of the IBM-Motorola relationships included such technologies as etching and lithography techniques for chip making, mobile data networks, and new generations of microprocessors. Both IBM and Motorola are members of the U.S. semiconductor consortium, Sematech. In 1989, IBM and Motorola began to share the earliest versions of X-ray lithography technology used in currently produced semiconductors. Motorola was also the third "leg" of IBM's highly touted joint venture with Apple Computer to develop multimedia operating systems and advanced chip technologies.

During the early 1990s, all three firms attempted to develop a new operating system based on Motorola's 88000 series microprocessor. This new microprocessor, known as the Power PC, was expected to have many of the same capabilities as Intel's Pentium series of chips, but ultimately the three-way venture never experienced the same market penetration as Intel did. Although IBM and Motorola continue to work jointly on cutting-edge semiconductor technology, they have recently begun to take different paths in using the Power PC architecture for consumer electronics, telecommunications, and other applications. More recently, the two firms joined with Intel to work on even more advanced semiconductor capital equipment to produce chips for the current decade. By working with both Intel and Motorola, IBM hopes to sustain America's lead in developing the equipment and technologies that are needed for tomorrow's semiconductor industry.

Apple Computer. The relationship between Apple Computer and IBM was important because it showed the extent to which Big Blue was willing to work with a firm that was very different from itself. In July 1991, both companies formed two separate ventures. One venture, named Kaleida, was designed around operating software and emerging multimedia technology and enabled both firms to consolidate the industry's technical standards. The second venture, Taligent, joined with Motorola to develop a new line of Power PC microprocessors. These Power PC chips were originally developed to compete with Intel's Pentium chips and offer customers faster speed at lower cost. These alliances were designed to assist each partner to work to mutual benefit. For example, IBM was to have gained access to Apple's proprietary Macintosh operating system, while Apple received development help and a steady supply of chips for its new computers. Both Kaleida and Taligent endeavors were highly welcomed in the computer marketplace, where numerous customers were increasingly wary of Microsoft and Intel's growing dominance in Windows-driven software applications. Although the broad framework of cooperation was designed to counter some of Microsoft's dominant market position in PC software, both pillars of the alliance, Kaleida and Taligent, eventually dissolved throughout 1995 and 1996. Neither IBM, Apple, nor, to a lesser extent, Motorola were able to resolve some key differences about how best to manage the organization and operations of the alliance.

Perkin-Elmer, Silicon Valley Group, and Etec Systems. According to many observers, IBM took on a major role to help the United States preserve its high-technology manufacturing base from Japanese assault during the early 1990s. In late 1989, Perkin-Elmer, a leading maker of scientific instruments, put its critical semiconductor manufacturing equipment division on the sale block. Perkin-Elmer represented one of the last viable U.S. manufacturers of chip-making equipment. Its sale or transfer to foreign investors would hasten the erosion of U.S. manufacturing capability in this field.

In early 1990, IBM joined forces with DuPont to transfer Perkin-Elmer's photolithography division to the Silicon Valley Group, and the electron beam operation to Etec Systems, two smaller Silicon Valley firms that possessed cutting-edge technology vital to next-generation chip design and production at the time. IBM, DuPont, and three other domestic strategic investors were dominant co-owners of both Silicon Valley Group and Etec Systems. In effect, IBM's oversight of Perkin-Elmer's transfer of key manufacturing assets into the hands of other friendly, strategically aligned investors ensured that the United States retained a strong domestic manufacturing capability for semiconductor capital equipment. In January 2000, Etec Systems merged with Applied Materials, a leader in developing a broad line of semiconductor capital equipment that is used throughout the entire chip-making industry. In August 2001, ASM Lithography, a Dutch company that has become a leader in photolithography technology, acquired Silicon Valley Group. IBM had already developed strong relationships with both Applied Materials and ASM Lithography over the past few years.

Toshiba. Despite the fact that IBM sought to slow down the pace of Japanese gains in the United States, IBM also took steps to enlarge the scope of cooperation with some of its Japanese partners as well. Toshiba has become IBM's most important Japanese alliance partner. It has worked with Big Blue in a number of different ventures, ranging from mainframe computers to semiconductors to flat-panel displays. Flat-panel displays represent screens that use liquid-crystal display (LCD) and other means to generate digital images. These screens are used in notebook and palm-sized, hand-held computers. Ever since September 1989, IBM and Toshiba jointly manufactured active matrix and liquid-crystal display technologies in an ultramodern plant and fabrication facility in Japan. The development and manufacture of flat-panel displays are still extremely costly and difficult. Each screen uses over one million transistors to control the transmission of images back and forth between the screen and the computer. IBM's latest generation of Think Pad notebook computers employs advanced color screens developed and produced by this venture. In July 1992, IBM broadened the scope of its alliance with Toshiba to include the German firm Siemens. This three-way venture will design and manufacture 256-megabit chips in the United States. The $1 billion cost of designing the first chip is so expensive that no one firm can afford to undertake the project alone. In October 1996, this three-way venture was expanded to include long-time IBM partner Motorola. Now, this complex alliance includes four different partners with complementary skills to forge ahead with extremely costly chip development.

In another related venture signed in May 2001, IBM and Toshiba have agreed to work with Sony to build even faster computer chips. These chips are designed to operate at speeds of current supercomputers, and they will be used for next-generation multimedia and entertainment applications. IBM will work with both Japanese partners at one of its semiconductor laboratories in Austin, Texas.

Siemens. IBM's relationship with Siemens forms the nexus of Big Blue's position in Europe. Siemens is Germany's largest manufacturer of electrical equipment, semiconductors, automation equipment, and industrial components. By working together with Siemens, IBM was able to forestall massive Japanese penetration of the European computer and semiconductor markets as well. In 1989, IBM sold to Siemens its Rolm subsidiary, a manufacturer of PBX and telephone switching equipment. In January 1990, the two companies signed a pact to codesign and manufacture sophisticated memory chips. Siemens remains the fourth member of a complex, evolving relationship with Motorola and Toshiba that was formed in July 1992 to produce even more dense 256-megabit chips. Even today, IBM continues to work with Siemens' semiconductor unit, now known as Infineon Technologies.

Philips. In October 1994, IBM formed a joint venture with European consumer electronics giant Philips to codesign and coproduce new forms of microcontroller chips for use in television sets, CD players, stereos, and home appliances. By linking up with one of the world's biggest and most advanced electronics firms, IBM gains access to Philips's expertise in consumer products. The deal helps both companies learn how to develop new products and technological applications that will be important for the emerging multimedia industry. For IBM, this was an important deal since it enabled Big Blue to understand the kinds of chips that were needed for the fast changing consumer electronics industry.

Current Strategic Alliance Initiatives

Today, IBM's umbrella of strategic alliances covers almost every important technology and business application in the world. Now, many of IBM's alliances are designed to help the company become a leading provider of Internet-based products and services. In addition, some of IBM's newest alliances are helping Big Blue enter new industries as well.

Electronic Commerce. Toward the late 1990s, most of IBM's strategic alliance effort focused on working with companies to accelerate their efforts to engage in electronic commerce and other Internet-based applications. IBM works with partners as varied as Wal-Mart Stores, Japan Airlines, Baxter Healthcare, and dozens of financial services firms to manage their computer and electronic commerce operations. Moreover, IBM has become extremely adept in building core technology platforms that make Big Blue an attractive alliance partner. For example, IBM's latest Internet, Intranet, and server technologies have made it the center of numerous alliance efforts involving such e-commerce companies as Siebel Systems (to manage customer relationships), Peregrine Systems (e-commerce transactions infrastructure), I2 Technologies and Ariba (business-to-business transaction platforms), and Cisco Systems (joint marketing and supply of networking equipment).

Telecommunications. The telecommunications industry has also received much attention from IBM in the past few years. For example, in August 2000, IBM and Sprint announced they would jointly develop new wireless services that would enable corporate customers to perform a variety of different functions using their own Intranets. These services could include receiving e-mail, checking the status of orders, and working with customers through Sprint's wireless networks. In March 2000, IBM entered into an alliance with Qwest Communications to jointly host and manage other companies' on-line Web operations. In this deal, IBM provides the Web-hosting skills and servers that operate on Qwest's advanced fiber-optic data network. This alliance also helps IBM in Europe as well, since it includes Qwest's preexisting alliance partner, Dutch phone company KPN. In Japan, IBM also entered into a broad strategic alliance with Nippon Telephone & Telegraph, also known as NTT. In a ten-year agreement with NTT, IBM will provide much of the computer and Internet technologies needed to help NTT become a full-service provider of Internet applications to customers in Japan.

Smart Technologies. IBM continues to invest in strategic alliances that help the company learn new hardware-based technologies as well. IBM has also begun working with semiconductor giant Texas Instruments on multimedia and video chips. The company is also working with Scientific-Atlanta to design next-generation interactive television, set-top boxes designed to provide Internet and other forms of telecommunications access through cable television networks. It has also signed a variety of alliance agreements with LSI Logic and Kymata to develop next-generation communication chips using optics and other technologies. Likewise, IBM has begun working with Xilinx to develop new system-on-a-chip technology. With the Carrier unit of United Technologies, IBM will participate in designing new Web-enabled air-conditioning systems. Both IBM and Carrier will develop new technologies that allow customers to control their air-conditioning systems through the Internet—a valuable service for many customers that would like to better manage their electricity costs during the summer. In addition, Carrier's air conditioners would use IBM's "smart technology" that notify customers when important mechanical components or fluids need service. In more advanced versions of this technology, the air conditioner will send a diagnostic report to a Carrier service center, which in turn will contact the customer to schedule a maintenance checkup and preventive repair.

Health Care. IBM has also started to form alliances with companies in the medical device and health care fields as well. In January 2000, IBM signed a deal with Medtronic, Inc. IBM will jointly design the chips and wireless networks that will power Medtronic's future pacemakers and cardiac defibrillators. Medtronic hopes to use IBM's technology to develop pacemakers that would automatically notify a patient's doctor or the nearest hospital in case he or she suffers an early heart attack or other abnormality. By designing ultra-responsive pacemakers, Medtronic hopes to save most patients from even suffering a full-blown cardiac event.

In March 2001, Pfizer, a leading pharmaceutical firm, entered into a technology alliance with IBM to create new user-friendly Internet health sites that will enable patients to learn about new treatments and developments in health care. IBM will provide much of the infrastructure for the site, while Pfizer will provide the information and health-oriented knowledge that will be continuously updated.

Ongoing Relationships. IBM continues to use strategic alliances to enter other industries that are increasingly dependent on electronics, semiconductors, and software skills to compete in the future. With Nissan Motor, Nippon Kokan, and Sumitomo Metals, IBM jointly designs and maintains these companies' factory automation software. These alliances with Japanese auto and steel makers help IBM learn how its software and advanced computing systems can be used in many types of industrial applications, such as automotive design and temperature controls.

The Global Airline Industry[2]

During the 1990s, many airline companies have begun to form close strategic alliances with their counterparts from different parts of the world. As the demand for air transportation increases with global business growth, tourism, the rise of discretionary incomes, and the need for airfreight services, many airlines are seeking to extend their reach and revenue streams from domestic markets into new regions of the world. In particular, alliances among different airline partners have taken on greater impetus during the mid-1990s as many governments (particularly those in Europe) have encouraged a wave of consolidation to improve efficiency and to promote competition within the industry. Alliances have begun to pervade the airline industry as they have in the telecommunications, semiconductor, financial services, and pharmaceutical industries. In all of these industries, firms have begun to realize that building a large, critically massed network is key to establishing competitive advantage and market position. As no one airline can afford to reach and serve every market in every region on a cost-competitive basis, alliances among once-fierce rivals have begun to mushroom, especially in the highly lucrative trans-Atlantic market. Some of the most noteworthy trans-Atlantic alliances involving two or more partners are listed in Exhibit 9-2.

Global Strategic Alliances in the Airline Industry

EXHIBIT 9-2

Trans-Atlantic Linkages/Relationships

Airlines	Type of Alliance
• Northwest Airlines • KLM Royal Dutch Airlines	Full partnership (antitrust immunity) Wings alliance
• United Airlines • Lufthansa	Full partnership (antitrust immunity) part of Star Alliance
• Delta Air Lines • Swissair • Sabena • Austrian Airlines	Full partnership (antitrust immunity) Relationship unwound in 1998/1999
• Continental Airlines • Alitalia	Code sharing, joint marketing (antitrust issues pending)
• American Airlines • British Airways	Code sharing, joint marketing (antitrust request withdrawn)
• Delta Airlines • Air France • CSA Czech Airlines • Alitalia • Aero Mexico	Full partnership (antitrust immunity) Sky Team alliance

Globe-Spanning Linkages/Relationships

Airlines	Type of Alliance
• United Airlines • Lufthansa • Scandinavian Airline System (SAS) • Thai International • Varig Brazilian Airlines	Star Alliance: Code sharing, joint marketing; includes up to 17 partners in 2002
• American Airlines • British Airways • Cathay Pacific • Qantas Airways • Aer Lingus • Lan Chile • Finn Air • Iberia	Code sharing, joint marketing, arrangement for global flights. New alliance now known as **one**world.
• Northwest Airlines • Continental Airlines • Japan Air System	Code sharing for Trans-Pacific flights

Although most airlines continue to retain their own corporate identities and marketing programs, the massive growth of strategic alliances in this industry has meant that most airlines became highly interdependent on their alliance partners in order to reach different markets around the world. Thus, individual airline companies are becoming a part of a larger airline alliance network.

From Code Sharing to Combined Operations

Airline alliances once started as simpler "code-sharing" arrangements that enabled cooperating partners to sell each other's seats using the same ticket for a passenger. When conceived in the early 1990s, code-sharing arrangements were an extremely important development in the industry, since they allow airlines to rationalize their passenger flights and airline capacity to maximize the number of revenue-miles per flight. In effect, airlines working together in code-sharing arrangements could streamline and improve the profitability of their operations by coordinating different schedules and ticket pricing for various markets. Airlines would link up and share their flight codes through central computer reservation systems in such a way that the passenger's ticket reflected a single itinerary that might include a flight that is on an airplane owned by an alliance partner. However, beyond that of selling seating capacity, code-sharing alliances are relatively simple mechanisms, since most code-sharing arrangements precluded the airline partners from more closely coordinating their schedules or pricing structures.

In the mid-1990s, however, airline alliances evolved from simpler code-sharing arrangements toward much closer, more intricate joint alliance planning between partners. In 1992, the U.S. Department of Transportation in a landmark decision granted antitrust immunity to Northwest Airlines and KLM Royal Dutch Airlines that enabled the two companies to coordinate their trans-Atlantic flights as if they were one single entity. This move helps both carriers reduce their costs significantly. This decision set the pattern for more sophisticated alliances that allowed partners to unite their entire fare structures, flight schedules, marketing initiatives, frequent flier programs, baggage handling facilities, and time and gate slots at different airports. These partnerships have worked to create significantly easier international connections for passengers traveling from one region to another, and it brought nonstop service to new, interior markets that were previously required to fly passengers to another "departing hub" or "gateway" location before they could actually catch their international flight. In recent years, governments have heretofore approved of such expanded partnership arrangements because there are more choices of international routings served through multiple hubs, thus preserving competition among competing airline alliances. The net effect of these alliance-driven, combined operations is to give partners an ability to leapfrog into new markets that they previously could not have served because of government regulations, pricing difficulties, overwhelming market dominance by a local carrier, or the high cost of establishing infrastructure at a newly served airport. These alliances provide the basis for a global network without the associated costs of high capital investment. Alliances receiving antitrust immunity are the only way that airlines can become even more global in their reach, particularly when there are still numerous government restrictions imposed by many nations.

Network versus Network

Airlines were forming alliances and combining their operations at a dizzying pace in the late 1990s. Northwest Airlines and KLM are working to extend their core Detroit–Amsterdam passenger routes to extend farther into continental Europe and the United States. These have included such other gateways as Minneapolis, New York, and Seattle-Tacoma. At one point, Delta Air Lines worked very closely with partners Swissair, Sabena, and Austrian Airlines to provide frequent nonstop service from New York, Atlanta, Cincinnati, and Salt Lake City to several European locations. However, this series of relationships eventually dissolved, and Delta began working with Air France to form a new trans-Atlantic network relationship, which recently won antitrust immunity. Delta's former alliance partners could not provide the kind of high-frequency flight schedules that were needed to battle those of American Airlines and United Airlines. Now, United Airlines closely coordinates its flight schedules and pricing closely with Lufthansa to gain access to Northern Europe and the rest of the continent. In May 1996, American Airlines sought governmental permission to enter into a broad-ranging alliance with British Airways to create a new global airline network. Far more vast than the Northwest–KLM or the previous Delta–Swissair–Sabena–Austrian Airlines alliances, the proposed American–British alliance would overshadow the existing trans-Atlantic division of labor among competing alliances in terms of sheer size of the parents, projected number of passengers carried, and the stranglehold that both American and British Airways would control at London's key Heathrow Airport. In linking up with British Airways, American gains the ability to ticket its customers for travel beyond Heathrow and into the continent. American is currently second to United in serving the trans-Atlantic market and cannot extend its reach to such cities as Rome, Budapest, Vienna, Athens, or any other points beyond without a partner. British Airways, on the other hand, seeks American as a partner because it offers a strong passenger network into much of the United States and Latin America, where American has been steadily gaining strength against many of the nationally based local airlines. The vast scale of the proposed American–British Airways alliance has prompted numerous protests from other competing airline partners, such as United Airlines and Lufthansa, which demand greater access to Heathrow and other European hubs before they will approve of the deal. Even five years after the original petition was filed with the U.S. and British governments, neither British Airways nor American Airlines has received full antitrust immunity for their coordinated trans-Atlantic schedules. In January 2002, the two carriers decided not to petition their respective governments for antitrust immunity.

The proliferation of alliances in the profitable trans-Atlantic market is giving way to more complex, multipartner operations that are now linking up partners from different parts of the world into a series of interwoven code-sharing and joint marketing arrangements. These broader, multiairline alliances have not yet received antitrust immunity for other markets, so their scope of coordination is somewhat more limited than that found in the core trans-Atlantic market. However, the trans-Atlantic alliance experiences for United Airlines, Delta Air Lines, and American Airlines have provided these carriers important experience and learning opportunities to broaden their relationships to other parts of the world where they have not intensively served before. From a competitive standpoint, these globe-spanning alliances will now pit entire global networks of airline alliances against other rival alliances to capture customers and market shares. Thus, the industry is moving to a new form of jointly managed cooperation and competition between entire collections of firms.

For example, in May 1997, the newly created Star Alliance enlarges the existing United Airlines–Lufthansa alliance to include a code-sharing arrangement with Thai International, SAS, and Varig Brazilian Airlines. By June 2002, the original five-member Star Alliance grew to include seventeen members, including ANA of Japan, British Midland, Air Canada, and a number of different carriers serving the Pacific. Star Alliance strengthened the reach of Lufthansa and United, the biggest carriers, to gain better access to Southeast Asia, Scandinavia, Latin America, and now the Pacific. By significantly broadening what is already a powerful alliance, Lufthansa in particular gains a much larger share of the profitable long-haul traffic from Europe to the Far East, especially from business travelers who contribute a disproportionate amount of airline profits. Even now, Star Alliance is currently negotiating to expand its alliance membership to other carriers throughout the world. In late 2001, both United Airlines and British Midland were seeking to acquire antitrust immunity from the U.S. and British governments to allow even more integration among their flight routes, schedules, and pricing.

During the last few years, Delta Air Lines has tried to extend its trans-Atlantic alliance network to include Singapore Airlines to serve Southeast Asia but was unable to persuade Singapore to join its alliance configuration. At the same time, Delta began working with Air France to form the SkyTeam alliance, which is designed to counter rival trans-Atlantic alliances. Delta is looking to enter the Pacific and Far Eastern markets by including Korean Air into its SkyTeam network. On the other hand, Delta has made some major inroads into the Latin American market by working more closely to integrate its flight schedules with long-standing partner AeroMexico, which has also become part of SkyTeam. By late 2001, Delta and Air France successfully petitioned their respective governments to seek antitrust immunity. Antitrust immunity, similar to the kind that exists between Northwest and KLM, allows both carriers to coordinate the use of their aircraft, set prices, and determine the schedules between the two countries. As recently as 1998, Air France gained the right to fly and to land at any U.S. destination. New partners in the alliance include Alitalia and CSA Czech Airlines as part of SkyTeam. The combination with Delta will allow all partners to fly not only to each other's destinations but to other destinations as well.

Meanwhile, American Airlines has been forming relationships with a number of important carriers to both Asia and Latin America throughout the past few years. Most recently, American and British Airways announced that they would form a global partnership spanning Europe, North America, the Far East, and

Australia by forming a series of alliances with Cathay Pacific of Hong Kong and Qantas Airways of Australia. Cathay Pacific and American Airlines both need each other in particular because neither has the critical mass to serve North America or the Pacific respectively. In particular, Cathay Pacific has come under severe margin pressures recently with the economic recession now plaguing Southeast Asia. American, however, needs Cathay Pacific as a key partner to circumvent the need to fly to Tokyo before reaching other Asian destinations. In March 1999, American Airlines, British Airways, Canadian Airlines, Cathay Pacific, and Qantas Airways formally unveiled their globe-spanning **one**world alliance. **One**world is designed to help all five carriers (and future participants) reach parts of the world they were unable to access before. Newer partners also include Iberia (routes in Spain and Portugal), Finn Air (routes in Scandinavia), and Aer Lingus (Ireland). Some analysts believe that because American and British Airways did not receive antitrust immunity, the relationship between the two megacarriers may weaken in future years as both companies look for more suitable partners. For now, they remain committed to the **one**world alliance.

Introduction

This chapter shows how companies can use strategic alliances to learn and build new sources of competitive advantage. The role of strategic alliances in shaping corporate and business strategy has grown significantly over the past decade. In almost every industry, alliances are becoming more common as companies realize that they can no longer afford the costs of developing new products or entering new markets on their own. Alliances are especially prevalent in industries or technologies that change rapidly, such as semiconductors, airlines, automobiles, pharmaceuticals, telecommunications, consumer electronics, and financial services.[3] What is also interesting about strategic alliances is that we are now beginning to see intensely competitive rivals now working together, often in ways unimaginable even a few years back. For example, we are seeing fierce competitors such as Oracle and Sun Microsystems in the software industry teaming up to jointly design next generation software platforms that they hope companies will use to manage their electronic-commerce activities. On a broader global level, many U.S. and Japanese firms in the automobile and electronics industries have teamed up to develop new technologies, even as they compete fiercely to sell their existing products and enter each other's markets.

strategic alliances: Linkages between companies designed to achieve an economic objective faster or more efficiently than either company could do so alone; take the basic forms of licensing arrangements, joint ventures, or multipartner consortia.

Strategic alliances are linkages between companies designed to achieve an objective faster or more efficiently than if either firm attempted to do so on its own. The role of strategic alliances in shaping the future course of both industries and individual firms is likely to become even more profound in the next century. For both single-business and diversified enterprises, teaming and allying with other companies are becoming powerful vehicles for entering new markets, learning new technologies, and developing new products. Many companies have discovered that the costs of undertaking internal development programs, especially for new drugs or high-technology products, are extremely high and risky. Other companies want to grow and expand, but they realize that mergers and acquisitions can present significant difficulties related to integrating newly acquired companies or businesses. On the other hand, strategic alliances serve a vital role in extending and renewing a firm's sources of competitive advantage because they allow companies to limit certain kinds of risk when entering new terrain.

We begin by examining the environmental changes that prompt companies to enter into strategic alliances. Second, we consider the different types and benefits of strategic alliances. Third, we analyze the costs and risks of cooperation that underscore all strategic alliances. Finally, we focus on alliance-based implementation issues, examining how companies can balance cooperation and competition to maximize the benefits and minimize the costs of alliance-based activities.

Factors Promoting the Rise of Strategic Alliances

Alliances work to extend a firm's competitive advantage in several important ways. In many situations, firms enter into strategic alliances because an alliance can potentially provide benefits that are not possible through either internal development or external acquisition. Thus, companies form alliances to acquire some of diversification's benefits without assuming the full costs of going it alone. Alliances represent a potent alternative to internally formulated diversification strategies to enter new industries that companies pursue on their own. Unlike do-it-yourself internal development, a firm must work with a partner to develop new technologies and/or products. Also, unlike full-scale acquisitions, an alliance does not give a firm total control over its partner; the firm does not completely merge with its partner. In this sense, alliances serve as an intermediate or transitional step to enter new industries and markets. *Alliances can assist the firm's learning and diversification into new areas of activity.*

Strategic alliances can help firms extend and renew their sources of competitive advantage when expanding globally. The successful pursuit of global or multidomestic strategies often requires firms to establish operations in distant markets. Yet, these commitments in many cases are high risk, especially when companies are not familiar with the local environment. Alliances thus act as potential risk reduction vehicles for firms seeking to enter new markets that they do not know well. As such, firms may find that *alliances provide useful platforms to test their products in new markets* before they commit themselves to establishing their own self-contained units and subsidiaries in global markets. By teaming up with a partner that has more experience and knowledge about a particular market's conditions, a firm can better understand how to compete in a new region at lower cost and risk. Even companies that have already established their own operating subsidiaries in distant markets can benefit from strategic alliances. Working with a partner can help overcome or sidetrack other economic obstacles to further expansion.

Firms engage in strategic alliances for a number of reasons, but they all involve some form of *risk reduction*. Strategic alliances can help reduce the risk of (1) entering new markets, (2) shaping of industry evolution, (3) learning and applying new technologies, and (4) rounding out a product line. These categories are not mutually exclusive. In practice, many firms will employ strategic alliances in order to manage and deal with several overlapping types of risks.

New Market Entry

Companies have formed strategic alliances to speed market entry. In the global pharmaceutical industry, for example, Merck, Fujisawa, and Bayer aggressively cross-license their newest drugs to one another. These arrangements help all three firms reduce the high fixed costs of R&D and global distribution. Fujisawa distributes Merck's and Bayer's drugs in Japan, while Bayer does so for Merck and Fujisawa in Europe. In this way, all three firms avoid duplicating the high fixed costs of development, distribution, and marketing worldwide. Pharmaceutical firms will often work with one another in order to promote the fast distribution and acceptance of a new drug. For example, Pharmacia jointly markets its new pain-reducing drug Celebrex together with Pfizer. By combining their marketing programs and sales initiatives to jointly support Celebrex's rollout and distribution, Pharmacia can speed up market acceptance of its drug, especially as it competes against a similar offering from competitor Merck. The cooperation found between Pharmacia and Pfizer is just one of many strategic alliances among pharmaceutical firms that are designed to smooth market entry and to accelerate market acceptance of a new drug. These relationships are especially important for the drug companies as marketing costs are rising fast in this industry.

In the global automobile industry, companies such as Ford and Mazda or General Motors and Isuzu assist each other in entering new markets with new products. In fact, strategic alliances in the automobile industry have helped many companies to realign their operations in ways that allow them not only to enter new markets, but also to learn about what customers want from their products. As each company has learned that there is no such thing as a truly "world car," working with a partner is a must in order to understand the unique market and transportation conditions that surround how customers use vehicles. For example, General Motors helps Isuzu enter the small truck market in the United States and Asia, while Isuzu helps General Motors better understand how to distribute cars in the Japanese, Middle Eastern, and Southeast Asian markets, where Isuzu has longer experience and a better distribution base. Isuzu has effectively become GM's distribution and marketing spearhead in markets where GM is not a familiar brand.

In the beverage industry, Nestlé works with Coca-Cola to gain access to the other's distribution channels. This is a long-standing relationship that combines both companies' marketing and distribution clout in ways that enhance each firm's competitive position in businesses that are more central to them. Coca-Cola distributes Nestlé's line of fruit juices and coffees, while Nestlé works with Coke on other soft drink products distribution worldwide. Without teaming up, both companies would have to spend more time and resources on their own "reinventing the wheel" to enter certain market segments.

The rise of numerous alliances in the airline industry is directly related to partners' seeking access to serve new markets they previously could not enter. In particular, U.S. and European airlines have been rapidly teaming up with one another to serve the profitable trans-Atlantic market in such a way that they can reach into the European continent and the U.S. interior, respectively. Trans-Atlantic airline alliances enable partners to extend their reach without incurring a disproportionate high cost of capital investment. Likewise, many of the same U.S. carriers are beginning to formulate a broad range of alliances to help them enter promising trans-Pacific markets, especially Japan, China, and Southeast Asia, which U.S. airlines have typically had difficulty reaching (largely because of government regulations and agreements needed between nations to allocate flights).

Shaping of Industry Evolution

Strategic alliances can help shape what an industry may look like in the future. In the semiconductor and biotechnology industries, many firms have formed alliances to define emerging standards or new products. (See Exhibit 9-3.) For example, Lucent Technologies and Motorola began working with one another in 1998 to develop a new generation of digital signal processing (DSP) chips that is designed to power next-generation cellular phones and other consumer electronics. By working together, both Lucent and Motorola hope to be able to participate in a fast-evolving segment of the semiconductor industry where demand is expected to grow more quickly than that for traditional microprocessors.

Intel has also used strategic alliances to help shape industry standards in the process of becoming the leading producer and supplier of microprocessors to almost all of the world's personal computer manufacturers. Intel uses long-term supply arrangements with most PC makers in the world for its broad line of Pentium and Celeron-class chips. By locking in with its customers, Intel can control to a significant degree the kinds of hardware and software that will be used in the world's personal computers, regardless of which company finally assembles the product. To counter Intel's near-monopoly position in microprocessors, arch rival Advanced Micro Devices has worked with Motorola to introduce a new type of copper interconnect technology that is designed to accelerate the computing power of its Athlon and Duron-class chips. Advanced Micro Devices, long a laggard to Intel, has relied on alliances to help it learn new technologies and to gain access to vital production technologies. Even IBM has worked with AMD to build chips for several years during the 1990s. In the area of advanced microprocessors, IBM itself has used alliances to aggressively develop markets for its Power PC microprocessor architecture. In addition to using its powerful internal R&D to create ultrafast chips that consume very little power, IBM has formed alliances with Sony and Toshiba to develop a next-generation "super-

Representative Alliances in the Semiconductor Industry — EXHIBIT 9-3

Partners	Technology
Lucent Technologies Motorola	Digital signal processors (DSPs)
IBM Motorola Toshiba Siemens	256-megabit memory chips Advanced flash memories
Advanced Micro Devices Fujitsu	Advanced flash memories
Intel Sharp Corporation	Advanced flash memories
LSI Logic Micron Technology	Hybrid, embedded DRAM chips
Advanced Micro Devices Motorola	Copper deposition technology in chip circuitry
Intel Hewlett-Packard	64-bit Itanium microprocessor (Merced Project)
Lucent Technologies NEC Mitsubishi Electric	Custom-designed chips for communications equipment
Toshiba Samsung	Advanced memory chips
Philips Electronics STMicroelectronics Taiwan Semiconductor	.09-micron chip technology
IBM Xilinx	System-on-a-chip technology using Power PC architecture
Toshiba Infineon Technologies	Advanced DRAM chips
Intel Analog Devices	Advanced DSP chips

computer on a chip" technology. IBM is also working closely with Nintendo to develop and produce the microprocessors used for the Japanese video game company's game Cube. During the early 1990s, IBM teamed up with Motorola and Apple Computer to develop and produce an advanced line of chips that were originally designed to confront Intel head on in the personal computer business. However, this relationship has faded into the background as both Motorola and IBM devote more of their efforts to non-PC applications. Apple, however, has continued to work with Motorola and to use its microprocessors for its Macintosh PC systems.

In the desktop printing industry, Canon has become the world's largest supplier of "engines" that power laser printers. Throughout the 1980s and 1990s, Canon formed relationships with leading companies to build core components for desktop laser printers. By teaming up with Hewlett-Packard, IBM, and other manufacturers, Canon ensures that upward of 60 percent of the world's laser printers use a Canon-made "engine" to power the machine. Similarly, Microsoft has aims to become the leading supplier of the software and operating systems used on next-generation office equipment and even consumer electronics. Throughout the computer and server industries, it has formed numerous cooperative software agreements with hardware and software companies to ensure that future products use the Microsoft Windows or Windows NT operating systems as the dominant format. Microsoft has even formed alliances with competitors to ensure that the Windows operating system is well represented on all types of product offerings. In many ways, competitors were compelled to work with Microsoft because of the software giant's enormous market clout and customer acceptance of its products. However, Microsoft's use of strategic alliances was just one part of a larger case that the U.S. government brought against the company because of its alleged anticompetitive tactics. Nevertheless, in all of these examples, alliances have played an important role in helping firms establish an industry standard and gain a dominant position.

More and more frequently, teams of companies across different industries will compete against other teams to see which group will ultimately produce a dominant standard. For example, Toshiba, Matsushita, and Time Warner (now part of AOL Time Warner) cooperated extensively during the mid-1990s to design highly versatile, digital video disks (DVDs) for the consumer electronics industry. Sony and Philips Electronics had their own alliance to codesign and produce their respective version of DVD technology that used a different set of design tools and layers to record and store video and other forms of data. These DVDs have already begun to replace VCRs as the primary consumer electronics device to complement the television set in many homes. Both the Sony–Philips alliance and the Toshiba–Matsushita–Time Warner alliance produced numerous variations of DVD prototypes and software platforms before the two sides were able to come to a mutual understanding and agree on a common set of technical standards in early 1996. Both alliance teams realized that if they failed to come to an agreement early in the product development stage, then it was highly unlikely that consumers would buy either competing DVD standard, since movies made on one version of DVD were not compatible with the other.[4]

More recently, telecommunications equipment companies have begun working closely among themselves to design an industry standard for new types of wireless communications. Here, the alliance efforts have been somewhat more fragmented. During the late 1990s, Ericsson, Motorola, and Nokia joined forces to promote a new wireless standard known as Wireless Application Protocol (WAP). This standard was designed to enhance the creation of new technologies and applications for wireless Internet usage. Other companies, however, formed their own relationships to promote their vision of what wireless technologies should be able to do. Some of these technologies use different software algorithms to transmit digital information (e.g., TDMA vs. CDMA vs. GSM standards). For example, Qualcomm (U.S. based), Nokia (Finland based), Symbian (U.K. based), and even Microsoft worked with a broad array of their own partners to create the technology platform for what is known as 2.5G and 3G technologies (*G* stands for *generation*). These are technologies that allow video streaming, wireless Internet transmission, and even the use of digital cameras on next-generation cellular phones. In addition, these phones will be designed to work together with future personal digital assistants (PDAs), such as Palm's Palm Pilot line of products and Handspring's future Visor offerings.

Learning and Applying New Technologies

Companies form alliances to learn or to gain access to new technologies. In the telecommunications industry, for example, a broad array of alliances has arisen over the past few years as existing telephone networks quickly converge with new Internet-driven communications and computer technologies. For example, a number of new upstart firms that promise to offer faster, clearer, and multipurpose communications services (voice, video, data) along broadband networks have found important strategic partners with the capital and technology to invest in them. Until it became a publicly traded company in June 1999, Juniper Networks worked closely with IBM and other companies to develop an ultrafast, terabit capability (transmission speeds of one trillion bits per second) router that will transform much of current Internet and voice traffic. At that time, Juniper was an upstart in a field dominated by the likes of Cisco Systems, Lucent Technologies, Nortel Networks, 3Com Corporation, and other networking companies that were seeking to enter the telecom and broadband networking equipment area. Now, Juniper Networks has begun challenging market leader Cisco Systems to develop even faster routers that will power next-generation telecommunications and optical networks. More important, Juniper has even begun to develop its own technology that many telecommunications firms are currently reviewing for their own use. Nortel Networks even entered into a joint marketing alliance with Juniper in summer 2000 to sell its ultrafast routers to other telecommunications firms. Nortel will provide much of the marketing and distribution clout that Juniper currently lacks.[5]

In a similar vein, Alcatel worked with Xylan, a small networking firm, to learn how to design advanced data networking gear. In March 1999, after several successful joint projects, Alcatel acquired Xylan to complement its existing internal development efforts. Thus, alliances have served as important vehicles for a number of upstart firms and incumbent high-tech firms to learn and apply emerging technologies to the telecommunications industries and other broadband network markets. Moreover, alliances complement the internal development efforts of companies with strategic interests in the telecommunications industries. Companies such as Alcatel, Cisco Systems, IBM, Nortel Networks, Lucent Technologies, WorldCom, Siemens, and Hughes Network Systems stand to benefit from their relationships with smaller upstart firms that often need capital and distribution assistance. These small companies can provide the talent, insight, and "young blood" energy needed to succeed in highly volatile and fast-moving markets. On the other hand, the upstart firms can gain significant legitimacy and market confidence when giant firms invest and help with their technology development efforts.

This same rationale to learn new technologies and to tap into new sources of talent drives many pharmaceutical firms to establish close alliance relationships with young biotechnology firms. Exhibit 9-4 shows just a few of the hundreds of relationships that have taken root over the past several years. For example, Bayer AG of Germany entered into an alliance with Millennium Pharmaceuticals to develop cancer-fighting drugs based on recent discoveries of a new gene that causes tumors to form. Both Bayer and Millennium will work over a six-year period to use computers and other advanced techniques to speed up the discovery of new genetic-based treatments for everything from cancer to osteoporosis. In a related manner, AstraZeneca formed an alliance with Orchid BioSciences, a leading biotechnology firm that specializes in discovering the specific genetic proteins that may be important triggers for disease formation. Orchid's technology is designed to foster the creation of drugs that are unique to each individual human being, using genetic materials to deliver very specific treatments that limit side effects and other downside risks.

In these alliances, pharmaceutical firms have the resources, marketing, distribution, regulatory knowledge, and R&D facilities that almost all the small biotechnology firms lack. On the other hand, biotechnology firms, often founded by recently trained microbiologists, possess cutting-edge techniques that are of great interest to more mature drug companies. These techniques include the use of computer-generated software algorithms to map out the human genetic sequence (genomic technologies), protein synthesis (using amino acid technologies), and the design of new genetic engineering techniques that specifically isolate different sources of hard-to-treat diseases. Often, younger biotechnology firms will develop and use techniques that are so new that they are hard to replicate within the established procedures and development patterns found in many incumbent pharmaceutical firms. Thus, large drug companies will often enter into mutually benefiting alliances with biotechnology companies to jointly learn and develop exotic new drug and drug delivery technologies together.[6]

In another technology-driven industry, Mitsubishi, Fuji Heavy Industries, and Kawasaki Heavy Industries have long worked closely with Boeing to learn new assembly techniques used in the aerospace industry. These three Japanese companies serve as chief

EXHIBIT 9-4 Representative Alliances in the Biotechnology Industry

Partners	Technology/Product
Biogen SmithKline Beecham	Tissue regeneration
Amgen Kirin Brewery	Blood platelet growth factor
Onyx Pharmaceuticals Bayer AG	"Arrow" drug delivery technology
Chiron Novartis	Genetic mapping technology
Genentech Hoffman-LaRoche	Tissue plasminogen activator
Neurocrine Biosciences Eli Lilly	Corticotropin releasing factor (CRF) hormones
Agouron Pharmaceuticals Roche Holding, Ltd.	Anticancer drugs
Human Genome Sciences SmithKline Beccham	Genetic mapping technology
Millennium Pharmaceuticals American Home Products	Genetic mapping technology
Creative BioMolecules Biogen	Kidney treatments
Incyte Pharmaceuticals Monsanto	Genetic engineering software
Pioneer Hi-Bred DuPont	Genetically engineered seeds for agriculture
Bayer AG Millennium Pharmaceuticals	Genetically engineered cancer-fighting compounds
DuPont Monsanto	Genetically engineered corn seeds
AstraZeneca PLC Orchid Biosciences	Advanced single nucleotide polymorphisms (SNPs)

subcontractors to Boeing for key parts of commercial aircraft, such as the fuselage and tail sections. For example, Mitsubishi Heavy Industries assembles about 60 percent of the fuselage used in many Boeing aircraft. In addition, Boeing's relationship to all three companies has grown closer as they cooperate on studying new fuselage designs that use composite materials. All three Japanese firms have long-term ambitions to enter the commercial aviation industry. Realizing that these three firms could pose a potential long-term threat, Boeing carefully manages the degree of technological sharing it conducts with its Japanese partners. On the other hand, Boeing finds its Japanese partners to be useful teachers of lower-cost Japanese assembly and fabrication techniques that Boeing can then incorporate in its operations in the United States, especially as Boeing learns to adopt new streamlined manufacturing techniques that call for closer supplier relationships and the use of computer networks.[7]

IBM has teamed up with Motorola and Toshiba to further improve its semiconductor-manufacturing prowess in making superdense chips. IBM gains access to Toshiba's manufacturing and miniaturization skills and its expertise across a whole range of technologies, including flat-panel display screens and specialized skills used for making chips in consumer electronics. With Motorola, IBM learns how to design new products for emerging wireless technologies. Both IBM and Motorola work together to develop new X-ray photolithography techniques that neither company can afford on its own. This technology is an integral part of designing and producing new types of microprocessors and memory chips. By working with two partners simultaneously, IBM hopes to learn the best techniques and designs from both.

Rounding Out the Product Line

Some companies use strategic alliances to round out or fill their product line. See Exhibit 9-5 for an overview of alliances that are shaping the global automotive industry. For example, Ford has worked with Nissan Motor to build a new generation of minivans (known as the Mercury Villager or Nissan Quest). Neither Nissan nor Ford could afford the development cost of new minivans on its own. During the late 1980s, Ford had another long-standing joint venture with Mazda to coproduce the Ford Escort and Probe in Michigan. Although Ford no longer currently produces either model, the relationship with Mazda was extremely instrumental in helping Ford learn new manufacturing and quality improvement techniques from its Japanese partner. Mazda, in turn, gains access to Ford's popular line of recreational and sport utility vehicles, which Mazda did not produce on its own.

Representative Alliances in the Global Auto Industry — EXHIBIT 9-5

U.S. Unit/Product	Partner	Location of Manufacture
Chevy Cavalier	Toyota/GM	California
Ford Festiva	Kia Motors	South Korea
Mercury Tracer	Mazda	Engineered in Japan, manufactured in Mexico
Mercury Villager	Nissan	Japan and United States
Dodge & Plymouth Colt	Mitsubishi	Japan
Plymouth Laser	Mitsubishi	Illinois
Eagle Medallion	Renault	France
Eagle Summit	Mitsubishi	Japan
Chrysler	General Motors	Transmission in United States
Chrysler	BMW	Joint investment in Latin America
United Technologies	Nissan	Automotive components
DaimlerChrysler	Mitsubishi Hyundai	Advanced modular engines
Caterpillar	DaimlerChrysler	Medium-duty engines
General Motors	Toyota	Fuel cells and hybrid engine technology
General Motors	Isuzu	40% equity stake
General Motors	Fuji Motor	20% equity stake

The relationship between Mazda and Ford has actually become much more close and complex over the past few years, as Ford has taken over 33 percent of the Japanese firm and installed an American CEO at its helm. As Mazda struggled with its own efforts to compete with Toyota, Honda, and Nissan, Ford became a valuable partner to Mazda in rebuilding its finances and learning how to sell in the United States. Mazda has gained extensively as well from Ford's financial strength during economic recessions in Japan and Southeast Asia. In effect, Ford has taken over Mazda's financial operations but has given its Japanese partner considerable leeway in developing and refining its own distinctive engineering talent.

In the financial services industry, both Fidelity Investments and Charles Schwab & Co., two leading discount brokerage houses, have offered other mutual fund companies' offerings through their own fund distribution systems. This strategic move was especially important for Schwab, who as recently as 1996, generally avoided such cooperation for fear of cannibalizing its own products to its customers. Now, Schwab believes that cooperating with other fund companies (e.g., Stein Roe Mutual Funds, Janus Funds, Nations Funds, Berger Funds) works to mutual advantage because it enables Schwab to participate directly in timing the new funds' rollout, setting minimum balance requirements, and other marketing considerations. Schwab directly benefits from cooperating with other companies because not only does it receive a fee for helping with the funds' launch, but it also provides a wide variety of product and fund offerings to fill in the "shelf space" of Schwab's vast brokerage and fund distribution system. The alliance also gives Schwab a potentially powerful marketing message to its customers; that is, Schwab customers will gain first access to purchasing shares in new funds. Conversely, the other fund companies gain access to Schwab's vast customer database and can now launch new funds with an existing, solid critical marketing mass of potential buyers that may not have been easily accessed before.[8]

In Japan, Mitsubishi and Hitachi resell mainframe and notebook computers built by IBM to complement their existing products. These alliances are especially important for Hitachi, which recently announced that it would no longer produce its own line of IBM-compatible mainframe computers. IBM achieved low-cost volume production of mainframe computers in Japan to accomplish its goals of breaking into the Japanese market, and Hitachi needed IBM's Power PC semiconductor line to fulfill its own line of consumer electronics and computers. Over time, as the two companies diversified their operations into other lines of business, both Mitsubishi and Hitachi needed to fill out their mainframe product lines but did not have the manufacturing capacity or advanced semiconductor technology to do it on their own. Mitsubishi's ties with IBM have also grown recently as the two companies begin to cooperate on designing the chips needed for new types of hand-held computers. Hitachi has also recently committed itself to using more IBM-manufactured Power PC microprocessors in its line of personal computers and other electronic equipment. With both companies, IBM gains valuable partners that already control many of the distribution channels for computers and related products in Japan.

IBM also sells some equipment made by its Japanese alliance partners in the United States. With Mitsubishi, IBM codesigns a PDA device that it once sold together with Bell South. Both companies continue to cooperate in looking for new ways to sell next-generation Internet-driven consumer appliances. In addition, IBM also works closely with Japanese firms Ricoh and Toshiba to cooperate on designing new types of imaging and flat-panel display technologies. Both companies contribute valuable technical expertise to IBM's product development efforts.

Star Alliance, which encompasses United Airlines, Lufthansa, Thai International, SAS, Varig Brazilian Airlines, Air Canada, and a dozen other carriers, allows each partner to offer a truly global range of cities and service. The alliance helps each airline partner serve many parts of the world that it previously could not access without significant cost or lengthy government petitions and regulatory processes. Star Alliance enables each of its partners to develop and coordinate a unified marketing theme (worldwide travel to anywhere) that ideally is designed to transport passengers from any region of the world to another using an alliance member's aircraft. In this way, each member of the alliance benefits from providing services that capture the full stream of revenues from each paying passenger. This global network allows the participants of Star to better compete against the likes of similarly emerging alliance networks around the world.

Types and Benefits of Strategic Alliances

Firms can enter into a number of different types of strategic alliances. These could include comparatively simple, more "distant" arrangements in which firms work with one another on a short-term or a contractually defined basis. In these alliances, the two parties effectively do not combine their managers, value chains, core technologies, or other skill sets. Examples of such simpler alliance vehicles include licensing, cross-marketing deals, limited forms of outsourcing, and loosely configured customer-supply arrangements. On the other hand, companies may seek to partner more closely in their cooperative ventures. Such alliances combine managers, technologies, products, processes, and other value-adding assets in varying ways to bring the companies more closely together. Examples of alliance vehicles in this league include technology development pacts, coproduction arrangements, and formal joint ventures in which the partners contribute a defined amount of capital to form a third-party entity. Finally, in even more complex strategic alliance arrangements, partners can take significant equity-stake holdings in one another, thus approximating many organizational and strategic characteristics of an outright merger or acquisition.

We will focus on three broad types or vehicles of strategic alliances: (1) licensing arrangements, (2) joint ventures, and (3) cross-holding arrangements that include equity stakes and consortia among firms. Each broad type of strategic alliance is implemented differently and imposes its own set of managerial skills, constraints, and coordination requirements needed to build competitive advantage.

Licensing Arrangements

In most manufacturing industries, licensing represents a sale of technology- or product-based knowledge in exchange for market entry. In service-based firms, licensing is the right to enter a market in exchange for a fee or royalty. Licensing arrangements have become more prominent across both categories. In many ways they represent the least sophisticated and simplest-to-manage form of strategic alliance. Licensing arrangements are simple alliances because they allow the participants greater access to either a technology or market in exchange for royalties or future technology sharing than either partner could do on its own. Within the airline industry, for example, many of the code-sharing arrangements that allow airlines to sell each other's seats are somewhat akin to the licensing agreements found in manufacturing and service industries. The airlines do not coordinate any other activities beyond their computer reservation systems and ticketing codes to sell seats and to capture a percentage of the revenues.

Unlike joint ventures or more complex cross-holding/equity stake consortia, licensing arrangements provide no joint equity ownership in a new entity. Companies enter into licensing agreements for several reasons. The primary reasons are (1) a need for help in commercializing a new technology and (2) global expansion of a brand franchise or marketing image.

Technology Development. In many cases, firms have freely licensed their newest technologies or innovations to other firms. This situation usually occurs because the firm holding the license cannot, on its own, develop or exploit the technology to its fullest extent. For example, during the early 1990s, Sun Microsystems aggressively licensed its RISC-based microprocessor technology (known as Sparc and UltraSparc) to numerous electronics firms. Sun developed an extremely innovative computer architecture but does not have the manufacturing capacity to enter markets quickly on its own. Thus, Sun needs the help of firms such as Texas Instruments, Siemens, Philips, Fujitsu, and LSI Logic to manufacture its RISC-based chip more cheaply and quickly. Sun also benefits from these partners' access to large markets that are interested in Sun's innovations. TI and Fujitsu have emerged as key licensees of the Sun system. Both firms have moved to deepen and extend the nature of their relationship with Sun Microsystems.

Exhibit 9-6 gives an overview of how Sun Microsystems used licensing to build a global presence in the semiconductor industry rapidly. As stated in Exhibit 9-6, Philips helps Sun break into the European market for RISC-based chips. Philips holds a commanding position in many European markets for computers and consumer electronics, the products that are most likely to take advantage of RISC technology. TI and Fujitsu give Sun manufacturing muscle to build the chip quickly. At that time, Sun also maintained a series of cross-licensing arrangements with three smaller U.S. design firms—Bipolar Integrated, LSI Logic, and Cypress Semiconductor—to ensure access to even newer cutting-edge technologies. Sun collaborated with these design firms to promote and to learn advanced design skills used to make even faster chips for the future. As Sun's Sparc technology became an important player in designing next-generation servers to handle large databases, Sun has steadily realigned its alliance arrangements over the past several years. In order to gain volume production of its Sparc and UltraSparc chips, Sun has become much closer to Texas Instruments and Fujitsu to provide low-cost manufacturing facilities for its chips. In particular, Texas Instruments has effectively become Sun Microsystems' largest manufacturing partner that handles even critical design tasks for Sun's Sparc chips.

EXHIBIT 9-6 Sun Microsystems' Licensing Strategy in the Early 1990s

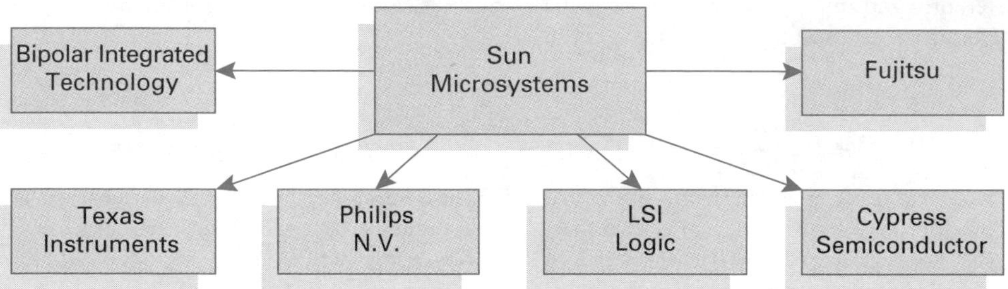

- Linkage with Philips gives Sun access to European market. Philips will specialize in RISC chips for consumer and telecommunications products.
- Linkage with Texas Instruments gives domestic credibility to new product design.
- Linkage with Fujitsu gives access to low-cost production.
- LSI Logic and other smaller firms provide for cross-licensing and exchange of ideas.

Because few firms can establish a commanding position in a new industry on their own, licensing becomes vital to building industry support. Firms want as many prospective users as possible to generate future sales and product applications. During the 1980s, Matsushita Electric of Japan licensed its VHS technology to anyone interested in building VCRs, including its rivals. Matsushita's liberal licensing policies allowed it to fill the distribution pipeline rapidly with the now famous VHS standard, eventually displacing Sony's Betamax system in the marketplace. During the 1990s, we witnessed much the same replay of licensing arrangements between the two different camps of firms that wanted to create and disseminate their own DVD technical standards and architectures for the post-VCR world of entertainment and consumer electronics. In a desire to avoid a replay of the Betamax-VHS wars of the 1980s, Matsushita, Toshiba, and Time Warner eventually cross-licensed their designs and specifications with those of Sony and Philips to prevent the emerging DVD market from cannibalizing itself as a result of product and technical incompatibilities in future products. Without a single DVD standard, consumers would be much more reluctant to buy DVD players that could not reliably play movies that were made by different companies.

Licenses are designed to keep the industry dynamic and to reduce the high fixed cost of duplication. For example, competitors in both the pharmaceutical and chemical industries freely exchange ideas and license their newest products to one another, since everyone has an interest in spreading out R&D and distribution expenses. On the one hand, all key industry players compete with one another, but on the other hand, they exchange information to maintain industry discipline and to further enhance their R&D competences.

Global Expansion. Many firms use licensing to gain fast market entry for existing products. For example, McDonald's, Anheuser-Busch, Frito-Lay International, Nestlé, KFC, and Coca-Cola view licensing as a valuable market entry tool. Licensing generates royalties and builds market share. It can also build a firm's standardized global image with comparatively little cost. At KFC, its licensing strategy provided fast entry into Japan's economy at reasonable cost. Without this licensing arrangement, KFC could not establish itself in Japan because of government regulations that prohibit foreign firms from entering Japan's restaurant businesses without a domestic partner. Coca-Cola works with a number of licensed franchisees to enter newly opened markets. The firm believes that franchising is an effective way to build market presence quickly, plus it provides access to local managers who are knowledgeable about market and competitive conditions.

In the airline industry, code-sharing arrangements help airline partners gain indirect access to new parts of the world and help them rationalize and streamline capacity. Code-sharing arrangements help increase an airline's revenue and indirectly increase its brand equity through alliance arrangements. In this sense, code sharing is equivalent to cross-marketing licensing arrangements found in many service industries, whereby partners cooperate to franchise, distribute, and divide the royalties/revenues by selling each other's products or offerings. By coordinating reservations and ticket codes, partners are able to sell seats on each other's planes and thus potentially capture more passengers who prefer an integrated travel itinerary rather than a series of tickets that must be exchanged with each airline separately.

Joint Ventures

Joint ventures are substantially much more complex than licensing arrangements. Unlike licensing, joint ventures involve the partners' creation of a third entity representing the interests and capital of the two or more partners. Partners contribute their own proportional amounts of capital, distinctive skills, managers, reporting systems, and technologies to the venture. Joint ventures often entail complex coordination between partners in carrying out value chain activities. In general, firms enter into joint ventures for four reasons: (1) seeking some degree of vertical integration, (2) needing to learn a partner's distinctive skills in some value-creating activity, (3) upgrading and improving internal skills, and (4) shaping future industry evolution.

Vertical Integration. Trying to attain the benefits of vertical integration (without the costs of doing it alone) is a critical reason why many firms enter joint ventures. Vertical integration is designed to help firms enlarge the scope of their operations within a single industry. Yet, for many firms, expanding their set of activities within the value chain can be an expensive and time-consuming proposition. Engaging in full vertical integration is especially risky for companies that compete in fast-changing industries. Joint ventures can help firms retain some degree of control over crucial supplies at a time when investment funds are scarce and cannot be allocated to backward integration. Also, joint ventures can assist firms to achieve the benefits of vertical integration without saddling them with higher fixed costs and risks. This benefit is especially appealing when the core technology used in the industry is changing quickly.

Joint ventures are prevalent in the global automotive industry, and also, in the petroleum and chemical industries. In the automotive industry, firms will often contract out production of key components to their partners in order to lower costs and to secure greater economies of scale. In the U.S. industry, the typical pattern during the 1980s and 1990s involved a U.S. firm working closely with a Japanese firm that possesses valuable experience in some critical manufacturing or technology-intensive task. In return, the Japanese partner gains access to the U.S. firm's distribution facilities and market. In many cases, the Japanese partner is better able to design new types of engines or electronics that U.S. consumers want, such as multivalve engines or advanced fuel injection systems that enhance performance. At the same time, U.S. automakers are often strapped for resources to invest in these technologies on their own. For example, General Motors uses joint ventures with Suzuki, Isuzu, and Toyota to produce many of its compact cars, including the Chevrolet Cavalier. DaimlerChrysler's U.S. unit relies on Mitsubishi Motors to produce a broad line of Chrysler, Plymouth, and Dodge cars in the subcompact and sports lines. In both cases, the U.S. firm has sought out a Japanese ally. The Japanese firm often commands superior manufacturing skills, quality processes, and fast changeover capability. In turn, Toyota, Isuzu, and Suzuki further reduce their own manufacturing fixed costs by producing for a U.S. company.

In the highly capital-intensive chemical and petroleum industries, joint ventures are becoming more common as firms seek to divvy up the high fixed costs required for managing ever more scale-intensive production processes. In both industries, production is highly dedicated and continuous in nature, meaning that it is difficult for firms on their own to build sufficient scale and profitability in products that often face highly volatile pricing and deep cyclical downturns when markets collapse. For example, Royal Dutch Petroleum's Shell unit and Texaco have worked closely to coordinate their production and marketing activities in the United States to rationalize their production capacity and thus lower costs.

In the airline industry, firms receiving antitrust immunity to coordinate their pricing, marketing, and scheduling operations in the trans-Atlantic market are effectively seeking the benefits of vertical integration without its commensurately high costs. By coordinating flight schedules and other key activities (e.g., baggage handling, landing slots in airports, vendor relations, crew facilities, ticket gates, and maintenance), partnering airlines can avoid duplicating some of the costly infrastructures that are needed each time they serve a new airport. Whether a plane is full or empty, the airline still incurs the costs of maintenance, crew handling, scheduling, and slot fees imposed by each airport. With an alliance, however, many of these fixed costs are shared, and capital investment for each partner is kept to a minimum.

Learning a Partner's Skills. Firms often enter into joint ventures to learn another firm's distinctive skills or capabilities in some key value-creating activity. In many high-technology industries, many years of development are required before a company possesses the proprietary technologies and specialized processes needed to compete effectively on its own. These skills may already be available in a potential partner. A joint venture can help firms learn these new skills without retracing the steps of innovation at great cost. For example, IBM entered into a venture with Toshiba to understand the technologies and manufacturing skills required for flat-panel display screens. IBM hopes to learn from Toshiba the critical miniaturization skills needed to make the screen's transistors that control the color displays in notebook computers. Mitsubishi and Hitachi, in turn, have a joint venture with IBM in Japan for mainframe computers. IBM makes the computers while its Japanese partners resell them under their own label.

Texas Instruments worked closely with Japanese partner Hitachi during the 1990s in designing and producing 16- and 64-megabit chips necessary for today's newest computers. By working with Hitachi, Texas Instruments hoped to learn the new types of etching and other fine manufacturing processes required for high-quality production of even denser chips. These relationships have helped TI become much more efficient in its semiconductor production expertise. In particular, these relationships were also useful in helping both companies transfer new sources of knowledge between each other when it came to testing and developing new types of chip manufacturing processes. Although the TI-Hitachi joint venture has recently ended, TI learned key manufacturing skills from its Japanese partner. The venture ended because of financial constraints and TI's decision to exit the memory chip business. TI now focuses its efforts on DSP chips that are the future for numerous applications in telecommunications, consumer electronics and other applications.

In another example, Mitsubishi Heavy Industries, Kawasaki, and Fuji have a complex joint venture with Boeing. These three Japanese firms manufacture key portions of aircraft fuselages and aircraft bodies for the U.S. firm. They contribute important fabrication skills in exchange for access to Boeing's distribution and global marketing network. The three Japanese firms hope to learn how Boeing organizes and sells its aircraft globally. Boeing seeks to improve its own highly refined assembly techniques with additional fresh insights from its Japanese partners.

Upgrading and Improving Skills. Joint ventures are instrumental in helping firms with similar skills improve and build upon each other's distinctive competences. Even though some of these joint ventures are likely to involve rivals competing within the same industry, companies may still benefit from close cooperation in developing an underlying cutting-edge technology that could transform the industry. The relationship between IBM and Siemens' Infineon Technologies unit in 16-megabit, 64-megabit, and 256-megabit memory chips is an example of a joint venture conceived to help each company upgrade and improve its skills in making more sophisticated semiconductors. Although IBM and Siemens' Infineon unit compete with each other in selling semiconductors to other companies, each partner still contributes engineering and manufacturing skills to accelerate the development of these chips. Both companies believe that sharing skills and technologies will enhance the competitiveness of their own products in the face of rising technological complexity and uncertainty. In a related example, Motorola's separate joint venture with IBM combines both partners' design and manufacturing strengths to improve semiconductor density and chip performance. Motorola and IBM can work together to make microprocessors and memory chips operate faster and store more capacity than if either firm were to do it alone.

Fuji Photo Film and Xerox formed a joint venture in photocopiers in the 1970s for similar reasons. Both companies wanted to improve their manufacturing prowess in low-end copiers. The two firms design, manufacture, and market small, low-end copiers through a separate, autonomous company named Fuji-Xerox, based in the Far East. Fuji-Xerox develops its own business strategy independently of its parent companies. Several analysts have commented that the Fuji-Xerox venture was instrumental in helping parent Xerox learn and apply Japanese manufacturing techniques to its other product lines. Xerox benefits from improving its manufacturing and quality control skills across all aspects of copier design and production. The joint venture helps Fuji learn and improve its lens-making operations for office equipment. Fuji-Xerox is now the technological center of developing state-of-the-art lasers, optics, and other finely machined office equipment for Xerox's operations worldwide, particularly in smaller-sized applications. Even though Xerox has recently suffered significant financial setbacks that resulted from internal organizational difficulties, it still relies heavily on Fuji-Xerox for new technologies and imaging skills.[9]

Shaping Industry Evolution. Firms can cooperate in a joint venture to develop and commercialize new technologies that may significantly influence an industry's future direction. For example, during the 1990s, AT&T (and later Lucent Technologies) worked closely with Zenith Electronics to design and produce the next generation of digital-based high-definition television (HDTV) technology. Together, they joined General Instrument, RCA, Philips, and NBC to commercialize and standardize today's emerging HDTV standards already found in different broadcasting markets. Thus, companies can ally with others in competing joint ventures in a race to develop the newest breakthrough technology or next-generation industry standard. Without using joint ventures, none of these companies would have been able to design and produce the next-generation HDTV standard in a timely manner. All of the companies involved in various aspects of HDTV development—AT&T, Zenith, General Instrument, RCA, Philips, and NBC—combined their various competing technologies into one Grand Alliance. The goal of this Grand Alliance, as it is formally known, is to gain agreement among all U.S. participants on a common digital standard for future HDTV broadcasts.

During the early 1990s, Texas Instruments formed a joint venture with Cyrix to design and produce new types of cutting-edge microprocessors and to influence the shape and power of future microprocessors in an evolving industry.* Neither TI nor Cyrix had much experience in producing microprocessors that could challenge market leader Intel. Together, however, they could pool their efforts to outflank Intel in designing a leaner, faster chip. Both companies hoped that the new chips would provide a viable competing product standard to Intel's microprocessors. The transfer and sharing of design and manufacturing skills contribute to improving both companies' competitiveness and chip-based design skills.

Corning Incorporated has formed alliances with more than twenty individual firms throughout the world. These joint ventures help Corning shape the evolving glass and advanced materials industry. Corning works with Samsung, Iwaki Glass, and Asahi Glass to design and produce advanced quality television tubes. In turn, each partner learns how to improve its own glass fabrication techniques. With Siemens of Germany, Corning has become one of the world's largest suppliers of fiber optics used in telecommunications. Most recently, it has investigated purchasing the optical fiber unit of competitor Lucent Technologies, which has struggled to realign its operations in the wake of declining demand in the telecommunications industry. Corning also has a separate joint venture with NGK of Japan. NGK is one of the world's largest auto parts makers (spark plugs) and has invested significant resources in commercializing advanced ceramics. In the future, some analysts believe that automotive engines may actually be made of ceramics rather than steel or aluminum. In each of Corning's joint ventures, a partner contributes a skill or market position that Corning does not have or could not develop quickly on its own.

The need to maintain industry dynamism and momentum in research is a motivating force that drives drug companies to engage in joint ventures, even when they compete in existing product lines. For example, the task of finding a drug that can kill the AIDS virus is so complex and daunting that many U.S. firms are seriously considering joint research ventures to pool their efforts. Competing chemical firms often team up in formal joint ventures to commercialize costly development processes. For example, U.S. chemical giant DuPont teamed up with Japanese firm Toray to accelerate the learning and transfer of new product applications for carbon fibers. Toray is the world's leader in producing carbon fiber and has utilized DuPont's original technology to build a strong market position in this critical field. Although originally pioneered for aerospace and defense applications, carbon fiber has begun to play an important role in many other industries. Today, many state-of-the-art golf clubs, other sporting equipment, and automotive parts are built from carbon fiber composite materials.

Cross-Holdings, Equity Stakes, Consortia, and Industry-Spanning Networks

The third broad category of strategic alliances includes some of the more complex forms of alliance arrangements. These alliances bring together companies in ways that are different from those found in licensing and joint venture mechanisms. Broadly amalgamated together as consortia and networks, these alliances represent highly complex linkages among groups of companies. Some of these linkages are financial, whereby companies own major equity stakes in one another. Other relationships involve complex sharing of technologies or other value-creating activities among different partners. Even other alliance arrangements are designed to facilitate knowledge sharing and the promulgation of technological standards to define an industry's basis for innovation and value creation. We use the terms *consortia* and *networks* to focus on three broad types of complex alliance evolution: (1) multipartner alliances designed to share an underlying technology, (2) formal groups of companies that own large cross-holdings and equity stakes in one another, and

* Cyrix later became part of National Semiconductor, which then sold it to Taiwan's Via Technologies in 1999.

(3) the rise of alliance networks that span an entire industry. In either case, these relationships represent the most sophisticated form of strategic alliance and involve complex coordination mechanisms that often go beyond the boundaries of individual firms.[10]

Multipartner Consortia. In the United States, Sematech represents the best example of a multipartner, technology-based consortia.[11] Based in Austin, Texas, Sematech involves more than fifteen U.S. firms interested in sharing ideas to promote new ways to manufacture semiconductors and chip-making equipment. Sematech aims to link up all participating U.S. semiconductor manufacturers to improve domestic design and manufacturing skills. Funded in part by the U.S. Defense Department, this multipartner arrangement is defined by the underlying need to upgrade the U.S. chip industry and protect it from Japanese competition. Members include smaller firms, such as Micron Technology, along with such giants as IBM, Lucent Technologies, Intel, Texas Instruments, and Motorola. Over the past decade, Sematech has been instrumental in helping U.S. firms learn and share new technologies and manufacturing skills that are vital to making even more dense memory chips and microprocessors. Sematech promotes specialization of chip-making skills among its member companies by encouraging interfirm sharing of new developments in advanced materials and new manufacturing techniques. This cooperative effort has helped its member companies become less dependent on Japanese chip-making equipment. In 1992, Sematech was also instrumental in helping several U.S. member companies secure domestic production facilities for flat-panel display screens used in laptop computers and flat-screen television sets. In 1994, the Clinton administration indicated the possibility of providing the funding necessary to create new U.S. consortia in other forms of advanced display electronics to counter the Japanese near-monopoly position in this technology. Today, Sematech is still committed to advancing next-generation technologies designed for even smaller and more densely packed semiconductors. Several member companies, particularly Intel, IBM, and Motorola, are investing heavily in a new manufacturing process known as extreme ultraviolet lithography (EUV) technology. This technique uses X-rays to generate the circuit patterns on silicon wafers that in turn represent the final semiconductor design for each layer of chip.

In Europe, several consortia have formed to protect and reinforce such industries as semiconductors, video display technologies, and aircraft. JESSI (Joint European Submicron Silicon Initiative) was organized in the 1990s to help European semiconductor manufacturers attain the manufacturing and design capabilities of U.S. and Japanese firms. It is Europe's equivalent to Sematech in the United States. JESSI includes such well-known European electronics firms as Siemens, Philips, and STMicroelectronics. Each member company contributes its expertise on some critical aspect of designing and manufacturing next-generation semiconductors. Another European consortium initiative, ESPRIT, is designed to advance the learning and application of new defense technologies among member companies.

Perhaps the most important European-based consortium to date is Airbus Industries. Conceived originally as a loosely organized, coproduction sharing consortium, Airbus has changed the nature of its alliance arrangement substantially in recent years. The Airbus consortium, once involving a cumbersome organizational arrangement among companies from four European companies, has now become a much more centralized company that reports along the lines of a single, integrated firm (parent company now known as EADS). Throughout its long history, Airbus brought together four European aerospace firms from Britain, France, Germany, and Spain. Each firm committed its entire aerospace business to a formal consortium arrangement. The goal of Airbus Industries has been to dethrone Boeing from its dominant position in the global commercial aircraft market. By pooling their member firms' resources, Airbus Industries has become a potent competitor for the U.S. giant. Without such pan-European cooperation, it is unlikely that any of the individual firms would have been able to challenge Boeing on a low-cost basis. Already, Airbus is making inroads in Boeing's North American markets (see Chapter 8). With the combination of its partners' resources and a new reporting structure, Airbus can engage in the kind of cross-subsidization strategies that are designed to probe and exploit Boeing's weaknesses in its worldwide markets.

Cross-Holding Consortia. Some of the more complex cross-holding alliance relationships are found in the Far East. Examples of cross-holding consortia include the large Japanese *keiretsus* and Korean *chaebols*. These collections of companies involve extensive equity cross-holdings among all of the member companies. Examples of Japanese keiretsus include Sumitomo, Mitsubishi, Mitsui, Dai-Ichi Kangyo, and Fuyo Groups.[12] Korean chaebols include Daewoo Group, Lucky-Goldstar, Sunkyong, Hyundai, and Samsung.

Two defining features of cross-holding consortia are building long-term focus and gaining technological critical mass among affiliated member companies. First, strong supplier–buyer relationships among keiretsu or chaebol members work to stabilize production volume and promote long-term focus. For example, producers of television sets or VCRs in this consortia arrangement could access the components needed for their products from other members in the consortia. This vertically integrated arrangement makes investment planning for high, fixed-costs investments easier and more predictable for the member firms. Because considerable sharing takes place among different member companies for key technologies, firms are able to cooperate in making huge, fixed costs investments; the consortia provide at least some degree of a "guaranteed" internal market for components or products to be used or sold by member companies.

Second, these consortia arrangements can provide member companies with the technological critical mass needed for investing in world-scale efficient plants. Take the case of semiconductors, for example. Since these devices are becoming the "brains" of many products ranging from television sets to cars and telephones, member companies that produce these products benefit from sharing the costs for a semiconductor plant that can serve all their needs. Instead of having each company build its own chip plant (with individually high fixed costs for each firm and lower economies of scale), the member companies contribute funds to build a more optimally sized plant that serves their collective needs, with correspondingly greater economies of scale and thus lower unit costs. Consequently, consortia arrangements allow firms to share the costs and develop the critical mass needed for building and running world-scale plants. The main drawback to these arrangements is that valuable capital is often tied up in investments that may be less productive or lacking the same depth of core competences as compared with a much more focused competitor. In addition, these cross-holdings may slow down a member firm's ability to react quickly to new developments.

In the last few years, the continued slowdown of the Japanese and South Korean economies has caused some of the major companies to rethink the way they manage this cross-holding arrangement. In particular, companies such as Toshiba, Mitsubishi, NEC, Hitachi, and Fujitsu have begun to sell some of their holdings in other companies, largely because they need the funds to invest in more central operations. Likewise, the South Korean government has issued a series of directives that companies such as Samsung, Lucky-Goldstar, Daewoo and Hyundai spin-off their noncore businesses in order to free up capital from unproductive uses. Both Japanese and South Korean cross-holding relationships represent large portions of each company's manufacturing base, and if their assets are not used productively, these alliances can actually hold back an entire nation's capacity to restructure and to grow. Because capital is tied up in relationships that are more tradition-bound, productivity of asset use has sagged in recent years. Another major factor that has accelerated the unwinding of some of these complex cross-holdings is the greater clamor that investors have been voicing for more "transparent" financial reporting of profitability and losses. Japanese and South Korean companies in the past have been able to occlude some of their financial reporting through alliance arrangements by transferring losses from one affiliate member's accounting books to another.

Industry-Spanning Alliance Networks. Competition and value creation in many industries now involve product and technology development that span multiple firms. In particular, breakthrough developments in high-technology industries and pharmaceuticals are often beyond the means and capability of an individual firm. As a result, firms in these and other industries are beginning to work more closely with one another than ever before. Oftentimes, a firm will work with a number of different partners to share knowledge, costs and risks, rather than just a single one. As a result, firms are finding themselves in a more complex alliance environment, where companies are forming a larger industry-wide network. More important, the growth of such alliance networks within and across industries means that each firm is now contributing its own distinctive competence in a way that requires it to *work interdependently* with other partnering companies, each of which will likely specialize in some value-creating activity.[13]

In what is perhaps the most complicated form of alliance evolution that has yet transpired, companies in many industries are now becoming members of what might be termed a larger knowledge-creating web. **Knowledge webs** are groups of companies that work together to shape the overall evolution of an industry. For example, in the wireless telecommunications industry, a wide range of companies, including Nokia, Motorola, Ericsson, Qualcomm, Symbian, Vodafone, Deutsche Telecom, Japan's NTT DoCoMo unit, and even Microsoft, are working to shape what could be the industry's next generation of wireless telephone and data communication systems. For example, NTT DoCoMo leads the world in developing and commercializing very user-friendly, next-generation wireless cell phones that can access the Internet, store MP3 music files, and even host a digital camera in which the user can then send images through wireless e-mail. Moreover, NTT envisions a digital wireless phone that handles voice recognition in order to avoid the use of cumbersome keypads to enter numbers or letters into the device. NTT's "I-mode" technology is expected to be a model for some of the newer 3G networks that are now in development.

knowledge web: A collection or group of companies that work in tandem to shape the evolution of an industry.

In industries that are characterized by fast change, high levels of uncertainty, and extremely high fixed costs, industry-spanning alliance networks are now becoming important forces that shape how the marketplace will evolve. These alliances are in some cases becoming so important that the development activities of the entire network are becoming more important than the actions taken by an individual firm working alone. Although becoming more common in such industries as multimedia, entertainment, software, personal computers and servers, telecommunications, consumer electronics, Internet access and health care, industry-spanning alliance networks also occur in other mature industries as well, such as those found in airlines and transportation companies. For example, individual railroad companies in the United States (e.g., CSX, Burlington Northern Santa Fe, Union Pacific) are now jointly working with container shipping companies (e.g., Denmark's Maersk, Japan's NYK and K-Line, Taiwan's Evergreen) to coordinate low-cost, global transportation of containers to anywhere in the United States and even around the world. Within the United States, the major railroad companies are now tying their schedules closely to automotive manufacturers who are now implementing just-in-time inventory systems (to reduce inventory). In addition, Burlington Northern Santa Fe is now closely coordinating its rail schedules to work in conjunction with the warehousing and shipping operations of United Parcel Service (UPS) to lower each firm's costs and improve delivery times. In general, U.S. railroad companies are now repositioning themselves to act as a full-service provider of documentation, shipping, customs clearance, and container tracking services that are tightly integrated with those of other firms around the world, including shipping, trucking, barge traffic, and even delivery.[14]

In the global airline industry, the number of industry-spanning networks has risen significantly in the past few years. Airline companies realize that they must form broader networks in order to capture the benefits of serving new markets without assuming even more fixed costs. For example, the relationship among American Airlines' **one**world alliance partners is growing closer whereby partners are now actively dividing the world among member airline carriers to maintain capacity and to stabilize costs. Also, the competing United- and Lufthansa-organized Star Alliance incorporates seventeen (and growing) members who work closely together to reach different parts of the world through active code-sharing activities that help lower costs. Although the vast majority of global airline alliances has not yet received the kind of broad antitrust immunity that allows for tight coordination as a single entity (as is the case with several trans-Atlantic arrangements), it is likely that more network alliance configurations will evolve over the next few years as carriers seek to establish a strong, integrated network in each regional market. On the other hand, even though there is a high level of interdependence among partners, alliance networks are not permanent relationships. For example, Delta Air Lines was not able to continue working with its original trans-Atlantic partners, Sabena, SwissAir, and Austrian Airlines for more than a few years. Although the three European firms served as a valuable linchpin in Delta's trans-Atlantic strategy, they were also smaller carriers that could not provide the same degree of shared scale and access that American Airlines found in British Airways or what United Airlines obtained with Lufthansa. Some observers have also noted that American Airlines worked behind the scenes to provide incentives to SwissAir and Sabena to switch their allegiance away from Delta and more toward American. Eventually, Delta began working with Air France, a large carrier that also needed a big trans-Atlantic partner.

Knowledge webs, on the other hand, are a highly complex variation of industry-spanning alliance networks because the primary contribution of each firm participating in the network tends to be innovation driven or related to knowledge creation of some type. In the telecommunications industry, for example, firms contribute their distinctive skills along such dimensions as software, algorithms, semiconductors, Internet browsers, voice recognition systems, video streaming, and even the actual "content" that could flow along future airwaves. Knowledge webs also characterize the nature of the entertainment industry, where broadcast networks interact heavily with film studios, production houses, Hollywood agencies, special effects firms, syndication firms, cable television systems, and even publishing firms.

co-opetition: The strategic situation whereby a firm cooperates and competes with another firm(s) at the same time. Firms in co-opetitive relationships often race with one another to learn each other's skills and to develop new sources of knowledge or value-creating activities.

One key characteristic that defines each firm's behavior in industry-spanning alliance networks, particularly knowledge webs, is that a participating company will actually cooperate and compete simultaneously with all of the partners in the web. Some researchers have also described this phenomenon as co-opetition.[15] **Co-opetition** refers to the strategic paradox in which a firm cooperates and competes with another firm at the same time. For example, in the fast-moving corporate server and data storage market, Sun Microsystems and EMC are both involved in a state of co-opetition. Sun Microsystems needs EMC's advanced data storage solutions in order to sell a full range of products to its corporate customers. EMC considers Sun Microsystems a critical partner that helps it sell more storage products. At the same time, however, Sun Microsystems competes with EMC to develop even newer forms of storage technology in order to achieve a breakthrough on some critical dimension that relates to the product's performance. Thus, both firms find themselves in a strategic paradox in which they actually need one another, but are taking steps to learn from each other in order to supplement their own internal development efforts to create the next breakthrough technology. Likewise, Intel and Microsoft are engaged in their own sort of co-opetition in the personal computer industry, in which both giants simultaneously work together to develop new PC offerings but also compete to see who can develop an innovation first (and therefore claim more profits from each personal computer that is sold).

In all types of knowledge webs, firms in an alliance network will race one another to contribute a new source of knowledge, capability, or skill in order to capture a disproportionately high level of profitability of the alliance network's products or services that are sold to customers. In other words, companies that can innovate faster than others will be in a better position to set the tone for the future path of product development within that industry. Companies hope to develop an architecture, a technology, a production process, or a product platform that becomes the basis for the industry's future standard. By setting a key standard, the innovating company can exert a disproportionate influence on the shape of future products that the industry will develop in ensuing years. For example, Microsoft has been extremely successful in making its DOS and Windows operating systems the de facto software standard of the personal computer industry. It is now seeking to dominate the market for corporate networks in the same way. Likewise, Intel hopes to parlay its success in microprocessors for personal computers into communication chips that dominate the Internet. In a similar vein, Matsushita Electric captured the dominant technological standard for videocassette recorders in the 1980s. Nokia hopes to do the same for next-generation 3G wireless networks by innovating a new wireless phone that contains its own Internet browser and video-streaming technology. Texas Instruments in the semiconductor industry is attempting to establish its dominance over DSPs, which will be the silicon brains of many future electronic and Internet products. All of these companies also work closely with other firms in order to better position themselves within their respective industries. Industry-spanning alliances help each of these firms to shape the evolution of their respective industries. At the same time, all of these firms will also compete with their partners to develop new sources of knowledge and to rush new products to market. Over time, the more dominant members of the alliance network will be able to reap a greater proportion of the alliance network's overall profitability from future products that are sold.

Risks and Costs of Strategic Alliances

Through alliances, firms can acquire new products, skills, and knowledge that are otherwise not available to them. Regardless of how the alliance is arranged (e.g., licensing, joint venture, equity stake, knowledge web), the firm faces a set of important potential trade-offs. Working with an alliance partner to learn and build new sources of competitive advantage, however, is not a cost-free proposition. Without clearly understanding the risks and costs inherent in alliances, cooperation may unintentionally damage a firm. In the worst case, loss of a firm's proprietary know-how or skills to a partner could create a new competitor.[16] Four general types of risks and costs are associated with alliances: (1) rising incompatibility between partners, (2) risk of knowledge or skill leakage, (3) risk of dependence, and (4) strategic control costs associated with day-to-day operational issues.

Rising Incompatibility of Partners

Even the best conceived alliances face the potential danger that partners may become incompatible over time. For example, firms that once needed each other to design a new product or to enter a new market may feel that their strategic interests no longer match as the market or industry evolves. When partners find that their long-term strategies have changed, they must then redefine the basis of the joint venture. In many situations, firms that once enjoyed a harmonious, close working relationship discover that changes in their strategies or industry conditions often resulted in growing incompatibility between their goals.

Consider the experience of Ford's long-standing joint venture with Volkswagen in Latin America. Through their seven-year-old joint venture known as Autolatina, Ford and Volkswagen coproduce a broad range of cars for the rising middle class in Brazil, Argentina, and other Latin American countries. The venture was significant to both Ford and Volkswagen, since it enabled them to develop the necessary critical mass of strength and skills to enter unknown and emerging markets. Autolatina allowed Ford and Volkswagen to share manufacturing, product development, and supply functions in Brazil and Argentina. The venture produced more than 750,000 cars to serve these two markets in 1993. However, the two firms have dissolved their venture in clashes over the best strategy to deal with the growing power of General Motors in Latin America. Moreover, Ford and Volkswagen have become reluctant to share their newest car designs and marketing strategies with each other.[17]

The gradual unwinding of the Kaleida and Taligent alliances among IBM, Apple Computer, and Motorola during the mid-1990s stemmed largely from the divergent strategic goals of the three companies. IBM entered both Kaleida and Taligent to tap into Apple Computer's expertise in order to push ahead Big Blue's growth objectives in the emerging multimedia arena. On the other hand, Apple Computer wanted a firmer commitment by IBM to use and market more aggressively its popular Macintosh line of computers through Big Blue's distribution system. IBM was less willing to commit to such a deep relationship largely because it was developing its own OS-2 line of software and operating systems to take on Microsoft's Windows technology. Moreover, IBM did not want to be put in a position where it felt it was constantly developing computer chips solely for Apple's internal use. Thus, IBM and Apple's strategic goals for Kaleida and Taligent eventually differed significantly as the relationship evolved.[18] On the other hand, IBM's relationships with Motorola have proven to be more stable, even if the two partners appear to be taking on a different track to their technology-driven alliance. Although the two companies appear to be moving in different ways now (IBM focusing on the Internet and Motorola focusing more on specialized chips and digital cellular phones), the companies still cooperate extensively on core semiconductor technology (developing new lithography techniques). Over time, one might expect that as IBM and Motorola develop their own distinctive strategies for navigating the semiconductor industry, the Power PC cross-marketing and licensing relationship will likely take a back seat as new microprocessors replace both companies' existing offerings.[19]

Rising incompatibility in developing strategies and objectives resulted in a serious rift between Texas Instruments and Cyrix during the 1990s as the two firms took diverging approaches to chip development over their several year-relationship to fight Intel jointly. Texas Instruments believed that Cyrix should rely exclusively on TI to produce the latest generation of Cyrix microprocessors. However, Cyrix wanted to work with a host of other chip companies to accelerate its own product-to-market development of new Cyrix-designed chips. TI felt that Cyrix had not delivered the newest chip designs as fast as promised, while Cyrix felt that TI had violated the small firm's proprietary design secrets. In turn, neither company had secured the design wins and recognition from the marketplace that would make for a significant challenge to Intel in the high-end microprocessor market. In March 1994, Cyrix entered into a separate manufacturing-based joint venture with IBM to produce a chip that would compete directly against Intel's Pentium line of microprocessors. In December 1994, TI and Cyrix settled a lawsuit that prohibited TI from manufacturing Cyrix's most important microprocessor chips. Cyrix, now a unit of Via Technologies of Taiwan, is currently in the midst of a new campaign against Intel with a new owning firm.

In the restaurant industry, a two-year joint venture between Arby's, a leading fast-food chain specializing in roast beef sandwiches, and ZuZu, an upstart Mexican restaurant chain, went sour in 1997 after the two companies could not agree on how best to coordinate their various menu items in different cities. Designed originally as a joint venture to bring together two companies that were struggling to define themselves in a saturating industry, the alliance intended to help both partners combine their talents and offerings for two distinctive market segments into one restaurant platform. Arby's originally needed ZuZu because its sales of roast beef sandwiches had plateaued, while it had plenty of seating capacity in many of its urban markets. ZuZu, on the other hand, found Arby's retailing and distribution system a real plus because it lacked the critical mass to "roll out" its offerings by itself. However, the venture collapsed for both operational and marketing reasons. From an operations perspective, Arby's restaurant crews were more used to processing, cooking, and serving food quickly—skills critical to serving customers in the fast-food segment. They were not able to cope with the more complicated and time-intensive ingredients required for ZuZu's nouveau Mexican cuisine, however. Also, Arby's food tends to be served in paper wrappers, while ZuZu's items typically came with metal utensils on a crockery plate designed to keep the food warm and fresh from the oven. Over time, managers in the venture realized that both Arby's and ZuZu were incompatible in terms of how they viewed their customers, food selection, and operational methods of preparation.[20]

Risk of Knowledge/Skill Drain

Many forms of cooperation require partners to share their knowledge and skills to develop a new technology or product. The central problem of sharing knowledge is the impossibility of strictly limiting how partners will use knowledge gained from cooperation. This problem is especially critical for firms that face industry convergence. For example, the computer, communications, and consumer electronics industries are growing more similar, which means that an alliance based on designing new types of computers will have an impact on communications devices as well. Consider the situation of Apple Computer. Apple's experimental product developed in the early 1990s combined a Macintosh computer, CD-ROM, and a screen that also receives television signals. This new Apple product merges technologies and skills required for competing in both the computer and consumer electronics businesses. However, Sony currently builds many of Apple's latest generation of laptop computers in a long-standing alliance. Sony has benefited substantially through its long-term relationship with Apple as it learns how to use Apple's distinctive consumer electronics skills and capabilities. This knowledge helped Sony enter the personal computer industry in the late 1990s. These skills are also instrumental to Sony's development of its Playstation line of video games. Apple does not possess manufacturing skills and distinctive competence to mass-produce laptop computers and display screens, so it remains vulnerable to potential encroachments by Sony into its market. Sony is thus in a superb position to learn and to see how Apple's latest product is likely to perform. Given Sony's distinctive competence in manufacturing high-quality television sets, Sony is potentially able to produce its own type of notebook computer that could be superior to that of Apple's. The close relationship with Apple has begun to pay major dividends for Sony as it looks beyond traditional consumer electronics to sustain growth. In 2000, Sony introduced its own line of ultrathin laptop computers that combine a fast Intel Pentium-class processor, an advanced flat-panel display screen, and a CD-RW/DVD drive that allows users to make their own CDs and even create their own movies with state-of-the-art graphics. This line of laptop computers, known as the Sony VAIO, is designed to complement Sony's other internal initiatives that will take the company into such new arenas as Internet-based entertainment. Sony's latest investments are envisioned to help computer users create their own digital films using Sony's multimedia film studio that is available on the company's Web site.

When IBM works together with Toshiba in designing flat-panel display screens used for laptop computers, IBM is limited in its ability to control how Toshiba uses the shared technology for other applications outside the venture. This joint venture, known as Display Technologies, Inc., is based in Japan, where Toshiba has a home field advantage in learning new technologies from IBM. Other applications in which Toshiba could apply IBM's technology include potential products such as flat-screen color television sets. Likewise, Toshiba cannot unconditionally limit IBM's use of what Big Blue learns from Toshiba in terms of new manufacturing technology and process improvement skills. IBM, in turn, could apply the new manufacturing skills that it learns from the joint venture to improve its cost position in developing new forms of hand-held computers that are not covered within the scope of the current alliance. By allying on a critical core technology of the future, neither IBM nor Toshiba can actually control the other firm's pace in using the technology to develop future commercial products. Recently, the two companies have differed in their strategic vision for that venture. Toshiba wants to use the displays for cellular phones and personal digital assistants—two products that are close to Toshiba's core strengths in consumer electronics and telecommunications. IBM, on the other hand, wants to use the venture's manufacturing capacity to produce displays for scientific instruments, laptop computers, and desktop computers—areas that are considered more crucial to IBM's core businesses. As the two companies diverge in how best to utilize their jointly owned plant's manufacturing operations, the Display Technologies venture itself may formally unwind, even though IBM and Toshiba continue to cooperate across a wide range of high-technology arenas.[21]

Firms taking part in a strategic alliance must therefore carefully identify and isolate what types of knowledge can be safely shared with a partner. They need to recognize that technologies previously developed for one set of products may later be applicable to other products as well. This likelihood is particularly strong in industries that are converging, or where future products increasingly use similar components or manufacturing skills. *A firm always runs the risk of giving the partner more insight into its knowledge base than intended.*

Risk of Dependence

Alliances can often make a firm too dependent on its partner.[22] This dependence can occur without the firm's awareness of the process. For example, many U.S. automakers believe that their joint ventures with Japanese and other firms have saved them time and money in their production of small cars. These alliances free up capital for other uses. Over time, however, firms can become overreliant on their partners to build new lines of cars for them. As a result, the firm's skills—especially those in manufacturing—can deteriorate, while those of the partner improve. In other words, a company that serves as a critical supplier of an underlying technology or production process to another firm will be able to exercise a high degree of control over its partner's activities. Thus, firms can find that alliances will "hollow out" their skills. This process is shown in Exhibit 9-7. Both General Motors and Chrysler experienced this problem in their automobile ventures with Japanese suppliers in the early 1990s. Chrysler, in particular, became highly dependent on Mitsubishi Motors for a steady supply of high-performance engines, transmissions, and other key components required for its subcompact and sports car lines, including its hot-selling Dodge Daytona, Dodge Stealth, Chrysler Laser, and Eagle Talon. Until recently, General Motors' entire Geo line of cars is manufactured by three different Japanese firms: Isuzu, Suzuki, and Toyota. Consequently, neither GM nor Chrysler was in a position to compete in this segment on its own because they lacked the critical manufacturing skills during the early 1990s.

EXHIBIT 9-7 Deepening Dependence on Alliance Partner

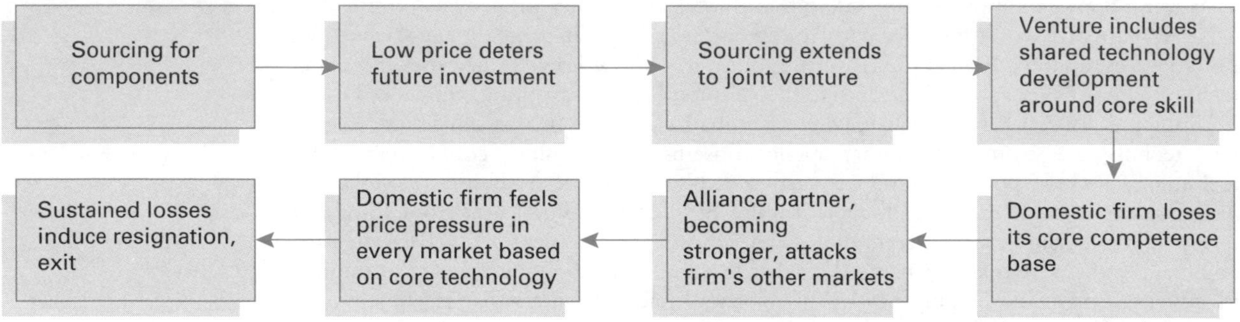

Sourcing for components → Low price deters future investment → Sourcing extends to joint venture → Venture includes shared technology development around core skill

↓

Domestic firm loses its core competence base → Alliance partner, becoming stronger, attacks firm's other markets → Domestic firm feels price pressure in every market based on core technology → Sustained losses induce resignation, exit

Process repeats itself across every firm competing in similar industry or line of business. Eventually, U.S. industry loses ground in cumulative effect.

The United States does not produce any of its own videocassette recorders or DVD players because U.S. consumer electronics firms have eagerly outsourced their manufacturing operations to Far Eastern companies. For example, all VCRs bearing the labels of General Electric, RCA, and Zenith Electronics come from such Japanese suppliers as Matsushita, Toshiba, and Hitachi, or Korean producers Lucky-Goldstar and Samsung. In turn, these same U.S. firms remain largely unable to compete in other consumer electronics, because the manufacturing skills required for televisions and VCRs are directly applicable to other uses. Once U.S. firms "surrendered" their VCR and other consumer electronics skills to their alliance partners, they faced an uphill battle to recapture control over critical value chain activities. As new Internet-based electronic appliances become more popular, U.S. firms will have difficulty serving this market without further relying on their manufacturing partners in the Far East and elsewhere. This means that U.S. firms will continue to be forced to share their profits in ways they may not have intended. Japanese, Taiwanese, and Korean companies appear likely to dominate Internet-based electronic appliances as they continue to invest in upgrading their manufacturing skills.

In the semiconductor industry, similar attempts by some U.S. firms to avoid building state-of-the-art chip fabrication facilities have made many companies dependent on Japanese, and especially Taiwanese suppliers for chips. For example, many midsized U.S. firms, such as Sun Microsystems and MIPS Technologies, depended on Fujitsu, Hitachi, and NEC for their manufacturing competence in producing new generations of RISC-based chips during the 1990s. The degree to which many U.S. semiconductor and personal computer firms are dependent upon Japanese sources of chip supply was starkly revealed in early 1993. A plant owned by Sumitomo Chemical that produced the specialty resin needed for making semiconductors caught fire and exploded. In turn, the spot market prices of memory chips for personal computers skyrocketed for six months afterward.

This pattern now appears to be repeating itself as Motorola and Lucent Technologies are now turning to Taiwan Semiconductor Manufacturing Company (TSMC) and United Microelectronics Company (UMC) to share in the costs of manufacturing leading-edge semiconductors. As the fixed costs of building new fabrication facilities continue to rise, outsourcing and alliances appear much more attractive to companies. Smaller U.S. firms, such as Altera, Broadcom, Nvidia, and Xilinx, use Taiwanese "chip foundries" as an explicit part of their strategy, since they are too small to invest in their own manufacturing facilities. However, continued and growing reliance on Taiwanese manufacturers by larger manufacturers such as Motorola and Lucent may damage their internal capability to master newer manufacturing processes that are required to enter new markets on their own.[23] On the other hand, both IBM and Intel are hoping to avoid such an outcome. These two giants continue to invest substantial sums in ultramodern manufacturing facilities. Intel alone spent $7.5 billion in 2001 on capital expenditures to build state-of-the-art facilities for its Pentium 4 chips. These investments ultimately enabled Intel to make newer classes of Pentium 4, Itanium, and other chips more efficiently—a critical factor in Intel's ability to remain competitive and even dominant in microprocessors.

Costs of Alliance Control and Operations

In day-to-day alliance operations, managers face three types of costs: (1) costs of coordination, (2) costs of learning, and (3) costs of inflexibility.

Costs of Coordination. Benefits of alliances can result only when the two partners work closely. Yet, working with an alliance partner can be a challenging and frustrating series of events, especially if the partner's values, organization, or operating methods are different from one's own. This may represent a significant latent challenge for airlines now engaged in multipartner alliances with firms from different parts of the world. Organizational cultures and styles are likely to clash as managers from separate regions come together. Strategies, budgets, plans, and product layouts must be carefully worked out and managed, as managers at Arby's and ZuZu came to realize belatedly. Managers must also hammer out such key issues as accounting formats and human resource practices within the alliance, including such questions as whether a manager works for one partner or the other and whether an assignment is temporary or permanent.[24] Such difficulties became apparent when managers from IBM, Toshiba, and Siemens got together to design and build 256-megabit chips. IBM managers felt that their colleagues from Toshiba were excessively group-oriented and wanted consensus on every step of the design and experimental process. Also, IBM managers felt that the German managers from Siemens were overly concerned with the costs and details of technical planning. Conversely, Japanese and German managers became frustrated with the apparent American penchant for taking on high-risk, uncertain experimental design approaches without getting approval from higher-up managers. Cooperation was also complicated by subtle differences in languages and in translation.

Cooperation is further inhibited by the natural reluctance of partners to divulge proprietary technology, knowledge, or skills to their partners. Such skills or technologies could later be used against the partner even as the alliance continues. For example, when General Motors teamed up with Japanese robot maker Fanuc, GM benefited in the short term from a low-cost supply of reliable robots and numerical control (NC) tools from its Japanese partner. Fanuc, on the other hand, learned from GM the core technologies to make its robots more advanced and "smarter" by assimilating GM's skills in sensor and vision systems, advanced software, machine language, computer systems integration, and other machine design concepts. Ultimately, Fanuc ended up competing against General Motors in selling industrial robots to other U.S. manufacturers, such as makers of construction equipment, farm equipment, and major home appliances. Fanuc was able to learn and apply skills from General Motors to make its own robots better than those of GM. Fanuc could then compete against other robotics companies with the technologies it acquired from GM. Now, Fanuc is believed to have as much as 75 percent of the world's market share for numerical control tools and other critical factory automation equipment.

Thus, the costs of coordinating and managing an alliance extend far beyond the simple management structure of the alliance. Coordination costs extend to the day-to-day management styles and issues surrounding the partnership. The struggles in getting partners to agree on management issues are often unforeseen. In addition, coordination involves deciding the degree of knowledge sharing as well. This is particularly true for firms that face issues of co-opetition when developing products in high-tech industries. Likewise, firms that participate in industry-spanning alliance networks or knowledge webs are particularly susceptible to difficulties in coordinating activities with other member firms. The real balance of power between partners is found in the knowledge flows between partners. Too much of a one-way knowledge flow to its partner could put a firm in a dangerously dependent position.

Costs of Learning. Firms must also concentrate on learning from their partners. This requires assuming the role of student rather than teacher. Firms cannot learn if they are smug or overconfident about what they can learn from their alliance partner. Korean firm Daewoo formed a joint venture with Caterpillar to learn how to make forklift trucks and other related construction equipment and machinery. Once Daewoo was able to master the design and production skills needed to make the equipment on its own, it bought out Caterpillar's interest in the venture and began competing against it in global markets. Samsung followed a similar series of events with U.S. forklift maker Clark Equipment. Apparently, neither Daewoo nor Samsung had expectations of working with their American partners over an extended period. Once they had learned what they needed, they bought out their partners. Both examples show that managers must take the initiative to learn new management techniques and skills from their partner quickly, while protecting their own core technology from excessive encroachment from an aggressive partner.

Learning means improving not only current products but also core skills, processes and technologies that may help the firm's competitiveness. This effort generates additional costs, since skill-based learning requires extra effort and attention to identify emerging or useful technologies and to bring them home effectively. To learn effectively, partners must be careful not to be overconfident when working with another firm. For example, in the 1970s, U.S. VCR manufacturer Ampex believed that it could "teach" Toshiba of Japan how to make better VCRs, since it possessed a proprietary magnetic head technology at the time. Ampex found over time that Toshiba not only learned how to make better VCRs but also improved on Ampex's video head design to improve the quality of Toshiba's own line of VCRs.

Learning is also much more difficult when managers are kept on alliance assignments for only a short period of time. Those managers do not have the time to establish informal contacts or to tap into the "grapevine" to learn new sources of information. When managers are rotated through the alliance too quickly, they lose the incentive to assimilate the necessary skills and technologies that will be useful to the parent firm when they return. Short-term assignments compromise managers' ability to learn new insights and skills from their partners. Much of this learning occurs informally as managers communicate with one another on a daily basis.

Costs of Inflexibility. Alliances paradoxically can constrain a firm's future strategy, despite offering immediate benefits of risk and cost reduction. Even the best negotiated contracts and arrangements cannot prespecify the future events that may disturb or change the conditions of the alliance. Thus, managers need to be flexible in dealing with various situations that are likely to arise when working with a partner. Long-standing alliances should be evolving relationships that reflect a close understanding of the partner's intentions and what the firm intends to gain from the alliance. Otherwise, alliances can actually limit the firm's ability to perform new sets of activities. In some instances, for example, alliances can limit the firm's ability to enter new markets where a partner is already situated. Consider the case of General Electric. GE cannot further enter and serve the medical equipment business in Japan without the help of its partner, Yokogawa Electric. The venture between GE and Yokogawa, known as GE Yokogawa, produces X-ray and CT (computer tomography) scanners for both the Japanese and other major markets around the world. However, Yokogawa acts as a "brake" on General Electric's speed and ability to maneuver, particularly if GE wants to use its Japanese manufacturing base to supply new markets. In a separate venture, GE works with Japanese giant Toshiba in several different ventures, including power generation equipment, power transmission equipment, and major home appliances. Toshiba has become an important partner for GE to sell major home appliances in the Japanese market. Yet, GE's alliance with Toshiba specifies what appliance distribution channels and what regional Japanese markets GE may enter. GE is limited in how far it can sell its major appliances to Japanese customers.

In May 1994, Rubbermaid ended a four-year-old joint venture with the Dutch chemical firm, DSM Group. Although Rubbermaid enjoyed a good working relationship with DSM, the European-based joint venture limited the degree to which Rubbermaid could act on its own in developing new markets for its popular houseware products. Rubbermaid wanted to invest in state-of-the-art manufacturing facilities to enter European segments faster. On the other hand, DSM, fearing the effects of a long European recession, wanted to cut back on further investment. After the joint venture ends, Rubbermaid (now a unit of Newell) will be free to compete in Europe without any restrictions imposed by its previous partner.[25]

Other day-to-day issues can collectively result in alliance inflexibility. Cash flow earned from a venture must be shared with a partner, such as between Fuji and Xerox. Jointly conducted research may lead to patents that require both partners to tell the other what their new products will be, as is the case in certain pharmaceutical and biotechnology alliances. Thus, alliances can lead the firm into a series of unanticipated obstacles. For example, the Kaleida and Taligent alliances between Apple and IBM to develop new operating systems and multimedia technologies for personal computers ran into a series of problems. Both IBM and Apple realized that they needed to cooperate closely to design a user-friendly operating system that could compete effectively against Microsoft's Windows and other new offerings. However, neither firm realized the degree of day-to-day negotiation that was required to reach consensus on key details of developing new types of software and multimedia computer formats. Long negotiations were needed to ensure that future products would be compatible with each firm's existing array of products. The time required for both firms to learn how to work with each other comfortably came at a high price, since the software industry is fast moving and product delays often mean potentially big losses of market share. Moreover, both IBM and Apple suffered from additional operating delays that resulted from the feeling that neither firm was willing to truly "commit" to the joint venture's final products.[26]

Balancing Cooperation and Competition

Alliances involve both benefits and risks. As such, all alliances involve careful assessment of unavoidable trade-offs. Many of the risks associated with alliances—knowledge/skill leakage, deepening dependence, and coordination costs—result when managers rush into alliances. The heaviest costs and highest risks of alliances manifest themselves when managers view alliances as a complete substitute for their own firm's internal development or global expansion strategy efforts. All too often, senior managers will regard alliances as a long-term "crutch" that enables them to avoid real commitments to developing the basics of a business. However, when managers use alliances as a substitute for internal development or market expansion efforts, they often feel they have surrendered control over their businesses. In fact, surrender more often than not results from business neglect and from misreading partners' strategic goals. Overreliance on alliances to learn, to build, and to extend new sources of competitive advantage can be a serious mistake. On the other hand, carefully designed and implemented alliance strategies can help firms attain many important benefits while limiting knowledge-sharing and competitive risks.

Western firms, with few exceptions, have been unable to use alliances as effectively as Japanese partners to learn new skills. They often become excessively dependent on their partners for key skills and products. Western managers fail to realize that cooperation and competition need to be balanced in a relationship. On the other hand, Japanese managers often run their alliances "in parallel" with internal development. For example, Toshiba works closely with IBM in developing newer models of flat-panel display screens for use in notebook computers. Yet, Toshiba ensures that it simultaneously has its own self-contained factory to apply the lessons from working with IBM to its own products. *Alliances work best when they are implemented in conjunction with the firm's own internal development and market expansion efforts.* A few basic guidelines managers can use to design effective alliances that protect and extend their firm's distinctive competence are described in the following sections.

Understand the Firm's Knowledge and Skill Base

The single most important step to prepare for an alliance is to understand how the firm's skills and knowledge contribute to competitive advantage. By knowing what skills are essential to the firm's future, managers can define the scope, goals, and limits of cooperation with a partner. First and foremost, companies must understand how their distinctive competence contributes to building competitive advantage. A firm's distinctive competence lays the foundation for learning and applying new technologies and core skills that are translated into new products. However, working with an alliance partner certainly exposes the firm's core skills and distinctive competence to some degree. All too many firms, such as General Electric, General Motors, and Chrysler, have failed to recognize how quickly critical skills and knowledge can leak to an alliance partner if management is not careful. This unintended transfer happens frequently when both senior management and the alliance manager do not protect the firm's distinctive competence. Despite its desire to work with more partners to reach new customers and markets, IBM has been extremely careful and deliberate in managing its growing array of alliances. IBM has long understood how mismanaged alliances can rapidly expose the firm's core skills and technologies to its partners. For example, IBM's joint venture with Toshiba in flat-panel screens has been conducted in a separate, jointly owned plant away from other IBM operations in Japan. This isolation limits how far Toshiba is able to "snoop" around or access other core IBM product development or technology areas and proprietary manufacturing processes. It also helps keep IBM attuned to its partner's interests and requests for technology. Despite the fact that the Display Technologies venture appears to be unwinding, both IBM and Toshiba will continue to make flat-panel displays for their own products for their own separate end markets. IBM is fully aware that as it renegotiates its relationship with Toshiba, the Japanese firm remains a potent, current competitor in other markets and products.

IBM's Microelectronics unit has generally preferred to work with domestic U.S. partners, such as Motorola, Novellus Systems, and Applied Materials, on critically sensitive technologies, such as photolithography and etching techniques used in making advanced semiconductors. Novellus Systems helped IBM become the first semiconductor manufacturer to substitute copper for aluminum in building the complex circuitry within microchips. IBM is a leading supporter of Sematech's efforts to deepen U.S. manufacturing skill in advanced chips. Working with domestic partners eases some of the costs of coordination. In recent years, IBM has also entered into a broad array of coproduction arrangements with a number of firms such as National Semiconductor, Transmeta, Cirrus Logic, Xilinx, and other smaller firms to help these companies gain access to vital manufacturing capabilities they do not have. It also enables IBM to compete indirectly with Intel by introducing new competitors' offerings of microprocessors into the PC industry where Intel has an overwhelming market position. At the same time, IBM has also begun working closely with Intel and Motorola to accelerate the development of newer X-ray and deep ultraviolet (DUV) lithography tools needed to push chip circuitry even further. This is another example where IBM, Intel and Motorola are working together in a co-opetitive relationship. Yet, neither firm wants to be overly dependent on Japanese and other suppliers of critical semiconductor capital equipment.[27]

In the past few years, IBM Microelectronics has expanded the reach of its alliances. In particular, IBM is using its technology-based strengths to enter a series of co-opetitive relationships with Japanese firms, once considered the primary threat to IBM's dominance in a broad array of businesses. These relationships are co-opetitive in nature because IBM realizes that even though it will share the costs in developing new chips with its Japanese partners, Big Blue cannot fully control how they will use their newly acquired skills to develop future products—some of which may compete with IBM's offerings in ways that no one could have predicted. In 1999, IBM became the primary manufacturing source to provide microprocessors for Nintendo's newest video game systems. In April 2001, IBM announced plans to work with Sony and Toshiba to build a new "supercomputer on a chip" for introduction in the latter part of this decade. By locating this venture in Austin, Texas, IBM is in a superior position to control the extent to which its partners can learn from IBM's core skills. Although Sony clearly wants to use this chip to further its own strategy for the multimedia and entertainment industries, IBM remains wary of Sony's renowned skills in manufacturing and thus wants to make sure that the consumer electronics giant does not get the upper hand in future semiconductor development. At the same time, IBM's relationship with Toshiba remains close, even though one of their oldest ventures that produce flat-panel displays may ultimately dissolve. Still, IBM has more strongly asserted its presence in the Japanese market, working with new firms across a broad array of products and services. IBM's newest semiconductor alliance—with Seiko-Epson of Japan—is designed to help both companies develop newer chips for Japan and other Asian markets.

IBM Microelectronics is also looking to serve as a "chip foundry" for other emerging semiconductor firms that do not have the capital or skills to engage in self-manufacture. IBM hopes to gain significant market recognition for its semiconductor prowess. In its most recent marketing campaign, IBM is now promoting its "Built with IBM Technology" logo in a move that imitates the Intel Inside campaign used in personal computers.

Choose Complementary Partners

Alliances are less likely to result in crippling dependence if firms are careful in selecting their partners. Alliances are apt to be smoother and less dangerous if two firms cooperate on a project that is not central to their interests or if they collaborate in a marketplace where their interests are not likely to collide. Partners with similar skills, technologies, and products/services designed for the same market or region often find themselves competing against each other relatively quickly. This development is most likely to occur when firms realize that their long-term goals may actually converge in the future, especially if the sharp distinction between industries or technologies begins to blur. Similarly, firms competing in the same marketplace or region will often find their partners becoming unintended competitors simply because their individual ambitions may override an earlier desire to cooperate. Consequently, co-opetition can ultimately become full-blown, direct competition. Thus, firms with complementary technological skills or firms that have complementary market strengths in different regions may make better partners because of the reduced potential for direct competition in end products and markets. The Nestlé and Coca-Cola alliance is an example of a complementary partnership that has worked well over the past few years. Nestlé has little interest in penetrating the soft drink market. Coca-Cola has few interests in the flavored drink and coffee segments. Yet, both firms have benefited from using each other's distribution channels and marketing programs. Both partners also strengthen themselves against other competitors in their respective markets.

The airline industry demonstrates the clear necessity of choosing partners that have complementary interests. Star Alliance, which encompasses United Airlines, Lufthansa, Scandinavian Airline System (SAS), Thai International, Air Canada, and Varig Brazilian Airlines, involves partners from different parts of the world that are seeking cooperation to enter each other's markets carefully. Each partner directly complements the others in terms of knowledge of local markets, best ways to deal with host governments in regulatory matters, and in providing key infrastructure (e.g., maintenance, aircraft service, crew handling facilities) at hub airports. Moreover, each airline is strong in one part of the world, but comparatively weak or nonexistent in the other parts. This makes the choice of complementary partners not only a necessity, but also a basis for longer-term, sustainable cooperation. Although airline alliances involving complementary partners can sometimes unwind (e.g., Delta Air Lines and Singapore Airlines), close coordination among partners to form trans-Atlantic, trans-Pacific, and even fully global networks helps each alliance member better serve its customers in those parts of the world where it has little previous experience. Still, alliance members will have to devote considerable effort to mesh and harmonize their disparate organizational cultures, styles, and decision-making processes.

Keep Alliance Personnel Long-Term

Learning and applying new skills and technologies requires patience and time. Thus, it is imperative that corporate managers keep their alliance personnel long-term. This step ensures that a sufficient "gestation" period occurs for effective learning and insight. Unfortunately, U.S. managers often perceive that alliance assignments are less valuable or "fast-track" than working in headquarters. Often, the alliance site is far from headquarters. Alliance assignments lack visibility to aspiring managers and offer little opportunity to network with other managers and superiors. These factors often bias U.S. companies toward short-term alliance assignments, which are viewed as tangential to the company's key activities. On the contrary, Japanese companies often commit their managerial and technical personnel to the life of the venture. This strategy ensures a vastly more receptive and fertile ground to learn their partner's skills. The managers' personal success now depends almost exclusively on what they can learn and bring back to the parent firm.

Ethical Dimension

The rise of strategic alliances should encourage managers to think about the ethical problems likely to emerge when undertaking such arrangements. Two dominant ethical issues surrounding strategic alliances are (1) balancing collaboration and competition within the alliance, and (2) the issue of loyalty among personnel assigned to an alliance.

Cooperation and Competition in Alliances

The formation of strategic alliances often raises a critical ethical question concerning the boundaries of cooperation and competition with partnering firms. On the one hand, strategic alliances are designed to give firms an opportunity to apply their distinctive skills and capabilities jointly to accomplish some objective (the collaboration side of alliances). On the other hand, alliances are also designed to help the firm learn from its partner new skills or technologies that it currently does not have (the competitive side of alliances). While alliances involve cooperation, a firm must set definite limits on how far it will go to cooperate with other partners. Firms need to protect their interests in an alliance by ensuring they do not "give away the store" in terms of losing control over their core technologies and proprietary knowledge. In other words, alliances involve a certain duality wherein partners work together (cooperate) on a certain objective but also attempt to learn new skills (compete). Thus, managing this tightrope balance with a partner involves a high degree of relationship building, while at the same time, communicating that certain areas are off limits for discussion.

Their day-to-day operations allow alliance partners to become more familiar with the habits and practices of their partners. This familiarity, in turn, enables them to build a stable relationship based on mutual respect and mutual benefit (cooperation). However, the workings of any alliance still depend upon a certain give-and-take quality to it, whereby partners trade information or technology in exchange for something of value from the partner (competition). Thus, every alliance in some sense has "two faces" to it. Genuine cooperation requires trust and stability to accomplish some jointly desired objective; learning from a partner requires negotiation or give and take that represents competition within the alliance. The ethical balance in alliances comes from a certain level of trust that partners build to ensure that they treat each other openly, while simultaneously not attempting to gain the upper hand on each other by demanding or covertly stealing technology that is clearly beyond the scope of the agreement.

Regardless of the alliance vehicle (licensing, joint ventures, networks, knowledge webs, consortia), firms always face the potential problem of partners attempting to take advantage of their relationship to learn or "steal" technology that was not part of the original arrangement. This ethical issue becomes paramount when firms are collaborating on large-scale projects that involve highly proprietary or emerging technologies representing many years of investment and effort. Unscrupulous partners can sometimes use alliances as a method to learn new technologies and processes from their partners "cheaply," thereby avoiding their own R&D to advance their efforts. This problem is likely to become more salient and problematic as firms become increasingly interwoven in alliances that bring in partners from other cultures and nations, where the ethical distinction between cooperation and competition may be much more blurred.

Alliance Personnel Issues

Another pertinent ethical issue is the staffing of alliances. Oftentimes, managers and technical personnel assigned to an alliance will experience a certain degree of confusion about where to place their loyalties. This problem will also affect their feelings toward their parent company and the alliance they are assigned to, particularly if they are to work with the alliance partner over a long time. Namely, are alliance personnel supposed to be loyal to their parent firm that assigned them there, or are they supposed to be loyal to the alliance as a new entity? Employees who think their primary loyalty should be with their parent firms may feel more prone to view the alliance as a "dispensable" vehicle, in which their only goal within the alliance is to learn as much as they can from the partner and then return to headquarters. On the other hand, employees who believe they must work more intimately with their partner's managers and employees may face the danger of "going native." In other words, people assigned to an alliance may begin to start thinking like their partners and to assimilate their partner's values and culture over time, particularly if they feel they have been neglected or forgotten by their parent firms. Employees may sometimes develop a new loyalty toward the alliance as an entity in its own right. Thus, senior managers must carefully evaluate these issues before assigning key personnel to an alliance. Staffing the alliance with too many people who are simply out to "get" the partner's technology or skills will destroy the fabric of trust within an alliance. However, sending out people to staff an alliance without giving them opportunities to return home will raise the potential of their "going native."

Summary

- Alliances represent a useful intermediate step for firms seeking to gain the benefits of diversifying into new areas of activity.
- Alliances can serve as a lower-risk vehicle for firms seeking to enter new markets as part of a measured strategy of global expansion.
- The need for some form of risk reduction promotes alliance formation. These risks include new market entry, industry evolution, learning and applying new technologies, and filling out a product line.

- Allying with other firms enables the company to secure added benefits, especially benefits from the opportunity to develop new products and technologies that are too costly for the firm to undertake by itself.
- Alliances come in three broad categories: licensing arrangements, joint ventures, and consortia. Each broader category, however, can be further divided into more specific types of strategic alliances (e.g., cross-marketing arrangements, coproduction, codevelopment pacts, equity stakes, etc.).
- Industry-spanning alliance networks are now taking on a greater importance in shaping the evolution of many new products and services, especially in entertainment, high-technology arenas, and health care.
- Firms that participate in industry-spanning alliance networks may find themselves members of a larger knowledge web. In this context, firms attempt to outrace one another to innovate new forms of technologies and knowledge to dominate the evolution of an industry. Frequently, firms will find themselves cooperating and competing with their partners at the same time.
- Managers must understand how their firm's distinctive competence benefits from working with a partner. Managers must also take steps to protect their firm's distinctive competence from excessive exposure to the firm's partners.
- All alliance configurations or forms impose risks. These risks are rising incompatibility of partners, knowledge/skill leakage to the partner, deepening dependence, and strategic control costs of coordination, learning, and inflexibility.
- Allying will be fruitful only to the extent that the benefits outweigh the costs.
- Understanding how the firm's skills and technologies relate to building competitive advantage is a vital step in defining the limits and scope of cooperation.
- Firms with complementary skills tend to make better alliance partners because they offer less potential for direct competition in end products or markets.
- Keeping alliance personnel long-term is critical to effective learning.
- All alliances involve a degree of collaboration and competition when working with a partner. Cooperating effectively to accomplish some desired objective requires relationship building and trust; however, learning new skills and technologies from a partner involves day-to-day negotiations and give and take that are more competitive in nature.

Exercises and Discussion Questions

1. Over the past year, the telecommunications industry has seen a large number of alliances formed between local telephone companies and other firms. Using the Internet, look up the Web site for Verizon Communications, a major local telephone company in many parts of the nation. What type of companies is Verizon allying with? What appears to be the rationale for Verizon's multiple array of alliances? Which ones appear to be complementary partners? Which ones appear to be technology development relationships?
2. Why is it important to understand the strategic motivations of a potential alliance partner? What are some things to consider when assessing the relative compatibility of a future partner?
3. Assume you are the CEO of a leading technology company. You are currently manufacturing state-of-the-art notebook computers and have a wildly successful brand name to your credit. A Japanese firm wishes to form an alliance with you. The proposed partnership would involve manufacturing a large portion of your notebook computers in Japan using the partner's factories and employees. The partner insists on using his or her factories in Japan because they have a reputation for quality products. What are some of the benefits and risks that you face in the relationship? How would you manage this relationship over the long term? Does manufacturing in Japan make a difference to your long-term competitive

advantage? What are some key issues you need to think about when entering the alliance?

Endnotes

1. Facts and data used for the IBM case are adapted from the following sources: "Low-Power Chip Developed by IBM Extends Battery Life," *Wall Street Journal*, October 12, 2001, p. B3; "IBM Sets Pact with Peregrine," *Wall Street Journal*, August 1, 2001; "Virage and IBM Agree to Broaden Partnerships on Digital-Video Products," *Wall Street Journal*, July 11, 2001; "IBM Gains Japan Airlines Work," *Wall Street Journal*, June 22, 2001; "IBM, Seiko Epson Negotiate to Form Asian Chip Venture," *Wall Street Journal*, May 24, 2001; "IBM, Toshiba Launch Talks to End Venture That Produces LCDs," *Wall Street Journal*, May 17, 2001; "IBM, Carrier to Unveil Joint Internet Venture in Air Conditioning," *Wall Street Journal*, April 9, 2001; "Joint Project to Develop Supercomputer on a Chip," *Semiconductor International*, April 1, 2001; "IBM Receives Sony Contract for New Chips," *Wall Street Journal*, March 12, 2001; "IBM, Cisco Extend Mobile Networking Alliance," *Fiber Optic News*, March 5, 2001; "IBM Will License LSI Chip Design for Digital Signals," *Wall Street Journal*, January 22, 2001; "IBM, Siemens Unit Form Joint Venture for Magnetic Chip," *Wall Street Journal*, December 7, 2000; "IBM and Kymata Develop Optical Chips for High Speed Networks," *Fiber Optic News*, December 4, 2000; "IBM Is Expected to Announce a Pact with NTT," *Wall Street Journal*, October 31, 2000; "Sprint, IBM Lotus to Jointly Develop Wireless Services," *Wall Street Journal*, August 23, 2000; "IBM Plans E-commerce Venture with Seven Other Firms," *Wall Street Journal*, June 8, 2000; "Qwest, IBM Plan to Build Internet Data Centers," *Wall Street Journal*, March 27, 2000; "IBM Takes Stakes in i2, Ariba in Sign of Business-to-Business Interest," *Wall Street Journal*, March 9, 2000; "Medtronic to Join Microsoft, IBM in Patient-Monitoring Devices," *Wall Street Journal*, January 24, 2000; "Xerox in Technology Alliance with IBM," *Wall Street Journal*, September 10, 1998, p. B6; "Applied Language, IBM Join to Offer Speech Products," *Wall Street Journal*, July 27, 1998, p. B4; "IBM Is Contracted to Make WinChip Microprocessors," *Wall Street Journal*, March 17, 1998, p. B6; "Sun and IBM, in Rare Cooperation, to Develop Java Operating System," *Wall Street Journal*, April 1, 1998, p. B2; "Advanced Micro Says IBM Has Been Hired to Make Its K6 Chips," *Wall Street Journal*, March 2, 1998, p. C16; "IBM Ready to Unveil Licensing Agreement with Adobe Systems," *Wall Street Journal*, February 19, 1998, p. B2; "IBM to Offer Kits to Design Chips That Use Copper," *Wall Street Journal*, October 27, 1997, p. B15; "IBM to Sell Relabeled 3Com Palm Pilot as Its First Digital Assistant," *Wall Street Journal*, September 23, 1997, p. B6; "IBM to Enter Market for TV Broadcasting Gear," *Wall Street Journal*, April 7, 1997, p. B5; "IBM to Launch Line of Workstations Using Intel Chips, Microsoft Software," *Wall Street Journal*, March 17, 1997, p. B9; "IBM, 3Com, Cascade Join On Networking Approach," *Wall Street Journal*, January 27, 1997, p. B12; "IBM Corp. Buys a Large Stake in NetObjects," *Wall Street Journal*, March 20, 1997, p. B6; "IBM Agrees to Allow Mitsubishi to Market Certain PowerPC Chips," *Wall Street Journal*, July 23, 1996, p. A4; "IBM Sets Pact to Resell Storage Devices Produced by Rival Storage Technology," *Wall Street Journal*, June 11, 1996, pp. A3, A4; "IBM Buys Stake in Firm Offering Videos on Demand," *Wall Street Journal*, November 16, 1994, p. B10; "Apple-IBM Goal of Universal Computer Faces Hurdles," *Wall Street Journal*, November 9, 1994, p. B4, "IBM and Philips Electronics Join in Chip Venture," *Wall Street Journal*, October 11, 1994, p. B3; "IBM, Apple to Announce Limited Pact for PCs Based on Common Technology," *Wall Street Journal*, October 28, 1994, p. A2; "Sega, IBM, Blockbuster to Test Electronic Distribution of Games," *Wall Street Journal*, June 1, 1994, p. B6. "IBM, Apple Computer, Scientific-Atlanta Plan Set-Top

Box Alliance," *Wall Street Journal*, May 24, 1994, p. B7; "The Vision Thing," *Forbes*, August 30, 1993, pp. 42–43; "IBM Targets Intel's Chip Monopoly with Computer Based on One of Its Own," *Wall Street Journal*, September 17, 1993, p. B2; "Again, IBM Divides to Conquer," *Business Week*, May 24, 1993, pp. 73–76; "Faith in a Stranger," *Business Week*, April 5, 1993, pp. 18–24; "IBM, Motorola Produce Chip Prototype, Showing First Result of Pact with Apple," *Wall Street Journal*, October 2, 1992, p. B6; "Talk about Your Dream Team," *Business Week*, July 27, 1992, pp. 59–60; "Breaking Up IBM," *Fortune*, July 27, 1992, pp. 44–53; "The New IBM," *Business Week*, December 16, 1991, pp. 112–120; "IBM and Apple Open New Front in PC Wars with Strategic Alliance," *Wall Street Journal*, July 5, 1991, p. A1; "What's Ailing Big Blue," *Business Week*, June 17, 1991, pp. 24–32.

2. Facts and data for the airline industry were adapted from the following: "For Once-Struggling Air France, a Surprising Comeback," *Wall Street Journal*, March 5, 2002, p. A13; "Collapse of Ansett Deal Affects Airbus, Star Alliance and Others in the Industry," *Wall Street Journal*, February 28, 2002, p. A15; "American Air, British Air Drop Plans for Venture," *Wall Street Journal*, January 28, 2002, pp. A3, A16; "Delta and Air France Set Initial Agreement under 'Open Skies' Deal," *Wall Street Journal*, October 22, 2001, p. B7; "Delta Air to Request Antitrust Immunity for Foreign Alliance," *Wall Street Journal*, August 15, 2001; "Alitalia Board Approves Bid to Forge Air Alliances," *Wall Street Journal*, July 10, 2001, p. A15; "AMR, British Air Renew Push for Alliance," *Wall Street Journal*, August 6, 2001; "More Airlines Will Crash If Mergers Are Blocked," *Wall Street Journal*, July 3, 2001; "Air New Zealand Spurns Qantas, Woos Singapore Airlines," *Wall Street Journal*, June 20, 2001; "American and British Air's Alliance Bids Again for Antitrust Immunity," *Wall Street Journal*, June 12, 2001; "Delta Instigates Broad Talks with 2 Airlines," *Wall Street Journal*, January 31, 2001; "American Air Says Huge Deal Helps Consumers," *Wall Street Journal*, January 11, 2001, pp. B3, B10; "Cathay Pacific May Join Alliance with British Air," *Wall Street Journal*, September 21, 1998, p. A22; "In Asia's Stormy Weather, Airlines Find Strength in Alliances," *Wall Street Journal*, August 19, 1998, p. A15; "United, Delta Air Unveil Big Alliance, Close Scrutiny by Regulators Expected," *Wall Street Journal*, May 1, 1998, p. A6; "American Airlines, US Airways Plan Marketing Accord to Vie with Rivals," *Wall Street Journal*, April 24, 1998, p. A4; "Lufthansa to Form Alliance with Japan's All Nippon Airways," *Dallas Morning News*, March 9, 1998, p. 7D; "Can Northwest's Service Match Continental in Alliance?" *Wall Street Journal*, January 30, 1998, p. B4; "Delta Loses Singapore Air as Partner in Its International Airline Alliance," *Wall Street Journal*, November 24, 1997, p. B14; "Lufthansa Looks to Broaden Its Alliance," *Wall Street Journal*, September 15, 1997, p. A18; "British Air and American May Alter Deal," *Wall Street Journal*, August 18, 1997, p. A10; "Northwest Air and KLM Are Near Pact That Would Resolve Alliance's Problems," *Wall Street Journal*, July 30, 1997, p. 8; "Five Airlines Unveil Expanded Alliance That Links Various Customer Services," *Wall Street Journal*, May 15, 1997, p. A8; "El Salvador's Taca, American Airlines to Form Alliance," *Wall Street Journal*, June 27, 1996, p. A12; "AMR and British Air to Share Profits as Well as Passengers, Form Alliance," *Wall Street Journal*, June 12, 1996, pp. A3, A4; "Airline Alliances to Alter Overseas Travel," *Wall Street Journal*, June 11, 1996, pp. B1, B4; "British Airways, AMR to Unveil Their Alliance," *Wall Street Journal*, June 10, 1996, p. A4; "U.S. Moves to Allow Delta, American to Form Close Links to Foreign Rivals," *Wall Street Journal*, May 22, 1996, pp. A2, A4.

3. A growing literature on strategic alliances has developed over the past ten years. Some of the representative research pieces include the following: A. Takeishi, "Bridging Inter- and Intra-Firm Boundaries: Management of Supplier Involvement in Automobile Product Development," *Strategic Management Journal* 22, no. 5 (2001): 403–434; J. E. Salk, and O Shenkar, "Social Identities in an International Joint Venture: An Exploratory Case Study," *Organization Science* 12, no. 2, (2001): 161–178; R. C. Schrader, "Collaboration and Performance in Foreign Markets: The Case of Young High-Technology Manufacturing Firms," *Academy of Management Journal* 44,

no. 1 (2001): 45–60; T. E. Stuart, "Interorganizational Alliances and the Performance of Firms: A Study of Growth and Innovation Rates in a High-Technology Industry," *Strategic Management Journal* 21, no. 8 (2000): 791–812; H. Merchant and D. Schendel, "How Do International Joint Ventures Create Shareholder Value?" *Strategic Management Journal* 21, no. 7 (2000): 723–738; A. C. Inkpen, "A Note on the Dynamics of Learning Alliances: Competition, Cooperation, and Relative Scope," *Strategic Management Journal* 21, no. 7 (2000): 775–780; A. Kaufman, C. H. Wood, and G. Theyel, "Collaboration and Technology Linkages: A Strategic Supplier Typology," *Strategic Management Journal* 21, no. 6 (2000): 649–664; T. Chi, "Option to Acquire or Divest a Joint Venture," *Strategic Management Journal* 21, no. 6 (2000): 665– 688; P. Dussauge, B. Garrette, and W. Mitchell, "Learning From Competing Partners: Outcomes and Durations of Scale and Link Alliances in Europe, North America and Asia," *Strategic Management Journal* 21, no. 2 (2000): 99–126; M. Koza and A. Y. Lewin, "The Co-evolution of Strategic Alliances," *Organization Science* 9, no. 3 (1998): 255–264; T. Khanna, "The Scope of Alliances," *Organization Science* 9, no. 3 (1998): 340–356; T. Khanna, R. Gulati, and N. Nohria, "The Dynamics of Learning Alliances: Competition, Cooperation and Relative Scope," *Strategic Management Journal* 19, no. 3 (1998): 193–210; A. C. Inkpen and A. Dinur, "Knowledge Management Processes and International Joint Ventures," *Organization Science* 9, no. 4 (1998): 454–468; S. Kumar and A. Seth, "The Design and Coordination and Control Mechanisms for Managing Joint Venture-Parent Relationships," *Strategic Management Journal* 19, no. 6 (1998): 579–600; R. Kumar and K. O. Nti, "Differential Learning and Interaction in Alliance Dynamics: A Process and Outcome Discrepancy Model," *Organization Science* 9, no. 3 (1998): 356–367; P. J. Lane and M. Lubatkin, "Relative Absorptive Capacity and Interorganizational Learning," *Strategic Management Journal* 19 (1998): 461–478; J. F. Hennart, D. J. Kim, and M. Zeng, "The Impact of Joint Venture Status on the Longevity of Japanese Stakes in U.S. Manufacturing Affiliates," *Organization Science* 9, no. 3 (1998): 382–395; R. N. Osborn and J. Hagedoorn, "The Institutionalization and Evolutionary Dynamics of Interorganizational Alliances and Networks," *Academy of Management Journal* 40, no. 2 (1997): 261–278; P. Dickson and K. M. Weaver, "Environmental Determinants and Individual-Level Moderators of Alliance Use," *Academy of Management Journal* 40, no. 2 (1997): 404–425; A. C. Inkpen and P. W. Beamish, "Knowledge, Bargaining Power, and the Instability of International Joint Ventures," *Academy of Management Review* 22 (1997): 177–202; P. F. Swan and J. E. Ettlie, "U.S.-Japanese Manufacturing Equity Relationships," *Academy of Management Journal* 40, no. 2 (1997): 463–479; J. F. Hennart and S. Reddy, "The Choice between Mergers/Acquisitions and Joint Ventures: The Case of Japanese Investors in the United States," *Strategic Management Journal* 18 (1997): 1–12; T. K. Das and B. S. Teng, "Between Trust and Control: Developing Confidence in Partner Cooperation in Alliances," *Academy of Management Review* 23, no. 3 (1998): 491–512; Y. L. Doz, "The Evolution of Cooperation in Strategic Alliances: Initial Conditions or Learning Processes?" *Strategic Management Journal* 17, Summer Special Issue (1996): 55–83; M. A. Lyles and J. E. Salk, "Knowledge Acquisition from Foreign Parents in International Joint Ventures: An Empirical Examination in the Hungarian Context," *Journal of International Business Studies* 27 (1996): 877–904; R. Gulati, "Does Familiarity Breed Trust? The Implications of Repeated Ties for Contractual Choice in Alliances," *Academy of Management Journal* 38, no. 1 (1995): 85–112; B. Gomes-Casseres, "Group versus Group: How Alliance Networks Compete," *Harvard Business Review* (July–August 1994): 5–10; R. M. Kanter, "Collaborative Advantage: The Art of Alliances," *Harvard Business Review* (July–August 1994) 96–108; N. Nohria and R.G Eccles, eds., *Networks and Organizations: Structure Form and Action* (Boston: Harvard Business Press, 1993); D. Mowery, ed., *International Collaborative Ventures in U.S. Manufacturing* (Cambridge, Mass.: Ballinger, 1988); J. Hagedoorn and J. Schakenraad, "The Effect of Strategic Technology Alliances on Company Performance," *Strategic Management Journal* 14, no. 4 (1994): 291–309; J. Bleeke and D. Ernst, *Collaborating to Compete* (New York: Wiley, 1993); A. Parkhe, "Messy Research, Methodological Predispositions, and Theory Development in International Joint

Ventures," *Academy of Management Review* 18, no. 2 (1993): 227–268; L. L. Blodgett, "Factors in the Instability of International Joint Ventures: An Event History Analysis," *Strategic Management Journal* 13 (1992): 475–481; D. Lei and J. W. Slocum, Jr., "Global Strategy, Competence-Building and Strategic Alliances," *California Management Review* (Fall 1992): 81–97; P. S. Ring and A. H. Van de Ven, "Structuring Cooperative Relationships between Organizations," *Strategic Management Journal* 13 (1992): 483–498; J. L. Badaracco, *The Knowledge Link: How Firms Compete through Strategic Alliances* (Boston: Harvard University Press, 1991); J. M. Geringer, "Strategic Determinants of Partner Selection Criteria in International Joint Ventures," *Journal of International Business Studies* 22 (1991): 41–62; G. Hamel, "Competition for Competence and Interpartner Learning within International Strategic Alliances," *Strategic Management Journal* 12 (1991): 83–103; D. Lei and J. W. Slocum, Jr., "Global Strategic Alliances: Payoffs and Pitfalls," *Organizational Dynamics* 1 (1991): 44–62; R. N. Osborn and C. C. Baughn, "Forms for Organizational Governance for Multinational Alliances," *Academy of Management Journal* 33 (1990): 503–519; B. Borys and D. Jemison, "Hybrid Arrangements as Strategic Alliances: Theoretical Issues in Organizational Combinations," *Academy of Management Review* 14 (1989): 234–249; G. Hamel, Y. Doz, and C. K. Prahalad, "Collaborate with Your Competitors and Win," *Harvard Business Review* (January–February 1989): 133–139; K. R. Harrigan, "Joint Ventures and Competitive Strategy," *Strategic Management Journal* 9 (1988): 141–158; B. Kogut, "Joint Ventures: Theoretical and Empirical Perspectives," *Strategic Management Journal* 9 (1988): 319–332; H. Thorelli, "Networks: Between Markets and Hierarchies," *Strategic Management Journal* 7 (1986): 37–51; K. Ohmae, *Triad Power: The Coming Shape of Global Competition* (New York: Free Press, 1985).

4. "Sony, Partners Plan Own Format on Rewritable Compact Disks," *Dallas Morning News*, August 14 1997, p. 2D.

5. See, for example, "Juniper Posts a $29.7 Million Net Loss, but Stock Nevertheless Jumps on Results," *Wall Street Journal*, October 12, 2001, p. B3; "Juniper, Sonus Share Converged Vision," *Fiber Optic News*, May 14, 2001.

6. Literally hundreds of biotechnology alliances have been formed over the past several years. See, for example, "Bayer, Millennium Say Genomic Drug That They Developed Fights Tumors," *Wall Street Journal*, January 11, 2001, p. B4; "AstraZeneca Forms Alliance with Orchid," *Wall Street Journal*, February 13, 2001, p. B6.

7. "Boeing Is Negotiating Wing-Parts Pacts with Japanese Firms for New Large Jet," *Wall Street Journal*, September 5, 1996, p. A4.

8. "Schwab Expands Role in Launching Other Firms' Funds," *Wall Street Journal*, July 21, 1998, p. C1, C25.

9. See "Seeking a Big Lift, Xerox to Launch Big Color Printer," *Wall Street Journal*, August 28, 2001, B1, B6; "Canon on the Loose," Forbes, July 23, 2001, pp. 68–69; "Xerox, Beset by Problems, Lost Ground to Rival Canon in 2000, Study Finds," *Wall Street Journal*, March 9, 2001, p. B6; "Xerox Nears Sale of Half Its Stake in Fuji Venture," *Wall Street Journal*, March 2, 2001, p. B6.

10. See, for example, "Y. L. Doz, P. M. Olk, and P. S. Ring, "Formation Processes of R&D Consortia: Which Path to Take? Where Does It Lead?" *Strategic Management Journal* 21 (2000): 239–266.

11. See, for example, L. D. Browning, J. M. Beyer, and J. C. Shetler, "Building Cooperation in a Competitive Industry: SEMATECH and the Semiconductor Industry," *Academy of Management Journal* 38, no. 1 (1995): 113–151. Also see W. J. Spencer and P. Grindley, "SEMATECH after Five Years: High Tech Consortia and U.S. Competitiveness," *California Management Review* 35 (Fall 1993): 9–32; C. H. Ferguson and C. R. Morris, *Computer Wars: How the West Can Win in a Post-IBM World* (New York: Times Books/Random House, 1993).

12. An excellent discussion of Japanese keiretsu may be found in C. H. Ferguson, "Computers and the Coming of the U.S. Keiretsu," *Harvard Business Review* (July–August 1990): 55–70; See also F. Kodama, *Emerging Patterns of Innovation* (Boston: Harvard Business School Press, 1995).

13. The concept of applying network-based theories from other disciplines can help contribute to our understanding of the dynamics of strategic alliances, particularly those involving multiple firms. An outstanding research piece that highlights some of these issues from a competitive perspective is D. R. Gnywali and R. Madhavan, "Cooperative Networks and Competitive Dynamics: A Structural Embeddedness Perspective," *Academy of Management Review* 26, no. 3 (2001): 431–445. Also see R. Gulati, N. Nohria, and A. Zaheer, "Strategic Networks," *Strategic Management Journal* 21 (2000): 203–215; R. Gulati, "Network Location and Learning: The Influence of Network Resources and Firm Capabilities on Alliance Formation," *Strategic Management Journal* 20 (1999): 397–420; T. Stuart, "Network Positions and Propensities to Collaborate: An Investigation of Strategic Alliance Formation in a High-Technology Industry," *Administrative Science Quarterly* 43 (1998): 668–698; B. Uzzi, "Social Structure and Competition in Interfirm Networks: The Paradox of Embeddedness," *Administrative Science Quarterly* 42 (1997): 35–67; J. Gimeno and C. Woo, "Economic Multiplexity: The Structural Embeddedness of Cooperation in Multiple Relations of Interdependence," *Advances in Strategic Management* 13 (1996): 323–361; W. W. Powell, K. W. Koput, and L. Smith-Doerr, "Interorganizational Collaboration and the Locus of Innovation: Networks of Learning in Biotechnology," *Administrative Science Quarterly* 29 (1996): 329–346.

14. See, for example, "Union Pacific Seeks to Boost Revenues in Unlikely Places," *Wall Street Journal*, October 16, 2001, p. B4.

15. See, for example, A. M. Brandenburger and B. Nalebuff, *Co-opetition: A Revolutionary Mindset That Combines Competition and Cooperation* (New York: Doubleday, 1996).

16. Issues and costs surrounding strategic alliances are further discussed in the following works: S. H. Park and G. R. Ungson, "Interfirm Rivalry and Managerial Complexity: A Conceptual Framework of Alliance Failure," *Organization Science* 12, no. 1 (2001): 37–53; J. J. Reuer and M. J. Leiblein, "Downside Risk Implications of Multinationality and International Joint Ventures," *Academy of Management Journal* 43, no. 2 (2000): 203–214; C. Saunders, M. Gebelt, and Q. Hu, "Achieving Success in Information Systems Outsourcing," *California Management Review* 39, no. 2 (1997): 63–79; P. C. Grindley and D. J. Teece, "Managing Intellectual Capital: Licensing and Cross-Licensing in Semiconductors and Electronics," *California Management Review* 39, no. 2 (1997): 8–41; S. H. Park and M. Russo, "When Competition Eclipses Cooperation: An Event History Analysis of Alliance Failure," *Management Science* 42 (1996): 875–890; B. Kogut and N. Kulatilaka, "Operating Flexibility, Global Manufacturing, and the Option Value of a Multinational Network," *Management Science* 40 (1994): 123–139; R. A. Bettis, S. P. Bradley, and G. Hamel, "Outsourcing and Industrial Decline," *Academy of Management Executive* (February 1992): 7–22; C. C. Snow, R. E. Miles and J. E. Coleman, "Managing 21st Century Network Organizations," *Organizational Dynamics* (Winter 1992): 5–20; D. Lei and J. W. Slocum, Jr., "Global Strategy, Competence-Building and Strategic Alliances," *California Management Review* (Fall 1992): 81–97; J. Bleeke and D. Ernst, "The Way to Win in Cross-Border Alliances," *Harvard Business Review* (November–December 1991): 127–135; D. Lei and J. W. Slocum, Jr., "Global Strategic Alliances: Payoffs and Pitfalls," *Organizational Dynamics* 1 (1991): 44–62; G. Hamel, Y. Doz, and C. K. Prahalad, "Collaborate With Your Competitors and Win," *Harvard Business Review* (January–February 1989): 133–139.

17. See "Ford and VW Part Company in Latin America," *Wall Street Journal*, December 2, 1994, p. A8.

18. "How Do Joint Ventures Go Wrong? Ask Kaleida," *Wall Street Journal*, November 22, 1995, pp. B1, B8. Also see "IBM, Apple, H-P to Disband Taligent; Big Layoffs Loom at Software Venture," *Wall Street Journal*, December 1, 1995, p. B5.

19. "Motorola, IBM to End Alliance on Design of PowerPC Chip Line," *Wall Street Journal*, June 12, 1998, p. B6.

20. "Mexican-Food Joint Venture Gives Arby's Indigestion," *Wall Street Journal*, August 12, 1997, pp. B1, B2.

21. See "IBM, Toshiba Launch Talks to End Venture That Produces LCDs," *Wall Street Journal*, May 15, 2001.

22. See, for example, R. B. Reich and E. D. Mankin, "Joint Ventures with Japan Give Away Our Future," *Harvard Business Review* (March–April 1986): 78–86.

23. See "Taiwan Semi to Spend Billions on Chip Plants," *Wall Street Journal*, October 26, 2001, p. A13; "Focus on Taiwan: UMC on the Move," *Semiconductor International*, September 1, 2001; "Taiwan's Manufacturers Climb the 'Food Chain,'" *Wall Street Journal*, December 13, 2000, p. B10.

24. See R. N. Osborn and C. C. Baughn, "Forms of Interorganizational Governance for Multinational Alliances," *Academy of Management Journal* 33 (1990): 503–519. Also, A. Parkhe, "Strategic Alliance Structuring: A Game Theoretic and Transaction Cost Examination of Interfirm Cooperation," *Academy of Management Journal* 36 (1993): 794–829.

25. "Rubbermaid Is on a Tear, Sweeping Away the Cobwebs," *Wall Street Journal*, September 8, 1998, p. B4; "Rubbermaid Ends Venture in Europe, Signaling Desire to Call Its Own Shots," *Wall Street Journal*, June 1, 1994, p. A4.

26. See, for example, "Apple-IBM Goal of Universal Computer Faces Hurdles," *Wall Street Journal*, November 9, 1994, p. B4.

27. See "Group of Tech Companies, 3 Labs to Unveil Chip-Making Machine," *Wall Street Journal*, April 11, 2001, p. B6.

PART 3

Organizing for Advantage

CHAPTER 10

Designing Organizations for Competitive Advantage

Chapter Outline

What You Will Learn

- Why strategy implementation is important
- How strategy implementation contributes to a firm's competitive advantage
- Why organizational issues are a significant part of strategy implementation
- How organizational structure lays the foundation for strategy implementation
- The broad types of organizational structures that companies are likely to use
- Why no single type of organizational structure is likely to fit all companies

Ford Motor Company[1]

Following more than ninety years of growth, Ford Motor Company has become one of the largest manufacturers of automobiles in the world (2000 revenues of $180.6 billion, profits of $3.4 billion). Throughout its long history, Ford has prided itself on its innovation and the creative flair used to design some of the world's most popular and best-selling lines of cars. For example, in the late 1960s, Ford revolutionized automobile design with its original Mustang sports car that took the world by storm. Other legendary Ford nameplates developed during the 1960s and 1970s, such as the Thunderbird (T-Bird), Fairlane, Galaxy, Mustang, Taurus, Explorer, and Lincoln Continental, remain distinctive in the annals of U.S. automobile manufacturing history.

All of the three major U.S. automobile companies (Ford, General Motors, and Chrysler) grew very fast in the twenty years that followed World War II. The American automotive industry was expanding rapidly not only in the United States but also around the world. General Motors and Ford especially invested heavily in their European operations after the war because of the rapidly growing economic prosperity of those markets, the sophistication of their customers, and the fact that countries such as France, Germany, and Italy had a strong base of engineering talent that made many European car companies significant competitors (e.g., BMW, Daimler-Benz, Fiat, Ferrari, and Renault). Throughout the 1960s and 1970s, both GM and Ford set up product development centers and factories in Europe to begin designing and developing cars for different national markets by tapping into the strong pool of local engineering talent and expertise. Ford, in particular, devoted a considerable amount of effort and resources to building a large European operation that would design and develop new automotive technologies and products that appealed to a very distinctive set of preferences, tastes, weather conditions, driving habits, and operating requirements that were more specific to a European environment. Because European roads tend to be more narrow than American roads, and road conditions often varied significantly from one region to another, cars targeted for European customers often required a different set of design, manufacturing, and performance requirements than cars sold in U.S. markets. In particular, engines, transmissions, suspension, safety features, and other components manufactured for European cars often had very different design and manufacturing specifications from those used for cars designed for American markets. In addition, cars developed for a European customer base often focused on maximizing fuel efficiency and economy, since gasoline costs were significantly higher than those in the United States. Thus, European cars typically housed a smaller, more fuel-efficient (and oftentimes more powerful) engine than those found in American cars. Also, European transmissions and suspensions were often "tighter" than those found in U.S. cars, meaning that the car gave a feeling to the driver that it would "hug" the road more closely. This was an especially important design feature, since narrow European roads and frequent bad weather spells meant that drivers would potentially encounter a high range of different and possibly hazardous driving conditions, especially in different countries. Thus, the designs, components, and operating requirements for European cars were often very different from those that guided automobile development and manufacture for cars in U.S. markets.

Early Organizational Structure

To manage the significant differences in the way cars are designed, developed, and manufactured in the United States and Europe, Ford employed a geographical division form of organization for over four decades. Ford's European operations were responsible for all aspects of automotive development, manufacture, and sales in Europe. In turn, Ford's North American headquarters was responsible for developing, manufacturing, and selling cars in the United States and elsewhere. In this way, Ford Europe and Ford North America operated autonomously from one another. For all practical purposes, Ford Europe acted as if it were almost a completely separate car company from Ford North America. Each part of the company designed and implemented its own set of product development centers, design centers, factories, and purchasing operations according to its respective market needs. Within the United States, however, Ford utilized a product division structure to manage two separate car divisions, Ford and Lincoln/Mercury. Each of these product divisions offered a line of cars tailored for a different market segment (Ford—smaller and midsize cars; Lincoln/Mercury—larger, luxury cars; light trucks; medium trucks). Ford's sales to the Asia/Pacific region were quite small after the war, so this region reported directly to North American headquarters through a small international division.

Over time, the long separation of Ford Europe from Ford North America resulted in extensive duplication of effort and activities between the two operating units. In many cases, the same Ford car design developed in the United States was often completely reengineered from the ground up in Europe, thus consuming significant design time and development effort to reach the market. Even auto parts and components made in the United States became increasingly incompatible with the separate design and manufacturing specifications created by Ford Europe. The number of product components and parts grew astronomically, creating an enormously complex supply and inventory system for the company. More important, the separation of European and American operations also meant that innovations created in one part of the world could not be readily transferred to the other. For example, design innovations and improvements in fuel-efficient engines made by Ford Europe were not readily adapted by Ford North America during the 1970s. Also, steady improvements in the introduction of new paint and assembly techniques in Ford's U.S. automobile plants did not flow to Ford's European operations, thus leaving the company in a situation where experience, talent, and skills in one part of the world could not readily be used in another.

This separate division of effort between the two regions made it difficult for the entire company to respond quickly to the onslaught of better quality, lower-cost Japanese car imports in the U.S. and European markets during the past two decades. Moreover, even the same model name used for a Ford car had very different components, design specifications, and even target markets between the two parts of the company. For example, the Ford Escort in the United States during the 1980s and 1990s appealed to a market segment that is interested in basic transportation with few of the features that are found in midsize or other performance-oriented models. On the other hand, the Ford Escort in Europe is a midrange family car that typically comes with a full range of options absent on the U.S. model. This duplication of design, development, and manufacturing activities between the two regions carried over to the entire range of Ford's products. Moreover, maintaining fully autonomous vehicle design and development centers in Europe meant that Ford's overall cost structure became bloated and a real burden on financial performance during the same time period. Duplication of design and development activities became so profound during the 1980s that at one point, the company realized that it had over eighty-two different automobile models, none of which shared even the same size radiator cap. Thus, the separation of Ford Europe from Ford North America represented an organizational approach that the company could no longer afford, especially as the automobile industry itself became more global in scope.

Creating a Global Organization

In April 1994, then-CEO Alex Trotman put forth a new organizational architecture for the entire company. Known as Ford 2000, the company's reorganization combines its European and North American automotive operations into one unit. By integrating these once-separate divisions into a single unit, Trotman hoped to transform Ford into a much more nimble company that can compete with fast-moving Japanese and other competitors around the world. This single automotive division was organized around five product vehicle development centers, four in the United States and one in Europe. Each vehicle development center was responsible for a particular type of vehicle platform (e.g., small car, midsized car, luxury car, sport utility vehicle, commercial truck) that would then be developed and sold around the world under its authority. Under this new structure, for example, the European vehicle development center focused on designing small, front-wheel, fuel-efficient cars that can be sold in any global market that wants that type of car. Midsize and larger cars, trucks, and sport utility vehicles were developed in Ford's four vehicle development centers based in the United States. Each of these vehicle development centers had direct oversight of product design, engineering, manufacture, and marketing for various car or truck models that fell under its platform category.

The objective of the reorganization was to create a company in which global product teams had the capability to design around a central type of car platform a series of car models that can then be sold around the world with minor modifications. As the organizational realignment unfolded, Ford's engineers and technical staff had two types of responsibilities: an individual expertise in a given technical or functional area (e.g., engines, powertrains, suspensions, or cooling systems) and a vehicle platform center to which they belonged (small car, midsized car, luxury car, sport utility vehicle, or commercial truck). Ultimately, managers reported to their superiors in the vehicle platform center under which they were assigned. The general thrust of the organization was to create a set of vehicle and component designs that would lower the economic and organizational costs of rolling out new models. Instead of designing two separate lines of Taurus midsized cars for sale in the United States and Europe, the company sought to create one basic midsized vehicle platform in North America and then modify it for individual markets anywhere around the world. Conversely, Ford's European vehicle development center for much of the 1990s concentrated its efforts on designing all of Ford's small-car needs and then modifying them according to road conditions and customer needs in individual markets as well. If everything went to plan, CEO Trotman envisioned that Ford's small-car engineers (based in Europe) would take the lead in designing and developing Ford's entire line of small vehicles for all of Europe, the United States, and other worldwide markets using the same basic vehicle platform template.

To prepare Ford for its organizational realignment, Trotman's senior management team aggressively invested in new vehicle platforms that carried over more parts from one model to another. For example, the Lincoln LS luxury car uses many of the same powertrain and chassis components that are found on the Lincoln Town Car, Continental, and even Jaguar XJS lines of cars. Also, the company invested heavily in new types of computer-assisted design and manufacturing (CAD/CAM) technologies that enable engineers to test design prototypes for vehicle ruggedness, reliability, and performance before they are actually produced in the factory. Many of Ford's late 1990s initiatives capitalized on using Ford's corporate Internet investments to link up with suppliers in order to streamline the time needed to jointly test and work on new car designs (often called an extranet, to reflect a dedicated Internet connection between a company and its suppliers and distributors). Ford's corporate intranet (designed to link up all parts of the company internally) also served a valuable role in helping to link up different parts of the company to communicate more quickly and to coordinate key tasks such as budgeting, product development, and sharing of marketing ideas. The intranet also helped streamline manufacturing time. Once an underlying platform met the company's stringent quality, safety, operating, and manufacturability requirements, engineers in the factory were then able to download design data and other bits of information directly from the development center into the factory, thus saving considerable amounts of time and engineering effort.

This powerful combination of using more common vehicle platforms, computer-integrated manufacturing, and the use of Internet technologies to manage various tasks laid the foundation for Ford's productivity gains over General Motors during the late 1990s. These investments also enabled Ford to significantly reduce the number of basic automotive platforms from twenty-four to sixteen yet increase the number of actual car models from those platforms by over 50 percent. By 2001, Ford was able to slice down the development time of a new car (from drawing board to dealer showroom) from ten years to thirty months. By using the same basic platform for a variety of different car models, Ford obtained major gains in efficiency and productivity by spending much less time and money on redesigning each model separately every year. In addition, using the Internet to work with suppliers to design and build more common parts has begun to produce significant savings for Ford in terms of both cost and development time.

Adjusting to New Competitive Realities

The transformation of Ford to become an even more efficient and agile producer of cars and trucks continues into the new millennium, although with a significantly different turn. Under Jacques Nasser (who took over as CEO in 1997), Ford began aggressively seeking to grow in all automobile categories, both in the United States and abroad. With the global automobile industry consolidating, Ford has begun to make some major moves that will begin to give it significant new strength in Europe and Asia. In January 1999, for example, Ford paid $6.45 billion to purchase the automobile businesses of Volvo of Sweden, thus helping Ford compete more effectively in the upper range of the midsized car market. The acquisition of Volvo is important to Ford because it allows the company to gain access to many innovations in safety, ergonomics, and advanced manufacturing techniques developed by the Swedish firm. (Ford, however, did not elect to purchase the truck division of Volvo). With the acquisition of Volvo, Ford is much better positioned to compete in Europe against the likes of DaimlerChrysler and the newly formed alliance between France's Renault and Japan's Nissan Motor Company. The acquisition of Volvo complements Ford's European buyout of Jaguar and Aston-Martin earlier in the 1990s. Many analysts believe that Ford will manage Volvo in such a way that it will preserve its European heritage and styling, while adapting Volvo's assets to help Ford compete better around the world.

In Asia, Ford's growing strength in marketing, financial management, and technology has given it the upper hand in working with its Japanese partner Mazda. In the late 1990s, Ford took on a de facto controlling interest in Mazda by owning 33 percent of the Japanese firm and by placing many Americans in the most senior management positions within the Japanese company. Many analysts have commented that Ford's closer relationship and cash injection into Mazda saved the Japanese firm from the brink of potential financial disaster with the downturn in the Japanese and Southeast Asian economies. In March 1999, Ford announced that it would work much more closely with Mazda to codevelop a new line of car platforms that would enable both companies to accelerate their product development times and simultaneously share key product components to gain even greater economies of scale. In effect, Mazda has become an important Ford affiliate in helping the U.S. auto giant become more competitive in the Far East.

Even though Ford secured major increases in productivity and cost savings by developing a shared set of automotive platforms to serve all of its world markets, there were limits in the gains that the company could ultimately achieve. The notion of a "world car" that could appeal to many different buyers and driving needs proved difficult to attain, mostly because customers became increasingly savvy about what features they wanted in their cars. Moreover, many of Ford's competitors, including General Motors, DaimlerChrysler, Toyota, Honda, Nissan Motor, and Hyundai, were attempting to undertake many of the same organizational changes that Ford initiated. In addition, cars from different manufacturers increasingly looked similar, regardless of their nameplate and identity. By 2000 and 2001, Ford found it difficult to sustain its major productivity gains over arch rival General Motors, who had actually caught up with Ford on some key measures of factory efficiency. Other automotive companies were beginning to implement many of the same Internet-based initiatives that Ford had deployed earlier in the decade. Ford also faced an extremely difficult and costly year in 2001 as it struggled to deal with a long-standing controversy over the safety of its Explorer sport utility vehicle. Many of these vehicles experienced catastrophic rollover accidents, particularly when driven with Firestone tires. The exact source or cause of these rollovers is still largely unknown. Even though Firestone admitted to some manufacturing problems in a plant that produces tires for the Explorer, Ford's quality image suffered. In addition, Ford incurred substantial costs involved in a nationwide recall of the Explorer to replace all of the Firestone tires that came with the vehicle.

Equally significant, Ford is fine-tuning its organizational realignment to accommodate the new competitive realities facing the company. Demand for a truly "world car" proved illusive, since younger and wealthier customers wanted to buy cars that reflected their own tastes and personalities. This meant that even though Ford could continue to build powertrains, engines, and other components that could be shared among different vehicles, the external look and "feel" of the car became even more important to buyers. As part of Ford's strategic and organizational change, the company is now relying more heavily on its portfolio of brands to serve a different type of market segment. For example, the Volvo brand is positioned as a maker of safe, family-oriented cars; Jaguar captures the feel of British elegance; Land Rover is sold to those who want luxurious off-road capabilities; and Lincoln-Mercury is aimed at U.S. buyers who want larger, more comfortable performance cars.

Now, U.S.-based senior management is giving their regional managers in Ford Europe more autonomy to better serve European customers. In a partial reversal of Trotman's original Ford 2000 organizational shift, CEO Nasser wanted to ensure that Ford can design and develop the cars that suit the tastes and driving needs of different markets. At the same time, he was pushing through Ford's shared platform and Internet-based initiatives to keep the company's product development costs under control. Nasser believed that the Internet can do much to link up the company's vast procurement, product development, manufacturing, and marketing operations in ways that were not possible as recently as five years ago.

Likewise, Ford is moving to share more costs and product designs with its core base of suppliers. Ford wants suppliers to take on a greater role in helping the company slice even more development time for future car products. During the latter part of 2001, Ford was also focusing its efforts to restore momentum to its North American and European car operations. This means that while the company will continue to develop new powertrains, engines, and chassis components that will be shared among different models, each region will have more say in how best to develop their own regional markets to suit the needs of more demanding customers.

Introduction

So far, we have focused on ways a firm can build and extend its sources of competitive advantage. We have analyzed how companies from various industries formulate specific strategies to create new sources of value from their activities. However, strategy formulation is only part of the equation in developing competitive advantage. Once a particular strategy has been chosen, the firm must then devote considerable effort to ensure that managers and employees are united in their efforts to execute the strategy. Managers must see that individual activities within an organization work together to help achieve competitive advantage. This task is referred to as strategy implementation.

This chapter is the first of two that focus on the ingredients of effective strategy implementation. In its simplest definition, **strategy implementation** refers to converting strategies into desired actions and results. In a broader sense, strategy implementation is concerned with efforts to build a more effective organization.[2] Understanding strategy implementation is crucial because the success of any organization depends on how well people work together to translate strategies into action. Managers and employees are the ultimate source of a firm's competitive advantage, because competitive advantage arises only when managers and employees in an organization work together in an integrated manner to achieve high performance. Thus, the issues of strategy implementation and competitive advantage are inextricably linked.

strategy implementation: The process by which strategies are converted into desired actions.

As seen from the Ford Strategic Snapshot, strategy implementation is really an ongoing process. Strategy implementation thus requires an effective way to organize people so that they can perform their jobs to their best of abilities. Equally important, each individual's work and output should support the overall strategy and direction of the organization. This is a much more difficult task than first appears. Therefore, this chapter will focus exclusively on the "architecture" of designing an organization. What are the basic frameworks and designs that organizations can use to help guide their people's efforts and work to support the overall strategy?

We begin by providing some reasons why strategy implementation is an imperative issue. Effective strategy implementation occurs when people from different parts and activities of an organization work and act together to achieve the desired strategy. In the second section, we focus exclusively on the topic of organizational structure. We look at how a firm may select a particular organizational structure to support its strategy. In the third section, we examine how firms with extensive global operations may modify their organizational structures. Finally, we revisit Ford to see how it has used specific organizational structures to support their strategies.

Why Study Strategic Implementation?

Strategy implementation is an important topic for managers and employees at all levels to understand. Successful strategy implementation depends on both a well-managed organization and a solid base of committed, competent personnel. Management can formulate any number of strategies to build competitive advantage, but the success of any given strategy is only as good as the organization and the people behind it. Without a solid base of competent people who understand and support the firm's strategy, it remains nothing more than words on paper. The effectiveness of implementation ultimately determines the success or failure of any given strategy.

Strategy Implementation and the Firm's Managers

A key implementation task for senior managers is to design an organization that allows people to use their talents, capabilities, and insights to the fullest in supporting the firm's strategy. Companies, especially large companies, are complex organizations composed of many functions, activities, businesses, and, most important, people. Many people, through no fault of their own, will not always understand the value and role of how individual parts of the organization contribute to the firm's overall strategy. Through a well-designed organization, senior managers can guide and channel their people's efforts to work together in an integrated, cohesive manner that best supports the firm's strategy. Building an organization in which many people work together smoothly is not an easy task.

First, managers themselves must take steps to carefully understand how different types of strategies will require specific organizational configurations or designs to achieve successful implementation. Just as every firm's strategy is likely to be distinctive, so will be its need for an appropriately fitting organization. This total view of the organization—structure, systems, staff, and culture—represents the bricks and mortar that implement and sustain a strategy. Each firm will likely require a customized set or arrangement of organizational "building blocks" that best fit its strategy. In other words, the choice of how to design and build an organization is inextricably linked with the firm's strategy. For example, firms whose business units are pursuing low-cost leadership strategies will require a type of organizational framework unlike that of businesses competing through differentiation or focus. Conversely, highly diversified firms will not require the same type of organizational setup as those firms that are less diversified. Effective strategy implementation depends on a *close fit or alignment between the firm's strategy and the shape or structure of the organization supporting it. Strategy and organization are coupled together.*

Second, managers must ensure that their choice of an organizational setup is internally consistent. In other words, all ingredients of the organization must fit tightly together, in much the same way as the parts of a high-performance combustion engine do. Organizational consistency means that the *various components of an organization fit together and make logical sense.* All parts of the organization must be arranged, put together, and fine-tuned in a coherent way to make strategy implementation smooth and powerful. Implementation, as an ongoing task, requires management to monitor how well the firm's many functions, activities, and people are coordinated smoothly to support a given strategy. This task is almost equivalent to an onboard automobile computer that monitors and controls the various parts of the engine—the fuel/air mixture, the temperature, the RPMs, and the idle speed—all of which must work together to achieve balance, control, and fast response to provide smooth performance.[3]

Strategy Implementation and the Firm's Employees

For employees, their value to the firm hinges directly on how well they understand and support the firm's strategy in the conduct of their own jobs. Talented and capable employees are the bedrock of any organization. These employees are people who work on a daily basis to translate the firm's strategy into tangible products or services for customers. Equally important, employees represent much more than simply a company's head count or staff. They represent vital sources of knowledge and are the "eyes and ears" of the organization.

Employees' close and continuing contact with customers and operational activities makes them a wellspring of knowledge and ideas for the firm. Their daily contact with customers gives them an edge over senior managers in sensing whether the firm appears to be moving in the right direction. These same competent people can quickly identify potential areas of improvement among the firm's activities. For example, factory workers on an assembly line are in a perfect position to spot potential weaknesses and defects in an aircraft or automobile. They are also the people who would be most likely to know how best to deal with the problem and suggest ways for improvement. Japanese companies are legendary in the efforts they take to listen and gather ideas from their employees. Employees are the source of continuing quality and process improvement in Japanese factories.

Thus, strategy implementation in its most effective form is a joint effort. Ideally, managers and employees work together in understanding and supporting the firm's strategy to the best of their efforts. Together, managers and employees represent the social mosaic or "fabric" of the firm. They are also the *organizational memory that has an enduring quality*. Sustained strategy implementation is more than selecting the right type of organizational framework; it is managers and employees working together in a clear and coherent direction. Successful implementation depends on the coordinated efforts of many people from all parts of the firm.

A Framework for Designing Organizational Structure

The basis for successful strategy implementation rests on designing an effective organization. People working within an organization must be able to understand how their actions interrelate with the actions of others to support and execute the firm's strategy. Yet, in many instances, talented people in even the best-managed firms are sometimes left groping to understand their own roles in supporting the firm's strategy. Organizational structure is vital in clarifying the roles of managers and employees that hold the company together.

Although the word structure often conjures up images of rigid control and tight rules, the concept of organizational structure is actually much richer. Designing an appropriate structure that tightly fits and supports the firm's strategy is one of senior management's primary tasks. In some ways, the choice of organizational structure is so important and enduring to the firm that it can markedly influence the way the firm will formulate and implement strategies in later time periods.

structure: The formal definition of working relationships between people in an organization.

Structure refers to the formal definition of working relationships within an organization. It is a vital component in any organization and serves a twofold purpose. On the one hand, structure distinguishes and separates the specific tasks that make up the firm's activities: what people should do. On the other hand, structure provides the basis to integrate these tasks into a coherent whole: how people should work together. *Structure balances the need for separating and integrating tasks within an organization.*[4]

Structure is vitally concerned with the *relationships among activities*. Grouping together critical core activities into organizational units forms the basis for a sustainable strategy. In this way, management can better understand the ingredients of what constitutes the major sources of its competitive advantage. A well-designed structure that facilitates the execution of the firm's central value-adding activities can greatly assist management to build and extend the firm's distinctive competence into new areas of activity in later time periods. Firms will choose a structure that best suits their particular grouping of activities. Consider the Strategic Snapshots of Nordstrom, Inc., and Tyco International from our previous chapters. The highly refined and nurtured differentiation-based strategy that Nordstrom pursues in retailing is quite different from the widely diversified posture of Tyco International. One thus will expect that the organizational structure needed to support Nordstrom's strategy will be quite different from one chosen by Tyco.

Thus, *any given strategy will require a particular form of organizational structure to best lend support to implementation*. In other words, the firm's strategy is a key driver of how senior managers choose to organize and group their key value-adding activities and tasks. The strategy a firm selects will, in large measure, determine the grouping of activities and tasks, the choice of practices and procedures to attain consistency of performance, and the delegation of authority within the firm. Once a firm's organizational structure is in place, however, it can be extremely costly to modify or replace it.

Basic Ingredients of Organizational Structure

Three important ingredients, or dimensions, compose organizational structure: (1) specialization, (2) standardization, and (3) centralization. Each of these ingredients of organizational structure influences how managers and employees interact (see Exhibit 10-1).

Key Dimensions of Organizational Structure — **EXHIBIT 10-1**

Specialization

- Matching activities with people who are best able to perform them
- Found at all levels within an organization

Standardization

- Practices, procedures, and guidelines that provide the basis for consistent performance
- Focused on achieving internal order within a given structure

Centralization

- Delegation of authority throughout the organization's ranks

Specialization

Specialization refers to identifying and assigning particular activities or tasks to the appropriate individuals, teams, or units capable of performing them. When used effectively, specialization enables an organization to divide many activities and tasks and allocate them to those people best equipped to handle them. The dimension of specialization can be found at all levels within an organization.

specialization: The assignment of particular tasks and activities to those people who are best able to perform them.

Every company uses the concept of specialization in some way. For example, within an automotive factory, welders perform only those tasks that relate to welding; assemblers do their jobs by putting the parts of the car together; painters work the specialized machinery that paints each car to a glowing finish. The skills of painters are different (specialized) from those of assemblers. In a fashion salon, customers can also find specialization at work. For example, some stylists are particularly skilled at cutting and shaping hair to current styles or perms, other stylists are better trained at choosing the right mix of dyes to modify hair color according to a customer's skin complexion or tone, while other stylists specialize in care for the hands and feet as manicurists and pedicurists. People conduct particular activities according to their skills and capabilities.

Specialization is also found when we examine larger units of a firm. For example, an automotive manufacturer may decide to group all of its assembly activities in one part of the factory, while placing the specialized paint machinery in another. On an even larger scale, the same automotive company can group all of its assembly operations in one unit that reports to senior management, while placing all of its engine-manufacturing operations in another specialized unit dedicated to producing engines. In the hair salon example, a company such as Supercuts could group all of its U.S. salons and shops in one unit, while placing all of its Latin American salons in another unit. Supercuts may choose to do this because the fashion and hair-styling requirements of U.S. customers (time spent on makeup, time spent on perms, type of shampoos used, type of advertising) may vary from those of Latin American customers. Thus, for Supercuts as a company, dividing up its markets may help management better understand specific market conditions. Specialization is vital to any organization, because it matches activities with people and units best able to perform them.

Standardization

standardization: The process of defining the organization's work practices and procedures so that people can repeatedly perform them at a given level or measure of performance.

Standardization is the process of defining the organization's work, procedures, and practices in such a way that people do their jobs in a consistent manner. Standardization is concerned with achieving internal order and performance within a given structure. The concept of standardization focuses on ensuring that people, teams and larger units perform "up to a given standard." It is found in many forms and at all levels, even within a single company. For example, standards for quality and ethical behavior exist at the personal level, while financial performance standards are used for larger units in a company. Regardless of level, the purpose behind standardization is to attain and to measure consistency of performance.

Standardization can take the form of rules, practices, procedures, and the criteria by which people are evaluated and measured on their performance. For example, the quality of welding and assembly in the automobile factory will be evaluated according to exacting, precisely defined measures of the car's fit, while the quality of a paint job will be assessed according to the luster and consistency of the car's appearance. In the fashion salon example, hair stylists are evaluated according to a quite challenging set of standards—those of the customer. Customers can tell whether their hair "looks and feels right" when they look in the mirror. Yet, in both the car factory and fashion salon examples, a defined set of practices, procedures, and criteria is used to measure and ensure consistent performance.

The concept of standardization also applies to larger units within a company. Here, the focus of standardization tends to be on gauging consistency of financial or operating performance. For example, a division in an automobile company producing luxury cars is likely to have a different standard for profitability as compared to a division producing subcompact, economy cars for young people in their first jobs. For example, at Ford, senior managers will probably hold the division producing luxury cars to a higher standard of profitability than the division producing economy cars for a less wealthy group of customers. Thus, *standardization is concerned with organizational practices, procedures, and criteria that provide the basis for consistent performance.*

Centralization

centralization: The degree to which senior managers have the authority to make decisions for the entire organization.

Centralization refers to the degree to which senior managers have the authority to make decisions for the entire organization. Delegating authority to lower-level personnel is an important aspect of organizational structure because it involves choosing which people have the right to decide and act. In a highly centralized organization, senior management retains most of the authority to decide how subunits will act. Senior managers in a centralized company decide strategy and objectives, even for smaller subunits within the firm. In contrast, a highly decentralized organization places wide discretion with lower-level managers and employees. Senior management plays a lesser role in setting goals and objectives for the company's subunits. By delegating authority to lower-level managers and personnel, senior management can harness the decision-making capabilities of many people throughout the company. Companies differ widely in the amount of authority they delegate to lower-level subunits. For example, in chemical and pharmaceutical companies such as Dow, DuPont, Monsanto, American Home Products, Merck, Schering-Plough, and Pfizer, top managers make many key decisions and communicate them to lower-level managers and employees. On the other hand, many high-tech and software firms such as Microsoft, Adobe Systems, Apple Computer, Hewlett-Packard, and Sun Microsystems prefer a high degree of decentralization that encourages their lower-level managers to make decisions on their own. *Centralization is concerned with the degree of delegation of authority throughout the organization's ranks.*

Broad Forms of Organizational Structure

In the preceding section, we examined the three basic ingredients of any organizational structure. Specialization deals with how managers assign activities and tasks to the people, teams, or units best capable of performing them. Standardization involves the practices, procedures, and criteria used to attain and ensure consistent performance. Centralization concerns the delegation of authority throughout the organization. These three ingredients can be combined in many different ways to build the right type of organization to implement strategy. Activities and tasks to achieve specialization can be divided in many ways. Also, managers can utilize any number of practices, procedures, and criteria to achieve consistent performance. In addition, senior managers have few predetermined limits as to how they may wish to decentralize and delegate authority. The interaction of these three ingredients—specialization, standardization, and centralization—will vary according to the firm's strategy. Accordingly, managers need to find the right combination of specialization, standardization, and centralization to implement their firm's strategy most effectively.

Four common combinations of these elements are (1) functional, (2) product, (3) geographic, and (4) matrix structures. Each of these broad structures involves different choices with respect to specialization, standardization, and centralization to implement a given strategy.[5]

Functional Structures

In a functional structure, each subunit is assigned responsibility for firmwide activities related to a particular function. Functions are the broad tasks that every organization performs to create value: production, marketing, engineering, finance, human resources. **Functional structures** group managers and employees according to their areas of expertise and the resources they use to perform their jobs. For example, in a functional structure, all company manufacturing activities are assigned to the same subunit regardless of where they are conducted or to what products they apply; all company marketing activities are grouped under another subunit that deals solely with marketing issues; all company development and engineering activities are grouped in a common subunit, and so on (see Exhibit 10-2).

functional structure:
An organizational structure that groups managers and employees according to their areas of expertise and skills to perform their tasks.

Diagram of a Typical Functional Structure — **EXHIBIT 10-2**

Corporate

R&D | Production/Operations | Marketing | Sales | Service

- Each function is responsible for its own set of tasks and activities.
- Each function has its own set of goals and objectives that require coordination with other functions.

A functional structure permits the firm to achieve a high degree of specialization in key value-adding activities. Functional structures are usually found in firms engaged in high-volume production of a single or narrow range of products or services. Thus, functional structures are particularly useful in supporting *low-cost leadership strategies*. Technical competence and specialization of skills in value-adding activities are concentrated in each of the functions. Grouping activities by way of a functional structure is efficient and cost-effective when technical, marketing, or product development expertise is scarce. Functional structures exhibit a high degree of standardization of procedures. Tight cost control, frequent detailed reports on operating efficiency, and well-defined assignment of responsibilities are the hallmarks of a functional structure in firms seeking to lower their costs. Operating practices, such as quality improvement and efficient flow of work, tend to follow strict procedures within each function. In addition, functional structures in low-cost leadership firms tend to be highly centralized. Top management monitors, oversees, and makes decisions concerning all of the functional activities occurring within the firm.

The functional structure can also be used to support *differentiation strategies*, but its application in such a setting is unlike its use in firms practicing low-cost leadership strategies. Recall that differentiation strategies place a high premium on quality, strong marketing skills, creative flair, innovative technologies, and often a distinctive company reputation. Firms practicing differentiation can therefore use a functional structure to develop especially distinctive or specialized marketing or R&D skills. Production efficiency, while important to firms that practice differentiation, is less likely to be as critical as other issues such as product design, marketing capabilities, and innovative technologies. Instead, these latter areas of activity are likely to receive continuous attention from top management.

Functional structures are particularly common in the petroleum, mining, and other resource-extractive industries. These firms organize their value-adding activities according to the specific stages of exploration, production, refining, distribution, and marketing. ExxonMobil, ChevronTexaco, Phillips Petroleum, and other large oil companies use a functional structure to organize their petroleum-based activities. Functional structures are also common in other firms that have high levels of vertical integration. Steel, glass, aggregates (e.g., gravel, rock), and rubber companies have traditionally relied on functional structures to manage the stages of production, refining, and fabrication of their products. Companies in the telecommunications industry also frequently use a functional structure, because it allows them to achieve low-cost, efficient management of their transmission operations. All of the local "Baby Bell" (or Regional Bell Operating Companies) firms, such as SBC Communications, Bell South, and Verizon, typically employ a functional structure to manage their telephone operations. A functional structure is a very efficient vehicle to coordinate activities, such as repair, installation, and switching for homes and businesses.

Functional structures are particularly suitable for firms that are small. They are equally suitable for firms that do not diversify into new businesses or areas of activity. In other words, functional structures support the needs of a single-business firm quite well. A functional structure consumes little overhead because it has only one general manager and one set of functional managers that oversee activities for the entire firm (high centralization). When businesses are very small or confine their activities to a narrow range of products/markets, functional structures work well to concentrate expertise (high specialization and standardization). For example, small food-processing firms, such as bakeries and canneries, often organize functionally for these reasons.

Advantages of Functional Structures. Functional structures provide economies of scale for management and administration of each function; therefore, they are excellent in reducing overhead costs for a firm. Functional structures hold down administrative costs because everyone in a department shares the training, experience, and resources devoted to a particular function. In addition, senior management can easily identify and promote those people who have the necessary technical expertise to manage their particular function. A key advantage of the functional structure is the high degree of centralized decision making it allows within each functional area. Functional structures are simple structures and are highly suitable for small firms, less diversified firms (big and small), and growing start-up firms. For large companies, such as those in the petroleum and telecommunications industries, functional structures are excellent in supporting high-volume, low-cost dedicated production or operations. Functional structures support large economies of scale for each functional activity.

Disadvantages of Functional Structures. The Achilles' heel of a functional structure is the difficulty it poses for coordination, especially if the firm expands into a broad range of products. When a functional structure is used, individuals within functional units will tend to develop loyalty to their specialties, which frequently makes them unwilling to accommodate the needs of other functional units. Consider, for example, a proposal by marketing personnel to expand a company's product line. Such a change will complicate the tasks of manufacturing personnel by increasing the number of designs, components, equipment variations, and production setups they must handle. Manufacturing personnel are therefore likely to object to such a change. Thus, a big disadvantage of the functional structure is that each function is likely to have its own set of values, priorities, goals, and even time perspectives on what constitutes an urgent versus routine matter. This narrowness often limits functional managers' perspective concerning the entire firm's operations. Functional managers may generally place their priorities above that of others for additional resources—sometimes to the detriment of the entire firm. (See Exhibit 10-3 for a summary of advantages and disadvantages of a functional structure.)

Key Characteristics of a Functional Structure — EXHIBIT 10-3

Advantages

- Economies of scale in administrative costs/activities
- Good for small-sized firms
- Easy to identify talent
- Fosters high centralization of decision making
- Promotes high task and activity specialization
- Supports a low-cost leadership strategy
- Supports vertical integration in a business
- Best for undiversified firms

Disadvantages

- Coordination difficulties arise when firm diversifies
- Difficult for each function to accommodate needs of other functions
- Divergent goals and objectives based on each function
- Inflexible with broad-based global or multidomestic strategies
- Needs extensive modification to support differentiation strategies
- Poor fit for highly diversified firms

In some ways, management control that spans functional activities may be difficult to achieve, because no common performance criteria are available by which to measure, for example, marketing effectiveness and manufacturing efficiency. Measuring performance involves comparing apples and oranges in the sense that each function is unlike the other. Although performance standards are easy to set and measure within a function, they do not mix well when comparing across functions.

Product Divisions

product divisions: The most basic form of product structure, in which each division houses all of the functions necessary for it to carry out its own strategy and mission.

As a firm expands into new products, businesses, or areas of unrelated activity, the functional structure often loses many of its advantages. High product diversity often leads to serving many types of customers and involves the firm in multiple technologies. In response to these developments, senior management will often utilize a **product divisional** structure. Product divisions are structures that divide the organization into self-contained units responsible for developing, producing, distributing, and selling their own products and services for their own markets (see Exhibit 10-4).

EXHIBIT 10-4 Diagram of a Typical Product Division Structure

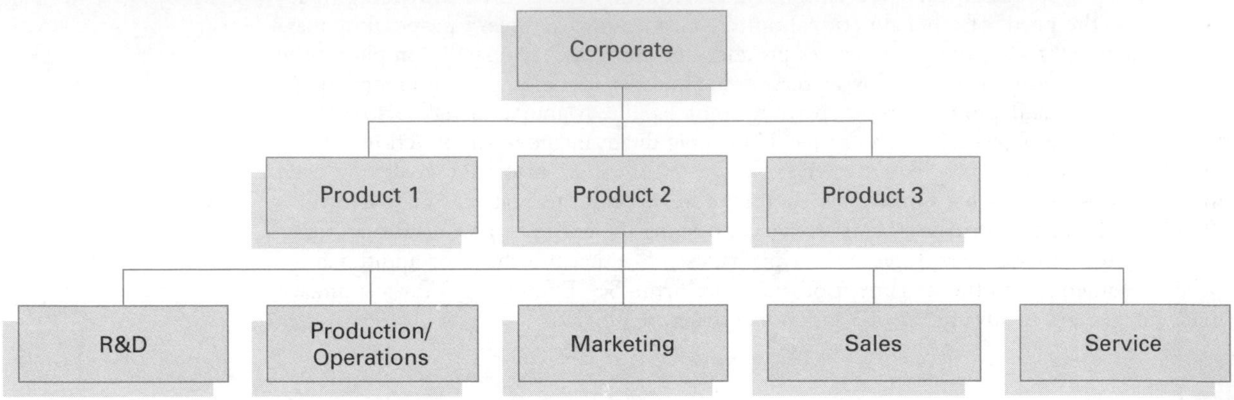

- Each division is self-contained and responsible for its own products and markets it serves.
- Each division contains its own set of functions.

A product division structure establishes a separate organizational unit (and management team) for each product (or group of related products) in the firm. Product divisions are the most commonly used organizational structures in large U.S. corporations. Most companies in the Fortune 500 have expanded into new businesses at some point and exhibit some degree of related or unrelated diversification. Product division structures tend to fit companies exhibiting wide diversification because each individual business unit is likely to face a different set of product, technology, market, and customer requirements.[6]

Product divisions in effect represent small, self-contained businesses within a company. Although a large company can have many product divisions, these divisions tend to remain fairly autonomous. Thus, managers and individuals assigned to a particular product division often become expert about that division's products and markets. Still, each division reports to senior management. Each product division also contains its own functional specialists and resources that are usually organized into departments. These functional departments are designed to support the needs of various products within the division. Most product divisions are evaluated on the basis of their own financial performance and the competitive success of their products. Consequently, each product division has the opportunity to develop its own distinctive competence or sources of competitive advantage for its own products.[7]

Product divisions display a high level of specialization based on the products the firm develops and produces. Unlike functional structures, in which specialization is based on operational activities and tasks, product divisions are organized in such a way that managers and employees become specialists and experts about the products they develop, produce, and sell. A product structure, therefore, encourages tailoring functional activities to the needs of particular products. A purely functional structure, by contrast, does not encourage such emphasis. Since managers of functional subunits are functional specialists, they have less detailed understanding of individual products. A product structure is therefore especially desirable when functional activities must be readily adapted to facilitate a product's competitive success in the marketplace.

Product divisions also differ from functional structures in terms of how performance is measured. Product divisions are evaluated on the basis of their profit contributions to the entire corporation. Since each division represents a product or group of similar products, senior management can easily isolate the financial performance of each division according to some benchmark or performance standard (usually a rate of return on investment or assets). In many cases, divisions are evaluated according to the performance criteria that best support that division's business strategy. Thus, individual divisions may be evaluated along different performance criteria, even within the same company. Consequently, senior management has great leeway in applying performance standards across divisions. For example, at General Electric, the standard for profitability may be quite high for mature businesses, such as lightbulbs. Because GE lightbulbs are well established in the marketplace, senior management may place a high priority on the lightbulb division to earn a big return on investment. On the other hand, GE's senior management may consider using another performance standard for a fast-growing business, such as medical equipment or plastics. In these businesses, GE must continue to invest large sums of money building new factories and laboratories. Consequently, these divisions may be evaluated along other performance criteria, such as growth in market share or number of customers added.

Although product structures allow senior management to mix and match standards to measure financial performance, senior management may still need to establish corporate-wide guidelines, practices, and procedures to ensure consistency of actions across divisions, say, in ethical areas and quality standards. Leading-edge companies that practice total quality management, such as Motorola, Honeywell, General Electric, Texas Instruments, and IBM, all use product division structures. Standards for product and service quality are uniformly understood, practiced, and applied across all divisions.

Some firms using product divisions display a high degree of centralization, with senior management closely monitoring and even participating in the shaping of business unit or product strategy. For example, at Motorola, senior managers often work closely with managers in the semiconductor and memory products divisions to plan production schedules and product rollouts for new types of chips. Senior managers, often with strong backgrounds in electronics, play a direct and major role in shaping the decisions and actions of individual product divisions. Other firms using product divisions may be much more decentralized. For example, at PepsiCo, senior management requires each division (soft drinks and Frito-Lay snack foods) to achieve a prespecified measure of profitability but leaves the operating details up to the divisions' managers. PepsiCo management makes few decisions about product offerings, timing of rollout, discounts, promotions, and other details specific to the division. Thus, the use of product division structures by themselves does not reveal much about the degree of centralization.

Advantages of Product Divisions. Product divisions offer enormous advantages in allocating, assigning, and defining the responsibilities required for each product or group of products. It allows managers to concentrate their expertise on their assigned products lines or markets. In addition, each product division has its own self-contained functional departments designed to support the needs for individual products. Thus, product divisions allow for considerable specialization that enables firms to develop a base of managerial and technical expertise for each product. A big advantage of the product division is that it enables senior management to locate and identify the costs, profits, and potential problems accurately within each line of business.

Product divisions also tend to help managers develop a cross-functional perspective that is important to achieving fast response. Since each product division has a self-contained set of functional departments, managers tend to learn fast and know what it takes to coordinate these functional departments effectively to build competitive advantage.

Product division structures are also excellent mechanisms by which to train and develop future senior and general managers, since this type of structure holds each division manager accountable for results of an entire business. Thus, opportunity for advancement presents considerable incentive for division managers to learn how to manage their businesses effectively.

Organizing along a product division format gives senior management considerable flexibility in rearranging the shape of the company's portfolio of businesses. Management can decide to sell different pieces of the company that are underperforming or do not have attractive prospects for the future. Since product divisions are self-contained units that house their own functions and centers of expertise, senior management can more readily put divisions on the block for sale if they no longer fit the company's long-range strategy.

Disadvantages of Product Divisions. Several important disadvantages are associated with product divisions. First is the potential for inefficient use of functional resources. Remember that each product division has its own self-contained set of functional departments. If a firm's products are actually quite similar in terms of development, production, or marketing, multiple functional departments duplicate time and effort across divisions that may be striving to accomplish the same objective.

Second, a product division structure duplicates administrative, management, and staff activities. Since each product division by design is highly autonomous, high overhead costs are associated with this structure. Each division is likely to possess its own administrative setup, including accounting and other staff functions.

Third, firms using product divisions tend to measure individual divisional performance by way of quantitative financial measures. This emphasis could induce a significant bias toward short-term thinking. Since division managers must meet a certain level of financial return (return on investment, assets, or sales), they may be inclined to run the business "according to the numbers." This may cause them to delay important investment in new process technologies, R&D, or other future sources of competitive advantages because of the daily short-term pressures to produce. Divisional managers may reinterpret "competitive advantage" as current return on investment, as opposed to building and applying new skills or capabilities that may not come to full fruition until much later. Thus, product division structures may instill a short-term orientation in divisional managers that, if uncontrolled, could lead to steady deterioration of overall corporate competitive advantage and distinctive competence.

Finally, product division structures may indirectly encourage an excess of internal competition between divisional managers. Since product divisions within the same company are often highly autonomous, their financial performance is easily compared, one against the other, by senior management. Divisional managers may attempt to outdo each other in trying to beat some performance target or goal, particularly when the potential for bonuses and future promotions is based on current divisional performance. This possibility is especially pronounced when division managers know that senior management may sell off divisions of the company that appears to be underperforming. Internal competition may also strongly discourage managers from working together on joint investment activities or "megaprojects" that could help all divisions involved.[8] (See Exhibit 10-5 for a summary of advantages and disadvantages of a product division structure.)

Variants of the Product Division Structure. Many U.S. companies have attempted to modify their product division structures in response to some of the disadvantages noted above. Three important modifications involve the use of strategic business units, groups or sectors, and the conglomerate or holding company structure. Related diversification firms tend to use the strategic business unit and group/sector modifications, while companies pursuing unrelated diversification tend to rely on the conglomerate, holding company structure.

strategic business unit: Form of organization that often represents larger product divisions or collections of smaller product divisions under one reporting relationship.

Strategic business units, or SBUs, represent a collection of individual product divisions that produce related or similar products (see Exhibit 10-6). SBUs are used by related diversified companies such as General Electric, American Express, Citigroup, Motorola, Texas Instruments, DuPont, IBM, Kellogg, Pfizer, and Honeywell to manage the great expanse of products and businesses under their umbrella. If these companies were to use a pure product division structure for each type of product they produce, they would have literally hundreds of product divisions that would report to senior management at corporate headquarters. This vast number would make it extremely cumbersome for senior management to understand and monitor what is going on in each business. The SBU concept, on the other hand, attempts to identify and group together similar product divisions that share an underlying common characteristic, such as technology used, customer served, etc. By shrinking a hundred different product divisions into ten SBUs, for example, senior management can monitor and oversee operations more easily and effectively.

Key Characteristics of Product Division Structures — EXHIBIT 10-5

Advantages

- High autonomy of divisions for each product/business
- Allows for specialization based on products/markets
- Enhances and supports needed change in products
- Allows for easy measurement of financial performance
- Standardizes performance measurement
- Cross-functional perspective
- Supports highly diversified strategies (related and unrelated)

Disadvantages

- Duplicates functions within each product division
- Duplicates administrative and staff functions
- Leads to short-term thinking if not careful
- Promotes high internal competition between divisional managers
- May under-invest in firm's core competence and skills; discourages companywide "mega" projects

Diagram of a Strategic Business Unit Structure — EXHIBIT 10-6

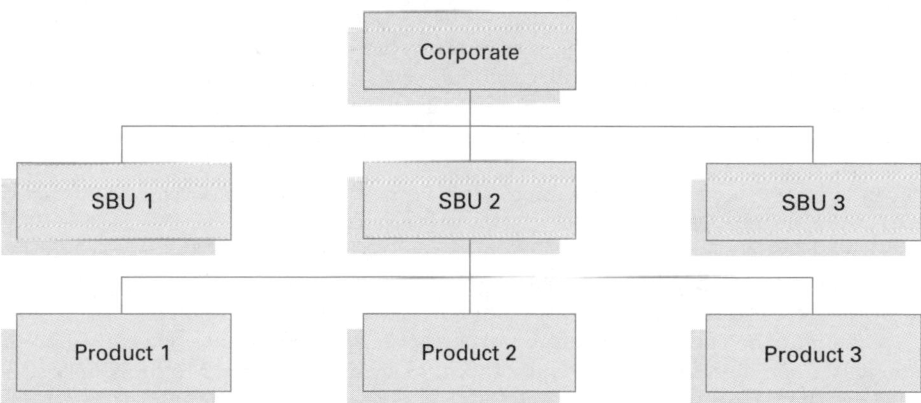

- The SBU structure is a collection of product divisions that produce related or similar products.
- Supports related diversification because similar products that are grouped together share a common underlying technology, market, skill, or resource.

In theory, SBUs attempt to group several product divisions to achieve important operational synergies. First, SBUs can enhance the prospects for sharing and transferring activities between businesses in related diversified firms. Second, by putting together divisions that share similar technological or market characteristics, the SBU form may reduce the potential for excessive internal competition. In turn, skillful use of the SBU concept may encourage divisional managers to undertake joint investment projects that help each division accomplish some objective that it could not accomplish alone. For example, Motorola uses a modified SBU structure to manage its highly diverse semiconductor and electronic components business. If Motorola were to employ a product division for each type of electronic component or product it produced, there would be dozens of product divisions and managers. Instead, Motorola groups its microprocessor and memory product divisions together under one larger SBU that is responsible for overseeing and monitoring the performance of these different product lines. This SBU shares a common manufacturing technology that is essential to producing state-of-the-art chips for many different kinds of customers. Whether chips are used in automobile engines or in personal computers, they are likely to share some common core technologies, competences, and production processes.

In practice, though, the SBU concept in many companies has not overcome an important deficiency of the product division structure—that of short-term orientation by managers. Both divisional and SBU managers still face the same intense pressures to perform, as the product and SBU structures make it easy for senior management to isolate and pinpoint financial performance. Even worse, in some cases, the SBU concept may aggravate the tendency toward short-term thinking, since it enables senior management to allocate cash and other resources more easily by dealing with groups or clusters of divisions, instead of many separate divisions working by themselves. Even though the SBU concept was originally designed to help senior managers build closely related clusters of divisions, in practice SBUs suffer from the same potential for short-term thinking that occurs with conventional product divisions.[9]

In the case of Ford, the company's recent reorganization in its Ford 2000 program places a great emphasis on utilizing a variant of the strategic business unit type of structure to help the company achieve greater economies of scale and cost efficiencies in designing the next generation of high-technology automobile. By organizing itself into five different vehicle platform centers, Ford hopes to improve the speed, innovation, and quality of automotive products that it develops and produces. In effect, each of Ford's five vehicle platform centers corresponds to an SBU dedicated to a particular type of vehicle platform design. Within each vehicle platform center (e.g., midsized cars), a number of different vehicle models (e.g., Taurus, Sable, Crown Victoria, and Mercury Marquis) will share similar types of designs, components, and manufacturing needs that are housed within that vehicle platform center. In turn, these different vehicle models will be organized into separate product divisions responsible to the vehicle platform center (SBU) to which they report. This arrangement enables Ford to develop different kinds of expertise for each SBU. For example, requirements for competing in the small car vehicle platform center is likely to be quite different from that needed to compete in the sport utility vehicle segment in terms of market served, number of available options, engine types used, and the kind of suspension and powertrain developed. By using SBUs, Ford will be able to develop individual vehicle platform strategies for each particular market.

group or sector: A larger version of the SBU structure that often houses many different SBUs under one reporting relationship.

Groups or sectors occur when companies go beyond the SBU concept to form large collections of SBUs. For example, TRW and United Technologies Corporation use the broader organizing concept known as the sector or group (see Exhibit 10-7). Companies sometimes use groups or sectors to tie together separate SBUs into one larger unit that represents a common industry or type of technology. For example, Motorola links up its SBUs that are related to electronics under one larger semiconductor products sector. Motorola's semiconductor sector contains all the core skills and technologies used in production and product design applications.

The group and sector concept, however, still displays the same fundamental limitations and disadvantages found in product divisions and SBUs. Sectors are simply groups of SBUs (composed of product divisions) lumped together in a grander unit. Groups and sectors add another layer of management between senior managers and SBU general managers. Although they are designed to help further ease senior management's need to understand the various businesses and technologies within the company, they are extremely costly to operate. In effect, they add a third layer of management between the product division and senior management (with SBU and group/sector layers in the middle). In the 1990s, many companies, such as General Electric and Honeywell, have moved away from using groups and sectors for this reason. GE found that this additional layer of management generated enormous administrative, staffing, and overhead costs. Instead, GE relies primarily on the simpler SBU concept to organize its many lines of businesses.[10]

conglomerate: Firm that practices unrelated diversification.

Conglomerate structures represent the last important modification of the pure product division structure (see Exhibit 10-8). In contrast to the SBU and group or sector organization, the conglomerate structure emphasizes an extremely lean administrative staff at corporate headquarters.[11] Companies such as Textron, Tyco International, Allegheny Teledyne, and other firms known to pursue unrelated diversification strategies use the hold-

Diagram of a Sector/Group Structure

EXHIBIT 10-7

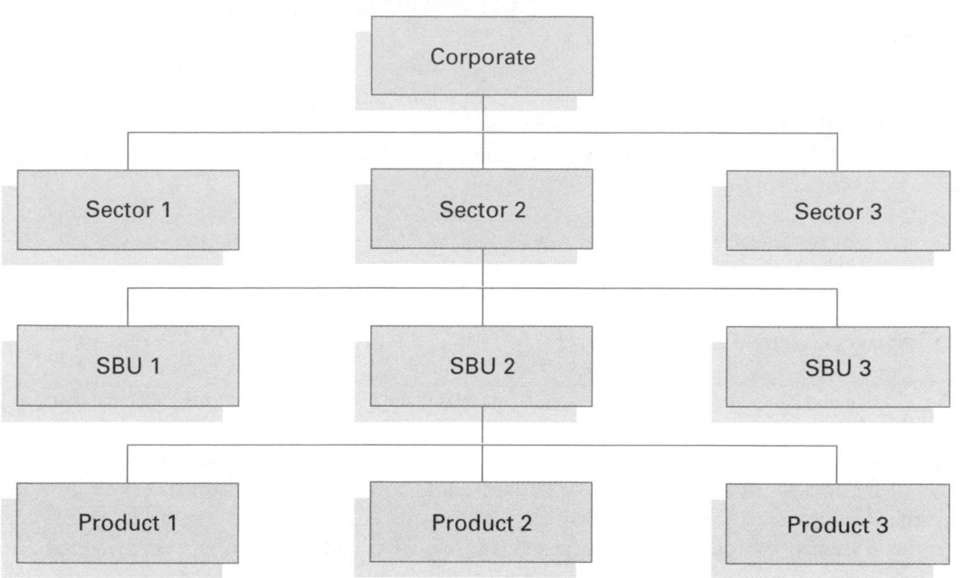

- Sector or group structures tie together different SBUs that represent a common industry, technology, or critical skill.
- Sectors help senior management get a handle on broad-based, related diversification. They are, however, costly to operate because of several layers of management.

Diagram of a Conglomerate/ Holding Company Structure

EXHIBIT 10-8

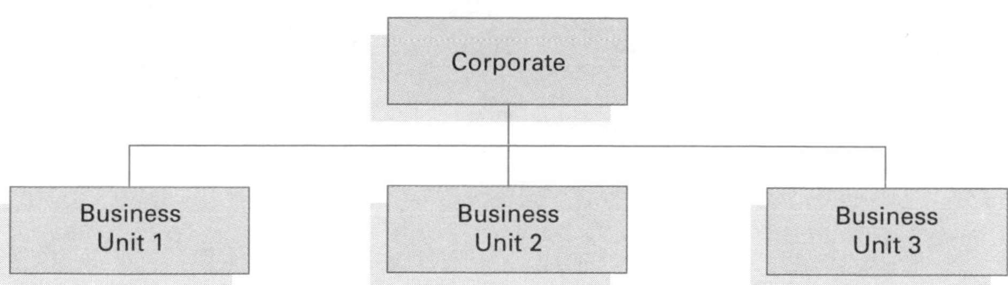

- Each business unit is managed independently of the others. Each business unit is also a company that can be easily sold off.
- Extremely lean corporate and administrative staff means few overhead costs.
- Supports unrelated diversification very well.

ing company structure to keep overhead costs low. Most firms using this very lean structure contain no groups or sectors or even SBUs.

Conglomerates are often called *holding companies* in the sense that the lines of business currently under the corporate umbrella can be readily sold to a willing buyer (an advantage for organizing businesses by way of product divisions). Conglomerate firms "hold" these assets until they are ready to sell them. Product division managers within the conglomerate holding company structure are given high autonomy and significant leeway to run their businesses in ways they see fit. In fact, divisional autonomy is likely to be greater in the holding company structure than in SBU or group/sector structures. In turn, however, divisional managers are under extreme pressure to perform, especially to provide high cash flow and fast return on investment. Companies such as Tyco International, ITT, Textron, and Allegheny Teledyne are known for actively selling and acquiring divisions to improve overall corporate profitability. For example, ITT has sold off more than 240 different lines of businesses (including Hostess Twinkies and makers of perfume) over the past twenty or more years to boost total corporate returns. Another conglomerate, Textron, has sold more than twenty-four businesses from utensils to steel mills over the past decade as well.[12]

Geographic Division Structures

Some firms operate in a number of geographic regions. For example, many fast-food chains fall in this category, as they must prepare food, serve it, maintain facilities, run local promotions, and perform other activities in many different restaurant market locations. Such firms often find the functional structure and the product division structure cumbersome because they provide for no direct way to coordinate activities within geographic regions. Functional and product structures also do not lend themselves well to developing expertise about what it takes to compete in a specific geographic region. A **geographic division** structure helps firms organize activities operated in many locations. Also known as *place or area structures*, geographic division structures allow firms to develop competitive advantage in particular regions according to that area's customers, competitors, and other factors. Many organizations use a geographic structure, such as the federal government, UPS, FedEx, and other delivery services. Restaurant chains, grocery stores, department stores, airlines, and other similar businesses also tend to employ geographic structures to organize activities (see Exhibit 10-9).

geographic division: An organizational form that divides and organizes the firm's activities according to where operations and people are located.

A geographic structure sets up a separate organizational subunit and management team for each region served by the firm. Geographic structures display a high level of specialization based on the markets the firm serves. If each unit is in close contact with its mar-

EXHIBIT 10-9 Diagram of a Typical Geographic Structure

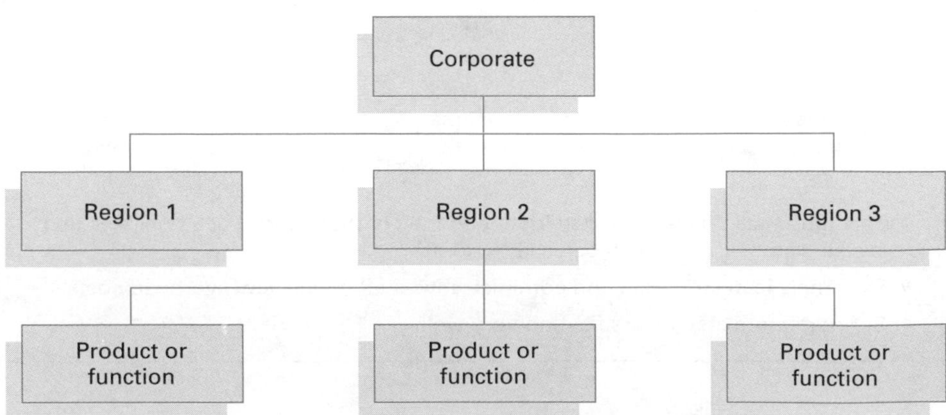

- Geographic structures are excellent in responding to the needs of local, regional markets.
- Geographic structures have their own self-contained product and/or functional structures to meet the operation and marketing needs of that region's customers.
- These structures promote a high level of decentralization.

ket, it can adapt readily to changing environmental demands. As is the case with product divisions, geographic divisions also contain all of the necessary functional activities (again, organized in departments) to achieve the company's objectives for that region. Geographic structures encourage rapid change in functional activities to adapt products and services to local markets. Thus, each region possesses its own administrative, marketing, financial, manufacturing, R&D, and other value-adding activities necessary to support a given regional strategy.[13]

Geographic division structures, like product division structures, are extremely versatile. Thus, the practices, procedures, and performance criteria used can vary according to regional competitive conditions, as well as the order of priorities senior management attaches to each region. Managers in geographic division structures are evaluated according to the financial performance of their particular region or market. For example, managers just starting to operate in one region may be evaluated on measures such as market penetration and market share. On the other hand, managers operating in more established markets are likely to be evaluated according to return on investment. In other words, geographic division structures lend themselves well to individualized measures and standards of financial performance because the subunits are self-contained divisional units. Consequently, senior management can vary the choice of standards used to assess divisional performance according to market conditions.

One of the most important reasons why firms organize geographically is to get closer to their customers. In turn, this closeness often encourages a high degree of decentralization, with regional and subregional managers enjoying considerable authority and leeway to run their operations. Although senior management may require each region to perform up to some level, it often leaves the details of managing operations to regional division heads.

One drawback of organizing geographically is that managers operating in a geographic structure often feel little need to coordinate their actions with managers in other regions. This drawback can be serious if companies need to protect a quality image across regions (as do fast-food chains, rental car firms, haircut and beauty salon chains, and travel agencies).

In practice, organizing geographically gives senior management enormous discretion to divide up or to consolidate the various subunits of a geographical structure. Regions may be defined as small subunits, such as the individual counties and states within the United States, or quite large subunits covering entire countries and even continents. Firms can even organize geographically based on similar market characteristics that span regions and continents. For example, a firm could divide up the world according to similarities in tastes, incomes, buying habits, or any combination of demand factors. Consequently, many multinational firms often turn to geographic structures to coordinate their global expansion and operations. For example, until recently, Procter & Gamble organized its operations around the world under a modified form of a geographic/regional structure for similar reasons. Detergents (e.g., liquid Tide) and shampoos often need specific blends and mixtures to accommodate local conditions, such as water hardness and purity, advertising campaigns, pricing flexibility, and distribution channels. Customers in different regions often demand variations in product design (as they do in Ford's automobile business). This feature is especially important when we examine the impact of the various organizational structures on global operations in a later part of this chapter.

Advantages of Geographic Structures. Firms using geographic structures develop functional capabilities within each region. A geographic structure facilitates timely adaptation of a firm's activities to local conditions without requiring managers to go beyond that region for resources. Organizing geographically can be a major source of strength when firms want to stay closely attuned to customers' needs. A key advantage of the geographic structure is that it puts the firm's operations close to its customers or suppliers. For manufacturing activities, it means that the firm may be able to source lower-cost labor and other supplies to achieve competitive advantage; locating near suppliers has been particularly beneficial for textile and garment manufacturers that have built sourcing operations in the Far East and Latin America. In other cases, locating near the customer means better response and service. Both FedEx and UPS have organized their operations geographically to improve customer service and competitive advantage.

Another advantage of organizing geographically is that it develops extremely seasoned managers who are aware of what it takes to compete in a given region. Geographic structures promote excellent specialization and knowledge about particular markets. Managers of geographic subunits generally reside in the regions they oversee, so they become familiar with local labor practices, governmental requirements, and cultural norms. Such individuals are ideally suited to supervise local operations. Subunit managers in functional and product structures, by contrast, generally reside at company headquarters. They are often less able to provide effective supervision of distant operations.

A final advantage of the geographic structure is its flexibility. Senior management can easily consolidate smaller regions to become bigger ones. Conversely, it is easy to divide up a large region into a series of smaller ones as market conditions change or fragment.

Disadvantages of Geographic Structures. A major disadvantage of the geographic structure is that it duplicates in each geographical region all of the functional activities needed to serve a particular region. Organizing geographically fragments functional activities by allocating a portion of each to a different geographic region. Such fragmentation reduces a firm's ability to achieve economies of scale.

A geographic structure may also promote conflict between regional managers and corporate headquarters. By inserting geographic managers between functional managers and senior managers, this structure removes senior management from direct involvement in the company's operations. This separation can result in disagreement over objectives between regions and corporate headquarters.

Finally, geographic structures may suffer an important disadvantage when it comes to setting standards for quality and image across markets or regions. For example, McDonald's, Wendy's, Burger King, and 7-Eleven prefer to organize their operations geographically so as to best serve their customers. On the other hand, they also insist that all regional managers and operators produce and serve their products at a quality standard that is uniform across regions. Managers in geographically organized firms may have to develop extensive rules and regulations to ensure quality across regions. For example, Domino's Pizza has numerous rules and procedures to ensure pizza quality, pizza temperature, and driver safety in all regions of the United States. (See Exhibit 10-10 for a summary of advantages and disadvantages of geographic structures.)

EXHIBIT 10-10 Key Characteristics of Geographic Structures

Advantages

- High specialization according to market needs
- High autonomy from other geographic units
- Promotes a high degree of decentralization
- Fast response to market needs
- Highly flexible structure; easy to create smaller geographic units
- Allows for full use and development of local talent/managers
- Excellent support for multidomestic strategies

Disadvantages

- Duplicates functions within each region
- Places coordination demands on senior management
- Needs other support measures to ensure high quality and uniform image
- May not work well in fast-changing, technologically-intensive businesses or industries

Matrix Structures

The vast majority of U.S. companies have organized around a product division structure or modification of such (SBUs, groups and sectors, or conglomerate/holding company). Recall that product divisions (or modifications of them) help senior management to group activities according to products. Nevertheless, some U.S. firms continue to use a functional or geographic structure to meet their special strategic situations.

In a small number of firms, however, senior management has chosen what is known as a matrix structure. **Matrix structures** organize activities along multiple (two) lines of authority. Instead of organizing solely along a functional or product structure, a firm using a matrix structure requires lower-level managers to report to two bosses. Matrix structures are designed to help coordinate functional, product, and regional activities across divisions or other subunits. In effect, a firm using a matrix structure may have both a product division working together with and overlaying a functional structure (or even geographic structure in some cases). Most U.S. firms using a matrix structure have combined a basic product division structure with that of a functional structure. Thus, two lines of authority and reporting relationships exist: one based on product and the other based on function.[14] (See Exhibit 10-11.)

matrix structure: An organizational form that divides and organizes activities along two or more lines of authority and reporting relationships.

Matrix structures became popular during the 1960s and 1970s as aerospace firms found that building new types of technologically advanced aircraft required extensive coordination between functions (engineering, production, fabrication, advanced materials, testing, assembly, distribution) and the product divisions that eventually sold the final aircraft product to specific markets (small aircraft, small corporate jets, large jetliners, specialized military aircraft). Aerospace companies such as Boeing, Lockheed-Martin, and Northrop Grumman all have utilized some variation of a matrix structure to handle the high-tech development activities common with new types of aircraft.

Diagram of a Typical Matrix Structure **EXHIBIT 10-11**

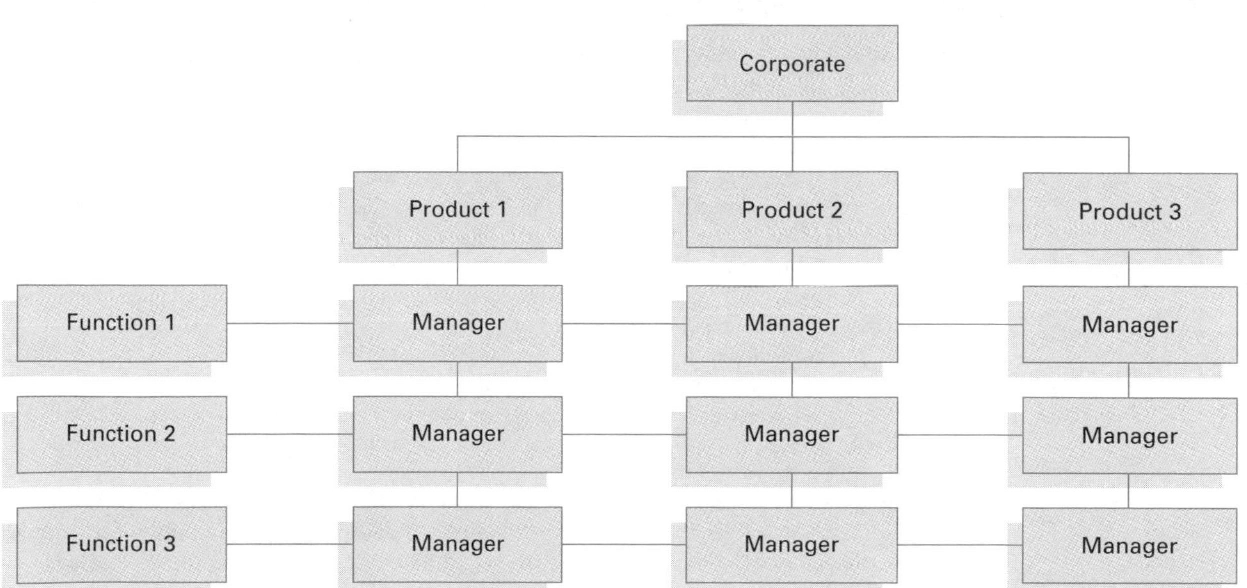

- Each lower-level manager reports to two bosses—one product division superior and one functional superior.
- Although they promote technology sharing, matrix structures are extremely costly and difficult to manage.
- Matrix structures lost favor over the 1980s; most companies that adopted them ultimately switched to another structure.

Matrix structures work to combine two lines or authority into one system. Thus, all matrix structures require lower-level managers to report to two immediate superiors representing different product, regional, or functional orientations. The term matrix came about from the criss-crossing of reporting relationships, as shown in Exhibit 10-11. Matrix structures may overlay a product division with a geographic division, or it may blend a product division with a functional structure.

In most U.S. firms using them, matrix structures attempt to capture the benefits of both the product division structure and the functional structure, while minimizing the disadvantages that are found in each. Matrix structures in their ideal form enable the firm to benefit from specialization of both function and product. The key benefit of using matrix structures is that information flows both vertically (within a given function from employee to manager to senior manager) and horizontally (across managers with comparable rank, authority, and responsibility) between divisions. Matrix structures thus try to remove some of the organizational barriers that impede fast information flow and transfer of knowledge or technical skills between product groups that use a common underlying technology. The ideal matrix organization is one where information flows smoothly and unimpeded between divisions (horizontally) and within divisions (vertically).

Advantages of Matrix Structures. Matrix structures work best when firms confront an environment in which product and technological change occurs rapidly. In addition to the aerospace industry, many other industries face such high change, including advanced composite materials, electronics, and communications equipment. Matrix structures also work best when functional resources and technical expertise are scarce but must be spread across product divisions that share a common core technology or distinctive competence.

Matrix structures in their smoothest implementation allow for considerable flexibility of operations, movement of people between formal divisions, and fast flow of technologies from the lab to the final product. Matrix structures tend to work best when they are focused on a particular project that has a time deadline. Senior managers can freely move highly skilled people from function to division and vice versa according to the timetables of specific product development needs. In addition, matrix structures also provide a strong basis for interdepartmental and interdivisional cooperation.

Disadvantages of Matrix Structures. The single biggest disadvantage of matrix structures is that they are extremely cumbersome and costly to manage. If managers do not know how to manage and run a matrix structure, the firm is saddled with the disadvantages of both the product division and the functional structure. From a financial standpoint, a matrix structure imposes high administrative costs because two lines of authority, accounting systems, reporting systems, and other support staff must be duplicated. In other words, a matrix organization would have to support two parallel sets of administrative staffs.

Equally important, matrix structures in practice can actually inhibit fast response and quick adaptability if managers are unable to work in such a structure. Imagine the following dysfunctional matrix structure used in a large electronics firm. The product divisions (or SBUs) operate independently of one another with an excessively short-term financial orientation, while managers in the functional structures jealously hide and restrict their technical expertise from each other and from other divisions. Functional managers will not work with product division managers and vice versa. Information and technical expertise does not flow from one division or structure to another; instead, managers impede information flows to protect themselves. Thus, in the worst case, matrix structures can induce organizational paralysis as managers from individual divisions and functions fail to cooperate. In effect, a matrix structure that is poorly implemented will achieve none of the special benefits for which it was designed.

Matrix structures impose a high human cost on the managers who must report to two bosses. Most lower-level managers who report to one boss or superior generally will have developed the interpersonal skills and ability to work with that person in planning subunit strategy or in resolving conflict and other issues. When the same lower-level manager must report to a second superior (from either functional or geographic structures), then that manager must now deal with two people who have their own personalities, styles, and agendas. Moreover, lower-level managers must balance priorities and assess which of the two superiors is really more powerful than the other. In effect, matrix structures can induce considerable personal stress in lower level managers and overwhelm their ability to do their jobs.

An issue related to stress in lower-level managers is that matrix structures may indirectly encourage a high level of political behavior and maneuvering in firms. Conflict is likely to arise between managers' and employees' loyalty to either functional or product division superiors. By their very nature, matrix structures are designed to encourage dual loyalties and responsibilities. In practice, however, few managers can really handle the day-to-day "balancing act" of working easily across divisional lines.

In practice, the disadvantages and high personal stress found in matrix structures often outweigh the advantages. During the 1980s, many U.S. firms outside the aerospace and high-tech industries experimented with using a matrix structure to improve coordination of activities across functions and divisions. Companies such as Dow Chemical, Digital Equipment, Citigroup, and IBM all attempted to adopt some type of matrix structure. Most, however, have retreated from it because of the difficulties noted earlier. (See Exhibit 10-12 for a summary of advantages and disadvantages of a matrix structure.)

Key Characteristics of Matrix Structures — EXHIBIT 10-12

Advantages

- Promotes sharing of key resources and skills
- Enhances fast change and flexibility
- Helps when resources are scarce
- Allows for transfer and movement of people
- High specialization along key activities and products

Disadvantages

- Very high cost structure
- Slows down decision making in practice
- Lower level managers often unable to feel comfortable in this structure
- High tension and stress
- Could generate conflict between superiors who are the "arms" of the matrix

Organizing for Global Operations

So far, we have concentrated on the broad organizational structures that firms can use to support strategy implementation. Firms using a functional structure group activities by function. Product division structures group activities by product. Geographic division structures organize by region or market. Matrix structures combine two of the other structures (usually product and function) in attempting to gain the benefits of both. All these structures have been used in some form by U.S. firms as they seek to build and extend their sources of competitive advantage. However, when firms seek to expand operations globally, these structures are often modified in varying degrees because of the market-specific economic, technological, and competitive factors that accompany global operations.

Effective global expansion requires senior management to identify and match the firm's strategy with its organizational structure. On the one hand, the decision to expand globally is theoretically not that much different from expanding domestically. However, the additional economic factors that come into play with global expansion (growing similarity of demand patterns, rising economies of scale, product perishability, new distribution channels, opportunities for cross-subsidization) make choosing the right, or best-fitting, organizational structure a somewhat more complex task than choosing an organizational structure solely to manage domestic operations. Problems of distance and distribution channels, competing in new markets, and different types of competitors arise. As firms of all sizes become increasingly involved with global expansion and operations, an organizational structure that can best accommodate smooth domestic and international operations must be chosen.

Firms expanding globally often use some variation of a basic organizational structure, including (1) international division structure, (2) worldwide product division structure, (3) worldwide geographic structure, (4) worldwide functional structure, (5) worldwide matrix structure, or (6) some hybrid combination known as a mixed structure.[15] Let us briefly highlight the basic features of each structure and examine how well it supports the implementation strategies of international expansion.

International Division Structures

The international division structure represents one of the easiest ways to organize for global operations. As the name suggests, all of the firm's nondomestic operations simply report to an international division. Domestic operations and sales are separated from foreign operations (see Exhibit 10-13).

EXHIBIT 10-13 Diagram of an International Division Structure

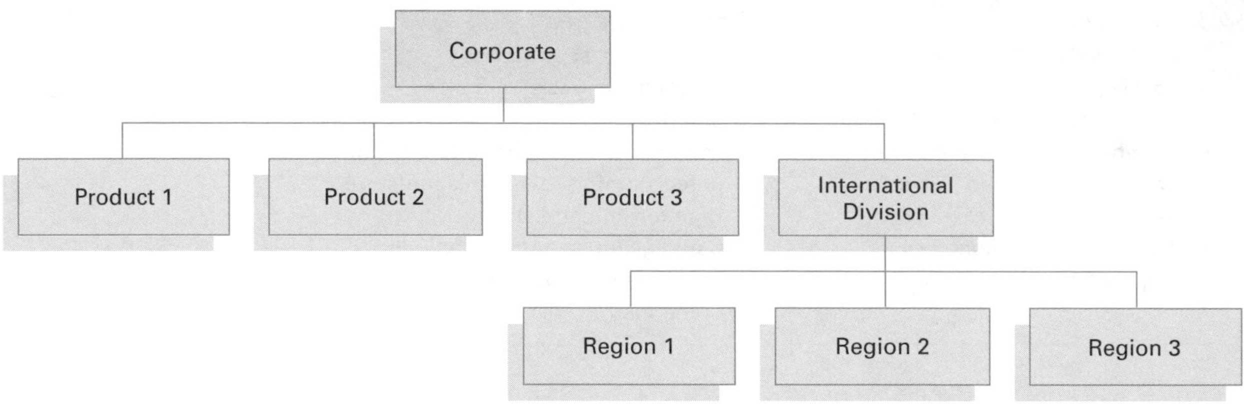

- International division structures are excellent to support a firm's early global expansion efforts.
- These structures promote a high level of specialization for overseas knowledge and activities.

Those that use the international division structure most extensively first begin to invest and to conduct operations outside their home country. More often than not, firms using the international division structure have a relatively low percentage of sales from abroad. The international division enables senior management to house all of its internationally seasoned and knowledgeable managers in one unit. This attractive feature of an international division helps the firm achieve a critical mass of knowledge about competing abroad that otherwise might be diffused throughout the rest of the company. Almost every firm in the Fortune 500 at one point or another has used the international division structure when it first ventured abroad.[16]

A current example of the international division in practice is that of General Motors in the United States. Most of General Motors' revenues come from car and truck sales located in the United States, yet the firm has begun to expand abroad in a major way, particularly in Europe and the Far East. Since GM's international operations represent a small but growing percentage of total sales, the international division structure fits GM's strategy well. Managers who run GM's operations in Asia, Latin America, Europe, and Australia report to superiors who are located in a separate division away from domestic operations.

These international division managers then report to senior management. The primary advantage of the international division structure is that it facilitates the accumulation of a critical mass of knowledge about global operations and local markets in one unit. The international division, which remains separate from domestic operations, is autonomous and free to formulate its own set of strategies to enter and develop new markets abroad.

The most important disadvantage facing the international division is its general unsuitability for managing large global operations. In other words, when a firm's global expansion is successful and becomes a significant portion of total revenues, the international division often cannot handle the huge volume of information and resources needed to conduct and coordinate global operations. It is no accident that General Motors has faced serious difficulties coordinating its international and domestic operations. As the company depends increasingly on automotive sales from emerging markets in the Far East and elsewhere, the international division becomes less suitable for managing an increasingly global company. Thus, international divisions are best suited to firms that have fairly small operations abroad. Most U.S. firms that have built large and prosperous international operations have moved away from using the international division structure to support their global strategies. Once the firm shifts away from the international division, it usually adopts either a worldwide product division structure or a worldwide geographic structure.

Worldwide Product Divisions

Worldwide product divisions are extremely common for firms that have a large portion of their revenues and operations occurring outside their home country. Many U.S. firms use a worldwide product or SBU structure to organize their global operations once they have disbanded their international division structure. The key distinction between a domestic product division and a worldwide product division is that the manager of the latter has global responsibility for all of the division's or SBU's products. This type of structure is especially well suited to the firm that is highly diversified with products that require little modification for the local market. Worldwide product or SBU structures work best in high-tech or scale-intensive industries. Products there often face homogeneous demand characteristics and require little or only moderate customization in local markets, but they also demand state-of-the-art manufacturing facilities and use proprietary technologies or design skills based on expensive R&D costs. The worldwide product or SBU structure assigns key functional activities to products. As a consequence, the worldwide product or SBU structure is best suited for those firms pursuing a global strategy. Examples of companies that have given worldwide authority to their product division or SBU managers include General Electric, United Technologies, and Texas Instruments. In fact, most large U.S. firms in the Fortune 500 that use product or SBU structures assign worldwide responsibility to these managers.

Implementation of Global Strategies. A worldwide product or SBU structure has several advantages over an international division structure. It helps facilitate communication of product planning on a global basis, which is an essential activity for firms pursuing a global strategy. Product or SBU structures help ensure consistency in pricing, quality, delivery, and service on a worldwide basis. For many classes of industrial, intermediate, or component products, worldwide product or SBU structures promote efficient production and distribution of products to large buyers that operate on a global basis. Products that can be easily shipped from one region to another must be priced on a global rather than a local basis. Otherwise, a temporary price reduction in one region will prompt customers in higher-price locations to shift purchases to the region with temporarily lower prices. For example, Japanese chip makers use worldwide product structures to avoid this problem. In another industry, both Caterpillar and Komatsu—two leading firms that produce construction and earth-moving equipment—use a worldwide product structure to centralize pricing to avoid market distortions caused by foreign exchange fluctuations.

Economies of Scale. A product structure facilitates large-scale operation of activities associated with each product by assigning them to a single subunit. This advantage of a product structure is especially valuable when functional activities of each business are highly susceptible to economies of scale and experience. Performing functional activities on a large scale will then yield significant cost savings. In fact, many global competitors in such industries as steel, fiber optics, cell phones, automobiles, semiconductors, and consumer electronics need to build huge factories to achieve economies of scale. Many companies in these industries use a product division structure to facilitate the building of scale-intensive factories that serve markets around the globe. For example, Philips Electronics of the Netherlands has steadily adopted a worldwide SBU structure to implement full-blown global strategies in its array of diversified businesses. This structure enables Philips to build critical mass and economies of scale in such related businesses as semiconductors, computers, lighting, compact discs, consumer electronics, and medical equipment. By relying on SBUs with global capabilities and responsibilities, Philips can build scale-intensive plants that allow the company to compete with large Japanese firms (Sony, Hitachi, Toshiba, Matsushita) in high-tech products, such as high-definition televisions, VCRs, DVDs, semiconductors, office equipment, and home appliances. In September 1998, Philips closed down an additional 100+ plants around the world in order to gain even greater economies of scale to compete in newer high-tech markets. This restructuring continues Philips's transformation from a once-staid multidomestic firm into a more cohesive global company. Even in 2001, Philips remains in the midst of its transformation. The company has decided to shut down even more plants operating in its far-flung worldwide empire, and it has begun to look for alliance and merger partners to build up its core electronics and technology-driven businesses.[17]

Ford's reorganization into five vehicle platform centers reflects some of the pressing needs to achieve economies of scale as the company seeks to remove redundancies and the high costs of its previously fragmented operations. As each vehicle platform center becomes responsible for product design, development, manufacturing, and planning on a worldwide basis, global economies of scale become more feasible. Moreover, scale becomes important in helping Ford lower the costs of purchasing components and parts from a consolidating supplier base as well.

Worldwide Geographic Division Structures

Some firms expanding abroad may opt for the worldwide geographic structure when their overseas operations become a substantial portion of their total sales. Oftentimes, U.S. firms will move from an international division structure to a worldwide geographic structure as a matter of course; senior management breaks up a big, cumbersome international division into a series of smaller regional divisions.

Worldwide geographic structures, in principle, are quite similar to the geographic structures discussed earlier. The primary difference is that distinct parts of the world represent lines of authority, rather than parts of an individual country or region. As may be expected, managers in a worldwide geographic structure have authority for all markets that compose their individual region. The worldwide geographic structure is especially well suited to firms with products that require extensive modification or local production to serve local markets. Thus, worldwide geographic structures are excellent in supporting those firms that pursue multidomestic strategies.

Implementation of Multidomestic Strategies. The worldwide geographic structure offers considerable capability and support for firms facing the need to introduce and modify products rapidly for local markets. The need for such adaptation can arise from many sources. For instance, firms that compete in the food processing, beverage, personal care, and textile industries (all of which require multidomestic strategies for competitive advantage) often utilize some version of a geographic structure. Competitive advantage in these industries depends on fast response, intensive product customization and local production—all key characteristics that favor a multidomestic strategy, and therefore a geographic structure. For example, Nestlé of Switzerland uses a regional structure to encourage managers to adapt its food, candy, and other nutrition products to local regulations, preferences, and distribution channels found in their operating areas. The high perishability of food requires Nestlé to build production and distribution facilities for its various food businesses in the regions in which they sell these products.[18]

Extreme Differences in Distribution Channels. Distribution channels may differ from country to country (an early feature of Ford's European operations, Coca-Cola's soft drink business, and Procter & Gamble's personal care products). This entails local adjustment of a firm's marketing and selling activity. A firm's preferred advertising medium may be unavailable in some countries. It will then need to vary its advertising approach and marketing mix from country to country. Large multinational banks (Citigroup, J. P. Morgan Chase, Sumitomo, and Paribas) tend to favor geographic/regional structures. This choice helps them better understand the lending needs of their local customers and local banking regulations.

Worldwide Functional Structures

In some companies, global expansion requires few modifications to their existing organizational structure. For example, firms in the petroleum and other resource-extractive industries continue to undertake their same extractive, refining, production, fabrication, and distribution activities, whether mines and refining facilities are located in the United States or elsewhere. Thus, some firms that expand globally will organize their global operations under a worldwide functional structure. ExxonMobil, ChevronTexaco, Royal Dutch Shell, and other petroleum firms use a worldwide functional structure to organize their global operations. The functional structure suits these firms extremely well, since the high level of vertical integration means that senior management must be able to closely monitor and understand all of the activities that contribute to refining and distributing the end product. This structure varies little from the basic functional structure outlined earlier in the chapter.

Worldwide Matrix Structures

A small number of firms from the United States, Europe, and the Far East utilize a worldwide matrix structure, which blends a worldwide product division structure with a worldwide geographic structure. Firms that use such a structure hope to achieve low-cost economies of scale with rapid adaptation to local markets. As mentioned previously, the matrix structure is complicated, and it takes talented managers—at all levels—to understand and implement it smoothly.[19] Firms that use worldwide matrix structures attempt to achieve the benefits of global and multidomestic strategies while avoiding some of their disadvantages.

One company that has used a worldwide matrix structure successfully so far is Asea-Brown-Boveri (ABB). ABB is dedicated to producing world-class products at low cost. It puts equal emphasis on understanding each customer's needs. ABB relies on its regional managers to understand the details of competing in individual markets. On the other hand, ABB depends on its worldwide product managers to achieve the kind of low-cost economies of scale to compete against similar global competitors. ABB thus places its managers in a constant balancing act. Regional managers know how to get government approvals and market opportunities for ABB's wide line of high-tech products. Product managers understand the technical specifications for building robotics, power generation systems, and high-speed trains. Coordinating the market-oriented needs of regional managers with the production-oriented tasks of product managers is the basis for ABB's worldwide matrix. While regional country managers in individual ABB companies can customize product offerings to varying degrees, they are still dependent on low-cost production and development that occurs in the product arm of the matrix. This balancing act is costly for

ABB, however. Managers must attend frequent meetings and travel extensively to meet their counterparts to design joint marketing and product development initiatives. Moreover, managers must be especially sensitive to leading and managing a wide array of different national cultures that are represented throughout the entire ABB organization. Although ABB continues to rely heavily on this complex organizational structure, the company is facing renewed competitive pressures from General Electric and Siemens as these two companies continue to pursue the same markets and customers that ABB wants to serve.[20]

Worldwide Hybrid or Mixed Structures

In an effort to gain the benefits of functional, product, and geographic structures, some firms devise hybrid arrangements that combine elements of each. The purpose of combining into **hybrid (or mixed) structures** is to achieve more benefits than any one structure could provide alone.

hybrid (or mixed) structures: Combining different basic organizational structures to attain the benefits of more than one.

Strategic Application to Ford Motor Company

Now, let us review our discussion of organizational structures and apply it to the Ford Motor Company.

The company's program known as Ford 2000, or the transformation of Ford that began under then-CEO Alex Trotman, reflected the growing need of the company to compete increasingly on a global basis during the mid-1990s. This shift was necessary for Ford to improve its communications and ability to share costs among different parts of the company. By the late 1990s, Ford's earlier preference for a geographic form of organization gave way to a modified SBU/product-based organization that shared increasingly worldwide responsibility for product development. Ford's prior division of the company into separate Ford Europe and Ford North America components (with the rest of the world reporting to Ford North America through an international division structure) reflected not only the fragmented and geographically dispersed nature of the auto industry four decades ago, but also the significant differences in product designs, driving habits, automotive technologies, innovations, and manufacturing approaches between the United States and Europe.

As Ford and other auto manufacturers came under growing pressure to accelerate the design of new car models, to introduce cutting-edge technologies (e.g., safety, fuel efficiency, high performance) into their products, and to lower the costs of product development, the previous use of a geographic division structure proved less useful in implementing a strategy that required a more consistent, global approach. By relying on its earlier geographic structure for a long time, Ford's cost structure became extremely bloated as product development costs across two continents resulted in separate car models that did not share similar designs, parts, components, or manufacturing. However, each separate part of the company, Ford Europe and Ford North America, felt growing pressure to reduce their costs and to improve product quality as Japanese and other competitors gained significant market share in both continents.

The objective of Ford 2000 was to transform the company from a geographically oriented company (with significant duplication of effort and costs across regions) into a reorganized company that is capable of designing a series of new car models around a common vehicle platform (with reduced duplication and greater use of similar components and parts). This new organization design persisted in its original form for much of the past nine years. Ford organized itself along five vehicle platform centers (four in the United States, one in Europe), each of which dedicates itself to a particular type of vehicle design (e.g., small car, midsized car, luxury car, sport utility vehicle, commercial truck) that then can be modified for sale and use in any part of the world. For example, requirements for designing new small car models fell under Ford's small car vehicle platform center (which is now based in Europe). This center worked to ensure that all of Ford's small cars, no matter where they may ultimately be sold, are designed and manufactured according to vehicle platform specifications laid out by it. Therefore, each of Ford's vehicle platform centers has been analogous to an SBU, in which all of the specific car models that borrow on the platform's underlying design will be housed. Each of these vehicle platform centers also assumed an increasingly worldwide role and responsibility for product development under the original tenets of the Ford 2000 program. Moreover, within the broader vehicle platform center, each specific car model operated as if it were a smaller product division that was responsible for all the activities needed to support it. To achieve significant cost reduction and faster product development, car models that are similar to one another in terms of design, engineering, manufacturing requirements, and technical features began to share all of the functions provided by the vehicle platform center.

The need to capture greater economies of scale in product development, manufacturing, and purchasing was a major factor in compelling CEO Trotman to reorganize the company with such urgency in the mid-1990s. This massive reorganization of Ford occurred at a time during which many aspects of the automobile industry were becoming increasingly global in nature (e.g., R&D, manufacturing requirements, purchasing). This means that future sources of competitive advantage will require a capability to build numerous models of new cars from the same basic platform. In addition, reliance on this modified SBU structure allows Ford to acquire new technologies and even car companies to complement its existing product development efforts and lines of cars. The inclusion of Aston Martin, Volvo, Land Rover, and even Mazda into Ford's global product development network enables Ford to leverage skills and technology from one part of the world to improve product development and skills elsewhere. Likewise, by managing Volvo and Mazda as Ford affiliates, the company preserves the distinctive qualities and skills that make these two companies leaders in their technical areas.

Under CEO Jacques Nasser, Ford's push to redesign its organization took a significantly different look. First, Nasser invested heavily in new Internet-based technologies to speed up communications among different parts of the company. The Internet has become the nerve center that links every part of the company together and can provide real-time information about orders, markets, factory capacity utilization, and a host of other data that once took weeks if not months to collect. Equally important, Ford also uses the Internet as a way to share costs, data, and product designs with its closest suppliers to further streamline the amount of time required to build a new car. The Internet allows Ford to work on a real-time basis with key suppliers to test new product and component designs before they hit the manufacturing floor. CEO Nasser also invested in new manufacturing technologies that enhance Ford's flexibility and agility to change car models quickly on the assembly with substantially less downtime than in previous years.

From an organizational perspective, Ford appears to be retreating somewhat from the original blueprint of Ford 2000. CEO Nasser, facing the realization that a truly "world car" is an illusion, gave his regional managers more autonomy to develop their markets in the manner they best see fit. On the one hand, Nasser insisted that the company build its cars from a common set of powertrain, engine, and chassis platforms that facilitate cost reduction and economies of scale. On the other hand, he appreciated the fact that customers are much more savvy and demanding from what they want from their cars. Cars no longer serve the purpose of basic and safe transportation; they have become important vehicles to express their owners' personalities and tastes. In addition, customers perceive certain brands to reflect a different kind of ownership experience (e.g., Volvo with safety, Aston Martin with elite cars, Jaguar with elegance). Thus, trying to push a standardized approach to product design across all regions of the world would ultimately compromise the value of some of Ford's recent acquisitions and cherished brands. Thus, even though engineering and product development remain organized along the vehicle platform format (which corresponds to the SBU structure), Nasser's recent decision to give more autonomy to Ford's regional managers strongly suggests that Ford's current organizational structure is one that more closely approximates a worldwide hybrid or mixed structure. Whether this organizational arrangement will persist many years into the future is unknown.

In summary, Ford is currently in the midst of an important organizational realignment. At the time, CEO Alex Trotman's 1994 decision to reorganize the company along broad product lines helped bring about significant economies of scale, cost savings, and the use of automotive platforms that allow for the use of shared technologies and components. However, it appears (in hindsight) that Ford overestimated the degree to which customers would be willing to buy into a "world car" model. The "world car" would differ little from one market to another. By the late 1990s, Ford under Jacques Nasser moved to restore some of the autonomy of its regional managers, especially in Europe, where major acquisitions of Volvo and Aston Martin are designed to help the company compete with specialized brands that emphasize safety, luxury, and other desired attributes.

The current organizational structure will likely shift again once Ford Motor Company best gauges the extent of knowledge and technology sharing that it will undertake among its divisions. This shift is likely to continue well into 2002 and 2003 as a new cadre of senior management takes over at Ford. In October 2001, William Clay Ford replaced Jacques Nasser as CEO of the company. William Clay Ford, who is a great-grandson of the company's founder, will seek to strengthen the company's relationships with its suppliers and dealers, while at the same time incorporate new technologies into future lines of cars and trucks.

No Single Structure Is Perfect

As mentioned earlier in this chapter, no single structure is appropriate for implementing all strategies. Each firm's strategy requires an appropriate organizational structure to provide the foundation for smooth strategy implementation. Even two similar firms, competing in the same industry with a similar set of products, technologies, and markets, may find that a structure that works for one firm may need some modification in another.

Choosing the right structure is critical because switching from one structure to another is a laborious and costly process. Oftentimes, a structure chosen to support one strategy will become less useful as the organization is forced to deal with new developments, such as changing markets, technologies, and cost structures. For example, Exide Corporation, a leading U.S. manufacturer of industrial and automotive batteries, faced many of the same organizational dilemmas that confronted Ford Motor Company. Under CEO Robert Lutz, Exide moved away from a country-centered organization (geographic divisions) to one that emphasized reporting along different lines of battery products (product divisions). However, this realignment caused numerous problems for Exide. Managers clashed over who would report to whom. More important, managers were confused about how best to meet and satisfy customers' needs. European managers, in particular, had developed close relationships with key automotive customers that spanned many decades and personal friendships. On the other hand, the new battery-centered organization required German and other European marketing managers to transfer their accounts to a new set of managers who reported directly to a superior who oversaw a specific battery line. This caused numerous problems and confusion for customers, who did not know how best to receive help with their accounts. Regional managers lost direct contact with the customers and suppliers with whom they had worked for a long time. On the other hand, product managers now faced the difficulty of attempting to modify battery sizes and power requirements for uses in different regions of the world. Product managers did not have the knowledge that resides in regional managers' minds; regional managers in turn were unwilling to help product managers gain access to their customer relationships. Turf battles roiled Exide over the past few years, and more than half of Exide's Europe-based managers resigned. Finally, the company settled on a mixed geographic/product division structure that attempts to capture the benefits of both organizational formats.[21]

Other companies facing similar challenges in redesigning their organizations include Procter & Gamble, which is currently undertaking an initiative known as "Organization 2005." This P&G realignment is designed to help the company gain more economies of scale and efficiencies as the consumer products giant tinkers with its traditional reliance on a country and region-centered form of organization. Within P&G, some managers feel that the company will ultimately abandon its geographic lines of reporting in favor of global SBUs that oversee an entire product category (e.g., paper goods, beauty care, pet foods, hygiene products). In 2001, P&G felt the same disarray and loss of talent as managers become frustrated with the details of implementing such a broad organizational shift.

Yet, *choosing the right structure is a necessary but not sufficient condition to implement strategy*. Selecting an organizational structure is much like deciding on the best "architecture" for a building. Architecture can provide the basic design, outline, and shape of the final building, but it requires a lot of mortar to keep the bricks solid and tightly held together. Organizational structure may be thought of as the framework on which bricks are laid into place. But bricks alone are not enough. As the Ford, Exide Corporation, and Procter & Gamble examples reveal, organizational changes without other steps are detrimental to competitive advantage. However, failing to realign the organization in the wake of changes in strategy, customer needs, and technological developments can ultimately prove just as harmful. Changing the organizational chart is reshuffling the bricks without factoring in the effects on people and morale. Mortar is necessary and comes in the form of other organizational support mechanisms that hold the bricks in place. These support mechanisms are also known as organizational design practices. The components of these support mechanisms include elements such as control systems, personal styles, corporate culture, and shared values. They all play influential roles that can mitigate some of the disadvantages of relying on structure alone. In the next chapter, we will examine these design practices in more detail.

An Overview of Organizational Structure

Obviously, choosing the right organizational structure to support strategy implementation is a complex task. Understanding the differences between various types of structure is essential because each offers certain strengths and weaknesses in supporting strategy implementation. No single organizational structure is suitable for all strategies. Any given strategy requires a particular kind of structure to achieve high performance. Finding the right match of strategy with organizational structure is a key task facing senior management. Securing the right match creates a strong foundation upon which senior managers, lower-level managers, and employees can work together to implement the firm's strategy.

Firms that are small or exhibit little diversification often find the functional structure the best match for their strategies. Functional structures allow for the development of specialized knowledge, technologies, and skills required to produce the end product or service. Functional structures also allow senior management to centralize key decisions and to closely monitor the firm's activities. Functional structures also fit the needs of vertically integrated companies, since the stages or activities that make up the final product can be divided and specialized into functional units.

Diversified firms often find the product division structure (or modifications of it) best matched to their corporate strategies. Product divisions offer firms considerable flexibility and specialization concerning products or groups of products. These divisions encourage divisional managers to become experts concerning their products and the technologies behind those products. Product divisions also allow senior managers to isolate and identify key strengths, weaknesses, and the financial performance of each division.

Related diversified firms, or those that attempt to build synergies among their products and businesses, often use a modification of the product division, such as strategic business units (SBUs) or groups and sectors. Unrelated diversifiers are more likely to use a modification of the product division known as the conglomerate or holding company structure. All product division structures (including these modifications) suffer from the disadvantage of encouraging a short-term financial orientation in their managers, which can lead to deterioration of the firm's competitive advantage if senior management is not careful.

Some firms organize their operations geographically because of the need to get closer to their customers. Geographic structures encourage fast response to changes in local markets and tend to be highly decentralized.

Matrix structures combine two of the structures already mentioned. Although matrix structures may enhance internal communication and flexibility, in practice they are difficult to apply and costly to operate.

Firms expanding globally use some variation of organizational structure to manage the special conditions of going abroad. Firms in the early stage of global expansion tend to use international division structures. Firms with multidomestic strategies prefer geographic structures to organize their overseas operations, while firms with global strategies are more likely to use a worldwide product division structure to support implementation.

Ethical Dimension

Establishing divisions to accommodate diversification separates senior management from individuals who actually operate the firm's businesses. Oftentimes, diversified firms have layers of management that make it difficult for the CEO to monitor the individual actions of each business unit. The CEO's task in setting the boundaries for proper behavior becomes more complicated. Ultimately, the CEO is still responsible for the ethical behavior and potential transgressions that may occur deeper within the organization. For example, Salomon Brothers' CEO John Gottfreund was forced to resign over a U.S. Treasury bond-trading scheme that involved several groups of bond traders in 1991. He was even forced to give up the cash and other bonuses that he thought Salomon Brothers owed him before he was relieved from duty. Even though the CEO was unaware of the transgressions occurring at the time, he was ultimately held accountable for the actions of his subordinates.

Similarly, the American public often holds CEOs accountable for the ethical breaches by employees that occur far beyond the immediate supervisory scope of the CEO. For example, AT&T's CEO publicly apologized to concerned groups in the United States for several employees' racist, cartoonlike depictions of African American employees in the company magazine in early 1993. Thus, the CEO frequently becomes a "lightning rod" for public outcry or indignation over the actions of the company's employees.

On the other side of the Pacific, Japanese executives often assume personal responsibility for problems or damages that their firms may have imposed on their customers or other bystanders. When a Japan Air System plane crashed into a mountain in rural Japan in the late 1980s, the CEO publicly resigned to express his deepest remorse and sorrow over the incident. Even though the CEO had no knowledge of any particular event that may have caused the accident, he felt it necessary to resign to preserve Japan Air System's reputation and the "company's face" in the public's eye.

Thus, CEOs will continue to face growing public scrutiny of their company's operations and behavior, no matter where such actions occur within the company. The CEOs' essential task of setting proper ethical and behavioral guidelines is no less significant when they are managing large numbers of employees dispersed among many organizational subunits around the globe.

Summary

- Strategy implementation is a vital issue because any strategy is only as good as the effort behind it to move it forward.
- Strategy implementation is intimately concerned with building the right kind of organization that can support a chosen strategy.

- One of the most important organizational building blocks that is needed to implement strategy is organizational structure.
- Organizational structure has three dimensions: specialization, standardization, and centralization. The four broad types of organizational structure that companies can use to support their strategies include functional structures, product division structures, geographic division structures, and matrix structures.
- A functional structure promotes company-wide scale in carrying out each functional activity; a product structure facilitates scale in performing activities associated with each product; and a geographic structure promotes responsiveness in operating activities in each geographic region. A matrix structure is a combination of two of the three structures already mentioned.
- These three basic structures—functional, product, and geographic—also promote the firm's distinctive competences in other areas. Thus, a functional structure conserves scarce general management talent; a product structure fosters ability to adapt a company's activities to the needs of specific products; a geographic structure promotes both the adaptability of a firm's activities to needs of geographic regions and the effective supervision of local activities.
- Strategies to expand the firm's operations globally also depend on the appropriate organizational structure. Global organizational structures include international division; worldwide product, geographic, or functional structures; or worldwide matrix and hybrid mixed structures.
- Worldwide product structures best support global strategies; worldwide geographic structures best support multidomestic strategies.

Exercises and Discussion Questions

1. Many companies in the United States have undergone significant restructuring and reengineering initiatives to improve their organizational capabilities. What are some of the drawbacks of traditional, functional structures that have previously been in place in many of these companies, especially those with a growing line of products and services? How well does a functional structure support a company that seeks to diversify into new industries and lines of business?
2. The Internet, e-mail, and other computer-driven technologies have become a powerful set of internal communications tools for many companies. How do you see the Internet's role in helping compensate for some of the trade-offs of conventional organizational structures? How can companies use the Internet to improve the quality and speed of information flow in their companies?
3. Many companies are now seeking to expand their operations globally. Which organizational structures best support different types of global expansion strategies? What are some economic factors and considerations that should influence the choice of organizational structure?

Endnotes

1. Data and material for the Ford case were adapted from the following sources: "Nice Guy, Knows Karate." *Forbes*, April 15, 2002, pp. 57-60; "Ford Plans Tall Sedan to Follow Taurus," *Wall Street Journal*, March 28, 2002, p. A4; "A Stalled Revolution by Nasser Puts a Ford in the Driver's Seat," *Wall Street Journal*, October 31, 2001, pp. A1, A8; "Ford's Jacques Nasser Is Ousted as CEO," *Wall Street Journal*, October 30, 2001, p. A3; "Ford's CEO Takes More Steps to Refocus on Company's Core Automotive Business," *Wall Street Journal*, October 12, 2001, p. A3; "Ford Plans Extensive

Restructuring of Operations," *Wall Street Journal*, August 20, 2001, p. A4; "Ford: Why It's Worse Than You Think," *Business Week*, March 20, 2001, pp. 80-90; "Ford's Gamble on Luxury," *Business Week*, March 5, 2001, p. 69; "Ford, Navistar Are Teaming Up to Build Medium-Duty Trucks for Commercial Use," *Wall Street Journal*, February 12, 2001, p. A10; "Ford Says Last Year's Quality Snafus Took Big Toll—Over $1 Billion in Profit," *Wall Street Journal*, January 12, 2001, pp. A3, A6; "Ford Exec Blasts Auto Industry, Challenges Peers," *Dallas Morning News*, January 5, 2001, p. 4D; "Ford Europe's Stuck in a Quagmire; Will Cutting Prices Give It Traction?" *Investor's Business Daily*, October 23, 2000, p. A1; "Ford in Japan: Long and Winding Road," *Wall Street Journal*, October 11, 2000, p. A21; "Ford and Mazda Plan to Develop Engines That They Will Share," *Wall Street Journal*, March 31, 1999, p. A10; "Out with Ovals, in with Safety Features," *Dallas Morning News*, March 30, 1999, p. 14D; "A Swedish Tiger in Ford's Tank," *Business Week*, February 8, 1999, p. 40; "Installation of a New Leadership Team Gives Ford an Edge over Its Competitors," *Wall Street Journal*, September 14, 1998, p. A3; "If Ford Can Do It, Why Can't GM?" *Business Week*, June 29, 1998, p. 36; "Ford Borrows a Better Idea," *Business Week*, June 8, 1998, p. 42; "Ford's Chief Sees Flat Prices, with Cost-Cutting the Surest Way to Boost Income," *Business Week*, May 4, 1998, p.159; "Too Many Models, Too Little Focus," *Business Week*, December 1, 1997, p. 148; "Alex Trotman in the Passing Lane," *Business Week*, July 28, 1997, p. 42; "Ford Realigns Ranks, amid Restructuring of Parts, Development," *Investor's Business Daily*, November 11, 1996, p. A3; "Autos: Get Big or Get Out," *Business Week*, September 2, 1996, p. 60; "All Ford Needs Is a Minor Tune-Up," *Business Week*, November 16, 1995, p. 104; "Ford's Really Big Leap at the Future: It's Risky, It's Worth It, and It May Not Work," *Fortune*, September 18, 1995, p. 134; "Alex Trotman's Daring Global Strategy," *Business Week*, April 3, 1995, p. 94; "Ford Chairman Trotman Outlines Plan to Expand Sales, Challenge GM's Lead," *Wall Street Journal*, May 13, 1994, p. A4; "Ford's Trotman Gambles on Global Restructuring Plan," *Wall Street Journal*, April 22, 1994; "Ford to Unify Global Development Effort," *Investor's Business Daily*, April 21, 1994, p. A4; "Ford to Realign with a System of Global Chiefs," *Wall Street Journal*, March 31, 1994, p. A3.

2. A recent research study that examined the relationship between different organizational processes with strategies is S. W. Floyd and P. J. Lane, "Strategizing throughout the Organization: Managing Role Conflict in Strategic Renewal," *Academy of Management Review* 25, no. 1 (2000): 154–177. See also L. J. Bourgeois and D. Brodwin, "Strategic Implementation: Five Approaches to an Elusive Phenomenon," *Strategic Management Journal* 5 (1984): 241–264; J. Galbraith and R. Kanzanjian, *Strategy Implementation: The Role of Structure and Process* (St. Paul, Minn.: West, 1985); J. Frederickson, "The Strategic Decision Process and Organizational Structure," *Academy of Management Review* 11 (1986): 280–297; D. Nadler and M. Tushman, *Strategic Organization Design* (Boston: Scott, Foresman, 1987); D. C. Hambrick and A. A. Cannella, Jr., "Strategy Implementation as Substance and Selling," *Academy of Management Executive* 3 (November 1989): 278–285. Also see J. R. Galbraith and D. A. Nathanson, *Strategy Implementation: The Role of Structure and Process* (St. Paul, Minn.: West, 1978), for a discussion of the key issues behind implementation.

   Works examining the concept of organizational structure include some of the following: L. W. Fry and J. W. Slocum, Jr., "Technology, Structure and Workgroup Effectiveness: A Test of a Contingency Model," *Academy of Management Journal* 17 (1984): 221–246; C. C. Miller, W. H. Glick, Y. D. Wang, and G. P. Huber, "Understanding Technology-Structure Relationships: Theory Development and Meta-Analytic Theory Testing," *Academy of Management Journal* 34 (1991): 370–399; J. M. Pennings and F. Harianto, "Technological Networking and Innovation Implementation," *Organization Science* 3 (1992): 356–382; D. Miller, "The Architecture of Simplicity," *Academy of Management Review* 18 (1993): 116–138; C. Gresov, H. A. Haveman, and T. A. Oliva, "Organization Design, Inertia and the Dynamics of Competitive Response," *Organization Science* 4 (1993): 181–208; H. L. Boschken, "Strategy and Structure: Reconceiving the Relationship," *Journal of Management* 16 (1990): 135–150. See also M. A. Hitt, R. E. Hoskisson and H. Kim, "International Diversification: Effects of Innovation and Firm Performance in Product-Diversified Firms," *Academy of Management Journal* 40, no. 4 (1997): 767–798, for an excellent discussion and overview of the impact of different kinds of structural modifications used to implement diversified and global strategies. Also see S. E. Human and K. G. Provan, "An Emergent Theory of Structure and Outcomes in Small-Firm Strategic Networks," *Academy of Management Journal* 40, no. 2 (1997): 368–403.

Also see R. Sabherwal, R. Hirschheim, and T. Goles, "The Dynamics of Alignment: Insights from a Punctuated Equilibrium Model," *Organization Science* 12, no. 2 (2001): 179–197; R. T. Keller, "Cross-Functional Project Groups in Research and New Product Development: Diversity, Communications, Job Stress, and Outcomes," *Academy of Management Journal* 44, no. 3 (2001): 547–556; H. K. Steensma and K. G. Corley, "Organizational Context as a Moderator of Theories on Firm Boundaries for Technology Sourcing," *Academy of Management Journal* 44, no. 2 (2001): 271–291; R. G. McGrath, "Exploratory Learning, Innovative Capacity, and Managerial Oversight," *Academy of Management Journal* 44, no. 1 (2001): 118–133; J. Sandberg, "Understanding Human Competence at Work: An Interpretive Approach," *Academy of Management Journal* 43, no. 1 (2000): 9–25; G. Lorenzoni and A. Lipparini, "The Leveraging of Interfirm Relationships as a Distinctive Organizational Capability: A Longitudinal Study," *Strategic Management Journal* 20, no. 4 (1999): 317–338; M. S. Kraatz, "Learning by Association? Interorganizational Networks and Adaptation to Environmental Change," *Academy of Management Journal* 41, no. 6 (1998): 621–643.

3. See, for example, Q. N. Huy, "In Praise of Middle Managers," *Harvard Business Review* 79, no. 8 (September 2001): 72–81. Also see J. H. Davis, F. D. Schoorman, R. C. Mayer, and H. H. Tan, "The Trusted General Manager and Business Unit Performance: Empirical Evidence of a Competitive Advantage," *Strategic Management Journal* 21, no. 5 (2000): 563–576; J. E. Dutton, S. J. Ashford, R. O'Neill, E. Hayes, and E. Wierba, "Reading the Wind: How Middle Managers Assess the Context for Selling Issues to Top Managers," *Strategic Management Journal* 18 (1997): 407–425; C. G. Smith and R. P. Vecchio, "Organizational Culture and Strategic Management: Issues in the Management of Strategic Change," *Journal of Managerial Issues* 5 (1993): 53–70; B. Wooldridge and S. Floyd, "The Strategy Process, Middle Management Involvement and Organizational Performance," *Strategic Management Journal* 11 (1990): 231–241; W. Guth and I. MacMillan, "Strategy Implementation versus Middle Management Self-Interest," *Strategic Management Journal* 7 (1986): 313–327.

4. Numerous classic works examine the concept of structure. Some of them include the following: P. Lawrence and J. Lorsch, *Organizations and Environment* (Homewood, Ill.: Irwin, 1967); J. D. Thompson, *Organizations in Action* (New York: McGraw-Hill, 1967); D. S. Pugh, D. J. Hickson, C. R. Hinings, and C. Turner, "The Context of Organization Structure," *Administrative Science Quarterly* 13 (1968): 65–105; M. Aiken and J. Hage, "The Organic Organization and Innovation," *Sociology* 5 (1971): 63–82; L. B. Mohr, "Organizational Technology and Organizational Structure," *Administrative Science Quarterly* 16 (1971): 444–459; J. Child, "Predicting and Understanding Organizational Structure," *Administrative Science Quarterly* 18 (1973): 168–185; A. H. Van de Ven and A. Delbecq, "A Task Contingent Model of Work Unit Structure," *Administrative Science Quarterly* 19 (1974): 183–197; H. K. Downey, D. Hellriegel, and J. W. Slocum, Jr., "Environmental Uncertainty: The Construct and Its Application," *Administrative Science Quarterly* 20 (1975): 313–327; J. D. Ford and J. W. Slocum, Jr., "Size, Technology, Environment and the Structure of Organizations," *Academy of Management Review* 2 (1977): 561–575; H. Mintzberg, *The Structuring of Organizations* (Englewood Cliffs, N.J.: Prentice-Hall, 1979); J. L. Pierce and A. L. Delbecq, "Organizational Structure, Individual Attitudes and Innovation," *Academy of Management Review* 2 (1977): 26–37; J. Hage, *Theories of Organization* (New York: Wiley, 1980).

5. See, for example, A. D. Chandler, *Scale and Scope* (Boston: Harvard University Press, 1990). Also see J. D. Ford and J. W. Slocum, Jr., "Size, Technology, Environment and the Structure of Organizations," *Academy of Management Review* 2 (1977): 561–575, for a discussion of how specialization, centralization, and standardization can differ among basic organizational structures. For a recent examination on the implications of choosing different organizational structures, see the following representative research piece: K. Atuahene-Gima and A. Ko, "An Empirical Investigation of the Effect of Market Orientation and Entrepreneurship Orientation Alignment on Product Innovation," *Organization Science* 12, no. 1 (2001): 54–74.

6. A landmark work that examines the product division structure is J. Lorsch and S. Allen, *Managing Diversity and Interdependence* (Boston: Division of Research, Harvard Business School, 1973). Also see R. Rumelt, *Strategy, Structure and Economic Performance* (Boston: Harvard Business School Press, 1974).

7. R. E. Hoskisson, "Multidivisional Structure and Performance: The Contingency of Diversification," *Academy of Management Journal* 30 (1987): 625–644.

8. See, for example, M. A. Hitt, R. E. Hoskisson, and R. D. Ireland, "A Mid-Range Theory of the Interactive Effects of International and Product Diversification on Innovation and Performance," *Journal of Management* 20 (1994): 297–326; R. E. Hoskisson, R. A. Johnson, and D. D. Moesel, "Corporate Divestiture Intensity in Restructuring Firms: Effects of Governance, Strategy, and Performance," *Academy of Management Journal* 37 (1994): 1207–1251; R. E. Hoskisson, M. A. Hitt, and C. W. L. Hill, "Managerial Incentives and Investment in R&D in Large Multiproduct Firms," *Organization Science* 4 (1993): 325–341; R. E. Hoskisson, M. A. Hitt, and C. W. L. Hill, "Managerial Risk Taking in Diversified Firms: An Evolutionary Perspective," *Organization Science* 2 (1991): 296–314; M. A. Hitt, R. E. Hoskisson, and R. D. Ireland, "Acquisitive Growth and Commitment to Innovation in M-Form Firms," *Strategic Management Journal* 11 (1990): 29–47.

9. An excellent discussion of the shortfalls of using SBUs to organize global-scale businesses is G. Hamel and C. K. Prahalad, "Strategic Intent," *Harvard Business Review* (May–June 1989): 63–76.

10. "Allied-Signal's Chairman Outlines Strategy for Growth," *Wall Street Journal*, August 17, 1993, p. B4; "Allied-Signal Streamlines into a Startling Turnaround," *Wall Street Journal*, May 20, 1992, p. B4.

11. R. A. Pitts, "Strategies and Structures for Diversification," *Academy of Management Journal* 20 (1977):197–208; N. A. Berg, "What's Different about Conglomerate Management?" *Harvard Business Review* 47 (1969): 112–120.

12. For example, see "ITT to Spin Off Rayonier Paper Unit, Concentrate on Its Higher Return Lines," *Wall Street Journal*, December 9, 1993, p. A4; "Allied-Signal Agrees to Buy Textron Unit," *Wall Street Journal*, May 13, 1994, p. A6. Also see "A New Mix: Conglomerates Make a Surprising Comeback—With a '90s Twist," *Wall Street Journal*, March 1, 1994, pp. A1, A6.

13. J. D. Daniels, R. A. Pitts, and M. J. Tretter, "Organizing for Dual Strategies of Product Diversity and International Expansion," *Strategic Management Journal* 6 (1985): 223–237. Also see M. A. Hitt, R. E. Hoskisson, and H. Kim, "International Diversification: Effects on Innovation and Firm Performance in Product-Diversified Firms," *Academy of Management Journal* 40, no. 4 (1997): 768–798; S. Tallman and J. T. Li, "Effects of International Diversity and Product Diversity on the Performance of Multinational Firms," *Academy of Management Journal* 39, no. 1 (1996): 179–196.

14. W. F. Joyce, "Matrix Organization: A Social Experiment," *Academy of Management Journal* 29 (1986): 536–561. Also see E. Larson and D. Gobeli, "Matrix Management: Contradictions and Insight," *California Management Review* 29 (Summer 1987):

126–138. An excellent book that discusses how the matrix organization works is S. Davis, *Matrix* (Reading, Mass.: Addison-Wesley, 1977).

15. C. A. Bartlett and S. Ghoshal, *Managing across Borders: The Transnational Solution* (Boston: Harvard Business School Press, 1989). Also see J. D. Daniels, R. A. Pitts, and M. J. Tretter, "Organizing for Dual Strategies of Product Diversity and International Expansion," *Strategic Management Journal* 6 (1985): 223–237.

16. W. G. Egelhoff, "Strategy and Structure in the Multinational Corporations: A Revision of the Stopford and Wells Model," *Strategic Management Journal* 9 (1988): 1–14. Also see C. A. Bartlett, "MNCs: Get Off the Organizational Merry-Go-Round," *Harvard Business Review* (March–April 1983): 138–146.

17. See, for example, "Philips Plans to Unveil Digital Videodisc Machine," *Wall Street Journal*, August 24, 2001, p. B7.

18. See, for example, "Nestlé's Brand Building Machine," *Fortune*, September 19, 1994, pp. 147–156.

19. For a discussion of the use of matrix arrangements in multinational enterprises, see S. M. Davis and P. R. Lawrence, *Matrix* (Reading, Mass.: Addison-Wesley, 1977); R. Pitts and J. Daniels, "Aftermath of the Matrix Mania," *Columbia Journal of World Business* 19, no. 2 (1984): 48–54. Also see Bartlett and Ghoshal, *Managing across Borders*; L. R. Burns and D. R. Wholey, "Adoption and Abandonment of Matrix Management Programs: Effects of Organizational Characteristics and Interorganizational Networks," *Academy of Management Journal* 36 (1993): 106–138; L. R. Burns, "Matrix Management in Hospitals: Testing Theories of Matrix Structure and Development," *Administrative Science Quarterly* 34 (1989): 349–368; C. Bartlett and S. Ghoshal, "Matrix Management: Not a Structure, a Frame of Mind," *Harvard Business Review* (July–August 1990):138–147.

20. See, for example, "ABB, Alstom to Pool European Power Business," *Wall Street Journal*, March 24, 1999, p. A19; "Asea Brown Boveri to Pay $1.5 Billion for Elsag Bailey," *Wall Street Journal*, October 15, 1998, p. A18; "ABB Restructures Its Management, Business Segments," *Wall Street Journal*, August 13, 1998, p. A8; "Europe Inc. Muscles Aside the U.S. and Japan in Asia," *Wall Street Journal*, October 2, 1997, p. A19; "Westinghouse: Traveling Light," *Business Week*, June 30, 1997, p. 48; "New Company, Same Ambition: Build a Global Giant," *Business Week*, May 12, 1997, p. 60; "ABB Names New Chief at Swiss Operations," *Wall Street Journal*, January 12, 1997; "ABB Overhauls Management Structure in Effort to Improve Its Global Position," *Wall Street Journal*, August 24, 1993, p. A5; W. Taylor, "The Logic of Global Business: An Interview with ABB's Percy Barnevik," *Harvard Business Review* (March–April 1991): 90–105.

21. See "Place vs. Product: It's Tough to Choose a Management Model," *Wall Street Journal*, June 27, 2001, pp. A1, A4.

CHAPTER 11

Attaining Integration for Advantage

Chapter Outline

What You Will Learn

- The concept of organization design practices
- Why organization design practices are crucial in helping the firm achieve integration
- Why many companies are moving to a "networked" organization
- The evolving virtual organization design
- The broad types of reward systems used by many companies
- How corporate culture can contribute to competitive advantage
- The dangers of relying too long on established organizational practices and corporate cultures

Disney World[1]

The Disney World complex near Orlando, Florida, is the largest family entertainment facility in the world. Disney World covers an area in excess of twenty-eight thousand acres and employs more than thirty-three thousand people. A central feature of this huge facility is the Magic Kingdom Park, a vast assortment of rides and amusements with such exotic terrain as the Celestial Heavens, the Amazon River, Dinosaur Land, the Grand Canyon, Tom Sawyer's Cave, and the Bottom of the Sea. Most children who have not been to the park aspire to go sometime during their lives. Disney World has always remained a top vacation spot for children and adults alike. Disney's world-renowned Florida park is only one part of the larger Disney Corporation, which has similar park operations in Anaheim, California, and affiliates in Europe and Japan. The towering Cinderella's Castle in the Magic Kingdom of each Disney park in Florida, California, France, and Japan clearly stands out as more than simply an emblem of the Disney Corporation. The Magic Kingdom also symbolizes a place where dreams of happiness come true.

Disney has more than twenty-three million visitors at its Florida location annually. The park's underlying mission is to generate special emotions: pleasure, delight, release, adventure, and excitement, even fear. These emotions are what customers receive in exchange for the more than $1 billion they spend annually at the Disney facility. In this sense, Disney's distinctive competence is more than providing a pleasurable vacation spot or entertainment; Disney is in the business of providing emotional experiences.

These special feelings are produced in part by the park's unusual physical decor that is designed and landscaped to take guests into authentically depicted jungles, swamps, caves, and seas. The park's restaurant pavilions also play a role; they depict the architectural styles of many nations and serve food of almost every imaginable regional type. However, the real key to Disney's magic is the park's employees. As attendants, tour guides, entertainers, and custodians, these individuals are almost continuously in contact with customers. Since the special atmosphere of fantasy and escape that customers experience is determined to a great extent by the way employees act, Disney exerts deliberate effort to control and influence employee behavior. Specific methods Disney uses to achieve this objective include socialization, job training, performance measurement, and rewards.

Socialization

All recruits undergo one and a half days of formal training called "Traditions I." Its main purpose is to imbue new employees with the company's key values. Recruits are given an overview of the company's distinguished history and are introduced to the philosophy of its illustrious founder, Walt Disney. The company's four main "disciplines"—safety, courtesy, show, and efficiency—are described and their central importance emphasized. Associates are introduced to the special vocabulary Disney uses to reinforce its central "entertainment experience" mission. For example, recruits are told that they are "cast members," not employees; have "roles," not jobs; wear "costumes," not uniforms; and serve "guests," not customers. Recruits are provided a wealth of detail about the park itself so that they can later deal effectively with guests' questions concerning the exact location of facilities, hotels, and even car parking sections. Training in guest courtesy is mandatory for all Disney employees. More important, each employee is expected to understand what customers expect to see and what Disney wants its guests to experience. For example, telephone operators learn how to "put a smile in their voice." Disney park cast members often engage in extensive role-playing sessions designed to improve their skill in handling customers who become lost or afraid. For example, friendly characters in Donald Duck and Mickey Mouse costumes help small children find their parents. These extensive measures are designed to instill Disney's central values in its entire staff. People working in the park are expected to behave in a manner consistent with Disney's basic principles.

Job Training

Recruits designated for positions as operators of the park's many theme "adventures" are carefully trained to carry out their respective assignments. As a first step, each individual must master a job description manual—sometimes exceeding thirty pages in length—detailing the specific behaviors necessary for the operator's role. Job manuals prescribe the dialogue operators should deliver, called the "spiel," and even provide the specific variations that are permissible. Having mastered the manual associated with a role, recruits must then rehearse their roles under the close guidance of a trainer until a high level of proficiency is achieved. Only then is an individual permitted to move "on location" into the park.

Performance Measurement

Because employees are widely dispersed throughout the park, managers cannot easily observe cast members' behavior directly. Managers, however, need to acquire knowledge of employee behavior to reward employee achievement properly. Therefore, Disney takes great effort to obtain this information. One source of such information is letters from guests; the park receives tens of thousands each year. All letters received each week are summarized in a "guest comment report" that is then widely distributed to managers and supervisors. It classifies guest comments as either compliments or complaints and indicates where possible the specific park location to which each comment applies. Managers also obtain information about employee performance from daily inspections of park activities conducted by the park's Industrial Engineering Department. Data collected by this unit are compiled in show quality reports, waiting time studies, and other documents and distributed regularly to managers and employees throughout the park.

Rewards

The park's hourly employees earn compensation comparable to the pay received by other employees in the Orlando area. Consequently, most people do not regard monetary rewards as their sole source of motivation. Many of these individuals want to work at Disney simply because of the fun and experience it provides. Working in a show business atmosphere and making friends with other employees and customers are important for many young people who spend a couple of years at Disney. People who have worked for Disney often feel they have learned special people skills that will last their lifetimes.

Cisco Systems[2]

Cisco Systems is one of the world's leading technology companies. The company is a leader in developing computer routers, switches, networking gear, and leading-edge telecommunications equipment that are at the heart of the Internet. When the company first went public in early 1990, few people had ever heard of the company, and even fewer knew about the products that Cisco designed and sold. In fact, most people hardly ever see an actual product developed by Cisco Systems, since routers and switches are usually found in computer and telecommunication servers and networks that serve to direct the flow of data to desktop computers in businesses and other organizations. Yet, without networking products made by companies such as Cisco Systems, the Internet would not be nearly as advanced, fast, and versatile as it is today.

By the late 1990s, many people had come to view Cisco Systems as synonymous with the Internet. At the end of 2000, Cisco had become a $20 billion company, and many of its competitors envied and imitated its organizational model. In fact, until the recent downturn that afflicted the economy in 2001, Cisco Systems had continuously grown at rates exceeding 20 and even 30 percent each year. Its computer networking gear is considered some of the most advanced products available, and Cisco has become an important rival to Lucent Technologies, Nortel Networks, and Ciena Corporation in selling cutting-edge technologies to telecommunications firms that are upgrading their own transmission infrastructure. In 1998 and 1999, Cisco developed and sold over 80 percent of the networking gear used to transmit and direct Internet traffic. At one point in March 2000, the company had become the most valuable company in the world with a market capitalization close to $550 billion. By April 2001, Cisco still had over $17 billion in cash, no debt, and still earned a profit for the year (although much less than in previous years because of the economic downturn). The company still has an overwhelming market share for all key networking gear products that are needed to power the Internet.

Cisco's meteoric rise to technological preeminence over the past decade is due in part to the company's leading-edge technologies and its ability to innovate rapidly. Equally important, Cisco Systems from its earliest days relied on a different organizational model that allowed it to become a highly agile yet focused competitor. At the same time, Cisco became extremely profitable because it did not have the same degree of fixed costs in manufacturing plants that saddled many of its competitors, including Alcatel, Lucent Technologies and Nortel Networks. Moreover, Cisco believes that it needs to be able to respond quickly to its customers' changing needs, especially in the telecommunications industry where technology moves fast. On the other hand, Cisco Systems was also able to grow its revenue astronomically by acquiring dozens of companies each year to fill out its product line. Since Cisco does comparatively little internal R&D on its own, the company depends heavily on its newly acquired talent and skills to sustain its high rate of product innovation and market growth. Some of the most defining characteristics of Cisco's approach to organizing its people and activities are described in the following sections.

Near Total Reliance on Suppliers and Manufacturing Partners

One of the most important hallmarks of Cisco's organizational model is its almost total reliance on its suppliers and manufacturing partners to build, assemble, test, and even deliver Cisco's entire line of products. In fact, most of the high-tech components and chips that go into Cisco's products are manufactured by third-party companies that specialize in a particular network component or assembly of the final product. These chips and components are then assembled into Cisco's final end products. Over the past decade, Cisco has established strong working relationships with these contract manufacturers that have become an integral part of Cisco's web of suppliers. These suppliers include such companies as Solectron, Flextronics, and Sanmina-SCI, which are able to produce vast quantities of key components for Cisco's networking gear at low cost. Cisco relies so heavily on its manufacturing partners that it even teaches them how to perform quality control according to Cisco's high standards. Cisco also delegates to its manufacturing partners highly intricate, customized product designs that fit each customer's unique specifications. As Cisco's manufacturing partners become more sophisticated in their capabilities, they are also better able to help Cisco become more flexible and agile in responding to fast-changing technologies. By 2000, these manufacturers have become so important to Cisco that they now build more than 60 percent of Cisco's products and will even ship them directly to customers' locations. These relationships help Cisco become one of the most efficient companies in managing its inventory and in reducing the amount of fixed costs required to produce more complex products. Equally important, Cisco has been able to shrink delivery times to customers from ten weeks to three weeks in most cases.

Fast Product Design Capability

Another important facet of Cisco's organizational model is the company's renowned capability to design new generations of networking equipment faster than its rivals can. To make sure that Cisco can build the right products for its customers, the company actively encourages its key enterprise and telecommunications customers to work directly with Cisco's designers and engineers to test new product designs. Although Cisco has a wealth of talent that it acquired through scores of acquisitions, the company believes that product development and innovation should focus on a customer's specific technology needs. Cisco actively woos its customers for ideas, suggestions, criticisms and other input to sharpen its product development skills. Cisco CEO John Chambers is well known throughout business circles for visiting customers and treating them as long-standing partners. In fact, Cisco fervently believes that much of the company's product development activity should be performed in conjunction with its customers, since they can provide unique yet realistic insights into how products should perform. Cisco asks its customers what kinds of products and technologies they feel they will need in future years. More important, Cisco wants to use customers' input as the basis for exceeding their expectations with next-generation products that are specifically made for each customer's needs. Customers can work in person with Cisco's engineers or directly with the company through the Internet. Cisco even allows its customers to design and order products through its Web site, where customers can check on the status of their orders through a real-time, continuously updated database that is tied in with Cisco's manufacturing partners. By encouraging customers to use the Internet, Cisco also listens directly to their complaints and suggestions on how best it can improve future networking gear to make it easier to use and less costly to install.

Retention of People from Acquisitions

CEO John Chambers also believes that for Cisco to remain on the cutting edge of technology, the company should seek new ideas and technologies from wherever they may be developed. This has led Cisco on a massive buying spree of many leading-edge companies that possess brilliant design and engineering talent throughout the 1990s. Ultimately, Cisco is always on the prowl for new talent. It wins by telling its soon-to-be acquired companies that Cisco will make it a leader in its technology field. Cisco has grown so successfully through its acquisitions that comparatively few of its products are "home grown." In fact, CEO Chambers feels that acquisitions, if done correctly, can help Cisco fill gaps in its product line more quickly than through internal R&D. Many corporate executives and analysts believe that Cisco Systems is one of the few companies that have been successful in retaining the people that it acquired through buyouts of companies. Cisco makes sure that when it buys companies, they share some important characteristics: (1) ambitious and talented engineers, (2) products or technologies that complement Cisco's own offerings, and (3) management who tend to stay and become important team leaders within Cisco after the buyout is completed.

Cisco has been especially successful in retaining people after making an acquisition because it not only offers generous compensation but also encourages newly acquired talent to become project leaders within Cisco. Senior managers that accompany the acquisition are asked to stay as well; in fact, CEO Chambers sets up a direct reporting relationship where newly acquired managers are able to oversee many of the same talented people they worked with before the acquisition. Cisco wants to harness the ambition and energy of newly trained engineers to run important technology products within the company. This helps Cisco improve its own knowledge and skill base over time. As these project leaders become important contributors to Cisco's growth and innovation, they also can rise to senior management levels very fast. Over time, as newly acquired talent becomes more familiar with Cisco's way of doing business, they in turn are able to manage entire Cisco departments or business units to find new opportunities for the future.

Introduction

This chapter is the second of two that focus specifically on how a well-designed organization lays the foundation for effective strategy implementation. Chapter 10 focused on the issue of organizational structure and how different organizational structures have particular advantages and disadvantages in supporting strategy implementation. It stressed that no single structure is perfect. Moreover, changing the organizational structure is a long process that involves significant cost and trade-offs. Each firm needs a custom-designed organization to match its specific strategy.

As mentioned in Chapter 10, a big part of strategy implementation is designing the right kind of organization that best fits and supports the firm's strategy. Still, no matter what structure management ultimately chooses, it comes with an ongoing need to monitor and "fine-tune" the organization to make sure people from all parts of it can work together smoothly. Recall that we compared an organization to a high-performance engine. The engine has many supporting components and sensors that control fuel/air mixture, temperature, idle speed, and power. When all components of a high-performance engine are working together, the result is smooth performance, balance, fast response, and control. Likewise, firms need additional mechanisms beyond structure to provide smooth performance within their organization. These additional mechanisms are called *organizational design practices*. In this chapter, we examine how senior managers use organizational design practices to support and fine-tune their firm's implementation efforts.

The first part of this chapter examines some new approaches developed by leading firms to deal with some of the disadvantages of existing organizational structures. In fact, many companies, large and small, have begun investigating and shifting away from their long-standing reliance on traditional organizational structures to support their strategies.

Instead, a growing number of companies are in the midst of utilizing important variants of some of the structures discussed in chapter 10. We will examine the concepts of "networked" and even "virtual" forms of organization, two topics of rapidly growing interest. The *networked organization* represents an attempt by firms to make their organizational structures more responsive to changes in the environment. A *virtual organization* represents a completely new form of organization whereby people from many different locations perform their tasks and activities in such a way that they are linked together on a real-time basis. Virtual organizations rely heavily on the use of computer networks to coordinate and link up disparate subunits, activities, locations, and even customers and suppliers to communicate and act together effectively. We then proceed to examine key organizational design practices that senior management can use to fine-tune their firm's strategy implementation. The key design practices we will analyze include reward and performance evaluation systems, shared values, and corporate culture.

Flexibility and Stability: Finding a Balance

Recall that every firm's internal organization is likely to be unique. In practice, the shape and architecture of each company's organization are heavily influenced by past decisions, the dominant technology or product design that shaped the company's business, the personality of the managers involved, as well as the evolution of the firm's strategy over time. An organizational structure that works well for one firm will likely require significant modification and adjustment before it can work for another firm.

As we enter this new millennium, we are in the midst of an organizational transformation. Rapid technological change, the emergence of new products and markets, globalization, and the need to keep people productive are among the many tensions forcing senior management to make their organizations more flexible. Percy Barnevik, former CEO of Asea-Brown-Boveri (ABB), stated the crux of the problem: "We want to be global and local, big and small, radically decentralized with centralized reporting and control. If we resolve those contradictions, we create real organizational advantage."[3] In both new and existing companies, management is experimenting with a wide array of new organizational formats and management practices. These practices are designed to make firms more responsive and flexible in every aspect of their operations and activities, regardless of function, product, or region. The resulting trend is toward a more flexible and agile organization combining the benefits of existing structures while reducing some disadvantages of rigidity and slow responsiveness. In reality, many organizations have begun moving away from relying on many of the traditional organizational structures that were highlighted in Chapter 10. Even ABB, which has long been considered an excellent model of organizational balance, is now beginning to shift away from relying on its traditional matrix structures to become more agile and flexible.[4]

Efforts to achieve both flexibility and fast response, on one hand, and efficiency and stability, on the other, have led many firms to experiment with new organizational concepts. Firms can modify their existing organizational structures to become more responsive and agile at any level or size. In fact, organizations are attempting to become more "loosely coupled" to manage operations. **Loosely coupled** means a deemphasis on internal vertical integration to perform every aspect of producing a good or service. A key facet of loose coupling is that firms are moving away from relying on traditional organizational structures to manage their activities.[5] Instead, firms are relying far more heavily on working with customers, suppliers, and alliance partners to perform many value-creating activities that they once performed in-house. Thus, firms moving toward a loosely coupled organizational format are attempting to achieve a broad division of labor with other firms. This means that firms are becoming increasingly more specialized in those activities they choose to perform. At the same time, they must communicate more frequently with customers, suppliers, and alliance partners in order to synchronize their activities and to share information.

loose coupling: An organization design and structure that fosters a balance between the need to centralize and decentralize activities.

Exhibit 11-1 portrays the extent to which firms can choose to become more or less loosely coupled. On the left side of Exhibit 11-1, firms can choose to perform most, if not all, of their value-creating activities in-house. This heavy emphasis on internal vertical integration means that the firm must coordinate all of its value-creating activities among many subunits. The traditional organizational structures described from the previous chapter provide the basic framework for strategy implementation and reporting relationships among the firm's people. As a firm chooses to become loosely coupled, it can move toward becoming a networked organization, or even a virtual organization that is portrayed on the far right side of Exhibit 11-1. In the virtual organization, the firm is seeking to become extremely specialized in what it does. Often, the firm will perform only one or two tasks and outsource all of its remaining activities in order to keep vertical integration to a minimum. Let us now examine some of the key characteristics of both the networked and virtual organizational forms.

Different Configurations of Broad Organization Designs — **EXHIBIT 11-1**

• Traditional Organizations	• Network Organizations	• Virtual Organizations
Emphasis on vertical integration in product, area, functional structures; fosters high stability	Emphasis on high responsiveness and partnering; balances stability with flexibility	Emphasis on extreme specialization; tight focus on one or two key activities

Moving to a Networked Organization

All companies seek to combine the stability and efficiency of their existing structures with a capability for fast response and flexibility. However, relying on traditional organizational structures to attain such a balance is a very difficult, if not impossible, task. As we have seen from Chapter 10, many companies such as Ford, Exide, ABB, and Procter & Gamble have incurred significant costs as they realign their organizational structures to accommodate and implement a shift in strategy. Other companies are looking beyond traditional organizational structures to find the right balance between flexibility and stability. Broadly speaking, an increasing number of companies are trying to become "networked" organizations. **Network organizations** are firms that attempt to balance their reliance on performing value-creating activities in-house with an emphasis on becoming more responsive and open to the environment.[6]

network organization: Organizational format in which firms try to balance their reliance on performing internal value-creating activities with the need to stay responsive and open to the environment.

Although network organizations still rely on conventional structures to provide the basic architecture of the firm, they differ from traditional firms in several important ways. The three primary characteristics of a networked organization are (1) semipermeable boundaries, (2) reliance on external alliances, and (3) an organizational focus on core processes and technologies. These characteristics are outlined in Exhibit 11-2.

Semipermeable Boundaries

Conventionally organized firms employ a strict division of tasks and activities along well-defined functional, product, or geographic lines. Although conventional structures may facilitate senior management's task of monitoring and measuring subunit performance, they

EXHIBIT 11-2 Characteristics of the Network Organization

Semipermeable Boundaries
- Looser organizational "walls"
- Faster information flow among subunits

Alliances and Partnering
- Divide up the industry value chain
- Specialize among partners

Focus on Core Processes/Technologies
- Specialization along a core activity
- Redefining ways to create value in core activity

tend to isolate individual subunits from each other. Thus, conventional structures create "walls" or boundaries between subunits that slow down information flow and impede the firm's responsiveness to environmental change. Network organizations differ from traditional firms in that their structures have semipermeable boundaries. Semipermeable boundaries mean that assignment of tasks, activities, and responsibilities is less strict along functional, divisional, or geographic lines within the organization. In other words, network firms aim to keep the subunits of conventional structures more open and flexible and to loosen the functional and divisional boundaries that separate and isolate the subunits of the firm. **Semipermeable boundaries** are preferred in network organizations because they help information flow faster. Still, network organizations do not completely abandon conventional organizational structures. Functions and divisions are not eliminated; only the walls or boundaries that separate subunits from one another are eased and rendered more flexible to accommodate new sources of information, thus enhancing the firm's responsiveness to environmental changes and new customer needs.

semipermeable boundaries: Flexible separations between organizational subunits across which communication, knowledge, and information flow more readily.

In the 1990s, Corning Incorporated redesigned its organizational structure to make its divisions more flexible. One of the most important steps in this direction was Corning's move to relax some of the formal boundaries that prevent the domestic product divisions from working closely with geographic divisions operating outside the United States. With its domestic product divisions working independently and separately from geographic divisions, Corning was previously unable to take quick advantage of newly emerging market opportunities for many of its products. In many of Corning's technologically advanced businesses such as fiber optics, catalytic converters, biotechnology testing equipment, and advanced materials, fast response to the needs of global customers and low-cost production achieved by combining manufacturing of numerous subunits are necessary to sustain competitive advantage. During the 1990s, Corning's CEO James Houghton spent considerable time and effort convincing product division and regional managers of the need to communicate and cooperate more extensively with each other. Since much of Corning's growth now occurs outside the United States, regional managers located abroad increasingly need the product and technological expertise housed in Corning's domestic product divisions. Corning's senior management has exerted great effort to make its organizational boundaries more semipermeable, thereby significantly boosting the firm's competitiveness in commercializing new products faster for customers around the world.

Other firms in the United States are attempting similar organizational changes to make their structures more semipermeable. For example, industrial giants Honeywell and United Technologies have restructured their operations several times throughout the past decade in order to become more responsive to their customers' needs. Both Honeywell and United Technologies compete with each other (as well as with General Electric) to meet the demanding needs of key customers in the aerospace, automotive, building controls, and industrial equipment businesses. As their customers become more technologically savvy, Honeywell and United Technologies need to be able to "turn on a dime" to meet their ever more specific and exacting requirements. Both companies have "delayered" their organizations by removing some of the sector and group reporting levels between key SBUs and senior management. Now, more SBU managers report directly to senior management. At the same time, Honeywell and United Technologies are attempting to reduce the functional boundaries that separate R&D from manufacturing and marketing within SBUs to cut down on the amount of time needed for product development.

Reliance on External Alliances

Network organizations also differ from conventional firms by relying more extensively on strategic alliances to become more responsive to external change. Compared with traditional firms, network organizations do not seek to maintain full control over all assets and value-adding activities required to produce a product or service. Thus, network firms do not seek complete control over the entire value chain. They place less emphasis on attaining full vertical integration. Strategic alliances represent a key external dimension of a network organization. These benefits include reduced risks in entering new markets, participating in new industries, learning and applying new technologies, and achieving faster product development. Firms often form networks of alliances to access the distinctive competences and skills of alliance partners. When properly managed, alliances can also provide considerable flexibility. By working closely with a partner, the firm does not have to commit its own valuable resources to attaining full control (or integration) over key value-adding activities. Firms that cooperate closely can divide up value chain activities according to their own distinctive competences and ability to contribute. In many cases, network organizations use strategic alliances as more formal extensions of long-standing supplier–customer relationships. By closely integrating the activities of both suppliers and customers, firms using network organizations have broken down the once-distant walls that traditionally kept them separated from their key partners and customers.

Let's revisit Corning to see how it has been able to use alliances successfully to achieve faster response and to build new sources of competitive advantage. Corning formed a series of alliances in several parts of the world to enter new markets and to develop new products faster. For example, in the Far East, Corning teamed up with Asahi Glass of Japan and Samsung of Korea to build television tubes. Since the majority of the world's production of television sets and other consumer electronics occurs in the Far East, Corning's alliances give the company an inside track in working with key players in this industry. In Europe, Corning has worked for a long time with Siemens of Germany to codevelop and produce ultrafine fiber optic cable and components for the telecommunications industry. The two companies formed a joint venture known as Siecor, which became a major powerhouse in advanced telecom equipment. Corning provided the expertise in glass and advanced materials; Siemens provided advanced manufacturing technology and access to the growing European market. The alliance was so successful that both companies benefited greatly from each other's contribution. In 2000, however, Siemens sold its half-interest in Siecor to Corning as the German giant sought more focus on its core power generation, industrial equipment, and medical equipment lines of business. Thus, alliances have enabled Corning to attain many of the benefits of learning and working with its partners, while positioning the company into a strong leading role in key growth industries for the future.

Organizational Focus on Core Processes and Technologies

The third key dimension of a network organization is its emphasis on organizing around core processes and technologies. **Core processes and technologies** are the key levers that form the underlying basis of the firm's distinctive competence and critical value-adding activities. The network firm attempts to combine the low-cost efficiency of the functional structure with the high degree of autonomy found in product divisions and the responsiveness of geographic structures. Moreover, the network firm tries to accomplish this task without using a cumbersome matrix structure. In effect, network firms move toward

core processes and technologies: The key levers or drivers that form the basis of a firm's distinctive competence and critical value-adding activities.

organizing themselves along their core processes and sources of distinctive competence as opposed to strictly relying on function, product, or region. The core processes, skills, and technologies that make up the firm's distinctive competence become the basis for specializing, prioritizing, and delegating activities within the network firm.

While all traditional structures in part are organized around some type of underlying process, these processes are usually specific to a subunit's particular needs (subunit specialization). Core processes, on the other hand, are key activities and technological drivers that cut across all divisions, whether based on product or geography. Core processes are not the same as functions such as engineering, manufacturing, and marketing; they represent a common skill or technology that all of the firm's subunits use in varying degrees to develop systemwide competitive advantage (or organization-wide specialization). Core processes and technologies could include, for example, the cross-docking distribution system that Wal-Mart uses so effectively to compete against other retailers and department stores, the miniaturization and microelectronics skills that Sony uses to produce new generations of televisions and Walkmans quickly, or even the satellite-based transmission network that FedEx and UPS use to coordinate overnight delivery operations. Many core processes and technologies, including those listed earlier, are cross-functional in nature; that is, they overlay product development, engineering, manufacturing, marketing, and distribution activities. Organizing around a core process involves bringing together various functions to accelerate information flow. Network organizations use the *concept of core processes and technologies as the basis for deciding which activities are truly vital.* Vital activities are conducted in-house or in conjunction with close alliance partners. Nonvital, or tangential, activities are outsourced to other firms.

Disney uses the concept of core processes to organize its Magic Kingdom and other amusement park operations. A core process for Disney is close and friendly customer contact. All activities within Disney's amusement parks are organized and positioned in such a way that guests are treated exceptionally well. Almost every possible guest need or request has been anticipated in advance: park rides and events are organized around considerations of human comfort and convenience; so are information booths, kiosks that sell ice cream, camera film, and souvenirs, and first aid kits that are located throughout the parks. Disney is customer service at its ultimate. Although every Disney amusement park contains vital functions (engineering, operations, maintenance and repair, sales), Disney's approach to customer service blends all functions into a defining core process. The overriding priority placed on fast and friendly customer service transcends the parochial interests of each of the individual functions. In fact, a growing number of firms from other service industries are studying the Disney approach to organizing its core activities around the customer. By making friendly customer service its core process, Disney lays the foundation for its distinctive competence-providing memorable emotional experiences, or the special "Disney Magic."

The concept of core processes and technologies is not limited to for-profit organizations in industry. Hospitals, for example, are becoming networked organizations as well. Core processes and technologies for large hospitals include delicate surgery, emergency trauma, burn units, oncology, and specialized treatment centers. On the other hand, hospitals are beginning to view certain medical procedures as increasingly noncore, such as routine examinations, day surgery, testing, diagnostics, and even advanced imaging (MRI and CAT scans) techniques that can be performed more cheaply in specialized, nonhospital facilities on an outpatient basis. The massive growth of medical and professional offices in plazas surrounding hospitals reveals the extent to which hospitals have begun relying on physicians and key service providers whose practices and offices are becoming loosely coupled with those of hospitals' core activities.

Moving to a Virtual Organization

The need for fast response has not been limited to companies that compete in the fast-moving high-tech and health care industries. In fact, many companies in a broad array of industries are finding that they must become even more specialized and focused in their strategies and activities in order to respond quickly and effectively to their customers' needs. While network organizations can help many firms become more responsive and open to the environment, some firms are choosing to become even more agile in their operations. In the most extreme form of loose coupling, these firms are becoming virtual organizations. In the broadest sense, a **virtual organization** seeks to coordinate and link up people and activities from many different locations to communicate and act together, often on a real-time basis. In many instances, a virtual organization encompasses not only the firm's own people but also those of suppliers, customers, and even alliance partners to create value together. Often, people in virtual organizations will work so closely with suppliers and customers that the firm will have effectively transformed itself into a complex network or web of value-creating activities.

virtual organization: An organizational format that coordinates and links up people and activities from different locations to communicate and act together, often on a real-time basis.

In many high-tech industries, virtual organizations rely heavily on internal computer networks, or even the Internet, to provide instantaneous communications and access to people who may be in many different locations, perhaps even around the world. However, firms do not have to be exclusively in high-tech industries to capture some of the benefits of the virtual organization format. Organizations in other industries or professional fields can still apply the underlying virtual organization concept in order to achieve speed, agility, and fast response. Although firms in many industries will claim "to be going virtual," the precise shape and look of the virtual organization will depend on how it is used in a specific industry. The virtual organization format will evolve to accommodate the particular types of products, services, technologies, and processes that are at the basis for defining what people will do and how their work is coordinated.[7]

The production of movies in the entertainment industry, for example, has long displayed many characteristics of a virtual organization. Filmmakers, directors, producers, actors, agents, makeup artists, costume specialists, special-effects artists, technicians, and lawyers come together from many different companies and agencies to produce a film. Although they are all independent economic entities, they closely coordinate and communicate among one another to produce a film according to very exacting specifications. After film production is complete, these contributors disband and then regroup, often with different people, to produce another film with a different set of actors, producers, directors, technical specialists, and so forth. Thus, the entertainment industry is actually composed of many different specialist firms, each of which is highly dependent on the people, knowledge, skills, and inputs of other firms to create a product that is often beyond the scope and capability of any given firm alone. Working together with people from different mind-sets, backgrounds, expertise, and age groups has become a vital core competence for entertainment-based firms that must undertake such a complex coordination task. At the same time, these firms must stay especially receptive to new ideas, technologies, creative techniques, and market trends that might become the basis for future films.

Health care is another industry where the virtual organization concept is becoming the primary mode by which hospitals, primary care doctors, nurses, surgeons, specialists, and other skilled personnel provide quality medical care. Consider the situation in which a person must undergo surgery for a medical condition. The patient will work closely with his or her primary care physician to select the most appropriate means of treatment and care. Often, the physician will then refer the patient to a specialist who can provide a second opinion, as well as much more detailed information and diagnosis about his or her condition. The patient will also consult with prospective surgeons to understand what type of care is needed before and after surgery, and to select the surgeon with whom he or she feels most comfortable. Once the patient is admitted into the hospital, key aspects of the virtual organization come into play. Nurses will take a blood sample for laboratory testing to make sure the patient has no other medical condition that may interfere or complicate his or her surgery. Radiology technicians will sometimes take X-rays of the patient to verify the position of the patient's internal organs. An anesthesiologist will work together with the surgeon—both of whom will require the help and skills of critical care nurses who are able to respond quickly to sudden changes in the patient's condition during surgery. Nurses provide a critical linchpin of care before, during, and after surgery. Some nurses work exclusively in surgery; others specialize in intensive care units or in emergency room care. Once the patient leaves surgery, his or her surgeon, primary care physician, nurses, dietitians, and other skilled personnel will communicate and interact among each other to make sure that the patient is on the road to recovery. All of these skilled medical personnel have the patient's interest at heart; at the same time, these skilled medical people are independent economic entities that work for a different organization in many cases. Surgeons typically manage their own specialty practices; primary care physicians are either independent doctors or belong to an independent physician practice (IPP) that organizes multiple doctors in one office; nurses usually work for the hospital; anesthesiologists maintain their own specialty offices; while radiologists and laboratory technicians may work for the hospital or, in some cases, for an outside private firm that has a long-term contract with the hospital. Thus, a complex task such as surgery requires people with distinctive, specialized skills from different locations to come together and contribute their knowledge and output to ensure that a patient is treated successfully.

In addition, many other aspects of modern medical care already exhibit and implements many aspects of a virtual organization. For example, X-ray and other advanced forms of mammography that help detect the early stages of breast cancer in women represent diagnostic techniques that occur increasingly outside the hospital or the physician's office. In many cities, mammography has become a mobile activity, with specialized vans designed to provide convenient and low-cost screening to women in malls, offices, and even grocery stores at certain times of the year. Thus, mammography comes directly to the female customer, and physicians or radiologists who are in different locations read the X-rays and communicate their findings directly with the patient. The management of some chronic disease conditions is becoming a virtual activity, as patients start to link up their blood pressure measuring devices with new electronic appliances that connect to the Internet. These new devices allow patients to transmit their pressure readings directly to their physician's office, where the readings are stored in the patient's records.

In the most technology-intensive application of the virtual organization concept, physicians from many locations around the country, and, in some cases, around the world are now providing second opinions by reading X-rays, CT scans, and MRI images that are digitally stored, transmitted, and displayed on computers linked to the Internet. Doctors can communicate with one another on a real-time, instantaneous basis through video-conferencing technologies that allow them to participate in making a diagnosis and to share information as if they were all conferring together in the same room.

Thus, the concept of coordinating the actions and contributions of people with different capabilities from different locations to focus on a core task captures the essence of a virtual organization. Such coordination is a complex, ongoing task that places enormous emphasis on effective and open communication. Yet, the concept of a virtual organization is still evolving. Although research on virtual organizations is a relatively recent academic endeavor, the virtual organization does appear to share the following three characteristics: (1) high specialization of knowledge, (2) rapid assembly/disassembly of project-based teams, and (3) ability to interconnect quickly with other firms. These characteristics are outlined in Exhibit 11-3.

High Specialization of Knowledge

One of the hallmarks of the virtual organization is that firms will focus on one or two core value-creating activities to drive their strategy and organization. Although firms

EXHIBIT 11-3 Key Characteristics of Virtual Organizations

- High specialization of knowledge
- Rapid assembly/disassembly of project teams
- Ability to interconnect quickly with other firms

adopting a network organization format also attempt to limit their scope of vertical integration, those using the virtual organization format choose to become distinctive and highly specialized in an even narrower range of activities. Typically, firms will concentrate their resources to dominate a central knowledge-driven activity or capability within an industry. For high-tech firms, examples of these activities include product or process design, highly refined manufacturing skills, or specialized marketing skills. Yet, professional-service firms that utilize a virtual organization format will also become highly specialized, such as the "boutiques" found in advertising and financial services industries, "specialty practices" in different fields of medicine (e.g., radiology, oncology, plastic surgery), and even narrow fields of specialization in law (e.g., patents, corporate litigation, bankruptcy, estate planning). Thus, building up a core capability or skill in a central knowledge-based activity allows the virtual firm to become an important participant in influencing or directly providing a given product or service to customers in the industry, especially in the earliest stages of the product's or service's life cycle.

This is a major reason why Cisco Systems focuses only on product development and customer relationships as its two core activities. On the one hand, Cisco wants to make sure it stays on the cutting edge of new product design and development activities by cultivating new talent wherever it comes from. On the other hand, Cisco listens closely and works intimately with its customers to ensure that they receive the best possible technology the fastest possible way. Cisco's network gear, and levels of customer service, often set the standard for other competitors to imitate. On the other hand, Cisco delegates almost all of its manufacturing operations to its partners who are better able to manage this function.

In a broader sense, firms that adopt the virtual organization format must ensure that they continue to invest in upgrading and refining their knowledge base and human capital. Organizing on a virtual basis allows firms to compete on the basis of agility and nimbleness and to transfer knowledge rapidly into valuable products and services. This means that virtual organizations will likely do best in more formative industries experiencing high growth rates and rapid product change. Although a distinctive level of specialization gives the firm considerable negotiating power with its suppliers, customers, and other partners, its knowledge base faces the ongoing risk of becoming obsolete if there are new entrants or competitors that can match the firm's resources and skill level. Moreover, since firms using the virtual organization format will outsource all of their noncore activities, they typically will not have the same size or degree of staying power as compared with larger, more vertically integrated firms if they must conduct a prolonged price war in the industry. For example, the very distinctive offerings of boutique firms in advertising and financial services, as well as the unique skills of physicians who practice in specialized fields of medicine, face potential imitation and even low-cost competition by other providers when their skills and knowledge become much more commonplace within their respective professions. Thus, as an industry or field of practice begins to enter maturity, the virtual organization will face growing dangers of being "outmuscled" by larger firms that will likely compete on the basis of low-cost leadership and economies of scale that are important drivers of competitive advantage for standardized products or services. Consequently, virtual organizations need to ensure that they cultivate the kinds of human resource practices that promote innovation, experimentation, and a willingness to risk. Since the firm's knowledge base almost entirely resides in its people's minds, the virtual organization is only as competitive as the quality and resourcefulness of the people that work in it.

This is a key factor behind Cisco's competitive success in growing so fast in the computer networking gear industry. Cisco takes careful steps to ensure that it is able to retain the engineers and senior managers when it acquires small companies with promising technologies. CEO John Chambers realizes that if Cisco is not able to hold onto these key people, then the company's long-term competitive posture suffers.

Rapid Assembly/Disassembly of Project Teams

Another important facet of the virtual organization is the ability to assemble people with different insights into project-based teams that work exclusively on a given product, service, or technology. When a given project is completed (e.g., developing a new product or process), these teams will just as quickly disassemble. People are then assigned to another project, where they may likely work with another group of people who bring a different set of skills according to what the new project needs. Therefore, virtual organizations depend heavily on facilitating and managing lateral relations among people who bring a different perspective to a project. **Lateral relations** means coordinating work and communication among people who are at the same reporting level within the organization.[8] For example, lateral relations in project-based teams might require people from engineering, manufacturing, marketing, sales, and finance to work together to share information and to communicate freely in order to develop a product or service. Project-based teams in virtual organizations place a high premium on fostering open communications among people from wherever they may be located. However, it is important that the people who work on these project-based teams possess strong interpersonal and relationship skills so that work proceeds smoothly. People with different insights and backgrounds need to be able to work smoothly together and to communicate their views effectively in order to respond quickly to customer demands or fast-changing technologies. This is especially important as project-based teams in a number of industries begin to expand membership to include personnel from the firm's suppliers and customers as well. When project-based teams combine individuals from suppliers and customers, they can promote even faster product and technology development and new insights. The interest and use of project-based teams will grow as more firms harness Internet-driven technologies to link up with their suppliers and customers. With the advent of the Internet in particular, project-based teams can very well include people who are geographically distant from one another.

lateral relations: Coordinating work and communications among people who are at the same reporting level within the organization.

Cisco's product development activities focus on using project teams that are able to share and bring together different insights and technologies to create new product concepts faster. Many of Cisco's project teams will also include key personnel from its customers, who provide the needed "reality check" to make sure that products are not designed overly complex. Moreover, Cisco has begun using the Internet as a means to create virtual product teams whereby project engineers from different locations can use the company's internal network to share knowledge and data in order to work on a new router or switch together.

Certainly, the Internet plays a major role in enhancing lateral relations and spawning project-based teams. In fact, a growing number of industries use project teams that actually involve coordinating the work of people who are located around the world. In the software industry, for example, project-based teams will frequently bring together designers and engineers from the United States, India, Israel, and even Russia to share insights in how best to create a new software program. AT&T, Sun Microsystems, Intel, Hewlett-Packard, Texas Instruments, and Microsoft are just a few companies that have organized software development project teams on a virtual basis. Project members work together by sharing their designs and knowledge through the Internet and through videoconferencing that let people communicate openly. Japanese companies such as Hitachi, NEC, and Matsushita Electric are beginning to implement their own versions of project teams that include software engineers from China to accelerate their own product development for telecommunications and semiconductors.

Yet, virtual project teams are rising in importance in almost every technical and professional endeavor. Managers, copyeditors, and designers in the advertising industry are now relying on highly flexible project teams that are dedicated to serving the needs of a given client. People interact not only within the firm but also with the client through the Internet and videoconferencing to determine which advertising message and copy is best suited for the client. In the aerospace industry, engineers are sharing their designs with key suppliers to assess which types of engines, airframe designs, and metallurgical alloys are needed for next-generation aircraft. Even in the field of medicine, specialty physicians and surgeons are now able to consult and work with one another through the Internet on how best to treat an individual patient's specific condition. This rising phenomenon is expected to bring a broad array of medical talent and insights ultimately to serve the patient through virtual means as well, and it is becoming known as *telemedicine*.

Ability to Interconnect Quickly with Other Firms

Finally, firms adopting the virtual organization format need to work and coordinate activities with a wide variety of different suppliers, customers, and partners. Equally important, these firms have to be able to connect and link up with other firms quickly, as well as to adjust easily to different product development time schedules, product development practices, design formats, communication patterns, customer order fulfillment systems, and process technologies. In other words, virtual organization firms must work "seamlessly" with other companies and adjust quickly to their methods, practices and processes. Using a metaphor from the personal computer and electronics industries, we might even go as far to say that companies using a virtual organization format need to make themselves "plug-compatible" with other firms. Just as a personal computer can accommodate such add-on products as scanners, digital cameras, MP3 players, zip drives, CD burners, and joysticks to play video games with little difficulty, firms competing with a virtual organization format need to be able to rapidly adjust and connect their skills, knowledge base, and activities with those of their suppliers, customers, and other partners. Virtual firms therefore need to make themselves flexible and compatible with the operational approaches, knowledge bases, and communication patterns of other firms. Thus, *virtual organizations are designed to promote faster coordination and communications not only within the firm but also among firms.*

Across many industries, we are seeing how companies are using the virtual organization format to become more actively involved with their suppliers, customers, and partners. In the semiconductor industry, many so-called "fabulous fabless" companies have achieved significant competitive advantages by cultivating their specialized design expertise. Companies such as Altera, Broadcom, Xilinx, and others are leaders in designing next-generation communications chips, but they outsource all of their manufacturing to such Taiwanese chip foundries as Taiwan Semiconductor Manufacturing and United Microelectronics, which in turn do very little product design work. Even pharmaceutical companies such as Pfizer and GlaxoSmithKline are using some aspects of the virtual organization format. Drug companies are phasing out their own internal production of basic chemical compounds that are used in their pharmaceuticals, relying on such companies as DSM Catalytica to produce them. In addition, many drug companies are also starting to work closely with specialized research firms to test and market new drugs. Companies such as Quintiles Transnational and Covance are two specialists that do little else than manage the clinical trials of pharmaceutical companies' drugs in the development pipeline. Even the large automotive companies are beginning to rely on their key suppliers to design and even manufacture major portions of each car or truck's interior. In fact, General Motors has shifted some one thousand of its own engineers to work at the firm's major suppliers. These auto suppliers will in turn begin training GM's engineers and workers to make components that will eventually be assembled in GM's products.

Cisco Systems has purposely designed its organization to be flexible to work together with an ever-expanding array of suppliers and customers. Cisco's product design data and ordering systems are closely meshed with those of key manufacturers, such as Flextronics and Solectron. When a customer orders a specific network router or switch, the information is fed directly into Cisco's order fulfillment system through the Internet. In turn, Cisco transmits this information to its manufacturing partners, who respond by informing Cisco when the order is likely to be ready for delivery. In most cases, the manufacturing partner will actually ship the finished product directly to the customer's location, where Cisco personnel will work with customer to provide installation and support.

Consider again the example of Amazon.com. In many ways, Amazon.com has built important sources of virtual advantage (e.g., speed, fast response) by way of its modified virtual organization format. Amazon.com owns its own warehouses to stock inventory but prefers to rely on its suppliers and logistics/delivery firms to provide fast replenishment of books, CDs, and videos to fill its customers' orders. Amazon specializes in gathering information from its customers so that it can provide personalized recommendations and solutions to people who visit its Web site. On the other hand, Amazon does not perform every aspect of its retailing and distribution activities. People at Amazon.com are as likely to work together with the company's suppliers and partners as they do among themselves. Amazon seeks to build close and lasting relationships with a vast number of different publishers, distributors, manufacturers, "brick-and-mortar" retailers, and logistics/delivery firms to ensure fast delivery of products to customers who order them. At the same time, however, Amazon has the ability to interconnect quickly with other companies who want to become part of Amazon's Internet-based system. One of the major reasons why Amazon.com has become such a dominant Internet-based retailer is because of its capability to serve as the "hub" that links up publishers, distributors, and even other retailers (e.g., Toys "R" Us) with logistics firms (e.g., UPS) to ensure speedy and smooth fulfillment of customers' orders. Thus, Amazon is able to build significant competitive advantage by way of its central position in a larger web of interconnected firms. Dell Computer in the personal computer industry also exhibits some important attributes of the virtual organization. By developing a flexible supply chain strategy with key manufacturers of computer peripherals, microprocessors, storage devices, disk drives, and software providers, Dell can easily customize a computer to any customer's specifications. More important, Dell can perform this task with little additional coordination cost or expense to the customer.

Organization Design Practices

organization design practices: Support mechanisms that facilitate the implementation of a strategy within the framework of a given structure.

A growing number of companies are making important modifications to their organizations to respond more effectively to changes in their competitive environments. Organizational mechanisms serving this end are also called organization design practices. **Organization design practices** are the means by which a firm implements strategy within the framework of its structure. Organization design practices (or support mechanisms) thus help complement the key role of organizational structure in implementing a firm's strategy. Organization design practices will be found in any firm—no matter if it relies on a traditional organizational structure, a networked organization form, or a virtual organization form as well. These design practices are easier to change and adjust than structure and to fine-tune to fit the needs of the firm's particular strategy. While every structure gives rise to its own set of disadvantages, organization design practices possess the ability to work around some of these disadvantages. In well-managed companies, senior management can use effective design practices to enhance decision making, information flow, and smoother strategy implementation.

Many kinds of design practices are used to supplement organizational structure. Some of the most important design practices include reward and performance evaluation systems, and shared values and corporate culture (see Exhibit 11-4). In the next sections, we explore these key organization design practices. Collectively, they represent the mortar that seals together the organization so that it can fully implement its strategy.

Reward and Performance Measurement Systems

A firm's reward system represents a powerful means of implementing strategy. The reward system defines the relationship between the firm and its employees by specifying the values and behaviors it desires from them. Reward systems in many cases are even more effective design tools than organizational structures to enhance desired performance. A company's reward system addresses the following two questions: What behaviors, practices, and outcomes should be rewarded? What should be the type and amount of our rewards? Since reward systems focus on incentives that motivate people's performance, they are an essential, if not the central issue in organization design. A firm's rewards should be designed to offer the most appropriate and effective incentives that will engender high performance.

Some Key Organization Design Practices — EXHIBIT 11-4

Reward and Performance Evaluation Systems

- Hierarchy-based systems
- Performance-based systems
- Impact on corporate performance

Shared Values and Corporate Culture

The two major kinds of reward systems are (1) hierarchy-based reward systems and (2) performance-based reward systems.[9]

Hierarchy-Based Systems

The hierarchy-based system puts a premium on the supervisor's subjective evaluation of the subordinate's performance. Numerous qualitative factors, such as team performance, cooperation with other people or units, long-term relationships with suppliers and customers, joint efforts and projects among people and divisions, and personal management styles and abilities, are often just as important as quantitative measures of performance, such as return on investment (ROI), production volume, or market share (see Exhibit 11-5).

Reward Systems: Key Characteristics of a Hierarchy-Based System — EXHIBIT 11-5

- Close superior-subordinate relationships
- Extensive use of subjective and objective criteria to measure performance
- Superiors will guide the career and actions of subordinates
- Emphasis on group and team efforts and results
- Emphasis on long-term thinking and actions that help the organization
- Supports differentiation strategies at the business unit level
- Supports related diversification and global strategies at corporate and business levels

Close Superior–Subordinate Relationship. The most important characteristic defining the hierarchy-based reward system is the relationship between superior and subordinate. The hierarchy-based system measures individual performance at a specified time interval, usually every year. These measures of performance contain both quantitative aspects and subjective, qualitative judgments made by superiors. Employees are informed of their performance, usually in the form of both formal feedback from the superior, as well as informal comments throughout the given time period. Often, superiors will take on the role of a mentor. Superiors will guide the career paths and steps of their subordinates to ensure that all employees know how to best implement the firm's strategy. Managers using hierarchy-based reward systems will often take advantage of their continuing contact with subordinates to transmit and teach the firm's key values and ideals. In this sense, hierarchy-based reward systems, by fostering close superior–subordinate contact, are excellent vehicles to transmit core organizational values and ideals to all employees. **Socialization**, or the process of instilling core values and beliefs in people, is a natural outcome of the hierarchy-based reward system. People in hierarchy-based reward systems often strongly identify with

socialization: The process by which shared values and ways of behaving are instilled in new managers and employees.

the organization. They feel that their efforts to work across formal organizational boundaries are recognized and rewarded.

Emphasis on Group or Team Efforts. Hierarchy-based reward systems place a great premium on group efforts and results, as opposed to individual results, in assigning bonuses and promotions. Often, corporate- or systemwide performance measures are given considerable weight in devising the formula for allocating individual bonuses. The hierarchy-based system considers team-based efforts and team output as primary benchmarks in assigning rewards and emphasizes the crucial nature of a long-term perspective, systemwide thinking, and cooperation. Hierarchy-based systems, because of their reliance on close superior–subordinate relationships and preference for team-based performance measures, tend to promote managers from within the firm.

Many of Disney's organizational practices within its amusement parks closely approximate a hierarchy-based reward system. Disney places heavy emphasis on a socialization process that helps each individual employee understand the company's long-standing values and ideals. Individual recruits must make significant efforts to fit within the company's values. Teamwork is placed at a premium. Training is based on two objectives: understanding the different functions within the park and understanding the company's values and approaches to customer service. Managers work closely with employees in making sure they fully comprehend their roles in working with other employees and Disney's customers. People who work at Disney do so partly for the money but also to learn important people skills.

Link with Strategies. Within a business unit or single-business firm, hierarchy-based systems tend to work best in firms practicing *differentiation*. Differentiation strategies that put a strong premium on high quality, solid marketing skills, creative flair, and highly innovative engineering require people who can work together. At companies such as Black and Decker, Cross Pens, or Citizen Watch, joint projects often cut across functions. Technological or quality-based leadership demands people who can perform under a variety of conditions and can cooperate closely with suppliers and customers. The subjective evaluation criteria characteristics of hierarchy-based reward systems encourage these attributes. Quality, engineering, and other marketing tasks often do not lend themselves well to strict, concrete measures of output. Moreover, quality-based strategies take time to develop and implement. Differentiation strategies need a longer-term outlook than do low-cost strategies, which tend to emphasize strict cost controls.

Hierarchy-based reward systems are also helpful for firms implementing *related diversification* and *global strategies*. Related diversifiers, such as Hewlett-Packard and many other electronics firms, need to ensure that their different subunits (divisions or SBUs) organize their activities around a crucial distinctive competence or central technology. To nurture the success of related diversification, senior management often uses a hierarchy-based reward system to ensure that managers and employees are rewarded for efforts that span across divisions or SBUs. In other words, related diversifiers need to make sure their managers and employees have sufficient incentive to think and act in ways that promote systemwide competitive advantage. Hierarchy-based reward systems are designed to promote cooperation across business units. These systems have worked well for such successful related diversifiers as DuPont, Dow Chemical, H. J. Heinz, IBM, and Motorola.

Firms that implement global strategies also tend to use a hierarchy-based reward system. Recall that global strategies require firms to coordinate subsidiaries and subunits tightly, no matter where they are located. The hallmarks of a global strategy, such as product standardization, economies of scale, and cross-subsidization, all require a reward system that promotes systemwide, global thinking. Companies using a hierarchy-based system to support their global strategies include Boeing, Pfizer, Novartis, Merck, Toyota, Matsushita Electric, IBM, Whirlpool, and Sony. Many European industrial and financial giants have long used a hierarchy-based system to promote people from within and to transfer them across subsidiaries across different parts of the world. Such companies include Allianz, Aventis, Deutsche Bank, Dresdner Bank, ICI, Nestle, Philips Electronics, and Unilever. The strong emphasis on teamwork, joint tasks and efforts across subunits, and close superior–subordinate relationships in hierarchy-based systems support the global strategy well.

Performance-Based Systems

The alternative to a hierarchy-based reward system is a performance-based system. As the name suggests, the performance-based reward system puts a great premium on quantitative measures of performance, such as ROI and market share. In contrast to the hierarchy-based reward system, the performance-based system assigns overwhelming priority to tangible measures of output and results (see Exhibit 11-6).

Reward Systems: Key Characteristics of a Performance-Based System

EXHIBIT 11-6

- Superior-subordinate relationships not typically close
- Emphasis on tangible, concrete measures of output or performance
- Focus on individual, not group, measures of performance
- Bonuses are a big portion of total compensation
- Enhances individual initiative, entrepreneurial thinking, and personal efforts to excel
- Supports low-cost leadership strategies at the business unit level
- Supports unrelated diversification and multidomestic strategies at the corporate and business levels

Concrete Measures of Performance. In the performance-based system, promotion and bonuses are based exclusively on the degree to which subordinates meet well-defined output and performance standards. Performance evaluation occurs frequently and formally in this system. Unlike the hierarchy-based system, qualitative and informal measures are not considered important to the process. The hallmark of the performance-based reward system is its emphasis on a distant, almost "market-based" approach between superior and subordinate. A market-based approach means that superiors measure their subordinates as if they were external contractors or agents. In other words, a subordinate's loyalty and affiliation with the firm contribute little to the manager's assessment of employee performance; both older and younger subordinates are expected to meet the same concrete, direct measures of performance. Consequently, little of the close personal interaction or relationship between superior and subordinate found in hierarchy-based systems is fostered in performance-based systems. The superior's personal care and mentoring that determine the subordinate's career path in the hierarchy-based system are replaced with the performance-based, "numbers-only" approach to rewards.

Emphasis on Individual Performance. Rewards in a performance-based system are strictly allocated according to individual results; team and cross-unit or corporate performance results are deemphasized. A concern for the development of the individual and that person's career path falls by the wayside, overshadowed by individual results. Performance-based systems often have an "up-or-out" nature to them—people are expected to perform at a high level; those who cannot do so are asked to leave the organization. On the other hand, the performance-based system does tend to reward generously; individual bonuses, which represent the essence of the system, can often amount to the equivalent of a year's salary. From an organization-wide perspective, performance-based systems reinforce a different set of values, such as individual initiative, entrepreneurial thinking, and personal effort. Performance-based systems do not attempt to socialize managers and employees.

Consistent with this lack of socialization are the lack of managerial prerequisites and other "symbols" of group identity or affiliation. In performance-based systems, promotion from within the ranks is not considered a priority. Every person's individual potential for promotion is assessed solely according to well-defined measures of output. Many managers in leading firms that use performance-based systems (Cendant, PepsiCo, Tricon Global Restaurants, Electronic Data Systems, Borden, AOL Time Warner) tend to come from outside.

Link with Strategies. Within a business unit or a single-business firm, performance-based reward systems work well to support *low-cost leadership strategies*. Low-cost leadership strategies emphasize intense supervision of people, task specialization, process engineering skills, and products designed for easy manufacture and distribution. As compared with differentiation strategies, low-cost strategies place less emphasis on creative flair, strong marketing skills, and innovative product designs. The need for subjective measurement of each individual's performance is therefore reduced. Rather, low-cost leadership strategies require tight cost controls, frequent reports on output and production rates, and well-defined responsibilities that tend not to span functions. Large, integrated steel and aluminum companies such as U.S. Steel, Bethlehem Steel, and Alcoa tend to use performance-based reward systems when evaluating functional or other subunit managers. Likewise, major airline carriers in the United States such as American Airlines, United Airlines, and Continental Airlines typically use rigid performance-based reward systems to evaluate people. CEOs of these airline companies know that they are competing in a nasty, often brutal business where cost containment is an absolute necessity for competitiveness. The high cost of acquiring and maintaining large aircraft fleets, as well as centralized hub-and-spoke airline hub systems, demand an unyielding eye to manage the bottom line. All of these steel and airline firms face very high fixed costs and operate in industries with little opportunity to practice differentiation. Their senior managers feel little need to cultivate a close relationship between superiors and subordinates. Performance-based systems, with their emphasis on tangible measures of performance, thus fit the needs of low-cost strategies quite well.

Performance-based reward systems are also suitable for firms practicing *unrelated diversification* and *multidomestic strategies*. Recall that conglomerate-based firms actively acquire and sell unrelated businesses across industries. When measuring performance, they place a high premium on financial measures of individual division or SBU performance. Unlike related diversifiers, unrelated firms such as Textron, Tyco International, Allegheny Teledyne, and ITT are made up of businesses that share no distinctive competence. Senior managers can therefore evaluate performance solely according to financial criteria. Businesses (and their managers/employees) that make the grade are kept within the corporate portfolio; those that fail to do so are sold. Tyco International, in particular, is well known for laying off thousands of employees after making an acquisition to ensure that businesses perform up to their targeted numbers. This kind of "market-based" approach is practiced in rewarding the firm's people as well; managers at Tyco can make several times their base salary if they exceed the performance standards given to them.

Firms that pursue multidomestic strategies of global expansion also tend to use some variant of the performance-based reward system. Unlike their global strategy counterparts, firms that practice multidomestic strategies tend to view the world as separate, discrete markets. Because their operations are not based on a common underlying technology and are separated from one another by distance and distinct local conditions, their individual performance is easy to gauge and measure. Subsidiaries and product brands are typically evaluated according to local profitability and market share measures. Companies using some format of a performance-based system to support their multidomestic strategies include PepsiCo, General Mills, Philip Morris, and other consumer packaged goods firms. Yet, firms pursuing multidomestic strategies are flexible in their use of the performance-based reward system. Remember that multidomestic strategies, even with their emphasis on treating each market separately, still need to develop and cultivate a shared corporate image worldwide. A shared image helps link up the multidomestic firm's numerous subsidiaries. Thus, even though senior managers will assess the performance of their subunits through largely quantitative means, they must balance such measures with informed subjective judgment as well.

Also, management must be careful not to alienate critical people in local markets. Senior managers therefore still need to encourage some degree of close superior–subordinate relationships.[10]

Performance Measurement at the Corporate Level

Denominator Management. Most corporate managers use financial measures such as ROI to some extent when assessing divisional performance. Corporate managers need to realize that divisional managers can often manipulate the numbers that determine such measures. Such a subterfuge is more popularly known as *denominator management*. Remember that all financial return measures are calculated by dividing profitability by assets or investments to come up with a final figure (e.g., ROI = return/investment). Denominator management occurs when managers try to understate the value of the assets or investment contained within their division. By shrinking the denominator, managers try to appear to be performing better than they really are. In the worst situation, divisional managers, if left unmonitored, may actually choose not to invest in their business over time. By not investing, the denominator will never grow. Yet, the business presents the illusion of competitiveness and high profitability. The end result is that a division or business unit may look financially attractive on paper but conceal deep problems that may fester for a long time. Ultimately, these problems can grow so severe as to pose a danger to the entire company.

Consider Westinghouse Electric's series of disasters that the company faced when it did not have an adequate appreciation of how managers could use financial ratios to "manage performance" of their respective units. Westinghouse took big hits in its financial services unit in the early 1990s and in its robotics unit in the 1980s. The lack of sufficient effort by senior management to evaluate each SBU's performance in a balanced way resulted in severe problems for Westinghouse. Westinghouse's management relied on quantitative data submitted by divisional managers as the sole barometer of unit performance. Emphasis was placed on using performance-based reward systems, which fit Westinghouse's almost conglomerate-like corporate strategy. However, the crucial flaw in Westinghouse's performance-based system was that senior management paid little attention to how managers were actually determining the numbers for each division. Over time, denominator management became the basis for implementing divisional strategies. Senior management paid little attention to how the numbers were devised. The result was that individual managers within each of Westinghouse's divisions did anything they could to generate "the right numbers." The problems that festered in the financial services subsidiary during the 1990s acted like a ticking time bomb. In the end, senior management's inattention cost the firm well over $3 billion in write-offs.

Westinghouse's checkered history of facing numerous difficulties in its multiple lines of business eventually resulted in an erosion of the firm's long-term competitiveness. Facing much tougher competition from the likes of General Electric, Siemens, Toshiba, ABB, and other similar firms, Westinghouse continued to diversify into numerous industries to avoid some of these competitive pressures. Ultimately, the firm eventually purchased CBS Corporation, a leading broadcaster that has since been purchased by Viacom in early 2000. Ironically, many of Westinghouse's previous business units are now thriving. These include Knoll Group, a leading designer of office furniture, as well as the avionics and defense electronics businesses, which are now part of Northrop Grumman. Westinghouse's electrical distribution and controls business is a strong contributor to Eaton Corporation, a diversified firm with many industrial lines of business.[11]

Early detection of potentially dangerous actions and denominator management of the sort engaged by Westinghouse's SBUs is necessary, especially in firms that practice conglomerate or unrelated diversification strategies. Corporate managers must delve deeply into the operations of each business to understand how the numbers are derived. They must assess various factors affecting each business, such as the risk associated with divisional decisions and the degree of internal investment. Such assessments naturally entail a high level of informed judgment. Still, they are necessary to limit some of the toxic side effects of relying on numbers alone.[12]

Shared Values and Corporate Culture

Yet another means of supporting effective strategy implementation is to instill a well-defined set of shared values and corporate culture within the firm. Deeply held shared values can strongly influence implementation of strategy. Shared values and corporate cultures help implement strategy by shaping the behavior of managers and employees.[13]

shared values: The basic norms and ideals that guide people's behaviors in the firm and form the underpinning of a firm's corporate culture.

corporate culture: The system of unwritten rules that guide how people perform and interrelate with one another.

Shared values lay the foundation for the norms and ideals that guide behavior. Related to the concept of shared values is the concept of corporate culture. **Corporate culture** is the embodiment of shared values. It is the system of norms and unwritten rules that guide people in how they should act and interrelate with one another. Corporate culture is the company's "personality." Culture represents the way of thinking and doing things within the company. In this sense, corporate culture causes employees to "internalize" the firm's values. Both shared values and their embodiment in corporate culture work to influence behavior on a day-to-day basis. Shared values and corporate cultures in organizations represent a big part of the mortar that binds together the bricks of a firm. They hold people together and give them a sense of belonging and purpose. All these intangibles provide vital support to strategy implementation efforts throughout the organization.[14] Once shared values become part of the rubric of the corporate culture, they serve as psychological rudders, guiding employees to behave in ways that are congruent with the company's interests. Corporate culture thus provides a common, but distinctive, way of seeing, processing, interpreting, and acting on information.

Characteristics of Shared Values That Define Culture

To develop a distinctive corporate culture, the values that define a firm's culture should be (1) simple and clear, (2) crystallized at the top, and (3) consistent over time. All of these characteristics represent important ingredients of the mortar that holds the organization together (see Exhibit 11-7).

EXHIBIT 11-7 Ideal Key Characteristics of Shared Values

- Simple to understand
- Crystallized at the top
- Consistent over time
- Examples

McDonald's → QSCV
Southwest Airlines → Fun, warm, friendly
Wal-Mart → Friendly service and low prices
Motorola → Quality is key

Simple and Clear Values. Values must be simple and clear so they can be understood and practiced by everyone. If values are to convey the same meaning, ideas, and sense of purpose to all employees within the firm, they must be identifiable to individuals from various backgrounds. The values must reflect some general belief about the company's commitment to a particular ideal or how the company's existence creates a unique identity that makes it distinctive from other competitors. Values that are explicit and give a sense of belonging, purpose, or self-confidence provide an *esprit de corps*, and assist managers in better understanding, cooperating, and relating to one another.

At McDonald's Corporation, the firm follows what it calls "QSCV" as the basis for defining its value system. Quality, service, cleanliness, and value are the four elements of QSCV that define the practices of every McDonald's restaurant, no matter where it is located worldwide. The best-quality ingredients in the food that McDonald's serves, the fastest possible service to its customers, the highest standards of cleanliness for its restaurants, and good value for the price together define McDonald's key values. The beauty of QSCV is that everyone in the company, from cook to manager, understands each element. QSCV requires no explanations and no complex interpretations. QSCV serves as the internal guidepost that channels the activities of employees in every McDonald's restaurant. It is the foundation for McDonald's relationships with its suppliers as well and has long been the basis for its corporate mission.

Crystallized at the Top. The most enduring values are those found and practiced at the top of the organization. Senior managers must believe, uphold, and practice the same values they expect their subordinates to follow. When people throughout the company can see their senior managers personally embody and practice the company's values, they will know what behaviors and actions will be consistently rewarded over time.

For example, many leading companies with high customer satisfaction ratings are the same firms in which the CEO and other senior managers practice customer service. At Southwest Airlines, for example, longtime CEO Herb Kelleher makes it a personal point to serve beverages and snacks to customers who fly on Southwest's planes. One day a week, Kelleher dresses in a sportshirt and shorts (just like the rest of Southwest's flight attendants) and goes down the aisle telling jokes as he hands out drinks and snacks. Sometimes, Kelleher will wear outrageous clothes to create a stir within the plane. By doing so, Kelleher exemplifies Southwest Airlines' core values of warmth, friendly service, and fun. Kelleher believes that only through friendly customer service can Southwest Airlines keep its customers on its short-haul routes. Through his actions, Kelleher conveys to employees his belief that customers on Southwest should have fun as they receive great value. Other Southwest Airlines senior managers are required to practice these same customer service values by serving customers in airplanes as well. Although Kelleher retired from Southwest in early 2001, his senior management team has emphasized that they will continue to foster and nurture Southwest's fun-loving and customer-caring culture. One of the emerging challenges that Southwest Airlines will likely face in the near future is the risk that its fun-loving, treat-workers-as-family culture may begin to fray at the edges as the company grows and expands operations throughout the United States. Over time, if Southwest Airlines eventually becomes more of a "professionally managed" company, then we can expect that its ability to sustain its unique culture will become even more difficult. This will become especially so if senior management becomes more "distant" from its workers, and they do not personally practice the same values that Herb Kelleher long pushed for.[15]

Consistent over Time. Values must be consistent and stable over time to preserve their integrity and to be effective in implementing strategy. Consistency is essential to making sure that the values are well cherished, unspoiled, and almost "pristine." Values that are constantly redefined, reinterpreted, and changed lose their meaning.[16] When values have little current relationship to a firm's strategy and no real roots in the organization, their importance will diminish in the eyes of managers and employees. Values that are timely must also be timeless. Many highly successful firms practice a consistent set of values over an extended period of time. McDonald's QSCV works anywhere, anytime. In fact, for McDonald's, its enduring QSCV values have reinforced its competitive advantage and reputation in the face of ongoing wars with Burger King and other fast-food outlets. Extensive training helps instill these values into all McDonald's personnel. When customers visit a McDonald's restaurant, the food quality, cleanliness, service, and value pricing policies tend to be consistent nationwide. Customers of Burger King, which has a much looser set of values and organizational practices, often experience less consistency. In many instances, the lack of a well-defined, consistent set of shared values at Burger King has resulted in high personnel turnover, even at senior management levels. Burger King's corporate owner, Diageo PLC, has been looking to sell the fast-food restaurant unit over the past several years but has not been able to find a buyer at the right price.

Values such as hard work, friendship, and genuine concern for the customer and for other employees inspire many of Wal-Mart's key practices. At companies such as 3M, Nokia, Intel, and Motorola, innovation is a timeless value that is constantly reinforced in these firms' day-to-day practices. Managers encourage their technical personnel to experiment and to develop new technologies or novel products using whatever conventional or unorthodox techniques may work. In fact, 3M actively cultivates "legends" about renegade engineers who managed to invent hugely successful products in the face of difficult bureaucratic constraints.

Consider the illustration of Disney again. From the 1960s to the present, Disney strongly emphasized the goal of ensuring that amusement park customers have as much fun and excitement as they can imagine. This guiding purpose and corporate value remains as true today as it was in the past. "Disney Magic" is a timeless concept that defines the company's strategy. This value also lays the foundation for the training and socialization process in which every employee must participate upon being hired.

Methods of Transmitting Shared Values

Shared values can be transmitted and learned in a number of ways (see Exhibit 11-8). Two of the most important mechanisms are (1) myths and legends and (2) socialization processes.

EXHIBIT 11-8 Ways to Transmit Shared Values

Myths and Legends
- Develop internal folklore
- Heighten awareness of key cherished values

Socialization
- Learning "proper" behaviors and ways of doing things
- Extensive mentoring and coaching

Myths and Legends. A common method of transmitting values is recounting stories involving individuals who have accomplished great feats on behalf of an enterprise. Over time, such accounts often develop a life of their own, embellishing the exploits of protagonists in much the same way that myths and legends exaggerate the feats of ancient heroes. Despite—or perhaps because of—this exaggeration, such stories can have a powerful effect in securing employee commitment to shared values. Legends are often passed on through storytellers who help maintain cohesion and unity of effort. Sometimes these myths and legends are used to convey an important message about what it takes to succeed within the company.

Consider the case of 3M, for example. It has achieved a stunning record of successful new product introductions, many pioneered by low-level "champions" deep within its organization. To encourage the perseverance needed to realize such achievement, stories about successful past champions have become an integral part of 3M's folklore. These legends have become so enduring that people use them as guides to their own efforts. One story that has taken on mythical proportions describes an engineer who, many years ago, became so interested in a project that he often worked on it rather than on assigned tasks. When his supervisor objected, he persisted whenever he could steal a moment and began coming in on Saturdays to work on his project. His supervisor soon objected to these weekend activities on the grounds that they consumed raw materials and tied up test equipment. But the engineer persevered, even secretly obtaining a lab key when his own was taken away. The engineer was eventually caught and fired, but he was so convinced of the project's worth that he kept working on it in his own garage.

This myth, as with many used by companies to communicate key values, has a positive ending. Months later, having perfected and market tested his invention, the engineer was able to interest one of 3M's top executives in his idea. Soon thereafter, the product was introduced to the market and in time it became one of the company's most successful (though no one ever knew exactly which product it was). This achievement led to the engineer's ultimate reemployment at a substantial increase in compensation. This legendary success story has been so widely cherished, repeated, and practiced at 3M that people now believe the story can apply to any of 3M's leading-edge, innovative products.

Socialization. Another vehicle that transmits shared values is socialization, which can serve to influence the way employees behave. In most companies, socialization occurs through extensive training and development programs. Learning the proper behaviors, routines, and the path to success in an organization helps socialize people. Companies with shared values develop their own ways to socialize their people. Usually, socialization takes place through extensive training, mentoring, coaching, and pointing out past successful role models from the company's history.

Socialization processes are especially prevalent in large professional-service firms. Accounting, advertising, law, and management consulting firms often possess their own set of special values and professional cultures. Newly hired professionals are often extensively trained and mentored by senior managers to ensure that they have "learned the ropes" of how to perform and behave. Instead of relying on formal training programs, professional-service firms practice intensive mentoring of newly hired trainees. Mentoring, coaching, and advising help transmit core values, operating practices, and the right behaviors to people over time. In many ways, young employees act as "apprentices" with older mentors who spearhead the socialization process.[17]

Japanese firms explicitly use the socialization process as a key vehicle to develop and foster corporate loyalty. Companies such as Sony, Toshiba, Mitsubishi, Hitachi, and Matsushita Electric take newly hired college graduates and train them in all aspects of proper corporate behavior and values. Managers show these graduates all the details of how to perform, how to make budgetary requests, and even what phrases to use to address a superior or a customer. Also, newly hired personnel are given tours of the company's key plants and an overview of the firm's corporate strategy. In this way, people become thoroughly familiar with the company's mission and shared values. Over time, a "company" man or woman is created.

Unilever uses an elaborate socialization process to create its own distinctive global culture that spans six continents. A European-based company that sells soap, foods, shampoos, and other packaged goods in numerous markets, Unilever employs extensive training and development to instill the company's operating practices and a corporate culture based on flexibility, cooperation, and consensus. Every new management trainee is assigned to a group of twenty-five to thirty people recruited for similar-level management positions. By focusing its efforts on training groups and teams of managers at the same stage of career development, Unilever infuses in them a feeling of shared experience and camaraderie. This exchange is especially important in a company that hires from so many cultures. The role of training to socialize managers is so important at Unilever that insiders have joked that the company is really a management-training center financed by soap and margarine. Extensive training, managerial rotation across assignments, frequent committee meetings, and executive retreats all work to bond Unilever's managers.[18]

Disney uses a special vocabulary to communicate key values to employees. Its use of the word *guests* to indicate customers, for example, connotes hospitality, personal warmth, and genuine interest not motivated by pecuniary gain. These values are precisely what it wants employees to internalize. Disney employees are instructed to use this special vocabulary as part of their socialization process. Extensive training and role playing are additional techniques that Disney employs to socialize its employees. Still another Disney method of communicating shared values is public celebration of achievements made possible by faithful adherence to key values.

Corporate Culture and Strategy Implementation

Each company is likely to have its own set of shared values and corporate culture; but whatever the shared values and corporate culture may be, they influence strategy implementation in two general, yet crucial ways:

- They provide the invisible mental and behavioral framework that guides the actions of managers and employees.
- They enable people to better relate to one another, while making the company distinctive from its competitors.

Well-defined and widely understood values lay the foundation for smoother strategy implementation, because people are likely to have a common set of operating assumptions and responses when dealing with environmental changes. Shared values put strategy implementation on an elevated plane, driven by the degree of common ground that transcends organizational structure and formal procedures.

Corporate Culture as Competitive Advantage. In many successful companies, a distinctive corporate culture has become a competitive advantage in itself. Corporate cultures based on timeless and widely shared values often provide an important mental basis for fast response, flexibility, and risk taking that spans organizational and geographic boundaries and "walls." A distinctive corporate culture acts as an "invisible structure" that represents a powerful competitive advantage.[19] Remember that a corporate culture shapes the norms, behaviors, and unwritten rules that employees follow. Culture that influences behavior, in turn, influences performance. A strategy is more likely to succeed if it is promoted throughout the firm in ways that are consistent with the corporate culture. Corporate culture is an invisible asset that helps unify the firm and keeps managers and employees from straying too far. It is an intangible, but powerful, resource that provides an underlying focus and common problem-solving approach for the firm's people.[20]

Distinctive corporate cultures are especially important to companies with extensive global operations. As noted in Chapter 8, Coca-Cola gives its managers and subsidiaries a high degree of leeway to formulate and implement marketing strategies for their particular regions. Moreover, the numerous affiliated companies—distributors, wholesalers, and bottlers—that supply and distribute Coke's products come from every part of the world. Keeping this giant, diverse group of people together and unified in purpose is no easy task. Organizational structures and reward systems help but cannot substitute for Coke's core values and a global image that span many cultures and beliefs. Quality, fun, joy, and refreshment represent core values that define the way Coke views itself. These values form the invisible bond that ties together Coke's numerous subsidiaries and relationships around the world. Not surprisingly, they are also the basis for Coke's distinctive global image.

Double-Edged Sword. A set of shared values and corporate culture may also inhibit fast response to a changing environment. Over time, a long-standing way of doing something, such as developing products, improving process technologies, or selling to customers can "imprint" itself into the company's culture. Oftentimes, the particular way a company does things becomes the underlying dominant reference point for undertaking future projects. Moreover, this dominant reference point or way of thinking makes itself felt in the corporate culture. *A dominant design or approach leads to a dominant mind-set.* This often results in strong corporate cultures that support an existing competitive advantage but also lead to difficulties in learning and building a new competitive advantage when the environment demands it. Even when the company is able to learn a new technology or product design, it may be difficult to exploit it fully within the context of its corporate culture and way of thinking.

For example, Procter & Gamble, a leading firm in the personal-care products industry, is trying to reinvent its culture to encourage a high level of diversity, experimentation, and willingness to engage in higher-risk projects. Throughout most of its history, Procter & Gamble has prided itself on developing and refining a culture that subtly encouraged a high degree of conformity and set of behaviors and norms that molded each manager and employee's viewpoints. As P&G's operations become more global and faster product innovation becomes more important to building competitive advantage, the corporate culture that supported P&G for so long became a gradual hindrance to bolder experimentation and risk taking. According to senior management, although P&G actively recruits job candidates from a variety of economic and ethnic backgrounds, over time all of these people begin to sound alike, think alike, and even look alike. To ensure that the firm stays innovative, senior management is hoping to transform P&G's culture into one that encourages both consistency of behaviors and "a tendency for rebellion."[21]

The transformation of IBM into a high-tech developer of new Internet-based electronic-commerce tools, advanced semiconductors, storage devices, ultrasophisticated disk drives, and other computer peripherals required Big Blue to change its internally focused culture gradually to one that was more customer-responsive over an extended period of time. Consider the numerous difficulties IBM has encountered in its mainframe computer business. The explosive growth of IBM's mainframe computer business during the 1960s through the late 1980s helped infuse a highly elaborate "mainframe" culture throughout the company. This culture embodied values and practices such as exclusive relationships with customers, technological leadership based on proprietary machines and software, and close cooperation among IBM business units. Within IBM, mainframe computers were known as "Big Iron," signaling that powerful computers process and transmit information in much the same way that railroads transported goods in the nineteenth century. This culture helped IBM totally dominate U.S. and global markets for mainframe computers.

Over time, this culture began to overshadow other IBM businesses, such as personal computers, Internet-driven business solutions, semiconductors, advanced network systems, and software development. Because of this mainframe culture, problems and issues in other businesses were approached from the mainframe point of view. In fact, senior management took drastic steps to protect the flagship mainframe business and culture—even going so far as to delay commercialization of competing technologies, such as RISC. However, competitive success in rapidly evolving personal computers, Internet-driven solutions, electronic-commerce technologies, and software requires fast market response, aggressive risk taking, and constant new product development as opposed to proprietary machines, technology, and software. Technological leadership and customer service as applied to mainframe computers—bigger proprietary machines, extended leasing and service agreements, and exclusive relationships with customers—did not apply to these new areas. Competitive success in personal computers, electronic commerce, Internet-driven solutions, and other fast-moving businesses required a culture radically different from IBM's mainframe-driven culture. Thus, the corporate culture and behaviors that emanated from IBM's mainframe business may have greatly impeded IBM's ability to detect and to respond to the fast growth in the personal computer industry. As a result, IBM in some ways is still playing catch-up to more agile competitors such as Apple Computer, Dell Computer, EMC, Hewlett-Packard, and Sun Microsystems.[22]

The transformation of IBM into a more nimble, agile competitor remains an ongoing process. Although it continues to enjoy modest growth in its traditional mainframe computer business, IBM's most recent strategic initiatives include much more focus on four core areas: microelectronics, components, e-commerce solutions, and advanced software. In the microelectronics and component businesses, IBM is an acknowledged global innovator and leader in many areas, including semiconductors, flat-panel display technologies, advanced disk drives, and state-of-the-art electronics. Most recently, IBM has begun to parlay these component-based strengths as a way to become a key supplier to many firms in the PC and other industries. For example, in March 1999, IBM signed a $16 billion long-term supply pact with Dell Computer in which Big Blue will provide the PC maker with state-of-the-art semiconductor and display technologies to meet Dell's needs. Some analysts believe that IBM is shrewdly positioning itself in a way to begin outsourcing most of its own PC development to Dell in the event that IBM continues to lose money in this business. In that same month, IBM entered into another long-term supply agreement with EMC, a leading innovator in data storage technologies and software. Many analysts believe that IBM will continue to grow its components business by offering to supply advanced technologies and manufacturing capabilities to both its rivals and newly emerging firms.

In the e-commerce solutions and software businesses, IBM has become much more aggressive in developing new technologies to help companies establish viable competitive market space positions using the Internet. IBM's deep technical expertise allows it to compete against the likes of Electronic Data Systems (EDS) and Computer Sciences Corporation (CSC) to win lucrative outsourcing contracts from large companies, airlines, and other organizations. It has begun to form important alliance relationships with Ariba, I2 Technologies, Commerce One, Oracle, and other firms that develop business-to-business software and Internet platforms. IBM is a key player in working with a host of firms in the airline, financial services, health care, and retailing industries to manage their computer, Web-hosting, and even inventory management systems. In its software unit, IBM has become an important partner to such companies as Hewlett-Packard, and especially Sun Microsystems, to promote the use of Java and related Jini software for Internet and other consumer electronics applications. IBM itself has been actively acquiring innovative software developers, such as Lotus Development and Tivoli—two companies that are vital in helping IBM establish a stronger position in the relational database market. Many analysts believe that IBM's growth in all of these businesses has well positioned the firm to become a leading player across all of these arenas, particularly as more firms use the Internet to develop their own "brick-and-click" strategies.

These initiatives reveal some of the growing dilemmas that will continue to haunt IBM. On the one hand, mainframe computers exert a disproportionate influence on IBM in terms of revenues, profits, and corporate culture influence. Yet, on the other hand, components, e-commerce, and software represent the current vision for IBM's future. How well IBM is able to manage and navigate the ongoing tension between these two broad initiatives will largely shape the company's ability to compete in the early part of the next decade.

Thus, shared values and corporate cultures can prove to be a double-edged sword. On the one hand, they provide the invisible bond and implicit guidance of behavior that make strategy implementation easier. On the other hand, they can impede a firm's ability to detect and respond to new developments in the environment. Managers will often "see" things through the lenses of an established culture.[23] They will then "interpret" new developments in terms of the existing culture, frequently viewing them as threats to the culture. This rigid view can work to slow down the company's recognition of a growing threat.

Keeping the Organization Vital. Firms with distinctive corporate cultures that match their strategies possess a huge advantage over competitors that do not enjoy such a match. Yet, distinctive corporate cultures can in some instances impede a firm's ability to respond to new developments and changes. Companies, as with people, often need a shake-up to keep themselves from becoming too complacent over time.

Hiroyuki Itami, a leading Japanese management scholar, notes that firms must sometimes take steps to prevent themselves from becoming too insular or protected by their cultures. Itami suggests that firms undertake a process of "creative tension," in which senior management deliberately chooses a small-scale new strategy that stretches the boundaries of organizational consensus and current behaviors.[24] **Creative tension** seeks to introduce new activities, ideas, and ways of thinking to the company's people. Careful use of creative tension can help managers think beyond the confines of their existing operating procedures, learned behaviors, and existing culture. For example, a new product strategy that uses an untried or novel technology or entry into a new market whose characteristics are unfamiliar to the firm can help stimulate creative tension. On the one hand, the chosen strategy should not be too radically different from the firm's traditional strategy; otherwise, managers and employees are likely to reject the idea outright. On the other hand, the cho-

creative tension: A process in which senior management systematically attempts to encourage people to think about new strategies and directions, which prevents the firm from becoming complacent.

sen strategy should not be so familiar that it fails to create a reasonable level of creative tension. Too easy a consensus means that the strategy is not sufficiently novel. In its ideal form, a "creatively tense" strategy should pit old and new ways of thinking against each other to generate sparks. The new strategy should not initially involve the entire organization, but rather a portion of its operations with the expectation that its effects will later spread systemwide.

For example, Microsoft's currently limited efforts to enter the emerging interactive cable television and entertainment fields to further deploy new forms of Internet-driven technology demonstrate a good example of creative tension. As a software company, Microsoft's culture puts a premium on individual creativity, flexibility, confrontation, and aggressive risk taking. These values have helped Microsoft's people excel in designing and quickly producing successive waves of new software that are the foundation for numerous applications. Yet, the evolving multimedia, cable interactive television, and Internet-related distribution fields may require new types of operating software beyond the current software platforms developed at Microsoft. Microsoft sensed that multimedia technologies and applications are bound to grow and impact the company at some point in the future. To learn more about potential Internet software and technology-based applications, Microsoft has entered a series of small-scale joint projects with General Instrument, Intel, Hewlett-Packard, WebTV Networks, RealNetworks, Comcast, AT&T, and even rival AOL Time Warner to see how multimedia and interactive television are likely to evolve. These projects are sufficiently different from Microsoft's core PC-based software business to promote creative tension within Microsoft. Yet, these small-scale projects are not so unrelated as to distract Microsoft from its core business. In fact, as the Internet becomes the dominant driver of information and content over personal computer networks and corporate intranets, Microsoft is taking the necessary steps to help position itself for the next wave of competition in this evolving industry. By participating directly in these emerging technologies, Microsoft has taken steps to prevent itself from being shut out of what appears to be a promising new industry that has exploded with high-speed Internet access.

An Overview of Organization Design Practices

In this chapter, we have focused on some of the key organization design practices that senior management can use to support strategy implementation. Most of these design practices are used to supplement the "architecture" of the firm's organization structure.

Clearly, effective strategy implementation requires a balanced set of organizational elements. A firm cannot rely solely on organizational structure to provide the means for implementation. Organization design practices, serving as important support mechanisms, work to overcome some of the inherent disadvantages of organization structures. To deal with the inherent rigidities of functional, product, and geographic structures, many firms have attempted to loosen their basic structures by using an evolving concept based on the principle of loose coupling. Two of the more salient aspects of loose coupling include network and virtual organization forms. Three characteristics define the network organization: semipermeable boundaries, reliance on external alliances, and an organizational focus on core processes and technologies. Semipermeable boundaries mean that the boundaries or "walls" between organizational subunits are loosened to encourage faster information flow. External alliances help firms achieve task specialization with their partners and enable them to divide up value-adding activities. An organizational focus on core processes and technologies can help firms decide which activities are truly vital.

Reward systems are the set of incentives used to generate high performance. Reward systems come in two forms: hierarchy-based systems and performance-based systems. Hierarchy-based systems place a high premium on close superior–subordinate relationships, on team and group efforts over individual effort, and on extensive use of subjective, informed judgment to evaluate performance. Performance-based systems place a premium on individual effort and results and evaluation of individuals based on concrete, tangible measures of performance.

Shared values and corporate culture help shape the behavior and actions of individuals within a firm. Shared values and corporate culture work to influence people's thought processes and how people use information. When appropriately matched with strategy, distinctive corporate cultures can serve as a real source of competitive advantage. On the other hand, strong cultures can also serve to impede recognition of new environmental developments. Occasionally, companies need to shake up their organizations to keep their cultures from becoming too stagnant. Strategies that promote creative tension can be used to achieve this goal.

Ethical Dimension

Measures described in this chapter help motivate employees to achieve organizational goals. Unfortunately, the motivation generated by these measures is sometimes so powerful that employees resort to unethical means to achieve desired ends. This result can lead to a host of problems, including product recalls, injunctions, fines, criminal penalties, and permanent loss of reputation.

Sears, Roebuck experienced some of these difficulties in 1993 following discovery by California authorities that several of its auto repair shops had engaged in a deliberate practice of misdiagnosing autos brought in for repair.[25] By performing expensive repair work that was not needed, these units improved their financial performance. However, the eventual discovery of this practice proved costly to Sears in settlement charges and damaged reputation. Intense motivation to achieve financial objectives appears to have been a factor inducing Sears's employees to engage in this unethical behavior.

To avoid this kind of activity, top managers must institute explicit measures to encourage employees to behave ethically when carrying out their duties. Among the many measures top managers can employ to encourage ethical behavior are (1) development of a corporate credo, (2) careful indoctrination of employees on ethical matters, (3) strong personal support of ethical values, and (4) institution of an ethically relevant control system (see Exhibit 11-9).

Corporate Credo

A useful first step in promoting ethical behavior is clarification of the standards by which to judge behavior. Many firms achieve such clarification by issuing a written "credo" articulating such standards. Johnson & Johnson, for example, has long published such a document (see Exhibit 11-10). It spells out the company's basic responsibilities to its customers, employees, communities, and stockholders. While this statement does not indicate precisely how employees should behave in each specific instance, it does communicate the basic principles that should guide their behavior. A document of this kind is a useful first step in encouraging employees to behave in ethical ways.

Indoctrination

Employees will embrace a corporate credo only if they accept as valid and important the standards it articulates. To achieve such acceptance, top managers must provide employees with opportunity to discuss and debate a company's credo. Senior-level managers in particular must be given such opportunity, since other employees will get their cues about what is ethically acceptable largely by the example set by executives.

Johnson & Johnson (J&J) offers its executives this kind of opportunity by scheduling periodic two-day "challenge meetings" at which approximately twenty-five senior man-

Implementation Methods to Encourage Ethical Behavior

EXHIBIT 11-9

- Corporate credo that defines ethical values
- Thorough instillation and training of values
- High-level support of ethical values
- Ethically relevant control systems

Corporate Credo of Johnson & Johnson

EXHIBIT 11-10

We believe our first responsibility is to the doctors, nurses, and patients, to mothers, and all others who use our products and services. In meeting their needs, everything we do must be high quality. We must constantly strive to reduce our costs in order to maintain reasonable prices. Customers' orders must be serviced promptly and accurately. Our suppliers and distributors must have an opportunity to make a fair profit.

We are responsible to our employees—the men and women who work with us throughout the world. Everyone must be considered as an individual. We must respect their dignity and recognize their merit. They must have a sense of security in their jobs. Compensation must be fair and adequate, and working conditions must be clean, orderly, and safe. Employees must feel free to make suggestions and complaints. There must be equal opportunity for employment, development, and advancement for those qualified. We must provide competent management, and their actions must be just and ethical.

We are responsible to the communities in which we live and work and to the world community as well.

We must be good citizens—support good works and charities and bear our fair share of taxes. We must encourage civic improvements and better health and education.

We must maintain in good order the property we are privileged to use, protecting the environment and natural resources.

Our final responsibility is to stockholders. Business must make a sound profit. We must experiment with new ideas. Research must be carried on, innovative programs developed, and mistakes paid for. New equipment must be purchased, new facilities provided, and new products launched. Reserves must be created to provide for adverse times.

When we operate according to these principles, the stockholders should realize a fair return.

Source: Johnson & Johnson Company.

agers debate each element of J&J's credo. One key result of these discussions is better understanding of the practical benefits resulting from ethical behavior. CEO Ralph Larsen stresses such benefits, claiming, "The Credo shouldn't be viewed as some kind of social welfare program. It's just plain good business."[26]

Full CEO Support

To facilitate acceptance of a corporate credo by lower-level employees, top managers must demonstrate their own strong personal support for it. They can convey such support in many ways. One simple but powerful method is simply to allocate substantial personal time to ethical matters. At Johnson & Johnson, for example, the company's CEO or president personally attends each "challenge meeting" described above. The willingness of these two senior executives to devote their personal time to this activity demonstrates the significance they attach to ethical matters. A CEO can also show support for ethical values by referring frequently to them when talking with employees. J&J's CEO regularly does this when making speeches to J&J employees. Perhaps the most powerful way CEOs can support ethical values is to adhere to them scrupulously in their own behavior. This has been a big part of Southwest Airlines' secret in keeping its unique, fun-loving culture so cherished and practiced by managers and employees throughout the organization. Herb Kelleher has long believed that he should practice what he preaches about making Southwest Airlines a company that respects the needs of its people and its customers. Indeed, without such adherence, other measures instituted to promote ethical behavior will have little impact, since employees will quickly see them as hypocritical.

Control Systems

To exercise proper control in the ethical area, a top manager needs information about any ethical breaches that may occur within the organization. Such information cannot be easily obtained because employees often go to considerable length to cover it up. Top managers deal with this problem in a variety of ways. Virtually all top managers make efforts to gather information about ethical behavior during their routine supervisory contacts with subordinates. Some institute additional measures such as a toll-free or Internet-accessed hotline that employees can use to report suspected ethical violations by peers. Increasingly, boards of directors also take the initiative in this area by establishing board-level ethics committees responsible for investigating and reporting ethical violations.

Information gathered through these methods will have little impact on employee behavior unless those who violate ethical norms are systematically sanctioned. A senior manager must therefore be willing to discipline violators, even to the extent of dismissing them from the organization for serious ethical misconduct. Warren Buffet, often referred to as Wall Street's "Mr. Clean," did not shrink from such action when called in to deal with Salomon Brothers' government bond–trading scandal. As Salomon Brothers' new CEO, he not only dismissed the head of the department responsible for government bond trading but "accepted resignations" from the firm's chairman, vice chairman, and president as well.[27]

Summary

- Environmental forces are leading many firms to adopt a loosely coupled organizational approach. Two of the more salient examples of this include a networked organization and the virtual organization.
- Reward systems are the set of incentives used to attain high performance and strategy implementation.
- Hierarchy-based reward systems encourage close superior–subordinate interaction, place a premium on team and group results over individual results, and use a high degree of informed subjective judgment to assess performance.
- Performance-based systems focus on tangible, concrete measures of output and results. They generally do not encourage close interactions between superiors and subordinates. Individual effort and results are the primary means to evaluate people.
- Shared values define the norms and ideals of the firm. Corporate culture is the embodiment of the firm's shared values.
- Distinctive corporate cultures can provide an important source of organizational competitive advantage. They can also impede the firm's ability to detect and respond to new environmental developments.

Exercises and Discussion Questions

1. Using the Internet, look up the Web sites for Southwest Airlines and American Airlines. Can you gauge the differences in corporate cultures between the two

firms as evidenced by how they portray themselves on their respective Web pages? What images does Southwest Airlines hope to convey through its Web site? Are these images different from those of American Airlines?

2. Using the Internet, look up the Web site for Korn/Ferry International, the world's largest executive search firm. How has Korn/Ferry used the Internet to develop new types of products and services to help companies meet their staffing needs? Do you see the Internet helping you attain some of your immediate job or career objectives?

Endnotes

1. Data for this Strategic Snapshot were adapted from the following sources: "Disney's Mickey Mensa Club," *Business Week*, March 8, 1999, pp. 108–110; "Disney Reorganizes Its Park Operations in Aggressive Plan to Expand Overseas," *Wall Street Journal*, December 14, 1998, p. B4; "Disney, Using Cash and Claw, Stays King of Animated Movies," *Wall Street Journal*, May 16, 1994, pp. A1, A4; "Going It Alone: Disney Stands Aside as Rivals Stampede to Digital Alliances," *Wall Street Journal*, September 24, 1993, pp. A1, A5; "Disney Training Works Magic," *HR Magazine* (May 1992): 53–57; "Kingdom's Magic Really Isn't," *Industry Week*, April 6, 1992, p. 6; "Building Morale at Disney Resort," *Lodging Hospitality* (March 1992): 26; "Mickey's Midlife Crisis," *Forbes*, May 13, 1991, pp. 42–43; "A Strategy for Service—Disney Style," *Journal of Business Strategy* (September-October 1991): 38–43; "Reality Intrudes into the Magic Kingdom," *The Economist*, April 21, 1990, pp. 71–72; "Disney Is Looking Just a Little Fragilistic," *Business Week*, June 25, 1990, pp. 52–54; "Making Magic: The Disney Approach to People Management," *Personnel* (December 1988): 28–35; "The Mouse That Soared," *Forbes*, January 8, 1990, p. 160; "Mickey Mouse's Sharp Pencil" *Forbes*, January 7, 1991, p. 39; "Creativity with Discipline," *Forbes*, March 6, 1989, pp. 41–42.

2. Data for the Cisco Systems Strategic Snapshot were adapted from the following sources: "Why Cisco's Comeback Plan Is a Long Shot," *Business Week*, May 21, 2001, p. 42; "Cisco Fractures Its Own Fairy Tale," *Fortune*, May 14, 2001, pp. 105–112; "Behind Cisco's Woes Are Some Wounds of Its Own Making," *Wall Street Journal*, April 18, 2001, pp. A1–A8; "How Cisco Makes Takeovers Work with Rules, Focus on Client Needs," *Investor's Business Daily*, November 20, 2000, p. A1; "Cisco Not the Top Choice of Every Network Builder," *Investor's Business Daily*, November 13, 2000, p. A6; "Cisco Keeps Growing, but Exactly How Fast Is Becoming an Issue," *Wall Street Journal*, November 3, 2000, pp. A1, A12; "Juniper Taking a Fast Route in Its Battles with Cisco," *Investor's Business Daily*, October 16, 2000, p. A6.

3. See W. Taylor, "The Logic of Global Business: An Interview with ABB's Percy Barnevik," *Harvard Business Review* (March–April 1991): 90–105.

4. See, for example, "As Orders Slump, ABB Speeds Plan to Cut Jobs, Debt," *Wall Street Journal*, October 25, 2001, p. A16; "New ABB Chairman Unveils Overhaul, Reacting to Rival GE," *Wall Street Journal*, January 12, 2001, p. A16.

5. An excellent research piece that discusses the notion of loose coupling is K. E. Weick, *The Social Psychology of Organizing* (Reading, MA: Addison-Wesley, 1979). Also see an earlier landmark organizational theory piece by M. S. Granovetter, "The Strength of Weak Ties," *American Journal of Sociology* 78 (1973): 136–138.

6. The research literature on network organizations has grown considerably in recent years. Listed here are some representative works that have identified and developed taxonomies or other measures for understanding network-based forms across a variety of settings: D. R. Gnyawali and R. Madhavan, "Cooperative Networks and Competitive Dynamics: A Structural Embeddedness Approach," *Academy of*

Management Review 26, no. 3 (2001): 431–445; R. T. Sparrowe, R. C. Liden, S. J. Wayne, and M. L. Kraimer, "Social Networks and the Performance of Individuals and Groups," *Academy of Management Journal* 44, no. 2 (2001): 316–325; A. Madhok and S. Tallman, "Resources, Transactions and Rents: Managing Value through Interfirm Collaborative Relationships," *Organization Science* 9, no. 3 (1998): 326–339; J. Sydow and A. Windeler, "Organizing and Evaluating Interfirm Networks: A Structurationist Perspective on Network Processes and Effectiveness," *Organization Science* 9, no. 3 (1998): 265–284; R. N. Osborn and J. Hagedoorn, "The Institutionalization and Evolutionary Dynamics of Interorganizational Alliances and Networks," *Academy of Management Journal* 40, no. 2 (1997): 261–278; K. Smith, S. Carroll and S. Ashford, "Intra- and Interorganizational Cooperation: Toward a Research Agenda," *Academy of Management Journal* 38 (1995): 7–23; J. M. Pickering and J. L. King, "Constructing the Networked Organization: Content and Context in the Development of Electronic Communications, *Organization Science* 6, no. 4 (1995): 475–500; K. Provan, "Embeddedness, Interdependence, and Opportunism in Organizational Supplier-Buyer Networks," *Journal of Management* 19 (1993): 841–856; A. Larson, "Network Dyads in Entrepreneurial Settings: A Study of the Governance of Exchange Processes," *Administrative Science Quarterly* 37 (1992): 76–104; C. C. Snow, R. E. Miles, and H. J. Coleman, Jr., "Managing 21st Century Network Organizations," *Organizational Dynamics* (Winter 1992): 5–20; R. E. Miles and C. C. Snow, "Causes of Failure in Network Organizations," *California Management Review* (Summer 1992): 53–73; H. Bahrami, "The Emerging Flexible Organization: Perspectives from Silicon Valley," *California Management Review* (Summer 1992): 33–52; J. C. Jarillo, "Comments on Transaction Costs and Strategic Networks," *Strategic Management Journal* 11 (1990): 497–499; J. C. Jarillo, "On Strategic Networks," *Strategic Management Journal* 9 (1988): 31–41; R. E. Miles and C. C. Snow, "Network Organizations: New Concepts for New Forms," *California Management Review* (Spring 1986); B. Kogut, W. Shan, and G. Walker, "Competitive Cooperation in Biotechnology: Learning through Networks?" in *Networks and Organizations: Structure, Form and Action*, ed. N. Nohria and R. Eccles (Boston: Harvard Business School Press, 1993), 348–365; A. Larson, "Network Dyads in Entrepreneurial Settings: A Study of the Governance of Exchange Relationships," *Administrative Science Quarterly* 37 (1992): 76–104; W. E. Baker, "Market Networks and Corporate Behavior," *American Journal of Sociology* 96 (1990): 589–625; G. Walker, "Network Position and Cognition in a Computer Software Firm," *Administrative Science Quarterly* 30 (1985): 103–130; R. G. Eccles and D. B. Crane, "Managing through Networks in Investment Banking," *California Management Review* 30, no. 1 (1987): 176–195.

7. A growing amount of research interest is beginning to flourish on virtual organizations. Some of the more representative research pieces include the following: M. L. Maznevski and K. M. Chudoba, "Bridging Space over Time: Global Virtual Team Dynamics and Effectiveness," *Organization Science* 11, no. 5 (2000): 473–492; G. DeSanctis and P. Monge, "Communication Processes for Virtual Organizations," *Organization Science* 10, no. 6 (1999): 693–704; M. K. Ahuja and K. M. Carley, "Network Structure in Virtual Organizations," *Organization Science* 10, no. 6 (1999): 741–757; R. Kraut, C. Steinfield, A. P. Chan, B. Butler, and A. Hoag, "Coordination and Virtualization: The Role of Electronic Networks and Personal Relationships," *Organization Science* 10, no. 6 (1999): 722–740; H. W. Volberda, "Toward the Flexible Form: How to Remain Vital in Hypercompetitive Environments," Organization Science 7 (1996): 359–374; R. Benjamin and R. Wigand, "Electronic Markets and Virtual Value Chains on the Information Superhighway," *Sloan Management Review* 35 (1995): 62–72; H. C. Lucas and J. Barudi, "The Role of Information Technology in Organizational Design," *Journal of Management Information Systems* 10 (1994): 9–23.

A book that examines the competitive dimension of virtual organizations is S. Goldman, R. Nagel, and K. Preiss, *Agile Competitors and Virtual Organizations: Strategies for Enriching the Customer* (New York: Van Nostrand Reinhold, 1995).

8. See, for example, R. T. Keller," Cross-Functional Project Groups in Research and New Product Development: Diversity, Communications, Job Stress and Outcomes," *Academy of Management Journal* 44, no. 3 (2001): 547–556; K. Lovelace, D. L. Shapiro and L. R. Weingart, "Maximizing Cross-Functional New Product Teams' Innovativeness and Constraint Adherence: A Conflict Communications Perspective," *Academy of Management Journal* 44, no. 4 (2001): 779–793; R. Reagans and E. W. Zuckerman, "Networks, Diversity and Productivity: The Social Capital of Corporate R&D Teams," *Organization Science* 12, no. 4 (2001): 502–517; I. Bouty, "Interpersonal and Interaction Influences on Informal Resource Exchanges between R&D Researchers across Organizational Boundaries," *Academy of Management Journal* 43, no. 1, 2000): 50–65; K. Kusunoki, I. Nonaka, and A. Nagata, "Organizational Capabilities in Product Development of Japanese Firms: A Conceptual Framework and Empirical Findings," *Organization Science* 9, no. 6 (1998): 699–718. Also see J. Lipnack and J. Stamps, *Virtual Teams: Researching across Space, Time and Organizations with Technology* (New York: Wiley, 1997); D. Denison, S. L. Hart, and J. Kahn, "From Chimneys to Cross-Functional Teams: Developing and Validating a Diagnostic Model," *Academy of Management Journal* 39, no. 5 (1996): 1005–1023; M. D. Aldridge and P. M. Swamidass, *Cross-Functional Management of Technology* (Chicago: Irwin, 1996).

9. See, for example, J. Kerr and J. W. Slocum, Jr., "Managing Corporate Culture through Reward Systems," *Academy of Management Executive* 1, no. 1 (1987): 99–110. This is an excellent article that portrays the key differences between hierarchy-based and performance-based reward systems. Recent work examining the nature of different reward systems on strategy implementation includes the following select works: H. G. Barkema and L. R. Gomez-Mejia, "Managerial Compensation and Firm Performance: A General Research Framework," *Academy of Management Journal* 41, no. 2 (1998): 135–145; T. M. Welbourne, D. E. Johnson, and A. Erez, "The Role-Based Performance Scale: Validity Analysis of a Theory-Based Measure," *Academy of Management Journal* 41, no. 5 (1998): 540–555; H. Tosi, J. P. Katz, and L. R. Gomez-Mejia, "Disaggregating the Agency Contract: The Effects of Monitoring, Incentive Alignment, and Term in Office on Agent Decision Making," *Academy of Management Journal* 40 (1997): 584–602; R. D. Naker, S. Y. Lee, G. Potter, and D. Srinivasan, "Contextual Analysis of Performance Impacts of Outcome-Based Incentive Compensation," *Academy of Management Journal* 39, no. 4 (1996): 920–948; J. M. Pennings, "Executive Reward Systems: A Cross-National Comparison," *Journal of Management Studies* 30 (1993): 261–281; L. R. Gomez-Mejia, J. Tosi, and T. Hinkin, "Managerial Control, Performance and Executive Compensation," *Academy of Management Journal* 30 (1987): 51–70; R. S. Schuler and S. A. Jackson, "Linking Competitive Strategies with Human Resource Management Practices," *Academy of Management Executive* 1, no. 3 (1987): 207–219.

   Also see D. Lei, J. W. Slocum, Jr., and R. W. Slater, "Global Strategy and Reward Systems: The Key Roles of Management Development and Corporate Culture," *Organizational Dynamics* (Winter 1990): 27–41. This article focuses on the interrelationships among various global strategies with reward systems to implement them. A full-blown study that examines the relationship between diversification strategy and reward systems is J. L. Kerr, "Diversification Strategies and Managerial Rewards: An Empirical Study," *Academy of Management Journal* 28 (1985): 155–179. Another study is that by D. Norburn and P. Miller, "Strategy and Executive Reward: The Mis-Match in the Strategy Process," *Journal of General Management* 6 (Summer 1981): 17–27.

10. Reward systems also exert a strong influence on the firm's culture and even its "organizational climate." See, for example, J. W. Slocum, Jr., and E. Jackofsky, "A Longitudinal Study of Organizational Climates," *Journal of Organizational Behavior* 9 (1988): 319–334, for a thorough coverage of what constitutes "organizational climate." Also see J. W. Slocum and W. Joyce, "Strategic Context and Organizational

Climate," in *Organizational Climate and Culture*, ed. B. Schneider (San Francisco: Jossey-Bass, 1990), 130–150.

11. See, for example, "Whatever Happened to the Old Westinghouse?" *Wall Street Journal*, October 30, 1998, p. B1; "Westinghouse Power Unit Is Purchased from CBS," *Wall Street Journal*, August 21, 1998, p. C14; "CBS to Sell Nonmedia Lines to Consortium," *Wall Street Journal*, June 29, 1998, p. A4; "How Westinghouse's Famous Name Simply Faded Away," *Wall Street Journal*, November 20, 1997, p. B6; "Westinghouse to Focus on Broadcasting," *Wall Street Journal*, November 17, 1997, p. A3; "Westinghouse to Buy American Radio," *Wall Street Journal*, September 22, 1997, p. A3; "For Old Westinghouse, Spinoff Is Life-or-Death Test," *Wall Street Journal*, November 13, 1996, p. B4; "Westinghouse, Infinity Deal Sets Stage for Other Radio Groups Seeking Merger," *Wall Street Journal*, June 21, 1996, p. A3; "Juicing Up Westinghouse," *Business Week*, January 15, 1996, p. 40; "Westinghouse Plans Write-Off of $906 Million," *Wall Street Journal*, January 12, 1994, pp. A3, A4; "Westinghouse Sees 3rd-Quarter Profit Falling 50% on Cleanup Unit Weakness," *Wall Street Journal*, September 20, 1993, p. B6; "Westinghouse Plans to Sell Unit to Eaton Corporation," *Wall Street Journal*, August 12, 1993, p. A3; "Westinghouse: More Pain Ahead," *Business Week*, December 7, 1992, pp. 26-28; "Behind the Mess at Westinghouse," *Fortune*, November 4, 1991, pp. 93–99; "Westinghouse Posts a Loss of $1.48 Billion for Quarter," *Wall Street Journal*, October 8, 1991, p. A3; "Westinghouse Move into Robotics, Shows Pitfalls of High-Tech Field," *Wall Street Journal*, May 14, 1984, p. 37; "Can You Be Sure, If It's Westinghouse?" *Forbes*, June 6, 1983, pp. 52–59.

12. The eventual difficulties that result from "managing by the numbers," or denominator management, are elaborated in C. K. Prahalad and G. Hamel, *Competing for the Future* (Boston: Harvard Business School Press, 1994).

13. The research literature examining organizational culture issues is vast. See, for example, M. J. Hatch, "The Dynamics of Organizational Culture," *Academy of Management Review* 18 (1993): 657–693; J. E. Sheridan, "Organizational Culture and Employee Retention," *Academy of Management Journal* 35 (1992): 1036–1056; J. *Martin, Cultures in Organizations: Three Perspectives* (New York: Oxford University Press, 1992); W. F. Joyce and J. W. Slocum, Jr., "Strategic Context and Organizational Climate," in *Organizational Climate and Culture*, ed. Schneider, 130–150; G. S. Saffold, "Culture Traits, Strength and Organizational Performance: Moving beyond 'Strong' Culture," *Academy of Management Review* 13 (1988): 546–588; W. G. Ouchi, "Markets, Bureaucracies and Clans," *Administrative Science Quarterly* 25 (1980): 129–141; A. Pettigrew, "On Studying Organizational Cultures," *Administrative Science Quarterly* 24 (1979): 570–581; E. Abrahamson and C. J. Fombrun, "Macrocultures: Determinants and Consequences," *Academy of Management Review* 19 (1994): 728–755; C. R. O'Reilly, "Corporations, Culture and Commitment: Motivation and Social Control in Organizations," *California Management Review* 32 (1989): 9–25; R. H. Kilmann, M. I. Saxton, and R. Serpa, eds., *Gaining Control of the Corporate Culture* (San Francisco: Jossey-Bass, 1990); S. Cartwright and C. L. Cooper, "The Role of Culture Capability in Successful Organizational Marriage," *Academy of Management Executive* 7 (1993): 57–70; J. P. Kotter and J. L. Heskett, *Corporate Culture and Performance* (New York: Free Press, 1992); J. R. Harrison and G. R. Carroll, "Keeping the Faith: A Model of Cultural Transmission in a Formal Organization," *Administrative Science Quarterly* 36 (1991): 552–582; S. A. Sackmann, "Culture and Subcultures: An Analysis of Organizational Knowledge," *Administrative Science Quarterly* 37 (1992): 140–161; N. Nohria and S. Ghoshal, "Differentiated Fit and Shared Values: Alternatives for Managing Headquarters–Subsidiary Relations," *Strategic Management Journal* 15, no. 6 (1994): 491–502.

14. For excellent discussion of this subject, see T. Peters and R. Waterman, *In Search of Excellence* (New York: Harper & Row, 1982). Chapter 9 of this work, entitled "Hands-On, Value-Driven," is particularly useful.

15. See "The Chairman of the Board Looks Back," *Fortune*, May 28, 2001, pp. 62–79.

16. See, for example, J. J. Jermier, J. W. Slocum, Jr., L. W. Fry, and J. Gaines, "Organizational Subcultures in a Soft Bureaucracy: Resistance behind the Myth and Facade of an Official Culture," *Organization Science* 2 (1991): 170–194.

17. See, for example, B. E. Ashforth and A. M. Saks, "Socialization Tactics: Longitudinal Effects on Newcomer Adjustment," *Academy of Management Journal* 39, no. 1 (1996): 149–178; J. A. Chatman, "Matching People and Organizations: Selection and Socialization in Public Accounting Firms," *Administrative Science Quarterly* 36 (1991): 459–484; G. R. Jones, "Socialization Tactics, Self-Efficacy, and Newcomers' Adjustments to Organizations," *Academy of Management Journal* 29 (1987): 262–279.

18. See, for example, F. A. Maljers, "Inside Unilever: The Evolving Transnational Company," *Harvard Business Review* (September–October 1992): 46–52.

19. See H. Itami, *Mobilizing Invisible Assets* (Cambridge, Mass.: Harvard University Press, 1987), for an excellent discussion of how corporate cultures are invisible assets.

20. See J. Barney, "Organizational Culture: Can It Be a Source of Sustained Competitive Advantage?" *Academy of Management Review* 11, no. 3 (1986): 480–481.

21. See "New CEO Preaches Rebellion for P&G's 'Cult,'" *Wall Street Journal*, December 11, 1998, pp. B1, B4.

22. "Is Gerstner Too Cautious to Save IBM?" *Fortune*, October 3, 1994, pp. 78–90.

23. See, for example, M. A. Hitt and B. Tyler, "Strategic Decision Models: Integrating Different Perspectives," *Strategic Management Journal* 12 (1991): 327–351.

24. H. Itami, *Mobilizing Invisible Assets* (Cambridge, Mass.: Harvard University Press, 1987), 153–155.

25. "California Accuses Sears of Bilking Auto Service Customers," *National Petroleum News* (August 1992): 21–22.

26. "Leaders of the Most Admired," *Fortune*, January 29, 1990, p. 50.

27. A. Kilpatrick, *Warren Buffett: The Good Guy of Wall Street* (n.p.: Donald Fine, 1992), 181.

PART 4

Sustaining and Renewing Advantage

CHAPTER 12

Cooperation and Autonomy: Managing Interrelationships

Chapter Outline

What You Will Learn

- The importance of interrelationships in sustaining competitive advantage
- The need to balance cooperation and autonomy in supporting interrelationships
- Factors that promote the need for greater cooperation
- Factors that promote the need for greater autonomy
- The concept of "technology fusion"
- Sources of internal resistance to organizational change

The 3M Company[1]

Perhaps one of the best-known companies in the United States, 3M has long prided itself on its capability for fast innovation and the creation of many new technologies. Customers all around the world value 3M's broad array of such top-quality products as Scotch tape, Post-It Notes, weather-stripping products, Scotchgard fabric protectants, and a broad array of technical products for the chemical, paint, medical device, and electronics industries. By the end of 2000, 3M produced revenues of $16.7 billion, and earned $1.78 billion in profits. Over its long history, 3M had pioneered over a hundred different core technologies that spawned tens of thousands of highly innovative products. Most recently, 3M has even produced some core breakthroughs that are found even in fiber optic networks and advanced medical applications. 3M's ability to create new products quickly has become so legendary that the company is frequently seen as a model of corporate innovation.

The company was founded in the early part of the twentieth century to manufacture sandpaper and other abrasive products that were used in the woodworking, automotive, and repair businesses. 3M's scientists and salespeople initially struggled with the company's first attempts to make sandpaper, since it was difficult to coat the abrasive mineral powders and grit onto the paper with a high degree of consistency. Under the direction of William McKnight, the man most often credited with helping 3M to grow in its formative years, the company built its own laboratory to generate ideas and new techniques to improve the quality of sandpaper. Improvements in the design and production of sandpaper resulted in new types of sandpaper (e.g., coarse-grained, medium-grained, fine-grained) that could be used for a variety of different products (e.g., woods, metals, porcelains). Customers in different industries began to use 3M's sandpaper for a variety of different uses. Feedback from customers also helped 3M to develop ideas for new products. Within a few years, scientists at 3M's lab created masking tape, Scotch tape, and other innovative products that were soon to power the company's fast growth. All of these abrasive and tape products laid the foundation for 3M's growing technical and marketing expertise with adhesives and coatings.

Under McKnight's direction, 3M instituted some key policies that were designed to promote innovation and creative thinking. McKnight and his management team genuinely believed that 3M needed to foster and promote innovation on a continuous basis. Innovation led to new opportunities for both personal and corporate growth. In the late 1930s, 3M created a Central Research Laboratory whose purpose was to stimulate creative thinking and experimentation that would help the company grow. More important, 3M's organization encouraged people from all parts of the expanding company to communicate with one another on a frequent basis. Scientists working on different projects were encouraged to share their knowledge through group meetings as well as through company-sponsored technology forums that promoted free-flowing discussions. As the company grew and more labs were created, management wanted to ensure that scientists working on one project could communicate with their counterparts working on different projects. The continuous exchange of knowledge produced an intellectual ferment at 3M. By sharing knowledge and viewing the work of his or her colleagues, a scientist could gain new insights into how a technology might be developed or better refined. More important, by expanding his or her horizon, a scientist might be able to discover a technical idea or breakthrough that might not have otherwise occurred. 3M also promoted communications and informal idea exchanges that went beyond the labs of scientists and engineering peers. The company actively encouraged scientists to communicate with people from marketing and manufacturing to discuss new product designs, manufacturing feasibility, customer needs, and the like. Over time, 3M's salespeople provided critical data and product feedback to technical personnel in design and manufacturing; in turn, 3M's scientists often visited customers to see how their products were working.

Translating Innovation into New Products

One of 3M's earliest strategies could be summarized as "unintentionally discovering new niches." 3M's senior management believed that people with interesting ideas should be free to pursue and develop them, even to the point that successful ideas could become freestanding businesses. In fact, by the 1940s, 3M even formalized a policy that researchers could spend up to 15 percent of their time to work on projects or ideas that were purely of individual interest. By promoting such personal entrepreneurship, the company could harness the power of individual creativity with the technical resources of 3M's expanding network of laboratories. For example, scientists working with 3M's original sandpaper and tape products eventually pioneered such innovations as automotive trim, weather stripping, upholstery, and even Scotchgard fabric protection. Other scientists also discovered such breakthrough 3M products as surgical masks and filters from working on their own personal projects. Thus, many of 3M's businesses originally started as novelty ideas that eventually found a ready market, even though there was no formal "strategic plan" to identify and target these markets initially.

To ensure that 3M could sustain such a high level of individual creativity and innovation-driven growth, 3M became one of the first companies to form product divisions that could devise their own strategies to grow as they saw fit. In fact, within a few decades, 3M had spawned dozens of different divisions, each of which possessed its own laboratory, manufacturing operation, and sales force. When a division got too big and managed an expanding number of products, 3M's senior management would carve out a separate new division to sharpen the focus on innovating and creating new products. This policy of spawning new divisions at one point resulted in several dozen 3M divisions, with each one working on its own product and market ideas. At the same time, however, senior management insisted that the entire company be able to freely share core technologies and breakthroughs that were developed in any part of 3M. For example, one division's development of advanced thin-film adhesives that ultimately proved to be a failure for high stress industrial applications later became the basis for 3M's wildly popular Post-It Notes in another division. Conversely, fiber technologies that lay the foundation for 3M's mask products also created opportunities to develop specialized filters and membranes in another division. Thus, individual creativity and innovation, when combined with active sharing of core technologies and knowledge throughout 3M, powered the company's annual double-digit growth rate for many years until the 1980s.

3M also fostered a number of highly innovative reward systems to stimulate individual creativity and product innovation. The company rewarded scientists not only through monetary means, but also through recognition of individual achievement. Top scientists were inducted into a corporate "hall of fame," where they were encouraged to provide guidance and ideas to younger scientists in different divisions. Equally important, 3M fostered a series of legends and myths throughout the company. These myths would often focus on an individual scientist's stubbornness and persistence to develop a new technology or product idea, even in the face of skepticism or resistance from management. Many of these myths would center on how an individual's personal fight led to the creation of new products that no one could have ever anticipated. At the same time, to promote an egalitarian perspective that cherished each individual's unique contribution, 3M recognized and promoted people from all parts of the company that played important roles in producing and distributing 3M's products to its customers.

Sustaining Growth in a Massive Company

By the 1980s, 3M's growth had slowed down considerably. Although 3M continued to foster individual creativity and innovation, revenue and earnings growth became more difficult as the company expanded into many new areas and markets. In many ways, 3M became a victim of its own success. At one point in the late 1970s, 3M managed dozens of autonomous divisions—each of which oversaw hundreds of different products. However, as competition intensified and the cost of capital grew in the 1980s, 3M undertook a series of important organizational changes during the decade.

For the first time in its history, 3M began to reorganize its many divisions into broader sectors. Divisions sharing a similar set of core technologies were thus grouped into one sector, while other divisions sharing a different set of core technologies were placed into another sector. The management of R&D also changed at 3M. The world-renowned Central Research Laboratories focused on "blue sky" projects, or basic scientific research that had no immediate commercial application. In turn, each sector had its own laboratories that focused on developing and refining an underlying set of core technologies. At the level of individual divisions, these laboratories became responsible for working on product ideas that could be translated into new products more quickly.

Important organizational changes occurred in other areas of 3M as well during the

1980s and 1990s. To promote greater economies of scale and cost savings, senior management created centralized manufacturing units that produced products for a number of different divisions. Thus, many divisions lost their traditional control and oversight over their own resources. Even the marketing function changed at 3M. Instead of creating highly specialized, product-specific marketing teams that belonged to each division, the company reorganized the sales force in order to promote cross-selling of 3M's products across different divisions. Over time, 3M's highly autonomous divisions faced significant internal tensions as managers learned to adapt to a new organizational approach. The nature of the divisions themselves was changing. Instead of forming a new division to work on its own new product idea, senior management moved in the direction to make each division more internally efficient and productive. In turn, scientists believed they had somewhat less scope of freedom to experiment with their own ideas, while manufacturing and marketing people felt uncomfortable in their newer, broader roles of working across divisions. Reward systems also appeared to change, as senior management placed somewhat greater emphasis on teamwork and fast results, as opposed to individual achievement based on personal growth or creativity. Throughout the 1990s, many observers noted that 3M was becoming more focused and growing its revenues faster, but at the expense of the free-wheeling, informal, and personal culture that once drove the company during its earlier days.

Introduction

As we have seen from our earlier chapters, finding the right fit between a firm's strategy and its organizational structure and design is an ongoing challenge. In practice, all companies will continue to search for the right balance that helps them build and sustain their competitive advantage. This task is even more challenging when one considers that the competitive environment for most firms has also become significantly more complex.

In this chapter, we focus on the issue of how senior managers can balance the need for interdivisional cooperation and strong divisional autonomy within the organization. Finding the right balance, or strategic alignment, between cooperation and autonomy is crucial. Firms compete as collective entities of people, businesses, and bundles of resources. Achieving a careful alignment between cooperation and autonomy determines how well firms manage the interrelationships of activities among their subunits. Interrelationships refer to value-adding activities, skills, technologies, or resources that are shared among the firm's subunits.[2] Interrelationships result when the firm's business units, divisions, or other subunits work with one another to build and sustain sources of *competitive advantage for the entire firm*. On the one hand, many firms may find that a high level of cooperation among business units or divisions is required to build and to sustain key sources of competitive advantage. On the other hand, some firms may find that fostering a high level of business unit or divisional autonomy is more essential to their competitive success. Thus, there is no blanket solution or answer that will work for each and every firm without considering the specific situations facing it.

Managing interrelationships is a delicate task. Even when a firm has selected an organizational structure that seems to best fit its overall strategy, senior managers need to carefully balance divisional cooperation and autonomy to promote interrelationships. Interrelationships are horizontal in nature, in that they involve value-adding activities that cut across divisions and businesses. Successful management of interrelationships that span divisions depends on how well senior management can "tilt" or align the firm toward the right balance of cooperation and autonomy. Managing this alignment effectively requires the firm to put in place key organization design practices that can shift the firm toward greater autonomy or greater cooperation over time.[3] Successful identification and management of interrelationships is thus key to building a coherent corporate-wide source of competitive advantage.

We begin by showing how a firm can use its organizational structure and supporting design practices to promote cooperation or autonomy. We then consider how a firm's strategy should influence the balance it strikes between these opposing organizational orientations. Finally, we consider developments that can oblige a firm to shift its organizational emphasis toward either greater cooperation or greater autonomy, and we examine likely sources of resistance to shifts of this kind.

Achieving Strategic Alignment within the Organization

A variety of organizational structures and design practices can affect the degree to which cooperation or autonomy is promoted within the firm. Exhibit 12-1 portrays how a firm can position itself along a continuum ranging from high levels of cooperation to high levels of autonomy. Let us examine how each of these organizational practices influences the tilt toward cooperation or autonomy.

Spectrum of Cooperation versus Autonomy **EXHIBIT 12-1**

	Cooperation ⟵⟶	Autonomy
1. Distinctive Competence	Shared and developed among SBUs	Competence specific to each division or SBU
2. Structure	Sizable corporate staff; large divisions, SBUs, sectors	"Lean" corporate staffs; small divisions, holding company format, or geographic structures
3. Staffing	Use of off-line coordinators and task forces	Lean or nonexistent use of coordinators; little corporate involvement
4. Reward and Performance Measurement Systems	Performance measured in a balanced way; rewards based in part on subjective measures and on overall performance of the enterprise (hierarchy-based)	Performance measured objectively; rewards based entirely on performance of own division (performance-based)
5. Shared Values and Corporate Culture	Subunits are members of a team; strong values emphasize belonging and cooperation among subunits	Subunits are rivals competing for top performance; strong divisional identity and emphasis on individual performers
6. Managerial Rotation	Frequent rotation of managers to promote systemwide view	Infrequent rotation of managers preserves autonomy

Distinctive Competence

The nature of a firm's distinctive competence plays an important role in influencing the degree of cooperation or autonomy required to sustain competitive advantage. Clearly, a distinctive competence that extends across multiple lines of businesses or subunits heightens the need for cooperation to sustain corporate-wide competitive advantage. Distinctive competences, skills, or technologies that are shared systemwide call for greater interunit cooperation, particularly within firms that emphasize internal development of new technologies and skills. Knowledge about products, technologies or customer needs developed by one business unit can often help another unit's competitiveness if there is an organizational mechanism to promote such sharing. More generally, a high level of cooperation is necessary when business units may be able to share activities that promote systemwide economies of scale or experience curve effects.

Conversely, a distinctive competence that is internal to any one particular division and not easily shared with other units heightens the need for autonomy. Fast response tends to be more important than scale economies. Firms whose competitive advantage is derived from fast response, creativity, and product customization are likely to give their divisional managers greater decision-making power. Competences, skills, and technologies that are not easily shared systemwide require increased divisional autonomy to sustain competitive advantage at the divisional level.

Organizational Structure

As mentioned in Chapter 10, modifications of the basic product division structure can do much to promote greater cooperation. For example, placement of strategic business units (SBUs) into groups and sectors will generally enhance cooperation. Product divisions facing similar markets or using similar technologies or joint production facilities are likely to cooperate more when they are placed within the same SBU. Matrix structures, despite their numerous disadvantages, also engender high levels of cooperation among divisions or subunits.

On the other hand, the conglomerate or holding company structure enhances divisional autonomy. Conglomerate structures emphasize a lean staff with few management layers between divisions and corporate headquarters. They make no attempt to group or link business units together under larger SBUs. The conglomerate structure facilitates a high level of autonomy, enabling division managers to run their own operations. As noted in Chapter 7, firms such as Tyco International and Textron give their business units great leeway in planning and implementing individual division strategies.

Geographic structures by their very nature promote a high degree of subunit autonomy. Recall that geographic structures work best when one market is unlike the next and when local conditions (requiring product customization and modifications) weigh heavily in strategy. Within this context, the use of a geographic structure facilitates the high degree of autonomy needed to build competitive advantage at local levels. Geographic structures thus promote the fast response capabilities needed to adapt to local market requirements and changes.

Off-Line Coordinators

A firm can increase cooperation among divisions by assigning individuals or committees outside the formal hierarchy to coordinate activities among subunits. These individuals and groups, often experienced managers and staff personnel, are referred to as **off-line coordinators**. The job of an off-line coordinator is to ensure that the firm's interrelationships are coordinated across divisional boundaries. Off-line coordinators help oversee the tasks of sharing resources, technologies, and skills among businesses. They are "off-line" in the sense that they are responsible only to corporate headquarters and thus do not owe an allegiance to any one business unit or division. These coordinators must work extensively with personnel within subunits to achieve informal cooperation. Off-line coordinating committees typically include all managers of a firm whose products have some bearing on the skill or resource that is being shared.

off-line coordinators: Individuals and groups, often experienced managers and staff personnel, outside the formal hierarchy who coordinate activities among subunits.

informal integrators: People who act as internal "referees" to resolve disputes and conflicts between divisional managers.

Another device for increasing cooperation is use of informal integrators. Informal integrators serve a role similar to that of off-line coordinators. **Informal integrators** act as internal "referees" to resolve disputes and conflicts between divisional managers. Conflict may result from divisions pursuing different strategies and goals. For example, at Procter & Gamble, corporate facilitators encourage autonomous brand management teams to share their knowledge of competitors and retailers with other teams. P&G managers are initially reluctant to share their ideas and insights, since many of them compete for the same shelf space in grocery stores and other outlets. However, P&G facilitators work to persuade managers to share their insights by providing strong internal incentives for working together, such as opportunities to lead the development and marketing of new products. Facilitators also emphasize that sharing does not necessarily result in cannibalization, loss of prestige, or loss of market share for any concerned manager.

In a similar vein, 3M used its own variation of off-line coordinators to instill a high degree of knowledge sharing among its many divisions. In 3M's earlier days, scientists often served in this capacity when they worked across different divisions to promote the development of new technologies. However, the use and role of off-line coordinators at 3M shifted when the company sought to induce a higher degree of cooperation among its many divisions during the 1980s and 1990s. 3M encouraged key managers to serve as off-line coordinators when the company periodically reviewed the potential for increased economies of scale and the physical sharing of manufacturing assets among different divisions to reduce the company's overall cost structure.

Yet another device for fostering cooperation among subunits is the use of internal task forces. **Internal task forces** serve as bridges that forge stronger interrelationships among divisions. Companies such as Honeywell, Chaparral Steel, Citizen Watch, Kodak, Motorola, Nissan, and Procter & Gamble use internal task forces to achieve smoother coordination of design and manufacturing of products among divisions. For example, Motorola encourages its division managers in R&D, manufacturing, and marketing to serve on temporary task forces. These task forces then plan new strategies for sharing technologies and production resources for individual products. This joint effort helps accelerate time-to-market for new products and facilitates sharing of insights that may be valuable in designing new products that no one manager may have thought of individually.

internal task forces: Groups that serve as bridges that forge stronger interrelationships among divisions in an organization.

NEC of Japan uses many corporate-sponsored product-planning committees and forums to identify core technologies that could serve as the basis for building systemwide interrelationships. It also uses both off line integrators and product forums to encourage cooperation between businesses. Off-line integrators play an essential role in reconciling the disparate needs of many businesses on a daily basis. From a corporate perspective, the purpose of numerous NEC product and technology development committees is to identify new sources of potential interrelationships. These NEC committees investigate, for example, how new semiconductor-based technologies can be applied across computers, communications, and consumer electronics. NEC's committees show how the innovations of one business unit can be used to fertilize new products and markets in other divisions. They also try to convince divisional managers of the merits of sharing resources and ideas, and of the benefit they can derive from innovations from other parts of the company.

While off-line coordinators and internal task forces are used in many types of companies, they can be particularly helpful whenever a high level of coordination among functions, divisions, or business units is desired. They are particularly suitable when outright consolidation of existing divisions and/or business units is unwarranted because opportunities for cooperation are too few to warrant full-scale consolidation or when combined entities would be too large for effective supervision. Off-line coordinators and internal task forces offer ways to foster cooperation without drastically altering the firm's divisional structure. Extensive use of off-line coordinators will tilt a company's organization toward the left of the continuum shown in Exhibit 12-1; conversely, general avoidance of using such coordinators will tilt it toward the right.

Reward and Performance Measurement Systems

Hierarchy-based reward systems, with their emphasis on close superior–subordinate relationships, work well to promote cooperation and interrelationships among subunits.[4] Recall that hierarchy-based systems use informed subjective criteria and judgment to evaluate performance. Qualitative and quantitative performance metrics are used. Oftentimes, division managers are evaluated according to both corporate, systemwide measures of performance and the performance of their own subunits.

On the other hand, performance-based reward systems facilitate high divisional autonomy. Recall that performance-based systems focus predominantly on objective, narrowly defined measures of output and results. Bonuses and promotions are based on achievement of individual divisions, with little attention paid to subjective factors, such as cooperation across subunits. Many attributes of performance-based reward systems were in place at 3M during its earlier years when the company intentionally placed a premium on individual achievement and creativity.

Shared Values and Corporate Culture

Shared values and corporate cultures that cherish a sense of corporate-wide feeling and belonging encourage systemwide cooperation and building of interrelationships. Companies such as Motorola, IBM, and Unilever teach and promote values that orient managers to think of the company's larger interests before those of their divisions. This emphasis on the overall company makes identifying and building useful interrelationships an easier task.

On the other hand, values that cherish individual initiative and strong independence foster divisional autonomy. At companies such as Johnson & Johnson (J&J) and PepsiCo, values based on risk taking and initiative spur competition among divisions, regions, and product brands. Systemwide cooperation is not considered nearly as critical as local initiative to build and sustain competitive advantage. J&J allows its fifty-plus business units to cultivate distinctly separate cultures. This autonomy fosters strong initiative and risk taking at the divisional level.

Managerial Rotation among Business Units

The degree to which firms actively rotate their managers across business units may also influence the cooperation/autonomy balance.[5] Transfer of managers throughout the company can instill an appreciation for systemwide cooperation and thinking. Managers who serve in different SBUs or divisions throughout their careers are better able to understand and build interrelationships. On the other hand, firms that keep their managers and personnel in the same business unit or division for long periods foster personal commitment and loyalty to the division, as opposed to the company. Managers then feel fewer obligations to share resources or ideas with their counterparts in the company, especially if managers are competing against each other for promotions and rewards.

Thus, firms can use many different organization design practices to promote cooperation or autonomy. The way a firm uses such practices will position it somewhere along the continuum shown in Exhibit 12-1.

Factors Promoting Closer Cooperation among Business Units

A high level of interdivisional cooperation is necessary to identify and to build systemwide, corporate-level interrelationships. This cooperation is particularly important for firms that have a distinctive competence, technology, or skill that spans multiple business units. Numerous developments can increase the need for such cooperation. Among the more important are (1) changes in the way customers use products, (2) technological convergence, (3) the rise of multipoint competition, (4) reduced emphasis on acquisitions, and (5) increased global expansion activity (see Exhibit 12-2).

Change in Product Usage

Closer divisional coordination is desirable when customers begin to view a firm's products as parts of a larger, integrated system. Consider, for example, the developments

Developments Prompting Need for Greater Coordination among Businesses

EXHIBIT 12-2

- Customers begin using formerly discrete products together in systems.
- Technologies of different products converge.
- Multipoint competition is on the rise.
- Acquisitions play a less important role in diversification.
- Global expansion increases.

now occurring in the broader consumer electronics, computers, communications and entertainment industries. Semiconductors, or powerful computer chips, are now at the heart of many devices that make communications and entertainment possible, especially such products as wireless telephones and video game consoles. For a company such as Sony Corporation, management must ensure that it is able to design and produce key electronic components that will serve to power next-generation consumer electronics and new gadgets. Now, Sony's newest lines of PlayStation 2 and 3 video game consoles incorporate many features that allow users to play DVDs, surf the Internet, and even perform tasks associated with early personal computers. This development means that business units within Sony must now cooperate to share costs, to fund R&D investments jointly, and to design even more futuristic products that bring together the expertise and knowledge from different parts of the company.

In the United States, Hewlett-Packard during the 1980s and 1990s experienced a situation whereby many of its products became more integrated or linked together through a common technology. Customers in industrial, medical, and scientific fields initially used Hewlett-Packard's electronic test and measurement equipment as free-standing units. In other words, electronic measuring instruments were not linked or hooked up to any other product. Now, industrial and medical users incorporate these devices into more complex systems linked by computers, microprocessors, and fully integrated testing and analysis systems. Even newer versions of Hewlett-Packard's products enable customers to harness the power of the Internet to transmit scientific data from one location to another.

Hewlett-Packard's engineering workstations also now serve as the "brains" or "nerve center" for many design and testing activities that used to be performed independently. For example, individual scientists, engineers, and development people in the aerospace industry previously designed new aircraft parts and subassemblies on their own. Some scientists worked in the lab; others worked closer to the factory floor. There was little effort to coordinate their work together, resulting in long delays in project testing and completion. Now, aerospace scientists using H-P's workstations can design, test, and modify their aircraft concepts all at once. This all-in-one capability makes it easier for users of H-P's equipment (firms in the aircraft industries) to cut down their own product development time. For Hewlett-Packard, this development has greatly expanded the need to build interrelationships and increase cooperation among the company's various business units. H-P divisions now need to cooperate on product design (to ensure compatibility of H-P products from separate divisions), component design (to manufacture compatible parts more easily for various H-P subsystems), sales (to enable the company to sell systems rather than individual products), marketing (to ensure proper pricing and advertising), and customer service.

Other industries facing similar transformations in product usage include the machine tool industry, which is becoming increasingly driven by computers and software. During the 1970s, factories used lathes, machine centers, and other tools as stand-alone operations. Stand-alone operations meant that none of the individual work centers were designed to communicate or link up with other parts of the factory. Materials and components moved from one end of the factory to the other with little coordination, other than that provided by human scheduling. Now, the rise of bar-coding methods, machining cells, servomechanics, and automated insertion equipment makes factories highly integrated operations. These techniques make great use of advanced software to help control and streamline operations. For example, computerized tracking systems often control the movement of inventory, work-in-process, and product changeover when goods move from one machining center to another within the factory.

As a consequence, companies in the machine tool industry have been obliged to undertake steps to ensure that their machinery and other tools work in tandem to give the customer a clean, smoothly running "package" of equipment. In fact, many machine tool producers, such as Cincinnati Milacron of the United States and Fanuc of Japan, are now taking steps to ensure that the software programs used to manage their systems are capable of fully linking with those of other suppliers and customers through advanced telecommunications and Internet-based networks.

Technological Convergence

Convergence of once-distinct technologies can also increase the need for subunit cooperation. Consider the recent developments in semiconductors, for example. Many formerly distinct products (cameras, microwave ovens, printers, personal computers, Internet-related appliances, telephones, calculators, and musical instruments) now incorporate powerful semiconductors in their design. These products are thus becoming technologically more similar, since they increasingly share a common core competence or skill. Circuit boards and semiconductor designs used for one product can often be easily modified for incorporation in another product. The growing reliance on these modular electronic components hastens the convergence of numerous products based on a core electronic or chip-based technology.

Recognizing this trend, Casio of Japan has focused on innovating new products based on using microelectronics to develop new controller chips that power its watches, calculators, and musical instruments. Casio watches and calculators often use the same types of liquid-crystal displays and timing mechanisms found in other Casio products, such as flat-screen television sets and video games. As these products embody a greater degree of technological content, Casio has now taken this electronics-based expertise to develop a series of new Internet-driven palm-sized network computer appliances that use a streamlined version of Microsoft's Windows CE program to provide paging and e-mail capabilities to people on the move. This palm-sized personal digital assistant (PDA), known as Cassiopeia, is designed to compete with similar offerings from 3Com, Palm, Handspring, IBM, Sharp, Sony, and other firms seeking to develop new forms of digital wireless communications that are also compatible with personal computers and other network appliances. The high-tech content in all of these products is compelling these firms to innovate and develop new forms of advanced technologies and capabilities to harness new sources of convergence.

In another example, Japanese optical equipment makers Canon and Nikon are using innovative lens and optical-based technologies to design office equipment, color copiers, laser printers, and even ultrasophisticated semiconductor photolithography equipment. Office copiers, cameras, printers, microscopes, semiconductor capital equipment (steppers), and laboratory-based testing equipment all draw on these two companies' extensive experience with precision engineering and manufacturing of lenses, mirrors, small lasers, and other optics-based technologies.

The Otis, Hamilton Sundstrand, Sikorsky, Carrier, and Pratt and Whitney divisions of United Technologies are also experiencing some degree of technological convergence. The elevators, helicopters, air-conditioning units, and building systems produced by these units are making increasing use of new closed-loop electrical designs, hydraulics, sensors, and microprocessor-based control systems. With the introduction and greater use of advanced electronics and control devices in new designs, these products have become "smarter" over time. For example, in many Sikorsky helicopter or Pratt and Whitney jet engines, centrally controlled microprocessors and sensors closely monitor and manage these systems' operations according to weather, altitude, weight load, and other critical factors. In United Technologies' Carrier division, entire buildings are now designed to be "intelligent," meaning that a central building control system handles numerous functions, such as security, heating, air conditioning, fire detection, and sprinkler systems. Building control systems now possess avionics-like technologies, servomechanical control systems, artificial intelligence, and advanced displays similar to those found in commercial and military aircraft. The use of new "smart technologies," such as advanced semiconductors and sensors that warn a customer of a pending mechanical failure helps Carrier develop a reputation for superior customer service. The skills required for Carrier to design and construct an intelligent building control system for its customers come not only from Carrier but also from other divisions, such as Otis and Pratt and Whitney. Otis has mastery of the controls needed to make elevators function smoothly, while Pratt and Whitney and Sikorsky possess the electronics and systems integration/control expertise to make the entire system "smarter" and more responsive. Most recently, in 2001, United Technologies has been pushing through new programs to enhance the company's overall productivity and growth rate. The company has invested significant resources to move into more service-oriented businesses to support its key customers in the aerospace and building controls businesses. In addition, such a move will help United Technologies' earnings become less cyclical over time.[6]

Industry Convergence. In a broader sense, technological convergence has begun to pervade and even redefine the structure of entire industries. Consider, for example, the rapid growth of the Internet that is cutting a wide swath across almost every industry in the United States. The Internet has already begun to link up telecommunications, data networking, and cable television with computers, consumer electronics, interactive television sets, and even PDAs to provide a whole new range of services. These services include on-line retailing, financial services, travel planning, buying a car, and other new capabilities. As the Internet continues to pervade and redefine more industries, companies such as IBM, Intel, Motorola, Yahoo!, AT&T, AOL Time Warner, Viacom, Comcast, Vivendi Universal, Hewlett-Packard, Microsoft, General Electric, Scientific Atlanta, and Walt Disney envision a day when customers can use their hybrid personal computer/television sets as multifunctional devices that enable on-line shopping, communications, interactive television, digital video recording, MP3 jukeboxes, and other features. This future hybrid digital television, and/or set-top box, and/or personal computer is expected to serve as the heart of a series of network appliances that will combine the traditional features of television sets and personal computers with those of telephones, fax machines, and even home security and temperature control systems. Thus, once separate and distinct industries, such as consumer electronics, telecommunications, personal computers, entertainment, and on-line services, are beginning to come together. This means that firms such as AOL Time Warner, IBM, and Microsoft will increasingly need to encourage their business units to cooperate and jointly plan strategies and investments to serve customers from industries that are converging over time.

Design and Engineering. Growing technological applicability of advanced materials, precision engineering, lasers, and semiconductors, to name a few areas, are making it possible for design and development skills to cut across many products and businesses. Many companies are realizing that emerging technologies and core competences can be used to create a wide array of new, previously unforeseen products that utilize similar design skills, creative insights, product development techniques, and process technologies to create systemwide advantage. For example, Hitachi contends that investment in scientific research for advanced materials, lasers, and ultraminiaturized electronics will eventually translate into new core technologies and become distinctive competences for the future. These technologies will serve as the basis for many next-generation products, such as magnetic levitation trains, engineered plastics, exotic synthetic fibers, and new forms of communications and computing gear. These new product design concepts and engineering skills now form the basis for Hitachi's vision of a broad series of distinctive competences across many new technologies. In turn, these technologies are also beginning to shape how products are designed and developed across Hitachi divisions. Thus, Hitachi's emerging distinctive competences are no longer confined to one division but instead are used across many. Consequently, heightened cooperation among SBUs and divisions is important to harness the potential of new technologies that cannot be developed in any one Hitachi SBU or division alone.

Manufacturing Capability. The rise of computer-integrated manufacturing (CIM) and flexible manufacturing systems (FMSs) also hastens technological convergence and the need for interdivisional cooperation.[7] CIM and FMS now make it possible to produce a growing variety of products using the same factory equipment. In other words, factories themselves are becoming "smarter" and more "flexible" by accommodating a higher degree of product variety than they could in the past. The greater use of new information-coding techniques, advanced software, and other computer technologies means that many factories will become much more responsive and capable of faster change to serve new market demands and niches. Over time, companies from a growing number of industries, ranging from plastics to automobile parts and even to textile manufacturers, are using advanced, flexible manufacturing equipment to accelerate product development and to produce products that are sold by other divisions. Because of this development, companies will find it easier to produce a group of related products using the same manufacturing technology and equipment. This manufacturing-driven source of convergence makes sharing and interdivisional cooperation essential to building corporate-wide economies of scale in key manufacturing-based, value-adding activities.[8]

The Rise of Multipoint Competition

Many firms are competing not only with individual products but with entire lines of business. This development is known as multipoint competition.[9] Multipoint competition forces a company to attack and defend along its entire product line, rather than to fight for individual market positions separately. In other words, multipoint competition occurs when companies commit their entire product line to attack or defend against other competitors with similar market positions. Multipoint competition is not product versus product, but rather groups of products versus groups of products. A firm's entire array of businesses is deployed to keep a competitor off balance.

An example of multipoint competition is the series of ongoing battles between H. J. Heinz and Stouffer Foods in the frozen foods and microwave dinner entrées segments. Each company attempts to periodically outflank and destabilize the other. Multipoint competition is best described as punch and counterpunch along an entire front or market. For example, Heinz will often lower the price on its Weight Watchers frozen foods products to gain additional market share and penetration from Stouffer Foods' microwave dinner entrées. In response, Stouffer counters Heinz's thrust with its own riposte in prepared foods, an attack focused directly on Heinz's well-entrenched position in such ready-to-use foods as ketchup, sauces, and dry-food preparations. Thus, both H. J. Heinz and Stouffer Foods use multipoint competition to engage in a series of "outflanking" attacks, where a thrust into a competitor's product line causes a competitor to deliver a counterpunch elsewhere. Multipoint competition is becoming common in many consumer goods and financial services industries. It is especially prevalent in foods and personal care products, where many companies have sizable market shares across families of products. Procter & Gamble, Colgate-Palmolive, and Johnson & Johnson all practice multipoint competition against each other along such products as disposable diapers, toothpastes, mouthwashes, personal care items, and lotions. Firms engaged in such competition need close cooperation among their business units.

The evolution of British conglomerate EMI over the past twenty years reveals the difficulty of battling competitors who are skilled in multipoint competition. EMI in the 1970s was a leading innovator of the CAT scanner, a computerized X-ray machine that could provide three-dimensional images of the human body. Yet, EMI's dominant business at the time was music, entertainment, and defense-oriented electronics. Although EMI's CAT scanner was a product leader for several years, eventually other companies such as General Electric, Toshiba, and Philips Electronics were able to displace EMI from the business. These companies enjoyed technological, production, and distribution-based interrelationships among their businesses that enabled them to employ multipoint competition strategies against EMI's more limited range of medical equipment offerings. Over time, GE, Toshiba, and Philips were able to outflank and outmaneuver EMI in later generations of medical equipment. EMI was unable to develop and implement the multipoint competition strategy needed to compete in the medical equipment industry. By 1989, EMI had sold off most of its defense electronics, medical equipment, and other technology-intensive businesses to General Electric and other European and Japanese firms. EMI's senior management concluded that the company could not compete effectively in these global businesses that depended heavily on fostering close interrelationships among divisions and SBUs. Currently, EMI's core businesses are situated solely in the music and entertainment industries. The transformation of EMI is continuing as the company considers strategic options that may include divesting itself of other peripheral businesses. As recently as January 2001, EMI almost merged with the Warner Music unit of AOL Time Warner to create a global media and music entertainment juggernaut. However, European regulators did not permit the merger to proceed because of antitrust concerns. Another merger attempt with Germany's Bertelsmann AG went awry in May 2001 as well. Still, many analysts believe that EMI's senior management remains prepared to sell the entire company to another entertainment or media company for the right price.[10]

Reduced Emphasis on Acquisitions

A firm that acquires new businesses to enlarge the scope of its operations will normally need to give a high level of autonomy to its divisions. Because many conglomerate firms (Textron, Litton, Allegheny Teledyne, Tyco International, Tenneco) use acquisitions to reshuffle their mix of businesses periodically, they give managers of individual businesses the leeway they need to run their own operations in the manner they see fit. Also, high levels of autonomy are needed to retain acquired managers. On the other hand, if a firm later shifts to internal development as the primary means of entry into new areas, the need for high levels of divisional autonomy is reduced. As the corporate focus shifts to internal development of new businesses, then cooperation becomes crucial in building the interrelationships that sustain competitive advantage.

During the 1980s, a growing amount of corporate diversification activity occurred by way of internal development of new products and technologies. This trend toward related diversification has obliged many firms to increase cooperation among SBUs and divisions. Consider conglomerates that were prevalent during the 1970s. Such firms began their existence as acquirers of unrelated businesses. Senior management of these companies therefore initially offered divisions high levels of autonomy. Many of these firms eventually discovered that the benefits of unrelated diversification were insufficient to offset the attendant costs. (See Chapter 7 for a full discussion of this trade-off.) With rising capital costs and the possible prevalence of a "conglomerate discount" weighing on their stock prices, a number of these firms eventually sold off their peripheral and poorly performing businesses and began pursuing a more related diversification strategy. This shift strategy has compelled them to implement a corresponding shift in management practices that foster higher levels of interdivisional cooperation.

The evolution of earlier conglomerate firm Gulf and Western into entertainment giant Viacom is a case in point. In 1980, it owned a wide array of businesses, including apparel, typewriters, gas stations, machinery, financial services, and chemical products. During the late 1980s, Gulf and Western sold off many of these businesses to focus primarily on its publishing (Simon and Schuster) and filmmaking operations (Paramount Productions). It even changed its name to Paramount Communications to reflect this sharply redefined corporate focus on entertainment, before it merged with Viacom, a leading television syndication company. Viacom, the current entity, is now investing heavily to secure a leading position in the fiercely competitive entertainment industry. It is balancing both internal development (the creation of new blockbuster movies through Paramount Pictures) and carefully focused external acquisitions in its corporate strategy. Most recently, Viacom acquired CBS Corporation to secure another outlet for its content production and distribution-based strategy. Viacom is probably well known to consumers through its various cable television offerings such as Nickelodeon, Showtime, and MTV. This new focus also gives Viacom a better opportunity to exploit emerging technological convergences provided by new multimedia, publishing, and Internet-driven technologies (interactive television, online retail services, information retrieval services, electronic commerce, pay-per-view television). These developments have obliged Viacom to shift the balance toward greater cooperation as it strives to become an important player in creating and delivering "content" for the evolving entertainment, and even broader multimedia industry.[11]

Even nonconglomerate firms continue to shed divisions or activities that no longer fit well with their core businesses. Many companies in the packaged foods industry have realigned their operations to enhance their corporate focus. Companies such as General Mills, ConAgra, and Hershey Foods have sold off less related businesses to allocate more resources for internal growth. At one point in its history, for example, General Mills owned a variety of businesses, including some in the chemical, fashion, jewelry, toy, and retailing industries. General Mills at one point even owned restaurant chains, such as The Olive Garden and Red Lobster. However, during the 1980s and 1990s, General Mills spun off many of these assets to concentrate more on its food-related businesses. The company realized that competing in the restaurant business (with its high personal service orientation) required core competences unrelated to those used in making breakfast cereals (with its focus on packaging, advertising, retail distribution, and new product development). Enduring synergies between the two businesses were illusionary. General Mills had struggled unsuccessfully to blend the packaged food culture with the restaurant culture.[12] With its current emphasis on internal development rather than acquisitions, General Mills is encouraging more cooperation among its subunits.

Increased Global Expansion Activity

Yet another development that has caused many large firms to seek greater divisional cooperation is increased global expansion activity. Whether the expansion occurs through global or through multidomestic strategies, corporate pursuit of growth abroad will tend to increase the need for communication and cooperation across business units. This need will be particularly pressing for those firms pursuing global strategies involving high levels of cross-subsidization. Recall that firms with global strategies use cross-subsidization to seek fast market presence and to destabilize other global competitors in contested markets. Effective pursuit of cross-subsidization tactics often requires close coordination and cooperation across divisional lines to attain scale economies and shared learning.

When compared with global strategies, multidomestic strategies generally need more autonomy at divisional and subsidiary levels to develop competitive advantage in local end markets. High levels of autonomy are needed to develop the fast response capabilities of subsidiaries serving diverse markets. Nevertheless, firms pursuing multidomestic strategies will find that some level of cooperation will be necessary across products and businesses, even those that share no tangible interrelationships, such as production or R&D. For companies such as Coca-Cola, Procter & Gamble, Henkel, Unilever, Anheuser-Busch, and McDonald's, a multidomestic strategy still depends on cultivating and projecting a well-defined corporate image. This image is an intangible asset, which becomes a vehicle that eases entry into new markets. Thus, policies concerning product and service quality, training procedures, and product development practices require some degree of coordination and cooperation across subsidiaries and businesses.

Factors Promoting Greater Unit Autonomy

Other developments can oblige a firm to move toward the right of the continuum shown in Exhibit 12-1 to increase divisional autonomy rather than cooperation. Developments frequently necessitating a shift in this direction are (1) increased acquisition activity, (2) the need to avert creeping bureaucratization, and (3) environmental turbulence (see Exhibit 12-3).

Developments Prompting Need for Greater Subunit Autonomy

EXHIBIT 12-3

- Acquisition activity increases.
- Creeping bureaucratization endangers firm's ability to respond to market and industry changes.
- Environmental turbulence requires faster response time.

Increased Acquisition Activity

If a firm with a highly cooperative organization decides to increase acquisition activity, it will generally need to shift its organization toward greater autonomy. This adjustment helps create an internal environment that is more compatible with the needs of managers of acquired businesses. Divisional autonomy is needed to ensure that creativity, knowledge, management practices, and a distinctive culture are not suffocated from excessive efforts to induce cooperation right after acquisition. Excessive emphasis on a cooperative mode can also alienate acquired managers, resulting in demoralization and desertions.

For example, the British firm Hanson PLC engaged in a wide array of acquisitions in the United States during the late 1980s. It acquired U.S. companies that produce industrial materials, such as brick makers, chemical firms, lumber firms, and cement producers. To keep its various acquired business units vibrant and competitive, Hanson gives high levels of autonomy to its U.S. managers. Hanson believes that excessive corporate interference will destroy the individual initiative of its acquired units to pursue opportunities in their own respective markets. In addition, few technological or production-based interrelationships exist between Hanson's various businesses.

Sony's purchase of Columbia Pictures and Matsushita Electric's acquisition of MCA Universal Film studios in California are well-publicized accounts of Japanese electronics giants acquiring entertainment firms in the United States during the late 1980s. Both Sony and Matsushita felt they needed to acquire filmmaking studios in the United States to bolster their presence in the increasingly global entertainment industry. Yet, neither Sony nor Matsushita Electric really possesses any knowledge or skills directly applicable to producing popular and successful films. For both Japanese giants, few real opportunities to build and manage interrelationships between the film and the electronics business were available. Nevertheless, both Sony and Matsushita believed that films and television shows would form the "software" that could be shown on Japanese-made televisions and VCRs for global distribution and provide the basis for future content that would flow along new telecommunications networks.

To ensure that both Columbia Pictures and MCA continue to produce blockbuster movie hits, Sony and Matsushita gradually delegated all key decision-making processes concerning filmmaking and entertainment to their U.S. affiliates. Filmmaking represents a completely unique set of operating procedures, cultures, and distinctive competences, which is unlike the set used in making consumer electronics. Filmmaking is personality driven and relationships oriented, while consumer electronics depends on engineering and manufacturing skills. Japanese executives believe they can benefit more from their acquisitions by not interfering in the day-to-day and even month-to-month decision making of their U.S. operations. By playing more of an investor role than an active manager role, Sony and Matsushita feel they will be better able to retain the U.S. creative talent necessary for future successful movies and development of entertainment ideas. Attempting to force tangible interrelationships on their U.S. filmmaking affiliates would ultimately destroy the value of their acquisitions.[13] Even with a high degree of managerial distance/autonomy between the electronics side of each firm and the acquired filmmaking units, both Sony and Matsushita lost considerable sums of money in attempting to integrate (however carefully) the two parts of the company. In November 1994, Sony took a massive $3 billion write-off on its purchase of Columbia Pictures. In April 1995, Matsushita decided that its ownership of

MCA Universal was no longer economically justified. The company sold 80 percent of MCA Universal to Seagram, a leading distillery and beverage producer that had big ambitions to enter the entertainment industry. Seagram also found that managing such complex businesses as entertainment, record labels, and film production required very different skills, competences, and mind-sets than those needed for its traditional beverages and distilled liquor businesses. Seagram, in turn, finalized a deal to sell all of its entertainment and record label music assets (e.g., Universal Music, PolyGram Records) in 2000 to Vivendi, a French company that also has major aspirations to expand in the entertainment industry.

Need to Avert Creeping Bureaucratization

As firms grow and hire more employees, many add intermediate managerial layers between corporate and operating levels. They also increase the number of rules and reporting procedures affecting budget requests for divisional and subunit activities. As a result of these changes, proposals must pass through an increasing number of organizational levels before being approved. They must also satisfy a greater number of constituents. In addition, approval from a top management group that is further removed from the action is less certain. All too often, these added requirements interfere with effective decision making, leading to decisions that poorly reflect the competitive realities of market changes. Even when sound decisions are produced, the time needed to reach them is often excessive, which, in turn, causes delays in instituting new technology, introducing new products, and exploiting new markets.

One common solution to this problem is to increase subunit autonomy. Giving divisions greater authority to make decisions affecting their businesses speeds up the decision-making process. It avoids the necessity of approving decisions at many higher levels. Autonomy puts decision making in the hands of individuals closest to the action. Increased autonomy thus raises the likelihood that decisions will reflect the true realities of the environment that surrounds the business. Conversely, excessively tight or interwoven interrelationships among divisions may ultimately slow down their response time as cumbersome procedures, rules, and practices burden divisional management.

All of the big U.S. automakers—General Motors, Ford, and DaimlerChrysler—have experienced the problem of cumbersome procedures. During the 1970s, strong domestic market conditions facilitated the creation of new layers of management and corporate staffs. These thick layers of management unfortunately insulated senior management from the desires of consumers who wanted better and smaller cars during the latter part of that decade. Not until the late 1980s did the Big Three automakers get serious about restructuring their operations to give their product managers more autonomy and leeway in making decisions about cars that better suited consumers' tastes.

In the late 1980s, Alcoa also attempted to delegate more decisions to its operating managers. This giant aluminum and metals processing company once had more than five layers of corporate management review every decision made by its divisions. However, general managers of Alcoa's twenty-plus units now report directly to the CEO without having to go through group- and sector-level executives. Division managers now have direct spending authority up to $5 million, with all higher funding requests sent directly to the CEO. The objective of Alcoa's internal restructuring was to promote individual initiative and faster response and decision making at all levels of the company.

In the late 1990s, Royal Dutch Shell Group engaged in a worldwide restructuring designed to make itself more agile and nimble in the wake of the consolidating global petroleum industry. In the past, each of Shell's five operating divisions (exploration and production, oil products, natural gas, coal, and chemicals) operated under several senior managers who in turn reported to a corporate committee that had ultimate decision-making power. Managing each of these five businesses through a complicated, consensus-oriented committee structure made it difficult for Shell to make decisions quickly and to isolate easily the performance of each business unit. With this restructuring, each business unit will be managed by its own CEO who in turn will be responsible for his or her own business performance. Shell's senior management wants to remove the committee structure so that information and decisions can be more quickly felt within each organization.[14]

Environmental Turbulence and Change

Growing bureaucratization creates special challenges for firms operating in industries experiencing rapid environmental change. Their businesses must make quick decisions or lose out to more nimble competitors, particularly in industries that appear to be fragmenting or "disaggregating" into smaller segments or niches. The need for divisional autonomy is then particularly strong, even when the firm has built close interrelationships across divisions in an earlier period.

Texas Instruments (TI) experienced this need in the mid-1990s. More agile and leaner Japanese and Korean competitors eroded large portions of TI's market share and technological leadership in memory chips. At an industry level, Japanese and Korean producers such as Hitachi, Toshiba, NEC, Mitsubishi Electric, and Samsung Electronics were able to outproduce TI and other U.S. firms in successive generations of standardized memory chips that are the basis for many consumer electronics, personal computers, and office equipment products. In addition, the broader semiconductor industry showed signs of becoming more turbulent and fragmented, as large U.S. manufacturers shifted their production emphasis away from making standardized memory chips to more profitable customized microprocessors, analog and mixed signal chips, controller chips, and application-specific (ASIC) integrated circuits. Customized microprocessors, in particular digital signal processors, were becoming more profitable than standardized memory chips for many U.S. firms, since U.S. design and product innovation skills were significantly better than that of their Japanese and Korean counterparts. Each of these separate lines of products, such as ASICs and digital signal processors (DSPs), demands fast innovation and speedy development time to respond to new market opportunities to use these chips. Fast response and agility have become as important as production-based interrelationships to compete in various semiconductor segments and niches that are becoming more customer-specific and targeted. In response to the need for faster responsiveness, Texas Instruments sold off its memory chip division to Micron Technology, and TI is now concentrating its efforts on developing and dominating the DSP chip market, as well as strengthening its position in the analog chip segment. DSP chips are becoming increasingly important components for use in digital wireless phones, telecommunications, Internet appliances, consumer electronics, automotive, and other critical applications. Competitive advantage in the DSP chip market requires a fast innovation and response capability that can quickly shift according to specific customer needs.

Many other developments can increase the rate of environmental change, thereby augmenting the need for division autonomy. For example, vigorous new rivals may enter a market. Rivals may increase or concentrate their innovative effort to redefine the industry (e.g., new restaurant concepts or software designs). New technologies may emerge to change products and processes (e.g., the way plastic syringes have replaced glass syringes in the medical equipment business). Government regulations limiting competition may be relaxed, thus accelerating entry and the creation of new market segments (e.g., mutual funds and cash management accounts in the financial services industry, or the creation of competitive local access providers in the newly deregulated telecommunications industry). Developments such as these are now occurring in the United States in the financial services, electric utilities, health care, and telecommunications industries. They raise competitive pressure and require faster decision making, thereby increasing the need for subunit autonomy. Firms experiencing such developments must adapt by increasing the autonomy they accord their subunits. In the restaurant and snack food industries, for example, firms are increasingly jockeying for even smaller market niches. The rise of niches within niches (e.g., ethnic foods, regional taste differences, new product derivatives and substitutes) makes it difficult for long-standing firms to continue to operate in a centralized manner as they did in the past. As a result, the Frito-Lay unit of PepsiCo is given free rein to experiment with its snack food offerings. Frito-Lay managers can experiment with new product concepts, such as the type of corn, tortilla, and potato chips marketed in specific regions of the United States. Imposing interrelationships across PepsiCo's businesses would undermine the fast response and individual initiative needed to compete in the fast-changing snack food and beverage industries.

Many of IBM's recent restructuring moves reflect the company's need for greater flexibility and faster response. Its recent management under CEO Louis Gertsner

(1993–2002) pursues the philosophy that business units should possess more autonomy to enter new markets and learn new technologies without having to go through a lengthy review process at corporate headquarters. Already, IBM's microelectronics, personal computer, storage devices, multimedia, Internet commerce, network systems, software, and computer peripheral businesses are acting much more like independent businesses that are free to respond to price cuts and rival new product ideas without clearing decisions with IBM's executive committee. This autonomy helps breathe new life into the various IBM divisions and thus invigorates faster response to the customer's needs.

Even software giant Microsoft is not immune from the need to stay nimble and agile in the wake of new developments in the software, Internet, and entertainment industries. Microsoft is facing a growing array of new competitors seeking to displace its Windows-based operating system from personal computers and network servers. Even more dangerous to Microsoft is the belief that new forms of software will be made free over the Internet, such as the new Linux operating system and different variants of Sun Microsystems' Java programming language. At the same time, Microsoft feels it needs to be as agile as many Internet portal companies (e.g., Yahoo!, AOL Time Warner, EarthLink) to become a viable player in the world of digital media and entertainment. To ensure that Microsoft remains vigilant and agile to respond to new competitors' moves, the company announced in April 1999 a broad restructuring plan that would divide the company into five separate business units, each of which would enable its managers and technical staff to become more autonomous and responsive to a specific group of customer needs. In many ways, this reorganization was badly needed at a time when Microsoft has grown so fast and so big that it became difficult to manage a variety of different fast-changing customer needs quickly. These five business units include the business and enterprise division, the developer group, business productivity group, the consumer and e-commerce group, and a unit dedicated to promoting new versions of Windows for consumer electronics applications. Each of these new businesses will also be given broad leeway to form alliances with other companies to help deflect Microsoft's growing array of competitors in its core software, Internet and emerging digital media businesses.

As Microsoft's realignment takes shape, some patterns appear to be emerging. Each of the divisions is organized not only in response to specific customer needs but also to help Microsoft gain better focus and agility in dealing with a particular set of competitors who are also targeting the same market segment. For example, the business and enterprise division is designed to directly confront challenges by Sun Microsystems' Java programming language and the emerging Linux operating system software. Thus, it would not be surprising to see this unit engage in a number of alliances with other software developers in an effort to slow down the growth of Java in corporate and consumer applications. The business productivity unit will focus on developing newer versions of Office 97 and 2000 software that are needed by corporate customers and their knowledge workers. This unit also is charged with developing new software that will blunt the impact of IBM's newest versions of Lotus Notes and Domino intranet software. Finally, the new consumer and commerce group is empowered to take on the Internet portals, such as Yahoo! and AOL Time Warner, to promote the economic viability of Microsoft's own Internet strategy based on the Microsoft Network (MSN). Microsoft is also leading a new software development effort known as Hailstorm. This project is designed to help Microsoft strengthen its position in the Internet access and service businesses by tying its Windows and other platforms with easy-to-use advanced browsers and other 'Net-driven technologies. Already, we are beginning to see Microsoft form a broad array of alliances with entertainment, telecommunications, cable, broadcasting, and digital media companies to sustain the viability of its new Internet-based content and distribution efforts.

Technology Fusion

An increasing number of companies, particularly Japanese, are beginning to invest in both older and new technologies to build new forms of competitive advantage. When companies seek to combine existing and emerging technologies to develop previously unforeseen products, they attempt to achieve "technology fusion." **Technology fusion** is the blending, or fusing together, of many sources of technology to create new, higher-order products.[15] The basis of technology fusion is that new products are not derived from a single source of technology but rather from multiple sources. Companies engaged in technology fusion must be particularly nimble in shifting the balance of cooperation and autonomy in a timely way.

technology fusion: The blending, or fusing together, of many sources of technology to create new, higher-order products.

Yet, it is not only Japanese companies that have led major efforts to build competitive advantage based on technology fusion. In fact, 3M already was a pioneer in developing its own variation of technology fusion as far back as fifty years ago. 3M's original skills in developing sandpaper eventually led the way to conceiving such products as masking tape, Scotch tape, and other related products. Together, all of these initiatives resulted in 3M's accumulation of deep skills and knowledge in the fields of coatings and abrasives. From these original two core technologies, 3M eventually entered into such seemingly unrelated products as ribbons, surgical masks, weather-stripping products, reflective lighting panels, advanced membranes, and even thin-film coatings used for electronic applications. By 2000, 3M has continued to invest in and develop a broad array of core technologies (including such new areas as surfactants, electronic filaments, filters) that are at the heart of many new products. Some of 3M's newest products include transdermal patches (used to slowly absorb medications into the human skin over an extended period), as well as optical coatings that are essential to the functioning of optical fiber telecommunication networks. Thus, 3M has been and remains a leader in developing and "fusing" a broad array of core technologies (both advanced and mature) to create a series of entirely new lines of products and businesses.

Developing Advanced, Hybrid Core Technologies

In the 1990s, however, Japanese companies had made significant bets on attempting to develop technology fusion–based strategies to enter new markets. Consider, for example, the case of Hitachi. Hitachi has invested heavily in such cutting-edge technologies as biotechnology, artificial intelligence, advanced materials, semiconductors, and lasers. Hitachi also protects and uses its older technologies based on power transmission and industrial equipment applications. Each of these technologies, both cutting-edge and mature, has considerable potential on its own to produce a wide array of products. On the other hand, if scientists at Hitachi can fuse together several different technologies (e.g., biotechnology with semiconductors), then it may be possible to produce a breakthrough product that combines ingredients from both types of expertise. Fusing biotechnology with semiconductors may produce a customized, genetically engineered device that can accelerate genetic mapping of the human body and other living organisms. The combination of biotechnology with advanced materials might produce other kinds of breakthroughs. Engineers could conceivably combine biotechnology techniques with new advanced composites to produce a flexible metal/composite alloy that resists rust, corrosion, and extreme heat. Hitachi executives believe the company must continue investing in a wide array of existing and new technologies to attain such technology fusion. These technologies, while appearing to be completely unrelated to one another, may actually lend themselves to productive combinations that were previously unforeseen. This process requires a delicate mixture of creativity and sustained investment in R&D and other technology-intensive activities.

Numerous Japanese companies, in particular, are engaging in technology fusion strategies. For example, companies such as Matsushita, NEC, Fanuc, Toshiba, and Mitsubishi are designing new products based on a technological concept known as mechatronics. **Mechatronics** refers to the fusion of precision, mechanical engineering skills with microelectronics. One goal of mechatronics is to produce micromotors and robots small enough to fit within human blood vessels. These micromotor-powered robots can then be inserted into the human body to help control bleeding or to remove plaque from arteries. On a larger scale, mechatronics is a fused technology that may produce new generations of

mechatronics: Refers to the fusion of precision, mechanical engineering skills with microelectronics.

robots that can wash windows on skyscrapers, scrape rust and barnacles off ships, remove toxic waste materials from hazardous or contaminated sites, and even engage in deep-sea, ocean-based mining or tunneling.

Olympus Optical Company of Japan is engaging in technology fusion to develop products for the next millennium. Olympus is best known to most people as a producer of quality cameras and laboratory equipment. Olympus Optical is investing heavily in seven key areas of technology: optics, information processing, microelectronics, advanced materials, medical equipment technology, precision engineering, and biotechnology. Olympus seeks to combine and complement these seven technologies in varying ways to devise entirely new, previously unforeseen products. For example, the precision engineering skills used to build the self-focusing, zoom lens in Olympus's popular 35mm SLR cameras are now envisioned for use in advanced microsurgery tools. The technology currently used in a camera's zoom lens that enables it to focus on a distant object can be applied to enable a doctor to locate and remove hard-to-reach damaged tissues within the human body. This technique, known as *minimally invasive laparoscopic surgery*, helps the patient recover faster without the trauma of traditional open-wound surgery. Olympus now works with the Ethicon Endo-Surgery Division of Johnson & Johnson in developing a new generation of microsurgery tools. These advanced microsurgery tools are already helping women avoid the pain and agony of undergoing conventional biopsies to detect potentially early stage breast diseases. On another front, Olympus seeks to combine information processing and digital compression technologies with advanced optics to create new head-mounted displays, which are the beginning of products based on virtual reality. These innovative products are likely to be widely used for entertainment, industrial design, simulation training, interior decoration, and medical applications by the end of the decade. In all of these examples, Olympus is pursuing technology fusion to blend existing and emerging technologies to create advanced hybrid products.

Although Japanese companies have aggressively pursued strategies to exploit technology fusion, many U.S., European, and Korean companies also have the ingredients necessary to undertake their own versions of technology fusion. For example, Motorola has combined wireless technologies with semiconductors to produce cellular phones. In another example, several small U.S. biotechnology companies are experimenting with designing integrated circuits based on enzymes rather than silicon materials. By using limitless combinations of amino acids to store data, these small U.S. firms are pushing the scientific frontier forward in the field of nanoelectronics, or nanotechnology. Nanoelectronics attempts to achieve the harnessing of electrical current at an even more miniaturized level than microelectronics; it is based on developing new forms of current transmission using scientific disciplines at the chemical, molecular, enzymatic, or protein level. Nanoelectronic devices may even displace the use of silicon-based semiconductors in the future; they are seen as especially important tools to help design ultratiny medical devices and instruments that can treat diseased arteries and other organs. U.S. scientists have already developed molecular logic circuits that represent a form of "organic transistors."[16] European giants ABB, Philips Electronics, and Siemens also appear to have the broad range of technologies necessary to pursue their own types of technology fusion strategies. For example, Siemens is combining its strengths in factory automation with software to design prototypes of new energy-efficient trains. Korean giant Samsung is attempting to merge semiconductors with video displays to create robots that use advanced vision systems. These robots may then be able to detect minute cracks and flaws in painted surfaces (automobiles) and structures (bridges and concrete beams). All of these combinations represent innovative ways to achieve technological fusion.

Organizational Alignment to Support Technology Fusion

Technology fusion has important implications for managing the balance between cooperation with autonomy (Exhibit 12-4). The development of creative product ideas, experimentation with cutting-edge technologies, and customization of products to markets all require high levels of autonomy. Business units or divisions are often in a better position

Technology Fusion and the Balance between Cooperation and Autonomy

EXHIBIT 12-4

Need for Cooperation ⟷	Need for Autonomy
• Economies of scale	• Creative product ideas
• Shared R&D costs	• Experimentation
• Joint production efforts	• Customization of products
• Tight management of interrelationships	• Understanding needs of local end markets
• Search for internal synergy	• Search for new market opportunities
• Sharing of ideas	• Free thinking

"Fusion" occurs as the company develops and blends new technologies with existing ones to create higher-order products.

to know which products appear to have a higher chance of success in the external market. In turn, however, the development and production of breakthrough products based on combining new and existing technologies requires significant economies of scale, proprietary R&D, and tight management of interrelationships across SBUs, all of which call for increased cooperation. As new products based on the fused technology are developed, a shift back to autonomy is needed to ensure that the new technology is applied effectively to specific markets. Thus, senior management in companies seeking to pursue technology fusion must periodically shift the balance between cooperation and autonomy to encourage actions and behaviors within the organization to accomplish development, production, and marketing most effectively. This task is not an easy one, even for Japanese companies.

3M's highly refined and balanced approach to organization design enabled the company to sustain a very successful technology fusion strategy over many decades. On the one hand, 3M implemented a number of policies designed to promote individual creativity, experimentation, free thinking, and innovation. 3M's reward systems were specifically designed to recognize scientists and other personnel for their willingness to "go against the grain" and take on highly uncertain projects. More important, 3M encouraged its scientists to work on projects of genuine personal interest—going as far as to let scientists use corporate labs and equipment for their own purposes. To promote the fast translation of ideas and concepts into winning products, 3M deliberately kept the size of its product divisions small. In fact, 3M would even carve out new divisions from divisions that had become too large to breathe new life into promising technologies and products under development.

At the same time, however, 3M also instituted a number of corporate policies that were designed to promote the free flow and sharing of knowledge and core technologies among divisions. New product or technological breakthroughs belonged to the entire company. In other words, scientists could freely borrow and use innovations and technologies that other scientists and divisions had developed for products in other parts of the company. Yet, to encourage individual creativity, 3M recognized, rewarded, and promoted those scientists and technical personnel who had a great impact on developing technologies that the entire company could use. In addition, 3M was an early leader in promoting a culture of informal networks where scientists could freely discuss and exchange their ideas. As the company became larger, 3M instituted technology sharing forums where scientists could visit with their counterparts from labs that were increasingly dispersed throughout the nation. 3M's senior management never dismissed the potential of any technology or product idea—even those that proved to be initial failures. New product ideas that proved a failure in one industry could represent an opportunity for growth in a completely different industry. For example, one 3M division's failure to develop an easy-to-use, sticky coating application for an industrial customer led to the creation of the enormously successful Post-It Notes for an entirely different consumer market. By explicitly encouraging the sharing of knowledge and skills, 3M laid the foundation for successful cross-pollination of ideas that are at the basis for technology fusion.

As 3M entered the 1990s, the company felt the underlying tension that accompanied a recent shift towards more cooperation among its many divisions. To this day, 3M remains in a careful "balancing act": the company continues to value the individual and his or her ability to be creative and innovative. Yet, 3M feels enormous pressure to streamline its operations and to achieve economies of scale, particularly in those mature core technologies that initially appear to have little remaining potential for fast growth. While scientists are still given a moderate degree of free rein and even monetary resources to pursue their own interesting projects, 3M has begun to reorganize its manufacturing and marketing functions to attain cost efficiencies and greater corporate productivity. Accordingly, reward systems at 3M have also shifted towards evaluating divisions on how well they are able to cooperate in seeking greater efficiencies in key activities that are shared across units. Under its most recent CEO, W. Jack McNerney (a veteran executive from General Electric), the company is pushing forward the development of new technologies, especially those with medical and telecom applications. At the same time, 3M is investigating how to better utilize its vast wealth of patents, proprietary knowledge and technologies to resuscitate growth in its more traditional, mature markets. There is little doubt that the new CEO will likely set high financial benchmarks for all of 3M's divisions to reach. Many analysts believe that McNerney will call for a thorough evaluation of the competitiveness of each 3M division. Whether 3M will shift back to an organizational posture that promotes greater unit autonomy remains an open question for the company's immediate future.

The issue of finding the right alignment to support technology fusion is no less difficult for Japanese companies. Consider again the case of Hitachi. On the one hand, senior management must give Hitachi's business units enough latitude to develop their own product ideas and insights based on their own experience. This objective calls for divisional autonomy. On the other hand, Hitachi's business units must always think of how to achieve internal sources of synergy with other divisions. This objective requires cooperation to build interrelationships. Divisional managers must constantly balance the need for creativity and autonomy in their own operations with the corporate goal of building technology-driven interrelationships systemwide. Hitachi must also balance a corporate culture that encourages free thinking and individuality with another set of norms that constrains business units from going too far on their own. This ongoing tension between cooperation and autonomy even extends to Hitachi's R&D labs and manufacturing functions. Scientists are free to investigate any technological breakthrough or idea that comes to mind, but they must share their ideas and results with scientists from other parts of the company. Thus, technology fusion exacts a high organizational cost, requiring a firm to engage in a constant "balancing act" between cooperation and autonomy.

The Problem of Internal Resistance

A minor shift in the balance or alignment between cooperation and autonomy can often be achieved without a great deal of organizational disruption. However, a major shift of this kind is much more difficult to bring about. Such a change can have a traumatic effect on members of an organization, causing breaks in long-standing routines and personal relationships, erosion of power bases, eclipsed status, and even the elimination of jobs. Affected individuals will naturally resist changes leading to these outcomes. This resistance can impede (even sabotage) an effort to achieve the kind of shift discussed here. Top managers interested in bringing about a shift from cooperation to autonomy or vice versa need to identify likely resistance and take steps to deal with it. We first consider the likely sources of resistance to such shifts (see Exhibit 12-5 for a summary) and then examine measures to deal with this kind of resistance.

Reactions to Shifts in Cooperation versus Autonomy EXHIBIT 12-5

Reaction	Support	Opposition
Shift to cooperation	Corporate managers	Subunit managers
Shift to autonomy	Subunit managers	Corporate managers

Resistance to Greater Cooperation

A shift in organization design practices toward the left of the continuum shown in Exhibit 12-1 reduces divisional autonomy. Divisional managers will therefore generally resist it. The strength of their resistance will vary across divisions. Stronger subunits will generally oppose such a shift as best as they can. In most situations, they have the least to gain from increased cooperation. Weaker subunits sometimes are more favorably disposed, since increased cooperation may enable them to obtain more help from powerful units. Corporate staffs are likely to support changes to enhance cooperation. They then become referees of conflicts between subunits, and their stature will grow as emphasis on cooperation increases.

Resistance to Greater Autonomy

Divisional managers will generally applaud a shift in organization design practices toward the right of the continuum shown in Exhibit 12-1. Autonomy increases their independence and latitude of operation. Some weaker subunits may object to such a move, fearing it will relieve pressure on stronger units to assist them and will compel them to compete on their own. Corporate staff personnel will also generally oppose a shift in this direction, fearing it will undermine their influence over a company's operations. Moreover, moves toward greater autonomy are often a harbinger of major corporate staff cuts.

Dealing with Resistance to Change

In practice, significant resistance to shifts in an organization's alignment between cooperation and autonomy is common. If not effectively countered, resistance can delay and even erode the firm's competitive advantage as its environment changes. At the same time, a major shift in the balance between cooperation and autonomy also presents an opportunity for a firm to rethink its way of doing things. Environmental turbulence and the emergence of new technologies can become valuable catalysts that stimulate learning and new management practices. They force corporate managers to undertake a series of overlapping steps that include sensing a need for change, building awareness of this need, fostering debate, creating consensus, assigning responsibility, and allocating resources. These steps are part of a process designed to encourage people initially opposed to change to embrace a new arrangement. We will examine these and other related issues in the next chapter.

Ethical Dimension

Clearly, each company must find its own proper balance between cooperation and autonomy needed to sustain competitive advantage. Building and managing interrelationships that span a firm's divisions or business units is a task that demands considerable judgment from senior management. Encouraging divisions that were once highly autonomous to cooperate and build interrelationships with each other requires considerable persuasion and negotiation. Convincing divisions accustomed to high levels of cooperation to act more like free-standing units when bureaucracy or environmental turbulence sets in can be equally difficult. In many cases, senior management must intervene directly to shift the balance between cooperation and autonomy to a new equilibrium. This kind of intervention often raises difficult ethical questions.

Consider the dilemma that now confronts IBM as it tries to induce greater divisional autonomy among its many technology-based businesses. IBM has long been regarded as a model company that could develop new generations of "blue-sky" technologies and wildly successful products. In recent years, however, IBM has faced a combination of creeping bureaucracy, fragmentation of the computer industry, and a steady shift away from mainframe computers. Managing highly interwoven relationships among various IBM businesses has become correspondingly less important to the company's competitive success than developing fast responsiveness to new market niches. The rise of new competitors armed with new technologies and products has meant that IBM has had to undertake a series of unpopular layoffs. It has also forced a change in many cherished IBM values. Most recently, CEO Lou Gertsner initiated a redefinition of IBM's core values and organizational design practices. Gertsner wants IBM managers to feel urgency and to adopt a crisis mentality. In his previous management positions at American Express and R. J. Reynolds, Gertsner developed a reputation for being able to slash through corporate red tape and cumbersome bureaucratic procedures in overhauling slow corporate cultures.

Yet, IBM has long been a company that positioned itself toward the far left of the spectrum of Exhibit 12-1. As a leading-edge company, IBM practiced full employment, high wages, and a strong corporate culture that fostered technological leadership. IBM's focus on building strong interrelationships across divisions ultimately led to management by committee. Now, IBM wants to become more responsive to its rapidly changing environment and to instill higher levels of divisional autonomy. The task of doing so continues to challenge new CEO Sam Palmisano and tens of thousands of current IBM people. A marked shift in the balance from cooperation toward autonomy means that divisions must become more accountable for their own profits and losses. While autonomy enhances individual creativity, it also requires people to redefine the way they approach risk. This shift requires new attitudes as IBM begins to emphasize strategic alliances (see Chapter 9), entry into emerging businesses (e.g., microelectronics, consumer electronics, multimedia, storage devices, and computer software), and fast decision making to cut down product development time. Thus, IBM is still currently searching for a new "heart and soul" as it adapts to changes unlike any others in its history. Even though the company has scored important successes in developing a wide array of even newer technologies, IBM's transition remains an ongoing process.[17]

The changes currently taking place at IBM and at numerous other U.S. (and even, more recently, at Japanese and Korean) companies raise questions about how managers should deal with their employees' expectations, values, and behaviors in the wake of organizational shifts. A shift toward cooperation or autonomy usually requires an adjustment in personal managerial style and way of thinking for both senior and divisional managers. Senior managers must deal with divisional and functional managers—and all employees—in an open manner that best smooths this transition. Questions will arise about such issues as people's ability to adjust to the shift and how to deal with a potential excess of managers and employees, retraining, job security, and other very human concerns. These concerns are particularly acute when top management attempts to shift the balance swiftly from one end of the spectrum in Exhibit 12-1 to the other. A shift of this kind forces a company to redefine its core values, causing frequent trauma to many parts of the organization.

Fine-Tuning a Delicate Balance

Striking the right balance between cooperation and autonomy is a complex task. Yet, attaining strategic alignment between these opposing orientations is vital to build and sustain strong competitive advantage. Senior management can realign the "tilt" between cooperation and autonomy by using many of the organizational structures and design practices discussed in earlier chapters (shown in Exhibit 12-1). However, senior management must place as much importance on the means used to accomplish this shift as on the desired outcome.

Developments such as changes in product use, technological convergence, the rise of multipoint competition, reduced emphasis on acquisitions, and increased overseas activity expand the need for heightened cooperation among divisions. Other developments (an increased emphasis on acquisitions to enter new markets, the need to avert creeping bureaucratization, and increased environmental turbulence) all point to the need for greater divisional autonomy.

Technology fusion is a new concept that refers to the blending of technologies to achieve higher-order products. Although this concept was initially conceived to describe the technology-driven strategies of Japanese companies, many U.S., European, and Korean firms are currently undertaking their own versions of technology fusion. Firms practicing technology fusion need to shift the balance constantly between cooperation and autonomy. These ongoing shifts are required to foster both systemwide interrelationships (cooperation) and individual creativity (autonomy).

A number of different organizational design factors can be used to adjust and modify the relationship between cooperation and autonomy. These include choice of organizational structure, reward systems, and staffing considerations. Off-line coordinators, internal task forces, and committees represent additional ways to achieve a higher level of cooperation among divisions. Senior management at corporate headquarters usually sponsors the use of coordinators and task forces to encourage conflict resolution and idea sharing among divisional managers. Coordinators and task forces can be used to supplement other design practices, such as consolidation and grouping of divisions into larger units.

Summary

- Firms experiencing change in the way their products are used, technological convergence, growth in multipoint competition, reduced emphasis on acquisitions, and increased global expansion often need to increase cooperation among their subunits.
- Increased acquisition activity, the need to avert creeping bureaucracy, and environmental turbulence raise the need for greater subunit autonomy.
- Corporate managers can shift the balance between cooperation and autonomy through organizational structures and design practices as shown in Exhibit 12-1. The implementation of reward systems, staff policies, and various types of corporate cultures can influence the tilt toward increased cooperation or increased autonomy.
- Technology fusion is the blending of technologies to create higher-order products.
- A frequent shifting of the emphasis between cooperation and autonomy is needed to achieve technology fusion.
- Senior management interested in shifting the balance between cooperation and autonomy must identify likely sources of resistance to such a move and institute an organizational change process to overcome such resistance.

Exercises and Discussion Questions

1. Over time, as industries tend to become more consolidated as they mature, which way do you think most companies will tilt in their organizational balance: more cooperation among subunits or more autonomy? When companies aim for greater cooperation, what is the impact on their ability to develop products faster and to

become more responsive to their customers? When companies tilt toward greater autonomy, what do you think the impact will be on their overall cost structure? Do you see any other organizational designs that may help companies attain the best of both worlds, so to speak?

2. Consider yourself a general manager of a large strategic business unit (SBU) of a highly diversified company. You traditionally enjoyed a high degree of freedom in setting your own unit's strategy and performance targets. Senior management, however, has decided to seek greater economies of scale for the entire company. How do you think such a shift will affect your traditional approach to managing your SBU? What are some arguments that you could propose to senior management to delay the effects or impact of such a shift? Conversely, how would you prepare your own staff and colleagues for the inevitabilities of such a shift? What would be some arguments and ideas that would help you manage your own personnel's ability to adjust to the shift?
3. For the past several years, a number of companies in the entertainment and media industries have grown extensively by acquisition (e.g., Viacom's purchase of CBS, Disney's purchase of ABC, Vivendi Universal's purchase of USA Networks). What does senior management hope to gain from making these purchases? If they emphasize cost savings through internal sharing of resources, what would be some likely effects on these newly acquired units? Likewise, if senior management encourages their newly acquired units to enter new markets as they see fit, would they emphasize more cooperation or autonomy?

Endnotes

1. A variety of data sources were used for the 3M Corporation Strategic Snapshot. Some of the most recent ones include the following: "3M: A Lab for Growth," *Business Week*, January 21, 2002, pp. 50–51; "At Minnesota Mining and Manufacturing, Hope Grows for a Payoff in Health Care," *Wall Street Journal*, December 10, 2001, p. B7B; "Eli Lilly, 3M Sign Deal on Herpes Treatment in Advanced Trials Phase," *Wall Street Journal*, October 9, 2001; "3M Cuts Back Earnings Forecast Again, Cites Slow Growth Abroad," *Wall Street Journal*, July 3, 2001, p. A3; "Spreading the GE Gospel—As 3M Chief, McNerney Wastes No Time," *Wall Street Journal*, June 5, 2001, pp. A1, A6; "McNerney: A Short Jump from GE to 3M," *Business Week*, December 18, 2000; "3M's Next Chief Plans to Fortify Results with Discipline He Learned at GE," *Wall Street Journal*, December 6, 2000; "Minnesota Mining & Catchall: 3M Has Sexy Technology and Sleepy Earnings," *Forbes*, September 4, 2000; "Scotchgard Line of 3M to End Most Products," *Wall Street Journal*, May 17, 2000; "3M and Taiwan Manufacturers to Slash Fiber LAN Cost," *Fiber Optics News*, May 15, 2000; "3M: The Heat Is on the Boss," *Business Week*, March 15, 1999; "3M Offers Fiber-to-the-Desk System," *Fiber Optics News*, February 2, 1998; "PolyCom, 3M in Joint Venture," *Wall Street Journal*, January 20, 1998; "Solectron, 3M, Xerox, Merrill Win Baldriges," *Wall Street Journal*, October 16, 1997; "3M Offers Fiber Management System," *Fiber Optics News*, October 7, 1996; "3M Introduces Cable-Pulling Lubricant, PC-Compatible Fiber Test System," *Fiber Optics News*, June 3, 1996; "Campaign to Sell 3M Name," *Wall Street Journal*, May 14, 1996; "High-Tech Tape Unravels at 3M," *Business Week*, November 27, 1995; "Thank You, 3M," *Forbes*, September 25, 1995; "The Drought Is Over at 3M," *Business Week*, November 7, 1994. An excellent overview of how 3M currently formulates strategies at the business unit level is found in G. Shaw, R. Brown, and P. Bromiley, "How 3M Is Rewriting Business Planning," *Harvard Business Review* 76, no. 3 (May–June 1998): 41–50.
2. See M. E Porter, *Competitive Advantage* (New York: Free Press, 1985).

3. See, for example, S. Ghoshal and C. A. Bartlett, "Changing the Role of Top Management: Beyond Structure to Processes," *Harvard Business Review* (January–February 1995): 86–96.

4. See, for example, V. Govindarajan and J. Fisher, "Strategy, Control Systems and Resource Sharing," *Academy of Management Journal* 33 (1990): 259–285.

5. See, for example, A. Edstrom and J. Galbraith, "Transfer of Managers as a Coordination and Control Strategy in Multinational Organizations," *Administrative Science Quarterly* 22 (1977): 248–263.

6. See, for example, "Can UTC Get Back on Its Flight Path?" *Business Week*, November 5, 2001, pp. 98–99.

7. Advanced manufacturing technologies can significantly enhance strategic flexibility and give rise to numerous opportunities for interdivisional cooperation. See, for example, J. D. Goldhar and M. Jelinek, "Plan for Economies of Scope," *Harvard Business Review* (November–December 1983): 141–148; M. Jelinek and J. D. Goldhar, "The Strategic Implications of the Factory of the Future," *Sloan Management Review* 25 (1984): 29–37; J. R. Meredith, "The Strategic Advantages of the Factory of the Future," *California Management Review* 29, no. 3 (1987): 27–41; P. Nemetz and L. Fry, "Flexible Manufacturing Organizations: Implications for Strategy Formulation and Organization Design," *Academy of Management Review* 13, no. 3 (1988): 627–638; G. I. Susman and J. W. Dean, "Strategic Use of Computer-Integrated Manufacturing in the Emerging Competitive Environment," *Computer-Integrated Manufacturing Systems* 2, no. 3 (1989): 133–138; D. Lei and J. D. Goldhar, "Multiple Niche Competition: The Strategic Use of CIM Technology," *Manufacturing Review* 3, no. 3 (1990): 195–206; R. Parthasarthy and S. P. Sethi, "The Impact of Flexible Automation on Business Strategy and Organizational Structure," *Academy of Management Review* 17, no. 1 (1992): 86–111.

8. See, for example, "The Latest Big Thing at Many Companies Is Speed, Speed, Speed," *Wall Street Journal*, December 23, 1994, pp. A1, A7.

9. For a full discussion of multipoint competition, see M. E. Porter, *Competitive Advantage* (New York: Free Press, 1985). Also see A. Karmani and B. Wernerfelt, "Multiple Point Competition," *Strategic Management Journal* 6 (1985): 87–96; F. L. Smith and R. L. Wilson, "The Predictive Validity of the Karnani and Wernerfelt Model of Multipoint Competition," *Strategic Management Journal* 16, no. 2 (1995): 143–160; W. P. Barnett, "Strategic Deterrence among Multipoint Competitors," *Academy of Management Proceedings* (1991): 7–10; M. J. Chen and I. C. MacMillan, "Nonresponse and Delayed Response to Competitive Moves: The Roles of Competitor Dependence and Action Irreversibility," *Academy of Management Journal* 35 (1992): 539–570; F. L. Smith and R. L. Wilson, "The Predictive Validity of the Karnani and Wernerfelt Model of Multipoint Competition," *Strategic Management Journal* 16 (1995): 143–160; M. A. Peteraf, "Intraindustry Structure and Response towards Rivals," *Managerial and Decision Economics* 14 (1994): 519–528; W. P. Barnett, "Strategic Deterrence among Multipoint Competitors," *Industrial and Corporate Change* 2 (1993): 249–278. Also see J. Gimeno and C. Y. Woo, "Multimarket Contact, Economies of Scope, and Firm Performance," *Academy of Management Journal* 42, no. 3 (1999): 239–259; J. Gimeno, "Reciprocal Threats in Multimarket Rivalry: Staking Out 'Spheres of Influence' in the U.S. Airline Industry," *Strategic Management Journal* 20, no. 2 (1999): 101–128; R. G. McGrath, M. J. Chen, and I. C. MacMillan, "Multimarket Maneuvering in Uncertain Spheres of Influence: Resource Diversion Strategies," *Academy of Management Review* 23, no. 4 (1998): 724–740; W. Boeker, J. Goodstein, J. Stephan, and J. P. Murmann, "Competition in a Multimarket Environment: The Case of Market Exit," *Organization Science* 8 (1997): 126–142; P. M. Parker and L. H. Roller, "Collusive Contact in Duopolies: Multimarket Contact and Cross-Ownership in the Mobile Telephone Industry," *Rand Journal of Economics* 28 (1997):

304–322; J. Gimeno and C. Y. Woo, "Hypercompetition in a Multimarket Environment: The Role of Strategic Similarity and Multimarket Contact in Competitive De-escalation," *Organization Science* 7 (1996): 322–340; J. A. Baum and J. J. Korn, "Competitive Dynamics of Interfirm Rivalry," *Academy of Management Journal* 39 (1996): 255–291.

10. See "EMI's Levy to Stress Stars, Internet in New Post," *Wall Street Journal*, October 16, 2001, p. B6; "Twice Jilted, EMI Faces the Music Alone," *Wall Street Journal*, June 6, 2001, p. B2; "Thorn-EMI Sheds Its Ambitions to Be a World High-Tech Power," *Wall Street Journal*, June 8, 1989, p. A15.

11. See "Viacom to Expand Its Online Presence with New Internet Unit, Radio Purchase," *Wall Street Journal*, February 23, 1999, p. B2; "Viacom's Itty-Bitty, Synergistic, Billion-Dollar Franchise," *Fortune*, November 23, 1998, pp. 223–226; "Video Unit May Help Viacom While Asia Creates Drag on Seagram, Disney," *Wall Street Journal*, July 17, 1998; "Media Boldly Going Where Others Are Bailing Out," *Business Week*, April 6, 1998, p. 46; "Paramount Puts a Glint in Redstone's Eye," *Business Week*, March 3, 1997, p. 72; "Nothing Spectacular on TV? It's Showtime for Web Users," *Investor's Business Daily*," January 9, 1997, p. A6.

12. See "General Mills to Spin Off Restaurants in Effort to Focus on Its Core Business," *Wall Street Journal*, December 15, 1994, pp. A3, A9.

13. See, for example, "Tradition Be Damned," *Business Week*, October 31, 1994, pp. 108–112.

14. See "Shell Shifts Top Division Management as It Moves toward Wide Restructuring," *Wall Street Journal*, December 11, 1998, p. A13.

15. An excellent discussion of technology fusion is found in F. Kodama, "Technology Fusion and the New R&D," *Harvard Business Review* 70 (July–August 1992): 70–78; F. Kodama, *Emerging Patterns of Innovation* (Boston: Harvard Business School Press, 1995).

16. See, for example, "Scientists Build Molecular Logic Circuits," *Wall Street Journal*, November 9, 2001, p. B3.

17. See "Out of the Box: Intel and IBM Fight for the Post-PC Future," *Forbes*, April 15, 2002, pp. 207-215; "The Future of IBM," *Fortune*, February 18, 2002, pp. 60–70; "IBM's New Boss," *Business Week*, February 11, 2002, pp. 66–72; "IBM Gains in Battle with BEA over Software," *Wall Street Journal*, November 1, 2001, pp. B6, B7; "IBM Unveils High-End Computer Server," *Wall Street Journal*, October 4, 2001, p. B7; "These Days Big Blue Is about Big Services, Not Just Big Boxes," *Wall Street Journal*, June 11, 2001, pp. A1, A10; "IBM to Unveil a Push into Wireless Internet with Product Rollout," *Wall Street Journal*, October 30, 2000, p. B2; "Gertsner Is Struggling as He Tries to Change Ingrained IBM Culture," *Wall Street Journal*, May 13, 1994, pp. A1, A5.

CHAPTER 13

Managing Strategic Change: Building Learning Organizations

Chapter Outline

What You Will Learn

- Why companies need to think about change
- The concept of a learning organization
- The key practices found in learning organizations
- Why static organizations have difficulty in responding to change
- The steps senior managers use in dealing with resistance to change

Sony Corporation[1]

Sony Corporation is one of the world's most consistently successful innovators of consumer electronic products. For the fiscal year that ended on March 31, 2001, Sony reported total revenues over $58 billion, with over $134 million in profits. Despite facing an economic slowdown in both its home Japanese market and the United States, Sony has consistently surprised and delighted consumers with superbly designed, user-friendly, high-technology products year after year. Many of its legendary innovations (the pocket-sized transistor radio, Walkman portable radio/cassette player, videocassette recorder [VCR], Trinitron system color television set, camcorder, compact disc [CD] player, and now personal computers, MP3 players, DVDs, and digital cellular phones) have become staples throughout the world. In addition, its most recent innovations, such as the Mini Disc (a miniature version of the portable CD player), the Palmtop (a hand-held computer designed to compete with the Palm Pilot), the PlayStation series of video game systems, Cybershot digital filmless cameras (using charged-coupled devices [CCDs] and flash memories), and the Data Discman (an electronic book that displays thousands of texts stored on a removable disc), are just beginning to make consumer inroads throughout Europe, the United States, and Japan. Sony is also in the lead to develop Internet-driven products and services, such as subscription services in digital music, interactive games and movies, and even interactive television.

Equally important, but less apparent, Sony is also an active supplier and participant in shaping the next generation of office equipment, notebook computers, advanced integrated circuits, ultrathin display materials, and other multimedia technologies currently under development. Sony has benefited from technological and market-based changes by learning and leading, rather than following competitors in the innovation race. It also has major ambitions to develop next-generation technologies that will be at the heart of new Internet-based appliances and even entertainment. In 1989, Sony purchased Materials Research Corporation, a leading U.S. supplier of manufacturing equipment and advanced materials for the semiconductor industry. During the 1990s, Sony became an important player in the global film and entertainment industry through its purchase of Columbia Pictures and CBS Records. For much of the past decade, Sony has remained an important manufacturing partner to Apple Computer, helping the U.S. firm design and manufacture a novel line of personal computers. In recent years, Sony has begun investing heavily in developing the "content" and communications sides of its business, especially by forming exploratory strategic alliances with a variety of Internet-based companies. For example, in two separate alliances formed in 2001, Sony and AOL Time Warner agreed to cooperate on the joint development of new Internet-driven consumer appliances. These include new Internet browsers that work on interactive televisions, as well as future digital cameras and camcorders. Sony and AOL also have been working to link the PlayStation 2 video game system onto the Internet. Users of the PlayStation 2 game console will then be able to communicate with each other through America Online's Instant Messenger and other e-mail systems. Also in 2001, Sony and Ericsson have pooled their assets and technologies together to gain the critical mass necessary to become even larger players in the wireless telecommunications industry. The joint venture between the two companies is designed to prevent Nokia from becoming the overwhelmingly dominant firm in the mobile handset business. The combination of investments in internal innovation, acquisitions, and strategic alliances should help Sony attain its long-term goal of transforming itself into an integrated electronics, entertainment, and content company.

How has Sony achieved such stunning success as an innovator of bold new products? The answer lies in its use of organizational practices that foster continuous learning. Companies that seek to learn and embrace new technologies and approaches to doing things are better able to innovate and build competitive advantage. Successful learning at Sony uses several steps: (1) allocation of resources for innovation and experimentation, (2) extensive decentralization of operations, (3) a bias against overspecialization, (4) frequent rotation of employees, (5) use of multiple product development teams, and (6) a balance between psychological and monetary rewards.

Resource Allocation

Recently, Sony has spent more than $1.8 billion annually for new product development (about 3 to 4 percent of total revenues), and employs more than nine thousand engineers and scientists devoted to such effort—almost 10 percent of its total workforce. Competitors such as Matsushita Electric, Sanyo, Sharp, Motorola, Nokia, and General Electric greatly admire its formidable commitment and capability in product R&D. Sony has been able to use its skills to cut significantly the amount of time needed for developing next-generation products.

Extensive Decentralization

Sony's operations are divided into twenty-three separate business groups, each responsible for a particular product line. In addition, the company also supports hundreds of development teams that can work across divisional lines on innovation projects. These project teams, typically organized around product development tasks and spanning functions, help bring multiple perspectives and approaches to thinking about and commercializing a new product. Equally important, these teams serve a vital integrative function that helps to unify the company's many decentralized operations into moving along a central direction. This combination of extensive decentralization and special teams creates many relatively small centers of decision making throughout the company.

Bias against Specialists

Like other Japanese companies, Sony recruits extensive technical talent at Japan's major universities. However, it does not necessarily pursue students with the highest grades. Instead, Sony seeks people who are *neyaka* (which roughly translates as "open-minded, optimistic, and wide ranging in interests") because Sony managers believe these traits foster continual learning and innovation. Conversely, they believe an overly specialized orientation hampers innovation. As company founder Ibuka puts it, "Specialists are inclined to argue why you can't do something, while our emphasis has always been to make something out of nothing." Sony's commitment to openness to new ideas depends on a diversity of backgrounds among its personnel. This diversity provides the fertile learning ground for Sony to test and commercialize new product concepts.

Frequent Rotation of Staff

Engineers in the company may seek new assignments anywhere in the organization, often without first notifying their supervisor. If an individual locates an attractive new position, the employee's boss is expected to cooperate in the transfer. This practice, which Sony refers to as "self-promotion," causes fairly frequent movement of technical talent within Sony's organization. Such movement infuses development teams with periodic new arrivals who bring fresh ideas and heightened enthusiasm.

Multiple Experiments

Sony often assigns several teams, each pursuing a different technology, to work on the same development problem. For example, five teams worked at various times on the company's CD player and later the MiniDisc project. The use of multiple experiments adds an element of healthy competition to the development process. It increases the likelihood that Sony will emerge as a leader in successful new technologies. Moreover, working with different technologies helps Sony learn which products are more likely to be easily manufactured and improved over time. By working with different designs and seeing how a customer will likely use a product from different angles, Sony can continuously improve its products over time by incorporating new features and streamlined designs. This additional development information gives Sony a market edge over its competitors.

Balance of Psychological and Monetary Rewards

Sony avoids paying monetary rewards such as bonuses and salary increases for technical achievement. Instead, it relies primarily on non-monetary rewards in a variety of forms to inspire creative effort. Perhaps most important, Sony gives engineers a great deal of leeway in selecting the development projects they will work on. The excitement of development work then provides its own psychological reward. Sony also allows individuals who originate new product ideas to supervise the teams formed to conduct the development work. This practice sometimes produces project leaders who are younger and less highly paid than the team members they supervise. Yet, it supplies a powerful incentive toward creative effort by enabling the company's most creative engineers to lead the development effort. Another device Sony uses to foster creativity is a technical fair sponsored annually by its corporate research department. The three-day event, open only to company employees, provides engineers and scientists an opportunity to display projects to their peers and the company's most senior executives, who make a point of visiting each display. This practice provides substantial psychological rewards for creative efforts and helps cross-pollinate ideas among project teams and business groups.

Introduction

As demonstrated in the cases and examples given in this text, most industries and their competitive environments are rapidly changing. Rapid change is not confined to high-technology or knowledge-intensive industries such as semiconductors, computers, health care, financial services, entertainment, software, biotechnology, and advanced materials. Many once-stable industries such as automobiles, banking, insurance, steel, retailing, publishing, food processing, and even hospitals now face the need to adapt to change quickly. With change comes the necessity of learning new skills and developing new sources of competitive advantage. Thus, all types of firms (large and small, established and new entrant, diversified and single-business) cannot rely on their existing sources of competitive advantage for survival; they must be able to learn and create new ones as their environments change. Building and sustaining competitive advantage in the midst of rapid change requires the organization to learn new technologies, new markets, and new ways of managing. *In the future, the only truly sustainable source of competitive advantage will be the organization's ability to change and learn new skills.*[2]

Successful organizational learning demands management's focused effort. Often, learning new skills and technologies can be a traumatic experience. The large-scale, ongoing restructurings of firms such as AT&T, IBM, Sears, Fidelity Investments, JCPenney, United Technologies, and Eastman Kodak are just a few examples in which one can see the dramatic effects of rapid environmental change. However, bringing about organizational change that facilitates learning is not an easy task. Managers and employees at all levels frequently resist the process of change, since it may alter their existing practices and web of relationships. Senior managers who seek to induce organizational changes that promote the learning of new skills and distinctive competences must therefore be sensitive to potential resistance. Their challenge is to take steps that encourage lower-level managers and employees to join and facilitate needed changes. We explore this challenge in the present chapter.

learning organizations: Firms that view change as a positive opportunity to learn and create new sources of competitive advantage.

The first part of this chapter focuses on how top managers can help their firms become learning organizations.[3] **Learning organizations** are firms that view change as a positive opportunity to learn and create new sources of competitive advantage. We focus on various organizational practices that promote this kind of proactive, change-oriented learning. Although instilling new forms of learning can be a difficult task, companies that are successful in doing so can better adjust and thrive in a rapidly changing environment.

The second part of the chapter examines the difficulty of implementing change in firms that have not yet become full-blown learning organizations. Not all firms in every industry face the same degree of rapid change, and change can occur at varying rates across different industries. Yet, it is likely that all firms in all industries will inevitably face the need to learn and create new sources of competitive advantage or, at a minimum, understand how to improve their existing sources of competitive advantage. Thus, senior management must tackle the challenge of promoting and implementing change in an increasing number of industries and must often do so in the face of manager and employee resistance to such efforts. We examine some sources of resistance to change and discuss how senior managers can muster support for organizational change.

Characteristics of Learning Organizations

Some firms possess characteristics that greatly enhance their capabilities to adapt to rapid change. Exhibit 13-1 highlights key organizational practices that contribute to a firm's potential for learning: (1) frequent rotation of managers, (2) continual training of personnel, (3) decentralization of decision making, (4) encouragement of multiple experiments, (5) high tolerance for failure, and (6) openness and diversity of many viewpoints. These practices encourage managers to be truly open to ideas that identify trends and generate choices. Under these conditions, adapting to the environment becomes easier and more likely to succeed.

Management Practices of Learning Organizations **EXHIBIT 13-1**

Frequent Rotation of Managers

Managers new to their positions are less likely to be wedded to a particular set of values or way of operating than individuals who have held the same position for many years. Long-standing managers of a department are likely to be proponents of their department's current strategy and, therefore, emotionally tied to its success. Over time, these individuals have a tendency to become less accepting of new strategies, approaches, and ways of doing things. For example, at companies such as Eastman Kodak, Polaroid, Timex Watch Company, and Merrill Lynch, managers who stayed with their respective lines of business were often unable to understand the nature of the changes facing their products and technologies; change became more difficult when managers were locked into a particular "lens" and functional perspective through which they defined and solved problems.

One organizational practice that enhances a firm's ability to change is periodic rotation of managers throughout the firm. Rotating managers across business lines exposes them to experiences, perspectives, functional skills, and competences that were developed elsewhere. Managerial rotation also promotes the building of interrelationships and synergies that span departmental and divisional lines. At Sony, managerial rotation infuses managers with new insights and ideas and gives them greater awareness of a wide range of technologies and products that consumers may want. Managers are thus able to see how employees from other departments work together smoothly to get new products to market fast. In turn, they become more aware of their own competitive environment. Frequent managerial rotation greatly enhances Sony's ability to adapt to environmental change.

General Motors' Saturn operation practices managerial rotation to encourage its people to visit other parts of the factory. Rotating both managers and employees throughout Saturn's many work areas helps convince people of the need to do their best in producing quality products. This system enables Saturn employees to see how their efforts and work contribute to the entire car's production and assembly. Managers and employees also learn multiple sets of skills that are used in auto manufacturing and assembly. In turn, the quality of the car improves, and people learn and share manufacturing insights and skills throughout the factory.[4]

Continual Training of Personnel

An insidious source of resistance to change is fear that change will render obsolete many managers' and employees' current skills, promotion opportunities, and career paths. Regular training and development through which managers and employees learn new skills lessen such fears and thus reduce resistance to change. Many researchers and analysts have noted that continuous training is one key pillar of Japanese firms' success in learning new technologies to develop fresh products quickly.[5] Sony and many other Japanese firms view training as an ongoing investment in corporate-wide continuous improvement. Companies can undertake continuous improvement (discussed more extensively in Chapter 14) when their employees are not afraid to suggest and implement changes. Finding ways to do things better helps the whole company improve. Sony's long string of product successes is due in part to a strong commitment to training and development of both personal and technically oriented skills. This training contributes to lower cost, higher quality, better morale, more openness in thinking about problems, and even entirely new product ideas. Most important, by encouraging its employees to learn new skills, Sony reduces employees' fear of change.

Sony maintains an internal training program designed to impress young Japanese employees with the firm's newest technologies. It also instills the company's management procedures, corporate values, and operating practices. Additionally, Sony trains its managers extensively to prepare them for overseas assignments. Overseas customs and practices are taught regularly. In particular, by sending highly talented, young managers to places such as the United States, Latin America, and Europe, Sony is able to see firsthand the emerging lifestyle and technology-driven trends that may first start in other markets. In turn, by actively researching and listening to what future consumers want from their products, Sony's managers can then develop those products that it thinks will capture people's desires. This type of training helps Sony's managers spot new trends and potential opportunities in consumer electronics markets and understand what each market wants in Sony's products.

Decentralization of Decision Making

Lower-level managers, sales representatives, and front-line employees are much closer to the action than most senior managers. They are therefore often the first to become aware of potential new developments and changes. A firm can improve its responsiveness by pushing decision-making responsibility down to these individuals; therefore, a firm should practice some degree of decentralization wherever possible. Careful decentralization facilitates organizational change and learning because it encourages managers and employees to participate in making decisions that directly affect them. It also gives them room to experiment with new methods they feel are appropriate. Yet, decentralization should not go so far that it results in duplication of activities across businesses, the dilution of a well-defined corporate mission and culture, or other inefficiencies. When carefully implemented, decentralization increases the number of employees who can deal with change, and mobilizes the energies of many people. Making the right level of decentralization work requires trust among managers and employees throughout the company. If managers cannot trust their employees or vice versa, then unfettered decentralization can cause numerous problems for the firm.

Well-thought-out decentralization works to promote change and learning because the flow of information is less likely to be distorted.[6] People on the front line (especially marketing, sales, customer service) are constantly exposed to numerous sources of timely information vital to detecting potential developments or opportunities. On the other hand, thick layers of management (particularly in companies organized along strictly functional lines for long periods of time) often distort or delay information flows. Managers tend to "reinterpret" information from their employees and pass it on in a distorted form to their superiors.

Of course, decentralization must be balanced with a strong sense of shared values to promote change and learning. Decentralization frees up the creative energies of managers and employees but can result in chaos if people do not share some common goals and values. Although Sony delegates responsibility widely, the firm carefully impresses upon its people the company's innovation-driven creed and goals. This combination allows Sony's employees to learn and apply new ideas in ways that are consistent with Sony's goals. A major part of Sony's decentralized organization is its use of small project teams that can move from one part of the company to another. These teams have the authority to make changes to improve the quality or efficiency of operations. Project teams help other department and business managers coordinate product development and use of new technologies. They also serve a vital purpose of moving across different functions and departments, thereby promoting active cross-pollination of ideas and skills throughout the company. Sony's flexible and fast-moving project teams thus provide the basis for building strong interrelationships among business units. These interrelationships facilitate the sharing of know-how and skills systemwide.

Johnson & Johnson is another example of how effective decentralization can foster the creation of new sources of competitive advantage. J&J's senior management has divided the company into more than fifty operating divisions (or "companies") that produce everything from surgical sutures to Tylenol, anesthesia, advanced surgical implements, medical instruments, diagnostic equipment, toothbrushes, baby oils, shampoos, and blood monitors. J&J's senior management believes in giving each division the power to do whatever is needed to succeed in its market. This high degree of decentralization has enabled J&J business units to become some of the most successful innovators and marketers in the United States, although the company may be becoming overstretched in recent years. The CEO of Johnson & Johnson compares his role to that of an orchestra conductor: he gives his players inspiration and direction, but his subordinates get complete freedom to execute the desired objective.[7]

Kodak's ongoing problems with its core photography and imaging operations stem partly from insufficient decentralization. After eleven restructurings over the past two decades, Kodak still has great difficulties in encouraging a high level of autonomy and responsiveness to market change. Despite holding numerous patents in the field of chemical and digital imaging, Kodak still appears unable to harness fully the knowledge of its product development teams to create new products faster and better. Kodak struggles with decentralization because the company lacks a well-defined, concrete mission that its people can follow in their day-to-day projects. A lack of a common focus, combined with a seemingly low urgency to learn new skills related to digital imaging, has also contributed to Kodak's problems.

Encouragement of Multiple Experiments

Developing new products and technological processes are often complicated tasks. Sometimes several initiatives need to be tried simultaneously to determine which is better. Running multiple projects reduces the likelihood that a superior approach will be overlooked. As separate groups or teams work on a solution to the same problem, people develop skills and insights that can prove useful in thinking about future products. In other words, companies need to "parallel-process" their efforts to learn new technologies and develop new products. Parallel processing enables a firm to see which technologies, product standards, marketing approaches, and management methods work best. This approach harnesses a healthy degree of internal competition with a dual focus on continuous improvement and search for best designs and best value. In turn, people are exposed to different ways of thinking about and doing things.

Sony's legendary success with its portable Walkman radio/cassette player reveals the enormous power of experimentation in producing breakthrough products. Several project teams worked on this project, helping determine which format would be the most desirable to consumers and the most easily manufactured. Sony has used numerous parallel project development teams to work on other promising technologies, such as miniaturized compact and optical disks, hand-held color televisions, and small video camcorders that automatically adjust the lens for better picture quality.

Multiple experiments are one key to Honda's enormous success in developing a broad range of engine technologies for automobiles, motorcycles, lawn mowers, power boats, and power generators. Honda keeps an "idea file" that includes numerous prototypes and designs for models previously developed but never produced. Many of these ideas have later become the basis for motorcycles, automobiles, and lawn mowers when opportunities opened up.[8] Oftentimes, ideas developed in one business unit to serve a particular customer have had considerable future, unanticipated value serving Honda's customers in another market.

Timex's early unwillingness to experiment with innovative applications may have shut the company out from new generations of products. The company's cadre of mechanical engineers was unable to assimilate electronic displays and other new technologies in watch designs, because they saw mechanical springs and gears as superior to emerging electronic technologies being developed by other companies. For example, competing manufacturers such as Citizen Watch, Seiko, Casio, and Texas Instruments were already producing watches made with electronic components, which were often derived from other product applications, such as calculators and measuring instruments.

High Tolerance for Failure

If people are punished for working on projects that eventually are not selected, then few will be willing to take on risky projects in the future. Firms must be careful not to discourage people associated with projects that do not work out if they want to sustain high creativity. Instead, senior managers should continue to reward them if their efforts are meaningful and reasonable. This approach ensures that employees receive the encouragement they need to "venture off the beaten path" when exploring new solutions.

Many innovative companies, including Sony, IBM, and 3M, have experienced failures, some of them rather large. For example, during the 1980s, Sony pioneered a new digital camera called the Mavica. The company believed the public was ready for a new filmless camera that could take clearer pictures faster. Yet, the Mavica was ahead of its time and few consumers were interested, so Sony withdrew the product. Not until the mid-1990s did Sony reintroduce the Mavica and the even more improved Cybershot digital camera system. This product is now a real winner in the marketplace. Sony now leads in the development of even more advanced imaging and storage technologies that are designed to help even the beginner take pictures that approach professional quality. Even with this early failure, Sony gained many insights into digital technology that led to new generations of compact disk players, Minidiscs, advanced integrated circuits, DVDs, digital phones, and network appliances. Sony did not penalize its managers or employees for this product's failure. Instead, it gave these individuals important positions in which they could borrow upon their newly acquired experiences and skills. They were encouraged to apply their expertise to designing new products and technologies. Ultimately, Sony is now well positioned to compete across a whole spectrum of digital imaging technologies for use in advanced consumer electronics applications.

IBM is another company that traditionally has not punished its people for a given product's failure. For example, IBM entered the home market for personal computers with the PS/1 model in the mid-1980s. Unfortunately, this product was severely underpowered and lacked many practical applications for home use. Customers could not use it very easily to manage their home finances, play computer games, or create their own stationery. IBM withdrew the product from the market and concentrated on improving the product's power and versatility. Managers involved with this product were not punished but instead were given new marketing and development assignments for a new line of business and home computers. These newer models (many labeled under the Aptiva brand) now enjoy considerable market success. IBM's continued reliance on these people to design more advanced types of personal computers has helped retain valuable experience and insight that the company used to revitalize its personal computer business.

3M is another company that seeks to utilize failures as a way to create new technologies and market opportunities. The company has long believed that it is far better to encourage people to make mistakes and stumble, rather than to wait too long before other competitors pounce on new market ideas. 3M's senior management has long believed that scientists need to keep their fertile minds active, and explicitly allow them to work on projects that may have no immediate payoff. During the 1990s, 3M instituted programs to provide internal grants of as much as $50,000 for scientists to work on individual special projects. Product and technology failures are legendary at 3M for creating new applications elsewhere. For example, one 3M division developed an easy-to-apply sticky coating for the aerospace industry. Unfortunately, the coating did not meet the aerospace customer's exacting needs. However, with a slight modification of the coating's chemical properties, another 3M division was able to pioneer today's wildly popular Post-It Notes. In fact, many of 3M's products resulted when scientists either failed in an initial experiment or accidentally "stumbled" onto something that turned out to be a future winner.

At Sony, IBM, and 3M, managers are encouraged to learn from their experiences instead of being fired for their decisions. Failures are defined as part of the learning process and personal growth. The knowledge gained by personnel associated with failures became instrumental in developing new products that helped the company enter other markets. In other companies, the very prospect of failure causes organizational paralysis rather than growth.

Openness and Diversity of Viewpoints

True openness by managers to new ideas, suggestions, and criticisms is rare in most firms. Openness means not only a willingness to listen to new ideas and face reality but also encouragement of a diversity of viewpoints and perspectives throughout the firm. Openness demands that managers suspend their need for control. The need for constant and direct control often limits the potential for effective learning, since it suppresses people from bringing up contrary viewpoints, "bad news," or alternative problem solutions that may cause internal political problems. Excessive control sharply narrows the manager's attention to short-term objectives. For example, if managerial attention is riveted solely to quantitative performance measures such as return on investment (ROI), managers will be less attuned and sensitive to environmental developments with potential long-term impact. During the 1980s and 1990s, managers at Westinghouse Electric were so obsessed with "making their numbers" that they even went so far as to undertake actions that ultimately resulted in the financial collapse of several Westinghouse business units. Moreover, managers fixated on control are often unable to draw useful suggestions and ideas from their employees, many of whom may be afraid of their superiors. Control usually focuses managers' attention on immediate details, taking the time and effort that managers need for discovering and understanding important long-term trends.

Another essential ingredient to openness is the ability to understand diverse perspectives and viewpoints. Managers must be able to appreciate other people's values, backgrounds, and experiences as being no less important than their own. In other words, true openness means a willingness to accept and listen to other people's ideas and perspectives. Although Sony tried to understand and shape the motion picture and entertainment industry through its initial acquisition of Columbia Pictures in 1989, the company soon discovered that many of its highly successful management techniques and insights learned from the electronics business had little direct applicability to the entertainment side of the firm. After a few difficult years in the early 1990s, Sony now applies a policy of openness to managing its Columbia Pictures unit in California. Realizing that filmmaking and electronics are two distinct industries, Sony encourages Columbia's film producers, studio managers, and technical talent to share their viewpoints with Sony's managers. This communication helps Sony's senior management understand the specific filmmaking problems and issues that differ from issues involved in making electronics-based products. Instituting these changes became especially urgent when Sony at first did not grasp the fundamental differences in operational procedures, management practices, and attitudes that defined and separated the two businesses and their respective mind-sets.[9]

Asea-Brown-Boveri (ABB) also practices a policy of being open to many viewpoints. This European producer of power generation equipment and machine tools believes that each market in which it operates is unique and that managers must therefore be open to their customers' and local personnel's specific requests. Products and technologies are customized to each market. ABB's managers often work directly with their customers to get a better feel for their special needs. Internally, ABB relies on lower-level managers and employees within each national market to suggest ideas on how best to deal with competitors and government regulations. By listening to customer and employee suggestions, ABB's managers gain insights into how to make their products better and what competitors are offering. This openness helps ABB become a better competitor.

The hidden belief that one's own background or experience is superior to another's seriously hinders learning. This phenomenon is especially dangerous for firms whose top management is overly represented by a particular function. For example, engineering-dominated firms, such as Raytheon, Rockwell International, and Texas Instruments, have experienced difficulty in entering the consumer market for such products as calculators, digital watches, and personal computers. TI's inability to view marketing as a function equal in importance to engineering and production is partly to blame. Consequently, TI developed consumer products (calculators, personal computers) in the same way it developed products for the government and other large companies. The result was a series of consumer products that were overpriced and lacking many user-friendly features. Resources that TI allocated to the consumer market were not as great as those dedicated to industrial markets that were more familiar to its senior managers. As a result, TI's managers were unable to get a feel for the consumer market.

Implementing Change in Static Organizations

A handful of firms have fully incorporated the practices described in the preceding sections into their management systems. Because of their ability to create new sources of competitive advantage rapidly, these learning organizations can adapt quickly to environmental change. On the other hand, many companies perceive change as a threat to their existing sources of competitive advantage and established procedures. In these firms, managers often resist efforts to change. Exhibit 13-2 presents a spectrum of how firms differ in their adaptability and responsiveness to change.

static organizations: Firms that have adapted extremely well to a particular environment but lack the ability to respond quickly to change.

Learning organizations such as Sony are found on the far right side of Exhibit 13-2. In learning organizations, managers view change as an opportunity for improvement and renewal of competitive advantage. At the far left are firms that have not adopted the organizational practices that promote learning and change but instead focus on doing better what they are already doing. Such firms we call "dinosaur" or static organizations.[10] **Static organizations** are akin to dinosaurs in that they have adapted themselves well to current environmental conditions but have little ability to change. They have a management system

Adaptability to Corporate Change — EXHIBIT 13-2

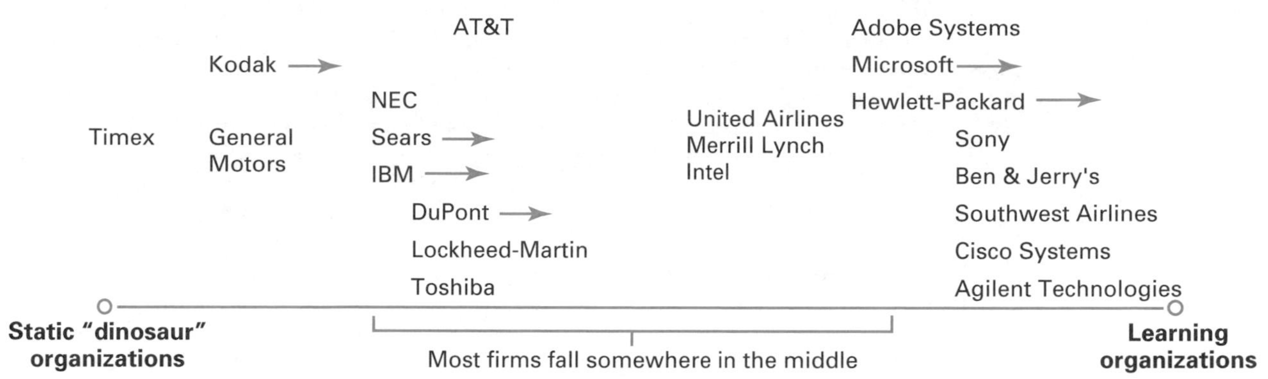

well attuned to a particular environment. These firms are often wedded to a particular technology, distribution channel, or other way of doing things that makes them vulnerable to new products or new competitors. Such firms often perform well for a considerable period of time but tend to become insular and averse to change. Their senior management loses the ability to see the ripples of change occurring in both the immediate competitive environment and the larger general environment. Managers at all levels within the firm become more inwardly focused rather than understanding what customers, competitors, and new entrants may be doing in the marketplace. In effect, their existing sources of competitive advantage have become extremely brittle and inflexible and thus especially vulnerable to new entrants, new products developed by competitors, or new technologies developed elsewhere in the industry (or beyond). As a result, when their competitive environments eventually change, they lack the ability to readily adapt.

For example, companies such as American Express, General Motors, JCPenney, and Sears during the late 1980s displayed many characteristics of a static, dinosaur-like organization. Each company was superbly adapted to its own previous low-change environment. In the automotive and retailing industries, GM, JCPenney, and Sears considered themselves as "definers" and incumbent leaders of industries they thought would not change very quickly. Yet, these companies came close to extinction because of rapidly changing environments brought about by new entrants, new technologies, and shifting customer needs. General Motors steadily lost market share to both Japanese imports and domestic competitors from 1983 to 2001, dropping from 50 percent of the U.S. market to a low of somewhere around 27 percent. The company struggled to reverse its slide by investing in advanced manufacturing technologies, robotics, software, acquisitions of Electronic Data Systems (EDS) and Hughes Aircraft, accelerated product development, quality improvement programs, and new car designs. Yet, despite all of these massively expensive undertakings, thick layers of bureaucratic management impeded fast information flow and made GM unresponsive to its customers' needs. To this day, although it made tremendous advances with its Saturn operation and its newly revived truck and sport utility vehicle (SUV) product lines, some doubt persists as to whether General Motors can sustain its recent pace of productivity/quality improvements. Nevertheless, it has shortened the time of new car model development by including suppliers, customers, and people from every function on its product development teams. GM also started practicing continuous improvement by asking its suppliers for ways to improve its manufacturing operations and reduce its inventory costs.[11]

Sears faced the same kind of problem in the retailing industry. Confronted with new "boutique" retailers and "category killers" such as Benetton, Abercrombie & Fitch, The Limited, and The Gap and new broad-line competitors such as Wal-Mart Stores, Sears was unable to provide the wide variety of products demanded by younger generations of consumers. Boutique retailers and category killers focus their efforts on specific niches. Their dedicated focus enabled them to command much higher customer loyalty and superior margins. Sears even lost ground to other main-line department stores and larger, megaretailers such as Federated Department Stores and Wal-Mart Stores, respectively. These retailers were better able to provide brand-name merchandise at lower prices. Now, Sears appears to be in the midst of earning higher levels of profits and attracting new types of customers that previously shopped at its competitors. Sears is selling many popular brand-name consumer electronics and household appliances in addition to its own popular Kenmore appliance line. It has stopped selling high-cost, low-turnover household furniture items that consume an inordinate amount of space at its stores. Its fashions are becoming more up-to-date and cater to a younger audience.[12]

The majority of companies are located somewhere in the middle of the spectrum shown in Exhibit 13-2. Change can and does occur in these firms but not without varying degrees of resistance and difficulty. However, most companies need to change or adapt within a short period of time. Rapid environmental change, if unanticipated, can seriously erode the value of a firm's distinctive competence and other sources of competitive advantage. For example, Eastman Kodak faces competitors capable of rapidly innovating new digital and electronics-based products that threaten its core film products. Kodak's skills and technologies used to make chemical-based film are not very transferable to producing digital-based imaging products. The distribution channels for electronics-based products (e.g., large specialized retailers and the Internet) are unlike those used to sell film (drug, grocery, and convenience stores). Thus, Kodak faces a different environment from the one in which it is used to competing. However, Kodak does have many promising technologies that will enable it to compete more effectively in the new environment. Convincing its own people that change and redirection are necessary to Kodak's survival is the critical task facing senior management. At Kodak and other firms facing similar pressures to change, senior management must play active roles in bringing about needed modifications.

Consequently, a static or slowly changing organization faces a significant challenge. Caught between the proverbial rock and a hard place, a static organization must often adapt quickly to an environmental development or be left behind in the wake of more nimble competitors. Yet, it may lack many of the organizational practices that enhance its ability to learn. Furthermore, the learning practices described previously often require considerable time to take effect. For example, several years at the very least may be required to generate value from a program of management rotation. All too often, a static organization requires even more rapid adaptation or it will lose its competitive position. It is easy to imagine how change can be so fast in some industries (e.g., software, semiconductors, Internet, financial services, and entertainment) that a change program initiated in one time period may already be obsolete before it is fully embraced by the organization. To bring about change in a static organization, senior managers must take a much more active role in the change process than is necessary in a learning organization. The following section identifies some of the obstacles senior management experience in trying to carry out this role. In a two-part discussion, we first discuss the resistance that senior managers of a static organization often encounter when attempting to bring about change. Then we describe a series of steps managers can take to overcome such resistance.

Resistance to Change in Static Organizations

Senior managers interested in promoting change in static organizations often possess insufficient knowledge to determine precisely how a firm should respond. They therefore need help designing and implementing a change program from managers and employees who have more specialized knowledge in specific areas. The need for such assistance is particularly great if a senior manager has been brought in from outside the company and possesses little industry experience. A senior manager interested in bringing about change in a static organization faces another kind of obstacle. Such an individual must also rely on managers and employees to implement the new response once it has been developed. Consequently, senior management needs the support of managers and employees in designing a change initiative and in implementing it. Unfortunately, managers and employees in static organizations often withhold such support. Among the most common reasons for withholding support are (1) lack of awareness of the need to change, (2) lack of interest in the opportunity that environmental change presents, and concern about (3) incompatibility, (4) cannibalization, and (5) personal loss (see Exhibit 13-3).

Common Reasons for Organizational Resistance to Change — EXHIBIT 13-3

- Lack of awareness of need to change
- Lack of interest in opportunity for change
- Incompatibility of change with existing values or interests
- Fear of cannibalization
- Fear of personal loss

Lack of Awareness

An appreciation of the need to change often requires a broad view of both the competitive and general environments. Managers and employees, especially functional managers and technicians preoccupied with their daily operating tasks, are often too focused on current activities to develop this kind of perspective. Therefore, people become overly shortsighted and too narrowly focused to be aware of potential changes over the horizon. As a result, they often fail to appreciate the need for change, especially if change means learning new methods, processes, or techniques that are significantly different from what they currently practice. The recent challenges facing companies as wide ranging as Eastman Kodak, Timex, Sears, Merrill Lynch, and companies in the music industry showed how people can become riveted to an earlier product, technology, way of serving a customer, or problem-solving approach.

Lack of Interest

Even when managers and employees recognize the need for change, they often perceive it as having only marginal impact on them. This kind of reaction is common even with new developments that could have severe consequences for the firm. It often occurs when a firm's own business is growing rapidly. Energies remain fully engaged with the firm's current activities. People also tend to ignore developments that represent transient or relatively small opportunities for expansion. Too often, an unproven or unorthodox approach is dismissed because of people's inability to understand the nature of the change.

Unfortunately, arrogance becomes a significant barrier to understanding the implications of new developments. For example, many once-existing U.S. companies in the consumer electronics industry, such as RCA, Philco, Motorola, General Electric, and Zenith, did not perceive the Japanese quality and low-cost advantage in making color televisions until it was too late. U.S. firms did not believe that Japanese manufacturing skills would help

Japanese products penetrate the U.S. market, where domestic firms had long commanded a strong market position. Japanese success in this activity underscores the vital roles of openness and experimentation to promote learning and competitive advantage.

Incompatibility with Cherished Values

Firms frequently develop their own sense of shared values and corporate culture that define the company's outlook and future strategies over time. In many cases, strongly held values or corporate culture can become significant obstacles to change. Managers and employees oppose new strategies, products, or approaches that appear to conflict with established practices. Strong corporate culture can often have the unintended effect of filtering out and neutralizing badly needed information and trends from the environment, since people are not used to thinking about their company's strategy and operations from a totally different perspective.

Consider the recent experience of Japanese computer and consumer electronics giant Nippon Electric Corporation (NEC). NEC invested heavily in its own proprietary personal computer (PC) software language. The company assigned great value to internal development of all key parts of its computers, including the software. Using an IBM-, Apple-, or Microsoft-based software operating system would violate NEC's cherished value of independence and self-directed innovation. Now, NEC is still reeling from tremendous competition from U.S.-based personal computer companies, such as Compaq Computer, Dell Computer, Apple, and even IBM itself, in its own home market. Japanese consumers, preferring the greater flexibility and software availability of IBM and Microsoft-based systems, are pushing NEC to adopt a more common computer software standard. NEC is only gradually shifting its strategy to incorporating Windows and other operating systems on its machines.[13] Even now, the company is still struggling with its computer business, and it has recently decided to shut down the production of some computer lines to refocus its efforts.

Fear of Cannibalization

Cannibalization is one of the greatest fears that prevent companies from investing in new technologies or products before competitors compel them to do so. Developing new products that are distinct from those of the firm's current lineup means admitting the possibility that alternative or substitute products do indeed exist. Facing the threat of substitute products or radically new product concepts is hard for any company to do. On the one hand, it means recognizing that the firm's strategic approach, assumptions, distinctive competences, and investments up to this point could quickly become obsolete. On the other hand, it may also require that the firms' people learn an entirely new set of skills and technologies to compete effectively in the new environment.

For example, by developing the personal computer and newer computer networking technology, IBM was forced to acknowledge that its core mainframe business would eventually face significant decline. Within IBM, people vigorously resisted this move, from fear that growing sales of emerging technologies would cannibalize sales of the firm's traditional products. The dominant approach that IBM used to develop, manufacture, sell, and service mainframe computers became part of the dominant mind-set of the entire firm. Anything that threatened IBM's dominance in the business was either dismissed (because IBM was too big), or ignored (because of a lack of understanding or urgency). Ironically, IBM during the early 1970s was the inventor of the RISC microprocessor used in smaller computers, but failed to commercialize it because of its likely impact on mainframe sales. Instead, recent sales gains by Hewlett-Packard, Sun Microsystems, and even Intel have grabbed big portions of the specialized RISC-based computer and workstation market.

In addition, industry leaders and other established firms generally enjoy higher profit margins in their traditional businesses than in newly emerging markets that they begin to explore (or prospect). This financial reality adds to the fear of cannibalization. For example, the Big Three U.S. automakers failed to innovate fast enough in smaller subcompact cars during the 1970s. Their hesitation to invest in worker training and to learn new assembly techniques accelerated Japanese import penetration into the United States. One can only hope that the Big Three will avoid these same steps when it comes to adopting new types of automotive technologies such as advanced fuel cells, batteries, and advanced materials and electronics. Fear of cannibalizing existing film sales remains a significant factor that holds Eastman Kodak back from vigorously developing new digital-imaging products; Kodak's new digital technologies threaten to erode its high margins in traditional chemical-based films.[14]

Fear of Personal Loss

Fear of personal loss is perhaps the most significant obstacle that prevents firms from becoming successful learners. The fear of restructurings that would eliminate entire divisions and businesses, along with all of the people involved, makes corporate change painful. Strategic change greatly impacts the personal well-being of employees in many ways. It alters how they interact with others and affects their bases of power. Also, change may render obsolete their skills, reduce their career opportunities, and even cost them their jobs. In recent years, numerous firms (General Motors, AT&T, Boeing, Nortel Networks, Lucent Technologies, Merrill Lynch, Sears, American Airlines, Union Pacific, United Technologies, and Texas Instruments) have been forced to lay off thousands of employees. Concern about layoffs often leads people to resist strategic change vigorously. For example, the United Auto Workers union has consistently fought General Motors' efforts to reclassify jobs to stream line the number of workers needed to produce cars and engaged in a costly strike against GM in 1998. This strike revolved around what GM could and could not do to outsource production to other nonunion U.S. plants or even foreign subsidiaries. Certainly with the ongoing downturn in the Japanese and Southeast Asian economies, Japanese and Korean firms, once greatly feared by U.S. competitors, are not immune to this problem either. Given the current global recession affecting their industries, many Japanese (e.g., Hitachi, Toshiba, NEC, Mitsubishi, and Mazda) and Korean (e.g., Lucky-Goldstar, Ssangyong, Samsung, Hyundai, and Daewoo) firms are extremely reluctant to undertake the kind of massive corporate restructurings that may endanger people's jobs. Even Japan's top semiconductor manufacturers, once greatly feared by U.S. companies, now face the prospect of letting go thousands of managers and employees as they seek to redirect their businesses to new growth opportunities.[15]

Change Steps

Senior managers implementing new initiatives in static organizations must deal with the issues of resistance brought about by the factors described in the preceding paragraphs. Some sources of resistance, such as fear of personal loss, remain extremely difficult, if not impossible, to resolve. However, these factors can also serve as important markers of where the firm needs to focus its change efforts. Also, the need for restructuring and decisive action opens up opportunities to make change and learning an integral part of the firm. To implement change effectively in static organizations, senior managers need to build commitment for some kind of change program or initiative.[16] Key steps in the process of building such commitment include (1) sensing the need for strategic change, (2) building organizational awareness of this need, (3) stimulating debate about alternative solutions, (4) strengthening consensus for a preferred approach, (5) assigning responsibility for implementation, and (6) allocating resources to sustain the effort (see Exhibit 13-4). These steps are especially valuable for firms that have just begun to recognize environmental developments that are starting to erode their existing sources of competitive advantage.

EXHIBIT 13-4 Key Steps to Implement Strategic Change

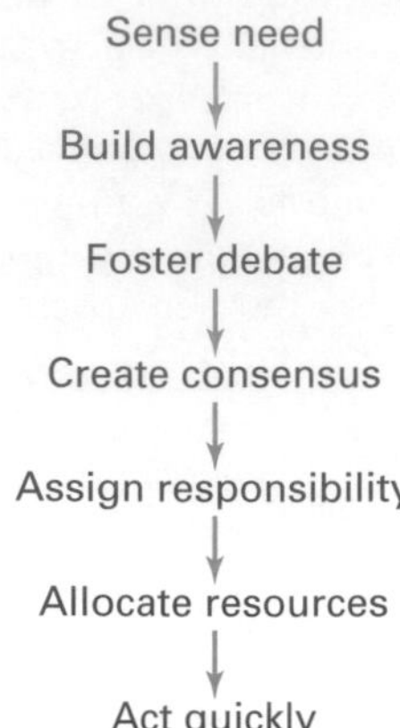

Sense the Need for Strategic Change

To fulfill their roles as change agents, members of senior management must develop an early awareness of the need for change. Information leading to such awareness can come from a variety of sources. Functional managers (vice presidents of manufacturing, marketing, and other departments) are one common source. A senior manager is likely to have frequent contact with such people during the course of everyday activities. During these interactions, valuable information about potential changes will sometimes come up. However, information supplied by these individuals will rarely be complete. For example, functional managers typically see only a portion of the firm's overall environment. They often suffer from specialty biases, especially in firms that do not have a well-developed system of managerial rotation and development. Thus, senior management should not rely exclusively on subordinates for information about environmental developments.

Another potential source of information about environmental developments is a firm's strategic planning process. Formal planning processes, however, can be real mixed blessings. On the one hand, they help managers identify near-term changes and the rise of potential competitors or new markets. On the other hand, planning processes can sometimes instill a rote method of analysis that can dangerously blind the firm to radical types of change. This danger results from reliance on the previous period's results as the basis for future assumptions within the planning process. Planning also tends to be dominated by managers in charge of major functions. As a consequence, planning reviews often become little more than a projection of historic trends and a rededication to past practices. Thus, a company's planning process can oftentimes be unreliable as a source of information about new developments, and certainly not a stimulant for creative thinking.

To secure reliable information about developments, senior managers generally need to spend time talking to people outside their own firms. A wide variety of external sources can be useful. Customers can provide especially valuable information about emerging product and service needs. For example, Canon successfully entered the U.S. copier and office equipment markets by asking secretaries what attributes they prefer in photocopiers. By building a reliable machine that did not require expensive maintenance, Canon was able to displace Xerox as market leader in the smaller and medium-sized copier categories. Information about new technologies and production techniques can often be acquired from suppliers. Suppliers are often more aware of shifts in the cost and availability of raw materials and of components that are likely to be introduced in new products. Benchmarking (a topic discussed in Chapter 14) provides an important source of information about the firm's practices and competitiveness vis-à-vis its competitors. Another source of information is scientific and professional associations, which may know more about developments in product and manufacturing technologies. Lobbyists who are typically aware of pending governmental regulations may also be a useful source of information. Examining the actions of competitors in closely related fields gives managers an additional lens through which to monitor the environment. These are just a few of the external sources of information available to top management. Outsiders still have their own biases but can provide fresh perspectives not available from within the firm.

Build Awareness of Need to Change and Learn

Once top managers have gained a general idea of the kind of change required, they must begin to build awareness of this need among employees in the firm, particularly among subordinates who possess expertise needed to shape a proper response, since such individuals have the power either to promote or to derail it. Senior management's objective at this point must be to target such individuals and encourage them to think about and evaluate important environmental developments and their significance for the firm.

Senior managers can take specific, direct steps to build an awareness for the need for change. An immediate step is to share their concerns verbally with lower-level managers and employees during routine contacts with them. These conversations will stimulate people's thoughts about possible change without raising anxieties too quickly. This step also reinforces the vital role of trust in airing problems and working through them. As they listen to people throughout the ranks, senior managers can surmise who is likely to support and oppose needed changes. Sharing information and establishing trust are critical in helping senior management build support for change.

A useful next action is to establish a task force to study the possible need for change more systematically. The group's composition must be carefully determined so that enough supporters are included to ensure that an initiative moves forward. A few opponents should also be included, however, in the hope that their interaction with supporters will convert them. Also, opponents often present arguments that have considerable merit. Failure to consider the value of these arguments only solidifies the opponents' resistance and raises the fear level among employees. This failure damages much of the firm's effort to instill new practices that promote learning. Opponents with special expertise may be able to contribute a unique perspective that turns out to be instrumental in solving problems.

Foster Debate

Stimulating debate about alternative solutions is essential, and a diversity of perspectives is vital to prevent the debate from being a one-sided exercise. Debate encourages new thinking that may produce insights not forthcoming from previous meetings. These debates also contribute to building a commitment to new goals. A task force can be useful in fostering healthy debate as well. By including proponents of several approaches, top management can ensure that the task force examines various solutions. Sometimes more than one task force can be formed to explore potential solutions. The results can then be compared at a later date to determine which approach is superior.[17]

Multiple teams are especially useful when new technology is involved. Diversity of ideas raises the chance that both the best and worst aspects of each alternative are brought to light. Bringing customers into the discussion is worthwhile, since they are the best judges of whether a new or modified product idea will work. Highly innovative companies such as McDonald's, Procter & Gamble, and Cisco Systems mandate customer participation when developing new products or service offerings. Customers test and comment on new product prototypes. For example, McDonald's numerous successes with different types of hamburgers and breakfast offerings were tested with customers in trial runs. The fat-free McLean Deluxe underwent extensive consumer testing in the mid-1990s to determine what customers liked best about the product.

Create Consensus

As results from debates come in, evidence will accumulate in favor of a particular approach. This evidence will itself help create consensus about the direction change should take. It will rarely persuade all parties, however, and some skeptics are likely to remain. Since resistance from such people can undermine further progress, a firm's management must strive to convert or at least neutralize these remaining "foes." Steps to do so can be extremely precarious, however, especially when the firm wants to become more open. Retaining entrenched opponents to a change initiative can result in further trouble. On the other hand, removing them too quickly without debate and consideration can seriously demoralize people, raising fears instead. Personal judgment, ethics, and leadership become vital guideposts at this stage.

Fortunately, opponents to a new initiative can often be converted by milder measures. Time alone can do much to transform opponents into allies. By giving an organization plenty of time to prepare for the new approach, management can provide opportunities for troubled or fearful personnel to work through resentment and frustration. At this stage, continuous training and management development can reap big dividends in implementing change. By teaching new skills to people threatened by a new approach, management can eliminate fear—one of the major sources of resistance to transformation. The reduction of fear can make employees valuable contributors to the change process. Companies can also take other steps to signal the positive effects of change. A change in the location of company headquarters or in a company's name can help signify the higher aspirations and positive benefits of change.

For example, the strategic integration and redirection of the Avco subsidiary after its takeover by Associates First Capital relied on many of these steps. Associates First Capital (now part of Citigroup) solicited Avco managers' and employees' ideas and feelings concerning what the company should do to compete in its many commercial and credit card businesses. By directly helping people recognize the certainty of change and finding a new role for them, management was able to reduce skepticism among Avco employees. Associates First Capital also hosted discussion groups in locations distant from the workplace as yet another vehicle for overcoming resistance to proposed change. Most likely, the enthusiasm of employees in favor of change worked to convert less enthusiastic members within focus and discussion groups.

Assign Responsibility

Once the appropriate response to an environmental change has been determined, responsibility for carrying it out must be assigned. Two basic approaches are available. First, a new effort toward change can be placed within an existing department. Second, it can be set up as a newly autonomous unit. The first approach will generally be less costly in the short run, since it enables a new activity to draw on resources and expertise of an existing unit. However, the new effort may lose urgency when the existing unit has priorities that lie elsewhere. To ensure that an initiative receives proper attention, it may need to be established as a separate unit headed by someone who has only its welfare in mind.

Who should be selected to administer such a unit? Candidates who have championed a new initiative in the past should be candidates for this position. Their past advocacy is testimony to their belief in the effort's worth, and it raises the likelihood that the initiative will receive the attention it needs to prosper. Also, longtime champions often possess skills needed to make the effort succeed. Motorola has used this approach successfully in implementing new manufacturing technologies to make quantum leaps in quality improvement during the 1990s. Previous process champions have been asked to participate and to initiate changes required to make new factories work.

Allocate Resources

A variety of resources may be needed to carry out a new initiative. For example, cash may be needed to develop a new technology, construct a prototype product, or conduct market research. Technical personnel and legal assistance may also be required. Management must ensure that sufficient resources are available for the initiative. Otherwise, the initiative will atrophy for lack of sustenance. Allocating these resources is the final step of the change process.

From Static to Learning Organizations

For the majority of firms that are not yet full-blown learning organizations, change can be a difficult and painstaking proposition. The difficulty is particularly acute in firms that have grown accustomed to environments with few competitors and stable technologies. However, few companies operate any longer within this type of no-change or even low-change competitive environment. Most firms increasingly face environments where rapid change is commonplace. Companies from every industry—financial services, hospitals, semiconductors, retailing, and every type of manufacturing—now face the onslaught of more agile competitors and ever-faster changing customer needs and technologies. Even those firms that once dominated their industries—Sears in retailing, Merrill Lynch in brokerage services, Procter & Gamble in personal care products, Intel in semiconductors, Kellogg in breakfast cereals, and Frito-Lay in snack foods—need to "reinvent" themselves periodically to learn new skills and approaches to serve their markets. Thus, static organizations are compelled to institute management practices that make adaptation to rapid change less difficult and even widely accepted by all of its people.

The Transformation of General Electric

If there has been one company over the past two decades that has instilled the idea of change as part of its corporate culture, it is General Electric—especially under the leadership period of CEO John "Jack" Welch (1981–2001). General Electric is America's most valuable company, as defined by its market capitalization. Part of the reason that investors have viewed GE so positively in recent years is directly attributable to the aggressive actions that Welch and his management team have taken to ensure that GE remains agile, lean, and noncomplacent about its competition. Yet, the transition from static organization to learning organization at General Electric has certainly proven to be a complex and difficult task.

Before Welch was brought into the company in 1981, GE was profitable and grew slowly each year. Its home appliances, aircraft engines, lighting, plastics, consumer electronics, and motors businesses, for example, were largely mature, profitable, and ripe for global competition. Each business unit was finely attuned to competing in its own environment, with competition and technology fairly predictable and stable. It has taken close to two decades for Welch and his management team to implement many new management practices that make change an accepted part of working at GE. Exhibit 13-5 shows the implementation of numerous changes that have pushed GE more toward a learning organization.

One of Welch's first steps was to make GE a "boundaryless" organization.[18] A **boundaryless organization** means that people in one department or division talk with people in other departments/divisions to share ideas, resources, and insights. In its most ideal form, a boundaryless organization encourages people to learn from one another, no matter where they may be located within or outside the organization. People should be free to learn and adapt the best ideas to improve their businesses. These ideas can come from people from other levels or places within the organization (internally), or from customers, suppliers, and even competitors (externally). A boundaryless organization means that people should be willing to listen and implement new ways of doing things, no matter where they originated.

boundaryless organization: An organization design in which people can easily share information, resources, and skills across departments and divisions.

Removing or reducing formal department-divisional boundaries is an important first step in becoming a learning organization. Welch believed that making GE boundaryless would pave the way to building an organization that could change faster and begin to learn new skills. Welch needed to uproot and replace deeply ingrained practices and habits that inhibited change. To accomplish his goal, Welch dissolved many layers of management that

EXHIBIT 13-5 Corporate Transformations in the 1990s: Making General Electric Boundaryless

1980	1986	1988–1992	1994 →
• GE vulnerable to change	• Reduce number of peripheral businesses	• Form strategic alliances	• Reduce SBU walls even more
• Slow growth	• Sell nonperforming assets	• "Work Out"	• Invest in Asia/Europe
• Average earnings	• Break down strong SBU lines	• Team with suppliers/ customers	• Foster continual training and development
• Big bureaucracy	• Acquire strong performers elsewhere	• Share knowledge and skills across GE's SBUs	• Encourage best practices and benchmarking
• High divisional walls	• Delayer management hierarchies	• Promote those who take risks	• Promote common vision
• Lots of protected turf	• Adopt new reward systems	• Invest in streamlined product development time	• Hire people with entrepreneurial tendencies
• Resistance to change			• "Six Sigma"

separated employees from managers and each other. Some of the efforts that Welch and his team took during the early 1980s resulted in large layoffs; the business press started calling the CEO "Neutron Jack" for his massive firings that left GE significantly depopulated in many business units. Despite heavy criticism, Welch moved to make each and every GE business unit much leaner and more agile over time. Each and every GE business was expected to become either "Number One or Number Two" in its respective industry. Those businesses that could not make the cut were sold. Even such well-known businesses as consumer electronics, small appliances, industrial controls, and broadcasting equipment were eventually divested. Within the four years that he was CEO, Welch sold off over a hundred different GE businesses—all of them slow growers or unprofitable. By selling some of the businesses that served as icons of the old GE, Welch sent a very clear message that no business is sacred from the need to change.

At the same time, GE acquired numerous other companies that helped surviving GE businesses to attain a number one or two position in its industry. For example, in 1986 GE completed the acquisition of RCA, a leading industrial and broadcasting company that also owns the NBC network. Since Welch took over, GE has made hundreds of acquisitions, usually of smaller companies, to bolster GE's growth rate and market share. Despite frequent communications to managers and employees that GE needed to change, Welch faced a difficult road. His efforts initially encountered significant resistance from lower-level managers who feared that change would erode their power bases. Many veteran GE managers left; others were asked to join management development programs designed to convince them of the need to change.

Welch later instituted other practices designed to enhance the firm's capacity for change. These include extensive managerial rotation and training programs to promote openness and idea exchange at all levels of the company. The company maintains an executive and employee development facility in Crotonville, New York. Every day, GE managers and employees enter courses and other training programs designed to keep them aware of environmental developments and the need to change. In the late 1980s, General Electric instituted a company-wide program known as "Work Out." Everyone is encouraged to participate in an ongoing internal overhaul of the company to locate and remove hidden inefficiencies and wasteful practices. People with the best and most workable suggestions are given authority to implement their recommendations.

To this day, General Electric is still working to make continuous learning and improvement a key part of its organizational practices. Boundaryless thinking has become an important part of GE's corporate culture. GE is now in the midst of a massive quality improvement program known as "Six Sigma." Using a program that is similar to Motorola's own quality initiative, GE is attempting to revamp all of its operations and core processes to promote those practices that best support and improve quality. The objective of Six Sigma is to identify and eliminate all sources of waste, thus unleashing even greater improvements in quality and productivity. Each and every GE employee is expected to undergo a series of classes regarding Six Sigma, until they graduate with a "black belt" in process improvement.

GE is becoming much more aggressive in its efforts to expand into new markets around the world, as well as into new service-based businesses. For the past six years, GE has placed a high priority on investing in Asia, with the explicit goal of making Asian consumers aware of GE's wide range of quality products and services, especially in Japan. At the same time, GE is moving to expand its service-based businesses to bolster the profitability of its manufacturing-based businesses. Such GE businesses as Aircraft Engines, Medical Systems, Power Systems, Lighting, Plastics, and Transportation Systems are moving to become even closer to their customers by setting up service operations directly on their customers' sites. For example, GE Transportation Systems is now beginning to work closely with the largest railroad companies in the United States (e.g., Union Pacific, Burlington Northern Santa Fe, CSX, Norfolk Southern) to provide immediate and on-site maintenance and repair work for their locomotives.[19]

In September 2001, Jack Welch retired from his CEO position at General Electric after twenty years of service. His replacement, Jeffrey R. Immelt from GE Medical Systems, has an even more challenging task facing him. Under Welch's stewardship, GE grew its earnings from \$1.5 billion in 1980 to \$12.7 billion in 2000. Revenues since 1981 have also quintupled to \$130 billion. When Welch took over in 1981, GE's market capitalization was \$13 billion (the nation's seventh most valuable company at the time). In early 2002, GE is worth over \$400 billion.[20] Many analysts now wonder how long GE can continue to grow its earnings and market capitalization, despite all that Jack Welch and his team have done over the past twenty years. Even the new CEO notes that his primary task at GE is to promote the development of new ideas, and Immelt will continue to push the company's growth into new types of service businesses. Prior to assuming the CEO's job, Immelt had already shown that he could lead change at GE Medical Systems. Under his leadership, GE Medical Systems made dozens of acquisitions and innovated many new products. He is also known for being a "high contact person" with customers and employees. Immelt believes in personally updating employees each week about GE's latest developments—new products developed, missed opportunities, nuggets for new ideas—through the company's internal e-mail system. E-mail is actually sent in five languages, sometimes even a dozen, to ensure that it reaches everybody around the world in GE's vast empire.[21]

An enduring legacy of Jack Welch is the growing number of former GE managers who now preach many of the same ideas. Executive search firms actively seek to hire away dozens of top GE managers each year for companies in every industry that seek to reinvent themselves in the way that GE did. These ex-GE managers are now transforming other companies. The choice of Jeffrey Immelt to become the new CEO of General Electric has also triggered an exodus of many leading GE managers who competed for the top job. In turn, however, these ex-GE alumni are now beginning to transform the companies that hired them in mid-2001. For example, firms such as Albertsons, The Home Depot, 3M, and Conseco now have their own CEOs who once worked closely with Welch to transform GE for much of the 1990s. All of these managers are now committed to making their companies leaders in their respective industries by instilling many of the same practices they pushed forth at GE.[22]

Embracing Change as a Way of Life

Perhaps the most important legacy that Jack Welch has left for both GE and management in general is the need for constant change.[23] Welch understood that for companies to learn and build new sources of competitive advantage, *a business within an industry must change and reinvent itself faster than the rate* at which the industry is changing. In other words, competitive advantage at the business unit level stems from the actions of each individual business to embrace and utilize change to create new opportunities at a rate faster than that which competitors, customers, and suppliers are changing. At the corporate level, competitive advantage comes when the entire organization is able to leverage new ideas, skills, technologies, and insights in ways that other competitors cannot. By doing those things that competitors cannot imitate, the company becomes increasingly distinctive. Distinctiveness, in turn, leads to stronger sources of competitive advantage—which ultimately translates into higher sustained profitability.

Undoubtedly, the issue of learning and change is highly complex. Yet, even such relatively new and agile companies as Cisco Systems and Microsoft are making change part of their culture. More than ever, Cisco Systems realizes that it, too, must devise new strategies to change its operations and new product development approaches as the telecommunications and computer networking industries' growth rates slow down. Throughout the 1990s, Cisco consistently grew its revenues and earnings over 25 percent per year. In 2000 and 2001, the company suffered a series of financial blows as telecom customers canceled their orders for next-generation optical networking equipment. Under CEO John Chambers, Cisco realizes that it must learn new skills and ideas to compete effectively. Even Chambers has admitted that as companies become larger, the more difficult it is to innovate.[24]

Promoting the need for learning and embracing change within a company is a tough sell, even for the best leaders. Its treatment in this chapter is at best rudimentary, since so many human relationship issues are involved. Many of the measures discussed in this chapter represent only the first steps of learning and change. Yet, they are applicable to all firms that find change at their doorstep. The rise of new technologies, markets, and competitors will surely accelerate the tempo of change in all industries.

Ethical Dimension

Building organizations capable of adapting to rapid change require senior managers to cultivate a true sense of openness and legitimacy toward diverse viewpoints. As we move into the twenty-first century, growing numbers of firms will face the need to adapt and change rapidly in the wake of environmental developments. While senior managers begin to restructure their organizations to adapt to environmental change, they must also consider two key ethical questions surrounding organizational issues. Although the ramifications of these questions are extremely complex and defy easy answers, it is worthwhile for managers to consider (1) how to use diversity to enrich the firm's knowledge base and (2) how to help employees cope with change.

Using Diversity to Enrich the Firm's Knowledge Base

Diversity of people, issues, and ideas provides strength to firms that know how to treat their people openly and with respect. In the future, few firms will be competing in slowly changing or no-change environments. Companies over time will need to learn new technologies, skills, capabilities, and human relationship skills to compete in fast-changing global environments where managers must be able to tap into a host of insights and ideas supplied by their organizational members, no matter who they are or where they are from.[25] A firm's future source of competitive advantage will increasingly be drawn from its people—people who are more diverse, agile, and mobile than ever before. Already, scores of U.S. companies such as AT&T, Hewlett-Packard, Intel, Microsoft, Sun Microsystems, and Texas Instruments are aggressively tapping into new sources of global talent. These firms are establishing operations and direct Internet-based forms of communications to work with key talent, no matter where they are located (e.g., China, Russia, Israel, India, Taiwan, Malaysia, Singapore). By the next century, the workforce will be more global as well, with companies tapping into the unique strengths of different regions and comparative advantages around the world, especially through corporate information networks based on Internet technology.[26] General Electric has already taken great strides in this direction, by linking up all of its business units with customers, suppliers, and employees around all of GE's vast global operations. The Internet will do much to shrink the geographic distances that once separated the far-flung subsidiaries and talents of people among subsidiaries, alliance partners, suppliers, and customers. On the other hand, firms that ignore or denigrate people with diverse or unorthodox ideas may be sabotaging their own future capacity for change. Few companies will remain insulated from technological change, the pressures of globalization, or the opportunities and challenges posed by diversity.

Consider how Texas Instruments uses its diverse workforce as a source of competitive advantage. TI is one of the world's leading producers of semiconductors, electronic components, and defense equipment. It views its diverse global workforce as key to its competitive advantage. The semiconductor and electronics industries are coming under the twin pressures of global competition and faster technological change. Texas Instruments' recent restructuring of its internal operations enables it to adapt to these changes by drawing on the unique insights and capabilities offered by its diverse global workforce to accelerate design and production time of its products. TI has software engineers working in India, production and process engineers in Japan, design engineers throughout Europe, and a host of operations throughout North America—all connected to one another by way of satellite or Internet transmission technology. To accelerate product development and commercialization, TI links its various engineers and technical staff around the world via a satellite-based communication system through which people can talk with their counterparts in other TI locations at any time during the day. As U.S. engineers and managers sleep, their colleagues in India are actively working on new software programs and chip designs. They, in turn, forward their communications and ideas to the United States through the Internet. When U.S.-based managers and employees go to work, the information from India is already there in their e-mail.

More important, TI encourages its numerous professional staff groups to work jointly on project development teams, with each team preferably staffed by a representative from each of TI's key geographic markets or areas. These teams travel worldwide to work on projects that draw upon their collective expertise. In this way, TI's project teams draw upon the distinctive skills, insights, and ideas from many persons and regions to look at a problem from numerous perspectives. This advantage would not exist had the company relied solely on its U.S.-based personnel to take the lead in key projects.

Helping Employees Cope with Change

Unfortunately, many people within static organizations lack the ability to change as quickly as the environment demands. This issue poses a growing dilemma for senior managers of many of today's blue-chip companies. New technologies or younger staff are replacing many of their older, seasoned, and experienced employees. On the other hand, top managers often feel that the attributes possessed by older employees, who helped the company to grow and prosper in earlier days, may now limit these people's ability to learn new technologies and skills.

For example, consider the situation faced by operators at telecommunications giant AT&T. The rise of computer-based telephone systems that allow customers to place their own long-distance calls without the help of an operator has effectively made many of AT&T's current operators unnecessary. Unfortunately, many of the people who currently staff these functions originally entered the company with limited education and skills. Although AT&T was able to provide them with a steady income and numerous benefits for many years, these operators face increasing obsolescence as newer systems are developed. Thus, management at AT&T faces a difficult choice. It can offer programs to retrain its operators to perform other functions, but this task would be expensive. On the other hand,

AT&T can simply fire vast numbers of operators as their union contracts expire in subsequent years. While doing so would save the company some labor expenses in the short term, it could demoralize employees in other parts of the company who also fear introduction of new technologies in the workplace. Thus, helping workers cope with the inevitable changes brought on by new technologies or environmental developments must be a prime task for top management.

Summary

- Building a learning organization helps firms create new sources of competitive advantage. As environments change more quickly, organizations must be able to reconfigure their products and technologies faster.
- Management practices that promote learning include (1) frequent rotation of managers, (2) continual training of personnel, (3) decentralization of decision making, (4) encouragement of multiple experiments, (5) high tolerance for failure, and (6) openness to diverse perspectives.
- Most firms are not yet learning organizations. For these firms, implementing change can be difficult because of varying levels of resistance. In the most extreme case, firms may look like "dinosaur" organizations.
- Dinosaur organizations are extremely well tuned and adapted to a no-change or even low-change environment. These firms are wedded to a particular technology, product design, or distribution channel. They are most vulnerable to new competitors or other environmental developments.
- Managers and employees often resist initiatives designed to enhance the organization's ability to adapt to change. Managers and employees resist change for many reasons; they (1) lack awareness of the need to change, (2) lack interest in the opportunity that change presents, (3) feel that an initiative is incompatible with cherished values, (4) fear cannibalization, and (5) worry about personal loss. The last factor is often the most troublesome.
- Senior managers interested in implementing a change initiative must undertake steps to overcome resistance. Often, opponents to change can become persuaded over time to see the necessity and merits for change if there is sufficient openness in the organization.
- Senior managers are responsible for creating a setting conducive to expressing various perspectives and arguments for and against change. Key steps in this process are (1) sensing the need for change, (2) building organizational awareness of this need, (3) stimulating debate about alternative solutions, (4) strengthening consensus for a preferred approach, (5) assigning responsibility for implementation, and (6) allocating resources to sustain the effort.
- A boundaryless organization means that people in one department or division talk with people in other departments or divisions. Removing barriers to communication represents an important step in helping firms make change and learning a part of their daily practice.

Exercises and Discussion Questions

1. There is no doubt that change is a difficult process in any organization, particularly one with a proud history. What do you believe are some of the basic reasons that change is difficult to implement? How does a company's success in a previous time period, ironically, make it even more difficult to change?
2. In recent years, a number of well-known U.S. companies have gone into bankruptcy or failed (e.g., Kmart, Montgomery Ward, National Steel). From an orga-

nizational perspective, what are some of the reasons that static or dinosaur organizations face even greater hurdles and obstacles to implement change? In your judgment, is change easier to implement at higher or lower levels within the organization? What are some steps that could promote change at the more senior levels within the organization? Likewise, what are some steps that could facilitate change at middle and lower levels within the organization as well?

3. As the chapter notes, very few companies possess all of the qualities that characterize a learning organization. In your judgment, how can firms become more effective in promoting their ability to learn? Should they look toward their competitors, their customers, or even firms in other industries for new ideas?
4. Over the long term, is learning easier to promote when a company is at the growth or mature stage of the product life cycle?

Endnotes

1. Facts and data for this case were adapted from the following sources: "Can Sony Regain the Magic?" *Business Week*, March 11, 2002, pp. 72–80; "In This Game, Microsoft Is More David Than Goliath," *Business Week*, November 19, 2001, p. 46; "Sony's Caution in Past Allows New Boldness," *Wall Street Journal*, November 19, 2001, pp. B1, B4; "AOL and Sony Plan Alliance to Develop Web Technologies for Consumer Devices," *Wall Street Journal*, November 13, 2001, p. B3; "Sony Agrees to License Video Recording," *Wall Street Journal*, October 19, 2001; "Sony: Losing the Magic Touch?" *Business Week*, October 15, 2001; "Sony Game Unit Invests in Square, Preparing for Fight with Microsoft," *Wall Street Journal*, October 10, 2001, p. B3; "Sony, Ericsson Mix Technology, Marketing Savvy," *Wall Street Journal*, October 9, 2001; "Sony Has Device to Enliven Home Entertainment," *Wall Street Journal*, August 23, 2001, p. B1; "Outfox the Xbox," *Forbes*, August 6, 2001, pp. 44–46; "Yahoo! and Sony Reach E-Commerce and Marketing Pact," *Wall Street Journal*, August 1, 2001; "New Sony Appliance Doesn't Match Compaq in Price and Simplicity," *Wall Street Journal*, July 19, 2001, p. B1; "Sony to Unveil Online Music Studio," *Wall Street Journal*, June 18, 2001, p. B6; "Sony, RealNetworks Form a Partnership," *Wall Street Journal*, May 16, 2001; "Sony, AOL Join Up to Link PlayStation 2 to Internet in Move to Outflank Microsoft," *Wall Street Journal*, May 15, 2001, pp. A3, A8; "Sony, Once Again, Unveils Broad Corporate Overhaul," *Wall Street Journal*, March 30, 2001, p. A13; "Sony's Boogie Knight," *Fortune*, March 19, 2001, pp. 105–115; "IBM Receives Sony Contract for New Chips," *Wall Street Journal*, March 12, 2001; "Sony to Unveil 40-Inch Flat-Glass Tube Television," *Wall Street Journal*, January 15, 2001, p. B2; "How Much Is That Robot in the Window?" *Business Week*, November 27, 2000; "The Only Game in Town: Sony's PlayStation 2 Smokes the Competition," *Fortune*, November 13, 2000; "Godzilla Needs Batteries," *Forbes*, September 18, 2000, pp. 66–69; "Sony Gets Real Personal," *Business Week*, September 11, 2000; "Sony, Universal Plan Music Venture for the Internet," *Wall Street Journal*, May 3, 2000; "Sony Music, BMG Entertainment Plan to Start Selling Digital Music on Web," *Wall Street Journal*, April 7, 2000; "Sony Creates Company to Target the Market for Broadband Services," *Wall Street Journal*, February 24, 2000; "Inside Sony, a Clash over Web Music," *Wall Street Journal*, January 26, 2000, pp. B1, B4; "How Sony Turned a Skinny Laptop into an Unlikely PC Success," *Wall Street Journal*, November 12, 1999; "Sony's CEO Management Style Wasn't Made in Japan," *Wall Street Journal*, October 7, 1999; "Sony Unveils Price Cuts for PlayStation Package," *Wall Street Journal*, August 26, 1998, p. B4; "Sony Modifies Camera with Revealing Feature," *Wall Street Journal*, August 13, 1998; "Dumb Appliances Smart Up a Bit," *Business Week*, August 10, 1998, p. 13; "Consumer Electronics: Matsushita: The Electronic Giant Wakes Up," *Business Week*, July 20, 1998, p. 120; "Sony Puts Expertise in Style and Ingenuity behind Flashy Portable," *Wall Street Journal*, June 18, 1998, p. B1; "The Games Sony Plays," *Business Week*, June 15, 1998, p. 128; "How Sony Created

a Monster," *Fortune*, June 8, 1998, p. 162; "Sony Again Attempts to Sell its Mini-CD, Focusing on Recording," *Wall Street Journal*, May 28, 1998, p. B1; "A Sharper Look for Those Tiny Screens," *Business Week*, May 5, 1998, p.158; "Microsoft, Sony Agree to Work Together to Link Consumer-Electronics Devices," *Wall Street Journal*, April 4, 1998, p. B6; "Sony Hits a Campaign Trail to Sell Public on MiniDiscs," *Investor's Business Daily*, April 1, 1998, p. A8; "Sony's U.S. Electronics Unit Readies New, $30 Million MiniDisc Campaign," *Wall Street Journal*, February 2, 1998, p. B12; "Sony Plans to Purchase 5% Stake in Next Level," *Wall Street Journal*, January 5, 1998, p. A3; "Dictate at Will, Download When Convenient," *Business Week*, December 15, 1997, p. 138; "Sony Says It's Weighing Digital Moves and Hires Blackstone Group to Assist," *Wall Street Journal*, November 21, 1997, p. B9; "Sony Profits Jump on Strong Sales of Electronics Gear," *Wall Street Journal*, October 31, 1997, p. B6; "Let Your Laptop Do the Navigating," *Business Week*, October 6, 1997, p. 23; "Sony, Sharp, Philips Form Display Venture," *Wall Street Journal*, July 31, 1997, p. B12; "Digital Video's Next Generation?" *Business Week*, June 16, 1997, p. 141; "Sony Turns to PC Market to Revive Its Sales Growth," *Investor's Business Daily*, April 16, 1997, p. A6; "Nintendo Catches Up to Sony in Market for Most-Advanced Video-Game Players," *Wall Street Journal*, February 3, 1997, p. B3; "TV and PC: Tying the Knot," *Business Week*, October 28, 1996, p. 31; "Sony, Discovery Agree on Store," *Wall Street Journal*, October 22, 1996; "Sony Unit to Enter U.S. Paging Field with Novel Offer," *Wall Street Journal*, September 17, 1996, p. B8; "Key Firms Launching Digital Video Disks Reach Licensing Pact," *Wall Street Journal*, September 16, 1996, p. B7; "Toshiba Joins Sony in Race for U.S. Home PC Market," *Investor's Business Daily*, September 10, 1996, p. A8; "Qualcomm-Sony Venture Wins 2 Orders for PCS Phones Valued at $850 Million," *Wall Street Journal*, June 21, 1996, p. B7; "Sony Launches Portable Products for Video CD Line," *Wall Street Journal*, June 4, 1996, p. B3; "Sony's New World," *Business Week*, May 27, 1996, p. 36; "Sony and Intel Plan to Make a Home PC That Will Take on the Industry," *Fortune*, December 11, 1995, p. 27.

Sony's particularly successful endeavor in compact disc (CD) players is discussed in T. Shibata, "Sony's Successful Strategy in Compact Discs," *Long-Range Planning* (August 1993): 16–21. Sony's growing relationship with Apple is covered in "Apple's Japanese Ally," *Fortune*, November 4, 1991, pp. 151–152. A detailed discussion of Sony's philosophy and the experiences of the company's cofounder and current chairman, Akio Morita, is found in *Made in Japan* (New York: Dutton, 1986), and A. Morita, "Partnering for Competitiveness: The Role of Japanese Business," *Harvard Business Review* (May–June 1992): 76–83.

2. A growing research literature on organizational learning examines the relationship of organizational practices and the organization's ability to change. Suggested references for further reading include the following: C. Argyris and K. A. Schon, *Organizational Learning: A Theory of Action Perspective* (Reading, Mass.: Addison-Wesley, 1978); C. M. Fiol and M. A. Lyles, "Organizational Learning," *Academy of Management Review* 10 (1985): 803–813; G. Huber, "Organizational Learning: The Contributing Processes and the Literatures," *Organization Science* 2, no. 1 (1991): 1–18; J. S. Brown and P. Duguid, "Organizational Learning and Communities of Practice: Toward a Unified View of Working, Learning, and Innovation," *Organization Science* 2 (1991): 40–57; and A. Van de Van and D. Polley, "Learning While Innovating," *Organization Science* 3 (1992): 92–116. Readers may also want to consider P. M. Senge, *The Fifth Discipline* (New York: Doubleday, 1990), and B. Levitt and J. G. March, "A Model of Adaptive Organizational Search," *Journal of Economic Behavior and Organization* 2 (1988): 307–333. An evolving typology of the different forms of organizational learning can be found in D. Miller, "A Preliminary Typology of Organizational Learning: Synthesizing the Literature," *Journal of Management* 22 (1996): 485–505.

A recent review of the key issues surrounding organizational change can be found in A. Pettigrew, R. W. Woodman and K. S. Cameron, "Studying Organizational Change and Development: Challenges for Future Research," *Academy of Management*

Journal 44, no. 4 (2001): 697–714; L. Heracleous and M. Barrett, "Organizational Change as Discourse: Communicative Actions and Deep Structures in the Context of Information Technology Implementation," *Academy of Management Journal* 44, no. 4 (2001): 755–778; B. L. Kirkman and D. L. Shapiro, "The Impact of Cultural Values on Job Satisfaction and Organizational Commitment in Self-Managing Work Teams: The Mediating Role of Employee Resistance," *Academy of Management Journal* 44, no. 3 (2001): 570–579. Some important empirical studies studying organizational learning and its antecedents have emerged in the past few years. Representative works include the following: J. B. Thomas, S. Watts Sussman, and J. C. Henderson, "Understanding 'Strategic Learning': Linking Organizational Learning, Knowledge Management and Sensemaking," *Organization Science* 12, no. 3 (2001): 331–345; F. Vermeulen and H. Barkema, "Learning through Acquisitions," *Academy of Management Journal* 44, no. 3 (2001): 457–476; R. G. McGrath, "Exploratory Learning, Innovative Capacity, and Managerial Oversight," *Academy of Management Journal* 44, no. 1 (2001): 112–133; D. Z. Levin, "Organizational Learning and the Transfer of Knowledge: An Investigation of Quality Improvement," *Organization Science* 11, no. 6 (2000): 630–647; H. W. Volberda, "Toward the Flexible Form: How to Remain Vital in Hypercompetitive Environments," *Organization Science* 7, no. 4 (1996): 359–374; B. L. Simonin, "The Importance of Collaborative Know-How: An Empirical Test of the Learning Organization," *Academy of Management Journal* 40, no. 5 (1997): 1150–1174; W. W. Powell, K. W. Koput, and L. Smith-Doerr, "Interorganizational Collaboration and the Locus of Innovation: Networks of Learning in Biotechnology," *Administrative Science Quarterly* 41 (1996): 116–145; R. M. Grant, "Prospering in Dynamically Competitive Environments: Organizational Capability as Knowledge Integration," *Organization Science* 7, no. 4 (1996): 375–387; E. Bruderer and J. V. Singh, "Organizational Evolution, Learning, and Selection: A Genetic-Algorithm-Based Model," *Academy of Management Journal* 39, no. 5 (1996): 1322–1349; J. M. Pennings, H. Barkema, and S. Douma, "Organizational Learning and Diversification," *Academy of Management Journal* 37 (1994): 608–640; H. Barkema, O. Shenkar, and J. M. Pennings, "Foreign Entry, Cultural Barriers, and Learning," *Strategic Management Journal* 17 (1996): 151–166; A. Parkhe, "Interfirm Diversity, Organizational Learning, and Longevity in Global Strategic Alliances," *Journal of International Business Studies* 22 (1991): 579–601.

3. This section is adapted from M. McGill, J. W. Slocum, Jr., and D. Lei, "Management Practices in Learning Organizations," *Organizational Dynamics* (Summer 1992): 5–17; D. A. Garvin, "Building a Learning Organization," *Harvard Business Review* (July–August 1993): 78–91; K. Jones and T. Ohbora, "Managing the Heretical Company," *McKinsey Quarterly* 3 (1990): 20–45; C. Argyris, "Education for Leading-Learning," *Organizational Dynamics* 22, no. 2 (1993): 5–17; M. E. McGill and J. W. Slocum, Jr., *The Smarter Organization* (New York: Wiley, 1994); D. Miller, *The Icarus Paradox: How Exceptional Companies Bring about Their Own Downfall* (New York: Harper Business, 1990); J. W. Slocum, Jr., M. E. McGill, and D. Lei, "The New Learning Strategy: Anytime, Anything, Anywhere," *Organizational Dynamics* 23, no. 2 (1994): 33–48; C. Argyris, "The Executive Mind and Double-Loop Learning," *Organizational Dynamics* 11, no. 1 (1982): 5–22.

Also see M. Marquardt and A. Reynolds, *The Global Learning Organization* (New York: Irwin, 1994); E. C. Nevis, A. C. DiBella, and J. M. Gould, "Understanding Organizations and Learning Systems," *Sloan Management Review* 36, no. 2 (1995): 73–85; I. Nonaka, "A Dynamic Theory of Organizational Knowledge Creation," *Organization Science* 5 (1994): 14–37; D. Levinthal and J. G. March, "The Myopia of Learning," *Strategic Management Journal* 14 (1993): 95–112; B. Kogut and U. Zander, "Knowledge of the Firm, Combinative Capabilities and the Replication of Technology," *Organization Science* 3 (1992): 383–397; A. Van de Van and D. Polley, "Learning While Innovating," *Organization Science* 3, no. 1 (1992): 92–116. R. Stata, "Organizational Learning—The Key to Management Innovation," *Sloan Management Review* 30, no. 3 (1989): 63–74.

4. See "GM: It'll Be a Long Road Back," *Business Week*, August 17, 1998, pp. 38–39; "GM Chairman Plans Sweeping Changes," *Wall Street Journal*, August 6, 1998, pp. A3–A6; "GM's Aurora," *Business Week*, March 21, 1994, pp. 88–95; "Saturn," *Business Week*, August 17, 1992, pp. 86–89; "GM's $11 Billion Turnaround," *Fortune*, October 17, 1994, pp. 54–70.

5. See, for example, H. Itami, *Mobilizing Invisible Assets* (Cambridge, Mass.: Harvard University Press, 1987), and W. Ouchi, *Theory Z: How American Business Can Meet the Japanese Challenge* (Reading, Mass.: Addison-Wesley, 1981), for an early overview and discussion of the high-premium Japanese firms place on continuous training.

6. See, for example, T. Peters, "Rethinking Scale," *California Management Review* 35, no. 1 (1992): 7–29.

7. See "Johnson & Johnson Is on a Roll," *Fortune*, December 26, 1994, pp. 178–195.

8. See T. Hout, M. E. Porter, and E. Rudden, "How Global Companies Win Out," *Harvard Business Review* (September–October 1982): 98–106; C. K. Prahalad and Y. Doz, *The Multinational Mission* (New York: Free Press, 1987); and "A U.S.-Style Shakeup at Honda," *Fortune*, December 31, 1991, pp. 115–122.

9. See, for example, "Sony Overhauls the Management Team at Its Troubled Hollywood Film Studio," *Wall Street Journal*, October 9, 1996, p. B6; "Sony's Studios Face a Future of Uncertainty," *Wall Street Journal*, November 22, 1994, pp. B1, B6; "Sony Finally Admits Billion-Dollar Mistake: Its Messed-Up Studio," *Wall Street Journal*, November 18, 1994, pp. A1, A10; "Levine Bets Doubters He Can Revive Sony Pictures," *Wall Street Journal*, February 21, 1995, pp. B1, B4.

10. See, for example, D. Dougherty and C. Hardy, "Sustained Product Innovation in Large, Mature Organizations: Overcoming Innovation-to-Organization Problems," *Academy of Management Journal* 39, no. 5 (1996): 1120–1153; E. E. Lawler III and J. R. Galbraith, "Avoiding the Corporate Dinosaur Syndrome," *Organizational Dynamics* 23, no. 2 (1994): 5–17; W. Weitzel and E. Johnson, "Reversing the Downward Spiral: Lessons from W. T. Grant and Sears Roebuck," *Academy of Management Executive* 5, no. 3 (1991): 7–22; E. C. Shapiro, *How Competitive Truths Become Competitive Traps* (New York: Wiley, 1991); "History Is Full of Giants That Failed to Adapt," *Forbes*, February 28, 1994, pp. 73–78.

11. See, for example, "Wide Gap Exists between GM, Rivals in Labor Productivity, Report Says," *Wall Street Journal*, July 16, 1998, p. A4.

12. See, for example, "Sears to Overhaul Stores, Change Format, Cut 5,000 Jobs in Move to Boost Profits," *Wall Street Journal*, October 25, 2001, p. B3; "Sears and Lowe's Widen Their Lead in Appliances," *Wall Street Journal*, September 11, 2001; "Sears Tests Limited-Ware Stores," *Wall Street Journal*, May 11, 2001; "Fashion Victim: Sears Apparel Sales Keep Unraveling," *Wall Street Journal*, April 30, 2001, p. B1; "Sears' New CEO Has Handle on Finance, But May Need to Master Merchandising," *Wall Street Journal*, September 12, 2000.

13. See "Japan's PC Market Bows to U.S. Makers as NEC Stronghold Continues to Loosen," *Wall Street Journal*, February 14, 1995, p. B4.

14. See "Kodak to Reorganize Its Business Again," *Wall Street Journal*, November 15, 2001, p. B12.

15. See "Japan Chip Makers Suffer from 'Structure,'" *Wall Street Journal*, November 13, 2001, p. A18.

16. The discussion in this section draws heavily on James Brian Quinn's excellent treatment of this subject in *Strategies for Change: Logical Incrementalism* (Homewood, Ill.: Irwin, 1980). These ideas, although frequently drawn from firms competing in low-change environments, are also applicable as initial steps to firms considering change

in fast-changing environments. An enhanced and more elaborate discussion of these ideas can be found in M. Goold and J. B. Quinn, "The Paradox of Strategic Controls," *Strategic Management Journal* 11 (1990): 43–57.

17. James Brian Quinn refers to such comparisons as "shoot-outs" (p. 126) in *Strategies for Change: Logical Incrementalism* (Homewood, Ill.: Irwin, 1980).

18. For an excellent discussion of GE's transformation and the leadership of GE's CEO Jack Welch, see N. M. Tichy and S. Sherman, *Control Your Destiny or Someone Else Will* (New York: Doubleday, 1993); R. N. Ashkenas and T. Jick, "From Dialogue to Action in GE Work-Out," in *Research in Organizational Change and Development*, vol. 6, ed. W. A. Pasmore and R. W. Woodman (Greenwich, Conn.: JAI, 1992), 267–287; L. Hirschhorn and T. Gilmore, "New Boundaries of the Boundaryless Company," *Harvard Business Review* (May–June 1992); "GE: Keep Those Ideas Coming," *Fortune*, August 12, 1991, pp. 41–49; N. M. Tichy, "GE's Crotonville: A Staging Ground for a Corporate Revolution," *Academy of Management Executive* 3, no. 2 (1989): 99–106; "GE Goes to Wall Street," *Fortune*, May 26, 1986; "Can Jack Welch Reinvent GE?" *Business Week*, June 30, 1986, pp. 62–67; "The Mind of Jack Welch," *Fortune*, March 27, 1989, pp. 39–50. An excellent discussion of the change process at both GE and other large U.S. firms can be found in F. J. Aguilar, *General Managers in Action* (New York: Oxford University Press, 1994).

19. See "GE Digs into Asia," *Fortune*, October 2, 2000, pp. 165–178.

20. See "Why Jack Welch's Brand of Leadership Matters," *Wall Street Journal*, September 5, 2001, pp. B1, B10.

21. See "What's So Great about GE?" *Fortune*, March 4, 2002, pp. 65–67; "At GE, New Pride in the Peacock," *Business Week*, November 19, 2001, pp. 79–81; "Welcome to the Frying Pan, Jeff," *Business Week*, October 8, 2001, pp. 82–84; "GE Foresees Growth Despite Big Hit from Terrorist Attack," *Wall Street Journal*, September 24, 2001, p. B4; "It's All Yours, Jeff. Now What?" *Fortune*, September 17, 2001, pp. 64–68; "GE's Immelt Frets over Economy, Not Icons," *Wall Street Journal*, September 5, 2001, pp. B1, B11; "GE's Jeffrey R. Immelt," *Investor's Business Daily*, November 28, 2000, p. A4.

22. See, for example, "Tidying Up at Home Depot," *Business Week*, November 26, 2001, pp. 102–104; "At Honeywell, It's Larry the Knife," *Business Week*, November 26, 2001, pp. 98–100.

23. See "The Welch Legacy: Creative Destruction," *Wall Street Journal*, September 10, 2001, p. A18.

24. See "A Do-It-Yourself Plan at Cisco," *Business Week*, September 10, 2001, p. 52.

25. See O. C. Richard, "Racial Diversity, Business Strategy, and Firm Performance: A Resource-Based Perspective," *Academy of Management Journal* 43, no. 2 (2000): 164–177.

26. Research in the area of virtual teams is growing. See, for example, M. L. Maznevski and K. M. Chudoba, "Bridging Space over Time: Global Virtual Team Dynamics and Effectiveness," *Organization Science* 11, no. 5 (2000): 473–492.

CHAPTER 14

Redefining Advantage

Chapter Outline

What You Will Learn

- Why organizations constantly reshape themselves to compete in the future
- The key role of total quality management (TQM) and continuous quality improvement (CQI) programs in redefining advantage
- What business process reengineering is
- Manufacturing and information-driven technologies that are changing the competitive landscape
- What it will be like to work in tomorrow's organization

Charting the Future at Nokia[1]

One of the world's leading providers of digital wireless phones, Nokia has made great strides toward becoming a household name in the United States and around the world. Based in Helsinki, Finland, Nokia has become extremely adept at designing and manufacturing an ever-expanding variety of mobile phones that have set the standard for performance, design, versatility, and looks in global markets. Considered by many analysts as the technology leader in developing current and next-generation digital phone and mobile Internet networks, Nokia is gearing itself up to become a potent force in other businesses as well, including software, color display screens, Internet browsers, and much of the hardware needed to deploy "broadband" telecommunications networks. By the end of 2000, Nokia generated over $26 billion in revenues and over $3.5 billion in profits for an industry that is now attracting dozens of rivals from the United States, the Far East, and even from parts of the developing world. Yet, Nokia's stunning growth and performance comes at a time when the market for wireless phones appears to be fast maturing. As Nokia can no longer count on double-digit sales gains from selling wireless phones, the company must now consider new strategies and actions to learn, build, and renew its sources of competitive advantage.

Although Nokia is now investing in new technologies and production processes to strengthen itself for future competition, the company is no stranger to reinventing itself. Started in 1966 as a diversified Finnish conglomerate, Nokia originally managed such diverse businesses as forestry products, paper goods, rubber, and even color television sets. Under CEO Jorma Ollila, who took over the top job in 1992, Nokia made a concerted decision to focus exclusively on wireless phones, which Ollila and his management team believed had a bright future. The company divested itself of all of its remaining businesses and proceeded to invest in state-of-the-art manufacturing plants that could churn out brand-new phones twenty-four hours a day, six days a week. Unlike many other companies that chose to outsource the majority of its production, Nokia believes that it should design and build its own factories to become the lowest cost producer in the world. By controlling its own production, Nokia can speed up the process in which a newly designed phone can be ready for manufacture. For other companies that choose to outsource most of their phone production, it can take upward of a month to prepare a production line for a new model. By contrast, at one of Nokia's most advanced factories in Finland, the company only needs four days, not five weeks, to ramp up to full production of a new phone model.

To ensure that the company's designers, engineers, manufacturing people, and sales force work together, Nokia uses a novel organizational format that combines people from different functions into flexible product teams. These product teams share knowledge and insights to accelerate time-to-market. Equally important, when designers and engineers are at the early stages of creating a new phone line, people from manufacturing are already at work figuring out how best to manufacture the phone at the lowest possible cost. In addition, manufacturing specialists provide critical data and feedback to the designers and engineers on different ways to improve the phone's design for smoother and easier production.

As Nokia begins to manufacture phones in different parts of the world, the company has also taken significant steps to work more closely with its key suppliers. For example, at a new plant under construction in China, Nokia is working with IBM, Philips Electronics, Sanyo, and other companies to build next-generation phones using a just-in-time manufacturing system. Under ideal conditions, Nokia is hoping to build phones for the huge Chinese market with almost no inventory in the production system. As demand for one particular phone model surges, the factory will be able to reconfigure its production line quickly to take advantage of growing sales. When demand slows down, the factory will also be able to retool itself in preparation for another line of phone products under development. By working closely with suppliers, Nokia also wants to ensure that its partners do not get caught with large amounts of inventory that they cannot easily sell. To make this vision a reality, Nokia is relying on its key suppliers for real-time information about the production status and unit cost of the phone's components and parts. Likewise, Nokia will instantaneously inform its suppliers of emerging trends and changes in market demand based on the latest retail sales results. In this way, both Nokia and its suppliers will be less likely to find themselves with large inventories of components or phones that do not sell well.

Nokia's management realizes that as new competitors enter the digital phone market (e.g., Sony, Samsung), it will face growing price pressures that will lower its profit margins. To counter this trend, Nokia is aiming to build its brand image around the world, as well as new low-cost factories that can help the company survive potentially severe price wars. To promote the style and quality of Nokia's phones, the company is also promoting its leading-edge digital phone as a new fashion accessory. Senior management hopes that as phones become more popular around the world, new customers will buy Nokia phones to make a fashion statement as much as to place a phone call.

Yet, despite the growing ubiquity of Nokia's digital phones around the world, there is another side to the Finnish giant. Nokia is also a major player in developing and installing the infrastructure and the telecom networking equipment that are at the backbone of next-generation wireless Internet transmission. This is the equipment that Internet service providers (ISPs) deploy to enable customers to surf the Web from their digital phones in the near future. To sustain the high growth of digital phones, Nokia has also reinvented the very concept of a mobile phone. Its advanced product line, the Nokia 7650 series, incorporates a large color screen and a built-in digital camera. Equally important, the 7650 phone can send pictures, sounds, and text to other digital phones or even Web sites as well. The 7650 phone also reveals just how strong Nokia has recently become in the field of advanced multimedia software, a skill area that the company only began investing in just a few years ago.

Other Nokia phones remain just as advanced. For example, its 9210 Communicator line of phones works with a color screen that is far more brilliant than those offered by Mitsubishi Electric, Microsoft, and even Hewlett-Packard. The 9210 Communicator also offers wireless Internet access, e-mail capability, a video player, word processing, spreadsheet programs, and even a personal digital assistant/organizer. This last feature also reveals Nokia's long-term ambition to take on such companies as Palm and Handspring in the fast growing market for personal digital assistants (PDAs). Within the 9210 Communicator, Nokia has also introduced a new type of power management system that allows the user to talk between four to ten hours without recharging the battery. In addition, despite the numerous features that Nokia offers in the 9210 Communicator, the device looks like a sleek phone, rather than a clunky electronic device that is hard to carry or use.

Nokia envisions that software will be the next core technology that the company must develop in order to stay ahead of its competitors. As phones become more versatile and allow different forms of communication (e.g., voice, video, music, data, text), Nokia feels that it must become the leader in the key technologies that support each application. The company is also making a push toward becoming a next-generation Internet portal company through its Club Nokia wireless Internet site. Customers subscribe to Club Nokia simply by owning a Nokia phone. Members are then able to surf the Web through Nokia's custom-designed Internet site and send e-mail and other messages through Nokia's browser and software. Club Nokia offers members the opportunity to personalize their phones, such as composing their own distinctive rings, creating their own choice of icons on the phone, and even customizing pictures that can be sent to their Nokia Picture Messaging-enabled phones. This last feature combines many functions found in early versions of digital cameras.

Nokia's broadest technology-based initiative is its push toward 3G networks. 3G refers to "third generation," which describes the technology that allows phones to carry voice, data, text, video, and other information either in real-time or as stored information. The underlying premise of 3G is that next-generation phone users will do much more than talk into their phones. To handle this growing range of multimedia applications, Nokia believes that an entirely new telecommunications and digital infrastructure is needed to handle fast-moving transmissions. The company is creating a comprehensive new set of technical standards that aims to provide wireless Internet and communications access to any user at anytime anyplace around the world.

To remain on the forefront of new technology, Nokia has also begun investing in new start-up companies to keep abreast of the latest developments. In 1998, the company created a new unit called Nokia Ventures, whose purpose is to identify and incubate new ideas—both within the company and from outside. Since its inception, Nokia Ventures has invested in over twenty-five different companies around the world to learn more about developments in mobile communication technology. Based in Menlo Park, California, Nokia Ventures has recently begun investing in new markets, such as Israel, where there is a considerable experience and talent base in software engineering. The company believes that Nokia Ventures can serve as a "greenhouse" for venturing and learning new ideas. This greenhouse also includes the Nokia Entrepreneurial Web—a new type of network organization designed to promote the exchange of business ideas among scientists and other personnel. Some of the technologies that Nokia Ventures has recently targeted include Internet security systems, new types of color display screens, and mobile alert messaging. In June 2000, Nokia Ventures invested in a small British start-up known as Categoric Software Corp., a company that developed an innovative type of software that provides instantaneous mobile messaging. Nokia believes that its new venture will help the company not only gain exposure to the new skills it must learn to stay competitive but also create entirely new markets and industries for the Internet economy.

A core pillar behind Nokia's enormous technological success is the company's longstanding belief in promoting the self-worth of any individual. Even though Finns dominate the company's senior management and engineering staff, Nokia views itself "as a multicultural organization doing business in a multicultural environment." Nokia believes that it must hire people from different parts of the world because people from different regions view and address problems from different perspectives. Putting people together on Nokia's teams enables the company to gain from a wide-ranging set of ideas and viewpoints that would not have been possible if the company confined itself to its Northern European region.

Introduction

During the past several years, senior management has come to realize that competitive advantage is often fleeting. New products, modern plant and equipment, and breakthrough technologies are all too readily copied by competitors or rendered obsolete by environmental change. More important, organizations depend on their people for competitive advantage. Key sources of knowledge, skills, technologies, and insights depend on assets that have two feet, and are free to move around from company to company in most cases. As a result, physical sources of competitive advantage often provide no more than a temporary boost. More and more firms are recognizing that to stay ahead of their competitors, they must continuously redefine their sources of competitive advantage.

In this chapter, we examine four approaches that leading-edge firms are currently taking to achieve this end. These routes to continuous redefinition of competitive advantage are (1) implementing total quality management programs, (2) reengineering business processes, (3) using computer-integrated manufacturing, and (4) harnessing the power of the Internet to transform the way they do business. Over time, many of these cutting-edge ideas and programs will become commonplace, and they, too, will raise the bar for what organizations must do in future time periods. In fact, some companies are so far advanced in their strategies to grow and renew themselves that they are leaders of their industries. Unfortunately, all too many companies have a more spotty record in learning from the industry leaders to remake themselves. Thus, staying in advance of the competition and keeping abreast of all emerging developments in the environment remain essential for firms that wish to stay competitive for long periods of time. Will there be new ideas, technologies, insights, and approaches to renewing competitive advantage in the future? Absolutely. Our goal in this chapter is to highlight some of the major initiatives that have fundamentally altered the competitive landscape in the past several years. After describing these initiatives, we then show how these efforts are changing the way firms organize themselves to compete. Later, we will examine some trends that seem to be emerging in the early part of this decade.

Total Quality Management Programs

U.S. managers have realized quality's importance in redefining competitive advantage.[2] During the early 1980s, many U.S. firms earned reputations for shoddy quality and defective products. At that time, much of this notoriety was deserved. Now managers view the task of improving product and service quality as one of their most critical and ongoing concerns. Many experts believe that Japan's single-minded commitment to superior quality was instrumental in enabling it to dominate global markets in cars, electronics, computers, watches, and cameras. Building quality products and service is no longer a secondary issue. Now, manufacturers from many parts of the Far East, Southeast Asia, and other parts of the developing world realize the critical impact of quality on the competitiveness of their products. This issue has become even more imperative as companies in Taiwan, Korea, Malaysia, Singapore, and elsewhere now feel the onslaught of price-based competition from even larger emerging competitors such as China and India. The quality movement is even making itself felt in the health care industry, as hospitals seek to improve patient care, reduce medical errors, and lower the costs of delivering top-notch treatments. Thus, the quality movement that once was confined to large portions of heavy manufacturing and high technology industries is now found everywhere. Total quality management (TQM) is vital to survival.

Providing quality products or services is a key factor in building and reinforcing a firm's competitive advantage. Many of the most admired companies in *Fortune* magazine's annual survey are those associated with quality products. Firms producing quality products are often leaders in their industries. Quality thus enhances a company's reputation. For example, the quality products and quality-based practices of such firms as Motorola, Intel, General Electric, Newell-Rubbermaid, and Maytag make them the envy of firms all over the world.

From a historical perspective, perhaps the man most commonly associated with quality improvement is W. Edwards Deming. Deming's name is synonymous with one of the world's leading quality experts.[3] He believes that most quality problems stem from management processes, not from shoddy labor. Deming is the man who first introduced total quality management (TQM) to Japanese managers during the early 1950s. At a time when U.S. firms would not listen to his recommendations, Deming received a warm reception in Japan. Their managers were so taken with his ideas that they established the now-famous Deming Prize. This honor is awarded annually to a firm that produces the best quality product on a number of dimensions. Deming's quality principles embrace both statistical process controls and continuous training of all employees. **Statistical process controls** (SPCs) use statistics to measure and control a production process. SPCs are often in the form of quality control charts that measure the percentage of defects occurring in a production process at any given time.

statistical process controls:
The use of statistics to measure and control a production process, often with the desired intent of achieving high product conformity.

Using SPCs to monitor and guarantee quality is often not enough, however. Deming's most important and lasting contribution is not the use of SPC charts for their own sake. More important, a quality perspective and thorough indoctrination about the key role of quality is vital throughout the entire firm to ensure that people think and practice quality procedures all the time. This view that quality products must come from quality thinking and quality practices remains Deming's key legacy. All employees and managers must pursue quality in their daily practices. Deming's TQM principles have become standard in many U.S. firms over the past ten years. Quality is a leading tool in helping many firms redefine their competitive advantage.

Principles of Quality

A defect-free product or service should exhibit quality along several measures.[4] Although many consultants and authors have their own concepts of quality, they generally include the following aspects:

1. *Conformity:* Products should be made according to exacting specifications and beat current industry standards. This aspect of quality in conformity means that the firm should try to match and exceed the standards of the industry's best producer.
2. *Functionality:* Products or services should perform as intended.
3. *Reliability:* Products or services should have consistent and steady performance over their extended use.
4. *Durability:* Products or services should last. The life of the product, in particular, should extend past that of previous models.
5. *Serviceability:* Products should be easily repaired if needed; sources of error in services should be identified and corrected.
6. *Aesthetics:* The product should look and feel good.
7. *Customer responsiveness:* Customers should receive courtesy and attention from the product or service provider. Customer focus is vital if firms are to learn what customers need. This emphasis on customer focus applies to both current and future products. Without a customer orientation, products and services are a shot in the dark.

total quality management: The cultivation and practice of quality in every person's tasks and activities throughout the organization.

This extended definition of quality underscores the view that firms cannot simply use statistical process controls alone. Use of SPCs does not allow management to proclaim a total quality commitment. Quality control charts do little if a product or service has been poorly designed in the first place. Defect-free production is just the first step toward total quality management. Instead, TQM embraces both an internal and external view. **Total quality management** is the cultivation of quality ideas and methods in every person's task and activities. It seeks to instill in every person the idea that quality is essential to competitive advantage. *Total quality management is a philosophy; it is a continuous process and not an end in itself.* Even more important, TQM's focus on customer-defined quality is key to sustaining competitive advantage. The customer's desires are key to determining every aspect of total quality management.

Quality means not only carefully measuring and controlling the firm's operations but also ensuring that all activities satisfy the customer. The "total" part of TQM includes the broader idea of the firm's internal processes, its suppliers, and, most important, its customers. Quality is only as good as how the customer perceives it. In fact, most of the preceding quality attributes depend on the customer's perspective, rather than on internal defect-free measures. *Customer focus must drive quality improvement programs.* Firms committed to quality must design and provide products and services from the customer's perspective. Only then can managers get a handle on what customers really want. Better understanding of the customer helps distinguish the firm from its competitors. All seven quality attributes help firms make their products special and distinctive. Yet, as we have seen in previous chapters, competitors are always on the move, seeking to overtake a firm's initial advances in product design and ways to satisfy customers. As a competitive weapon, total quality management requires continuous, ongoing efforts to stay ahead of competitors in satisfying and anticipating customers' needs. Equally important, TQM requires managers and employees from every part of the organization to look for ways to leapfrog over the competition.

Throughout much of the past decade, Motorola has pursued this multilevel customer-driven approach to quality. "Total Customer Satisfaction" teams work to ensure that customers get what they want, when they want it. Motorola considers customer focus vital. It seeks customer input to design better products and to gain insights about competitors. Motorola's Six Sigma program (started in the mid-1980s to enter the Japanese market) also aims to reduce defects dramatically with every new product. Motorola's cellular phones and pagers are known for their durability, ease of use, aesthetics, and leading-edge technology. The products have a truly distinctive feel to them. In addition, the company charges less for each successive product generation. Motorola achieves these results by continuously training its people in quality improvement techniques. The training not only reduces defects but also encourages simpler manufacturing methods. Motorola's people feel they are really building something special. Thus, Motorola's commitment to quality is twofold:

Quality is built into the product and into the firm's daily practices. This philosophy makes Motorola's products distinctive from those of competitors. To foster this quality commitment, Motorola spends significant sums annually on training. Still, the benefits it reaps far outweigh the cost. Training people to think, live, and breathe quality prevents substantial problems later on. Most important, skilled and committed people are motivated to deliver their best when they know that quality is rewarded. Yet, even pursuing these quality-based measures is still not a foolproof shield against competitors. In recent years, Motorola has faced even tougher competition from the likes of Nokia, Ericsson, Samsung, and other companies that are driving product design and quality standards higher. Motorola's Six Sigma program has been so successful that other companies have started their own version of it, including GE, Honeywell, and Texas Instruments.

During the 1970s, the U.S. automakers violated almost every aspect of quality as defined by Deming. Most cars were shoddy and did not perform up to expectations. For example, doors did not fit hinges smoothly and consistently. Paint would peel a few years later. Engines would often not start or contained mismatched parts. Dealers often treated customers rudely and were inattentive to their needs. Cars from separate divisions, especially at GM, lost their distinctive feel and touch. At one point, consumers could not tell a Cadillac from a Chevrolet. In fact, the Cadillac Cimarron was built on the same chassis used for the Chevrolet Cavalier during the mid-1980s to reduce costs. Consequently, U.S. automakers experienced dramatic losses in their market positions. Chrysler and Ford almost went bankrupt in 1980. As the automakers eventually learned, quality improvement efforts (when implemented systemwide) can actually lower production costs over time. During the early 1980s, managers in many industries believed that building a higher quality product would always cost more than building an average quality one. This belief is not valid. In fact, more and more companies report that quality improvement actually reduces long-term production costs. By doing things right the first time, firms dramatically lower costs due to reduction in warranty obligations, replacements, complaints, scrap, and rework. Low quality imposes the highest cost of all: loss of reputation and greater risk aversion on the part of the customer. Still, the lesson has not resonated well with all firms in every industry; all too often, quality has become a buzzword that masks a superficial series of initiatives that produce very little lasting commitment.

Continuous Quality Improvement

As mentioned previously, firms should approach TQM as a continuous process and an ongoing investment in their operational activities. In a broader sense, firms need to practice continuous quality improvement in all of their activities. **Continuous quality improvement** (CQI) is the deliberate and methodical search for better ways of doing things.[5] The goal of CQI is exceeding current industry standards and trying to set new ones. The continuous development of problem identification and resolution skills is critical to sustaining and creating new sources of competitive advantage. Japanese automakers, for example, use CQI to go beyond customers' current needs and desires. CQI must be an integral part of a firm's strategy to refine and renew its distinctive competence. Improvement extends to all aspects of a firm's activities and relationships. It can and should involve suppliers, customers, and especially employees. The notion that continuous quality improvement should extend to involve suppliers becomes particularly relevant as many firms start organizing and outsourcing their activities on a virtual basis.

continuous quality improvement: The deliberate and methodical search for better ways of improving products and processes.

At Honda, for example, CQI means reducing the roughness and vibration at successively higher levels of tolerance in every new car model. Windshield designs are improved each year to make assembly easier and faster. Windshields are also shaped better to keep wind noise out and air drag low. Engine layout is continually modified to make self-service and maintenance more convenient and faster. Engines are mounted and balanced with new types of frames and mountings to keep the car's performance even. These continuous quality improvement practices make Honda's cars extremely desirable to its customers. Continuous quality improvement also makes current models significantly better than those of just a few years ago. One can assume from recent history that Honda's continuous improvement strategy is based on making the hot-selling features on today's Accord the basis for the lower-priced Civic a few years later.[6] In other words, what is cutting-edge in the Accord now becomes standard in the lower-end Civic tomorrow (trickle-down technology).

The proactive discovery and removal of potential quality defects has risen to a real science at Caterpillar, the largest manufacturer of construction and earth-moving equipment in the world. Caterpillar realizes that it faces ongoing competition with such tough rivals as Komatsu, Hitachi, and other manufacturers seeking to sell state-of-the-art equipment to governments and large corporate customers around the world. In addition to competing on the basis of low cost, Caterpillar also has made continuous quality improvement an overriding priority for R&D spending. For example, Caterpillar's latest equipment uses electronic sensors to monitor oil pressure, temperature, viscosity, and contaminants in its hydraulic systems. No matter where the equipment may be used around the world, the sensors, connected to the Internet through wireless technologies, are able to relay critical data about potential mechanical breakdowns and the equipment's wear rate by satellite to Caterpillar's headquarters in Illinois. By having real-time information about the working status of its equipment, Caterpillar can proactively respond and meet its customers' needs for absolutely fail-safe products in advance of an actual breakdown.

In a similar vein, the Carrier unit of United Technologies has begun working with IBM to develop versions of this smart technology that will enable future air conditioners and refrigeration units to inform customers of potential mechanical breakdowns in advance of their occurrence. In fact, some of the newest applications of smart technology will even schedule preventative maintenance calls if the sensors detect some critical part or component is likely to fail in the future. IBM is also beginning to offer versions of this smart sensor technology to major home appliance manufacturers.

By their very nature, continuous improvement efforts have a strong internal focus. However, the ultimate objective is to ensure that products and services match and exceed the offerings made by competitors. An integral part of CQI is benchmarking, in which firms deliberately search for the best practices, techniques, and ideas that other companies have used to improve their own operations and products. **Benchmarking** is the systematic identification, examination, and implementation of alternative practices and techniques that other firms (often outside the industry) use to achieve excellent performance. It is a multistep process in which the firm doing the benchmarking seeks to learn and incorporate process refinements, even if the model firm is different from its own. First, the firm identifies those processes within its own organization that need improvement or attention. Second, managers try to locate other firms that are particularly distinctive or excellent in performing or managing those processes. Third, the benchmarking firm contacts the managers of the model companies to learn from their experiences, problems, and solutions. Finally, the benchmarking firm tries to duplicate successful practices or processes that seem to lead to higher performance and better quality.

benchmarking: A firm's process of searching for, identifying, and using ideas, techniques, and improvements of other companies in its own activities.

Benchmarking is an important part of quality improvement efforts, since it enables companies to shorten the time needed to learn and introduce important process changes and refinements. Many companies from a variety of industries, such as Xerox, Ford, CIGNA, UnitedHealth Group, Intel, Corning, and Caterpillar, use benchmarking as a key quality improvement tool. Fidelity Investments, for example, at one point even visited specialized machine tool manufacturers and transportation companies to better understand how to improve its own logistics and massive mail delivery operation. Fidelity wanted to see how other leading-edge companies using advanced processing technologies can help it ensure that customer accounts and new information are not lost in its own internal handling processes.

An important effect of continuous quality improvement is that new insights and approaches will often make current product and process designs obsolete. When firms practice CQI, they lessen the likelihood that competitors can easily imitate their product designs. Moreover, CQI efforts help people gain insights and learn new methods to improve job performance. These steps enable firms to improve and to deepen their distinctive competence.

Building a Quality Culture

When management makes quality part of the firm's daily practice, it creates the basis for more enduring competitive advantage. A quality-based culture is unique to each firm. TQM and CQI transform a firm into a moving target. As mentioned before, competitors can quickly copy technologies and a firm's product designs. But they cannot readily imitate the depth of training, organizational learning, and employee insights that make distinctive continuous improvement practices part of the firm's day-to-day fabric. Pulling out the threads of a tightly interwoven organizational fabric tells competitors little about how everything fits together. Treating employees and customers well is vital to weaving this quality-based fabric tightly into enduring competitive advantages. "Tightly woven" competitive advantage makes it harder for competitors to woo away customers and employees. The following paragraphs describe several companies that have created this type of tightly woven quality-based culture.

To serve its customers better than its competitors, Fidelity Investments has spent millions of dollars on employee training and new technology to serve its customers instantaneously. Fidelity, the largest mutual fund company in the United States, believes that each representative must have tools and training to work with customers on an individual basis. Customers often call at a rate of three hundred thousand per day. Operators aim to serve each one within thirty seconds. A sophisticated computer-controlled phone system switches customers to specific locations nationwide to reduce waiting time. Computer networks also store brokerage, retirement, and other account information for fast access. Training is a key part of Fidelity's customer-based quality strategy. Service is personalized as much as possible. Representatives learn how to deal with customers and are educated in Fidelity's broad range of funds and services. All of a customer's account records can be accessed immediately on a computer screen. This ability allows the service representative to answer questions and to process transactions rapidly. In the past decade, Fidelity Investments has outpaced its competitors in growth, and new technologies have contributed substantially to this result. This investment has helped Fidelity also become a leader in distributing other fund companies' products over its Fidelity Funds Network, which enables Fidelity's customers to purchase mutual funds from other competing companies through a single account. In the late 1990s, this same push to enhance customer service spurred Fidelity Investments to develop a highly sophisticated and easy-to-use Web site that enables account holders to service their own accounts anytime and from anywhere. To encourage customers to become more proficient in managing their own accounts, Fidelity's Web site offers a broad range of financial planning tools that will even help a beginner get a superior grasp on how to manage his or her money and future investment plans. The Web site also allows people to trade stocks and other securities at a deep discount compared with the rates that customers would be charged if they spoke with a live personal representative. By helping customers help themselves, Fidelity not only captures more customers but also lowers some of its own costs through advanced technology. The firm also sees its growing technological capabilities as a key competitive weapon to jockey with such other rivals as E*Trade, Ameritrade, and Charles Schwab—all of which have used the Internet to carve out their own position in the financial services industry.

One company that had made a big turnaround because of its recent quality-driven practices is Ford Motor Company. In 1980, the company was teetering on the edge of bankruptcy. By 1986, it succeeded in turning out a winning design known as the Ford Taurus/Mercury Sable. The key to Ford's renaissance rested in its employee involvement (EI) quality programs. Special purpose teams were set up to find out what customers really wanted in the car. Suppliers were brought in at the earliest design stage. Tests were run to ensure that all specifications were met or exceeded. Dealers were trained to work with younger, wealthier buyers, who often preferred Japanese imports because of their perceived superior value. Most important, Ford learned how to build cars from the customer's perspective. Customer's preferences determined what the carmaker would do internally with factory procedures and work processes. To sustain its quality and continuous improvement efforts, Ford undertook a major reorganization in the mid-1990s to integrate its vast engineering, production, and supply operations into a more cohesive system worldwide.

Xerox is a special example of how a single-minded focus and commitment to quality can turn a company around. In 1980, Xerox was fast losing market share to Japanese competitors in all of its product categories. Over the following seven years, under then-CEO David Kearns, the company made quality practices part of daily life at Xerox. This was not an easy task. Employees did not feel their efforts meant anything. Customers were alienated from the company. Factories often turned out shoddier products with each new generation. However, by making customer satisfaction a key priority, Xerox began to turn itself around. To this day, Xerox tries to stay very close to its customers. Surveys are sent out frequently to customers, asking them to evaluate Xerox's service. Complaints and requests are processed immediately through a centralized toll-free number. Xerox wants to make sure that it has a one-call, one-person problem resolution system. Service people are expected to call customers after problems are fixed. One hundred percent satisfaction has become a corporate-wide fixation. In 1989, Xerox won the Malcolm Baldrige Quality Award. Now, Xerox is a leader in many new "document" technologies that involve digital imaging, printing, networks, copiers, and information technologies that enable its corporate customers to lower the cost of their operations and to improve their ability to store information.[7]

Have U.S. firms learned their lessons? In recent years, the success rate appears somewhat mixed. On the one hand, all of the U.S. automakers have made significant strides in reducing the quality and productivity gap with factories from Japan and Germany. In a very important measure of quality, the number of defects reported by customers purchasing U.S.-built vehicles has steadily gone down every year for most of the past decade. On the other hand, there have been some slip-ups. Ford noted that quality problems cost the manufacturer over $1 billion in 2000, with numerous recalls made for a number of different model vehicles. In many of these instances, Ford took a major step in announcing a series of recalls to ensure customer safety, as was the case with the tires found on the Ford Explorer SUV. Yet, Ford had to settle with a California court over the issue of possible defects in ignition modules that could potentially cause some of its cars to stall with no warning to the driver.

General Motors is steadily closing the quality gap with many of its domestic and foreign competitors, but some analysts and auto designers claim that it is still difficult for GM to design cars with distinctive features. For example, the recent Cadillac Catera was considered underpowered and somewhat bland for the premium price that GM wanted to charge. Even GM's legendary Saturn unit is facing tougher competition from reinvigorated competitors from Japan and Korea.

Even Xerox is currently facing renewed difficulties in battling Japanese competitor Canon for color copiers, printers, and large document imaging and processing systems. During the late 1990s, Xerox stumbled on an internal reorganization that contributed to some early difficulties related to rolling out new products and servicing customers' needs. This misstep cost Xerox dearly as Canon started encroaching on the U.S. firm's market share. The lesson remains clear now as it was in earlier days: *total quality management must remain a constant top priority in every organization that seeks to earn its customers' purchases and loyalty.*

Reengineering: Business Process Design

reengineering: The complete rethinking, reinventing, and redesign of how a business or set of activities operates.

Corporate management has undertaken another organizational practice to renew competitive advantage known as reengineering. **Reengineering** is the complete rethinking and redesign of the way business activities are performed. It is also known as business process design.[8] While the concept of reengineering has been around for almost a decade, firms continue to rethink and reinvent the steps, procedures, and processes for all of their activities. Reengineering attempts radical changes to obtain breakthrough results in performance. In many ways, reengineering extends beyond TQM and continuous improvement and asks a more fundamental question: If we had to start over, what could we do better?

Companies that reengineer their processes start from the perspective of the customer. It is a "clean sheet" approach to asking the most basic questions about the business: How would we organize activities? What activities would we perform? Are there inefficiencies that we can prevent? How do we build quality into the process from day 1? Business processes crucial to the design, manufacture, and delivery of a product are identified and reviewed for every possible improvement. They are rethought, reinvented, and reworked to provide quantum leaps in productivity, turnaround, and cost efficiency. Unnecessary processes are eliminated. The essence of reengineering is to force the firm to select those activities it can do best. Reengineering can help a firm identify practices and reinforce core processes that contribute to its distinctive competence. Any activity that falls short of meeting the central question "If we start over, can we do this better?" is modified or eliminated.

New technologies, particularly computer-based information systems, have made reengineering a vital necessity for firms that compete on the basis of time. **Competing on time** means speeding up the time needed to innovate new products and get them to market faster than competitors.[9] In many fast-moving industries, being able to compete on time is the only way to capture the attention and market share of customers who are increasingly accustomed to seeing companies introducing new product designs and features at ever-faster rates. For example, Nokia, Sony, Ericsson, Samsung, and Motorola are continuously racing one another to roll out an even smaller, more versatile digital phone that promises even faster Internet access as phone prices continue to decline.

competing on time: Speeding up the time needed to innovate new products and get them to market faster than competitors.

Factors behind Reengineering

The surging interest in reengineering stems from three environmental developments: (1) shorter product life cycles, (2) greater information intensity, and (3) hidden costs of inefficiency.

Shorter Product Life Cycles. In many industries, the product life cycle has become increasingly compressed. For example, all of the digital phone manufacturers realize that the life cycle for each digital phone product generation is now about six months. This shortened cycle compels the company to innovate quickly and, more important, to deliver a new product or service rapidly to the customer. Laptop computers, networking equipment, PDAs, consumer electronics, video game consoles, semiconductors, software, and medical diagnostic equipment are also fast-changing products. Companies in these industries are accelerating to market new product versions to preempt competitors' offerings. Obsolescence often occurs within months rather than years. Consider the situation confronting Nokia in the digital wireless phone business. Each new generation of mobile phone incorporates state-of-the-art technology, only to become obsolete within a year. In 2001, comparatively few phones allowed users to surf the Web through wireless Internet technologies. By 2003, such technology has become commonplace. Also, many future phones will likely contain digital cameras, MP3 players, and advanced software that will allow users to engage in all sorts of multimedia applications. Thus, Nokia must invest heavily to remain on the cutting edge of new technologies that render each generation of mobile phone obsolete at an accelerating rate. In another example, at the beginning of 2001, Intel's latest microprocessor design featured a processing speed of 1.4 gigahertz (that's 1.4 billion calculations a second). By the end of 2001, Intel already had a 3.0-gigahertz model planned for production for early 2003. Design, production, and marketing activities must be organized for fast response and fast delivery. Rapid innovation has now become an important source of competitive advantage.

Information Intensity. The growing use of computers and databases allows for the storage of vast amounts of information, much more than was previously possible on paper. The proliferation of computers has changed the way many industries compete. Speed in identifying information has become essential to holding new customers. For example, hospital management, financial services, and telecommunications are three industries in which computers have redefined operations.

Throughout the United States, hospitals of all sizes are adopting new computerized technologies that allow them to manage and track patient records closely to avoid errors in providing quality care. Previously, patient records were stored in hard-copy forms, written by hand. Now, new technologies enable the storage of patient records in digital form, so that nurses, physicians, and skilled caregivers do not have to waste precious time searching for key information about the patient (e.g., allergies, drug interactions, physician history, previous treatments, vaccinations, etc.). Some hospitals are even adopting sophisticated pharmacy-dispensing technologies that promise to eliminate potential dosage and drug-related errors in providing medications to patients during their hospital stay. Such technology not only enhances the quality of patient care but also eases the record-keeping tasks and stress levels confronting care providers.

At Fidelity Investments, for example, advanced Internet-driven computer networks have eliminated the need for cumbersome paperwork sent through the mail and processed manually, thereby reducing delays in working with individual customers. By making all of its forms available through its secure Web sites, Fidelity also makes it easier for customers to open accounts from the comfort of their homes or from anywhere else they may be. The rise of this information intensity is not confined to services. Motorola's sales representatives for custom pagers are tied into a wide-ranging computer network. Hand-held computers transmit customer needs and specific orders directly into the factory. At many companies, sales representatives enter their forecasts directly on a real-time basis using the Internet. This allows the company to track instantaneously what products are needed and how best to price them.

Hidden Costs of Inefficiency. Many firms, even in slower-changing industries, remain burdened with high costs of internal inefficiency. Inefficiencies resulting from poor inventory control and order fulfillment errors are potential sources of alienation and loss of customers. Piles of paperwork slow down response time to customers or patients, create costly mismatches between supply and demand, and cost the firm or hospital lost opportunities to offer speedy service. However, automation and new technologies are often bandages for poorly designed processes and procedures that bleed cash. Yet, major gains in customer service, product development time, and production cycle time are possible when managers rethink processes with a "clean sheet of paper." Hidden costs stemming from bad habits can insidiously erode profitability. Inefficient procedures, if truly unneeded, should be eliminated. They work to erode a firm's competitive advantage.

General Electric, by embracing its own Six Sigma program, has tackled the problem of hidden sources of inefficiency head-on. Since 1995, GE has empowered and encouraged all of its employees and managers to identify and isolate what they believe to be inefficient or wasteful practices that detract from the company's profitability. By training and allocating resources to its Six Sigma program throughout the company, GE has been able to locate and remove "hidden factory" after "hidden factory" that represented underused equipment or inefficient procedures that detracted from full-capacity utilization. According to the company, each hidden factory thus represented a source of capital or asset base that was not previously used to its fullest extent. In effect, GE's reengineering and Six Sigma program enabled the company to save capital expenditures and to squeeze much more productivity out of its existing assets.

Steps of Reengineering

Although each company will likely formulate its own reengineering strategy and approach, there are several core steps involved in any such effort. Managers undertaking the task of reengineering need to address the following key issues: (1) defining purpose and need, (2) organizing around results and outcomes, and (3) linking up directly with suppliers and customers. Ideally, reengineering enables firms to undertake quantum leaps in cost reduction and quality improvement through a clean-sheet approach that greatly reduces downtime, waste, error, and work-in-process.

Defining Purpose and Need. Reengineering is all about process. Many processes are located deep within the firm. The first step managers need to take is to ask the most basic question: How should we perform activities if we began all over again? By asking this question, managers and employees acknowledge the need for a clear vision of their firm or business strategy. In answering the question, managers come to realize that reengineering occurs deep within the firm. Thus, activities that concern workflow, information flow, decision making, facilities layout, and distribution channels receive most of the reengineering effort. Yet, redesigning processes is pointless without understanding how processes contribute to a firm's strategy. Reengineering to achieve breakthrough speed and delivery is pointless when customers no longer want your products. In other words, strategy, customer needs, and processes must work together to create competitive advantage.

Organizing around Results and Outcomes. Central to all reengineering activities is the need to refocus managerial and employee attention around outcomes and final results rather than functional tasks. Historically, most manufacturing and marketing activities were designed around specific tasks and functions. As a consequence, high manufacturing efficiency meant producing according to such internal measures as workflow, information updates, turnaround, work-in-process, and inventory. These internal measures may have little bearing on the final outcome, however. Products still may not suit customers' needs even when they are produced efficiently.

Consider again how hospitals are forced to reengineer many of their activities to provide top-quality, patient-focused care. To ensure that patients, who are often intimidated and scared, receive the best possible treatment and stay, many hospitals are now beginning to treat their patients as "guests." In previous years, doctors, nurses, anesthesiologists, and other care providers would each successively ask a patient for his or her medical history, not realizing how frustrating and annoying it is for the patient to keep answering the same questions over and over again. This information-based problem resulted when hospitals traditionally organized their information and records along internally driven functional or departmental lines, rather than putting the patient's concerns first. In many hospitals now, medical and patient records are taken only once as the patient is admitted. Also, patients are made to feel more special as caregivers learn about their particular concerns, dietary needs or preferences, and other personal considerations. Hospitals are also taking the lead in helping patients learn to care for themselves once they get home through continuing education programs. These programs are designed to help patients live more fulfilling and healthy lives as they continue to recover.

Reengineering forces manufacturing and other functions to organize around an external outcome, customer need, or end result. In other words, value-adding activities in the reengineered firm are measured on how well the firm performs along an *external measure of effectiveness rather than an internal measure of efficiency*. Instead of thinking of their roles as defined by tasks, employees define their roles in terms of results, outputs, or outcomes. Organizing along core processes may still occur, but it is not the end objective of reengineering efforts. Reengineering's ultimate focus is on achieving effective external outcomes.

In the reengineered firm, examples of possible external outcomes or measures of performance include the following: faster throughput, faster cycle time, zero inventory, accelerated development time, and total customer satisfaction. These desired end results are then measured against those of similar or better competitors. Using such measures can help a firm size up how distinctive it is from its competitors. Success on external process measures such as these directly contributes to the bottom line, as waste and other previous bad habits are steadily eliminated.

For individual employees, reengineering means focusing their efforts according to some desired end result or external measure as well. People's jobs in a reengineered environment demand multiple skills and talents as opposed to functionally defined tasks for a single, repetitive purpose or job. For many companies, sales representatives now take steps to ensure that products are designed and manufactured according to the customer's exact specifications. To accomplish this task, a sales representative must feel comfortable with the language and techniques used in design, manufacturing, inventory, distribution, and order control. At Fidelity Investments, customer service representatives work to ensure completion of every step in setting up accounts. Their jobs are designed around fulfilling every stage of the process: giving the customer an account number, setting up a computer file, ensuring the flow of funds, confirming transactions, and providing information about investment products.

Linking Up with Suppliers and Customers. Another key step of successful reengineering is tying the firm's activities closely with suppliers and customers. This step has become almost a standard practice in almost every firm in every industry. In particular, the introduction of the Internet and other types of intranets or virtual private networks (VPNs) has effectively compelled every firm to become more closely linked with key suppliers and customers, if only to hasten order processing and identification of customers' needs. Corporate networks (e.g., intranets, extranets) are becoming more tightly linked with those of suppliers and customers, thus enabling all parties to share ideas and product design data early on. This set of interfirm relationships becomes especially important as firms continue to organize their value-creating activities on an increasingly virtual basis. By delegating and sharing key value-creating activities with suppliers and customers, firms must become more efficient in their own resource allocation to ensure that they remain agile and nimble to compete. Thus, reengineering hastens the "virtualization" of many firms.

In effect, reengineering attempts to break down the previous practices that separate people, both within and outside the firm. Suppliers and customers become more tightly linked partners. The closer relationships between firms and their suppliers means that each individual partner can specialize in an activity or task that it is best suited for. This, in turn, means that key suppliers can perform many of the tasks that the firm once did on its own. For example, many key suppliers in the automobile industry, such as Breed Technologies, Magna International, Honeywell, TRW, Johnson Controls, Mark IV Industries, Federal Mogul, Echlin, SPX, Dana, and Borg-Warner, are now engineering and building entire subassemblies and components for General Motors, Ford, and DaimlerChrysler, often by utilizing virtual project teams. These activities were once performed by the automakers themselves.

Working with suppliers and customers may occur through external alliances or through sophisticated Internet-based networks. Reengineering these relationships allows greater supplier and customer involvement in a firm's activities. It also often leads to more specialization among partners, with each one performing a smaller subset of activities with a dedicated focus, often resulting in the formation and spread of virtual organizations (see Chapter 11). Firms become more directly tied into key customers' ordering systems, enabling customers to receive what they want when they want it. This increases customer satisfaction and reduces costs simultaneously.

Benefits of Reengineering

just-in-time: Sophisticated approach to inventory management in which firms receive material from their suppliers when it is needed.

Firms engaged in reengineering often adopt just-in-time inventory (JIT) management. JIT inventory is one key benefit of reengineering. **Just-in-time** refers to sophisticated techniques of inventory control whose ultimate objective is to reduce the amount of time and resources allocated to managing inventory and work-in-process. In the ideal JIT environment, inventory approaches zero. Suppliers and firms produce according to what their customers need at any given moment in time. The benefits of using JIT to build close linkages between suppliers and customers are sometimes dramatic. In the best-running firms, JIT can make order turnaround almost immediate. Inventory costs, a huge burden on many firms, often become negligible. Product changeover is faster, and product modifications are easier.

Effective implementation of JIT systems requires bringing all key suppliers and customers on board to create new product designs and processes. From day 1, suppliers help establish the design standards and manufacturability of new parts or products. Customers explain what they want and how the product or service should perform. Collective insights from these various parties cut waste of resources and remove delays and errors that previously cost precious response time. Just-in-time thinking and practices helped Chrysler (now part of DaimlerChrysler) reengineer many of its operations to become leaner in the wake of severe Japanese competition. During the 1990s, Chrysler sliced the development time of its LH car line from five years to three. Using what it calls a "platform" team structure, Chrysler removed organizational barriers between people. Chrysler brought suppliers and customers on board to discuss new product ideas from the beginning. JIT removed the need to carry a huge inventory of parts. Managers and employees from engineering, design, manufacturing, marketing, and distribution were organized into small teams. These teams focused on getting measurable results at each stage of the design process. These results formed the basis for subsequent improvement in designing later-model cars. The Dodge Viper, Chrysler Concorde, Chrysler 300M, and Jeep Grand Cherokee are direct results of the newly reengineered Chrysler platform. In fact, during the mid-1990s, the Dodge Viper set a product development speed record—eighteen months from product concept to dealer delivery. Other models, such as the Intrepid, Neon, and Eagle Vision, came out under budget and exceeded many product performance specifications. In turn, this accelerated pace of product development has now become the benchmark standard for every competitor to beat in the automotive industry. Now, auto firms are looking to shorten this process to as little as five months.

Nokia is currently adopting many of its own just-in-time techniques to ensure that it remains competitive in the mobile phone business. In particular, Nokia is beginning to work more closely with key suppliers to ensure that phone parts and components are delivered to Nokia's manufacturing facilities when they are needed, even on a daily basis. To sustain its dominant market position, Nokia wants to eliminate as much inventory as possible from its manufacturing system in order to lower its costs even further. Key suppliers such as IBM, Philips Electronics, and Sanyo are compelled to upgrade their own operational and manufacturing activities to meet Nokia's stringent cost and delivery requirements.

Streamlining and reengineering operating processes have substantially reduced costs at managed care/insurance firm CIGNA and at telecommunications equipment giant Lucent Technologies. At CIGNA, reorganizing information and paperwork flow around clients has made it possible for every customer service representative to access each person's record immediately via computer. Gone are the days when a patient or customer request for information took more than a week to process. Paperwork shuffles and delays are eliminated. Other managed care and insurance firms are moving in the same direction, and some are even leading the effort to win over customers through superior information-based service. For example, WellPoint Health Networks and UnitedHealth Group are also investing in many of the same information technologies that CIGNA continues to deploy. All three managed care/insurance firms hope to streamline their own paperwork and bureaucracy costs that once saddled their internal systems. Although some of these new efforts have proved daunting, the ultimate goal has been to reduce the paperwork and high cost of managing patient files. Thus, many reengineering principles work for service businesses equally well. During the mid-1990s, Lucent Technologies' telecom networking equipment business successfully implemented a new process management and quality improvement system. This effort vastly improved the software used in complex digital-based phone system switches. By introducing a new series of steps to make software, Lucent dramatically cut its development costs, shortened development time, and improved quality—all at the same time.

These examples demonstrate the significant benefits of successful reengineering. Companies are finding that reengineering streamlines many formerly slow and cumbersome processes. Other processes are simply eliminated. Most important, customer response and delivery times improve. Turnaround time for production goes down. Reducing the number of processes increases quality and responsiveness. When every activity is organized around some well-defined external goal, increased customer satisfaction, faster throughput, reduced cycle time, and faster innovation often result. Such benefits contribute to competitive advantage in measurable ways.

Costs of Reengineering

While reengineering can work wonders, it can also introduce its own set of problems. First, many firms attempting reengineering may not have thought through the entire effort. Firms may reengineer activities or even entire businesses that are no longer actually needed. For example, reengineering Texas Instruments' personal computer business would be a moot point, since TI has no market demand for its personal computers.

Second, reengineering exacts a potentially huge toll on employees. By streamlining, eliminating, and compressing activities, firms often create an excess of workers, which leads to layoffs. For example, efforts to reengineer AT&T's long-distance business may seal the fate of many of the company's telephone operators. If AT&T fully implements an automated network system, customers will no longer need operators except for special circumstances, such as overseas calls and collect calls.

Third, reengineering is an expensive process. Job descriptions must be rethought and rewritten. People need to be trained to think and act to achieve new, externally oriented outcomes. Entirely new computer systems are often needed to replace outmoded or slow-moving activities. Managers must initiate extensive changes in accounting, financial reporting, supplier relations, shipping, customer service, installation, customer support, and facilities management. Equally important, top management must rethink and redesign incentive systems to match the goals of reengineering—a much more complex task than it first appears. *Reengineering involves not only processes but also mind-sets.* These problems help explain why reengineering has worked for only about half the firms trying it.[10]

Reengineering in the Future

Firms are likely to continue to strive for major improvements in the way they do business. Advances in technology and management techniques will push firms to become more competitive. Firms will use reengineering to make their operations more distinctive and leaner. Thus, reengineering will remain an important topic, although the terms used to describe the process may change over time. A key issue will be finding new ways to involve employees more extensively. Reengineering will be a tough issue for many companies as employees realize that their jobs may be at stake in the effort. Companies such as Nokia, Fidelity Investments, CIGNA, and the Chrysler unit of DaimlerChrysler have found that reengineering their business processes has generated spectacular results, significantly enhancing their competitive advantage. However, reengineering's impact on large numbers of employees without multiple skills persists as a weighty question.

Computer-Integrated Manufacturing Technology

Over the past fifteen years, new manufacturing technology has begun to redefine the industrial landscape. The rise of computer-integrated manufacturing (CIM) and flexible manufacturing systems (FMSs) is changing the way firms produce and assemble products. Modern CIM- and FMS-based plants can now produce a far greater range of products at lower unit costs than previously. In the past, factories that operated without CIM and FMS faced a "productivity paradox."[11] This **productivity paradox** refers to a basic economic trade-off concerning production. Factories could produce more of the same product at decreasing unit cost. Or they could produce a greater number of different products at higher unit cost. Increased efficiency thus inevitably led to a decrease in variety. This trade-off deterred managers from using their factories to introduce a greater variety of newer products. The factory itself therefore became a barrier to innovation.

productivity paradox: The economic trade-off that managers must make when using traditional manufacturing technology: to achieve low-cost production, flexibility and variety of production are sacrificed.

In this section, we examine how CIM and FMS technologies have overcome this problem by changing the nature of modern production. In the best-running factories today, innovation, productivity, low cost, high quality, and high variety all come together in one system. State-of-the-art factories not only use computers to manage key scheduling and operational tasks, but also harness the power of the Internet to directly tie production with sales forecasts and even specific customized orders for individual customers. The brains and nerve center of the modern factory has moved away from physical hardware to leading-edge software, skills, and Internet-driven technologies to make manufacturing a much more agile, nimble, and flexible corporate resource. These assets now give firms an unparalleled flexibility to produce more varieties of products at lesser cost with greater ease.

Modern manufacturing has redefined the notion of competitive advantage. CIM and FMS, complemented with new ways to utilize the Internet for fast responsiveness, have recast manufacturing into a new platform for rapid innovation. Fast innovation is now possible in the factory, not just in the lab or with a customer. As a consequence, manufacturing now plays an even more significant role in redefining competitive advantage. We examine the impact of CIM and FMS on the way manufacturing is performed, on strategy, and on employee training and skills.

Manufacturing's Transformation

When firms adopt CIM and FMS, their factories become computer controlled. These computer-driven factories employ a common database that links all parts of the factory—design, manufacturing, fabrication, and other activities—into one integrated system. In other words, the computer defines the process and, through CIM, creates a factory-based information system. Factories using CIM and FMS can avoid the costly delays previously associated with product changeovers and the introduction of product variety. The single biggest impact of CIM and FMS technology is elimination of the trade-off between cost and variety. The plant floor is now capable of providing a high degree of variety while still operating at low unit cost. CIM and FMS have changed manufacturing in the following ways:

1. *Rapid response:* Factories can now respond quickly to changes in market demand, product design and mix, output rates, and demand surges. Production becomes much more closely tied to demand. In the best factories, production is tailored to an individual's customized and personalized order.
2. *Flexibility:* Factories can now handle an expanding variety of product designs and families without significant increase in unit cost. In other words, the cost of retooling and resetting equipment to handle different products is reduced. A greater variety of products is produced as easily as long runs of a single product.
3. *Accelerated throughput:* Higher speed is now possible through "smart" sensors, bar coding, software, and less in-process inventory. Factory "bottlenecks" no longer slow down customer delivery and special product requests.
4. *Lower fixed costs:* Because CIM and FMS can efficiently produce a greater variety of products, they can lower the firm's overall fixed costs. These technologies have made it possible for one set of factories to produce products for several different business units. In addition, factories experience less downtime, since machines can be used to produce numerous products for different markets. This time savings slices the cost of operations dramatically (see Exhibit 14-1).

At Motorola, for example, pagers and wireless Web devices are assembled in Boca Raton, Florida, in a fully automated, highly flexible CIM-based system. Advanced CIM technologies at Motorola include robots, automated materials-handling systems, and flexible assembly tools. These tools can be changed automatically from one type or shape of pager to another as needed. Orders are entered electronically into the CIM system's central computer. No paperwork is needed. The computer electronically scans and reads the customer's specifications, sorts out the appropriate components, and assembles the final pager—all in minutes.

Another example of CIM/FMS technology dramatically enhancing flexibility is the Ingersoll Milling Machine Company. Ingersoll uses an advanced CIM system that links design with manufacturing and process control. Ingersoll's CIM system can machine more

EXHIBIT 14-1 The Rise of Advanced Manufacturing Technology

Traditional Technology Can Be Characterized by

- Economies of scale as the basis for manufacturing activities
- Learning curve based on repetition, single product
- Task specialization and rigidity to improve productivity
- Long lead times for change

Which Lead to

- Centralization
- Large plants
- Standard product design and long product life cycles
- Low rate of change and high stability
- Inventory used as a buffer

In Contrast, the CIM Factory Is Characterized by

- Economies of scope as the economic driver of manufacturing
- Truncated product life cycle
- Multimission facilities
- Product flexibility and variety
- Rapid response to change

Which Lead to

- Decentralization
- Disaggregated capacity and small size
- Flexibility and shorter life cycles
- Inexpensive surge and turnaround ability
- Many custom products

than twenty-five thousand different prismatic parts used for specialized machine tools and motor controls. Seventy percent of its production occurs in lot sizes of one. Half of the different parts this machine can make will never be made twice. Unit production cost is approximately the same as for a long run of a single standard part.

The $10 million flexible machining system of Vought Corporation (now part of Lockheed Martin) began operations during the mid-1980s. This advanced technology allows the aerospace maker to produce some six hundred designs of specialized aircraft parts using the same equipment—even one design at a time in random sequence. This FMS is expected to save Vought over $25 million annually in machine costs by performing, in seventy thousand hours, work that would have taken more than two hundred thousand hours by conventional machining methods.

Impact of New Manufacturing on Strategy

The redefinition of manufacturing capabilities will change the way manufacturing fits into business strategy. CIM complements the new practices of total quality management and reengineering. Firms are just beginning to feel the impact of CIM technology on their factory operations. Computer-controlled machine tools can work just as well making one hundred units of a single design as one hundred units of different designs. For a growing number of companies, manufacturing one unit or manufacturing many is now economically the same. Businesses using CIM/FMS technology can now build competitive advantage on variety, customization, and speed of response without sacrificing low cost and high quality.[12]

The use of advanced manufacturing technology means that the experience curve concept will apply not just to a single product but to a range of products. Flexible factories enable firms to design new products and enter new markets with little additional setup cost. Mass customization, as discussed in Chapter 4, is rapidly becoming a competitive reality for every firm implementing these new manufacturing systems. Fast product design and rapid time-to-market will provide entirely new ways to compete, enabling firms to respond to the needs of not just smaller segments but also *individual customers*. Through the use of Internet-based ordering systems, low-cost customization will become a standard competitive tool for firms in every industry. To take full advantage of this new technology's promise, interdivisional cooperation among business units will become more important, since expensive CIM equipment must often be shared among businesses. Also businesses will need to incorporate manufacturing as a specific priority in their own Internet-based investments as they continue to mesh their own activities with those of key suppliers. The Internet will enable firms to tie their manufacturing operations not only with customers but also with critical suppliers to ensure that key parts and components are scheduled according to what the customer wishes. Business units will need to manage these highly flexible facilities jointly (with sister units and with suppliers) to lower their own production costs and improve product turnaround.

One key result of CIM is that *design and manufacturing will become much more closely linked.* New computer-assisted design (CAD) tools will be able to test new product ideas and prototypes immediately. The resulting designs, stored as program files in the CIM computer, allow for immediate ramp-up of production when needed. The trend of compressing design with manufacturing will make factories unable to accommodate these changes obsolete. Already, we are beginning to witness the full blossoming of closer design–manufacturing linkages in the aerospace and automotive industries. Boeing's numerous suppliers of fuselages, airframes, wing assemblies, and hydraulics are using sophisticated CAD networks to test their designs in real time. Once these stringent tests are certified, new designs are forwarded electronically through computer networks directly to factories (at both Boeing and other suppliers) for quick manufacture and easier assembly.

This same trend is already present in Nokia's operations. Design, engineering, and manufacturing activities are tightly interwoven so that each department can provide fast feedback to one another on how best to improve the quality and manufacturability of a new line of wireless phone. Manufacturing personnel at Nokia are expected to inform designers and engineers on how to improve a phone's underlying shape or other design characteristics so that it can be manufactured more consistently and with fewer glitches. Conversely, designers and engineers bring manufacturing people on board immediately when Nokia plans to develop another product line. By working with manufacturing personnel early on in the design process, Nokia designers and engineers can learn what kinds of costs are likely to be involved as the phone moves from testing into full production.

U.S. automakers are beginning to fully implement sophisticated CAD systems in both their factories and development centers to slash the development time needed for new components, subassemblies, and exterior automobile designs. The computers used in these systems are able to simulate a variety of different stress, harshness, vibration, roughness, and other driving conditions so that high-performance prototypes can be designed on a computer screen before they are actually built in physical form. Once a prototype is accepted, the design data (in digital form) are directly forwarded to the factories' computers for further engineering and manufacturing refinements. These computer networks have enabled General Motors, Ford, and DaimlerChrysler to test a variety of alternative designs rapidly to ensure they meet cost and quality objectives.

Another result of CIM is that *technology will accelerate the pace of technology and industry convergence*. CIM enables firms to produce a growing number of products in the same factory. Flexible factories capable of producing components for personal computers, for example, can easily produce related products for a number of other industries, such as consumer electronics and office equipment.[13] For example, Motorola's automated equipment for producing circuit boards allows it to build printed electronics panels for many products and components. Automated factories produce a wide range of power systems and packages for computers, two-way radios, switching equipment, and other communications devices. Motorola's newest semiconductor plants are capable of turning out many different types of custom-made chips on the same production line.

Impact of New Manufacturing on Employees

The introduction of radically new technology into the factory workplace generally has dramatic effects on employees. Highly routine, rote, mind-numbing operations are giving way to unmanned systems that perform the work of previously unskilled or semiskilled labor. To succeed in the new CIM factory, employees will need multiple sets of skills to compete. Factory jobs in the past were specialized and narrowly defined. Workers were often unable to work on other factory jobs that needed different skills. Formal workplace rules and strictly defined tasks limited employees' ability to do other tasks.

The rise of CIM means that employees will have to engage in a much greater variety of activities. Fewer workers will be needed, but those retained will have to learn many types of skills. Workers will need a better understanding of computer technology; they must know how to use software and how to adapt the system to changing products that come through the factory. These requirements put a premium on organizing employees into cross-functional teams that can work with numerous products and manufacturing processes. Cross-functional teams include people from design, manufacturing, and marketing who work together on a focused project. The teams need to be small and versatile enough to learn and apply new skills quickly. They must also move from one part of the factory or firm to another as needed.

Tomorrow's factory workers will differ substantially from their predecessors. More than likely, they will look more like *technicians or knowledge workers*. Formal job classifications will matter little. Factories will use decreasing amounts of physical, unskilled labor. The proportion of direct labor in a product's cost will decline even further than it has already. Many firms across a wide array of industries are already experiencing these developments. For example, skilled technicians and engineers have already begun to replace hundreds of semiskilled workers in Motorola's automated plants. Production of Motorola's chips, phones, and pagers is increasingly automated. In another example, ultramodern Japanese factories at Fanuc, a maker of machine tools, need only two workers per shift to staff an entire factory. Robots and computer-controlled machines do the rest. Fanuc leads the world in the production of highly sophisticated numerically controlled (NC) machine tools and robotics that are found in factories and assembly lines all around the world. Fanuc's dominance of this business stems not only from its continuous investment in new manufacturing technology but also from fiercely dedicated employees able to perform a wide range of highly sophisticated technical tasks involving design, engineering, and manufacturing activities in cross-functional teams. These teams work without close supervision of management to improve the factory's productivity and to find new ways of performing work at lower cost. Even such a dominant giant as Fanuc must continue to invest in training and upgrading its managers' and employees' skills. Currently, Fanuc is in the midst of developing new technologies that seek to transform its numerically controlled machine tools into more flexible, robotically managed automation systems. These newest robotic systems require advanced skills and technologies in such areas as artificial intelligence, machine vision systems, software engineering, electronic sensors, and even ergonomics. Meeting the needs of demanding customers in such industries as appliances, aerospace, transportation, and heavy manufacturing means that Fanuc must continue to invest in new forms of knowledge and human resources to stay on top of the machine tool business.

Revisiting the Internet and Competitive Advantage

Throughout this book, we have discussed the emergence of the Internet as a powerful information and computer-based tool and distribution channel that is transforming the way firms in many industries are doing business. In many ways, the omnipresence of the Internet is changing the fundamental way many businesses are thinking about how to create and deliver value to their customers, as we have seen in chapter 5. In industries such as financial services and travel planning, the Internet has already become an indispensable tool that enables customers to link up directly with brokerage firms, airlines, car rental agencies, and other entities. Many firms in manufacturing industries (e.g., Cisco Systems, Intel, General Electric) are already using the Internet to link their operations and marketing activities directly with their customers. By 2003, for example, some analysts expect that Intel will generate more than 75 percent of its revenues through the Internet. Firms in the automotive industry (e.g., GM, Ford Motor, and DaimlerChrysler) are beginning to use the Internet as a tool to establish virtual supply chains with key suppliers to reduce work-in-process and large finished goods inventories. Although the Internet has made its presence felt in the U.S. economy for only a few years now, it already appears to be influencing strategy in several key ways. Even though Chapter 5 discussed the broader implications of the Internet on competitive strategy, let's reexamine some of the more salient aspects of the Internet on how firms will build new sources of competitive advantage.

Compressing the Value Chain

First and foremost, the Internet enables firms to establish direct links to almost anybody anywhere and to deliver new products and services at very low cost. The major challenge that the Internet poses to established brick-and-mortar businesses is that it enables innovative upstart firms to circumvent existing barriers to entry in many industries. We have already seen how the Internet has already markedly transformed the retailing and music industries in just the past few years. Using the Internet, many companies (e.g., Amazon.com, Vehix.com, Di-Tech.com) are finding they can establish a direct link to their customers and suppliers to perform transactions on a real-time basis. The Internet also enables firms to bypass many existing distribution channels (e.g., wholesalers, value-added resellers, and even retailers) to reach customers directly. This enables some firms to pass impressive cost savings directly to the customer (e.g., Amazon.com in book and music retailing). It is now even possible to do much of the "legwork" of purchasing a car over the Internet. For example, Web sites such as automallusa.com, Vehix.com, and autobytel.com, enable customers to preselect the type and model of car they want, the options they want to go with the car, and the dealer in a geographic area who is likely to have the lowest prices. Thus, the Internet is already serving as a giant, cyberspace-based "auction house" that compels firms to compete with one another on many price and product attributes. The result will likely be significant compression of current value chain configurations found in many industries today as firms find new ways to squeeze cost out of the system.

The Internet lends itself to immediate, real-time learning about and adjustment to customers' needs. Learning and product/service development cycles are becoming much shorter as a result. This new development compels firms to become leaner in how they gather, synthesize, use, and disseminate information within the organization. Fast processing and synthesis of information to detect new market trends and emerging customer needs will become a new type of core competence that firms must learn. Firms that learn the fastest and are most willing to experiment with new product and service offerings will become the best equipped to compete using the Internet. The faster a company learns, the more quickly it will be able to create new products and services for Internet customers. This in turn enables the company to capture a growing base of customers, thus allowing it to learn even more from the marketplace.[14]

A major byproduct of the growth of the Internet is that it is now possible for some firms to serve customers as effectively over the computer as with an actual salesperson. Sophisticated Web pages that offer customers a full array of product, service, and pricing information can perform many of the tasks that traditionally were associated with personalized selling. Thus, even the basic notion of how to sell to a customer will now come under great reexamination. For companies such as Amazon.com, Fidelity Investments, Charles Schwab, and Southwest Airlines, the Internet provides the foundation and tools for customers to become more empowered to perform transactions on their own. These companies even encourage the broader notion of customer empowerment by providing significant incentives for customers to perform on-line transactions.

The Internet's growth enables firms to broaden and deepen their relationships with customers through mass customization of an expanding array of product/service offerings (as discussed in Chapters 4 and 5) and through inexpensive e-mail transmission of offerings to customers (e.g., new product catalogs directly to customer's e-mail sites or home pages). Already, visitors to many companies' Web pages find they can search for products and components by part number, product use, size, cost, and other criteria that the computer can directly screen through advanced search algorithms. This capability enables customers to place an order for parts or services and pay for them electronically. Customers of firms such as United Parcel Service (UPS) and FedEx can even track the status of their orders and know when a critical package delivery has been made. Thus, an increasing number of companies use the Internet to provide new services inexpensively and even personalize their offerings to repeat customers. And this is just the beginning. Over time, we can expect to see many firms begin to link up their core manufacturing operations with the Internet. Customers will demand the ability to place their own tailor-made requests into the factory or operations center through the Internet, and receive their customized products securely and quickly.

Building Virtual Supply Chains

The Internet also enables firms to work more closely with suppliers further back in the value chain. The automotive industry is an area where large manufacturers (e.g., Ford) are using the Internet to work with key suppliers to design new automobile components jointly. For example, designs for new automotive parts are created at one supplier. It then forwards the design's technical specifications and other data electronically to the automotive firm through corporate intranets and extranets that prevent outsiders from eavesdropping or snooping on proprietary information. The automotive firm then uses the supplier's data to test the component in a variety of simulation exercises for different car models and driving conditions. The results of these experiments and tests are then returned to the supplier for additional improvements. The cumulative effect of using the Internet to create such virtual supply chains greatly slices the amount of development time and resources needed to create next-generation designs. As discussed in Chapter 11, the organizing of value-creating activities along a virtual basis means that suppliers, firms, and customers must be able to freely exchange information, insights, and ideas to create new products and services quickly. Virtual project teams will span firms and include suppliers and, in many cases, even customers as part of the product or service design and creation process. Previously, designing and producing a new line of cars required upward of five years. Already, automakers are reducing the development cycle to under twenty months by using new Internet-driven information and manufacturing technologies. The Internet's facilitation of virtual supply chains enables firms to collaborate more effectively across a broader range of key suppliers using similar types of design software protocols to link up their operations. As supply chains become more virtual and information based, so will the need for firms to understand how best to organize their knowledge and other value-creating activities with suppliers and customers.

Competitive Dynamics and the Internet

Broadly speaking, the Internet will cause almost every firm in every industry to rethink its relationships with distributors, retailers, and the end customer. If the book and music industries (e.g., record label companies) are harbingers of what is likely to come, then the Internet will hasten *consolidation* of many industries. As the Internet becomes more pervasive in every industry, the more innovative firms will seize the initiative in redefining what customers can expect in terms of value, pricing, delivery, and customization. Companies that use the Internet to listen to their customers and design products specifically for them will steadily accumulate market share from competitors that are slow to react. Over time, the number of competitors within an industry may drop as the winners continue to grab market share away from weaker firms. Although this process has always occurred in every industry for many decades, the Internet will likely hasten the process of "shaking out" weaker competitors who suffer declining market share. As the weaker firms' market shares decline, they cannot afford to invest in the newer technologies that allow them to reach and serve customers with innovative approaches. As customers steadily gravitate toward the faster-growing firms, the winners accumulate more economies of scale that, in turn, support further investments in new technologies. In both the book and music industries, for example, we are beginning to see the rapid pace of consolidation whereby those companies that can harness the power of the Internet (e.g., Amazon.com, Vivendi Universal, Sony, Bertelsmann AG) to reach new customers are steadily changing customers' expectations, as well as the competitive dynamics of the business. Amazon.com has fundamentally changed the nature of book retailing. Many smaller traditional book retailers have folded up operations in the past decade, as customers become more comfortable purchasing books through the Internet. Likewise, the advent of digital music formats has caused significant disarray in the music industry, and the number of major record label companies has shrunk to five in recent years.

Ironically, established brick-and-mortar businesses that may have not been the first to adopt the Internet but that aggressively embrace it as part of their total competitive strategy may be in the best position to benefit if and when their respective industries consolidate. First, such businesses are likely to have accumulated significant economies of scale and experience (see Chapter 3) about how best to compete in their respective industry. They also likely have significant assets already in place that an upstart Internet firm will have to create from the ground up. Equally important, their brand identities are likely to offer competitive advantage and some initial defensive value, especially to customers who may at first be risk-averse to using the Internet. However, these preexisting advantages will dissipate over time if the established firm does not learn to compete with an Internet upstart that cleverly redesigns the industry's value chain from a novel perspective. Because the Internet dramatically changes the nature and cost of distribution and customer benefits, established firms must embrace the Internet early to help make on-line customer service a vital and complementary part of the way they do business. Thus, established businesses that quickly embrace and deploy the Internet can still effectively riposte new upstart firms and defend their competitive positions.

For example, UPS and FedEx have used the Internet to enable customers not only to track their shipped packages' location but also to set up their own product catalogs on the Web. Both firms are using the Internet as a means to deepen their relationships with customers, with the result that both companies now offer not only package delivery but also sophisticated sources of information that assist customers in a variety of ways.

Charles Schwab, a leading discount brokerage firm, is using the Internet to create a very strong competitive position in the on-line brokerage segment of the industry. In 1996, Schwab's exposure to the Internet was close to zero. By 1999, Schwab was trading more than $5 billion in securities every week on its Web site—more than half of the firm's entire trading volume. Already, these numbers have made Schwab the leading on-line brokerage firm, with about 30 percent market share. Schwab believes that an important customer benefit of on-line trading is that it delivers personalized information and service in real time at virtually no additional cost to the firm. Schwab's tremendous growth on the Internet also complements the existing services that it already delivers to customers. On its Web site, customers can look up real-time quotes, news, historical financial data, and stock charts, and they can use personalized financial software to do sophisticated planning. Not to be outdone, arch rival Fidelity Investments has deployed a wide array of similar financial planning and trading tools on the Internet to retain its customers. Both companies have realized the need to add powerful Internet capabilities to their traditional channels, not only because their main rival has done so but also to prevent their customers from defecting to such upstart firms as E*Trade and Ameritrade, which can offer Internet trading capabilities without Charles Schwab's or Fidelity Investments' existing fixed costs and investments. For both Charles Schwab and Fidelity Investments, the Internet has become a vital tool that complements their existing business practices and enables them to learn new sources of competitive advantage.[15]

Land's End uses the Internet successfully not only to present a huge digital product catalog in cyberspace but also to offer its Web page as a personalized service tool. This Internet-based tool enables customers to store vital information (e.g., family members' birthdays, future graduation dates, anniversaries, etc.). Once this information is entered, Land's End will then e-mail the customer a notice two weeks in advance of a forthcoming event and suggest a gift that might best suit the occasion. The company will even ship gifts directly to recipients using information provided in advance by the customer.

The Organization of Tomorrow

Firms will organize and conduct their activities in the next century in a dramatically different way than they do today. Senior management will increasingly realize that their employees hold the secret to tomorrow's sources of competitive advantage. Physical sources of competitive advantage, such as new products, factories, and distribution channels, will continue to play a role. However, as competitors become better organized, the basis of redefined competitive advantage is the ability of an organization to change and learn.

Tomorrow's firms will continue to undertake many of the quality improvement, reengineering, and new manufacturing practices described in this chapter to sharpen and renew their competitive advantage. Yet, the common denominator behind all these new practices is substantially greater reliance on employees for their ideas, insights, and skills. Competitive advantage and competitive success will increasingly depend on how well firms work with and treat their employees. Companies can no longer afford to treat their people as replaceable expenses in an income statement or as liabilities on a balance sheet. Employees are not robots, and they cannot be expected to perform highly rote, mind-numbing tasks in a fast-changing environment. Instead, success from new technologies, methods, and other advances will increasingly depend on the employees' knowledge, skills, and ability to adapt. *Future sources of competitive advantage will come from the firm's ability to help its employees learn and grow.*

A firm's future success in developing new products, entering new markets, and applying new technologies will depend on how well trained and motivated its employees are. Leading firms such as General Electric, Fidelity Investments, Cisco Systems, Ford, and AT&T have already grasped this essential truth. Employees are taking the lead in redefining these firms' sources of competitive advantage. And they are doing so in a radically different kind of organization, commonly referred to as the horizontal organization.[16] A **horizontal organization** replaces the strict separation of design, manufacturing, marketing, and other activities with small cross-functional teams and close relationships with suppliers and customers. In fact, the horizontal organization may leapfrog over the current trend toward networked organizations and even full-blown virtual organizations (discussed in Chapter 11) by relying on small, flexible teams to replace many aspects of formal organizational structures and practices. The horizontal organization appears to go even further than the networked organization in making the entire firm boundaryless. Three important characteristics of the horizontal organization distinguish it from today's firms: (1) using cross-functional teams, (2) partnering with suppliers and customers, and (3) treating employees as partners.

horizontal organization: An organization design in which teams and small units replace the strict separation of functional activities such as design, manufacturing, marketing, finance, distribution, sales, and service.

Using Cross-Functional Teams

cross-functional teams: Small units that work across a wide range of functions, technologies, products, and services based in different parts of the firm.

Cross-functional teams are small units that work across a wide range of technologies, products, or services. People from design, manufacturing, marketing, finance, and accounting work together on a focused project or problem. These teams are highly flexible and can work on activities or tasks located anywhere within the organization. They work among themselves and have the authority to make changes necessary to accomplish their goals. The power of small teams derives from their ability to foster communication and rapid learning. Organizing people into self-directed teams of seven to ten people, for example, encourages the free flow of ideas and discussion of many alternative solutions. Problems are discussed forthrightly without the need to hide information from managers. This fresh approach to organizing encourages people to be open and creative and to learn from each other. Equally important, it enables people to apply their skills and see the results of their work directly. Since teams are often free to move anywhere within the company, they are a major feature of the boundaryless organization.[17]

Eastman Kodak and Motorola are two firms that have used cross-functional teams with great success. Eastman Kodak first tried cross-functional teams when it wanted to resuscitate its black-and-white film division. Saddled with inefficient work rules and obsolete procedures and faced with growing foreign competition, this division reorganized itself into a series of small teams. Known as "Team Zebra," this effort turned around the fortunes of Kodak's black-and-white film business in less than a year. Teams were organized around specific sources of inefficiency or work dysfunction involving such issues as cycle time, on-time delivery, customer service, and product development. Black-and-white film products went from being over budget and inefficient to under budget and lean in two years. Response time to customers was also cut in half. Now Kodak is forming small teams to work on emerging products and processes, including digital technologies.

Motorola uses dozens of project teams to coordinate activities among its many design units and plant facilities. One of these—the "Bandit" team—is devoted to improving the customized production of pagers. Faster responsiveness is the unchanging goal for this team. Other teams work on specific projects, such as accelerating product development time in designing new chips and cellular phones. Teams are continually trained in new techniques and skills when they need them. Workers learn statistical process control methods. New employees are specifically taught quality control, flexible manufacturing, and new types of assembly techniques.

By making extensive use of such teams, firms are transforming the way they organize themselves. Exhibit 14-2 shows how the future firm will look compared to today's organizational format. The organization of tomorrow, composed almost entirely of teams and small subunits, will work on specific projects or issues that define a firm's distinctive competence in some way. Organizing strictly along functions such as design, manufacturing, marketing, and finance restricts the flow of information and ideas throughout the company, which in turn inhibits learning and prevents people from seeing the results of their work. Each time information flows through multiple layers of management, the quality of the transmitted information becomes distorted. Because of distortion, senior management often receives only a partial account of what actually happens in the market or on the factory floor. Tomorrow's firm will look much *flatter*, and it may not even fit a conventional organizational chart. In a flatter organization activities are compressed into smaller, more flexible work teams. These organizations will have significantly fewer management layers between employees and top managers. As indicated in the Kodak and Motorola examples, such companies will be a collection of many small, fast-learning, highly focused teams. The ultimate horizontal organization may do away entirely with traditional subunits that represent particular types of functions.

Partnering with Suppliers and Customers

Companies in the future will take the team concept that they use internally and apply it to their customers and suppliers. **External partnering** involves customers and suppliers much more directly with the firm's value-adding activities, often through virtual organizational formats. Partnering may involve formal strategic alliances or close Internet-driven, supplier–buyer relationships that evolve over time. Customers and suppliers will become much more involved in decision making concerning the firm's operations, product development, and distribution. As suppliers take on more important work that firms used to do, this external partnering will steadily dilute the boundaries between firms over time. The involvement of suppliers and buyers substantially reduces waste, cycle time, and development time for new products. However, these relationships will also pose a significant coordination cost on both firms and their suppliers to ensure that activities work closely together.

external partnering: The process of including suppliers and customers in the firm's set of value-adding activities, often through virtual organizational formats.

Greater involvement by suppliers and customers will mean that the employees of such partners will often serve on a firm's internal cross-functional teams. As Exhibit 14-3 shows, many of the firm's activity centers will include customers and suppliers. Partnership

EXHIBIT 14-2 From a Vertical Organization to Cross-Functional Teams

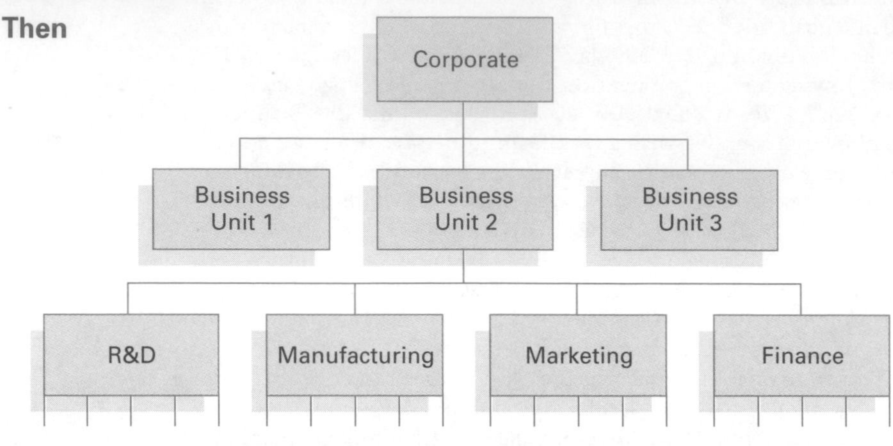

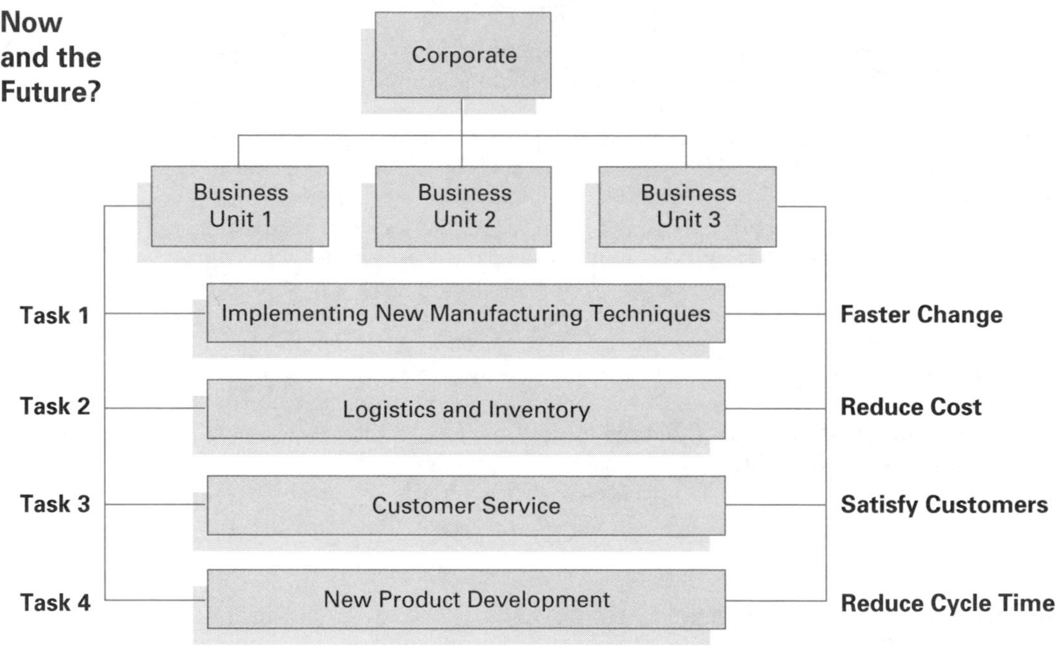

relationships are likely to become deeper and more intricate over time. Some supplier-based partnerships may grow to become more formal strategic alliances. These alliances may even involve a firm's buying significant equity stake holdings in their suppliers. Even without formal strategic alliances, customers and suppliers will form Internet-driven relationships to work on key products, markets, and technologies. In other situations, suppliers will often send key personnel to work on-site with their biggest and most important customers to handle all of their requests. At many firms, for example, suppliers already have established an office at their customer's location. For example, Procter & Gamble has a subsidiary office located in Bentonville, Arkansas—the site of Wal-Mart Stores' corporate headquarters. P&G maintains this office directly in conjunction with Wal-Mart's ordering and supply chain operations to ensure that the retailing giant receives all of its critical products, inven-

Transition to a Horizontal Organization — EXHIBIT 14-3

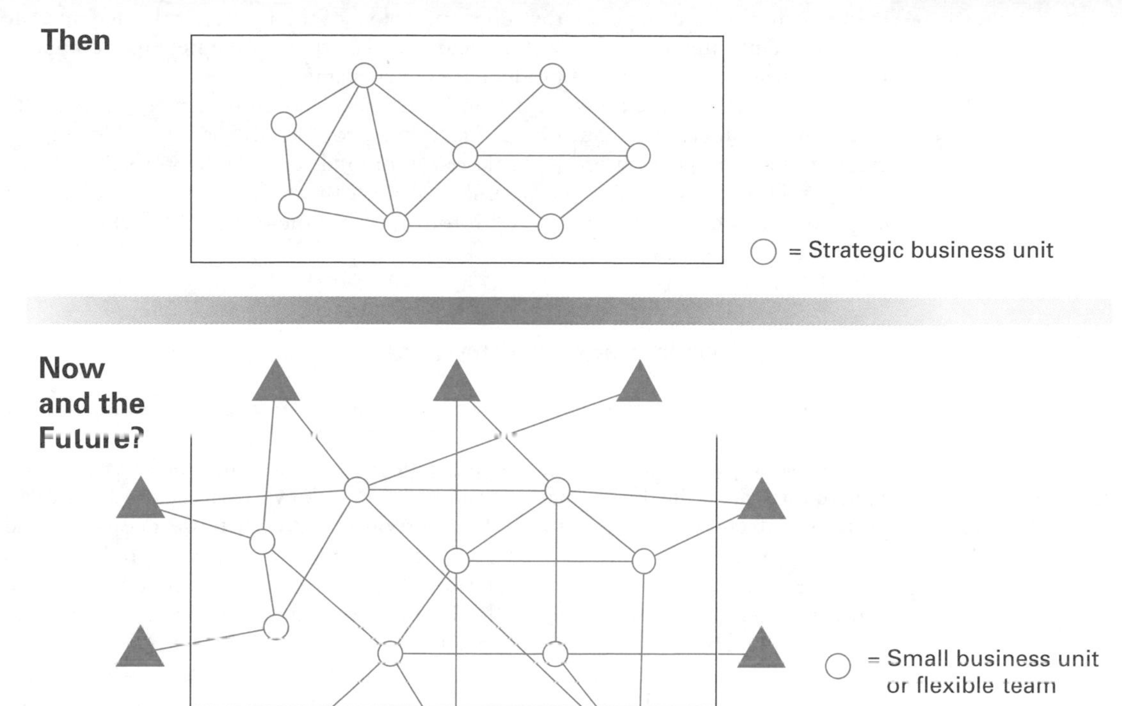

tory management, and billing services needed. In a similar vein, chemical giant DuPont works very closely with key automotive customer General Motors. The relationship is so close that DuPont actually owns and manages the paint shop facilities that are located within General Motors' automobile assembly plants. GM works on fabricating, building, stamping, and assembling the cars; DuPont's paint facilities provide the galvanized coatings and paints needed to give GM's cars their final finish.

In the semiconductor industry, chip equipment giants Applied Materials, Novellus Systems, and KLA-Tencor work directly with the technical personnel of such companies as Intel, Texas Instruments, IBM Microelectronics, Micron Technology, and other semiconductor manufacturers to ensure that their sophisticated and expensive equipment are used to their fullest capacity. Technical personnel from Applied Materials have taken on a greater role in making sure that Texas Instruments is able to maximize the capacity utilization of Applied's newest chip fabrication and processing equipment. Over time, many analysts feel that chip manufacturers in the semiconductor industry will increasingly rely on companies such as Applied Materials and Novellus Systems to perform much of the process management and improvement work that companies once performed themselves. This type of relationship in which suppliers work directly with the customer at the latter's location is becoming more commonplace in every industry. This proximity helps the customer get immediate attention and helps suppliers determine future needs. Suppliers have begun to work closely with customers in improving their own quality and streamlining their processes as well.

Eastman Kodak, for example, has already experienced many of these changes. Kodak is working with a number of partners, such as Intel and Motorola, to design and supply a new generation of digital filmless cameras for the consumer market. The new device is designed to help both casual and professional photographers take pictures in new ways by storing imaging on flash memory cards or even computer disks. The images will purportedly become as rich and fine as those taken with conventional photography but give users the opportunity to manipulate the tones and colors of the image. Both Intel and Motorola are important suppliers of key semiconductor-based technologies and components in Kodak's efforts to develop and produce these new cameras.

Motorola works closely with many of its key chip customers, such as Ford Motor Company and high-tech giant Philips Electronics. Ford needs custom-made chips and microcontrollers to operate more sophisticated automobile engines. Motorola's embedded microcontrollers can serve this purpose. Philips Electronics also uses Motorola's specialized chips to run its compact disc players. Motorola designs these embedded chips according to Philips' power specifications.

Treating Employees as Partners

empowerment: Delegation of decision-making authority and responsibility to those people most directly involved with a given project or task.

Most important, firms will need to treat their own people increasingly as partners. Managers must view employees as inherently capable of learning new skills and interested in personal improvement. People who are empowered to do things on their own and know their efforts are valued will make great strides to achieve their goals. **Empowerment** places the decision-making authority and responsibility with those people most directly concerned with a given project or task. Empowerment is a critical ingredient in the success of small teams. The power of small teams lies in their ability to renew everyone's focus and rivet attention on achieving results. People treated as genuine partners will look forward to their jobs. They will be receptive to learning new skills that help their work. Empowered teams will have the capacity to continually find new ways to speed work flow. Self-management will be as important as supervised management, perhaps even more so.

Employees who are treated as partners are the best renewable source of competitive advantage. However, companies need to ensure that they design incentive, performance measurement, and reward systems that support their employees' efforts. Reward systems must tie in closely with the firm's overall strategy and mission, as well as with their employees' unique set of skills and insights. This is a challenging, ongoing task, since it means that senior management must constantly communicate with the employees about what they expect from them and, more important, what employees can expect from their efforts on the job. A key part of the reward system must be to encourage and cultivate new skills and ideas that result from continuous learning. Firms will be in a better position to adapt and change when people are willing to learn new things. Redefining advantage has two aspects: continuous improvement of the firm's existing sources of advantage and building new sources of advantage. Improvement in both areas depends on how effectively people can learn and change with the environment.

The ideas presented in this chapter reflect what is already occurring in many companies today. Quality improvement, reengineering, flexible manufacturing, horizontal organizations, and cross-functional teams are realities that currently exist in the workplace. An employee's ability to identify and associate with these concepts will directly influence his or her future success. Only by mastering these concepts will today's employees be able to adapt to the changing workplace of tomorrow.

Summary

- Firms need to redefine their competitive advantage continuously. This process involves two steps: (1) making one's competitive advantage distinctive from other firms and (2) organizing in ways that allow employees to identify and build new sources of advantage for the future.

- Total quality management, reengineering, flexible manufacturing, and Internet-centered activities are four important management practices that help firms preserve and reinforce their distinctiveness.
- Firms that make quality part of their daily routine can improve continuously over time.
- Reengineering involves asking the question "If we had to start over, what would we do differently?" Firms that reinvent their business processes are asking themselves this question. Activities they can do better, they keep; nondistinctive activities are eliminated.
- Flexible manufacturing uses computers to enable factories to produce a greater variety of products at low unit cost.
- Horizontal organizations rely on small teams to run their operations. Organizing horizontally helps firms build future sources of competitive advantage.
- The essence of the horizontal organization is the cross-functional team. Cross-functional teams work best when they are small. They encourage people to gain insights, to share ideas, and to learn new skills.
- Treating employees as partners is the best source of future competitive advantage. People can always learn new things. Only when they learn effectively can machines and processes be improved.

Endnotes

1. Data and facts for the Nokia Strategic Snapshot were adapted from the following sources: "Nokia, Rivals in Telecom Gear Transmit Clear Messages of a Struggling Sector," *Wall Street Journal*, March 13, 2002, pp. A3, A6; "Nokia Rocks Its Rivals," *Fortune*, March 4, 2002, pp. 115–118; "Nokia Aims to Be a Force in Software with Handset Debut," *Wall Street Journal*, November 20, 2001, p. B6; "Nokia Acquires Maker of Networking Gear in $421 Million Deal," *Wall Street Journal*, July 26, 2001; "Clash of the Titans: Microsoft and Nokia Take Aim at the Mobile Net," *Business Week*, July 9, 2001; "Nokia Extends Lead on Cellphone Rivals," *Wall Street Journal*, June 1, 2001; "Nokia to Develop Games for Wireless Devices," *Wall Street Journal*, May 17, 2001; "Damn the Torpedoes" *Business Week*, May 14, 2001, pp. 99–109; "Telecom Firms Take Steps to Survive Stiff Competition," *Wall Street Journal*, March 28, 2001; "Outsourcing Alone Won't Save Nokia's Rivals," *Business Week*, February 12, 2001; "Nokia Warns of a Slowdown in Sector as It Posts Profit Exceeding Expectations," *Wall Street Journal*, January 31, 2001, pp. A3, A8; "Nokia's Color Screen Technology May Beat Microsoft's to Market," *Wall Street Journal*, January 15, 2001, p. A19; "Nokia Unveils Mobile Computer with Color Screen," *Investor's Business Daily*, November 22, 2000, p. A10; "Strong Culture Helped Nokia Earn Top Spot," *Investor's Business Daily*, November 16, 2000, p. A8; "Much of Finland Coasts on Nokia's Success," *Wall Street Journal*, October 30, 2000; "Nokia's Costly Stumble," *Business Week*, August 14, 2000; "India's Technology Whizzes Find Passage to Nokia," *Wall Street Journal*, August 1, 2000, pp. B1, B12; "Finland's Nokia to Increase Investment in Start-Ups with 2nd Venture Fund," *Wall Street Journal*, July 3, 2000, p. B7; "Make Room for Nokia's Jorma Ollila," *Business Week*, July 3, 2000; "RealNetworks, Nokia Team Up to Add 'Streaming' Software to Wireless Phones," *Wall Street Journal*, June 29, 2000; "Nokia Fights for Toehold in Japan's Cell-Phone Market," *Wall Street Journal*, June 26, 2000; "Nokia's Secret Code," *Fortune*, May 1, 2000; "Nokia Widens Lead in Cell-Phone Market," *Wall Street Journal*, February 8, 2000; "Next Up for Cell Phones: Weaving a Wireless Web as Nokia Sees It," *Fortune*, October 25, 1999; "Nokia Cell Phones to Use 3Com's Palm Software," *Wall Street Journal*, October 14,1999; "Nokia Picks Intel to Supply Set-Top Boxes," *Wall Street Journal*, October 12, 1999; "Nokia Shoots for the Stars with New Phone," *Wall Street*

Journal, August 24, 1999; "Nokia Gets New World Order," *Wall Street Journal*, July 28, 1999; "Now Nokia Is Net Crazy," *Business Week*, April 5, 1999; "Has the Market Topped? Has Nokia?" *Fortune*, March 1, 1999.

2. Research and work on quality improvement are steadily growing. Some good recent sources include the following: G. J. Young, M. P. Charns, and S. M. Shortell, "Top Manager and Network Effects on the Adoption of Innovative Management Practices: A Study of TQM in a Public Hospital System," *Strategic Management Journal* 22, no. 10 (2001): 935–952; T. J. Douglas and W. Q. Judge, Jr., "Total Quality Management Implementation and Competitive Advantage: The Role of Structural Control and Exploration," *Academy of Management Journal* 44, no. 1 (2001): 158–169; B. Victor, A. Boynton, and T. Stephens-Jahng, "The Effective Design of Work under Total Quality Management," *Organization Science* 11, no. 1 (2000): 102–117; C. Shea and J. Howell, "Organizational Antecedents to the Successful Implementation of Total Quality Management," *Journal of Quality Management* 3 (1998): 3–24; J. Westphal, R. Gulati, and S. Shortell, "Customization or Conformity? An Institutional and Network Perspective on the Context and Consequences of TQM Adoption," *Administrative Science Quarterly* 42 (1997): 366–394; M. Uzumeri, "ISO 9000 and Other Metastandards: Principles of Management Practice?" *Academy of Management Executive*, 11, no. 1 (1997): 21–36; T.Y. Choi and O. C. Behling, "Top Managers and TQM Success: One More Look after All These Years," *Academy of Management Executive* 11, no. 1 (1997): 37–38; R. Reed, D. J. Lemak, and J. C. Montgomery, "Beyond Process: TQM Content and Firm Performance," *Academy of Management Review* 21, no. 1 (1996): 173–202; J. Motwani, V. Sower, and L. Brashier, "Implementing TQM in the Health Care Sector," *Health Care Management Review* 21, no. 1 (1996): 73–80; T. Powell, "Total Quality Management as Competitive Advantage: A Review and Empirical Study," *Strategic Management Journal* 16 (1995): 15–37; J. Hackman and R. Wageman, "Total Quality Management: Empirical, Conceptual, and Practical Issues," *Administrative Science Quarterly* 40 (1995): 309–342; S. Sitkin, K. Sutcliffe, and R. Schroeder, "Distinguishing Control from Learning in Total Quality Management: A Contingency Perspective," *Academy of Management Review* 19 (1994): 537–564.

Also see, for example, J. Belohlav, "Quality, Strategy, and Competitiveness," *California Management Review* (Spring 1993): 55–58; R. E. Cole, P. Bacdayan, and B. J. White, "Quality, Participation, and Competitiveness," *California Management Review* (Spring 1993): 68–81; D. A. Garvin, "How the Baldrige Award Really Works," *Harvard Business Review* (November–December 1991): 86–95; D. Kearns, "Leadership through Quality," *Academy of Management Executive* (May 1990): 86–89; J. M. Juran, *Juran on Leadership and Quality* (New York: Free Press, 1989); S. Mizuno, *Management for Total Quality* (Cambridge, Mass.: Productivity Press, 1988); W. E. Deming, *Out of the Crisis* (Cambridge, Mass.: MIT Center for Advanced Engineering Study, 1986); G. Taguchi, *Introduction to Quality Engineering* (Tokyo: Asian Productivity Institute, 1986); N. Mann, *The Key to Excellence: The Story of the Deming Philosophy* (Los Angeles: Prestwick, 1985); P. Crosby, *Quality Is Free* (New York: McGraw-Hill, 1979); T. C. Powell, "Total Quality Management as Competitive Advantage: A Review and Empirical Study," *Strategic Management Journal* 16, no. 1 (1995): 15–38; B. A. Spencer, "Models of Organization and Total Quality Management: A Comparison and Critical Evaluation," *Academy of Management Review* 19, no. 3 (1994): 446–472; J. W. Dean, Jr., and D. E. Bowen, "Management Theory and Total Quality: Improving Research and Practice through Theory Development," *Academy of Management Review* 19, no. 3 (1994): 392–418; R. K. Reger, L. T. Gustafson, S. M. DeMarie, and J. V. Mullane, "Reframing the Organization: Why Implementing Total Quality Is Easier Said Than Done," *Academy of Management Review* 19, no. 3 (1994): 575–584; S. Shiba, A. Graham, and D. Walden, *A New American TQM* (Portland, Ore.: Productivity, 1994).

3. W. E. Deming, *Out of the Crisis* (Cambridge, Mass.: MIT Center for Advanced Engineering Study, 1986); R. S. Schuler and D. L. Harris, "Deming Quality Improve-

ment: Implications for Human Resource Management as Illustrated in a Small Company," *Human Resource Planning* 14 (1991): 191–208; A. Gabor, *The Man Who Discovered Quality: How W. Edwards Deming Brought the Quality Revolution to America* (New York: Times Books, 1990); K. Yoshida, "Deming Management Philosophy: Does It Work in the United States as Well as in Japan?" *Columbia Journal of World Business* 24, no. 3 (1989): 10–17; W. B. Gartner and M. J. Naughton, "The Deming Theory of Management," *Academy of Management Review* 13 (1988): 138–142; W. E. Deming, *Quality, Productivity and Competitive Position* (Cambridge, Mass.: MIT Center for Advanced Engineering Study, 1982); W. E. Deming, *Elementary Principles of the Statistical Control of Quality* (Nippon Kagaku Gigutsu Remmei: Japanese Union of Science and Engineering [JUSE], 1951).

4. Various measures have been used to assess quality. These listed here are adapted from D. A. Garvin, "Competing on the Eight Dimensions of Quality," *Harvard Business Review* (November–December 1987): 101–109; P. E. Plesk, "Defining Quality at the Marketing/Development Interface," *Quality Progress* (June 1987): 28–36; D. A. Garvin, "What Does Product Quality Really Mean?" *Sloan Management Review* (Fall 1984): 25–39.

5. M. Imai, *Kaizen: The Key to Japan's Competitive Success* (New York: McGraw-Hill, 1986); K. Suzaki, *The New Manufacturing Challenge: Techniques for Continuous Improvement* (New York: Free Press, 1987); G. Taguchi, *Introduction to Off-Line Quality Control* (Tokyo: Japanese Standards Association, 1979).

6. K. B. Clark and T. Fujimoto, "The Power of Product Integrity," *Harvard Business Review* (November–December 1990): 107–118.

7. See, for example, "Xerox Recasts Itself as Formidable Force in Digital Revolution," *Wall Street Journal*, February 2, 1999, p. A1, A10; "Back in Focus," *Forbes*, June 6, 1994, pp. 72–76; "Can Xerox Duplicate Its Glory Days?" *Business Week*, October 4, 1993, pp. 56–58; J. S. Bowen and E. Walton, "Reenacting the Corporation: Organizational Change and Restructuring of Xerox," *Planning Review* (September–October 1993): 5–8; R. Howard, "The CEO as Organizational Architect: An Interview with Xerox's Paul Allaire," *Harvard Business Review* (September–October 1992): 106–119.

8. Reengineering is a recent topic. Good leading sources include T. Davenport, *Process Innovation: Reengineering Work through Information Technology* (Boston: Harvard Business School Press, 1992), and M. Hammer, "Reengineering Work: Don't Automate, Obliterate," *Harvard Business Review* (July–August 1990): 104–113. Also see, "Reengineering: The Hot New Management Tool," *Fortune*, August 23, 1993, pp. 41–48; G. Hall, J. Rosenthal, and J. Wade, "How to Make Reengineering Really Work," *Harvard Business Review* (November–December 1993): 119–131; M. Hammer and J. Champy, *Reengineering the Corporation* (New York: Harper Business, 1993); "Reengineering the Corporation," *World Executive's Digest* (July 1993): 16–23.

9. One classic piece in this area on time-based competition is G. Stalk, "Time: The Next Source of Competitive Advantage," *Harvard Business Review* (July–August 1988): 41–50. Also see K. M. Eisenhardt and S. L. Brown, "Time Pacing: Competing in Markets That Won't Stand Still," *Harvard Business Review* 76 (March–April 1998): 59–69.

10. See "Reengineering: The Hot New Management Tool," *Fortune*, August 23, 1993, p. 41; "Re-engineering Gives Firms New Efficiency, Workers the Pink Slip," *Wall Street Journal*, March 16, 1993, pp. A1, A11.

11. For a full discussion of the productivity paradox, see W. Abernathy, K. B. Clark, and A. M. Kantrow, *Industrial Renaissance* (New York: Free Press, 1983); W. Skinner, "The Productivity Paradox," *Harvard Business Review* (July–August 1986): 55–60; J. D. Goldhar, "In the Factory of the Future, Innovation Is Productivity," *Research Management* (March–April 1986): 26–33; R. Jaikumar and R. Hayes, "Manufacturing's

Crisis: New Technologies, Old Organizations," *Harvard Business Review* (September–October 1988): 77–85; D. Lei and J. D. Goldhar, "Multiple Niche Competition: The Strategic Use of CIM Technology," *Manufacturing Review* (September 1990): 195–206.

12. See, for example, B. J. Pine, *Mass Customization* (Boston: Harvard Business School Press, 1993); A. T. Talysum, M. Z. Hassan, and J. D. Goldhar, "Uncertainty Reduction through Flexible Manufacturing," *IEEE Transactions on Engineering Management* EM-34, no. 2 (May 1987): 85–91.

13. See, for example, "Brave New Factory: From the Line to the Supply Chain, All Goes on Autopilot," *Business Week*, July 23, 2001; "Heroes of U.S. Manufacturing: America Remains the World's Top Industrial Power with the Help of Innovators Like These," *Fortune*, March 19, 2001; "Cutting Edges: Better Machine Tools Give Manufacturers Newfound Resilience," *Wall Street Journal*, February 15, 2001, pp. A1, A8. An early pictorial that describes the impact of computers and flexible automation in a variety of industrial product settings is found in "The Digital Factory," *Fortune*, November 14, 1994, pp. 92–110.

14. See, for example, D. B. Yoffie and M. A. Cusumano, "Judo Strategy: The Competitive Dynamics of Internet Time," *Harvard Business Review* 77 (January–February 1999): 70–82; J. F. Rayport and J. J. Sviokla, "Exploiting the Virtual Value Chain," *Harvard Business Review* 73 (November–December 1995). Also see "The e-Corporation," *Fortune*, December 7, 1998, pp. 80–102.

15. See, for example, "Schwab Puts It All Online," *Fortune*, December 7, 1998, pp. 94–100.

16. Descriptions of the evolving horizontal organization can be found in F. Ostroff and D. Smith, "The Horizontal Organization," *McKinsey Quarterly* 1 (1992): 148–168; K. Jones and T. Ohbora, "Managing the Heretical Company," *McKinsey Quarterly* 3, 1990): 20–45; J. R. Galbraith, *Competing with Flexible Lateral Organization* (Boston: Addison-Wesley, 1994); E. E. Lawler III, *The Ultimate Advantage* (San Francisco: Jossey-Bass, 1992); R. Charan, "How Networks Reshape Organizations—For Results," *Harvard Business Review* (September–October 1991): 104–115; L. Hirschhorn and T. Gilmore, "The New Boundaries of the 'Boundaryless' Company," *Harvard Business Review* (May–June 1992): 104–115; J. R. Katzenbach and D. K. Smith, "The Discipline of Teams," *Harvard Business Review* (March–April 1993): 111–124; J. P. Womack and D. T. Jones, "From Lean Production to the Lean Enterprise," *Harvard Business Review* (March–April 1994): 93–105.

Some additional recent work in this area includes the following examples: R. Wageman, "How Leaders Foster Self-Managing Team Effectiveness: Design Choices versus Hands-On Coaching," *Organization Science* 12, no. 5 (2001): 559–577; D. R. Denison, S. L. Hart, and J. A. Kahn, "From Chimneys to Cross-Functional Teams: Developing and Validating a Diagnostic Model," *Academy of Management Journal* 39, no. 4 (1996): 1005–1023; D. T. Hall, "Protean Careers of the 21st Century," *Academy of Management Executive* 10, no. 4 (1996): 8–16; R. E. Miles, C. C. Snow, J. A. Mathews, G. Miles, and H. J. Coleman, Jr., "Organizing in the Knowledge Age: Anticipating the Cellular Form," *Academy of Management Executive* 11, no. 4 (1997): 7–24; T. T. Baldwin, C. Danielson, and W. Wiggenhorn, "The Evolution of Learning Strategies in Organizations: From Employee Development to Business Redefinition," *Academy of Management Executive* 11, no. 4 (1997): 47–58; J. R. W. Joplin and C. S. Daus, "Challenges of Leading a Diverse Workforce," *Academy of Management Executive* 11, no. 3 (1997): 32–47.

17. A growing stream of research has begun examining the growth of cross-functional teams in a variety of settings. Some of the representative works include the following: J. A. Chatman and F. J. Flynn, "The Influence of Demographic Heterogeneity on the Emergence and Consequences of Cooperative Norms in Work Teams," *Acad-*

emy of Management Journal 44, no. 5 (2001): 956–974; M. Hoegl and H. G. Gemuenden, "Teamwork Quality and the Success of Innovative Projects: A Theoretical Concept and Empirical Evidence," *Organization Science* 12, no. 4 (2001): 435–449; K. Lovelace, D. L. Shapiro, and L. R. Weingart, "Maximizing Cross-Functional New Product Teams' Innovativeness and Constraint Adherence: A Conflict Communications Perspective," *Academy of Management Journal* 44, no. 4 (2001): 779–793; R. T. Keller, "Cross-Functional Project Groups in Research and New Product Development: Diversity, Communications, Job Stress, and Outcomes," *Academy of Management Journal* 44, no. 3 (2001): 547–556; B. L. Kirkman and D. L. Shapiro, "The Impact of Cultural Values on Job Satisfaction and Organizational Commitment in Self-Managing Work Teams: The Mediating Role of Employee Resistance," *Academy of Management Journal* 44, no. 3 (2001): 557–569; G. L. Stewart and M. R. Barrick, "Team Structure and Performance: Assessing the Mediating Role of Intrateam Process and the Moderating Role of Task Type," *Academy of Management Journal* 43, no. 2 (2000): 135–148; P. M. Swamidass and M. D. Aldridge, "Ten Rules for Timely Task Completion in Cross-Functional Teams," *Research-Technology Management* 39, no. 4 (1996): 12–13; R. A. Lutz, "Implementing Technological Change with Cross-Functional Change with Cross-Functional Teams," *Research-Technology Management* 37, no. 2 (1994): 14–18; D. G. Ancona and D. F. Caldwell, "Demography and Design: Predictors of New Product Team Performance," *Organization Science* 3 (1992): 321–341.

Glossary

A

Activity Ratios measures used to assess the efficiency of a firm's use of assets (e.g., sales divided by assets).

Area Structures an organizational form that divides and organizes the firm's activities according to where operations and people are located (also known as place structures, geographic divisions).

B

Backbone a high-speed transmission line (often of fiber-optic cable) that forms a critical pathway in a telecommunications network. Backbones represent the most important building blocks of modern telephone and Internet-based networks.

Backward Integration a strategy that moves the firm upstream into an activity currently conducted by a supplier (see vertical integration; forward integration).

Bandwidth the defined range of frequencies used by a transmission signal to carry voice, video, data, or other information. The need for greater bandwidth is a fundamental constraint that limits the speed with which all types of information (voice, video, data) is transmitted across the Internet and other networks.

Barriers to Entry economic forces that slow down or prevent entry into an industry.

Benchmarking a firm's process of searching, identifying, and using ideas, techniques, and improvements of other companies in its own activities.

Boundaryless Organization an organization design in which people can easily share information, resources, and skills across departments and divisions.

Bureaucratization the gradual process by which information flow becomes steadily slower within the firm.

Business Managers people in charge of managing and operating a single line of business.

Business Strategy plans and actions that firms devise to compete in a given product/market scope or setting; addresses the question "How do we compete within an industry?"

Business System the subset of value chain activities that a firm actually performs.

C

CAD/CAM Network the linking up of multiple design and manufacturing activities (both within and across) firms through the use of complex networks of computers. CAD stands for computer-assisted design; CAM stands for computer-assisted manufacturing.

Capability Drivers the basic economic and strategic means by which a firm builds an underlying source of competitive advantage in its market or industry. Examples of basic capability drivers include first-mover advantages, economies of scale, experience effects, and interrelationships among business units.

Centralization the degree to which senior managers have the authority to make decisions for the entire organization.

Chaebol a complex arrangement in which Korean firms (often family-owned) assume equity stakes and other ownership positions to maintain a web of companies.

Collaboration cooperation between partners that is often short-term or limited in scope. Collaboration is actually another form of competition between partners seeking to learn and absorb skills from one another.

Comparative Financial Analysis the evaluation of a firm's financial condition across multiple time periods.

Competence-Changing Technology a technology that markedly changes or redefines the structure of an industry; often new processes or innovations that disrupt and erode the market for existing products.

Competing on Time speeding up the time needed to innovate new products and get them to market faster than competitors.

Competitive Advantage allows a firm to gain an edge over rivals when competing. Competitive advantage comes from a firm's ability to perform activities more distinctively or more effectively than rivals.

Competitive Environment the immediate economic factors—customers, competitors, suppliers, buyers, and potential substitutes—of direct relevance to a firm in a given industry (also known as industry environment).

Competitor Intelligence Gathering scanning specifically targeted or directed toward a firm's rivals; often focuses on a competitor's products, technologies, and other important information.

Composite Material a new material made from a distinct combination of metal, polymers, or ceramics that offers great strength and endurance; examples include carbon fibers and graphite used in tennis rackets and golf clubs.

Computer-Integrated Manufacturing (CIM) the use of modern computer and information technologies that closely link up design and marketing activities with those of manufacturing.

Conglomerate Discount an empirical finding of what a conglomerate firm's stock is worth because the market believes management is destroying the value of its individual businesses.

Conglomerates firms that practice unrelated diversification (see unrelated diversification; holding company structure).

Continuous Quality Improvement the deliberate and methodical search for better ways of improving products and processes.

Convergence the blurring of industry boundaries in such a way that the economic and competitive factors shaping one industry begin to influence the evolution of another. Convergence tends to occur most often when the characteristics of a product or service begin to substitute or complement those of an existing offering (e.g., Internet and the personal computer, Internet and financial services).

Co-Opetition the strategic situation whereby a firm cooperates and competes with another firm(s) at the same time. Firms in co-opetitive relationships often race with one another to learn each other's skills and to develop new sources of knowledge or value-creating activities.

Core Processes and Technologies the key levers or drivers that form the basis of a firm's distinctive competence and critical value-adding activities.

Corporate Culture the system of unwritten rules that guide how people perform and interrelate with one another.

Corporate Managers people responsible for overseeing and managing a portfolio of businesses within the firm.

Corporate Restructurings steps designed to change the corporate portfolio of businesses to achieve greater focus and efficiency among businesses; often involve selling off businesses that do not fit a core technology or are a drag on earnings.

Corporate Strategy plans and actions that firms need to formulate and implement when managing a portfolio of businesses, an especially critical issue when firms seek to diversify from their initial activities or operations into new areas. Corporate strategy issues are key to extending the firm's competitive advantage from one business to another.

Cost Driver a technological or economic factor that determines the cost of performing some activity.

Creative Tension a process in which senior management systematically attempts to encourage people to think about new strategies and directions, which prevents the firm from becoming complacent.

Cross-Functional Teams small units that work across a wide range of functions, technologies, products, and services based in different parts of the firm.

Cross-Subsidization using financial, technological, and marketing resources from one market to fight a competitor in another; involves extensive use of "parry and thrust" tactics to gain new market positions.

Cumulative Volume the quantity that a firm has produced since the beginning of that activity, up to this point in time.

Current Ratio a measure used to assess a firm's ability to make payments to its short-term creditors; current assets divided by current liabilities.

Customer Intimacy a deep knowledge of what motivates a customer to buy; often used in the context of fostering a high degree of communication with the customer to earn his or her loyalty.

Customer-Defined Quality the best value a firm can put into its products and services for the market segments it serves. Customer-defined quality is more important to competitive strategy than what the firm thinks its quality should be.

D

Debt Ratio a measure of a firm's leverage; the amount of debt it possesses divided by stockholder equity.

Defending an activity designed to help the firm shield or insulate itself from environmental change (see prospecting).

De-Integration the process by which a firm becomes less vertically integrated, often by selling off those activities that it once performed in-house.

Delayering the removal of excess levels of management that impede fast information flow within the firm.

Development Policies the training and skill improvement guidelines or practices used by a firm to cultivate its people.

Differentiation competitive strategy based on providing buyers with something special or unique that makes the firm's product or service distinctive.

Digital a method used to capture or represent information by discrete or individually unique signals (usually bits of binary data).

Digitization the conversion of information into binary form (0s and 1s). Digitization is a key reason why information-based industries are rapidly moving to the Internet.

Disintermediation the bypassing of middlemen and other economic entities that once separated firms from their customers.

Distinctive Competence the special skills, capabilities, or resources that enable a firm to stand out from its competitors; what a firm can do especially well to compete or serve its customers.

Diversification a strategy that takes the firm into new industries and markets (see related diversification; unrelated diversification).

Diversified Firm a firm that operates more than one line of business. Diversified firms often operate across several industries or markets, each with a separate set of customers and competitive requirements (also known as a multibusiness firm). Firms can differ in the degree or extent of their diversification.

Downscoping the reduction of a firm's wide spanning corporate diversification by shrinking the scope of activities it performs.

Downstream Activities economic activities that occur close to the customer but far away from the firm's suppliers. Examples include outbound logistics, distribution, marketing, sales, and service (see also upstream activities).

E

e-Business the use of Internet-based technologies to transform how a business interacts with its customers and suppliers.

Economies of Experience cost reductions that occur from continuous repetition of activities that allow for improvement with each successive act (also known as experience curve effects or learning curve effects).

Economies of Scale the declines in per-unit cost of production or any activity as volume grows.

Economies of Scope an economic characteristic that results when production of two or more goods can be done more efficiently with one set of assets than from separate assets dedicated to each product.

Empowerment delegation of decision-making authority and responsibility to those people most directly involved with a given project or task.

Environment all external forces, factors, or conditions that exert some degree of impact on the strategies, decisions, and actions taken by the firm.

Environmental Scanning the gathering of information about external conditions for use in formulating strategies.

Ethical Dilemmas difficult choices involving moral, legal, or other highly delicate issues that managers must weigh and balance when considering the needs of various stakeholders. Ethical dilemmas work to shape and sometimes constrain a firm's ability to take certain actions.

Exit Barriers economic forces that slow down or prevent exit from an industry.

Experience Curve Effects cost reductions that occur from continuous repetition of activities that allow for improvement with each successive act (also known as economies of experience or learning curve effects).

External Partnering the process of including suppliers and customers in the firm's set of value-adding activities, often through virtual organizational formats.

F

Fiduciary Responsibility the primary responsibility facing top management—to make sure the firm delivers value to its shareholders, the owners of the firm.

First-Mover Advantages the benefits that firms enjoy from being the first or earliest to compete in an industry.

Flexible Factories production facilities capable of producing a variety of products, often by using state-of-the-art computer technologies to promote fast changeover of designs and tools (see flexible manufacturing).

Flexible Manufacturing the ability of equipment in factories to change easily from the production of one good to another (see flexible factories).

Focus Strategies competitive strategies based on targeting a specific niche within an industry. Focus strategies can occur in two forms: cost-based focus and differentiation-based focus.

Forward Integration a strategy that moves the firm downstream into an activity currently performed by a buyer (see vertical integration; backward integration).

Full Integration vertical integration that seeks to control every activity in the value chain. In full integration, firms bring all activities required to design, develop, produce, and market a product in-house (see partial integration).

Functional Structure an organizational structure that groups managers and employees according to their areas of expertise and skills to perform their tasks.

G

General Environment the broad collection of forces or conditions that affect every firm or organization in every industry (also known as macroenvironment).

Generic Strategies the broad types of competitive strategies—low-cost leadership, differentiation, and focus—that firms use to build competitive advantage (see low-cost leadership, differentiation, focus strategies).

Geographic Division an organizational form that divides and organizes the firm's activities according to where operations and people are located.

Global Strategy a strategy that seeks to achieve a high level of consistency and standardization of products, processes, and operations around the world; coordination of the firm's many subsidiaries to achieve high interdependence and mutual support.

Globalization viewing the world as a single market for the firm; the process by which the firm expands across different regions and national markets. On an industry level, globalization refers to the changes in economic factors, such as economies of scale, experience, and R&D, that make competing on a worldwide basis a necessity.

Goals the specific results to be achieved within a given time period (also known as objectives).

Group or Sector a larger version of the SBU structure that often houses many different SBUs under one reporting relationship.

H

Harvesting the systematic removal of cash and other assets from a slow-growth or declining business; may be thought of as "milking" a business before it loses all its value.

Hierarchy-Based Reward System a type of compensation structure that encourages close superior-subordinate relationships, an emphasis on group achievement, use of both qualitative and quantitative measures of performance, and promotion from within (see performance-based reward system).

Holding Company Structure a lean form of a product division structure used by conglomerates in unrelated diversification (see conglomerates, product division, product structure, unrelated diversification).

Hollow Out the process by which a firm becomes steadily less competitive as a result of delegating its core value-adding activities to other firms.

Homogeneity of Demand similarity of demand patterns and wants across customers, regardless of where they are located.

Horizontal Organization an organization design in which teams and small units replace the strict separation of functional activities such as design, manufacturing, marketing, finance, distribution, sales, and service.

Hybrid (or Mixed) Structures combining different basic organizational structures to attain the benefits of more than one.

Hybrid Products products that result from combining or fusing together different sources of technologies (see technology fusion).

I

Industrial Espionage systematic and deliberate attempts to learn about a competitor's technologies or new products through secretive, and often illegal, ways.

Industry Attractiveness the potential for profitability when competing in a given industry. An attractive industry has high profit potential; an unattractive industry has low profit potential.

Industry Environment the immediate economic factors—customers, competitors, suppliers, buyers, and potential substitutes—of direct relevance to a firm in a given industry (also known as competitive environment).

Industry Initiative the ability of a firm to shape, influence, or introduce new product ideas, standards, or technologies within an industry.

Industry Structure the interrelationship among the factors in a firm's competitive or industry environment; configuration of economic forces and factors that interrelate to affect the behavior of firms competing in that industry.

Inertia the difficulty that established firms face when trying to adjust to change; inhibits fast response to new developments in the environment

Informal Integrators people who act as internal "referees" to resolve disputes and conflicts between divisional managers.

Intangible Assets resources based on skills or other hard-to-imitate assets that are not physical in form; examples include brand equity, fast product development, management techniques, proprietary means of developing knowledge, innovation, and so forth.

Internal Task Forces groups that serve as bridges that forge stronger interrelationships among divisions in an organization.

International Division a structure by which all of the firm's managers and employees in nondomestic activities report to a single senior manager who is separate from other domestic divisional managers; a structure traditionally used by firms that are starting to increase their overseas operations.

Internet the enormous collection of interconnected networks that share the similar use of transmission and delivery protocols (TCP/IP). The Internet evolved from early government-related programs to construct a huge network of research centers, universities, and government installations that would link up computer systems together.

Interrelationships the sharing of activities, technologies, skills, and resources among a firm's subunits, particularly divisions or strategic business units (SBUs).

Invisible Assets intangible sources of competitive advantage such as brands, images, corporate cultures, knowledge, and organizational practices that are hard for competitors to imitate and duplicate.

J

Joint Ventures a form of strategic alliance in which partners work closely—usually through a third company that is set up by both partners—to pursue a mutually shared interest.

Just-in-Time sophisticated approach to inventory management in which firms receive material from their suppliers when it is needed.

K

Keiretsu a complex arrangement in which firms take equity stakes in one another as a long-standing strategic alliance; used in Japan to link up many different companies.

Knowledge Web a collection or group of companies that work in tandem to shape the evolution of an industry.

Knowledge-Based Assets intangible assets such as reputation, brand names, scientific skills, or quality techniques that are hard-to-imitate and critical to making a firm's distinctive competence valuable.

Knowledge-Based Competition economic competition and competitive advantage derived from the creation and use of new forms of knowledge, skills, and technologies.

L

Lateral Relations coordinating work and communications among people who are the same reporting level within the organization.

Learning Curve Effects cost reductions that occur from continuous repetition of activities that allow for improvement with each successive act (also known as economies of experience or experience curve effects).

Learning Organizations firms that view change as a positive opportunity to learn and create new sources of competitive advantage.

Liquid Crystal Displays (LCDs) a display technology that consists of three parts: two glass substrates, a liquid crystal (made from a chemical compound) in the middle, and an electronic device that changes or "stimulates" crystals to produce different colors. LCD technology allows visual display of numbers, images, or other data through the use of crystal, as opposed to conventional tube technology.

Liquidity the ability of a firm or business to pay or meet its obligations (e.g., debt payments, accounts payable) as they come due. The more liquid the firm, the easier its ability to meet these obligations.

Location of Activities the physical place where an economic, value-adding activity occurs. Location can be an important source of competitive advantage for some types of firms.

Loose Coupling an organization design and structure that fosters a balance between the need to centralize and decentralize activities.

Low-Cost Leadership a competitive strategy based on the firm's ability to provide products or services at lower cost than its rivals.

M

Macroenvironment the broad collection of forces or conditions that affect every firm or organization in every industry (also known as general environment).

Mass Customization the capability to produce a growing variety or range of products at reduced unit costs. Mass customization is a strategic competitive weapon that helps firms to expand the range of their product offerings and modifications without incurring the high costs of variety.

Matrix Structure an organizational form that divides and organizes activities along two or more lines of authority and reporting relationships.

Mechatronics refers to the fusion of precision, mechanical engineering skills with microelectronics.

Microchip a flat semiconductor device in which tiny (often microscopic) amounts of chemical elements are deposited, etched, and sealed to create integrated circuits. Microchips lay the foundation for the semiconductor industry.

Microprocessor a microchip that performs arithmetic, control, and logic-based operations; used as the central processing unit of personal computers and workstations.

Minimum Efficient Scale (MES) level of production volume that a factory must reach before it achieves full efficiency.

Mission describes the firm or organization in terms of its business. Mission statements answer the questions "What business are we in?" and "What do we intend to do to succeed?" Mission statements are somewhat more concrete than vision statements but still do not specify the goals and objectives necessary to translate the mission into reality (see vision; goals; objectives).

Mixed Structures combining different basic organizational structures to attain the benefits of more than one (also known as hybrid structures).

Modularity an element of product design that allows for the mixing and matching of different components and parts that all share the same interface or means of connecting with one another. A product exhibits modularity if its constituent parts can be rearranged among themselves or with additional parts that share the same pattern of linkage.

Multibusiness Firm a firm that operates more than one line of business. Multibusiness firms often operate across several industries or markets, each with a separate set of customers and competitive requirements (also known as a diversified firm). Firms can possess many business units in their corporate portfolio.

Multidomestic Strategy a strategy that seeks to adjust a firm's products, processes, and operations for markets and regions around the world; allows subsidiaries to tailor their products, marketing, and other activities according to the needs of their specific markets.

Multipoint Competition a form of economic competition in which a firm commits its entire product line against a similarly endowed competitor's array of products.

N

Nanotechnology science and technology based on combining different types of amino acids or molecules to create new types of enzymatic-based circuits and other miniaturized products.

Network Effects an economic condition in which the value of a product or service rises as more people utilize it.

Network Organization organizational format in which firms try to balance their reliance on performing internal value-creating activities with the need to stay responsive and open to the environment.

O

Objectives the specific results to be achieved within a given time period (also known as goals). Objectives guide the firm or organization in achieving its mission (see vision; mission).

Off-Line Coordinators individuals and groups, often experienced managers and staff personnel, outside the formal hierarchy who coordinate activities among subunits.

Organization Design Practices support mechanisms that facilitate the implementation of a strategy within the framework of a given structure.

Outsource the use of other firms to perform value-adding activities once conducted in-house.

P

Partial Integration vertical integration that is selective about which areas of activity the firm will choose to undertake. In partial integration, firms do not control every activity required to design, develop, produce, and market a product (see full integration).

Performance-Based Reward System a type of compensation structure that puts a premium on a high level of individual performance, a strong reliance on bonuses as part of total compensation, and a relative de-emphasis on close superior–subordinate relationships (see hierarchy-based reward system).

Peripheral Businesses business units or divisions that are not central to the firm's core set of activities, skills, or technologies.

Perishability the loss of economic value that occurs when a product or service is not used within a given time period, often used to describe the ease with which a product spoils or decays; a major economic consideration that promotes the use of multidomestic strategies.

Personalization the creation of a unique mix or set of products and services catered to a specific individual's needs.

Pirating hiring individuals from a competitor specifically to gain their knowledge (also known as raiding).

Place Structure an organizational form that divides and organizes the firm's activities according to where operations and people are located (also known as area structures, geographic structures).

Primary Activities economic activities that relate directly to the actual creation, manufacture, distribution, and sale of a product or service to the firm's customer (see support activities).

Process Development the design and use of new procedures, technologies, techniques, and other steps to improve value-adding activities.

Product Development the conception, design, and commercialization of new products.

Product Differentiation the physical or perceptual differences that make a product special or unique in the eyes of the customer.

Product Divisions the most basic form of product structure, in which each division houses all of the functions necessary for it to carry out its own strategy and mission.

Product Realization the product development process, beginning with product idea and concept and ending with production and distribution.

Product Structure an organizational structure that divides the firm into self-contained units able to perform all of their own activities independently; examples include product divisions, strategic business units (SBUs), sectors or groups, and conglomerate/holding company formats.

Productivity Paradox the economic trade-off that managers must make when using traditional manufacturing technology to achieve low-cost production, flexibility and variety of production are sacrificed.

Prospecting an activity designed to help the firm search, understand, and accommodate environmental change; a proactive attempt by a firm to make an environmental change favorable to itself (see defending).

R

Raiding hiring individuals from a competitor specifically to gain their knowledge (also known as pirating).

Rapid Prototyping a design technology that accelerates the testing of new product concepts, ideas, and designs, often through the use of computer modeling techniques.

Ratio Analysis the use of a proportion of two figures or numbers that allow for consistent comparison of performance with other firms.

Reengineering the complete rethinking, reinventing, and redesign of how a business or set of activities operates.

Related Diversification a strategy that expands the firm's operations into similar industries and markets; extends the firm's distinctive competence to other lines of business that are similar to the firm's initial base (see related industry; unrelated diversification).

Related Industry an industry that shares many of the same economic, technological, or market-based drivers or characteristics as another.

Resource-Based View of the Firm an evolving set of strategic management ideas that place considerable emphasis on the firm's ability to distinguish itself from its rivals by means of investing in hard-to-imitate and specific resources (e.g., technologies, skills, capabilities, assets, management approaches).

Resource Sharing the transfer of skills, technologies, or knowledge from one business to another; vital to building synergy in related diversification.

Return on Assets net income divided by total assets.

Return on Capital net income divided by total capital.

Return on Equity net income divided by stockholder equity.

Return on Investment net income divided by total investment.

Revitalization the process of renewing a company's sources of distinctive competence and competitive advantage.

Rightsizing shrinking of the firm's workforce and resource commitment to the firm's businesses.

S

Scope of Operations the extent of a firm's involvement in different activities, products, and markets.

Sector a larger version of the strategic business unit (SBU) that often houses many SBUs under one reporting relationship; sometimes called a group (see group, strategic business unit (SBU), product division, product structure).

Semiconductor electronic device containing many transistors that serve different switching functions on a small chip, usually made of silicon, germanium, or gallium arsenide. Each transistor, in itself, can serve as a switch, amplifier, or oscillator. Semiconductors are vital to the function of many consumer and industrial products. (The term semiconductor actually refers to a type of material or substrate that is part insulator and part conductor.)

Semipermeable Boundaries flexible separations between organizational subunits across which communication, knowledge, and information flow more readily.

Shared Values the basic norms and ideals that guide people's behaviors in the firm and form the underpinning of a firm's corporate culture.

Single-Business Firm a firm that operates only one business in one industry or market (also known as an undiversified firm).

Socialization the process by which shared values and ways of behaving are instilled in new managers and employees.

Specialization the assignment of particular tasks and activities to those people who are best able to perform them.

Spin-Off a form of corporate restructuring that sells businesses or parts of a company that no longer contribute to the firm's earnings or distinctive competence.

Standardization the process of defining the organization's work practices and procedures so that people can repeatedly perform them at a given level or measure of performance.

Static Organizations firms that have adapted extremely well to a particular environment but lack the ability to respond quickly to change.

Statistical Process Controls the use of statistics to measure and control a production process, often with the desired intent of achieving high product conformity.

Strategic Alliances linkages between companies designed to achieve an economic objective faster or more efficiently than either company could do alone; take the basic forms of licensing arrangements, joint ventures, or multipartner consortia.

Strategic Business Unit form of organization that often represents larger product divisions or collections of smaller product divisions under one reporting relationship.

Strategic Groups the distribution or grouping of firms that pursue similar strategies in response to environmental forces within an industry. Firms within the same strategic group will tend to compete more vigorously with one another than with firms from other strategic groups.

Strategic Management Process the steps by which management converts a firm's values, mission, and goals/objectives into a workable strategy; consists of four stages: analysis, formulation, implementation, and adjustment/evaluation.

Strategy refers to the ideas, plans, and support that firms employ to compete successfully against their rivals. Strategy is designed to help firms achieve competitive advantage.

Strategy Implementation the process by which strategies are converted into desired actions.

Structure the formal definition of working relationships between people in an organization.

Support Activities economic activities that assist the firm's primary activities (see primary activities).

Switching Costs costs that occur when buyers or suppliers move from one competitor's products or services to another's.

SWOT Analysis shorthand for strengths, weaknesses, opportunities, and threats; a fundamental step in assessing the firm's external environment; required as a first step of strategy formulation and typically carried out at the business level of the firm.

Synergy an economic effect in which the different parts of the company contribute a unique source of heightened value to the firm when managed as a single, unified entity.

Systemwide Advantage the building and sustaining of competitive advantage across multiple business units to achieve corporatewide strengths.

T

Technological Convergence growing technological similarity of products and businesses, such as components, designs, and production processes, among once-distinct industries.

Technology Fusion the blending, or fusing together, of many sources of technology to create new, higher-order products.

Terrain the environment (or industry) in which competition occurs. In a military sense, terrain is the type of environment or ground on which a battle takes place. From a business sense, terrain refers to markets, segments, and products used to win over customers.

Total Quality Management the cultivation and practice of quality in every person's tasks and activities throughout the organization.

Transaction Costs economic costs of finding, negotiating, selling, buying, and resolving disputes with other firms (e.g., suppliers and customers) in the open market.

Turnover Ratios measures that assess the speed with which various assets (inventory, receivables) are converted into cash.

U

Undiversified Firm a firm that operates only one business in one industry or market (also known as a single-business firm).

Unrelated Diversification a strategy that expands the firm's operations into industries and markets that are not similar or related to the firm's initial base; does not involve sharing the firm's distinctive competence across different lines of business (see related diversification; related industry).

Upstream Activities economic activities that occur close to the firm's suppliers but far away from the consumer. Examples include inbound logistics, procurement, manufacturing, and operations (see also downstream activities).

V

Value Chain an analytical tool that describes all activities that make up the economic performance and capabilities of the firm; used to analyze and examine activities that create value for a given firm.

Value-Added/Weight Ration a key economic factor that influences the globalization of industries; high value-added/weight promotes global strategies; low value-added/weight ratios promote multidomestic strategies.

Value engineering process by which each step in engineering and product development activities directly contribute to the value of the final product.

Vertical Integration the expansion of the firm's value chain to include activities performed by suppliers and buyers; the degree of control that a firm exerts over the supply of its inputs and the purchase of its outputs. Vertical integration strategies and decisions enlarge the scope of the firm's activities in one industry.

Virtual Advantage a type of competitive advantage based on speed, fast turnaround, and deep knowledge of customers' needs to create value faster than competitors can do, often by focusing on a few core value-adding activities

Virtual Organization an organizational format that coordinates and links up people and activities from different locations to communicate and act together, often on a real-time basis.

Vision the highest aspirations and ideals of a person or organization; what a firm wants to be. Vision statements often describe the firm or organization in lofty, even romantic or mystical tones (see mission; goals; objectives).

Name Index

n = found in notes

Company and Product Index

n = found in notes   italic page number = found in an exhibit

Subject Index

n = found in notes   italic page number = found in an exhibit

Robert A. Pitts
David Lei

Strategic Management

Building and Sustaining Competitive Advantage

3e

Strategic Management, 3e reveals to you how firms build, extend, organize and sustain a competitive advantage with a focus on seven key themes: distinctive competence, quality, globalization, change, internet, innovation and ethics. Authors David Lei and Robert Pitts take an applications-oriented approach in which a company's strategic position or dilemma is dissected and analyzed in such a way that all key concepts and ideas are brought to bear for the reader. The third edition has been updated to include the most timely and relevant examples and topics possible, including a new chapter 5 on the applications and implications of the Internet for strategic management.

Enrich your course with these products available from South-Western:

- *Global Corporate Management in the Marketplace: An Online Simulation in Business Strategy* by Ernest R. Cadotte
- *Strategic Management in the Marketplace: An Online Simulation* by Ernest R. Cadotte
- *Strategize! Experiential Exercises in Strategic Management* by Siciliano & Gopinath
- *The Global Business Game, Release 2.0: A Simulation in Strategic Management and International Business* by Joe Wolfe

You may also easily create a customize[illegible] this text through Thomson Custom Publish[illegible] [illegible]ese products and custom cases, visit http:/[illegible]

THOMSON
SOUTH-WESTERN

Join us on the Internet
Management - http://management.swcollege.com
South-Western - http://www.swcollege.com

ISBN 0-324-11689-6